Twentieth-Century Literary Criticism

Guide to Gale Literary Criticism Series

For criticism on	Consult these Gale series
Authors now living or who died after December 31, 1999	*CONTEMPORARY LITERARY CRITICISM (CLC)*
Authors who died between 1900 and 1999	*TWENTIETH-CENTURY LITERARY CRITICISM (TCLC)*
Authors who died between 1800 and 1899	*NINETEENTH-CENTURY LITERATURE CRITICISM (NCLC)*
Authors who died between 1400 and 1799	*LITERATURE CRITICISM FROM 1400 TO 1800 (LC)* *SHAKESPEAREAN CRITICISM (SC)*
Authors who died before 1400	*CLASSICAL AND MEDIEVAL LITERATURE CRITICISM (CMLC)*
Authors of books for children and young adults	*CHILDREN'S LITERATURE REVIEW (CLR)*
Dramatists	*DRAMA CRITICISM (DC)*
Poets	*POETRY CRITICISM (PC)*
Short story writers	*SHORT STORY CRITICISM (SSC)*
Black writers of the past two hundred years	*BLACK LITERATURE CRITICISM (BLC)* *BLACK LITERATURE CRITICISM SUPPLEMENT (BLCS)*
Hispanic writers of the late nineteenth and twentieth centuries	*HISPANIC LITERATURE CRITICISM (HLC)* *HISPANIC LITERATURE CRITICISM SUPPLEMENT (HLCS)*
Native North American writers and orators of the eighteenth, nineteenth, and twentieth centuries	*NATIVE NORTH AMERICAN LITERATURE (NNAL)*
Major authors from the Renaissance to the present	*WORLD LITERATURE CRITICISM, 1500 TO THE PRESENT (WLC)* *WORLD LITERATURE CRITICISM SUPPLEMENT (WLCS)*

ISSN 0276-8178

Volume 127

Twentieth-Century Literary Criticism

**Criticism of the
Works of Novelists, Poets, Playwrights,
Short Story Writers, and Other Creative Writers
Who Lived between 1900 and 1999,
from the First Published Critical
Appraisals to Current Evaluations**

Janet Witalec
Project Editor

GALE®

THOMSON
GALE

Detroit • New York • San Diego • San Francisco • Cleveland • New Haven, Conn. • Waterville, Maine • London • Munich

Twentieth-Century Literary Criticism, Vol. 127

Project Editor
Janet Witalec

Editorial
Jenny Cromie, Scott Darga, Kathy D. Darrow, Julie Keppen, Ellen McGeagh, Linda Pavlovski

Research
Nicodemus Ford, Sarah Genik, Tamara C. Nott, Tracie A. Richardson

Permissions
Shalice Shah-Caldwell

Imaging and Multimedia
Leitha Etheridge-Sims, Lezlie Light, Luke Rademacher, Robyn Young

Product Design
Michael Logusz

Composition and Electronic Capture
Carolyn Roney

Manufacturing
Stacy L. Melson

LIBRARY OF CONGRESS CATALOG CARD NUMBER 76-46132

ISBN 0-7876-5941-x
ISSN 0276-8178

Printed in the United States of America
10 9 8 7 6 5 4 3 2 1

Contents

Preface vii

Acknowledgments xi

Literary Criticism Series Advisory Board xiii

Preface

Since its inception more than fifteen years ago, *Twentieth-Century Literary Criticism* (*TCLC*) has been purchased and used by nearly 10,000 school, public, and college or university libraries. *TCLC* has covered more than 500 authors, representing 58 nationalities and over 25,000 titles. No other reference source has surveyed the critical response to twentieth-century authors and literature as thoroughly as *TCLC*. In the words of one reviewer, "there is nothing comparable available." *TCLC* "is a gold mine of information—dates, pseudonyms, biographical information, and criticism from books and periodicals—which many librarians would have difficulty assembling on their own."

Scope of the Series

TCLC is designed to serve as an introduction to authors who died between 1900 and 1999 and to the most significant interpretations of these author's works. Volumes published from 1978 through 1999 included authors who died between 1900 and 1960. The great poets, novelists, short story writers, playwrights, and philosophers of the period are frequently studied in high school and college literature courses. In organizing and reprinting the vast amount of critical material written on these authors, *TCLC* helps students develop valuable insight into literary history, promotes a better understanding of the texts, and sparks ideas for papers and assignments. Each entry in *TCLC* presents a comprehensive survey on an author's career or an individual work of literature and provides the user with a multiplicity of interpretations and assessments. Such variety allows students to pursue their own interests; furthermore, it fosters an awareness that literature is dynamic and responsive to many different opinions.

Every fourth volume of *TCLC* is devoted to literary topics. These topics widen the focus of the series from the individual authors to such broader subjects as literary movements, prominent themes in twentieth-century literature, literary reaction to political and historical events, significant eras in literary history, prominent literary anniversaries, and the literatures of cultures that are often overlooked by English-speaking readers.

TCLC is designed as a companion series to Gale's *Contemporary Literary Criticism,* (*CLC*) which reprints commentary on authors who died after 1999. Because of the different time periods under consideration, there is no duplication of material between *CLC* and *TCLC*.

Organization of the Book

A *TCLC* entry consists of the following elements:

- The **Author Heading** cites the name under which the author most commonly wrote, followed by birth and death dates. Also located here are any name variations under which an author wrote, including transliterated forms for authors whose native languages use nonroman alphabets. If the author wrote consistently under a pseudonym, the pseudonym will be listed in the author heading and the author's actual name given in parenthesis on the first line of the biographical and critical information. Uncertain birth or death dates are indicated by question marks. Single-work entries are preceded by a heading that consists of the most common form of the title in English translation (if applicable) and the original date of composition.

- A **Portrait of the Author** is included when available.

- The **Introduction** contains background information that introduces the reader to the author, work, or topic that is the subject of the entry.

- The list of **Principal Works** is ordered chronologically by date of first publication and lists the most important works by the author. The genre and publication date of each work is given. In the case of foreign authors whose works have been translated into English, the English-language version of the title follows in brackets. Unless otherwise indicated, dramas are dated by first performance, not first publication.

- Reprinted **Criticism** is arranged chronologically in each entry to provide a useful perspective on changes in critical evaluation over time. The critic's name and the date of composition or publication of the critical work are given at the beginning of each piece of criticism. Unsigned criticism is preceded by the title of the source in which it appeared. All titles by the author featured in the text are printed in boldface type. Footnotes are reprinted at the end of each essay or excerpt. In the case of excerpted criticism, only those footnotes that pertain to the excerpted texts are included.

- A complete **Bibliographical Citation** of the original essay or book precedes each piece of criticism.

- Critical essays are prefaced by brief **Annotations** explicating each piece.

- An annotated bibliography of **Further Reading** appears at the end of each entry and suggests resources for additional study. In some cases, significant essays for which the editors could not obtain reprint rights are included here. Boxed material following the further reading list provides references to other biographical and critical sources on the author in series published by Gale.

Indexes

A **Cumulative Author Index** lists all of the authors that appear in a wide variety of reference sources published by the Gale Group, including *TCLC*. A complete list of these sources is found facing the first page of the Author Index. The index also includes birth and death dates and cross references between pseudonyms and actual names.

A **Cumulative Nationality Index** lists all authors featured in *TCLC* by nationality, followed by the number of the *TCLC* volume in which their entry appears.

A **Cumulative Topic Index** lists the literary themes and topics treated in the series as well as in *Classical and Medieval Literature Criticism, Literature Criticism from 1400 to 1800, Nineteenth-Century Literature Criticism,* and the *Contemporary Literary Criticism* Yearbook, which was discontinued in 1998.

An alphabetical **Title Index** accompanies each volume of *TCLC*. Listings of titles by authors covered in the given volume are followed by the author's name and the corresponding page numbers where the titles are discussed. English translations of foreign titles and variations of titles are cross-referenced to the title under which a work was originally published. Titles of novels, dramas, nonfiction books, and poetry, short story, or essay collections are printed in italics, while individual poems, short stories, and essays are printed in roman type within quotation marks.

In response to numerous suggestions from librarians, Gale also produces an annual paperbound edition of the *TCLC* cumulative title index. This annual cumulation, which alphabetically lists all titles reviewed in the series, is available to all customers. Additional copies of this index are available upon request. Librarians and patrons will welcome this separate index; it saves shelf space, is easy to use, and is recyclable upon receipt of the next edition.

Citing *Twentieth-Century Literary Criticism*

When writing papers, students who quote directly from any volume in the Literary Criticism Series may use the following general format to footnote reprinted criticism. The first example pertains to material drawn from periodicals, the second to material reprinted from books.

George Orwell, "Reflections on Gandhi," *Partisan Review* 6 (Winter 1949): 85-92; reprinted in *Twentieth-Century Literary Criticism,* vol. 59, ed. Jennifer Gariepy (Detroit: The Gale Group, 1995), 40-3.

William H. Slavick, "Going to School to DuBose Heyward," *The Harlem Renaissance Re-examined,* ed. Victor A. Kramer (AMS, 1987), 65- 91; reprinted in *Twentieth-Century Literary Criticism,* vol. 59, ed. Jennifer Gariepy (Detroit: The Gale Group, 1995), 94-105.

Suggestions are Welcome

Readers who wish to suggest new features, topics, or authors to appear in future volumes, or who have other suggestions or comments are cordially invited to call, write, or fax the Project Editor:

Project Editor, Literary Criticism Series
The Gale Group
27500 Drake Road
Farmington Hills, MI 48331-3535
1-800-347-4253 (GALE)
Fax: 248-699-8054

Acknowledgments

The editors wish to thank the copyright holders of the criticism included in this volume and the permissions managers of many book and magazine publishing companies for assisting us in securing reproduction rights. We are also grateful to the staffs of the Detroit Public Library, the Library of Congress, the University of Detroit Mercy Library, Wayne State University Purdy/Kresge Library Complex, and the University of Michigan Libraries for making their resources available to us. Following is a list of the copyright holders who have granted us permission to reproduce material in this volume of *TCLC*. Every effort has been made to trace copyright, but if omissions have been made, please let us know.

COPYRIGHTED MATERIAL IN *TCLC*, VOLUME 127, WAS REPRODUCED FROM THE FOLLOWING PERIODICALS:

American Literary Realism, v. 25, Spring, 1993; v. 32, Fall, 1999; v. 32, Winter, 2000. All reproduced by permission.—*American Literature*, v. 62, June, 1990. Copyright June 1990, Duke University Press. All rights reserved. Reproduced by permission.—*American Transcendental Quarterly*, v. 13, March, 1999. Reproduced by permission.—*Arizona Quarterly*, v. 40, Summer, 1984 for "A Note on Kate Chopin's 'The White Eagle,'" by Joyce Coyne Dyer. Reproduced by permission of the publisher and the author.—*Chicago Daily Tribune*, v. xciii, September 22, 1934. Copyright 1934, renewed 1962. Reproduced by permission.—*Explicator*, v. 45, Fall, 1986; v. 52, Spring, 1994. Both reproduced by permission.—*Genders*, July, 1989 for "Personal Property: Exchange Value and the Female Self in 'The Awakening'" by Margit Stange. Reproduced by permission of the publisher and the author.—*Kenyon Review*, v. 13, Winter, 1951. Copyright © 1951, renewed 1979 by Kenyon College. All rights reserved. Reproduced by permission.—*Michigan Quarterly Review*, v. 34, Fall, 1995 for "Cinema, Psychoanalysis, and Hermeneutics: G. W. Pabst's 'Secrets of a Soul,'" by Ira Konigsberg. Reproduced by permission of the author.—*The Mississippi Quarterly*, v. 47, Spring, 1994. Reproduced by permission.—*Modern Drama*, v. 3, February, 1961; v. 16, December, 1973. Both reproduced by permission.—*The Nation*, vol. 136, June 28, 1933; vol. 139, August 8, 1934. Both reproduced by permission.—*New German Critique*, v. 50, Spring, 1990. Reproduced by permission.—*New Republic*, v. 104, February 3, 1941. © 1941, renewed 1968 The New Republic, Inc./v. 167, December 9, 1972; v. 168, June 23, 1973. © 1972, 1973 The New Republic, Inc. All reproduced by permission of *The New Republic.*—*New York Herald Tribune Books*, April 5, 1931; May 7, 1933. Copyright 1931, renewed 1959; Copyright 1933, renewed 1961 *The New York Times*. Both reproduced by permission.—*New Yorker*, v. 49, August 20, 1973. Reproduced by permission.—*The North American Review*, vol. 231, 1931. Reproduced by permission.—*Novel, A Forum on Fiction*, v. 20, Spring, 1987. Copyright NOVEL Corp. © 1987. Reproduced by permission.—*Saturday Review of Literature*, v. 11, August 4, 1934; v. 23, February 1, 1941. © 1934, renewed 1962; © 1941, renewed 1968 General Media International, Inc. Both reproduced by permission.—*Screen*, v. 24, July, 1983. Reproduced by permission.—*Sight and Sound*, v. 45, Spring, 1976. Reproduced by permission.—*Southern Literary Journal*, v. 18, Fall, 1985; v. 23, Spring, 1991; v. 29, Fall, 1996. Copyright 1985, 1991, 1996 by the Department of English, University of North Carolina at Chapel Hill. All reproduced by permission.—*Southern Quarterly*, v. 37, Summer, 1999. Reproduced by permission.—*Southern Studies*, v. 20, Winter, 1981 for "Symbolic Setting in Kate Chopin's 'A Shameful Affair,'" by Joyce Dyer; v. 24, Spring, 1985 for "Techniques of Distancing in the Fiction of Kate Chopin," by Joyce Coyne Dyer; v. 26, 1987 for "Kate Chopin's 'The Awakening': An Assault on American Racial and Sexual Mythology," by Anna Shannon Elfenbein. All reproduced by permission of the authors./v. 1, Summer, 1990; v. 2, Fall-Winter,1991; v. 4, Winter, 1993. Both reproduced by permission.—*The Spectator*, vol. 149, November 18, 1932; vol. 152, June 8, 1934. Both reproduced by permission.—*Studies in American Fiction*, v. 23, Spring, 1995; v. 24, Spring, 1996. Copyright © 1995, 1996, Northeastern University. Both reproduced by permission.—*Studies in Short Fiction*, v. 33, Spring, 1996. Reproduced by permission.—*Times Literary Supplement*, May 5, 1931; October 20, 1932; December 12, 1934. © The Times Supplements Limited 1931, 1932, 1934. All reproduced by permission.—*Women's Studies*, v. 13, 1986. Reproduced by permission.

COPYRIGHTED MATERIAL IN *TCLC*, VOLUME 127, WAS REPRODUCED FROM THE FOLLOWING BOOKS:

Berman, Russell A. From *Cultural Studies of Modern German: History, Representation, and Nationhood.* The University of Wisconsin Press, 1993. Copyright © 1993 by The University of Wisconsin Press. All rights reserved. Reproduced by permission.—Burgess, Anthony. From *The John Collier Reader.* Alfred A. Knopf, 1973. Copyright © 1973 Estate of An-

Literary Criticism Series Advisory Board

The members of the Gale Group Literary Criticism Series Advisory Board—reference librarians and subject specialists from public, academic, and school library systems—represent a cross-section of our customer base and offer a variety of informed perspectives on both the presentation and content of our literature criticism products. Advisory board members assess and define such quality issues as the relevance, currency, and usefulness of the author coverage, critical content, and literary topics included in our series; evaluate the layout, presentation, and general quality of our printed volumes; provide feedback on the criteria used for selecting authors and topics covered in our series; provide suggestions for potential enhancements to our series; identify any gaps in our coverage of authors or literary topics, recommending authors or topics for inclusion; analyze the appropriateness of our content and presentation for various user audiences, such as high school students, undergraduates, graduate students, librarians, and educators; and offer feedback on any proposed changes/enhancements to our series. We wish to thank the following advisors for their advice throughout the year.

Kate Chopin
1851-1904

(Full name Katherine O'Flaherty Chopin) American novelist, short story writer, and essayist.

For additional information on Chopin's life and works, see *TCLC,* Volumes 5 and 14.

INTRODUCTION

A popular local colorist during her lifetime, Chopin is best known today for her psychological novel *The Awakening,* (1899) which depicts a woman's search for spiritual and sexual freedom in the repressive society of late-nineteenth-century America. When *The Awakening* appeared, critical and public indignation over the novel's frank treatment of guiltless adultery caused Chopin to abandon her literary career, and the novel itself was forgotten for several decades. Since the 1950s, however, serious critical attention has focused on the pioneering psychological realism, symbolic imagery, and artistic integrity of the work.

BIOGRAPHICAL INFORMATION

Born in St. Louis, Missouri, in 1851, Chopin was the daughter of a prominent businessman and his wife. Her father died when Chopin was four years old, and her childhood was profoundly influenced by her mother, grandmother, and great-grandmother, women descended from French Creole pioneers. Chopin also spent time with her family's Creole and mulatto slaves, whose dialects she mastered, and she read the works of Walter Scott, Edmund Spenser, and other writers who were not represented among the encyclopedias and religious books in the family library. Despite her bookish nature, Chopin was an undistinguished student at the convent school she attended. She graduated at age seventeen and spent two years as a belle of fashionable St. Louis society. In 1870 she married a wealthy Creole cotton magnate, Oscar Chopin, and moved with him to New Orleans. For the next decade, Chopin pursued the demanding social and domestic schedule of a wealthy New Orleans wife, the recollection of which would serve as material for *The Awakening.* By 1880, however, financial difficulties made it necessary for Chopin's steadily growing family to move to Cloutierville in Natchitoches Parish, located in Louisiana's Red River bayou region. There Chopin's husband managed the family plantations until his death in 1883. Afterward Chopin insisted on assuming her husband's managerial responsibilities, which brought her into contact with almost every aspect of the family business and every segment of the

community. She was particularly intrigued by the French Acadian, Creole, and mulatto sharecroppers who worked the plantations. The impressions she gathered of these people and of Natchitoches Parish life were later reflected in her fiction.

In the mid-1880s Chopin sold most of her property and left Louisiana to live with her mother in St. Louis. Family friends, who had found her letters entertaining, encouraged Chopin to write professionally, and she soon began writing short stories. These early works show the influence of her favorite authors, especially the French writers Guy de Maupassant, Alphonse Daudet, and Molière. At this time Chopin also read the works of Charles Darwin, Thomas Huxley, and Herbert Spencer in order to keep abreast of trends in scientific thinking, and she began questioning the benefits of certain mores and ethical constraints imposed by society on human nature. After an apprenticeship marked by routine rejections, she published the novel *At Fault* in 1890. This work displayed many of the shortcomings of a first novel and failed to interest readers. Chopin had also begun to publish short stories in the most popular

American periodicals. With the publication of the collections *Bayou Folk* (1894) and *A Night in Acadie* (1897), her growing reputation as a skillful local colorist was established. In 1899 Chopin completed her ambitious novel *The Awakening,* which was received with hostility by critics despite general acknowledgment of Chopin's mature writing skills. Chopin's reputation as a writer was severely damaged by the negative reception of *The Awakening;* she had difficulties finding publishers for her later works and was ousted from local literary groups. Demoralized, she wrote little during the rest of her life. She died of a cerebral hemorrhage in 1904.

MAJOR WORKS

The short stories collected in *Bayou Folk* and *A Night in Acadie* established Chopin as an important writer of local-color fiction. Set primarily near Natchitoches Parish, these tales of Creole and Cajun life are noted for meticulous descriptions of setting, precise dialect, and an objective point of view. Although they sometimes have a slick quality, the stories in *Bayou Folk* and *A Night in Acadie* attempt honest examinations of sexuality, repression, freedom, and responsibility—themes Chopin was to explore more fully in *The Awakening.*

The Awakening is considered Chopin's best work as well as a remarkable novel to have been written during the morally uncompromising era of 1890s America. Psychologically realistic, *The Awakening* is the story of Edna Pontellier, a conventional wife and mother who experiences a spiritual epiphany and an awakened sense of independence that change her life. The theme of sexual freedom and the consequences women must face to attain it is supported by sensual imagery that acquires symbolic meaning as the story progresses. This symbolism emphasizes the conflict within Pontellier, who realizes that she can neither exercise her newfound sense of independence nor return to life as it was before her "awakening." For example, the sexual candor of the Creole community on Grand Isle, the novel's setting, is contrasted with the conventional moral strictures of New Orleans; birds in gilded cages and free-flying birds are juxtaposed; and the protagonist selects for her confidantes both the domesticated, devoted Adele Ratignolle and the passionate Madame Reisz, a lonely and unattractive pianist. The central symbol of the novel, the sea, also provides the framework for the main action. As a symbol, the sea embodies multiple pairs of polarities, the most prominent being that it is the site of both Edna Pontellier's awakening and of her suicide at the end of the narrative.

CRITICAL RECEPTION

After the initial furor over *The Awakening* had passed, the novel was largely ignored until the 1930s, when Daniel S. Rankin published a study of Chopin's works that included a highly favorable assessment of the book. During the succeeding decades, critical debate surrounding *The Awakening* has focused on Chopin's view of women's roles in society, the significance of the main character's awakening and her subsequent suicide, and the possibility of parallels between the lives of Chopin and her protagonist. George Arms, for instance, has contended that Chopin was a happily married woman and devoted mother whose emotional life bore no resemblance to that of Edna Pontellier, while Chopin's principal biographer, Per Seyersted, has noted her secretive, individualistic nature and her evident enjoyment of living alone as an independent writer. Priscilla Allen has posited that male critics allow their preconceptions about "good" and "bad" women to influence their interpretations of Chopin's novel, arguing that they too often assume that Edna Pontellier's first priority should have been to her family and not to herself. Like Allen, Seyersted brings a feminist interpretation to *The Awakening* and points out that the increasing depiction of passionate, independent women in Chopin's other fiction supports the theory that she was in fact concerned about the incompatibility of motherhood and career for women living during the late nineteenth century.

Once considered a minor author of local-color fiction, Chopin is today recognized for her examination of sexuality, individual freedom, and the consequences of one's actions—themes and concerns important to many later American writers. While her psychological examinations of female protagonists have made *The Awakening* and several of Chopin's stories seminal works in the development of feminist literature, her writings also provide a broad examination of societies that stifle self-expression, illustrating, as Peggy Skaggs has observed, that "having a secure place . . . is not enough in life; that one's sexual nature is a powerful part of the self, whether feminine or masculine."

PRINCIPAL WORKS

CRITICISM

Emily Toth (essay date fall-winter 1976)

SOURCE: Toth, Emily. "Kate Chopin's *The Awakening* as Feminist Criticism." *Southern Studies* 2, nos. 3-4 (fall-winter 1991): 231-41.

[*In the following essay, originally published in 1976, Toth argues that* The Awakening *belongs to the didactic feminist tradition of women's literature.*]

The title of this essay is bound to annoy some readers. *The Awakening*'s not about "Women's Lib," they may argue. It's a skillfully written novel, not a tract. It's a work of art, not a polemic. Or—as some critics have claimed—it's not really about women at all, but about the universal, existential human condition, loneliness and alienation.[1]

But Edna Pontellier is a woman, and what happens to her would not have happened to a man. *The Awakening* is a story of what happens when a woman does not accept her place in the home. The novel moves us because it illustrates the need for women's psychological, physical, social, and sexual emancipation—the goals of feminists in the twentieth century as well as the nineteenth. In its picture of the particular limitations placed upon women, the novel belongs to the tradition of feminist criticism a century ago, a tradition which embraces both fiction and social commentary. It is a tradition which literary historians still generally ignore.

What I call feminist criticism, or the criticism of women's limited roles, is not new to the nineteenth century. In the fourteenth century, Christine de Pisan wrote *Le Duc des Vrais Amants* to attack the double standard in love and sex, as embodied in the system of courtly love. In the seventeenth century Anne Bradstreet, the first American poet, complained in the *Prologue to the Tenth Muse* that her contemporaries failed to take her seriously because of her sex. Nor were other women poets, unknown today, silent about prejudices against them and women in general.[2]

A more systematic criticism of women's role in society begins in 1791, the year Mary Wollstonecraft wrote *A Vindication of the Rights of Woman*. She argued that women's weaknesses stem from deprivation: lack of experience and education, repression of individual talents. Wollstonecraft's work inaugurated more than a century of ferment over what was termed "the Woman Question."

Countless other critical works followed, especially in the latter part of the nineteenth century. Some of the more influential include Margaret Fuller's *Woman in the Nineteenth Century* (American, 1844), John Stuart Mill's *On the Subjection of Women* (English, 1869), August Bebel's *Die Frau und der Sozialismus* (German, 1883), and Charlotte Perkins Gilman's *Women and Economics* (American, 1898).

All these feminist critiques are compendia, covering the situation of women in the physical, psychological, sociological, and economic spheres. All support greater independence for women. Wollstonecraft and Fuller are the most idealistic and utopian; Mill is a liberal who stops short of such radical changes as easy divorce and the entry of large numbers of women into "male" professions. Bebel and Gilman are materialists, socialists who see change in the "sexuo-economic relation" (Gilman's phrase) as essential to any other changes on women's condition. Only Bebel gives more than cursory attention to poor and working-class women. Yet the similarities among these critics are far more evident than their differences.

What unites these books is a concern for women's escape from confinement, in all spheres of her life. And escape from confinement is the overriding theme of *The Awakening*, a book which demonstrates Kate Chopin's close connections with the ideas of feminist social critics. While there is no proof that she read feminist social commentaries, she did read wisely, in several languages. Moreover, the ideas expressed by feminist critics were part of the cultural milieu of her day, part of the Woman Question. Even if she had not embraced feminist ideas, she could not be untouched by them.

In *The Awakening*, Kate Chopin transforms the insights of feminist critics into fiction. Her translation involves a movement from the abstract to the concrete. Instead of an idea, she presents a character; instead of a generalization, she makes a case study. In a number of ways, Edna Pontellier is the embodiment of nineteenth-century feminist criticism. In *The Awakening*, Kate Chopin uses directly the ideas of Gilman, Mill, and Bebel, and makes of *The Awakening* both a synthesis and crowning achievement of feminist consciousness at the turn of the century.

Edna Pontellier of *The Awakening* is twenty-eight years old and married to a New Orleans businessman twelve years her senior. During a summer at Grand Isle, she has a sensuous awakening. The sea, sand, and sky provide a seductive background; the Creoles, especially the mother-woman Adèle Ratignolle, encourage her to overcome her reserved Kentucky Presbyterian ways. Edna begins to examine her place in the universe.

She learns to swim, and she becomes attracted to Robert Lebrun, a young man (26) who flirts with her in the Creole fashion. She becomes more and more discontented with her role as wife and mother of two young sons. Sensing that their growing psychological intimacy is dangerous, Robert leaves immediately for Mexico, ostensibly on business. Soon afterwards, the Pontelliers return to New Orleans for the winter.

Edna continues to question her purpose in life. She becomes friendly with the disagreeable pianist, Mademoiselle Reisz, who is close to Robert and shares his letters with Edna. She begins to paint, and drops her social obligations. While her husband is away on a business trip, she moves out of his house into a small home of her own. And her awakened sensuality leads her to begin an affair with a roue, Alćee Arobin. She feels no shame, no remorse: only a greater intensity of passionate desire than she had ever felt before.

Robert returns from Mexico. Although he tries to avoid seeing Edna, they meet twice by chance. He confesses his love for her, but seems shocked at her independent behavior. Her sensual responsiveness seems to surprise him: she touches and kisses him before he makes any move toward her. Her announcement that she is not her husband's property, but gives herself as she chooses, seems to frighten Robert. Then Edna is suddenly called away to assist Adèle Ratignolle, who is about to give birth to her fourth child. The conventional word used for giving birth has a particular irony: it is Adèle's "confinement."

When Edna returns, after witnessing a scene of "torture" that caused in her an inward revolt against woman's lot, she finds only a parting note from Robert: "Good-by—because I love you."[3] Edna does not sleep that night. Confronting her destiny, she refuses to sacrifice her "self." She realizes that Arobin and Robert are both meaningless to her, and the children (who are supposed to give significance to a woman's life) are antagonists she must elude, to avoid "the soul's slavery" (999).

She returns to Grand Isle, the site of her mental and physical awakening. Shedding all her clothes on the beach, she swims until her strength is gone and death overtakes her.

Kate Chopin's critics found the novel immoral and condemned the book and its author, primarily for her expression of female sexuality. Very hurt by the book's reception, Chopin wrote only a few more stories before her early death in 1904, at the age of 53. Apart from the sexual awakening, however, she was not expressing uncommon thoughts, for the theme of confinement was treated thoroughly by feminist critics.

Confinement is both a process and a state, and it begins very early in a girl's life. Charlotte Perkins Gilman describes the process in *Women and Economics*.

> Each woman born . . . has had to live over again in her own person the same process of restriction, repression, denial; the smothering 'no' which crushed down all human desires to create, to discover, to learn, to express, to advance. Each woman has had, on the other hand, the same single avenue of expression and attainment; the same one way in which alone she might do what she could, get what she might. All other doors were shut, and this one always open; and the whole pressure of advancing humanity was upon her."[4]

Writing a year or two before *The Awakening*, Gilman describes through a general social commentary the process of confinement Edna underwent as a child. The only visual image we have of Edna's childhood is a description she gives Adèle Ratignolle of

> . . . a summer day in Kentucky, of a meadow that seemed as big as the ocean to the very little girl walking through the grass, which was higher than her waist. She threw out her arms as if swimming when she walked, beating the tall grass as one strikes out in the water.

(896)

In Edna's description of herself as a young girl, the child is active, in control of her body. She strikes out at her environment; it does not mold her. She is outdoors, not confined in the home. The analogy to the ocean and swimming suggests no restrictions—and anticipates Edna's emancipation and death.

Where was Edna going then? Adèle asks. Edna does not recall, and adds, "My sun-bonnet obstructed the view." (896) It should be noted that bonnets, parasols and gloves are very much a part of a lady's apparel in *The Awakening,* for fair skin is part of the bourgeois ideal of beauty. These accessories protect her from the sun, but also insulate her from a life of the senses. Edna's freeing herself from her role is paralleled in clothing. Our first view of her is a view of an advancing parasol, seen by her husband. As she reconsiders her life, she finds herself "daily casting aside the fictitious self which we assume like a garment with which to appear before the world" (939). At the end of the novel Edna has cast aside all confinements, all garments, and stands naked at the sea. During her final swim she recalls "the blue-grass meadow that she traversed when a little child, believing that it had no beginning and no end." (1000).

In Edna's answer to Adèle, the sunbonnet may be read as a sign that Edna was undergoing the process of confinement required for a young girl. The bonnet restricts her ability to discover, to advance. Both literally and symbolically, she cannot see where she is going.

She tells Adèle that "I could see only the stretch of green before me, and I felt as if I must walk on forever, without coming to the end of it. I don't remember whether I was frightened or pleased" (896). She confides to Adèle that "sometimes I feel this summer as if I were walking through the green meadow again; idly, aimlessly, unthinking and unguided" (897). Edna seems to prefer the freedom of the child, before the process of confinement begins in earnest, before all doors but one are closed. Yet she recognizes that one may be "frightened" by freedom.

Gilman's "same single avenue"—a clearly-defined, restricted space—contrasts sharply with Edna's "stretch of green," or unlimited territory. Both are metaphors for a condition in life: a state of confinement or a freedom to choose.

In the past, Edna soon learned that "All other doors were shut" (in Gilman's words) except the door to "the same single avenue of expression and attainment." As an adolescent, Edna was infatuated with a cavalry officer, with the fiance' of another young woman, and with a great tragedian. All of these were hopeless from the start; yet they reveal that by her adolescent years Edna could no longer see her fate as an unlimited meadow. Instead, her future would be embodied in a man. Her only choice, her only avenue, would be her choice of that man.

Edna learned as a young woman to say to herself what Gilman calls "the smothering 'no.'" Society (or Gilman's "pressure of advancing humanity") begins the process of conditioning, but then each woman lives "over again in her own person" her confinement. Edna keeps to herself her inward disturbances, and expects to lead the dual life, "that outward existence which conforms, the inward life which questions" (893). She completes for herself the process of "restriction, repression, denial" begun by society: giving up her dreams, she accepts the "single avenue."

When she marries Léonce Pontellier, she does not love him, but "his absolute devotion flattered her" (898). Yet her marriage is a form of rebellion, a last attempt at evading the "smothering 'no'"—for her father and her sister Margaret, her surrogate mother, feel "violent opposition" to her marriage with a Catholic (898). Edna's choice seems to be an attempt to widen her avenue.

After her wedding, however, Edna expects to be a dignified matron, "closing the portals forever behind her upon the realm of romance and dreams" (898). "Portals" is simply a more romantic term to show that, as Gilman states, "All other doors were shut, and this one always open." The door as an image of enclosure is conventional, virtually a dead metaphor; but it is noteworthy that it appears in both Gilman and Chopin to allude to the same critical choice in a young woman's life.

Edna's illusions do not die. They merely go underground, to surface again with her attraction to another man, Robert. In modern terminology, Edna has not been completely conditioned to the female role. In Kate Chopin's imagery, Edna prefers the ocean of green grass.

Gilman's picture of the *process* of confinement is the most telling among nineteenth-century feminist critics. But John Stuart Mill gives the best portrayal of the *state* of confinement experienced by the bourgeois woman, especially the wife.[5] Several key passages in *On the Subjection of Women* anticipate *The Awakening.* Mill argues, as does Chopin, that women need to free their bodies from physical limitations and to liberate their energies from confinement to domestic duties.

Mill is aware of the relationship between mind and body, and between social customs and behavior. He answers the complaint that women are too changeable and uncertain to be suited for anything but domestic life by arguing that

> Much of all this is the mere overflow of nervous energy run to waste, and would cease when the energy was directed to a definite end. Much is also the result of conscious or unconscious cultivation; as we see by the almost total disappearance of 'hysteria' and fainting-

fits, since they have gone out of fashion. Moreover, when people are brought up, like many women of higher classes . . . a kind of hot-house plants, shielded from the wholesome vicissitudes of air and temperature, and untrained in any of the occupations and exercises which give stimulus and development to the circulatory and muscular system . . . it is no wonder if those of them who do not die of consumption, grow up . . . without stamina to support any task, physical or mental, requiring continuity of effort. But women brought up to work for their livelihood show none of these morbid characteristics. . . . Women who in their early years have shared in the healthy physical education and bodily freedom of their brothers, and who obtain a sufficiency of pure air and exercise in after-life, very rarely have any excessive susceptibility of nerves which can disqualify them for active pursuits.[6]

Mill argues, then, that physical exercise is essential to mental well-being; that work cures nervous susceptibility and inability to concentrate; that much of women's weakness is traceable to customs of the day. All three of these points are illustrated in *The Awakening,* through the three main female characters: Edna, Mademoiselle Reisz, and Madame Ratignolle.

Throughout much of the novel, Edna is characterized by a kind of lassitude, a torpor: she spends an inordinate amount of time sleeping or eating[7]; she abandons herself, as she tells Adèle, as if she were still the child in the unlimited meadow. All summer she has tried and failed to learn to swim. But one night in the moonlight she succeeds. She gains an outlet for her energies.

> "She was like the little tottering, stumbling, clutching child, who all of a sudden realizes its powers, and walks for the first time alone. . . . She could have shouted for joy. . . .

"A feeling of exultation overtook her, as if some power of significant import had been given her to control the working of her body and soul. She grew daring and reckless, overestimating her strength. . . ." She swims out toward the sea, and "As she swam she seemed to be reaching out for the unlimited in which to lose herself" (908).

The language is the antithesis of confinement: "powers," "control," "daring," "reckless," "overestimating," "unlimited." As she exults in pushing her body to its limits, Edna senses a liberation of both body and soul. This is her first awakening in the book, the first answer to her questions about her place in the universe.[8] The freedom of her body enlarges her vision of herself.

The physical exercise and the life outdoors awaken her sensuality: her pleasure in her own body is one of the forces impelling her toward the affair with Alcée Arobin. She no longer accepts woman's "crushing 'no'"; instead she seeks an intensity of experience. Her growing desire for physical independence leads her to move from her husband's house, which stands for a confinement of her body. Her learning to swim is indeed like a baby's first step. In the last scene in the novel, she is naked and feels "like some new-born creature" (1000).

Mademoiselle Reisz and Madame Ratignolle are counterparts to Edna, representing two different directions in which the newly-awakened Edna might use her energies. Mademoiselle Reisz has overcome the limitations of the female role through meaningful work, illustrating Mill's point that directing one's energies to a definite end cures any "nervous susceptibilities." She is an unpleasant and assertive little woman, no longer young, lacking any feminine tentativeness of manner. Her independent status gives her strength and the right to her eccentricities: although she is both ugly and outspoken, her splendid piano-playing entrances Edna. Later Mademoiselle Reisz talks with Edna abut the need for "the soul that dares and defies" (946). Edna thinks about her own painting as a possible way of defining herself through work—but she lacks the commitment to be that courageous soul.

Madame Ratignolle illustrates Mill's third point, that much of women's weakness is traceable to the customs of the day. Adèle is the complete "mother-woman," the antithesis of Mademoiselle Reisz in her joyful absorption in others: her husband, her three young children. Voluptuously beautiful, golden-blonde, she is a madonna fluttering with protective wings about her children. She is constantly concerned with her "condition," her latest pregnancy. She uses is as an occasion to be a coquette.

Although she is in robust health, she prefers to lean on a man's arm when she walks. She lets everyone know that the doctor forbade her "to lift so much as a pin!" (892). In one scene she complains of faintness. Edna bathes her face with cologne; Robert fans her; and the narrator reports that "The spell was soon over, and Mrs. Pontellier could not help wondering if there were not a little imagination responsible for its origin, for the rose tint had never faded from her friend's face" (892).

Edna's thoughts are traitorous, but they are also John Stuart Mill's. Mary Wollstonecraft, too, was aware of the effect that fashions in female behavior had on women's apparent health. She writes in *A Vindication of the Rights of Women* that a wife might even "condescend to use and feign a sickly delicacy in order to secure her husband's affection."[9]

Mill and Chopin portray fainting as a feminine wile in a more sympathetic way. To Mill, it is a result of society's definition of women as weak creatures; to Chopin, it is the manifestation of Adèle's good-natured and total acceptance of what is expected from women. In both writers, women's weakness is a result of conformity; women's strength, a result of struggle against confinement. Madame Ratignolle absorbs the female role; Mademoiselle Reisz transcends it; Edna is trapped between the extremes incarnated in her two friends.

Edna ultimately believes herself incapable of escaping woman's state of confinement. Escaping through a man

would simply be choosing the same avenue: "Today it is Arobin, tomorrow it will be some one else" (999). Neither the liberation of the soul through painting nor the liberation of the body through sensuality is enough: she lacks that "continuity of effort" which Mill finds lacking in most "women of the higher classes." Her vagueness, her dreamy purposelessness illustrate his description of bourgeois woman's untrained, hot-house existence. Edna Pontellier is the concrete embodiment of Mill's ideas.

These examples from Gilman and Mill should suggest some connections that can be drawn between the feminist analysis in nineteenth-century social criticism and that found in fiction of the same era. Other significant parallels may be seen between *The Awakening* and works of feminist critics.

For instance, Mill's description of the married woman who is expected to "have her time and faculties always at the disposal of everybody," who "must always be at the beck and call of somebody, generally everybody" (211) anticipates Léonce Pontellier's demands for attention and the children's demands for bon-bons.

There is also a connection with Gilman's criticism of men and women who are "over-sexed": in her definition, too involved in the specialized tasks allotted to their gender. Both "mother-women," like Adèle Ratignolle, and businessmen immersed in their work, like Léonce Pontellier, are illustrations for her criticism.

Gilman was strongly opposed to gratification of sensual appetites, but not all feminist critics agreed with her. Some of the writers even excuse adultery in women, in a somewhat limited fashion. Mary Wollstonecraft, for instance, feels that given women's education toward pleasing men, women no longer young nor beautiful may find themselves with an unsatisfied need for "gallantry" and "conquests": hence, a desire for other men's approval and attention when those of their husbands are lacking (60-61, 137). But her discussion really centers around the need for male approval, not the need for sexual pleasure or variety.

Among the major feminist critics, only August Bebel, in *Die Frau und der Sozialismus,* provides an unambiguous and positive view of female adultery. He argues that a sexually-unfulfilled spouse has the right to seek satisfaction outside marriage, that nature should not be thwarted, and that sexual abstinence in women may lead not only to hysteria, but to insanity. He makes no strong distinctions between love and lust.[10] Nor does Edna Pontellier, although respectable women were supposed to embrace the one and shun the other. Bebel is hardly typical of even the most radical critics in the Victorian era, but his ideas suggest that Kate Chopin was not utterly alone in her thinking.

The connections between nineteenth-century feminist critics and such important writers of fiction as Kate Chopin, Charlotte Bronte and George Eliot have barely been touched. Literary criticism has too often confined itself to texts defined strictly as "literary," excluding social criticism from consideration. Students of social history have too often ignored fictional materials.

A work like *The Awakening* functions not only as a story, but also a critique. When we can see more clearly its place in nineteenth-century social criticism, we can understand more easily its impact on its original readers and its meaning for us as part of our widening knowledge of women's past. Because it expands our field of vision, *The Awakening* is the best kind of feminist criticism.

Notes

1. The argument that *The Awakening* is universal rather than female in application is almost a convention in Chopin criticism. Merrill Maguire Skaggs argues, for instance, that the novel is an expose' neither of the "new woman" nor of the Creoles, "but rather of any society in which the rights of one individual are automatically less than those of another." See *The Folk of Southern Fiction* (Athens: University of Georgia Press, 1972), p. 188. For similar arguments, see also John R. May, "Local Color in *The Awakening*," *Southern Review* 6 (Autumn 1970), pp. 1031-40; Michael D. Reed, "Social Convention and Passional Nature in Kate Chopin's *The Awakening*," paper given at the Modern Language Association convention, 1974.

2. Christine de Pisan, *The Book of the Duke of True Lovers,* trans. Alice Kemp-Welch (London, 1908); Anne Bradstreet, "The Prologue" in *The Women Poets in English: An Anthology,* ed. Ann Stanford (New York, 1972): 46-47. *The Women Poets in English* contains the works of numerous forgotten feminist critics, including Rachel Speght, Katherine Philips, Joan Philips, and Mary Lee, Lady Chudleigh.

3. Kate Chopin, *The Awakening* in *The Complete Works of Kate Chopin,* ed. Per Seyersted (Baton Rouge, 1969): 995, 997. Further references to this edition will be cited by page number in the text.

4. Charlotte Perkins Gilman, *Women and Economics* (New York, 1966): 70-71.

5. Although Mill wrote *On the Subjection of Women,* he explains in his autobiography that it was "enriched" by his daughter's ideas, and that "all that is most striking and profound belongs to my wife," Harriet Taylor Mill. Bebel also gives credit to his wife for helping him with his work. The women critics (Wollstonecraft, Gilman, Fuller) give no particular credit to men in their lives, presumably because they have lived what they are writing about.

On the Mills, see Alice Rossi, "Sentiment and Intellect" in *Essays on Sex Equality* by John Stuart Mill and Harriet Taylor Mill (Chicago, 1970), esp. p. 57. For Bebel's debt to his wife, see his *Aus Meinem Leben* (Stuttgart, 1910): 180.

6. *On the Subjection of Women,* in Rossi, 194. Other references to this edition will be cited by page number in the text.

7. Edna's sleeping and eating are analyzed in two recent articles. See Ruth Sullivan and Stewart Smith, "Narrative Stance in Kate Chopin's *The Awakening,*" *Studies in American Fiction* (September 1973): 62-75 and Cynthia Griffin Wolff, "Thanatos and Eros: Kate Chopin's *The Awakening,*" *American Quarterly* 25 (October 1973): 499-71.

8. Learning to swim is not, however, classified as an awakening in Otis B. Wheeler's "The Five Awakenings of Edna Pontellier," *Southern Review* 11 (January 1975): 118-128. Wheeler is more interested in awakenings which involve directly Edna's rejection of female social roles.

9. Mary Wollstonecraft, *A Vindication of the Rights of Women* (New York, 1967): 62. Other references to this edition will be cited by page number in the text.

10. August Bebel, *Die Frau und der Sozialismus* (Berlin, 1946): 132, 156, 158, 162.

Joyce Dyer (essay date winter 1981)

SOURCE: Dyer, Joyce. "Symbolic Setting in Kate Chopin's 'A Shameful Affair.'" *Southern Studies* 20, no. 4 (winter 1981): 447-52.

[*In the following essay, Dyer discusses the ways in which Chopin's use of setting in "A Shameful Affair" prefigures the symbolism of* The Awakening.]

"A Shameful Affair," written on June 5th and 9th of 1891, represents an exciting thematic prelude to *The Awakening.* In it Mildred Orme, for a moment in her life at least, trades volumes of Ibsen and Browning for the broad, brawny shoulders of Fred Evelyn, a farmhand. She suffers more from guilt than Edna Pontellier seems to. Nevertheless, she makes discoveries about her physical nature that are as overwhelming, forceful, and important as Edna's. She awakens eight years before Chopin's best-known heroine. She prepares the way.

"A Shameful Affair" anticipates *The Awakening*'s technique as well as theme. The story explores Mildred's desires symbolically. The setting—the lush Kraummer farm on the Iron Mountain—is as important to our understanding of Mildred Orme's awakening as the sea, the night, and the Grand Isle oaks are to our understanding of Edna Pontellier. The Kraummer farm, where Mildred Orme spends a summer, is indeed "no such farm as one reads about in humorous fiction."[1] Images of fertility—undulating wheat fields and streams of clear water full of fish—continually remind us of the force and insistency of Mildred's passion. In each of the story's three sections, Chopin juxtaposes or integrates lush descriptions of nature with scenes in which Mildred Orme discovers what James E. Rocks calls "the violent physical and mental effects of repressed desire."[2] **"A Shameful Affair,"** then, introduces us to a technique—the extensive and elaborate use of symbolic setting to describe the unconscious—that permits subtle exploration of Mildred's desires and later helps to make *The Awakening* one of the unique and vital novels of the nineteenth century.

Mildred Orme, as Chopin's mildly ironic attitude toward her suggests, knows far less about herself than she thinks she does. In the story's first sentence, the reader finds this twenty-year-old bronze-haired beauty sitting in the "snuggest" corner of the Kraummer's big front porch, content. Mildred Orme has chosen not to accompany the rest of her family to Narragansett, hoping to find time in this safe and restful ("snug") retreat to pursue "exalted lines of thought" (p. 133). She lounges in her "agreeable corner" (p. 131) reading Ibsen and Browning. Mildred believes that her reading and twenty years of experience have given her considerable wisdom. Already she has refused six offers of marriage and formed her philosophy: life is a tedious affair. Certain of her superior nature and intellect, Mildred views the farmhands as members of a different species: intellectually inferior, coarsely mannered, gracelessly inarticulate.

Mildred soon begins to recognize that she still has much to learn about her biology. Chopin's description of the Kraummer farm prepares us for this recognition. Early in section i, Chopin introduces symbols of natural growth and fertility, symbols that will help us understand the force that drives Mildred toward Fred Evelyn. Chopin's juxtaposition of the images with Mildred's own first sensations of desire suggests that the reproductive urge drives all life. In the second paragraph of the first section, Chopin writes:

> Here were swelling acres where the undulating wheat gleamed in the sun like a golden sea. For silver there was the Meramec—or, better, it was pure crystal, for here and there one might look clean through it down to where the pebbles lay like green and yellow gems. Along the river's edge trees were growing to the very water, and in it, sweeping it when they were willow.
>
> (p. 131)

The wheat is ripe. Here, observes Chopin, were "swelling acres." The grain is so thick that when it waves, the fields look sea-like. Trees are so abundant that they grow to the very edge of the water and beyond. Overgrown branches of willows scrape the surface of the river. The wheat is ready for harvest. The willows continue to grow and thrive, nourished plentifully by the Meramec's water.

Two paragraphs after this description, Mildred's previous contentment is violently disturbed by the presence of Fred Evelyn. Mildred feels strangely uneasy after an accidental meeting with this man. Although he detests Ibsen and Tolstoi ("he doesn't read 'in books'—says they are spectacles for the short-sighted to look at life through" [p. 135]), Mildred finds him overwhelmingly attractive. He is tanned from outdoor work, young, and strong. "He had nice blue eyes. His fair hair was dishevelled. His shoulders were broad and square and his limbs strong and clean. A not unpicturesque figure in the rough attire that bared his throat

to view and gave perfect freedom to his every motion" (p. 131). She decides she will honor him with a smile, but he never looks her way. Slighted, Mildred convinces Mrs. Kraummer to ask Fred to take her to church. Fred, however, has already made plans to go fishing and refuses. Mildred fails to understand why she is vexed by being snubbed by one so far below her, "a tramp, perhaps" (pp. 132-33). Nevertheless, she cannot ignore or forget Fred. The conditions are now exactly right for Mildred's awakening: "It was summer time; she was idle; she was piqued" (p. 132).

Chopin begins section ii with another description of the Kraummers' wheat. This time Mildred (who, like the wheat, is ripening) merges with the grain. On Sunday, the day after the first encounter with Fred, Mildred walks through the bending, heavy wheat toward the river. For a moment, Mildred and the grain coalesce, forming a single image reminiscent of J. G. Frazer's Corn Goddesses—Demeter and Persephone of Greece and the Corn-Mother and Corn-Maiden of northern Europe and North America: "High above her waist reached the yellow grain. Mildred's brown eyes filled with a reflected golden light as they caught the glint of it" (p. 133). Her eyes "reflect" the force of the wheat—the "golden light" that radiates from it. She even looks like a fertility goddess: "Her straw hat had slipped disreputably to one side, over the wavy bronze brown bang that half covered her forehead. Her cheeks were ripe with color that the sun had coaxed there; so were her lips" (p. 133).

The reader watches Mildred's passion unfold through the dramatic and symbolic fishing scene that follows in the same section. Mildred's impatience with the fish symbolically indicates her sexual impatience. Fred, who, like Hemingway's Nick Adams and Jake Barnes, has apparently gone fishing because he has found that "Eden without Eve is not only possible but preferable,"[3] is interrupted by Mildred as she emerges from the wheat, "holding tight to the book she had brought with her" (p. 133). Fred continues to fish after Mildred arrives, but his tireless patience with the fish annoys Mildred. She wonders how long, how many hours, he can sit still, waiting for a fish to bite his hook. Mildred wants to catch the fish to symbolically satisfy her sexual urge. Her need is urgent and immediate. She wants something to happen; she wants to change a situation that is beginning to "pall." She convinces Fred to let her hold the pole. As we might expect, a fish immediately clings to her hook, and Mildred is "seized with excitement upon seeing the line dragged deep in the water" (p. 134). Fred, not as sexually eager as Mildred, shouts, "Wait, wait! Not yet" (p. 134), but Mildred has her way.

Ironically, Fred Evelyn is now awakened by Mildred's excitement. As he grasps her pole to prevent her from drawing the fish, he starts violently "at finding himself so close to a bronze-brown tangle that almost swept his chin—to a hot cheek only a few inches away from his shoulder, to a pair of young, dark eyes that gleamed for an instant unconscious things into his own" (p. 134). Mildred's dark eyes still reflect the glint of the wheat and gleam "unconscious things" into Fred's own eyes, secrets long buried or never known. For a moment, both Fred and Mildred give way to the impulses they share with the wheat. Fred kisses Mildred; bewildered, "she did not know if it was ten times or only once" (p. 134). Then, suddenly, they separate and run from each other. Fred Evelyn disappears down the field path. Mildred, ashamed and confused, wonders if she should tell the Kraummers about the kiss that still burns her lips. She decides, as rationally as she can, to consider the situation calmly at a later time.

Chopin begins section iii by noting how confused Mildred is by her new physical turmoil. Because her previous sanity has been disturbed, Mildred begins to wonder if she is mad. Indeed, why should a kiss—something she thought she had long ago outgrown—be so delicious? "The sweet trouble of it banished sleep from her pillow" (p. 135), notes Chopin. The phrase "sweet trouble" well represents Mildred's state. Ambiguously, the forces that upset and confuse her bring both sweetness and trouble, both pleasure and shame. The "sweet trouble" continues to bother Mildred even after she discovers that Fred Evelyn is not a poor illiterate, but a member of her own social class who enjoys spending summers doing unconventional jobs.

It is appropriate that Mildred Orme and Fred Evelyn meet a final time amidst the wheat, for the wheat has consistently informed us that physical forces have led to Mildred's confusion and awakening. "In the gathering twilight she walked again through the wheat that was heavy and fragrant with dew" (p. 135), notes Chopin. Although Mildred never senses that the heavy, fragrant grain throbs with the same forces that pulsate within Mildred herself, she does sense that something she cannot stop is at work inside of her. As she sees Fred Evelyn approaching, Mildred knows that she cannot run away as a small child might. She must face her emotions. As Fred begins to apologize, to call himself "the most consummate hound that walks the earth" (p. 136), she urges him to remain quiet. She wants to forget what happened on the Meramec's bank. But Mildred Orme's final words let Fred and the reader understand that although she will try to repress the incident, Mildred will no longer foolishly think of herself as a woman who cannot be touched by passion. She promises to forgive him "Some day . . . some day—perhaps; when I shall have forgiven myself" (p. 136). Fred is puzzled by her words. Suddenly, a "quick wave came beating into his brown throat and staining it crimson, when he guessed what it might be" (p. 136). She had wanted that kiss more than anything in her life. And she knew it.

Why did Chopin decide in 1891 to let the Southern landscape give us information about Mildred Orme's unconscious? Why did she continue to use the technique in stories throughout the 1890s such as **"A Harbinger," "Caline," "Azélie," "La Belle Zoraïde," "At Chênière Caminada," "A Respectable Woman," "Vagabonds," "The Storm,"** and **"A Vocation and a Voice"**? Why did she rely on it so heavily in ***The Awakening***? Because

Chopin never discussed or tried to justify her use of symbolic settings (except indirectly, when she said that the excessive regional delight of James Whitcomb Riley, Mrs. Catherwood, and Lew Wallace for "native streams, trees, bushes and birds, the lovely country life about them" produced "too sentimental songs," not art ["The Western Association of Writers," p. 691]) we can only guess. Perhaps she sensed that it was artistically efficient. With it she could achieve the indirection and variety necessary to create "subtle, complex, true" portraits of men and women ("The Western Association of Writers," p. 691).

One may hypothesize that perhaps Chopin's use of terrain symbolic of the unconscious was dictated by the censoring instinct. The 1890s, a decade that chose James Whitcomb Riley as its favorite poet and Reverend Charles M. Sheldon's *In His Steps* as its best-selling novel, would not tolerate an explicit discussion of the subconscious. R. W. Gilder, *Century*'s editor and the decade's literary spokesman, for example, consistently forced Chopin to soften her realism with idealism and to "sweeten" her heroines. One might guess that Chopin may have discovered that by using symbolic settings she could explore "unacceptable" impulses in a form "acceptable" both to her publishers and to herself.

Perhaps Chopin also sensed that by using symbolic descriptions she would not alienate readers who demanded and praised local color regionalism. Readers who wanted to find verisimilitude in her fiction *could* find it. Many of Chopin's symbolic nature descriptions were so lovely and "realistic" that they superficially resembled the non-functional descriptions of Ruth McEnery Stuart about the splendors of Brake Island, of Alice French about the scenic autumn beauty in the Black River bottoms, and of Mary Noailles Murfree about the majesty of the Tennessee Mountains. She was careful to use native flowers, trees, and landscape. Chopin's stories DID satisfy the regional curiosity of readers of Edward King's *The Great South,* Charles Nordhoff's *The Cotton States in the Spring and Summer of 1875,* and the magazine articles of Charles Dudley Warner, Rebecca Harding Davis, and Lafcadio Hearn.

Or, perhaps Chopin chose the technique for some other reason. Maybe she recognized that the technique was one of self-effacement and protection. She could always answer her critics with the phrase, "Sex is in your mind." On the other hand, possibly Chopin, like Hawthorne, Poe, Emerson, Whitman, and Melville, actually felt that nature was practically sentient—or, at least, closely related to the mind and soul of man. Finally, maybe the technique was far less the result of conscious decisions than the above explanations suggest. Perhaps it was simply a part of her instinctive, personal style.

For whatever reason, Chopin found early in her career a technique that served her well. In ***The Awakening*** the Meramec becomes the Gulf of Mexico, the fields of wheat become orange groves, water oaks, and acres of camomile.

The symbolic power of the Grand Isle symbols increases: Edna's sea awakens both soul and body. Although the landscape in **"A Shameful Affair"** is neither as exotic nor as symbolically complex as the landscape in *The Awakening,* it is vitally important to her 1891 short story and to the development of her symbolic technique. Without the careful descriptions of the Kraummer farm, **"A Shameful Affair"** would be interesting, but not as subtle and artistically satisfying as it is in its present form. And *The Awakening*? Without such early experiments with symbolic descriptions, one wonders if Chopin's 1899 novel would have been the same.

Notes

1. *The Complete Works of Kate Chopin,* Per Seyersted, ed. (Baton Rouge, Louisiana, 1969), I: 131; hereafter cited parenthetically.

2. "Kate Chopin's Ironic Vision," *Revue de Louisiane* 1 (1972), 116.

3. Arthur Waldhorn, *A Reader's Guide to Ernest Hemingway* (New York, 1972), 107.

Joyce Coyne Dyer (essay date summer 1984)

SOURCE: Coyne Dyer, Joyce."A Note on Kate Chopin's 'The White Eagle.'" *Arizona Quarterly* 40, no. 2 (summer 1984): 189-92.

[*In the following essay, Dyer analyzes the symbolism in Chopin's little-known late story "The White Eagle."*]

Few critics discuss Chopin's fiction written after April 1899—the publication date of *The Awakening*—with any degree of seriousness. Kenneth Eble writes that her last stories "lack distinction."[1] Per Seyersted regrets the "tame," uncourageous nature of the bulk of her final manuscripts.[2] And Robert Arner observes, "Only a few of her final tales are worth serious discussion."[3] Certainly one aspect of Chopin's fiction that suffers in her late stories is her imagery. Unlike the metaphors in *The Awakening* (as well as in several excellent stories) that enhance and often expand theme and meaning, those in her final short stories most frequently function either to decorate a sentence or to provide a convenient backdrop.

In **"The Wood-Choppers"** (October 1901), for example, Chopin describes a storm very unlike the one in her masterful 1898 story (**"The Storm"**). It adds melodrama rather than psychological insight. The rain that pelts "upon the shingle roof"[4] and the mud that creeps up Léontine's ankles fail to become metaphors for the young girl's unconscious, as they do in stories such as **"The Storm"** and **"Vagabonds."** The driving rain only intensifies the pathos of Léontine's immediate predicament: since the local wood-chopper has not come to cut firewood, she must carry a stout heart and cut it herself, cut it so that her poor, white-haired, "feeble-looking and much bent" (p. 675) mother

might avoid a fatal chill. In the dashing rain, a rich man, Mr. Willet, conveniently appears to rescue both Léontine and her mother from their "downpour" of ill luck. And in **"Polly,"** a story that ends with the embarrassingly trite injunction "Polly, put the kettle on!" (Seyersted notes the irony that these were the final words Chopin gave to the public),[5] banal, superfluous images decorate her prose. For instance, Chopin comments that after Polly's sisters receive new books bought for the girls by Polly herself, they "hovered over the books like bees over a clover path in June" (p. 683). Such examples, unfortunately, are far too plentiful and easy to find in Chopin's work between November 1899 and 1903.

"The White Eagle," however, a story about a woman who develops an unusual relationship with a cast-iron bird, suggests that at least at one time after *The Awakening* Chopin was eager to explore the variety of symbolism that today makes *The Awakening* so remarkable. The white eagle that dominates Chopin's May 9, 1900, story is an image that recalls the symbolic ambiguity and density of Edna Pontellier's ocean.

The eagle is wonderfully ambiguous. In some ways it represents the past of the woman in the story, her youth and the dreams it once held. When the woman was a child, the eagle had sat on the lawn of her parents' estate and "sheltered . . . [her] unconscious summer dreams" (p. 671). After her parents died and her brothers and sisters parted, the girl took the white eagle and moved it to her new lodgings. It was the only remainder from her childhood that the girl had. "People," says Chopin, "wondered at the young woman's persistence in carting him about with her when she moved from place to place" (p. 672).

But the eagle also becomes a substitute for the lover the woman never has. "No mate came to seek her out" (p. 672), we learn, except the eagle. As she grows older, "she fancie[s] the white eagle blink[s] at her from his sombre corner on the floor, an effect produced by remnants of white paint that still stuck in his deep eye sockets" (p. 672). She seldom leaves her room, preferring to spend most of her time sewing at her machine and watching the eagle. But only death brings consummation and union. Just before her final breath, the woman has a vision: "The eagle had blinked and blinked, had left his corner and come and perched upon her, pecking at her bosom" (p. 672). After she dies, a relative decides to use the bird as the woman's tombstone marker. The woman and the bird are at last physically united.

The eagle, too, seems intended to remind us of the woman's static condition. Like the bird, the woman spreads her wings but never takes flight. She was young and vital once, but she never knew how to direct her energy. She never married, she never made friends, she never enjoyed her days. Like the cast-iron eagle, she is all frozen potential. Years of bending over her sewing machine in a stuffy room cause the woman to acquire the eventual posture of the bird. The eagle, sinking deeply into the woman's grave, "dipped forward as if about to take his flight. But he never does" (p. 673). Nor does the woman.

But this brief analysis does not exhaust the symbolic implications of the white eagle. The symbol defies quick translation. For example, there are suggestions of supernatural properties in Chopin's remark, "That was the last she knew of her white eagle in this life" (p. 672). Other times, the bird seems to possess some great, mysterious knowledge we can only guess at. It has a "venerable" head and wears "an expression which, in a human being, would have passed for wisdom" (p. 671). Also, Seyersted notes that the eagle appears to be the woman's "alter-ego."[6] Indeed, there seems adequate evidence for his observation: the woman begins, uncannily, to look and behave more and more like her grotesque companion ("Her hair began to grizzle. Her skin got dry and waxlike upon her face and hands"; "she uttered a shriek in the night" [p. 672]). Peter James Petersen chooses to call the story "reminiscent of Flaubert's '*Un coeur simple,*' in which a woman who is systematically deprived of human contact sublimates all her longings in her relationship to a parrot, which is stuffed after it dies."[7] Too, the eagle, a flesh eater, a bird of prey, might be thought of as Death's messenger, if not Death himself. His corner is "gloomy" and he waits patiently for the woman to grow old. And, one wonders, as he must about Melville's whale, why is the eagle white?

The sea in *The Awakening* and the strange bird in **"The White Eagle"** resist paraphrase. They invite speculation, encourage wholesome intellectual puzzlement, and remind the reader that very few characters and situations, in life and fiction, are as simple as they may first appear. But the images also produce some regret in Chopin devotees. They serve as evidence that if Chopin had lived longer, if she had received some slight encouragement from contemporary reviewers of her 1899 novel, she might have chosen to further develop the richly ambiguous symbol and, perhaps, to write fiction like, if not greater than, *The Awakening* and **"The White Eagle."**

Notes

1. Kenneth Eble, "A Forgotten Novel: Kate Chopin's *The Awakening,*" *Western Humanities Review,* 10 (1956), 261.

2. Per Seyersted, *Kate Chopin: A Critical Biography* (Baton Rouge: Louisiana State University Press, 1969), p. 182.

3. Robert Arner, "Music from a Farther Room: A Study of the Fiction of Kate Chopin," Diss. Pennsylvania State University 1970, p. 229.

4. *The Complete Works of Kate Chopin,* ed. Per Seyersted (Baton Rouge: Louisiana State University Press, 1969), II, 674; hereafter cited parenthetically.

5. Seyersted, p. 185.

6. Seyersted, p. 184.

7. Peter James Petersen, "The Fiction of Kate Chopin," Diss. The University of New Mexico 1972, p. 263.

Lawrence Thornton (essay date 1984)

SOURCE: Thornton, Lawrence. "*The Awakening*: A Political Romance." In *Unbodied Hope: Narcissism and the Modern Model,* pp. 63-80. Lewisburg: Bucknell University Press, 1984.

[*In the following essay, Thornton examines Edna Pontellier's growing awareness of politics in Creole society in* The Awakening.]

> The food of hope
> Is meditated action; robbed of this
> Her sole support, she languishes and dies.
>
> —Wordsworth, *The Excursion*

I

Anyone familiar with *The Awakening* knows that it echoes characters and events in *Madame Bovary,* but Chopin's indebtedness to Flaubert stops short of merely imitating the problems Flaubert imagined for his heroine. First of all, while Edna Pontellier and Emma Bovary are both narcissists, Edna becomes aware of political crises related to her position within Creole society that sharply distinguish her from Emma, who responds to French provincial society only as a mirror of her romantic fantasies. Secondly, Edna's existential crisis lasts much longer than Emma's short and brutal confrontation with reality. In addition to her political theme, Chopin carefully and almost leisurely explores the shocks to the romantic consciousness which were briefly glimpsed at the end of *Madame Bovary.*

The similarities and differences in aims become immediately apparent through a comparison of two important passages. Twelve pages into *The Awakening* we encounter the well-known evocation of the sea that becomes a central motif in the novel:

> The voice of the sea is seductive; never ceasing, whispering, clamoring, murmuring, inviting the soul to wander for a spell in abysses of solitude; to lose itself in mazes of inward contemplation.
>
> The voice of the sea speaks to the soul. The touch of the sea is sensuous, enfolding the body in its soft, close embrace.[1]

These sentences are reminiscent of the exchange of platitudes between Léon Dupuis and Emma Bovary which moves from shared clichés about reading to Léon's avowal of great passion for sunsets and the seashore:

> "Oh, I love the sea!" said Monsieur Léon.
>
> "And doesn't it seem to you," continued Madame Bovary, "that the mind travels more freely on this limitless expanse, of which the contemplation elevates the soul, gives ideas to the infinite, the ideal?"[2]

The sea symbolizes imagination in both passages, but there is a considerable difference between Emma's superficial response to received ideas, and Edna's romantic but serious exploration of her own soul. Emma's naïveté is nowhere more evident than in this confession to Léon that the sea is a catalyst to the "ideal" world of sentimental Romanticism. In *The Awakening,* however, the emphasis falls on the seductive, isolating effects of "inward contemplation." Whereas Flaubert is interested in exposing the dry rot of Romanticism, Chopin is concerned with a woman whose susceptibility to Romantic codes ultimately gives way to at least a partial understanding of the lie that animates her visions. Edna's knowledge of the deliquescent nature of Romantic ideals also informs her view of personal freedom, and thus takes her story in another direction from Emma's.

That direction leads to an irresolvable conflict between Edna's vision of herself as an independent woman and the social forces of Creole Louisiana near the end of the nineteenth century. Throughout *The Awakening,* Chopin shows how Edna is deceived both by her private vision and by the society she discovers during the summer on Grand Isle. The hopes she begins to entertain about a new life spring from a congeries of sentimental ideals galvanized by Robert Lebrun, a "blagueur" (p. 12) who devotes himself to a different woman each summer. Edna's friend, Adele Ratignolle, sees the danger Robert poses to someone as impressionable as Edna and asks him to "let Mrs. Pontellier alone" (p. 20), which he declines to do, even after Adele tells him that "she is not one of us; she is not like us. She might make the unfortunate blunder of taking you seriously" (p. 21). The deceptiveness Adele recognizes in Robert mirrors the deceptiveness of Creole society which seems to accord women greater latitude than it is willing to grant. That women could smoke cigarettes, listen to men tell risqué stories, and read French novels soon appears as only a veneer covering a solidly conventional society that titillated itself with flourishes of libertinism.[3] For, despite their apparent standing within the Creole world (a standing, it should be noted, gained solely through marriage), women are presented as an oppressed class. Edna's gradual understanding of her oppression becomes part of the conceptual framework of her overall rebellion, and so, along with my analysis of the consequences of Romantic Imagination, I want to show how Chopin shapes her materials through detailed social description and social interpretation.

Because of the social conventions that prescribe behavior in her world, Edna has nowhere to go, succumbing to the promises of Romanticism while living in a society that will not tolerate the terms she sets for her own freedom. Although she manages by sheer force of will to free herself from the oppressive marriage with Léonce, Edna does not experience freedom; instead, she finds herself trapped by her romantic visions and by what Léonce calls *les convenances.* If *The Awakening* were only another examination of narcissism and the romantic predictions of a bourgeois woman, it would simply repeat the material Flaubert renders in his great novel. Chopin is not Flaubert, but within the range of her talent she treats questions about Romanticism, narcissism, and women's independence that

are essentially political and thus considerably different from those raised in *Madame Bovary.* Moreover, we care about Edna Pontellier in ways that we cannot care about Emma Bovary because Edna's intimations of an autonomous life force us to consider the problems of freedom and oppression within society, while Emma's whole life revolves around sentimental fatuities. If Edna at times seems predictable and even tiresome, these characteristics are countered by Chopin's subtle rendering of the process of "inward contemplation" that leads Edna to an understanding of an insurmountable social dilemma which can only be escaped in death.

II

For roughly the first half of the novel Chopin subordinates the political implications of Edna's predicament to the solitude and tentative self-exploration that begins to occupy her heroine during the summer idyll on Grand Isle. In the opening scenes Edna's undefined sense of longing is symbolized by the voice of the sea, which encourages the soul "to lose itself in mazes of inward contemplation," so that the relationships between Edna's isolation, her Romantic sensibility, and the social significance of her situation do not emerge with any clarity until the guests at Madame Lebrun's establishment gather for an evening of entertainment. Even then, there is no specific statement to link the motifs together; what Chopin gives us instead is the motif of music, which indirectly leads to images of flight and escape. As Mademoiselle Reisz begins to play the piano, Edna recalls the pleasure she derives from listening to her friend Adele when she practices. One piece Adele plays Edna calls "Solitude": "When she heard it there came before her imagination the figure of a man standing beside a desolate rock on the seashore. He was naked. His attitude was one of hopeless resignation as he looked toward a distant bird winging its flight away from him" (pp. 26-27). The image of the bird does not assume its full significance as a unifying symbol for another sixty pages when Edna remembers a comment of Mademoiselle Reisz's as she and Alcée sit before the fire in the "pigeon house": "When I left today," she tells him, "she put her arms around me and felt my shoulder blades, to see if my wings were strong, she said. 'The bird that would soar above the level plain of tradition and prejudice must have strong winds. It is a sad spectacle to see the weaklings bruised, exhausted, fluttering back to earth'" (p. 82). As the reader knows, escape from the labyrinth of self or tradition demands a cunning Edna does not possess. This failure is made explicit on the final page of the novel when she returns to *Chênière Caminada:* "A bird with a broken wing was beating the air above, reeling fluttering, circling disabled down, down to the water" (p. 113). Trapped in romantic longings whose objects are always vague and shifting in her mind's eye, and in a culture whose codes of duty and responsibility make escape impossible for even the most reluctant of "mother-women" (p. 10), Edna's fate is clearly foreshadowed in the imagery of defeated flight Chopin weaves into *The Awakening.*

At this point, we need to ask why, in a novel that addresses a woman's fate in society, Chopin chose a male figure to symbolize her heroine's solitude. The reason stems from Chopin's having realized that, on an unconscious level, Edna can only imagine a man in a position suggesting freedom and escape. His failure represents Edna's projection of herself onto the imagined figure. This view is consonant with the rest of the novel where we see that only men are free to act as they like and to go where they want: Robert to Mexico, Léonce to New York, Alcée from bed to bed. Whether it is Grand Isle, *Chênière Caminada,* or New Orleans, men escape, women remain. The New Woman Edna feels emerging from her "fictitious self" (p. 57) demands the prerogatives of men, but in making these demands she can only be destroyed by overreaching in a society that has no place for her.

But there are other reasons beyond the fact that there was little hope for independent women in New Orleans at the turn of the century that must be considered in an account of Edna's failure. Simply put, she cannot see beyond the Romantic prison of imagination. To illustrate her myopia, Chopin introduces Mademoiselle Reisz, whose clarity of mind offers a striking contrast to the essentially abstract nature of Edna's quest. Through music she discovers a kindred spirit in Edna, whose vision of the naked man occurs shortly before the musician plays a Chopin impromptu that arouses Edna's passions and brings her to tears. "Mademoiselle Reisz perceived her agitation . . . She patted her . . . upon the shoulder as she said: 'You are the only one worth playing for. Those others? Bah!'" (p. 27). She realizes that for her young friend music is the correlative of passion just as it is for her, but once their relationship develops Mademoiselle Reisz discovers that Edna's sensitivity does not encompass the discipline or the clarity of vision requisite to either the artist or the rebel. This is made clear one afternoon when Edna explains that she is becoming an artist. The older woman responds harshly, saying that "you have pretensions, Madame," pointing out that "to succeed, the artist must possess the courageous soul . . . that dares and defies" (p. 63).

Mademoiselle Reisz is to Edna what Marlow and Stein are to Lord Jim: a romantic who has found a "way to be" that does not compromise her ideals. Like Marlow and Stein again, she functions as a mentor who recognizes Edna's potentiality for independence while understanding that her impressionable young friend must learn to see more clearly in order to achieve what she wants and avoid disaster.

Once they have begun to meet in New Orleans, the musician's misgivings about Edna's ability to find her way in a new Romantic world are expressed in another kind of music. Edna demands to see a letter Robert has written to Mademoiselle Reisz, hoping that she will find some mention of herself. That she is overwhelmed by Robert and misled by their relationship troubles the older woman, and her sense of impending disaster leads her to weave fragments of Wagner's *Liebestod* into the Chopin piece she has been playing. This double theme of Romantic life and death becomes part of the atmosphere of the city, floating "out upon the night, over the housetops, the crescent of the moon, losing itself in the silence of the upper air" (p. 64). Like Stein's great speech on the destructive element that presents the positive and negative aspects of Romanticism, Mademoiselle Reisz's music symbolizes the antithetical modes of Romance represented by Chopin and Wagner, and her evocation of Tristan and Isolde becomes an important part of *The Awakening*'s imagery of destruction.

Mademoiselle Reisz functions as the only example of a free, independent woman whose hardiness Edna must emulate if she is to succeed and soar above "tradition and prejudice." There is no question that the older woman provides Edna with a more viable model than Adele Ratignolle who is, after all, trapped without even knowing it. Mademoiselle Reisz's apartment becomes a refuge for Edna and the pianist comes closer than anyone else to making contact and supplying advice that could be helpful as Edna tries to find a place for her new self in the world. Nevertheless, her role in the novel is problematic, for she is an imperfect model whose positive qualities are balanced by abrasiveness and egocentrism. Chopin calls attention to the musician's idiosyncrasies when she introduces her into the story. Robert has gone to ask her to play for his mother's guests and finds her in one of the cottages: "She was dragging a chair in and out of her room, and at intervals objecting to the crying of a baby, which a nurse in the adjoining cottage was endeavoring to put to sleep. She was a disagreeable little woman, no longer young, who had quarreled with almost every one, owing to a temper which was self-assertive and a disposition to trample upon the rights of others" (p. 26). Later, at Edna's dinner party, "Mademoiselle had only disagreeable things to say of the symphony concerts, and insulting remarks to make of all the musicians of New Orleans, singly and collectively" (p. 87). While Edna instinctively rebels against the larger social dictates of Creole society, those social graces that express less overwhelming *convenances* are still important to her, so that her amusement at her friend's disdain of conventions does not mean that she intends to imitate her. More subtly, Mademoiselle Reisz fails as a model because at this point Edna's passions, unlike her friend's, cannot be sublimated to music, but need physical expression. Like all her friends, Mademoiselle Reisz is eventually left behind as Edna increasingly dissociates herself from society and moves further into the mazes of solitude.

The musical motif in *The Awakening* provides specific dramatic referents to Edna's emotional states, but her imaginative life belongs to the realm of fantasy. Following her swim in the Gulf, Edna wants to think about her double experience of freedom and the "vision of death" (p. 29) that came to her in the water. Robert suddenly appears and Edna finds herself explaining that she has been overwhelmed by powerful experiences she does not understand: "There must be spirits abroad tonight," she muses, half-seriously. Picking up the cue, Robert invents a Gulf spirit who has searched for "one mortal worthy to hold him company, worthy of being exalted for a few hours into the realms of the semi-celestials" (p. 30). Robert does not understand Edna's experiences, nor does he particularly care to; his interests are in the direction of establishing himself in Edna's imaginative life. Whether by intention or pure chance, his words do enter her consciousness so that the Gulf spirit becomes a symbolic presence for Edna on Grand Isle and later in New Orleans.

In fact, the next section of the novel is given over to an elaboration of the fantastic. In the course of exposing the structure of fiction devoted to the unreal, Tzvetan Todorov cites the following comment by Olga Riemann: "The hero (of a fantastic tale) continually and distinctly feels the contradiction between two worlds, that of the real and that of the fantastic, and is himself amazed by the extraordinary phenomena which surround him."[4] What Edna experiences during the next few days approximates this situation very closely, for Robert's invention of the Gulf spirit and Edna's vigil before the sea that night lead to an awareness of a "contradiction between two worlds," particularly when she wakes up the next morning:

> She slept but a few hours: They were troubled and feverish hours, disturbed with dreams that were intangible, that eluded her, leaving only an impression upon her half-awakened sense of something unattainable. The air was invigorating and steadied somewhat her faculties. However, she was not seeking refreshment or help from any source, either external or from within. She was blindly following whatever impulse moved her, as if she had placed herself in alien hands for direction, and freed her soul of responsibility.
>
> (P. 33)

Like a princess in a fairy-tale, Edna awakens to an enchanted world where the old rules of reality no longer seem valid.

The immediate result of her new perspective is to propose taking a boat trip to *Chênière Caminada* with Robert, and from the moment of their departure to the island the day contains experiences suggesting that reality had been altered. For example, as they sail toward the island, "Edna felt as if she were being borne away from some anchorage which held her fast, whose chains had been loosening— had snapped the night before when the mystic spirit was abroad, leaving her free to drift whithersoever she chose to set her sails" (p. 35). Soon after they reach the island Edna takes a nap. When she awakens, she tells Robert that "the whole island seems changed. A new race of beings must have sprung up. . . ." (p. 38). Later that afternoon she and Robert listen to one of Madame Antonie's stories about the Baratarian pirates. As she speaks, "Edna could hear the whispering voices of dead men and the clink of muffled gold" (p. 39). The fantasy continues during the return trip to Grand Isle, for Edna believes that "misty spirit forms were prowling in the shadows and among the reeds, and upon the water phantom ships [were] speeding to cover" (pp. 39-40). Edna recreates the atmosphere of these imaginary encounters at the dinner party she gives for her father when she tells the story "of a woman who paddled

away with her lover one night in a pirogue and never came back. They were lost amid the Baratarian Islands, and no one ever heard of them or found a trace of them from that day to this" (p. 70). It should be clear that the day Edna and Robert spend on *Chênière Caminada* is filled with examples of "extraordinary phenomena."

The fantastic is implied in Chopin's early evocation of the sea, just as it is in Edna's visions of the unbinding of chains, pirate ships, and the lovers who disappear somewhere in the Baratarian Islands, freed forever from the mundane world of responsibility. Taken together, these events establish the atmosphere of Edna's mind, the mood of her thought. In this regard, it is important to see that *The Awakening* does not force the reader "to hesitate between a natural and a supernatural explanation of the events described";[5] only Edna hesitates between the fanastic and the real. The reader becomes increasingly aware of the ironic presentation of events, as well as the distance opening between Edna and reality.

Edna cannot actualize the self that increasingly absorbs her attention because that imagined self has no substance. Even when she is most deeply immersed in her newly discovered world, none of her visions of her self, or of a future, achieve clarity. In this respect, there is a distinction between Edna and Emma Bovary that should be explored. Emma constructs extremely detailed imaginary worlds for herself and Léon, Rodolphe, and Largardy from the raw materials of sentimental literature, images of Parisian social life, and the drama that unfolds before her on the stage of the Rouen Opera House. But her world begins and ends in that matrix of images, which to her are "pictures of the world." While Robert, in the guise of demon lover, appears in several of Edna's visions, she does not create detailed alternatives to the dreary life she has shared with Léonce. The reason should be clear enough: Edna's awakening corresponds with the attentions she receives from Robert who reifies the "realms of romance" anesthetized by Léonce, but her ultimate desire is for freedom to do as she likes, not, like Emma's, to find the man of her dreams. Thus, the journey into the Baratarian Islands she imagines with a demon lover is less important than her perception that she is "free to drift whithersoever she chose to set her sails."

III

The motifs of music and fantasy that I have discussed so far shape *The Awakening*'s themes of marriage, sexuality, and liberation. For the moment, I want to consider these themes separately in the order I have just mentioned, since that order corresponds to the direction of Edna's growth. Later, I will discuss them as a synthesis, a single perspective on the conditions of Edna's life, and by extension, that of women in Creole society.

All of these themes are announced in the first scene of the novel. Edna and Robert have just returned from a walk on the beach when Léonce remarks on Edna's tan, looking at her as "at a valuable piece of personal property which has suffered some damage" (p. 4). At the same time, Edna surveys her hand "critically," remembers her rings given over to Léonce for safekeeping, and takes them back. The conflict between freedom and oppression, the problem of narcissism, and Edna's retreat from and return to the symbols of marriage are neatly set out in three sentences. But there is more here, for marriage already appears to be incompatible with Edna's solipsistic character. From this muted beginning, marriage becomes the great fact of the novel, inescapable and monolithic, repeatedly described as oppressive, the source of ennui, and the means by which women are brought to suffer the pain of childbirth, the "torture" of nature as Edna perceives it while watching over Adele Ratignolle's *accouchement.*

We encounter a complex manifestation of Edna's feelings about marriage later that night after Léonce has returned from billiards at Klein's Hotel. She and Léonce have had a disagreement about the care of the children and Edna begins to cry, overcome by vague feelings that cancel any memory of her husband's former "kindness": "An indescribable oppression, which seemed to generate in some unfamiliar part of her consciousness, filled her whole being with a vague anguish. It was like a shadow, like a mist passing across her soul's summer day. It was strange and unfamiliar; it was a mood" (p. 8). This unspecified malaise is an inseparable part of marriage, producing a mood like a "shadow" or a "mist," phenomena that can obscure the outline of things, perhaps even obscure the self. These images soon become part of *The Awakening*'s symbolic design, for by suggesting that marriage obscures the essential self, they establish quite early one of Chopin's central political concerns. They allow us to see how Edna is oppressed by the facts of marriage and by her temperament in much the same way that the scene at the Banneville grove, where the wind coaxes a murmuring sound from the trees, symbolized Emma's ennui and disillusionment over her marriage to Charles.

The suggestion of obscurity and isolation that emerges from Edna's reverie reappears when Chopin writes that, "Mrs. Pontellier was not a mother-woman . . . one who idolized their children, worshipped their husbands, and esteemed it a holy privilege to efface themselves as individuals and grow wings as ministering angels" (p. 10). Adele Ratignolle is the type of such selfless creatures: "There are no words to describe her save the old ones that have served so often to picture the bygone heroine of romance and the fair lady of our dreams" (p. 10). What does Chopin mean to suggest by saying that there are no words to describe such women? Primarily, I would argue, that this epitome of the "mother-woman" is an anachronism, even though the beaches at Grand Isle are covered with them and they exemplify society's vision of woman's function. By saying that there are only the old words to describe Adele, Chopin subtly links her to the received ideas of woman's role in society. The "mother-woman" is a fiction. The old words have created a woman who fulfills "our" expectation and these words, associated with ro-

mance and dream, have created the self-image in which women like Adele bask. The point is that the essential self of both kinds of women is obscured, first by the institution of marriage, which separates the inner from the outer self, and second by the myths of womanhood that equate effacement of self, even the abjuring of self, with ideal and natural behavior. Thus both the romantic woman and the woman who mirrors the romantic clichés of a society's myths are blighted by the very terms of marriage.

But one of the novel's most interesting themes becomes apparent when we realize that, despite her rebelliousness, the associations Edna brings to marriage as a young woman can never be fully escaped. This is the case despite Léonce's lack of anything like the vigor of her youthful romantic fantasies that culminated in her infatuation with a "great tragedian" whose picture she kept and sometimes kissed. In fact, her entrapment is partly the result of the blandness she experiences with Léonce:

> Her marriage to Léonce Pontellier was purely an accident, in this respect resembling many other marriages which masquerade as decrees of Fate. It was in the midst of her secret great passion that she met him. He fell in love, as men are in the habit of doing, and pressed his suit with an earnestness and an ardor which left nothing to be desired. He pleased her, his absolute devotion flattered her. She fancied there was a sympathy of thought and taste between them in which fantasy she was mistaken.
>
> (P. 19)

Edna then comes to see her marriage, with its initial vague resemblance to her adolescent longings, as a step into the "world of reality," the act of a mature woman who will leave behind forever the "realm of romance and dreams." It is not long before she finds herself forced to confront realities that are clearly antithetical to her modest expectations: "She grew fond of her husband, realizing with some unaccountable satisfaction that no trace of passion or excessive and fictitious warmth colored her affection, thereby threatening its dissolution" (pp. 19-20). So marriage for Edna devolves to fondness, and the absence of passionate emotion seems to guarantee stability.

The stultifying effects of the relationship with Léonce—the price Edna and all other wives pay for stability—are quickly developed. When she visits Adele in New Orleans, "the little glimpse of domestic harmony which had been offered her, gave her no regret, no longing. It was not a condition of life which fitted her, and she could see in it but an appalling and hopeless ennui" (p. 56). In response to Léonce's entreaties for her to attend her sister's wedding, she says that "a wedding is one of the most lamentable spectacles on earth" (p. 6). Later, her awareness of having become a possession increasingly grates on Edna's sense of her individuality, and she gives her opinion of men who treat her as an object near the end of the novel during a conversation with Robert. "You have been a very, very foolish boy," she says,

> wasting your time dreaming of impossible things when you speak of Mr. Pontellier setting me free! I am no longer one of Mr. Pontellier's possessions to dispose of

or not. I give myself where I choose. If he were to say, 'Here, Robert, take her and be happy, she is yours,' I should laugh at you both.

(Pp. 106-7)

Earlier, when Edna first began to express her independence by ignoring the custom of her Tuesday at homes, Léonce responded by saying, "I should think you'd understand by this time that people don't do such things; we've got to observe *les convenances*" (p. 51). Léonce's comment cuts to the heart of what Edna rebels against; for her, marriage has come to seem like only one more convention within the myriad social forms that have become oppressive to her. Although she feels that marriage is "not a condition of life which fitted her," that she is no longer a possession, the facts of her life argue against her interpretation of it. Margaret Culley stresses Edna's delight in her independence as an element of the novel's tragedy. Referring to her comment about no longer being a possession of any man's, Culley says that "we glimpse the ecstasy of the discovery of the power of the self and the refusal to abjure it."[6] But there is a considerable distance between what Edna says and does that makes Culley's assessment more optimistic than the situation warrants. Surely the "delight [Edna] takes in her solitary self"[7] measures the distance between her imagination and reality in a painfully ironic way. Regardless of what she thinks, the shadow cast on Edna's soul by the convention of marriage and society cannot be escaped. Her decision to take her own life acknowledges the impossibility of returning to marriage, or of finding satisfaction in her solitude. It is the logical culmination of despair engendered by the loss of stability and her awareness of never being able to find a substitute for it in her affair with Alcée, or anyone else.

IV

Edna is deceived by the promises of sex just as she is misled by the conventions of marriage, but even though she delights in the adulterous pleasures discovered with Alcée, *The Awakening* is not an erotic novel. Lazar Ziff sees the true significance of her sexuality when he writes that Edna "was an American woman, raised in the Protestant mistrust of the senses and in the detestation of sexual desire as the root of evil. As a result, the hidden act came for her to be equivalent to the hidden and true self, once her nature awakened in the open surroundings of Creole Louisiana."[8] Ziff's observation alludes to the "shadow" Jung characterized as "a moral problem that challenges the whole ego personality, for no one can become conscious of the shadow without considerable moral effort. To become conscious of it involves recognizing the dark aspects of the personality as present and real. This act is the essential condition for any kind of self-knowledge."[9] Ironically, Edna's discovery of the "dark aspects" of her "true self" leads to increased self-knowledge, which isolates her from human contact, rather than providing a means by which she could experience emotional and physical gratification.

Such reflexiveness is clearly illustrated in the affair with Arobin. Edna has agreed to go to the races with Alcée and

Mrs. Highcamp and later, when he takes her home, we are told that she "wanted something to happen—something, anything; she did not know what" (p. 75). Like Rodolphe when he first meets Emma, Alcée senses an easy conquest. All he has to do is fulfill her expectations:

> His manner invited easy confidence. . . . They laughed and talked; and before it was time to go he was telling her how different life might have been if he had known her years before. With ingenuous frankness he spoke of what a wicked, ill-disciplined boy he had been, and impulsively drew up his cuff to exhibit on his wrist the scar of a saber cut which he had received in a duel outside of Paris when he was nineteen.

(P. 76)

This apocryphal story of Alcée's past as a hero out of the pages of Dumas provides the opportunity for an even bolder gesture: "He stood close to her, and the effrontery of his eyes repelled the old, vanishing self in her, yet drew all her awakening sensuousness" (p. 76). Here Alcée's melodramatic persona appeals to Edna for the same reason she was drawn to the cavalry officer and the tragedian—he embodies the "realm of romance" left behind with her marriage and reawakened by Robert.

What follows is as inevitable as Rodolphe's success with Emma, for what Edna wants is an opportunity to express the "animalism" that "strove impatiently within her" (p. 78). A mutual seduction follows "the first kiss of her life to which her nature had really responded" (p. 83). However, despite this expression of freedom, which was clearly inevitable, when Arobin leaves later that night "there was an overwhelming feeling of irresponsibility. There was the shock of the unexpected and the unaccustomed." There was also something more important:

> Above all, there was understanding. She felt as if a mist had been lifted from her eyes, enabling her to look upon and comprehend the significance of life, that monster made up of beauty and brutality. But among the conflicting sensations which assailed her, there was neither shame nor remorse.

(P. 83)

The mist "lifted from her eyes" is the same mist Chopin refers to in the passage dealing with the "vague anguish" Edna discovers in marriage. What Edna understands here is that she has been liberated from the kind of life for which she is "not suited," from marriage and from the shadow marriage cast on her sexuality. At the same time, this scene reveals another important aspect of her character. Edna always greets each new experience hyperbolically and she is constantly duped by fresh promises. Her conviction that she can now "comprehend the significance of life" is only another example, since her understanding fades with the waning of her enthusiasm about her passional self. She has learned nothing that could help her escape from the solitude steadily encroaching on her inner life.

The affair with Alcée becomes part of an emerging pattern of longing and restlessness which recalls the shadows and mists of her earliest sense of oppression. At the farewell party she gives to her old life on Esplanade Street such unfocused yearning is obvious:

> . . . As she sat there amid her guests, she felt the old ennui overtaking her; the hopelessness which so often assailed her, which came upon her like an obsession, like something extraneous, independent of volition. It was something which announced itself; a chill breath that seemed to issue from some vast cavern wherein discords wailed. There came over her the acute longing which always summoned into her spiritual vision the presence of the beloved one, overpowering her at once with a sense of the unattainable.
>
> (P. 88)

The sense of ennui returns us to the bedroom of her cottage on Grand Isle where she wept without knowing why, and felt a "vague anguish" whose source was inexplicable. The only substantial difference between the passage above and Edna's earlier encounters with hopelessness is the vision of the "beloved one" who is obviously "unattainable." Clearly, her vision has been enlarged while the conditions of her life remain as they were on the night the novel opens.

Thus every detail in *The Awakening* contributes to a growing impression that Edna's beginning is her end. Ten pages into the novel, Chopin writes that "Mrs. Pontellier was beginning to realize her position in the universe as a human being, and to recognize her relations as an individual to the world within and about her" (pp. 14-15). Yet, a sentence later, in a paragraph introducing the first reference to the sensuous voice of the sea, the narrator warns that "The beginning of things, of a world especially, is necessarily vague, tangled, chaotic, and exceedingly disturbing. How few of us ever emerge from such beginnings! How many souls perish in the tumult!" The voice of the sea, as well as the Gulf spirit, hold out to Edna a promise that cannot be fulfilled. When the voice is heard once again on the last page it echoes the earlier promise of the sea, but concludes on the word "solitude," and the invitation to Edna's soul to "lose itself in mazes of inward contemplation" is replaced by the image of the "bird with the broken wing." Moreover, between these images of the sea framing the novel we see other motifs and themes also turning away from the promises they held out for Edna to their beginnings: the positive suggestiveness of Chopin's impromptu is transposed to Wagner's evocation of the dying Isolde; the fantastic worlds of *Chênière Caminada* and Grand Isle become the house on Esplanade Street; the sexual passion with Alcée deliquesces into loneliness; and the promise of Robert's attention on Grand Isle turns into his farewell letter.

It is Robert's letter that finally shatters Edna's illusions of escape. After sitting up all night thinking about it, her dilemma finally becomes clear:

> She had said over and over to herself: 'To-day it is Arobin; tomorrow it will be some one else. It makes no difference to me, it doesn't matter about Léonce Pon-

tellier—but Raoul and Etienne!'. . . . There was no human being whom she wanted near her except Robert; and she even realized that the day would come when he, too, and the thought of him would melt out of her existence, leaving her alone. The children appeared before her like antagonists who had overcome her; who had overpowered and sought to drag her into the soul's slavery for the rest of her days. But she knew a way to elude them.

> (P. 113)

Edna now understands that Alcée, Robert, and her own sexual awakening belong to a metaphor for the unattainable. Her life has no direction, her world no form, and the emptiness she has come to feel is Chopin's comment on the "realms of romance."

But this is not the end. Edna's void is suddenly filled with a vision of her children, which not only takes her back to her beginning, but also becomes the sign of her "soul's slavery." Regardless of her casual attention to them, and her attempts to break away from marriage, they have always been there. Once, Edna said to Adele Ratignolle that "I would give up the unessential; I would give my money, I would give my life for my children; but I wouldn't give myself" (p. 48). That was when their antagonism was veiled. During her vigil, Edna has come to realize that it is Raoul and Etienne, not Léonce, who bind her to the ennui of a life that does not fit her. And so it is a double vision Edna experiences; she understands the mendacity of her "spiritual vision" and also that the "soul's slavery" her children would drag her back to is too great a price to pay now that she has tasted freedom, however confusedly. The agony she feels has a moral basis because she realizes that continuing to live as she must in a world circumscribed by *les convenances* could only destroy her children, and that realization adds considerably to her stature.

Defeated by the lies of romance and the facts of *les convenances,* Edna's return to the seashore at *Chênière Caminada* is accompanied not by thoughts or Robert or Alcée, but by the overwhelming pressure of Léonce, Raoul, and Etienne. As she swims out to sea, her mind is filled with sounds from her youth, above all the clang of the cavalry officer's spurs. We are left, as Edna dies, to meditate on that sound with intimations of a world that vanished as she reached out to grasp it.

Chopin's novel is prophetic of concerns that Virginia Woolf, Dorothy Richardson, and other women novelists would explore in the next quarter-century; were it not for her blindness to alternatives at the end, her virtual isolation, Edna might have grown up to keep company with Mrs. Dalloway and Mrs. Ramsey, and to achieve a sense of identity similar to theirs. Though my argument in this book depends on (among other things) the persistence of a fictional critique of Romantic Idealism that extends well into our own time, it is important to see that Kate Chopin's treatment is idiosyncratic and focused on its debilitating effects not only on a single character but also on all women caught in the rigidities of a social system like that of Creole Louisiana. And this leads to an interesting irony that emerges from the conjunction of the two previous studies of female characters and the chapter that follows on *Lord Jim.* The "realms of romance" explored by Chopin and Flaubert are unquestionably destructive, and both novelists show that romance was the preeminent form of thought, the matrix of identity, available to women in the nineteenth century. Emma and Edna, because of their narcissism, are not free to choose another mode of thought, but it should be kept in mind that Jim and the other male characters at least have available to them other means of achieving identity or establishing personality. No novel considered here is so bleak as Chopin's in this regard, for she shows us that the illusions of romance were the dead end of identity for nineteenth-century women. As we will see in the next chapter, it is just the potential, the freedom to disabuse himself of similar illusions, that makes Conrad's Jim such a problematic case.

Notes

1. Kate Chopin, *The Awakening,* ed. Margaret Culley (New York: Norton, 1976), p. 15. Hereafter cited in the text.

2. Gustave Flaubert, *Madame Bovary,* ed. Paul de Man (New York: Norton, 1965), p. 58.

3. In *The American 1890's: Life and Times of a Lost Generation* (New York: Viking, 1966), Lazar Ziff makes the following comments about Creole society: "The community about which she wrote was one in which respectable women took wine with their dinner and brandy after, smoked `cigarettes, played Chopin sonatas, and listened to the men tell risqué stories. It was, in short, far more French than American. . . . [T]hese were for Mrs. Chopin the conditions of civility, and, since they were so French, a magazine public accustomed to accepting naughtiness from that quarter and taking pleasure in it on those terms raised no protest. But for Mrs. Chopin they were only outward signs of a culture that was hers and had its inner effects in the moral make-up of her characters" (p. 297). For a more general examination of the social contexts of fiction than I can explore in this space see Georg Lukács, *The Historical Novel* (London: Merlin Press, 1962), and Ian Watt, *The Rise of the Novel* (Berkeley, Calif.: University of California Press, 1965).

4. Tzvetan Todorov, *The Fantastic: A Structural Approach to a Literary Genre,* trans. Richard Howard (Cleveland, Ohio: The Press of the Case Western Reserve University, 1973), p. 26.

5. Todorov, p. 33.

6. Margaret Culley, "Edna Pontellier: 'A Solitary Soul,'" in *The Awakening,* p. 228.

7. Culley, p. 228.

8. Ziff, p. 304.

9. C. G. Jung, *Psyche and Symbol,* ed. Violet S. de Laszlo (New York: Doubleday Anchor Books, 1958), p. 7.

Joyce Coyne Dyer (essay date spring 1985)

SOURCE: Coyne Dyer, Joyce. "Techniques of Distancing in the Fiction of Kate Chopin." *Southern Studies* 24, no. 1 (spring 1985): 69-81.

[*In the following essay, Dyer discusses Chopin's technique of appealing to her readers' prejudices to openly discuss in her short stories topics that were normally considered taboo at the time.*]

Chopin often made the prejudice of her Southerners (Creoles and Acadians) the subject of her fiction. Madame Carambeau, for instance, "detested dogs, cats, organ-grinders, white servants and children's noises. She despised Americans, Germans and all people of a different faith from her own."[1] Prejudice often became not only Chopin's topic, but also, curiously, her technique. Chopin relied, almost cynically it seems, on the prejudices of her readership and critics to allow her to talk about female sexuality in a way that otherwise might have been considered offensive or "vulgar." Along with other important techniques we will examine, Chopin's probably quite conscious method of ascribing strong sexual desire—a trait we know she thought universal—to Indians, gypsies, madwomen, Negroes, and social outcasts provided her with comfortable distance from a message too powerful for her time. The uncivilized or insane could be expected to behave in course, wild, and "unnatural" ways; fringe members of society could be portrayed differently from people in the mainstream of a civilized community. What could a proper white Southern woman possibly have in common with a Naomi Mobry, a Zoraïde, or a Juanita?

In Chopin's earliest short story about female sexual desire, **"Mrs. Mobry's Reason"** (January 10, 1891), the author equates Naomi Mobry's lust with the final stages of her developing madness. Chopin carefully, symbolically, defines and describes the progressive stages of Naomi's growing insanity, distancing Naomi, step by step, from the region of "normal" emotions and desires. The story, which contains a strong hint of the situation in Ibsen's *Ghosts,*[2] proves a fine introduction to one technique of reticence, self-effacement, and subterfuge that would serve Chopin well throughout the 1890s.

Naomi Mobry, daughter of Editha Payne, a woman who knew about the inherited madness in her family and should, perhaps, never have married, never have borne children, is seen in an early section of **"Mrs. Mobry's Reason"** as an unusually sensitive young woman. While she talks with her supercilious twenty-two-year-old cousin Sigmund, Naomi subtly discloses her heightened sensitivity to the colors of nature. Shortly after Sigmund naively proposes that Naomi read more and take a course at the university to enable her "to define the quality in Chopin's music that charms [her]" (72), Naomi assures her cousin that she would rather romp through the hills than sit closeted in a stuffy room. Exhibiting what Sigmund calls "a veritable savage eye for pure color" (73), Naomi describes the fields and hills which she loves.

What color! Look, now, at the purple wrapping those hills away to the east. See the hundred shades of green spreading before us, with the new-plowed fields between making brown dashes and patches. And then the sky, so blue where it frames those white velvet clouds. They'll be red and gold this evening.

(73)

Naomi's preference for the hills, for the earth and nature, and her ecstatic sensitivity to color begin to hint at her sensuous nature. Curiously, Naomi chooses the "raw" colors, like the Impressionists Chopin referred to in her review "'Crumbling Idols' by Hamlin Garland" (undated). Even the color purple is alluded to by Chopin in her review, the very color Naomi admires: "[Garland] admits," she writes, "that he himself has discovered certain 'purple shadows' by looking at a stretch of sand, with his head turned top-side down!" (694) Though others may not, like Naomi and Garland, see the purple which wraps the hills or casts shadows on the sand, or admire the red and gold that accompany the evening, the Impressionistic vision is not thought to be insincere by Chopin. We might guess that the author was using Naomi's description, her choice of colors, to reveal a temperament unafraid of moral and social pressure, unafraid of what the truth might bring: a temperament not unlike that of the daring Impressionists Chopin discusses, "with their individualism; their abandonment of the traditional and conventional in the interest of 'truth'" (694). It was, after all, a temperament not unlike Chopin's own.

As Naomi proceeds to describe her unusual sensitivity to sound, we continue to sense her powerful, sensuous attraction to the earth and natural force. Her initial comment about the subject seems ordinary: "There's nothing that has the meaning for me in this world that sound has" (73). Musicians, singers, and conductors have all made similar remarks. However, as she continues to speak, we realize that it is not the sounds of instruments and human voices that obsess her. The sounds of the earth itself fascinate and haunt her. She hears symphonies played by the wind. She muses, "I wonder if anyone else has an ear so tuned and sharpened as I have, to detect the music, not of the spheres, but of the earth, the subtleties of major and minor chord that the wind strikes upon the tree branches" (73). She even lets Sigmund know that she can hear the rhythmical breathing of the earth. "Have you ever heard the earth breath, Sigmund?" (73), she asks. After she notes the amazement in Sigmund's eyes, she senses the peculiarity and strangeness of her question. In order to change the subject, she merrily challenges her cousin to a mock duel. The real, recognizable, "ordinary" sounds of "the clink and scrape of the slender steels" replace the remote, unnatural sounds Naomi has been describing. Both Sigmund and his cousin temporarily need to hear a familiar noise that returns them to the comfortable realm of safe experience.

Naomi's reactions to sun and heat in section iii also might be read as suspiciously sexual. Naomi's increasing madness, again, continues to serve as the deceptive guise that allows Chopin to record the shocking. Sigmund believes that he and Naomi are falling in love in a purely romantic sense. Indeed, he finds "nothing so good to look upon as Naomi's brown [eyes]" (76) as he and the girl boat along the Meramec. Though to an onshore observer they might look like the boy and girl in a conventional romance, Naomi does not find the scene or the experience as idyllic and refreshing as Sigmund does. The sun intensifies her longing for her cousin. Chopin notes that Naomi is bothered by the "hot and lurid" (76) sun, words that suggest both the flamelike glow of the sun itself and the violent passion Naomi feels. The two have to glide under the shade of willow trees to avoid the sun's penetrating rays. Sigmund was "filled with wonder at the sweet trouble which stirred [Naomi] when she caught his gaze and answered it" (76). As Chopin's symbolism has indicated, Naomi's trouble is hardly as "sweet" as Sigmund thinks. She grows irritated when Editha asks her what is the matter. "I'm sure I don't know, mamma," she sharply replies. "This heavy heat would make anyone's blood run a little sluggishly" (77). Naomi's sexual desire, symbolized by her response to sun and heat, further detaches her from normal things around her.

In section iv, Naomi's reactions to the sun become even more telling. Unlike Charles Farady's uncomplicated reaction to the sun in **"A Point at Issue!"** (August, 1889), Naomi's reaction defines intricate components of her mental breakdown—or, as we now might recognize, of her sexual development. In this section, Naomi's full sexual energy is released at the very moment Chopin ushers her into madness. "I went in the boat," she tells Sigmund after he locates her sitting by the river's edge, "and when I was out there in the middle of the stream—listen, Sigmund—the sun struck me upon the head, with something in its hand—no, no, not in his hand—And after that I didn't care, for I know everything now" (78). The sun's stroke has freed her to express her sexual fondness for Sigmund. She can now passionately kiss him and confess her desire. "Ah, Sigmund," she cries out, "this is just as I was dreaming it this morning when I awoke. Then I was angry because you were sleeping off there in your room like a senseless log, when I was awake and wanted you. And you slept on and never came to me" (78). But the sun's stroke has, simultaneously, finalized her madness. Naomi can no longer recognize the peculiarity of her statements as she once could when she told Sigmund about hearing the earth breath. "I know what the birds are saying up in the trees," she tells her cousin, "like Siegfried when he played upon his pipe under a tree, last winter in town. I can tell you everything that the fishes say in the water. They were talking under the boat when you called me—" (78).

But the knowledge of the sun, the knowledge of her passion, is too bright, too intense for Naomi's day. Even Sigmund, who for a moment moves his "wooden" arms that hang at his sides to embrace her, kisses her only once—"he sought no further kiss" (78). Naomi's insights are now too candid and her spirit too erotic for people such as Sigmund to understand, or even for Naomi herself to comprehend. As Susan Wolstenholme has noted, Naomi and Sigmund have reversed sex roles: "Naomi plays what would conventionally be the male role in the relationship by initiating activities and even making sexual advances."[3] The intensity and confusion of her vision, a vision as we see, closely connected to her discovery of "abnormal" sexual and sensuous craving, burns the very light out of her eyes. Naomi will never again be able to return to the world her cousin inhabits. In the final sequence of the story, we see Naomi sitting upon a lounge, playing like a little child with scraps of paper that she tears and places in rows upon the cushion beside her.

It is significant, as well, to look closely at the frame Chopin provides for Naomi Mobry's story. The piece begins and ends with scenes that focus on Editha Payne Mobry, Naomi's mother. Chopin uses her, as she does her daughter, to talk about passion in a permissible way. The mother confesses her crime to John Mobry at the story's end: "[Madness] has been in the blood that is mine for generations, John, and I knew it, and I married you" (79). With terror in her eyes, she continues, "Oh, God! if it might end with me and with her—my stricken dove! But, John . . . Edward has already a child. Others will be born to him, and I see the crime of my marriage reaching out to curse me through the lips of generations that will come" (79). Editha's crime, her sin, like Naomi's madness, is carefully associated with desire and lust; its consequence and Editha's remorse make its discussion allowable.

In section i, Chopin records details of Editha and John's courtship. We see, through them, that Editha's weakness is more than that of simply wanting what other young girls were thought to desire: a safe marriage, a home. Editha agrees to John's offer, after three years of obstinate refusal, because of her passionate sexual need for John Mobry. She weakens "in the springtime and under the blossom-laden branches of an apple tree" (71). "Chance," we are told, "brought him to her that spring day out under the blossoms, at a moment when inward forces were at work with her to weaken and undo the determination of a lifetime" (71). The apple tree, of course, recalls the original Garden, the original sin and sexual shame, but the equation of Editha's "sin" with sexual passion increases as we observe the symbolism Chopin uses to define her response to the world and to men. The images surrounding the discussion of her "sin" are the very images that surround the discussion of Naomi's madness. The common images suggest the common sexual content of both women's experiences. Sensuous imagery is important to both accounts; perhaps even more important, the sun, with its heat and intensity, becomes the figure central to the experiences of both females. Editha, we are told, looked away from John for a moment before accepting his long-standing proposal, "far away across the green hills that the sun had touched and quickened, and beyond, into the impenetrable mist" (71).

Chopin, then, avoids making a threatening statement about female passion in "Mrs. Mobry's Reason." Editha Payne is punished for her "sin"; Naomi cannot be held responsible for aberrant sexual behavior that is inextricably connected with her madness, can she? And yet, as we have seen, although Chopin evasively avoids offending, she still manages to make a forceful, stunning statement about the erotic. Wolstenholme suggests that "Mrs. Mobry's Reason" suffers from Chopin's making Editha Payne's "crime" the giving way to her desire and passion for a good man; such behavior is, the critic notes, "rarely a crime in a Chopin story." "The punishment fate metes out is disproportionate to the crime," Wolstenholme feels, whereas in Ibsen's *Ghosts* Mrs. Alving's sin is proportionate to her betrayal of her own desires and feelings.[4] Perhaps the inconsistency Wolstenholme notes was intended by Chopin: in such an early piece she might have felt a special need to distort her true judgment of female passion in order to allow her simply to broadcast its presence. Chopin's inconsistency might be seen as still another way she veils herself from direct responsibility for objectionable remarks and conclusions.

"A Lady of Bayou St. John" and "La Belle Zoraïde," stories written a month apart (August and September 1893) and both included in *Bayou Folk*, have a strong dependence on techniques of distancing, including Chopin's reliance on stereotypical racial attitudes as well as her use of connections between two stories, connections that offer sexual information but are so subtle they might be missed. In "A Lady of Bayou St. John" we meet Madame Delisle, a very young woman whose husband, Gustave, "was away yonder in Virginia somewhere, with Beauregard" (298), fighting for the Confederates in the Civil War. The story deals primarily with Madame Delisle's perverse, romantic loyalty to the dead (after her husband is killed in battle, she erects an altar to his memory, letting that memory "crowd and fill [her] life" [301] for the remainder of her days). This behavior is an essential psychological mystery in the narrator's exploration of what she calls "that psychological enigma, a woman's heart" (302). At first the story seems to resemble other Chopin stories about characters who live in the past: "Ma'ame Pélagie," "The Return of Alcibiade," "The Bênitous' Slave." But there is something else enigmatic—and disturbing—about Madame Delisle's psyche: suggestions about her sexual nature are included. As we will see, the most powerful statement about her sexuality, ironically, appears not in "A Lady of Bayou St. John," but, rather, in a later piece, "La Belle Zoraïde," that seems not to be about Madame Delisle at all.

Robert Arner has noted that in "A Lady of Bayou St. John" "Mrs. Chopin was not ready to say yet what she saw [in a woman's heart]."[5] However, Chopin does not feel timid about recording the presence of male passion in her story. Sepincourt—a Frenchman who visits Madame Delisle during Gustave's absence, falls in love with her, and vigorously proposes that she and he hurry off to Paris—Chopin comfortably, graphically describes his desire. We see it "in the glance that penetrated [Madame Delisle's] own; in the quiver of his sensitive lip and the quick beating of a swollen vein in his brown throat" (299). Chopin's description of Madame Delisle's own sexual response is less direct. Reading a letter from the Frenchman, Madame Delisle discovers it to be "a voice from the unknown, like music, awaking in her a delicious tumult that seized and held possession of her whole being" (300). She kisses him many times when he visits next, agreeing "in a fainting voice that he could scarcely hear" to go with him—"Anywhere, anywhere" (300). The embrace, the kisses, and her words (delivered, Chopin suggests, on the very verge of a swoon) remind us, in subtle ways, more of the typically romantic woman in nineteenth-century fiction than of some of Chopin's more daringly presented passionate females. The possibility of continued sexual exploration ends altogether with the next stroke of Chopin's pen. "But she did not go with him," the narrator explains. "Chance willed it otherwise. That night a courier brought her a message from Beauregard, telling her that Gustave, her husband, was dead" (300). We hear no more about Madame Delisle's emerging sexuality.

As has been mentioned, the "delicious tumult" hinted at in **"The Lady of Bayou St. John"** is, cleverly, defined in more exact terms—terms approximately as direct as those used by the author in her description of Sepincourt—in **"La Belle Zoraïde."** The story is a tale told by Manna-Loulou, Madame Delisle's Negro servant, and seems to have relatively little to do with Madame Delisle herself. We know the story must have been told before the proposal by Sepincourt. Before his arrival, we learn in **"A Lady of Bayou St. John,"** Madame "could not fall asleep at night unless old black Manna-Loulou sat beside her bed and told her stories" (298). After he lets his passion for her be known and she experiences the fright of her new feelings of love, Madame Delisle does not want Manna-Loulou by her side: "She would not hear Manna-Loulou's stories. She wanted to be alone, to tremble and to weep" (299-300). The reference to Manna-Loulou is so brief and so casual that it would be easy to miss it altogether or to ignore its significance. Yet, we cannot fully appreciate what Chopin is telling us about Madame Delisle's sexuality without understanding the association between Madame's reluctance to hear Manna-Loulou's tale, expressed in **"The Lady of Bayou St. John,"** and the specific content of one such tale told by the Negro servant in **"La Belle Zoraïde."**

"La Belle Zoraïde" is a tale rich with disguised and veiled parallels. Robert Arner has noted one such significant ambiguity: "the teller of the tale and her listener stand in precisely the same relationship to each other as Zoraïde and Madame Delarivière do: slave-mistress." Arner perceptively asks, "Is the story intended as an act of rebellion, however non-violent, by Manna Loulou?"[6] Another parallel of importance also quietly begins to surface between Zoraïde's situation and that of Madame Delisle.

In **"La Belle Zoraïde,"** as Per Seyersted observes, Chopin examines "the theme of activated passion." Zoraïde, he

writes, "catches fire."[7] But she is a Negro, and her passion, therefore, is permissible. The dark, sexual content—the account of Zoraïde's desire for Mézor, Doctor Langlé's servant—is announced through a description of the night that precedes the commencement of Manna-Loulou's storytelling. "The summer night was hot and still" (303) the story begins. This stillness and heat are the sort that precede a storm—a release of energy. Symbolically, the heat and stillness suggest that a release of sexual energy is also about to occur. The heat makes a riverman lazy and languorous and causes "a lover's lament for the loss of his mistress" (303) to form upon his lips. Chopin stresses that "not a ripple of air swept over the *marais*" (303). She also emphasizes the unusual darkness of the night, hinting at mystery. "Yonder, across Bayou St. John," she observes, "lights twinkled here and there in the darkness, and in the dark sky above a few stars were blinking" (303).

Although the stillness, heat, and darkness of this night are not mentioned again after Manna-Loulou begins narrating, the reader quickly senses that in the Negro servant's story he will discover the "release" of tension and energy that the night images foreshadow. Indeed, the stillness breaks when Zoraïde sees Mézor dance the Bamboula in Congo Square, "the sensual nature of [which dance] caused its prohibition."[8] Zoraïde, Chopin tells us with language far more explicit than that used to describe Madame Delisle's desire for Sepincourt, feels the music's primitive rhythms and longs to touch Mézor's body, "bare to the waist, . . . like a column of ebony, . . . [and glistening] like oil" (304). She desires this man "from the moment she [sees] the fierce gleam of his eye, lighted by the inspiring strains of the Bamboula, and [beholds] the stately movements of his splendid body swaying and quivering through the figures of the dance" (304).

Mézor, unlike M'sieur Ambroise, the mulatto "with his shining whispers like a white man's" (304) whom Zoraïde's mistress, Madame Delarivière, wants her to marry, is a figure of immense sexuality. He stands "as straight as a cypress-tree and as proud looking as a king" (304). When he is not dancing in Congo Square, he is hoeing his master's sugar cane, "barefooted and half naked" (305). Zoraïde cannot resist his appeal; though prohibited by her mistress from seeing him again, she disobeys and bears his child.

But Chopin has carefully distanced us from Zoraïde's behavior. Zoraïde is not a civilized white Southerner; she is, rather, a Negro and, later, like Naomi, a madwoman. Making the lovers both Negro (Zoraïde the color of *cafe-au-lait* and Mézor of ebony) makes the explicitness of the narrator's remarks more acceptable: Negroes, to nineteenth-century Southerners, were thought, primarily, to be sexually different from whites—promiscuous, primitive, lustful, fierce. Chopin even has the narrator who frames the story, Manna-Loulou (a woman "herself as black as the night" [303]), disapprove of Zoraïde's behavior, reinforcing many of the prejudices of white Southerners and moving us another step away from Chopin's true assessment of the situation. "But you know how the negroes are, Ma'zélle Titite," Manna-Loulou says, smiling sadly as she seems to support the common prejudice about racial sexuality. "There is no mistress, no master, no king nor priest who can hinder them from loving when they will. And these two found ways and means" (305). Zoraïde and Mézor's behavior was not offensive because the color line permitted a strikingly different sexual code. Too, we find that Zoraïde, heartbroken because of her mistress's lie that her baby had died, becomes mad, forever clasping a rag bundle to her breast. She becomes "Zoraïde la folle" (307), and, as with Naomi Mobry, we have even more difficulty recognizing her mental state as in any way approximate to our own.

Chopin has even more carefully distanced us from the important parallel between Zoraïde and Madame Delisle that, when recognized, allows us to see that Zoraïde's eroticism is shared by Madame. The similarity between what Zoraïde felt and Madame Delisle was feeling becomes evident only if, after reading both stories, we remember Zoraïde's refusal to have Manna-Loulou continue with her nightly ritual of storytelling. One must have read **"The Lady of Bayou St. John,"** and read it carefully, to discover the connection Chopin is making. From **"La Belle Zoraïde"** alone we have no suggestion that the feelings Manna-Loulou ascribes to Zoraïde are shared by Madame Delisle, a young, wealthy, white Southern woman, but in Madame's refusal to listen further, we find the specific nature of the "delicious tumult" Madame Delisle experiences defined. Had Madame Delisle, after the overtures of Sepincourt, in some way sensed a parallel between her new sexual excitement and Zoraïde's? Was she afraid to admit it? Did she vaguely fear that Manna-Loulou's stories would give her own feelings too much clarity and intensity? Certainly Madame Delisle's sacrifice of self and passion to the memory of Gustave suggests that the guilt of her momentary desire for a man not her husband was of an extreme variety. Once again, Chopin avoids a direct message in favor of ambiguity, apparent stereotyping, and the most subtle sorts of clues.

We find similar as well as new techniques to establish distance from the truth of female passion in **"Juanita"** (July 26, 1894). The Juanita figure, we know, was a real person in Chopin's life, the daughter of the local postmaster in Sulphur Springs, Missouri.[9] Chopin revised this story for *Moods* magazine from a diary entry about Annie Venn, the original **"Juanita."**[10]

Although **"Juanita"** appeared first as a diary item, we cannot help but guess that Chopin began consciously working toward narrator distortion as she began to see the potential of her observations. We know this happened with **"Cavenelle,"** and we know that no matter how true events are that appear in Chopin's first person stories (of which there are remarkably few), the narrator often is treated with mild or intense irony. Seyersted, for example, observes that **"Vagabonds,"** as the manuscript at the Missouri Historical Society indicates, "describes an actual in-

cident in the life of Kate Chopin, the Cloutierville widow."[11] Yet we have seen, with the help of critics of **"Vagabonds,"** that the storekeeper is hardly Kate Chopin: she is, rather, a repressed woman overly concerned about respectability and unaware of her true desires.[12]

The narrator of **"Juanita"** is "respectable" as well. She does have a sense of humor, though often at others' expense. She laughs at Juanita's appearance and peculiar taste in men. She thinks of herself as superior to the low-life behavior of Rock Spring's (originally Sulphur Spring's) town character. "For my part I never expected Juanita to be more respectable than a squirrel; and I don't see how any one else could have expected it" (368), she concludes.

Chopin's use of a distorted first person is an especially fine and effective distancing procedure, perhaps in some ways even more ambiguous and interesting than a Manna-Loulou type frame. Chopin, ironically, gains distance from the Juanita figure and her peculiar sexual behavior and preferences by associating herself closely with the details of Juanita's history. Disapproval of a character's behavior by the supposed "author" of an autobiographical fragment would naturally be more forceful and convincing than that of a storyteller who is named and apparently fictional, a Manna-Loulou. Chopin avoids the imputation that she approves of or understands Juanita's behavior by telling us, *herself,* that Juanita is no more moral than a squirrel. This assessment of Juanita's peculiar conduct would have been shared by countless numbers of Chopin's readers.

Another device Chopin uses here is similar to a distancing procedure described in the discussion of the previous short stories. **"Juanita,"** like **"La Belle Zoraïde,"** is coupled with a companion piece. That companion piece, **"The Night Came Slowly,"** lets us know more about the true identity of the narrator (and Chopin's hidden comment about female sexuality) as **"The Lady of Bayou St. John"** lets us know more about Madame Delisle and her obvious similarity to Zoraïde. Again, Chopin cleverly keeps part of the truth buried in a separate story, away from the reader's immediate experience.

"The Night Came Slowly" was originally, like **"Juanita,"** a diary entry. Written two days before the Annie Venn account, it was published with **"Juanita"** under the title **"A Scrap and a Sketch."**[13] In it we find the use of the first person, but the voice of the "I" in Chopin's "scrap" is very different from that of the "I" in **"Juanita."** This is the voice of a woman strongly drawn to the sensuous. Though the sensuous in the piece is never directly equated with sexual awareness and desire, the language the narrator uses to describe her feelings is lush, provocative, mysterious, and interestingly metaphoric. The charm of the night to which she abandons herself is "soothing and penetrating" (366). The wind is called "the caressing wind" (366). It curiously "rippled the maple leaves like little warm love thrills" (366). This narrator casts aside respectability with disdain. "Why do fools cumber the

Earth!" she asks excitedly. "It was a man's voice that broke the necromancer's spell. A man came to-day with his 'Bible Class.' He is detestable with his red cheeks and bold eyes and coarse manner and speech. What does he know of Christ?" (366) She confidently concludes, "I would rather ask the stars: they have seen him" (366). The thoughts might have been Edna's own as she fled the church of Our Lady of Lourdes on the Chênière Caminada for Madame Antoine's.

It is the person who can respond sensuously (and, it is hinted, sexually) who is happiest and closest to wisdom and fulfillment. Or so we learn in **"The Night Came Slowly."** The mood of the piece and its message—so much closer to Chopin's prevalent thesis throughout her canon—informs our reading of **"Juanita,"** but only if we recognize that here is another instance of Chopin's subtle pairing of stories that appear, on first look, to have little to do with each other but, more closely examined, become absolutely inseparable, providing essential—and, perhaps, to many, objectionable—information in a highly discreet and wonderfully clever way. Juanita, though apparently far less articulate than the narrator of **"The Night Came Slowly,"** shares her fondness for and attraction to nature and the life of the senses. She has an "inflamed moon-face" (368); she spends her time when living with her parents close to the earth, "preparing vegetables for dinner or sorting her mother's flower-seed" (367), and she wanders frequently with her curious lover from the village to the secretive woods, a journey familiar to that of many of Hawthorne's outcasts.

Chopin adds still another technique to make Juanita's behavior seem irregular, to distance her from the normal and the ordinary. An effect comparable to the use of Negroes in **"La Belle Zoraïde"** and a madwoman in **"Mrs. Mobry's Reason"** is achieved by making Juanita the grotesque town character. Her appearance, her choices, her actions are so bizarre that we immediately see little of ourselves in her. She is enormous. She stands five-feet-ten and weighs over two-hundred pounds. Her wardrobe consists of a single garment—a soiled calico "Mother Hubbard." Yet, men literally swarm around her, as they do Hemingway's enormous Alice in "The Light of the World." Young and old, "They hung on her fence at all hours; they met her in the lanes; they penetrated to the store and back to the living-room" (368). She becomes involved with a number of attractive suitors: a rich South Missouri farmer and a Texas millionaire who owns a hundred white horses, one of which "spirited animals" (368) Juanita, significantly, begins to ride in her village.

Juanita's final choice is neither the wealthy farmer nor the Texas tycoon. In a passage highly reminiscent of Flannery O'Connor's "Good Country People," we learn that Juanita has chosen a puny, helpless, poor, ragged, one-legged man. Juanita tries to seel subscriptions to buy him a "cork-leg" (originally a "wooden" leg in the diary version [1018]). She also, later, produces a baby, "whose father, she announced, was her husband, the one-legged man" (368). No

one could ever prove a marriage had occurred: "the story of a wandering preacher was told; a secret marriage in the State of Illinois; and a lost certificate" (368), but the propriety and appearance of her relationship with the one-legged man concerns Juanita not at all. Villagers, including the narrator, become accustomed to the common sight of Juanita mounting her husband upon a sorry-looking pony and leading it by the bridle into the woods—where Juanita "lavishes the wealth of her undivided affections upon the one-legged man" (368).

We have only to glance quickly through a list of Chopin's other stories to see that techniques discussed here, especially social and racial stereotyping, were used with uncommon frequency. In **"Vagabonds"** (Dec. [2?], 1895) and **"A Vocation and a Voice"** (November 1896) vagabonds and gypsies inform us about the instinctive life. In **"Loka"** (April 9-10, 1892) it is an Indian girl who desires to flee irresponsibly to the woods as she sniffs the sassafras leaves and "pungent camomile" (215), unlaces and removes her brogans, and stands "a-quiver, panting, ready for flight" (215). Calixta in **"At the 'Cadian Ball"** (July 15-17, 1892) is Spanish: "that little Spanish vixen" (219), Chopin calls her.[14] In **"Fedora"** the titular figure is an extremely repressed woman seen by all around her as a sorry, pathetic, narrow-visioned spinster.

And in *The Awakening* there is some veiling. For example, Chopin conveys sexual knowledge through the use of lush, symbolic landscape descriptions; through the appearance of minor characters, such as Tonie and Gouvernail, whose relationships with women in earlier stories quietly, silently inform the novel; through the omission of poetic lines, a technique also important to our understanding of **"A Respectable Woman"**; and through the creation of Mariequita, another Spanish girl, as a symbol of the fully sensuous life. However, Edna herself is not Spanish. Nor is she a Negro, an Indian, a madwoman, or a town character like Juanita, she was too much like her readers for them to permit her erotic, sensual, shameless behavior.

In *The Awakening* there could be no doubt about Chopin's true message: female passion is universal, touching all equally, overwhelming women of every economic and social class, every race. But Chopin, like Edna, was to learn that society would not tolerate such unconventional and bold remarks. Contemporary reviews of the novel, now so familiar, condemned Chopin's masterpiece as "vulgar,"[15] and "not healthy."[16] The reception, as we now know, "froze the creative impulse within her,"[17] "killed her literary creativity."[18] Chopin knew the novel, with its directness, was a risk, but she probably thought that her public, like Chopin herself, was ready to look into the very face of truth. Perhaps by her use of distancing techniques throughout the 1890s Chopin hoped, in an artistically interesting way, to prepare her readers, her critics, and herself for the powerful, more direct message of her 1899 novel. Unfortunately, only she was ready to walk closer to the universal truth of female sexuality in 1899.

Notes

1. Kate Chopin, "A Matter of Prejudice," in *The Complete Works of Kate Chopin,* ed. Per Seyersted (Baton Rouge, 1969), I, 282; hereafter works from volumes I and II of this edition will be cited parenthetically.

2. For a thorough discussion of the Ibsen parallel (as well as the story's debt to Wagner's *Ring* cycle) see Susan Wolstenholme, "Kate Chopin's Sources for 'Mrs. Mobry's Reason,'" *American Literature,* 51 (January 1980), 540-43.

3. Ibid., 541.

4. Ibid., 543.

5. "Music from a Farther Room: A Study of the Fiction of Kate Chopin," Diss. The Pennsylvania State University 1970, 77.

6. Ibid., p. 91.

7. *Kate Chopin: A Critical Biography* (Baton Rouge, 1969), 108-09.

8. Workers of the Writers' Projects Administration in the State of Louisiana, *Louisiana: A Guide to the State* (New York, 1941), 98.

9. Per Seyersted, *Kate Chopin: A Critical Biography,* p. 217.

10. Kate Chopin, *A Kate Chopin Miscellany,* ed. Per Seyersted and Emily Toth (Natchitoches, 1979), 99.

11. *Kate Chopin: A Critical Biography,* p. 217.

12. See Robert Arner, "Characterization and the Colloquial Style in Kate Chopin's 'Vagabonds,'" *Markham Review,* 2 (May 1971), 110-12; Joyce Coyne Dyer, "Night Images in the Work of Kate Chopin," *American Literary Realism, 1870-1910,* 14 (Autumn 1981), 224-25.

13. Per Seyersted, *Kate Chopin: A Critical Biography,* 217.

14. Chopin may have sensed that her later description of Calixta in "The Storm" was even too powerful to be veiled by her Spanish heritage. "When [Alcée] touched her breasts they gave themselves up in quivering ecstasy, inviting his lips" (595), she had written. The author never tried to publish the piece because, as Seyersted noted, she was "quite aware of how daring she had been in this tale" (*Kate Chopin: A Critical Biography,* p. 164).

15. "Fiction," *Literature,* 4 (23 June 1899), 570.

16. "Notes from Bookland," St. Louis *Daily Globe-Democrat,* 13 May 1899.

17. "Kate Chopin (O'Flaherty)," *American Authors, 1600-1900: Biographical Dictionary of American Literature* (New York, 1938), 156.

18. Per Seyersted, *Kate Chopin: A Critical Biography,* 183.

Wayne Batten (essay date fall 1985)

SOURCE: Batten, Wayne. "Illusion and Archetype: The Curious Story of Edna Pontellier." *Southern Literary Journal,* 18, no. 1 (fall 1985): 73-88.

[*In the following essay, Batten examines Chopin's ambiguity of meaning regarding the notion of illusion in* The Awakening.]

Near the end of *The Awakening,* the protagonist is summoned by her friend Adèle Ratignolle, who is in labor for her fourth child. Although Edna herself has two children, the spectacle of childbirth leaves her shaken, and the kindly Doctor Mandelet insists on walking her home. Both the Doctor and Adèle know that Edna has moved out of her husband's house and possibly returned the attentions of the roué Alcée Arobin, and they may suspect, as the reader knows, that she is about to consummate her long-incubating passion for Robert Lebrun. The trouble, the Doctor tells Edna, is that

> "youth is given up to illusions. It seems to be a provision of Nature, a decoy to secure mothers for the race. And Nature takes no account of moral consequences, of arbitrary conditions which we create, and which we feel obliged to maintain at any cost."
>
> "Yes," she said. "The years that are gone seem like dreams—if one might go on sleeping and dreaming—but to wake up and find—oh! well! perhaps it is better to wake up after all, even to suffer, rather than to remain a dupe to illusions all one's life."[1]

Of the commentators who for various reasons have extolled Edna's quest for selfhood, none notice, in this crucial interchange when Edna refuses professional help, that she and the Doctor are speaking at cross-purposes.[2] If by "illusions" they mean not, loosely, "misconceptions" or "delusions," then they are speaking of the distorting power of imagination, of how certain images harmfully influence perception. But the Doctor is asserting that romantic fictions actually assist instinctual "Nature" to entrap women in the condition which Adèle has just exhibited at its severest, while Edna can only be referring to the habits and assumptions that have sustained her conventional marriage to Léonce Pontellier at the cost of her own passionate nature, which has only recently been awakened. Given the unfailing precision and *sang-froid* of Kate Chopin's writing, it seems likely that the confusion points to a serious rather than a merely accidental ambivalence.

Doctor Mandelet's diagnosis was the subject of two letters which Kate Chopin purportedly received from London in the autumn of 1899, in the midst of a general outcry against the novel. Rankin, Chopin's first biographer, reprints both letters in full.[3] Lady Janet Scammon Young wishes that Mandelet had advised Mr. Pontellier not to "fancy that because you have possessed your wife hundreds of times she necessarily long ago came to entire womanly self knowledge—that your embraces have as a matter of course aroused whatever of passion she may be endowed with." Had Pontellier helped Edna to distinguish between love and passion, Lady Janet continues, Edna need not have died, but could instead have enriched her marriage with "her passional nature." With her letter Lady Janet encloses one from Dunrobin Thomson, a consulting physician who warns that "the especial point of a wife's danger when her beautiful, God given womanhood awakes, is that she will save her self-respect by imagining herself in love with the awakener." If, on the contrary, again assisted by her husband, "she knows perfectly well that it is passion; if she esteems and respects her passional capacity as she does her capacity to be moved by a song or a sonnet, or a great poem, or a word nobly said—she is safe." Edna, accordingly, could have learned that the fantasies she constructs with Robert Lebrun do not render his attraction fundamentally different from the unembellished lure of Arobin; for, although illusions can dress up passion to look like love, the "passional capacity" can be safely recognized by associating it, not love, with the excitement of music and other arts. Yet Edna's fantasies contain something essential to her, and her imagination is not the free agent that Doctor Thomson would wish. It would be of the greatest interest to have Doctor Thomson's reaction to the contrary case of Emma Bovary, whose faith in romantic illusions renders any reconciliation between her passionate nature and her real world impossible.

Chopin's second biographer, Per Seyersted, adds still another dimension to the problem of illusion. Writing seventy years after the fact, Seyersted was unable to verify that either Lady Janet or Doctor Thomson ever existed, so that although the letters are preserved at the Missouri Historical Society, "we cannot quite exclude the possibility that they may have been falsifications."[4] Did the author, stunned and perhaps embarrassed by the effluvia cast by critics upon her somewhat self-indulgent and certainly libidinous protagonist, deviously compose these laudatory missives herself, maintaining that "the essence of the matter lies in the accursed stupidity of men"? Or did Father Rankin, who interviewed many of Chopin's circle and whose research notes were unaccountably lost, intentionally foist bogus documents upon the public, which in 1932 might bring up the old charge of scurrility, requiring a rebuttal stronger than any he could otherwise supply? Whoever abused the limits of illusion in the case, the letters give thoughtful responses to the question of why Edna dies and what could have prevented "that last clean swim." And while both letters maintain that Doctor Mandelet gives inadequate treatment to Edna's problem, they also point to the suggestive power of illusion for both cause and cure.

Edna's illusions fall into three categories: those suggested to her by other characters, those she creates, and the images associated with her by the author. The third group is equivalent to Edna's real experience, to objective rather than subjective material, a distinction sometimes deliberately blurred by the impressionistic narrative technique but no less crucial for understanding her plight. When Edna, despondent after Robert's withdrawal and apparent abandonment on the night of Mme. Ratignolle's *accouchement*, casts aside her bathing suit, she feels "like some new-born creature, opening its eyes in a familiar world that it had never known" (p. 189). The birth image and the paradoxical feeling of returning to a place and knowing it for the first time are Edna's, but the attendant images are provided by the narrator. Incantatory passages are repeated from chapter six, early in the novel, but now the "seductive" voice and the "soft, close embrace" of the sea are more sinister. The soul is again drawn "to wander in abysses of solitude," but the earlier "to lose itself in mazes of inward contemplation" is dropped from the phrase (pp. 25, 189). Similarly, the wavelets, which "coiled back like slow, white serpents" on the night Edna learns to swim, have become shackles, "coiled like serpents about her ankles" (pp. 47, 189). During labor Mme. Ratignolle's braided hair is "coiled like a golden serpent" (p. 180). Much earlier, the reptilian image appeals to Edna, as she considers Robert's suggestion that they visit Grande Terre, to "climb up the hill to the old fort and look at the little wriggling gold snakes, and watch the lizards sun themselves" (p. 58). The powerful serpent image or *uroboros* thus surfaces at moments of seduction, childbirth, and death, but only under Edna's control in the first instance. Finally, as Edna begins to swim, she remembers her first exhilarating swim and the sea-like bluegrass meadow where she wandered as a child, "believing that it had no beginning and no end" (p. 190). More memories come as she swims until, on the threshold of eternity,

> Edna heard her father's voice and her sister Margaret's. She heard the barking of an old dog that was chained to the sycamore tree. The spurs of the cavalry officer clanged as he walked across the porch. There was the hum of bees, and the musky odor of pinks filled the air.
>
> (p. 190)

These final images, though consisting of Edna's early memories, have the focus and sensory immediacy of illusions, completing the cycle of life by approximating Edna's return to significant moments in her childhood.

In her analysis, Cynthia Griffin Wolff posits that Edna's childhood shows the development of a schizoid personality, a self-enclosed and self-protective psyche that fears and avoids real intimacy.[5] Less convincingly, Wolff argues that this solipsism protects an infantile, oral fixation, and that Edna's fascination with the sea betrays a longing to return to the gratifying "oceanic" state of the infant still at one with the mother, still immersed in the amniotic fluid. To make a watertight case, Wolff must ignore several important considerations; Edna, for example, does not perversely leave Robert but is instead called away by the imperious Mme. Ratignolle, who with maddening clairvoyance has perceived that neither he nor Edna may quite live up to the Creole code of conduct. More importantly, Edna's last sensations do not accord with a "regression, back beyond childhood, back into time eternal."[6] Instead, they leave her at a time in childhood having special significance for her, which she has in part confided to Mme. Ratignolle in an earlier scene:

At a very early age—perhaps it was when she traversed the ocean of waving grass—she remembered that she had been passionately enamored of a dignified and sad-eyed cavalry officer who visited her father in Kentucky. She could not leave his presence when he was there, nor remove her eyes from his face, which was something like Napoleon's, with a lock of black hair falling across the forehead.

(p. 31)

Edna was subsequently infatuated with a young man engaged to her sister's friend, and still later, as a young woman, "the face and figure of a great tragedian began to haunt her imagination and stir her senses" (p. 32). Wolff shows that this succession of love-objects, each one more illusory than the one previous, naturally leads Edna to marry Pontellier, because "a husband who evoked passion from her might lure the hidden self into the open, tempting Edna to attach her emotions to flesh and blood rather than phantoms."[7] After hearing Edna's confidences, however, Mme. Ratignolle is sufficiently uneasy to warn Robert to "let Mrs. Pontellier alone" (p. 35). What finally does and does not happen between Edna and Robert can be understood less as a flight from the realities of flesh and blood than as the result of difficulties with the "phantoms" themselves.

Little Edna was enamored of a man, not an illusion, so intensely that "she could not leave his presence when he was there, nor remove her eyes from his face." The Freudian critic might well point out that the cavalry officer was a friend of her father and thus a suitable person to whom Edna could transfer powerful Oedipal longings. The other recurring image from this time, the endless sea-field, gives the child a sense of freedom (especially from the gloomy Presbyterianism of her stern father) but also suggests the danger of becoming lost. The overwhelming emotions attached to the officer carry the same threat. In her next phase, in early puberty, Edna is drawn to a man she can safely identify as lover and husband, though not *her* lover and husband. With the tragedian Edna brings to bear a repertoire of romantic illusions which, unlike Emma Bovary before her, she never imagines her own husband can fulfill. This third, precociously cynical stage, this dissociation of imaginary from actual experience, breaks down in the course of the novel, and Edna finds no means of regaining her equilibrium. Her dilemma is sketched in her contrasting responses to music. When Mlle. Reisz plays, Edna is shaken by passions lashing her "as the waves daily beat upon her splendid body" (pp. 44-45). Previously she has responded to music as she does to the more prosaic performances of Mme. Ratignolle. A piece Edna calls "Solitude" causes her to visualize

the figure of a man standing beside a desolate rock on the seashore. He was naked. His attitude was one of hopeless resignation as he looked toward a distant bird winging its flight away from him.

(p. 44)

This foreboding constellation brings together three sets of images: birds, sea, and mysterious male figures, each am-

bivalent with longing and danger. James H. Justus comments: "The picture itself can be seen as a transsexual projection: the naked man is Edna as well as the vaguely identified, wished-for, would-be lover: a kind of redaction of the twenty-eight swimmers plus one in Walt Whitman's *Song of Myself.*"[8] It is also likely that the lost man is a transmuted memory of her first, powerful attachment. Here, however, the male principle, wisdom, or Zeus, is in flight from the *animus* figure, who is left at the mercy of the waves, the undifferentiated sea of the unconscious. The passions aroused by Mlle. Reisz's music are safely contained in the medium of art, but when Edna brings them to her actual experience the attenuation of her imaginative faculty will prove more serious.

The imagination becomes attenuated when it ceases to mediate between the inner world of the psyche and the external world of society, marriage, and morality. The fantasy life may become hyperactive, but rather than compensating the psyche for its loss of actuality it expresses the true nature of the problem, reinforcing the message of recurring dreams. On the night of Edna's first, exhilarating swim, she finds herself in a new, more powerful position in relation to her world. Expanding on her comment that "it is like a night in a dream," Robert playfully associates her new skill with folklore:

On the twenty-eighth of August, at the hour of midnight, and if the moon is shining—the moon must be shining—a spirit that has haunted these shores for ages rises up from the Gulf. With its own penetrating vision the spirit seeks some one mortal worthy to hold him company, worthy of being exalted for a few hours into realms of the semicelestials. His search has always hitherto been fruitless, and he has sunk back, disheartened, into the sea. But tonight he found Mrs. Pontellier. Perhaps he will never wholly release her from the spell. Perhaps she will never again suffer a poor, unworthy earthling to walk in the shadow of her divine presence.

(pp. 49-50)

Robert offers Edna a way to understand her excitement. The archetypal Gulf spirit only appears at times of crucial change, governed by the lunar, dream-like aspect of consciousness. He arises from the sea as the woman's *animus* arises from the unconscious at a moment when a new, more comprehensive organization of the psyche has become possible. Like the Gulf spirit, however, the *animus* presents a corresponding threat: the woman's subliminal, male identity, with its direct access to the unbounded unconscious, will dominate the psyche, eventually extinguishing the ego-consciousness; the woman is possessed by the archetype, who "will never wholly release her from the spell." The usual defense is either to repress the instinctual life altogether or, as Robert unwittingly implies, to project the archetype onto a real man, to "suffer a poor, unworthy earthling to walk in the shadow of her divine presence." This form of projection, though dangerous itself, at least opens the way through dialog to a relationship in which the transcendent figures are beneficially contained.[9] Receptive to Robert's imaginative suggestions,

Edna seems clearly on the path of projection, and when they return from the beach before the rest of the party the silence between them is "pregnant with the first-felt throbbings of desire" (p. 51).

Edna and Robert amplify their shared images during a trip by sailboat to Chêniére Caminada the next day, ostensibly to attend mass. Recalling the "mystic spirit" Edna now feels "free to drift whithersoever she chose to set her sails" (p. 58). Previously, Edna's confidences to Mme. Ratignolle had begun with her confession that "the sight of the water stretching so far away, those motionless sails against the blue sky, made a delicious picture that I just wanted to sit and look at" (p. 29). Now a participant, Edna is drawn to Robert's entreaties to take her sailing in his own pirogue, and she is delighted at the suggestion that her Gulf spirit will help her find buried treasure. Like Robert's "little wriggling gold snakes" and Edna's vision of "watching the slimy lizards writhe in and out among the ruins of the old fort," pirate gold becomes a metaphor for illicit sexual gratification:

> "I'd give it all to you, the pirate gold and every bit of treasure we could dig up. I think you would know how to spend it. Pirate gold isn't a thing to be hoarded or utilized. It is something to squander and throw to the four winds, for the fun of seeing the golden specks fly."
>
> "We'd share it, and scatter it together," he said. His face flushed.
>
> (pp. 58-59)

Small wonder, after this, that Edna finds the atmosphere in church "stifling" and leaves before the end of mass. The renegades find harbor at a nearby cottage, she "in the very center of the high, white bed," he reclining "against the sloping keel of the overturned boat" just outside the bedroom (pp. 61-62). Refreshed, Edna consumes a bit of bread and wine, then plucks an orange and throws it at Robert, who is sufficiently seduced to insist on delaying their return until night. After hearing their hostess tell legends of the Baratarians, Edna and Robert sail home by moonlight, while the narrator records that "misty spirit forms were prowling in the shadows and among the reeds, and upon the water were phantom ships, speeding to cover" (p. 65). The impersonal narrative voice thus confirms what will prove to be the furthest extent to which the lovers can actualize their fantasies. Robert, who has perhaps pandered his illusions more effectively than he anticipated, decides the next day to begin his fortune-seeking trip to Mexico, a project he had postponed numerous times before. The dreamspinner turns and escapes into the commercial, material world. Surprised and hurt, Edna finds his move "perfectly preposterous and uncalled for" (p. 74).

Edna possesses now a complex of images of special significance for her: Gulf spirit, moonlit expeditions, sails on open sea, pirates, buried treasure, phantom ships, mists, a cloud of gold dust thrown "to the four winds." Building upon the actual setting at Grand Isle and neighboring is-lands, these images contain as their nexus the *animus* in the form of demon lover, the woman's spirit-ravisher, illicit lover of body and soul. Robert's initial withdrawal frustrates Edna in the normal course of projecting the affect-laden archetype, who remains tied up in her framework of illusions and therefore insusceptible to dialog. During Robert's long absence, Edna consolidates her illusory resources. Her father visits, providing "a welcome disturbance," revealing that his stern religion and patriarchal attitudes are matched, significantly, by his love of horse racing, his attractive bronze complexion, his white, silky beard and hair, and his habit of staying drunk all day with "numerous 'toddies'" of his own concoction (pp. 113, 115). After a particularly exciting day at the races, Edna and her father join her husband and Doctor Mandelet for dinner. Over the wine the talk turns to recollection and story telling, Pontellier and Edna's father leading the way by telling stories of more interest to themselves than to the hearers. The Doctor appears no "happier in his selection, when he told the old, ever new and curious story of the waning of a woman's love, seeking strange, new channels, only to return to its legitimate source after days of unrest" (p. 117). Edna, in particular, is unimpressed by this case history, relevant though it may be to her own predicament. Instead,

> She had one of her own to tell, of a woman who paddled away with her lover one night in a pirogue and never came back. They were lost amid the Baratarian Islands, and no one ever heard of them or found trace of them from that day to this. It was a pure invention. She said that Madame Antoine had related it to her. That, also, was an invention. Perhaps it was a dream she had had. But every glowing word seemed real to those who listened.
>
> (p. 117)

Dreams are often the medium through which the ego can glimpse *animus,* and Edna's frequent sleep or drowsiness has been commented on.[10] The expedition which she and Robert never carried out has gained an archetypal immediacy, as "every glowing word seemed real" even to the male listeners. But here the trip ends, not with the lovers scattering gold together, but with disappearance and probable death. Consciously, Edna continues to develop her attachment to Robert, but unconsciously she feels that this romance cannot be reconciled with the known world. After hearing Edna's tale, the Doctor recognizes that her latency leaves her open to impersonal eroticism: "I hope to heaven it isn't Alcée Arobin" (p. 118)

The common cultural cognate for Edna's complex illusion is best exemplified in the group of ballads known as "The Daemon Lover" or "James Harris," in which a woman abandons her husband and children to answer the call of her former lover, who appears at her window after a long absence at sea and tempts her with the promise of riches.[11] In an early, lengthy version, the lover is a spirit "much like unto a man," but in later, shorter variations he is a devil replete with cloven foot; and rather than merely disappearing the woman is drowned or carried to hell aboard his golden ship. Oral tradition appears to have developed the disastrous consequences of the woman's departure from her proper role as wife and mother, though the cautionary note is offset by the lurid effects of the devil's blandishments. Any sacrifice of social identity naturally bodes great risk, and when Edna moves out of her husband's grand house to the tiny "pigeon-house" she jeopardizes what she terms "illusions," the social role and support system which her own paradigm may not adequately supplant. Her step toward greater independence and fulfillment, then, is also a move to act out the archetypal story of the woman governed by *animus.* Edna's disregard for the consequences and contingencies of violating convention indicates that her new illusions will mediate with the social world as poorly as her previous "illusions" mediated latent aspects of her psyche. Her certitude in this line of action is charged with mystification. In response to Doctor Mandelet's offer of help, she explains:

> "Some way I don't feel moved to speak of things that trouble me. Don't think I am ungrateful or that I don't appreciate your sympathy. There are periods of despondency and suffering which take possession of me. But I don't want anything but my own way."

> (p. 184)

Minutes later, when Edna is about to enter the house where she believes Robert is waiting for her, "she could picture at that moment no greater bliss on earth than possession of the beloved one" (p. 185). A second time, however, Robert proves elusive, if not illusory; longing to possess, Edna is herself possessed. Jung writes that the woman at this stage

> becomes wrapped in a veil of illusions by her demon-familiar, and, as the daughter who alone understands her father (that is, is eternally right in everything), she is translated to the land of sheep, where she is put to graze by the shepherd of her soul, the animus.[12]

In compensation for this peril, *animus* is also a psychopomp, who "gives to woman's consciousness a capacity for reflection, deliberation, and self-knowledge."[13] Unable to free herself of her "veil of illusions" through relationship with Robert, on whom she could project her overwhelming *animus,* Edna is left a prey to its negative effects, impersonal and hapless sexuality: "Today it is Arobin; tomorrow it will be someone else" (p. 188). Correspondingly, the obligations which Edna casts aside are not supplanted by experiences of relatedness through which the self gains meaning and stability; hence the capacity for self-knowledge becomes a void, prey to illusions made fascinating by the archetype.

But Edna's "veil," woven of dream, fantasy and folklore, gains a still deeper archetypal reference through a set of images applied to her, images which associate her with both Venus and Psyche. Recalling Mrs. Pontellier's last dinner party in her husband's house, Victor Lebrun says that "Venus rising from the foam could have presented no more entrancing a spectacle than Mrs. Pontellier, blazing with beauty and diamonds at the head of the board" (p. 186). This appearance of seductive, god-like self-sufficiency ironically belies what Edna is feeling at the party, when she simultaneously longs for Robert and is overpowered by a sense of the unattainable. Victor's description does, however, accord with Robert's earlier conjecture that Edna "will never again suffer a poor, unworthy earthling to walk in the shadow of her divine presence." The divine aura, the effulgence of reified archetype, actually makes the woman fragile. The perilous cross between mortal and divine is the subject of the myth of Psyche, in which Eros himself serves as *animus,* holding Psyche captive in his sumptuous palace, visiting her bed nightly, but adjuring her never to look upon him.[14] At first it is Venus who, angered by the tributes paid to Psyche's merely mortal beauty, represents the malignant power of archetype; when Psyche brings forth her concealed lamp and discovers the beauty of Eros, he punishes her by taking flight, leaving her so bereft that her first impulse is to fling herself into a river to die.[15] This crucial phase of the myth is the subject of **"Psyche's Lament,"** one of Kate Chopin's early poems. The second stanza

> O sombre sweetness; black enfolden charms,
>   Come to me once again!
> Leave me not desolate; with empty arms
>   That seeking, strive in vain
> To clasp a void where warmest Love hath lain.[16]

expresses a passionate longing for the lost Eros, with no suggestion that he might be recovered. Here, in contrast to the myth, the "cursed lights" have only destroyed a sensual paradise, not opened the way to conscious love. The ambivalence of this moment is central to Edna's tragedy. Arobin's is "the first kiss of her life to which her nature had really responded. It was a flaming torch that kindled desire" (p. 139). The light of Psyche's lamp transforms Eros from the serpent she expected to the most ravishing of lovers; after intercourse with Arobin, Edna "felt as if a mist had been lifted from her eyes, enabling her to look upon and comprehend the significance of life, that monster made up of beauty and brutality" (p. 140). Edna cannot "imagine herself in love" with Arobin, however, and therefore the light, figurative and literal, cannot survive Robert's farewell note. After receiving it "She did not sleep. She did not go to bed. The lamp sputtered and went out" (p. 185). The narrator's images of illumination from torch or lamp reveal Edna to be a type of Psyche thwarted. In the brief chapter which introduces the incantatory personification of the sea, the narrator has warned: "A certain light was beginning to dawn dimly within her—the light which, showing the way, forbids it" (p. 25).

One alternative open to Edna is to become herself a creator and manipulator of illusion in the self-conscious and socially recognized role of artist. Although she "handled her brushes with a certain ease and freedom" indicating "natural aptitude" (p. 22), she has difficulty making the transition from amateur to professional. The discipline she needs has not been part of her upbringing; but training and practice might supply this deficiency were it not for more elusive problems confronting the dabbler who would be artist. The first of these emerges when Edna attempts a portrait of Mme. Ratignolle:

> The picture completed bore no resemblance to Madame Ratignolle. She was greatly disappointed to find that it did not look like her. But it was a fair enough piece of work, and in many respects satisfying.
>
> Mrs. Pontellier evidently did not think so. After surveying the sketch critically she drew a broad smudge of paint across its surface, and crumpled the paper between her hands.
>
> (p. 22)

Clearly, the narrator does not share the evaluation made by the two women, and Edna's perfectionism may not be very distant from her friend's desire for a product that is representational rather than otherwise "satisfying." The scene suggests that Edna has neither resolved the inevitable tension between illusion and reality, nor learned to inhabit the hinterland between the two, a place more essential to the artist than the convenient "atelier" where Edna daydreams. Another aspect of Edna's limitations arises in her relationship with Mlle. Reisz, who is unquestionably an artist. When in a later scene Edna laughingly speaks of becoming an artist, Reisz tells her she has "pretentions," for the artist in addition to "absolute gifts" must, in order to succeed, "possess the courageous soul . . . The brave soul. The soul that dares and defies" (pp. 105-106). On another visit Reisz feels Edna's shoulder blades to see if her wings are strong, adding, "the bird that would soar above the level plain of tradition and prejudice must have strong wings. It is a sad spectacle to see the weaklings bruised, exhausted, fluttering back to earth" (p. 138). The imagery here recalls Edna's vision of a bird in flight from a male figure and anticipates the actual, wounded bird which flutters into the sea moments before the end. As conceived and represented by Mlle. Reisz, the Romantic artist must be opposed and superior to society, heroic and solipsistic. Quarrelsome, ugly, wearing an emblematic bunch of artificial violets in her hair, the little pianist shows the disfigurement which her kind of specialized isolation entails.[17] Artistry thus presents danger as great as any Edna could encounter in employing her skills toward greater self-knowledge.

Whether Edna fails or refuses to sublimate her newfound, passionate nature through the medium or art, her plight shows the difficulty of finding a social role adequate to her needs. Society in this novel offers women only one role, and Edna is not a "mother-woman." With mild sarcasm the narrator explains: "They were women who idolized their children, worshiped their husbands, and esteemed it a holy privilege to efface themselves as individuals and grow wings as ministering angels" (p. 16). In her study of nineteenth-century American culture, Ann Douglas maintains that this maternal mystique served largely unacknowledged purposes:

> The cult of motherhood, like the Mother's Day it eventually established in the American calendar, was an essential precondition to the flattery American women

were trained to demand in place of justice and equality. It offered them, of course, a very genuine basis for self-respect. It gave them, moreover, an innate, unassailable, untestable claim to charismatic authority and prestige, a sanction for subjectivity and self-love.[18]

While men in *The Awakening* enjoy their careers in business or the professions, the matriarchy has ascendancy over the personal sphere, with the result that in respectable relationships men seem to have difficulty conceiving of women in other than maternal terms. When Edna resists her husband's selfish demand that she wake up and listen attentively to his account when he returns late from his gambling party, he retaliates by accusing her of neglecting their children. Even Robert, who helps to formulate Edna's erotic fantasies, had attended sometimes a girl or widow, but "as often as not it was some interesting married woman" (p. 20). His great hope on his return from Mexico is that Pontellier will set Edna "free" to become a wife and, inevitably, a mother all over again. Despite the practicality of its basis, the matriarchy is not independent of illusion, for like other complex roles it draws upon imagination. The prime embodiment of "mother-woman" is, of course, Mme. Ratignolle:

> There are no words to describe her save the old ones that have served so often to picture the bygone heroine of romance and the fair lady of our dreams . . . the spun-gold hair that comb nor confining pin could restrain; the blue eyes that were like nothing but sapphires; two lips that pouted, that were so red one could only think of cherries or some other delicious crimson fruit in looking at them.
>
> (p. 17)

Again the narrator simultaneously employs and debunks standard images, suggesting both their usefulness and their deficiency. In the Creole society into which Edna has married the charismatic mother image gains its ultimate, paradoxical power through association with Roman Catholic iconography. Posing for her portrait Mme. Ratignolle is "like some sensuous Madonna" (p. 22) wearing her favorite color, white. The imagery continues with the Farival twins (whom Mlle. Reisz, significantly, despises), "girls of fourteen, always clad in the Virgin's colors, blue and white, having been dedicated to the Blessed Virgin at their baptism" (p. 41). The logical disparity between "mother-woman" and virgin is dissolved in the figure of Mary, who expresses her consummate motherhood without the aid of mere men. In light of the miraculous mother, an archetype fully as powerful as the demon lover, the narrator wonders if Edna's growing recognition of "her relations as an individual to the world within and about her" is "perhaps more *wisdom* than the Holy Ghost is usually pleased to vouchsafe to any woman" (p. 25, italics mine).

Although in their final conversation Edna and Doctor Mandelet have differing referents in mind for "illusions," the problem addressed is the same: what to do when illusions fail, when the psyche is left unprotected against particularities of time and place over which it has no more control than do the caged or stricken birds that appear at beginning and end. Worse still to live unshielded from full knowledge of this entrapment. The circle closes about Edna as she discerns that, all illusions aside, Adèle's final admonishment to "think of the children" bears a moral weight from which she cannot escape. She is overwhelmed, finally, not only by transcendent forces but also by the orientation of her society toward them, which reinforces the increasing autonomy of her fantasy life and frustrates her need to actualize vital aspects of her psyche through a meaningful and viable relationship with another. Among her last thoughts she acknowledges that husband and children are part of her life, "but they need not have thought that they could possess her, body and soul" (p. 190). Her flaw is that she counters this absolutism with her own by refusing, despite her reply to Doctor Mandelet, to live and suffer knowledge. In this respect she resembles Madame Bovary, who is similarly cornered by a network of circumstances and who dies in recoil from the painful recognition of her failure.[19] In contrast, Edna's struggle achieves Promethean dimensions because her fascination with *animus* both charts a crucial phase of psychic development and brings her into opposition with the sexless mother archetype which commands her social world. Her tragedy arises, however, less from the archetypes themselves than from the perilous nature of illusions which, clashing, rend for a moment to reveal the real world which is the perogative of the tragic protagonist, through suffering, to know.

For Edna, then, truth to her inmost nature and to the forces of individuation demands that she complete the transition from illusion to reality, that she finish the story she and Robert began on the night of her first long swim. If she cannot go forward, she can return to the erotic darkness which Psyche laments, to her first demon lover, to the point when past and present, illusion and reality, thought and sensation merge in the blissful embrace of *animus,* the shepherd of her soul. "The spurs of the cavalry officer clanged as he walked across the porch. There was the hum of bees, and the musky odor of pinks filled the air."

Notes

1. Kate Chopin, *The Awakening* (New York: Avon Books, 1972) 184. Subsequent references will be given parenthetically in the text. Per Seyersted's edition in *The Complete Works of Kate Chopin* can be found in libraries but is relatively rare.

2. For example, Ottavio Mark Casale, "Beyond Sex: The Dark Romanticism of Kate Chopin's *The Awakening*," *Ball State University Forum* 19.1 (1978): 76-80, places the novel in the tradition of Emerson, Hawthorne, and Melville; Donald A. Ringe, "Romantic Imagery in Kate Chopin's *The Awakening*," *American Literature* 43 (1972): 580-588, relates the novel's transcendentalist concept of self-discovery to the sea imagery; Susan J. Rosowski, "The Novel of Awakening," *Genre* 12 (1979): 313-332, compares Edna with other female protagonists of the bildung-

sroman type and links sea and meadow as images of escape from finitude; I am especially indebted to Lawrence Thornton, "*The Awakening*: A Political Romance," *American Literature* 52 (1980): 50-66, who shows Edna's conflict with Creole culture, its dependence on illusion, and the moral aspect of her sexual awakening; Nancy Walker, "Feminist or Naturalist: the Social Context of Kate Chopin's *The Awakening*," *The Southern Quarterly* 17.2 (1979): 95-103, also deals with conflict between cultures but stresses the novel's adherence to naturalist conventions in representing the sexual basis of Edna's enlightenment; Priscilla Allen, "Old Critics and New: The Treatment of Chopin's *The Awakening*," *The Authority of Experience: Essays in Feminist Criticism,* ed. Arlyn Diamond and Lee R. Edwards (Amherst: University of Massachusetts Press, 1977) 224-238, gives a useful, if somewhat polemical, review of earlier treatments of Edna; Allen finds emphasis on sexual awareness reductive and suggests, instead, that Edna's is a tragic struggle for freedom, for "full integrity, full personhood—or nothing" (p. 238).

3. Quotations from the Young and Thomson letters in Daniel S. Rankin, *Kate Chopin and Her Creole Stories* (Philadelphia: University of Pennsylvania Press, 1932) 178-182.

4. Per Seyersted, *Kate Chopin: A Critical Biography* (Oslo: Universitetsforlaget; Baton Rouge: Louisiana State University Press, 1969) 179.

5. In "Thanatos and Eros: Kate Chopin's *The Awakening*," *American Quarterly* 25 (1973): 449-471. Wolff is seconded by Ringe's essay on the question of Edna's solipsism and possessiveness, though he attributes these qualities to a Romantic vision of the emerging self. James H. Justus, "The Unawakening of Edna Pontellier," *The Southern Literary Journal* 10.2 (1978): 107-122, similarly attributes Edna's apparent regression to an actual increase in self-awareness which cannot find mature expression.

6. Wolff, p. 471.

7. Wolff, p. 452.

8. Justus, p. 116.

9. On the phenomenon of *animus* see Emma Jung, *Animus and Amina,* trans. Cary F. Baynes and Hildegard Nagel (1957; Zurich: Spring Publications, 1978); and C. G. Jung, *Aion: Researches into the Phenomenology of the Self,* vol. 9, pt. 2 of *The Collected Works of C .G. Jung,* trans. R.F.C. Hull, 2nd ed., Bollingen Series 20 (Princeton: Princeton University Press, 1968) pars. 1-67. On the problem of containment and projection see also Jung's discussion of marriage in *The Development of Personality,* vol. 17 of *The Collected Works* (1954) pars. 324-345.

10. Especially by George Arms, "Kate Chopin's *The Awakening* in the Perspective of Her Literary Career," *Essays on American Literature in Honor of*

Jay B. Hubbell, ed. Clarence Gohdes (Durham: Duke University Press, 1967) 215-228; by Ringe; and by Robert S. Levine, "Circadian Rhythms and Rebellion in Kate Chopin's *The Awakening,*" *Studies in American Fiction* 10 (1982): 71-81.

11. Eight versions of the ballad are given in *The English and Scottish Popular Ballads,* ed. Francis James Child, 5 vols. (1882-1898; New York: Dover Publications, 1965) 4: 360-369. Child records that an "Americanized version" of this ballad was printed at Philadelphia and cited in *Graham's Illustrated Magazine* for September, 1858 (p. 361). Given the widespread oral tradition of the tale, however, Kate Chopin need not have had any specific text in mind when she wrote her novel.

12. *Aion,* par. 32.

13. *Aion,* par. 33.

14. The standard psychological explication of this myth is Erich Neumann, *Amor and Psyche: The Psychic Development of the Feminine—A Commentary on the Tale by Apuleius,* trans. Ralph Manheim, Bollingen Series 54 (Princeton: Princeton University Press, 1971). For application to female protagonists of fiction, *Lee R. Edwards, "The Labors of Psyche: Toward a Theory of Female Heroism,"* *Critical Inquiry* 6 (1979): 33-49.

15. Neumann, p. 100, comments on Psyche's suicidal reactions to the enormity of archetypal experience.

16. *The Complete Works of Kate Chopin,* ed. Per Seyersted, 2 vols. (Baton Rouge: Louisiana State University Press, 1969) 2: 727.

17. The short story "Lilacs" shows the author's interest in the suggestiveness and emblemism of flowers. The pianist's hair ornament recalls the withered violets of Ophelia, while the pinks associated with the cavalry officer are *dianthus,* flower of the god Zeus or Eros.

18. *The Femininization of American Culture* (New York: Alfred A. Knopf, 1977) 75.

19. The comparison with Flaubert accords with the findings of Eliane Jasenas, "The French Influence in Kate Chopin's *The Awakening,*" *Nineteenth-Century French Studies* 4 (1976): 312-322.

Martin Simpson (essay date fall 1986)

SOURCE: Simpson, Martin. "Chopin's 'A Shameful Affair.'" *Explicator,* 45, no. 1 (fall 1986): 59-60.

[*In the following essay, Simpson discusses images of nature and society in "A Shameful Affair."*]

Mildred Orme, in Kate Chopin's **"A Shameful Affair,"** is a socially conventional and sexually repressed young woman who has come to the Kraummer farm to escape the sexual demands that were made on her in civilized, urban society. Chopin uses fertile nature imagery to show Mildred being drawn out of the realm of sheltered social convention and into a natural world that is rich with sensuous physical surroundings. Here Mildred is forced to recognize and struggle with her sexuality.

Mildred is obviously a young woman who has continually repressed the sexual side of her nature. She is attracted to Fred Evelyn from the first time she sees him and goes out of her way to get his attention. After he has refused her request to drive her to church, she walks down to the river where she knows he will be fishing. She knows he will be alone, because earlier "all the other farmhands had gone forth in Sunday attire" (150). Even though it is obvious to the reader that Mildred is pursuing Fred, she conceals this knowledge from herself. She labels Fred as a "clumsy farmhand" and notes quite inaccurately that "farmhands are not so very nice to look at" (148). After she has had her sexual nature awakened by his kiss, she tells herself that the desire she feels for him is a "shameful whim that chanced to visit her soul, like an ugly dream" (152). Mildred has been able to avoid facing her sexual repression in the past only because she has been away in a civilized, urban environment where social conventions have allowed her to keep men at arm's length. She has "refused [her] half dozen offers" (149) and ironically has come to the farm to seek "the repose that would enable her to follow exalted lines of thought" (150).

The imagery that Chopin uses to describe the farm and Mildred's relation to it reveals that Mildred has entered a sensuous environment that she is trying to resist by clinging to symbols of civilization. The farmhouse itself, as a man-made structure, can be considered an island of civilization amidst the "swelling acres [of] undulating wheat" that "gleam in the sun like a golden sea" (148) and connote pulsating fertility. At first Mildred remains "seated in the snuggest corner of the big front porch of the Kraummer farmhouse," behind her "Browning or her Ibsen" (148), which conveys the image of someone who is trying to isolate herself intellectually in a farmhouse that is itself isolated in an ocean of natural fertility.

Mildred has to abandon her island of civilized social convention when she becomes interested in Fred Evelyn, and nature begins to take its effect on her when she does. She must go down a "long, narrow footpath through the bending wheat" (150) to encounter Fred at the river. This footpath is like a tunnel through the "yellow wheat" that reaches "high above her waist" (150) on either side, which suggests the nearly overwhelming aspect of the fecundity that is almost enveloping her. Mildred's close contact with her sensuous surroundings causes her own repressed sexuality to come to the surface. Her brown eyes become "filled with a reflected golden light" (150) from the wheat as she passes through it, and her lips and cheeks become "ripe with color that the sun had coaxed there" (150). Nature has now begun to erode the self-control that Mildred has exercised over her passions.

Mildred's losing battle against the effects of the fertility around her is conveyed through Chopin's inspired use of imagery during the scene at the river. While she is watching Fred fish, Mildred is standing very still and "holding tight to the book she had brought with her" (150). The book is a sort of life-preserver (a repression-preserver, rather), a symbol of civilization and social restraint. When she "carefully" lays the book down and takes into her hands the phallic fishing pole that Fred gives her, she has given in to her sexual instincts. The voluntary act of setting aside the book and picking up the pole symbolically foreshadows her willing participation in the passionate kiss that follows.

After she has unwittingly and temporarily surrendered to her sexual desires at the river, Mildred once again retreats into her customary repressive behavior. When she feels the first moment of shame after Fred has kissed her, she determines to return to her room in the farmhouse. She will be isolated from nature there, and she can "give calm thought to the situation, and determine then how to act" (151). Only when she is back on the "very narrow path" through "the wheat that [is] heavy and fragrant with dew" (153) is she able to admit to herself what Chopin has already shown to the reader in the scene at the river: she is partly responsible for Fred's impulsive kiss. Being greatly disturbed at this knowledge, she tells Fred that she hopes to someday be able to forgive herself (153).

Chopin's theme in **"A Shameful Affair,"** the enlightened idea that sexual repression is harmful, is brought out by her contrasting images of civilized society and liberating natural fecundity. Mildred's consistent retreat from sexuality, associated with symbols of societal repression, causes her to become a troubled and confused young woman. She will never be a complete and healthy human being, Chopin is saying, until she comes to terms with the "golden, undulating sea" of her passions.

Reference

Chopin, Kate. "A Shameful Affair." *The Awakening and Selected Stories of Kate Chopin.* ed. Barbara H. Solomon. (New York: Signet, 1976) 148-53.

Carole Stone (essay date 1986)

SOURCE: Stone, Carole. "The Female Artist in Kate Chopin's *The Awakening*: Brith and Creativity." *Women's Studies,* 13, nos. 1-2 (1986): 23-32.

[In the following essay, Stone views Chopin's birth imagery in The Awakening *as symbolic of the birth of Edna Pontellier as an artist.]*

When Kate Chopin's *The Awakening* was published in 1899 critics attacked its depiction of a heroine who sought sexual pleasure outside of marriage and condemned Chopin for "failing to perceive that the relation of a mother

to her children is far more important than the gratification of a passion which experience has taught her is . . . evanescent."[1] But *The Awakening* is even more radical in its treatment of motherhood because it questions the assumptions that childbirth and child care are a woman's principal vocation, and that motherhood gives pleasure to all women.

In Chopin's era childbirth was considered a woman's noblest act; to write of it otherwise was unacceptable. Thus, the clinical details of pregnancy and birthing remained largely unwritten. As Dr. Mandelet tells Edna in *The Awakening.* "The trouble is that youth is given up to illusions. It seems to be a provision of Nature to secure mothers for the race."[2] But Dr. Mandelet's insight is rare for a man because he is a physician. By shattering the illusion that giving birth is a glorious experience, Chopin attacks the patriarchal structure which denies women control of their bodies. In addition, however, she goes beyond naturalism in her use of the birth motif. On the symbolic level birthing is a metaphor for the rebirth of the book's protagonist, Edna Pontellier, as artist. The novel can be read as a depiction of the growth of the female artist, a *bildungsroman,* in which birth is emphasized as unique to the female experience.

Many recent critics of *The Awakening* fail to see Edna's growing sense of power and control as signs of progress toward a new self-definition. They view her as a woman deluded by romanticism who is unable to make a conscious choice, such as the decision to become an artist, because her instincts are regressive. Cynthia Griffin Wolff, for example, considers Edna passive, an artist at the mercy of her work. Further, she finds that for Edna birth is a pyschic trauma awakening her to the impossibility of total fusion with another.[3] Another critic, Suzanne Wolkenfeld, considers that Edna's "experience of rebirth is not directed toward new life, but backward to the womb."[4] And James Justus observes that Edna's "awakening is not an advance towards a new definition of self but a return to the protective self-evident identity of childhood,"[5] while Donald A. Ringe considers Edna's romanticism part of a voyage of transcendental self-discovery, but concludes that Chopin "allows her character no limitless expansion of self."[6] A more recent critic, Carole Christ, views Edna's awakening in a positive light, seeing her evolving sense of self as spiritual rebirth. However, Christ, too, finds Edna ultimately socially defeated in spite of the very important fact that this heroine grows as an artist.[7]

In this essay I will argue that Edna's memories of her childhood, her immersion in the sea, and her search for a mother figure are emblems of regression in the service of progression toward an artistic vocation. Rather than returning to the dependency of childhood, she goes forward to a new conception of self, a definition of herself as artist. Further, I will suggest that Edna's romanticism is positive because it catalyzes her imaginative power. As the final step forward functioning as an autonomous human being, moreover, she sees through the delusion of romantic love after confronting the horror of giving birth.

Edna's artistic birthing is shown through the contrasting characters of two women, Adèle Ratignolle, a "mother-woman," and Mme. Reisz, a pianist. As Per Seyersted has observed, "the novel covers two generations and births . . . a finely wrought system of tensions and interrelations set up between Edna's slow birth as authentic and sexual being and the counterpointed pregnancy and confinement of Adèle."[8] Adèle embodies female biology, always talking of her condition, for she has a baby about every two years. Adèle's opposite, Mme. Reisz, a serious artist, is unmarried. She exemplifies the solitary life of the dedicated artist.

A third influence on Edna's artistic development is Robert LeBrun, a young Creole man who, because he has not yet assumed the masculine values of his society, can be a friend to Edna as her husband cannot. He teaches her to swim, furthering her autonomy, and with his easy way of talking about himself, encourages her self-expression. Because he has aroused sexual desire in her, she eventually has an affair with another man, Alcée Arobin, an affair which functions as a rite of passage to sexual autonomy.

Each of these three figures has positive and negative qualities that help and hinder Edna's struggle to be creative. Adèle Ratignolle, a sensuous woman, awakes Edna to the sensuality of her own body. Also Adèle's candor in talking about such subjects as her pregnancy helps Edna to overcome her reserve. Furthermore, Adèle encourages her to express thoughts and feelings she had kept hidden, even from herself. For example, at Adèle's urging to say what she is thinking as they sit together by the sea, Edna recalls "a summer day in Kentucky, of a meadow that seemed as big as the ocean to the very little girl . . . She threw out her arms as if swimming when she walked, beating the tall grass as one strikes out in the water." (17) When Edna says that she feels as if this summer is like walking through that meadow again "unguided," Adèle strokes her hand, and we see that in fact, though not an artist, it is she who guides Edna toward warmth, openness, and creativity. For Edna's memory is an important step in the growth of her power of free association, necessary in the creative process.

In these early scenes by the sea Chopin also establishes the sea as a central symbol for Edna's birthing of a new self. The connection in her mind between the grass and the sea foreshadows the autonomy she achieves by learning to swim, as well as her final walk into the sea at the book's end. Symbolically, the sea is both a generative and a destructive force in *The Awakening*; it represents danger inherent in artistic self-expression—losing oneself in unlimited space—as well as the source of all life, facilitating rebirth, so that Edna in her first moments of being able to swim feels like a child who has learned to walk. The ocean has also been seen as a symbol of woman or the mother in both her benevolent and terrible aspects. Madame Ratignolle, in association with the sea, represents the benevolent mother who nurtues Edna and even inspires her to paint. Adèle seems to her, as she is seated on the beach, like "some sensuous Madonna," and she paints her picture.

At this beginning point in her artistic development Edna thinks of herself as a "dabbler." However, though Edna has had no formal training, Chopin establishes the fact that she is talented for "she handled her brushes with a certain ease and freedom which came not from a long and close acquaintance with them but from a natural aptitude." (12) We also see early on that Edna has the capacity for self-criticism as "after surveying the sketch critically, she drew a broad smudge of paint across its surface and crumpled the paper between her hands." (12) Later when Edna's critical faculties are turned against conventional values of home, husband, and family in the direction of autonomy, Adèle will show the negative side of her mothering qualities. By constantly reminding Edna of her duty to her children, she binds her to society's rules and impedes her creative growth.

In these early scenes at Grand Isle where Edna's struggle to be an artist is beginning, Robert is another source of imaginative power. As she paints Adèle's portrait, he encourages her with "expressions of appreciation in French." While this may simply be Creole flattery, it is more encouragement than she has ever received from her husband. Like Adèle, he is sensual, and as she paints he rests his head against her arm. He also speaks about himself freely, telling her of his plans to go to Mexico. Under his influence she speaks to him about her life, and it is he who awakens her to the passions of her body. A few weeks after the painting scene on the beach, Chopin again uses the sea as a symbol of growth, and again in connection with Robert. One evening he proposes a night swim and we see him lingering behind with the lovers, "and there was not one but was ready to follow when he led the way." (28) Robert's appearance is associated frequently with lovers; he becomes Cupid who awakens Edna to the force of Eros. This evening she learns to swim and feels herself "reaching out for the unlimited in which to lose herself." (30) Loss of boundaries suggests orgiastic union which foreshadows Edna's final merging with the sea. Significantly, that evening as she lies in a hammock, an image of love-making, she feels herself "pregnant with the first felt throbbing desire" (32) for Robert.

When her husband returns later she refuses to go inside when he asks her to. By now she has achieved mastery over her body by learning to swim and mastery over her environment by challenging his authority. She now has to achieve mastery over her imagination, but at this point can only "blindly follow whatever impulse moved her." (34) Next morning, without much thought, she asks a servant to tell Robert she wishes him to take the boat with her to Cheniere for Mass. Walking to the wharf, there are, as always when Robert appears, lovers who already stroll "shoulder to shoulder." Edna's imagination is subsumed by the romance phase of her creative growth as she spends an idyllic day with Robert. This chapter could be considered an epithalamion which, like Edmund Spenser's, is governed by the position of the sun during each part of the marriage day. On the boat trip, "The lovers were all along. They saw nothing, they heard nothing." (36) Edna and

Robert became like the lovers, infatuated with each other, as the sun was high up and beginning to bite." (36)

Edna grows tired in church during Mass, and we see her reject another of society's institutions of authority in favor of the natural force of Eros. Robert takes her to the home of Madame Antoine where Edna partially removes her clothes and while Robert waits for her outside, lies down "in a strange, quaint bed, with its country odor of the laurel, lingering about the sheets and mattress." (39) The laurel, expressive of victory and celebration, is a tree sacred to Apollo, and since the sun charts the course of this harmonious day, the association is clear. The festival being celebrated is a mock wedding, and the hammock which Edna slept in the night before has been replaced by the marriage bed.

Edna wakes to an Edenic world of simple pleasure and magical properties. Beside her bed are bread and wine, symbolizing communion. Outside she picks an orange from a tree in a natural paradise where, Robert tells her, she has slept for a hundred years while he guarded her. As the day ends they watch the sun "turning the western sky to flaming copper and gold," (41) as Madame Antoine tells them stories. She represents the oral tradition of art, a simple phase which Edna can enjoy and emulate. On the boat trip back, Edna hears "the whispering voices of dead men and the click of muffled gold." (42) This day is the high point of romance in Edna's imagination, and she will return to it in her memory as she paints, and as she repeats Madame Antoine's stories.

The woman who represents a structured form of art is Mme. Reisz, the true artist Edna wishes to become. While Madame Ratignolle plays the piano solely for the pleasure of her family, Mme. Reisz plays Frederic Chopin with great feeling and art. Before hearing Mme. Reisz play, music had evoked pictures in Edna's mind. After listening to her play, Edna's passions are aroused. But like such nineteenth century female artists as Emily Dickinson, Mme. Reisz is unmarried, childless, eccentric in manner and in dress, and alienated from society. She cannot serve as a role model for Edna. Nevertheless, Edna's creative development continues. After the family's return to New Orleans, she takes up her painting once more in spite of her husband's admonishment that she "not let the family go to the devil" while she paints. She works with "great energy and interest" though she feels she is not accomplishing anything. Often she sings "Ah tu savais," the song Robert sang on Grand Isle, and she recalls:

> the ripple of the water, the flapping sail. She could see the glint of the moon upon the bay, and could feel the soft, gusty beating of the hot south wind. A subtle current of desire passed through her body, weakening her hold upon the brushes and making her eyes burn.
>
> (62)

On the one hand romance limits her work, but on the other hand it is a source of inspiration.

There are factors beyond Edna's control, however, which limit her development. Gilbert and Gubar, in a discussion of the woman writer in patriarchal society, describe "the loneliness of the female artist, her feelings of alienation from male predecessors coupled with her need for sisterly precursors and successors, her urgent need for a female audience."[9] Certainly this describes Edna's situation as she seeks out her two contrasting women friends for validation, Mme. Reisz and Adèle Ratignolle. She brings her paintings to Adèle even though she knows in advance, "her opinion in such a matter would be next to valueness . . . but she sought the words of praise and encouragement that would help her to put heart into her venture." (59) Adèle, true to her character as a "mother-woman," tells her that her talent is immense, and Edna is pleased even though she recognizes "its true worth." She receives a much harsher judgement of her artistic capacity from Mme. Reisz. In reply to the question of what she has been doing, Edna tells her "I am becoming an artist" and her friend says, "Ah! an artist. You have pretensions, Madame." (68) Sensing the insecurity which keeps her from total commitment to art, Mme. Reisz warns, "To be an artist includes much; one must possess many gifts—absolute gifts—which have not been acquired by one's own effort. And moreover, to succeed the artist must possess the courageous soul." (68)

But there is much evidence to show the growth in Edna's capacity to be an artist. She is learning to enjoy solitude, and her teacher, an art dealer, observes that her work "grows in force and individuality." At a dinner party she tells the Baratarian story she heard from Madame Antoine, and her imagination has grown so much that she makes "every glowing word seem real" to her listeners. Shortly after, she moves out of her husband's house, using money from an inheritance and from the sale of her paintings, into a smaller house of her own. Edna's little house, like Woolf's "room of one's own," is a symbol for growing psychic and financial independence. In addition, even more important than these actions, Edna has defined herself as an artist. Jokingly she says to Mme. Reisz, "You see that I have persistence. Does that quality count for anything in art?" (68) Indeed it does. Edna paints even though she lacks the serious criticism from others that could help her shape her art and despite the fact that she misses the support of women artists who understand the special obstacles that impede female creativity.

Two events occur almost simultaneously at the novel's climax, events which portray the forces that finally defeat Edna's search for artistic wholeness. One is her witnessing of Adèle's suffering in child-birth and the other is Robert's admitting that he loves her and wants to marry her. Edna has gone to Adèle, leaving Robert just after he tells her he has dreamed of marrying her if her husband will free her. She has replied that she is no longer one of Mr. Pontellier's possessions to be given away. When she returns from Adèle's he is gone, having explained in a note that he has left not because he doesn't love her but because he does. Robert has been deeply connected to her sexual growth, which in turn affected the growth of her imagination. Through him she has begun to transfer the authenticity of her romantic vision to her paintings. Now, romantic illusions shattered, she loses the catlyst for her art.

The other illusion that is shattered is that of childbirth being a moment of joy. Edna does not remember her own pain when she gave birth, since she was chloroformed. Now, seeing Adèle's pain, she recognizes that she cannot rebel against nature. Adèle's parting words "think of the children" remind her of her mother-role which conflicts with her new-found freedom. Chopin was far ahead of her time in exposing the myth of bearing children as a woman's ultimate fulfillment, calling Adèle's "acouchement" a scene of torture. Almost a century later Sylvia Plath was to use the same image in *The Bell Jar* by describing the delivery room as "some awful torture chamber."[10] And a doctor tells Plath's protagonist Esther, just as Dr. Mandelet told Edna, "They oughtn't to let women watch. You'll never want a baby if you do. It'll be the end of the human race."[11]

The next morning Edna returns to Grand Isle and walks to her death in the sea. Is her suicide triggered by Adèle's suffering in childbirth? By the knowledge that it is futile to rebel against biology? Does she kill herself because Robert has left her? Or because she has failed to become an artist? Edna drowns herself because she cannot live as a conventional wife or mother any longer, and society will not accept her newfound self. The solitude she enjoys makes for artistic growth, but she is bound to children, home, social duty. She will not sacrifice her new autonomy because, as Anne Jones points out, "she will not relinquish the core of her vision, which is not finally romance, but rather her own autonomous being . . . so she freely goes to the sea, losing her life. But she does not lose her self."[12]

By beginning and ending *The Awakening* with the sea Chopin gives the book a wholeness that Edna cannot find in her life. Furthermore, Chopin's themes of sea/mother, love/lover, self/birth, sexuality/creativity are joined as Edna's birth of a new self is juxtaposed against Adèle's giving birth to another. In a moment of liberty she stands naked on the beach feeling like "some new-born creature" before entering the sea which becomes the universal Great Mother. To be sure, Chopin uses one image of defeat, the "bird with the broken wing," which Edna sees "reeling, fluttering, circling, disabled down down to the water." (124) This was the image used by Mlle. Reisz when, as if predicting Edna's fall she said, "it is a sad spectacle to see the weakling bruised, exhausted, fluttering back to earth." (89) But how strong must a woman be at this time in order to maintain her artistic vocation without any support from community? Certainly Mlle. Reisz has given Edna no encouragement, so Edna thinks of how she would have laughed at her, of Robert who would never understand, and of her children who "sought to drag her into the soul's slavery." (123)

Yet Edna's final moment is one of autonomous sexuality, as the world of her imagination resonates with fertility—

"There was the hum of bees, and the musky odor of pinks filled the air." (125) Chopin repeats the description of the sea which describes Edna's first swim, "The touch of the sea is sensuous, enfolding the body in its soft, close embrace," (124) and with this symbolic closure portrays Edna becoming whole in the only way she can, by immersion in the universal sea of love. But how can Edna's death be positive? Many critics think it is not.[13] Wolff, for example, uses it as further evidence of Edna's regressive instincts.[14] Christ believes that while the ending of the novel was realistic for its time, suicide as a resolution cannot satisfy women now.[15] Nevertheless, Edna Pontellier succeeds in giving birth to a new self even though the fact that she can not live on earth as this new self is tragic. The triumph of *The Awakening* lies in Chopin's depicting, when others did not, the conflicts faced by women who wish to become artists. Courageously, she built in her novel a bridge from past to future so that women might find their way across. Like her heroine, she too was a *pontellier*, a bridge-maker.

Notes

1. C. L. Deyo, "The Newest Books," St. Louis *Post-Dispatch,* May 20, 1899, quoted in Kate Chopin, *The Awakening,* an authoritative text, Context, Criticisms (New York, Norton, 1976), p. 149.

2. Kate Chopin, *The Awakening & Selected Stories of Kate Chopin* (New York: The New American Library, 1976), p. 120. All quotes are cited from this edition,

3. Cynthia Griffin Wolff, "Thanatos and Eros: Kate Chopin's *The Awakening,*" *American Quarterly* XXV (Oct. 1973), printed in *The Awakening,* ed. Culley, p. 212, 217.

4. Suzanne Wolkenfeld, "Edna's Suicide: The Problem of the One and the Many," in *The Awakening* ed. Culley, p. 223.

5. James Justus, "The Unawakening of Edna Pontellier." *Southern Literary Journal,* X (Spring, 1978), p. 112.

6. Donald A. Ringe, "Romantic Imagery in Kate Chopin's *The Awakening,*" *American Literature,* 43 (January, 1972), reprinted in *The Awakening,* ed. Culley, p. 206.

7. Carol P. Christ, *Diving Deep and Surfacing: Women Writers on Spiritual Quest* (Boston: Beacon Press, 1980), p. 35.

8. Per Seyersted, *Kate Chopin: A Critical Biography* (Baton Rouge: Louisiana State University Press, 1969), p. 153.

9. Sandra Gilbert and Susan Gubar, *The Madwoman in the Attic: The Woman Writer and the Nineteenth Century Literary Imagination* (New Haven: Yale University Press, 1979), p. 50.

10. Sylvia Plath, *The Bell Jar* (New York: Harper & Row, 1971), p. 53.

11. Plath, p. 53.

12. Anne Goodwyn Jones, *Tomorrow Is Another Day: The Women Writer in the South, 1859-1936* (Baton Rouge: Louisiana State University Press, 1981), p. 169.

13. Wolkenfeld sums up critical views of Edna's suicide in *The Awakening,* ed. Culley. Those cited who hold negative views are Donald S. Rankin, George M. Spangler, and Cynthia Griffin Wolff.

14. Wolff, in *The Awakening,* ed. Culley, p. 218.

15. Christ, p. 39.

Patricia S. Yaeger (essay date spring 1987)

SOURCE: Yaeger, Patricia S. "'A Language Which Nobody Understood': Emancipatory Strategies in *The Awakening*" *Novel* 20, no. 3 (spring 1987): 197-219.

[*In the following essay, Yaeger argues that language, not sexual liberation, is the element that makes* The Awakening *a "transgressive" novel.*]

Despite the academy's growing commitment to producing and publishing feminist interpretations of literary texts, insofar as feminist critics read Kate Chopin's *The Awakening* as a novel about sexual liberation, we read it with our patriarchal biases intact. Of course *The Awakening*'s final scene is breath-taking; Edna Pontellier transcends her circumscribed status as sensual entity—as the object of others' desires—and stands before us as her own subject, as a blissfully embodied being: ". . . she cast the unpleasant, pricking, garments from her, and for the first time in her life she stood naked in the open air, at the mercy of the sun, the breeze that beat upon her, and the waves that invited her."[1] It is because of this new dignity and visibility Chopin gives to women's desires that *The Awakening* has been celebrated as one of the great subversive novels—a novel belonging to the tradition of transgressive narratives Tony Tanner describes in *Adultery in the Novel.* But in this essay I will suggest that Tanner's ideas are inadequate to account for the real transgressive force of Chopin's novel. Instead, I want to locate this force in Chopin's representation of a language Edna Pontellier seeks but does not possess, in her representation of "a language which nobody understood."[2]

In *Adultery in the Novel* Tanner explains that eighteenth- and nineteenth-century novels derive a "narrative urgency" from their power to interrupt the status quo by representing characters or ideas which impinge on society's stability. While most bourgeois novels affirm marriage, the nuclear family, or genealogical continuity as the source of social stability, these same novels gather momentum by representing "an energy that threatens to contravene that stability of the family on which society depends": an energy frequently embodied in the adulterous woman.[3] While

prostitutes, orphans, adventurers, and other marginal characters dominate the early phases of the novel and disrupt its representations of family stability with a raw transgressive force, Tanner suggests that in the novel's later incarnations this same energy is embodied in the motive or act of adultery. "Marriage, to put it at its simplest . . . is a means by which society attempts to bring into harmonious alignment patterns of passion and patterns of property" (15).

According to Tanner, marriage and adultery are central to the bourgeois novel because marriage mediates between the opposed demands of private desire and public law. "If society depends for its existence on certain rules governing what may be combined and what should be kept separate, then adultery, by bringing the wrong things together in the wrong places (or the wrong people in the wrong beds), offers an attack on those rules, revealing them to be arbitrary rather than absolute" (13). This is a fine observation, and resembles the critique Edna Pontellier applies to her husband and children while contemplating suicide. But Edna's critique of her position within the nuclear family, her sense of herself as someone who should not be regarded as her husband's or children's property, is only a part of her story: her realization does not begin to explain the forces in her society that resist critique. While the adulterous impulses of the novelistic heroine challenge one form of patriarchy, I want to suggest that they enhance another: the power of woman's "extra-marital" desire does not have the revolutionary power Tanner predicates.

Obsessed with the other, murdered, ostracized, or killed by her own hand, the adulterous woman is caught in an elaborate code that has already been negotiated by her society. Her actions may be defined as abnormal, but they are only mildly transgressive; adultery remains well within the arena of permissible social trespass. Edna Pontellier falls in love with Robert Lebrun precisely *because* this possibility is inscribed within her, because adulterous desire is covertly regarded in her society as a path for woman's misconduct: such desire continues to involve an obsessional valorization of the masculine.

> Edna often wondered at one propensity which sometimes had inwardly disturbed her. . . . At a very early age . . . she remembered that she had been passionately enamored of a dignified and sad-eyed cavalry officer who visited her father in Kentucky. She could not leave his presence when he was there, nor remove her eyes from his face, which was something like Napoleon's.
>
> (18-19)

Participating in the bourgeois family is one expression of the romantic obsession that shapes and destroys the bourgeois heroine. Participating in licentious desire for a man other than her husband is simply another. At the Pontelliers' dinner party early in the novel we can see how this desire remains within the schema of approved social narratives:

The Colonel, with little sense of humor and of the fitness of things, related a somber episode of those dark and bitter days, in which he had acted a conspicuous part and always formed a central figure. Nor was the Doctor happier in his selection, when he told the old, ever new and curious story of the waning of a woman's love, seeking strange, new channels, only to return to its legitimate source after days of fierce unrest. It was one of the many little human documents which had been unfolded to him during his long career as a physician. The story did not seem especially to impress Edna.

(70)

With his generous construction of what is and is not "legitimate," the doctor has told a story in Tanner's "New Testament tradition." According to Tanner, Christ is the ideal narrator, the narrator who, when "confronted with the woman taken in adultery," tries to make the "would-be lawgivers aware of her problematical reality, calling into question both the impersonal application of the law and the justification and rights of the would-be legislators. Effectively this implies the disintegration of society-as-constituted" (14). But what else might it imply? Christ, despite his distinct "femininity," and Mandelet, despite his generosity, still claim jural power by virtue of their gender; their acts and judgments do not imply "the disintegration of society as constituted," but rather its "fatherly" reformation, since these paternal figures define—if not society's center—then its gentlemanly margins. In their "generous" revisions of law we find the same plot transferred to another patriarchal economy. Neither Christ nor Dr. Mandelet suggests a revision of the traditional heterosexual plot which, while it may or may not involve marriage, always involves a hierarchical reading of woman's relation to man.

Tanner has more to say; he argues that even "without anything or anyone necessarily having changed place or roles (in social terms), the action of adultery portends the possible breakdown of all the mediations on which society itself depends, and demonstrates the latent impossibility of participating in the interrelated patterns that comprise its structure" (17). This apocalyptic view of transgression is appealing, but wrong. For Edna, the thought or practice of adultery seems revolutionary but is actually a conservative gesture within the larger scheme of things, another mode of social acquiescence.[4] The most radical act of trespass Chopin's novel describes is not Edna's propensity to fall in love, or even the way she acts after falling, but the fact that she is disturbed by her own obsessions.

Before her romance with Lebrun intervenes, Chopin's novel holds Edna's awakening open for us as an extraordinary event that Chopin refuses to attach—except peripherally—to Lebrun until we have witnessed Edna's preliminary attempts at self-dialogue and self-knowledge. We should therefore take exception to Tanner's paradigm, his notion that adultery

> introduces an agonizing and irresolvable category—confusion—into the individual and thence into society itself. . . . If society depends for its existence on certain rules governing what may be combined and what should be kept separate, then adultery, by bringing the wrong things together in the wrong places (or the wrong people in the wrong beds), offers an attack on those rules, revealing them to be arbitrary rather than absolute. In this way, the adulterous woman becomes the "gap" in society that gradually extends through it. In attempting to ostracize her, society moves toward ostracizing itself.

(12-13)

Society may read itself through the absence of the adulterous woman, but she, being absent, cannot read herself. It is the absence of such critique and not the absence of adultery that allows the maintenance of a sex/gender system that remains repressive and hierarchical and victimizes women by making them not only wives, but objects of romantic or domestic narratives. *The Awakening*'s most radical awareness is that Edna inhabits a world of limited linguistic possibilities, of limited possibilities for interpreting and re-organizing her feelings, and therefore of limited possibilities for action. In Edna's world what sorts of things are open to question and what things are not? Although Edna initially attempts to move into an arena in which she can begin to explore feelings which lie outside the prescribed social code, finally she can only think about herself within that code, can only act within some permutation of the subject-object relations her society has ordained for her.

If this is so, can we still define *The Awakening* as one of the grand subversive novels, as a novel belonging to a great tradition of emancipatory fiction? We can make such claims for *The Awakening* only if Chopin has been successful in inventing a novelistic structure in which the heroine's very absence of speech works productively, in which Edna's silence offers a new dialogic ground from which we can measure the systematic distortions of her old ground of being and begin to construct a new, utopian image of the emergence of women's antithetical desires. Does Chopin's novel offer such utopian structures?

"She had put her head down on Madame Ratignolle's shoulder. She was flushed and felt intoxicated with the sound of her own voice and the unaccustomed taste of candor. It muddled her like wine, or like a first breath of freedom" (20). What are the conditions that permit Edna to feel intoxicated with the sound of her own voice, to experience this "unaccustomed taste of candor" in conversation with a friend? These feelings are customary, this rapture quite ordinary, in fictions by men. "The earth is all before me," Wordsworth insists in *The Prelude*. "With a heart / Joyous, nor scared at its own liberty, / I look about; and should the chosen guide / Be nothing better than a wandering cloud, / I cannot miss my way. I breathe again!"[5] We know, of course, that Wordsworth has it wrong, that he has miles to go before he discovers anything remotely resembling liberty. Intoxicated by his own voice, thrilled at the prospect of articulate freedom, Wordsworth still claims prophetic powers; he permits his mind to wander and releases his voice to those "trances of thought and mountings of the mind" which hurry toward him. This makes gorgeous poetry, but for whom does it speak? Such moments are rarely recorded by women writers either on their own behalf or on behalf of their fictional heroines. In the scene in *The Awakening* where Edna returns to the beach from her unearthly swim, it is Robert Lebrun who speaks for her, who frames and articulates the meaning of her adventure, and the plot he invents involves a mystical, masculine sea-spirit responsible for Edna's sense of election, as if romance were the only form of elation a heroine might feel. Edna repudiates Robert's story: "'Don't banter me,' she said, wounded at what appeared to be his flippancy" (30). And yet Robert's metaphors quickly become Edna's own:

> Sailing across the bay to the *Chênière Caminada*, Edna felt as if she were being borne away from some anchorage which had held her fast, whose chains had been loosening—had snapped the night before when the mystic spirit was abroad, leaving her free to drift whithersoever she chose to set her sails. Robert spoke to her incessantly . . .
>
> (35)

The tension between Edna's imagined freedom and Robert's incessant speech is palpable, but unlike the speech of Edna's husband, Robert's words invite dialogue: "'I'll take you some night in the pirogue when the moon shines. Maybe your Gulf spirit will whisper to you in which of these islands the treasures are hidden—direct you to the very spot, perhaps.' 'And in a day we should be rich!' she laughed. 'I'd give it all to you, the pirate gold and every bit of treasure we could dig up.'" (35). Not only is Robert's vision one that Edna can participate in and help to create, but it is also like a fairy-tale: romantic, enticing, utopian. As a "utopia" Robert's vision is not at all emancipatory; it offers only the flip side, the half-fulfilled wishes of an everyday ideology.

> *"How many years have I slept?" she inquired. "The whole island seems changed. A new race of beings must have sprung up, leaving only you and me as past relics. . . ."*
>
> *He familiarly adjusted a ruffle upon her shoulder.*
>
> *"You have slept precisely one hundred years. I was left here to guard your slumbers; and for one hundred years I have been out under the shed reading a book. The only evil I couldn't prevent was to keep a broiled fowl from drying up."*
>
> (38)

This comic repartee is charming: as Foucault explains in *The Order of Things*, utopias afford us special consolation. "Although they have no real locality there is nevertheless a fantastic, untroubled region in which they are able to unfold; they open up . . . countries where life is easy, even though the road to them is chimerical. . . . This is why utopias permit fables and discourse: they run with the very grain of language and are part of the fundamental dimension of the *fabula*."[6] What Robert Lebrun offers Edna is a

continuing story, a mode of discourse which may be chimerical, but unlike Edna's talk with her husband is also potentially communal. This discursive mode cannot, however, invite its speakers to test the limits of their language; instead, it creates a pleasurable nexus of fancy through which Edna may dream. Freed from the repressive talk of her husband, Edna chooses another mode of oppression, a speech-world that offers space for flirtation that Edna finds liberating. But this liberation is also limiting, a form of stultification, and in exchanging the intoxicating sound of her own voice as she speaks on the beach for Robert's romantic voice, Edna Pontellier's growing sense of self is stabilized, frozen into a mode of feeling and consciousness which, for all its promise of sexual fulfillment, leaves her essentially without resources, without an opportunity for other internal dialogues.[7] We may see *The Awakening* as a novel praising sexual discovery and critiquing the asymmetries of the marriage plot, but we must also recognize that this is a novel in which the heroine's capacities for thought are shut down, a novel in which Edna's temptations *to think* are repressed by the moody discourse of romance. In fact, the novel's explicitly utopian constructs partake of this romance framework; they do not function transgressively. Does Chopin offer her heroine—or her reader—any emancipatory alternative?

Let us begin to answer this question by considering a moment from Lacan's essay "From Love to the Libido"—a moment in which Lacan turns upon his audience and denies that we can ever define ourselves through another's language.

> What I, Lacan . . . am telling you is that the subject as such is uncertain because he is divided by the effects of language. Through the effects of speech, the subject always realizes himself more in the Other, but he is already pursuing there more than half of himself. He will simply find his desire ever more divided, pulverized, in the circumscribable metonymy of speech.[8]

The hearing of a lecture, the writing of a psychoanalytic text, the reading of a novel: these are moments of self-divisiveness, of seeking what we are in that which we are not. It is this drive toward self-realization in the speech of the other that we have begun to discover in *The Awakening*. Chopin's novel focuses from its beginning on the difficulties we have maneuvering within the precincts of language. It opens with an exotic and showy image: "A green and yellow parrot, which hung in a cage outside the door, kept repeating over and over: *Allez vous-en! Allez vous-en! Sapristi!* That's all right!" (3) The parrot's speech is nonsensical, and yet it illuminates its world in an intriguing way. An amalgam of English and Creole, this exotic speech alerts us to the fact that the parrot inhabits a multilingual culture and suggests the babble and lyricism bred by mixing world views. But in addition to giving us a glimpse of the worlds we will encounter within the larger novel, these opening paragraphs make enigmatic statements about our relation to language itself; they open up an intriguing linguistic matrix.

> Mr. Pontellier, unable to read his newspaper with any degree of comfort, arose with an expression and an ex-

clamation of disgust. He walked down the gallery and across the narrow "bridges" which connected the Lebrun cottages one with the other. . . .

He stopped before the door of his own cottage, which was the fourth one from the main building and next to the last. Seating himself in a wicker rocker which was there, he once more applied himself to the task of reading the newspaper. The day was Sunday; the paper was a day old.

(3)

In contrast to the giddy plurality of the parrot's speech, Mr. Pontellier's meditations are redundant and single-minded. Chopin asks us to associate his propriety with the backward tug of words which are "a day old" and already emptied of meaning.[9] The parrot, on the other hand, speaks a language emptied of meaning but full of something else. "He could speak a little Spanish, and also a language which nobody understood, unless it was the mockingbird that hung on the other side of the door, whistling his fluty notes out upon the breeze with maddening persistence" (3). Repetitive, discontinuous, incomprehensible: the speech of this parrot points to an immediate contrast between everyday speech and a more extraordinary speech world. The parrot mixes modes of speech at random; its polyvocal discourse directs our attention to a potential lack of meaning in words themselves—to a register of meaning beyond the reach of its language which is paradoxically articulated in *The Awakening* as "a language which nobody understood."

In reading the parrot's speech we are in the vicinity of what Lacan calls "metonymy":

A lack is encountered by the subject in the Other, in the very intimation that the Other makes to him by his discourse. In the intervals of the discourse of the Other, there emerges in the experience of the child something that is radically mappable, namely, *He is saying this to me, but what does he want?*

In this interval intersecting the signifiers . . . is the locus of what, in other registers of my exposition, I have called metonymy. It is there that what we call desire crawls, slips, escapes, like the ferret. The desire of the Other is apprehended by the subject in that which does not work, in the lacks of the discourse of the Other, and all the child's whys reveal not so much an avidity for the reason of things, as a testing of the adult, a *Why are you telling me this?* ever-resuscitated from its base, which is the enigma of the adult's desire.

(214)

Reading Chopin's text we find ourselves, from our first overhearing of the parrot's empty speech, in the position of the child who asks "Why?" but unlike the child we can begin to formulate an answer. The register of desire—of something not described within language but premised and promised there—is provided for us in the "empty" referents of the parrot's speech and its highly charged iterations of the mockingbird's song. It is this enigmatic "language" Mr. Pontellier attempts to shun as he navigates his

newspaper and the "bridges" connecting the coherent and well-mapped spaces between the cottages. But it is in the unmapped spaces, the spaces between words, the unspoken sites of desire that Edna Pontellier initially resides, and in order to understand how this transgressive impulse is structured into Chopin's novel we need to see that Chopin herself has divided the linguistic topography of *The Awakening* in to an extra-linguistic zone of meaning imaged for us at the beginning of the novel in the speech of the parrot, a "language which nobody understood," and a countervailing region of linguistic constraints imaged for us in Mr. Pontellier's speech.

Although Lacan's reading of "metonymy" helps us to identify this linguistic topography, the novel's missing register of language should not be confused with the irrecoverable "lack" that Lacan defines at the heart of discourse, or the psychic dyslexia in which Kristeva says "Woman" resides. Although "the feminine," in Kristeva's early essays, is said to be synonymous with the a-linguistic ("What I mean by 'woman' is that which is not represented, that which is unspoken, that which is left out of namings and ideologies"[10]), I want to suggest that Edna's absent language is not a manifestation of women's permanent expulsion from "masculine speech" but of what Jean-François Lyotard calls *"le differend."*

Lyotard explains that "in the *differend* something 'asks' to be put into sentences, and suffers the wrong of not being able to be at the moment. . . . It is the concern of a literature, of a philosophy, perhaps of a politics, to testify to these *differends* by finding an idiom for them."[11] Chopin testifies to these *"differends"* by using the metaphor of an absent or displaced vocality ("the voice of the sea," the multivoiced babble of the parrot) to emphasize Edna's need for a more passionate and intersubjective speech that would allow Edna to revise or rearticulate her relations to her own desire and to the social reality that thwarts this desire. This is to argue that *The Awakening* is a text that asks for another idiom to fill in the unspoken voices in Edna's story: an idiom that contemporary women writers and feminist critics have begun to provide.[12] Thus Edna Pontellier speaks an unfinished discourse that reaches out to be completed by other speaking human beings: her "lost" speech—represented by her own speech fragments, by the sibilant voice of the sea and the chatter of the trilingual parrot—is not unfinished on an a-historical, metaphysical plane. Instead, Chopin's displaced metaphors of vocality help us to envision for her heroine a more radical speech situation, a linguistic practice that would reach out to the *"differend,"* to a politics that is not yet a politics, to a language that should be phrased but cannot yet (or could not then) be phrased.[13] In this reading of Chopin's text the emancipatory moments in *The Awakening* do not consist of those instances of adulterous desire that drive Edna toward the transgressive side of the marriage plot. Instead, such emancipatory moments are contained in those unstable instances of self-questioning and dialogue with herself and with other women that the novel's romance plot helps to elide.

Before looking more closely at the way the "*differend*" operates in Chopin's novel, let us consider the moment of Edna's awakening in more detail. On the evening when Edna first begins, consciously, to recognize her powers and wants "to swim far out, where no woman had swum before" (28), her experience is one of multiple moods, of emotions which seem confused and inarticulate: "A thousand emotions have swept through me to-night. I don't comprehend half of them. . . . I wonder if any night on earth will ever again be like this one. It is like a night in a dream. The people about me are like some uncanny, half-human beings. There must be spirits abroad to-night" (30). Sensing the extraordinary reach of her feelings, Lebrun answers in kind:

> "There are," whispered Robert. "Didn't you know this was the twenty-eighth of August?"

> "The twenty-eighth of August?"

> "Yes. On the twenty-eighth of August, at the hour of midnight, and if the moon is shining—the moon must be shining—a spirit that has haunted these shores for ages rises up from the Gulf. With its own penetrating vision the spirit seeks some one mortal worthy to hold him company, worthy of being exalted for a few hours into realms of the semi-celestials. His search has always hitherto been fruitless, and he has sunk back, disheartened, into the sea. But tonight he found Mrs. Pontellier. Perhaps he will never wholly release her from the spell. Perhaps she will never again suffer a poor, unworthy earthling to walk in the shadow of her divine presence."

> (30)

While Robert Lebrun may have "penetrated her mood," he has also begun to alter its meaning. Edna's experience has been solitary and essentially mysterious; her swim has been a surpassing of limits, a mythic encounter with death—an experience suffused with metaphor, beyond comprehension. Robert's words do not begin to encompass its meaning, but he does attempt to communicate with her, to understand her mood. And since Edna lacks an alternative register of language to describe her tumultuous feelings, Robert's conceit soon becomes her own; his language comes to stand for the nameless feelings she has just begun to experience. Just as Edna's initial awakening, her continuing journey toward self-articulation and self-awareness is initially eccentric and complex, so this journey is finally diminished and divided, reduced in the romantic stories that she is told and the romantic stories she comes to tell herself, to a simplistic narrative that falsifies the diversity of her awakening consciousness. From this perspective, the pivotal event of Chopin's novel is not Edna's suicide, nor her break with her husband, but her openness to Robert Lebrun's stories, her vulnerability to the romantic speech of the other which has, by the end of the novel, become her speech as well:

> "I love you," she whispered, "only you; no one but you. It was you who awoke me last summer out of a life-long, stupid dream. Oh! you have made me so unhappy with your indifference. Oh! I have suffered, suf-

fered! Now you are here we shall love each other, my Robert. We shall be everything to each other. Nothing else in the world is of any consequence. I must go to my friend; but you will wait for me? No matter how late; you will wait for me, Robert?"

> (107)

Edna's final retelling of her story is not an accurate self-portrait, but a radical betrayal of the "awakening" that emerges at the novel's beginning. This initial "awakening" does not involve the violent triangulation of adultery, romance, and erotic story-telling, but the exploration of a discontinuous series of images that are promisingly feminocentric. In fact, what is disturbing about Edna's last speech to Robert is its falsification of her story, its naming of Lebrun as author of her growth, as source of her awakening. For what this last speech denies is the essential strangeness of Edna's initial self-consciousness, the tantalizing world of unvoiced dreams and ideas that Edna encounters at the novel's inception. By the end of the novel Edna has drifted into a system of self-explanation that—while it seems to account for her experience—also falsifies that experience by giving it the gloss of coherence, of a continuous narrative line. Edna's thoughts at the beginning of the novel are much more confused—but they are also more heterogeneous and promising.

In the opening scenes of *The Awakening* this struggle among different social possibilities, among diverse points of view, fails to take place as explicitly realized dialogue. Even Edna's husband does not have the power to challenge the voices which annoy him, but only "the privilege of quitting their society when they ceased to be entertaining." "The parrot and the mocking-bird were the property of Madame Lebrun," Chopin tells us, "and they had the right to make all the noise they wished" (3). The detail seems trivial, but it is worth noting that just as Mr. Pontellier's reaction to the parrot's nonsensical speech is defined in terms of his relation to the parrot as someone else's possession, so his wife is defined in terms of property relations as well. "'What folly to bathe at such an hour and in such heat! . . . You are burnt beyond recognition,' he added, looking at his wife as one looks at a valuable piece of personal property which has suffered some damage" (4). In Pontellier's linguistic world, the roles of speaker and listener are clearly defined in terms of social and material hierarchies. Edna Pontellier is someone her husband feels free to command and free to define, but she is not someone to whom Mr. Pontellier listens:

> "What is it?" asked Pontellier, looking lazily and amused from one to the other. It was some utter nonsense; some adventure out there in the water, and they both tried to relate it at once. It did not seem half so amusing when told. They realized this, and so did Mr. Pontellier. He yawned and stretched himself. Then he got up, saying he had half a mind to go over to Klein's hotel and play a game of billiards.

> (5)

When Pontellier—feeling "very talkative"—returns from Klein's hotel late at night, he blithely awakens his wife to converse.

He talked to her while he undressed, telling her anec-dotes and bits of news and gossip that he had gathered during the day. From his trousers pockets he took a fistful of crumpled bank notes and a good deal of silver coin, which he piled on the bureau indiscriminately with keys, knife, handkerchief, and whatever else hap-pened to be in his pockets.

(7)

Pontellier expects his words to have the same weight as his silver; the only difference is that he dispenses his language with greater abandon. But Edna Pontellier inhabits a speech-world very different from her husband's, a world oddly bereft of his cultural symbols. "Overcome with sleep," she continues dreaming as he speaks and answers him "with little half utterances." For her husband, Edna's separateness is maddening. Her words, like the words of the parrot Pontellier cannot abide, seem nonsensical; her "little half utterances" suggest a replay of the early morning scene on the beach. But this time the hierarchies are played out in earnest, and Pontellier reacts to his wife's inattention with a burgher-like furor. Nominally concerned for his children, he stalks to their rooms, only to find them inhabiting their own bizarre speech-worlds: "He turned and shifted the youngsters about in bed. One of them began to kick and talk about a basket full of crabs" (7).

While *The Awakening* traces the closure of its own intervals of desire and self-questioning, Chopin is also engaged in the radical mapping of those moments of speech in which our desires begin to address us. If the socio-symbolic world we inhabit encourages us to displace unspoken polyphanies with repetition, with customary stories, with narrative lines, the force of *The Awakening*'s subversive nocturnes, its metonymic intervals, belies the permanence of Pontellier's social forms and suggests a linguistic counterplot which glitters through the text with disarticulate meaning. The child's response throws his father's patriarchal assumptions into even higher relief when Pontellier responds to his son's "utter nonsense" by chiding his wife: "Mr. Pontellier returned to his wife with the information that Raoul had a high fever and needed looking after. . . . He reproached his wife with her inattention, her habitual neglect of the children. If it was not a mother's place to look after children, whose on earth was it?" (7). When Pontellier uses his power of speech to awaken his wife and to define her, Edna answers with deliberate silence. But when Pontellier drifts off to sleep, this silence loses its power. "Turning, she thrust her face, steaming and wet, into the bend of her arm, and she went on crying there, not caring any longer to dry her face, her eyes, her arms. She could not have told why she was crying." What is remarkable about this episode is Chopin's emphasis on the unspoken, the unsayable:

An indescribable oppression, which seemed to generate in some unfamiliar part of her consciousness, filled her whole being with a vague anguish. It was like a shadow, like a mist passing across her soul's summer day. It was strange and unfamiliar; it was a mood. She did not sit there inwardly upbraiding her husband, lamenting at

Fate, which had directed her footsteps to the path which they had taken. She was just having a good cry all to herself. The mosquitoes made merry over her, biting her firm, round arms and nipping at her bare insteps.

(8)

The oppression Edna feels is not merely "indescribable" and "vague," it also comes from an "unfamiliar" region of consciousness and can only be described through analogy. Edna's mood closes as swiftly as it has opened: "The little stinging, buzzing imps succeeded in dispelling a mood which might have held her there in the darkness half a night longer" (8). The biting mosquitoes add an ominous note and operate upon Edna like her husband's alien language; it is as if their determined orality forecloses on Edna's own right to speak.

In the morning the talk between wife and husband is amicably re-established through an economic transaction: "Mr. Pontellier gave his wife half the money which he had brought away from Klein's hotel the evening before" (9). When Mr. Pontellier responds with the appropriate cultural symbols, Edna is as trapped as she was in her conversations with Robert; she can only voice gratitude. "'It will buy a handsome wedding present for Sister Janet!' she exclaimed, smoothing out the bills as she counted them one by one. 'Oh! we'll treat Sister Janet better than that, my dear,' he laughed, as he prepared to kiss her good-by" (9). This happiness continues when Mr. Pontellier returns to New Orleans. The medium of this continued harmony is something oral or edible, something, like language, that Edna can put in her mouth:

A few days later a box arrived for Mrs. Pontellier from New Orleans. It was from her husband. It was filled with *friandises*, with luscious and toothsome bits—the finest of fruits, *patés*, a rare bottle or two, delicious syrups, and bon-bons in abundance.

Mrs. Pontellier was always very generous with the contents of such a box; she was quite used to receiving them when away from home. The *patés* and fruit were brought to the dining-room; the bonbons were passed around. And the ladies, selecting with dainty and discriminating fingers and a little greedily, all declared that Mr. Pontellier was the best husband in the world. Mrs. Pontellier was forced to admit that she knew of none better.

(9)

Chopin's description of Edna's acquiescence, her praise of her husband, is edged with an undeclared violence; Edna is "forced to admit" what she does not feel. But what else could she say? "Mr. Pontellier was a great favorite, and ladies, men, children, even nurses, were always on hand to say good-by to him. His wife stood smiling and waving, the boys shouting, as he disappeared in the old rockaway down the sandy road" (9). Edna has no words for describing her intricate feelings, and if she did, who would listen? She could only speak in a private "language which nobody understood, unless it was the mocking-bird that hung on the other side of the door, whistling his fluty notes out upon the breeze . . ."

In her essay on *The Awakening* Cynthia Griffin Wolff argues that Edna's central problem is psychological, that once her "hidden self" has begun "to exert its inexorable power" we can see that Edna's "libidinal appetite has been fixated at the oral level."[14] I have begun, in contrast, to suggest that Edna's problem is linguistic and social, that her "orality" is frustrated, exacerbated by her social milieu. Wolff insists on the correspondence between Edna's "preoccupation with nourishment" and an infantile, "orally destructive self, a limitless void whose needs can be filled, finally, only by total fusion with the outside world, a totality of sensuous enfolding" (208, 211). She explains that this totality "means annihilation of the ego." But we have seen that Edna's need for fusion, her preoccupation with nourishment or oral surfeiting, does not arise from Edna's own infantility but from social prescription. Married to a Creole, Edna does not feel at home in his society, and she feels especially ill at ease with the Creole manner of speech. If the gap between Creole and Anglo-American cultures gives Edna a glimpse of the inadequacies of each, Edna's inability to deal fluently in the language her husband and lovers speak remains a sign of her disempowerment. As she sails across the bay with Robert to the *Chênière Caminada,* he flirts with a "young barefooted Spanish girl" named Mariequita. Mariequita is coy and flirtatious; she teases Lebrun and asks him sweet, ribald questions:

> Edna liked it all. She looked Mariequita up and down, from her ugly brown toes to her pretty black eyes, and back again.
>
> "Why does she look at me like that?" inquired the girl of Robert.
>
> "Maybe she thinks you are pretty. Shall I ask her?"
>
> "No. Is she your sweetheart?"
>
> "She's a married lady, and has two children."
>
> "Oh! well! Francisco ran away with Sylvano's wife, who had four children. They took all his money and one of the children and stole his boat."
>
> "Shut up!"
>
> "Does she understand?"
>
> "Oh, hush!"
>
> (34)

The scene is gay, but Mariequita's questions are filled with foreboding. Robert's knowledge of several languages, his power to control what others hear and speak, is a sign of his "right" to preside in a context where "no one present understood what they said" (34).

In a conversation with Alcée Arobin later in the novel we see how the paths for women's self-expression are continually limited. As Edna begins to explore her own devi-

ance from social codes, Alcée Arobin usurps her role as story-teller; he begins to define her himself:

> "One of these days," she said, "I'm going to pull myself together for a while and think—try to determine what character of a woman I am; for, candidly, I don't know. By all the codes which I am acquainted with, I am a devilishly wicked specimen of the sex. But some way I can't convince myself that I am. I must think about it."
>
> "Don't. What's the use? Why should you bother thinking about it when I can tell you what manner of woman you are." His fingers strayed occasionally down to her warm, smooth cheeks and firm chin, which was growing a little full and double.
>
> (82)

The text moves from an emphasis on Edna's power of thought and speech to an emphasis on her erotic power, her flesh, as Arobin reasserts the old codes and "feeds" her with stories. Earlier in the novel Adele Ratignolle is similarly primed. Counselling Robert Lebrun to leave Mrs. Pontellier alone, Madame Ratignolle is rebuked for her efforts to speak: "'It isn't pleasant to have a woman tell you—'" Robert Lebrun interrupts, "unheedingly, but breaking off suddenly: 'Now if I were like Arobin—you remember Alcée Arobin and that story of the consul's wife at Biloxi?'" Lebrun's speech operates not only as a form of entertainment, but as a form of repression. "And he related the story of Alcée Arobin and the consul's wife; and another about the tenor of the French Opera, who received letters which should never have been written; and still other stories, grave and gay, till Mrs. Pontellier and her possible propensity for taking young men seriously was apparently forgotten" (21). Lebrun dismisses Madame Ratignolle's concern for Edna and reminds us that the women in Chopin's novel taste little if any verbal freedom. Visiting the Ratignolles Edna observes that

> The Ratignolles understood each other perfectly. If ever the fusion of two human beings into one has been accomplished on this sphere it was surely in their union.
>
> . . .
>
> Monsieur Ratignolle . . . spoke with an animation and earnestness that gave an exaggerated importance to every syllable he uttered. His wife was keenly interested in everything he said, laying down her fork the better to listen, chiming in, taking the words out of his mouth.
>
> (56)

If Edna "is remarkably vulnerable to feelings of being invaded and overwhelmed," if, as Wolff insists, "she is very much at the mercy of her environment," this is because her environment *is* invasive and overwhelming, not only limiting her self-expression to acts of eating, but also rewarding women who, like Madame Ratignolle, are dutifully "delicious" in their roles, who put men's words in their mouths, who have "eaten" their husbands' language.

We have established that *The Awakening* revolves around the heroine's limiting life in the courts of romance and describes, as well, a frightening antagonism between a feminine subject and the objectifying world of discourse she inhabits. "The letter was on the bookshelf. It possessed the greatest interest and attraction for Edna; the envelope, its size and shape, the postmark, the handwriting. She examined every detail of the outside before opening it" (47). What men say, what they write grows more and more portentous, and the cumulative weight of their saying is often the same: "There was no special message to Edna except a postscript saying that if Mrs. Pontellier desired to finish the book which he had been reading to her, his mother would find it in his room, among other books there on the table" (47). The world of alien discourse seems omnipresent in the novel, and when Edna tries to make her own mark, her efforts are fruitless. "Once she stopped, and taking off her wedding ring, flung it upon the carpet. When she saw it lying there, she stamped her heel upon it, striving to crush it. But her small boot heel did not make an indenture, not a mark upon the little glittering circlet" (53). In frustration Edna seizes a glass vase and flings it to the hearth. "She wanted to destroy something. The crash and clatter were what she wanted to hear" (53). If *The Awakening* can be defined as an emancipatory text, if it voices a conflict between men's speech and the speaking of women, this is a conflict articulated as a struggle between men's normative language and something unvoiced and enigmatic—a clatter, a "language which nobody understood." Edna's anger is speechless; her gesture all but impotent, for when a maid sidles into the room to clean up the glass she rediscovers her mistress's cast-off ring: "Edna held out her hand, and taking the ring, slipped it upon her finger" (53).

It is, in fact, only women of property like Madame Lebrun, the owner of the summer resort where the Pontelliers are staying, or artists like Mademoiselle Reisz who have the power of public expression. But Mademoiselle Reisz (who would seem, initially, to offer Edna another model for female selfhood) is surprisingly complicitous in limiting Edna's options. We find the strongest image of her complicity midway through the novel when she hands Edna the letter from Robert and asks Edna to read it while Mademoiselle Reisz plays heart-rending music. "Edna did not know when the Impromptu began or ended. She sat on the sofa corner reading Robert's letter by the fading light." As Edna reads Mademoiselle plays like a manic cupid, gliding "from the Chopin into the quivering lovenotes of Isolde's song, and back again to the Impromptu with its soulful and poignant longing" (64). The music grows fantastic; it fills the room, and Edna begins to sob "as she had wept one midnight at Grand Isle when strange, new voices awoke in her." Now she hears one voice only and this voice has an oppressive material weight. "Mademoiselle reentered and lit a candle. Robert's letter was on the floor. She stopped and picked it up. It was crumpled and damp with tears. Mademoiselle smoothed the letter out, restored it to the envelope, and replaced it in the table drawer" (64). Like Mr. Pontellier's crumpled bank notes and small change, the letter has come to possess its own objectivity, its own material power. But if this is a letter that Made-

moiselle Reisz can exchange for the pleasure of Edna's visit, it also represses her particular sonority. Mademoiselle Reisz's music is replaced by Robert's tune: "Robert's voice was not pretentious. It was musical and true. The voice, the notes, the whole refrain haunted her memory."

The speech of the masculine "other" becomes, for Edna Pontellier and the women in her society, an arena of self-loss and inner divisiveness. Madame Lebrun's expressions, like Edna's, remain vestigial, enigmatic. Her sewing machine echoes the "clatter" of Edna's broken vase.

> "I have a letter somewhere," looking in the machine drawer and finding the letter in the bottom of the work-basket. "He says to tell you he will be in Vera Cruz the beginning of next month"—clatter, clatter!—"and if you still have the intention of joining him"—bang! clatter, clatter, bang!
>
> "Why didn't you tell me so before, mother? You know I wanted—" Clatter, clatter, clatter!
>
> (23)

If Madame Lebrun does not possess Alcée Arobin's power of definition, she does possess his power of interruption, and the noise of her sewing machine half-prepares us for her jibe at her younger son: "Really, this table is getting to be more and more like Bedlam every day, with everybody talking at once. Sometimes—I hope God will forgive me—but positively, sometimes I wish Victor would lose the power of speech" (42).

Translated into the language of the other, Edna's own story fails to materialize. But what might it have looked like? What is the rhythm and content of Edna's speech when she is neither speaking like her father or lover nor to him? First, we have seen that Chopin plays with the hiatus between the stories Edna inherits and what, in Edna, is heterogeneous to these stories, but is not bound by them. In *The Awakening* a story or framing device is frequently set against a "remainder" or supplement of meaning not encompassed within that frame. This remainder, this "excess" of meaning represents a "*differend*" which challenges the framing story's totalizing power, its explanatory validity. (Adorno puts this another way in his *Negative Dialectics*: "A matter of urgency to the concept would be what it fails to cover, what its abstractionist mechanism eliminates, what is not already a case of the concept.")[15] It is never a question of Edna's transcendence of local mythology, but rather of a negative and dialectical play between myth and that which resists mythic closure:

> "Of whom—of what are you thinking?" asked Adele of her companion. . . .
>
> "Nothing," returned Mrs. Pontellier, with a start, adding at once: "How stupid! But it seems to me it is the reply we make instinctively to such a question. Let me see . . . I was really not conscious of thinking of anything; but perhaps I can retrace my thoughts."
>
> "Oh! never mind!" laughed Madame Ratignolle. "I am not quite so exacting. . . . It is really too hot to think, especially to think about thinking."

Clearly Adele Ratignolle's dislike of "thinking" is normative in Edna's society and acts as near-absolute rule. But Edna ventures into areas of the mind that are not well mapped, into memories excluded from Adele Ratignolle's cultural typology. And in thinking of "Nothing," something old and familiar emerges:

> "But for the fun of it," persisted Edna. "First of all, the sight of the water stretching so far away, those motionless sails against the blue sky, made a delicious picture that I just wanted to sit and look at. The hot wind beating in my face made me think—without any connection that I can trace—of a summer day in Kentucky, of a meadow that seemed as big as the ocean to the very little girl walking through the grass . . . She threw out her arms as if swimming when she walked, beating the tall grass as one strikes out in the water. Oh, I see the connection now!"
>
> "Where were you going that day in Kentucky, walking through the grass?"
>
> . . .
>
> "Likely as not it was Sunday," she laughed, "and I was running away from prayers, from the Presbyterian service, read in a spirit of gloom by my father that chills me yet to think of."
>
> (17-18)

As practitioners of free association and students of Freud we may see little that is remarkable in Edna's response. But this is to underestimate the radical quality of her awareness, to dismiss its acrobatic integrity. It is as if Chopin is aware, as Edna is only naively, that the mind wants to go beyond itself, to go toward extremes, to test the accuracy of its own boundaries. Even as the social order demands a closing of ranks—a synthesis or yoking together of disparate ideas in such a way that their disparity grows invisible—the individual has the capacity to challenge her own syntactic boundaries. Edna's talks with Madame Ratignolle present us with a radical example of thought as disconnection, of Edna's capacity to separate ideas from one context to pursue them in another. This is the precondition for dialectic, the capacity for critique that Hegel defines in his *Phenomenology*:

> The activity of dissolution is the power and work of the *Understanding,* the most astonishing and mightiest of powers, or rather the absolute power. The circle that remains self-enclosed and, like substance, holds its moments together, is an immediate relationship, one therefore which has nothing astonishing about it. But that an accident as such, detached from what circumscribes it, what is bound and is actual only in its context with others, should attain an existence of its own and a separate freedom—this is the tremendous power of the negative; it is the energy of thought, of the pure 'I'.[16]

What does this "power of the negative" mean for Edna, and what does it do for her? The images she conjures up seem aimless and accidental, beyond further synthesis, beyond dialectic. But this is precisely their virtue.

In escaping her father's old sermons, Edna strikes out into new physical space; she veers toward an arena of free feeling not designated by the pater-familias. Similarly, in walking to the beach, Adele Ratignolle and Edna have slipped momentarily outside the zone of paternal definition. "In some unaccountable way they had escaped from Robert," Chopin explains (15). The problem, of course, is that their escape is *literally* unaccountable, that outside the other's language they enter the arena of "Nothing," of a language which nobody speaks. And yet in talking with Adele Ratignolle Edna begins to see connections she has not seen before; her thoughts become unsystematic—they go forward before going astray. "Thought," as Maire Jaanus Kurrik suggests, "must admit that it is not only cogency but play, that it is random and can go astray, and can only go forward because it can go astray. Thought has an unshielded and open aspect, which is unsystematic, and which traditional philosophy has repressed for fear of chaos."[17] She adds that thought must "abdicate its idea of hegemony and autarky, and practice a disenchantment of the concept, its transcendence," if it is to challenge its own preconceptions (221). Edna is not so self-conscious about the nature of her thinking, but as her mind plays over the past in a random and heterodox fashion, we can recognize in her thoughts the potential disenchantment of the concept that most binds her, the concept of an obsessive attachment to men, of a romantic and excessive bondage to father-like figures. The image of the beloved cavalry officer that Edna remembers is followed by a series of images or memories of men who have "haunted" Edna's imagination and "stirred" her senses. These broken images come to her not as images of love, but as sources of puzzlement, disaffection, and wonder. Edna is open to thinking about the mystery of her affections; she notes in past amours an obsessive quality that demands perusal.

But something prevents Edna from thinking further, from becoming fully aware of the conditions which bind her. In this instance the conversation between Edna and Adele is interrupted; as they converse on the beach their voices are blurred by "the sound of approaching voices. It was Robert, surrounded by a troop of children, searching for them" (20). Unable to continue their conversation, interrupted in the very moment when Edna had begun to feel "intoxicated with the sound of her own voice . . . the women at once rose and began to shake out their draperies and relax their muscles," and Madame Ratignolle begins to lean "draggingly" on Robert's arm as they walk home (20).

Thought should, perhaps, be "unshielded" and "open"; if thinking is to occur at all the mind must open itself to what is playful, random and unsystematic. But thought can only go so far afield before it ceases to be thought at all; as Hegel suggests, mind or spirit possesses its power only "by looking the negative in the face, and tarrying with it. This tarrying with the negative is the magical power that converts it into being" (19). And this "tarrying with" is something that occurs over time and in a community of speakers; it is not the product of an instant. What prevents Edna's "tarrying with" the negative is not her own inadequacy or some incapacity inherent in speech as such, but Edna's lack of a speech community that will encourage these new speculations, her lack of a group of fellow speakers who will encourage the growth of her thought and its translation into praxis. Though Madame Ratignolle is sympathetic and offers Edna both physical solace and a sympathetic ear, open conversation between them is rare; they speak different languages. "Edna had once told Madame Ratignolle that she would never sacrifice herself for her children, or for any one. Then had followed a rather heated argument." Edna finds herself speaking a language as impenetrable to others as the parrot's babble: "The two women did not appear to understand each other or to be talking the same language" (48). The pull of the libidinal speech-world Edna shares with Robert, then, is immense. (Robert, Chopin explains, "talked a good deal about himself. He was very young, and did not know any better. Mrs. Pontellier talked a little about herself for the same reason. Each was interested in what the other said" [6]). What emerges from their conversation is not a critique of society, however, but gay, utopian play, a pattern of speech in which Edna is once again caught within the semiotic, the bodily residues of her social code, and is not permitted the range of meaning or the control over culturally established symbols that Robert Lebrun is able to command.

Given the power that Robert (and the romance plot itself) exerts over Edna's ordinary patterns of associative thinking, it is worth noting that Chopin's novel ends in a more heterogeneous zone, with Edna's attention turned neither toward Robert nor her husband and children, but toward her own past:

> She looked into the distance, and the old terror flamed up for an instant, then sank again. Edna heard her father's voice and her sister Margaret's. She heard the barking of an old dog that was chained to the sycamore tree. The spurs of the cavalry officer clanged as he walked across the porch. There was the hum of bees, and the musky odor of pinks filled the air.
>
> (114)

This lyrical ending is as enigmatic as the novel's beginning; it might be read as a regression toward oral passivity: toward an infantile repudiation of the validity claims, the social responsibilities adult speech requires. But I would suggest this extralinguistic memory comes to Edna at the end of her life because it is in such a sequence of images, and not the language of Robert Lebrun, that Edna can find the most accessible path to her story—that even in death Edna is seeking (as she sought on the beach) a path of emancipation; she is seeking a register of language more her own.

At the end of the novel as Edna swims out to sea and tries to address Robert once more, she falls again; she finds herself trying to speak a language no one understands. "'Good-by—because, I love you.' He did not know; he did not understand. He would never understand" (114). The story that Edna has told herself about her affection for Robert is inadequate. Close to death, she turns her mind toward the blurred edge of her womanhood, and the novel ends as it has begun, with a medley of distinct and disconnected voices. Here they represent a point of possible origin; they trace that moment in time when, still experiencing the world as a multitude of sounds, Edna's attention begins to shift from the plural voices of childhood toward the socially anticipated fulfillment of her sexual rhythms, toward the obsessive "clang" of the cavalryman's spurs. Just as the novel begins with the parrot's strange speech, with an order of speaking that satirizes and escapes from the epistemological confines of the heroine's world, so Edna's own awakening begins with and returns at her death to the rich and painful lure of desires that are still outside speech and beyond the social order. We must look again at this excluded order of meaning.

In *The Order of Things* Michel Foucault describes the discontinuity and disjunction he feels in perusing a list of incommensurable words or objects encountered in a story by Borges. Foucault experiences the variable terms of this list as "monstrous" and unnerving—Borges' reader is presented with an "order of things" which refuses orderly synthesis. This mode of disorder Foucault defines as a "heteroclite," a state in which "things are 'laid', 'placed', 'arranged' in sites so very different from one another that it is impossible . . . to define a *common locus* beneath them all" (xvii-xviii). In the opening sentences of **The Awakening** the parrot's speech presents us with a similar confusion. Here different syntactic and semantic units from different language systems mingle but refuse to cohere, and we find ourselves contemplating a potential "heterotopia," a discontinuous linguistic space in which the communicative function of language itself is called into question. These discontinuous linguistic spaces, these "heterotopias," are disturbing "because they secretly undermine language . . . because they shatter or tangle common names, because they destroy 'syntax' in advance, and not only the syntax with which we construct sentences but also that less apparent syntax which causes words and things . . . to 'hold together'" (xviii). The opening sentences of Chopin's text have a similar effect upon their reader.[18] In the discrepancies between different languages and the fractioned idioms these languages produce, we are presented with several categories of words and of things that cannot be held, simultaneously, in consciousness. The novel begins by challenging orthodoxy; it posits a world of saying in which ordinary ways of looking at things are called into question.

Chopin's novel pushes us from its beginning toward an arena of speech which asks us to become aware of disjunctions between the disorder of words and the social order, between our usual perceptions and the world these perceptions are designed to organize. The potent, possible syntheses between the self and its world—the syntheses the symbolic order insists we believe in—are challenged and in their place we discover a universe that is anomalous, asynchronic, confusing: a world not so much out of joint as out of its inhabitants' thought, a world outrageously unthinkable. Chopin insists that Mr. Pontellier's manner of organizing himself within this world is to ignore its arch nonsense, to cling to its objects for fetishistic support. He reads his newspaper, fingers his vest pocket: "There was a ten-dollar bill there. He did not know: perhaps he would return for the early dinner and perhaps he would not" (5). Within the novel an extraordinary register of speech is always opening up and then quietly shutting down—a closure which returns us, inevitably, to the circumscribed world of other people's objects and other people's speech, to a linear world in which the intervals of desire are stabilized by cultural symbols that determine the perimeters of self-knowledge.

Chopin makes us aware that the world her novel is designed to represent is itself a heteroclite; her text points to a discrepancy between one kind of social order and its possible others. "It is here," as Foucault says in *The Order of Things,* in the region where the heteroclite becomes visible,

> that a culture, imperceptibly deviating from the empirical orders prescribed for it by its primary codes, instituting an initial separation from them, causes them to lose their original transparency, relinquishes its immediate and invisible powers, free itself sufficiently to discover that these orders are perhaps not the only possible ones or the best ones; this culture then finds itself faced with the stark fact that there exists, below the level of its spontaneous orders, things that are in themselves capable of being ordered, that belong to a certain unspoken order . . .

(xx)

To argue that Edna Pontellier commits suicide because she lacks a language, because of this "unspoken order," seems a cruel oversimplification of her character and of her material situation. And yet at the end of *The Awakening* we are, like Edna, subjected to a multiplication of points of view and can see no way to contain this multiplicity within the novel's heterosexist milieu. To argue that Edna lacks a language, then, is not only to say that culture has invaded her consciousness, has mortgaged her right to original speech, but that Edna's language is inadequate to her vital needs, that it is singular when it should be plural, masculine when it should be feminine, phantasmic when it should be open and dialectical. And what becomes clear by the novel's end is that Robert Lebrun has served as an iconic replacement for that which Edna cannot say; his name functions as a hieroglyph condensing Edna's complex desires—both those she has named and those which remain unnameable.

In *Powers of Horror* Julia Kristeva suggests that "phobia bears the marks of the frailty of the subject's signifying system," and Edna's love for Robert—although it is not phobic as such, reproduces this frailty as symptom; when Edna seeks nothing but the speech of her beloved, it makes her "signifying system" frail.[19] Edna Pontellier has no language to help her integrate and interrogate the diversity of her feelings; she experiences neither world nor signifying system capacious enough to accommodate her desires. But by the end of the novel these contradictory desires become noisy, impossible to repress. As Edna helps Adele Rati-

gnolle through a difficult childbirth the romantic interlude that Edna has shared with Robert becomes faint; it seems "unreal, and only half-remembered" (108), and once again language fails her. When Dr. Mandelet asks if she will go abroad to relax, Edna finds herself stumbling for words: "'Perhaps—no, I am not going. I'm not going to be forced into doing things. I don't want to go abroad. I want to be let alone. Nobody has any right—except children, perhaps—and even then, it seems to me—or it did seem—' She felt that her speech was voicing the incoherency of her thoughts, and stopped abruptly" (109). After watching Adele give birth and listening to her painful repetitions ("Think of the children, think of them"), Edna begins to re-experience the bodily sensations and feelings for her children that she has repressed; her extra-marital desires grow more tumultuous. Once more her sentences split with the weight of this conflict, and as Mandelet tries to put them together, as he offers to "talk of things you never have dreamt of talking about before," Edna refuses his kind and magian powers, just as, in childhood, she refused her father's chill summons to prayer. She gives herself, instead, to the "voice" of the sea, to that sibilance in which every name drowns. And her mind returns to what she can claim of her childhood, to the story she told Adele Ratignolle on the hot summer beach.

Kristeva has suggested that we consider "the phobic person as a subject in want of metaphoricalness" (37), and I have suggested that the same becomes true of a woman in love, a woman who becomes the subject of her culture's romantic fantasies. "Incapable of producing metaphors by means of signs alone," Kristeva argues,

> [this subject] produces them in the very material of drives—and it turns out that the only rhetoric of which he is capable is that of affect, and it is projected, as often as not, by means of *images.* It will then fall upon analysis to give back a memory, hence a language, to the unnamable and namable states of fear, while emphasizing the former, which make up what is most unapproachable in the unconscious.

(37)

I am not suggesting that Edna is in need of a Freudian or even a Kristevan analysis. I am suggesting instead that we can locate the power of the novel's final images in Edna's desire "to give back a memory, hence a language," to that within her which remains nameless.

> There is a fact which our experience of speech does not permit us to deny, the fact that every discourse is cast in the direction of something which it seeks to seize hold of, that it is incomplete and open, somewhat as the visual field is partial, limited and extended by an horizon. How can we explain this almost visual property of speaking on the basis of this object closed in principle, shut up on itself in a self-sufficient totality, which is the system of *langue?*[20]

The "voice" of the sea Edna tries to embrace is more than a harbinger of death, more than a sign of dark and unfulfilled sexuality; the novel's final images frame and articulate Edna's incessant need for some other register of language, for a mode of speech that will express her unspoken, but not unspeakable needs.

Notes

1. Kate Chopin, *The Awakening,* ed. Margaret Culley (New York: Norton, 1976), p. 113. All further references will be cited in the text.

2. For readings of Edna that celebrate her sexual awakening, see, for example, Per Seyersted's emphasis on "Edna's slow birth as a sexual and authentic being" (153) in *Kate Chopin: A Critical Biography* (New York: Octagon, 1980), pp. 134-63, and Sandra M. Gilbert's excellent "The Second Coming of Aphrodite: Kate Chopin's Fantasy of Desire" in *Kenyon Review* (Summer 1983), pp. 42-66. Gilbert's enthusiastic description of Edna as a "resurrected Venus . . . returning to Cyprus . . . a radiant symbol of the erotic liberation that turn-of-the-century women had begun to allow themselves to desire" (58, 62), endows Edna with an archetypal complicity in erotic myth that Chopin herself takes pains to critique. For a reading that is less passionate than Gilbert's but truer to the novel's sexual ambiguities, see Paula Treichler's "The Construction of Ambiguity in *The Awakening*: A Linguistic Analysis," in *Women and Language in Literature and Society,* ed. Sally McConnell-Ginet *et al.* (New York: Praeger, 1980), pp. 239-57.

3. Tony Tanner, *Adultery in the Novel: Contract and Transgression* (Baltimore: Johns Hopkins University Press, 1979), p. 4. All further references will be cited in the text.

4. For a similar view of Tanner's work and an extended critique of the ways in which critics have refused to see the difference between "transgression" and real social change, see Allon White's "Pigs and Pierrots: The Politics of Transgression in Modern Fiction" in *Raritan* (Summer 1982), pp. 51-70.

5. William Wordsworth, *The Prelude* in *Selected Poems and Prefaces: William Wordsworth,* ed. Jack Stillinger (Boston: Riverside, 1965), p. 193.

6. Michel Foucault, *The Order of Things: An Archaeology of the Human Sciences* (New York: Vintage, 1973), p. xviii. All further references will be cited in the text.

7. Gilbert argues that Robert's telling of these "wistful adult fairy tale[s]" (53) aids in reproducing a modern Aphrodite's birth from the foam—a birth in which Edna is "mystically and mythically revitalized." Gilbert imagines that Robert's words are without distorting power because she envisions Grand Isle as a woman's world, a colony situated "outside patriarchal culture, beyond the limits of the city where men make history. . . . Here power can flow from outside . . . from the timelessness . . . that is free of

historical constraints" (51). The point of my essay is that these "historical constraints" invade Edna's fantasies of "timelessness" as insistently as they invade Mr. Pontellier's city life.

8. Jacques Lacan, *The Four Fundamental Concepts of Psycho-Analysis,* ed. Jacques-Alain Miller, trans. Alan Sheridan (New York: Norton, 1978), p. 188. All further references will be cited in the text.

9. Edna is also associated with old print. Early in the novel Adele Ratignolle "brought the pattern of drawers for Mrs. Pontellier to cut out, a marvel of construction, fashioned to enclose a baby's body so effectually that only two small eyes might look out from the garment, like an Eskimo's." This is a world where characters are cut to fit the language they speak, where Edna's manufacture of a pattern for her children's garments can be read as a parable for her condition within language: "Mrs. Pontellier's mind was quite at rest concerning the present material needs of her children . . . but she did not want to appear unamiable and uninterested, so she had brought forth newspapers which she spread upon the floor of the gallery, and under Madame Ratignolle's directions she had cut a pattern of the impervious garment" (10).

10. Julia Kristeva, "Interview-1974," trans. Claire Pajaczkowska, *m/f* (5/6 1981), p. 166.

11. Jean-François Lyotard, *Le differend* (Paris: Minuit, 1983), p.30. All further references will be cited in the text. This translation is from Peter Dews' "The Letter and the Line: Discourse and its Other in Lyotard," in *Diacritics* (Fall 1984), p. 49. See also in the same issue "Interview," trans. Georges Van Den Abbeele, pp. 16-21, and David Carroll's "Rephrasing the Political with Kant and Lyotard: From Aesthetic to Political Judgments," pp. 74-87.

12. See, for example, Margaret Culley's "Edna Pontellier: 'A Solitary Soul'" in her edition of *The Awakening;* Susan J. Rosowski's "The Novel of Awakening" in *The Voyage In: Fictions of Female Development,* ed. Elizabeth Abel, Marianne Hirsch, and Elizabeth Langland (Hanover: University Press of New England, 1983); Paula Treichler's "The Construction of Ambiguity in *The Awakening*: A Linguistic Analysis" in *Women and Language in Literature and Society,* ed. Sally McConnell-Ginet, Ruth Borker, and Nelly Furman (New York: Praeger, 1980); Anne Goodwyn Jones' "Kate Chopin: The Life Behind the Mask" in *Tomorrow Is Another Day: The Woman Writer in the South, 1859-1936* (Baton Rouge: Louisiana State University Press, 1981); and Sandra M. Gilbert's "The Second Coming of Aphrodite: Kate Chopin's Fantasy of Desire," in *Kenyon Review* (Summer 1983), pp. 42-66.

13. Gilbert wants to discover a more definite, definable symbolic matrix than Chopin's novel provides. Still, her essay itself is a beautiful testimonial to the "dif-

ferend" in Chopin's novel. Gilbert finds *The Awakening* prophetic, and argues that Chopin's novel calls out toward new paradigms: Edna "is journeying not just toward rebirth but toward a regenerative and revisionary genre, a genre that intends to propose new realities for women by providing new mythic paradigms through which women's lives can be understood" (59). But Gilbert argues that this transformation actually occurs as Edna swims "out of one kind of novel—the work of Eliotian or Flaubertian 'realism' she had previously inhabited—and into a new kind of work, a mythic/metaphysical romance that elaborates her distinctively female fantasy of paradisiacal fulfillment and therefore adumbrates much of the feminist modernism that was to come within a few decades" (52). In other words, Gilbert experiences the novel primarily through its *differend,* through the future discourse it calls toward. This may distort Gilbert's reading of Chopin, but it transforms her essay into a form of feminist myth-making that uplifts and inspires.

14. Cynthia Griffin Wolff, "Thanatos and Eros" in *The Awakening,* ed. Margaret Culley, (New York: Norton, 1976), p. 208. All further references will be cited in the text.

15. Theodor W. Adorno, *Negative Dialectics,* trans. E. B. Ashton (New York: Continuum, 1983), p. 8.

16. G. W. F. Hegel, *Phenomenology of Spirit,* trans. A. V. Miller (London: Oxford University Press, 1977), pp. 18-19.

17. Maire Jaanus Kurrik, *Literature and Negation* (New York: Columbia University Press, 1979), p. 221. Kurrik's ideas have been useful throughout in helping me come to terms with Edna Pontellier's way of thinking. See also Adorno's *Negative Dialectics,* pp. 3-57.

18. I have focussed on the opening sentences, but this sense of the "heteroclite" pervades Chopin's text. The most bizarre and recurrent instance of a set of characters who simultaneously inhabit Mr. Pontellier's world and live in some other, incommensurable realm is the pair of lovers and their surreal duenna:

> The lovers were just entering the grounds of the pension. They were leaning toward each other as the water-oaks bent from the sea. There was not a particle of earth beneath their feet. Their heads might have been turned upside-down, so absolutely did they tread upon blue ether. The lady in black, creeping behind them, looked a trifle paler and more jaded than usual.

(22)

19. Julia Kristeva, *Powers of Horror: An Essay in Abjection,* trans. Leon S. Roudiez (New York: Columbia, 1982), p. 35. All further references will be cited in the text.

20. Lyotard, *Le differend,* p. 32. This translation is from Peter Dews' "The Letter and the Line: Discourse and its Other in Lyotard," in *Diacritics* (Fall 1984), p. 41.

Anna Shannon Elfenbein (essay date 1987)

SOURCE: Elfenbein, Anna Shannon. "Kate Chopin's *The Awakening*: An Assault on American Racial and Sexual Mythology." *Southern Studies,* 26, no. 4 (1987): 304-12.

[*In the following essay, Elfenbein contends that Chopin challenged American racist and sexist notions about sexuality in* The Awakening.]

Kate Chopin's *The Awakening* (1899) shocked its nineteenth-century readers by presenting without comment the adultery of Edna Pontellier, a wealthy, white American wife and mother adrift in Creole society. The shock was so great that the novel went unread for almost sixty years. Recent critics have tended to blame the literary double standard, which prohibited female authors at the turn of the century from broaching topics available to male authors, for the opprobrium Chopin suffered. But it was the cultural chauvinism of Chopin's contemporaries that was primarily responsible for their adverse reaction to *The Awakening.*

For much of Chopin's audience the troublesome issue of female desire was resolved through a racist conception of passion and purity according to which passion was projected onto "dark" women, while purity was reserved exclusively for "white" women. This conception manifests itself in the comments of early reviewers of *The Awakening.* W. M. Reedy, publisher of the *Mirror* and responsible for introducing some of Maupassant's provocative pieces to America, voiced the objections of many of his American confreres when he condemned Chopin for permitting her heroine, a "real American lady," to "disrupt the sacred institutions of marriage and American motherhood without repentance." Reedy was willing to accept a "woman sinner on American soil if she was a 'foreigner'"[1] or a member of the lower class, like Stephen Crane's Maggie, Frank Norris's Trina, or Theodore Dreiser's Carrie,[2] but not if she was white and upper-class, like Edna Pontellier.

Chopin's contemporaries were dismayed by *The Awakening* because its sexual realism assaulted American sexual-caste mythology. Profoundly subversive and courageous, the novel collapsed the traditional categories that had long segregated "dark" women and "white" women in American literature and advanced a new conception of female desire that was color-blind and democratic. Exploiting the complex social milieu available to her as a New Orleans author and deploying a multi-racial cast of female characters, who share to varying degrees Edna Pontellier's awakened sensuality, Chopin violated the expectations of her genteel readers by showing that sexual passion is no respecter of class or caste boundaries.

The complex social milieu Chopin depicted also distinguishes *The Awakening* from Flaubert's *Madame Bovary,* to which it has frequently been compared.[3] Instead of the bourgeois aspirations to social status of an Emma Bovary, Chopin's Edna experiences ambivalence toward the sensuality of the New Orleans Creoles. Her disorientation concerning the behavior appropriate for privileged white women in Creole society is perceived by Adèle Ratignolle, the exemplar of white Creole femininity, when she warns Robert Lebrun, who has been pursuing Edna in a conventional Creole way, that Edna "'is not one of us; she is not like us. She might make the unfortunate mistake of taking you seriously.'"[4] Edna does make this mistake, and because her status as a privileged white woman depends upon her compliance with an elaborate system of racial and sexual rules that constrict the sexual expression of white women, her awakening and her noncompliance threaten a social order she fails to understand. Constricted by class and caste bias and her propensity to see everything only as it impinges on her own emotional life, Edna's view of her world is not large enough to accommodate her discovery of the common sexual ground of women's experience.

As Edna veers from the path charted for privileged white women, she is contrasted with the other women characters in the novel, characters who occupy an unchanging space in the patriarchal society Chopin describes. Critics of the novel have of course discussed the contrast between Edna and Adèle Ratignolle and Mademoiselle Reisz, a pianist, noting that these women present mutually exclusive options for Edna. They have also examined Chopin's ironic coupling of a pair of lovers with a lady in black who tells her rosary while shadowing them and Edna. However, in focusing on this dark lady, presumably a white widow, and the lovers, they have neglected to note Chopin's implicit comparison of Edna with women of color or ambiguous race who make up the novel's gallery of "dark" women.[5] Peripheral and incompletely realized as characters, these dark women in **The Awakening** add richness and complexity to the novel, making it possible for Chopin in her depiction of Edna, whose character is so much at odds with conventional views of woman's nature, to subvert literary stereotype and popular prejudice. A matrix of diverse female types, "white" and "dark," surrounds Edna, who sees other women only in the way convention dictates.

Although Chopin may have shared to a degree the racist assumptions of American culture of her period, the novel's realistic treatment of Edna's interaction with these women exposes the sex and caste prejudices of Creole society—a society itself the object of slur and stereotype in American society at large. In so doing, Chopin challenged the biases of the novel's contemporary detractors, who recognized too well the racial implications of the novel, and its current rediscoverers, who, in emphasizing the novel's depiction of sexism, see only a portion of the picture of a sexist, racist society that Chopin drew with compelling accuracy. At the center of this picture, Edna progresses toward discovery of "her position in the universe" (893), but her way is doubly barred, for sexual *and* racial prohibitions block her as they block the other women in the novel.

Chopin's realism repeatedly captures the racism as well as the sexism of Edna's acquaintances. Swerving toward so-

cial satire in a dinner-table scene that reinforces our sense of the provinciality of her Creole characters, Chopin presents the diners' alarm and prurient interest when they learn that Robert Lebrun, the elder son of their hostess, plans to live and do business in Mexico. Any reader who has been privy to ethnic jokes in similar situations may squirm at Chopin's description of the round-table speculation that follows the news of Robert's departure, culminating in Adèle Ratignolle's request "that Robert . . . exercise extreme caution in dealing with the Mexicans . . . a treacherous people, unscrupulous and revengeful. She trusted she did them no injustice in thus condemning them as a race" (924). The discussion concludes with the testimony of Victor Lebrun, who assures all who will listen that Mexicans, especially Mexican women, about whom he implies intimate knowledge, are happy, childlike people.

Victor, the younger son in the Lebrun family, embodies the racist and sexist prejudices of his society, asserting his importance by badgering the black women of the Lebrun household or by bragging of his sexual prowess. The "droll" (924) stories he tells of his conquests and the demeaning treatment he accords the domestics who serve his family pass without notice in Edna's crowd, where such extremes of male self-assertion are sanctioned. Victor's behavior, an adolescent and therefore comic version of male practice in Edna's society, fuses sexual and racial exploitation, assorting Chopin's cast of women characters according to their conventional service functions. Edna fails repeatedly to hear Victor's "highly colored story" of adventures he "wouldn't want his mother to know" (942). Presumably these adventures also take place with women whom he wouldn't want his mother to know.

Edna, Madame Lebrun, and the other white women in the novel accept the presence of such dark rivals as they do the services of dark menials without reflection and without criticizing the habits of their men. Madame employs a little black girl to "work the treadle" of her machine: "The Creole woman does not take any chances which may be avoided of imperiling her health" (901). Edna, marked by her Presbyterian prudery as an outsider in the sensuous and expressive society of the Creoles, awakens too late to the absurdity of racial divisions of labor that do not protect white women from the biological perils women share. Deceived by the seeming candor of Creole society concerning sex, she recoils from Adèle Ratignolle's "harrowing story of one of her *accouchements*," which withheld "no intimate detail" from a mixed audience at table, and from Robert's "droll" stories related to an amused audience of married women (889). The meaning of Adèle's "harrowing" story and of Robert and his brother Victor's "droll" stories escapes Edna, who fails to understand, until too late, their applicability to her own situation as a woman. Edna's failure to see compounds her failure to hear. Her negative view of those whose stigmatized status she shares retards the intellectual and emotional development she requires for survival.

The "Solitary Soul" of Chopin's original title for the novel, Edna stands apart from both the white and dark women in

New Orleans, though she is implicated in the strict separation of female roles and races there. Edna fails repeatedly to hear, see, or emphatize with others. Her "obstructed" (896) vision eliminates the possibility of transcendence of the fixed roles available to women in her society, though her "natural aptitude" (891) as a portrait painter might have allowed transcendence had she had the critical vision Chopin herself demonstrates in drawing her. However, because Edna is merely narcissistically involved with her art, she effaces her portrait of Adèle Ratignolle in irritation when Adèle objects that it doesn't look like her and irritation commands the dark women of the Pontellier household to pose. Having discovered that the maid's back and shoulders are "molded on classic lines" (940) and that the maid will not object to an unflattering or inaccurate portrait as Adèle has objected, Edna captures only a conventional view of her woman sitter. She must fail as an artist because she lacks the ability to see anything but a highly stylized image such as the image of "Solitude" she envisions when Adèle plays a favorite piano solo. To Edna, "Solitude" must be a male figure. Poised beside a desolate rock on the seashore, watching a distant bird winging its flight away from him, this male figure is a synthetic and sentimental type, epitomized by nineteenth-century calendar art and by the works of Maxfield Parrish.[6] Although Edna responds more authentically to the music of Mademoiselle Reisz, her response is emotional rather than intellectual and fails to free her from the distorted perspective her society affords women of her social class.

Edna's class consciousness and her incapacity for transcendence appear in her blindness to the quotidian presence of dark women in her world, blindness that establishes her inability to escape those patriarchal imperatives regarding sex and woman's place that her sensual nature leads her to violate. Edna's unthinking reliance on values that will ultimately require her suicide appears in her failure to perceive these women or their significance. Alienated from her role as a mother by the quadroon nurse, who cares for her two sons with "fictitious animation" (935), and unable to take off her wedding ring or shatter a vase without being interrupted by a maid, who silently hands the ring back to her, Edna feels herself alone and exceptional. She wants "to swim far out, where no woman had swum before" (908), but in the end she drowns herself like many other nineteenth-century heroines in no-exit situations.

Edna is not the only woman in *The Awakening* who fails to make common cause with other women. For the other women in the novel establish no more than the shallowest of female relationships. Ironically, it is Edna who feels the claims of sisterhood most acutely, forgoing the long-awaited consummation of her passion for Robert Lebrun to attend Adèle when her friend sends word that she is in labor. Watching Adèle, who is transformed by travail, her face "drawn and pinched, her sweet blue eyes haggard and unnatural" (994), Edna confronts the facts of life that privileged women see only at rare moments. In contrast, Josephine, the attending "griffe"[7] nurse or midwife, refuses

"to take too seriously . . . a situation with which she [is] so familiar" (994). Each woman is isolated in this experience that women share: Adèle, awaiting the male doctor, the audience for her grand performance, feels abandoned and neglected. Josephine works hard to maintain her professionalism and patience. Edna recoils from the scene of "torture" (995) so reminiscent of her own experiences of childbirth, fleeing the labor room and later deciding, like other white heroines in Southern fiction, that "To-morrow would be time to think of everything" (997).

The marked separation of the women in this scene underlines Chopin's consistent treatment of class and caste divisions among women in the novel, divisions she realistically portrays and implicitly calls into question. The staging of such separation is most evident in the foregoing scene, and in two other scenes in the novel that depict Mariequita, a peripheral but essential "dark" woman character whom Edna fatally misperceives. Mariequita's response mirrors Edna's, reflecting the class and caste antagonism that divides women from each other and from true self-knowledge. Although racism and sexism in Creole society and in the society in which Edna was born mandate a difference between women of Edna's class and Mariequita's caste, Chopin juxtaposes Edna and Mariequita, blurring the racial categories established by men to control the sexuality of women and exposing the flawed vision of these two victims of such distinctions.

It is no accident that Robert and Victor Lebrun, whose surname reinscribes their "dark" proclivities, court both Edna and Mariequita or that Mariequita appears at two crucial junctures in the story to underscore the unacknowledged importance of dark women in Edna's world. In the Chênière Caminada episode that juxtaposes the limiting facts of life and the romantic fantasies Edna and Robert weave for each other, Mariequita appears, "making 'eyes'" (915) at Robert. Although Edna views Mariequita as stereotypically "dark" and carefree, it is Edna who is on a fool's errand and Mariequita who has business to transact. Separated from Mariequita by class, purpose, and language but *not*, quite obviously, by gender and sexuality, Edna is unable to understand Mariequita's amused banter in Spanish to Robert about the lovers in the boat. Edna's view of Mariequita is fragmented, focusing as it does on apparent irrelevancies such as the "sand and slime between her brown toes" (914) rather than on the telling interaction between Robert and this young woman with whom he shares a language closed to Edna.

Later in this episode, Edna anatomizes her own body as she awakens to her sensuality and looks "at her round arms . . . as if [they] were something she saw for the first time." It is the whiteness of her skin, "the fine, firm quality and texture of her flesh" (918), that is stressed here, as in an earlier episode when her husband Leonce looks at her tanning skin "as one looks at a valuable piece of personal property which has suffered some damage," and she responds by surveying her "hands, strong, shapely hands . . . drawing up her lawn sleeves about the wrists" (882).

The connection between Edna's badge of class, white skin, and her status as a married lady is forged here with a re-signed closural gesture, as she "silently reache[s] out to [Léonce], and he, understanding, [takes] [her] rings from his vest pocket and drop[s] them into her open palm" (882). Edna's fragmented body is not unified until the end of the novel, when she emerges "naked in the open air, at the mercy of the sun, the breeze that beat upon her, and the waves that invited her." At this moment, she, like Mariequita, stands barefoot in the sand, "the foamy wave-lets curl[ing] up to her white feet, and coil[ing] like serpents about her ankles" (1000).

The Chênière Caminada episode in which Mariequita first appears prepares for her reappearance in the final scene of the novel, linking Edna to a class of women convention-ally assumed to differ from privileged women. This link-age is sustained through recurrent mention of dark women with flashing eyes who satisfy their desires without suffer-ing the social ostracism Edna must suffer if she "swims out where no [white] woman had ever swum before." On the return from Chênière Caminada, Robert teaches Edna a romantic little air, *Ah! si tu savais!*—"Ah, if you knew what your eyes tell me!" Edna, who has dark and passion-ate eyes, parrots the words, failing to perceive the ironic connection between the lyrics of this refrain, Mariequita's eye-play, and the flashing eyes of other dark women in the novel. Although haunted by the melody, Edna refuses to confront the truth embodied in its lyrics until the end of the novel, when she flees her discovery of the impersonal and ephemeral nature of sexual passion.

Edna's first intuition of this truth comes when Robert re-turns from Mexico with a memento (aptly Freudian)—a finely embroidered tobacco pouch. When Edna, who has indulged in a brief consolation affair with Alcée Arobin, a notorious roué, questions Robert about this gift from his Vera Cruz "girl" and about the women of Mexico "'with their black eyes and their lace scarfs'" (985), she betrays the limited range of her worldly experience. Robert's re-sponse shows his worldly wisdom, as does his blasé atti-tude toward the experience. Although Robert's experience contrasts with Edna's naivete, they both recognize the in-significance of the affairs they have enjoyed while apart. His callous assertion that the Vera Cruz girl "'wasn't of the slightest importance'" (985) and that "'There are some people who leave impressions not so lasting as the imprint of an oar upon the water'" (985) accords with Edna's claim that Alcée Arobin's photograph means nothing to her. The untimely interruption of this interchange by Alcée himself adds another voice to the tasteless, chauvinistic discussion of the dark women of Mexico, whom Alcée characterizes as "'Stunning girls'" (985). Although Edna fails to see that her own status as an object of male pos-session is no different from that of women who serve as objects of male passion, she realizes that Robert, who shares a male language with Arobin that is as closed to her as was Mariequita's Spanish, "had seemed nearer to her off there in Mexico" (987). Arobin's pointed request that Edna convey his regards to Mr. Pontellier when she writes

puts her in her place, which differs from that of the dark women under discussion only in the strictly artificial or le-gal sense agreed upon by men.

The ability of men like Robert and Alcée to assert their mastery of women in such discussions confirms Edna's powerlessness to change her lot by allying herself with men. The end of the novel, which presents Mariequita once more, suggests Edna's powerlessness to change her lot by allying herself with women. When Edna walks as though catatonic past Mariequita and Victor to her death, she cannot really see Mariequita, nor can she be seen by her. Edna's hard-won understanding of her sexual nature thus remains bounded by race and class prejudices, which are signaled by the fact that here as in the beginning she is called "Mrs. Pontellier"[8] and by the fact that here as in the Chênière Caminada episode, she is unable to interact with Mariequita except by casting herself once more into the social role that she has sought to escape. Thus, she in-trudes upon Victor and Mariequita and gives them orders for a supper she never intends to eat. In this, her last so-cial act as Mrs. Pontellier, Edna betrays once more the conventional attitudes of her class, which dictate suicide, the socially correct choice for a respectable white woman who has strayed from her role as wife and mother. Through food, the emblem of her subjugation and her self-indulgence throughout the novel, Edna insists on service from Victor and Mariequita, the dark woman who will provide a plausible story to account for her "accidental drowning."

Held in reserve until this final scene and sketched once again with minimal but telling strokes, Mariequita re-sponds to Edna according to convention. Even Edna's sus-picious appearance at Grand Isle before the summer ses-sion cannot crack the class code that disables both women. Both are centered on themselves and must act out the roles they have been assigned, roles that satisfy neither but maintain the patriarchal order. Thus, Edna ignores Mariequita, addressing her remarks to Victor. And Mariequita feels jealous of Edna, believing the myth of a woman "who gave the most sumptuous dinners in America, and who had all the men in New Orleans at her feet" (998). Such a belief, so at variance with the truth, suggests the romantic illusions that will survive Edna to perpetuate male control. Because Mariequita lives on to tell Edna's story—and to get it all wrong—and because Mariequita's story is so clearly the one Victor has told her to maintain his power over her, Edna's partial knowledge of the sexual realities concealed by romantic fictions dies with her.

The true story, Kate Chopin's story of Edna's awakening, however, remains to cancel those romantic fictions that lead Edna astray. The inevitable consequence of her initial belief in her ability to venture further than other women of her class and of the caste, and of the class consciousness she shares with other privileged women, Edna's suicide indicts both sexism and racism. For Edna, and Edna alone among the women in the world of the novel, awakens to the truth about her own sexuality and that of other women, a truth concealed by romantic, racist fictions. Through Edna's awakening and her suicide, through her "obstructed vision" of the sexual realities that impinge on the lives of all women, Chopin took her stand against the sexual stereotypes that deny women, including Edna and the other women in the novel, not only the freedom and the opportunity but even the ability to experience and express their diversity.

Notes

1. Quoted by Per Seyersted, *Kate Chopin: A Critical Biography* (Baton Rouge, 1969), 114.

2. Edna Pontellier is unique because her creator was a woman and because she [Edna] is a white, upper-class wife and mother. Stephen Crane's Maggie, Hamlin Garland's Rose, Theodore Dreiser's Carrie, and Frank Norris's Trina manifest passion, but only Edna possesses an independent sense of herself as a sexual being; and she defies race, class, and sex conventions regarding woman's sexual nature.

3. It is worth noting that Chopin's debt to Flaubert's *Madame Bovary* is less than has been suggested by those who draw analogies between Edna Pontellier's situation and Emma Bovary's. Significantly, Emma is surrounded by male characters, while Edna is surrounded by a gallery of female types, white, black, and racially mixed.

4. Kate Chopin, *The Awakening,* in *The Complete Works of Kate Chopin,* Vol. II, ed. Per Seyersted (Baton Rouge, 1969), 900. All subsequent references to *The Awakening* will be parenthetically cited in the text.

5. This critical neglect is merely one case in point of white solipsism. In *Ain't I a Woman: Black Women and Feminism* (Boston: South End Press, 1981), Bell Hooks [Gloria Watkins] indicts white critics in general for making black women invisible in their readings of literature.

6. James H. Justus, "The Unawakening of Edna Pontellier," *The Southern Literary Journal* 10 (Spring, 1978), 107-22. Justus perceives that the male image originates in romantic iconography but fails to see that it has more than a personal reality for Edna, since it suggests her programming by her culture, a programming she shares with other women encouraged to visualize themselves as men in order to attain vicarious individuality.

7. This is the term for an individual of mixed black and native American ancestry.

8. In "The Construction of Ambiguity in *The Awakening*: A Linguistic Analysis," *Women and Language in Literature and Society,* Sally McConnell-Ginet, Ruth Borker and Nelly Furnam, eds. (New York, 1980), 239-57, Paula A. Treichler notes that Edna achieves individuality in the course of the novel and becomes identified to the reader as Edna. Treichler asserts that by the final chapter Edna has fully achieved her identity, but "the real Edna is elsewhere" (254). The use of Edna's married name in the final chapter, however, also suggests that in commiting suicide Edna is behaving as she has been programmed to behave. She is following the only path open to women of her class who experience sexual passion outside of marriage.

Barbara C. Ewell (essay date 1988)

SOURCE: Ewell, Barbara C. "*The Awakening* in a Course on Women in Literature." In *Approaches to Teaching Chopin's The Awakening,* edited by Bernard Koloski, pp. 86-93. The Modern Language Association of America, 1988.

[*In the following essay, Ewell explains her approach to teaching* The Awakening.]

The Awakening may be the quintessential text for a course in women's studies. Greeted with polite dismay at its publication in 1899, revived and hailed as a lost classic sixty years later on the crest of the most recent women's movement, the novel offers a paradigmatic tale of a woman's abortive struggle toward selfhood in an oppressive, uncomprehending society. Who could ask for a more rousing exemplar of the fate of women who seek personal integrity in a world that reduces womanhood to role-playing? Or, for that matter, of the fate of women writers who dare to reveal the "life behind the mask" of conventional propriety? The stories of Edna and her author are the real stuff of consciousness-raising. And consequently, often without trying, sometimes even actively resisting, I have found *The Awakening* emerging as a touchstone if not the resonant centerpiece of my course on women in literature.

The centrality of *The Awakening* has been consistent over ten years of teaching the course, primarily in the South: to young sophisticates of a women's college, to the more provincial young people of a rural state university, or, most recently, to the professional adult students of a liberal arts college in a major city. Variations of student responses do occur, of course, but a common identification with the southern landscapes hardly accounts for students' consistent and riveted fascination with Chopin's novel.

These southern, and thus relatively conservative, contexts have also shaped my own rather traditional approach to the course itself. Women in Literature, as I teach it, is an intensive study of novels, short stories, poems, and occasionally plays by women. Partly in deference to student interest and, until recently, to the dearth of handy texts, the bias has been toward nineteenth- and twentieth-century British and American writers. Of late, *The Norton Anthology of Literature by Women* and my own expanded reading have encouraged the inclusion of many earlier and more international works, though I persist in avoiding translations. My usual practice is to assign one or two nineteenth-century novels—Austen's *Pride and Prejudice,* a Brontë novel (*Jane Eyre* or *Villette* work well), a selection from Wollstonecraft; then Chopin's ***The Awakening,*** often preceded by regional short stories by Jewett, Chopin, and Freeman; sometimes Wharton's *The House of Mirth,* Woolf's *Room of One's Own* and *To the Lighthouse* or *Orlando,* Hurston's *Their Eyes Were Watching God,* Plath's *The Bell Jar* (less and less), a Lessing novel (*The Golden Notebook* or *Memoirs of a Survivor*); sometimes Welty's *Delta Wedding* or Rhys's *Wide Sargasso Sea* (excellent with *Jane Eyre*), Angelou's *I Know Why the Caged Bird Sings,* Morrison's *Sula* or *The Bluest Eye*; and from time to time, Atwood's *Surfacing,* Ellen Douglas's *A Lifetime Burning,* Brown's *Rubyfruit Jungle,* Jong's *Fear of Flying,* Rebecca Hill's *Blue Rise,* or some other contemporary work that has piqued my—or other reviewers'—interest. In addition to the six to eight novels finally chosen, we often read selections from a short-fiction or drama anthology and always spend several weeks with an anthology of poetry.

My aims in this course are perhaps apparent from the reading list—to expose students to some of the great British and American works by women that focus on female concerns: marrying, dealing with social roles, discovering sexuality, developing selfhood. I emphasize the "other" perspective that women have on their lives, the way stereotypes disintegrate when one sees this other point of view, and the peculiar constraints women must face and resolve. These thematic approaches seem appropriate in a course frequently elected by non-literature majors, but the texts themselves are studied principally as aesthetic rather than cultural documents.

The susceptibility of ***The Awakening*** to the approaches of women's studies is clear even in the biographical introduction with which I try to begin any new text. These life sketches, which are pointedly not going to be "on the test," encourage students to appreciate not only the very human creators of these wonderful textures and narratives but also—I hope—the pleasures of knowing some things solely for their own sake. Chopin's biography, which I know better than most other biographies of women writers, is an especially good instance of a writer whose life and fiction interact in oblique, but perhaps typically female, ways. The fairly conventional patterns of her youth in St. Louis and adulthood in New Orleans and in the Cane River country, for example, are broken by her widowhood in midlife and the writing career that followed. Chopin's fictional exploitation of these settings is fairly obvious, but students are also always intrigued by the contradictions of her apparently happy marriage to Oscar and Edna's less fortunate relationship with Léonce, factors that underline the inventive dimensions of art. The scandalized reaction to ***The Awakening*** is also instructive, focusing for students the differing historical realities of the novel and preparing them better for the social inhibitions that later limit Edna's alternatives. Finally, Chopin's response to the rejection of her work and the oblivion of the novel after her death are poignant examples of the power of the criti-

cal industry to suppress or neglect whatever voices that unsettle its complacent self-conceptions. That particular lesson usually has considerable impact.

Having thus established some biographical context for the novel, I generally turn to the students to discover what their initial impressions of and reactions to the novel have been. I am rarely disappointed. ***The Awakening*** has always seemed to me easy to teach precisely because it does elicit such various—often passionate—responses. It is difficult, I think, not to read Edna's story without some response: outrage, disgust, pity, wonder, terror. All these good old Aristotelian cathartic emotions are particularly elicited by the ending: why did Edna kill herself? what does it mean that she did? More often than not in this initial discussion, students bring up most of what I consider the significant elements of an interpretation—Edna's relations with others, men and women; her role as mother and wife; her notions of self and sexuality; the role of setting—and thus set the stage for my eventual comments. But the students' engagement is itself a liberating classroom experience. Many who had never ventured any opinion suddenly become vociferous defenders—or protesters—of Edna's fate. And frequently, their involvement with this text frees them to express themselves on other texts as well. Of course, that kind of engagement is central to a women's studies class, which, in the best traditions of liberal education, proposes to examine the moral and personal relevance of historical texts.

The pertinence of Edna's dilemma—how to be an individual in a society that insists she play specific roles—is certainly a key to its fascination since it uniquely engages both younger students (who are much involved in articulating their selves) and older students (who are well aware of the compromising forces of social reality). But in presenting the terms of that dilemma, Chopin exposes a number of specifically female concerns, issues that are inevitably the focus of women's studies: the nature of female sexuality, the conventional opposition of romance and passion, the moral isolation of women in patriarchal systems, the role of female friendship, the importance of the body and the physical world to self-realization, the ambivalence toward children and childbearing. One good approach to many of these matters—which also helps to define Edna's dilemma and thus to interpret the novel's disturbing ending—is a close scrutiny of chapter 6, the first and most deliberate of Chopin's editorial intrusions. Not only does the chapter articulate the nature of Mrs. Pontellier's crisis— "to realize her position in the universe as a human being, and to recognize her relations as an individual to the world within and about her"—but it also epitomizes the features of that crisis. The "two contradictory impulses," for example, that Edna obeys in first refusing and then following Robert to the beach underline the spontaneity of her awakening; a corresponding ambivalence is reflected in the image of the "certain light" that both shows the way and then forbids it. Edna's irrational and moody behavior is thus shown to be a function of deep and deeply uncomprehended recognitions about her "position in the universe as a human being." While these observations help to explain Edna's erratic and impulsive, almost involuntary quest, Chopin also insists on the unsettling uniqueness of Edna's awareness—"a ponderous weight of wisdom to descend upon the soul of a young woman of twenty-eight." This characteristically wry irony is immediately followed by the narrator's sympathetic regard for anyone expecting to survive such interior chaos. Edna's moral isolation as a woman—not to mention as a Protestant and a Kentuckian in this Catholic Creole society—is thus made a prominent and ominous element of her self-awakening. The sensuality that for women is often a path to awareness is also beautifully evoked here, coupled with its major symbol, the sea. A lyric refrain personifies the sea as lover, whose initial invitation to solitude and reflection conceals depths that Edna has only begun to plumb. A comparison of the initial version with the altered repetition in the final pages offers a dramatic instance of the subtleties of Chopin's style even as it underlines the real possibilities of choice that do remain for Edna, if only for the short space of the novel.

Although all these seminal elements can be made the focus of critical discussion, the sensuality of the passage seems to me particularly useful in launching an examination of the overall role of setting—especially of the sea. The alternation between Grand Isle and New Orleans clarifies the conflicts Edna experiences between the sensuous and physical realities that awaken her self and the strict social conventions that have previously defined her. A good place to focus on the specific role of the sea is Edna's learning to swim. Paula A. Treichler has a fine analysis of the ambiguity of the language in this passage and its relevance to female perceptions of power, but most students quickly grasp there the metaphoric power of Edna's struggles with the sea and the prescient vision of death her conquest of its forces eventually yields. The ensuing battle of wills on the gallery with Léonce and his efforts to enforce his sexual desires on her only emphasize Chopin's narrative skills and her ability to mingle event and symbol provocatively.

But it is Edna's own character that most clearly embodies the complexity of women's choices in a world defined by male concerns. The ambivalence, for example, highlighted in chapter 6 recurs both in decisions Edna makes later and in the figure that she poses to the reader. Exploiting that duality in classroom discussions is a good way, I find, to dramatize the difficulty of "objective" judgments or even of moral absolutes. Such an approach calls into question not only the conventional structures of Edna's society but our complicity with them—challenges to our assumptions about reality, which are obviously basic to Chopin's intent in this novel as well as central to the perspectives of women's studies. It is useful at this point, then, to pose to students two possible views of Edna: is she a hopeless, irresponsible romantic, revenging herself on the universe, or a purposeful individual, seeking selfhood, but lacking any real alternatives? Although such formulations oversimplify the matter, they do provide a basis for discussion and a

means of understanding both Edna's personal dilemma and ours in attempting to comprehend its significance. The evidence for either perspective is persuasive; witness the available criticism of the novel. Edna's natural sensuality, for example, her "sensuous susceptibility to beauty," is everywhere: from her admiration of Adèle to her awareness of her body, especially at Chênière Caminada, to her recurrent eating and sleeping and dreaming in the novel. While this affinity for the physical implies very female concerns, if not some substantiality in her self-awakening, evidence for her romanticism is also powerful: her adolescent fantasies about unattainable men, her prosaic and thus "real" marriage to Léonce, and her general equation of "life's delirium" with the desirable and the ephemeral and of reality with the mechanical and endless. At the same time, Edna declares her need for self-determination and quite consistently abandons Léonce's house and money in her effort to cast "aside that fictious self which we assume like a garment with which to appear before the world" (19). In contrast, she does not think very much or very clearly about her predicament; Adèle calls her an unthinking child, and even en route to her suicide she appears to have no definite insight or plan.

But the central ambivalence in Edna and the critical issue for nineteenth-century women focuses on her understanding of love and passion. The crucial passage here is another (though less intrusive than the first) editorial chapter, chapter 28, recounting Edna's response to Arobin's passionate embraces. Like most nineteenth-century women, for whom sexual passion was deemed at least unladylike if not downright vitiating, Edna had learned as a child to confuse sexual passion with romance. In Arobin's purely physical attractions, the separateness of these experiences is revealed. The mist is "lifted from her eyes, enabling her to look upon and comprehend the significance of life, that monster made up of beauty and brutality." As Edna's illusions about sexual passion begin to fall away, she understands more clearly what she wants, not from Arobin, but from Robert—a romantic, physical relationship, the consummation of body and soul, self and other. Her romantic, adolescent dreams of fulfillment—"life's delirium"—now disclose their physical component, sexual desire. But what Edna has yet to understand is that physical passion, real contact with real people, has concrete consequences. The complications of that insight are the crux, not only of Edna's dilemma, but, as Chopin saw, of the contemporary woman, attempting to forge a realistic, implicitly modern perspective on the dissolving paradigms of Victorian culture. This crisis of sexual identity, posed so prominently and disturbingly in the life of a woman, is a central issue of the age, forming a primary if often unacknowledged undercurrent of realist fiction in Chopin's time. But Chopin's explicitly feminine perspective challenges those paradigms more profoundly and thus more threateningly than any vision before that of the modernists themselves.

This female perspective is similarly apparent in Chopin's treatment of Edna's women friends. Adèle Ratignolle and Mlle Reisz are Edna's primary confidantes and models;

she admires and loves them both and values their counsel. At the same time, Chopin exposes their insufficiency as models and embodies in them aspects of Edna's basic conflict between her romantic desires and her longing for self-sufficiency. Adèle's romantic beauty, her absorption in the role of "mother-woman" are attractively conventional, but Edna cannot sacrifice "the essential" for the sake of such blissful immersion in others' needs. Similarly, Mlle Reisz possesses the courageous soul of independence—the essential self Edna cherishes—but Edna cannot bear the pianist's lonely solitude or the lack of romance in her life. Chopin creates in these two women rich models of the limited alternatives late nineteenth-century America offered women. The different responses they elicit from that society (as well as from Edna)—its benevolent protectiveness toward Adèle or its condescending tolerance of Mlle Reisz—are instructive. A significant insight of women's studies has been the power of roles—of social structures—to determine personal choices, complicating the search for self (a sympathetic quest, particularly for adolescents), especially a search as undirected and unhappy as Edna's.

But it is Edna's final awakening that centers this novel in a course about women. For the real complication of sexual identity and selfhood for women remains the responsibility for children. Edna's climactic recognition begins with her unexpected meeting with Robert at Catiche's garden café and their return to the "pigeon house" where they finally confess their love (36). But Edna's response to Robert's "mad" dreams of divorce is a dramatic measure of how far even an errant soul like Edna's can go toward insight and freedom. No one can any longer set her free, she explains to a stunned Robert: "I give myself where I choose." But Chopin brilliantly interrupts any reply Robert might offer with a knock on the door and Adèle's request for her friend's presence at her imminent labor and delivery. Not only does Edna's departure reveal the priority of her friendship with Adèle over her tryst with Robert, but that seemingly chance intrusion on their imminent sexual encounter is also a summons to recognition. Precisely as Edna is about to realize "life's delirium"—the merging of passion and romance with Robert—its results, especially before effective and widespread birth control, are vividly recalled to her: children. That relation of passion and children, which for women remains the chief issue of sexuality, is more fully expounded in Edna's conversation with Dr. Mandelet, who understands "intuitively" the sources of Edna's dismay (38). Romance is an illusion, and, deliberately confused with passion for young Victorian girls, it becomes "a decoy to secure mothers for the race"; but the children that result from that illusory confusion are real responsibilities, whose rights even Edna cannot ignore or "trample on." To awaken thus, as she must, to these bitter facts of life is to incur responsibility for one's choices, even ignorant choices; it is to recognize one's position in the universe as a responsible individual and to relinquish the romantic dream of union with others—the very dream that had led to that self-recognition—at the very moment when selfhood had made communion really possible. And

though Edna tries to defer this unpleasant recognition, Robert's pusillanimous note—"I love you. Good-by—because I love you" (38)—which confirms his own inability to deal with real consequences, leaves her no choice.

But Edna's return to Grand Isle is as ambivalent as her spiritual path. I find it a lively exercise to review with students her final deliberations, especially her focus on her children, whom she will not allow "to drag her into the soul's slavery" but who are still the only ones that "matter" (39). The wonderfully complex tone of that final passage, with its insistence on Edna's despair and its symbolic bird with a broken wing, coupled with the deeply attractive imagery of birth and the sensuous pleasure of the sea, only heightens the ambivalence of Edna's plight. But it also provides excellent material for either side of the debate that, we hope, is now raging in the classroom about whether Edna's deed is justifiable or even defensible. Appropriately, too, children become the key element in such a discussion—as children have always been in the seemingly endless—if not timeless—debate about the nature and place of women in human being.

If the classes on *The Awakening* have gone well, many inhibitions are dissipating both in the classroom and in the informal journals that I have found a vital writing component of a women and literature course. When students have to articulate their thoughts and feelings about texts and discussions—even, perhaps especially, negative ones—classroom participation is dramatically improved, in both quality and quantity. Moreover, rewarding students for at least trying to see the moral and political as well as intellectual pertinence of these texts to their lives reinforces the sense of literary engagement that I want to encourage. Indeed, the many unresolvable and emotionally confusing issues raised in such a class almost require this expressive outlet. But the other well-known function of journal writing is its usefulness in generating formal papers. While I generally do not assign research papers in this course, I do ask for at least two short essays. And *The Awakening,* which evokes such strong responses, also provides very manageable material for analysis, especially for a first paper, when student insecurities loom large. Assignments on the role of setting, the use of female models or foils, image patterns (birds, the sea, eating and sleeping), and the function of minor characters have all proved fairly successful. Broader topics are also possible, such as the conflicts of women and society, the ambivalences of childbearing, the portrayal of men, the alienation of the outsider, female friendships, the value of suicide, or the nature of freedom or of female sexuality.

Though, as I have tried to suggest, *The Awakening* broaches many issues central to the perspectives of women's studies, the crucial value of the novel in a classroom remains for me its ability to generate excitement and real involvement with a text. Throughout my years of teaching the novel, those responses have varied, but they remain intense. Younger, less sophisticated students, for example, who still believe the world is their liberated oyster, seem more intransigent toward Edna's suicide (why didn't she just move away? elope with Robert? get a job?) and less forgiving of her abandonment of her children, who, for these students, are still part of a misty, happy future. To such students, Chopin can teach tolerance and empathy. Many black women, especially older ones, who have a long heritage of overcoming vastly greater obstacles than Edna's, are frankly disgusted with her cowardice (white ladies just don't know what real trouble is!). Chopin's gift to them can be renewed confidence in their own powers and traditions. Edna's problems perhaps find greatest understanding among other older, middle-class women, who have known the bittersweet burdens of children and who recognize the silent, choking restrictions of bourgeois respectability. But most students, while they may not agree with Edna or may even find her weak and foolish, as perhaps Chopin's ironic distances suggest she is, rarely fail to see the poignance of her dilemma. They recognize, as Chopin obviously intended us to, that weak and confused as Edna may be, her conflict with an uncomprehending society has a piercing and resonant reality. And while even Chopin withholds her judgment on its outcome, none of us is rendered exempt from evaluating its causes or its complex components of sex, freedom, and the demands of society and selfhood. Such engagement, of course, is the manifest goal of women's studies and, indeed, of all effective learning and teaching.

Cristina Giorcelli (essay date 1988)

SOURCE: Giorcelli, Cristina. "Edna's Wisdom: A Transitional and Numinous Merging." In *New Essays on The Awakening,* edited by Wendy Martin, pp. 109-48. Cambridge: Cambridge University Press, 1988.

[*In the following essay, Giorcelli argues the Chopin's ambiguities in* The Awakening *support both her own and her protagonist's "cyclical view of existence."*]

The human being who has a soul does not obey anyone but the universe,"[1] wrote the French poet Gabriel Germain. Readers of Kate Chopin's *The Awakening* keep asking themselves whether the protagonist, Edna Pontellier, abandoning herself to the waters of the Gulf of Mexico at the end of the book, obeys the universe and therefore the needs of her soul; or whether, "idly, aimlessly, unthinking and unguided"—as she has lived for twenty-eight years—she simply lets herself be carried into the unknown "rapt in oblivious forgetfulness." The question of whether Chopin intends Edna's disappearance to be regarded as a victory (the mythical apotheosis of her integrity, whatever its cost)[2] or a defeat (the inevitable outcome of her hubris, whatever its motivation).[3]

The ending is indeed ambiguous because it is "open" and technically "circular." We do not actually "see" Edna drown but see her instead surrounded by and bathed in symbols of fertility and immortality (the sea, the sun,

bees). To this extent, the ending is open. At the same time, it is technically circular because the narrative movement in the last chapter reverts to the very beginning of the book, which is set on the sensuous, promising Gulf of Mexico. The close thus presents an equivocal "solution." There is the implied suicide, but Edna may have begun to live at another level of existence.

Since the critical discovery of the book in the 1960s, the elusiveness of its ending and the puzzling treatment of its protagonist's personality have caused critics to examine it mainly from two stances. From a feminist point of view, Edna's plight is that of a woman who finally begins "to realize her position in the universe as a human being, and to recognize her relations as an individual to the world within and about her." Although her spiritual and social quest is not represented as successful,[4] it is regarded as attesting to the New Woman's awareness of her right to be herself and even, when necessary, to take her own life as the ultimate statement of self-assertion. From the point of view of stylistic coherence,[5] however, the message of *The Awakening* is blurred by the dichotomies and ambiguities that pervade the entire narration. The author's wavering hold on surface and underlying meanings, ironic and serious tones, direct and indirect statements indicates a refusal to take sides and baffles judgment.

The Awakening escapes basic, clear-cut definitions from the viewpoint of both its technique and its theoretical allegiance to one or another literary mode (realism, naturalism, symbolism). Is it a novel or an extended short story? Does Chopin intend to deal with the spiritual growth and deep transformation of her protagonist, or does she intend to disclose the pitiful fatuity and inevitable failure of human aspirations? With regard to the more technical problem, the main character is psychologically, emotionally, and socially drawn in terms so stark as almost to oversimplify her case. Moreover, information about the other characters or the background situation is presented in an apparently casual and indefinite manner. As far as the more theoretical purposes are concerned, rather than either turning into a socially accepted self or helplessly suffering the insults of malevolent chance, Edna is steeped in ontological ambivalence. She seems only intermittently to be able to take a firm grasp of the world. If at times "she felt as if a mist had been lifted from her eyes, enabling her to look upon and comprehend the significance of life, that monster made up of beauty and brutality," at other times she is confused and hesitant. She muses, "if one might go on sleeping and dreaming—but to wake up and find—oh! well! perhaps it is better to wake up after all, even to suffer, rather than to remain a dupe to illusions all one's life."

The book's meaning and structure may be better recognized and valued if one takes a many-sided perspective and allows a number of options to coexist and play off against one another. Such a reading does not choose between or reconcile dualities, but holds them in what Richard Wilbur, in another context, calls "honed abeyance." The conclusion would then acquire another, further significance. If the open and circular ending eludes our expectations as to the meaning of Edna's final plunge, it might be seen as purposely flexible. Chopin matches the structure with the thematic content of the book: a cyclical view of existence.

The complex and composite subject presented in the narrative is appropriately introduced by the linguistic features of its title.[6] Syntactically, as it consists of an -*ing* clause, it is a blend of nominal *and* verbal functions. Semantically, it designates a border condition that, while linking two (or three) opposing ones (sleeping and/or dreaming versus waking up), partakes of both and points to a form of semi-somnambulism, to living and acting in the dark. This vacillating, shady situation and action may be interpreted in terms of both its physical and its metaphorical (spiritual, intellectual, sexual) meaning. Since the narration centers on Edna, who is descended from Kentucky Presbyterians, a subtle (if partially blasphemous) religious reference might be inferred from the title as well. Edna's awakenings, from sleep to life and from dreams/reveries to rationality, endow the narration with a vague sense of transience. Her prevailing and pervasive characteristic is one of potentialities not wholly actualized, of stages not entirely reached, of thoughts not distinctly formulated, of emotions not openly recognized.

From the outset, Edna is described as possessing liminal features.[7] She is difficult to figure in traditionally structured categories or even to be appraised by readers and fellow characters. Perhaps only Dr. Mandelet understands her. This wise and sympathetic old man invites her confidence ("I don't want you to blame yourself, whatever comes. Good night, my child")[8] and may be regarded as the foil to her self-centered and rigid father. If his paternalistic and positivistic outlook forces upon her an evaluation of reality that smothers her imaginative flutterings ("youth is given up to illusions. It seems to be a provision of Nature, a decoy to secure mothers for the race"), he is also the only character who offers to comfort and assist her in her despair. Mandelet possesses "anointed eyes," implying that he is gifted with a "divine" attribute: He sees far into the unseen. (His name, incidentally, sounds like and contains a pun on "Mandalay," the mystic bay of Burma, a symbol of Eastern wisdom.) But Edna's distinctive condition is to be isolated and incapable of limiting (or unwilling to limit) the extent of her finally assumed independence.

All that concerns Edna is marked by an essential state of "inbetweenness." She can be defined mainly by approximation and is not integrated into any milieu: neither in the one in which she was raised nor in the one in which she lives. Physically she is "rather handsome than beautiful"; her eyes are "yellowish brown," "about" the color of her hair; her eyebrows are "a shade darker." Her figure is characterized by a "noble beauty" and a "graceful severity," where the chiasmus of the adjectives bridges distances and mitigates polarities. In short, Edna is "different from the crowd." Religiously, as a child, she ran away "from prayers, from the Presbyterian service" and, as an adult, again on a Sunday, she leaves the "stifling atmosphere" of the Catholic mass. Intellectually she is caught between an "outward existence which conforms" and an "inward life which questions." Emotionally she is torn by conflicting "impulses" and she feels either "happy" or "unhappy," she is either "kind" or "cold" (Chap. 26). Although there were traces of French blood in her, we are told at the beginning of the narrative that they "seemed to have been lost in dilution"; ethnically and genetically, we might say, she is elusively complex.

In a society regulated by convention, dress and comportment are of utmost importance. It is revealing that, whereas the Creole women around her wear either white (Adele Ratignolle and Madame Lebrun) or black (the enigmatic "lady in black" and Mademoiselle Reisz) garments and ornaments, Edna, at Grand Isle, unites the opposites, wearing a white muslin "with a waving vertical line of brown running through it" and, in New Orleans, she puts on a blue dress with a red silk handkerchief around her head and a golden satin gown.[9] The color symbolism is unmistakable: Edna's white, which points to a transfiguration of being, is brought down to "earth" by brown (her eyes and hair), which indicates matter and sadness; blue and red represent her countertendencies toward abstraction and sexuality; and gold is the symbol of the fully realized, supreme essense.[10] As far as behavior is concerned, at the beginning of the story, although her Creole, "feminine" friend Adele is cautious about exposing her skin to the strong rays of the sun, Edna does not protect hers at all, disclosing her defiant disregard of southern womanly taboos ("You are burnt beyond recognition," her husband had angrily exclaimed in Chapter 1, not realizing that a new, phoenixlike identity was about to rise out of her "ashes"). Above all, not fully understanding the Creole code, she makes the "unfortunate blunder" of falling in love with Robert, thus living out dramatically a relationship originally meant to be taken only as pleasantly courteous. Spatially as well, Edna cannot be surrounded by fixed, socially controlled, enclosed places. As a child, in her native Kentucky, she had walked "diagonally" (along the longest and thickest, the most toilsome but most exalting, route) across a field of bluegrass. As a grown woman in New Orleans she takes extended walks, preferring "to wander alone into strange and unfamiliar places"—a mimesis of her conditions—rather than staying at home, the home of which she says: "It never seemed like mine." She needs open, preferably vast, spaces: a meadow, the beach, the streets of a large city. Since it is the tendency of her nature to escape structured categories, her ambivalence is underlined by the characteristics of the places where events occur. She begins to understand her real self at Grand Isle, a summer resort between the city and the sea. When she feels the first "throbbings of desire" for Robert, she spends a day with him at a yet more distant and smaller island, Chenière Caminada as if she needed to retreat to a wilder, more secluded and separated area where fantasies might reign more freely and where the two of them might pose as the living characters of a revisited fairytale. After her return to New Orleans, viewing her neighborhood with the outlook of an outsider, she judges it "very French, very foreign."

In all respects, Edna is a stranger who lives on the periphery of (in between) two ways of life—the American and the Creole, the strictly Puritanical and the sensuously Catholic—and two sets of conventions—the reserved and the exuberant. At the same time, Edna lives spiritually and logistically outside the social institution that tends to define her. She does not follow her husband to New York; she leaves her husband's house; she entrusts her children to the care of her mother-in-law. Presumably expressing the opinion of Creole society, Adele aptly observes, "She is not one of us; she is not like us." Edna is considered to be and feels different; she finds the world around her not only "alien" but even "antagonistic."

Similarly, in the temporal dimension, the narration emphasizes the liminal time of day, the period of darkness between one day and another. In the first section of the book, situated at Grand Isle and consisting of sixteen chapters, events are grouped under six time sequences: The first (Chaps. 1-3) covers the period from one Sunday morning to Monday morning; the second (Chaps. 4-6) from an afternoon to the night of the same day; the third (Chaps. 7-8) from one morning to luncheon of the same day; the fourth (Chaps. 9-14) from a Saturday night (August 28) to Sunday night; the fifth (Chap. 15), one evening and night; and the sixth (Chap. 16), one morning in September (characteristically, a liminal month). According to the traditionally accepted[11] four divisions of the day cycle (morning, midday, afternoon, and evening/night), mornings and evenings/nights seem to be in balance (five recurrences each).[12] The most momentous events occur during the evenings/nights. On the first Sunday night (Chap. 3), Edna is abruptly awakened and upset by her husband, thus disclosing the discontent beneath the smooth surface of her married life. On the occasion of Edna's late afternoon swim in the ocean, Chopin comments fervently on Edna's quest (Chap. 6). On a Saturday evening, Edna swims far out alone for the first time and feels she is "reaching out for the unlimited in which to lose herself," thus realizing her potential for autonomy. Later that night, for the first time since her marriage six years before, she resists her husband's "compelling wishes" with determination. On the following late Sunday afternoon, at Chenière Caminada, she wakes up like Sleeping Beauty, after a long sleep (of "a hundred years," as Robert/Prince Charming tells her), to live a few hours of perfectly idyllic harmony (the most extended period in the book) in a magic atmosphere. On an evening, finally, Edna learns that Robert is leaving for Mexico and realizes that, through him, she is losing "that which her impassioned, newly awakened being demanded."

In this first section of the book, the actual time covered by the narrative is about four unconsecutive days between the middle of August and the middle of September. Semantic and thematic linguistic references link the sequences to one another;[13] each sequence (except for the fourth) starts with the day subdivision following the one that ends the previous sequence.[14] The impression of a fluid, languorous, but compact stretch of time is thus effectively created. Only the fourth sequence stands out from the third and fifth, and breaks this contiguous and predictable succession of the day cycle phases: It begins and ends at night, whereas Chapter 8 ends at luncheon and Chapter 15 starts in the evening. Covering a very important lapse of time, in which Edna learns how to swim—that is, how to enter the fluid element itself—and her feelings for Robert coalesce into a deep infatuation, it fits her character that this sequence is circumscribed by darkness.

The second section of *The Awakening* is situated in New Orleans and contains twenty-two chapters. The actual time span covered by the narrative is about five months—roughly from the end of September to the middle/end of February, which is the end of winter in this region. Since this second section runs approximately only one-third longer than the first one, time is often fragmented into sporadic but significant events, which are rarely temporally tied to the preceding or following ones. No succession of the day's four solar subdivisions is to be consistently found between one chapter and the next. Darkness prevails throughout. The section starts on an evening (Chap. 18) and ends at night (Chap. 38). The critical events that affect the protagonist happen in the evenings/nights: the third (and last) quarrel with her husband (Chap. 17), her first visit to Mademoiselle Reisz, the pianist, who plays a crucial role in the story (Chap. 21); dinner during which Dr. Mandelet realizes that Edna vibrates with life and is ready for change, and in which she recounts the just invented (and "open") anecdote of the two lovers who disappeared in a pirogue; the sense of absolute freedom and rest she experiences when everybody (the four men in her life: her father, husband, and two sons) leaves her and, alone, she reads Emerson (Chap. 24); Alcée's kiss, which affects her like "a flaming torch"; her regret that "it was not the kiss of love which had inflamed her" (Chap. 28); her sumptuous dinner party in which, as will be shown, so much is revealed (Chap. 30); the beginning of her affair with Alcée that very night (Chap. 31); her first kissing of Robert (Chap. 36); her assistance during Adele's childbirth and her realization that a woman's independence is hindered by the existence of her children (Chap. 37). Finally, that very night, there is the shattering of all her dreams and illusions by the farewell note from Robert. In ten chapters the main action occurs in the evenings/nights (Chapters 17, 21, 23, 27, 28, 30, 31, 34, 37, 38) and in six (Chapters 20, 24, 25, 26, 33, 36) it starts in the afternoon. Only in Chapters 18, 22, 29, and 35 do events occur in the mornings, and in two chapters (19 and 32) they cover diverse days and times.

In the third section, which consists only of Chapter 34, the action rapidly returns to Grand Isle for the span of half a day and the time is toward noon, the moment of fullest sun and splendor.

Edna's inner crisis comes to a head because of her infatuation/love for Robert, who shares some of her physical and psychological characteristics, which are achieved both by making her more masculine and him more feminine. "In coloring he was not unlike his companion," writes Chopin. "A clean-shaved face made the resemblance more pronounced."[15] Psychologically, too, Robert tends to be passive and "childish."[16] A gallant with a reserved and delicate personality, he is so affected by the world around him that his eyes, rather than possessing a color and an expression of their own, "gathered in and reflected the light and languor of the summer day." Affinities between them—if one wants to push speculations beyond the text—date from long before their first meeting at Grand Isle: Edna and Robert were both orphans (of mother and of father, respectively) and had been brought up by the one parent who—from the evidence given in the case of the former and from what we learn in the case of the latter—did not seem to have much in common with or to have a preference for them: Edna's older sister, Margaret, is pictured as being as stern as their father, the colonel (Chap. 7 and, in passing, Chap. 22); Mademoiselle Reisz says that Aline Lebrun loves Robert's brother, Victor, more than him.

At the outset of their relationship at Grand Isle, Edna and Robert share a similar way of amusing themselves (Chaps. 1 and 2) and, above all, a propensity to conjure up and become attuned to fairy-tale situations (Chaps. 12 and 13). In Chapter 1 Chopin shows them facing each other while sitting on the step of a porch (a liminal place), and again in Chapter 4 they hold the same position. They are indeed mirror images—or doubles—of one another, thus disclosing both their haunting death instinct and their desire for immortality. When Edna sees and confronts Robert after his return from Mexico, she repeats almost verbatim[17] the sentence with which he summarizes his past months' experiences. She does this in order for him to realize (although he does not) how in harmony they have been, notwithstanding their separation. Only apparently, however, are her additions to his sentence *minor* specifications ("Caminada," "sunny," "with a little more comprehension than") or reservations ("still"). In effect, they indicate how attentive she has been to the events that stirred her life from the summer on. In particular, when talking of their fairytale interlude, she gives the magic little island (Grand Terre) its complete name to emphasize its importance in her life. She describes the old fort as "sunny" to convey to him some of her own feelings of that memorable day when she had thought that "she would like to be alone there with Robert, in the sun," the symbol of plenitude. Informing him that in the city she had tried to give her life meaning by working, she asserts that the occupation she had undertaken was not just "mechanical." But immediately afterward she has to admit that she has not succeeded in her intent, possibly because—as we know from previous authorial comments—she is "devoid of ambition, and striving not toward accomplishment." Even if they share many characteristics, then, Robert, after five months and a sojourn abroad, is very much the same man he was when he

left: timid, tied to the rules of his milieu. Edna, on the other hand, has tested herself in new personal as well as professional directions and has begun to realize that dreams and fantasies should not be fettered by institutional forms. At their second encounter she can "maternally" reproach him by saying: "You have been a very, very foolish boy, wasting your time dreaming of impossible things. . . . I give myself where I choose."

Their state of in-betweenness is further exemplified by Edna's and Robert's being the middle members of a feminine and a masculine triad. (Three is a recurrent number throughout the narration.)[18] Edna is both pulled toward and repulsed by Adele Ratignolle—the devoted mother, the Madonna, the Queen—on the one side, and, on the other, by Mademoiselle Reisz—the devoted pianist, the disagreeable and ugly spinster. As a girl, Edna had been caught between two very dissimilar, strongly defined, assertive sisters: Margaret, who was "matronly and dignified" and Janet, who was "a vixen." Now she is attracted by Adele and Mademoiselle Reisz for different reasons. Dissimilar as they are, Adele, sensuous and placid, helps Edna think of herself as a "woman," whereas Mademoiselle Reisz, malicious and imperious, "seemed to reach Edna's spirit" through her "divine art," thus helping her to think of herself as an "individual."

Robert stands between and is juxtaposed to both Leonce Pontellier, the acquisitive businessman and boring husband, and Alcée/Victor, the physically attractive and morally unscrupulous men about town. Robert shares features with and is different from both: Like Leonce, he is dependable and conventional, but he is also imaginative and agreeable. Like Alcée/Victor, given his resemblance to Edna, he is handsome (though his physical aspect is never fully described) and successful with women, but he is also a tactful gentleman.

Both Edna and Robert represent transitional states of being, states marked by ontological mobility and epistemological vagueness. Edna is often defined by negations (or, as we have indicated, by approximations). Psychologically, her husband thinks that she is "not a mother-woman." She feels "not thoroughly at home in the society of Creoles" because she is "not accustomed to an outward and spoken expression of affection." Deprived of a mother, Edna could not fully be a daughter and is not moved by any sisterly affection. She refuses to attend her younger sister's wedding. She is also prone to abandon her responsibilities as a wife: After the third quarrel with her husband, she flings her wedding ring upon the carpet and stamps her heel upon it (Chap. 17); she is intensely, but even in her own eyes only occasionally, a mother, "fond of her children in an uneven, impulsive way" and "It was with a wrench and a pang that Edna left her children. . . . All along the journey homeward their presence lingered with her like the memory of a delicious song. By the time she had regained the city the song no longer echoed in her soul."

Only "half" of Edna is where the whole person should be: She is often "half-awake"; she feels "half-hearted"; she traces "half remembered experiences"; she cherishes the "half-darkness" of her garden; she can at times only "half comprehend" what is said. She is also "absent-minded" and lacking in "forethought," because she acts upon impulses and whims, which she only "half" knows. In this, too, she differs greatly from the Creole attitude toward life which seems to be marked by a monotonous consistency (Leonce's devotion, Chap. 3) and an annoying persistence (Adele's conversation, Chap. 4). Further, Edna possesses only half of what, according to Mademoiselle Reisz, is needed to be an artist: the natural talent but not "the courageous soul. . . . The soul that dares and defies." She seeks a total (spiritual, intellectual, sexual) love relationship, but is torn between a romantic fantasy (Robert "had seemed nearer to her off there in Mexico") and an erotic liaison (after sensuously responding to Alcée's first kiss, she regrets that "it was not love which had held this cup of life to her lips"). Stamped by ambivalence, she is portrayed in her final act as still both dying and alive.

Edna's mind and body are literally trying to catch up with each other. Following the exaltation provoked by her first solitary swim, walking home, she feels "as though her thoughts were elsewhere—somewhere in advance of her body, and she was striving to overtake them." Upon leaving Adele's house, before her final plunge into the sea, she again feels "as if her thoughts had gone ahead of her and she was striving to overtake them." At the beginning and toward the end of the narrative, these two comments underline Edna's still unachieved completeness of being. Only in the water does she experience a fusion of body and soul, because in the formal-informal element she loses her *principium individuationis* and her physical self seems to become as light and free and "weightless" as her spiritual self.

Edna's "symbol" is the maze suggested, first, by the depths of the sea (Chap. 6) and, later, by the "deep tangle" of the garden outside her New Orleans house. In Chapter 7, and briefly again in Chapter 34, the sea is specifically related to the "green" Kentucky meadow of "blue grass." After her last quarrel with her husband, she finds solace in looking out at "the dusky and tortuous outlines of flowers and foliage. She was seeking herself and finding herself in just such sweet, half darkness which met her moods." Through the adjectives, "green" and "blue," two expanses (the *blue* sea and the *green* garden) are connected with the third one (the *green* meadow of *blue* grass): It is only when these two colors (the natural and the spiritual) merge that Edna feels happy ("entertained") and would like to remain in that situation, as in a labyrinth, "forever."

Linguistic structures underscore the thematic ambiguity of the book. An adverbial clause is often used to approach, albeit tentatively, Edna's inner self: "as if" (or "as though"). In trying to define what Edna thinks or, more frequently, what Edna feels,[19] Chopin often reverts to this hypothetical, circuitous, basically unreal adverbial clause to relate her character's inner world to the outside one. "As if" establishes, according to Vaihinger's analysis, "an

apperceptive construct under which something can be subsumed and from which deductions can be made," although what is stated in the conditional clause is considered unreal. This formula posits the "subjective" validity (and not the objective significance) of judgment, since the assumptions are presented as only imaginary.[20] Thus, for instance, Chopin informs us that Edna's eyes would be held on an object "as if lost in some inward maze of contemplation or thought." Edna tells Adele that on that momentous summer day in Kentucky, when walking through the meadow of blue grass, she threw her arms out "as if swimming." The day she goes to Chenière Caminada with Robert, she acts "as if she had placed herself in alien hands." When she visits Madame Ratignolle with her sketches and drawings, she confesses that she feels "as if I wanted to be doing something," and, when alone in her husband's house, she is overcome by exultation and walks through it "as if inspecting it for the first time." On melancholy days it seems to her "as if life were passing by, leaving its promise broken and unfulfilled." After her reaction to Alcée's kiss she feels "as if a mist had been lifted from her eyes." When by chance she meets Robert for the second time in New Orleans, in the cafe in the little garden, she reacts "as if a designing Providence had led him into her path." After kissing Robert, she looks into his face "as if she would never withdraw her eyes more." Edna's epistemological self is presented as so frail in its relationship with reality that she cannot conceive real analogies or draw actual equivalences; she can articulate only hazy, tentative comparisons that seem to have no objective significance and to be rooted in no objective reality. The validity, the expediency of such significances and such realities, is, however, admitted by the very possibility (or necessity) of the comparisons themselves. Edna's cognitive process is thus based on *fiction*; she approaches reality through a potentially rich but dangerously indirect method. She yearns for abstractions, for illusions created by her "mythical" impulse: "the abiding truth," "the unlimited in which to lose herself," "life's delirium," "the unattainable."

Transitional states are inevitably states of inner and outer ambiguity. In her quest for her true self, Edna loses, or enhances with the addition of the opposite ones, her original gender connotations and social attributes. At Grand Isle she becomes so attached to Adele Ratignolle—who possesses "grace and majesty" and speaks "the law and the gospel"—that she looks at her "like a faultless Madonna," with the feeling with which, in Provençal times, a man would have looked at a woman. Adele is even described as "the fair lady of our dreams," with "spun-gold hair," blue eyes that resemble "sapphires," and lips "so red one could only think of cherries." To such a goddess or fairytale figure, Edna cannot but be tied by the subtlest of bonds, or what "we might as well call love." As Edna conquers areas within and outside herself for the expression of her individuality (she goes out freely, she paints, she shuns her obligations, she lives alone, she takes a lover whom she does not love, she is ready to start an affair with another one whom she loves), she gradually abandons the prescribed "womanly" manners. She talks "like her father," she drinks like a man ("She drank the liquor from the glass as a man would have done"), she twice defines her own attitude as "unwomanly," and, taking the initiative, *she* kisses her beloved Robert. Symbolically, at the end of the narrative, she stands alone in the nude, on the seashore, like the man whose figure her mind had once evoked when listening to a piece of piano music: "There came before her imagination the figure of a man standing beside a desolate rock on the seashore. He was naked. His attitude was one of hopeless resignation as he looked toward a distant bird winging its flight away from him." Becoming independent and living freely entails, for Edna, possessing and developing androgynous characteristics. Chopin seems here to imply that an up-to-date goddess and a fairytale or romance protagonist should be both feminine and masculine (not like Adele, who, being only "feminine," is a "bygone heroine").

In her first published short story, **"Wiser Than a God"** (1889), Chopin had pitted the artistic profession against family life. Paula Von Stoltz,[21] the main character, thinking of these two vocations as mutually exclusive, chooses to become a famous pianist, that is—paraphrasing the words of the epigraph[22]—to "be wise" *rather than* "to love."

In *The Awakening,* to love/to be in love is a means *toward* becoming wise, a stage toward realizing one's "position in the universe," toward metamorphosing into the "god" who is possibly the only being capable of matching these two faculties. Having started her quest with the desire to love and to be loved, Edna ends it by subsuming her capacity to live and becoming wise. In her last moments, when she is back on the beach at Grand Isle, she realizes that, although she would like to have Robert near her, "the day would come when he, too, and the thought of him would melt out of her existence, leaving her alone." But her love is, at last, directed to the prime sources of being: the sea and the sun, that is, both to the ambivalent, mediating agent that includes the formal and the informal and to the all-encompassing spirit of creation. In this final scene she is indeed both the real woman and the imagined man. And since she feels like "some new-born creature opening its eyes in a familiar world that it had never known," her/his plight becomes that of reconciling opposites, of coming to terms with mysterious essences (a "familiar" and yet "never known" reality), by achieving plenitude. By overcoming gender restrictions, by breaking all barriers, by identifying life and death, Edna attains, at the very end, a precarious, quasi-divine wholeness.

Symbols of negative meaning are interspersed with positive ones. Edna is not, like Paula Von Stoltz, wiser than a god, but for a short while she is as wise as the gods/goddesses who might also love. First by emphasizing Edna's similarity to Robert and then by making her drop all social, "feminine" niceties, Chopin creates an androgynous being whose dynamic tension must be kept in balance. Such a complex and compound entity alone can master, in her/his awareness (and with the complicity of the indeterminate ending), inner and outer limits. Through her an-

drogyny Edna succeeds in achieving the wholeness of a composite unity, both integral and versatile, both necessary and free. Triumphing over sex and role differentiations ontologically implies subjugating that which substantiates but curtails, and ethically it entails mastering the grim unilaterality of responsibility. The bourgeois crisis[23] that Edna endures—the discrepancy between duty toward others and right toward herself, between social demands and personal yearnings, between repressive order and chaotic freedom—may be overcome in the grasped fullness of her dual being.

If we are tempted to regard Edna's last gesture as narcissistic (the drowning and the water symbolism imply as much), the fact that she abandons her self points rather to a reaching out for, an attainment of, more self. She merges with that supreme reality and *other* cosmos that has "no beginning and no end," in which opposites are not so much reconciled as potentially summed up, and birth, death, rebirth are endlessly recycled in the Heraclitean flux. At this point she can cast "the unpleasant pricking garments from her." Although "faded," these garments stand for the worn-out social rules and the hypocritical allure behind moralistic conventions, and even for the illusion of completeness through sexual encounters ("pricking"). On the verge of attaining wholeness, Edna can throw aside "that fictitious self which we assume like a garment with which to appear before the world." These garment metaphors take on greater drama from the fact that clothes metaphors play so large a role in the narration. After Robert's departure for Mexico, her existence had already appeared to her "like a faded garment which seems to be no longer worth wearing." And after having assisted Adele—when she still believes that Robert is waiting for her at home—she regards the turmoil of her fierce emotions as "a somber, uncomfortable garment, which she had but to loosen to be rid of." By divesting herself of all her garments—her bathing suit, but also her "outer" fictitious self, her past experiences and her wrenching emotions—she frees herself from her physical life, logical thoughts, and subconscious perceptions, as well as from external hindrances, in order to enter a condition of authenticity and joy in the water under the sun. Through a baptismal immersion in the sanctifying waters of inner grace, and in the face of immortality symbolized by the bees and sun, she is platonically recapturing that lost innocence that is her soul,[24] cloaked and hampered by the body and its trappings. The scene and the imagery recall those at Christ's baptism on the Jordan (Matt. 3:16-17). Unlike the episode in the Gospel, however, there is here no saintly witness, no official recognition, to testify to Edna's essence, and the bird hovering above has "a broken wing" and is therefore not an adequate symbol of the divine. Once again, Edna retains her ambiguity by being *alone* to intuit and interpret the cosmic event of which she is the protagonist: her super-natural awakening.

Only twice before, in the first section at Grand Isle, had Edna been shown on the beach in the morning: in Chapter 7, in which she discloses moments of her inner life to Adele for the first time, and in Chapter 16, in which, under Mademoiselle Reisz's eyes, she plunges and swims "with an abandon that thrilled and invigorated her." In both cases the combination of water and sun prompts important insights into herself: By recalling an episode of her childhood, she realizes her propensity to abandon herself to a vast natural solitude (the meadow of bluegrass). By reacting with a plunge in the water to an unpleasant piece of gossip (in the past, Robert had been interested in Mariequita, the pretty and spontaneous, "natural" Spanish girl), she again abandons herself to another vast natural solitude (the sea). At the end, not only does she identify sea and meadow ("the water was deep, but she lifted her white body and reached out with a long, sweeping stroke. . . . She went on and on . . . thinking of the bluegrass meadow"), but she lets herself be seduced by the sensuous "touch of the sea" under the sun, that is, under the most powerful symbol of intuitive knowledge, of the spirit in its highest individual realization, in its "illumination."[25] Since, moreover, the sun, like the sea, symbolizes the beginning and the end of all, we are confronted with a scene in which each distinct element and their combination underscore the notion of an eternal cycle of birth, death, and rebirth. No longer under the influence of the moon, the passive and "feminine" symbol[26]—and, incidentally, also a symbol of death—Edna is here in conjunction with the sun, the golden divinity, the symbol of eternal life. The influence of the moon, which had presided over her gradual development, is thus overcome. In this final scene, at the "mercy" of the sun, if her body will die, her Life will not perish.

Encircled by the night, she for a while arises to the sun's level during her farewell dinner party (Chap. 30). Wrapped in the golden "shimmer" of her satin gown, at the head of a table covered with pale yellow satin and adorned both by "massive brass candelabra, burning softly under yellow silk shades" and by yellow roses, with champagne glittering in the crystal glasses, Edna suggests "the regal woman, the one who rules, who looks on, who stands alone."[27] In the profusion of gold that is the sun's basic attribute, one may say that she represents the sun/Apollo's nightly counterpart (the moon/Artemis). In the crucial Chapter 10, while going to the beach the night in which she learns how to swim, she already misses Robert "just as one misses the sun." Not in juxtaposition to, however, but in merging with those parts of being that compose her unity will Edna finally attain a sense of completeness.

In the last scene, no longer attached to ephemeral life, Edna enters a love relationship with the sun and the sea, the primal elemental factors; after experiencing "how delicious" it feels to stand naked under the sky, she lets herself be embraced by the water. In the process of attaining fulfillment with Nature, with the Emersonian Not-Me, with the universe, the reality of her life is left behind and the people she was related to (sons, husband, friends, relatives, beloved one, and even her secretly treasured first love) become distant and meaningless. Back at Grand Isle, finally rejecting both absolute renunciation (in the first section of the book represented by the lady in black) and

juvenile fulfillment (previously incarnated by the two young lovers), she opts for absolute fulfillment.

It is consistent with what we regard as the author's deliberate decision not to propose definitive answers and not to assign precise and restricting qualities to Edna that the book ends when she is achieving the wholeness for which she craves. For this reason, although in the last scene Edna is imbued with a mystic aura, negative or deathly forces are also at work: Mademoiselle Reisz's sneer, her father's and her sister Margaret's (undoubtedly harsh) voices, the barking of an old dog (the animal psychopomp), the sycamore tree (which traditionally protects the souls of the dead),[28] the metallic, hideous clang of the cavalry officer's spurs. To the end Edna must remain poised between contrary visions, messages, and meanings in order to retain her polyvalent nature. Her wanderings do not end because the maze, her symbol, has led her into the cavern where she undergoes a change of heart and where a superior *being* emerges. The only "cavern" she had been familiar with is one "wherein discords wailed." In this last scene, therefore, in the composite center of her being, Spirit and Nature, Reason and Understanding, I and Not-I do merge for a chronologically brief, but symbolically infinite, time. In this merging, Edna joins the source of *Being*. She lives and dies within the twisting labyrinth, which stands for the perennial cycle of life—death—rebirth. The process of becoming—following the two main patterns of the labyrinth—is, indeed, infinite like the spiral, and perpetually returning on itself like a braid.[29] The ambiguous ending permits an open and intersected interpretation: Death and life may be regarded as phases of a single existence, either of which will be superseded by the other.

From a rationalist outlook, by presenting both of these possibilities concurrently, Chopin has courted misunderstanding. Her transcendentalist influences, however, justify her diffidence toward ordinarily accepted standards of judgment and solely rational explanations. In her epistemological relativism, she allows neither naturalistic conditions nor purely logical procedures to account for the mysterious complexities of life. As she had once written: "truth rests upon a shifting basis and is apt to be kaleidoscopic."[30]

Whitman's impact on Chopin has already been analyzed, particularly on her imagery and symbolism.[31] What must be noted is her debt to Emerson and the transcendentalists with respect to her sense of human beings as intermediaries between myth and consciousness, between the projections of their "divine" unconscious (dreams, visions, intuitions) and their interpretations of such projections, by which "Feeling is converted into thought; intuition, into insight."[32] In this perspective, human beings serve a dynamic function of intercommunication and interchange, and perform a role that shuns the law of conceptual logic as well as the gratifications that come from strict definitions. This inner potential connects the individual with those dried-up ("shrunk") powers that, as Emerson claims in *Nature*, had once peopled the cosmos with gods born of his/her unconscious "overflowing currents. Out from him sprang the sun and the moon; from man, the sun; from woman, the moon. The laws of his mind, the periods of his actions externalized themselves into day and night, into the year and the seasons."[33]

In a very unobtrusive and apparently unconscious manner, Chopin appears to have seized upon mythic figures to help unravel both the complexity and the mystery of human existence. As with so many artists, gods and goddesses are thus employed by her as hypostases of a higher unity. Writers often resort to myths not as ways to escape history, but as structures "for dealing with shared crisis of self-definition in the face of the unknown";[34] in such cases, myths offer them the opportunity of "naming the unknown."[35] Chopin may have kept a related group of myths (and of gods and goddesses) more or less intentionally[36] in mind—without meticulously following them in every detail—to depict her protagonist's mystifying identity. The mythical content may also account for the open ending.[37]

Edna's spiritual tendencies are hinted at from the beginning of the book. The first thing we know about her is that she possesses a physical emblem of spirituality, "strong, shapely hands." (One recalls Mandelet's "anointed eyes": His name may refer also to the French word for hand.) Leonce Pontellier, who considers his wife "a valuable piece of personal property," regards his possessions as "gods." Furthermore, the images of portals and of a temple are employed to convey what marriage was for Edna: "As the devoted wife of a man who worshiped her, she felt she would take her place with a certain dignity in the world of reality, closing the portals forever behind her" (Chap. 7). And again: "Within the precincts of her home she felt like one who has entered and lingered within the portals of some forbidden temple." But she, the pantheistic goddess, suffocates "inside" the *reality* of married life, conceived of as a temple that entombs her. She has to fling open the portals onto *realities* of dreams to be herself, to capture her divinity: "Edna began . . . to feel again the realities pressing into her soul." Her dreaming and daydreaming indicate a preference for the inner world and are conducive to tearing down those barriers that, in the "awakened" state, do not allow her archetypal models to surface. Thus, mythic and fairytale figures perfectly suit Edna, who has become the heroine of her dreamed about, compelling romance from the moment when the "mystic spirit" brought her to the "realms of the semicelestials."

In the languorous tempo and hazy atmosphere of the first section of the book, and in the fragmented tempo and tense atmosphere of the second section, there are two moments (Chapters 13 and 30) in which the protagonist is not only different from but "above" all the other characters.

In Chapter 13 Edna acts and speaks like fairytale princesses—like Sleeping Beauty or Snow White: "The whole place was immaculately clean, and the big, four-posted bed, snow-white, invited one to repose. It stood in a small side room. . . . Edna, left alone in the little side room, loosened her clothes. . . . [She] stretched herself in the

very center of the high, white bed. How luxurious it felt to rest thus in a strange, quaint bed." Later, she speaks like Sleeping Beauty: "How many years have I slept?" she inquired. "The whole island seems changed. A new race of beings must have sprung up, leaving only you and me as past relics." "You have slept precisely one hundred years." In both fairytale heroines, the awakening to individuality (and to sexuality) occurs after a period of withdrawal from active life.

At another time (Chap. 30) Edna takes on attributes of Persephone, the queen of the underworld, the goddess who crosses continuously the threshold of life and death: the sceptre (suggesting the regal woman who rules), a tiara of diamonds ("Something new, Edna?" exclaimed Miss Mayblunt, with lorgnette directed toward a magnificent cluster of diamonds that sparkled, that almost sputtered, in Edna's hair, just over the center of her forehead"), the pitcher (Edna does not actually pour the libations, but cocktails and champagne enrich and brighten her table), the color yellow.

The most important connection between the two fairytale princesses and the mythic queen is that both Snow White/ Sleeping Beauty and Persephone share the motif of the long sleep, similar to death (for the Greeks, Sleep and Death were divine brothers). Edna sleeps and often takes naps even during the day, as if to balance her sleeping and waking hours. The two princesses and Persephone, after a period of sleep and isolation, will awake (be reborn) and experience joy and completeness, either with the prince or with the mother. In the last scene, after her long phase of semiactivity and narcissistic "contemplation of the self"[38]—of semisomnambulism—Edna is finally enjoying ecstasy in Nature. The two fairytales may be regarded as the popular version of the myth of Persephone,[39] who lives, in some variants, six months on earth (from March—approximately the month in which Edna returns to Grand Isle—to August—the month in which Edna first appeared at Grand Isle) and six months in Hades (from September to February, the time Edna spends in New Orleans). In both the fairytales and the myth, the theme is that of cyclical birth—death—rebirth.

In Chapter 30, however, a number of reticulated suggestions are offered to give substance and depth to the mythical figure of Persephone. At Edna's dinner party, oriental refinements are conjured up to create a voluptuous setting: the music of mandolins (an instrument that derives from the oriental lute and, incidentally, contains another reference to the hand, and therefore to spirituality), the perfume of jessamines (the Arabic flower), the splash of a fountain (the heart of the Arabic garden).[40] In this context, Victor, Robert's younger brother, a "*tête montée*," is expressly depicted as Dionysus, the oriental-Greek god of "intoxicated delight."[41] On his black curls, in fact, is laid a garland of roses (not of ivy, however—but roses are possibly more suggestive) and "his dusky eyes glowed with a languishing fire." One of the women guests drapes a white silk scarf "across the boy in graceful folds," and another one makes him sip champagne from a glass brought to his lips. At this moment of the night, a "mystic cord" seems to pass around Edna's guests and "jest and laughter" bind them together in a sort of repressed bacchanal. (By these hints Chopin suggests a Swinburnean atmosphere.)[42]

Through his physical appeal and the impetuousness of his nature, Victor gains Edna's and the other women's sympathies. Up to that point in the narrative he has played a minor role: He has mainly been shown bickering with various people: his mother, Mr. Farival (Chap. 15), and—as Madamoiselle Reisz recounts—with Robert (Chap. 16). Victor is now at the center of everybody's attention and turns into "a vision of Oriental beauty." The oriental (sensual, exotic, even cruel)[43] role is so well enacted by him that in the last chapter of the book, at Grand Isle, he teases Mariequita and makes her jealous of his acquaintances and deeds in the city by telling her that the women at Edna's feast were "youthful houris."

Dionysus is the chthonian god of oriental origin who, like Persephone, stands for the two main cycles of nature: death and rebirth, winter and spring, barrenness and fertility. Indeed, in the Orphic tradition, he was believed—as Dionysus Zagreus—to be the son of Zeus and Demeter, Persephone's mother. He, the divine child, the twice born, belongs to both the world and the underworld; he is the god of duality. Dionysus is, in his masculine and feminine nature, a formidable synthesis of opposites[44] and a link between disparate realities. He represents paradox and the embrace of mad ecstasy that occurs when death and life meet.[45] One of his familiar settings is the sea, and the sea is Victor's special domain, since he spends most of the year at Grand Isle. Dionysus/Victor has, therefore, affinities with Persephone (and the "semicelestial" Ariadne)/Edna.

It has been stated before that Robert and Edna share important psychological and physical traits and that they function in similar ways within the narrative. If Edna possesses and brings into play characteristics usually considered masculine, Robert possesses feminine ones. He is youthful and attractive, but he is also endowed with self-control and balance. In a phrase, he represents the man of conscience. From the mythological point of view, Robert (whose name in German etymology means "bright") is thus comparable to Apollo, the ambidextrous god of circular completeness (symbolized by the sun disc). Confronted with Dionysus, Apollo stands as his opposite, but also as his complement. They epitomize "the eternal contrast between a restless, whirling life and a still, far-seeing spirit."[46] At Delphi the two gods were celebrated as juxtaposed divinities: Apollo during the solar months, Dionysus in the winter. Moreover, Dionysus excites some of the very faculties that Apollo guards: prophesying, singing, playing musical instruments. Robert confesses that in Mexico "Something put into my head that you cared for me, and I lost my senses," thus guessing the truth, and after the trip to Chenière Caminada, he sings the melody "Si tu savais" with a voice that is "not pretentious" but "musical and

true." In the summer, at Grand Isle, we see little of Victor; in the winter, except at the end, when spring is advancing, Robert is away in Mexico.

Dionysus is often represented as accompanied by processions of Maenads and satyrs; on three occasions (Chaps. 9, 15, 30) Victor is portrayed at the dinner table, surrounded by a big, vociferous company of men and women. Victor is the only man, in addition to Robert, to walk with Edna under her sunshade (Chap. 20), thus showing a certain degree of possible intimacy with her.[47]

The bond that unites Victor, Robert, and Edna is subtle but so strong that when, at the party, Victor kisses the palm of Edna's hand, she is moved because "The touch of his lips was like a pleasing sting." Robert will react in a similar way when Edna kisses him: "She leaned over and kissed him—a soft, cool, delicate kiss, whose voluptuous sting penetrated his whole being." The "sting" of a wasp or bee, combined with "pleasing" and "voluptuous," suggests a masochistic combination of pain and delight, Thanatos and Eros. The bee, incidentally a solar symbol, is identified with Persephone's mother (Demeter), and represents the resurrection of the soul and the sacred Word (significantly, the bee reappears at the very end of the book). Victor, Edna, and Robert, therefore, share the same divine substance, the Spirit.[48]

Victor (Latin, "winner") is the youngest of the men to flirt with Edna: He is nineteen, Alcée's age when he was wounded in a duel in Paris. The two men personify, in fact, the impetuous roué, the "wicked, ill-disciplined boy," who completely fulfills the demands of his temperament (the number nineteen, as the result of the sum of ten and nine, indicates both a complete cycle and full human satisfaction).[49] "Alcée" may refer to Alcaeus, the Greek poet who celebrated convivial and physical pleasures, and his surname, Arobin, sounds like "Arab" and points toward exoticism and sensuality.

In *Die Geburt der Tragödie (The Birth of Tragedy)* (1872), Nietzsche had ascribed the conditions of great art (as those operative in Greece in the fifth century B.C.) to a blending of the Apollonian and the Dionysian principles, the former described as the world of visions and rapt repose and the latter as the world of voluptuousness and strenuous becoming. Even if Chopin did not know Nietzsche's work,[50] these mythological dichotomies were widely discussed,[51] and indeed seem to be incarnated in the two Lebrun brothers. (Their surname refers to matter and sadness, to earth and death.) One may also hazard that in the serene contemplation and joyful ecstasy of her final musical[52] and dramatic merging, Edna symbolizes their union.

Dionysus and Persephone are like the children of Demeter, and Dionysus and Apollo are, respectively, a chthonian and a solar double. In our context, if Victor and Edna are similar because both are defined as impetuous (Chaps. 30 and 32), Robert and Edna are more than just doubles of one another. They are similar and *almost* coeval: We are obliquely informed[53] that he is twenty-six, whereas, when the narration starts, Edna is twenty-eight. They may thus bring to mind the famous divine twins, Apollo and Artemis, who were born of Leto under a palm tree. When, in the first scene of the book, Edna and Robert are together, she is fanning herself with a palm leaf (Chap. 2).

In several traits Edna may be linked to Persephone, the queen of Hades. In her beauty and fertility she is a chthonian Aphrodite, who, in turn, is an immortal Ariadne (even the name of the daughter of Minos of Crete is associated with that of the love goddess).[54] In other traits, however, she may be regarded as being analogous to Artemis, the virgin goddess. Artemis is associated with the moon and has a virginal, independent nature. Edna is represented mainly during the dark times of the day and declares that she will not be hampered by her children: "I would give up the unessential; I would give my money, I would give my life for my children; but I wouldn't give myself." Artemis, moreover, delights in wild nature and performs the function of protectress of childbirth. Edna likes open, solitary, "uncivilized" places and rushes to assist Adele at the end, notwithstanding the presence of Robert in her house. Not being a mother-woman, Edna's two past experiences of childbirth seem to her "far away, unreal, and only half-remembered" (Chap. 36). It is as if, like most goddesses (Hera, for instance), after her own childbirths, she had returned to a virginal state: She tends toward a life of complete independence and craves "solitude" (Chaps. 4, 6, 9, 10, and 34). Artemis loves dogs; at the beginning of her experience of marital independence Edna plays with her children's little dog (Chap. 24) and at the end she hears the barking of an old dog (Chap. 39). In her desire to cast manners and obligations aside, Edna may thus be considered wild and ruthless, like Artemis. Finally, Artemis, the Lady of Clamors, is associated not only with Apollo but also (like Ariadne) with Dionysus,[55] thus bringing Edna, Robert, and Victor mythologically even closer together.

In trying to account for all the aspects of such an elusive character as Edna, we realize that neither Persephone nor Artemis entirely encompasses her. Yet another goddess, the one who completes the triad of the virginal ones, is necessary: Athene (who, being present with Artemis at Persephone's abduction, indicates her affinity with them). To adopt Richard Ellmann's term, Chopin does not proceed "singlemythedly." The reference to so many contiguous archetypes may be justified by the composite nature of Edna's personality, which, to be fully accounted for, needs a plurality of figures. But they are tightly connected to one another, notwithstanding their particularities.

Dumezil has maintained that a tripartite system representing the three functions of productivity, force, and sovereignty is to be found in Indo-European myths.[56] In our text, productivity would be embodied in Persephone, force in Artemis, and sovereignty in Athene. Athene is characterized by a complete independence of humanity. Edna says to Robert, "I give myself where I choose," and in the last scene she thinks, "Today it is Arobin; tomorrow it will

be someone else." Athene, like Artemis, performs the role of protectress of childbirth, but, above all, of the arts. Edna is endowed with gifts as a painter. Furthermore, Athene embodies the inner tension of being both a virgin and a mother. Such an anti-thetical condition is well represented by Edna's split between the psychological and the physiological levels of her existence. Masculine maiden and virgin mother, Athene is essentially androgynous and, as such, all the more similar to Edna. The goddess is often associated with the snake or serpent, a symbol of autochthony and a messenger between the underworld and human reality.[57] This reminds us of Edna's first swim, when the sea "swelled lazily in broad billows that melted into one another and did not break except upon the beach in little foamy crests that coiled back like slow, white serpents." In the final scene too, "The foamy wavelets curled up to her white feet, and coiled like serpents about her ankles." The serpent represents rebirth, renewal, and spiritual enlargement in the inner world.

Another animal sacred to Athene is the horse, which is also one of Apollo's attributes (a further, indirect connection with Robert). Chopin writes that "There were possibly a few track men out there who knew the race horse as well as Edna"; and when Dr. Mandelet compares her to "some beautiful sleek animal waking up in the sun," he may be thinking of a horse. Athene has connections both with Dionysus, to whom according to one tradition, she was related,[58] and with her half-brother Apollo, who, according to another secret tradition,[59] was thought of as her son by Hephaistos. In the richness of her multiple aspects, Athene is thus involved with the two main mythical figures behind the two most important male characters in the novel.

Athene is intimately bound to Persephone. In fact, the owl, a symbol of wisdom, is an animal they share.[60] After her first quarrel with her husband at Grand Isle, when Edna goes out on the porch and first becomes aware of "some unfamiliar part of her consciousness," all is silent around her "except the hooting of an old owl." The similarity between Athene and Persephone is attested to by still another symbol of fertility: the pomegranate for Athene and the orange (the internal structure of which is similar to that of the pomegranate) for Edna. On two eventful occasions she is pictured among the orange trees. First, in Chap. 13, she appears four times among or under the orange trees, to emphasize the abundance of feeling that takes hold of her at Chenière Caminada (the first part of the island's name may recall the oak and its mushroom, symbols of longevity and of regeneration through death).[61] Later, in Chap. 36, while sitting under the orange trees of the small cafe in the garden, Edna meets Robert just before their reciprocal declaration of love in her pigeon house.

The plurality of mythical figures needed to portray such an elusive character as Edna points to the discontinuities of the self that, according to Bloom,[62] typically characterize American romanticism. At the same time, however, Chopin seems to direct attention to the most discerning elements that link these figures to one another in order to lend Edna her many-sided uniqueness. Athene is, for instance, the protectress of feminine handiworks, in patriarchal times represented by the spindle or the needle. In popular fairytales these are often fairies' or witches' tools. In "Sleeping Beauty," the princess pricks her finger with the old woman's spindle in the tower and falls asleep. At the opening of "Snow White," after pricking her finger with a needle, the queen longs for a child to whom she indeed gives birth not very long after. The sexual implications of these tools[63] stress the role of Athene and of middle-aged or old women as go-betweens (midwives) in a psychological (as well as a physical) sense. Such females may display either the positive or the negative sides of womanhood, like the seven good fairies versus the eighth, wicked one in "Sleeping Beauty" or the queen mother versus the wicked stepmother in "Snow White."

In *The Awakening,* two women without men (a widow and a spinster) are invested with a similar function. Aline Lebrun and Mademoiselle Reisz live in high, tortuous, dark, gothic eyries. Madame Lebrun's room at Grand Isle "was situated at the top of the house, made up of odd angles and a queer, sloping ceiling" and Mademoiselle Reisz's apartment in New Orleans is under a roof and is full of "dingy" windows, which admit "a good deal of smoke and soot"; from them "the crescent of the river" and "the masts of ships and the big chimneys of the Mississippi steamers" can be seen. These two women are the benevolent fairy and the malevolent witch, respectively: Madame Lebrun is always dressed in white, works at her sewing machine with the determination with which Mademoiselle Reisz practices her piano art, and is still "a fresh, pretty woman." Although of little importance in the narrative, Madame Lebrun is the mother of the two most important men and the one who, by providing Edna with Mademoiselle Reisz's address, indirectly favors Edna's and Robert's meeting in New Orleans. Mademoiselle Reisz, by contrast, is always dressed in black and, without being malevolent (although her surname rhymes with "vice"), is certainly wry, critical, and prophetic. Soot and chimneys belong to witches as well as to her, as does the shining crescent. But it is "the crescent of the river" and not of the moon. This shift underlines the fact that Mademoiselle Reisz cannot be associated with the most pregnant symbol of woman's fertility. Witches' horror of water (therefore of the spiritual element) is also characteristic of her: "Mademoiselle Reisz's avoidance of the water had furnished a theme for much pleasantry." Her physical aspect, moreover, is rather grotesque: "Her laugh consisted of a contortion of the face and all the muscles of the body," her hands have "strong, wiry fingers." She is so small and deformed that at Edna's dinner party she has to be "elevated upon cushions," and when she sits at the piano, "the lines of her body settled into ungraceful curves and angles." She always wears "a batch of rusty black lace with a bunch of artificial violets pinned to the side of her hair." Like witches, Mademoiselle Reisz is ageless and might be as old as her furniture, "dingy and battered from a hundred years of use" (the number underlines the mythic time in which she, like a character in a fairytale, lives).[64] Everything in her points toward the magic being who stirs up hidden forces. It is, for instance, after Reisz's playing of the piano that Edna, passionately moved by it, swims for the first time alone. It is she who quiets Edna's troubled soul with her music. She is the first to tell Edna that Robert is in love with her and, finally, she sharply conveys to her that Robert is not the person whom she should love: "If I were young and in love I should never deem a man of ordinary caliber worthy of my devotion." Conversely, it is to Mademoiselle Reisz that Edna first discloses both her desire to leave her husband's house and her resolution "never again to belong to another than herself"; moreover, it is to her that Edna first confesses her love for Robert (Chap. 26).

Mademoiselle Reisz is thus a conjurer and a *ficelle,* a necessary link that accounts both for Edna's gradual awareness of her aspirations and for the progress of the action. (Edna will meet Robert again in Mademoiselle Reisz's apartment.) She may be connected to Athene (and Edna) because, in her dark side, the goddess wears the head of one of the gorgons, the terrible Medusa, on her aegis, her shield. Mademoiselle Reisz's head is obviously not covered with serpents, but the author insists on her unusual millinery, her only characterizing ornament.[65] If, with her talent and her dedication, Mademoiselle Reisz stands for the spiritual urge forward, this urge, as in the case of the gorgon, is perverted by an excessive, presumptuous, ultimately self-destructive turning on itself.[66]

Since the pursuit of a rigid coherence is advocated by Chopin neither in professional nor in family life, Adele, too, takes on for a while the semblance of Medusa in the last scene in which she appears—that of the delivery of her child: "Her face was drawn and pinched, her sweet blue eyes haggard and unnatural. All her beautiful hair had been . . . coiled like a golden serpent." Even Adele, the tender mother, the sweet and sympathetic Madonna, who, as Demeter tried to protect Persephone, would like to protect Edna ("In some way you seem to me like a child"), shows her dark side. Demeter, too, becomes Demeter Erynnis.[67]

In Athene/Medusa, therefore, the three different characters of Edna, Mademoiselle Reisz, and Adele merge, at least temporarily. So that if we might have been tempted to detect in the characterization of Mademoiselle Reisz and, to a lesser extent, of Aline Lebrun traces of the old patriarchal prejudice that rejects women without men as anomalies, with Adele as Medusa as well, another subtle indication can be inferred: In a repressive society,[68] sooner or later, continuously or occasionally, womanhood as such is destined to be regarded, even by a woman artist, as frightening (possibly because the female Medusa forces men and women to look at themselves and realize their true nature). By drawing a many-sided character like Edna, Chopin has bridged the gap between the two more stereotyped opposing figures of Adele and Mademoiselle Reisz, while imbuing them with unexpected, linking attributes.

Other evidence throws light on the controversial meaning of the book. Pallas Athene is the moon[69] (and, as such, is connected with Artemis) and represents the lunar cycle. The Panathenaea Festival, which every four years celebrated magnificently the protectress of Athens, could begin on the twenty-eighth of the month dedicated to her.[70] When *The Awakening* begins, Edna is twenty-eight, and the only precise date in the whole narration is that of Edna's first swim: August 28. Twenty-eight is the number that indicates the lunar months and is closely related to the female. It is the arithmetic sum of the first seven numbers and represents a complete cycle, totality, eternal life, thus fitting the etymology of Edna's name, which means "rejuvenation" in Hebrew[71] (and is close to Erda, the German earth goddess). Through a perennial cycle of birth-death-rebirth she is, therefore, true to her name. What is of special interest to us is that twenty-eight points to a dynamic perfection.[72]

August 28 is also, however, the day on which the Christian calendar celebrates Saint Augustine, the Church doctor who would have agreed with the Holy Spirit in not vouchsafing to any woman a significant amount of wisdom (to paraphrase Chopin's words in Chapter 6). Augustine, as we know, was deeply influenced by Plotinus's *Enneads*, which identified the content of true wisdom in self-direction and self-awareness in knowledge of the Good. In Plotinus's thinking, when man reaches freedom in the One, he is freed from all dependence, from all individuality: The return to unity marks his return to transcendent independence when he is finally alone with the Alone,[73] when he attains "self union." Only by transcending oneself, by becoming all things, through a pantheistic union with the Universal Being does one attain infinity, perfection. Augustine insists on the gulf (the word, so rich in metaphorical meanings, makes us think of the Gulf at Grand Isle) between man and God, but retains the neoplatonic belief that redemption as well as regeneration proceeds by turning inward upon oneself and that obligation to God entails a desire for self-fulfillment. He maintains that duty and self-interest ultimately coincide, because love of self and love of God, even if they exist separately, are coextensive.[74]

In the mystery surrounding Edna's last act, one may detect concepts and posit hypotheses that afford a multilateral dimension to her instinctual decision, especially since, when walking toward the sea, "She was not dwelling upon any particular train of thought." Even the fact that the narrative ends with Chapter 39 may offer a subject for speculation. The result of thirteen multiplied three times, this number symbolizes a dynamic, limited, and relative system tending to the acquisition of a more forceful potentiality. Being elevated to the third power, the system strives toward perfection, totality.[75]

With her inner and outer liminality, her search for existential fulfillment and her multifaceted, goddesslike traits, Edna entices us, moves us. Whatever judgment we will pass on her struggle for independence and self-realiza-tion—that is, no matter how doomed from the start is this bourgeois myth propounded by a society that then denies it for women—through her final sensuous and mystic ecstasy, seeking immersion in her environment, she either purges herself of her narrowly conceived individualism or exorcises the isolation into which she was cast.[76] Rather than living as under a "narcotic"—etymologically associated with "sleep" and with Narcissus—she breaks the isolation of her existence, sublimates her instincts by directing them toward the Ideal, and joins the universe.

Edna's plight is constrained by neither social circumstance nor obstacle. She is left free to do as she pleases: She has no husband, no children, no relatives, no acquaintances, no society either, overtly to malign or brutally to hamper her. From the aesthetic point of view, the writer neither attempts to project an intriguing situation by adopting involuted narrative structures nor does she care to reveal to the fullest extent her characters' deepest psychological instincts and motivations. Yet we are conquered by Edna's *naiveté*[77] and by the sheer honesty of her timeless, solitary quest.

Notes

Cristina Giorcelli, a graduate of Bryn Mawr, is Professor of American Literature at the University of RomeThree. She has written extensively on W. Irving, E. A. Poe, H. Melville, H. James, S. Crane, E. Wharton, G. Stein, W. C. Williams, L. Zukofsky. Since 1980, she directs the Anglo-American section of the quarterly journal *Letterature d'America*. She is also editor of a series on *Abito e Identita (Clothing and Identity)*.

1. Gabriel Germain, *Chants pour l'Ame de l'Afrique* (Paris: Debresse, 1956), p. 89: "L'homme qui a une âme n'obéit qu'à l'Univers."

2. In Chapter 32, the protagonist feels that "She began to look with her own eyes; to see and to apprehend the deeper undercurrents of life. No longer was she content to 'feed upon opinion' when her own soul had invited her."

3. In Chapter 38, Edna says: "I don't want anything but my own way."

4. Carol P. Christ, *Diving Deep and Surfacing: Women Writers on Spiritual Quest* (Boston: Beacon Press, 1980).

5. George M. Spangler, "Kate Chopin's *The Awakening*: A Partial Dissent," *Novel* 3(3) (Spring 1970):249-55; and Jane P. Tompkins, "*The Awakening*: An Evaluation," *Feminist Studies,* 3(3-4) (Spring-Summer 1976):22-9.

6. The title of the book was actually meant to consist of both the present one and the one that the author had originally proposed to the publisher: *A Solitary Soul.* Per Seyersted, *Kate Chopin: A Critical Biography* (Baton Rouge: Louisiana State University Press, 1969), p. 221, n. 38.

7. See Victor W. Turner, "Betwixt and Between: The Liminal Period in Rites de Passage," in *The Forest of Symbols: Aspects of Ndembu Ritual* (Ithaca, N.Y.: Cornell University Press, 1967), and also "Passages, Margins, and Poverty: Religious Symbols of *Communitas*" in *Dramas, Fields, and Metaphors: Symbolic Action in Human Society* (Ithaca, N.Y.: Cornell University Press, 1974). To be liminal entails achieving a new state of being, a new spiritual *communitas,* whereas to be marginal implies being permanently excluded, an absolute "other." It is the aim of this chapter to try and demonstrate that Edna belongs to the liminal.

8. For instance, Edna thinks of herself as a child and as childish (Chaps. 7, 19, 35, 39), and is defined as a child by Adele Ratignolle (Chap. 33), by Doctor Mandelet (Chap. 38), and by the author (Chap. 10).

9. Edna wears the red silk handkerchief on her head after having kissed Alcée, that is, after having begun to break the moral code of her class. The sexually free Spanish girl, Mariequita, is the only other character to wear a red piece of clothing, in fact, a red kerchief on her head (Chap. 12).

10. For a discussion of the meaning of these colors, see Jean Chevalier and Alain Gheerbrant, *Dictionnaire des Symboles* (Paris: Laffont, 1969), pp. 107-9, 126, 111-12, 663-5, 564-6, respectively.

11. Ibid., p. 436.

12. Five mornings are expressly mentioned: the Sunday morning at the beginning of the story; the following Monday morning (Chap. 3); one morning (Chap. 7); one Sunday morning (Chap. 12); one morning (Chap. 16). Five evenings/nights are accounted for: the first Sunday night (Chap. 3); one evening (Chap. 5); one Saturday night, August 28 (Chaps. 9, 10, 21); one Sunday night (Chap. 14); one evening and night (Chap. 15).

13. The first sequence is connected to the second one by both a linguistic and a thematic reference ["A few days later a box arrived for Mrs. Pontellier from New Orleans" (Chap. 3), and "She was sitting there the afternoon of the day the box arrived from New Orleans" (Chap. 4)]. The second sequence is connected to the third one by the use of an identical background: the sea at Grand Isle. (At the end of Chapter 5 Edna swims in the sea, and in Chapter 6 the author comments on her swimming. At the beginning of Chapter 7, while contemplating the sea, Edna starts thinking about herself, thus beginning to realize the nature of her personality.) The fourth sequence appears to be tenuously connected to the one that precedes it (at the beginning of Chapter 9 the author informs us that the time is a Saturday night "a few weeks after the intimate conversation held between Robert and Madame Ratignolle," which occurred in Chapter 8). This sequence is not linked to the following one. The fifth sequence is tied to the sixth one by a thematic reference—in Edna's flashback—to Robert's leaving "five days ago" (Chap. 16).

14. The first sequence ends (Chap. 3) in the morning (and an afternoon is anticipated); the second sequence starts (Chap. 4) in the afternoon and ends (Chap. 6) at night; the third sequence starts (Chap. 7) in the morning and ends (Chap. 8) at luncheon; the fourth sequence, instead, starts (Chap. 9) at night and ends (Chap. 14) at night; the fifth sequence starts in the evening and ends at night (Chap. 15); the last sequence (Chap. 16) starts in the morning.

15. Edna notices that his hair is "the color of hers" (Chap. 33).

16. Adele Ratignolle says to Robert: "You speak with about as little reflection as we might expect from one of those children down there playing in the sand" (Chap. 8). The author comments, "He was childishly gratified to discover her appetite" (Chap. 13). Later Edna defines him as "a foolish boy" (Chap. 34). When Robert is not in the company of women, he likes to be with children (Chaps. 2 and 7).

17. Robert says: "I've been seeing the waves and the white beach of Grand Isle, the quiet, grassy street of the Chenière, the old fort at Grand Terre. I've been working like a machine and feeling like a lost soul. There was nothing interesting." Edna says: "I've been seeing the waves and the white beach of Grand Isle, the quiet, grassy street of the Chenière Caminada, the old sunny fort at Grand Terre. I've been working with a little more determination than a machine, and still feeling like a lost soul. There was nothing interesting."

18. For instance, three are the quarrels between Edna and her husband (Chaps. 3, 11, 17); three are her visits to Mademoiselle Reisz (Chaps. 21, 26, 33); three times the lady in black appears with the lovers (Chaps. 7, 8, 15); three times she appears with the lovers and Mr. Farival (Chap. 12). Three times the twins play the piano (Chaps. 1, 2, 9). Before marrying, Edna had experienced three infatuations (Chap. 7). Robert speaks three languages (Chap. 2). Linguistically, too, the narration is dotted by triads: When Edna is shattered by the news that Robert is going to Mexico, she desperately wonders how he could leave so suddenly, "as if he were going over to Klein's or to the wharf or down the beach." The colonel reproaches Edna for her "filial," "sisterly," and "womanly" wants (Chap. 24); Arobin may be met at "horse courses," "operas," or "clubs" (Chap. 25). Robert sweetens his coffee with three lumps of sugar (Chap. 36). Celina's husband is defined as "a fool, a coward, and a pig" (Chap. 39). Three is the first perfect number, which represents totality, the achievement of divine Unity, the participation of humanity in the invisible world. It is also associated with the search for one's biological and sexual identity.

19. In several cases the adverbial clause, when referring to Edna, is preceded by the verb "to feel." For instance: "I felt as if I must go on forever" and "I feel this summer as if I were going through the green meadow again" (Chap. 7); "a feeling of exultation overtook her as if some power of significant import had been given her to control the working of her body and her soul" (Chap. 10); "Edna felt as if she were being borne away from some anchorage which had held her fast" (Chap. 12); "she felt as if she were thoroughly acquainted with him" (Chap. 23); "I feel as if I had been wound up to a certain pitch—too tight—and something inside of me had snapped" (Chap. 31).

20. Hans Vaihinger, *The Philosophy of "As if"* (London: Routledge and Kegan Paul, 1968), pp. 93, 95.

21. This young woman, whose vocation is to become a concert pianist, and Mademoiselle Reisz do not bear French surnames. Perhaps on account of their exacting calling, the author prefers to assign them ancestry different from that of most of the other, more "easygoing," characters.

22. "To love and be wise is scarcely granted even to a God."

23. In Adorno's dialectical analysis, the narrowly conceived *principium individuationis* is one of the myths of bourgeois ethics that, distancing "truth" and "freedom" from the social context and imbuing authenticity with "religious authoritarian pathos without the least religious content," further alienates the "monadological" individual. Theodor W. Adorno, *Minima Moralia,* trans. E. F. N. Jephcott (London: Verso, 1978), pp. 152-5. These Marxist observations may be of help insofar as they emphasize how tightly *The Awakening* is connected to the bourgeois tradition and culture.

24. The word "soul" occurs more than twenty times in the narrative, four times in each of the following chapters: 6, 21, 39; in this last, the contexts in which the word was used in the previous two chapters are repeated.

25. Chevalier and Gheerbrant, *Dictionnaire des Symboles,* pp. 710-14.

26. Ibid., pp. 474-8.

27. In Sandra M. Gilbert's "The Second Coming of Aphrodite: Kate Chopin's Fantasy of Desire," *Kenyon Review* 5(3) (Summer 1983), Gilbert argues that Chopin is portraying in Edna a *fin-de-siècle* Aphrodite, thus "exploring a vein of revisionary mythology allied not only to the revisionary erotics of free love advocates like Victoria Woodhull and Emma Goldmann but also to the feminist theology of women like Florence Nightingale . . . and Mary Baker Eddy" (61).

28. Chevalier and Gheerbrant, *Dictionnaire des Symboles,* pp. 197-201, 728.

29. Ibid., pp. 445-7.

30. Kate Chopin, "Emile Zola's '*Lourdes*'" (1984) in *The Complete Works of Kate Chopin,* ed. Per Seyersted, 2 vols. (Baton Rouge: Louisiana State University Press, 1969), Vol. 2, p. 697.

31. See Seyersted, *Kate Chopin,* pp. 86, 151; Lewis Leary, "Kate Chopin and Walt Whitman" in *Southern Excursions: Essays on Mark Twain and Others* (Baton Rouge: Louisiana State University Press, 1971), p. 170; Joan Zlotnick, "A Woman's Will: Kate Chopin on Selfhood, Wifehood, and Motherhood," *Markham Review* 3 (October 1968):1-5; Gregory L. Candela, "Walt Whitman and Kate Chopin: A Further Connection," *Walt Whitman Review* 24(4) (December 1978):3.

32. Jeffrey Steele, "Interpreting the Self: Emerson and the Unconscious," in *Emerson, Prospect and Retrospect,* ed. Joel Porte (Cambridge, Mass.: Harvard University Press, 1982), p. 102.

33. *The Collected Works of Ralph Waldo Emerson,* ed. Robert E. Spiller and Alfred R. Ferguson (Cambridge, Mass.: Harvard University Press, 1971), vol. I, p. 42.

34. Estella Lauter, *Women as Mythmakers, Poetry and Visual Art by Twentieth-Century Women* (Bloomington: Indiana University Press, 1984), p. 8.

35. Albert S. Cook, *Myth and Language* (Bloomington: Indiana University Press, 1980), p. 1.

36. A. Pratt maintains that women writers often resort to myths as acts of discovery prompted by imagination and intuition. Annis Pratt, *Archetypal Patterns in Women's Fiction* (Bloomington: Indiana University Press, 1981). In the plan of studies of Chopin's convent school, mythology was one of the subjects taught. Louise Callan, *The Society of the Sacred Heart in North America* (New York: Longmans, 1937), pp. 735-6.

37. Myth has, among its features, that of being an "expanding contextual structure." Eric Gould, *Mythical Intentions in Modern Literature* (Princeton, N.J.: Princeton University Press, 1982), p. 177.

38. Bruno Bettelheim, *The Uses of Enchantment. The Meaning and Importance of Fairy Tales* (New York: Knopf, 1977), p. 226. Chopin is obviously indebted to the romantic tradition on sleep and dreams. She could not have known Freud's *Die Traumdeutung (The Interpretation of Dreams),* which appeared in 1900 and was not translated into English until 1913, yet her work shows a profound sensitivity to the nature of the unconscious.

39. Marie L. von Franz, *The Feminine in Fairy Tales* (Irving: University of Dallas, 1972), pp. 18-43. The following Jungian analysis is based on the conviction that—as Bickman observed—Jungian psychology completes the movement of American romanticism

and turns "metaphysics into a phenomenology of consciousness. The most striking activity in American Romanticism is that . . . of the imagination exploring those areas where ideas are felt as well as thought, and where spiritual aspirations and sexual desires are discovered to spring from the same inner dynamics." Martin Bickman, *The Unsounded Centre: Jungian Studies in American Romanticism* (Chapel Hill: University of North Carolina Press, 1980), p. 39.

40. Curiously, when looking at the garden earlier (Chap. 17), Edna had not mentioned this fountain. Chopin's narrative method is often based on reticence and understatement. For example, one learns the names of Edna's children (Raoul and Etienne) in Chapters 3 and 14, respectively; again, only in the last chapter does one first learn that during the previous summer, Edna had always tripped over some loose planks in the porch.

41. Walter F. Otto, *Dionysus, Myth and Cult* (Dallas: Spring Publications, 1981), p. 65.

42. Margaret Culley, "Edna Pontellier: A Solitary Soul," in *The Awakening, An Authoritative Text, Contexts, Criticism,* ed. M. Culley (New York: Norton, 1976), p. 227. See also Gilbert, "The Second Coming of Aphrodite," 61.

43. Victor, who insists on singing the song Edna does not want to hear, provides the disruptive climax of the party.

44. Otto, *Dionysus, Myth and Cult,* p. 136.

45. Ibid., p. 137.

46. Ibid., p. 208.

47. Edna appears under the sunshade twice with Robert (Chaps. 1 and 12) and once with Adele (Chap. 7).

48. Chevalier and Gheerbrant, *Dictionnaire des Symboles,* pp. 1-2.

49. Ibid., pp. 292-3, 531-3.

50. In *Kate Chopin, A Critical Biography,* Per Seyersted never mentions Nietzsche as a possible influence on Chopin. But Daniel S. Rankin in *Kate Chopin and Her Creole Stories* (Philadelphia: University of Pennsylvania Press, 1932, p. 174) suggests that this novel may have been indebted to Gabrielle D'Annunzio, as well as to other representatives of European aestheticism. Specifically, he mentions *The Triumph of Death* (translated into English in 1896), which shows the impact of Nietzsche and of Wagner. In both novels there is indeed a strong emphasis on the power of music to move and to reveal the inner world of every human being. Incidentally, in a book published posthumously in 1901, *Der Wille zur Macht (The Will to Power),* Nietzsche writes that Dionysus is the epitome of "transitoriness" and declares that he can be interpreted "as enjoyment of productive and destructive force, as *continual creation.*" Friedrich Ni-

etzsche, *The Will to Power,* ed. Walter Kaufmann (New York: Vintage Books, 1968), p. 539, sects. 1049, 1885-6. It is, of course, too early to speak of a Nietzschean influence here. Although Nietzsche's books began appearing in the 1870s, his influence on Anglo-American culture did not commence until 1896, when, newly translated in Britain, his works started to be known. Patrick Bridgwater, *Nietzsche in Anglosaxony* (Leicester: Leicester University Press, 1972), p. 150. For further reference, see Stephen Donadio, *Nietzsche, Henry James, and the Artistic Will* (New York: Oxford University Press, 1978). Nietzsche is linked to American culture through his devotion to Emerson. From 1862 and for more than a quarter of a century, "Emerson was the object of Nietzsche's continuing interest." Herman Hummel, "Emerson and Nietzsche," *New England Quarterly* 19 (1946):73. It is possible that the occasional Nietzschean theme in Chopin is actually Emersonian and one acquired on native ground.

Note that Walter Pater, too, had studied the figure of Dionysus as the expression of a power that is "bringing together things naturally asunder, making, as it were, for the human body a soul of waters." W. Pater, "A Study of Dionysus," in *Greek Studies, A Series of Essays* (London: Macmillan, 1922), p. 29.

51. For a complete bibliography of Nietzsche, see Herbert W. Reichert and Karl Schlechta, *International Nietzsche Bibliography* (Chapel Hill: University of North Carolina Press, 1968).

52. Kate Chopin, *The Awakening,* ed. with an introduction by Lewis Leary (New York: Holt Rinehart, 1970), pp. 12-13.

53. In Chapter 5 the author gives us his age indirectly: We have to make an addition (fifteen plus eleven) in order to know it. Edna's age, instead, is stated twice (Chaps. 6 and 30).

54. Otto, *Dionysus, Myth and Cult,* pp. 181-8.

55. Ibid., p. 92. Incidentally, Ariadne (who, like Persephone, Artemis, and Aphrodite, belongs to the element of moisture, Becoming, and death) had, like Edna, two sons.

56. Georges Dumezil, *Myths et Epopée,* 3 vols. (Paris: Gallimard, 1968).

57. Karoly Kerenyi, *Athene, Virgin and Mother in Greek Religion* (Zurich: Spring Publications, 1978), pp. 17, 55-7. Given Chopin's familiarity with the poetry of A. C. Swinburne, see his "Erechtheus."

58. Ibid., p. 47.

59. Ibid., p. 54.

60. Ibid., p. 32.

61. Chevalier and Gheerbrant, *Dictionnaire des Symboles,* p. 169.

62. Harold Bloom, *Poetry and Repression: Revisionism from Blake to Stevens* (New Haven, Conn.: Yale University Press, 1976), p. 255. The critic maintains that "The Emersonian or American Sublime . . . differs from the British or the Continental model not by a greater or lesser degree of positivity or negativity, but by a greater acceptance or affirmation of discontinuities in the self."

63. Von Franz, *The Feminine in Fairy Tales,* p. 38.

64. The number ten (or its multiples: one hundred, one thousand, ten thousand) is frequently employed in the book. Ten designates a totality in movement, a return to unity, an alternation, or better, a coexistence, of life and death. Chevalier and Alain Gheerbrant, *Dictionnaire des Symboles,* pp. 292-3.

65. To signify the alliance between rationality and vital powers, all pagan mother-goddesses carry the serpent as an attribute (Isis, Demeter, Athena, Cybele). In Christian iconography, the serpent is, instead, crushed under Mary's foot. In Medusa the serpents stand for perverted power. See S. Freud's essay "The Uncanny" (1919) and Tobin Siebers, *The Mirror of Medusa* (Berkeley: University of California Press, 1983).

66. Chevalier and Gheerbrant, *Dictionnaire des Symboles,* pp. 388-9.

67. Carl G. Jung and Karoly Kerenyi, *Essays on a Science of Mythology, The Myth of the Divine Child and the Mysteries of Eleusis,* Bollingen Series (Princeton, N.J.: Princeton University Press, 1973), p. 126. Edna and Adele are designated as "cruel" by Robert (Chap. 36) and Doctor Mandelet (Chap. 38), respectively.

68. A. Goodwin Jones, *Tomorrow Is Another Day: The Woman Writer in the South, 1859-1936* (Baton Rouge: Louisiana State University Press, 1981), p. 173-7.

69. Kerenyi, *Athene, Virgin and Mother in Greek Religion,* p. 59.

70. Ibid., pp. 40-1. Incidentally, the month dedicated to Athene corresponds to our mid-July-mid-August period, roughly both the month in which *The Awakening* begins and the "eighth" one in our calendar.

71. A similar meaning (rejuvenation, cyclical restoration) is involved in Edna's desire to eat fish. In fact, by taking her last "swim" she may become like a fish, and further, take on the nature of the supreme christological symbol. On the other hand, the fish may also symbolize her sensitivity, inconstancy, and desire to let herself go. Chevalier and Gheerbrant, *Dictionnaire des Symboles,* pp. 617-19.

72. Ibid., pp. 806-7 and 411-12. Twenty-eight, being also the sum of twenty and eight, stands for God, the primary Unity, and for resurrection and transfiguration. Twenty-eight is also the sum of the years of the Farival twins, who seem to be perfectly symmetrical (Chap. 9) and, therefore, indicate the possibility of surmounting multiplicity by attaining unity through a balanced duality. Twenty-eight, finally, designates Adam Kadmon, the Universal Man.

73. Plotinus, *The Enneads,* trans. Stephen MacKenna, rev. B. S. Page (London: Faber and Faber, 1956), particularly Enneads IV and VI.

74. See Oliver O'Donovan, *The Problem of Self-Love in St. Augustine* (New Haven, Conn.: Yale University Press, 1980). Such concepts may have been handed down to Kate Chopin through Emerson, or she may have absorbed them through her Catholic unbringing. To the impact of Augustine's doctrines (and of Plotinus's pantheism) on Puritan theology and, through it, on transcendentalism, Perry Miller has devoted numerous essays. His "From Edwards to Emerson" is precious, even if it studies a chronologically more limited span of theological thought. Perry Miller, *Errand into the Wilderness* (Cambridge, Mass.: Harvard University Press, 1956).

75. Chevalier and Gheerbrant, *Dictionnaire des Symboles,* pp. 766, 772-5.

76. Siebers, *The Mirror of Medusa,* pp. 57-86.

77. See Ruth Sullivan and Stewart Smith, "Narrative Stance in Kate Chopin's *The Awakening,*" *Studies in American Fiction* 1(1) (Spring 1973):62-75; Cynthia Griffin Wolff, "Thanatos and Eros: Kate Chopin's *The Awakening.*" *American Quarterly* 25(4) (October 1973):449-71; and Allen F. Stein, "Kate Chopin's *The Awakening* and the Limits of Moral Judgment," in *A Fair Day in the Affections: Literary Essays in Honor of Robert B. White, Jr.,* ed. Jack D. Durant and M. Thomas Hester (Raleigh, N.C.: Winston Press, 1980).

Elaine Showalter (essay date 1988)

SOURCE: Showalter, Elaine. "Tradition and the Female Talent: *The Awakening* as a Solitary Book." In *New Essays on The Awakening,* edited by Wendy Martin, pp. 33-57. Cambridge: Cambridge University Press, 1988.

[*In the following essay, Showalter examines the ways in which Chopin defied the female literary tradition with* The Awakening.]

"Whatever we may do or attempt, despite the embrace and transports of love, the hunger of the lips, we are always alone. I have dragged you out into the night in the vain hope of a moment's escape from the horrible solitude which overpowers me. But what is the use! I speak and you answer me, and still each of us is alone; side by side but alone."[1] In 1895, these words, from a story by Guy de Maupassant called "Solitude," which she had translated for a St. Louis magazine, expressed an urbane and melancholy wisdom that Kate Chopin found compelling. To a woman who had survived the illusions that friendship, romance, marriage, or even motherhood would provide lifelong companionship and identity, and who had come to recognize the existential solitude of all human beings, Maupassant's declaration became a kind of credo. Indeed, *The Awakening,* which Chopin subtitled "A Solitary Soul," may be read as an account of Edna Pontellier's evolution from romantic fantasies of fusion with another person to self-definition and self-reliance. At the beginning of the novel, in the midst of the bustling social world of Grand Isle, caught in her domestic roles of wife and mother, Edna pictures solitude as alien, masculine, and frightening, a naked man standing beside a "desolate rock" by the sea in an attitude of "hopeless resignation" (Chap. 9). By the end, she has claimed a solitude that is defiantly feminine, returning to the nearly empty island off-season, to stand naked and "absolutely alone" by the shore and to elude "the soul's slavery" by plunging into the sea's embrace (Chap. 39).

Yet Edna's triumphant embrace of solitude could not be the choice of Kate Chopin as an artist. A writer may work in solitude, but literature depends on a tradition, on shared forms and representations of experience; and literary genres, like biological species, evolve because of significant innovations by individuals that survive through imitation and revision. Thus it can be a very serious blow to a developing genre when a revolutionary work is taken out of circulation. Experimentation is retarded and repressed, and it may be several generations before the evolution of the literary genre catches up. The interruption of this evolutionary process is most destructive for the literature of a minority group, in which writers have to contend with cultural prejudices against their creative gifts. Yet radical departures from literary convention within a minority tradition are especially likely to be censured and suppressed by the dominant culture, because they violate social as well as aesthetic stereotypes and expectations.

The Awakening was just such a revolutionary book. Generally recognized today as the first aesthetically successful novel to have been written by an American woman, it marked a significant epoch in the evolution of an American female literary tradition. As an American woman novelist of the 1890s, Kate Chopin had inherited a rich and complex tradition, composed not only of her American female precursors but also of American transcendentalism, European realism, and *fin-de-siècle* feminism and aestheticism. In this context, *The Awakening* broke new thematic and stylistic ground. Chopin went boldly beyond the work of her precursors in writing about women's longing for sexual and personal emancipation.

Yet the novel represents a literary beginning as abruptly cut off as its heroine's awakening consciousness. Edna Pontellier's explicit violations of the modes and codes of nineteenth-century American women's behavior shocked contemporary critics, who described *The Awakening* as "morbid," "essentially vulgar," and "gilded dirt."[2] Banned in Kate Chopin's own city of St. Louis and censured in the national press, *The Awakening* thus became a solitary book, one that dropped out of sight, and that remained unsung by literary historians and unread by several generations of American women writers.

In many respects, *The Awakening* seems to comment on its own history as a novel, to predict its own critical fate. The parallels between the experiences of Edna Pontellier, as she breaks away from the conventional feminine roles of wife and mother, and Kate Chopin, as she breaks away from conventions of literary domesticity, suggest that Edna's story may also be read as a parable of Chopin's literary awakening. Both the author and the heroine seem to be oscillating between two worlds, caught between contradictory definitions of femininity and creativity, and seeking either to synthesize them or to go beyond them to an emancipated womanhood and an emancipated fiction. Edna Pontellier's "unfocused yearning" for an autonomous life is akin to Kate Chopin's yearning to write works that go beyond female plots and feminine endings.

In the early stages of her career, Chopin had tried to follow the literary advice and literary examples of others and had learned that such dutiful efforts led only to imaginative stagnation. By the late 1890s, when she wrote *The Awakening,* Chopin had come to believe that the true artist was one who defied tradition, who rejected both the "convenances" of respectable morality and the conventions and formulas of literary success. What impressed her most about Maupassant was that he had "escaped from tradition and authority . . . had entered into himself and looked out upon life through his own being and with his own eyes."[3] This is very close to what happens to Edna Pontellier as she frees herself from social obligations and received opinions and begins "to look with her own eyes; to see and to apprehend the deeper undercurrents of life" (Chap. 32). Much as she admired Maupassant, and much as she learned from translating his work, Chopin felt no desire to imitate him. Her sense of the need for independence and individuality in writing is dramatically expressed in *The Awakening* by Mademoiselle Reisz, who tells Edna that the artist must possess "the courageous soul that dares and defies" (Chap. 21) and must have strong wings to soar "above the level plain of tradition and prejudice" (Chap. 27).

Nonetheless, in order to understand *The Awakening* fully, we need to read it in the context of literary tradition. Even in its defiant solitude, *The Awakening* speaks for a transitional phase in American women's writing, and Chopin herself would never have written the books she did without a tradition to admire and oppose. When she wrote *The Awakening* in 1899, Chopin could look back to at least two generations of female literary precursors. The antebellum novelists, led by Harriet Beecher Stowe, Susan Warner, and E. D. E. N. Southworth, were the first members of these generations. Born in the early decades of the nineteenth century, they began to publish stories and novels in the 1850s and 1860s that reflected the dominant expressive and symbolic models of an American woman's culture. The historian Carroll Smith-Rosenberg has called this culture the "female world of love and ritual," and it was primarily defined by the veneration of motherhood, by intense mother-daughter bonds, and by intimate female friendships. As Smith-Rosenberg explains: "Uniquely female rituals drew women together during every stage of their lives, from adolescence through courtship, marriage, childbirth and child rearing, death and mourning. Women revealed their deepest feelings to one another, helped one another with the burdens of housewifery and motherhood, nursed one another's sick, and mourned for one another's dead."[4] Although premarital relationships between the sexes were subject to severe restrictions, romantic friendships between women were admired and encouraged. The nineteenth-century ideal of female "passionlessness"—the belief that women did not have the same sexual desires as men—had advantages as well as disadvantages for women. It reinforced the notion that women were the purer and more spiritual sex, and thus were morally superior to men. Furthermore, as the historian Nancy F. Cott has argued, "acceptance of the idea of passionlessness created sexual solidarity among women; it allowed women to consider their love relationships with one another of higher character than heterosexual relationships because they excluded (male) carnal passion."[5] "I do not believe that men can ever feel so pure an enthusiasm for women as we can feel for one another," wrote the novelist Catherine Sedgwick. "Ours is nearest to the love of angels."[6] The homosocial world of women's culture in fact allowed much leeway for physical intimacy and touch; "girls routinely slept together, kissed and hugged one another."[7] But these caresses were not interpreted as erotic expressions.

The mid-nineteenth-century code of values growing out of women's culture, which Mary Ryan calls "the empire of the mother," was also sustained by sermons, child-rearing manuals, and sentimental fiction.[8] Women writers advocated motherly influence—"gentle nurture," "sweet control," and "educating power"—as an effective solution to such social problems as alcoholism, crime, slavery, and war. As Harriet Beecher Stowe proclaimed, "The 'Woman Question' of the day is: Shall MOTHERHOOD ever be felt in the public administration of the affairs of state?"[9]

As writers, however, the sentimentalists looked to motherhood for their metaphors and justifications of literary creativity. "Creating a story is like bearing a child," wrote Stowe, "and it leaves me in as weak and helpless a state as when my baby was born."[10] Thematically and stylistically, pre-Civil War women's fiction, variously described as "literary domesticity" or the "sentimental novel," celebrates matriarchal institutions and idealizes the period of blissful bonding between mother and child. It is permeated by the artifacts, spaces, and images of nineteenth-century American domestic culture: the kitchen, with its worn rocking chair; the Edenic mother's garden, with its fragrant female flowers and energetic male bees; the caged songbird, which represents the creative woman in her domestic sphere. Women's narratives were formally composed of brief sketches joined together like the pieces of a patchwork quilt; they frequently alluded to specific quilt patterns and followed quilt design conventions of repetition, variation, and contrast. Finally, their most intense representation of female sexual pleasure was not in terms of heterosexual romance, but rather the holding or suckling of a baby; for, as Mary Ryan points out, "nursing an infant was one of the most hallowed and inviolate episodes in a woman's life. . . . Breast-feeding was sanctioned as 'one of the most important duties of female life,' 'one of peculiar, inexpressible felicity,' and 'the sole occupation and pleasure' of a new mother."[11]

The cumulative effect of all these covert appeals to female solidarity in books written by, for, and about women could be a subversive critique of patriarchal power. Yet aesthetically the fiction of this generation was severely restricted. The sentimentalists did not identify with the figure of the "artist," the "genius," or the "poet" promulgated by patriarchal culture. As Nina Baym explains, "they conceptualized authorship as a profession rather than a calling. . . . Women authors tended not to think of themselves as artists or justify themselves in the language of art until the 1870s and after."[12] In the writing of the sentimentalists, "the dimensions of formal self-consciousness, attachment to or quarrel with a grand tradition, aesthetic seriousness, are all missing. Often the women deliberately and even proudly disavowed membership in an artistic fraternity."[13] Insofar as art implied a male club or circle of brothers, women felt excluded from it. Instead they claimed affiliation with a literary sorority, a society of sisters whose motives were moral rather than aesthetic, whose ambitions were to teach and to influence rather than to create. Although their books sold by the millions, they were not taken seriously by male critics.

The next generation of American women writers, however, found themselves in a different cultural situation. After the Civil War, the homosocial world of women's culture began to dissolve as women demanded entrance to higher education, the professions, and the political world. The female local colorists who began to publish stories about American regional life in the 1870s and 1880s were also attracted to the male worlds of art and prestige opening up to women, and they began to assert themselves as the daughters of literary fathers as well as literary mothers. Claiming both male and female aesthetic models, they felt free to present themselves as artists and to write confidently about the art of fiction in such essays as Elizabeth Stuart Phelps's "Art for Truth's Sake".[14] Among the differences the local colorists saw between themselves and their predecessors was the question of "self-ishness," the ability to put literary ambitions before domestic duties. Although she had been strongly influenced in her work by Harriet Beecher Stowe's *Pearl of Orr's Island,* Sarah Orne Jewett came to believe that Stowe's work was "incomplete" because she was unable to "bring herself to that cold selfishness of the moment for one's work's sake."[15]

Writers of this generation chose to put their work first. The 1870s and 1880s were what Susan B. Anthony called "an epoch of single women,"[16] and many unmarried women writers of this generation lived alone; others were involved in "Boston marriages," or long-term relationships with another woman. But despite their individual lifestyles, many speculated in their writing on the conflicts between maternity and artistic creativity. Motherhood no longer seemed to be the motivating force of writing, but rather its opposite. Thus artistic fulfillment required the sacrifice of maternal drives, and maternal fulfillment meant giving up artistic ambitions.

The conflicts between love and work that Edna Pontellier faces in *The Awakening* were anticipated in such earlier novels as Louisa May Alcott's unfinished *Diana and Persis* (1879) and Elizabeth Stuart Phelps's *The Story of Avis* (1879). A gifted painter who has studied in Florence and Paris, Avis does not intend to marry. As she tells her suitor, "My ideals of art are those with which marriage is perfectly incompatible. Success—for a woman—means absolute surrender, in whatever direction. Whether she paints a picture, or loves a man, there is no division of labor possible in her economy. To the attainment of any end worth living for, a symmetrical sacrifice of her nature is compulsory upon her." But love persuades her to change her mind, and the novel records the inexorable destruction of her artistic genius as domestic responsibilities, maternal cares, and her husband's failures use up her energy. By the end of the novel, Avis has become resigned to the idea that her life is a sacrifice for the next generation of women. Thinking back to her mother, a talented actress who gave up her profession to marry and died young, and looking at her daughter, Wait, Avis takes heart in the hope that it may take three generations to create the woman who can unite "her supreme capacity of love" with the "sacred individuality of her life."[17] As women's culture declined after the Civil War, moreover, the local colorists mourned its demise by investing its traditional images with mythic significance. In their stories, the mother's garden has become a paradisal sanctuary; the caged bird a wild white heron, or heroine of nature; the house an emblem of the female body, with the kitchen as its womb; and the artifacts of domesticity virtually totemic objects. In Jewett's *Country of the Pointed Firs,* for example, the braided rag rug has become a kind of prayer mat of concentric circles from which the matriarchal priestess, Mrs. Todd, delivers her sybilline pronouncements. The woman artist in this fiction expresses her conflicting needs most fully in her quasi-religious dedication to these artifacts of a bygone age.

The New Women writers of the 1890s no longer grieved for the female bonds and sanctuaries of the past. Products of both Darwinian skepticism and aesthetic sophistication, they had an ambivalent or even hostile relationship to women's culture, which they often saw as boring and restrictive. Their attitudes toward female sexuality were also revolutionary. A few radical feminists had always maintained that women's sexual apathy was not an innately feminine attribute but rather the result of prudery and repression; some women's rights activitists too had privately confessed that, as Elizabeth Cady Stanton wrote in her diary in 1883, "a healthy woman has as much passion as a man."[18] Not all New Women advocated female sexual emancipation; the most zealous advocates of free love were male novelists such as Grant Allen, whose best-seller, *The Woman Who Did* (1895), became a byword of the decade. But the heroine of New Woman fiction, as Linda Dowling has explained, "expressed her quarrel with Victorian culture chiefly through sexual means—by heightening sexual consciousness, candor, and expression."[19] No wonder, then, that reviewers saw *The Awakening* as part of the "overworked field of sex fiction" or noted that since "San Francisco and Paris, and London, and New York had furnished Women Who Did, why not New Orleans?"[20]

In the form as well as the content of their work, New Women writers demanded freedom and innovation. They modified the realistic three-decker novels about courtship and marriage that had formed the bulk of midcentury "woman's fiction" to make room for interludes of fantasy and parable, especially episodes "in which a woman will dream of an entirely different world or will cross-dress, experimenting with the freedom available to boys and men."[21] Instead of the crisply plotted short stories that had been the primary genre of the local colorists, writers such as Olive Schreiner, Ella D'Arcy, Sarah Grand, and "George Egerton" (Mary Chavelita Dunne) experimented with new fictional forms that they called "keynotes," "allegories," "fantasies," "monochromes," or "dreams." As Egerton explained, these impressionistic narratives were efforts to explore a hitherto unrecorded female consciousness: "I realized that in literature everything had been done better by man than woman could hope to emulate. There was only one small plot left for herself to tell: the *terra incognita* of herself, as she knew herself to be, not as man liked to imagine her—in a word to give herself away, as man had given himself away in his writings."[22]

Kate Chopin's literary evolution took her progressively through the three phases of nineteenth-century American women's culture and women's writing. Born in 1850, she grew up with the great best-sellers of the American and English sentimentalists. As a girl, she had wept over the works of Warner and Stowe and had copied pious passages from the English novelist Dinah Mulock Craik's *The Woman's Kingdom* into her diary. Throughout her adolescence, Chopin had also shared an intimate friendship with Kitty Garasché, a classmate at the Academy of the Sacred Heart. Together, Chopin recalled, the girls had read fiction and poetry, gone on excursions, and "exchanged our heart secrets."[23] Their friendship ended in 1870 when Kate Chopin married and Kitty Garasché entered a convent. Yet when Oscar Chopin died in 1883, his young widow went to visit her old friend and was shocked by her blind isolation from the world. When Chopin began to write, she took as her models such local colorists as Sarah Orne Jewett and Mary Wilkins Freeman, who had not only mastered technique and construction but had also devoted themselves to telling the stories of female loneliness, isolation, and frustration.

Sandra Gilbert has suggested that local color was a narrative strategy that Chopin employed to slove a specific problem: how to deal with extreme psychological states without the excesses of sentimental narrative and without critical recrimination. At first, Gilbert suggests, "local color" writing "offered both a mode and a manner that could mediate between the literary structures she had inherited and those she had begun." Like the anthropologist, the local colorist could observe vagaries of culture and character with "almost scientific detachment." Furthermore, "by reporting odd events and customs that were part of a region's 'local color' she could tell what would ordinarily be rather shocking or even melodramatic tales in an unmelodramatic way, and without fear of . . . moral outrage."[24]

But before long, Chopin looked beyond the oddities of the local colorists to more ambitious models. Her literary tastes were anything but parochial. She read widely in a variety of genres—Darwin, Spencer, and Huxley, as well as Aristophanes, Flaubert, Whitman, Swinburne, and Ibsen. In particular, she associated her own literary and psychological awakening with Maupassant. "Here was life, not fiction," she wrote of his influence on her, "for where were the plots, the old fashioned mechanism and stage trapping that in a vague, unthinking way I had fancied were essential to the art of story making."[25] In a review of a book by the local colorist Hamlin Garland, Chopin expressed her dissatisfaction with the restricted subjects of regional writing: "Social problems, social environments, local color, and the rest of it" could not "insure the survival of a writer who employs them."[26] She resented being compared to George Washington Cable or Grace King.[27] Furthermore, she did not share the female local colorists' obsession with the past, their desperate nostalgia for a bygone idealized age. "How curiously the past effaces itself for me!" she wrote in her diary in 1894. "I cannot live through yesterday or tomorrow."[28] Unlike Jewett, Freeman, King, or Woolson, she did not favor the old woman as narrator.

Despite her identification with the New Women, however, Chopin was not an activist. She never joined the women's suffrage movement or belonged to a female literary community. Indeed, her celebrated St. Louis literary salon attracted mostly male journalists, editors, and writers. Chopin resigned after only two years from a St. Louis women's literary and charitable society. When her children identified her close friends to be interviewed by her first biographer, Daniel Rankin, there were no women on the list.[29]

Thus Chopin certainly did not wish to write a didactic feminist novel. In reviews published in the 1890s, she indicated her impatience with novelists such as Zola and Hardy, who tried to instruct their readers. She distrusted the rhetoric of such feminist bestsellers as Sarah Grand's *The Heavenly Twins* (1893). The eleventh commandment, she noted, is "Thou shalt not preach."[30] Instead she would try to record, in her own way and in her own voice, the *terra incognita* of a woman's "inward life" in all its "vague, tangled, chaotic" tumult.

Much of the shock effect of *The Awakening* to the readers of 1899 came from Chopin's rejection of the conventions of women's writing. Despite her name, which echoes two famous heroines of the domestic novel (Edna Earl in Augusta Evans's *St. Elmo* and Edna Kenderdine in Dinah Craik's *The Woman's Kingdom*), Edna Pontellier appears to reject the domestic empire of the mother and the sororal world of women's culture. Seemingly beyond the bonds of womanhood, she has neither mother nor daughter, and even refuses to go to her sister's wedding.

Moreover, whereas the sentimental heroine nurtures others, and the abstemious local color heroine subsists upon meager vegetarian diets, Kate Chopin's heroine is a robust woman who does not deny her appetites. Freeman's New England nun picks at her dainty lunch of lettuce leaves and currants, but Edna Pontellier eats hearty meals of paté, pompano, steak, and broiled chicken; bites off chunks of crusty bread; snacks on beer and Gruyere cheese; and sips brandy, wine, and champagne.

Formally, too, the novel has moved away from conventional techniques of realism to an impressionistic rhythm of epiphany and mood. Chopin abandoned the chapter titles she had used in her first novel, *At Fault* (1890), for thirty-nine numbered chapters of uneven length, ranging from the single paragraph of Chapter 28 to the sustained narrative of the dinner party in Chapter 30. The chapters are unified less by their style than by their focus on Edna's consciousness, and by the repetition of key motifs and images: music, the sea, shadows, swimming, eating, sleeping, gambling, the lovers, birth. Chapters of lyricism and fantasy, such as Edna's voyage to the Chenière Caminada, alternate with realistic, even satirical, scenes of Edna's marriage.

Most important, where previous works ignored sexuality or spiritualized it through maternity, *The Awakening* is insistently sexual, explicitly involved with the body and with self-awareness through physical awareness. Although Edna's actual seduction by Arobin takes place in the narrative neverland between Chapters 31 and 32, Chopin brilliantly evokes sexuality through images and details. In keeping with the novel's emphasis on the self, several scenes suggest Edna's initial autoeroticism. Edna's midnight swim, which awakens the "first-felt throbbings of desire," takes place in an atmosphere of erotic fragrance, "strange, rare odors . . . a tangle of the sea-smell and of weeds and damp new-ploughed earth, mingled with the heavy perfume of a field of white blossoms" (Chap. 10). A similarly voluptuous scene is her nap at Chenière Caminada, when she examines her flesh as she lies in a "strange, quaint bed with its sweet country odor of laurel" (Chap. 13).

Edna reminds Dr. Mandalet of "some beautiful, sleek animal waking up in the sun" (Chap. 23), and we recall that among her fantasies in listening to music is the image of a lady stroking a cat. The image both conveys Edna's sensuality and hints at the self-contained, almost masturbatory, quality of her sexuality. Her rendezvous with Robert takes place in a sunny garden where both stroke a drowsy cat's silky fur, and Arobin first seduces her by smoothing her hair with his "soft, magnetic hand" (Chap. 31).

Yet despite these departures from tradition, there are other respects in which the novel seems very much of its time. As its title suggests, *The Awakening* is a novel about a process rather than a program, about a passage rather than a destination. Like Edith Wharton's *The House of Mirth* (1905), it is a transitional female fiction of the *fin-de-siècle,* a narrative of and about the passage from the homosocial women's culture and literature of the nineteenth century to the heterosexual fiction of modernism. Chopin might have taken the plot from a notebook entry Henry James made in 1892 about "the growing divorce between the American woman (with her comparative leisure, culture, grace, social instincts, artistic ambition) and the male American immersed in the ferocity of business, with no time for any but the most sordid interests, purely commercial, professional, democratic and political. This divorce is rapidly becoming a gulf."[31] The Gulf where the opening chapters of *The Awakening* are set certainly suggests the "growing divorce" between Edna's interests and desires and Leonce's obsessions with the stock market, property, and his brokerage business.

Yet in turning away from her marriage, Edna initially looks back to women's culture rather than forward to another man. As Sandra Gilbert has pointed out, Grand Isle is an oasis of women's culture, or a "female colony": "Madame Lebrun's pension on Grand Isle is very much a woman's land not only because it is owned and run by a single woman and dominated by 'mother-women' but also because (as in so many summer colonies today) its principal inhabitants are actually women and children whose husbands and fathers visit only on weekends . . . [and it is situated,] like so many places that are significant for women, outside patriarchal culture, beyond the limits and limitations of the city where men make history, on a shore that marks the margin where nature intersects with culture."[32]

Edna's awakening, moreover, begins not with a man, but with Adele Ratignolle, the empress of the "mother-women" of Grand Isle. A "self-contained" (Chap. 7) woman, Edna has never had any close relationships with members of her own sex. Thus it is Adele who belatedly initiates Edna into the world of female love and ritual on the first step of her sensual voyage of self-discovery. Edna's first attraction to Adele is physical: "the excessive physical charm of the Creole had first attracted her, for Edna had a sensuous susceptibility to beauty" (Chap. 7). At the beach, in the hot sun, she responds to Adele's caresses, the first she has ever known from another woman, as Adele clasps her hand "firmly and warmly" and strokes it fondly. The touch provokes Edna to an unaccustomed candor; leaning her head on Adele's shoulder and confiding some of her secrets, she begins to feel "intoxicated" (Chap. 7). The bond between them goes beyond sympathy, as Chopin notes, to "what we might well call love" (Chap. 7).

In some respects, the motherless Edna also seeks a mother surrogate in Adele and looks to her for nurturance. Adele provides maternal encouragement for Edna's painting and tells her that her "talent is immense" (Chap. 18). Characteristically, Adele has rationalized her own "art" as a maternal project: "she was keeping up her music on account of the children . . . a means of brightening the home and making it attractive" (Chap. 9). Edna's responses to Adele's music have been similarly tame and sentimental. Her revealing fantasies as she listens to Adele play her easy pieces suggest the restriction and decorum of the female world: "a dainty young woman . . . taking mincing dancing steps, as she came down a long avenue between tall hedges"; "children at play" (Chap. 9). Women's art, as Adele presents it, is social, pleasant, and undemanding. It does not conflict with her duties as a wife and mother, and can even be seen to enhance them. Edna understands this well; as she retorts when her husband recommends Adele as a model of an artist, "She isn't a musician and I'm not a painter!" (Chap. 19).

Yet the relationship with the conventional Adele educates the immature Edna to respond for the first time both to a different kind of sexuality and to the unconventional and difficult art of Mademoiselle Reisz. In responding to Adele's interest, Edna begins to think about her own past and to analyze her own personality. In textual terms, it is through this relationship that she becomes "Edna" in the narrative rather than "Mrs. Pontellier."

We see the next stage of Edna's awakening in her relationship with Mademoiselle Reisz, who initiates her into the world of art. Significantly, this passage also takes place through a female rather than a male mentor, and, as with Adele, there is something more intense than friendship between the two women. Whereas Adele's fondness for Edna, however, is depicted as maternal and womanly, Mademoiselle Reisz's attraction to Edna suggests something more perverse. The pianist is obsessed with Edna's beauty, raves over her figure in a bathing suit, greets her as "ma belle" and "ma reine," holds her hand, and describes herself as "a foolish old woman whom you have captivated" (Chap. 21). If Adele is a surrogate for Edna's dead mother and the intimate friend she never had as a girl, Mademoiselle Reisz, whose music reduces Edna to passionate sobs, seems to be a surrogate lover. And whereas Adele is a "faultless madonna" who speaks for the values and laws of the Creole community, Mademoiselle Reisz is a renegade, self-assertive and outspoken. She has no patience with petty social rules and violates the most basic expectations of femininity. To a rake like Arobin, she is so unattractive, unpleasant, and unwomanly as to seem "partially demented" (Chap. 27). Even Edna occasionally perceives Mademoiselle Reisz's awkwardness as a kind of deformity, and is sometimes offended by the old woman's candor and is not sure whether she likes her.

Yet despite her eccentricities, Mademoiselle Reisz seems "to reach Edna's spirit and set it free" (Chap. 26). Her voice in the novel seems to speak for the author's view of art and for the artist. It is surely no accident, for example, that it is Chopin's music that Mademoiselle Reisz performs. At the *pension* on Grand Isle, the pianist first plays a Chopin prelude, to which Edna responds with surprising turbulence: "the very passions themselves were aroused within her soul, swaying it, lashing it, as the waves daily beat upon her splendid body. She trembled, she was choking, and the tears blinded her" (Chap. 9). "Chopin" becomes the code word for a world of repressed passion between Edna and Robert that Mademoiselle Reisz controls. Later the pianist plays a Chopin impromptu for Edna that Robert has admired; this time the music is "strange and fantastic—turbulent, plaintive and soft with entreaty" (Chap. 21). These references to "Chopin" in the text are on one level allusions to an intimate, romantic, and poignant musical *oeuvre* that reinforces the novel's sensual atmosphere. But on another level, they function as what Nancy K. Miller has called the "internal female signature" in women's writing, here a literary punning signature that alludes to Kate Chopin's ambitions as an artist and to the emotions she wished her book to arouse in its readers.[33]

Chopin's career represented one important aesthetic model for his literary namesake. As a girl, Kate Chopin had been a talented musician, and her first published story, **"Wiser Than a God,"** was about a woman concert pianist who refused to marry. Moreover, Chopin's music both stylistically and thematically influences the language and form of *The Awakening.* The structure of the impromptu, in which there is an opening presentation of a theme, a contrasting middle section, and a modified return to the melodic and rhythmic materials of the opening section, parallels the narrative form of *The Awakening.* The composer's techniques of unifying his work through the repetition of musical phrases, his experiments with harmony and dissonance, his use of folk motifs, his effects of frustration and delayed resolution can also be compared to Kate Chopin's repetition of sentences, her juxtaposition of realism and impressionism, her incorporation of local color elements, and her rejection of conventional closure. Like that of the composer's impromptu, Chopin's style seems spontaneous and improvised, but it is in fact carefully designed and executed.[34]

Madame Ratignolle and Mademoiselle Reisz not only represent important alternative roles and influences for Edna in the world of the novel, but as the proto-heroines of sentimental and local color fiction, they also suggest different plots and conclusions. Adele's story suggests that Edna will give up her rebellion, return to her marriage, have another baby, and by degrees learn to appreciate, love, and even desire her husband. Such was the plot of many late-nineteenth-century sentimental novels about erring young women married to older men, such as Susan Warner's *Diana* (1880) and Louisa May Alcott's *Moods* (1882). Mademoiselle Reisz's story suggests that Edna will lose her beauty, her youth, her husband, and children—everything, in short, but her art and her pride—and become a kind of New Orleans nun.

Chopin wished to reject both of these endings and to escape from the literary traditions they represented; but her own literary solitude, her resistance to allying herself with a specific ideological or aesthetic position, made it impossible for her to work out something different and new. Edna remains very much entangled in her own emotions and moods, rather than moving beyond them to real self-understanding and to an awareness of her relationship to her society. She alternates between two moods of "intoxication" and "languor," expansive states of activity, optimism, and power and passive states of contemplation, despondency, and sexual thralldom. Edna feels intoxicated when she is assertive and in control. She first experiences such exultant feelings when she confides her history to Adele Ratignolle and again when she learns how to swim: "intoxicated with her newly conquered power," she swims out too far. She is excited when she gambles successfully for high stakes at the race track, and finally she feels "an intoxication of expectancy" about awakening Robert with a seductive kiss and playing the dominant role with him. But these emotional peaks are countered by equally intense moods of depression, reverie, or stupor. At the worst, these are states of "indescribable oppression," "vague anguish," or "hopeless ennui." At best, they are moments of passive sensuality in which Edna feels drugged; Arobin's lips and hands, for example, act "like a narcotic upon her" (Chap. 25).

Edna welcomes both kinds of feelings because they are intense, and thus preserve her from the tedium of ordinary existence. They are in fact adolescent emotions, suitable to a heroine who is belatedly awakening; but Edna does not go beyond them to an adulthood that offers new experiences or responsibilities. In her relationships with men, she both longs for complete and romantic fusion with a fantasy lover and is unprepared to share her life with another person.

Chopin's account of the Pontellier marriage, for example, shows Edna's tacit collusion in a sexual bargain that allows her to keep to herself. Although she thinks of her marriage to a paternalistic man twelve years her senior as "purely an accident," the text makes it clear that Edna has married Leonce primarily to secure a fatherly protector who will not make too many domestic, emotional, or sexual demands on her. She is "fond of her husband," with "no trace of passion or excessive or fictitious warmth" (Chap. 7). They do not have an interest in each other's activities or thoughts, and have agreed to a complete separation of their social spheres; Leonce is fully absorbed by the business, social, and sexual activities of the male sphere, the city, Carondelet Street, Klein's Hotel at Grand Isle, where he gambles, and especially the New Orleans world of the clubs and the red-light district. Even Adele Ratignolle warns Edna of the risks of Mr. Pontellier's club life and of the "diversion" he finds there. "It's a pity Mr. Pontellier doesn't stay home more in the evenings," she tells Edna. "I think you would be more—well, if you don't mind my saying it—more united, if he did." "Oh! dear no!" Edna responds, "with a blank look in her eyes. 'What should I do if he stayed home? We wouldn't have anything to say to each other'" (Chap. 23). Edna gets this blank look in her eyes—eyes that are originally described as "quick and bright"—whenever she is confronted with something she does not want to see. When she joins the Ratignolles at home together, Edna does not envy them, although, as the author remarks, "if ever the fusion of two human beings into one has been accomplished on this sphere it was surely in their union" (Chap. 18). Instead, she is moved by pity for Adele's "colorless existence which never uplifted its possessor beyond the region of blind contentment" (Chap. 18).

Nonetheless, Edna does not easily relinquish her fantasy of rhapsodic oneness with a perfect lover. She imagines that such a union will bring permanent ecstasy; it will lead, not simply to "domestic harmony" like that of the Ratignolles, but to "life's delirium" (Chap. 18). In her story of the woman who paddles away with her lover in a pirogue and is never heard of again, Edna elaborates on her vision as she describes the lovers, "close together, rapt in oblivious forgetfulness, drifting into the unknown" (Chap. 23). Although her affair with Arobin shocks her into an awareness of her own sexual passions, it leaves her illusions about love intact. Desire, she understands, can exist independently of love. But love retains its magical aura; indeed, her sexual awakening with Arobin generates an even "fiercer, more overpowering love" for Robert (Chap. 28). And when Robert comes back, Edna has persuaded herself that the force of their love will overwhelm all obstacles: "We shall be everything to each other. Nothing else in the world is of any consequence" (Chap. 36). Her intention seems to be that they will go off together into the unknown, like the lovers in her story. But Robert cannot accept such a role, and when he leaves her, Edna finally realizes "that the day would come when he, too, and the thought of him, would melt out of her existence, leaving her alone" (Chap. 39).

The other side of Edna's terror of solitude, however, is the bondage of class as well as gender that keeps her in a prison of the self. She goes blank too whenever she might be expected to notice the double standard of ladylike privilege and oppression of women in southern society. Floating along in her "mazes of inward contemplation," Edna barely notices the silent quadroon nurse who takes care of her children, the little black girl who works the treadles of Madame Lebrun's sewing machine, the laundress who keeps her in frilly white, or the maid who picks up her broken glass. She never makes connections between her lot and theirs.

The scene in which Edna witnesses Adele in childbirth (Chap. 37) is the first time in the novel that she identifies with another woman's pain, and draws some halting conclusions about the female and the human condition, rather than simply about her own ennui. Edna's births have taken place in unconsciousness; when she goes to Adele's childbed, "her own like experiences seemed far away, unreal, and only half remembered. She recalled faintly an ec-stasy of pain, the heavy odor of chloroform, a stupor which had deadened sensation" (Chap. 37) The stupor that deadens sensation is an apt metaphor for the real and imaginary narcotics supplied by fantasy, money, and patriarchy, which have protected Edna from pain for most of her life, but which have also kept her from becoming an adult.

But in thinking of nature's trap for women, Edna never moves from her own questioning to the larger social statement that is feminism. Her ineffectuality is partly a product of her time; as a heroine in transition between the homosocial and the heterosexual worlds, Edna has lost some of the sense of connectedness to other women that might help her plan her future. Though she has sojourned in the "female colony" of Grand Isle, it is far from being a feminist utopia, a real community of women, in terms of sisterhood. The novel suggests, in fact, something of the historical loss for women of transferring the sense of self to relationships with men.

Edna's solitude is one of the reasons that her emancipation does not take her very far. Despite her efforts to escape the rituals of femininity, Edna seems fated to reenact them, even though, as Chopin recounts these scenes, she satirizes and revises their conventions. Ironically, considering her determination to discard the trappings of her role as a society matron—her wedding ring, her "reception day," her "charming home"—the high point of Edna's awakening is the dinner party she gives for her twenty-ninth birthday. Edna's birthday party begins like a kind of drawing-room comedy. We are told the guest list, the seating plan, the menu, and the table setting; some of the guests are boring, and some do not like each other; Madame Ratignolle does not show up at the last minute, and Mademoiselle Reisz makes disagreeable remarks in French.

Yet as it proceeds to its bacchanalian climax, the dinner party also has a symbolic intensity and resonance that makes it, as Sandra Gilbert argues, Edna's "most authentic act of self-definition."[35] Not only is the twenty-ninth birthday a feminine threshold, the passage from youth to middle age, but Edna is literally on the threshold of a new life in her little house. The dinner, as Arobin remarks, is a *coup d'état,* an overthrow of her marriage, all the more an act of aggression because Leonce will pay the bills. Moreover, she has created an atmosphere of splendor and luxury that seems to exceed the requirements of the occasion. The table is set with gold satin, Sevres china, crystal, silver, and gold; there is "champagne to swim in" (Chap. 29), and Edna is magnificently dressed in a satin and lace gown, with a cluster of diamonds (a gift from Leonce) in her hair. Presiding at the head of the table, she seems powerful and autonomous: "There was something in her attitude which suggested the regal woman, the one who rules, who looks on, who stands alone" (Chap. 30). Edna's moment of mastery thus takes place in the context of a familiar ceremony of women's culture. Indeed, dinner parties are virtual set pieces of feminist aesthetics, suggesting that the hostess is a kind of artist in her own sphere, someone whose creativity is channeled into the production of social and domestic harmony. Like Virginia Woolf's Mrs. Ramsay in *To the Lighthouse,* Edna exhausts herself in creating a sense of fellowship at her table, although in the midst of her guests she still experiences an "acute longing" for "the unattainable" (Chap. 30).

But there is a gap between the intensity of Edna's desire, a desire that by now has gone beyond sexual fulfillment to take in a much vaster range of metaphysical longings, and the means that she has to express herself. Edna may look like a queen, but she is still a housewife. The political and aesthetic weapons she has in her *coup d'état* are only forks and knives, glasses and dresses.

Can Edna, and Kate Chopin, then, escape from confining traditions only in death? Some critics have seen Edna's much-debated suicide as a heroic embrace of independence and a symbolic resurrection into myth, a feminist counterpart of Melville's Bulkington: "Take heart, take heart, O Edna, up from the spray of thy ocean-perishing, up, straight up, leaps thy apotheosis!" But the ending too seems to return Edna to the nineteenth-century female literary tradition, even though Chopin redefines it for her own purpose. Readers of the 1890s were well accustomed to drowning as the fictional punishment for female transgression against morality, and most contemporary critics of *The Awakening* thus automatically interpreted Edna's suicide as the wages of sin.

Drowning itself brings to mind metaphorical analogies between femininity and liquidity. As the female body is prone to wetness, blood, milk, tears, and amniotic fluid, so in drowning the woman is immersed in the feminine organic element. Drowning thus becomes the traditionally feminine literary death.[36] And Edna's last thoughts further recycle significant images of the feminine from her past. As exhaustion overpowers her, "Edna heard her father's voice and her sister Margaret's. She heard the barking of an old dog that was chained to the sycamore tree. The spurs of the cavalry officer clanged as he walked across the porch. There was the hum of bees, and the musky odor of pinks filled the air" (Chap. 39). Edna's memories are those of awakening from the freedom of childhood to the limitations conferred by female sexuality.

The image of the bees and the flowers not only recalls early descriptions of Edna's sexuality as a "sensitive blossom," but also places *The Awakening* firmly within the traditions of American women's writing, where it is a standard trope for the unequal sexual relations between women and men. Margaret Fuller, for example, writes in her journal: "Woman is the flower, man the bee. She sighs out of melodious fragrance, and invites the winged laborer. He drains her cup, and carries off the honey. She dies on the stalk; he returns to the hive, well fed, and praised as an active member of the community."[37] In post—Civil War fiction, the image is a reminder of an elemental power that women's culture must confront. *The Awakening* seems particularly to echo the last lines of Mary Wilkins Freeman's "A New England Nun," in which the

heroine, having broken her long-standing engagement, is free to continue her solitary life, and closes her door on "the sounds of the busy harvest of men and birds and bees; there were halloos, metallic clatterings, sweet calls, long hummings."[38] These are the images of a nature that, Edna has learned, decoys women into slavery; yet even in drowning, she cannot escape from their seductiveness, for to ignore their claim is also to cut oneself off from culture, from the "humming" life of creation and achievement.

We can re-create the literary tradition in which Kate Chopin wrote *The Awakening,* but of course, we can never know how the tradition might have changed if her novel had not had to wait half a century to find its audience. Few of Chopin's literary contemporaries came into contact with the book. Chopin's biographer, Per Seyersted, notes that her work "was apparently unknown to Dreiser, even though he began writing *Sister Carrie* just when *The Awakening* was being loudly condemned. Also Ellen Glasgow, who was at this time beginning to describe unsatisfactory marriages, seems to have been unaware of the author's existence. Indeed, we can safely say that though she was so much of an innovator in American literature, she was virtually unknown by those who were now to shape it and that she had no influence on them."[39] Ironically, even Willa Cather, the one woman writer of the *fin-de-siècle* who reviewed *The Awakening,* not only failed to recognize its importance but also dismissed its theme as "trite."[40] It would be decades before another American woman novelist combined Kate Chopin's artistic maturity with her sophisticated outlook on sexuality, and overcame both the sentimental codes of feminine "artlessness" and the sexual codes of feminine "passionlessness."

In terms of Chopin's own literary development, there were signs that *The Awakening* would have been a pivotal work. While it was in press, she wrote one of her finest and most daring short stories, **"The Storm,"** which surpasses even *The Awakening* in terms of its expressive freedom. Chopin was also being drawn back to a rethinking of women's culture. Her last poem, written in 1900, was addressed to Kitty Garesché and spoke of the permanence of emotional bonds between women:

"TO THE FRIEND OF MY YOUTH"

It is not all of life
To cling together while the years glide past.
It is not all of love
To walk with clapsed hands from the first to last.
That mystic garland which the spring did twine
Of scented lilac and the new-blown rose,
Faster than chains will hold my soul to thine
Thro' joy, and grief, thro' life—unto its close.[41]

We have only these tantalizing fragments to hint at the directions Chopin's work might have taken if *The Awakening* had been a critical success or even a *succès de scandale,* and if her career had not been cut off by her early death. The fate of *The Awakening* shows only too well how a literary tradition may be enabling, even essential, as well as confining. Struggling to escape from tradition, Kate Chopin courageously risked social and literary ostracism. It is up to contemporary readers to restore her solitary book to its place in our literary heritage.

Notes

1. Guy de Maupassant, "Solitude," trans. Kate Chopin, *St. Louis Life* 12 (December 28, 1895), 30; quoted in Margaret Culley, "Edna Pontellier: 'A Solitary Soul,'" in *The Awakening,* Norton Critical Edition (New York: Norton, 1976), p. 224.

2. See the contemporary reviews in the Norton Critical Edition, pp. 145-55.

3. "Confidences," in *The Complete Works of Kate Chopin,* ed. Per Seyersted (Baton Rouge: Louisiana State University Press, 1969), Vol. II, p. 701.

4. Carroll Smith-Rosenberg, *Disorderly Conduct: Visions of Gender in Victorian America* (New York: Knopf, 1985), p. 28.

5. Nancy R. Cott, "Passionlessness: An Interpretation of Victorian Sexual Ideology, 1790-1850," *Signs* 4 (1978):233.

6. Catherine Maria Sedgwick, manuscript diary, quoted in Cott, "Passionlessness," 233.

7. Smith-Rosenberg, *Disorderly Conduct,* p. 69.

8. See Mary P. Ryan, *The Empire of the Mother: American Writing about Domesticity* (New York: Haworth Press, 1982).

9. Harriet Beecher Stowe, *My Wife and I,* quoted in Mary Kelley, *Private Woman, Public Stage: Literary Domesticity in Nineteenth-Century America* (New York: Oxford University Press, 1984), p. 327.

10. Ibid., p. 249.

11. Mary P. Ryan, *Womanhood in America from Colonial Times to the Present* (New York: Franklin Watts, 1983), p. 144.

12. Nina Baym, *Women's Fiction: A Guide to Novels by and about Women in America 1820-1870* (Ithaca, N.Y.: Cornell University Press, 1978), p. 32.

13. Ibid., p. 32.

14. Elizabeth Stuart Phelps, "Art for Truth's Sake," in her autobiography, *Chapters from a Life* (Boston: Houghton Mifflin, 1897).

15. Sarah Orne Jewett, *Letters,* ed. Annie Adams Field (Boston: Houghton Mifflin, 1911), p. 47; quoted in Josephine Donovan, *Sarah Orne Jewett* (New York: Frederick Ungar, 1980), p. 124.

16. Susan B. Anthony, "Homes of Single Women," 1877, quoted in Carol Farley Kessler, "Introduction" to Elizabeth Stuart Phelps, *The Story of Avis* (repr. New Brunswick, N.J.: Rutgers University Press, 1985), xxii.

17. Phelps, *The Story of Avis,* pp. 126, 246.

18. Elizabeth Cady Stanton, diary for 1883, quoted in Cott, "Passionlessness," 236 n. 60.

19. Linda Dowling, "The Decadent and the New Woman in the 1890s," *Nineteenth-Century Fiction* 33 (1979):441.

20. Frances Porcher, "Kate Chopin's Novel," *The Mirror* (May 4, 1899) and "Books of the Day," *Chicago Times-Herald* (June 1, 1899), in Norton Critical Edition, pp. 145, 149.

21. Martha Vicinus, "Introduction" to George Egerton, *Keynotes and Discords* (repr. London: Virago Books, 1983), xvi.

22. George Egerton, "A Keynote to *Keynotes,*" in *Ten Contemporaries,* ed. John Gawsworth (London: Ernest Benn, 1932), p. 60.

23. Per Seyersted, *Kate Chopin: A Critical Biography* (New York: Octagon Books, 1980), p. 18.

24. Sandra Gilbert, "Introduction" to *The Awakening and Selected Stories* (Harmondsworth: Penguin, 1984), p. 16.

25. "Confidences," in Chopin, *Complete Works* Vol. II, pp. 700-1.

26. "Crumbling Idols," in Chopin, *Complete Works,* Vol. II, p. 693.

27. Seyersted, *Kate Chopin,* p. 83.

28. Ibid., p. 58.

29. Ibid., p. 209, n. 55.

30. "Confidences," in Chopin, *Complete Works,* Vol. II, p. 702.

31. Henry James, November 26, 1892, quoted in Larzer Ziff, *The American 1890s* (New York: Viking, 1966), p. 275.

32. Gilbert, "Introduction," p. 25.

33. Thanks to Nancy K. Miller of Barnard College for this phrase from her current work on the development of women's writing in France. I am also indebted to the insights of Cheryl Torsney of the University of West Virginia, and to the comments of the other participants of my NEH Seminar on "Women's Writing and Women's Culture," Summer 1984.

34. Thanks to Lynne Rogers, Music Department, Princeton University, for information about Frédéric Chopin.

35. Gilbert, "Introduction," p. 30.

36. See Gaston Bachelard, *L'eau et les rêves* (Paris, 1942), pp. 109-25.

37. Margaret Fuller, "Life Without and Life Within," quoted in Bell G. Chevigny, *The Woman and the*

Myth (Old Westbury, N.Y.: Feminist Press, 1976), p. 349. See also Wendy Martin, *An American Triptych: Anne Bradstreet, Emily Dickinson, Adrienne Rich* (Chapel Hill: University of North Carolina Press, 1984), pp. 154-9.

38. "A New England Nun," in Mary Wilkins Freeman, *The Revolt of Mother,* ed. Michele Clark (New York: Feminist Press, 1974), p. 97.

39. Seyersted, *Kate Chopin,* p. 196.

40. "Sibert" [Willa Cather], "Books and Magazines," *Pittsburgh Leader* (July 8, 1899), in Norton Critical Edition, p. 153.

41. Chopin, *Complete Works,* Vol. II, p. 735.

Nancy Walker (essay date 1988)

SOURCE: Walker, Nancy. "The Historical and Cultural Setting." In *Approaches to Teaching Chopin's The Awakening,* edited by Bernard Koloski, pp. 67-72. The Modern Language Association of America, 1988.

[In the following essay, Walker explores ways to incorporate Chopin's New Orleans Creole setting into classroom discussion of The Awakening.*]*

One dimension of Kate Chopin's *The Awakening* likely to be overlooked in the classroom is the richness of the historical and cultural background against which the novel takes place. New Orleans Creole culture in the late nineteenth century constituted a world unto itself—a set of traditions, mores, and customs unlike any other in America. Indeed, Chopin's descriptions of this culture serve as more than mere backdrop; the contrast between Edna's upbringing in Kentucky and the Creole society of Léonce Pontellier creates a subtle but persistent thread in the novel, one that helps to explain Edna's restlessness and alienation from the society around her. Approaching the novel as—at least in part—an account of the clash between the dominant southern culture in which Edna was raised and the New Orleans Creole subculture in which she finds herself after her marriage allows students not only to better understand a part of American cultural history but also to see Edna as a woman influenced by her past as well as by the events and surroundings of her present.

As Per Seyersted's biography and the letters and diary entries in the *Kate Chopin Miscellany* make clear, *The Awakening* is far from autobiographical. Kate Chopin and Edna Pontellier were the products of very different backgrounds, and that difference influenced their individual responses to the mores and values of New Orleans Creole culture toward the end of the nineteenth century. Whereas Edna has come to her marriage directly from the stern Protestantism of her father's home, Chopin grew up immersed in the cosmopolitan life of the Creoles in both St. Louis and New Orleans. Chopin's maternal grandfather, Wilson Faris, was a Kentuckian, a circumstance that, though it may well have contributed to Chopin's understanding of southern life east of the Mississippi River, had little effect on the atmosphere in which she was raised. In addition, Chopin had traveled extensively before she settled in New Orleans, and her perspective on cultural variety was far wider than that of Edna. On her way to New York to embark on a several-month honeymoon tour of Europe, Chopin commented favorably on Cincinnati and its beer gardens but was not at all pleased by Philadelphia, which she described as a "gloomy puritanical looking city" (Seyersted and Toth 68). The breadth of Chopin's experience with travel and reading—especially by the time she wrote *The Awakening* in her mid-forties—distinguishes her from the unworldly Edna and provides her with a far greater sense of cultural relativism.

The setting of the novel derives from Chopin's residence in New Orleans from 1870 to 1879 as well as from earlier visits there with her family. Born in St. Louis to an Irish-Catholic father and a French-Creole mother, Kate O'Flaherty married Oscar Chopin, a Creole from Natchitoches, Louisiana, and the couple settled in New Orleans, where Oscar became a cotton merchant. The Chopins lived in what was known as the "American" part of the city, an area now known as the Garden District, across Canal Street from the French Quarter. Constantinople Street and Louisiana Avenue, where the Chopins had successive residences, formed part of a burgeoning suburb outside what most long-time residents considered "real" New Orleans: the Vieux Carré. In fact, Per Seyersted, Chopin's biographer, mentions that Oscar Chopin's father, who had come to Louisiana from France and had clung to his French heritage, disliked the fact that the couple chose to live in the American section of the city (37). Nevertheless, Kate Chopin explored New Orleans with a freedom unusual for women in the 1870s and became well acquainted with the colorful mixture of cultures and the bustle of trade in this port city.

Between 1860 and 1880, the population of New Orleans grew from 168,675 to 216,090 (nearly half of the residents were black), and the city was at that time "the only metropolis in the South" (Ezell 232). Founded in 1718, it was also one of the oldest cities in the southern part of the country. Age and size had their negative effects on life in New Orleans in the 1870s. Because the city lacked an adequate system of sanitation and stood below sea level, its narrow streets were filled with human and animal wastes and garbage; and epidemics of yellow fever, smallpox, and cholera were common, largely due to the miasmal swamps immediately adjacent to the city. The yellow fever epidemic of 1878, for example, claimed the lives of more than four thousand New Orleans residents. In an attempt to escape this threat, the wives and children of many Creole families, including those of Oscar Chopin, spent their summers on Grand Isle, which, because it is an island in the Gulf of Mexico about fifty miles south of New Orleans, enjoys gulf breezes that virtually remove the fever-carrying mosquitoes.

It is in this languid, semitropical setting that Chopin places the beginning and the ending of *The Awakening.* Because Grand Isle's summer population was almost entirely Creole, Edna is first shown here immersed in a culture with which she feels at odds and yet to which she is strongly attracted. Unlike Kate Chopin, who grew up speaking French and who managed to charm her Gallic father-in-law, despite his displeasure with her half-Irish heritage, Edna was born to a Kentucky Presbyterian family with values far removed from those of the warm, easygoing Creoles. Early in *The Awakening.* Edna recalls a day in her childhood when she felt a pleasant sense of escape from the rigidity of her home, and she says to Mme Rati-gnolle, "Likely as not, it was Sunday, . . . and I was running away from prayers, from the Presbyterian service, read in a spirit of gloom by my father that chills me yet to think of" (7). Although Edna's family subsequently moved to Mississippi, her severe Calvinistic Protestant background underwent no apparent change, and she is again reminded of it in the novel when her father comes to New Orleans to visit. She is relieved when he finally leaves, taking with him "his padded shoulders, his Bible reading, his 'toddies' and ponderous oaths" (24).

Differences in values and behavior between the Catholic French Creoles of New Orleans and the Kentucky Presbyterians during the years before and after the Civil War could hardly have been more striking. Religious and political forces combined in the early years of the nineteenth century to alter southern Protestantism in ways that created a gulf between it and both Catholicism and northern Protestantism. As Ezell points out in *The South since 1865,* the "Great Revival" of 1800 strengthened evangelical Protestantism among the middle and lower classes of the South. Although this revival spirit initially fostered democratic and even liberal social attitudes, beginning in the 1830s northern criticism of the South—especially of the system of slavery—caused an increasing conservatism among southern Protestants that eventually led to the splitting of most denominations into northern and southern branches. "A great resurgence of religious orthodoxy began to regiment thought to protect Southern vested interests. . . . Liberalism brought threats to the *status quo*; therefore, Southern reaction was conservative in religion as well as in politics" (341). Edna's Kentucky Presbyterian father, who had been a colonel in the Confederate army, is a member of the generation of southerners who were most directly affected by this intense conservative trend in both religious and social attitudes.

The Catholic church, in contrast, was largely unaffected by the wave of southern conservatism in the middle years of the nineteenth century, and the Creoles of southern Louisiana, although many of them owned slaves, preserved through the century virtually the same traditions and social attitudes that they had developed during the years since their settlement of the area in the early eighteenth century. New Orleans, during the period of Chopin's residence there, was dominated by Creole culture, and the Creoles, who had developed a highly sophisticated society, were notably hostile toward the backwoods "Americans" who poured into this major port city with boatloads of timber, furs, and tobacco. To the refined Creole, these hunters and farmers seemed crude, dirty, and socially backward, and although they came down the Mississippi from a variety of states, Kentuckians must have seemed particularly offensive, because the Creoles calle all these outsiders "Kaintocks" (Chase 80).

From its street names and architecture to its Mardi Gras celebrations, New Orleans, under the influence of the Creoles, more nearly resembled a southern European than an American city. Edward King, a contemporary observer writing in *Scribner's Monthly* in 1873, stresses the European atmosphere of French New Orleans:

> Step off from Canal Street, that avenue of compromises which separates the French and the American cities, some bright February morning, and you are at once in a foreign atmosphere. Three paces from the corner have enchanted you; the surroundings of a Southern-American commonwealth have vanished; this might be Toulouse, or Bordeaux, or Marseilles.
>
> (10)

Long before the advent of jazz, music was an important part of the city's cultural life, and the French Opera House was the first in the country to stage productions of Wagner (Seyersted 42). Unconstrained by the Puritanism of their Protestant neighbors, for whom life was serious business, the Creoles played as hard as they worked. Indeed, to those from other parts of the country, Creole life seemed almost sinfully sensuous. Seyersted quotes Lafcadio Hearn, the author, who moved to New Orleans in 1877, as saying, "work . . . in this voluptuous climate . . . is impossible" (41). What appeared to some to be a hedonistic way of life, coupled with the Creole institution of concubinage with quadroon and octoroon women, gave New Orleans a reputation as a sinful city. As Clement Eaton notes in *A History of the Old South,* "Americans who came down the Mississippi were shocked at the Creole Sundays, when the Sabbath day was devoted to pleasure and commerce. Furthermore, these Latins were passionately fond of gambling, lotteries, and dancing" (183). Even those Americans living as neighbors to the French Creoles were vexed at their self-sufficiency, their lack of interest in political affairs. As Edward King describes the situation, "they seem as remote from New York and Washington as if limitless oceans rolled between" (12).

In keeping with this atmosphere of social freedom, women in Creole culture, as is evident in *The Awakening,* were far less affected by the Victorian strictures that dictated the behavior of middle-class women in other parts of the country. Although they tacitly supported a sexual double standard by their acceptance of their husbands' part-Negro mistresses and were legally as powerless as other women, Creole women participated fully in the sensuous atmosphere that surrounded them: drinking wine, enjoying music and literature, wearing bright colors, and entertaining lavishly. Well-educated, especially in the arts, these women were acquainted with literary trends, and many were accomplished musicians and painters. Although Creole culture was patriarchal in the extreme, women enjoyed life in ways that those subjected to Edna's father's "gloom" could not.

Teaching *The Awakening* with an awareness of the religious and social differences in Kate Chopin's cultural milieu enriches students' reading of the novel. It also removes Chopin from the narrow designation of "regionalist" or "local colorist" to which she has often been confined and demonstrates her understanding of the larger cultural patterns and problems of the late nineteenth century. Certainly Edna Pontellier's brave if doomed attempts at self-definition remain the central issue of the novel, but complicating those attempts are the romanticism that results from her rebellion against her rigid Presbyterian background and her inability to adjust that romanticism to the reality of her present environment.

Early in the novel, Chopin makes clear Edna's distance from the mores of the Creoles summering at Grand Isle: "Mrs. Pontellier, though she had married a Creole, was not thoroughly at home in the society of Creoles; never before had she been thrown so intimately among them. . . . A characteristic which distinguished [the Creoles] and which impressed Mrs. Pontellier most forcibly was their entire absence of prudery" (4). Edna is shocked by Mme Ratignolle's detailed recounting of her childbirth experiences, and she reads "in secret and solitude" an unnamed novel that the others read and discuss openly (4). The gossipy, confidence-sharing ways of the Creoles does not merge easily with Edna's Presbyterian reserve—"Mrs. Pontellier was not a woman given to confidences" (7)—yet she is seduced by the easy relations of this culture: "That summer at Grand Isle she began to loosen a little the mantle of reserve that had always enveloped her" (7). Significantly, Chopin places the Pontelliers' New Orleans residence not in the Garden District, the "American" part of the city, but on Esplanade Street (actually, Avenue), at the edge of the French Quarter. Chopin had been familiar with this neighborhood since before her marriage, since it was noted for its grassy promenades where the part-black mistresses of white gentlemen strolled, often with their illegitimate offspring, just minutes from their homes on streets with such names as "Desire" and "Good Children." Edna is thus immersed physically in the Creole world, both on Grand Isle and in New Orleans.

Edna's early desire to escape the grimness of her Kentucky home has led to her marriage to Léonce. Beneath her reserve lies a strain of romanticism and rebelliousness that early in her life manifested itself in imagined attachments to a series of unavailable men: the "dignified and sad-eyed cavalry officer," the young man in Mississippi who was engaged to someone else, and finally the "great tragedian" whose picture she kept on her desk. Chopin makes it clear that Edna's marriage is not the result of any such grand passion: "Her marriage to Léonce Pontellier was purely an accident" (7). One of her motives for marrying him, in fact, is her desire to flout the wishes of her father, who violently opposes her marrying a Catholic. Even after her marriage, her stern father attempts to dictate her values and her behavior. Though proud of her artistic talent, he takes credit for it, "convinced as he was that he had bequeathed to all of his daughters the germs of a masterful capability" (23). The Colonel disagrees with Léonce's rather liberal treatment of Edna's "moods":

> "You are too lenient, too lenient by far, Léonce," asserted the Colonel. "Authority, coercion are what is needed. Put your foot down good and hard; the only way to manage a wife. Take my word for it."
>
> The Colonel was perhaps unaware that he had coerced his own wife into her grave.
>
> (24)

Caught between the Puritanical sternness of her father's world and the relaxed familiarity of Creole culture, Edna can belong fully to neither. Mme Ratignolle recognizes Edna's position as an outsider early in the novel when she exhorts Robert Lebrum to stop flirting with her: "She is not one of us; she is not like us. She might make the unfortunate blunder of taking you seriously" (8). Edna does, of course, take Robert seriously, just as he takes seriously her status as a possession of her husband, even though she tries to counteract this assumption toward the end of the novel: "I give myself when I choose. If he [Léonce] were to say, 'Here, Robert, take her and be happy; she is yours,' I should laugh at you both" (36). Robert cannot understand this freedom, and so he does the "honorable" thing by leaving. And having effectively left her husband, Edna can imagine no future; therefore, she swims into the Gulf of Mexico.

Readers of *The Awakening* have tended, correctly, to see Edna as a "misfit" in several ways. She is not a "mother-woman" like Mme Ratignolle, nor is she a self-fulfilled artist like Mlle Reisz. She tries to be an artist—with Mlle Reisz's encouragement—but tragically, considering the milieu, fails for lack of sufficient talent and commitment. She feels unconnected to her marriage and wants independence, but divorce is not an option and she does not have the means to be financially independent. In these respects she is a woman who does not belong to her time, but it is equally important to realize that she does not belong to her place.

Margit Stange (essay date July 1989)

SOURCE: Stange, Margit. "Personal Property: Exchange Value and the Female Self in *The Awakening*." *Genders*, no. 5 (July 1989): 106-19.

[*In the following essay, Stange discusses representations of the female self in* The Awakening.]

In the beginning of *The Awakening*, New Orleans stock-broker Leonce Pontellier, staying with his wife, Edna, at an exclusive Creole family resort, surveys Edna as she walks up from the beach in the company of her summer flirtation, Robert Lebrun. "'You are burnt beyond recognition' [Leonce says], looking at his wife as one looks at a valuable piece of personal property which has suffered some damage."[1] Leonce's comment is the reader's introduction to Edna, whose search for self is the novel's subject.[2] To take Leonce's hyperbole—"you are burnt beyond recognition"—as literally as Leonce takes his role as Edna's "owner" is to be introduced to an Edna who exists as a recognizable individual in reference to her status as valuable property. This status appears to determine Edna's perception of herself: in response to Leonce's anxiety, Edna makes her first self-examination in this novel about a heroine who is "beginning to realize her position in the universe as a human being, and to recognize her relations as an individual to the world within and about her" (15). Edna, having been told "you are burnt beyond recognition,"

> held up her hands, strong, shapely hands, and surveyed them critically, drawing up her lawn sleeves above the wrists. This reminded her of her rings, which she had given to her husband before leaving for the beach. She silently reached out to him, and he, understanding, took the rings from his vest pocket and dropped them into her open palm. She slipped them upon her fingers.
>
> (4)

In the context of the property system in which Edna exists as a sign of value, Edna's body is detachable and alienable from her own viewpoint: the hands and wrists are part of the body yet can be objectified, held out and examined as if they belonged to someone else—as indeed, in some sense that Leonce insists upon very literally, they do belong to someone else. Edna's perception of her own body is structured by the detachability of the hand and arm as signs of Leonce's ownership of her. Her hands also suggest the possibility of being an owner herself when they make the proprietary gesture of reaching out for the rings that Leonce obediently drops into the palm (this gesture of Edna's contrasts with a bride's conventional passive reception of the ring). The hands are the organs of appropriation; Elizabeth Cady Stanton, in a speech on female rights given in 1892, argued that "to deny [to woman] the rights of property is like cutting off the hands."[3] In having Edna put on the rings herself (a gesture Edna will again perform at a moment when she decisively turns away from her domestic role), Chopin suggests that the chief item of property owned by the proprietary Edna is Edna herself. Thus the opening scene foreshadows the turning point of the plot at which Edna, deciding to leave Leonce's house, resolves "never again to belong to another than herself" (80).

"Self-ownership" was a central project of feminist reformers of the second half of the nineteenth century. In the lexicon of late nineteenth-century women's rights reformers and feminist free love advocates, the term *self-ownership,* when applied to women, had a specific sexual meaning. First popularized by Lucinda Chandler in the 1840s and widely used by the feminist reformers who followed her, self-ownership signified the wife's right to refuse to have sex with her husband. According to Chandler, the practice of self-ownership would mean that "the woman . . . has control over her own person, independent of the desires of her husband."[4] Self-ownership was closely linked with "voluntary motherhood" and thus became a program for putting woman in control of sex and reproduction. "Self-ownership," writes historian William Leach, "meant that woman, not man, would decide when, where, and how the sexual act would be performed. . . . It also meant that woman, not man, would determine when children would be conceived and how many."[5] Self-ownership became central to feminist ideology of the second half of the century. According to Linda Gordon, by the mid-seventies, advocacy of so-called voluntary motherhood—woman's "right to choose when to be pregnant"—was shared by "the whole feminist community."[6]

This feminist community, in contradiction of its advocacy of choice and control for women, was unanimously opposed to the use of birth control devices. This opposition was shared by suffragists, moral reformers, and free love advocates alike. Various kinds of contraceptive technology were accessible to middle-class women. However, as historian Gordon notes, nineteenth-century birth control practice was determined by ideology rather than the availability of technology. In the prevailing ideology of even the most radical feminist reformers, motherhood was an inextricable part of female sexuality.[7] Why did feminists, whose goal was to win for women the civil and proprietary rights that would make them equal to men, choose to deny women the freedom to have sex without pregnancy? As Gordon points out, the linkage of self-ownership with reproduction certainly reflects the reality of many women's lives, which were dominated by multiple births and the attendant realities of risk, disease, and pain.[8] Some of the resistance to birth control technology, Gordon suggests, was motivated by material conditions: birth control devices, by separating sex from reproduction, appeared to threaten the family structure that provided most middle-class women their only social standing and economic security.[9] But even among those reformers who were not concerned with upholding the family (free love advocates and nonmarrying career women, for example), there was a strong resistance to contraception—a resistance that amounts to a refusal to separate motherhood from female sexuality.

To put voluntary motherhood practiced without birth control devices at the center of self-ownership is to make motherhood central to a woman's life and identity. The capacity to bear children is the sexual function that most dramatically distinguishes the sexual lives—and the day-to-day lives—of women from those of men. The ban on contraceptive technology enforces a lived distinction between male and female sexuality: without effective contraception, sex for a woman always means sex *as* a woman because it means a potential pregnancy. The opposition to contraceptive technology (as well as the idealization of motherhood of which it is a part) reflects a commitment to the sexualization of female identity. Through the practice of self-ownership, this differentiated sexuality with motherhood at its core becomes the possession that a woman makes available or withholds in order to demonstrate self-ownership. To ask why the feminist reformers opposed contraceptive technology is, then, to ask how motherhood functions in the construction of the self-owning female self. In making motherhood a central possession of the self, the feminists were defining that self as sexual and as female. The possession of this sexualized self through self-ownership amounts to the exercise of a right to alienate (confirmed by a right to withhold). This selfhood, then, consists of the alienation of female sexuality in a market. Charlotte Perkins Gilman, in her 1899 critique of this sexual market, attacked it as a market in which "he is . . . the demand . . . she is the supply."[10] The feminists' opposition to birth control technology reflects a commitment to this market: underlying their construction of female selfhood is the ideology of woman's sexual value in exchange.

Chopin's dramatization of female self-ownership demonstrates the central importance of the ideology of woman's value in exchange to contemporary notions of female selfhood. If, as Stanton declares in the speech on female selfhood quoted above, "in discussing the rights of woman, we are to consider, first, what belongs to her as an individual," what Edna Pontellier considers as her property is, first, her body.[11] Her body is both what she owns and what she owns with. She begins to discover a self by uncovering her hands and "surveying them critically" with her eyes, thus making an appropriative visual assessment of herself as a proprietary being. Her hands and eyes will serve her in her "venture" into her "work" of sketching and painting (54-55). Thus her hands, by remaining attached (and not cut off like those of the woman who is denied the rights of property), serve her visual appropriation of the world and provide the first object of this appropriation: her own body.

Edna's hands appear in two states: naked and sunburned, and ringed. In the first state, they are conventionally "unrecognizable" as signs of her status as Leonce's wife. Sunburned hands, by indicating the performance of outdoor labor, would nullify Edna's "value" as a sign of Leonce's wealth. In the terminology of Thorstein Veblen's turn-of-the-century analysis of the ownership system, Edna is an item of "conspicuous consumption" that brings "reputability" (a degree of status) to Leonce. Such status-bearing wealth must be surplus wealth: useful articles do not serve to advertise the owner's luxurious freedom from need. Edna must, then, appear to be surplus—she must appear to perform no useful labor.[12] The rings—showy, luxurious, useless items of conspicuous consumption *par excellence*—restore her status as surplus. Yet this status is also constituted by the sight of her hands without the rings: the significance of the sunburned hands quickly collapses into the significance of the ringed hands when the sunburned, naked hands "remind" both Leonce and Edna of the ringed, value-bearing hands. And Edna's sunburn is directly constitutive of her "value," for it results from her conspicu-

ous, vicarious consumption of leisure on Leonce's behalf (what Veblen calls "vicarious leisure"): she has been enjoying a holiday at the respectable, luxurious resort frequented by Leonce's Creole circle.

Thus Edna's hands appear in their naked and exposed state as a reminder of Leonce's property interests while they also, in this state, suggest an identity and proprietary interests of her own. The appropriative survey of the female body as a sign of male ownership continues to engage Edna: her visual fascination fastens on the hands and body of her friend Adele Ratignolle, whose "excessive physical charm" at first attracts Edna (15). Edna "like[s] to sit and gaze at her fair companion." She watches Adele at her domestic labors. "Never were hands more exquisite than [Adele's], and it was a joy to look at them when she threaded her needle or adjusted her gold thimble . . . as she sewed away on the little night drawers" (10). Here, the hands are the organs of labor—but again, gender determines possessive status. Adele's hands are perfectly white because she always wears dogskin gloves with gauntlets (16). The femininity of the laboring hands, their luxuriously aesthetic and spectacular quality, conspicuously signifies that the value of Adele's labor does not stem from production for use: Edna "[can]not see the use" of Adele's labor (16). Adele's laboring hands signify her consecration to her "role" within the family, and they are marked with the gold of a thimble as Edna's are marked with the gold of a ring.

In their white, "exquisite" beauty, Adele's hands are stably—organically—signs of her status as wealth. When Adele jokes "with excessive naiveté" about the fear of making her husband jealous, "that made them all laugh. The right hand jealous of the left! . . . But for that matter, the Creole husband is never jealous; with him the gangrene passion is one which has become dwarfed by disuse" (12). (This ownership is not reciprocal: the question of jealousy pertains only to the husband; the wife's jealous, proprietary interest in her husband is not evoked.) Adele's entire presence is a reminder of the property system in which woman is a form of surplus wealth whose value exists in relation to exchange. A woman of "excessive physical charm," Adele is luxuriously draped in "pure white, with a fluffiness of ruffles that became her. The draperies and fluttering things which she wore suited her rich, luxuriant beauty" (15-16). Her body is as rich, white, and ornamental as her clothes: she appears "more beautiful than ever" in a negligee that leaves her arms "almost wholly bare" and "expose[s] the rich, melting curves of her white throat" (55).

In her rich and elaborate yet revealing clothing, Adele is excessively covered while her body, already a sign of wealth, makes such coverings redundant. Adele appears as a concretized *feme covert*. Under the Napoleonic Code which was still in force in Louisiana in the 1890s, wives were legally identical with their husbands; being in *coverture,* they had no separate legal or proprietary identity and could not own property in their own right.[13] Adele's beauty is her conspicuousness as a form of wealth: her looks are describable by "no words . . . save the old ones that have served so often to picture the bygone heroine of romance." These words—"gold," "sapphires," "cherries or some other delicious crimson fruit"—construct femininity as tangible property. The value of the woman is emphatically defined as social wealth that exists as an effect of the public circulation of the tropes—"the old [words] that have served so often"—that identify her as beautiful. Her beauty is the product and representation of its own circulation. Adele's "excessive physical charm" is a kind of currency that makes her the "embodiment of every womanly grace and charm" (10).

It is in public display that Adele's beauty manifests itself. The sight of woman as social wealth is the starting point of Edna's self-seeking. "Mrs. Pontellier liked to sit and gaze at her fair companion as she might look upon a faultless Madonna" (12). An amateur artist, Edna finds such "joy" in looking at Adele that she wants to "try herself on Madame Ratignolle" (13). Adele, "seated there like some sensuous Madonna, with the gleam of the fading day enriching her splendid color" (13), appears to Edna as a particularly "tempting subject" of a sketch. This sketch becomes the second sight that Edna "surveys critically" (the first being her hands); finding that it "[bears] no resemblance to Madame Ratignolle" (and despite the fact that it is "a fair enough piece of work, and satisfying in many ways"), Edna enforces her proprietary rights in regard to the sketch as she smudges it and "crumple[s] the paper between her hands" (13). Edna is inspired to make another try when she visits Adele at home in New Orleans and finds her again at her ornamental domestic labor (Adele is unnecessarily sorting her husband's laundry). "Madame Ratignolle looked more beautiful than ever there at home. . . . 'Perhaps I shall be able to paint your picture some day,' said Edna. . . . 'I believe I ought to work again'" (55). The sight of Adele at home inspires Edna to do the work that will help her get out of the home. Later she will leave Leonce and support herself on the income from her art and from a legacy of her mother's.

In her insistence on owning her own property and supporting herself, Edna is a model of the legal opposite of the *feme covert*—she is the *feme sole*. Thus Chopin connects her to the Married Women's Property Acts, property law reforms instituted in the latter part of the century that gave married women varying rights of ownership. Edna comes from "old Presbyterian Kentucky stock" (66). Kentucky belonged to the block of states with the most advanced separation of property in marriage. In fact, Kentucky had the most advanced Married Women's Property Act in the nation, granting married women not only the right to own separate property and make contracts, but the right to keep their earnings.[14]

Thus Chopin connects Edna to the feminist drive for women's property rights. Elizabeth Cady Stanton, in her speech on female selfhood quoted above, makes possessive individualism the first consideration among women's rights:

"In discussing the rights of woman, we are to consider, first, what belongs to her as an individual."[15] Chopin suggests that what a woman owns in owning herself is her sexual exchange value. The *feme covert,* in being both property and the inspiration to own, allows Edna to be a *feme sole.* The self she owns can be owned—is property—because it is recognizable as social wealth. Adele, who concretizes the status of the woman and mother as domestic property, makes visible to Edna the female exchange value that constitutes a self to own. Thus Edna's possessive selfhood looks "back" to the chattel form of marriage, valorizing (in a literal sense) the woman as property. In Adele, the "bygone heroine," Edna finds the capital which she invests to produce her market selfhood.

The way that Edna owns herself by owning her value in exchange is a form of voluntary motherhood: "Edna had once told Madame Ratignolle that she would never sacrifice herself for her children, or for any one. Then had followed a rather heated argument." In this argument Edna "explains" to Adele, "I would give my life for my children; but I wouldn't give myself." Adele's answer is, "a woman who would give her life for her children could do no more than that. . . . I'm sure I couldn't do more than that." Withholding nothing, Adele cannot conceive of giving more than she already gives. Edna cannot at first identify what it is she has chosen to withhold: "I wouldn't give myself. I can't make it more clear; . . . it's only something which . . . is revealing itself to me" (48).

The self at first exists in the presumption of the right to withhold oneself as a mother. But Edna, like the feminist advocates of self-ownership, soon determines that voluntary motherhood means withholding herself sexually. After her first successful swim (during which she experiences a moment of self-support and the absolute solitariness of death), she stays on the porch, refusing Leonce's repeated orders and entreaties to come inside to bed (32). Later Edna stops sleeping with her husband altogether, so that Leonce complains to the family doctor, "she's making it devilishly uncomfortable for me . . . She's got some sort of notion in her head concerning the eternal rights of women; and—you understand—we meet in the morning at the breakfast table" (65). It is by withholding herself sexually, then, that Edna exercises the "eternal rights of women" in insisting that she has a self and that she owns that self.

The freedom to withhold oneself has its complement in the freedom to give oneself. No longer sleeping with—or even living with—her husband, Edna declares herself free to have sex with whomever she chooses. She tells Robert, "I am no longer one of Mr. Pontellier's possessions to dispose of or not. I give myself where I choose" (107). Edna supposes that her self-giving is chosen because she has presumed the choice of not giving—she has made her motherhood voluntary. Adele, in contrast, is the mother who never withholds and thus cannot choose but to give. Will and intention seem to be with Edna, whereas Adele exercises no will (and has no self). Yet Adele's giving is not an involuntary and therefore selfless reflex, but a consciously and intentionally developed identity. Adele is Grand Isle's greatest exponent of the "role" of "mother-woman," a role that is produced through deliberate public staging (10). First presented to Edna as a beautiful vision of the "Madonna," Adele produces her maternity through public discourse. Her children are "thoughts" brought out in speech: Adele "thinks" (out loud) of "a fourth one" and, after giving birth to it, implores Edna, in a phrase that Edna will not be able to get out of her mind, to "think of the children, oh think of them" (110).

"Madame Ratignolle had been married seven years. About every two years she had a baby. At that time she . . . was beginning to think of a fourth one. She was always talking about her 'condition.' Her 'condition' was in no way apparent, and no one would have known a thing about it but for her persistence in making it the subject of conversation" (11). Adele produces her "role" of "mother-woman" by thinking and provoking thought, but it is impossible to determine whether Adele thinks about getting pregnant; whether, that is, she practices self-ownership and voluntary motherhood by withholding herself from sex. The two-year intervals between her pregnancies might result from chance, or they might represent intentional spacing that keeps Adele in or nearly in the "condition" that provides her identity. This ambiguity characterizes the "condition" of motherhood that Adele is "always" producing for herself. Motherhood is a "role" and therefore consciously produced and paraded. Yet the intention and will that are used to stage the role conflict with its content, for the role of mother demands selflessness: the mother-women of Grand Isle "efface themselves as individuals" (10). Motherhood is never voluntary or involuntary. If motherhood is a social role that Adele intentionally inhabits, it is also a condition that she can never actually choose, since intending to become pregnant cannot make her so. Thus, motherhood has a kind of built-in selflessness that is dramatically expressed in the scene when Adele, who is usually in control of her presence, becomes pathetically hysterical and paranoic during labor and childbirth. Here, Adele's intentional embrace of motherhood gets its force from the unwilled nature of the "torture" that it attempts to appropriate. Hardly able to speak after her ordeal in childbirth, Adele whispers in an "exhausted" voice, "think of the children, Edna" (109).[16]

Adele and Edna embody the two poles of motherhood: Adele is the "mother-woman" and Edna is "not a mother-woman" (15, 10). The axis of motherhood gives Edna her original sense of identity. What makes her "not a mother-woman" is her refusal to "give" herself for her children. Unlike Adele, Edna does not embrace the role. Her motherhood seems arbitrary, externally imposed and unwilled, "a responsibility which she had blindly assumed." She is "fond of her children in an uneven, impulsive way. She [will] sometimes gather them passionately to her heart; she [will] sometimes forget them" (20). Her "half-remembered" experience of childbirth is an "ecstasy" and a "stupor" (109, 108). Edna's refusal to give herself as a mother,

rather than making her the controller and proprietor of her life, entails the passivity of thoughtlessness. In refusing to be a mother-woman she absents herself from the motherhood that is thus all the more arbitrarily thrust upon her.

Indeed, Edna is inescapably a mother. Motherhood is what Edna withholds and thus she, too, is essentially a "mother-woman." Adele's presence is a provocation and reminder of the self-constituting function of motherhood. Adele's selflessness is an inducement to Edna to identify a self to give. For Edna, who "becom[es] herself" by "daily casting aside that fictitious self which we assume like a garment with which to appear before the world" (57), the friendship with Adele is "the most obvious . . . influence" in the loosening of Edna's "mantle of reserve" (57, 14-15). The Creole community recognizes no private sphere. Adele's sexual and reproductive value is already located in the sphere of public exchange (or, the public is already like the private: the Creoles are like "one big family") (11). In this Creole openness, Edna is inspired to resituate her sexual exchange value in an economy of public circulation.

"The candor of [Adele's] whole existence, which every one might read," is part of a Creole lack of prudery that allows for the open circulation of stories about sex and childbirth. With "profound astonishment" Edna reads "in secret and solitude" a book that "had gone the rounds" and was openly discussed at table. "Never would Edna Pontellier forget the shock with which she heard Madame Ratignolle relating to old Monsieur Farival the harrowing story of one of her *accouchements,* withholding no intimate detail. She was growing accustomed to like shocks, but she could not keep the mounting color back from her cheeks" (11). The candor of Adele's motherhood provokes blushes that simultaneously constitute Edna's reserve and "give her away" to the public. Her body, whether sunburned or blushing, is red from an exposure that privatizes and valorizes that body as her domestic, private attributes—sexuality, modesty, reproduction—are manifested as social value.

Adele has nothing to hide because her body underneath her clothes is manifestly social wealth. Her bareness is as ornamentally "beautiful" as her ornamented, clothed self. The reserved, private, domestic self of Adele reveals itself to Edna as the valuable product of circulation, and this revelation prompts Edna to explore her own possessive privacy. She becomes aware of having "thoughts and emotions which never voiced themselves. They belonged to her and were her own" (48). Her erotic longings belong in this category. "Edna often wondered at one propensity which sometimes had inwardly disturbed her without causing any outward show or manifestation on her part" (18). This is a propensity to become silently infatuated with various men. These "silent" possessions of the self are owned in a way most clearly illustrated in the story of Edna's greatest infatuation, whose object was a "great trage-dian."

The picture of the tragedian stood enframed upon her desk. Anyone may possess the portrait of a tragedian without exciting suspicion or comment. (This was a sinister reflection which she cherished.) In the presence of others she expressed admiration for his exalted gifts, as she handed the photograph around and dwelt upon the fidelity of the likeness. When alone she sometimes picked it up and kissed the cold glass passionately.

(19)

Edna's comment upon the fidelity of the likeness recapitulates the book's opening, in which Leonce's anxiety about Edna's lapse from recognizability, and his restoration of her recognizability via the wedding rings, consists of a discourse that constantly remembers and reinscribes her as a sign of him in his proprietary office. Her "fidelity" in this marital, possessive sense is her recognizability as such a sign. Edna's photograph is to Edna as Edna is to Leonce. It represents her possessive identity, her selfhood as an owner (thus there is a mirrorlike quality in the "cold glass" which shows her herself kissing herself). The photograph embodies and reflects Edna's erotic desire for the tragedian. It objectifies her sexuality in an image that is handed around, praised for its "fidelity," and kissed in private.

Like Adele, the photograph concretizes erotic value that is both publicly produced and privately owned. The erotic availability and desirability of the actor whose photograph "anyone might possess" is a product of reproduction and circulation, as Edna's own kisses are incited by and followed by the circulation of the object. The mode of owning it is "handing it around" while she praises the "fidelity" of the likeness. That is, she assumes an individual possessive relationship to the photograph only in the context of its possession by any number of other owners, whose possession produces the "sinister reflection" of her own possessive, cherishing privacy. But Edna's position as an owner is not that of Adele's husband—or of her own. Edna gives up possession in order to have this possessive relationship. In praising the "fidelity of the likeness" she does not praise its likeness to her but emphasizes that the photograph represents and thus "belongs to" its original—a man whose inaccessibility makes her infatuation "hopeless." Edna can see her photograph as property only by seeing it as male property—just as her own hands, in their function as signs of Leonce's ownership of her, appear detachable and therefore ownable. Yet the absence of Edna in what the photograph represents allows her to imagine a possessive self that is somehow hidden and concealed—and therefore her own. Alone with her photograph, she imagines it circulating. Circulating it, she is able to imagine being secretly alone with it. In her ownership of the photograph, Edna establishes her possessive relationship to her sexuality.

"I am no longer one of Mr. Pontellier's possessions to dispose of or not. I give myself where I choose," says Edna to Robert (106-107). She has withheld herself from her husband in order to give herself. Instead of being property "to dispose of or not," she intends to be property that is necessarily disposed of. The forms of value in which Edna exchanges herself are the duties and functions of the woman and wife—female sexual service, motherhood, and the performance of wifely domestic/social amenities. Edna reprivatizes and reserves this value by giving up her social and domestic duties as the lady of the house, by moving out of the impressive family home into a private domestic space, the "pigeon house" (91), and by withholding sex from her husband. This reserved self is what she gives away at her "grand dinner," when she launches her sexual exchange value into wider circulation.

> Whatever came, she had resolved never again to belong to another than herself. "I shall give a grand dinner before I leave the old house!" Edna exclaimed.
>
> (80)

At the dinner, the "glittering circlet" of Edna's wedding ring (57) is now her crown.

> "Something new, Edna?" exclaimed Miss Mayblunt, with lorgnette directed toward a magnificent cluster of diamonds that sparkled, that almost sputtered, in Edna's hair. . . .
>
> ". . . a present from my husband. . . . I may as well admit that this is my birthday. . . . In good time I expect you to drink my health. Meanwhile, I shall ask you to begin with this cocktail, composed . . . by my father in honor of Sister Janet's wedding."
>
> (86)

Her wedding rings had "sparkled," but the tiara (a conventional adornment of the "young matron") "sputters." This dinner marks the exploding of the intramarriage market, in which she repeatedly sells herself to the same man, into the public market, in which she circulates as the owner of her own sexual exchange value. In its very conception, the dinner collapses the private and public: "though Edna had spoken of the dinner as a very grand affair, it was in truth a very small affair and very select" (85). The absent beloved, Robert, is represented by Victor, his flirtatious younger brother. Flanking Edna are representatives of two modes of the market in sex value: Arobin, the gambler and playboy, represents adulterous and extramarital serial liaisons, while Monsieur Ratignolle enjoys the quasi-organic bond of Creole marriage.

The wealth of the Pontellier household is conspicuously displayed and offered to the guests. On the table "there were silver and gold . . . and crystal which glittered like the gems which the women wore" (86). The women, like the accoutrements, are presented as forms of wealth, and Edna is the queen among them. In her diamond crown, she both embodies and reigns over Leonce's riches. This dinner at which, like all women under exogamy, she leaves "the old house" is a version of the woman-giving potlatch, the marriage feast at which the father gives away the virgin daughter. The cocktail "composed" by the father for the daughter Janet's wedding is explicitly compared by Edna's lover Arobin to the gift of Edna herself: "it might not be amiss to start out by drinking the Colonel's health in the cocktail which he composed, on the birthday of the most charming of women—the daughter whom he invented" (87). Edna is thus the gift not just of Leonce, who makes her into a form of wealth by marking her as value, but of her father, too; that is, she is a bride. As a bride, she is an invention—man-made, brought into the world for, by, and on the occasion of the staging of ownership in the conspicuous consumption of a wedding/potlatch.

An "invention," Edna is thoroughly representational. As a sign of value she is hailed as a sign of her father's wealth of inventiveness in making signs/wealth. The dinner dramatizes the richness of her market-determined transformations: ceremonial drink, invention, queen, luxurious gift. To say that it is her "birthday" is to say that her self is born through exchange and consists of these multiple signs which circulate in the market. What Edna wears marks her as value:

> The golden shimmer of Edna's satin gown spread in rich folds on either side of her. There was a soft fall of lace encircling her shoulders. It was the color of her skin, without the glow, the myriad living tints that one may sometimes discover in vibrant flesh. There was something in her attitude, in her whole appearance . . . which suggested the regal woman, the one who rules, who looks on, who stands alone.
>
> (88)

The gold of her dress makes reference to the value in which she is robed. The lace "encircling" her shoulders refers to the skin which at the novel's opening effects Edna's transformation into "surplus." It is as if the lace is an extra skin—a conspicuously surplus skin—which in its decorative insubstantiality mirrors the meaning of Edna's skin. But the lace is not a true mirror. It points out the superior capacity of the "real" skin to change, to have "myriad tints" which allow it to be continually dissolved and recreated as a sign of value.

Edna as a sign of value is the referent of all the surrounding signs of value. She sits at the head of the table in her crown like "the regal woman, the one who rules, . . . who stands alone," as if she were the principle (and principal) of value that reigns over all its manifestations—the gold, silver, crystal, gems, and delicacies. Now Edna is like Adele, the regal woman who has the "grace and majesty which queens are . . . supposed to possess" (14). And like Adele, who is tortured and "exhausted" by childbirth, Edna experiences the complement of regal power in the exhausted passivity that overcomes her after the dinner, when the celebration of private wealth moves into the realization of value through the ceremonial enactment of breakage and loss.

Edna leaves the Pontellier house with Arobin, who pauses outside the door of the "old house" to break off a spray of jessamine, enacting this defloration. He offers it to Edna: "No; I don't want anything," she answers. Emptied, she says she feels as if "something inside of me had snapped." This metaphorical defloration empties Edna of the erotic desire whose ownership constitutes her selfhood. Edna's

shoulders are bare of the encircling lace and Arobin caresses them. Edna is passive, but Arobin feels the "response of her flesh," which, in its consecration to value, embodies the sexuality that is created in circulation. Now, after Edna's ceremonial "self-giving," this eroticism no longer constitutes a sensation that Edna can appropriate as her own desire (91).

The loss of the self in maternal bloodshedding is enacted at the end of the dinner when the ceremony changes from a potlatch to a sacred, sacrificial rite. The desirous Mrs. Highcamp crowns Victor with a garland of yellow and red roses, effecting his magical transformation into a bacchanalian "vision of Oriental beauty." One of the transfixed guests mutters Swinburne under his breath: "There was a graven image of Desire / Painted with red blood on a ground of gold." This "graven image," like Edna's photograph, reflects her desire. Victor publicly sings the secret song that expresses the production of Edna's "private" desire as a suspicious reflection of circulation, *si tu savais ce que tes yeux me disent* ("if you knew what your eyes are saying to me") (90). She reacts with such consternation that she breaks her wine glass, and the contents—either red or gold, like the roses and the graven image—flow over Arobin and Mrs. Highcamp. Arobin has consecrated the evening's drinks as analogues of Edna, who has invited the guests to "drink her health"—that is, drink *her*—on her "birthday." In involuntarily shattering the glass, which, like the "cold glass" covering the photo, contains a possessive reflection of her value, Edna shatters the "mantle of reserve," symbolically releasing the maternal blood that constitutes her value.

The maternal quality of her self-giving—its involuntary and selfless aspects—overwhelms Edna again some time after the potlatch when, just as she is about to "give" herself to Robert, Edna is called away to witness Adele enduring the agonies of childbirth. The sight of Adele's "torture" overwhelms Edna (as does Adele's exhausted plea to "think of the children"), leaving her "stunned and speechless" (109-111). When she returns to her little house, Robert is gone forever. Deprived of the chance to "give" herself to her desire, she spends the night thinking of her children. Later, she walks to the beach from which she will swim to her death "not thinking of these things" (113). Withholding herself from motherhood, insisting on her right to refuse to "sacrifice" herself for her children, Edna owns herself. In the logic of self-ownership and voluntary motherhood, motherhood is itself the ground on which woman claims ownership of her sexual value. Edna seizes the most extreme prerogatives of this self-ownership, withholding herself from motherhood by withholding herself from life and thus giving herself in a maternal dissolution.

Edna's death in the ocean dramatizes the self-ownership rhetoric of Elizabeth Cady Stanton. Stanton argues that "self-sovereignty" is the existential birthright of both women and men, for every human being "launched on the sea of life" is unique and "alone." But women's self-sovereignty specifically denotes sexual self-determination.[17]

And women—that is, mothers—earn a special presumptive self-sovereignty: "alone [woman] goes to the gates of death to give life to every man that is born into the world; no one can share her fears, no one can mitigate her pangs; and if her sorrow is greater than she can bear, alone she passes beyond the gates into the vast unknown."[18] At the moment of extreme maternal giving, the moment when motherhood takes her life, the woman owns her self by withholding herself from motherhood.

Notes

1. Kate Chopin, *The Awakening,* ed. Margaret Culley (New York: Norton, 1976), p. 4. All further references are given in the text and refer to this edition.

2. Many critics who have discussed the search for self-hood in *The Awakening* argue that Chopin opposes selfhood to socially imposed feminine roles that entail passivity, relative identity, and other-centeredness. See, for example, Per Seyersted, *Kate Chopin: A Critical Biography* (Baton Rouge: Louisiana University Press, 1969) and Margaret Culley, "Edna Pontellier: 'A Solitary Soul,'" in *The Awakening,* ed. Culley, pp. 224-228. Susan Rosowski and Cynthia Griffin Wolff argue that Chopin depicts the difficulty of resisting the infantilizing, fantasy-prone narcissism encouraged by the feminine role in order to achieve autonomy in the realm of the real. See Susan Rosowski, "The Novel of Awakening," *Genre* 12 (Fall 1979): 313-332, and Cynthia Griffin Wolff, "Thanatos and Eros: Kate Chopin's *The Awakening,*" *American Quarterly* 25 (October 1973): 449-471. Sandra M. Gilbert locates the achievement of selfhood outside of the existing, male-dominated social order. Chopin's heroine, Gilbert argues, achieves symbolic "rebirth" by departing for a mythical matriarchal realm. See Sandra M. Gilbert, "Introduction: The Second Coming of Aphrodite," in *The Awakening and Selected Stories* by Kate Chopin, ed. Sandra M. Gilbert (New York: Penguin Books, 1984), pp. 7-33.

3. Elizabeth Cady Stanton, "The Solitude of Self," in Ellen Carol DuBois, ed., *Elizabeth Cady Stanton, Susan B. Anthony: Correspondence, Writings, Speeches* (New York: Schocken, 1981), p. 249. In this speech Stanton gave in 1892 on the occasion of her regination from the presidency of the suffrage movement, Stanton argued for full civil rights for woman on the grounds of her aloneness and existential "self-sovereignty." In its argument and rhetoric, this speech of Stanton's is strikingly similar to Chopin's presentation of female selfhood (*The Awakening*'s original title was *A Solitary Soul*). Like the self Chopin's heroine discovers, Stanton's self is an absolute, possessive self whose metaphorical situation is that of a lone individual "on a solitary island" or "launched on the sea of life" (247-248). In Stanton and in Chopin, female subjectivity and women's rights are grounded in absolute selfhood. For an account of early English feminists' commitment to absolute selfhood, see Catherine Gallagher, "Embracing the Absolute: The Politics of the Female Subject in Seventeenth-Century England," *Genders* 1 (Spring 1988): 24-39.

4. Lucinda Chandler, "Motherhood," *Woodhull and Claflin's Weekly,* May 13, 1871. Quoted in William Leach, *True Love and Perfect Union: The Feminist Reform of Sex and Society* (London: Routledge and Kegan Paul, 1981), p. 89. Leach sees the drive for women's property rights as an attempt to codify self-ownership through property law. He writes, "Chandler believed so strongly in the principle of self-ownership that she wanted it fixed in the law; she joined the moral educationists of Washington in an attempt to repeal the law of couverture in the District of Columbia and to give every woman the 'legal . . . custody and control of her person in wifehood to govern according to her wisdom and instincts the maternal office and protect her child . . . from the dangers of selfish passion, alcoholism and vice'" (89).

5. Ibid.

6. Linda Gordon, *Woman's Body, Woman's Right: Birth Control in America* (New York: Penguin Books, 1974), p. 109. On voluntary motherhood, see Gordon, *Woman's Body,* chap. 5, "Voluntary Motherhood: The Beginnings of the Birth Control Movement," pp. 95-115. William Leach writes, "by the 1870s, self-ownership . . . had become the stock in trade of feminist thinking on birth control" (Leach, *True Love,* p. 92). Daniel Scott Smith notes that "the theme of the wife's right to control her body and her fertility was not uncommon" in Victorian America. Smith quotes Henry C. Wright as follows: "it is a woman's right, not her privilege, to control the surrender of her person; she should have pleasure or not allow access unless she wanted a child." Henry C. Wright, *Marriage and Parentage* (Boston: Bela Marsh, 1853), pp. 252-255, quoted in Daniel Scott Smith, "Family Limitation, Sexual Control and Domestic Feminism in Victorian America," in *Clio's Consciousness Raised,* ed. Lois Banner and Mary Hartman (New York, 1974), pp. 119-136, 129. Smith also quotes Dido Lewis on the advocacy of the Moral Education Society for the right "of a wife to be her own person, and her sacred right to deny her husband if need be; and to decide how often and when she should become a mother." Dido Lewis, *Chastity, or Our Secret Sins* (New York: Canfield Publishing Company, 1888), p. 18, quoted in Smith, "Family Limitation," p. 129.

7. Gordon, *Woman's Body,* pp. 106-111.

8. Ibid., pp. 109-111.

9. Ibid., p. 110.

10. Charlotte Perkins Gilman, *Women and Economics: The Economic Factor between Men and Women as a Factor in Social Evolution,* ed. Carl Degler (New

York: Harper and Row, 1966), p. 86. For a twentieth-century critique of the market in woman, see Gayle Rubin, "The Traffic in Women: Notes on the 'Political Economy' of Sex" in Rayna R. Reiter, ed., *Toward an Anthropology of Women* (New York: Monthly Review Press, 1975, 157-210) p. 177.

11. Stanton, "The Solitude of Self," p. 247.

12. Thorstein Veblen, *The Theory of the Leisure Class: An Economic Study in the Evolution of Institutions* (New York: Macmillan Company, 1899). Veblen argues that the purpose of the ownership of personal property is to achieve social status (or "reputability"); all property is a version of that original property whose "usefulness" was to serve as a trophy marking the "prepotence," or social superiority, of the trophy's owner (23, 29). Objects that are appropriated for use do not cause reputability or prepotence to accrue to their possessors, and such objects are not owned in the conventional sense but are instead subject to "use-appropriation" (23). Ownership, and the reputable self it produces, exists only when the community has reached a point of social and economic organization that allows for the production of a surplus. The first form taken by this "margin worth fighting for" is woman. The original form of ownership was the ownership of women by men. Veblen's account depends upon the idea that woman is already property, for the first ownership came about when the men of one tribe stole the women of another tribe in order to hold them as trophies (20, 23). To be a woman, then, is to be an object of exchange, a social product, surplus. In Veblen's famous characterization of the contemporary domestic ownership system, the bourgeois wife advertises her status as surplus in her role as the chief item of household property as she earns "reputability" for her husband through vicarious consumption and by performing vicarious leisure (usually in the form of nonproductive domestic and social functions) (65-67). This reading of Veblen suggests that ownership and the male selfhood it constitutes are produced by and reflect not the self but others, whose over-shifting perceptions and positions create and destroy the effect of reputability and thus of selfhood. Surplus is a product of social/economic organization; to own (surplus) is thus to establish a mediated relationship with the world. Like Veblen, Chopin pokes fun at the figure of the male owner whose relationship to the world is thus mediated. In the opening pages of *The Awakening,* Leonce rather ridiculously governs himself according to his notions of property rights; for example, he grants the caged birds the right to sing because they are owned by Mme. Lebrun and grants himself the right to retreat to "his own cottage" (3). The surplus and mediating character of personal property is manifested in the woman's femininity. While femininity reflects the oppressive system that makes woman property, for Edna, the unstable, non-

essential, and representative character of her status as Leonce's property becomes suggestive of the possibility of a self-determination that paradoxically remains within the bounds of the male ownership system: she can herself put her wedding rings on or take them off.

13. Margaret Culley, "The Context of *The Awakening,*" in *The Awakening,* ed. Culley, p. 118.

14. Leach, *True Love,* p. 175.

15. Stanton, "The Solitude of Self," p. 247.

16. Motherhood (which includes the abstention from motherhood) is thus a form of a speculative risk taking. The intention to become a mother is the kind of "weak" intention that Walter Benn Michaels connects with "acts that take place in the market, such as speculating in commodities." See chapter 7, "Action and Accident: Photography and Writing," in Walter Benn Michaels, *The Gold Standard and the Logic of Naturalism: American Literature at the Turn of the Century* (Berkeley: University of California Press, 1987), p. 237. Michaels argues that for the self in the market, "self-possession" and "self-interest" are grounded in "the possibility of intention and action coming apart" (244, 241). My discussion of the logic of voluntary motherhood—like Michaels's own example of Lily Bart as a self-speculating self—emphasizes that this self-interest is gendered. For women, self-speculation is sexual; that is to say that sexuality is the content of the female self in the market. Contrary to what Michaels claims, Lily is "a victim of patriarchal capitalism" in a way that the male entrepreneurs in the novel are not (240). The "voluntariness" of female self-speculation is merely an effect of the commodity system, which constructs value along the polarities of accessibility and rarity. The woman cannot choose whether to speculate or what to speculate in; by being a woman she is already sexually at risk. The speculative risk taken by Lily Bart in the marriage market includes the risk of withholding sexual accessibility from the market—a risk that results in her death (complete with hallucinated motherhood). "Voluntary motherhood" concretizes female self-speculation as the risk of pregnancy—which is the risk of life—and points to the enforced nature of female self-speculation by identifying all women as mothers.

17. Ellen Carol Dubois writes, "everywhere [Stanton] lectured, she held parlor meetings of women only on 'marriage and maternity.' . . . Her central point was that women ought to be able to control their own sexual lives, a right which she called 'individual' or 'self' sovereignty." Ellen Carol Dubois, Introduction in Stanton, *Elizabeth Cady Stanton,* p. 95.

18. Ibid., pp. 248, 251.

Ellen Peel (essay date June 1990)

SOURCE: Peel, Ellen. "Semiotic Subversion in 'Désirée's Baby.'" *American Literature* 62, no. 2 (June 1990): 223-37.

[*In the following essay, Peel provides a semiotic and political interpretation of "Désirée's Baby."*]

I

At first **"Désirée's Baby,"** published in 1893 by Kate Chopin, seems no more than a poignant little story with a clever twist at the end.[1] Yet that does not fully explain why the tale is widely anthologized, why it haunts readers with the feeling that, the more it is observed, the more facets it will show. In **"Désirée's Baby"** Chopin, best known as the author of *The Awakening,* has created a small gem, whose complexity has not yet been fully appreciated. As I explore that complexity, my broader goal is a theoretical one: I plan to show not only that a semiotic and a political approach can be combined, but also that they must be combined in order to do justice to this story and to others like it, stories that lie at the nexus of concerns of sex, race, and class.

A semiotic approach to the work reveals that, despite its brevity, it offers a rich account of the disruption of meaning, and that the character largely responsible for the disruption is Désirée Aubigny, who might on a first reading seem unprepossessing.[2] She is a catalyst, however, for the subversion of meaning. When the semiotic approach is supplemented by a political approach, it can be seen that, in particular, Désirée casts doubt on the meaning of race, sex, and class.[3] In this drama of misinterpretations, she undermines smugness about the ability to read signs, such as skin color, as clear evidence about how to categorize people.

The disruption culminates when Désirée, whom everyone considers white, has a baby boy who looks partly black. When she is rejected by her husband, Armand, she takes the infant, disappears into the bayou, and does not return. Armand later finds out, however, that he himself is black, on his mother's side. Désirée, though unintentionally, has devastated him by means of these two surprises, one concerning her supposed race and one concerning his own.

Using a combined semiotic and political approach, my analysis consists of four steps: I trace how the surprises to Armand disrupt signification; question whether they are actually as subversive as they first appear; shift the focus more definitively to Désirée to show how the story associates her with certain enigmatic, subversive absences; and, finally, discuss how the story criticizes, yet sympathetically accounts for, the limitations of Désirée's subversiveness.

The story takes place in an antebellum Creole community ruled by institutions based on apparently clear dualities: master over slave, white over black, and man over woman.

Complacently deciphering the unruffled surface of this symbolic system, the characters feel confident that they know who belongs in which category and what signifies membership in each category. Moreover, as Emily Toth has observed, in the story the three dualities parallel each other, as do critiques of their hierarchical structures.[4]

Within this system of race, sex, and class, the most complacent representative is Armand Aubigny. Confident that he is a white, a male, and a master, he feels in control of the system. In order to understand how his wife challenges signification, we must take a closer look at the surprises that Armand encounters.

The tale begins with a flashback about Désirée's childhood and courtship. She was a foundling adopted by childless Madame and Monsieur Valmondé. Like a queen and king in a fairy tale, they were delighted by her mysterious arrival and named her Désirée, "*the wished-for one,*" "*the desired one.*" She, like a fairy-tale princess, "grew to be beautiful and gentle, affectionate and sincere,—the idol of Valmondé." When she grew up, she was noticed by Armand, the dashing owner of a nearby plantation. He fell in love immediately and married her. She "loved him desperately. When he frowned she trembled, but loved him. When he smiled, she asked no greater blessing of God." They were not to live happily ever after.

Soon after the story proper opens, Armand meets with the first surprise. He, other people, and finally Désirée see something unusual in her infant son's appearance. She asks her husband what it means, and he replies, "It means . . . that the child is not white; it means that you are not white." Désirée writes Madame Valmondé a letter pleading that her adoptive mother deny Armand's accusation. The older woman cannot do so but asks Désirée to come home with her baby. When Armand tells his wife he wants her to go, she takes the child and disappears forever into the bayou.

Thus, Armand's first surprise comes when he interprets his baby's appearance to mean that the child and its mother are not white. What seemed white now seems black. Désirée, with the child she has brought Armand, has apparently uncovered a weakness in her husband's ability to decipher the symbols around him.

Ironically, Désirée's power comes from the fact that she seems malleable. Into an established, ostensibly secure system she came as a child apparently without a past. As a wild card, to those around her the girl appeared blank, or appeared to possess nonthreatening traits such as submissiveness. Désirée seemed to invite projection: Madame Valmondé wanted a child, Armand wanted a wife, and both deceived themselves into believing they could safely project their desires onto Désirée, the undifferentiated blank screen. Actually, however, her blankness should be read as a warning about the fragility of representation.

One aspect of Désirée's blankness is her pre-Oedipal namelessness. As a foundling, she has lost her original last name and has received one that is hers only by adoption. Even foundlings usually receive a first name of their own, but in a sense Désirée also lacks that, for her first name merely reflects others' "desires." In addition, namelessness has a particularly female cast in this society, since women, including Désirée, lose their last name at marriage. Namelessness connotes not only femaleness but also blackness in antebellum society, where white masters can deprive black slaves of their names. Although Désirée's namelessness literally results only from her status as a foundling and a married woman, her lack of a name could serve figuratively as a warning to Armand that she might be black.

But he sees only what he desires. Before the wedding he "was reminded that she was nameless. What did it matter about a name when he could give her one of the oldest and proudest in Louisiana?" On this virgin page Armand believes he can write his name, the name he inherited from his father or, more broadly, the patriarchal Name of the Father. In addition, as a father, Armand wants to pass on that name to his son. Before he turns against his wife and baby, she exclaims: "Oh, Armand is the proudest father in the parish, I believe, *chiefly because it is a boy, to bear his name*; though he says not,—that he would have loved a girl as well. But I know it isn't true. I know he says that to please me" (emphasis added).

The approaching downfall of Armand's wife, and hence of his plans for his name, is foreshadowed by the relationship between Désirée's blankness and another name, that of the slave La Blanche. The mulatta's name refers to the whiteness of her skin, but "*blanche*" can also mean "*pure*" or "*blank*," recalling Désirée's blankness. La Blanche is Désirée's double in several ways. Neither has a "proper" name, only a descriptive one. During the scene in which Armand rejects his wife, he explicitly points out the physical resemblance between the women:

> "Look at my hand; whiter than yours, Armand," [Désirée] laughed hysterically.
>
> "As white as La Blanche's," he returned cruelly. . . .

The story also links the two women through their children, for the mistress first notices her son's race when she compares him to one of La Blanche's quadroon sons. And perhaps Armand is the father of La Blanche's son.[5] The two women—and even their sons—may have parallel ties to Armand because of the possible sexual connection between slave and master. So much doubling hints that the slave's racial mix has foreshadowed that of the mistress.

Because La Blanche's name refers to her in the visual but not the racial sense, her appearance illustrates the contradiction of a racial system that is based on color but does not consider visual evidence conclusive. In this discourse a person who looks white but has a "drop" of black "blood" is labeled black. As Joel Williamson says, the "one-drop rule" would seem definitive but in fact leads to the problem of "invisible blackness."[6]

Miscegenation, which lies at the heart of the contradiction, marks the point at which sexual politics most clearly intersect with racial politics. Theoretically either parent in an interracial union could belong to either race. Nonetheless, "by far the greatest incidence of miscegenation took place between white men and black female slaves."[7] Even when the white man did not technically rape the black woman, their relationship tended to result from, or at least be characterized by, an imbalance of power in race, sex, and sometimes class. Ironically, descendants of such a union, if their color was ambiguous, embodied a challenge to the very power differential that gave birth to them.

"Désirée's Baby" calls attention to the paradoxes that result from miscegenation and the one-drop rule. La Blanche and Désirée look white but are considered black, while "dark, handsome" Armand—whose hand looks darker than theirs—is considered white. Désirée's entry into the symbolic system forces Armand to confront the contradiction he ignored in La Blanche, another white-looking woman. A form of poetic justice ensures that the same one-drop rule that enables him to keep La Blanche as a slave causes him to lose Désirée as a wife. After the first surprise, Armand sees Désirée's blankness as blackness, not *blancheness*.

It is crucial to note that Désirée is disruptive, not because she *produces* flaws in the signifying system but because she *reveals* flaws that were already there. Long before her marriage, for instance, Armand was considered white and La Blanche was considered black. In a sense, Désirée acts as a mirror, revealing absurdities that were always already there in the institutions but repressed. Her blankness has reflective power.

In another sense, Désirée's potential as a mirror was one of her attractions for Armand, for he wanted her to bear a child that would replicate him—in a flattering way. Armand blames and smashes the mirror that has produced a black reflection. An outsider observing Armand's generally harsh treatment of slaves might, however, see his baby's darkness as another instance of poetic justice, the return of the oppressed.

Similarly, if the baby's darkness comes from his mother, whom Armand dominates, then the child's appearance represents the return of another oppressed group, women. To reproduce the father exactly, the child would have to inherit none of his mother's traits. In a metaphorical sense the first surprise means that Armand learns that his son is not all-male but half-female. The infant is an Aubigny but has inherited some of Désirée's namelessness as well, for we never learn his first name (nor that of his double). More generally, paternal power, the name of the father, seems to have failed to compensate for the mother's blackness or blankness.

To blame someone for the baby's troubling appearance, Armand has followed the exhortation, "*Cherchez la femme*." In particular, he is looking for a black mother to blame. He is right to trace semiotic disruption to Désirée, but the trouble is more complex than he at first realizes.

The end of the story brings the second surprise—black genes come to the baby from Armand, through his own mother. Early on, readers have learned that old Monsieur Aubigny married a Frenchwoman in France and stayed there until his wife died, at which point he brought eight-year-old Armand to Louisiana. Only after Désirée and her baby have disappeared and her husband is burning their belongings, do he and the readers come across a letter from his mother to his father: ". . . I thank the good God for having so arranged our lives that our dear Armand will never know that his mother, who adores him, belongs to the race that is cursed with the brand of slavery." As Joseph Conrad suggested, the "heart of darkness" lies within the self: the letter unveils Armand's "dark, handsome face" to himself.

At this point, several shifts occur. One takes place between wife and husband. For Armand, his wife was originally a screen onto which he could project what he desired. When he found a black mark on the screen, he rejected it. Now he has learned that the mark was a reproduction of his own blackness. The mark, which he considers a taint, moves from her to him.

Another shift takes place between sons and fathers. As Robert D. Arner implies, Armand at first rejects his baby for being the child of a white man and a black woman but then finds that the description fits himself.[8] With blackness, the half-female nature attributed to the baby has also moved to Armand. An intergenerational shift occurs between women as well as men, for the role of black mother has gone from Armand's wife to his mother.

Thus two surprises have profoundly disturbed Armand. As in the Hegelian dialectic of master and slave, these two surprises have shaken the structure of white over black, male over female, and master over slave. Armand, the figure who seemed to belong to the dominant race, sex, and class, is shown to be heir to blackness and femaleness and to belong to the group "cursed with the brand of slavery." The repressed has returned and drained meaning from the established system of signification.

II

Nevertheless, these surprises are less subversive than they first appear. The fact that they shake Armand's concept of meaning and punish his arrogance does not mean that they actually change the inequality of power between the sexes, between the races, or between the classes, even on his plantation. Armand might be less sure of his ability to tell black from white, but he probably will not free his slaves. Moreover, through the traumas experienced by Armand, the story invites readers to pity the suffering caused by inequalities of power but not to wonder how those inequalities could change. In other words, the surprises are more disruptive in a *semiotic* than a *political* sense; they endanger the system of *signification* more than the system of *domination*.

The text directs sympathy less toward black characters than toward characters on the margin between black and white. The story urges us to consider it a pity that Désirée and Armand, brought up as white, must undergo the trauma of receiving the news that they are black. But we are hardly urged to pity the much larger number of people who have lived as enslaved blacks since birth. The implication is that being black might deserve no particular sympathy unless a person was once considered white. The broader effects of race and its relation to slavery remain unexamined.

The problem arises in part because Chopin is using the Tragic Mulatto convention, which appears repeatedly in American literature.[9] It is often easy for white readers to identify with the Tragic Mulatto, because she or he is typically raised as white and only later discovers the trace of blackness. Yet the invocation of "tragedy" introduces problems, partly because it implies resignation to the inevitable. The very idea of a Tragic Mulatto also suggests that mulattoes may be more tragic, more deserving of pity, than people of purely black ancestry.

Moreover, the very notion of pity is inadequate as a political response and can even have a conservative effect. The limitations of pity are best observed by looking at the traces of sexism that, like traces of racism, appear as a residue in the text. The parallel between racism and sexism in the story is complicated, because *insufficient* concern for blacks and slaves corresponds to *excessive* concern for women. Excessive concern can be debilitating for women by defining them solely as victims.

When Désirée walks away, apparently to her death, the tale most strongly urges readers to show such concern for women. This arises because of the sympathetic way in which the entire story has represented her. She is good: "beautiful and gentle, affectionate and sincere." She is appealing: "'Armand,' she called to him, in a voice which must have stabbed him, if he was human." She is vulnerable: "Her hair was uncovered and the sun's rays brought a golden gleam from its brown meshes. . . . She walked across a deserted field, where the stubble bruised her tender feet, so delicately shod, and tore her thin gown to shreds." This doe-like character joins a long line of women who, by dying at the end of a story or a novel, call forth readers' tears. In particular, Tragic Mulattoes tend to be *mulattas.*

But scrutiny of such endings raises the discomfiting possibility that they rely on feminine vulnerability in order to move readers. A strong, rebellious, surviving heroine might not provide such tidily tragic closure. I am not suggesting that Désirée's pain should be presented less sympathetically; rather, I am questioning the implication that a less vulnerable woman would deserve less concern.

The connection of pity with race, class, and sex is noteworthy in the double of Désirée's baby—La Blanche's quadroon son. In contrast to Désirée's bruised feet, his bare feet are described merely as coming in contact with a polished floor, for the story presents only Désirée as suffering from the lack of sturdy shoes. Here the stress on feminine vulnerability combines with the acceptance of black slavery, as if it were a pity for a person such as Désirée to suffer: a member of the weak sex, someone who at least used to belong to groups that do not deserve such treatment—the race with "a golden gleam" in their hair and the class with the right to "tender feet."

For these reasons, even though the meanings of race, sex, and class are threatened by Armand's surprises, those two events do not seriously disturb the system of power relations. The story invites sympathy for Désirée partly on the sexist grounds that feminine women are weak and on the racist grounds that white members of the master class do not deserve to be treated like black slaves.

Twentieth-century readers may be troubled to find that Armand's surprises have a less subversive effect than at first seemed possible. The ideologies behind them can be better understood if placed in historical context. Because the story is set in the era of slavery, its verisimilitude would falter if Armand suddenly reformed and freed his slaves. We must also consider the era in which the story was written and originally read, for the late nineteenth century in the United States was marked by a rebounding prejudice against blacks. Attitudes towards women also differed substantially from those of the late twentieth century: even the women's movement drew on notions of female purity and martyrdom that sound strange today but were part of nineteenth-century discourse. Thus it would be anachronistic to expect more subversiveness from the traumas experienced by Armand.

III

Some of these problems can be mitigated, however, by thinking more carefully about the text—or rather about what is missing from the text. Shifting the focus more definitively to Désirée discloses certain enigmatic, disruptive absences.

Almost everyone who has written on the story has mentioned, favorably or unfavorably, the concluding revelation about Armand's mother. This final twist recalls the surprise endings of Guy de Maupassant, who strongly influenced Chopin.[10] While evoking sympathy for Désirée, the twist essentially turns backward to tradition and male power: the very presence of a plot twist may reflect Chopin's inheritance from de Maupassant, a literary forefather; in the ending the focus of narrative point of view is Armand, upholder of conservative values; and the female character earns sympathy largely through a sentimental convention—through powerless, victimized innocence. In fact, my discussion itself has so far concentrated on surprises undergone by Armand, a figure of male conservatism. I agree with Cynthia Griffin Wolff that we should cease analyzing the surprise ending and look elsewhere.[11]

Instead of concentrating on the ending, with its conservative, male orientation, we should turn to Désirée, who is absent from the ending. Although submissive, the young woman does have some power. Her boldest action is disappearance, but she does act. While she neither desires nor anticipates the havoc she wreaks, she does catalyze the entire plot.[12]

Through Armand, we have already started to see how the meanings of race, class, and sex are crumbling. Désirée offers two greater challenges to meaning, because she may not be wholly white and because she may not die in the bayou. These are enigmas, in the sense used in *S/Z*,[13] and they remain inconspicuously unsolved, both for readers and, apparently, for other characters. The enigmas are silent, formless absences that cannot be found in any specific location.

To begin with, Désirée may be black—and thus a black mother—after all. If she is black, that mitigates some of the racism I discussed earlier. Instead of being a white character who deserves sympathy for unjust treatment that includes the accusation of being black, she is a black character whose unjust treatment, minus the accusation, on its own account deserves sympathy. Whether or not Désirée is black, the impossibility of knowing her race reveals the fragility of meaning more than Armand's knowable race does. The *presence* of a traditional, *male*-oriented twist *located* at the end of the story veils a troubling, *female*-oriented *absence*—of knowledge based on skin color or on writing—that has *no particular location.*

Désirée is troubling in another way as well. The tale says, "She disappeared among the reeds and willows that grew thick along the banks of the deep, sluggish bayou; and she did not come back again," but it never actually says she dies. Just as it is possible that she is partly black, so it is possible that she (with the baby) is alive. If so, that survival mitigates some of the sexism I discussed earlier. Désirée deserves sympathy even if she does not pay for it with her life. In addition, if she does not kill herself, she is saying in effect that life is worth living even if she is black and has lost Armand's love. Indeed, by escaping she has freed herself from those who once projected their desires on her. Even if she does kill herself and her child in the bayou, it is significant that the deaths are absent from the text, because in this way the work allows some hope, however slight, for the race, class, and sex the characters represent. Like the impossibility of knowing Désirée's race, the impossibility of knowing her death offers a challenge to complacency about knowledge.

As the two unsolved enigmas suggest, the challenge to meaning, like Désirée, tends to operate negatively, through non-sense. She sometimes cries out unconsciously and involuntarily or remains completely silent. These traits appear in the scene where she notices her baby is black:

> "Ah!" It was a cry that she could not help; which she was not conscious of having uttered. . . .
>
> She tried to speak to the little quadroon boy; but no sound would come, at first. When he heard his name uttered, he looked up, and his mistress was pointing to the door.

She at first seemed no threat to the signifying structure she had entered, but the very inarticulateness of this blank card reveals that the system of signification sometimes breaks down.

By creating Désirée's enigmas—the possibility that she is black and the possibility that she and her baby are alive—Chopin to some extent resists the racism and sexism to which she was urged by much in her historical moment. It is important that the enigmas are not just difficult but decipherable puzzles that, when solved, would clearly state that Désirée was black and alive. Instead, the enigmas have the elusive indeterminacy typical of Désirée.

As we have seen, Armand first thinks his wife is white, but he decides he has misinterpreted her. He thinks his wife is black and solely responsible for their son's blackness, but again Armand finds he has misinterpreted. Although unsettling, both incidents leave intact the hope that knowledge can correct misinterpretations. Yet the absences associated with Désirée erode some of that semiotic hope. Because the readers—and probably the characters—never know whether she is partly black and whether she survives the bayou, the story throws into question the very possibility of knowledge, at least in some cases.

IV

It would be satisfying to end on that note, but I must add that Désirée still disrupts the practice of domination less than semiotic practice. While sympathetic to her, Chopin reveals the limitations of some of the character's values. Of course the author does not hold twentieth-century beliefs; yet she is far enough from Désirée's antebellum era to present a critique indicating that the young woman, as a product of her society, has internalized so many of its values that she can never fully attack it. Chopin subtly indicates that, in spite of the disruptiveness of Désirée's enigmas, her subversiveness remains limited, for three main reasons.

To begin with, Désirée is excessively dependent on the unconscious. She is "unconscious," in the sense that she is unaware. For example, Désirée is the last to realize that her child is not white, and it never occurs to her that her baby's blackness comes from her husband. On another level, she often seems unaware of herself, driven by her own unconscious. Her actions after discovering the baby's race seem trancelike, as if in a dream—or nightmare. And, as has been shown above, she sometimes cries out involuntarily. On still another level, Désirée's lack of political consciousness could also be seen as a kind of "unconsciousness." None of this detracts from her raw power, but uncontrollable power can be as dangerous to those who wield it as to others.

The second restriction on Désirée's subversiveness comes from a certain negative quality. Through her silence (and inarticulateness), through the story's silence about her enigmas, and through her final absence, she disrupts her

society's signifying system by revealing its contradictions and meaninglessness. She does destroy complacency about knowledge. Yet all this is not enough. Destruction often must precede creation but cannot in itself suffice. Désirée creates nothing but a baby, whom she certainly takes away, and perhaps kills.

Even Désirée's destructiveness is limited, for she possesses another negative trait: she is "essentially passive."[14] She is discovered by Monsieur Valmondé, she is discovered by Armand, she is filled with joy or fear by her husband's volatile moods, and, while lying on a couch and recovering slowly from childbirth, she is visited by Madame Valmondé. Désirée is immersed in her husband's value system and never stands up to him, not even to interpret the meaning of his dark skin or the baby's, much less to criticize his racism, his sexism, or his treatment of slaves. When she finally acts, she pleads ineffectually with her husband, writes ineffectually to her mother, and then takes the most passive action possible—she disappears. Like the suicide of Edna Pontellier in *The Awakening,* Désirée's disappearance is hardly a triumph.

The third weakness lies in Désirée's lack of a sense of political solidarity. She acts only individually or as part of a nuclear family, never as part of a broader group. She fails to acknowledge ties with anyone outside the family who belongs to her sex or to her newly attributed race and class. Her similarity to La Blanche, for instance, fills her with horror. In fact, in Désirée's final efforts to win back Armand she is seeking someone she thinks is her diametric opposite—a white male, assured of his place as master. The only exception to Désirée's final solitude is her baby. But even he cannot represent any kind of political bonding. Even if she does not murder him, nothing indicates that she sees him as linked to her in shared oppression.

Désirée's individualism resembles that of other characters.[15] For instance, the general condition of blacks and slaves never really comes into question. Madame Valmondé, like Désirée, regrets that one individual, Armand, treats his slaves cruelly, but not that he or other people own slaves in the first place. Instead of recognizing the institutional nature of exploitation based on race, class, and sex, Désirée and others seem to feel that problems stem from the lack of certain personal qualities, such as pity or sympathy. "Young Aubigny's rule was a strict one . . . and under it his negroes had forgotten how to be gay, as they had been during the old master's easy-going and indulgent lifetime." Indulgence rather than emancipation is presented as the alternative to Armand's harshness. In a similar vein, individualizing love is shown as the "antidote to the poison of Armand's racial abstraction."[16] His love for his wife and baby causes him to treat the slaves well for a while. This makes Désirée happy, but she does not question whether one man's moods should have such power over other people.

Chopin sympathetically but critically shows that her characters define problems in terms of the lack of individualistic qualities such as love and mercy, not in terms of the subordination of one group by another. I do not mean to say that individual virtues totally lack value, only that they may not suffice to solve certain problems. In short, though some characters feel pity for slaves, blacks, and women, the assumption that they are inferior goes unquestioned.

In this ideology, superiors should have a sense of *noblesse oblige,* but they remain superior. Concerning sex, race, and class, Désirée upsets systems of meaning but—by failing to connect the personal with the political—stops short of attacking hierarchical power structures. Disruption of meaning could lead to, and may be necessary for, political disruption, but Désirée does not take the political step.

Instead of attacking the meaningfulness of racial difference as a criterion for human rights, Désirée takes a more limited step: she reveals that racial difference is *more difficult to detect* than is commonly supposed. In this view, suffering can result if people classify each other too hastily or if, having finished the sorting process, people treat their inferiors cruelly. But the system of racial difference, with its built-in hierarchy, persists. In this system, superiority is still meaningful; the only difficulty lies in detecting it. It is no wonder that those viewed as inferior do not unite with each other.

Chopin presents these three reasons—unconsciousness, negativeness, and lack of solidarity—to help explain why Désirée does reveal her society's lack of knowledge but fails to change its ideological values, much less its actual power hierarchies.[17] She poses so little threat to the dominant power structures that she holds a relatively privileged position for most of her life. Yet subversiveness need not be bound so tightly to traits such as unconsciousness that make it self-limiting.

Désirée's semiotic subversiveness should be taken seriously. Her disruption of meaning may even be necessary, but Chopin skillfully suggests it is not sufficient.

Notes

1. "Désirée's Baby," in *The Complete Works of Kate Chopin,* ed. Per Seyersted (Baton Rouge: Louisiana State Univ. Press, 1969), I, 240-45. I would like to thank Robert D. Arner, William Bush, Gillian C. Gill, Margaret Homans, and Gila Safran-Naveh for their comments on this paper.

2. I am using "semiotic" to refer to the study of signs in the broad sense, to the study of the systems by which we create signification, decipher meaning, and gain knowledge.

3. I am using "political" in the broad sense to refer to concern with societal power relations, not just electoral politics.

4. "Kate Chopin and Literary Convention: 'Désirée's Baby,'" *Southern Studies,* 20 (1981), 203; and see

Robert D. Arner, "Kate Chopin," *Louisiana Studies,* 14 (1975), 47.

5. Cynthia Griffin Wolff, "Kate Chopin and the Fiction of Limits: 'Désirée's Baby,'" *Southern Literary Journal,* 10 (1978), 128.

6. *New People: Miscegenation and Mulattoes in the United States* (New York: Free Press-Macmillan, 1980), p. 98. To avoid confusion, I generally follow the terminology of the society shown in the story, using the one-drop rule in deciding how to refer to characters' race. I refer to "mulattoes" only when the context demands it. Important parallels exist between Chopin's story and *Pudd'nhead Wilson,* which Mark Twain published the next year. Eric Sundquist puts Twain's novel in historical context, explaining that the work both grows out of and protests against growing racism in the United States in the late nineteenth century, an era that sought to redefine "white" and "black" by concepts like the "one-drop rule" ("Mark Twain and Homer Plessy," *Representations,* No. 24 [1988], 102-28).

7. James Kinney, *Amalgamation! Race, Sex, and Rhetoric in the Nineteenth-Century American Novel* (Westport, Conn.: Greenwood, 1985), p. 19; see Winthrop D. Jordan, *White over Black: American Attitudes Toward the Negro, 1550-1812* (Chapel Hill: Univ. of North Carolina Press, 1968), p. 138; and Judith R. Berzon, *Neither White Nor Black: The Mulatto Character in American Fiction* (New York: New York Univ. Press, 1978), p. 9.

8. "Pride and Prejudice: Kate Chopin's 'Désirée's Baby,'" *Mississippi Quarterly,* 25 (1972), 133.

9. For more information on the Tragic Mulatto, see Berzon, pp. 99-116; Toth; Barbara Christian, *Black Feminist Criticism: Perspectives on Black Women Writers* (New York: Pergamon, 1985), pp. 3-4 and passim; and Jules Zanger, "The 'Tragic Octoroon' in Pre-Civil War Fiction," *American Quarterly,* 18 (1966), 63-70.

10. Per Seyersted, *Kate Chopin: A Critical Biography* (Oslo: Universitetsforlaget, 1969), p. 73; Wolff, p. 126.

11. Wolff, p. 125.

12. Arner makes a similar point ("Pride and Prejudice," p. 137).

13. Roland Barthes, *S/Z,* trans. Richard Miller (New York: Hill and Wang-Farrar, Straus and Giroux, 1974), pp. 209-10.

14. Barbara C. Ewell, *Kate Chopin* (New York: Ungar, 1986), p. 71.

15. Wolff makes a similar point (p. 127).

16. Arner, "Kate Chopin," p. 52.

17. The force of just one of the three influences can be seen by comparison with *Pudd'nhead Wilson.* Unlike

Désirée, Roxana is conscious and takes positive action, but both characters lack unity with a group. Roxana, who suffers from only one of the three disadvantages I have explained, still cannot manage to bring about notable subversion.

Douglas Radcliff-Umstead (essay date summer 1990)

SOURCE: Radcliff, Douglas. "Literature of Deliverance: Images of Nature in *The Awakening*." *Southern Studies* 1, no. 2 (summer 1990): 127-47.

[*In the following essay, Radcliff-Umstead explores the sociopolitical aspects of* The Awakening *as illustrated by Chopin's nature imagery.*]

Kate Chopin's novel **The Awakening** belongs to the nineteenth-century tradition of "literature of images" where description of nature relates to and advances the narrative's major themes and characterizations. The American novel shares with the works of authors like Chateaubriand, Balzac, Flaubert and Charlotte Bronte a similar emphasis on natural description as a primary instrument to express fundamental psychological and social conflicts.[1] As a female author portraying the revolt of her heroine against a restrictive society, Chopin employs nature to illustrate the entrapment of women under patriarchy and their battle to achieve deliverance.[2] Edna Pontellier, the protagonist of **The Awakening,** seeks to liberate herself from the traditional womanly roles of wife, mother or lover in order to experience an unbounded fullness of being. Rather than being a pictorial, decorative element, nature description in Chopin's novel is intrinsic to the development of plot, motives and point of view. Hers is a technique of focalization where images of nature convey the actual scene as physically viewed by certain characters and as mentally perceived by those same actors in the narrative. Behind the psychological portrait of the heroine in revolt against genteel bondage is a sociopolitical dimension to be represented in those focalizing natural descriptions. The goal of this essay will be to study the function of images of nature in **The Awakening** so as to explore the narrative's semiotic complexities.

Chopin builds the novel on the opposition between interiors and the exterior where the heroine struggles to escape an imprisoning reality. Doors, real or metaphorical, are always shutting to confine Edna (Toth, "Feminist Criticism," 246). The protagonist comes to discover the Otherness of both the physical and social worlds apart from an inner self of which she was scarcely conscious before the start of the novel's events.[3] Her spiritual awakening consists of gaining insight into a disquieting truth in her being while she recognizes in outer nature a sympathetic (although troubling) correspondence with her newly stirred emotions. There also arises an opposition in the cultural distance between Edna's Kentucky Presbyterian background and the values of the Louisiana Creole community where

the central character is an uneasy member as a result of her six-year marriage to the New Orleans broker Léonce Pontellier. That Creole society founds itself on racism (the labor of quadroons and "darkies" as children's nurses, cooks, maids, and servant-boys) and sexism, reducing adult females to the status of "mother-women." While Chopin records the racist situation without criticizing it, she makes of her novel a frontal assault on the male domination of women. Although Edna enjoys general acceptance and even sympathy among the Creoles, she considers herself a psychological and linguistic outsider in their Francophone company. As an anthropologist has analyzed the paradox of culture (Hall 87), the heroine is caught between her present status in a social system with its various demands (Tuesdays at-home for receptions, an air of solicitude in managing a household) and her past experience of Protestant self-reliance on a Kentucky horse farm and a Mississippi plantation. Edna would have to combat an image of the delicate and obedient Southern lady that had its origins in the rhetoric supporting slavery during the antebellum period when writers like George Fitzhugh upheld a social hierarchy where white women existed between white masters and slaves. According to Fitzhugh, "[A husband] ceases to love his wife when she becomes masculine or rebellious."[4] While conforming to the mores of Creole society does bring a sense of psychological security, the heroine rejects the spiritual desiccation caused by complying with custom, and she seeks to assert independence at the cost of being on the outside.

Even when the Creoles leave New Orleans for their summer vacations on Grand Isle (the setting at the novel's opening), they reproduce their urban environment there to make of the beach world a scene of social integration. Even amidst the apparently unlimited horizon and spaciousness of the seashore retreat, there predominates an impression of narrowness as vacationers must observe "*les convenances.*" Though living in cottages, the Creoles are connected to each other by narrow bridges linking the buildings together. They also dine at a common table where they practice their ceremonious rituals to complete their self-contained world. A spirit of remoteness also prevails on Grand Isle, a place so out of time that Sunday newspapers arrive late from town. But since the island stands between the restrictions of the city and the boundlessness of the sea, this enchanting setting on the Gulf of Mexico does stir in the protagonist feelings of revolt that no appeal to social convention will ever suppress. There by the sea Edna awakens for the first time to the contradiction between the outward demand for conformity and the inner desire to challenge convention: "the dual life—the outward existence which conforms, the inward life which questions" (277). The restless waves of the gulf illustrate the conflicting character of landscape in the novel that correspond to the currents of unresolved emotions in the heroine's heart.

Edna's movement toward self-realization becomes evident on a Sunday excursion to the small island Chênière Caminada in the company of her young admirer Robert Lebrun.

One of the customs of Creole society that always astonishes the protagonist with her Calvinist prudery is the chaste gallantry between married women and younger single males. As long as those relationships are conducted within the bounds of New Orleans propriety, no husband objects to the innocent attentions paid to his wife. But Chopin's novel studies exactly the psychological need to transcend arbitrary limits and the role that nature plays in promoting the escape from confining conditions. The passage by water to Chênière Caminada is a rite of liberation: "Sailing across the bay . . . , Edna felt as if she were being borne away from some anchorage which had held her fast" (299). As the phenomenologist Gaston Bachelard demonstrates in his text *Water and Dreams,* the principle of water is an ambivalent source of renewed life and menacing death. For freedom at sea also bears with it the danger of a bewildering sense of being lost, of drifting aimlessly. Here the seascape shows life's duality. The protagonist's break from a past of bondage to institutions and customs occurs when she hastily departs from the suffocating interior atmosphere of morning mass at the island's parish church. Society and the church are here fused to stifle genuine feelings of rebelliousness. Edna must flee the company of worshipers like the symbolic "lady in black" forever holding her velvet prayer-book in an attitude of deathlike mourning usually associated with the woman's closely following after two insouciant young lovers as if to suggest Thanatos in pursuit of Eros (Wolff 454). The hours that Edna and Robert spend wandering the Chênière Caminada and enjoying the hospitality of a humble cottage renew the pastoral tradition of the *locus amoenus*: the pleasant shelter of seeming eternal peacefulness (Curtius 195). But instead of suspending the novel's principal action, this pastoral interlude advances the heroine's sensual transformation. Although the landscape initially appeared caught in an unchanging sameness, upon Edna's "awakening" from slumber in the white purity of Madame Antoine's cottage she sees the island as if turned into a land of enchantment. Significantly the sheets of the white bed in Madame Antoine's rustic cabin are made fragrant by laurel, sacred to Apollo in this novel whose heroine will briefly be elevated in the brilliance of a fatal dawn to a state resembling that of a pagan goddess. The opposition between inner and outer vanishes magically (but only momentarily) in this bucolic episode where nature gently pervades the protective and nourishing shelter.

Upon awakening the protagonist brings to mind Sleeping Beauty having rested for a century in the guard of a faithful knight. For here Robert Lebrun, unlike Edna's husband, can share the radiance of the country setting because of his sensitive character. Whereas Léonce Pontellier thinks of land as a commodity to be exchanged for profit or to stand as a sign of material success, young Lebrun joins the heroine in appreciating the wondrousness of the island. While Edna earlier felt compelled to run from the artificially instituted church services, here she celebrates a natural mass by taking bread and wine (Casale 79). Going outside the cottage, the protagonist plucks an orange that she throws to Robert in a rite that leads to his illumination as he comes to her under the orange tree. The ambrosial fruit with its sweet fragrance and pungent taste is part of a moment of glowing light when nature calls Edna and Robert to the dream of a romantic union that will never be realized. In what began as a flight across a long line of gray, weather-beaten houses on a "low, drowsy island" (301) culminates in a meeting of souls during the sun's resplendent descent:

> It was very pleasant to stay there under the orange trees, while the sun dipped lower and lower, turning the western sky to flaming copper and gold. The shadows lengthened and crept out like stealthy, grotesque monsters across the grass.
>
> (304)

Stylistically the rather abstract "It was" construction serves to veil the slow movement of time and the advance of luminosity (Treichler 241). But with the coming of nocturnal shadows the reader of this landscape grows aware of a possible menace of bizarre monsters letting loose previously repressed and socially forbidden emotions. For Edna life itself will be the ultimate monster of beauty and brutality. The wondrous magic of the pastoral moment will pass to the fairytale nightmare of illicit and finally fatal romance. Reading an episode such as the outing to Chênière Caminada is never an isolated act since Chopin will later have Edna refer to Madame Antoine's tale of pirates on the Baratarian Islands. The excursion will forever stay with Edna, not only as a promise of love to be fulfilled but also as a vision of lovers lost sailing among those Baratarian Islands surrounded by treacherous currents.

Gardens also serve in this narrative as miniature examples of the *locus amoenus,* areas that can mediate between inside and outside, between city and country. The Lebrun townhouse on Chartres Street at first appears prison-like due to the iron bars before the front door and lower windows, but a side gate opens into a garden enclosed by a high fence. Even in late autumn the Lebrun garden remains a welcoming enclave with its civilized furnishings of wicker chairs, chaise lounge and table for refreshments in the afternoon. The immured garden is a zone of protection and repose. Although Edna ordinarily regards the Pontellier home as a place of alienation, her husband's most conspicuous possession, at certain moments when the other members of her family are away, she delights in strolling the damp garden walks and attending to trimming the plants: "The garden smelled so good and looked so pretty in the afternoon sunlight" (339). Fragrance and glowing light stimulate in her the vibrant sensations of a being first awakening to the earth's beauty. In this novel of emancipation the protagonist eventually assumes that attitude of sensuous availability to the outer world (instead of passive receptivity) that Chopin's contemporary André Gide called "*disponibilité*" in his poetic tract *Les Nourritures Terrestres.* But because the house on Esplanade Street seems to be a "forbidden temple" (352) erected in Léonce's idolatry of financial prosperity, Edna takes advantage of her husband's prolonged absence on a business trip to

New York to rent a small dwelling in the immediate neighborhood as a refuge from her social obligations. Ironically the heroine never comes to know in the tiny garden of her own home the ecstatic promise of a passionate rapport with Robert that she at last experiences by a chance meeting with him at a modest suburban garden restaurant:

> . . . a small leafy corner, with a few green tables under the orange trees. An old cat slept all day on the stone step in the sun, and an old *mulatresse* slept her idle hours away in her chair at the open window, till some one happened to knock on one of the green tables.
>
> (373)

Many of the elements of the episode at Madame Antoine's cottage are present here: orange trees, an atmosphere of slumber, checkered sunlight filtering through quivering leaves. Here as elsewhere in the novel the setting responds to Edna's tremendous need for nourishment and rest.[5] Both the cat and the rustic cook are somnolent guardians of this suburban oasis midway between the city and the country. Whereas other gardens have permitted Edna the privilege of communicating with her innermost thoughts, the restaurant garden offers her the opportunity for intimate directness with her beloved Robert to clear away the tensions caused by his abrupt departure during the summer at Grand Isle for a commercial venture in Mexico. The orange trees become emblematic of the forbidden love that they at last are about to acknowledge to each other. While one's private garden may be a site for establishing control over the physical world through horticultural labors, this garden restaurant in a public but relatively secluded location permits Edna and Robert to achieve briefly a loving closeness through the understanding that they finally reach. The refreshing enclosure of gardens verdant with hope makes possible the transparent immediacy of formerly repressed sentiments.[6]

Gardens and open fields both display the flowers whose bright colors and sweet fragrances arouse Edna to an awareness of her hidden self. Borders of yellow camomile mark the limit between the vacationers' cottages on Grand Isle and the seashore as if to indicate the dividing point between urban culture and the endless gulf. The heroine frequently picks flowers to decorate the interior of her home with their beauty, a blossoming loveliness with which she can be identified in her awakening and opening to new, powerful sensations.[7] Edna's closest female friend, the Creole Adèle Ratignolle, in the ebullient fullness of her role as a traditional mother-woman expecting still another baby, resembles the great, sweet roses adorning the hearth of her salon. Red and yellow roses also embellish the twenty-ninth birthday party that the heroine celebrates on the eve of her moving away from her husband's house. On that festive occasion a female guest crowns Robert's younger brother Victor with a garland of those roses as if he were Eros incarnate until Edna removes the wreath and flings it away:

> There was a graven image of Desire
> Painted with red blood on a ground of gold.
>
> (357)

The crown of victory truly belongs to the protagonist, not to any male pretender among her guests.

Of all the flowers mentioned in the novel the one most closely associated with the heroine is jessamine with its seductive fragrance that becomes the emblem of her "sensual development" (Dyer 192). Sprays of jessamine grow on the trellis by the front verandah of her townhouse for Edna to inhale the perfume and thrust the blossoms into the bosom of her white morning gown. That same, heavy fragrance predominates at the birthday party, engulfing the dining room through open windows. Shortly after the celebration the roué Alcée Arobin, soon to be the heroine's adulterous lover, offers her a sprig of jessamine that she refuses in continuing hesitation before erotic involvement. But Arobin fully recognizes how Edna is opening to sexual fulfillment: "He had detected the latent sensuality, which unfolded under his delicate sense of her nature's requirement like a torpid, torrid sensitive blossom" (373). For flowers symbolize in ambivalent fashion not only sensual awakening but also the protagonist's vulnerability to temptation that could compromise and destroy her. The polysemic role of flowers is evident within two pages of the text at the end of Chapter 17 and the start of the following chapter. As Edna gazes out at the garden of her home one bewitching night, she beholds:

> . . . the dusky and tortuous outlines of flowers and foliage. She was seeking herself and finding herself in just such sweet, half-darkness which met her moods.
>
> (318)

Amidst the flowers the heroine is becoming an "I" independent of her husband or any other man. Out in the flowering garden she might elude the prison of her domestic life (White 103). But also here emphasis falls on the entanglement of the plant life that threatens to endanger her in a new existence. On the very morning that Edna plucks the jessamine, a sense of alienation passes over her:

> The street, the children, the fruit vender, the flowers growing there under her eyes, were all part and parcel of an alien world which had suddenly become antagonistic.
>
> (319)

Chopin's narrative art consists in recapturing all the conflictual nature of the protagonist's being torn between the hope of enriching but menacingly entangling vital relationships. Like flowers, Edna possesses alluring beauty but also a fragility of being.

One of the few persons who perceived the heroine's vulnerability and encouraged her in facing herself and society is the often irascible pianist Mlle Reisz. When Edna informed the musician of her intentions to become a painter, Mlle Reisz cautioned her, ". . . to succeed, the artist must possess the courageous soul" (330). The flower that is associated with the pianist is violets, that she wears in a bunch on the side of her head. One critic finds violets to be emblematic of "rites of protection" since artists must be solitary creatures defending their absolute and original gifts from a Philistine world (Dyer 192). But Chopin also wishes to stress the shabbiness of the pianist's willful retreat from company by noting that the violets are artificial and well-worn. Not until Edna sends Mlle Reisz a fresh bunch of violets with black lace trimming for the birthday party does the lonely artist yield ever so slightly from her spiritual isolationism. In her small apartment the pianist tries to overcome the drabness of her private life by filling her windowframe with pots of rose geraniums. It is there by that window, when the apartment's tenant is away, that Edna is occupied with picking dry leaves from the geraniums just as in total surprise Robert enters there two days after his return from Mexico. The scene between the two has a quality later to be realized in films where the heroine tensely repeats Robert's elliptic and elusive answers to her probing questions while the reader seems to see a camera close-up shot of her nervously playing with the flowers: ". . . the reality was that they sat ten feet apart, she at the window, crushing geranium leaves in her hand and smelling them, he twirling around on the piano stool" (366). The anxious strain in their not-as-yet-confessed love for each other reveals itself in her angry hand movements with the flowers. Through color, fragrance, and leafy texture, flowers provide a varied imagery of temptation, menace, tension, disappointment and artistic aloofness.

In communicating from the interior to the exterior, windows can serve in the novel as symbols of expectation or of frustration (Brombert 57-61). Not only do windows permit a view to the outside, but they also allow light and nature's perfumes to pervade inner spaces. Through their exposure of the outer world, windows relieve the cluttered atmosphere of rooms full of ostentatiously expensive furnishings, as at the Pontellier house where in a rebellious mood Edna breaks a vase purchased by her husband and she calms down by looking out into the night. Sometimes a solitary window observation post offers a sense of peace and an impression of gaining control over circumstances, as with Dr. Mandelet, the family physician that Léonce Pontellier consults in husbandly concern over his wife's erratic behavior. This neutral but deeply reflective character enjoys his semi-retirement reading by his study's window and gazing out to the garden whose long expanse shelters the doctor's home from street traffic. The meditative serenity achieved by the physician at his window watch enables him to peer objectively but sympathetically into the hidden emotions of his troubled patients.

Windows also illustrate the ambivalence typical throughout this narrative. Mlle Reisz' top-floor apartment reveals a contrasting dinginess and almost transcendent feeling of release:

> There were plenty of windows in her little front room. They were for the most part dingy, but as they were nearly always open it did not make so much difference. They often admitted into the room a good deal of smoke and soot; but at the same time all the light and

air that there was came through them. From her windows could be seen the crescent of the river, the masts of ships and the big chimneys of the Mississippi steamers.

(328)

This whole passage rests on a series of oppositions: shabbiness versus enthralling perspective, grime versus the bright glow of daytime, the anti-social seclusion of an apartment reached by steep stairs versus the immediate contact with the vast outlying world of rooftops and river, the stasis of the interior setting and the dynamism of sea and river vessels. As an emancipated woman the artist Mlle Reisz controls her environment, where at her keyboard she nearly hypnotizes the protagonist by interweaving Wagner's "Liebestod" with an "Impromptu" by Frederic Chopin to express the destructiveness of passionate desire (Thornton 55). The light that the windows provide functions as a positive force, causing the heroine on her many visits to be invaded by a feeling of repose. While window views from on high may grant an aesthetic appreciation of present time and space, Chopin's art of ambiguity also represents how a window post can be a scene of frustration as already demonstrated by the strained reunion of Edna and Robert in Mlle Reisz's apartment upon his return from Mexico. Although characters may temporarily ease the anxiety in their hearts by looking beyond their narrow, closed existences, the privileged view from windows does not always liberate them from imprisonment.

Foremost among the spectacles seen from windows is the progress of the seasons, the major structuring device of this novel. More than from its formal arrangement into thirty-nine chapters, the narrative gains coherence from the underlying structure based on the change of seasons. Seasonal time, because of its cyclical rhythm, surpasses chronological time to take part in eternity (Poulet 377). But the round of seasons in *The Awakening* will never achieve its completion on account of the heroine's suicide. The seasons as qualities of human experience rather than an objective recounting of temperatures and climatic conditions prevail to express the drama of a woman coming alive to a physical world that she must quit rather than accept the daily compromises of society. At the novel's start summertime is more than a period of exhausting heat and biting mosquitoes but a state of mind full of undefined yearning and conflict:

> An indescribable oppression, which seemed to generate in some unfamiliar part of her consciousness, filled her whole being with a vague anguish. It was like a shadow, like a mist passing across her soul's summer day.

(270)

Here Chopin not only describes the Louisiana summer in the manner of a regional realist (the one degree of critical recognition that she received for many decades), but she also makes summer a metaphor of Edna's psychological turmoil. The heroine becomes an object passed across by the Southern summertime (Treichler 241). Marriage is the oppressive force obscuring the soul's bright summer day (Thornton 59, 62). A transparent existence in conformity with social conventions ends with the darkness of troubling inner questions. Seasonal moods point to the transformation taking place in the protagonist, who will never know another summer with its sultry hope for liberation from deadening customs.

Summer reaches its climax with the outing to Chênière Caminada, with a swift decline following upon Robert's sudden departure to Mexico and the subsequent breaking up of the vacationing colony for the return to New Orleans. Autumn settles gently upon the city, not as a season of natural crisis and deepening coloration but as a period of lingering warmth that permits entertaining on the verandah into November while giving pause to reflect on fundamental changes in attitude. In the eyes of acquaintances Edna appears a totally transformed being, made radiant in the glow of autumn afternoons (Ch. 20). Then winter strikes as a time of frigid invasion "when treacherous drafts came down chimneys and insidious currents of deadly cold found their way through key-holes" (272). Adjectives like "treacherous" and "insidious" represent the ethical qualities of a time of deceit and entrapment. Winter mists are perceptual screens that obscure reality and diminish hope. The gloom of winter skies causes Edna's artistic creativity as a painter to languish in the dark improvised studio at the Pontellier townhouse. Darkness objectifies the despair in the protagonist's heart during Robert's visit to Mexico. But the clouded atmosphere lifts at the thought of Lebrun's imminent return: "The murky, lowering sky, which had depressed her a few hours before, seemed bracing and invigorating as she splashed through the streets on her way home" (349). From swimming at Grand Isle during the summer Edna's principal recreation changes to walking throughout the autumn and winter in New Orleans (Treichler 246). Edna's radical changes in reacting to the wintry weather reflect the novel's basic stylistic ambivalence in the play of emotions from disappointment to expectation.

Wintertime proves to be a season of extreme decisions for Mme Pontellier, with her move from Léonce's house occurring in late January or early February (Ch. 32), the ensuing sexual liaison with Arobin, and the definitive departure of Robert after their confession of reciprocated love. Just before Edna learns of Lebrun's second flight from her, nature seems to smile at her with a deceptive spirit of hope:

> . . . the stars were blazing. The air was mild and caressing, but cool with the breath of spring and the night.
>
> (379)

For by the penultimate thirty-eighth chapter the early warmth of the southern springtime can be felt in the stellar brilliance of the night, yet with a tinge of coolness to restrain ardent emotions. On that delightful night Edna's strolling companion is Dr. Mandelet, on their way back from Adèle Ratignolle's delivery. The physician cautions Mme Pontellier that nature remains indifferent to the moral consequences of human decisions and actions. Although the point of view of Chopin's protagonist toward nature is to project her own emotions in its phenomena, outward physical nature pays no heed to the ardent sentiments and passions of the heroine or any other character. Then on coming to recognize the emptiness of false dreams of happiness with her beloved Robert, the heroine drowns herself at Grand Isle in the indifferently roseate dawn of an early spring day when the sun's heat belies the icy cold of the waters where she vanishes. Just as nature's dormant energies are about to burst forth in renewed vitality, Edna Pontellier elects to withdraw from its ceaseless round of promise and betrayal.

Throughout this narrative the heroine is constantly attempting to establish a space of her own. The move to the rented house constitutes just such an effort to define a sphere where she might be in full control, but the move represents a decline in the social hierarchy along with the opportunity for increased freedom of action. There are two episodes, however, in Chapters 23 and 25, when visits to the race track fire Edna with an enthusiasm that transforms her from morbid sullenness to vibrant animation. The equestrain setting is an environment of intermediate nature: outdoors with powerful and beautiful animals in competition, but absolutely human-made in construction and purpose with horses trained for the sport of humans. As a child of the Kentucky blue grass country Edna displays a close bond to the Confederate colonel father against whom she is usually in rebellion. Nearness to horses arouses an intense libidinal energy in her, to be associated with her adulterous lover Arobin and his high-spirited steeds (Dyer 195). In the thoroughly social arena of the race track Edna's expertise in equine matters puts her at an advantage over everyone else, men and women alike who struggle to hear her excited comments in the hope of emulating her good fortune in betting on the horses. Like some of the fastest running and most independent horses, the heroine has become full of mettle and somewhat unmanageable, to her husband's regret. Ambivalently the race track is a zone for the unleashing of primitive forces and at the same time an artificial showcase setting for the social elite to divert their idleness with gambling. Edna knows to the supreme degree the total sense of power and possession of her social group only when she is in that racing milieu.[8] When Dr. Mandelet sees Mme Pontellier at an intimate dinner party after the first visit to the race track, the physician marvels at her metamorphosis into an impassioned creature: "She reminded him of some beautiful, sleek animal waking up in the sun" (336). Through horses Edna comes into contact with the ultimate source of vital energy.

It is in fact the sun which in the novel symbolizes the warm release of sexual forces within the heroine. To overcome the chilly darkness of psychological conflict the protagonist seeks the illumination of both the sun and the moon. On rainy days she cannot pursue her painting, feeling deprived of the mellowing sunlight. To her the sun signifies hope, and she views Robert's absence for even a brief period as similar to a cloud's darkening a sunny day. During the time of her most intense activity as a painter Edna would occasionally conquer feelings of alienation and experience a state of spiritual transcendence:

> She was happy to be alive and breathing, when her whole being seemed to be one with the sunlight, the color, the odors, the luxuriant warmth of some perfect Southern day.

(324)

The sun plays an instrumental role in elevating her soul to know harmony with the physical universe. As the consequence of her struggle to win freedom she at times acquires a solar radiance that causes others like Mlle Reisz to associate her with the comforting rays of the sun: "Ah! Here comes the sunlight!" (346). But just as the myth of Hyacinth illustrates, the protective Apollo also possesses the power to destroy with his merciless heat. The adjective that in this novel most usually describes the sun's intense summer heat is "biting," to represent the star's ferocious force. As a model of urban circumspection Léonce scolds his wife for allowing the sun at Grand Isle to burn her beyond recognition,[9] and Robert is always trying to shield Edna with a sunshade. A parasol also serves to protect her from the intense light, but such "accessories" as sunshades and parasols block her view and cut her off from desired physical sensations (Toth, "Feminist Criticism," 245). The heroine's suicide will occur at the dynamic moment of sunrise over the Gulf of Mexico where in dying she will be spiritually reborn in the renewing solar rays.

Edna is just as much a creature of the night as a luminous figure of daylight. During that fateful summer on Grand Isle she learns to swim, taking lessons from Robert by moonlight. Both the moon and the swimming symbolize her initiation into an authentic eros that she never knew in her conjugal life. The moon constantly tempts the heroine to swim out into distant and strange waters whose mystery veils any threat of danger. When the moon casts its clarity over the restless gulf, it also brings Edna a sense of peace: "There was no weight of darkness; there were no shadows. The white light of the moon had fallen upon the world like the mystery and softness of sleep" (291-92). The impression here is that of the gentle, soft quality of the brilliant nocturnal scene that frees the world and its sensitive inhabitants of feelings of oppressiveness. The sun and moon are two vital principles of cosmic direction to guide the protagonist in her path of liberation. In **The Awakening** the moon is never that placid sphere described by the early nineteenth-century Italian poet Giacomo Leopardi as being indifferent to the sufferings and aspirations of humans trapped on earth. Instead, the moon restores Edna to the realm of romance and dreams that the spectacle of marriage took from her.[10] Under the mystic lunar rays bayou legends relate how spirits haunt the gulf's shores and cast their spells on elect souls like the protagonist. But in this novel's ambiguous moods even gentle moonlight may mark the sadness and pain of separation, as on the night of Robert's departure from Grand Isle when his

boatsman waits for the moon to illuminate their sailing back to the mainland. As various critics have noted (Dyer 199), the moon in Chopin's writings is an emblem of Woman and also here of enlightening truth. In the soft nocturnal light of the moon, as in the sun's biting rays, Edna Pontellier yearns to know the mystery of the infinite.

This novel emphasizes the horizon of the apparently boundless sea that forever lures the heroine in daylight and at night. Images of enclosure alternate with visions of infinity to characterize Edna's battle to escape the sterile stasis of life as mother and wife. The sea in this narrative possesses contrary human qualities of being restless, serene, inviting, endangering, invigorating and enervating. Its waters are always calling enticingly to the protagonist:

> The voice of the sea is seductive; never ceasing, whispering, clamoring, murmuring, inviting the soul to wander for a spell in abysses of solitude; to lose itself in mazes of inward contemplation.

(277)

Stress here falls upon the *sound* instead of the *sight* of the Gulf that insists in speaking in its multi-modulated voice to the just awakening heroine. Throughout the novel Chopin uses the refrain of the sea's voice with subtle variation to depict the "oceanic" yearnings of the protagonist toward a totally engulfing experience (Wolff 469). The image of "mazes" suggests the menace of labyrinths and caverns to annihilate Edna if she loses herself in the quest for deliverance. Her constant sleeping takes her to wander in mazes of romantic dreams away from mediocre waking reality. But in Edna's intense longing to end her social bondage the sea represents a vision of endless freedom.

For the protagonist her immersion in the waves of the Gulf not only leads to knowledge of the infinite but also of that solitary self that until the summer at Grand Isle she unconsciously repressed in conformity to the mores of late nineteenth-century American society. The sea does not just speak to Edna, but it also touches her quivering body with a sensuous caress that awakens her formerly dormant passionate spirit. The very person who teaches her to swim and who arouses dreams of romance in her, Robert Lebrun, shares her awareness of the sea's capacity for passion, recalling an earlier infatuation of his for Mme. Ratignolle one summertime vacation when the very waves sizzled at the contact with his body burning from frustrated desire. Only one character in the novel displays an aversion for the sea—Mlle Reisz, whose disliking for the water others attribute to her artistic temperament but whose private keyboard performances for Edna excite the most powerful emotions: ". . . the very passions themselves were aroused within her soul, swaying it, lashing it, as the waves daily beat upon her splendid body" (290). The association between the sea and the arts continues during the protagonist's pursuit of painting. Sometimes when working from an attractive female model, Edna would be stirred by a subtle narcissism inspired by the classic lines of her subject's body, her singing the haunting song "*Ah! si tu savais!*" and above all by remembering the sea: "She could again hear the ripple of the water, the flapping sail. She could see the glint of the moon upon the bay, and could feel the soft, gusty beating of the hot south wind. A subtle current of desire passed through her body, weakening her hold upon the brushes and making her eyes burn" (324). Painting, music, the whole range of sensations made available by the Gulf merge in a synaesthetic experience of a supreme *jouissance* joining orgasm and artistic creativity. Chopin's heroine anticipates that ecstasy which the present-day feminist writer Hélène Cixous celebrates when women learn to write with their bodies:

> I . . . overflow; my desires have invented new desires, my body knows unheard of songs. Time and again . . . I have felt so full of luminous torrents that I could burst . . .
>
> (876)

In learning to swim the protagonist moves on those very luminous torrents as her body becomes part of the natural flow in the Gulf's expanse. Mastering how to swim signifies her acquiring physical and spiritual strength (Spacks 74). But gaining the skill to swim deludes Edna into defying the power of the sea by going out alone far into the waters, although without her knowledge Léonce observes her patronizingly and protectively. For the threat of integration with the liquid whole is loss of self (Treichler 245). The sea's true invitation that Edna will eventually accept is death, the final spiritual elation that the heroine senses late at night when the waters sing a mournful lullaby to her. Leopardi's poem "The Infinite" similarly relates how thought is drowned in immensity and the soul undergoes a sweet shipwreck in the sea's infinity (cf. Ringe 583). In Chopin's novel the gulf is more than a decorative border or limit, more than a privileged state of containment (Jameson 210). The sea is the fatal challenge of the siren's song promising the deliverance of sweet annihilation.

Though an adult, Edna Pontellier must undergo a form of infantile regression in order to recapture a child's receptivity to physical experience. The ability to swim does not come easily to her, and she often thrashes about in the waves like a clumsy infant lacking basic motor skills. What the adult is seeking to know again is that impression of the infinite which she once felt as a child wandering in the high and spacious blue grass fields of her native state:

> . . . a summer day in Kentucky, . . . a meadow that seemed as big as the ocean to the very little girl walking through the grass, which was higher than her waist. She threw out her arms as if swimming when she walked, beating the tall grass as one strikes out in the water.
>
> (280)

The third-person reference to the little girl indicates a schizoid divisiveness menacing the heroine as she contemplates her past (Roscher 295). The image of the Kentucky meadow remained with Edna all her life, so that the effort of mastering how to swim compels her to reexperience the boundlessness of the grassy fields before a child struggling to make her way across vast spaces. Just as the high grass seemed to close in upon the child, the sea with the turmoil of its waves can engulf the adult swimmer. Both the grass in childhood and the sea in adulthood can overwhelm the solitary individual. The abysses of the sea's seductive invitation loom as womb-like enclosures for an infant or for the dead. That passionate "unity of emotions and will" (Treichler 244) achieved in learning to swim bears a deadly threat. As the heroine descends to the darkness of her desires, undefined caverns menace to entrap her. Death by drowning will take Edna back to the childhood moment in the meadow without beginning or end.

Suicide would lift Mme Pontellier out of the dark abysses of physicality to fly on the sunlit breezes of the infinite. Throughout the novel the image of birds symbolizes either captivity or the striving toward freedom. The book begins with the description of a caged parrot calling out to a Whitmanesque mockingbird an order of separation and resignation: "*Allez-vous-en! Allez-vous-en! Sapristi!* That's all right!" (265). In her marital condition Edna resembles a caged bird at first accepting the bars imprisoning her but longing to escape. Confined to the "cage of marriage" (White 98), initially she barely suspects a way of freedom. From time to time the plaintive refrain of an owl hooting amidst sheltering oak trees creates a haunting nocturne that expresses spiritual inquietude. On hearing a melancholy musical composition entitled "Solitude," the protagonist envisions a lonely young man standing naked on a shore and looking desolately at a distant bird flying out of sight. Neither the naked youth nor the heroine possess the wings to bear them to freedom.

Ironically the mother-women appear as bird-like angelic creatures whose wings flutter protectively around their young (Fletcher 123). When Edna tells Mlle Reisz of her decision to act freely of the opinion of others, the artist warns her about the problems involved in defying conventions: "The bird that would soar above the level plain of tradition and prejudice must have strong wings. It is a sad spectacle to see the weaklings bruised, exhausted, fluttering back to earth" (350). The heroine never rises to that declaration of inalienable human rights that Jane Eyre once stated in forceful reply to her being compared to a bird tearing its plumage in the imprisonment of a cage: "I am no bird; and no net ensnares me; I am a free human being with an independent will" (*Jane Eyre,* 270). When Edna does flee from Léonce's home, she calls her small rented dwelling the "pigeon house." It is in that tiny building where she holds her carnal liaison with Arobin and where she and Robert go to exchange a kiss and embrace of mutual love after their reconciliation at the suburban garden restaurant. But the "pigeon house" also becomes the site for the protagonist's disillusionment on returning there from Adèle's delivery to discover Lebrun's note of farewell in order to safeguard her reputation. On the morning of her suicide Edna sees a bird reeling in the air with a broken wing and moving slowly down to the sea. For while men can dream of birds with strong wings to take them to faraway shores, a solitary woman must seek another form of flight.

Throughout the novel Edna's increasing availability to sensations of the physical world finds expression in the adjective "delicious," the key seme for this narrative of discovery and deliverance. Not only are foods and beverages delicious, but so are the picture of the bay at Grand Isle, the refreshing waves of the gulf, the countryside for small children eager to be away from the monotonous pavements of the city, February days warm with the promise of summer, a scribbled note from one of Edna's infant sons, the memory of a familiar song and the dream of an impossible desire to taste life's delirium. Even a mother-woman like Adèle Ratignolle with her cherry lips looks delicious. Sometimes the adjective occurs three times on one page, only to be repeated on the following page. When the heroine returns to Grand Isle and stands naked at dawn before the sea, in her divestment of artificial garments and customs Edna knows the absolute deliciousness of rebirth to nature. Her dying in the bay recalls the ocean's final summons in Whitman's "Out of the cradle endlessly rocking" where the sea at daybreak whispers "the delicious word death." For a woman who once beheld with aversion the sand and slime between the toes of the sensuous Spanish servant-girl Mariequita, Edna now arrives at her own total contact with physical reality on that fatal shore with the delicious touch of her bare feet on the sand before she walks out into the water. Her cosmic yearning reaches its passionate consummation as she discovers what Rimbaud in *Une Saison en Enfer* calls eternity in the merging of the opposed forces of the sun and sea. Edna's willful death causes her to transcend the solely political implications of woman's revolt from social constrictions which only Dr. Mandelet with his sage detachment perceived as inspiring her flight from Léonce's control. She acquires the negative power of an awakening unto death by refusing to return to that shore of patriarchal reality (Watson 118). Woman's free role in or outside society must acknowledge that *She* is part of a natural order with birds, horses, the ocean, the sun, moon and waving meadows. Chopin's novel employs a narrative syntax based on images of nature to represent a heroine's delicious realization of her struggle for deliverance.

Notes

1. My methodological guide here is Doris Kadish's work on the relational reading of nineteenth-century European novels. The primary difference between Chopin's style and that of authors like Balzac, Chateaubriand and Flaubert (among those studied by Kadish for their development of images of nature as narrative strategy and not stylistic decor) is that the American writer uses greatly condensed descriptions in comparison to the lengthy and complex nature description of the European novelists. The first important attempt to relate Chopin to major European novelists was Emily Toth's doctoral dissertation.

2. Kristeva analyzes imprisonment in these terms, "The difficulty a mother has in acknowledging (or being acknowledged by) the symbolic realm—in other words, the problem she has with the phallus that her father or her husband stands for—is not such as to help the future subject leave the natural mansion" (13). Edna Pontellier originally rebelled against her father by marrying a Roman Catholic, and she will fight against her husband's attempts to reduce her to one of his precious possessions. In her Jungian analysis Marina Roscher attributes a demon of death to the animus that Edna's father imprinted upon his daughter (295).

3. Although I have reservations about his use of Erikson's rather sexist distinctions between "male outer space" and "female inner spaces," White's essay convincingly probes the polaritiies on which Chopin's novel is constructed. Lattin asserts that, "Chopin's characters cannot know themselves until they understand their surroundings" (225). May sees Edna as becoming a victim of the sensuousness of the Louisiana setting (1037). Ringe notes how Edna must become aware of what is not-herself: the physical world and other persons (582).

4. Leslie cites Fitzhugh in her study of pro-slavery rhetoric (42). White comments upon the continuity of patriarchal thought about woman's role by Southern writers well past the Civil War until the end of the century when Wilbur Fisk Tillett asserted in *The Century Magazine* that, "The Southern woman loves the retirement of her home . . ." (99). Walker argues that Edna's plight arises from her daily contact with the Louisiana Creole setting (97).

5. Arms comments how Edna's frequent sleeping reduces her "reawakening" to a form of death (219-20). In a psychoanalytical approach, Wolff sees the heroine's sleeping and eating patterns as part of her orally destructive personality (461-64).

6. Starobinski in studying Rousseau's narrative calls transparent those sites that lead to intimacy and immediacy (14).

7. Zlotnick views Edna as a newly blossomed flower, with dead leaves as remnants of a past time without meaning (no pagination). Dyer regards flowers as symbolic of carnal awakening in the heroine (72), as well as in other characters in Chopin's short stories. The novel ends with Edna's drowning and reliving the "musky odor of pinks" (384).

8. Gerrard observes how the protagonist associates Arobin with the strength and sensuality of horses (136).

9. Casale views Léonce as an inhabitant of the land, most at ease in New Orleans (79). Mr. Pontellier, who spends only weekends on Grand Isle where he frequents Klein's hotel to play billiards and talk about business with male friends, does swim, usually early in the morning before the sun bites. For Treichler the

heroine in swimming becomes both active subject and simultaneously passive object (256).

10. Zlotnick speaks of the moon's sexual-mystical influence on nature and compares the lunar role in D. H. Lawrence's *The Rainbow* and *Sons and Lovers* (no pagination).

References

Arms, George. "Kate Chopin's *The Awakening* in the Perspective of her Literary Career." In *Essays on American Literature in Honor of Jay B. Hubbell*. Ed. Clarence Gohdes. Durham: Duke UP, 1967. 215-28.

Bachelard, Gaston. *Water and Dreams*. Trans. Edith Farrell. Dallas: Pegasus, 1983.

Brombert, Victor. *The Novels of Flaubert: A Study of Themes and Techniques*. Princeton: Princeton UP, 1966.

Bronte, Charlotte. *Jane Eyre*. New York: The Modern Library, 1933.

Casale, Ottavio. "Beyond Sex: The Dark Romanticism of Kate Chopin's *The Awakening*." *Ball State University Forum*, 19 (1978), 76-81.

Chopin, Kate. *'The Storm' and Other Stories, with 'The Awakening'*. Old Westbury, N.Y.: Feminist Press, 1974.

Cixous, Hélène. "The Laugh of the Medusa." *Signs*, 1 (1976), 875-93.

Curtius, Ernst Robert. *European Literature and the Latin Middle Ages*. Trans. Willard R. Trask. Princeton: Princeton UP, 1953.

Dyer, Joyce. "Chopin's Use of Natural Correlatives as Psychological Symbols in her Fiction." Diss. Kent State University, 1977.

Fletcher, Marie. "The Southern Woman in the Fiction of Kate Chopin." *Louisiana History*, 7 (1966), 117-32.

Gerrard, Lisa. "The Romantic Woman in Nineteenth-Century Fiction: A Comparative Study of *Madame Bovary, La Regenta, The Mill on the Floss,* and *The Awakening*." Diss. University of California, Berkeley, 1979.

Hall, Edward T. *Beyond Culture*. Garden City, N.Y.: Anchor Books, 1977.

Jameson, Fredric. *The Political Unconscious*. Ithaca: Cornell UP, 1981.

Kadish, Doris Y. *The Literature of Images: Narrative Landscape from Rousseau to Flaubert*. New Brunswick: Rutgers UP, 1986.

Kristeva, Julia. *Powers of Horror, An Essay on Abjection*. Trans. Leon Roudiez. New York: Columbia UP, 1982.

Lattin, Patricia Hopkins. "The Search for Self in Kate Chopin's Fiction: Simple versus Complex Vision." *Southern Studies*, 21 (1982), 222-35.

Leslie, Kent Anderson. "A Myth of the Southern Lady: Antebellum Proslavery Rhetoric and the Proper Place of Women." *Sociological Spectrum*, 6 (1986), 31-49.

May, John R. "Local Color in *The Awakening*." *Southern Review*, 6 (1970), 1031-40.

Poulet, Georges. *Studies in Human Time*. Trans. Elliot Coleman. Baltimore: Johns Hopkins UP, 1956.

Ringe, Donald A. "Romantic Imagery in Kate Chopin's *The Awakening*." *American Literature*, 43 (1972), 580-88.

Roscher, Marina. "The Suicide of Edna Pontellier: An Ambiguous Ending?" *Southern Studies*, 23 (1984), 289-97.

Spacks, Patricia Meyer. *The Female Imagination*. New York: Knopf, 1975.

Skaggs, Peggy. *Kate Chopin*. Boston: Twayne, 1985.

Starobinski, Jean. *Jean-Jacques Rousseau: la transparence et l'obstacle*. Paris: Gallimard, 1971.

Thornton, Lawrence. "*The Awakening*: A Political Romance." *American Literature*, 52 (1980), 50-66.

Toth, Emily. "The Outward Existence which Conforms: Kate Chopin and Literary Convention." Diss. Johns Hopkins, 1975.

———. "Comment." *Signs*, 1 (1976), 1005.

———. "Kate Chopin's *The Awakening* as Feminist Criticism." *Louisiana Studies*, 15 (1976), 241-51.

Treichler, Paula A. "The Construction of Ambiguity in *The Awakening*." in *Women and Language in Literature and Society*. Ed. S. McConnell-Ginet, R. Borker and N. Furman. New York: Praeger, 1980, pp. 239-57.

Walker, Nancy. "Feminist or Naturalist: The Social Context of Kate Chopin's *The Awakening*." *Southern Quarterly*, 17 (1979), 95-103.

Watson, Barbara Bellow. "On Power and the Literary Text." *Signs*, 1 (1975), 111-18.

White, Robert. "Inner and Outer Space in *The Awakening*." *Mosaic*, 17 (1984), 97-109.

Wolff, Cynthia Griffin. "Thanatos and Eros: Kate Chopin's *The Awakening*." *American Quarterly*, 25 (1973), 449-71.

Zlotnick, Joan. "A Woman's Will: Kate Chopin on Selfhood, Wifehood, and Motherhood." *The Markham Review*, 3 (October 1968), no pagination.

Manfred Malzahn (essay date spring 1991)

SOURCE: Malzahn, Manfred. "The Strange Demise of Edna Pontellier." *Southern Literary Journal* 23, no. 2 (spring 1991): 31-9.

[*In the following essay, Malzahn examines the narrative of* The Awakening *for an explanation of Edna's motives for committing suicide.*]

For a long time, critics have been puzzled by the self-inflicted death of Edna Pontellier, the heroine of Kate Chopin's *The Awakening* (1899). At the end of her process of awakening, which begins with a summer infatuation and leads to a breakaway from the family home and from the role of wife and mother, Edna is not a victorious New Woman, leading an independent life of spiritual and sensual fulfillment. She is quite simply dead, to the relief of contemporary commentators such as the unnamed author of the "Book Reviews" column in *Public Opinion* of 22 June 1899, who presents himself as the representative of the general reading public when he asserts that "we are well satisfied when Mrs. Pontellier deliberately swims out to her death in the waters of the gulf."[1]

The reason given is that Edna comes across as an "unpleasant person,"[2] a selfish, adulterous woman for whom the author has failed to secure the reader's sympathy. This is a view based on a moral judgement about Edna's actions rather than a close reading of the novel. The fact that the heroine of the book is the one focal character whose thoughts and emotions are described at great length is proof enough of "an undercurrent of sympathy for Edna," which the more perceptive, though still disapproving, reviewer of the New Orleans *Times-Democrat* of 18 June detects.[3]

Besides, does Edna Pontellier really kill herself deliberately? The narrator suggests possible reasons in the final chapter, describing the heroine's thoughts in one of the moments of gloom to which she has been prone; however, there is a disclaimer following close upon the one phrase that definitely seems to hint at what is to follow. One would have expected a new paragraph to begin, as the narrative moves from flashback to actuality, from the preceding night to Edna's last day: the lack of such a caesura makes the juxtaposition all the more striking:

> Despondency had come upon her there in the wakeful night, and had never lifted. There was no one thing in the world that she desired. There was no human being whom she wanted near except Robert; and she even realised that the day would come when he, too, and the thought of him would melt out of her existence, leaving her alone. The children appeared before her like antagonists who had overcome her, who had overpowered and sought to drag her into the soul's slavery for the rest of her days. But she knew a way to elude them. She was not thinking of these things when she walked down to the beach.[4]

From this point onwards, there is no indication that Edna is acting with deliberate intent to end her life there and then. She puts on her swimming costume and leaves her clothes in the bath-house, just as if she were going for "a little swim, before dinner,"[5] as she declares she will. Previously she has announced that she is hungry and stated her preference for the evening meal. This is perceived as a sign of an undiminished healthy appetite by the same critic who plainly states two pages earlier that "Edna resolves to commit suicide," failing to remark upon her paradoxical behavior.[6] Is she intentionally deluding her addressee?

I would suggest another explanation for the contradiction. In the final chapter, Edna Pontellier is described as acting "rather mechanically."[7] The thinking is over and done, though after all the reflections of the previous night, Edna is not consciously carrying out a plan but, rather, absent-mindedly walking towards her death. She is like a somnambulist, mesmerised by her ultimate seducer, the sea, of which she would have been more wary if she—like the reader—had been made aware of the satanic quality in its voice by the plethora of sharp "s" sounds in the description:

> The water of the gulf stretched before her, gleaming with the million lights of the sun. The voice of the sea is seductive, never ceasing, whispering, clamoring, murmuring, inviting the soul to wander in abysses of solitude.[8]

There is no way around it: Edna Pontellier was misled, her awakening ends with the Big Sleep, whether this be Suzanne Wolkenfeld's "union with the One,"[9] or Christina Giorcelli's "absolute fulfillment."[10] Such recent evaluations of the novel's end, motivated by feelings diametrically opposed to those which early reviewers had towards the heroine, are equally prone to be blinkered. Ultimately, Edna's rebellion is a failure: she does not find a new place in society, having given up her old one for good. She is not an Adèle Ratignolle, who can content herself with being a leisured housewife and mother. Neither is she a Mademoiselle Reisz, capable of sublimating her desires in search for artistic achievement. She wants to follow her impulses and to be independent: the people around her, including her husband, let her have her way to an extent that shows an exceptional amount of tolerance, given the time and the place of the story. Still, she fails to find a new life worth living, and dies in a way which Dorothy Dix's Women's Page in the *Daily Picayune* of 8 October 1899 describes as a "coward's deed,"[11] and a typically male one at that.

I think that it is not the failure to see the duplicity inherent in the symbolic significance of the ending—after all, the symbolism is very hard to miss in any part of the book—which caused George M. Spangler to say that "Mrs. Chopin provided a conclusion for a novel other than the one she wrote."[12] Underlying this evaluation is the simple fact that he did not find a convincing reason for the suicide on the level of the narrated action. Edna's symbolic union with the elements is indeed suggested by the narrative, but it takes place in the mind of the reader and the critic. Edna herself does not think in such categories any more than Huck Finn is bothered by the metaphorical meaning of his journey down the river. In *The Awakening,* it is the narrator who interprets the heroine's thoughts, ever at pains to show the reader the limits of Edna Pontlllier's understanding.

The one hypothesis that Spangler has to offer for the ending of the novel drags in not only the narrator but the author herself. The wish to fend off the condemnation by narrow-minded moralists, he claims, may have led Kate Chopin to mete out a kind of "poetic justice"[13] that would drown all objections in a sea of tears, thus diminishing the figure of her heroine and her own artistic achievement while failing to achieve the desired effect on reviewers. It is possible that Chopin herself felt she had swum out too far in writing *The Awakening,* and that she was not just talking tongue-in-cheek when she wrote that by the time she had found out where the story was going, "the play was half over and then it was then too late."[14]

The writing of the novel proved to be, ultimately, the rebellious author's literary suicide. The parallels between Kate Chopin and Edna Pontellier are, however, limited. Most importantly, there is the question of artistic ambition, something Edna does not possess to a sufficient degree. In view of this, the identi-fication of the heroine with the author can only go as far as seeing Edna the free giver of love as one side of Chopin's personality, with Adèle Ratignolle the faithful wife, and Mademoiselle Reisz the celibate recluse representing the other two mutually exclusive roles. But even so, Edna Pontellier as a fictional character stands alone, and her actions must be explained in terms of her own mind.

The mind is largely dominated by instinct and impulse, messages from the center of her being, that elusive "self" which according to Edna is the only thing she will never give up. In her awakening, she does indeed become a more natural being, but her growing freedom from social restraints is accompanied by a growing subjection to moods changing with the weather and the time of day. "The weather [is] dark and cloudy," and she finds herself unable to paint;[15] her lover, Arobin, finds her in an exceptionally happy mood, sitting in front of the fire with the mere prospect of a barometric improvement. Her highs get higher and her lows get lower; she becomes as changeable and unpredictable as the elements, even acquiring a "seductive voice"[16] like the sea itself.

Now, we all know that the sea does not speak, and at the same time we are all too accustomed to metaphors which give it a voice. But this voice exists in the mind of the user of the metaphor, in our case, the narrator of the novel. The voice of the sea is described as the alluring, tantalizing, persistent utterance of a potentially dangerous natural force. If Edna has herself acquired such a voice at last, is not the suggestion even stronger that it was something within her which spoke to her in the first place? As a parrot will only reflect such language as it has been taught, the sea will only tell the listener what he or she wants to hear, and the message is ultimately that from a human being. In the case of the parrot, with which the story begins,[17] it may be one from another person; in the case of the sea, it can only be from oneself, or one's self. Edna begins indeed to become one with the elements: she can be the sea, her own destroyer, as well as she can be "the sunlight" to Mademoiselle Reisz.[18]

Edna's progressive identification with nature comes with the progress she makes toward the center of her being. But there seems to be a self-destructive force there, which is released as the heroine frees her self in freeing herself. When she takes that last swim in the ocean, she abandons herself to this force, whereas before, fear of death had intervened and kept her within reach of the shore as well as within reach of society.[19] Her liberation from fears of moral disapproval coincides with a liberation from the fear of death: in her striving for self-fulfillment she loses the instinct of self-preservation and follows another, darker impulse. She casts off her clothes and then even the swimming costume which she had put on out of habit. Standing naked in the sun, she feels like a completely natural being for the first time, "like some new-born creature, opening its eyes in a familiar world that it had never known."[20]

The image is of the animal kingdom; Edna has become "some . . . creature," an "it" rather than a "she." Consequently, she goes to drown herself with as much determination as a lemming, and with only marginally more awareness of the significance of her act. Her thoughts are kaleidoscopic recollections governed by childish logic that makes the ocean shrink to the size of the "bluegrass meadow"[21] of one of her early memories. Her satisfaction at the notion of escape from the tyranny of husband and children, and from the scorn of Mademoiselle Reisz, has an equally infantile ring. Only the thoughts of her beloved Robert and the sympathetic adviser Dr. Mandelet reawaken her for a moment, reintroducing the possibility of salvation, if not through love then through understanding. But the natural fear of dying returns too late and subsides as Edna's thoughts return to earlier memories.

Viewed in this light, the ending makes perfect sense within the symbolic structure of the novel. Edna sees a "bird with a broken wing . . . circling disabled down, down to the water,"[22] before she herself performs a similar motion. Though she lives in a "pigeon house,"[23] she is not the bird with strong wings, the one "that would soar above the level plain of tradition and prejudice,"[24] who could succeed against the odds, according to the pianist Mademoiselle Reisz. But again, it may all look meaningful enough from a critic's point of view; however, that does not mean that the internal narrative logic of the story is explained. Why did she do it? remains the question that still demands a satisfactory answer.

One possible answer is that Edna is just cracking up, that her husband in his well-meaning superficiality and naiveté has actually come fairly close to the truth when he tells the old family doctor that his wife is somehow "peculiar."[25] At least there are plenty of instances of behavior which may be regarded as evidence of a psychological disturbance. There is a quick succession of radically different moods with Edna, and at least one occasion when such a change is perceived by those in Edna's company as an embarrassment. This is the dinner party which she gives in the family home on the occasion of her twenty-ninth birthday. It is a fairly conventional affair apart from the absence of the husband, the atmosphere is jolly, the wine has been flowing, and then Robert's brother Victor is coaxed into singing a song:

"Ah! si tu savais!"

"Stop!" [Edna] cried, "don't sing that. I don't want you to sing it," and she laid her glass so impetuously and blindly upon the table as to shatter it against a carafe. The wine spilled over Arobin's legs and some of it trickled down upon Mrs. Highcamp's black gauze gown.[26]

It is not only Edna's rebellion against social conventions but also her erratic conduct that contributes to her growing isolation, and Doctor Mandelet, the physician who knows "that inner life which so seldom unfolds itself to unanointed eyes,"[27] comes to see the connection during another dinner party. Edna is a changed person, exuberant, radiant, but losing touch with reality, and thus the high flight foreshadows a long fall. On the night when Mandelet realizes this, Mrs. Pontellier presents herself as a capable inventor and teller of stories. She enthralls her audience, but at the cost of getting lost in her own inventions: it is certainly legitimate to see this as a reference to the dangers of Kate Chopin's own chosen calling, especially when one considers the number of times the word "fictitious" is used in a pejorative sense in the novel. As much as the author of her story, Edna is treading on thin ice. Her doom is sealed when "all sense of reality had gone out of her life; she had abandoned herself to Fate, and awaited the consequences with indifference."[28]

But her death is not brought on by fate, and neither is it merely the inevitable consequence of her own actions. The final departure of Robert, the man she loves, obviously has a lot to do with it, but equally important is the event which is reported in Chapter 27, the birth of a child to Edna's friend Adèle Ratignolle. Before venturing an explanation of the significance of this episode, I would like to quote a comment by Lewis Leary on the symbolic structure of the novel, which appears to me an adequate assessment: "Almost every incident or reference in *The Awakening* anticipates an incident or reference that follows it or will remind a reader of something that has happened before."[29]

There are plenty of prior references to children in the book, but only one to childbirth in an early chapter, when Edna is shocked by the frankness with which Creole women talk about pregnancy and birth even in the presence of men. Edna finds it hard to comprehend the "entire absence of prudery"[30] concerning matters of procreation. She is also, self-avowedly, extremely squeamish about blood and wounds; even touching a scar on Arobin's wrist is too much for her to bear.[31] When she is persuaded by Adèle to be with her at the birth, she stays and watches "with a flaming, outspoken revolt against the ways of Nature,"[32] finally being admonished by her friend to "think of the children."[33]

The births of her own two sons are by that time only dim memories of pain, the occasions almost devoid of meaning:

> She was seized with a vague dread. Her own like experiences seemed far away, unreal, and only half remembered. She recalled faintly an ecstasy of pain, the heavy

odor of chloroform, a stupor which had deadened sensation, and an awakening to find a little new life to which she had given being, added to the great unnumbered multitude of souls that come and go.[34]

The explicit use of the word "awakening" in this context is crucial. The awakening is not only a return from a sleeping to a fully conscious state, but a return to a changed reality, a different "little new life." In Edna's case, this may be herself, a rebirth of her as the "little unthinking child . . . walking through the green meadow,"[35] unconscious of danger. However, another possible meaning is that this "little new life" is another child to which Edna will give birth. She has been sleeping with Arobin, and there is at least the possibility that this has resulted in pregnancy. Before dismissing this as a far-fetched interpretation, one should consider that it would ultimately make sense of the ending: Edna revolts against Nature itself by destroying herself as a means of procreation, but ironically by following another natural impulse that is directed at self-destruction, the impulse that drives a lemming, or, in the vision of Edna herself, "humanity like worms struggling blindly towards inevitable annihilation."[36]

As an authorial comment, it appears to prove that Kate Chopin was indeed one who had chosen to "pluck from the Darwinian tree of knowledge and to see human existence in its true meaning."[37] From Edna's point of view, though, this is an instinctive vision coming from within. Edna has not read Darwinian theory, but half-consciously played with fire, half-conscious of the dangers of breaking social rules, but not of those incurred by tapping into forces hidden deep within her self. By doing so, she has taken on something bigger than she, something elementary, connected with the beyond into which she finally drifts. In the light of Kate Chopin's obvious interest in psychology, demonstrated in not only her fiction, but also her essays,[38] consider the following description by her contemporary William James:

> There is a continuum of cosmic consciousness, against which our individuality builds but accidental fences, and into which our several minds plunge as into a mother-sea or reservoir. Our "normal" consciousness is circumscribed for adaptation to our external earthly environment, but the fence is weak in spots, and fitful influences from beyond leak in, showing the otherwise unverifiable connection.[39]

To me, there is a commensurability between James's explanation and Kate Chopin's demonstration of the attraction and the danger of the "mother-sea." James locates this sea, the root of the danger, in the "beyond," in a manner that reminds one of ancient folk beliefs about werewolves and moonstruck people, as well as of H. P. Lovecraft stories. A Jungian might substitute "generic memory" for "cosmic consciousness," but in any case, it is clear that we are talking of the normally hidden depths within the human psyche. As a psychological novel, *The Awakening* is the story of an exploration of those depths by an explorer ill equipped for the journey. It is a tale of terror, all the more effective because it operates within the realm of the credible; the story of a woman who tries to discard a "fictitious self,"[40] only to find that she has unleashed forces beyond her control, as, in another sense, the author herself did by the publication of the novel, which ended her literary career in an environment where social and artistic freedom were particularly difficult to attain for a woman, even for one stronger than Edna Pontellier.

Notes

1. In Kate Chopin, *The Awakening: An Authoritative Text, Contexts, Criticism,* edited by Margaret Culley (New York: Norton, 1976), 151.

2. Culley.

3. Culley, 150.

4. Kate Chopin, *The Awakening: Introduction by Helen Taylor* (London: 1978), 188.

5. Taylor, 188.

6. Michael T. Gilmore, "Revolt Against Nature: The Problematic Modernism of *The Awakening,*" in Wendy Martin, ed., *New Essays on The Awakening* (Cambridge: 1988), 62.

7. Taylor, 188.

8. Taylor, 189.

9. "Edna's Suicide: The Problem of the One and the Many," in Culley, 223.

10. "Edna's Wisdom: A Transitional and Numinous Merging," in *New Essays on The Awakening,* 126.

11. "Women and Suicide," in Culley, 134.

12. "Kate Chopin's *The Awakening*: A Partial Dissent," in Culley, 187.

13. Culley, 189.

14. Author's note on *The Awakening,* in "Aims and Autographs of Authors," in Culley, 159.

15. Taylor, 123.

16. Taylor, 179.

17. Taylor, 5.

18. Taylor, 131.

19. Taylor, 48.

20. Taylor, 189.

21. Taylor, 190.

22. Taylor, 189.

23. Taylor, 142.

24. Taylor, 138.

25. Taylor, 110.

26. Taylor, 150.

27. Taylor, 118.

28. Taylor, 172.

29. "Kate Chopin and Walt Whitman," in Culley, 197.

30. Taylor, 19.

31. Taylor, 127.

32. Taylor, 182.

33. Taylor.

34. Taylor.

35. Taylor, 30.

36. Taylor, 97.

37. Per Seyersted, "Introduction," in *The Complete Works of Kate Chopin.* Edited and with an Introduction by Per Seyersted. 2 vols. (Baton Rouge: 1969), vol. 1, 23.

38. Seyersted, vol. 2, 691 ff.

39. "A Psychical Researcher," in John J. McDermott, ed., *The Writings of William James: A Complete Introduction* (Chicago: 1977), 798 ff.

40. Taylor, 96.

Catherine Morgan-Proux (essay date winter 1993)

SOURCE: Morgan-Proux, Catherine. "Athena of Goose? Kate Chopin's Ironical Treatment of Motherhood in 'Athénaïse.'" *Southern Studies* 4, no. 4 (winter 1993): 625-40.

[*In the following essay, Morgan-Proux argues that Chopin's apparent glorification of childbirth and motherhood in the story "Athénaïse" is ironic.*]

When Edna Pontellier leaves the childbirth scene in the penultimate chapter of *The Awakening,* stunned by the "scene of torture" that she has just witnessed, Doctor Mandelet articulates her thoughts: "Youth is given up to illusions. It seems to be a provision of Nature; a decoy to secure mothers for the race."(996)[1] He could not have described Athénaïse more accurately. My challenge in this paper is to demonstrate how, contrary to prevailing critical views, the apparent glorification of motherhood in the short story **"Athénaïse"** is pure irony. Edna's lucidity at the end of *The Awakening* is a striking contrast to what we see as Athénaïse's self-delusions, but the narrative stance that deflates—albeit covertly—the monolithic myth of motherhood is consistent with a general pattern in Chopin's fiction.

It has generally been agreed that **"Athénaïse"** relates the story of how a rebellious young wife, dissatisfied by the institution of marriage, is suddenly and overwhelmingly redeemed by pregnancy, which turns her into a mature woman and reconciles her to her estranged husband. The happy ending has been interpreted by critics as proof of Kate Chopin's belief in maternal instinct. Critics generally point out that its comment on motherhood is ultimately rather conventional and adheres to the nineteenth-century ideology of the sanctifying effect of pregnancy. This interpretation is tempting but misguided and fails utterly to take into account the subtle ways Chopin, in fact, subverts this ideology and challenges the very idea of maternal instinct.[2]

Irony is the literary device used *par excellence* by the short story writer, and we know that Maupassant, that master of the ironic *dénouement,* was one of Chopin's major influences.[3] However, the aspect of irony that is under discussion here is not the ironic twist at the end of the plot but rather "the awareness of a discrepancy or incongruity between words and their meaning, or between actions and their results, or between appearance and reality" (Cudden, 338). The use of irony is particularly relevant for this study in a number of ways. Firstly, it enriches our understanding of Chopin as a dialectical writer who prefers an interplay of narrative stances rather than authorial absolutism. Secondly, and more significantly, the very notion of disparity between words and meaning reflects the inherent split that deconstructionism has taught us is inherent in language. In language that aims to articulate the mother, the effect of this split is all the more evident, for as we shall see in Kristeva's theory of semiotics, patriarchal culture and its concomitant language has fixed maternity in a discourse of the cult of the mother, removing it from actual, lived experience.

In Chopin's fiction the discrepancies exposed by irony are subtle and have been a source of critical inquiry.[4] The first major dissertation on Kate Chopin,[5] by Emily Toth, analyzed the way she ostensibly conformed to existing literary traditions and prerogatives but at the same time developed strategies within those frames that enabled her to express her own artistic voice. It would seem that the same technique functions here. While outwardly celebrating marital and maternal joy in the story of Athénaïse in a way that would conform to the tastes of her nineteenth-century audience, and especially to the editors of *Atlantic* magazine which published the story,[6] Chopin also succeeds in creating irony that undercuts the nineteenth-century cult of motherhood.

Chopin's contemporary critics were so outraged by *The Awakening*'s frank treatment of female sexuality and what they consider a lack of moral integrity on the part of the protagonist that they seemed generally to overlook this realistic version of the experience of motherhood that undercuts the nineteenth-century ideal.[7] However, when one considers the quasi-universal reverence for motherhood that prevailed at this period and most particularly in the South, Chopin's words are outspoken ones indeed. All commentators of the Southern Lady make it quite clear that both models arise from a patriarchal society that seeks justification for its own existence. Even Cash labels this

myth-making process as "gyneolatry" (Cash, 86). Southern women's conduct was prescribed by the cult of domesticity, or, as Barbara Welter identifies it, the cult of true womanhood that defined a white woman as pious, pure, submissive and domestic.[8] Any challenge to the prevailing ideology that women's source of happiness was anything other than fulfilling a sacred mission to provide large numbers of healthy, morally upright children that would contribute to the prosperity of the region amounted to sacrilege. Any vision of childbirth and childbearing that cast doubt upon the idealized version and dared present the sometimes grim realities[9] that women faced must have been considered highly subversive. A "violation of Southern Womanhood was also, *ipso facto,* a violation of the South" (Jones, 11). Little wonder, then, that Chopin's treatment of pregnancy in "Athénaïse" requires at least a veneer of respectability for it to be accepted by potential editors and a largely conservative public.

The point is that if Athénaïse does indeed, through maternity, renounce her childhood to become a woman and take her place in adult society according to Freudian and Lacanian paradigm, her true growth as a woman is questionable. What makes this story so interesting is its Kristeverian suggestion that the social order reserves little place for the pre-symbolic mother and merely recognizes the culturally constructed, ideological mother, one that Athénaïse ultimately complies with. By the end of the story, we do not see Athénaïse as a fulfilled mother-to-be who is awakened to some mystical maternal knowledge but—to borrow the description made by the bank clerk—more as an immature "goose."

An intertextual reading of Chopin's work puts the reader on guard against making the quick assumption that **"Athénaïse"** amounts to a vision of motherhood as having a pacifying effect on impulsive emotions and entailing a restoration of normalcy and serenity. On the contrary, there is a strong pattern of anxiety associated with being a mother in Chopin's fiction where having children not only constrains but physically threatens women's lives. **"Désirée's Baby"** is a powerful reminder of how the nineteenth-century Southern Lady's primary function as a mother was to maintain the impeccable pedigree of the white family. When her husband suspects that Désirée may possibly have deviated from her duty, his accusation— later revealed to be unfounded—leads to her banishment and tragic end. **"La Belle Zoraïde"** is a painful demonstration of the paradox of the southern slave economy, which declared that the household duties of slave women were natural extensions of their roles as wives and mothers but demanded they answer to a master (or a mistress in this case) who would act according to imperatives that had no consideration for the slaves' own family.[10] The prerogatives of Madame Delisle who wants total devotion from her servant-companion are incompatible with La Belle Zoraïde's desires to start her own family. The depth of the deprivation that Zoraïde experiences when she is falsely told that her baby has died drives her to insanity. The nature of her dementia is particularly ironic: She is locked into a permanent state of taking care of her adopted rag doll baby and even fails to recognize her true child who is momentarily restored to her. **"Mrs. Mobry's Reason"** is a disturbing story that also links maternity to madness.[11] This time, anguish is not caused by the contradictory demands of a patriarchal society, nor even by nature itself but by a woman's secrecy about her medical condition. Here, it is a mother who knowingly passes on a hereditary illness to a daughter and perhaps to her son. This story conveys the idea that motherhood without a sense of responsibility—or even a voice—can have disastrous results. If it is true that this story refuses to adopt a moralistic tone and that Chopin's interest "is not so much in the hereditary madness as in the awakening love which brings it out" (Seyersted, 108), the reader is still left with the overwhelming sense of a mother's guilt who describes her act as a "crime" and a "curse" (79).

Other stories provide portraits of mothers whose experiences of childbearing has had a devastating effect on their bodies and their souls. The once coquettish Mentine in **"A Visit to Avoyelles,"** who has brought up four children, is a pitiful sight to her visitor and one-time paramour, Doudouce. Her change of appearance has become part of town lore. Her voice has become "shrill" from screaming at children and her figure is "misshapen" (229). Mrs. Sommers in **"A Pair of Silk Stockings"** has led such a self-effacing existence for her children that she has been starved of books and theater as well as food and clothes. Her wonderfully self-indulgent shopping spree during which she briefly becomes a subject again—she contemplates her limbs and realizes they are a "part of herself"—is all the more poignant because it is so pathetically limited in time and in scope.

The theme of motherhood in ***The Awakening,*** Chopin's masterpiece, is complex and challenging. The rich web of metaphors that evoke birth and regeneration provide much of the novel's exquisite poetry and sensuality.[12] Various stages of Edna's personal awakening, for example, are described in images of new life such as a child learning to walk, or renewed life: the sea sustains her like amniotic fluid. This pattern of images culminates in the powerful, final beach scene in which she sheds clothes like old skin as part of the process of giving birth to herself: "How strange and awful it seemed to stand naked under the sky! How delicious! She felt like some new-born creature, opening its eyes in a familiar world that it had never known" (1000).

However, this exultant, lyrical language finds its counterpoint in the raw realism that characterizes Edna's actual experience of mothering. The myth of the glorious and joyful mission of motherhood is seriously subverted by Chopin's heroine. In contrast to the devoted "mother-women" at Grande Isle who, loyal to the maudlin, self-sacrificing mother archetype, ministering like angels to their offspring, Edna's feelings towards her own children are void of sentimentalism and oscillate between the love of a "good enough mother" and plain resentment. She admits to her friend Adèle that she would give up her life but not her "self" for her children. In the end, she gives up both when she realizes that her own children, her "antagonists" (999) are the major obstacle preventing her from experiencing unconditional freedom. The childbirth scene itself is chilling in its realism. Adèle's labor is described as "torture" (995); Edna remembers her own labor as a chloroformed stupor and her newborn as one of "the great unnumbered multitude of souls that come and go" (994). Edna's rather cynical awakening to motherhood as a "decoy" after witnessing Adèle giving birth, referred to at the beginning of this discussion has a decidedly modern ring, is and prefigures Sylvia Plath: "They oughtn't to let a woman watch. You'll never want a baby if you do. It's the end of the human race," says a doctor to Esther, heroine of *The Bell Jar* (Plath, 53; Stone, 31).

Just how does this irony operate? Firstly, the irony of the protagonists' names sets the tone for the rest of the story. Emily Toth identifies the source of the heroine's name as Chopin's maternal grandmother, Mary Athénaïse Charleville Faris, who, like her fictional name-sake, went into marriage naively and was wounded by it (Toth, 18). However, like Per Seyersted, we are reminded of Athena, the Greek goddess whose characteristics include her triumphant independence from men (Seyersted, 114). A virgin goddess, "legend would submit her to no-one among the male gods" (Hopper, 5). The city's protectress, she is closely associated with urban, intellectual and civilized pursuits. Chopin's character would seem to stand as the antithesis of her mythical counterpart. Throughout the story, she relies heavily on men who supervise her every movement, including at the end of the story when she supposedly "knows her own mind." We realize that this portrayal of women reflects historical fact: a lady in the late nineteenth century seldom ventured out unaccompanied. But in Chopin's fiction heroines significantly find tremendous pleasure in finding freedom of movement: we remember Edna's joy at walking alone in the streets of New Orleans[13] and we recall Chopin's earliest sketch, **"Emancipation: A Life Fable,"** which tells the story of an animal who leaves his cage for the first time and, despite the risks of being outside, never returns to his home but instead joins the real world, "seeking, finding, joying, and suffering" (38). In this light, Athénaïse's unwillingness to chart her own itinerary is striking. As the story opens, we learn that she has left her husband to run back home to her parents, as she is prone to do, and Cazeau, as he thinks of "means to keep her home thereafter" (428), prepares to fetch her. Despite her resolve never to return with him, Athénaïse yields to his appeal, and realizing the "futility of rebellion against a social and sacred institution" (432), she does indeed return. Her next escape plan—to live in New Orleans—is masterminded by her brother, Montéclin, in whose hands she puts herself entirely: "Her only hope for rescue from her hateful surroundings lay in Montéclin. Of herself she felt powerless to plan, to act, even to conceive a way out of pitfall the whole world seemed to have conspired to thrust her" (436). Montéclin embraces the role of "*grand seigneur*" (441), coming to the assistance of his sister who has cast herself as a damsel in distress. He devises a plan that leaves nothing to chance and which Athénaïse follows "implicitly" (441).

Once installed in New Orleans, she places herself in a similar manner in the hands of another man—Gouvernail. All her needs, practical and emotional, are met by him. He runs errands for her, provides her with reading matter, consoles her when she feels lonely, and takes her on her first trip outside the boarding house. When it is time for her to leave the city, it is Gouvernail who takes her to the station, supervises her boarding the train, and, in effect, parcels her off back to her brother in a reverse trajectory of her arrival. She is conveyed from husband, to brother, to potential lover and back again with each man taking care of the logistics. We are left with an impression of dependency that jars with her mythical namesake, Athena the self-sufficient goddess.

Cazeau's name also seems to be used ironically. It would seem to stand for "caza" or chateau. His house, however, is no castle but bluntly described as "squat, square and one-story" (427). It is not much of a home either, with its "bare floor and huge rafters, and its heavy pieces of furniture that loomed dimly in the gloom of the apartment" (426). We realize early on that, in fact, this house is emblematic of Athénaïse's feelings of entrapment.

Gouvernail's name carries its share of irony, too, in this particular story. This French word suggests a rudder, an instrument used for steering. From our reading of other stories, we are aware that this "sensitive bachelor" (Dyer, 46-55) is indeed capable of changing direction in women's lives. In **"A Respectable Woman,"** for example, his sensuality awakens passionate impulses that have been dormant in Mrs. Baroda, who thereafter becomes a sexually active woman planting a long, languorous kiss on her husband's lips and looking forward to Gouvernail's next visit. In **"Athénaïse,"** our heroine appears distinctly indifferent to Gouvernail's amorous desires: she finds him weeping but does not investigate and she finds the touch of his hands merely "friendly" (450). He amounts to little more than a comfortable shoulder for her to cry on during periods of homesickness. Gouvernail is so totally absent from the watershed "annunciation" scene during which Athénaïse learns of her pregnancy, that she afterwards feels a little pang of guilt "for having forgotten him so completely" (453). So, in a curious turn of irony, the one whom we anticipated to be Athénaïse's "guide" or mentor turns out to be little more than a sub-plot character providing love interest in the narrative but not for our heroine.

To finish with the subject of names, it is perhaps possible that the third syllable of Montéclin's name also had an ironic twist. "Clin" evokes the French expression, "clin d'oeil" meaning a wink; a playful hint of connivance between narrator and reader as we recognize, like Montéclin does at the end of the story, that Athénaïse's happy reconciliation with the father of the child she is carrying is altogether a cliché and really rather "commonplace" (454).

The crux of the story is the "annunciation scene" during which Athénaïse, feeling "body-sick" (449) and "not herself" (451) goes to Sylvie, the fifty-year-old, portly quadroon proprietress of the boarding house, and learns that her unusual condition is due to the fact that she is pregnant. It is the pivotal event around which the narrative structure evolves. Yet, remarkably, it hangs upon an ellipsis. "Sylvie was very wise and Athénaïse was very ignorant" (451). On an immediate level, this phenomenon can be taken simply as poetic device that increases the dramatic intensity of the moment. In an extended interpretation of motherhood in Chopin's fiction, we see it as part of a pattern whereby motherhood escapes literary expression.

Most often this "annunciation scene" has been interpreted as marking an epiphany for our heroine who thereafter gains profound insight into the mystery of creation and matures into womanhood because of it. Certain allusions are made to the Biblical story: Athénaïse has been previously linked to Gabe or Gabriel and the effect of the good news upon her is a "miracle" (451). However, these references are perversions of the original annunciation. Black Gabe is no archangel on a holy mission to whisper the news of a future birth, but a runaway slave who pauses to take breath as he is brought back by his master, Cazeau's father. Likewise, the "miracle" of this annunciation does not lie in the fact that the future mother is a virgin but in the arousal of "her whole passionate nature" (451), announcing the beginning of Athénaïse's awareness of her sensual impulses. Hungry now with desire for Cazeau, she is satiated only by their reunion, "he felt the yielding of her whole body against him. He felt her lips for the first time respond to the passion of his own" (454). In a subtle subversion of the Christian story, the virgin has been supplanted by a sexually active mother who does not offer redemption for mankind but finds herself saving her own marriage.

Other elements of this scene invite us to consider it as a humorous parody of the Biblical text. For this part of the discussion, I am particularly indebted to Jacqueline Olson Padgett's article, "Kate Chopin and the Literature of the Annunciation, with a Reading of Lilacs." Padgett focuses on another short story, **"Lilacs,"** which she sees as drawing upon the details and symbols of the Annunciation story in a way that "mocks a tradition prizing virginity and separating the cloistered from the secular" (Padgett, 97). This interpretation enhances the reading of **"Athénaïse"** as a mockery of the patriarchal myth-making process that idealizes motherhood in order to maintain it (but which is far removed from the experience of mothering or the psyche of mothers).

Padgett helpfully points out the leitmotifs of Annunciation literature inspired by the Biblical text. She notes the dove representing the Holy Spirit; the fluttering of the wings of that dove and of the archangel Gabriel; the rush of wind as the dove and the angel intrude on and transform Mary's ordinariness; the evocation of a benign and purposeful God: the words spoken by Gabriel and Mary; music belonging to celestial harmony; and flowers like the Madonna or Annunciation lily suggestive of purity, fecundity and perfection. In Chopin's hands these determinants are given tongue-in-cheek treatment. The only birds that are present in this scene are as far removed from evoking the Holy Spirit as one could find: a "mocking bird that hung in a cage outside the kitchen door, and a disreputable parrot that belonged to the cook next door" (451). The rush of wind is more genteel than transformational: "the short uneven breathing that ruffled her bosom" (451). As opposed to heavenly harmony, we find "turmoil of her senses" (451) and the cacophony of a blasphemous dove-parrot that "swore hoarsely all day long in bad French" (451).[14] Athénaïse is associated not with flowers emblematic of fertility, but with an urban courtyard where she spends time "weeding and pottering" (451) in a rather desultory manner.

As Padgett remarks, "Annunciations . . . blend word and flesh, but they typically emphasize *word*" (Padgett, 98). It is all the more significant for the reading, then, that the word announcing Athénaïse's maternity is conspicuously absent, superseded by the sound of paternity. As Athénaïse repeats the name of the father she articulates her departure from the Imaginary and her initiation into the Symbolic Order of the Father. "She half whispered his name . . . She spoke it over and over, as if it were some new, sweet sound born out of darkness and confusion, and reaching her for the first time" (451). According to Lacanian theory, the Imaginary corresponds to the pre-Oedipal period when the child feels itself to be a part of its mother and cannot conceive of a state of separateness. The Oedipal crisis, brought about by the intervention of the father, marks the child's entry into the Symbolic Order. The acquisition of language is made possible by the loss of the mother which is internalized as a lack and the acceptance of the phallus as the representation of the Law of the Father.[15]

Re-reading the section of the story which immediately precedes the annunciation scene in the light of the Lacanian paradigm endorses the idea that Athénaïse undergoes this rite of passage to emerge as a speaking subject in a patriarchal order. Athénaïse contemplates herself in her mirror, thus gaining a unitary body image or "body ego" before the father intervenes to form a family triad. Significantly, Athénaïse's first act as speaking subject is to pen a letter which she does effortlessly, "with a single thought, a spontaneous impulse" (451), and she is filled with a desire to speak: "She wanted to talk to someone, to tell some person" (452). For the first time since her arrival at the boarding house, she steps into the public street, marking her entrance into the social world of adults. After gaining acceptance from her spiritual father—she is "God-blessed" (452) on the street corner—one of the first principles she practices is commerce. She goes to her husband's bank and demands money with confidence. The "air of . . . proprietorship" (452) that she acquires seems to be a convincing imitation of the men she has encountered whose relationships and behavior are often defined by money. The cause of Montéclin's hatred for Cazeau, for example,

is a grudge against the latter's refusal to lend him some money. Her other brothers, on the other hand, admire Cazeau for his business dealings with city merchants. Montéclin relishes his role of financial provider, paying for his sister's lodging in the city. As for Gouvernail, he enjoys "haggling" (444) over transactions with Sylvie. Moreover, when he takes Athénaïse out for dinner, the waiter receives Gouvernail and Athénaïse as a married couple, but, according to the narrator, this is an understandable error: "No wonder he made the mistake, with Gouvernail assuming such an air of proprietorship!" (447) Equally versed now in the handling of money, Athénaïse's parting gift to Pousette the maid is, appropriately enough, a silver dollar.

However, just as we detected irony in the narrator's treatment of the annunciation, we can't help but notice the derisive tone that permeates Athénaïse's entrance into womanhood. Religious sanction is bestowed upon her by an Irish oyster woman, a surprising representative of the church. She is carrying a fat, dirty baby that Athénaïse embraces. From the narrator's use of exclamation marks we deduce that she deigns to do so condescendingly: "She *even* kissed it!" (452, my emphasis)

Athénaïse herself is convinced that she has gained her place in society and has matured into womanhood. In a mental reply to the accusation from "[P]eople [who] often said that Athénaïse would know her own mind one day, which was equivalent to saying that she was at present unacquainted with it" (433), she is now able to declare, "No one could have said now that she did not know her own mind" (452). The final section of the story leaves us unconvinced. She carries herself with a "new dignity and reserve" (453) that would please her parents who were hoping that marriage (and concomitant motherhood) would "bring the poise, the desirable pose, so glaringly lacking in Athénaïse" (433). It seems to us that this is exactly what Athénaïse does, she strikes a pose. Assuming the part of a culturally constructed mother, she is necessarily fixed in the permanent childlike state which that culture confers upon her. If there is an evolution in Athénaïse, she changes from being a capricious child to a needy infant in precisely the way the southern myth conceived women: "constantly chaperoned, economically dependent, denied development" (Jones. 22).

The narrator has announced early on that if Athénaïse were to gain self-knowledge, "it would be by no intellectual research" but through the sensuality of nature, "as the song to the bird, the perfume and color to the flower" (433). After her enlightenment we could therefore anticipate an intense involvement with nature. However, even after her supposed awakening to passion, Athénaïse's relationship with nature seems rather tame. The sight of the country is merely a tonic or "balm" to her excited senses; she is "charmed" by the sugar plantations and rows of neat little (Negro) cabins "like little villages of a single street" (454)[17]. In fact, Athénaïse's vision of nature is truncated. In keeping with her culturally constructed role of wife and mother, she is drawn to what is cultivated or even domestic in the landscape and is out of touch with the darker forces of the wilderness. Her fancy caught by the grandeur of the houses, she sees only "sudden glimpses" of the bayou, "creeping sluggishly out from a tangled growth of wood, and brush, and fern, and poison-vines, and palmettos" (454). The accumulation of so many wild, even menacing plants suggests the uncontainability of nature and serves as a foil to our posing heroine. Athénaïse reverses the foreign, "complicated design" (453) of the sewing patterns from Sylvie but is unable to see the "tangled" undergrowth. Eventually, the landscape becomes "monotonous" (454) and she ends up closing her eyes and shutting herself off completely.

The final image of Athénaïse is like a self-styled tableau. She withdraws from her husband's embrace, "arrested" by the sound of a baby Negro crying in a faraway cabin. Her attention captured by the distant sound far from suggesting her connectedness with the world, seems more like another pose in keeping with her picturesque tastes. Her question, which forms the final lines of the story, only stresses her naïveté for us.[18]

Julia Kristeva's exploration of maternity offsets the Freudian and Lacanian emphasis on the father by emphasizing the importance of the maternal presence in the make-up of an individual before being necessarily repressed by the Oedipal crisis. She sees motherhood in terms of positionality or relativity; the patriarchal order, she argues, has separated it into an essence and fixed the concept of Mother. By way of illustration, in her analysis, "Motherhood According to Giovanni Bellini," she distinguishes two methods of representation of motherhood in Western culture: the idealized, fetishized Madonnas of Leonardo da Vinci and the iconographic configurations of Bellini in which she finds "a luminous spatialization, the ultimate language of jouissance" (Kristeva, 269) that corresponds to the maternal experience. Athénaïse's own form of self-representation—the poses she adopts—are borrowed from the cultural construct of a romanticized maternal image. Athénaïse, just like Adéle in **The Awakening,** is an example of the split between image and reality, object and subject, myth and experience that is inevitable in a patriarchal economy. In the later work, Chopin also portrays a heroine who wakes up to the inauthenticity of idealized motherhood. In her final swim in the ocean, Edna is able to shed herself of the figural and revive something of elusive, fragmentary pre-Oedipal mother.

Identifying irony as the dominant voice makes sense of this intriguing story. The use of irony suggests that the version of motherhood presented is not a universal, exclusive one and that the writer and reader are aware of discrepancies. Endowed with her knowledge of the Law of the Father, Athénaïse feels "as if she had fallen heir to some magnificent inheritance" (452), but the ironic tone that permeates the story invites us to wonder if she will not eventually feel the weight of paternal law that she, like the fallen Eve she identifies with, is the self-sacrificing

support. Chopin's statement on motherhood is a highly subversive one: culture must deify motherhood in order to maintain it and that genuine awakened passion—not awakened acquiescence to social order—is its natural expression. This interpretation also sheds light on Kate Chopin's treatment of motherhood in her fiction as a whole. The narrative distance that is set up by irony is symptomatic of the female writer's struggle to incorporate the mother into the text. Neither Athena nor goose, the pre-Oedipal mother while providing creative impetus, basically resists literary expression, like the sinuous bayou allowing only glimpses of herself through the text.[19]

Notes

1. All quotations from Chopin works in this article have been taken from Per Seyersted, ed., *The Complete Works of Kate Chopin* (Baton Rouge and London: Louisiana State University Press, 1969).

2. Bert Bender admits that Athénaïse's awakening to her biological destiny is not Kate Chopin's general solution to women's anxieties but suggests that it is the most socially acceptable one. "Kate Chopin's Lyrical Short Stories," *Studies in Short Fiction,* Vol. 11, (1974): 257-66. Larzer Ziff states that the plot is slightly daring but ends "conventionally" and that the reader gathers that Athénaïse's emotional maturity will continue to grow after giving birth. *The American 1890's: Life and Times of a Lost Generation* (Lincoln and London: University of Nebraska Press, 1966): 299. Robert Arner contends that the confirmation of her biological role as mother allows Athénaïse to accept her social role as wife. *Louisiana Studies,* Special Kate Chopin Issue (Spring 1975): 72. Barbara Ewell argues that Athénaïse gains a two-fold sense of self-recognition: firstly, the emotional fulfillment of motherhood and secondly, the self-possession that comes with sensuality. She concludes that this story is evidence that Kate Chopin is "sensitive to deeply satisfying pleasures of motherhood and the rich sensuality of reproduction." *Kate Chopin* (New York: Unger Publishing Company, 1986), 111.

3. As an exception, Emily Toth does point out the "ironically couched comments on marriage in general" in "Athénaïse." "Kate Chopin Thinks Back Through Her Mothers," *Kate Chopin Reconsidered: Beyond the Bayou,* eds., Lynda S. Boren and Sara deSaussure Davis (Baton Rouge: Louisiana State University Press, 1992), 19.

4. For a discussion of the influence of Maupassant on Chopin, see Jean Bardot, "L'Influence Française dans la Vie et l'Oeuvre de Kate Chopin," Ph.D. Thesis, Université de Paris IV, 1985-86, 172-219.

5. See, for example, James E. Rocks, "Kate Chopin's Ironic Vision," *Louisiana Review* (1972): 110-20.

6. Emily Toth, "That Outward Existence Which Conforms: Kate Chopin and Literary Convention," Ph.D. diss., Johns Hopkins University, 1975.

7. Elsewhere Toth points out that the only other two stories (out of more than a dozen submitted) that were accepted for publication by the rather conservative magazine *Atlantic* were "Tante Cat'rinette" (1894) and "Neg Creol" (1896, 1897). Both stories are based upon the conventional idea of slaves' loyalty to their white masters. "Chopin Thinks Back," 19-20.

8. One reviewer who did focus on Edna's role as mother concentrates on her deviance from society's set of priorities: "[Edna who] fails to perceive that the relation of a mother to her children is far more important than the gratification of a passion which experience has taught her is, by its very nature evanescent, can hardly be said to be very awake." *New Orleans Times Democrat*, reproduced in the Norton edition of *The Awakening: An Authoritative Text, Contexts and Criticisms*, ed. Margaret Culley (New York and London: Norton, 1976) 150.

9. For further discussion of the cult of domesticity, see Barbara Welter, "The Cult of True Womanhood: 1820-1860," *American Quarterly* 18 (1966): 151-74; Anne Firor Scott, *The Southern Lady: From Pedestal to Politics, 1830-1930* (Chicago: University of Chicago Press, 1970); Anne Goodwyn Jones, *Tomorrow Is Another Day: The Woman Writer in the South, 1859-1936* (Baton Rouge and London: Louisiana State University Press, 1981).

10. According to Sally McMillan, southern women were knowledgeable about the risks of childbirth and did express privately their apprehension. See *Motherhood in the Old South* (Baton Rouge: Louisiana State University Press, 1990), 55-56. See also, Anne Firor Scott, *The Southern Lady*, 64.

11. See chapter 4 of Elizabeth Fox-Genovese, *Within the Plantation Household: Black and White Women of the South* (Chapel Hill: University of North Carolina Press, 1988) for a discussion of gender conventions of the slave system.

12. See Susan Wolstonholme, "Kate Chopin's Sources for 'Mrs. Mobry's Reason,'" *American Literature*, 51.4 (1980): 540-43 for a discussion of Henrik Ibsen's *Ghosts* and Richard Wagner's *Ring* as possible influences.

13. For a fuller discussion of the birth metaphor in *The Awakening*, see Carole Stone, "The Female Artist in Kate Chopin's 'The Awakening': Birth and Creativity," *Women's Studies* 13 (1986): 23-32; Ivy Schwietzer, "Maternal Discourse and the Romance of Self-Possession in Kate Chopin's 'The Awakening,'" *Boundary* 2, 17.1 (1990): 158-86.

14. She tells Robert, "I always feel so sorry for women who don't like to walk; they miss so much—so many rare little glimpses of life; and we women learn so little of life on the whole" (990).

15. These birds remind us of the parrot and the mockingbird that hang outside the main house of Mme Lebrun's boarding house at Grand Isle in *The Awakening*. For a fascinating discussion of the psychoanalytical implications of their enigmatic form of communication, see Patricia Yaeger, "'A Language Which Nobody Understood': Emancipatory Strategies in 'The Awakening,'" *Kate Chopin: The Awakening* in series *Case Studies in Contemporary Criticism*, ed. Nancy Walker (Boston: Bedford Books of St. Martin's Press, 1993), 270-96.

16. For a clear exposition of Lacanian theory, see Toril Moi, *Sexual/Textual Politics: Feminist Literary Theory* (London and New York: Methuen, 1986), 99-101.

17. We are reminded of Leonce Pontellier's similar attitude towards Edna. He looks at her "as one looks at a valuable piece of personal property." *The Awakening*, 882.

18. This anodyne, picturesque vision of the southern landscape makes us think of the grandmother in Flannery O'Connor's *A Good Man is Hard to Find* who is charmed by the pickaninies she sees from the car window.

19. For an opposite view, see Ziff, 299, who states "the wife will go on growing in her attempts to discover her nature."

Works Cited

Arner, Robert. Special Kate Chopin issue. *Louisiana Studies: An Interdisciplinary Journal of the South*, 14.1 (1975): 11-139.

Bardot, Jean. "L'Influence Française dans la Vie et l'Ouevre de Kate Chopin." Ph. D. Thesis; Université de Paris IV, 1985-86.

Bender, Bert. "Kate Chopin's Lyrical Short Stories." *Studies in Short Fiction*, Vol. 11, 1974.

Boren, Lynda S. and Sara deSaussure Davis, eds. *Kate Chopin Reconsidered: Beyond the Bayou*. Baton Rouge and London: Louisiana State University Press, 1992.

Cudden, J. A. *A Dictionary of Literary Terms*. New York: Doubleday and Company Inc., 1976.

Culley, Margaret, ed. *The Awakening: An Authoritative Text, Contexts and Criticisms*. New York and London: Norton, 1976.

Dyer, Joyce. "Gouvernail, Kate Chopin's Sensitive Bachelor." *Southern Literary Journal*, 14.1 (1981): 46-55.

Ewell, Barbara. *Kate Chopin*. New York: Unger Publishing Company, 1986.

Fox-Genovese, Elizabeth. *Within the Plantation Household: Black and White Women of the South*. Chapel Hill: University of North Carolina Press, 1988.

Jones, Anne Goodwyn. *Tomorrow is Another Day: The Woman Writer in the South, 1859-1936*. Baton Rouge and London: Louisiana State University Press, 1981.

Hopper, R. J. "Athena and the Early Acropolic Partenos and Parthenon." *Greece and Rome*. Supplement to Vol. X. Clarendon Press, 1963.

Kristeva, Julia. *Desire in Language: A Semiotic Approach to Literature and Art*. Trans. Leo S. Roudiez; New York: Columbia University Press, 1980.

McMillen, Sally. *Motherhood in the Old South*. Baton Rouge and London: Louisiana State University Press, 1992.

Moi, Toril. *Sexual/Textual Politics: Feminist Literary Theory*. London and New York: Methuen, 1968.

Padgett, Jacqueline Olson. "Kate Chopin and the Literature of the Annunciation, with a Reading of Lilacs." *Louisiana Literature*, 2.1 (1994): 97-107.

Plath, Sylvia. *The Bell Jar*. New York: Harper and Row, 1971.

Rocks, James E. "Kate Chopin's Ironic Vision." *Louisiana Review*, 1 (1972); 110-20.

Seyersted, Per. *Kate Chopin. A Critical Biography*. Baton Rouge and London: Louisiana State University Press, 1969.

———, ed. *The Complete Works of Kate Chopin*. Baton Rouge and London: Louisiana State University Press, 1969.

Schweitzer, Ivy. "Maternal Discourse and the Romance of Self Expression in Kate Chopin's 'The Awakening'." *Boundary*, 2, 17.1 (1990); 158-86.

Scott, Anne Firor. *The Southern Lady: From Pedestal to Politics 1830-1930*. Chicago: University of Chicago Press, 1970.

Stone, Carole. "The Female Artist in Kate Chopin's 'The Awakening': Birth and Creativity." *Women's Studies*, 13 (1986); 23-32.

Toth, Emily, "That Outward Existence Which Conforms: Kate Chopin and Literary Convention." Diss., Johns Hopkins University, 1975.

———, "Kate Chopin Thinks Back through Her Mothers." *Kate Chopin Reconsidered: Beyond the Bayou*. Eds. Lynda S. Boren and Sara deSaussure Davis. Baton Rouge and London: Louisiana State University Press, 1992.

Welter, Barbara. "The Cult of True Womanhood 1820-1860." *American Quarterly*, 18 (1966): 151-74.

Wolstonholme, Susan. "Kate Chopin's Sources for 'Mrs. Mobry's Reason'." *American Literature*, 51.4 (1980); 540-43.

Yaeger, Patricia. "'A Language which Nobody Understood': Emancipatory Strategies in 'The Awakening'" in *Kate Chopin, The Awakening* in series *Case Studies in Contemporary Criticism*. Ed. Nancy Walker; Boston: Bedford Books of St. Martin's Press, 1993.

Ziff, Larzer. *The American Nineties: Life and Times of a Lost Generation*. Lincoln and London: University of Nebraska Press, 1966.

Dieter Schulz (essay date spring 1993)

SOURCE: Schulz, Dieter. "Notes toward a *fin-de-siècle* Reading of Kate Chopin's *The Awakening*." *American Literary Realism* 25, no. 3 (spring 1993): 69-76.

[*In the following essay, Schulz explores similarities between* The Awakening *and other works written at the end of the nineteenth century.*]

The ending of Chopin's **The Awakening** signals Edna Pontellier's failure to resolve the conflict between her urge toward self-realization and the constricting conventions of society. Most critics, as Elizabeth Fox-Genovese has remarked, treat the novel "as a problem novel that cries out for a 'solution.'"[1] They see Edna's conflict in cultural terms—in the framework of late Victorianism and the postbellum South—or as a version of the Romantic quest for transcendence. From these perspectives, Chopin's protagonist appears as either a failed New Woman or a failed Romantic, with the blame being variously placed on society or Edna or both.

Useful as these approaches are, they tend to obscure the literary dimension of Chopin's art. As we know from her biography, Chopin's taste was cosmopolitan. She was an avid reader of British, German, Italian, and, above all, French fiction, and she had a strong interest in music (notably Wagner) and the arts. According to Daniel Rankin, "[Chopin] absorbed the atmosphere and the mood of the ending of the century, as that ending is reflected in Continental European art and literature."[2] Rankin's reservations about what he considered to be the morbid elements in Chopin's novel should not blind us to the relevance of his insight. Taking my cue from the title of a recent collection of Chopin criticism, I wish to encourage readers and critics to go not only "beyond the bayou" but also beyond the U.S. by drawing attention to some of the international trends that intersect in **The Awakening**.[3] Published in 1899, the book is an important example of a *fin-de-siècle* sensibility. Chopin's original title was "A Solitary Soul." Edna's solitude bears strong resemblances to many other solitary figures in the literature and art produced around 1900. From a comparative perspective, **The Awakening** appears as a novel of moods rather than as a piece of social fiction; Edna's "problem" has the distinctive flavor of turn-of-the-century mood poetry and *art nouveau*.

A MOOD NOVEL

In an important interpretation of Chopin's novel, George Arms underscores the vagueness of Edna's rebellion and her tendency to lapse into sleep: "On the whole, as she reveals herself, her aimlessness impresses us more than her sense of conflict. [. . .] Edna appears not so much as a woman who is aware of the opposition of two ideals but rather as one who drifts—who finally, even in death, is drifting when she again recalls having wandered on the blue-green meadow as a little girl." Arms goes on to comment on Edna's "sleepiness from reading Emerson" and her "inordinate amount of sleeping throughout the novel, in spite of her underlying vitality."[4]

Shakespeare's *Midsummer Night's Dream* as well as Thoreau's *Walden* suggest that the fully realized self requires a double awakening: The first is a movement from everyday consciousness to a dream world; the second marks the completed initiation, the achievement of an authentic self.[5] Edna never moves beyond the first stage; she remains in a state of half-slumber. As her senses are awakened, her soul, as it were, sinks into her body. The result is a frame of mind that is close to somnambulism. Even when she appears to take note of her surroundings, Edna's gaze is inward rather than outward: "Mrs. Pontellier's eyes were quick and bright; they were a yellowish brown, about the color of her hair. She had a way of turning them swiftly upon an object and holding them there as if lost in some inward maze of contemplation or thought."[6] As her sensuality unfolds itself, she turns more and more inward: "Edna looked straight before her with a self-absorbed expression upon her face. She felt no interest in anything about her. The street, the children, the fruit vender, the flowers growing there under her eyes, were all part and parcel of an alien world which had suddenly become antagonistic" (54).

Edna's gaze combines an intense inner life with drowsiness and *ennui*. One of the earliest and most striking versions of this combination of inwardness and alienation was offered by Balzac in his description of the Marquise d'Aiglemont in *La Femme de trente ans* (1834):

> La marquise, alors âgée de trente ans, était belle quoique frêle de formes et d'une excessive délicatesse. Son plus grand charme venait d'une physionomie dont le calme trahissait une étonnante profondeur dans l'âme. Son œil plein d'éclat, mais qui semblait voilé par une pensée constante, accusait une vie fiévreuse et la résignation la plus étendue. Ses paupières, presque toujours chastement baissées vers la terre, se relevaient rarement. Si elle jetait des regards autour d'elle, c'était par un mouvement triste, et vous eussiez dit qu'elle réservait le feu de ses yeux pour d'occultes contemplations.[7]

Chopin was familiar with Balzac's writings, and the parallels are striking indeed, but an even more immediate model for Edna's pensive look may have been the Pre-Raphaelite portraits of women by Dante Gabriel Rossetti, William Morris, and Edvard Burne-Jones. Commenting on these portraits in 1900, Rudolf Kassner, one of the leading *fin-de-siècle* figures in Germany, was struck by the dreamy, melancholy expression and the peculiar sensuality of the women: Body and soul seem to have become one, or rather, the body has become a symbol of the soul; by the same token, these women exist in a sphere of their own,

unrelated to society, and separated even from the male who may have aroused their sensuality.[8] A key concept in Kassner's analysis is the notion of mood ("Stimmung"). The women depicted in Pre-Raphaelite painting and poetry embody a mood—a mysterious, unfathomable disposition of the psyche. Hugo von Hofmannsthal had made much the same point when he reported on the 1894 Vienna Exhibition. He marveled at the "soulfulness" in the eyes of Rossetti's and Burne-Jones' women; there was a depth and a mystery in these eyes, combined with melancholy, that provided a fitting emblem of the modern artist's sensibility.[9]

Mood was a central category in *fin-de-siècle* literature and art. In the writings of Oscar Wilde, Walter Pater, and Arthur Symons, mood advanced to a privileged concept. Reality was considered as a product of moods; hence poetry inevitably focused on a mood or several moods. According to Yeats' essay "The Moods," "[l]iterature differs from explanatory and scientific writing in being wrought about a mood, or a community of moods, as the body is wrought about an invisible soul."[10]

Edna's awakening involves both the discovery of a new inner life and an escape from ordinary, conventional reality. This nexus of intensity and alienation is characteristic of mood poetry. In his book on William Blake, Symons relates the modern idea of moods to Blake's concept of states: "By *states* Blake means very much what we mean by *moods,* which in common with many mystics, he conceives as permanent spiritual forces, through which what is transitory in man passes, while man imagines that they, more transitory than himself, are passing through him."[11] Mood thus provides the modern equivalent of transcendence. In German literature around 1900, mood became a privileged notion to suggest the blurring and expanding of perceptual boundaries. The early poetry of Hofmannsthal, Rilke, and Stefan George focuses on transitory psychic states in an effort to shift or indeed suspend the limitations of ordinary experience. As Helmuth Koopmann has pointed out, these poems project neither utopias nor artificial paradises, but an intra-psychic world of dreams and vague, floating desires. The process of transcendence, in short, is neither upward nor outward but inward into the recesses of the soul.

While the poets, thanks to the subjective quality of their genre, express powerful visions of great intensity, the prose writers, in contrast, tend to develop the escapist and self-defeating components of inward transcendence. In the early fiction of Thomas and Heinrich Mann, the clash of subjectivity with social norms leads to alienation and death. Withdrawal, defeat, and death are the inevitable consequences of the protagonists' adherence to their moods.[12]

From this perspective, *The Awakening* dramatizes less the failure of a would-be New Woman than the gradual, step-by-step deepening of a mood. If Chopin's protagonist challenges society in her final swim, she does so by remaining true to her dominant mood. Her psychic disposition involves an intense though vague fantasy life and, at the same time, a withdrawal from social obligations. If Edna's stance is affected by her being a woman and a wife, we should also recognize that her final gesture would have been understood by Thomas Mann's Aschenbach and many other solitary souls in turn-of-the-century literature.

<h3>NATURE AND SYMBOLISM</h3>

Edna's withdrawal from society is completed by her immersion in the natural element of water. Critics usually point to the Romantics and Walt Whitman as the chief sources of inspiration for Chopin's use of nature images.[13] The reference to the Romantic tradition is helpful but ultimately misleading. According to Benita von Heynitz, Chopin's treatment of nature and the relationship between the protagonist and nature has strong affinities with *art nouveau* or *Jugendstil*, a trend in turn-of-the-century art and literature that marks a departure from late Romanticism as well as *décadence* and anticipates elements of modernism and expressionism.[14]

The nature symbolism of *art nouveau* differs both from the romantic symbol with its ontological underpinning and from the objective correlative or modernism which cancels the expression of the subject. The fundamental assumption underlying Romantic nature imagery and symbolism is the ontological analogy between the human mind and nature. Due in part to the writings of Charles Darwin, this analogy collapsed in the second half of the nineteenth century. No longer in (even potential) harmony with nature, the self withdraws into an interior space. Nature continues to provide a wealth of imagery, but nature symbolism now serves as a *chiffre*—a kind of shorthand for subjective moods. No longer grounded in an ontology, the connection between mind and nature turns into a suggestive relationship anchored in the psychic state of the protagonist.[15]

Edna experiences the sea as alluring and threatening. Few readers will miss the crucial passage in Chapter 7, if only because it is repeated almost verbatim at the end of the novel:

> The voice of the sea is seductive; never ceasing, whispering, clamoring, murmuring, inviting the soul to wander for a spell in abysses of solitude; to lose itself in mazes of inward contemplation.
>
> The voice of the sea speaks to the soul. The touch of the sea is sensuous, enfolding the body in its soft, close embrace.
>
> (15)

Suicide by drowning was a popular motif in nineteenth-century fiction, particularly in novels dramatizing the plight of the "fallen woman." Another, and more pertinent, antecedent to Chopin's novel is Hawthorne's *Blithedale Romance* (1852): Perhaps for the first time in American fiction, drowning is stylized into an aesthetic act (albeit an abortive one) on the part of the woman.[16] The aesthetic potential of the motif was fully exploited in the second half of the century. John Everett Millais' famous Ophelia painting of 1852 inspired a host of literary responses, among them Rimbaud's equally famous "Ophélie" (1870).

While the many variations on the theme of the fallen woman explore the moral implications of the motif, artists and writers became more and more fascinated by what they perceived to be the aesthetic affinity between the female body and water. As the sinuous line replaced the techniques of impressionism as a structural device, painters developed the analogy between female and watery outlines to the point where body and element became fused into one. G. J. V. Clairin's *Wave* (1890) and Aristide Maillol's woodcut with the same title (1898) are only two of the most famous examples of what one could almost call an obsession in the artistic community. In 1889 Paul Gauguin painted Undine, the water spirit of German folklore who, after a temporary stay among ordinary mortals, returns to her watery realm. Undine became one of the most common motifs in 1890s painting and graphic art. The English translation of Friedrich de la Motte Fouqué's *Undine* (1811) was enthusiastically reviewed by Poe in 1839. On one of his tours of Great Britain, Theodor Fontane noted the extraordinary popularity of the romance in England.[17]

Kate Chopin owned a copy of *Undine*.[18] Like Undine, Edna retreats to the water after a disappointment in love. More importantly, ***The Awakening,*** much like the Undine versions in literature and the arts, suggests a natural affinity between woman and water—"natural" in aesthetic, indeed decorative, terms. As von Heynitz points out, the emphasis, in *art nouveau,* on naturalness marks an important departure from the Pre-Raphaelite and *décadence* renderings of the female body. The paintings of Rossetti, for instance, often seem to capture a moment of great expectancy; Kassner suggests that it is the moment before the woman is embraced by the male. Strongly tinged by the male gaze, some of Rossetti's women exude the allure and the threat of the *femme fatale*. One reviewer of ***The Awakening*** was obviously under the impression of this type of portrait when he felt reminded of "one of Aubrey Beardsley's hideous but haunting pictures with their disfiguring leer of sensuality [. . .]."[19] It is precisely this "leer of sensuality" that is missing from Chopin's protagonist. Thus the reviewer's remark alerts us to the distinctiveness of Edna's awakening. Chopin's treatment of Edna's sensuality is as far removed from the moralizing tradition of the "fallen woman" literature as it is from the lasciviousness of *décadence*. The emphasis she places on the healthiness and naturalness of erotic impulses puts her protagonist into the company of Undine and the numerous other mermaids that populate *art nouveau* literature and art.

Disappointed in her associations with men, Edna in the end withdraws into her natural element. Despite momentary doubts and regrets, her dominant mood appears to be one of exaltation. Written in highly sensory prose, the final scene of the novel projects a *Gesamtkunstwerk,* a synaesthetic experience combining visual, auditory, olfactory, and tactile sensations:

> Edna heard her father's voice and her sister Margaret's. She heard the barking of an old dog that was chained to the sycamore tree. The spurs of the cavalry officer clanged as he walked across the porch. There was the hum of bees, and the musky odor of pinks filled the air.

If this ending, as has been argued, amounts to a regression to childhood or a surrender to social forces,[20] we should also note that Edna's last swim has the distinct flavor of an experience of oneness and totality that was the highest goal of many *fin-de-siècle* artists and writers. Nature, in this context, has lost its status as a medium of transcendence in the Romantic sense. Water does serve a symbolic purpose, but it functions in a decorative way, not as an ontological analogue of the soul.

The next generation of writers would go on to employ nature imagery in straightforward mythic and archetypal terms. In modernist writing, nature is often correlated to the sub- and pre-conscious strata of the psyche. As the protagonist of D. H. Lawrence's "The Woman Who Rode Away" (1925) abandons her self-will in the Mexican wilderness, she achieves an archetypal consciousness.[21] Such a breakthrough is not for Edna Pontellier. Just as one should note Chopin's distance from Romantic pantheism, one should be wary of confusing her literary strategies with the modernist use of myth. Edna was no Venus or Psyche.[22] Chopin's sensibility was equally close to, but also equally remote from Romanticism and modernism. ***The Awakening*** absorbs elements of the former and anticipates features of the latter, but its "moment," as the publication date of the novel suggests, is in between. The novel expresses a turn-of-the-century sensibility that has an integrity of its own.

Notes

1. Fox-Genovese, "*The Awakening* in the Context of the Experience, Culture, and Values of Southern Women," *Approaches to Teaching Chopin's "The Awakening"*, ed. Bernard Koloski (New York: Modern Language Association of America, 1988), p. 34.

2. Rankin, *Kate Chopin and Her Creole Stories* (1932), rpt. in the Norton Critical Edition of *The Awakening*, ed. Margaret Culley (New York: Norton, 1976), p. 164.

3. *Kate Chopin Reconsidered: Beyond the Bayou*, ed. Lynda S. Boren and Sara deSaussure Davis (Baton Rouge: Louisiana State Univ. Press, 1992).

4. Arms, "Kate Chopin's *The Awakening* in the Perspective of Her Literary Career" (1967), rpt. in Norton Critical Edition of *The Awakening*, pp. 176-177.

5. See Andreas Höfele, "Erwachen in Shakespeares *A Midsummer Night's Dream*," *Archiv für das Studium der neueren Sprachen und Literaturen* 228 (1991)

41-51; Stanley Cavell, *The Senses of Walden*, expanded ed. (San Francisco: North Point Press, 1981), pp. 99-103.

6. *The Awakening*, Norton Critical Edition, p. 5. All further page references in the text are to this edition.

7. Balzac, *La Femme de trente ans*, ed. Maurice Allem (Paris: Garnier, 1965), p. 107.

> "The Marquise had reached her thirtieth year. She was beautiful in spite of her fragile form and extremely delicate look. Her greatest charm lay in her still face, revealing unfathomed depths of soul. Some haunting, ever-present thought veiled, as it were, the full brilliance of eyes which told of a fevered life and boundless resignation. So seldom did she raise the eyelids soberly downcast, and so listless were her glances, that it almost seemed as if the fire in her eyes were reserved for some occult contemplation."

(Honore de Balzac, *A Woman of Thirty* in *A Study of Woman*, Honore de Balzac in Twenty-five volumes, Vol. II [New York: Peter Fenelon Collier & Son, 1900], 407.)

8. Kassner, "Dante Gabriel Rossetti: Sonette und Frauenköpfe," *Sämtliche Werke*, ed. Ernst Zinn (Pfullingen: Neske, 1969), pp. 149-176.

9. Hofmannsthal, "Über moderne englische Malerei," *Die Präraffaeliten*, ed. Gisela Hönnighausen (Stuttgart: Reclam, 1992), pp. 367-372.

10. Quoted from Lothar Hönnighausen, *The Symbolist Tradition in English Literature: A Study of Pre-Raphaelitism and "Fin de Siècle"* (Cambridge: Cambridge Univ. Press, 1988), p. 94.

11. Quoted from Hönnighausen, *The Symbolist Tradition*, p. 94.

12. Koopmann, "Entgrenzung—Zu einem literarischen Phänomen um 1900," *Fin de siècle: Zu literatur und Kunst der Jahrhundertwende*, ed. Roger Bauer et al. (Frankfurt-am-Main: Klostermann, 1977), pp. 73-92.

13. See, e.g., Donald A. Ringe, "Romantic Imagery in Kate Chopin's *The Awakening*" (1972), rpt. in Norton Critical Edition of *The Awakening*, pp. 201-206; Joyce Dyer, "Symbolism and Imagery in *The Awakening*," *Approaches to Teaching Chopin's "The Awakening*," pp. 126-131.

14. Von Heynitz, *Literarische Kontexte von Kate Chopins "The Awakening*," Diss. University of Heidelberg, 1993, ch. 7. Originally limited to the arts, the terms *art nouveau* and *Jugendstil* have recently become accepted by literary historians as well. See Joachim W. Storck, "'Jugendstil'—ein literaturgeschichtlicher Epochenbegriff? Aspekte und Kriterien," *Im Dialog mit der Moderne: Zur deutschsprachigen Literatur von der Gründerzeit bis zur Gegenwart*, ed. by Roland Jost and Hansgeorg Schmidt-Bergmann (Frankfurt-am-Main Athenäum, 1986), pp. 106-130.

15. Hönnighausen, *The Symbolist Tradition,* p. 19.

16. On the theatrical elements in Zenobia, see Dietmar Schloss, "The Art of Experience in Hawthorne's *The Blithedale Romance*," *Amerikastudien* 36 (1991) 309-310.

17. On the paintings mentioned above see Jean-Paul Bouillon, *Der Jugendstil in Wort und Bild* (Stuttgart: Klett-Cotta, 1985), pp. 34-35, 98. On Fontane and *Undine* see Renate Schäfer, "Fontanes Melusine-Motiv," *Euphorion* 56 (1962) 69-104, esp. 72.

18. See her "List of Books" in *A Kate Chopin Miscellany,* ed. Per Seyersted and Emily Toth (Natchitoches, LA: Northwestern State Univ. Press, 1979), p. 88.

19. Rpt. in Norton Critical Edition of *The Awakening,* p. 152.

20. For representative examples of either view see Cynthia Griffin Wolff, "Thanatos and Eros: Kate Chopin's *The Awakening*" (1973), rpt. in Norton Critical Edition of *The Awakening,* pp. 206-218; Andrew Delbanco, "The Half-Life of Edna Pontellier," *New Essays on The Awakening,* ed. Wendy Martin (Cambridge: Cambridge Univ. Press, 1988), pp. 89-107.

21. Thomas Kullmann, "Exotic Landscapes and Borderline Experiences in Twentieth Century Fiction: D. H. Lawrence, Karen Blixen and Malcolm Lowry," *Anglistentag 1992: Proceedings* (Tübingen: Niemeyer, forthcoming). See also Michael T. Gilmore, "Revolt Against Nature: The Problematic Modernism of *The Awakening*," *New Essays on The Awakening,* pp. 59-87.

22. See the myth readings by Rosemary Franklin, Wayne Batten, and Sandra Gilbert listed in the "Bibliographical Essay" of Thomas Bonner's *The Kate Chopin Companion* (New York: Greenwood Press, 1988), p. 242.

Jack Branscomb (essay date spring 1994)

SOURCE: Branscomb, Jack. "Chopin's 'Ripe Figs.'" *The Explicator* 52, no. 3 (spring 1994): 165-66.

[In the following essay, Branscomb discusses the importance of time in "Ripe Figs."]

Kate Chopin's **"Ripe Figs"** (1:199), though one of the most interesting pieces in *A Night in Acadie* (1897), has received relatively little critical comment, possibly because of its brevity (under three hundred words) and its apparent simplicity. In the only extended treatment the story has received, Elaine Gardiner calls it "barely . . . a sketch" (379), although she effectively makes the case for its charm and its importance among Chopin's works. Like others who comment on the story (Ewell 100; Skaggs 27),

Gardiner emphasizes the importance of contrasts, natural imagery, and cyclical patterns in the plot and argues that the story presents a harmonious relationship between the representatives of youth and age within the natural cycles of human life. While acknowledging the importance of the motifs Gardiner points out, I shall argue that another sense of time is crucial in **"Ripe Figs"** and that the work is not so rudimentary as it may at first seem. Far more than a sketch, it subtly presents much deeper conflicts and richer themes than have hitherto been observed. The relationship between the two characters is less harmonious than Gardiner suggests, and the calendar of the church is as important to the story as the cycles of nature.

The plot of **"Ripe Figs"** is simple. A young girl, Babette, wants to visit relatives on the Bayou-Lafourche, "where the sugar cane grows" (1:199). Her godmother, Maman-Nainaine, says she may go when the figs ripen. Time passes slowly for the impatient girl, and when the figs finally are ripe she thinks they are late, while Maman-Nainaine is surprised at how early they are. Nevertheless, Maman-Nainaine says that Babette may go, and that she is to tell her Tante Frosine that Maman-Nainaine expects to see her (Frosine) "at Toussaint—when the chrysanthemums are in bloom" (1:199). The story is graceful and quietly humorous, and the theme of youth and age in relation to time is clearly conveyed.

Chopin gives Maman-Nainaine the last word in the story, and the crux of my argument lies in her concluding words about seeing Aunt Frosine at Toussaint. Gardiner, like most readers of the story, assumes that Toussaint is a place name. While this is indeed possible, it is far more likely, in the context of this time-ridden story, that Maman-Nainaine is using the French term for All Saints Day, November 1, as the time of the meeting to come. She thus reinforces her reference to a season in nature by naming a specific day in the religious calendar. Recognizing the time reference has important implications for the character of Maman-Nainaine and her relationship with her goddaughter, and for the theme of the story as a whole.

It is tempting to see Maman-Nainaine as embodying merely a benevolent aspect of the rhythms of nature—"the tranquil energy of nature's continuity," as Gardiner characterizes her (381). She does, after all, first tie Babette's visit to Bayou-Lafourche to the ripening of the figs, and when the fruit appears, she relishes it. However, through the specification of Toussaint, which was both a major feast and also a socially important day when families customarily met to visit family graves (Bonner 150), Chopin reinforces the dominant pattern of religious references made about Maman-Nainaine: She is Babette's godmother; she is stately, with patience like that of a statue of the Virgin; and her cap stands "like an aureole about her white, placid face" (1:199). The cumulative images and her naming of Toussaint suggest that she represents not just a mature phase of a natural cycle; she embodies even more a belief in the world of the spirit and an awareness of death that are unknown to the ripening girl. She knows that the chrysanthemum is the flower of the dying year, the time when the family reunites, not to eat the sugar cane of Bayou-Lafourche, but to commune with the dead.

Besides broadening the thematic concerns of the story, this aspect of Maman-Nainaine's personality contributes considerably to both the sense of conflict and the humor in the story. At first the conflict seems to involve merely the different perspectives of age and youth on the passage of time and the coming of maturity. Maman-Nainaine says that the girl may eat sugar cane at the proper season, when the figs ripen. Though the narrator says with mock naïvete, "Not that the ripening of figs had the least thing to do with it" (1:199), the common association of the fig with female sexuality suggests that Maman-Nainaine's restriction goes beyond a simple lesson in patience. Rather than being just markers of the seasons, as Gardiner suggests (381), the figs, like the chrysanthemums, are thus significant in themselves. When Babette produces the long-awaited figs for her godmother, Maman-Nainaine arches her eyebrows and says the fruit has ripened very early. She is perturbed at the disruption of her timetable for Babette, and her peeling "the very plumpest figs with her pointed silver fruit-knife" (1:199) sets a slightly ominous tone for the conclusion of the story. Her final instruction to Babette is therefore only partially an acquiescence in the girl's departure and all that it symbolizes; it is also a drily witty assertion of control and a veiled suggestion that though ripeness may be all, Babette's understanding of the nature of ripeness is incomplete. The reunion in the fall will come not just whenever the flowers of autumn choose to bloom, but on the appointed holy day, All Saints. The story thus concludes with the implication that there are other seasons than those of nature and that the desires of youth must be balanced by the deeper understanding of age.

Works Cited

Bonner, Thomas. *The Kate Chopin Companion.* New York: Greenwood, 1988.

Chopin, Kate. *The Complete Works of Kate Chopin.* Vol. 1. Ed. Per Seyersted. Baton Rouge: Louisiana State UP, 1969. 199. 2 vols.

Ewell, Barbara. *Kate Chopin.* Boston: Twayne, 1985.

Gardiner, Elaine. "'Ripe Figs': Kate Chopin in Miniature." *Modern Fiction Studies* 28 (1982): 379-82.

Skaggs, Peggy. *Kate Chopin.* Boston: Twayne, 1985.

David Steiling (essay date spring 1994)

SOURCE: Steiling, David. "Multi-Cultural Aesthetic in Kate Chopin's 'A Gentleman of Bayou Teche.'" *The Mississippi Quarterly* 47, no. 2 (spring 1994): 197-101.

[*In the following essay, Steiling discusses Chopin's use of irony to address regional and ethnic stereotypes in "A Gentleman of Bayou Teche."*]

"A Gentleman of Bayou Teche" by Kate Chopin is seldom read and has attracted virtually no critical attention, but the subject and design of this sketch amply demonstrate that its author understood how subcultures can be particularly sensitive to the way they are perceived and recorded by outsiders. This sketch shows that Chopin had thoughtfully considered how the drawing of "local" characters can easily be distorted into the creation of stereotypes. But Chopin, writing a hundred years ago, not only illustrates the problems of writing about regional American life but poses a solution to these problems that readers today might find extraordinary for its manifestation of current pluralist and multicultural ideals.

This sketch, along with Chopin's own remarks[1], clearly indicates her ambivalence toward the "local color school" of American writing. A certain amount of this ambivalence may reflect Chopin's perception of how the term "local color writing" was becoming a means of diminishing the work of women and regional writers of the period. What this sketch makes clear is that this ambivalence goes deeper and is a reaction to the ethical and aesthetic problems of representing distinct ethnic and regional cultures.

"A Gentleman of Bayou Teche" appeared in Chopin's first published collection, **Bayou Folk** (1894), and relates the story of Mr. Sublet, an artist visiting the Hallet plantation looking for "bits of 'local color.'" There Sublet is taken with the decidedly "local" appearance of a Cajun, Evariste Bonamour, and contracts to draw his picture, giving him two silver dollars to secure the contract. Evariste and daughter Martinette fail to make much sense of why Sublet wishes to draw Evariste dressed just as if he had emerged from the swamp, but Evariste gives the two dollars to Martinette to buy more substantial clothes for the winter. On her way to the store, Martinette stops to brag about the matter to Aunt Dicey, who reacts to the news by snickering at what she sees as the simplicity of Martinette and her father. In Aunt Dicey's view, Sublet intends to use the picture of Evariste to illustrate the "lowdown 'Cajuns o'Bayeh Teche!" Dicey recounts how Sublet's son had entered her cabin unannounced and asked to take her photograph while she was ironing. "I 'lowed I gwine make a picture outen him and dis heah flati'on, ef he don' cl'ar hisse'f quick," recalls Dicey. "An' he say he baig my pardon fo' his intrudement. All dat kine o'talk to a ole nigga 'oman! Dat plainly sho' he don' know his place."[2] Dicey comments that if she were to have her picture taken, she would want "'im to come in heah an' say: 'Howdy, Aunt Dicey! will you be so kine and go put on yo' noo calker dress an' yo' bonnit w'at you w'as to meein', an' stan' 'side f'om dat i'onin'boa'd w'ilse I gwine take yo' photygraph.'" Martinette believes Aunt Dicey's construction of Sublet's intention, and instead of going to the store returns home, ashamed.

The next day Martinette goes to the plantation house to return the money while her father goes fishing. Prevailed upon by Sublet to provide an explanation, Martinette finally blurts out, "My papa ent one lowdown 'Cajun. He ent goin' to stan' to have that kine o' writin' put down un'neath his picture!" (p. 299). Bolting from the house, Martinette runs into her father, who is ascending the steps bearing Sublet's son in his arms. Evariste has rescued the boy from the lake, where he had overturned in a pirogue. Sublet proposes to Evariste that he still draw his picture but subtitle it "a hero of Bayou Teche" (pp. 300-301), but Evariste demurs because to him saving the child was just an ordinary, not an extraordinary act. Sublet's host suggests a compromise whereby Sublet should draw the picture but Evariste would be allowed to title it. Evariste will return in his best pants and coat for the sitting, and the picture will be titled "Mista Evariste Anatole Bonamour, a gent'man of de Bayou Teche" (p. 303).

This tale is more than a sketch of the pride and nobility that lie beneath the facade of the impoverished Cajun, or even a well-observed study of class relationships in the bayou community; it is a narrative of the artist's relationship with the subject and a moral tale for the local colorist.

Chopin evokes the conventions of the local-color school in the plantation setting, the presence of the chivalric noble savage, and the use of dialect, but the reader is invited to see beyond these conventions through the narrative's irony. The evocation of the plantation as setting is completed in the picture of the household of Evariste, where pride and gentility are valued as highly as they are in the household of the landowner. Similarly the chivalric actions of Evariste and his daughter are contrasted to the rudeness, impetuousness, and thoughtlessness of Sublet and his son. But the effect of these simple strategies, combined with the action, is to focus the story, not on the account of the heroic act of the Cajun but on the education of the artist. While the reader is entertained by the eccentric detail of the speech and setting, this fascination is undercut by a growing awareness of how such regard is perceived by the subjects of that condescending, if well-intentioned, study.

Sublet and his son betray an ignorance of custom and local manners that results in near tragic consequences. The capsizing of the pirogue is an effective trope for the subtle balance required in navigating the cultural backwaters of the bayou, and tragedy is only averted by the knowledge, tolerance and diplomacy of the locals. The story is a warning to the writer/artist who would venture into the bayou after "bits of local color." The substance of the tale is that the rendering of individuals as "types" is a literary exploitation. Chopin seems determined to build on her association with the conventions of "local color" while disassociating herself from its exploitative qualities.

Of course Chopin manages in this tale to have it both ways. She shows us the petty one-up-manship between the classes in the community and the sometimes comical extremes of pride—for example, when Evariste traces imaginary characters on the tablecloth with an imaginary pen to simulate writing even though he can neither read nor write. But these pictures are balanced by their opposites: the ca-

sual, everyday heroism, the persistence of pride in self-image despite poverty. Chopin's central perception is of the need to be sensitive and respectful to the culture being observed. Anthropologists and folklorists of Chopin's day were learning the same lesson. What was to result was a new observational technique that emphasized tolerance and respect for cultural diversity, the foundation for today's pluralist and multicultural ideals.

It is in the title of the story that Chopin's fictional framework finds its distillation. The proposal she places in the mouth of the plantation owner is that finally the decision as to how to mediate the inherent differences between local and outsider, observed and observer, between the dominant and the sub-culture—the decision as to who or what is to control the image—must reside in the local, the subject, the subculture. The subject must be permitted to explain itself. This is the particular breakthrough embodied in this sketch. It shows that Kate Chopin could and did use the techniques of the local-color school to deconstruct and transcend the limitations of the local-color writer.

Notes

1. See Per Seyersted, Kate Chopin: A Critical Biography (Baton Rouge: Louisiana State University, 1980), p. 83.

2. Kate Chopin, "A Gentleman of Bayou Teche," Bayou Folk (Ridgewood, New Jersey: Gregg Press, 1967), p. 295.

Heather Kirk Thomas (essay date spring 1995)

SOURCE: Kirk Thomas, Heather. "Kate Chopin's Scribbling Women and the American Literary Marketplace." *Studies in American Fiction* 23, no. 1 (spring 1995): 19-34.

[*In the following essay, Thomas examines works in which Chopin satirized the life and career of the typical nineteenth-century American woman fiction writer.*]

"I want the book to succeed," Kate Chopin wrote in an 1894 diary entry about her short story collection, **Bayou Folk.** Five years later—despite disappointing reviews of her novel, **The Awakening**—she nonetheless queried her publisher, Herbert Stone, "What are the prospects for the book?"[1] Chopin's private and public writings confirm that she considered herself a professional writer. But her sense of herself as a woman writer, her comprehension of women's literary tradition, and her relationship with her literary foremothers—that "d_____d mob of scribbling women" Hawthorne lamented in the 1850s—are other, perhaps more interesting, questions.[2]

In *Private Woman Public Stage*, Mary Kelley documents the publishing travails of mid-nineteenth-century scribbling women, the "literary domestics" whose professional identities were upstaged by "their primary self-identification as private domestic women."[3] And in *Doing Literary Business,* Susan Coultrap-McQuin finds that Chopin's literary foremothers, despite formidable success and devout career commitment, "still had to contend with limiting stereotypes of women."[4] Thus it seems surprising that Chopin, who inherited these stereotypes when she began writing in the 1890s, would also propagate them. In three career-spanning works—**"Miss Witherwell's Mistake,"** *The Awakening,* and **"Elizabeth Stock's One Story"**—Chopin satirizes women writers in ways that strongly imply she wished to dissociate herself from the traditional female litterateur."[5] These caricatures provide insight not only into Chopin's own career but also into the status of the female professional writer in late nineteenth-century America.

Chopin specifically ridiculed women writers in only three works, but as Barbara Ewell notes, even her first novel At Fault (1890) managed to "manipulate effectively the techniques of romance [read women's popular fiction] to mock its conventions."[6] Elizabeth Ammons has proposed that Chopin belonged to a group of writers in the 1890s who desired to be "artists" as well as professionals. Breaking with the past, these women assailed "the territory of high art traditionally posted in Western culture as the exclusive property of privileged white men."[7]

In light of this premise, Chopin seems less atypical in her censure of scribbling women. Willa Cather, for example, claimed she expected little of women writers until they could produce "a stout sea tale, a manly battle yarn, anything without wine, women and love."[8] Ironically, Cather treated *The Awakening* to a similarly uncharitable review. Objecting to its "trite" retelling of Flaubert's *Madame Bovary,* Cather (in a revealing trope) compares Chopin's narrative decisions to a man acquiring a mate: "An author's choice of themes is frequently as inexplicable as his choice of a wife. It is governed by some innate temperamental bias that cannot be diagrammed. This is particularly so in women who write."[9]

Cather's criticism, however, might be considered poetic justice, since Chopin had herself dunned her sister scribblers. Her first parody of the literary woman, **"Miss Witherwell's Mistake,"** was completed in November 1889 at the beginning of her literary apprenticeship. Chopin's third published story, it appeared in February 1891 in the St. Louis magazine *Fashion and Fancy.*[10] Echoing the spirit of Hawthorne's oftquoted remark, **"Miss Witherwell's Mistake"** derides scribbling women's "trash" and mocks their female readers. The story recounts the career of Miss Frances Witherwell, an unmarried journalist of a seasoned age who contributes fiction and women's articles to a small-town newspaper, the "Boredomville Battery." Notwithstanding Chopin's gesture in christening her character "Wither-well," she also derides the female journalist's hackneyed production: flagrantly Southern "tale[s] of passion" and self-important essays like "The Wintering of Canaries," "Security Against the Moth" (*The Complete Works of Kate Chopin* [hereafter abbreviated as *CW*],

p. 59), and "The Use and Abuse of the Corset," the last title mockingly described as "an unusually strong thing . . . handled in that free, fearless, almost heroic style, permitted to so well established a veteran in journalism as Miss Witherwell" (*CW*, p. 63). The story also critiques Boredomville's matrons for their unconditional fidelity to the Woman's Page. These gullible readers are sheep naively "beholden to the spinster, Miss Witherwell" for her essay "A Word to Mothers" (*CW*, p. 59).

The story's plot revolves around Witherwell's wealthy niece, whose outraged father has forbidden her to marry the man she loves. Seeking her aunt's advice in her love affair, the niece pretends she requires a story resolution. Exceedingly dense about real lovers (the "mistake" of the title), Witherwell is nonetheless delighted to suggest a fictional solution. Chopin provides a deft satire of nineteenth-century critical schools with Witherwell's recommendation that in problems of the heart the hero must "perform some act to ingratiate himself with the obdurate parent." When the niece appropriately rejects her advice, Witherwell retorts: The poison of the realistic school has certainly tainted and withered your fancy in the bud. . . . Marry them, most certainly, or let them die" (*CW*, p. 65). Needless to say, the niece marries, but the story's conclusion authentically addresses the dilemma faced by women working in traditionally male fields. In a few years the new husband rises to editor-in-chief of the newspaper, although Witherwell herself held "a moneyed interest" (*CW*, p. 59). Witherwell's joy in her niece's happiness and her work on the paper seem sufficient reward. Flourishing her blue pencil and churning out her "brilliant articles for the Battery," she grows "older in years, but not in reality" (*CW*, p. 66). Presumably she still keeps a spotless house.

The tale's disparagement of women writers and their readers anticipates statements Chopin made nearly a decade later about her own, by then, relatively successful literary career. In an autobiographical essay appearing November 26, 1899, in the *St. Louis Post-Dispatch* (six months after the publication of *The Awakening*), Chopin describes her writing as an occupation she pursues only when not inclined "to struggle with the intricacies of a pattern" or "if the temptation to try a new furniture polish on an old table leg is not too powerful to be denied" (*CW*, pp. 721-22). Chopin clearly satirizes the notion that a woman writer's scrupulous housekeeping enhances her literary credentials. The early story **"Miss Witherwell's Mistake"** likewise substantiates Mary Kelley's position that in mid-century the "'female writer' was considered a contradiction in terms, that such a being was seen as unnatural, such a woman as unfeminine."[11] The proper sphere for a woman was the house. But since Boredomville can observe Miss Witherwell's "neat and pretty home," her domesticity apparently tenders proof that she holds "nothing in common with that oft-cited Mrs. Jelleby [sic], who has served not a little to bring the female litterateur into disrepute" (*CW*, p. 59).

Miss Witherwell, in fact, adores tidying up, professing that her "most pungent conceptions" were conceived whilst engaged in some such domestic occupation as sprinkling camphor in the folds of the winter curtains, or lining trunks with tarpaper, to prevent moths. And she herself tells of that poetic, enigmatic inspiration "Trust Not!" having flashed upon her, whilst she stood at the pantry-shelf washing with her own safe hands, her cut-glass goblets in warm soap-suds.

(*CW*, p. 59)

Chopin's lampoon of the Muse of Housekeeping parodies comparable representations in nineteenth-century women's fiction. Mrs. A. D. T. Whitney's novel *The Other Girls* (1873), for instance, describes a young servant girl who becomes a successful poet. Despite her new prosperity, the girl continues her employment because, as she informs her mistress, "The best and brightest things I've ever thought have come into my head over the ironing-board or the bread-making."[12] As a widow attempting to write in a household of six children, Chopin had surely encountered this archetypal female conflict between a woman's work and her workmanship. An anonymous poem that appeared in *St. Louis Life* a few months before the publication of **"Miss Witherwell's Mistake"** probably more accurately depicts Chopin's boisterous household and composition habits. Since the magazine's editor Sue V. Moore, Chopin's close friend and another scribbling woman, probably wrote the poem, the professional ironies are manifest:

> MRS. _____, OF ST. LOUIS.
> The novelist sat at her desk at work,
> Surrounded by scattered scraps of paper,
> And her little son tossed them all about,
> With merry skip and caper.
> Now struck by a thought he stops his play,
> "Mama," he cries, and his bright eyes glitter,
> "Do they call you literary because
> You work in such a litter?"[13]

Interestingly, the story's mockery of Miss Witherwell's literary product—those heady Southern romances and essays on corsets and canaries—might display Chopin's self-consciousness over her own recent endeavors. Her meticulous log-book records confirm that she too exploited Southern settings in her early fiction but, more significantly, that she earned nothing from her writings in 1890, the same year she published At Fault at her own expense (a route Hawthorne also pursued with Fanshawe). By the time **"Miss Witherwell's Mistake"** appeared in February 1891, from January through April that year Chopin had been translating essays from the French to sell to local newspapers—pieces whose irrelevant titles resemble Miss Witherwell's but delineate a more masculine turf: "The Shape of the Head"; "A Trip to Portuguese Guinea"; "A Visit to the Planet Mars"; "A Transfusion of Goatsblood"; "Revival of Wrestling"; and "Cut-Papier Figures."[14] Reconsidered in light of Chopin's artistic quandary in the initial years of her literary apprenticeship, **"Miss Witherwell's Mistake"** documents Chopin's quarrel with her readers and her exasperation with her stymied career. It also proclaims her distaste for the constrictive range of subjects and genres—domestic fictions, housekeeping essays, children's

literature—allotted to literary women. Chopin along with other "New Woman writers of the 1890s," in Elaine Showalter's assessment, "had an ambivalent or even hostile relationship to women's culture, which they often saw as boring and restrictive."[15] If Chopin's early experience with editorial rejection taught her what kind of women's writings sold, this story appears to dramatize her doubts that she wanted success at any price.

Chopin's next female journalist, Miss Mayblunt, appears nearly a decade later in **The Awakening.** Even less than a ficelle, Mayblunt does not figure in Barbara Solomon's extensive compilation of the novel's major and minor "foils" to Edna Pontellier.[16] In fact, Mayblunt's function in the narrative has remained something of a puzzle. The journalist's ironic characterization, however, suggests that Chopin might have intended Mayblunt as another avatar of **The Awakening**'s effaced narrator, the novelist herself If so, Mayblunt might personify Chopin's decade-long experience as the token "literary woman" at Louisiana and St. Louis soirees. Chopin's writings yield interesting precedents for this interpretation. Her review of the writer Ruth McEnery Stuart in the February 27, 1897, *St. Louis Criterion* is undoubtedly modeled after Chopin's own reception on her return visits to provincial Natchitoches parish, Louisiana. Chopin sarcastically quips that Stuart's literary genius has been "recognized throughout the length and breadth of these United States—everywhere, except in one small parish in Louisiana" (*CW*, p. 712). Chopin's 1899 autobiographical essay for the *Post-Dispatch* also expressed her exasperation with being treated as a dilettante: "How hard it is for one's acquaintances and friends to realize that one's books are to be taken seriously, and that they are subject to the same laws which govern the existence of others' books!" (*CW*, p. 722).

If the germ for Miss Mayblunt's characterization was Chopin's experience as St. Louis's or Natchitoches' token woman writer, then the mean-spirited passage introducing the journalist, a guest at Edna's bacchanalian banquet, becomes doubly ironic: Mayblunt is a woman "no longer in her teens, who looked at the world through lorgnettes and with the keenest interest. It was thought and said that she was intellectual; it was suspected of her that she wrote under a nom de gueree" (*CW*, p. 970).[17] Monsieur Gouvernail, a journalist "connected with one of the daily papers" (*CW*, p. 970), escorts Mayblunt to Edna's dinner; his accompaniment might even authenticate his female colleague's credentials.[18] At least when the banquet commences, the guests concede Mayblunt a modicum of expertise. Edna asks Mayblunt directly if the term "composed" might be used to describe a garnet-hued drink that her father concocted (*CW*, p. 971). Although asked a usage question, however, Mayblunt is not allowed to respond. Edna's lover Alcee Arobin interrupts, insisting that since Edna's father composed the cocktail, it should be drunk in honor of "the daughter whom he invented" (*CW*, p. 971). During the ensuing hilarity, Mayblunt fails to taste her drink, begging instead to contemplate its exquisite color. But Chopin makes the point in the exchange that it matters little whether Mayblunt was embarrassed by Arobin's earthy quip about Edna's conception, irritated by his implication that men "invented" women, or merely posturing as an artiste; a female journalist's opinions are superfluous. While Mrs. Merriman is "talking 'books' with Mr. Gouvernail and trying to draw from him his opinion upon current literary topics" (*CW,* p. 972), no one solicits Mayblunt's judgments. Universally ignored, she pretends to enjoy Mr. Merriman's boring business stories, so "lame and lacking point" (*CW,* pp. 971-72) that even his wife rarely allows their conclusion.

Like Miss Witherwell, Miss Mayblunt never rises above stereotype; even her name, "May-blunt," appears designedly allegorical, connoting subservience and tactlessness. Chopin further parodies the female journalist's insecurity when the guests, in a rare instance, include her in the conversation, and she obsequiously panders to her hostess. Celebrating Edna's amateur artistic talent over her own rhetorical skills, she gushes: "Oh! to be able to paint in color rather than in words!" (*CW,* p. 973).

Deborah E. Barker interprets Mayblunt as Chopin's version of the woman writer whose fiction "lacks color" or who fears "to enter fully the public sphere and use her own name for her writing."[19] But Mayblunt's demeanor remarkably resembles Chopin's in her 1899 autobiographical essay, in which she initially dismisses her writing as an ancillary whim but later asks to be taken seriously. If the successful Chopin hesitated to expose the scope of her ambitions to her St. Louis readers, Mayblunt's characterization suggests that Chopin acknowledged her own reticence and was able good-naturedly to mock her literary self as public persona. In fact, her private writings manifest a tenuous relationship with the public throughout her professional life. In a May 4, 1894, diary entry, for example, she deplores missing her weekly euchre club to promote her new collection *Bayou Folk*:

> I fear it was the commercial instinct which decided me. I want the book to succeed. But how immensely uninteresting some "society" people are! That class which we know as Philistines. Their refined voices, and refined speech which says nothing—or worse, says something which offends me.
>
> (*CM* [*A Kate Chopin Miscellany*], p. 89)

Despite Chopin's discomfort, her commercial instinct apparently drove her to give countless readings at local guilds, clubs, and private soirees. Five years after this diary entry, an 1899 Atlantic essay, **"In the Confidence of a Story-Writer,"** reiterates her uneasiness among the Philistines: "And very much out of place did I feel in these intellectual gatherings. I escaped by some pretext, and regained my corner, where no 'questions' and no fine language can reach me" (*CW,* p. 704).[20] Like Edna Pontellier, Mademoiselle Reisz, and Miss Mayblunt—*The Awakening*'s three alienated female artist-figures-chopin obviously knew the loneliness of the outsider.

Chopin's third woman writer appears in **"Elizabeth Stock's One Story,"** completed in March 1898, a few months after the publisher Way & Williams had accepted ***The Awakening.***[21] The sketch's anonymous narrator, a summer sojourner in the Missouri village of Stonelift, sifts through the papers of the lately deceased Elizabeth Stock. Formerly the village postmistress, Stock also enjoyed a local reputation as one "much given over to scribbling" (*CW,* p. 586). When the visitor—perhaps herself a successful literary woman in the manner of Jewett's narrator in *The Country of the Pointed Firs*—scrutinizes Stock's writings, she encounters only "scraps and bits of writing in bad prose and impossible verse" (*CW,* p. 586)." The single autobiographical manuscript she judges "a connected or consecutive narration" (*CW,* p. 586) discloses the creative confinement, paltry self-esteem, and general indigence of would-be scribbling women.

Stock's manuscript confesses that her lifelong dream is "to write stories." But when she asks her uncle (a man for whom she otherwise holds scant respect) to read her account of a local villager, he retorts, "I reckon you better stick to your dress making: this here ain't no story; everybody knows about old Si' Shepard" (*CW,* p. 586). Taking her uncle's criticism to heart, Stock fails to enter a short story contest because she fears that "the story had to be original, entertaining, full of action and Goodness knows what all. It was no use. I gave it up" (*CW,* p. 587). The one story she feels competent to relate is the angst-ridden story of her fall: "I feel as I'd like to tell how I lost my position [as postmistress], mostly through my own negligence, I'll admit that" (*CW,* p. 587). Stock's self-disparaging tale reveals her fierce dedication to her work, despite her dream of a literary life. But in an ironic twist of fate, she undermines her health after reading a postcard's urgent message and delivering it during an ice storm, and she loses her employment after resulting accusations that she reads people's mail. With this final calamity, she relinquishes all hopes of a writing career. Realizing that "the truth is, I got no more money, or so little it don't count" (*CW,* p. 591), she can no longer afford to dream[22].

According to Elizabeth Ammons, turn-of-the-century American women writers exposed in their fiction the link between institutional and sexual exploitation of women and "female muteness."[23] Chopin's story records Stock's analogous powerlessness and muteness when she loses her government position to the son of a wealthy St. Louisian. The resulting loss of income—far greater than that enjoyed by Freeman's starving New Englanders—signifies the literal end of Stock's independence. Chopin herself experienced financial instability both during her marriage to Oscar Chopin, a struggling Louisiana cotton factor, and afterward as a widow with six children. But Stock's unemployment silences her authorial voice.

Barbara Ewell finds that Stock represents "one of Chopin's strongest, most self-possessed females,"[24] but the story delivers a dismaying portrait of the rural woman with literary aspirations. Perhaps Chopin used the surname "Stock" to evoke the countless anonymous women who hoped their writing might pay the bills—isolated women awaiting acceptance from distant editors and eminent Eastern publishers.[25] The story attempts a rustic Missouri vernacular and includes a comic segment on Stock's difficulties with plot-making, but it is not a funny sketch.[26] Its initial paragraph divulges the protagonist's fate and voices, in the manner of a Greek chorus, her final tragic silencing:

> Elizabeth Stock, an unmarried woman of thirty-eight, died of consumption during the past winter. . . . The physicians say she showed hope of rallying till placed in the incurable ward, when all courage seemed to leave her, and she relapsed into a silence that remained unbroken till the end.
>
> (*CW,* p. 586)

Chopin's prologue echoes a newspaper obituary's stoicism but also marks, in a metafictional sense, the suppression of a culturally defeated female writer, one of the "Judith Shakespeares" later memorialized by Virginia Woolf. Despite the narrator's cynicism about Stock's literary potential, as an example of the scores of scribbling women who failed to reach an audience, this portrait stands as Chopin's most realistic and consequently compassionate depiction of the would-be female litterateur. Ten years earlier, Chopin had portrayed Miss Witherwell as a hopeless romantic but as an editor/writer fortunate enough to publish. By contrast, Stock's later and more darkly ironic characterization delineates an impoverished and lonely woman who fails as a writer because she is such a good reader"[27].

Chopin's three scribblers contribute meaningfully to our sense of her artistic development within her brief career. Miss Witherwell, Chopin's first female journalist, produces romantic fiction and didactic housekeeping articles devoured by loyal female fans. If Witherwell's characterization never rises above stereotype, it does record Chopin's aversion to the traditionally sentimental "schools" as well as to the genres commonly open to, even reserved for, scribbling women. Chopin also burlesques the female reader's interest in and expectations for the woman writer's private domestic life and exhibits a narrative confidence that an ideal reader would decipher her irony and share her disdain. In mocking Witherwell, Chopin manifests what she, as female "artist," is not. At the same time, her censure of scribbling women distances her from the previous mainstream of women professionals (in Nina Baym's characterization of that wave) and confirms she sought to identify with the realists whose membership, except for Easterners like Wharton, Jewett, or Freeman, was typically male.[28]

Created a decade after Witherwell, the fawning Miss Mayblunt serves as comic relief at Edna's banquet. An obsequious, nearly invisible literary woman, she is universally ignored by the other guests and never mentioned again after the gala. If she serves no obvious narrative function, perhaps she registers Chopin's own social experience as a public persona, perhaps a mocking admission (like Flaubert's): "Miss Mayblunt, c'est moi!" The novelist re-

inscribes her own name in the novel in selecting Frederic Chopin's music for Mademoiselle Reisz, the only artist who "dares and defies." A wry wink at the public's perception of female writers would be characteristic of Chopin's self-reflexive irony.

Chopin completed her third portrait, Elizabeth Stock, while awaiting publication of *The Awakening.* She undoubtedly suspected that the novel might become her magnum opus, capable of confirming or destroying her literary standing. **"The Haunted Chamber,"** a poem composed in February 1899 while awaiting or reading proofs of the novel, strongly suggests she anticipated mixed reviews:

> Of course t'was an excellent story to tell
> Of a fair, frail, passionate woman who fell.
> So now I must listen the whole night through
> To the torment with which I had nothing to do—

Whatever her suspicions about the novel, Chopin's confidence in its artistry tempered with the knowledge that its themes would outrage some reviewers might have furnished the germ for **"Elizabeth Stock's One Story"** and elicited its strong statement about female silence and professional disappointment.

"Kate Chopin's literary evolution," Showalter observes, "took her progressively through the three phases of nineteenth-century American women's culture and women's writing"; Chopin's career hinged on "the legacy of domestic fiction to work against, and the models of the local colorists and New Women writers with which to experiment."[29] In this light, Stock personifies Chopin's departure from the earlier literary domestics' sentimentalized depictions of rural life and female avocation. In their hands, Stock would have married the new postmaster or her longtime suitor, Vance Wallace, and sold stories to augment their livelihood. Her portrait also moves Chopin beyond the archetypal local colorist who would have returned Stock to her dressmaking and vegetable garden. Stock rejects marriage to Wallace (calling him "a fool"), accepts the new postmaster, and welcomes death: "I'd like to sit right on here," she concludes, "and forget every thing and go to sleep and never wake up" (*CW,* p. 591). Of Chopin's three scribbling women, only Stock's characterization anticipates modernist angst.

By contrast to Chopin's fictional portraits, her other writings accord her female colleagues more respect. She praised the work of Sarah Orne Jewett, Octave Thanet (Alice French), and Ruth McEnery Stuart, and considered Mary E. Wilkins Freeman "a genius."[30] Like other professional writers of her era, she also mentored would-be literary women, among them a neighbor, Mrs. Hull, who asked her advice about some manuscript stories. Unfortunately, Chopin found Hull's stories in "the conventional groove" (*CM,* p. 90), and she valued originality even more than she derided sentimentalism, perhaps an over-reaction since she also wrote romantic fiction herself.[31]

Chopin assiduously promoted her own literary career and could be tough on the competition. More fortunate in her career than Elizabeth Stock, Chopin nonetheless battled hard to win readers and establish her reputation as a woman of letters. Her professional ambitions were early and constant. She sent a copy of her first novel, *At Fault,* to William Dean Howells, gave numerous readings at clubs and guilds, and at her own expense travelled to New York, Boston, and Chicago in search of publishers.[32] Considering Chopin's own sacrifices, it is curious that she was so hard on female writers in her fiction. We might predict some sororal charity from the creator of the passionate Calixta in **"The Storm,"** the mysterious Mrs. Baroda in **"A Respectable Woman,"** and the joyously if only briefly emancipated Mrs. Mallard in **"The Story of an Hour."** In *Reinventing Womanhood,* however, Carolyn Heilbrun argues that some women who have successfully challenged male bastions act like "honorary males."[33] Once admitted to traditionally masculine spheres, they defend their territory from others of their sex, particularly from those they consider dilettantes. Chopin's desire to distance herself from traditional women's writing—conceivably her impulse in creating these three disparaging portraits—appears to link her to the ranks of these "honorary males." But whatever her design, her career-long practice suggests an ambivalence about her ambitions to be a serious writer. If Chopin's sense of the women's literary marketplace was bleak, she must have occasionally questioned the quality of her work when it sold. Recollecting Hawthorne's response to the triumph of women's "trash," her three characterizations also imply that she might have been uneasy when she did succeed. "Polly," Chopin's last published story before her untimely death in 1904, returns the female protagonist (who initially worked in a real estate office) to the kitchen, a more appropriate sphere for the literary domestics, and concludes with the nursery-rhyme cliche, "Polly, put the kettle on!" (*CW,* p. 684). Chopin no doubt tailored the story for the audience of *The Youth's Companion,* which had proved a reliable outlet for her local color and didactic fiction since the early 1890s.[34] But Miss Witherwell could have written "Polly" for the Battery.[35]

Viewed together within Chopin's extensive corpus, her three scribbling women chart the development of her literary life. Miss Witherwell represents a genre that Chopin obviously abhorred but still produced throughout the decade, either out of financial need or in order to keep her career alive; Miss Mayblunt symbolizes the writer as public personality, the commercial aspect of the marketplace that the serious artist instinctively resents; finally, Elizabeth Stock's portrayal immortalizes the failed literary woman who questions her talent, loses her reputation and health, and dies alone in "unbroken silence." Serving as negative foils for Chopin, these caricatures imply she experienced a distinctive and prolonged ambivalence about her career. They also suggest that other nineteenth-century literary women harbored significant doubts about their profession, which undoubtedly contributed to their competition within the marketplace.

In that sense, our reconsideration of Chopin's fiction is more meaningful than any final certitude vis-a-vis the impetus for these three portraits. In our rush to (re)judgment of nineteenth-century women writers, we must address their inadequacies along with their strengths. Chopin's fiction commonly effaces women of color. Her marked aversion to the women responsible for the enormous body of sentimental/popular literature functions as a comparable literary silencing. Chopin craved her own moment on the public stage, but cast as "artist" rather than as female scribbler. In her 1894 diary, with her career on the rise, she confessed her amusement when she met a woman who "hasnt the slightest idea that I write. Its delicious" (*CM,* p. 94).[36] But in **"A Reflection,"** composed six months after the publication of *The Awakening,* Chopin laments "being left by the wayside; left with the grass and the clouds and a few dumb animals" (*CW,* p. 622). "The Artist" in her clearly expects some recognition in the aftermath of her literary rebellion; for whatever reason, she never wrote as daringly again. If she resented being left behind, seemingly forgotten by the literary world, she might have pondered the scribbling women her own fiction endeavored to suppress. For these women's staunch conventionalism not only elicited her break with the past but also, as these three portraits imply, shaped her aesthetic future.

Notes

1. For Chopin's May 4, 1894, diary entry and her June 7, 1899, letter to Herbert S. Stone, see Per Seyersted, ed., *A Kate Chopin Miscellany* (Natchitoches: Northwestern State Univ. Press, 1979), pp. 89 and 137. Hereafter cited parenthetically as CM. An earlier version of this essay was presented at the American Literature II Section, "Doing a 'Man's' Job: Women and the Professions in American Realism" at the MMLA conference, November 1991; my thanks to Tom Quirk for suggestions for revision.

2. Hawthorne's complete remark was "America is now wholly given over to a d_____d mob of scribbling women, and I should have no chance of success while the public taste is occupied with their trash—and should be ashamed of myself if I did succeed." For his January 19, 1855, letter from Liverpool to William Ticknor, see *The Letters, 1853-1856,* ed. Thomas Woodson, James A. Rubino, L. Neal Smith, and Norman Holmes Pearson, in The Centenary Edition of the Works of Nathaniel Hawthorne, Vol. 17 (Columbus: Ohio State Univ. Press, 1987), p. 304.

3. Mary Kelley, *Private Woman Public Stage: Literary Domesticity in Nineteenth-Century America* (New York: Oxford Univ. Press, 1983), p. 189.

4. Susan Coultrap-McQuin, *Doing Literary Business: American Women Writers in the Nineteenth Century* (Chapel Hill: Univ. of North Carolina Press, 1990), p. 198.

5. Of the two short stories, only "Miss Witherwell's Mistake" appeared during Chopin's lifetime; it was not included in either of her story collections, *Bayou Folk* (1894) or *A Night in Acadie* (1897). For the bulk of Chopin's fiction, essays, and poetry, see *The*

Complete Works of Kate Chopin, ed. Per Seyersted Baton Rouge: Louisiana State Univ. Press, 1984), hereafter cited parenthetically as *CW.*

6. Barbara Ewell, *Kate Chopin* (New York: Ungar, 1986), p. 47.

7. Elizabeth Ammons, *Conflicting Stories: American Women Writers at the Turn into the Twentieth Century* (New York: Oxford Univ. Press, 1991), pp. 4-5. See also Dieter Schulz, "Notes Toward a fin-de-siecle Reading of Kate Chopin's *The Awakening,*" *ALR,* 25 (Spring 1993), 69-76.

8. Bernice Slote, ed., *The Kingdom of Art: Willa Cather's First Principles and Critical Statements, 1893-1896* (Lincoln: Univ. of Nebraska Press, 1966), p. 409.

9. Signed "Sibert" [Catherl, "Books and Magazines," *Pittsburgh Leader,* July 8, 1899, p. 6; reprinted in Kate Chopin, *The Awakening,* ed. Margaret Culley (New York: Norton, 1976), p. 153.

10. According to Chopin's records, the story was rejected by five other publishers before its appearance in Fashion and Fancy; hence Chopin might have revised the story along the way. Her two log books (1888-1902), which date her literary compositions, submissions, rejections, acceptances, and earnings, are at the Missouri Historical Society Archives in St. Louis.

11. Kelley, p. 190.

12. Reprinted in Ann Douglas Wood, "The Scribbling Women' and Fanny Fern: Why Women Wrote," *Hidden Hands: An Anthology of American Women Writers, 1790-1870,* ed. Lucy M. Freibert and Barbara A. White, 2nd ed. (New Brunswick: Rutgers Univ. Press, 1988), p. 363.

13. Anonymous, "To Mrs.———,of St. Louis," *St. Louis Life,* 2 (November 22, 1890), 9.

14. Of the six translations recorded in Chopin's log books, the *St. Louis Post-Dispatch* printed "The Shape of the Head," January 25, 1891; "Revival of Wrestling," March 8, 1891, signed "C"; and "How to Make Manikins" ("Cut-Papier Figures"), April 5, 1891. If the other three were published, they have not been located. See CM, p. 204.

15. Elaine Showalter, *Sister's Choice: Tradition and Change in American Women's Writing* (Oxford: Clarendon Press, 1991), p. 68.

16. Barbara Solomon, "Characters as Foils to Edna," in *Approaches to Teaching Chopin's* The Awakening, ed. Bernard Koloski (New York: Modern Language Association, 1988), pp. 114-19.

17. Chopin had published two stories herself under the pseudonym "La Tour": "Miss McEnders," completed March 7, 1892, and published March 6, 1897, in the St. Louis Criterion (*CW,* p. 1011) and "Fedora," completed November 19, 1895, and published February 20, 1897, also in the *Criterion* (*CW,* p. 1026).

18. Gouvernail, to whom Chopin gives the famous Swinburne lines at Edna's banquet, also appears in "A Respectable Woman" and "Athenaise."

19. Deborah E. Barker, "The Awakening of Female Artistry," in *Kate Chopin Reconsidered: Beyond the Bayou,* ed. Lynda S. Boren and Sara deSaussure Davis (Baton Rouge: Louisiana State Univ. Press, 1992), p. 70.

20. Since Chopin revised this essay several times between 1896 and the version published in the January 1899 *Atlantic,* presumably her dislike of society functions remained acute.

21. The story was not published during Chopin's lifetime, but her log book indicates it was to be included in a proposed collection, "A Vocation and a Voice," which likewise never found a publisher. In November 1898, *The Awakening* was transferred to Herbert S. Stone & Company, Chicago and New York, and published by them on April 22, 1899.

22. I read the narrator as female, although Chopin's description is ambivalent. By contrast, Elaine Showalter sees a "male editor, who may be either her nephew or her longtime suitor," *Sister's Choice,* p. 158.

23. Ammons, p. 5.

24. Ewell, p. 167.

25. For a superb treatment of the economic distress of nineteenth-century American women writers, see Virginia L. Blum, "Mary Wilkins Freeman and the Taste of Necessity," *AL,* 65 (1993), 69-94.

26. See Ewell, P. 166, who notes that Chopin shared Stock's problems with plot. For Chopin's literary impediments, see her October 1896 essay (published 1899), "In the Confidence of a Story-Writer", (*CW,* p. 704), and her November 26, 1899, essay, "On Certain Brisk, Bright Days" CW, p. 722).

27. I am indebted to an anonymous source for suggesting this nuance in Chopin's story.

28. Nina Baym, *Woman's Fiction: A Guide to Novels by and about Women in America, 1820-1870* (Ithaca: Cornell Univ. Press, 1978), on women's didacticism and sentimental fiction; see also Kelley and Coultrap-McQuin.

29. Showalter, pp. 69, 67.

30. In a May 12, 1894, diary entry, Chopin mentions both Jewett and Freeman: "I know of no one better than Miss Jewett to study for technique and nicety of construction. I don't mention Mary E. Wilkins for she is a great genius and genius is not to be studied. We are unfortunately being afflicted with imitations

of Miss Wilkins ad nauseum" (CM, p. 90). Chopin also admired Ruth McEnery Stuart's stories, which sound a "wholesome, human note," and especially her humor because it has "nothing finical or feminine about it" (*CW*, p. 711). Chopin credited Mary Halleck Foote with "excellent work" of a "fine literary quality, damaged somewhat by a too conventional romanticism," but a writer who, nonetheless, "knows her territory." Chopin also acknowledged the talents of Octave Thanet (Alice French), whose "heart is essentially with the plain, everyday people." For Chopin's remarks on Foote and Thanet, see Heather Kirk Thomas, "'Development of the Literary West': An Undiscovered Kate Chopin Essay," *ALR*, 22 (Winter 1990), 71-72.

31. Some examples of Chopin's more romantic fiction are the stories "Love on the Bon-Dieu" and "A Sentimental Soul"; the one-act play, "An Embarrassing Position"; and her first novel, *At Fault*. Most critics find her poetry, in general, egregiously sentimental.

32. For Chopin's trips to New York and Boston in May 1893, see CM, pp. 107-08. For a March 1898 trip to Chicago, see Per Seyersted, "Kate Chopin's Wound: Two New Letters," *ALR*, 20 (Fall 1987), 72, and Emily Toth, *Kate Chopin* (New York: William Morrow, 1990), pp. 305-06. In addition, a clipping from an unidentified newspaper of December 25, 1898 (describing Chopin's recent visit to Natchitoches Parish, Louisiana) claims she planned to spend "the rest of the winter [or the early months of 1899] in New York." For unknown reasons, Chopin never made this New York excursion. Clipping is in Melrose Scrapbook No. 69, Louisiana Room Archives, Eugene Watson Library, Northwestern Louisiana State University, Natchitoches.

33. Carolyn Hedbrun, *Reinventing Womanhood* (New York: Norton, 1979), p. 43.

34. Completed in January 1902, "Polly" appeared on July 3, 1902, in *The Youth's Companion* (*CW*, p. 1029). Chopin's first sale to this magazine was "For Marse Chouchoute," published on August 20, 1891; she sold at least eleven stories in total (see *CW*, pp. 1004-29).

35. Citing the commonly-held belief that "Chopin did not write much after *The Awakening* because the hostile reviews of the novel devastated her," Elizabeth Ammons concludes that she is "sure that is true" (p. 75). I argue elsewhere, however, that illness, rather than authorial depression after mixed reviews of her novel, caused Chopin to alter her impressionistic style and thematic focus in the declining years of her life. See Heather Kirk Thomas, "'What Are the Prospects for the Book?': Rewriting a Woman's Life," in *Beyond the Bayou*, pp. 36-57.

36. Reproduced from Chopin's May 28, 1894, diary entry, including punctuation errors.

Barbara Claire Freeman (essay date 1995)

SOURCE: Freeman, Barbara Claire. "*The Awakening*: Waking Up at the End of the Line." In *The Feminine Sublime: Gender and Excess in Women's Fiction*, pp. 13-39. Berkley: University of California Press, 1995.

[*In the following essay, Freeman explores the notion of the sublime in* The Awakening.]

> The sublime does not so properly persuade us, as it ravishes and transports us, and produces in us a certain Admiration, mingled with Astonishment and with Surprize, which is quite another thing than the barely pleasing, or the barely persuading: that it gives a noble Vigour to a Discourse, an invincible Force, which commits a pleasing Rape upon the very Soul of the Reader.
>
> (John Dennis, *The Grounds of Criticism in Poetry*)

> You can't make a political "program" with it, but you can bear witness to it.—And what if no one hears the testimony, etc.?
>
> (Jean-François Lyotard, *The Differend*)

> Love is lak de sea. It's uh movin' thing, but still and all, it takes its shape from de shore it meets, and it's different with every shore.
>
> (Zora Neale Hurston, *Their Eyes Were Watching God*)

> These waters must be troubled before they can exert their virtues.
>
> (Edmund Burke, *A Philosophical Enquiry into the Origin of our Ideas of the Sublime and Beautiful*)

Longinus cites only one female poet in his influential *Peri Hypsous* (On the sublime), the first-century treatise whose fame was revived by Boileau's French translation and commentary of 1674.[1] That poet, of course, is Sappho of Lesbos (early sixth century B.C.), and Longinus chooses her lyric *phainetai moi* to illustrate his view that literary excellence depends upon the writer's ability to harmonize differences and create an organic whole.[2] Anticipating the New Critic's demand that the perfect poem, like a "well-wrought urn" or "verbal icon," achieve the status of an autonomous unit, Longinus praises Sappho's ability "in selecting the outstanding details and making a unity of them" (10.1) as particularly exemplary of sublime writing. What is striking, however, is the disparity between Sappho's poem and Longinus' interpretation of it. Whereas the lyric describes an experience of total fragmentation when the speaker hears her lover's "sweet voice" (10.1), Longinus commends Sappho's skill in creating the illusion of wholeness: according to him, she is able to join diverse parts in such a way that "they co-operate to form a unity and are linked by the bonds of harmony" (40.1).

Given this poem's crucial role in establishing Longinus' account of the sublime, it is worth examining in some detail. I cite versions of the poem as it appears in two eminent and recent translations of Longinus, the first by D. A. Russell, the second by G. M. A. Grube.[3]

> To me he seems a peer of the gods, the man who sits
> facing you and hears your sweet voice
> And lovely laughter; it flutters my heart in my breast.
> When I see you only for a moment, I cannot speak;
> My tongue is broken, a subtle fire runs under my skin;
> my eyes cannot see, my ears hum; Cold sweat pours
>   off me; shivering
>   grips me all over; I am paler than grass;
> I seem near to dying; But all must be endured . . .

(10.2)

The translation in Grube's edition renders the last two stanzas as follows:

> Yea, my tongue is broken, and through and through
>   me
> 'Neath the flesh, impalpable fire runs tingling;
> Nothing see mine eyes, and a noise of roaring
> Waves in my ears sounds;
>
> Sweat runs down in rivers, a tremor seizes
> All my limbs and paler than grass in autumn,
> Caught by pains of menacing death, I falter,
> Lost in the love trance.

(10.2)

And here, in Russell's translation, is Longinus' commentary:

> Consider Sappho's treatment of the feelings involved in the madness of being in love. She uses the attendant circumstances and draws on real life at every point. And in what does she show her quality? In her skill in selecting the outstanding details and making a unity of them . . . Do you not admire the way she brings everything together—mind and body, hearing and tongue, eyes and skin? She seems to have lost them all, and to be looking for them as though they were external to her. She is cold and hot, mad and sane, frightened and near death, all by turns.

(10.1-3)

Longinus' insistence that the poem's sublimity resides in its representation of unity, its ability to connect disparate elements and "bring everything together," is especially puzzling given that Sappho seems so little concerned with univocity. Longinus values the poem because he believes it achieves precisely the opposite of what in fact it does: despite his assumption that its excellence depends upon Sappho's skill in replacing the diverse with the singular, there is little, if any, textual evidence for his celebration of homogeneity. Sappho juxtaposes such apparent dualisms as life and death, hot and cold, or sanity and madness not, as Longinus would have it, in order to create harmony, but rather to unsettle the notion of organic form upon which his notion of the sublime depends. Rather than unify the disparate, Sappho foregrounds the activity of self-shattering. Instead of warding off fragmentation, she insists upon it. It is as if the goal of Longinus' commentary

were to domesticate and neutralize the very excessiveness Sappho's text bespeaks.

My principal concern, however, is not with the strength or weakness of Longinus' literary criticism. I wish instead to examine the function Sappho's lyric plays in Longinus' treatise in order to suggest that his is a paradigmatic response to the irruption of a threatening and potentially uncontainable version of the sublime, one that appears to represent excess but does so only the better to keep it within bounds. The move Longinus makes in relation to Sappho is particularly instructive since, as we shall see, later theorists echo it time and time again. Longinus' commentary on Sappho plays a constitutive role in the sublime's theorization by shaping the ways in which the subject's encounter with excess, one of the sublime's most characteristic and enduring features, may and may not be conceptualized.[4] Neil Hertz's brilliant "Reading of Longinus," which is itself representative of late twentieth-century American theorists' commitment to a romantic (or Wordsworthian) sublime, continues this tradition by repeating the very same scenario.[5] Hertz not only recuperates an instance of difference in a literary text and reads it as forming a unified whole; perhaps more important, he constructs a theory of the sublime that perpetuates its tactic of exclusion.

This [essay's] exploration of significant misreadings in the history of the sublime, along with the role and place of gender in producing that history, will let us look at ways in which the sublime might be written otherwise, were that dimension not repressed. Kate Chopin's novel *The Awakening* amplifies and elucidates precisely those elements of the sublime that Sappho foregrounds and Longinus obscures. *The Awakening,* which stands at the dawn of twentieth-century American women's fiction and brings forward some of its basic preoccupations and themes, also suggests a particular version of the feminine sublime, here understood not as a transhistorical or universal category, but rather as the attempt to articulate the subject's confrontation with excess in a mode that does not lead solely to its recuperation. At stake in Chopin's novel is the very "transport" (*ekstasis*) Sappho inscribes, a "going close to death" that marks the limits of the representable. Here the sublime is no longer a rhetorical mode or style of writing, but an encounter with the other in which the self, simultaneously disabled and empowered, testifies to what exceeds it. At issue is not only the attempt to represent excess, which by definition breaks totality and cannot be bound, but the desire for excess itself; not just the description of, but the wish for, sublimity.

I

As Chopin remarks, "The beginning of things, of a world especially, is necessarily vague, tangled, chaotic, and exceedingly disturbing."[6] We begin with a discussion of Longinus not only because, as the author of the first treatise on the sublime, he defines the set of problems that will coalesce under this name, but because his treatment of

Sappho is paradigmatic of the kinds of disturbances that are at the very heart of the sublime's theorization. In order to grasp the significance of his response to Sappho, however, we need to understand Longinus' view of sublimity, the better to ask in what ways Sappho's lyric both exemplifies and undercuts it.

First and foremost, the sublime is a certain kind of linguistic event, a mode of discourse that breaks down the differences and involves a merger between speaker (or writer) and hearer (or reader). "Sublimity," according to Longinus, "is a kind of eminence or excellence of discourse" (1.3). It is not an essential property of language but rather makes itself known by the effect it produces, and that effect is one of ravishment; as Russell puts it, "whatever *knocks the reader out* is sublime" (xiii). Sublime language disrupts everyday consciousness: "great writing . . . takes the reader out of himself"; it "tears everything up like a whirlwind, and exhibits the orator's whole power at a single blow" (1.4).[7] The sublime utterance, which itself attempts to represent excess, also involves its production: it is accompanied by a threefold identification between speaker, message, and listener in which the latter comes "to believe he has created what he has only heard" (7.2). This identification displaces the identity of its participants and is characteristic of the moment of *hypsous,* that state of transport and exaltation that for Longinus is the mark of sublimity. One of the defining features of sublime discourse is its ability to blur customary differences between speaker and hearer, text and reader. As Suzanne Guerlac points out, "this paradoxical moment is presented by the text as being both the effect and the origin of the sublime, which engenders itself through 'impregnating' the soul of the listener."[8]

Unlike the listener's experience of discourse that seeks merely to please or to persuade, the effect of sublime language entails a certain loss of control. Longinus emphasizes that the sublime "produces ecstasy rather than persuasion in the hearer" and insists that this "combination of wonder and astonishment always proves superior to the merely persuasive and pleasant. This is because persuasion is on the whole something we can control, whereas amazement and wonder exert invincible power and force and get the better of every hearer" (1.4). The discourse of the sublime, then, is integrally bound up with the subject's responses to what possesses it, to the nature and effects of such a merger, and to the ways in which various forms of identification may be understood. At stake is the question of how to theorize ravishment.

Although Longinus never explicitly confronts this issue, his treatise suggests (or is most frequently read as if it suggested) that the moment of *hypsous* becomes a struggle for dominance between opposing forces, an almost Darwinian contest in which the strong flourish and the weak are overcome.[9] For the sublime not only produces an identification between speaker and audience but entails a modification in relations of power between the parties involved, and the diversity of ways in which such modifications may

be conceptualized is at the heart of critical debates regarding the sublime.[10] Bloom's theory of the anxiety of influence has as its origin Longinus' precept, itself borrowed from Hesiod, that "strife is good for men" (13.4). The orator attempts to possess the auditor in much the same way that the poet wishes to transport the reader; the view of creativity as bound up with the quest for mastery and ownership shapes Longinus' view of literary production itself. Poets struggle amongst themselves to best one another: even Plato would not have attained greatness without the need to show his superiority to his rival Homer, for he could not have "put such a brilliant finish on his philosophical doctrines or so often risen to poetical subjects and poetical language, if he had not tried, and tried, wholeheartedly, to compete for the prize against Homer, like a young aspirant challenging an admired master" (13.4). Many contemporary American theorists of the sublime reinforce this claim.[11] Thomas Weiskel, for example, insists that "discourse in the *Peri Hypsous (on Great Writing)* is a power struggle," while according to Paul Fry, "the Longinian sublime appears in a climate of antagonism, as rivalry between authors."[12]

But if the sublime is, to borrow Fry's phrase, always "a drama of power" and "a struggle for possession," I must stress what Longinus and the majority of his critics do not: that the kind of power at stake in Sappho's lyric differs in important respects from the other examples Longinus cites as illustrative of the sublime.[13] For Sappho's ode affirms a form of possession that redefines traditional modes of domination and relations of power. By exploring the differences between Sappho's ode and Homer's—since he is the other poet Longinus chooses to exemplify "excellence in selection and organization" (10.1)—we will see that Sappho's lyric offers an alternative to Longinus's belief that the sublime entails a struggle for domination in which one party submits to another, and that his misreading of Sappho has significant consequences for the sublime's theorization.

For Longinus, who believes that "sublimity will be achieved if we consistently select the most important of those inherent features and learn to organize them as a unity by combining one with another" (10.1), the ability "to select and organize material" is one of the factors that "can make our writing sublime" (10.1). Comparing Sappho's skillful description of "the feelings involved in the madness of being in love" (10.1) with Homer's talent for portraying storms, he especially praises the latter's skill in depicting "the most terrifying aspects" (10.3). And both poems provide impressive examples of realistic description. Sappho conveys precisely what "lovers experience" (10.3); "she uses the attendant circumstances and draws on real life at every point" (10.1); the result of her art is "that we see in her not a single emotion, but a complex of emotions . . ." (10.3). Indeed, their similar gift for accurate representation prompts Longinus' comparison of the two poets. Like Sappho, Homer is a genius because he is able to choose the details that will convey the essence of an experience. Longinus cites a passage in which Homer likens Hector to a storm at sea as exemplary:

He [Hector] fell upon them [the Greeks] as upon a
   swift
      ship falls a wave,
Huge, wind-reared by the clouds. The ship
Is curtained in foam, a hideous blast of wind
Roars in the sail. The sailors shudder in terror:
They being carried away from under death, but only
   just.

                                                    (10.5)

Sappho and Homer share the ability to select and combine
the most disparate elements of an awesome event in order
to present a complete, unified portrait of it. But Longinus
implies that the two poets have more in common than rhetorical or stylistic facility: he also suggests that each poet
is concerned to describe a version of the same experience,
as if the terror of almost dying at sea were the same as almost dying of love. This assumption, however, conflates
two very different kinds of near-death experiences and ignores a crucial distinction between the kind of death, or
perhaps more important, the kind of ecstasy, at stake. Sappho's and Homer's lyrics may be alike in that both depict
the speaker's encounter with death, but they do not exhibit
the same concern with self-preservation. While Homer
writes about escaping death, Sappho describes the process
of going toward it. And whereas the Homeric hero either
wins or loses, lives or dies, Sappho's protagonist can only
"win" by losing and "death" becomes one name for a moment of *hypsous* whose articulation eludes any literal description. Sappho, unlike Homer, is not concerned with
strife or combat, nor does her poem support the notion
that the sublime entails the defeat of death. Moreover, the
kinds of power relations about which she writes do not involve dominance, in which one identity subjugates another, but a merger in which usually separate identities
conjoin. Such a junction displaces the ordinary meaning of
"possession" wherein one either owns or is owned, and instead suggests that the poet/lover can possess that by which
she is also possessed.

Sappho's lyric thus articulates a version of sublimity that
differs radically from the Longinian sublime of power and
rivalry. In so doing, it foregrounds what Longinus and
subsequent theorists ignore: the deployment of agency to
intensify and underscore the wish for dispossession, and to
recognize in the scene of self-dispersal a site of self-
empowerment. What is particularly striking about the
poem, to echo Chopin's phrase, is Sappho's affirmation of
the need for "the unlimited in which to lose herself" (29).
But whereas Sappho's poem refuses any binary formulation of life and death, Longinus' commentary, like Homer's lyric, reinforces their separation, and we shall see that
Longinus' repression of a certain heterogeneous and irreconcilable desire has far-reaching consequences in the history of the sublime's theorization.[14]

II

It may seem a long way from Longinus' treatise to Neil
Hertz's *End of the Line: Essays on Psychoanalysis and the
Sublime* (1985), but Hertz's notion of the sublime, especially as evidenced by his well-known "Reading of Longinus" (first published in *Poétique* in 1973), is strikingly
congruent with Longinus'; and I have chosen to focus the
discussion of Sappho's lyric through a meditation upon
this essay not only because it exemplifies, if not defines,
an important moment in late twentieth-century American
studies of the sublime, but because Hertz's and Longinus'
responses to Sappho have significant affinities.

According to Hertz, the sublime moment involves a turn
or "transfer of power" (7), a crucial movement in which
the subject shifts "from being 'under death' to being out
from under death" (6). Precisely because no such "turn"
occurs in Sappho's poem, it is particularly surprising that
Hertz chooses her ode to support this account of the sublime. Although there is a marked difference between the
beginning and the end of the poem (the speaker, for example, begins by reporting specific sensations ["my eyes
cannot see, my ears hum"] and concludes by describing
general ones ["I am paler than grass; I seem near to
dying"]), such a progression bears no relation to the notion
of "the sublime turn" upon which Hertz insists. It is also
surprising that Hertz reverses the order of Longinus' text;
he quotes Homer's poem before beginning to discuss Sappho and then cites only the last stanza. Just as Hertz points
out that "Sappho's ode serves Longinus' purposes" (7), so
she serves his: reading her poem as if it were a microcosm
of Homer's lends credence to his view that the sublime
entails a chiasmatic reversal, a shift from "victimized
body" to "poetic force" (7). According to Hertz, what
Longinus writes of Homer—that he has "tortured the
words to correspond with the emotion of the moment" and
has "in effect stamped the special character of the danger
on the diction: 'they are being carried away from under
death'" (10.6)—is equally true of Sappho. Hertz thus ignores the crucial differences between the two poems and
reads Sappho's lyric as if, like Homer's, it celebrates a
"turning away from near-annihilation" (6), which, for him,
is the hallmark of the sublime. In a telling comparison,
Hertz compares Sappho's alleged turning away to two
lines from Wordsworth's *Prelude,* lines that will also figure in Hertz's subsequent "Notion of Blockage in the Literature of the Sublime" (1978): "Sappho's turn from being
'under death' to being out from under death . . . is, characteristically, the sublime turn (compare Wordsworth's
'my mind turned round / As with the might of waters')"
(6).[15] Hertz's agenda is to show that Longinus' treatise authorizes and endorses a basically Wordsworthian sublime
that, precipitated by a collision with mortality, celebrates
the self's triumph over anything that would undermine its
autonomy or interfere with its movement toward transcendence.

It is crucial both that Hertz establish the structure of the
sublime as a transfer of power and that he define this turn
as one of "disintegration and figurative reconstitution"
(14), a movement from chaos to unity. Insisting that "the
turn itself, the transfer of power, can take place only if
some element can shift its position from one side of the
scheme to the other" (7), Hertz reads Sappho's text "not

simply (as) a poem of passion and self-division but one which dramatizes, in a startlingly condensed fashion, the shift from Sappho-as-victimized-body to Sappho-as-poetic-force" (7). Hertz's insistence upon a clear and present difference between (defeated) "victimized body" and (triumphant) "poetic force" parallels his view that the sublime moves from a state of "disintegration" to one of "figurative reconstitution"; moreover, both distinctions endorse a view of the sublime as entailing the transcendence of an overwhelming obstacles or force. But is there any textual evidence that such a shift occurs? As we have seen, Sappho does not conceive of the speaker's experience in terms of victory or defeat, nor does the poem confirm Hertz's view that her body is "victimized." At the end of the poem the speaker proclaims herself "near to dying" (or in Grube's translation, "caught in the pain of menacing death"), yet neither phrase supports Hertz's contention that the poem illustrates "the transfer of power" or "shift from-body-to-force" that supposedly characterizes the sublime turn; neither attests to the essential turn "away from near-annihilation" that is indeed central to Homer's lyric. Sappho rather describes a kind of excess that cannot exist within Hertz's (or Longinus') conceptual framework.

If libidinal and linguistic energies are not quite the same, her poem implies, they may also be less neatly separable than Hertz might wish. In so doing the poem exhibits a sublime that, at once visceral and verbal, inscribes both "body" and "poetic force" without collapsing the difference between them. Hertz's contention that the sublime entails a transfer of power that progresses from defeat to victory (or from body to mind) thus upholds precisely the dualism Sappho's poem denies. An important question, then, is not simply what authorizes Hertz's characterization of Sappho's body as "victimized," but why he fails to see that her text resists and critiques such a theorization of sublimity? The relevance of gender to this question cannot be underestimated, and this issue comes to the fore in Hertz's second essay on the sublime, "The Notion of Blockage in the Literature of the Sublime" (1978). Published two years after Thomas Weiskel's influential *Romantic Sublime: Studies in the Structure and Psychology of Transcendence,* Hertz's "Notion of Blockage" examines what his earlier essay had overlooked: the notion of a potentially unrecuperable excess that, in Jacques Derrida's famous phrase, cannot "be brought back home to the father" (52).

In this new essay Hertz continues to emphasize that the sublime entails a transfer of power, a movement in which the self is first "checked in some activity . . . then released into another order of discourse" (44). Here, however, his explicit focus is the problem of excess raised both by the mind's movement of blockage and release at play in Kant's mathematical sublime and by Weiskel's psychoanalytic reading of Kant. For Weiskel as for Kant, the sublime arises from a moment when the self confronts and overcomes an obstacle or "blocking agent." Because Hertz wants to consider "both the role it (the moment of blockage) played in eighteenth- and nineteenth-century ac-

counts of the sublime and the fascination it still seems to exert on contemporary historians and theorists of literature" (41), he examines the function of "blockage" in texts on the sublime by Samuel Holt Monk and Weiskel. In each case a feminine figure (or traditional symbol of femininity such as water or chaos) becomes a metaphor for the obstacle or "blocking agent."[16]

The first indication of a relationship between femininity and the notion of blockage emerges in Hertz's discussion of Monk's magisterial study of the sublime. Monk begins "with a careful paraphrasing of Kant" (45) because the latter's paradigm of the sublime as a moment of blockage followed by a compensatory positive movement provides a defense against total immersion in the labyrinth of eighteenth-century speculation about the sublime. The sheer magnitude of writing about the sublime during this period is, in effect, a version of what it purports to describe: it would, Monk says, "be unwise to embark on the confused seas of English theories of the sublime without having some idea as to where we are going."[17] (Note the remarkable recurrence of images of the sea as metaphors for the sublime: Homer's "huge wave batters the ship, bringing the sailors close to death"; Sappho hears the sound of roaring waves as sweat runs rivers down her body; and in "The Notion of Blockage" Hertz remarks upon "the rising tide of academic publications" just before he cites Wordsworth's image of "the Fleet waters of a drowning world" [41].) We will return to the link between the sea and sublimity in connection with *The Awakening.* For the moment, it is important to remark that English theories of the sublime, here aligned with the threat of excess Monk attempts to ward off, are symbolized by femininity. Monk begins his introduction by likening speculation about the sublime to "the confused seas" and proceeds to compare it to a woman in disarray: "theories of beauty are relatively trim and respectable, but in theories of the sublime one catches the century somewhat off its guard, sees it, as it were, without powder or pomatum, whalebone and patches" (6). Perhaps English theories of sublimity, the confused seas, and a woman caught without makeup are, for both Monk and Hertz, parallel terms. Speculation about the sublime becomes the obstacle the scholar needs to overcome in order to construct its definitive study and, appropriately enough, a woman unfit to be seen presents herself as the appropriate symbol for this inhibiting, yet necessary, force.

Weiskel's study of the romantic sublime contains a similar movement of thought that represses femininity in order to construct identity. Whereas Monk relies upon Kant, Weiskel finds in Freud's Oedipus complex—the "structure beneath the vast epiphenomena of the sublime" (11)—means to chart a course upon the perilous seas. Because Kant's sublime is equivalent to the "moment in which the mind turns within and performs its identification with reason," the sublime moment "recapitulates and thereby reestablishes the Oedipus complex, whose positive resolution is the basis of culture itself" (93-94). Weiskel thus identifies Kant's notion of the moral law with the Freudian superego in which, as Hertz points out, "an identification with the father (is) taken as a model" (51). But Hertz also remarks Weiskel's suspicion that the Oedipus complex does not function as the "deep structure" (103) of the sublime, and that it wards off a terrifying heterogeneity for which the theory cannot account; indeed, Weiskel worries that he has "arrived at [the] model by pressing one theory and suppressing a multitude of facts for which it cannot account" (99). The Stolen Boat episode in *The Prelude* (1.357-400), in which the speaker suffers overwhelming remorse after Mother Nature persuades him to steal a boat in "an act of stealth / And troubled pleasure," leads Weiskel to conclude that the boy's guilt conceals "a deeper, original ambivalence" (102) that cannot be explained by the notion of "an ambivalent struggle against an essentially benevolent pedagogy" (102). "Could it be," he wonders, "that the anxiety of the sublime does not ultimately result from the pressure of the super-ego after all?" (103). It will come as no surprise that the frightening excess that, if unleashed, might block the theory's success is, for Weiskel as for Longinus, Monk, and Hertz, symbolized by the feminine.

The magnitude that cannot be "returned to the father" leads to the territory of the mother. Although Weiskel does not use the term "pre-Oedipal," his explanation for this new anxiety of the sublime calls up an invocation of the desire and terror at work in the (maternal) pre-Oedipal phase, in which the infant is still bound in symbiotic union with its mother:

> The very gratification of instinctual aims, in its quality of excess, alerts the ego to a danger. There is simultaneously a wish to be inundated or engulfed by pleasurable stimuli and a fear of being incorporated, overwhelmed, annihilated. This is hardly a rigorous formulation of the original "oral ambivalence," but it helps to account for the peculiar, ambivalent quality of the abyss image. . . . Our line of thought postulates a wish to be inundated and a simultaneous anxiety of annihilation: to survive, as it were, the ego must go on the offensive and cease to be passive. This movement from passive to active is technically a reaction formation, and the Oedipal configuration we have remarked thus appears as itself a defense against the original wish.
>
> (104-5)[18]

Becoming a self, in this scenario, requires a transfer of libidinal energy from the mother to the father, as if the mother were herself the threatening agent that, without paternal intervention, would interfere with the formation of the child's separate identity. Yet Weiskel does not remark that the shift from passive to active (or pre-Oedipal to Oedipal) is accompanied by a correlative shift in which the father replaces the mother, or that "survival" depends upon her repression. The excess that might have impeded the theory's performance again turns out to instantiate it, for Weiskel concludes that "though the sublime of magnitude does not originate in a power struggle, it almost instantaneously turns into one as the secondary Oedipal system takes over" (106). In every case, the gender of the blocking agent that seems to interfere with but in fact enables the sublime moment is feminine.

Given Hertz's attunement to the connections between issues of gender and motifs of scapegoating, it is surprising that he does not notice the reenactment within his own work on the sublime of the very strategies of repression he explores so astutely within the works of Monk and Weiskel. His conclusion regarding Weiskel's use of the pre-Oedipal phase and the scholar's wish for the moment of blockage are particularly instructive:

> We might even see in Weiskel's invocation of the [maternal] pre-Oedipal phases, in his interpretation of them as constituting the deep (hence primary) structure of the sublime and yet as still only a tributary of the Oedipal system into which it invariably flows, a more serious and argued version of Monk's joke about the woman not fit to be seen. The goal in each case is the Oedipal moment, that is, the goal is the sublime of conflict and structure. The scholar's *wish* is for the moment of blockage, when an indefinite and disarrayed sequence is resolved (at whatever sacrifice) into a one-to-one confrontation, when numerical excess can be converted into that supererogatory identification with the blocking agent that is the guarantor of the self's own integrity as an agent.
>
> (53)

Hertz and Weiskel employ similar strategies in their wish to bring the sublime safely back home to the father. Conceiving of excess only as a frightening (and feminine) other provides the occasion for a confrontation that enables the (masculine) self to confirm, or enhance, its own existence. Excess in such a formulation cannot be defined as heterogeneity, but rather is understood exclusively as a hostile, persecutory force; as in Longinus, the sublime becomes synonymous with the self's ability to master the other.

Although it is to Hertz's credit that his essays make explicit the rhetorical strategies by which such mastery is achieved, he fails to envision a sublime that does not depend for its construction upon the repression of excess. He concludes "The Notion of Blockage" with an alternative formulation of the sublime, "not the recuperable baffled self associated with scenarios of blockage, but a more radical flux and dispersion of the subject" (58), yet does so only the better to exclude the notion of this more "radical flux" in the very act of describing it: while "the moment of blockage might have been rendered as one of utter self-loss, it was, even before its recuperation as sublime exaltation, a confirmation of the unitary status of the self" (53). The second half of the sentence disqualifies the possibility the preceding phrase had seemed to affirm; the sublime "of utter self-loss" serves merely as the exception that confirms the theory's rule. Once again excess is thematized as a "blocking agent" that guarantees the self's own "unitary status." What seems to be the articulation of a problem functions as the form of its dismissal.[19]

Whereas Hertz appears to examine a kind of magnitude that cannot be read as "a confirmation of the unitary status of the self" (53) and one that, in Weiskel's phrase, does not "dramatize the rhythm of transcendence in its extremist and purest form" (22), his treatment of excess repeats and enacts the very movement it appears only to describe: the theorist *needs* a potentially uncontainable form of excess (or "blocking agent") in order that the model, by successfully defending against it, may strengthen and thereby confirm itself. The "common function of the moment of blockage in sublime scenarios" (60) is to legitimate differences, restore continuity, and ensure that the boundary between self and other will remain unblurred. And although Hertz may be correct to insist that while "some remarkable effects can be generated by crossing the line . . . the line needs to be established in order to be vividly transgressed" (59), we need to reassess a critical tradition that can consider the sublime exclusively in terms of a model of transgression. What notion of the sublime might ensue if one could no longer determine exactly where a line ends, or what crossing it entails?

It is not surprising that the specter of difference that haunts Weiskel and Hertz is one to which Hertz's reading of Sappho was blind: that of a kind of excess (and ecstasy) that not only cannot "be brought back home to the Father" (52) but that, within the terms of the tradition, is never addressed as such. The pages that follow attempt to redress this omission by attending to what the Longinian-Hertzian model of sublimity excludes. At issue is the articulation of a sublime that not only does not conform to the pattern of "preordained failure, and the consequent feeling of bafflement, and the sense of awe and wonder" that for Monk exemplifies "the sublime experience from Addison to Kant" (58) and that so many of its recent theorists continue to uphold, but to which writers such as Sappho bear witness without attempting to contain. It is this "more radical flux and dispersion" that Sappho describes and Chopin's novel affirms, for in *The Awakening* Edna Pontellier embraces the solubility Monk, Hertz, and Weiskel so fear. Faced with what Monk could theorize only as "the confused seas of the sublime" (6), she walks right in.

III

Words at their most sublime have the force and feel of water. The ocean is *The Awakening*'s central character, the axis around which the narrative turns. From the beginning it is represented as a linguistic presence, possessing a voice that speaks to Edna's soul. What it says simultaneously resists and impels symbolization. Unlike the green and yellow parrot whose voice inaugurates the novel by mechanically repeating the same unintelligible phrase and who, Chopin tells us, speaks "a language which nobody understood" (3), the sea speaks the language of the unsayable.[20] Its voice, "seductive, never ceasing, whispering, clamoring, murmuring, inviting the soul to wander for a spell in abysses of solitude; to lose itself in mazes of inward contemplation" (15), necessarily partakes of many tongues and reaches Edna "like a loving but imperative entreaty" (14). Perhaps because the ocean possesses a multitude of voices, the command it proscribes is never reducible to any single precept or act.

The sound of the ocean haunts the novel. Like a lover's half-forgotten touch, it betokens absence; indeed, it is a carrier of absence, giving Edna—or whoever hears it—access to a certain kind of knowledge. Hearing it, for example, implies the ability to hear the sound of "wake" within "awakening" and thus to recognize that the same word can signify both life and death, for "wake" simultaneously denotes consciousness of life and a funeral rite, a collective ritual for the dead. (There is a wake within *The Awakening*, but it takes place before Edna's death, at a feast she gives as a gift to herself.) That the same word has contradictory meanings, or means contradiction, points to the irreconcilable coexistence of opposites without the possibility of resolution. Signs of life are equally signs of death, and hearing the ocean's voice impels knowledge of their proximity.

Chopin consistently refuses a dualistic formulation of the relation between life and death, sleeping and waking, or pleasure and pain, and in so doing radically alters a Homeric (or romantic) view of the sublime in which the protagonist's encounter with a potentially overwhelming obstacle leads to heightened powers and a resurgence of life. Displacing the notion that the sublime attests to a polarization of opposites is the novel's insistence upon their co-implication. The voice of the sea indicates polarities only to combine them. Although, for example, Edna perceives the sea's touch as "sensuous, enfolding the body in its soft, close embrace" (15), its waves also "sway," "lash," and "beat upon her splendid body" (27). Chopin thus implies that what lulls may just as easily lash, that what soothes also inflames, and that nursery songs can kill.

Sappho's lyric and Chopin's novel both describe what occurs in response to hearing a beloved voice. In *The Awakening*, as in *phainetai moi*, hearing the other's voice makes something happen: it is a singular event that engenders shock or crisis. The novel's beginning thus reproduces Longinus' description of the unique relation between orator and auditor at play in the sublime, in which the hearer's (or reader's) identification with the speaker (or text) allows the latter to imagine that he "has created what he has merely heard" (1.4). The rapport between Edna and the ocean's voice replicates not only that between orator and auditor in the Longinian sublime, but that between lover and the beloved in Sappho's poem: hearing its address inaugurates a desire where previously there was none. In this case the reader hears through Edna's ears, and what she hears is the ocean.

Chopin's representation of the ocean continually emphasizes its independence from the domain of vision. It is significant, for example, that Edna hears it for the first time in total darkness. Wakened after midnight by the return of her husband, Léonce, Edna sits alone on the porch and suddenly hears "the everlasting voice of the sea, that was not uplifted at that soft hour," a voice that breaks "like a mournful lullaby upon the night" (8). Absence of light allows awareness of a kind of presence one does not need eyes to discern: the sea's "mournful voice" breaks like a lullaby, a song sung by mothers to comfort their children and send them to sleep, as if its capacity to offer solace suggests a relation between the representation of absence and a distinctly aural register.

Throughout the history of the sublime the sea has often served as its most appropriate, if not exemplary, metaphor; and it is worth recalling some traditional representations of this relation the better to understand just how dramatically Chopin's construction of the oceanic sublime differs from them. In both Longinus and Burke, the sea is a major source of sublime sentiment. For Longinus the ocean's majesty is self-evident: he holds that "a natural inclination . . . leads us to admire not the little streams, however pellucid and however useful, but the Nile, the Danube, the Rhine, and above all, the Ocean" (42, Russell). For Burke the ocean is so appropriate a symbol of sublimity that he chooses it to illustrate the precept that "whatever therefore is terrible, with regard to sight, is sublime too" (53). Our differing responses to the sight of "a level plain of a vast extent on land" and to the "prospect of the ocean" show that the latter "is an object of no small terror" in a way that the plain, despite its vastness, is not: the ocean's capacity to arouse terror is the source of both its power and its sublimity (53-54). In Schopenhauer the ocean actually outranks all other forms of natural display. Transfixed and uplifted by its sight, the "undismayed beholder" watches "mountainous waves rise and fall, dash themselves furiously up against steep cliffs, and toss their spray high into the air; the storm howls, the sea boils, the lightning flashes from black clouds, and the peals of thunder drown the voice of the storm and sea." Indeed, Schopenhauer holds that such oceanic immensity yields "the most complete impression of the sublime."[21] In each case, however, the ocean's sublimity is bound up with vision: the sea is something a detached observer looks at, usually from afar. That Edna is transfixed by the ocean's sound rather than its sight is important because here Chopin revises typical constructions of the oceanic sublime. Edna transgresses Kant's injunction that "we must be able to view (it) as poets do, merely in terms of what manifests itself to the eye [*was der Augenschein zeigt*]—e.g., if we observe it while it is calm, as a clear mirror of water bounded only by the sky; or, if it is turbulent, as being like an abyss threatening to engulf everything."[22] Edna's relation to the ocean would, according to Kant, be neither poetically nor philosophically correct: merely looking at the sea holds no particular interest for her. She has a natural, if untutored, aptitude for painting and "a serious susceptibility to beauty" (15), yet only the ocean's voice and touch affect her. Chopin's oceanic sublime is not something "we must regard as the poets do, merely by what the eye reveals," but rather functions as a mode of address.[23] As in Sappho, sublime encounters are occasioned by something heard.

Edna's first encounter with the sublime is marked by an identification with what she hears. The sound of the

ocean's "everlasting voice," which disrupts the everyday world she has taken for granted, speaks a language radically different from any she has previously heard and it leaves a mark: "an indescribable oppression, which seemed to generate in some unfamiliar part of her consciousness, filled her whole being with a vague anguish. It was like a shadow, like a mist passing across her soul's summer day" (8). Sound tears and Edna has been torn. Thus begins her awakening.

Learning to swim is merely its continuation. Although hearing the ocean's voice awakens her desire, Edna does not venture into it until she has been touched by another kind of sound, namely, by one of Chopin's preludes. Listening to music composed by the artist whose name replicates the author's own is a prelude to immersion in that which she has heard. Passion comes in waves that sway the soul, but sound also gives rise to waves and hearing them precedes Edna's awakening.

Toward the end of a festive midsummer soirée, Robert Lebrun arranges for Mademoiselle Reisz, a renowned but eccentric pianist, to play for the assembly. Hearing the prelude has a dramatic effect on Edna: usually music "had a way of evoking pictures in her mind" (26), but now she sees nothing; what she hears possesses and overcomes her. That Edna's most profound encounters are occasioned by what she hears suggests that hearing may entail entanglement in a way that seeing does not. For hearing, as Gerald C. Bruns reminds us, is not the spectator's mode:

> The ear is exposed and vulnerable, at risk, whereas the eye tries to keep itself at a distance and frequently from view (the private eye). The eye appropriates what it sees, but the ear is always expropriated, always being taken over by another ('lend me your ears'). The ear gives the other access to us, allows it to enter us, occupy and obsess us . . . hearing means the loss of subjectivity and self-possession . . . [and] puts us in the mode of being summoned, of being answerable and having to appear.[24]

Bruns's gloss on Heidegger's *On the Way to Language* also applies to Edna's response to Chopin: "the very first chords which Mademoiselle Reisz struck upon the piano sent out a keen tremor down Mrs. Pontellier's spinal column . . . she waited for the material pictures which she thought would gather and blaze before her imagination. She waited in vain. She saw no pictures of solitude, of hope, of longing, or of despair" (27).

How to say something that cannot be said, that confronts us with the inability to present it? The problem that has occasioned the discourse and theory of the sublime is the same as that posed by *The Awakening*: the difficulty of symbolizing an excess that resists visual or linguistic formulation but is there nonetheless. Edna's experience of what Hertz would call "blockage"—her inability to translate sense-impressions into images—calls for a radically different mode of perception, but one that does not lead to an enhanced sense of self. Adorno's conviction that music's value resides in its ability to call "for change through the cryptic language of suffering" is enacted by the prelude's effect on Edna: she trembles, chokes, is blinded by tears, and then, as if to seek deeper knowledge of the "cryptic language" she has heard, she learns to swim.[25] The figurative parallel between the prelude, whose notes arouse passion in her soul, and the ocean, whose waves like music beat upon her body, is established just before Edna, with the other guests, walks down to the ocean and swims for the first time.

Edna's first swim is neither an attempt to appropriate the ocean's power nor a submission to it. It does not represent a struggle for dominance over a force that, as in Homer, has the power to engulf her, but rather, as in Sappho, allows a relation to "the unlimited" in which she seeks "to lose herself" (29). Swimming offers a way of entering apartness; finding her "self" is, paradoxically, a matter of entering the water of the Gulf of Mexico and learning how to lose that which she has found:

> That night she was like the little tottering, stumbling, clutching child, who all of a sudden realizes its power, and walks for the first time alone, boldly and with over-confidence. She could have shouted for joy. She did shout for joy, as with a sweeping stroke or two she lifted her body to the surface of the water . . . she turned her face seaward to gather in an impression of space and solitude, which the vast expanse of water, meeting and melting with the moonlit sky, conveyed to her excited fancy. As she swam she seemed to be reaching out from the unlimited in which to lose herself.

> (28-29)

Learning to swim also entails awareness that the ocean can be lethal. Swimming too great a distance from the shore and at the limits of her strength, Edna experiences a "flash of terror"; "a quick vision of death" smites Edna's soul but she manages to regain the land.[26] She perceives her experience as an "encounter with death" (29) yet makes no mention of it.

Nor do most of Chopin's critics. For although, as Sandra Gilbert and Susan Gubar point out, "in the past few decades *The Awakening* has become one of the most persistently analyzed American novels,"[27] surprisingly few critics have discussed the role of the ocean and its voice, an omission made all the more startling given Chopin's insistence upon it.[28] Dale Bauer, Sandra Gilbert, Susan Gubar, and Patricia Yaeger discuss the ways in which the sea functions as a metaphor for Edna's awakening, yet none of these critics recognize that it is also a metaphor for language itself. Nor are they attuned to the ways in which Edna's newly awakened desire must also be understood as a desire for the sublime.

In "The Second Coming of Aphrodite: Kate Chopin's Fantasy of Desire," Gilbert and Gubar offer a meticulous and insightful interpretation of "oceanic imagery" in *The Awakening.* According to these persuasive critics, the sea provides an alternative to patriarchal culture: lying "beyond the limits and limitations of the cities where men make history, on one of those magical shores that mark the margin where nature and culture intersect" (102), it also provides an element "in whose baptismal embrace Edna is renewed, reborn" (103). For Gilbert and Gubar the novel not only tells the story of Edna's awakening and initiation into a "pagan paradise" in which "metaphorically speaking, Edna has become Aphrodite, or at least an ephebe of that goddess," but examines the consequences that "would have befallen any late-nineteenth-century woman who experienced such a fantastic transformation" (106). They propose that the novel be read as "a feminist myth of Aphrodite/Venus, as an alternative to the patriarchal Western myth of Jesus" (96), in which the Gulf, incarnated by the white foam of the sea from which the goddess emerges, is Aphrodite's birthplace. Just as Gilbert and Gubar find in Edna a modern Aphrodite, so they mythologize and idealize the sea and its "magical shores," for their apparent attentiveness to the ocean ignores the very register Chopin emphasizes—that of sound, not sight. Privileging vision, in this case the image of Venus rising from the waves rather than the voice of the ocean Edna hears, allows them to offer the comforting, if implausible, message that the embrace of Chopin's ocean promises only fulfillment, never terror, and that the one may be neatly separated from the other. Such an idealization upholds a vision of plenitude that a more sustained attention to the ocean's voice would function to resist. Chopin's construction of the ocean suggests not self-presence but self-dispersal; it invites the soul "to lose itself in mazes of inward contemplation" (15); and what it instills is the desire for loss.

Emphasizing only the sea's beneficent aspects, Gilbert and Gubar are able to put forward an entirely reassuring interpretation of it. Not only is Edna swimming "into a kind of alternative paradise"; the novel is itself "a new kind of work, a mythic/metaphysical romance that elaborates her female fantasy of paradisal fulfillment" (104). Their reading ignores not only the question but the consequences of asking what hearing the ocean's voice entails and enables a view of the novel's conclusion in which the ocean functions solely as a redemptive site, an "alternative paradise": "Edna's last swim may not seem to be a suicide—that is, a death—at all, or, if it is a death, it is a death associated with a resurrection, a sort of pagan female Good Friday that promises an Aphroditean Easter" (109). Gilbert and Gubar's commitment to a thematics of redemption mirrors Hertz's and Weiskel's treatment of the sublime as a sustained, if interrupted, progression toward transcendence. In each case what is envisioned is an ocean without undertow, a voice that is able to tell everything it knows, and the possibility of desire without loss.

For Dale Bauer, however, the ocean does not speak at all, an extremely surprising omission given that her Baktinian reading of the novel emphasizes such notions as "dialogue," "heteroglossia," and above all, "voice." In Bauer's view, Edna's relationship to the sea reflects her need to withdraw from a constraining and oppressive society and return "to a womb-like sea. Hers is also a retreat to the imaginary realm in which the only 'voice' with which Edna must contend is the sea's."[29] That Bauer puts the word "voice" in quotation marks is perhaps indicative of her own assumptions about language, namely that the domain of the unrepresentable and excessive, here symbolized by the sea, belongs to a "pre-linguistic, imaginary realm" (149) that has no relation to speech and language. Bauer's assurance that we can distinguish the cultural (or spoken) from the natural (or silent) elides Chopin's representation of the ocean as that which blurs the difference between the two. Whereas *The Awakening* foregrounds these issues, Bauer's reading precludes them. And whereas the sea as represented by Chopin conjoins realms usually assumed to be separate, Bauer reinstates the distinction the ocean's voice displaces. Her failure to hear is perhaps symptomatic of the view that language is, or ought to be, a site of plenitude, offering a realm in which everything can be said and nothing need go unheard. That language may possess a force that, as in Sappho, threatens to overwhelm the auditor and bring her close to death is perhaps something that current readings of *The Awakening* wish to avoid.

While Patricia Yaeger's "'A Language Which Nobody Understood': Emancipatory Strategies in *The Awakening*" is unquestionably the most sophisticated critical treatment of these issues, it nonetheless shares the assumption that language, in principle if not practice, should offer a refuge from, rather than an amplification of, the unsayable. According to Yaeger, Edna's quest is for an alternative form of communication, a speech and voice of her own. In this regard she compares the speech of the parrot to the voice of the sea: both are expressions of "the absent or displaced vocality" Edna seeks; both "emphasize Edna's need for a more passionate and intersubjective speech that will allow Edna to revise or rearticulate her relation to her own desire and to the social reality that thwarts this desire."[30] But whereas Yaeger conflates the voice of the parrot and that of the sea, I wish to emphasize their differences. While Yaeger finds in the parrot's nonsensical jabber and the sea's voice alike metaphors for "a potential lack of meaning in words themselves" (203)—meaning, that is, in the words available to Edna—I contend that the voice of the ocean attests to the incommensurable in a way that the parrot's mechanical babble does not, and that in so doing it depicts an alterity that is, strictly speaking, unsayable.

Yaeger is the only critic of *The Awakening* to find in Jean-François Lyotard's theory of "the differend" a useful way of explaining Edna's linguistic predicament and its outcome. And while I agree that "Edna's absent language is not a manifestation of women's permanent expulsion from 'masculine speech' but of what Lyotard calls '*le différend*'" (204), I disagree with her understanding of just what this concept implies. According to Lyotard:

> In the differend, something "asks" to be put into phrases, and suffers from the wrong of not being able to be put into phrases right away. This is when the human beings who thought they could use language as an instrument of communication learn through the feeling

of pain which accompanies silence (and of pleasure which accompanies the invention of a new idiom), that they are summoned by language, not to augment to their profit the quantity of information through existing idioms, but to recognize that what remains to be phrased exceeds what they can presently phrase, and that they must be allowed to institute idioms which do not yet exist.[31]

Lyotard employs the notion of the differend to describe practices that remain beyond the grasp of representation. Unlike Wittgenstein's injunction, "What we cannot speak about we must consign to silence," his goal is to make the presentation of the fact that the unpresentable exists as much the concern of a critical politics as of aesthetic practices. Lyotard's differend has much in common with his concept of the sublime.[32] For the differend, which entails both "the feeling of pain which accompanies silence (and of pleasure which accompanies the invention of a new idiom)" (13), foreshadows Lyotard's insistence that the sublime entails "the pleasure of a displeasure" (165) and recalls his famous definition of sublimity in *The Postmodern Condition*: "the real sublime . . . is an intrinsic combination of pleasure and pain: the pleasure that reason should exceed all presentation, the pain that imagination or sensibility should not be equal to the concept."[33] In *The Differend* pain accompanies silence while pleasure accompanies the invention of a new idiom, but for our purposes what matters is that the differend and the sublime both emphasize something that is fundamentally inexpressible.[34] Both concepts underscore the dimension within language that, like the voice of Sappho's beloved or Chopin's ocean, testifies to the unsayable. Both signify neither absence nor presence but rather the possibility of an absolute and untranslatable otherness.

Yaeger's essay precludes consideration of the single element upon which Chopin and Lyotard insist: the force of the incommensurable. Whereas Lyotard maintains that to testify to the differend is a matter of calling attention to the disjunction between radically heterogeneous genres of discourse, for Yaeger such testimony is equivalent to recovering the silence left by the ocean's, and Edna's, not yet articulate voice, and by replacing the unsayable with speech. According to Yaeger something crucial is missing and language—a new idiom—will repair the differend by putting speech in the place of silence. I would contend that the ocean's voice intensifies the hearer's relation to that which cannot be translated into speech, making audible an absence to which she must nonetheless bear witness. In *The Awakening* hearing entails the recognition that something remains to be said, and this linguistic residue exceeds what can be put into words. The search for new "idioms," then, is not simply a matter of putting speech in the place of silence, of filling in gaps and replacing absence with presence, but of attesting to an excess that resists the attempt to translate sheer heterogeneity into a univocal message. Chopin's evocation of the ocean functions as a differend not because it replaces a flawed or missing speech-act with a more successful one, but because it stresses the impossibility of paraphrasing the singularity and particularity of its voice, and thereby allows us to hear a silence that might otherwise have remained unheard.

IV

Critics of *The Awakening* continue to be perplexed by the nature of Edna's desire. As Walter Benn Michaels argues convincingly, what is most confusing about the novel is not that Edna's desires are frustrated, but rather that so many of them are fulfilled: as he points out, the narrative "is marked by Edna's inability . . . to reshape her own ability to get what she wants."[35] And Edna's wishes do appear to be granted without apparent effort on her part. She wants to become an artist and quickly finds a market for her work; longs for freedom from her husband, children, and domestic routine and soon has personal and financial independence; desires sexual adventures and has them; indeed, the only thing Edna wants and does not get is Robert's love, but the reader suspects that had he not left her she would have left him, that frustration rather than fulfillment conditions her desire. The view of Edna as suffering somewhat narcissistically from the "problem" of getting nearly everything and everyone she wants draws support from her own assessment of her capacity of desire: "there was no one thing in the world that she desired. There was no human being whom she wanted near her except Robert; and she even realized that the day would come when he, too, and the thought of him would melt out of her existence, leaving her alone" (113). Edna's world seems simultaneously to offer her nothing she can want at the same time that it satisfies her every whim, and Michaels's assessment of the novel's conclusion, in which he holds that Edna's suicide "may best be understood neither as the repudiation of a society in which one can't have all the things one wants nor as an escape from a society in which one can't want all the things one can have but as an encounter with wanting itself" (498), would appear irrefutable. I argue, however, that understanding Edna's desire within the context of the sublime offers an alternative to this interpretation.

What does "an encounter with wanting itself" entail? On the one hand, Michaels implies that such an encounter signals the death of desire. Getting what you want means no longer being able to want it, for desire's satisfaction implies its annihilation. Seen in this light, Edna's desire can be understood only as an addiction to the unavailable, as a never-ending quest for something new to want. But Michaels also suggests another interpretation of such an encounter, "in which the failure of one's desire for things and people need not be understood as exhausting all desire's possibilities" (498). Basing his second account upon Edna's remark to Dr. Mandelet that "I don't want anything but my own way," he implies that Edna's desire "can survive both the presence and the absence of any desirable things" (498) but is nonetheless doomed to failure because it is separated from the realm of subjects and objects. Seen in this light, Edna's problem is not her inability to desire, but her "submersion in it and idealization of it, an ideali-

zation that immortalizes desire by divorcing it both from the subject (which dies) and the object (which is death) that it seems to require" (498-99). In either case, for Michaels "an encounter with wanting itself" entails an encounter with death. The specificity of Edna's desire, however, redefines both of Michaels's accounts; Edna's "encounter with wanting itself" is unintelligible unless we explore what Michaels ignores: her wish for "the unlimited in which to lose herself." For although, as Michaels points out, "no body in Chopin can embody the infinite" (499), Edna desires precisely what she cannot embody.

What, or perhaps more important, *how* does Edna want? In *The Awakening* fulfillment entails not satisfaction but prolongation; it is neither a matter of getting what one wants (independence, money, sexual freedom, etc.) nor of removing desire from the realm of contingency. Rather, it involves a certain relation to excess, one that requires the representation or "embodiment" of that which one cannot possess. What Michaels fails to notice is that Edna's encounter with desire is simultaneously an encounter with language, here embodied by the ocean's voice, and that she wants the ocean's "everlasting voice" because it alone signifies that which is in excess of any boundary or limit. Like the bluegrass meadow that "she traversed as a child, believing that it had no beginning or end" (114), the ocean offers itself as sustaining a relation to that which she cannot represent. Given the choices available to her, the "fulfillment" of Edna's desire can only be merger, and presumably death, in the element that first awakened it. And although Edna wants to maintain a relation to what the ocean represents, her world offers nothing beyond the satisfaction of her demands. In this case, then, "desire gives birth to its own death" (496) because death within the force that awakened desire is all that remains for Edna to want. By the end of the novel there remains "no one thing in the world that she desired" (113)—a situation that comes about not because she is now incapable of wanting nor because she wants too much. The "object" of Edna's desire is neither a person nor a thing but a sustained relation to the ocean and everything it signifies.

To make what is unnameable appear in language itself— the desire at stake in the sublime is akin to Edna's desire for the ocean's voice: both defy the subject's representational capacities and can be signified only by that which, to borrow Lyotard's formulation, "puts forward the unpresentable in presentation itself," seeking "new presentations not in order to enjoy them but to impart a stronger sense of the unpresentable."[36] At issue is not a mastery of the ineffable, as in Hertz's and Weiskel's account of the romantic sublime, but rather an attestation to the unspeakable and uncontainable elements within language itself. This version of the sublime contests what Weiskel contends is the "essential claim of the romantic sublime: that man can, in feeling and speech, transcend the human" (3). Indeed, Edna wants the opposite: to find in "the unlimited" not a site of self-transcendence but rather a means of self-loss.

Edna's final swim—her going (and coming) "close to death"—must be understood both within the context of her initial encounter with the ocean and as the consequence of having awakened to desire in a social and political milieu that, as Gilbert and Gubar so rightly suggest, offers no means of articulating and sustaining her capacity for desire.[37] When, at the end of the novel, Edna tells Doctor Mandelet "perhaps it is better to wake up after all even to suffer, rather than to remain a dupe to illusions all one's life" (110), nowhere does her culture allow a means of representing her connection to the voice by which she has been called. In this context Edna's love for Robert bears no relation to his availability but rather results from his ability to manifest and facilitate her connection to the other. He is the only character attuned to Edna's need for the unlimited and until his departure for Mexico he is central to her intensifying relationship with it. Edna wants Robert because he sustains rather than satisfies her desire.

If Sappho's lyric ends by representing a merger that conflates the difference between any two sets of terms without at the same time annihilating their difference, so the end of *The Awakening* underscores the proximity and irreconcilability of opposites. Offering disparate accounts of Edna's walk into the ocean, Chopin first compares Edna to a crippled bird whose disabled wings make flying, or, in this case, living, impossible. Standing at the edge of the Gulf, Edna sees that "a bird with a broken wing was beating the air above, reeling, fluttering, circling disabled down, down to the water" (113), images that lead us to interpret Edna's last swim as a sign of her failure to survive in an oppressive world. But Chopin proceeds to suggest just the opposite. Before going into the sea, Edna removes her old bathing suit: she casts "the unpleasant, pricking garments from her, and for the first time in her life she stood naked in the open air, at the mercy of the sun, the breeze that beat upon her, and the waves that invited her" (113). Standing naked under the sky Edna feels "like some new-born creature, opening its eyes in a familiar world that it had never known," reversing the earlier connotation in which she saw that "all along the white beach, up and down, there was no living thing in sight" (113). As in Sappho's lyric, Chopin maintains the residue within language that is unhearable at the same time that she finds a new idiom for presenting its voice. But Edna's last walk into the ocean does not institute "a new idiom" in the sense that it puts speech in the place of silence (thus upholding the view that language is merely a vehicle of communication). Rather her response bears witness to the incommensurable voice she has heard. This is a "going close to death" that cannot simply be rendered by a phrase but to which phrases can testify nevertheless. Chopin's construction of the ocean's voice and the woman's response presents itself as one example of such an idiom: as a figure for the sublime, the ocean is also a figure for the unfigurable.

The novel's final paragraph, which describes Edna's last moments of consciousness, continues to foreground contradiction:

> She looked into the distance, and the old terror flamed up for an instant, then sank again. Edna heard her father's voice and her sister Margaret's. She heard the

barking of an old dog that was chained to the sycamore tree. The spurs of the cavalry officer clanged as he walked across the porch. There was the hum of bees, and the musky odor of pinks filled the air.

> (114)

Chopin insists upon the disparate. Images of triumph—looking into the distance, vanquishing "the old terror"—coincide with symbols of authority and oppression, and then give way to sensory impressions that can be construed in neither context: the "hum of bees, and the musky odor of pinks." As Jane P. Tompkins remarks:

> Contradictory signs are everywhere. . . . The sight of an injured bird implies defeat, but Edna's shedding of her bathing suit signals rebirth. The act of swimming out so far seems both calculated and almost unconsciously performed. Edna's final vision, as she goes under, is sensual and promising, Whitmanesque, but qualified by images of a chain and spurs.[38]

But whereas Tompkins chastises Chopin for leaving the reader at sea in ambiguity, Chopin's conclusion foregrounds the very incommensurability Edna desires but cannot represent. Concluding the novel by placing images that apparently exclude one another in a relation of mutual interdependence, Chopin refuses to satisfy the wish for a single or definitive interpretation of Edna's last act, and in so doing constructs a sublime in which there is no end of the line.

Notes

1. For a brief discussion of the text's authorship and history see *"Longinus" on Sublimity,* trans. D. A. Russell (Oxford: Clarendon, 1965), x-xii. See also the introduction and notes accompanying Russell's edition of the Greek text *"Longinus" on the Sublime* (Oxford: Clarendon, 1964). Following Neil Hertz, I have also consulted another recent translation, G. M. A. Grube's *Longinus on Great Writing* (New York: Bobbs-Merrill, 1957). Unless otherwise noted all further references to Longinus are to Russell's translation and occur in the text.

2. Sappho's famous ode is preserved only through inclusion in Longinus' treatise. For a discussion of Longinus' and Boileau's treatment of the poem, see Joan DeJean, *Fictions of Sappho: 1546-1937* (Chicago: University of Chicago Press, 1989), 84-87.

3. The reader may wish to read Sappho's ode in the original Greek and then compare Julia Dubnoff's literal translation of it with those provided by Russell and Grube:

> φαίνεταί μοι κῆνος ἴσος θέοισιν
> ἔμμεν' ὤνηρ, ὄττις ἐνάντιός τοι
> ἰσδάνει καὶ πλάσιον ἀδυ φωνεί-
> σας ὑπακούει
>
> καὶ γελαίσας ἰμέροεν, τό μ' ἦμὰν
> καρδίαν ἐν στήθεσιν ἐπτόαισεν,

ὠς γὰρ ἔς ς' ἴδω βρόχε' ὥς με φώναι-
ς' οὐδ' ἔν ἔτ' εἴκει,

ἀλλ' ἄκαν μὲν γλῶσσα †ἔαγε λέπτον
δ' αὔτικα χρῶι πῦρ ὑπαδεδρόμηκεν,
ὀππάτεσσι δ' οὐδ' ἔν ὄρημμ', ἐπιρρόμ-
βεισς δ' ἄκουαι,

†ἔκαδε μ' ἴδρως ψῦχρος κακχέεται† τρόμος δέ
παῖσαν ἄγρει, χλωροτέρα δε ποίας
ἔμμι, τεθνάκην δ' ὀλίγω 'πιδεύης
φαίνομ' †αι

ἀλλὰ πὰν τόλματον ἐπεὶ †καὶ πένητα†

That man to me seems equal to the gods,
the man who sits opposite you
and close by listens
to your sweet voice

and your enticing laughter—
that indeed has stirred up the heart in my breast.
For whenever I look at you even briefly
I can no longer say a single thing,

but my tongue is frozen in silence;
instantly a delicate flame runs beneath my skin;
with my eyes I see nothing;
my ears make a whirring noise.

A cold sweat covers me,
trembling seizes my body,
and I am greener than grass.
Lacking but little of death do I seem.

But all must be endured since . . .

I have relied upon the versions of Sappho that appear in Russell and Grube primarily because these are the translations Neil Hertz cites, and it is his particular reading of Sappho's lyric that is the object of this critique.

4. Peter De Bolla interestingly defines sublime discourse as discourse that produces the very excessiveness it purports to describe (*The Discourse of the Sublime: Readings in History, Aesthetics, and the Subject* [New York: Basil Blackwell, 1989], 12): "the discourse of the sublime . . . is a discourse which produces, from within itself, what is habitually termed the category of the sublime and in doing so it becomes a self-transforming discourse. The only way in which it is possible to identify this newly mutated discursive form is via its propensity to produce to excess. . . . Hence the discourse on the sublime, in its function as an analytic discourse or excessive experience, became increasingly preoccupied with the discursive production of the excess."

5. Neil Hertz, *The End of the Line: Essays on Psychoanalysis and the Sublime* (New York: Columbia University Press, 1985), 1-20. Subsequent references are to this edition and occur in the text.

6. Kate Chopin, *The Awakening,* ed. Margaret Culley (New York: Norton, 1976), 15. Subsequent references are to this edition and occur in the text.

7. Grube, *Longinus on Great Writing,* 4.

8. Suzanne Guerlac, *The Impersonal Sublime: Hugo, Baudelaire, Lautréamont* (Stanford: Stanford University Press, 1990), 3. Guerlac emphasizes that the Longinian sublime is not "merely rhetorical" but "occurs as a force of enunciation determined neither by subjective intention nor by mimetic effect" (11). Thus, she argues, "the Longinian emphasis on the act of enunciation, and, in particular, the call for the dissimulation of figurative language, is incompatible with the mimetic structure of metaphor that is at the basis of the analyses of the romantic sublime" (194). Unlike Weiskel, for whom the sublime functions as a transcendent turn, Guerlac finds in the sublime "the site within the metaphysical tradition, and within the tradition of aesthetics, of resistance to mimesis, to metaphorical recuperation or 'resolution' and to aesthetics" (194-95); see 182-93 for Guerlac's discussion of Weiskel's *Romantic Sublime* (which I cite in note 12).

9. Ronald Paulson ("Versions of a Human Sublime," *New Literary History* 16, no. 2 [Winter 1985]: 427) points out that while "studies of the sublime, from Burke to Monk and Hipple, used to focus on the enumeration of qualities in the sublime object or, more precisely, as they are reflected in the mind of the spectator . . . in the last decade, mediated by Nietzsche and Freud, by Harold Bloom and Thomas Weiskel, the focus has shifted to the agon between subject and object. The former is both/either a participant within a sublime confrontation and/or a spectator without."

10. Longinus' assumption that the sublime entails a transformation of conventional power relations anticipates Burke's famous dictum: "I know of nothing sublime which is not some modification of power" (Edmund Burke, *A Philosophical Enquiry into the Origin of our Ideas of the Sublime and Beautiful,* ed. Adam Phillips [Oxford: Oxford University Press, 1990], 59).

11. See in particular Harold Bloom, *The Anxiety of Influence* (New York: Oxford University Press, 1973). For Bloom the poet achieves sublimity only through overcoming the threat represented by the work of a "strong" precursor poet. In addition to Neil Hertz and Thomas Weiskel, recent proponents of this view include Marc W. Redfield who, in a provocative analysis of Fredric Jameson's notion of a postmodern sublime ("Pynchon's Postmodern Sublime," *PMLA* 104, no. 2 [March 1989]: 152), argues that the sublime moves "from a threatening diffusion of signs toward a more structured conflict, which enables a self

to prop itself up, so to speak, on its own anxiety, reading the confirmation of its existence in the image of its threatened destruction." In the same issue of the *PMLA,* R. Jahan Ramazani reaffirms the view that the sublime entails confrontation and/or struggle between opposing forces ("Yeats: Tragic Joy and the Sublime," *PMLA* 104, no. 2 [March 1989]: 164). Drawing upon the accounts of Hertz and Weiskel, he interprets the sublime "as a staged confrontation with death" in which "the anticipation of death gives rise to a counterassertion of life." For Ramazani "death precipitates the emotional turning called the sublime, although theorists of the sublime often refer to death by other names, or by what Kenneth Burke terms 'deflections': nothingness, castration, physical destruction, semiotic collapse, defeat by a precursor, and annihilation of the ego. Death is the recurrent obsession for these theorists, from Longinus to Heidegger and Bloom."

12. Thomas Weiskel, *The Romantic Sublime: Studies in the Structure and Psychology of Transcendence* (Baltimore: Johns Hopkins University Press, 1976), 5; Paul H. Fry, "The Possession of the Sublime," *Studies in Romanticism* 26, no. 2 (Summer 1987): 188.

13. Fry, "Possession of the Sublime," 189-90. See also Fry's discussion of Longinus' treatment of Sappho in "Longinus at Colonus," in *The Reach of Criticism: Method and Perception in Literary Theory* (New Haven: Yale University Press, 1983), 47-86.

14. A discussion regarding Longinus' commentary on Sappho occurs between Suzanne Guerlac and Frances Ferguson in *New Literary History* 16, no. 2 (Winter 1985), the issue entitled "The Sublime and the Beautiful: Reconsiderations." Although their dispute does not directly engage Sappho's portrait of desire or Longinus' reaction to it, it does address a closely related topic: the status of the subject and the kind of subjectivity at stake in the Longinian sublime. Does the sublime as represented by Longinus threaten or uphold the "unified self-identity of the subject" (275)? Guerlac and Ferguson propose very different answers, but both explore the question by examining Longinus' reading of Sappho.

In the article "Longinus and the Subject of the Sublime," Guerlac argues that theorists who emphasize pure "force of feeling" and who read Longinus from an exclusively phenomenological point of view "obscure a more radical force at work in the Longinian sublime, one which threatens the very notion of the subjectivity, or the unified self-identity of the subject" (275). Guerlac proposes to read *On the Sublime* "in terms of a 'rhetoric' of enunciation, instead of expression" in order to show that in the Longinian sublime "the subject of feeling, or the 'aesthetic' subject, is disrupted as well as the subject of certainty or the theoretical subject" (275). The success of Guerlac's argument depends upon her discussion

of Longinus' treatment of Sappho. She argues that what Longinus appreciates in the poem of Sappho "is clearly not a representation of unity, or of a unified body. The body is portrayed as broken, fragmented" (282). Rather, Longinus appreciates "the force of enunciation" through which Sappho is able to portray, and ultimately unify, the fragmented body. In Guerlac's view it is this "force of enunciation which unifies these fragments, combin[ing] them into a single whole; embodying the text and the body—which now serves as a figure for the unity of composition of the text" (282). Although Guerlac appears to challenge the notion that the sublime implies (or helps construct) a unified subject, she does not question the prevailing view that the Longinian sublime entails the achievement of textual unity or dispute his reading of Sappho's lyric. Like Longinus', Guerlac's reading represses Sappho's emphasis on semiotic and erotic transport and reiterates the view that the sublime text functions as an antidote to division. Guerlac's "force of enunciation" repairs, not underscores, fragmentation and helps to maintain textual unity, if it is not indeed equivalent to it. For if the effect of figurative language is to give the semblance of unity, how can it follow that "there is no stable ground or truth or sincerity in the event of sublimity, which, through a force of enunciation, disrupts the stable identity of the subject" (285)? Unity remains the master trope whether the "force of enunciation" or the subject produces it; Guerlac now ascribes to it the unity and power previously ascribed to the subject.

Guerlac fails to notice precisely what Ferguson remarks in her elegant article, "A Commentary on Suzanne Guerlac's 'Longinus and the Subject of the Sublime'": "the capacity of rhetoric to produce what we might call 'a subjectivity effect'" (292). Ferguson argues that although Guerlac substitutes rhetoric for subjectivity and ascribes to the former the function previously reserved for the latter, nothing has really changed. What difference, Ferguson asks, does it make if the *subject* is divided when *language* is not? "Figurativity thus comes in aid of the notion of unity, in substituting for the shattered bodily unity a figurative wholeness. What is thus disconnected in one register is unified in another" (293). While it would be extremely interesting to know Guerlac's response to Ferguson's remarks, particularly noteworthy in this context is that their debate centers on Longinus' reading of Sappho.

15. See Hertz, *The End of the Line,* 59.

16. For a study that explores the relation between gender, narrative, and a blocking agent or obstacle, see Theresa de Lauretis, "Desire in Narrative," in *Alice Doesn't: Feminism, Semiotics, Cinema* (Bloomington: Indiana University Press, 1984), 103-57. De Lauretis not only argues that narrative structure depends upon a certain sadism but holds that the subject of narrative, or mythical hero, is invariably gen-

dered as male, while the obstacle he encounters is female. According to de Lauretis, "the hero must be male regardless of the gender of the text-image, because the obstacle, whatever its personification, is morphologically female and indeed, simply, the woman" (118-19). By its very nature, then, "representation works to support the male status of the mythical subject" (140).

17. Samuel Holt Monk, *The Sublime: A Study of Critical Theories in Eighteenth-Century England* (1935; rpt., Ann Arbor: University of Michigan Press, 1960), 6. Subsequent references are to this edition and occur in the text.

18. According to Hertz, Weiskel locates in "the pre-Oedipal phases . . . the motivating power of the mathematical sublime, then sees them as rejoining a secondary system that is recognizably Oedipal and more clearly manifested in the dynamical sublime" (*The End of the Line,* 52).

19. Writing seven years after "The Notion of Blockage," Hertz concludes *The End of the Line* with an essay entitled "Afterword: The End of the Line" in which he returns to the previously unexamined question of gender that haunted his discussion of Longinus. Here Hertz inquires: "What comes *after* the end of the line . . . at the end of the line, who pays? and why?" (223). His afterword, however, enacts the very pattern of scapegoating he has already described. A discussion of the relation between gender and scapegoating in George Eliot's *Daniel Deronda* prompts Hertz to ask "how her [the Princess'] gender, her being 'The Mother,' [is] linked to her serving as scapegoat?" (229). His response is that exorcism of the princess allows Daniel to put "a pre-Oedipal mother aside when he enters the symbolic order and takes his place under the sign of his Jewish grandfather" (230). Pursuing the discussion of the pre-Oedipal stage that he had raised all too briefly in connection with Weiskel, Hertz interprets Julia Kristeva's "*L'abjet d'amour*" in a way that parallels his readings of Longinus and Kant. Just as Hertz interprets Kant's mathematical sublime through a Wordsworthian grid of blockage and release, now he reads Kristeva's concept of the non-object or "*abjet*" in terms of the mechanism of scapegoating he finds at work in *Daniel Deronda*. Whereas Kristeva's formulation of the *abjet might* have been understood not only as abjection but as the more "radical flux and dispersion of the subject" that Hertz describes in the essay on "The Notion of Blockage," he interprets it as a triumphant staving off of chaos, an instant in which the infant links itself with the paternal function. The casting out of the *vide,* of "that which could have been a chaos and which now begins to become an *abject*" (232), enables the infant's first sense of selfhood, and the movement Kristeva traces becomes a corollary to that at work in *Daniel Deronda*: "the casting out of the Princess, her abjection, is intended not to collapse the distance between author and sur-

rogate, but to stabilize it as a chosen separation and thus to ground the multiple gestures of mimesis that make up the novel" (233). The Oedipal moment of casting out differences and achieving an identification with the father, previously described as identical to the structure of the sublime, Hertz now locates at the heart of Kristeva's description of the pre-Oedipal stage. In Hertz's reading of Kristeva, the mother comes to serve the name and law of the father, recreating the same "end of the line scenario" that characterizes Hertz's treatment of Sappho. Once again Hertz evokes the possibility of an excess that cannot "be brought back home to the Father" but does so only the better to return it to him.

20. The phrase "language of the unsayable" derives from the title of the book edited by Sanford Budick and Wolfgang Iser, *Languages of the Unsayable: The Play of Negativity in Literature and Literary Theory* (New York: Columbia University Press, 1989).

21. "Selections from *The World As Will and Idea,*" Book 111, section 39, in *Philosophies of Art and Beauty: Selected Readings in Aesthetics from Plato to Heidegger,* ed. Albert Hofstadter and Richard Kuhns (New York: The Modern Library, 1964), 464.

22. Immanuel Kant, *Critique of Judgment,* section 29, trans. Werner S. Pluhar (Indianapolis: Hackett, 1987), 130. Subsequent references are to this edition and will appear in the text, along with German terms from the original (*Kritik der Urteilkraft,* ed. Wilhelm Weischedel [Frankfurt: Suhrkamp, 1974]) that I add to show that Kant talks about sacrifice and uses concepts of power and subordination to explain the function of the imagination. For an intriguing discussion of this passage, see Paul de Man, "Phenomenality and Materiality in Kant," in *Hermeneutics: Questions and Prospects,* ed. Gary Shapiro and Alan Sica (Amherst: University of Massachusetts Press, 1984), 132-35.

23. For an insightful discussion of the oceanic sublime, see Steven Z. Levine, "Seascapes of the Sublime: Vernet, Monet, and the Oceanic Feeling," *New Literary History* 16, no. 2 (Winter 1985): 377-400.

24. Gerald L. Bruns, "Disappeared: Heidegger and the Emancipation of Language," in *Languages of the Unsayable: The Play of Negativity in Literature and Literary Theory,* ed. Sanford Budick and Wolfgang Iser (New York: Columbia University Press, 1989), 127-28.

25. Theodore W. Adorno, cited in Bruns, "Disappeared," 144.

26. Edna's "flash of terror" of course recalls Burke's dictum that "terror is in all cases whatsoever either more openly or latently the ruling principle of the sublime" (*Enquiry,* 54). We focus upon Burke's sublime and his notion of terror in the following chapter.

27. Sandra M. Gilbert and Susan Gubar, *Sex Changes,* vol. 2 of *No Man's Land: The Place of the Woman Writer in the Twentieth Century* (New Haven: Yale University Press, 1989), 98. Subsequent references are to this edition and occur in the text.

28. Some of the influential readings of *The Awakening* that do not discuss the ocean's role or "voice" include Margaret Culley, "Edna Pontellier: 'A Solitary Soul,'" in her edition of *The Awakening,* 224-28; Anne Goodwin Jones, "Kate Chopin: The Life Behind the Mask," in *Tomorrow Is Another Day: The Woman Writer in the South, 1859-1936* (Baton Rouge: Louisiana State University Press, 1981), 135-82; Susan J. Rosowski, "The Novel of Awakening," *Genre* 12 (Fall 1979): 313-32; George M. Spangler, "Kate Chopin's *The Awakening*: A Partial Dissent," *Novel* 3, no. 3 (Spring 1970): 249-55; Margit Stange, "Personal Property: Exchange Value and the Female Self in *The Awakening,*" *Genders,* no. 5 (July 1989): 106-119: Ruth Sullivan and Stewart Smith, "Narrative Stances in Kate Chopin's *The Awakening,*" *Studies in American Fiction* 1, no. 1 (1973): 62-75; Lawrence Thornton, "*The Awakening*: A Political Romance," *American Literature* 52, no. 1 (March 1980): 50-66; Paula A. Treichler, "The Construction of Ambiguity in *The Awakening*: A Linguistic Analysis," in *Women And Language in Literature and Society,* ed. Sally McConnell-Ginet, Ruth Borker, Nelly Furman (New York: Praeger, 1980), 239-57; Otis B. Wheeler, "The Five Awakenings of Edna Pontellier," *Southern Review* 11, no. 1 (1975): 118-128; and Cynthia Griffin Wolff, "Thanatos and Eros," in Culley's edition of *The Awakening,* 206-18. For a reading that considers Chopin's treatment of Whitman, see Elizabeth Balken House, "*The Awakening*: Kate Chopin's 'Endlessly Rocking' Cycle," *Ball State University Forum* 20, no. 2 (Spring 1979): 53-58. For an overview of critical responses to *The Awakening* prior to 1977, see Priscilla Allen, "Old Critics and New: The Treatment of Chopin's *The Awakening,*" in *The Authority of Experience: Essays in Feminist Criticism,* ed. Arlyn Diamond and Lee R. Edwards (Amherst: University of Massachusetts Press, 1977), 224-38.

29. Dale Bauer, "Kate Chopin's *The Awakening*: Having and Hating the Tradition," in *Feminist Dialogics: A Theory of Failed Community* (Albany: State University of New York Press, 1988), 148. Subsequent references are to this edition and occur in the text.

30. Patricia Yaeger, "'A Language Which Nobody Understood': Emancipatory Strategies in *The Awakening,*" *Novel* 20, no. 3 (Spring 1987): 204. Subsequent references will be in the text.

31. Jean-François Lyotard, *The Differend: Phrases in Dispute,* trans. Georges Van Den Abbeele (Minneapolis: University of Minnesota Press, 1988), 13. Subsequent references are to this edition and occur in the text.

32. Ludwig Wittgenstein, *Tractatus Logico-Philosophicus,* trans. D. F. Pears and B. F. McGuinness (London: Routledge and Kegan Paul: 1961), prop. 7, 151.

33. "Answering the Question: What is Postmodernism?" in *The Postmodern Condition,* trans. Regis Durand (Minneapolis: University of Minnesota Press, 1984), 81. See also Lyotard's discussion of aesthetic pleasure and the sublime, "Complexity and the Sublime," in *Postmodernism: ICA Documents,* ed. Lisa Appignanesi (London: Free Association Books, 1989), 19-26. Here Lyotard emphasizes that "with the idea of the sublime, the feeling when faced with a work of art is no longer the feeling of pleasure, or not simply one of pleasure. It is a contradictory feeling, because it is a feeling of both pleasure and displeasure, together. . . . With the sublime, the question of death enters the aesthetic question" (22).

34. For Lyotard's discussion of the relation between an aesthetics of the sublime and questions of representation, see "The Sublime and the Avant-Garde," in *The Lyotard Reader,* ed. Andrew Benjamin, trans. Lisa Liebmann (Cambridge: Basil Blackwell, 1989), 196-211. Lyotard's most comprehensive discussion of Kant's sublime occurs in *Lessons on the Analytic of the Sublime,* trans. Elizabeth Rottenberg (Stanford: Stanford University Press, 1994). On Lyotard's notions of representation and postmodernity, see Bill Readings, *Introducing Lyotard: Art and Politics* (London: Routledge, 1991), 53-85; and David Carroll, *Paraesthetics: Foucault, Lyotard, Derrida* (New York: Methuen, 1987), 155-84.

35. Walter Benn Michaels, "The Contracted Heart," *New Literary History* 21, no. 3 (Spring 1990): 498. Subsequent references will be in the text.

36. Lyotard, *The Postmodern Condition,* 81.

37. Gilbert and Gubar, *No Man's Land,* 97.

38. Jane P. Tompkins, "The Awakening: An Evaluation," *Feminist Studies* 3, nos. 3-4 (Spring-Summer 1976): 24.

Cynthia Griffin Wolff (essay date spring 1996)

SOURCE: Griffin Wolff, Cynthia. "Un-Utterable Longing: The Discourse of Feminine Sexuality in *The Awakening.*" *Studies in American Fiction* 24, no. 1 (spring 1996): 3-23.

[*In the following essay, Wolff examines* The Awakening *in terms of nineteenth-century medical discourse on female sexuality.*]

Because novelists are particular about beginnings, we should notice that ***The Awakening*** opens with two things: sumptuous sensory images and an outpouring of babble—

words that resemble ordinary speech, but which really have meaning for no one, not even the speaker.

> A green and yellow parrot, which hung in a cage outside the door, kept repeating over and over:
>
> "Allez vous-en! Allez vous-en! Sapristi! That's all right!"
>
> He could speak a little Spanish, and also a language which nobody understood.[1]

Although an onlooker is able to enjoy this vivid scene, the parrot cannot; moreover, there is a sense of enigma (or fraud) about this bird who seems able to communicate, but is not. Indeed, the absolute discontinuity among the bird's "discourse," its exotic plumage, and its feelings (whatever they may be) is even more significant to the larger themes of the novel than the fact that he is caged. Or perhaps this very disconnectedness (and the bird's consequent isolation) defines the cage.

Critics admire the "modernism" of Chopin's work, the strong spareness of the prose and the "minimalism" of a narrative whose absences are at least as important as its action and whose narrator maintains strict emotional and moral neutrality. What we may not fully appreciate is the relationship between these elements and Edna Pontellier's personal tragedy, a relationship whose terms are announced by the apparent disarray of the novel's brilliant beginning. This is a tale about not speaking, about disjunction—about denials, oversights, prohibitions, exclusions, and absences. Not merely about things that are never named, but most significantly about stories that cannot be told and things that can be neither thought nor spoken because they do not have a name.

After about 1849, the notion of a "woman's sexual awakening" became, by definition, an impossibility—a contradiction in terms—because the medical establishment in America began to promulgate the view that normal females possessed no erotic inclinations whatsoever (and one cannot awaken something that does not exist). William Acton, the acknowledged expert on the nature of women's sexuality and author of "one of the most widely quoted books on sexual problems and diseases in the English-speaking world,"[2] wrote:

> I have taken pains to obtain and compare abundant evidence on this subject, and the result of my inquiries I may briefly epitomize as follows:—I should say that the majority of women (happily for society) are not very much troubled with sexual feeling of any kind. What men are habitually women are only exceptionally. It is too true, I admit, as the divorce courts show, that there are some few women who have sexual desires so strong that they surpass those of men, and shock public feeling by their consequences.[3]

Acton's work elaborated a comprehensive system of women's "inequality" to men; and it was so universally respected that his sentiments can be taken to represent opinions that were held throughout much of America during the second half of the nineteenth century. Certainly they define the attitudes of that stem Presbyterian world in which Edna Pointellier grew to maturity.[4]

In fact, Edna's particular religious background could not have been chosen casually by Chopin, for a woman reared in this faith during the 1870s and 1880s (the years of Edna's youth) would have been preternaturally susceptible to the most crippling elements of Acton's strictures.

American Calvinism always preached that although the woman was to be "regarded as equal to man. in her title to grace," she was nonetheless "the weaker vessel," and was thus obliged to pursue all endeavors as a "subordinate to the husband."[5] During the later nineteenth century, Presbyterianism was generally regarded as a conservative bastion for such ideas, and many Presbyterians themselves construed their mission as one of upholding precisely these conservative-religious values. Not surprisingly, then, beginning in the 1870s and continuing through the end of the century, the Presbyterian church in America suffered a crisis over the role of women that might well be defined by the question, "Shall Women Speak?"[6]

The embroglio began when a Newark clergyman invited two women into his pulpit to speak in favor of the Temperance Movement. Seeing an opportunity to reaffirm the precedent of women's "naturally" subordinate role, the Presbytery of Newark brought formal charges against the minister. In the minds of the accusers, the issue was far from narrow:

> "I believe the subject involves the honor of my God. . . . My argument is subordination of sex. . . . There exists a created subordination; a divinely arranged and appointed subordination of woman as woman to man as man. Woman was made for man. . . . The proper condition of the adult female is marriage; the general rule for ladies is marriage. . . . Man's place is on the platform. It is positively base for a woman to speak in the pulpit. . . . The whole question is one of subordination."[7]

For both the Puritan Fathers and their late nineteenth-century Calvinist descendants, the specter of a woman speaking out was portentous: at best, it was unsettling to the male hierarchy; at worst, it augured chaos. Suffragists could also discern the importance of this case, and the dispute among Newark Presbyterians became a notorious part of "the record of their struggle" and was widely publicized.[8]

This kind of "woman-problem" had first arisen in America when Anne Hutchinson "stepped out of the role the community defined for her," for "if a woman could instruct men, then all legitimate authority was in jeopardy."[9] The prototypical response had been formulated in Hutchinson's day: require women to assume their divinely ordained, subordinate position. Their failure to do so would result (so the argument ran) not merely in civil misrule, but in grotesque sexual misconduct. Thus in the Hutchinson case, the phantoms of both social turmoil and sexual license haunted the trial: "everywhere in the court examination, one finds the insinuation that Hutchinson is, like Jezebel, guilty of fornication."[10] Confronted with what they feared might become a similar provocation, the Presbyterian clergymen of Edna Pointellier's youth demanded that woman keep to their "natural sphere" of home, hearth, and motherhood. As for women's sexuality, William Acton was their more than sufficient spokesman.

All of Acton's formulations are sweepingly comprehensive and inescapably normative, and in this respect he greatly resembles the Puritans. He does not admit of gradations among women; nor does he entertain the possibility that additional data—testimony from women themselves, perhaps—might contradict or even emend his pronouncements. Instead, he presents his ideas as nothing less than a description of both a divinely ordained condition and a condition for middle-class respectability. He clearly considers the absence of passion in "normal women" to be a good thing (for its presence in a decent female would "shock public feeling"); and he refers dismissively to "prostitutes" and "loose, or, at least, low and vulgar women" whose strong libidinous drives "give a very false idea of the condition of female sexual feelings in general." In short, the innate frigidity of women signified a form of refinement and could be used as a touchstone for respectability.[11]

The official "scientific" and "medical" view can be stated quite simply: an average woman (a "decent" woman) possesses no sexual feelings whatsoever. Thus it is not enough to say that *The Awakening* is a novel about repression (that is, about a situation in which a woman possesses sexual feelings, but is prohibited from acting upon them). It is, instead, a novel about a woman whose shaping culture has, in general, refused her right to speak out freely; this is, moreover, a culture that construes a woman's self-expression as a violation of sexual "purity" and a culture that has denied the existence of women's libidinous potential altogether—has eliminated the very concept of sexual passion for "normal" women.

The consequences are emotionally mutilating (in the extreme case, some form of mental breakdown would result). In such a culture, if a "respectable" woman supposes herself to feel "something," some powerful ardor in her relationship with a man, she can draw only two possible inferences. Either her feelings are not sexual (and should not be enacted in a genital relationship), or she is in some (disgraceful) way "abnormal." Moreover, because there is presumed to be no such entity as sexual feelings in the typical woman, a typical (i.e. "normal") woman will literally have no words for her (nonexistent) feelings, will have access to no discourse within which these (nonexistent) passions can be examined or discussed, will be; able to make no coherent connection between the (unintelligible) inner world of her affective life and the external, social world in which she must live.[12] Finally, if she feels confusion and emotional pain, her culture's general prohibition against speaking out will make it difficult, perhaps impossible, to discuss or even reveal her discomfort.

Of course there was an escape hatch (infinitesimal and insufficient). After all, men and women did marry, did have sexual intercourse, doubtless did (sometimes) enjoy their love-making, and did (occasionally) find ways to discuss the intimate elements of their relationship. Indeed, the range of actual situations for females in America at the end of the nineteenth century—among various cultural groups, among diverse regions—was undoubtedly rather great. Yet the normative pronouncements regarding women's "proper" behavior in this age of Anthony Comstock (founder of the Society for the Suppression of Vice and the man who succeeded in having the Act which bears his name passed in 1873) were stringent—as were the assumptions about public behavior.[13]

The extent and resourcefulness of individual solutions to this situation must remain a mystery. However, the publicly approved forms of discourse for female desire are a matter of record. Medical and psychological experts concluded that although women had no sexual drives per se, they often possessed a passionate desire to bear children: such ardor was both "normal" and (inevitably) sexual. On these terms, then, sexual activity—even moderate sexual "desire"—was appropriate in "normal" women. However, a profound displacement or confusion was introduced by this accommodation: the language of feminine sexuality became inextricably intertwined with discourse that had to do with child-bearing and motherhood.

According to Acton (and others who followed his lead), nature itself had made the longing to have children the essential, causative force of a woman's sexual "appetite." Thus men and women were essentially different: men have sexual impulses and needs (and these are quite independent of any wish to sire offspring); women crave children (and consequently they might be said—very indirectly—to "want" sexual activity). "Virility" and "maternity" were defined as parallel instincts that were nonetheless fundamentally dissimilar; and a woman's possessing sexual ardor independent of her yearning for babies became a defining symptom of abnormality or immorality or both:

> It is to be expected, that, at the time when the man is physically in the fittest state to procreate his species, nature should provide him with a natural and earnest desire . . . to the commission of the act. . . . He now instinctively seeks the society of women. Intercourse with females increases his excitement, and all is ready for the copulative act. . . .
>
> He feels that MANHOOD has been attained, he experiences all those mysterious sensations which make up what we call VIRILITY. . . .
>
> This feeling of virility is much more developed in man than is that of maternity in woman.
>
> If the married female conceives every second year, we usually notice that during the nine months following conception she experiences no great sexual excitement. . . .

Love of home, of children, and of domestic duties are the only passions [women] feel. As a general rule, a modest woman seldom desires any sexual gratification for herself. She submits to her husband's embraces, but principally to gratify him; and were it not for the desire of maternity, would far rather be relieved from his attentions.[14]

Scholars have accepted almost as chiche the fact that in late Victorian America "motherhood" was exalted as an all-but-divine state. However, if we do not also understand the oblique (and contradictory) sexual implications of this cultural ideal, we may be unaware of the confusion and conflict it engendered.

This definition of feminine sexuality radically displaced a woman's passionate desires: unlike males, who were permitted to "possess" their sexuality and were consequently allowed to experience passion directly and as a part of the "self," females were allowed access to sexuality only indirectly—as a subsidiary component of the desire for children. It was literally unimaginable that any "decent" woman would experience sexual appetite as an immediate and urgent drive, distinct from all other desires and duties. In emotional terms, men "owned" their libido; however, women's libido was "owned" by their prospective children.[15]

Any woman would find this concatenation of denials and demands unbalancing; however, in Edna's case, the already vexed situation is heightened by a severe conflict of cultures. In a society where the actual experiences of women were diverse and the normative pronouncements were stringent, Chopin has constructed a novel where extremes converge to demonstrate the malignant potential of these normative attitudes, and she marks the summer at Grand Isle as the moment when crisis begins.

Reared as a Presbyterian in Kentucky, Edna has been married to a Creole for many years. Nonetheless, she has never-become "thoroughly at home in the society of Creoles; [and] never before had she been thrown so intimately among them" (pp. 27-28). It is not that these people do not have a rigorous sexual code: their customs follow the boundary conditions that Acton and his fellow theorists postulated. However, far from being Bible-bound, sober, and staid, so long as they remain within the rules of this code, Creoles permit themselves an extraordinary freedom of sensual expression. Thus a lusty carnal appetite in men is taken for granted. (Robert has his affair with the Mexican girl, everyone knows about it, and no one thinks to disapprove.) However, the case of Creole women is different, for their sexuality may exist only as a component of "motherhood." Nevertheless, so long as they accept this model, women, too, may engage in a sumptuous sexual life. Mme. Ratignolle, the "sensuous Madonna," embodies the essence of ardor and voluptuary appetite thus construed.

Such a system imposes penalties (Adele's accouchement is one specific marker for the price to be paid); however,

within these limiting conditions, the Creole world is more densely erotic than any community Edna has encountered. It revels frankly and happily in the pleasures of the flesh—not merely enjoying these delights with undisguised zest, but discussing them in public with no shame at all. Edna can recognize the inherent "chastity" of such people, but their habits nonetheless embarrass her profoundly:

> Madame Ratignolle had been married seven years. About every two years she had a baby. At that time she had three babies, and was beginning to think of a fourth one. She was always talking about her "condition." Her "condition" was in no way apparent, and no one would have known a thing about it but for her persistence in making it the subject of conversation.
>
> (p. 27)

A late twentieth century reader may innocently suppose that Adele's preoccupation is purely maternal. The full truth is quite otherwise: in the discourse of the day, Adele has elected to flaunt her sexuality—to celebrate both her ardor and her physical enjoyment. Robert enters the festive, flirtatious moment by recalling the "lady who had subsisted upon nougat during the entire—," and is checked only by Edna's blushing discomfort.

All such instances of candor unsettle Mrs. Pontellier.[16] This strange world, with its languorous climate and frankly sensuous habits, is a world where "normal," "respectable" women openly vaunt pleasures that are unfamiliar to Edna Pontellier. She is fascinated, stimulated, eventually profoundly aroused. And although she is bewildered by these new sensations, once having been touched by them, she becomes unwilling to pull away. Much of the novel, theft, is concerned with Edna's quest for a viable and acceptable mode of owning and expressing her sexuality: first by locating the defining boundaries for these feelings and thus being able to define and name what she feels inside herself; second by finding some acceptable social construct which will permit her to enact what she feels in the outside world and to make an appropriate, vital, and affirming connection between the "me" and the "not-me."[17]

Edna's easiest option is "collusion," to become a "mother-woman"; however, she rejects this role violently because Of the displacements and forfeitures that it would impose. If, like Adele, she were willing to disguise her erotic drives in the mantle of "motherhood," she might indulge the many delights of the body as Adele patently does. However, such a capitulation would not allow her really to possess her own feelings—nor even to talk about them directly or explicitly. It would maim the "self," not unify and affirm it: like Adele, Edna would be obliged to displace all of her sexual discourse into prattle about "the children" or her (pregnant) "condition," fettering her carnal desires to the production of babies; and part of what was really inside (that is, her sexual drive) would have been displaced on to something outside (society's construction of female appetite as essentially "maternal"). In the process, the authority and integrity of her identity would have been compromised, and instead of making contact with the outside world, she would be merged into and controlled by it. Edna loves her children and is happy to be a mother; however, she refuses to define her sexuality in terms of them.[18]

Thus Edna's rejection of this emotional mutilation lies behind the novel's many tortured examinations of her relationship to the children and informs such assertions as: "I would give up the unessential; I would give my money, I would give my life for my children; but I wouldn't give myself" (p. 67). Edna's children make very few actual demands upon her time or energy (and she has all the "childcare" one might desire). Thus the emphatic quality of her renunciation addresses not a real burden, but the internalized social directive. Renouncing what she can clearly recognize as an unacceptable violation of her emotional integrity is Edna's most confident step toward freedom.

She shrugs away from marriage for many of the same reasons, declaring that she will "never again belong to another than herself" (p. 100). The problem is neither immediate nor personal: it is not Leonce, per se, that Edna repudiates, but the warped forms of intimacy that he represents.[19] Like Adele, Leonce is acquainted with no discourse off eminine sexuality other than some variant on the language of "motherhood." This conflation is revealed in the first intimate scene between Leonce and Edna (Chapter 3). Leonce has returned from an evening of card-playing, jolly at having won a little money—"in excellent humor . . . high spirits, and very talkative" (p. 23). To be sure, he does not "court" his wife; yet he is scarcely brutal or coarse, and his gossipy, somewhat preoccupied manner as he empties his pockets might be that of any long-married man. Indeed, it is Edna's unapproachable manner that disrupts the potential harmony of the moment. There is nothing peculiar about the "action" of this scenario, nor is it difficult to read the subtext: Leonce would like to conclude his pleasant evening with a sexual encounter; his wife is not interested.

The real oddity has to do with language. Although the couple falls into a kind of argument over their differing inclinations, sex itself is never mentioned. Instead, when Leonce chooses to rebuke his wife (presumably for her passional indifference to him), he employs a vernacular of "motherhood" to do so. "He reproached his wife with her inattention, her habitual neglect of the children. If it was not a mother's place to look after children, whose on earth was it?" (p. 24). With this alienated discourse, neither party can talk about the real source of unhappiness, and sexual harmony within the marriage is threatened or compromised. Leonce at least has "acceptable" alternatives (for example, we should probably not suppose that he is celibate during his long absences from home). Edna has none—not even the satisfaction of being able to define the exact nature of her despondency.[20]

She generally shuns the effort to assert herself, and to a remarkable degree she has detached herself from language altogether. As Joseph R. Urgo has observed, "For the first six chapters of the novel, she says all of four sentences."[21] Moreover, although she has lived among the Creoles for many years, "she understood French imperfectly unless directly addressed" (p. 56). On this occasion, then, it is not surprising that she "said nothing and refused to answer her husband when he questioned her" (p. 24). This is her customary reaction. Although Chopin's narrator refrains from moralizing about Edna's predicament, she does give the reader information from which it is possible to extrapolate Mrs. Pontellier's reason.s for avoiding speech.

After her minor disagreement with Leonce, Edna begins to weep: "She could not have told why she was crying. . . . An indescribable oppression, which seemed to generate in some unfamiliar part of her conscious, filled her whole being with a vague anguish" (pp. 24-25). At the most literal level, Edna is absolutely unable to "tell" why she is crying: her deepest passions have no "true" name. Society has given them only false names, like "maternity"; and such a discourse of feminine sexuality both distorts a woman's feelings and compromises her authority over them. Thus Edna's recoil.from language—her refusal to comply with this misrepresentation—is a primitive effort to retain control over her "self."

> Even as a child she had lived her own small life all within herself. At a very early period she had apprehended instinctively the dual life—that outward existence which conforms, the inward life which questions.
>
> (p. 32)
>
> She had all her life long been accustomed to harbor thoughts and emotions which never voiced themselves. They had never taken the form of struggles. They belonged to her and were her own, and she entertained the conviction that she had a right to them and that they concerned no one but herself.
>
> (pp. 66-67)

Nor is it surprising that Edna has always been deeply susceptible to fantasies—to her inward "dreams" of the cavalry officer, of the engaged young man from a neighboring plantation, of the "great tragedian." A person can and does entirely possess the products of his or her own imagination because (like the passions which infuse them) they are a part of the self. Thus falling into fantasy becomes another way by which Edna seeks to maintain the integrity of self.

In some primitive way, silence also is Edna's only appropriate reaction to society's way of defining female sexuality: for if women were imagined to have no sexual feelings, not to speak would (ironically) be the way to "communicate" this absence. Yet not to speak has an annihilating consequence: it is, in the end, not to be—not to have social reality. One can never affirm "self" merely through silence and fantasy—can never forge that vital connection between the "me" and the "notme" that validates identity. (Even the "fantasy" of art is embedded in an act of communication between the "me" and the "not-me?") A "self can mature only if one strives to articulate emotions; learning to name one's feelings is an integral component of learning the extent and nature of one's feelings, and what is undescribed may remain Sways "indescribable"—even to oneself—"vague" and even "unfamiliar." Moreover, without some authentic, responsive reaction from another, no one can escape the kind of solitude that increasingly oppresses Edna during the summer of her twenty-ninth year.[22]

Indeed, the dispassionate tone of Chopin's novel may be related to the complexity of Edna's quest, for Edna cannot "solve" her problem without an extraordinary feat of creativity. She must discover not merely a new vernacular with which to name her feelings—not merely a new form of plot that is capable of containing them—but also an "audience" that both comprehends and esteems the story she might ultimately tell. Thus the true subject of *The Awakening* may be less the particular dilemma of Mrs. Pontellier than the larger problems of female narrative that it reflects; and if Edna's poignant fate is in part a reflection of her own habits, it is also, in equal part, a measure of society's failure to allow its women a language of their own.

Most immediately personal is Edna's enchantment with forms of "communication" that do not require words. She is entranced by the ocean because its "language" neither compromises nor distorts her most intimate passions. Yet it cannot allow her to assert and confirm "self"; for ironically, like society, the sea requires an immersion of "self" (and this is, perhaps, the reason Edna has feared the water for so long).

> Seductive; never ceasing, whispering, clamoring, murmuring, inviting the soul to wander for a spell in abysses of solitude; to lose itself in mazes of inward contemplation.
>
> The voice of the sea speaks to the soul. The touch of the sea is sensuous, enfolding the body in its soft, close embrace.
>
> (p. 32)

Music, also seems to have "spoken" to Edna, most often conjuring primly conventional emotional "pictures" in her mind. However, as soon as she stirs from her sensual torpor and discards the prim and the conventional, music begins to conjure something more violently demanding: "no pictures of solitude, of hope, of longing, or of despair. But the very passions themselves were aroused with her soul, swaying it, lashing it, as the waves daily beat upon her splendid body" (p. 45). Without the customary "pictures" to contain them, these emotions clamor for expression with an intensity that is all but unbearable.

It is troubling that the narrative formulations to which Edna is habitually drawn are so formulaic, that they decline to attempt some model of feminine initiative or some assertion of, explicitly feminine passion. She configures her outing with Robert as "Sleeping Beauty" ("'How many years have I slept?' she inquired" [p. 57]). Her dinner-table story is passive—the romance of a woman who was carried off "by her lover one night in a pirogue and never came back" (p. 90). And if, as Sandra Gilbert has argued, Edna presides over a "Swinburnian Last Supper" just before her death, this moment when the "old ennui" and "hopelessness" overtake her once again must be read not as a new birth of Venus, but as a poignant prefiguration of her return to that sea whence she came (p. 109).[23]

Yet troubling as Edna's habits of mind may be, Chopin also makes it clear that it would have taken more than daring ingenuity to alter her situation. The demand for women's rights alarmed sexual theorists, who construed all changes in the accepted paradigm as portents of anarchy:

> "The tendency of our generation [is] to break up old associations, and to be emancipated from the beliefs of our fathers. . . . This feeling crops out in publicly ridiculing marriage, dwelling on its evils . . . demanding 'women's rights.'"

Their response was to reaffirm the conventional life-story by insisting that women's dissatisfactions could be readily dismissed as nothing but an evidence of their innate inferiority.

> "In medical colleges, in medical books, in medical practice, woman is recognized as having a peculiar organization, requiring the most careful and gentle treatment. . . . Her bodily powers are not able to endure like those of the other sex."[24]

When Leonce begins to discern the differences in Edna's manner and takes his concerns to Dr. Mandelet, their conversation is uncannily similar to these nineteenth-century discussions of woman's nature.

> "She's odd, she's not like herself. I can't make her out . . . She's got some sort of notion in her head concerning the eternal rights of women." . . .
>
> "Woman, my dear friend," [the Doctor responds,] "is a very peculiar and delicate organism—a sensitive and highly organized woman, such as I know Mrs. Pontellier to be, is especially peculiar. . . . Most women are moody and whimsical."
>
> (pp. 85-86)

It would take invention and resolution indeed to counter such a confident weight of received opinion—more than most women (most people) possess.

If the power of Edna's narrative ability is insufficient to retaliate against such fettering force, her primary choice of "audience" merely recapitulates her other problems. Instead of perusing Robert's true nature, she fancies him to be the lover of her dreams. She does not heed the conventions within which their flirtation begins; instead (as Addle observes), she makes "the unfortunate blunder of taking [him] seriously" (p. 35). Nor does she very much attend to Robert's conversation; for although he has spoken enthusiastically of going to Mexico, his untimely departure catches her entirely by surprise. Thus the exact nature of their intimacy is always best for Edna when it must be inferred (because it has not been put into words):

> [Robert] seated himself again and rolled a cigarette, which he smoked in silence. Neither did Mrs. Pontellier speak. No multitude of words could have been more significant than those moments of silence, or more pregnant with the first-felt throbbings of desire.
>
> (p. 49)

Neither the reader nor Edna herself can know whose "desire" has been felt nor precisely what the object of this "desire" might be. However, the (almost overtly ironic) use of "pregnant" suggests that it is Edna, and not Robert, who has suffused this moment with unique intensity—and, most important, that she has not yet escaped all of those conventional constructions of female sexuality that bind it to maternity.

Mlle. Reisz and Alcee Arobin (characters in Edna's nascent narratives and audiences for them) both hold out the possibility that Edna might resolve her dilemma by usurping the prerogatives of men. Yet each offers a "solution" that would constrain Edna to relinquish some significant and valued portion of herself.

Ivy Schweitzer has observed that Mlle. Reisz, "a musician and composer, represents one extreme possibility; she exemplifies the artist with '. . . The soul that dares and defies' conventionality, transgresses boundaries, and transcends gender."[25] Mlle. Reisz also holds out the independence that men can achieve in a career. Yet Edna chooses not to follow this avenue; and Mlle. Reisz's admonition that the artist "must possess the courageous soul" (p. 83) may have been less of a deterrent than a statement about the example of that lady's own life. Fulfillment through aesthetic creativity appears to offer authentic expression to only one portion of the self. Mlle. Reisz "had quarreled with almost everyone, owing to a temper which was self-assertive and a disposition to trample upon the rights of others"; having no sensuous charm or aesthetic allure ("a homely woman with a small weazened face and body and eyes that glowed" [p. 44]), she presents a sad and sorry prospect of some future Edna-as-successful-artist. What woman seeking sexual fulfillment would willing follow the pathway to such a forfeiture of feminine sensuous pleasure as this?

Arobin offers the opposite. Something simpler, but equally wounding. Lust. Sex divorced from all other feelings. The expression of that raw libido that was presumed to be part of men's nature (as "virility"), but categorically denied as a component of the normal female. Yet Edna finds that limiting sexuality to this form of expression imposes a distortion fully as destructive as society's construction of "maternity."

Paobin pursues Edna by pretending that casual sexuality is some fuller, more "sincere" emotion (he is careful never to mention love). And although his practiced style invites "easy confidence," it is also filled with "effrontery" (p.

96)—with the desire to treat her as no more than a "beautiful, sleek animal waking up in the sun" (p. 90). His manher could seem "so genuine that it often deceived even himself"; yet "in her cooler, quieter moments," Edna recognizes that it would be "absurd" to take him seriously (p. 98). This form of eroticism explicitly excludes the integral complexity of Edna's unique "self": she might be anyone, any "sleek animal waking up in the sun," any woman whose "latent sensuality [would unfold] under his delicate sense of her nature's requirements like a torpid, torrid sensitive blossom" (p. 126). Thus the aftermath of their consummation is not an affirmation of identity for Edna, but another form of maiming—a cascade of simple sentences in largely parallel form to configure alienation and disintegration—the novel's shortest, most mutilated chapter. Less than half a page. These lay bare the harsh realities of existence, "beauty and brutality," and conclude with nothing but a "dull pang of regret because it was not the kiss of love which had inflamed her" (p. 104).

By the time Robert returns, Edna has all but exhausted the limited possibilities of her world; and if her first preference is once again to construe him as dream-like—"for he had seemed nearer to her off there in Mexico" (p. 124)—she has gained the courage to speak forbidden discourse in the hope of inventing a new kind of narrative. "I suppose this is what you would call unwomanly," she begins, "but I have got into a habit of expressing myself. It doesn't matter to me, and you may think me unwomanly if you like" (p. 127). They return to her little house, and when Robert seems to doze in a chair, she rewrites the sleeping beauty story by reversing their roles and awakening him with a kiss, "a soft, cool, delicate kiss, whose voluptuous sting penetrated his whole being. . . . She put her hand up to his face and pressed his cheek against her own. The action was full of love and tenderness" (pp. 128-29).

Reality is the realm into which Edna would lead Robert: a complex kingdom of sensuous freedom commingled with "love and tenderness," a place where man and woman awaken each other to share the "beauty and brutality" of life together in mutual affirmation. Each owning sexual appetite; both sharing the stem burdens of brute passion.

Edna is shocked, then, to discover Robert continuing to speak a language of "dreams": "I lost my senses. I forgot everything but a wild dream of your some way becoming my wife" (p. 129). Even worse, Robert's "dream" retains the confining accounterments of the narrative Edna has journeyed so far to escape. She wants a new paradigm; he merely wants to rearrange the actors of the old one, and Edna firmly rejects his falsifying, custom-bound notions: "You have been a very, very foolish boy, wasting your time dreaming of impossible things. . . . I give myself where I choose" (p. 129). When Robert responds with perplexity to this new assertion of autonomy, Edna is offered the opportunity to show him what fortitude might mean.

Female sexuality had been falsified by the construct of "maternity"; however, there was one barbarous component of femininity, one consequence of feminine sexuality, that even the mother-woman could never evade.

In the nineteenth century, with its still-primitive obstetrical practices and its high child-mortality rates, she was expected to face severe bodily pain, disease, and death—and still serve as the emotional support and strength of her family. As the eminent Philadelphia neurologist S. Weir Mitchell wrote in the 1880s, "We may be sure that our daughters will be more likely to have to face at some time the grim question of pain than the lads who grow up beside them. . . . To most women . . . there comes a time when pain is a grim presence in their lives."[26]

Having confronted the harsh "masculine" fact of unmitigated sexual desire, Edna entreats Robert to comprehend the inescapable pain and danger of the "feminine" by acknowledging the reality of childbirth. Having risked the scorn of being judged "unwomanly" by speaking her feelings and by awakening Robert with an act of love and passion conjoined, she asks him to demonstrate comparable courage. He, too, must leave dreams and half-truths behind, must comprehend the full complexity of her experience—both the brutality and the beauty—if he is to share in the creation of this new narrative of ardent devotion. "Wait," she implores, as she leaves to attend Adele; "I shall come back" (p. 130).

After the delivery, Edna's still-fragile emergent self is shaken. In response to Dr. Mandelet queries, she once again shrugs away from language: "I don't feel moved to speak of things that trouble me." Her desires continue to trail a fairy-tale hope of absolute happiness: "I don't want anything but my own way" (p. 132). Still her anticipated reunion with Robert fortifies her. She foresees the opportunity to resume their love-making: and she believes there will a "time to think of everything (p 133) on the morning to follow, a chance to fashion the story of their life together. However, she has refused to consider his weakness and his fondness for illusions. Thus she is unprepared for the letter she finds: "I love you. Good-by—because I love you" (p. 134). In the end, Edna has discovered no partner/audience with whom to construct her new naftative, and she cannot concoct one in solitude.

Nonetheless, she concludes with a narrative gesture of sorts—a concatenation of the parlance of "maternity." Perhaps it is a tale of the son, Icarus, defeated by overweening ambition: "A bird with a broken wing was beating the air above, reeling, fluttering, circling disabled down, down to the water" (p. 136). Perhaps a tale of babies: "Naked in the open air . . . she felt like some new-born creature, opening its eyes in a familiar world that it had never known" (p. 136). Most likely, it is a tragic inversion of the birth of Venus: "The touch of the sea is sensuous, enfolding the body in its soft, close embrace (p. 136).

So Edna has failed. Or rather, being a woman with some weaknesses and no extraordinary strengths, Edna has chosen the only alternative she could imagine to the ravaging

social arrangements of her day. (Only seven years earlier, "The Yellow Wallpaper" had attracted wide attention to the same stifling, potentially annihilating constructions of "femininity.") However, we must not overlook the fact that if her heroine faltered, Kate Chopin fashioned a splendid success. *The Awakening* is the new narrative that Mrs. Pontellier was unable to create: not (it is true) a story of female affirmation, but rather an excruciatingly exact dissection of the ways in which society distorts a woman's true nature. The ruthless contemporary reviews leave no doubt that Kate Chopin had invented a powerful (and thus threatening) discourse for feminine sexuality. And although the novel was forced to languish (Like yet another "sleeping beauty") largely unread for three quarters of a century, the current respect it enjoys is a belated affirmation of Kate Chopin's SUCCESS.

Notes

1. Kate Chopin, *The Awakening,* ed. Nancy A. Walker (New York: St. Martin's, 1993) p. 19. Hereafter cited parenthetically.

2. Carl N. Degler, *At Odds: Women and the Family in American from the Revolution to the Present* (New York: Oxford Univ. Press, 1980), P.250.

3. William Acton, *The Functions and Disorders of the Reproductive Organs in Childhood, Youth, Adult Age, and Advanced Life,* 4th ed. (Philadelphia: Lindsay and Blakiston, 1875), 162-63. We might be tempted to suppose that this attitude was in some essential way "Puritanical." However, since Carl Degler makes it clear that these explicit notions of women as totally devoid of passion entered American culture rather late, it is important to understand the distinction between the two attitudes. Puritans believed that women possessed sexual inclinations, but that these were a remnant of humankind's innate depravity. "Cases of adultery in 18th-century America also reveal the acceptance of the idea that women's sexuality could be strong," Degler points out, and "advice books of the early 19th century could also be quite explicit in describing women's sexual anatomy" (Degler, pp. 251-52). The late nineteenth-century theorists believed that women did not possess passion at all. In his book on prostition, Acton focuses entirely upon the urgency of the male's sexual desire and the absolute necessity of providing an "outlet" for it. William Acton, *Prostitution,* ed. Peter Fryer (New York: Praeger, 1968), pp. 198ff.

4. In depicting Edna's repressive background, Chopin identifies this Presbyterianism with Edna's suppression of overt, real-life sexuality. "During one period of my life," Edna tells Adele, "religion took a firm hold upon me; after I was twelve and until—until—why, I suppose until now, though I never though much about it—just driven along by habit" (p. 35). It is significant that the age Edna mentions is both the age at which girls begin to mature sexually and the age at which Carol Gilligan has found that many

women "lose their voice." Carol Gilligan, In *A Different Voice: Psychological Theory and Women's Development* (Cambridge: Harvard Univ. Press, 1982), pp. 12ff. Acton's views were not universally accepted, however. The aspiring middle and upper classes of urban areas were more inclined than others to accept his paradigm. See Ellen K. Rothman, *Hands and Hearts: A History of Courtship in America* (New York: Basic, 1984), pp. 87-177.

5. William Hailer, *The Rise of Puritanism* (New York: Harper, 1957), p. 121.

6. Lois A. Boyd, "Shall Women Speak?" *The Journal of Presbyterian History* 56 (1978), 281-94. See also Lois A. Boyd and Douglas Brackenridge, *Presbyterian Women in America* (Westport: Greenwood, 1983): "During the last two decades of the nineteenth century, the inherent conservatism of the Presbyterian church caused social customs and traditions to be modified only slowly and not without tension and turmoil" (p. 108).

7. Boyd, "Shall Women Speak?" p. 287, quoting from the proceedings of the case against Isaac McBride See in December 1876.

8. Boyd, "Shall Women Speak?" p. 291.

9. Amy Schrager Lang, *Prophetic Woman: Anne Hutchinson and the Problem of Dissent in the Literature of New England* (Berkeley: Univ. of California Press, 1987), pp. 42-43.

10. Lang, P. 43.

11. Acton's discussion of "nymphomania" reveals the era's obsessive need to control women's sexuality whenever it might be manifested—and especially to surpress any inclination toward masturbation (*On Organs,* 162-63). It is difficult to understand why anyone would suppose masturbation to present a problem in the "normal" woman (or girl) if a complete absence of sexuality is the "natural" condition for females. This entire discussion is interesting because it reveals the inherent confusions and contradictions of Acton's theories (and perhaps the contrary data provided by his actual medical practice).

12. Smith-Rosenberg's description of the treatment of "hysteria" gives a chillingly graphic account of society's need to subdue sexuality in women. See Carroll Smith Rosenberg, *Disorderly Conduct: Visions of Gender in Victorian America* (New York: Alfred A. Knopf, 1985), pp. 206-7, 211. Society's conviction that the irrational elements in women's nature (including her sexuality) must be controlled is everywhere evident in the contemporary discussions that Smith-Rosenberg cites. However, an even more urgent anxiety can be found (almost never entirely articulated)—namely, that if women really expressed sexual desire and achieved sexual pleasure, their demands might exceed the capacity of the relevant males to satisfy them.

13. Perhaps it is not surprising that during this extremely oppressive period, there was an equally extreme reaction; see Louis J. Kern, "Stamping Out the 'Brutality of the He': Sexual Ideology and the Masculine Ideal in the Literature of Victorian Sex Radicals," *ATQ* 5 (1991), 225-39. Yet the normative impact of the sex-radicals was negligible by comparison with the prudish impact of people like Comstock and Acton.

14. Acton, *On Organs,* pp. 123, 138, 164. Nancy Chodorow's observations concerning the consequences of this particular social construction of the "feminine" are pertinent to Chopin's novel; she ties no small portion of women's unhappiness to the fact that they are forced to "live through their children." *Feminism and Psychoanalytic Theory* (New Haven: Yale Univ. Press, 1989), p. 44.

15. It is interesting that the mores of this code did not make the woman's sexual drive some part of her husband's "property." Even Acton is clear that men should not engage in marital excesses and that a wife's reasonable reticence should be respected; this was one reason for his defense of legalized prostitution. Patricia Yeager discusses notions of property and ownership in this novel, tying them to linguistic problems. See Yeager, "A Language Which Nobody Understood," in Walker, esp. pp. 282ff.

16. "[She would never] forget the shock with which she heard Madame Ratignolle relating to old Monsieur Farival the harrowing story of one of her accouchements, withholding no intimate detail. . . . A book had gone the rounds of the pension. When it came her turn to read it, she did so with profound astonishment. She felt moved to read the book in secret and solitude, though none of the others had done so. . . . It was openly criticized and freely discussed at table" (p. 28).

17. See R. D. Laing, *Self and Others* (Harmondsworth: Penguin, 1971), pp. 17-53. Laing's analysis of "false-naming" illuminates how very little in Edna's life experience has facilitated the development of an authentic, socially confirmed sense of self.

18. Almost twenty years ago, I wrote an essay on this novel, "Thanatos and Eros: Kate Chopin's *The Awakening*" (repr. in Walker). What I am attempting here is not a fundamentally different reading of this novel (which still seems to me to present the tragic plight of a woman whose "identity" is never forged into a coherent, viable "self"), but a reading that traces the social or cultural origins of Edna's problem. In an interesting discussion of Edna's reading of Emerson, Virginia Kouisdis discusses Edna's determination to achieve a "unified self" from a somewhat different critical perspective: see Kouisdis, "Prison into Prism: Emerson's 'Many-Colored Lenses' and the Woman Writer of Early Modernism," in *The Green American Tradition: Essays and Poems for Sherman Paul,* ed.

Daniel Peck (Baton Rouge: Louisiana State Univ. Press, 1989), pp. 115-34.

19. Leonce is a literal-minded, rather dull man—too preoccupied with his business and too fond of his material possessions. Nonetheless, he is scarcely a tyrant; and if he regards Edna with an unduly proprietary air, he at least cares enough about her to seek help from Dr. Mandelet when their relationship is clearly foundering. A great many critics have focused upon his tendency to regard Edna as a piece of property. John Carlos Rowe's "The Economics of the Body in Kate Chopin's *The Awakening*," in Lynda S. Boren and Sara deSaussure Davis, *Kate Chopin Reconsidered: Beyond the Bayou* (Baton Rouge: Louisiana State Univ. Press, 1992), 117-42, is one of the most arresting and interesting of these. Rowe asks: "What does it mean to have a body? For Edna, and for Mme. Ratignolle, it is always someone else who possesses your body, and such 'possession' already signifies something other than your body: a 'wife,' a 'lover,' a white sunshade, a sunbonnet, children, heirs. In short, the body is exchangeable for something else, has been transformed into something else, has entered an economy in which it can be so changed" (p. 120).

20. Although Chopin's focus is on Edna, she allows the reader to see that Leonce is also maimed by this system; and in his case, too, the problem is one of distorted language. Presumably, he knows at least some of what he wants (more enthusiastic sexual response from his wife); however, he is prohibited from asserting his desires directly because no "decent" or "sensitive" husband would make explicit sexual demands of his wife (who presumably only tolerates his advances because she has an interest in bearing children). Leonce's dilemma has nothing at all to do with children; however, a discourse of "mothering" is all he is allowed if he wants to voice his disappointment. "It would have been a difficult matter for Mr. Pontellier to define to his own satisfaction or any one else's wherein his wife failed in her duty toward their children. It was something which he felt rather than perceived, and he never voiced the feeling without subsequent regret and ample atonement" (p. 26). The sad impasse between the couple is developed most fully in Chapter 11.

21. Joseph R. Urgo, "A Prologue to Rebellion: *The Awakening* and the Habit of Self-Expression," SLQ 20 (1987/88), 23.

22. Dale M. Bauer and Andrew M. Lakritz present an excellent discussion of the social and cultural dialogues whose presence and power inform this novel. They recognize the quasi-medical terminology that lies at the root of the problem, although they do not trace its origins. "*The Awakening* and the Woman Question," in Bernard Koloski, ed., *Approches to Teaching Chopin's* The Awakening (New York: Modern Language Association, 1988), pp. 47-52.

23. Sandra M. Gilbert, "The Second Coming of Aphrodite: Kate Chopin's Fantasy of Desire," *KR* 5 (Summer 1983), 44.

24. G. J. Barker-Benfield, *The Horrors of the Half-Known Life: Male Attitudes Toward Women and Sexuality in Nineteenth-Century America* (New York: Harper, 1976). pp. 206, 200, quoting John Todd, *Woman's Rights* (Boston: Lee and Shephard, 1867) and John Todd, *Serpents in the Dove's Nest* (Boston: Lee and Shephard. 1867).

25. Ivy Schweitzer, "Maternal Discourse and the Romance of Selt-Possession in Kate Chopin's *The Awakening*, "*Boundary 2* 17 1990), 172.

26. Smith-Rosenberg, p. 199.

Dara Llewellyn (essay date spring 1996)

SOURCE: Llewellyn, Dara. "Reader Activation of Boundaries in Kate Chopin's 'Beyond the Bayou.'" *Studies in Short Fiction* 33, no. 2 (spring 1996): 255-62.

[*In the following essay, Llewellyn examines Chopin's symbolic use of the physical setting of "Beyond the Bayou."*]

Boundaries exist everywhere in the worlds created within short stories and within the experience this genre offers the reader. Generally, we use the word "boundary" in the ordinary sense of demarcation, but I would like to suggest that we use it as a "term of art" in the study of short fiction. Without becoming overly technical, we can borrow from the mathematical notion of boundary as both limit and field. As a beginning I will show how these adjusted definitions give us some new leverage on a particular story by Kate Chopin, and on the nature of storyness itself. **"Beyond the Bayou"** is a rich illustration because it is about boundaries of the usual sort (physical, temporal, psychological) while it foregrounds the boundary conditions of the reader's experience.

Many writers have described a landscape of the mind, a spatial configuration of physical boundaries that metaphorically reveal a character's state(s) of mind. In **"Beyond the Bayou,"** Chopin chooses a marshy, sluggish body of water as the real and symbolic boundary for the storyworld in which her heroine La Folle exists. An introduction to the physical setting comes first in the story, as if an orientation to place were somehow more important than anything else. One might argue that any opening is just to "set the stage," but this cliche obscures the real function of any storyworld threshold, as Susan Lohafer demonstrates in *Coming to Terms with the Short Story*.[1]

At the very least one can say that Chopin wants the reader to notice the bayou, for it is mentioned not only in the title, but also in the first sentence of the story: "The bayou curved like a crescent around the point of land on which La Folle's cabin stood" (175). That the bayou is intended to be seen—and seen as a boundary—is clear from the way the shape of the bayou encloses the world where the character La Folle fives. Mental mapping is an immediate reader response to the narrator's description at this point. The physicality of the boundary is so clear here that the reader can sketch it.

Chopin strengthens this image of the bayou as a delimiting boundary by adding a growth of woods behind La Folle's cabin, to complete the encirclement of her environs:

> Between the stream and the hut lay a big abandoned field. . . . Through the woods that spread back into unknown regions the woman had drawn an imaginary line, and past this circle she never stepped. This was her only form of mania.
>
> (175)

Chopin seems to want the reader to "map" this region, as her choice of words suggests: The narrator speaks of "drawing an imaginary line." This physical boundary of the bayou is clearly meant to have a shaping effect—on La Folle's experience, on the reader's experience, and thus on the story itself.

The fines between the physical and the psychical boundaries are blurred, however, in this mental mapping. Even as the reader tracks the narrator's description of the physical landscape, so, too, she takes the character's perspective and experiences La Folle's perception of the psychical boundary, the point beyond which La Folle cannot go or beyond which she cannot function because she is terrified of crossing this boundary to her world.[2] The negative impact of this delimiting boundary is figuratively revealed in the barrenness of the enclosed field and by the threatening strangeness of the woods at the back of her cabin.

When considering the story as a spatial construct shaped by the bayou, the reader sees it as no accident that Bellissime, the white master's house, is at the farthest remove from the cabin of La Folle, a former slave, beloved though she is of his children. Here are dialectically opposed landscapes, a patterning frequently used in short stories and, here, helping to create cultural context. The very real physical distance and barrier between the two homesteads represent the also very real social, economic, and racial separations between the characters. It is also no accident that all the cabins in the quarters are clustered near the bayou; the inhabitants of these cabins—like La Folle, but to a lesser extent—are separated from the main house and kept near the bayou, the dividing line in this storyworld.

Individuation of consciousness in this story also serves to reinforce the divisiveness found in the story landscape. The limiting and shaping factor occurring from the individuation of consciousness is especially evident in La Folle's isolated character. She is always set apart—as her physical confines demonstrate. Separation is also revealed in the relationship between two characters. La Folle's relationship with both the young P'tit Maitre and Cheri, loving though it is, must span a gulf because of the social and economic differences as well as the physical distance between their homes. Separation may also be seen between a character and her community, as La Folle's separation from everyone "beyond the bayou" demonstrates, or as seen in her role as a black woman separated from the white family who live at Belissime, a place she could "never" visit.

The only real bridge across this chasm of individuation is through the reader's active participation in tracking the story. It is the reader who undergoes, like La Folle, that movement from closure to openness captured in the changing values of the bayou boundary. It is the reader who experiences La Folle's emotional trauma each time she confronts a bloody child. Chopin structures the time frames of these confrontations as temporal boundaries that further shape both La Folle's and the reader's experience.

The reader is introduced very simply to two parallel time frames: La Folle when she is past 35 and then La Folle as a child. This dual time frame allows the reader to register an emotional trauma from La Folle's childhood and, at the same time, an emotional limitation in her subsequent adult life. The reader enters the bayou-country storyworld through the narrator's auspices before, meeting the then 35-year-old La Folle ". . . fixed in her mania." Next the reader is introduced to the precipitating trauma La Folle experienced as a child, when she saw a young man she knew, covered in blood, being pursued from the "unknown" woods into the haven of her mother's cabin.

Chopin, or rather the narrator, summarily describes the impact on the small black child: "The sight had stunned her childish reason" (175). After this moment, the cabin and its immediate environs represent the only security La Folle knows, one she would not leave even as an adult. Yet always at her back are "the woods that spread back into unknown regions" from which the bloody young man had run, threatening psychological regions containing the terrors of her youth as well as (or having become perhaps) the "unknown."

The narrative strategy of embedding time frames creates a number of different effects as the reader activates each time frame. The reader activates the first time frame with the words, "She was now . . . ," the temporal marker now signaling time in the present. In this time frame, the reader tracks La Folle's perspective on her world where she is "a large, gaunt black woman, past thirty-five," living in isolation upon her point of land (175). It is an experience of barrenness, of fear, of a life lived in almost total isolation, broken only by visits from P'tit Maitre's children.

The second time frame is activated with another temporal marker, "It was when . . ."; the marker when places the reader in some past time. In this second time frame, experienced so dose upon the first time frame, the reader holds the perspective of the child Jacqueline while she watches a younger "P'tit Maitre, black with powder and crimson with blood stagger into the cabin of Jacqueline's mother, his pursuers close at his heels" (175). In the exterior time frame, the experiences of innocence and terror fuse into an immobility that is still evident in La Folle's adult time frame.

Taken simply as a structural device, the embedding of one time frame within another has the effect of compressing time for the reader, allowing the reader to trace "in a moment" the psychological scarring of the young black girl and the barren experience of the adult woman imprisoned by her fear. As a grown woman, La Folle has never crossed the bayou even though she loves the family of P'tit Maitre and is beloved by them. Nor does she cross the bayou when all the other slave quarters are moved across to the master's side of the river. Chopin describes La Folle's psychological trauma, its after-effect, and the community's consequent acceptance of it so matter-of-factly that all the drama seems simply part of the landscape, again blurring the distinction between the physical, temporal, and psychological boundaries.

Thus far, the boundaries being activated in the story function mainly in patterns of exclusion or compression. The bayou functions as an enclosing, even imprisoning force, while time serves to compress and consequently intensify the reader's experience. It is when the reader activates parallel experiential structures in the story that the boundaries begin to function most evidently in that manner peculiar to the short story.

In a dramatic parallel to her early experience, the adult La Folle is once more traumatized by the arrival of a bloody child. Cheri, her favorite of P'tit Maitre's children, shoots himself in the leg while hunting behind her cabin, again in the "woods that spread back into unknown regions." Alone with the wounded child whom she loves devotedly, and trapped by the physical and psychical boundary of the bayou, La Folle is confronted for the first time by the absolute limits of her existence: ". . . of the world beyond the bayou she had long known nothing, save what her morbid fancy conceived" (175). A grown woman, with "more physical strength than most men," La Folle is still prey to her fancies, and, holding the injured child, she stands by the bayou screaming for help.

Here is a nexus in the flow of time, a single moment in time that holds all other moments in careful balance and is the basis of all short stories. Will La Folle cross the bayou? Will she remain trapped in her fear? Finally, when no one responds to her cries, La Folle is forced by her fear for the child's safety, a fear larger and finally more powerful than her own fear of everything "beyond the bayou," to cross the almost dry stream-bed. La Folle faces the "[e]xtreme terror [that] was upon her" and runs across the bayou to take the child home, and, once the child is safe, collapses (177-78). The transcendence of her fear and her subsequent collapse mark a pivotal moment in the story.

When La Folle crosses the physical (spatial) boundary of the bayou, the boundaries of time are also transcended, for she is able to shed her past, or, at least, the traumatic effect of that past. La Folle's two confrontations with a bloody youngster create a dramatic parallel that allows the reader to comprehend two emotionally traumatic experiences, widely divergent in time, almost simultaneously. The story begins in the present and ends in the present, enclosing within that narrative time frame past events that have structured—or, at least, have affected—the present; the narrative flashback thus allows the reader to experience both time frames "at once."

This significant moment is a formative and transcendent one for La Folle that frees her from her earlier limits. Again we have that tension peculiar to the short story, a tension activated by the reader's crossing that bayou with La Folle. It is the same tension seen, for example, in Faulkner's stories—when one moment itself ultimately shapes the larger continuum of time implied in the storyworld, thus creating the singular integrity of the story.[3] La Folle's crossing of the bayou is of course a classic example of overcoming a fear by facing it. La Folle has crossed the extreme limit of her experiential domain because her love for Cheri, (and her fear for his safety) is larger than her fear of the "beyond," and once she crosses that boundary, she is no longer bound by her fears. When La Folle crosses the bayou, all the time frames come together and hinge upon that one moment. It is thus that the story coalesces, pulls in to this moment and takes on a singular integrity.

In dealing with symbolic values such as the bayou or the bloody child, it is necessary, I feel, to differentiate between the heuristic of boundary-created tensions and the standard notion of symbolic values. The first is a product of a text-processing approach and the second need not be. The primary difference is in the movement of the reader's awareness. Symbolic value may attach itself to any element in the text, a bloody child or the bayou itself, boundary or not. But when the reader's awareness must move between boundaries, whether spatial, temporal, or experiential, then that movement creates vibrations which themselves establish a network of tensions. It is the invocation of these tensions, rather than the more static evocation of associations, that I am attempting to model here.

For a more concrete look at the reader-activated, boundary-created tensions, we can examine different views of Chopin's storyworld. Two spheres of physical experience are available to La Folle in this story, each comprising the main realities of her life at different periods. The larger sphere, spatially depicted, radiates out from La Folle's cabin and includes the field in front, the woods in back, the bayou that virtually islands her land, as well as the land beyond the bayou where are found: first, the cabin quarters of P'tit Maitre's servants and then, at the farthest distance, Bellissime, the family home of the formerly slave-holding white family. In contrast, the inner concentric sphere includes only that space that lies inside the bayou, La Folle's cabin with its barren field in front.

When the time frames are activated, the bayou becomes part of a continuum rather than just a limit. One can consider the bayou functioning as a threshold into a larger domain of experience, or, perhaps, as a permeable membrane, shaping rather than confining some portion of the continuum of La Folle's experience (as well as the reader's). The notion of transcending to a larger field or continuum of experience is significant here. Even though La Folle's experiences had once been limited by the bayou, crossing the bayou expands her experiences in such a way that she can not only move beyond the bayou but also sees the world anew, where "the white, bursting cotton with the dew upon it, gleamed for acres and acres like frosted silver in the early dawn" (Chopin 261).

Her experience is remade. The world formerly forbidden to her by her fears is now a sensual delight for her: "When La Folle came to the broad stretch of velvety lawn that surrounded the house, she moved slowly and with delight over the springy turf, that was delicious beneath her tread" (179). An edenic expression of her newly-made experience continues:

> She stopped to find whence came those perfumes that were assailing her senses with memories from a time far gone.
>
> There they were, stealing up to her from the thousand blue violets that peeped out from green, luxuriant beds. There they were, showering down from the big waxen bells of the magnolias far above her head, and from the jessamine clumps around her.
>
> There were roses, too, without number. To right and left palms spread in broad and graceful curves. It all looked like enchantment beneath the sparkling sheen of dew.
>
> (179-80)

Chopin's spare prose shifts to a rich, flowery piling of sensual image upon sensual image, springing out at the reader in its abundance.

La Folle's embracing of this new world of rich, varied sensory experience provides the story's closure: "A look of wonder and deep content crept into her face as she watched for the first time the sun rise upon the new, the beautiful world beyond the bayou" (180). The world of "morbid fancy" has become a rich potential for delight, a representation of that notion in the definition of boundary that limit and potentiality are somehow intimately connected, perhaps even the same, that one is somehow a product of the other in a reflexive way. This final sentence in the story, with its implicit openness, is in direct contrast to the confining and binding description of the bayou found in the opening sentence discussed earlier.

Because the reading time between the first and last sentence is so short, the contrast between them is registered in a special way peculiar to the aesthetics of short stories. The reading experience conflates—yet contains—duration. Of course, there is a certain unidirectional flow to time in the story. It is, after all, the story of a woman's life. But, as with many stories, the reader's experience follows a pattern of flow different from just a chronological countdown. Although La Folle does move from childhood to adulthood within the story, the path that the reader follows is more circular, time turning back on itself and, paradoxically, only then being able to flow forward once again.

If we look at the time line of La Folle's life from the reader's perspective, a wave pattern is more apt for tracing that experience than outlining a straight linear progression, despite the very real presence of a cause and effect sequence to account for her trauma. The wave pattern of La Folle's life as the reader experiences it cannot flow simply from childhood to adulthood, because very early on that flow runs into an outside interference that results in an immobilizing trauma: the bloody child emerging from the "unknown woods." At that point, the energy and direction behind the flow of her life line is obstructed and the flow can only lap back upon itself. In fact, the energy of the flowing wave is almost canceled out, as can be witnessed in the barrenness of the enclosed field. It takes another outside influence, Cheri's accident, to open that channel and once again permit the flow of time. La Folle's life energy is diffracted. Her wave is freed and "passes into the region behind"—or beyond, we might say, given Chopin's title.[4] The bloody child image may resonate in the reader's experience as a classic image or symbol of rebirth, a way of returning to full knowledge of oneself, but it is a boundary marker of experience even as the bayou is. The reader is tensely caught up in La Folle's predicament and feels an appropriate release later when La Folle collapses after crossing the boundary of the bayou. The child has been merely an impetus to the awakening (or rebirth) of La Folle's emotional self, more symbolic than participatory. Here, perhaps, is a touch of the old notion of catharsis in these shared emotional confrontations and release, for the reader does track La Folle's emotions, but the reader's role also involves more than simple emotional identification.

It is in the reader's awareness that all the boundary conditions of the short story become activated, all within a very short span of reading time. It is in the reader's awareness that the compression or coalescence peculiar to the short story occurs. It is here that the dual meaning of boundary comes most into play. For it is the shift from limit to field or the manifold capacity of the short story to be both at once that creates the dynamic tension that pulls the story in on itself and into a short form. It is that sharply drawn tension between a single moment and its larger continuum. It is that singular nexus between potentiality and limit. The reader is pulled by the story into experiencing both the fullness and the limits of experience in a "single cognitive moment."

Chopin's narrative in **"Beyond the Bayou"** demonstrates the relationship between these two impulses of expansive field and narrowing limit. The narrative not only showcases the notion of boundary in its major symbol, but, at the same time, reveals the workings of boundary dynamics in terms of time and space and human experience. A reader experiences these boundary conditions in moving through the text. Like La Folle, the reader is then freed, freed to discern any number of readings within the texts, whether in psychological, socioeconomic, spiritual, phenomenological, or whatever other terms.

Notes

1. Susan Lohafer convincingly makes the case that the sentence unit is more important to the short story than to "either the most discursive poem or the most poetic novel."

2. Bower and Morrow, among others, discuss the dynamics of how a reader tracks a character's experience.

3. One notable example is when Isaac sees the "Grandfather" buck in Faulkner's story "The Old People."

4. In discussing the mechanics of a wave function, Giancoli describes the process of diffraction in which a wave that meets an obstruction passes around and into the region behind the obstacle.

Works Cited

Bower, Gordon H. and Daniel G. Morrow. "Mental Models in Narrative Comprehension." *Science* 5 Jan. 1990: 44-48.

Chopin, Kate. "Beyond the Bayou." *The Complete Works of Kate Chopin.* Ed. Per Seyersted. 2 vols. Baton Rouge: Louisiana State UP, 1969. 1: 175-80.

Faulkner, William. "The Old People." *Go Down Moses.* New York: Random, 1940. 163-87.

Giancoli, Douglas C. *Physics: Principles with Applications.* 2nd ed. Englewood Cliffs, New Jersey: Prentice, 1985.

Lohafer, Susan. *Coming to Terms with the Short Story.* Baton Rouge: Louisiana State UP, 1983.

Walter Taylor and Jo Ann B. Fineman (essay date fall 1996)

SOURCE: Taylor, Walter and Fineman, Jo Ann. "Kate Chopin: Pre-Freudian Freudian." *Southern Literary Journal* 29, no. 1 (fall 1996): 35-45.

[*In the following essay, Taylor and Fineman examine psychoanalytic elements in* The Awakening.]

As Kate Chopin's Edna Pontellier sits contemplating the sea in *The Awakening* (1899), her friend Adèle Ratignolle asks a simple question: "Of whom—of what are you thinking?" The question evokes a complex response. Edna replies that she was thinking of a day during her Kentucky childhood when she was walking through a meadow; to a "very little girl" that meadow "seemed as big as the ocean." And she remembers that she "threw out her arms as if swimming when she walked, beating the tall grass as one strikes out at the water." Now, at age 28, Edna does not remember why she was walking through that meadow, only that "I felt as if I must walk on forever, without coming to the end of it" (16-17).

Edna's feeling of euphoria, of a connection with matter which extends on to infinity, suggests what Freud was later to describe as the "oceanic state," a period of early childhood when the infant, unaware of the boundaries between her own body, her mother's, and her environment, identifies erotically with all three. Edna, who has lost her mother at an early age, is at the time of her memory long past the oceanic state, old enough to walk through the meadow alone.[1] What she is experiencing appears to be a "screen memory," a memory which masks an earlier memory; her walk through the tall, sea-like grass, moving caressingly as though to her dead mother's touch, reflects a wish both to return to the symbiosis of the "oceanic state" and to restore her mother's soothing arms. And most significantly, the memory of that grassy field surfaces in the adult Edna while she is talking with Adèle, a friend to whom she has given the patronizing label of "mother woman."

Too little attention has been paid to the significance of Edna's memory, which suggests a great deal about Chopin's remarkable understanding of depth psychology. Perhaps her most important achievement in *The Awakening*'s to have conceived, as Freud later did, the notion of an unconscious mind which dominates her character's actions. Edna is, in fact, the paradigm of a pioneering map of the human psyche for which Chopin, with her pre-Freudian perspectives, was forced to imagine both the contours and the vocabulary. It is a map which existed in no previous work of literature.[2]

From the opening pages of *The Awakening,* Edna's actions are shown to be controlled by unconscious forces. It is a given of modern psychodynamic child psychiatry that the early loss of a parent is an overwhelming determinant of adult character. Perhaps because the trauma of her mother's death is so deeply embedded in Edna's unconscious, Chopin chose not to dramatize the event directly; the text supplies only the information that her mother had "died when . . . [Edna and her sisters] were quite young" (17). But Edna's adult responses to this loss illustrate Chopin's acute understanding of the dynamics of repression and avoidance. Edna is able to retrieve her memory of the sea of grass only after a series of evasions. Her first response to Adèle's question is denial: she replies "with a start" that she is thinking of "nothing"—then quickly adds, "I was not really conscious of thinking anything." When she seeks consciously to "retrace her thoughts," she realizes this too is untrue. And when she finally admits she was thinking of that day in Kentucky, she is still unaware why; she insists that it is "without any connection I can trace," then contradicts herself by saying that it was "the hot wind [of the sea] beating in my face" that was the connection (16-17).

Edna's resistance to the memory thus attests to the scars the loss of her mother has created; but her trauma, Chopin is aware, concerns more than the loss of a parent. Childhood psychoanalytic psychology is clear on the point that any child would contrive reasons for such a loss and that such a child might blame the surviving parent; the younger the child, moreover, the more irrational might be the response. Edna's trauma is exacerbated by the fact that there may be an element of truth in such fantasies. In a passage remarkable for its directness, Chopin's narrator comments that Edna's dominating father "had coerced his own wife into her grave"—a fact of which her father himself "was perhaps unaware" (68).

If Edna's childhood memories of her mother remain only in screen memories, she is supremely conscious of her father, whose portrait is vividly detailed. A former Confederate colonel who tells war stories with himself as the hero, her father is a profane, hard-drinking, Bible-quoting Presbyterian who, her husband Léonce has heard, "used to atone for his week-day sins with his Sunday devotions" (63). His notion of marriage remains patriarchal and controlling. "You are too lenient" with Edna, he tells Léonce. "Authority, coercion are what is needed. Put your foot down good and hard. . . ." For the Colonel, that is "the only way to manage a wife" (68).

Still, despite the detail with which her father's portrait is realized, Edna's detached attitude indicates the familiar process of evasion at work. The narrator's comment that Edna is "not very warmly or deeply attached" to her only surviving parent seems calculatedly inadequate, as does Edna's response when he visits her in New Orleans. "She discovered that he interested her," the narrator relates, "though she realized that he might not interest her long." What that means to Edna at the time is that "for the first time in her life she felt as if she were thoroughly acquainted" with her father; yet when he leaves after a brief argument the narrator comments that she "was glad to be rid of [him] . . . with his padded shoulders, his Bible reading, his 'toddies' and his ponderous oaths" (65-66, 68).

Padded shoulders, toddies, oaths: these are vexations; what Edna has chosen not to be acquainted with, the text implies, is that these are symptoms of a poisonous family *gestalt* from which her sisters must have suffered as much as she. The most obvious result of her mother's death is that they have been raised in a repressively patriarchal, masculine-dominated home. The portraits of the sisters, again sketched only in the barest outline, suggest Edna's evasion of the problem. Edna has never been close to either sister. According to Léonce, the younger sister, Janet, "is something of a vixen" (63). Edna and Janet "had quarreled a good deal," the narrator relates, "through force of unfortunate habit"—a statement which suggests both are in some sense victims of the situation; but the mature Edna sees no reason to attend Janet's wedding. The older sister, Margaret, appears to have served as a rather unsympathetic mother-substitute for the two girls; she took over the role of housewife after their mother's death, and the situation has shaped her character. She is "matronly and dignified," the narrator relates, "probably from having assumed matronly and housewifely responsibilities too early in life"; thus "Margaret was not effusive; she was practical" (17). She also stands for the repressive qualities Edna and others associate with the father's Presbyterian religion. According to Léonce, "Margaret . . . has all the Presbyterianism undiluted" (63).

These teasing hints constitute all of the narrative's significant information about Edna's sisters; and again, Edna's bland disinterest suggests her deep-rooted repression of the traumas of her childhood. There is a story here that cries out for understanding: a three-daughter family presided over by a father who thinks "authority, coercion are what is needed" with a wife, who has "coerced" the mother into an early grave. In such a family it would be no wonder that a younger daughter was perceived as a "vixen" or that an older daughter, burdened with assuming a mother's role without a mother as a model, imitated the father's remote, authoritarian notion of parenthood. That Edna appears programmed to evade such understanding suggests much about the formation of her psyche. Scanty as this information is, however, Chopin has provided significant guidelines for Edna's emerging character. Not only has Edna suffered the loss of her mother, removing the model and primary identification figure, but the practical and (by inference) distant and effectively cold Margaret never offers a substitute object for feminine identification.[3] The youthful Edna has thus become fixed in her longing for and symbolic search for reunion with the lost mother.

Predictably, she is a lonely, bookish child who shrinks from familiarity with other girls. "Edna had had an occasional girl friend," the narrator comments, "but whether accidentally or not, they seemed to have been all of one type—the self-contained." It is equally suggestive that embedded in these early memories are fantasies which indicate a propensity to displace her libidinal needs onto a male other than her father. Another incident—"perhaps it was when she traversed the ocean of waving grass"[4]—is a childhood experience of fantasied love of a particular man: "a dignified and sad-eyed cavalry officer who visited her father in Kentucky." Edna "could not leave his presence . . . nor remove her eyes from his face" (17, 18).

Bereft of her mother, raised by a father who responds to femininity only by refusing to recognize it, Edna thus creates a fantasy of a man who affirms her as a female. This is, clearly, a defensive attempt at restitution, not only to be comforted by the erotic fantasy of the tender "sad-eyed cavalry officer," but to find a pre-oedipal object attachment as a restitution for the mother. This childhood fantasy, which soon "melted imperceptibly out of her existence" (31), resurfaces in another avatar when Edna is "a little miss, just merging into her teens." Her new focus is an "engaged young man" from a neighboring plantation whose fiancée is a friend of Margaret's; the result is predictably "bitter" because it provokes the realization that "she herself was nothing" to the young man (18). For Chopin, the situation is a paradigm of repression and self-devaluation. The two experiences have the common feature that the relationships are, *per se*, unrealizable. Moreover, Edna has now reconstructed an oedipal triangle, a reparative, defensive fantasy which allows her safely to yearn for the "engaged young man" and at the same time to consolidate further her self-image of nothingness and faulty feminine identity. In this way, the narrator comments, "at a very early period, she had apprehended instinctively the dual life—that outward existence which comforms, the inward life which questions" (14).

The situation foreshadows a final fantasied relationship, an imagined love affair with "the great tragedian." Never identified by name in the narration,[5] this misty figure, whose photograph she favors with secret kisses, has the added but inevitable feature that he is beyond any personal contact: a blank page on which to project her fantasies. As the narrator makes plain, Chopin is well aware of the reality of the needs that underlie such fantasies. "The persistence of the infatuation lent it an aspect of genuineness. The hopelessness of it colored it with the lofty tones of a great passion" (18).

It is Léonce Pontellier's misfortune—and Edna's—that she has chosen him as a player in her effort to repress these fantasies. "It was in the midst of her secret great passion [for the tragedian] that she met him," the narrator relates. When Léonce, twelve years older than Edna, falls in love with her, she decides that although "the acme of bliss, which would have been a marriage with the tragedian, was not for her in this world," still, "as the devoted wife of a man who worshiped her, she . . . could take her place . . . in the world of reality." Léonce, in short, has the misfortune to be cast in the role of "reality"; to Edna at the time of their marriage, he thus symbolizes the act of denial, "closing the portals forever behind her upon the realm of romance and dreams" (18-19).

The terms of Edna's marriage with Léonce are illustrated in the fact that she realizes "with some unaccountable satisfaction that no trace of passion or excessive and fictitious warmth colored her affection, thereby threatening its dissolution" (19). Léonce is a representation of the oedipal father of her fantasy, a displacement from the original father, safely defended against by the splitting off of sexual passion. He is also a narcissistic object choice; she is drawn to him because he is a man who "worshiped" her, thus placing her in the position of the woman who is admired and treasured. Edna, in choosing Léonce, has finalized her psychological split between "that outward existence which comforts" and "the inward life which questions."

Edna's "unaccountable satisfaction" thus consists in the fact that by choosing a man twelve years her senior, a substitute for her remote, passionless father, she appears to have sealed off the threat from her incapacity for a mature, post-oedipal male object attachment. But Chopin, aware of the ambiguities of repression and fixation, at least suggests another reason for that "unaccountable satisfaction": by choosing a man whose very existence drives her erotic projections underground, she protects those projections rather than banishing them, insuring their continuance as fantasies. No wonder that when Edna rejects her husband and her marriage, she turns to art as a possible replacement; not yet committed to painting, she has already created an extended sketch of that part of her experience which she has been fated consciously to evade and deny. And significantly, the immediate agent of Edna's awakening is not Robert Lebrun, to whom she ascribes it, but a woman who is also an artist, the pianist Mlle. Reisz.

Reisz strikingly resembles Edna's childhood girlfriends who were "all of one type—the self-contained." Like Edna, she is a woman alienated from Creole society, though for different reasons: the pianist is singularly unequipped with the physical and social charms society demands. A "homely woman, with a small weazened face," possessed of "absolutely no taste in dress," unmarried and "no longer young," Reisz could easily have become a basket case of inhibition and asexuality (25). Instead, she has channeled her deepest fantasies into art and creative expression, where she has succeeded brilliantly. Her success has allowed her a freedom possible for few women. She lives alone in her Bienville Street apartment. To many she is "a disagreeable little woman . . . who had quarrelled with almost everyone"; but this reputation, Edna understands, is in part "owing to a temper which was self-assertive" as well as to "a disposition to trample upon the rights of others" (25). Reisz's strength, in short, comes through as a social as well as an artistic triumph. In addition to talent, she tells Edna, "the artist must possess the courageous soul." For Reisz, that means "the brave soul. The soul that dares and defies" (61).

If this self-isolated woman has achieved such status, it is because her art has provided her a way to channel impulses that Edna has hitherto dealt with through evasion. But the way she speaks to Edna is not in words; it is through that art. "You are the only one worth playing for" (45), she tells Edna at Grand Isle. The irony of that statement is that her art conveys impulses Edna is ill-equipped to handle. What Edna hears is "an impress of the abiding truth" (44); and that truth is precisely the truth screened by her memory of that sea of grass. All summer, Robert has struggled, unsuccessfully, to teach her to swim. Her failures are clearly connected to her buried memories of the oceanic phase and the lost mother. "A certain ungovernable dread hung about her when in the water, unless there was a hand near by that might reach out and reassure her" (27). Reisz's music speaks to the source of these fears: ". . . the very passions themselves were aroused within her soul, swaying it, lashing it, as the waves daily beat upon her . . . body" (26). Now, having received the ocean-like "impress of the abiding truth" from another woman, she no longer needs the support of this nearby hand. She discovers that she has power over the sea.

The change signals a significant psychic event: a reunion with those forces the sea symbolizes. Edna literally shouts for joy: "A feeling of exultation overtook her, as if some power of significant import had been given her soul." And her response recalls the child's first discoveries of its ability to control its body in the outer environment: ". . . she was like the little tottering, stumbling, clutching child, who of a sudden realizes its powers, and walks for the first time alone." But predictably, her response also resembles a child's first ecstatic sense of omnipotence. She reacts both "boldly and with overconfidence," the narrator relates. "As she swam she seemed to be reaching out for the unlimited in which to lose herself" (27-28).

Edna's reaction illustrates another aspect of Chopin's perception of the psychology of loss. The fascination of memories of the oceanic state is that, because the child has not marked off the symbiotic boundaries between itself and others, the world of the self appears unlimited and grandiose. The irony of the adult's effort to recreate that world is that, while the movement of the psyche appears to be outward and assertive, it is in fact inward and repressive. As Edna swims outward toward the sea, she moves inward toward that childhood vision of the sea of grass. For the present, Edna manages to return safely to shore, but the problem remains.

For Chopin, the very definition of "awakening" can thus be understood as a reversal, as in dream work. Edna is, in fact, slowly but inexorably regressing toward attempted symbiotic union with the lost mother. Mlle. Reisz has been a transient revival of the maternal object, a woman who gives her music to Edna as a mother gives to and nurtures a beloved infant; but such restitutions for early lost love objects often cannot be sustained. Edna has no art to channel her passions as Mlle. Reisz has and no image of adult female conduct except the "mother women" she despises. "The past," she feels, "offered no lesson which she was willing to heed" (44).

Chopin's acute sensitivity to unconscious life shows brilliantly here; the past, for Edna, is bereft of a maternal feminine identification figure, leaving her only with unresolved pre-oedipal longings to *merge with* a love object, rather than to experience individuation and psychic autonomy. It is in this context that Edna's awakening focuses on two younger men who appeal to her thwarted adult female identity: Robert Lebrun and Alcée Arobin. Each affair, in its own way, is an effort to recreate the compensatory fantasies of her youth.

Her flirtation with Robert is another version of the hopeless love affairs with the cavalry officer, the engaged young man, and the tragedian: ". . . she recognized anew the symptoms of infatuation which she had felt incipiently as a child, as a girl in her early teens, and later as a young woman" (44). When Robert predictably yields to the mores of his society and rejects her—his parting note reads, "Good-by—because I love you" (106)—those fantasies are stripped away, baring the loveless narcissism of her affair

with Alcée Arobin. Alcée represents a further development in her regression and the gradual failure of her fragile defenses. There is none of the affective rapport she feels with Robert. Rather, he appeals to an "animalism that stirred impatiently within her"; "the touch of his lips upon her hands" acts "like a narcotic upon her" (75, 74). It is now clearer than ever that sexuality without loving is the splitting to which Edna has been doomed by the loss of the mother-infant attachment. This is her deepest pathology, and the proof of it is that with Alcée she is able to experience sexual arousal without true attachment to her love object.

Such is the final episode of Edna's ironic awakening: an explicitly sexual one to which her entire history has led her in her twenty-eighth year. It is not, however, the final jolt that edges Edna into despair. That is provided by the one individual who most truly has her interests at heart, the "mother woman" Adèle Ratignole. It is most suggestive that, as Edna sits on the beach and remembers that feminine sea of grass, Chopin has her in the company of the first mature feminine companion of her life.[6] A significant aspect of Edna's tragedy is that she will be unable to receive the mothering Adèle's friendship offers. The two friends quarrel over Edna's unwillingness to "sacrifice herself for her children": "a rather heated argument" in which they "did not appear . . . to be talking the same language" (46). Adèle sees Edna's lack of maturity clearly. "In some ways you seem to me like a child" (91), she tells her. But precisely because the two women are not talking the same language, the pregnant Adèle's affection turns tragic.

To draw Edna to an awareness of the need for such sacrifice, Adèle extracts a promise that Edna will attend her when her time comes. The move brings on the shock that finalizes Edna's regression. Summoned to Adèle's bedside, she experiences "a vague dread." Her memory reviews her own childbirth experiences, now apparently obscured by anesthesia and denial. "They seemed far away, unreal, and only half remembered." Fragmented memories surface. "She recalled faintly an ecstasy of pain," then, apparently, unconsciousness, followed by a very different—and ironic—"awakening" from the one aroused in her by Reisz's music and by Robert, "an awakening to find a little new life to which she had given being" (104). This curiously detached response reflects Edna's sense of alienation from her own children. Not surprisingly, the familiar process of avoidance sets in. "She began to wish she had not come," and she struggles to find an excuse to leave. She stays, however, and observes an event which traumatizes her. "With an inward agony, with a flaming, outspoken revolt against the ways of Nature, she witnessed the scene of torture." Adèle's final admonition, "Think of the children," only adds to the damage. When Edna at last departs she is "still stunned and speechless with emotion" (104). It is in this context that she returns home to find Robert's farewell note.

Edna's shock at the "scene of torture" is a complex matter, and critics have predictably disagreed about its significance. What is clear is that the incident shocks Edna into the self-knowledge that she cannot integrate the split in her personality: "the dual life—that outward existence which conforms" (housewifery, mothering) and "the inward life which questions" (independence, sensuality) (108). The result is that "she understood now clearly what she had meant long ago when she had said . . . that she . . . would never sacrifice herself for her children" (108). It is a climactic insight. As Edna's regression—with its consequent sense of emptiness and detachment from love objects—increases and overwhelms her, she realizes that she cannot find a loving attachment to Raoul and Etienne; in Nancy Chodorow's terms, she cannot "reproduce mothering" that she has never experienced. Those children now "appeared before her like antagonists who had overcome her; who had . . . sought to drag her into the soul's slavery for the rest of her days" (108).

Shocked into a final regressive state, Chopin's Edna commits suicide mechanically. She returns to the beach the next day believing that she has "done all the thinking which was necessary." As she stands naked on the shore she feels "like some new-born creature, opening its eyes in a familiar world that it had never known." But the infinity the ocean promises is what it has always been, an illusion. Edna's final thoughts are not of the sea which surrounds her, but of the day she walked through the grass remembering the oceanic feelings of infancy. "Edna heard her father's voice and her sister Margaret's. . . . The spurs of the cavalry officer clanged as he walked across the porch" (108-109). The final avatar of Edna's awakening reveals her desire to return to the oceanic phase of her childhood and the embracing arms of the lost mother. But the sea, like her lovers, betrays her at last; its image of infinity masks the destructive force of regression to the inner world of the infantile psyche.

There is, obviously, a great deal more to be said about Chopin's use of depth psychology in *The Awakening.* It is unfair to Chopin to claim for her a modern knowledge of psychoanalysis or to superimpose on her a twentieth-century vocabulary. Still, her understanding of Edna's psychology reveals her as a true pioneer. Psychoanalytic considerations saturate *The Awakening* to such a degree that it is impossible to visualize Edna's emergence, or her tragedy, without them. Years before her time, Chopin created in *The Awakening* a vision of the human psyche that included the unconscious mind and an entire structure of defense mechanisms. Through Edna Pontellier she constructed a central thesis that Freud was in the process of developing: that such unconscious motivations are the driving force in human behavior. And in doing so she anticipated, by three quarters of a century, studies of the effect of inadequate mothering or early mother loss such as that of Chodorow. That her originality has gone virtually unnoticed in this post-Freudian age is a testament to the accuracy of her observations.

Notes

1. Perhaps because Edna's memories of her mother are buried in her unconscious, Chopin never specifies the time sequence between the death of the mother and this childhood memory. Indications of the mother's presence are significantly missing, however, from the description of the day in Kentucky, or from subsequent discussions of her childhood.

2. The names of Freud, Bleuler, and other European psychiatrists of Chopin's time are notable in their absence from Emily Toth's 1990 biography. We know of no study that suggests specific influences of this nature. Cynthia Griffin Wolff's "Thanatos and Eros: Kate Chopin's *The Awakening*" uses Freud and Laing with insight to speculate about Edna's psychology but never considers the nature or the originality of Chopin's understanding.

3. As Nancy Chodorow succinctly puts it, "Women come to mother because they have been mothered by women" (*The Reproduction of Mothering* 211).

4. The word "perhaps" signals Edna's avoidance of the significance of the issue; but it also implies that she does connect the memories.

5. Culley writes that the tragedian is "probably Edmund Booth," emphasizing that "Chopin was a fan of the actor and in 1894 published a review of his letters entitled 'The Real Edmund Booth'" (18 n.).

6. Hence it is not surprising that when Adèle takes her hand in a moment of closeness, Edna finds the unexpected intimacy "a little confusing." She is, the narrator relates, "not accustomed to an outward . . . expression of affection" (17) from a woman, and in Adèle she has met the image of the adoring mother of her fantasies. Nor is it surprising that Edna—no stranger to the arts of evasion—reacts with ambiguity, saddling Adèle with the disparaging label of "mother woman," a term which suggests her own need to deprecate and deny what she has been deprived of.

Works Cited

Chodorow, Nancy. *The Reproduction of Mothering: Psychoanalysis and the Sociology of Gender.* Berkeley: U of California P, 1978.

Chopin, Kate. *The Awakening: An Authoritative Text.* Ed. Margo Culley. 2nd ed. New York: Norton, 1994.

Toth, Emily. *Kate Chopin.* New York: William Morrow, 1990.

Wolff, Cynthia Griffin. "Thanatos and Eros: Kate Chopin's *The Awakening. American Quarterly* 25 (October 1973), 449-71.

Sandra Gunning (essay date 1996)

SOURCE: Gunning, Sandra. "Rethinking White Female Silences: Kate Chopin's Local Color Fiction and the Politics of White Supremacy." In *Race, Rape, and Lynching: The Red Record of American Literature, 1890-1912*, pp. 108-35. Oxford: Oxford University Press, 1996.

[*In the following essay, Gunning analyzes Chopin's works for evidence of her views on racial violence and stereotypes.*]

> Harris & Page of course wrote from a different standpoint;—that of the white *gentleman* as I write from the standpoint of a white lady.
>
> —Grace King

In any discussion of late-nineteenth-century American and African American literary discourses on white supremacist violence, George Washington Cable, Thomas Dixon, Thomas Nelson Page, Ida B. Wells, Charles Chesnutt, Sutton E. Griggs, David Bryant Fulton, and even Pauline Hopkins must undoubtedly be included as prominent figures. Yet this standard list suggests that lynching and mob rule were of concern only to black and white male writers and to black women activists. Much work remains to be done in uncovering how white women participated in debates about white supremacist violence, whether as literary figures or as social reformers. The tradition of white female activism perfected during the antislavery movement culminated by the end of the century in women's efforts to secure temperance reform, to improve the social conditions of the poor, to "Americanize" immigrants, and especially to extend women's rights to include the vote, access to birth control, and higher education. Such widespread activity would surely have set the stage for white female commentary on white supremacist violence.[1]

Not surprisingly, white women ran the gamut of opinions for and against lynching. By the 1890s, one of the most notorious supporters of the idea of the black rapist was Rebecca Latimer Felton, wife of a Georgia minister-politician, an avid suffragist, a supporter of the temperance movement, and later the first woman to serve as a United States senator. Speaking in 1897 at the annual meeting of the State Agricultural Society of Georgia on ways to improve farm life, Felton urged rural whites to look to the protection of their women:

> I warned those representative men . . . of the terrible effects that were already seen in the corruption of the negro vote, their venality, the use of whiskey, the debasement of the ignorant and incitement of evil passion in the vicious. . . . A crime nearly unknown before and during the war had become an almost daily occurrence and mob law had also become omnipotent.

It was at the same meeting that she made her infamous plea to white men to "lynch a thousand times a week if necessary," provoking the ire of black and white men opposed to lynching, including the black editor Alexander

Manly from Wilmington, North Carolina, and Andrew Sledd, a white Southerner and a professor at Emory.[2] Felton's views were popular enough, however, for her to launch a lecture tour aimed at protesting what she saw as white male inaction in the face of black rape.

Because of her sympathy for Southern white supremacists, Frances Willard of the Women's Christian Temperance Union found herself embroiled with Ida B. Wells in a battle over her public reputation as a moral reformer. The furor arose over an 1890 newspaper interview given by Willard in which she described "great dark faced mobs whose rallying cry is better whiskey and more of it." Willard claimed that "[t]he safety of women, of childhood, of the home is menaced in a thousand localities at this moment, so that men dare not go beyond the sight of their own roof-tree."[3] During her first visit to England on an anti-lynching lecture tour, Wells publicly attacked Willard for this stand, a move that prompted the British temperance leader Lady Henry Somerset to publish a new interview with Willard to serve as a vindication. In the interview Willard stood by her belief that Southern families were menaced by blacks, a fact she had heard from "the best people I know in the South"; still, to mollify critics like Wells, she added at the same time that "no crime however heinous can by any possibility excuse the commission of any act of cruelty or the taking of any human life without due course of law."[4] Willard's WCTU eventually passed an anti-lynching resolution in 1893; and despite Wells's protests that Willard's earlier public utterances were tantamount to a support of white violence, the temperance reformer was staunchly defended by William Lloyd Garrison, Frederick Douglass, and Julia Ward Howe.

Compared to Willard, Chicago social worker and NAACP member Jane Addams was much less equivocal in her attack on lynching, publishing in the January 1901 issue of the *Independent* an indictment of mob rule called "Respect for Law." However, as Bettina Aptheker has pointed out, Addams did not reject the image of the black beast; rather, she saw lynching as an act that degraded white participants and enforced a disregard for legitimate institutions of law. Addams admitted that there was indeed "a peculiar class of crime [i.e. rape] committed by one race against another," but she argued "[t]hat the bestial in man, that which leads him to pillage and rape, can never be controlled by public cruelty and dramatic punishment, which too often cover fury and revenge." Addams went on to suggest that

> [b]rutality begets brutality; and proceeding on the theory that the negro is undeveloped, and therefore must be treated in this primitive fashion, is to forget that the immature pay little attention to statements, but quickly imitate what they see. The under-developed are never helped by such methods as these, for they learn only by imitation. The child who is managed by a system of bullying and terrorizing is almost sure to be the vicious and stupid child.[5]

Like Willard, Addams was horrified by mob rule; but she also gave credence to the white supremacist notion that "under-developed" black men were driven to rape white women, and that as moral beings blacks were severely handicapped. And again it was Ida B. Wells who responded to what she saw as serious moral lapses in white feminist argumentation on lynching, replying several months later to Addams's comments with her article "Lynching and the Excuse for It," also published in the *Independent*. While more respectful of Addams than she was of Willard, Wells nevertheless pointed out firmly that the belief in black rape was "the same baseless assumption which influences ninety-nine out of every one hundred persons who discuss this question" and urged that "misrepresentation should have no place in the discussion of this all important question, [and] that the figures of the lynching record should be allowed to plead, trumpet tongued, in defense of the slandered dead."[6]

Activists like Wells would fight for decades more to encourage many white women reformers to rethink their stance on white supremacy. The situation was made more difficult by the fact that, in their postbellum campaign, white women suffragists embraced a strategy of "expediency" under which they accommodated white supremacy in order to sign on Southern states behind the campaign for the woman's vote. In 1867, early in the post-Civil War campaign for suffrage, Elizabeth Cady Stanton argued that

> [w]ith the black man, we have no new element in government, but with the education and elevation of women, we have a power that is to develop the Saxon race into a higher and nobler life and thus, by the law of attraction, to lift all races to a more even platform than can ever be reached in the political isolation of the sexes.[7]

In terms of a white female organization dedicated to fighting white supremacist violence, Wells and others had to wait until 1930 for the founding of the Association of Southern Women for the Prevention of Lynching organized by Jesse Daniel Ames, herself a white suffragist. Ames's organization "represented an acceptance of accountability for a racist mythology that white women had not created but that they nevertheless served." Unlike earlier suffragists who had argued that "the Negro Problem" and the political and social advancement of women were completely separate issues, Ames saw lynching "not only as an obstacle to regional development and an injustice to blacks, but also an insult to white women."[8] Ames and her organization sought to work with black women against lynching; such interracial cooperation made her recognize more clearly that the practice of lynching was itself supported by stereotypes of black female promiscuity—a fantasy that shielded white men who raped black women.

The record left by Felton, Willard, Addams, and Ames suggests that white women reformers who were interested in improving race relations came late to a sophisticated analysis of white supremacist violence, which is why, for example, overtly anti-lynching works of fiction by white women writers seem so few and far between before 1920.[9] Thus, decades after the efforts of Wells and other black women, the May 1923 issue of *Century Magazine* contains the short story "Nemesis" by Virginia novelist Mary Johnston on the aftereffects of a lynching on a small Southern town. In the story Johnston acknowledges that lynching is less about black guilt (the story's lynchers never actually ascertain whether their victim is guilty) than it is about white male desire for revenge. A number of the lynch mob's leaders are in fact adopted sons of the South, hailing from New England, the Midwest, and the West, revealing Johnston's belief that the responsibility for white supremacist violence was national and not just Southern. The story ends when the ghost of the dead rape victim returns to admonish her husband for his role in the lynching: "John, don't ever say that you-all did that for me! If you're asking me—no! no! no! What good could it do you-all or me or him or anybody? It didn't please and it didn't serve—not anything—not anybody!"[10] Silenced first by the rape attack and then by the imposition of male narratives about black criminality, the woman rejects the crime of murder committed in her name as an act that serves no purpose for the protection of the white home and hearth. Curiously, though, Johnston only implies that the black man lynched is not guilty of rape.

Without disregarding the nature of white female political discourse on lynching and rape, it is equally important to identify how these topics surfaced in late-nineteenth-century white women's fiction, beyond the kind of direct commentary provided by Felton, Addams, Ames, or Johnston. In the field of black women's writing, for instance, only recently have critics paid any attention to how Pauline E. Hopkins explicitly addresses racial violence in *Contending Forces* (1900), a novel ostensibly designed to address issues of race, femininity, and domesticity. Instead of dismissing Hopkins's work as a novel of black manners marred by a "wild portrayal of injustice, cruelty, and brutality," scholars now recognize *Contending Forces*'s explicit contrast of the promise of black domestic life in America with the crisis of lynching and rape as Hopkins's challenge to readers to recognize that the social and political survival of blacks into the twentieth century depended on the defeat of white supremacy.[11]

Given the fact that turn-of-the-century white women writers—already negotiating traditional notions about what passed as suitable subject matter for the female author—were further constricted by the conservative tastes of publishers and public alike, can we also read white women's writing in the 1890s as similarly engaged with lynching and white supremacy through a certain kind of genteel discourse of fiction?[12]

This chapter sets forth a "rereading" of the recently canonized turn-of-the-century white woman writer Kate Chopin, as an attempt to expand the assumed record of American women's responses to lynching beyond the official utterances of the women who actually spoke out on the issue. Reclaimed by twentieth-century feminist scholars because of her iconoclastic representation of female sexual rebellion in *The Awakening* (1899), Chopin has always been portrayed as sympathetic to the New Woman movement at the turn of the century. On the subject of Chopin and white supremacy, critics uniformly turn to her 1893 short story **"Désirée's Baby"** to demonstrate her critique of nineteenth-century double standards of race and sexual conduct that governed the lives of white men and women. Still, though some attention has been paid to the ethnic contexts of her Southern fiction, little has been done to examine fully how the themes of female sexual liberation can be read specifically in the context of the racial politics of female containment inherent in the ideology of lynching. Similarly, more consideration is needed of how her local color fiction addressed not just miscegenation and black concubinage, but also the problems of regional recovery after the Civil War and Reconstruction, of white male aggression, and of white fantasies of black sexuality.[13] Unfortunately, the traditional simplification by white feminist critics and others of the term *woman writer* renders economic, racial, ethnic, and regional distinctions subordinate to gender, masking the unavoidable convergence of all five categories and severely limiting fuller critical discussion of Chopin and other white female writers within American literature.

As Anne Goodwyn Jones has suggested, even when we assume that "Chopin's concerns more centrally had to do with what she saw as the almost immutable and far from regionally limited relationship between woman and man, the symbols she chose to invest her subject with imaginative power come from her [S]outhern experience."[14] Thus, many of Chopin's short stories, as well as her first novel, *At Fault* (1890), evince a strong preoccupation with white adjustment in the wake of black emancipation, with the problem of internal ethnic and class divisions, and with the shift from rural to urban, from Southern to Northern bases of power.[15]

Chopin's fictional representation of the Reconstruction and post-Reconstruction social scenes are not designed to promote pro-black political activism, as in the case of some of the fiction by William Dean Howells or George Washington Cable. Hers are "thoroughly orthodox" late-nineteenth-century white attitudes toward African Americans; and in much of her work, images of "black suffering, slavery and oppression are all linguistically and thematically appropriated for white women."[16] However, her fiction's representation of white society as heterogeneous and at times violently divided bears some comparison to the conflicted responses to the stereotype of white unity that appear in Mark Twain's *Pudd'nhead Wilson* (1894) and later in the novels of Thomas Dixon. Also, since so many of Kate Chopin's stories are about white men as well as white women, the issue of white supremacy and its attendant violence surfaces as a subject not through the unambiguous lens of racial war, but subtly, within an often all-white context that has been carefully and imperceptibly "shaped and transformed by the presence of the marginalized."[17]

KATE CHOPIN AS WHITE SOUTHERNER

The "Southern experience" on which Chopin drew heavily to shape her white characters has the potential to complicate considerably how we read her representation of whiteness, and specifically of white masculinity. Unlike Thomas Dixon, Chopin was not reared in the shadow of the Ku Klux Klan, but both her childhood in St. Louis before the Civil War and her marriage to a racially loyal white Southerner tied her on the one hand to the memory of slavery, and on the other to the violence of white supremacy itself.

Chopin was born Catherine O'Flaherty in 1851 in St. Louis, Missouri. Her Irish father, a prosperous self-made merchant, died in a train accident when she was five. After her father's death, Kate O'Flaherty was raised exclusively by the independent women of her mother's family, presided over by Victoire Verdon Charleville, a descendent of the early creole settlers to the city. At the time of Chopin's childhood, St. Louis was technically Northern, but "having been settled by French [slaveholding] colonists from New Orleans" the city did possess a Southern as well as a frontier quality. Though many of its citizens did not own slaves, St. Louis had become a slave trading center, slave auctions taking place "[o]ccasionally . . . on the steps of the [city] Courthouse"; on the eve of the Civil War, the O'Flaherty household included six slaves.[18] Staunchly Confederate in sympathy, with slaveholding relatives living in Louisiana and a son fighting for the Southern cause, the O'Flahertys were disliked by the pro-Union faction in St. Louis and at one point in 1863 a Union flag was draped on their front porch. In what might be considered the only overtly political act of her life, thirteen-year-old Kate O'Flaherty angrily ripped the flag off her home; she narrowly escaped arrest by the pro-Union authorities of the city, but her act earned her the nickname of St Louis's. "Littlest Rebel."[19] The family survived the war, suffering some vandalism of their home, but also enduring the death their son George while he served in the Confederate army. And of course they were destined to lose their slaves, including one Louise, who was presumably Chopin's cherished black "mammy."[20]

Kate O'Flaherty's connection to the South was reaffirmed by her marriage to Louisiana-born Oscar Chopin in 1870. After a courtship and a wedding ceremony in St. Louis, and then a European honeymoon that coincided with the Franco-Prussian War, the Chopins returned to the United States late in the year to settle in New Orleans, where Oscar worked as a cotton factor. By 1879 he was experiencing financial difficulties, and he moved his large family (five sons) north to Cloutierville, a small village in Natchitoches Parish where he had purchased some land to argument the remains of his family estate. After bearing her sixth and last child in Cloutierville, Kate Chopin remained there with her husband until his death in 1882.

Oscar Chopin had never been successful as a businessman, and the newly widowed Kate had to resolve her husband's enormous debt in the midst of caring for six children. Undaunted by this challenge, she put the estate in order and in 1884 decided to move back to St. Louis to be with her mother. Thus it was in St. Louis, in the comfort of first and familiar surroundings, that Chopin drew on almost twelve years of life in Louisiana, publishing two novels and approximately a hundred stories about black and white women and men, and the complexities of sexuality, marriage, and maternity. She corresponded frequently with her in-laws in Cloutierville and kept up with the running of the Chopin estate, which was now rented out. She never returned to Louisiana for any extended period, and she died in St. Louis in 1904.

In terms of race relations, Louisiana had a unique history in the South. New Orleans, Chopin's home during the early years of her marriage, offered residents a rich mélange of French, African, Anglo, and Spanish cultures. While other Southern states during slavery enacted segregation and antimiscegenation laws, in Louisiana blacks and whites mixed freely in the Catholic Church, in the street, and at quadroon balls that still occurred after the Civil War; indeed there were even a few interracial marriages, despite the ban against such contact.[21]

Before the war, free blacks "owned real and personal property (including slaves), contracted legal marriages, testified against whites in courts of law, learned trades and professions, and participated in music and the arts."[22] Interestingly, free men of color had never been closely allied with black slaves. After emancipation, however, the fates of both the free *gens de couleur* and the exslaves were linked in the struggle for civil rights. According to John Blassingame, the ex-slave, as "the property the white man went to war to preserve, was the ubiquitous reminder of his folly, guilt, humiliation, and defeat. . . . Most whites were bewildered, angered, and humiliated by the change" in the status quo.[23] Thus, despite the seemingly liberal racial atmosphere of antebellum Louisiana, after the war the stage was set for violence as whites moved to regain control.

The worlds of New Orleans, Cloutierville, and the Cane River valley in which Kate Chopin set her local color stories had their own violent racial past, which undoubtedly become part of the fabric of both her Southern identity and her Southern writing. Indeed, as Helen Taylor asserts, "[s]he could hardly have been oblivious to the many class and race tensions in the area, or to the considerable shifts in economic and social power and influence" that marked the tumultuous years after the Civil War.[24] Before the war, her father-in-law, the French-born Dr. Jean Baptiste Chopin, had been a wealthy cotton planter with 94 slaves and more than 4,000 acres of land. Prior to the advent of Dr. Chopin, the land had been owned by Robert McAlpin, said to have been the model for Harriet Beecher Stowe's cruel slaveholder Simon Legree in *Uncle Tom's Cabin*. Comparison and confusion in the minds of local residents between the two was inevitable, since Dr. Chopin was notoriously cruel to both his slaves and his white wife.[25]

As a child Oscar Chopin had been unwilling to brutalize his father's slaves, but as an adult coming of age after the

Civil War he was clearly a devoted white supremacist, since in 1874 he enlisted in the Crescent City White League. The White Leaguers, whose members numbered among New Orleans's white elite, sought to oust the state's Republican administration, which was hated for favoring blacks. In the summer of 1874, the armed paramilitary White Leaguers—including Oscar Chopin—stormed City Hall to force the mayor's resignation, and a struggle with the city police ensued. Yet another company of white supremacists moved on the State House, expelling the Republication state government until federal troops reinstated it a week later. Despite nationwide indignation at the League's actions, the federal government did not prosecute the rebels. The "Battle of Liberty Place," as it was latter dubbed by New Orleans whites, resulted in the deaths of twenty people and the wounding of a hundred others.[26]

Oscar Chopin's affiliation with the White League would not have seemed out of place in the racially polarized context of Reconstruction. During this period, Louisiana creoles from all classes—especially in New Orleans—swelled the ranks of the state's many local white supremacist organizations such as the Innocents and the Ku Klux Klan. In 1868 almost half the white male population in many parishes of Louisiana belonged to the Knights of the White Camellia (KWC), an organization founded by the French creole Alcibiade DeBlanc that was pledged toward "the MAINTENANCE OF THE SUPREMACY OF THE WHITE RACE in this Republic."[27] The northern part of the state increasingly became a Klan stronghold; and in 1873, whites murdered 103 blacks in the town of Colfax.[28] Such violence continued through to the end of the century. In 1891 eleven Italian immigrants were lynched by a New Orleans mob after a court failed to convict them for the murder of a police officer. Lynching continued, and in 1898 blacks were disenfranchised with the inclusion of the "grandfather" clause in the state constitution. One of the most infamous race riots in American history occurred in 1900 in New Orleans—the same city Kate Chopin loved to roam during the 1870s, fascinated by the exotic presence of black culture.[29] The riot began with an altercation between black resident Robert Charles and the city police, and it finally exploded into a bloody white rampage against the city's black population that lasted for four days.[30]

Site of the Chopin family's ancestral home, Natchitoches Parish had a history consistent with the rest of the state, which meant that its black residents (60 percent of the parish's population) were consistently targeted by white supremacists. Cloutierville resident Phanor Breazeale left a "Statement on Reconstruction Natchitoches" that chronicled his and other white supremacists' criminal activities against blacks in the parish from 1872 to 1878, the year before Kate and Oscar Chopin moved north to the town.[31] Dispassionately and in chilling detail Breazeale describes white Democratic election fraud, the purpose of which was to counteract black Republican votes, and his own eager participation in the ambush and lynching of blacks.[32] In one anecdote Breazeale regrets only that, in attempting to lynch a black political activist, his comrades inadvertently murdered a harmless black sexton of the Episcopal church. Despite such "mistakes," Breazeale views his actions and those of other white terrorists with pride, carefully recounting his substantial role in the intimidation and harassment of an elected black official and his family. Ironically, Breazeale makes it clear in his narrative that the motives of such white "patriots" were purely to exercise political control and intimidation, not to protect white women, noting that though "the negro population on the west bank of Red River of ward 3 was enormously in the majority . . . they were good quiet citizens and obeyed the ladies looking after the crops for their absent husbands."[33] Breazeale eventually married Oscar Chopin's sister, and in later years he served as a friend and confidant to Kate Chopin, entertaining her with tales of his Reconstruction-era activities. According to some, Breazeale told Chopin the story that later became *The Awakening*. And, according to Emily Toth, Breazeale might have served as a model for the many attractive but ungovernable white male characters in Chopin's fiction.[34]

The turmoil of politically and racially violent Louisiana in Kate Chopin's lifetime surfaces obliquely in her fiction, mediated through localized representations of domestic disputes and rural community clashes among whites with differing class, regional, and ethnic affiliations (upper-class French creoles still living on the land, urban residents of New Orleans, lower-class cajuns, "American" whites).

CLASS, RACE, ETHNICITY, AND MALE AGGRESSION IN CHOPIN'S FICTION

In her discussion of pre-Civil War Afro-creole culture in New Orleans, historian Gwendolyn Midlo Hall asserts that the "Afro-creole culture of New Orleans has had a significant impact not only on blacks of Louisiana and Afro-American culture in the United States but on American culture in general."[35] Both the cultural and political conditions of black life had a continuing impact on white racial consciousness, and Chopin's literary imagination was undoubtedly shaped by her exposure to the political and cultural turmoil of the Reconstruction and post-Reconstruction eras. Thus her short stories often deploy a problematic, unresolved investigation of the limits of white action against the backdrop of increasingly prescriptive social roles for both blacks and whites.

As active characters, blacks are not central to Chopin's exploration of white Southern identities; however, the use of blackness, slavery, and Reconstruction as cultural and historical referents to locate and describe white social experience is crucial in her fiction. Chopin constructs blackness generally (although not exclusively) as benign, separate, and exotic rather than as monstrous. Most characterizations draw on the old standards of local color and plantation fiction: blacks like Old Uncle Oswald in **"The Bênitous' Slave"** and the servants in **"Old Aunt Peggy,"** **"Tante Cat'rinette"** and **"Nég Créol"** are quaint "darky" throwbacks to serene plantation days.

When she is critical of Southern culture, as in **"Désirée's Baby"** and **"La Belle Zoraïde,"** Chopin uses the stereotype of black sexual freedom as a metaphor to criticize hypocrisy over miscegenation and white refusal to come to terms with sexual passion. Chopin does not, however, advocate the abolition of Jim Crow. When the issue of integration surfaces, it is usually seen as an obnoxious act performed half-seriously by local whites who want to harass their own kind, as her novel *At Fault* and the story **"In and Out of Old Natchitoches"** demonstrate. Blacks in her fiction welcome separation, and mulatto characters in **"A Little Free Mulatto"** and **"In and Out of Old Natchitoches"** find peace and happiness in the little black enclave L'Isle des Mulâtres.[36]

When blacks and whites do meet, as long as social distinctions are upheld, they confront each other easily and without tensions, as in **"Ozème's Holiday."** While the cajun farmer Ozème vacations around the Cane River valley, he stops to nurse black Aunt Tildy's sick nephew and harvest her cotton before the rain. Working side by side in the field with Aunt Tildy, Ozème remarks jokingly: "I am watchin' you, ol' woman; you don' fool me. You got to work that han' o' yo's spryer than you doin', or I'll take the rawhide. You done fo'got w'at the rawhide tas'e like, I reckon" (*The Complete Works of Kate Chopin* [hereafter abbreviated as *CW*], 386).[37] Aunt Tildy is highly amused at this "reminder" of the old days, as the white man "Mista Ozème," who might have beaten her with impunity during slavery, does not mind helping her out of a bind after the Civil War.

Chopin's portraits of blacks are generally one-dimensional, but her representation of the internal world of white Southerners is always marked by an acute sensitivity to the heterogeneity of origins and experiences in terms of class, ethnicity, and generation. In contrast to the cajun farmer Ozème, members of the French creole planter class who bear allegiance to the Old South are almost overwhelmed by the historical turn of events. Such is the case in Chopin's story **"Ma'ame Pélagie"** where the main character, a former plantation belle, cannot exist outside of the memories of her family's past. For men of Ma'ame Pélagie's class, the difficulty of negotiating change expresses itself in community violence and self-destructive behavior, both of which from Chopin's point of view are counterproductive to the success of the postwar South.[38] The primary example of her complex attitude toward class and white male aggression appears in the saga of the Santien family whose fate Chopin outlines in several stories, including *At Fault*, **"In Sabine"** (1893), **"In and Out of Old Natchitoches"** (1893), and **"A No-Account Creole"** (1894)—works in which the contradictions around class and white male aggression generate their own particular discourse on whiteness.

Like the Chopins and their Cloutierville neighbors the Sampites, the fictional Santiens were wealthy creole planters before the war: "In the days of Lucien Santien and his hundred slaves, [the plantation] . . . had been very splendid in the wealth of its thousand acres. But the war did its work, of course. Then [his son] Jules Santien was not the man to mend such damage as the war had left" (*CW,* 82). The "damage" inflicted by the Civil War comes visibly in the loss of slaves, and the Santiens find themselves unable to manage under the economically altered conditions of the South. After the death of Jules, Madame Santien returns to her family in France, while her sons Hector, Placide, and Grégoire tend to what remains of the family estate, but to no avail.[39] According to Grégoire, "Hec, he took charge the firs' year an' run it in debt. Placide an' me did'n' have no betta luck the naxt year. Then the creditors come up from New Orleans an' took holt. That' the time I packed my duds an' lef'" (*CW,* 751). Eventually Hector chooses to live among the lowlife of New Orleans, and Placide earns the nickname of "a no-account creole" because of his lack of ambition and desultory attitude toward work. Only young Grégoire attempts to integrate himself within a postwar community when he goes to help out on the thriving plantation Place-du-Bois, owned by his young, recently widowed aunt Thérèse Lafirme.

The Santien brothers reference what Joseph G. Tregle calls the "myth" of the creole, a race that

> produced "the aristocracy of the region" through most of the nineteenth century, maintaining family circles renowned for haughty exclusivity as well as cultural refinement and worldly sophistication, the whole invigorated and sustained by fierce conceit of ancestry and a 'chivalry' which gave its inheritors certainty of their superiority over lesser breeds of men.[40]

Quick-tempered, arrogant, but made immensely attractive and sympathetic in Chopin's stories, the Santiens are romanticized in standard plantation fiction style as reminders of a more adventuresome, more passionate past. Thus, in **"A No-Account Creole,"** Grégoire's older brother Placide inhabits a bucolic world in a crumbling plantation house on his ruined, mortgaged land, content to spend his days doing odd jobs or wandering around the Red River. Though Chopin had originally conceived her story around the life and loves of a woman, Euphrasie Manton, the plot centers squarely on Placide's struggle with destiny and (dis)empowerment in his role as Euphrasie's discarded creole lover.[41] Indeed, Placide holds the story hostage when, gun in hand, he sets out to murder the yankified Offdean for taking possession of his family's land as well as of his childhood sweetheart. Bloodshed is narrowly averted when, as an ultimate demonstration that no one but a creole knows "how to love" (*CW,* 101), Placide decides to make the ultimate sacrifice and free Euphrasie from all romantic obligation.

Chopin's story would function simply as a romantic tribute to male heterosexual passion and the capacity for noble self-sacrifice, were it not for the fact that she places Placide's initial impulse toward murder within antebellum traditions of Southern honor and a legacy of white violence produced and nurtured by the South's defining history of slavery. Meanwhile, both Euphrasie and Offdean are products of an increasingly urban world, where to a great extent the social status of whites is fluid. Impor-

tantly, Placide's link to the antebellum past is enforced by the only moment of black narrative in the story. One of Santien's ex-slaves, La Chatte, recalls a chilling incident during her enslavement when a youthful Placide, intolerant of having his desires disregarded, forced La Chatte at gunpoint to drop her other chores and fix him a meal of coquignoles and coffee. During her entire time in the kitchen, until the meal's preparation was complete, Placide held the gun to her head. At the end of her story, La Chatte hints at even more such incidents with the patriarch Jules Santien. As a poverty-stricken black laundress on the decayed Santien estate, La Chatte calls to mind a disenfranchised black population whose collective memory speaks to the historical brutality of life under slavery, as well as to the dual hope and disappointment fostered by Reconstruction and the years beyond. Though each character references a separate group fear of disenfranchisement in both the story's present and its implied future, Placide's tragedy as a failed white man is made to displace that of La Chatte.

The anxiety over white failure engages with but is not analogous to the "failure" of blacks to move from slavery to freedom. Rather, the historical and political isolation suffered by white characters such as Placide both recalls and denies the isolation imposed on American blacks at the historical moment of the story's publication in 1894. Placide is celebrated on white ethnic terms as a romantic creole lover, but his final disqualification as an overly passionate suitor and an irresponsible landowner echoes both the sexual criminalization of black men as beasts/rapists under the regime of late-nineteenth-century white supremacy and their disenfranchisement as post-Civil War citizens. Thus, inasmuch as Placide's violence toward Offdean is not "racial" violence, it is racialized within the context of his past life as a slaveholder's son and of his present life as a white man who operates on his own codes of chivalrous conduct in an economically dynamic, biracial, multiethnic South. Placide's story also references that of countless black men in the South in that both he and his creed must be evacuated to make room for a presumably more acceptable type of lover and landowner in the New South. Thus, though Chopin's sympathetic focus in the story seems to leave room only for Placide, so that blackness can not function as more than a shadowy subtext for the narrative, her articulation of a white man's history in terms that might have been used to describe the fortunes of African American men underscores her dependence on racial discourses about blacks and whites as mutually constitutive, with or without the presence of black characters in her fiction.

This pattern of representation that demands a simultaneous referencing of black and white also marks Chopin's narrative strategy in *At Fault.* The novel's main focus is the romantic relationship between Thérèse Lafirme and David Hosmer, a St. Louis businessman who runs a timber mill on Thérèse's land. In this context Chopin seems to put aside the explosive issues of black suffrage, the Klan, and mob violence, focusing instead on the white domestic haven maintained by Thérèse, the enlightened female despot of Place-du-Bois.

At Fault adheres to the standard plot of the North/South reunion romance between Thérèse and Hosmer to signify the promise of Henry Grady's New South: the unity between Southern agricultural power and Northern commercial and business interests. The subplot of racial discontent and violence, however, belongs to two other significant characters: on the one hand Grégoire, who struggles to adapt to the world created by Thérèse and Hosmer; and on the other the destructive, pretechnocratic, mixed-blood character Joçint. Their struggle is figured in the context of a New South coming to terms with the railroad, industrial development by the Northern business establishment represented by Hosmer, and the sudden shift of a black population from slavery to wage labor.

The tension between antebellum white ideals and the postemancipation threat of "color" comes when Grégoire surprises Joçint in the act of burning down Hosmer's mill: instead of relying on more legitimate methods of punishment, the creole fatally shoots the arsonist. While Chopin unmistakably suggests that Grégoire's murderous impulse is horrifying, her narrative allows no sympathy for the victim. Rude, animalistic, and "extremely treacherous" (*CW*, 757) as a direct consequence of his Indian blood, the dark-skinned Joçint represents a version of the black beast stereotype of pro-lynching fiction.[42]

Donald Ringe has suggested that Chopin creates parallel figures in Grégoire and Joçint, figures whose "inner natures simply will not permit" assimilation into the postwar South.[43] However, as a creole Grégoire is allowed a certain heroic measure. As the unruly worker turned saboteur who refuses to adhere to the new order, Joçint and not Grégoire stands as the obstacle to national progress, and as such becomes the primary embodiment of evil in the novel's Southern white community—a fact that demands his extermination.[44] Consequently, as an act of salvation for the New South, Grégoire's murder of Joçint "is seen as less threatening and forgiven more easily by the whole community."[45] His act of racial aggression creates exactly the same effects that real-life acts of white terrorism such as the lynching, Klan rides, and race riots of the type engaged in by Chopin's husband and Phanor Breazeale were supposed to achieve: the black workers who have been pilfering from the Lafirme plantation regard the show of white power with awe and are suitably respectful of traditional racial hierarchies. Thus Chopin's failure to offer a complete condemnation of Grégoire suggests that, though she may not approve of white violence, she respects its usefulness.

While Chopin's characterization of Joçint is consistent with some aspects of white supremacist ideology, she disrupts at least some of the traditional racial assumptions around the black beast in order to re-vision gender and race politics among the white characters. For one thing, the subplot repudiates the specific notion of the black as

rapist, since Joçint is never a sexual threat to Thérèse. While the bloodshed in *At Fault* mirrors that of the real-life lynching of blacks, Chopin here implies in part that violence occurs, as even Thomas Dixon himself later acknowledged, "when the Negro ceases to work under the direction of the Southern white man."[46] Thus the conflict between Joçint and his white employers is figured primarily as a clash of racially determined goals over the use of land and labor, rather than as the rape and possession of the white female body. This presentation fractures the rhetoric of white supremacy that fused the objectified and disempowered white female body with the white nation. As a white woman who does not rely on the "necessary" protection of white men, Thérèse's self-sufficiency and independence (as well as her willingness to cultivate her love for the married Hosmer) mark her as the kind of dangerous woman the black beast stereotype was meant to corral.

The reformulation of Thérèse's role in the white South's social and political future articulates a new rhetoric of race, gender, and power that is further exemplified in the contrasts between Grégoire and Thérèse as managers of the land and its black labor force. As an example of the new order of white female management, Thérèse Lafirme handles her intractable black workers with a disciplined yet kindly hand, replacing the male violence of slavery days with her Southern knowledge of the "darky" character.[47] Though the novel begins after the Civil War and affords us little information about her life as a wife and slave mistress, Thérèse Lafirme's ability to weather successfully the era's changing economic and social conditions speaks to Chopin's revision of the myth of the Southern belle. Specifically Chopin replaces this myth with the idea of the Southern woman as the white man's equal in leadership and business acumen. The roots of such a revision had taken hold during the Civil War, when white plantation mistresses had been required to manage the slaves and land following the departure of their men to join the Confederate army. With her character Thérèse, Chopin argues for a trend identified by her contemporary Wilbur Fisk Tillett in which "a woman is respected and honored in the South for earning her own living, and would lose respect if, as an able-bodied woman, she settled herself as a burden on a brother, or even on a father."[48]

Significantly, *At Fault* demonstrates that Chopin is willing to challenge the politics of white supremacy only enough to liberate her white heroines, while embracing at the same time its structuring of race relations to consolidate Thérèse's power. Rather than embodying a besieged nation, Chopin's heroine thus becomes a feminized literalization of Grady's New South community spirit, a community that, when dealing with racial inferiors, relies not on "the cowardly menace of mask or shot-gun, but [on] the peaceful majesty of intelligence and responsibility, massed and unified for the protection of its homes and the preservation of its liberty."[49] Chopin's use of Grégoire confirms even Grady's admission that "under this fair seeming there is disorder and violence," but Chopin also uses Thérèse to signify an alternate reality that respects traditional racial codes and racial balances of power without losing sight of the Southern white need for black labor.[50] As Grady himself suggests in his manifesto *The New South,* Thérèse Lafirme's world "is simply the old South under new conditions."[51]

Grégoire clearly functions as a means of demarcating the space for the existence of a kind of Southern "New Woman," but he also exists to help refigure significantly the meaning of white violence. For one thing, his role as an anachronism of the antebellum South displaces contemporary white anxiety over lynching as a barbarous practice. Grégoire's aggression is depicted as tragic rather than as merely destructive, and he is doubly romanticized as a gentleman and a passionate suitor.

As she does with Placide, Chopin specifically accounts for Grégoire's predilection for violent racial control by linking his behavior to antebellum male models of white behavior: he is fascinated by the memory of McFarlane, the first owner of Place-du-Bois, whose exercise of complete control over the lives of his slaves made him "[t]he meanest w'ite man thet ever lived"; he "can't res' in his grave fur the niggas he's killed" (*CW,* 751).[52] Thus Grégoire's violence has no roots in the present political or domestic world of Place-du-Bois, and the racial and economic management of the South engineered by Thérèse and Hosmer is vindicated from its own historical submersion within a world of racial turmoil. Their system is based on a subjugation of black labor, but their dominance is masked behind the figure of Grégoire; white racial violence is accounted for as simply a declining problem of creole arrogance out-of-bounds, not a long-standing white antipathy to black economic and political rivalry that might extend into the twentieth century. So, the story implies, violence will disappear upon Grégoire's removal, rather than requiring a reform of black and white power relations.

While few scholars can conceive of naming Chopin, Thomas Nelson Page, and Thomas Dixon in the same breath, it is worth considering that Chopin shares these male writers' uneasiness with white violence. In his trilogy on the Ku Klux Klan, Dixon abhors the chaos of mob aggression, opting instead for the ritualized murder committed by his Klansmen, which he renders as almost a religious experience in its power to rejuvenate white masculinity. Page's *Red Rock: A Chronicle of Reconstruction* (1898) does feature anti-black violence after Reconstruction; but by the novel's end, blacks under white supervision are pressed into service on the frontier as Indian fighters for the U.S. Army, thereby transforming racial aggression into a necessary tool for territorial expansion. Indeed, Page is most like Chopin in his short story collection *In Ole Virginia* (1887), where white violence is romanticized as a pre-Civil War occurrence not against blacks but within the context of Civil War battles and duels. He confronts interracial violence in the ghost story "No Haid Pawn," but within an appropriately distancing context: his white hero, lost on a hunting trip, takes shelter in a haunted antebellum plantation and contemplates the deeds of the estate's long-dead West Indian (rather than American) slave owner, who was guilty of the vilest of deeds. Such a rescripting of the face of the South for a national audience would have minimized any white anxiety over the fifty to eighty blacks lynched yearly in the 1880s, and especially over anti-black riots that occurred in Carrollton, Mississippi, and Danville, Virginia, Page's home state.[53]

In keeping with the need to distance her vision of the postwar South from the reality of lynching and to secure racial boundaries, Chopin uses Grégoire's behavior to repudiate violence as a practice that might put whites in the position of imitating (and thus embodying) the moral deficiency of the racial Other. (And here Chopin seems to echo the rhetoric of Jane Addams discussed earlier.) As an "enlightened" intersectional coalition of white characters, Thérèse, David, and his sister Melicent Hosmer are disturbed by the fact that Grégoire does not "understand [why] . . . he should receive any thing but praise for having rid the community of so offensive and dangerous a personage as Joçint," and collectively they register an emotional shock at his complete "blind[ness] to the moral aspect of his deed" (*CW,* 824). The Northern characters exhibit a more extreme response. Indeed, Hosmer's inward abhorrence of the murder situates Grégoire in the same role of destructive animal inhabited by Joçint:

> Heredity and pathology had to be considered in relation with the slayer's character. . . . [Hosmer] was conscious of an inward repulsion which this action of Grégoire's awakened in him,—much the same as a feeling of disgust for an animal whose instinct drives it to the doing of violent deeds,—yet he made no difference in his manner towards him.
>
> (*CW,* 824)

In an outward show of racial solidarity with Thérèse's nephew, Hosmer is silent in front of black workers; but his private characterization of Grégoire draws again on the rhetoric of heredity and eugenics, and it registers a growing fear that violence achieves only the destruction of white morality.

As a potential mate for Grégoire, Melicent Hosmer responds to the young man with a kind of social segregation that mirrors general white hysteria over physical contact with black men. Immediately she makes plans to leave Place-du-Bois and berates Thérèse for tolerating Grégoire's presence after the murder:

> "I don't understand you at all, Mrs. Lafirme. Think what he's done; murdered a defenseless man! How can you have him near you—seated at your table? I don't know what nerves you have in your bodies, you and David. . . . Never! If he were dying I wouldn't go near him."
>
> (*CW,* 828)

Melicent is criticized throughout the novel for her distaste at being around black servants and her harsh judgment of

Southerners, yet her disciplined enforcement of proper separation between races and types stands in contrast to Grégoire's later undisciplined attempts at integration. Angered by Melicent and Thérèse's condemnation of Joçint's murder, Grégoire becomes a parody of the Northern integrationist when at gunpoint he forces his fellow townsmen to drink with blacks.[54] This chaotic, last-ditch attempt to reaffirm his power as an aristocrat only results in disruption of the community's moral and racial harmony, since whites, angered at this social imposition, begin to threaten the innocent black men Grégoire has ordered into the bar.[55] As the black workers remark, "Grégoir gwine be Grégoir tell he die" (*CW*, 833), so the only option is to expel him from Place-du-Bois.

Still, it is significant that, although Grégoire must be exiled, by the end of the novel he is reincarnated as a heroic ideal. When toward the end of the narrative Thérèse receives word that Grégoire has been killed in a Texas barroom brawl, all is forgiven as she and her workers grieve for him and revere his memory. This group includes even the black ferryman Nathan, "who had been one day felled to earth by a crowbar in Grégoire's hand, [and] had come himself to look at that deed as not altogether blamable in light of the provocation that had called it forth" (*CW*, 853). This ending makes sense given that Chopin, like her Northern contemporary Frances Willard, does not criticize Grégoire's racial attitude but rather his methods of racial control. Joçint is reprehensible because, as an Indian and a black, he is driven to impulsive destruction. Grégoire is reprehensible because his acts begin to imitate the violence, moral vacuity, and anti-progressivism of nonwhites. In their emotional restraint, their benevolent paternalism to blacks, their civilized acknowledgment of social rules, and their stand for modernization, Hosmer and Thérèse together represent for Chopin an alternative route for white development in the context of North/South social and economic alliances.

Chopin mythologizes aggression and white identity formation in the context of black slavery through the examples of Grégoire and Placide. Yet even as they are condemned for their violent outbursts and lack of self-discipline, theirs is "the only social class that Kate Chopin is really familiar with in this stratified society," and with which, through characters like Thérèse Lafirme, she finally identifies.[56] In *At Fault* Chopin deconstructs white supremacy's myth of the black rapist in order to free her white women characters from restrictive political roles, yet the fact that she does not completely condemn Grégoire's instinct for race protection suggests that she embraces the sense of entitlement offered by the validation of whiteness.

Such validation is exemplified in her short story **"In Sabine"** where Chopin—in tandem with many of her contemporaries—turns from the planter class to lower-class whites for a portrait of real white evil. The main character in "In Sabine" is again Grégoire Santien, whom Chopin uses this time not to demarcate white shortcomings but to make clear the class-bound dimensions of idealized whiteness.

"In Sabine" also functions as a commentary on ethnic division among whites themselves, specifically Americans and creoles in the context of increased anxiety over racial purity after emancipation.

In search of shelter near the Texas-Louisiana border in Sabine Parish, Grégoire encounters Bud Aiken, the "disreputable so-called 'Texan'" (*CW*, 326) who habitually abuses his cajun wife 'Tite Reine. In the context of his rejection by Thérèse and Melicent, Grégoire is mindful of the need to control his behavior in the presence of women and so chooses not to kill Aiken; instead Grégoire merely distracts him with a long poker game and liberal supplies of alcohol. Exhausted from hours of carousing, Aiken falls into a deep, drunken sleep, allowing Grégoire to put 'Tite Reine on a horse headed back to her family in adjacent Natchitoches Parish.

While Grégoire represents for Chopin the aristocratic white man made rigid by his adherence to past values, Bud Aiken signifies by both his alien class and his ethnic origins an even clearer notion of evil, a construction that affords Grégoire a certain absolution in the aftermath of Joçint's murder. As the enemy of the kind of refinement symbolized by Thérèse's new feminine South, Aiken treats Reine like a black slave, sending her "out into the field to pick cotton with old Uncle Mortimer" (*CW*, 331), the neighboring black sharecropper. Such an attempt to appropriate the lifestyle of a wealthy antebellum planter marks Aiken as a social upstart, while his enslavement of 'Tite Reine constitutes a corruption of the kinds of social relations epitomized at Place-du-Bois.

Reine's denigration in Aiken's household is rendered complete when, as she stares at Grégoire from the shock of seeing a familiar face from home, Aiken insults her racially: "'Well, is that all you got to say to my frien' Mr. Sanchun? That's the way with them Cajuns, . . . ain't got sense enough to know a white man when they see one'" (*CW*, 327). Chopin's depiction of Aiken's denigration of 'Tite Reine's ethnic identity and his literal enslavement of a white woman evoke the familiar nineteenth-century feminist representation of marriage as enslavement, and the paralleling of helpless femininity with disenfranchised blackness.[57] Indeed, Reine suspects that Aiken really wants her not as a wife but as a slave concubine:

> "sometime' he plague me mos' crazy; he tell me 't ent no preacher, it 's a Texas drummer w'at marry him an' me; an' w'en I don' know w'at way to turn no mo', he say no, it's a Meth'dis' archbishop, an' keep on laughin' 'bout me, an' I don' know w'at the truth!"
>
> (*CW*, 330)

Anna Shannon Elfenbein suggests that Reine's tale of white abuse is tantamount to a "denial [on Chopin's part] of the chivalrous claims of white men and their rationalization of lynch law as a means of dealing with the brute 'nigger'," demonstrating that "Chopin clearly anticipates the dawning racial awareness of white women" who would later agitate against lynching.[58] This idea seems confirmed by the actions of the story's only black character. As Reine tells the story, Bud "'would 'a' choke' me to death one day w'en he was drunk, if [black] Unc' Mort'mer had n' make 'im lef go—with his axe ov' his head'" (*CW*, 329-30). This scene of a black raising an axe against a white man might ordinarily result in a lynching. Yet Chopin revises the usual white construction of black violence to make it chivalric—not to point to blacks' capacity for heroism but rather to illustrate their imagined faithfulness to good whites (a fallback here on plantation fiction stereotypes). Mortimer is presented as asexual, a move that further draws on the plantation fiction stereotype of black men in order to underscore Aiken's capacity for lawless, abusive sexual desire. And since 'Tite Reine is abused by one white man only to be delivered by another in the form of Grégoire, her story functions less to revise the myth of the black beast for the benefit of African Americans, than to demarcate social and ethnic categories of whiteness.

Following the Louisiana Purchase in 1803, creole and American ethnic tensions had run high in Louisiana, a fact replicated in Chopin's designation of Aiken as the alien villain. According to historian Joseph Tregle, however, such tensions were severely altered after the Civil War because black emancipation brought (at least for a time) de jure black equality: "In the midst of this convulsion, the creole was caught up not simply in a general Southern explosion of antiblack fanaticism, but as well in a peculiar complication which once again set him apart." As Tregle suggests,

> [w]hereas once the danger confronting them had been humiliating loss of Gallic identity to a devouring Anglo-Saxon homogenization, now it was the infinitely more horrible possibility of being consigned to debased status in the "inferior" race, identified as half-brother to the black, a sort of mixed breed stripped of blood pride as well as of any claim to social or political preferment. . . . In such a manner was the cardinal tenet of the now familiar myth born: for those so threatened, henceforth to be creole was to be white.[59]

Traditionally cajuns were "rigorously excluded [from the creole world] having arrived in the colony not straight from the Continent but by way of Canada"; yet in spite of 'Tite Reine's class origins, because Chopin decries the sexual enslavement and "negroization" of her heroine, she proves Reine's value as a white woman and thus argues the case for her salvation.[60] Thus, the urgency to rescue the cajun 'Tite Reine is also the urgency to rescue the identity of nontraditional American ethnicities chafing under restrictive definitions of whiteness, without altering the racial designation of blackness as undesirable.

Ironically, in achieving its rescue of white womanhood from white men, "In Sabine" disturbs the white supremacist fantasy of a natural white masculine solidarity always activated when white women are in danger. Thomas Dixon articulates this fantasy in *The Leopard's Spots* (1902) when

he describes community reaction to the alleged black rapist: "In a moment the white race . . . [would be] fused into a homogeneous mass of love, sympathy, hate and revenge. The rich and the poor, the learned and the ignorant, the banker and the blacksmith, the great and the small, they . . . [would all be] one now."[61]

As Joyce Coyne Dyer and Robert Emmett Monroe suggest, Aiken may "represent the savage state that civilization must destroy, conquer and replace," and Grégoire's own submerged desires for 'Tite Reine tie him to Aiken, even as Aiken's class and ethnic differences serve to distance Grégoire from that desire.[62] With the "white" rapist directly represented as a mirror image of the white hero, Grégoire and Aiken exist as bifurcations of the same white male psyche, suggesting Chopin's implicit recognition that both the (white) male impulse to rescue and the (black) male impulse to rape are dual fictions arising out of conflicted white supremacist attitudes toward white women.

Dyer and Monroe also cite Grégoire's connection to Aiken in his sexual attraction to 'Tite Reine, as he recalls "her trim rounded figure; her piquant face with its saucy black coquettish eyes" (*CW*, 326).[63] But what establish Grégoire as Aiken's social and ethnic superior, what affirm his racial and moral purity, are both his designation of 'Tite Reine as white (and therefore deserving of his respect for her) and his refusal to act on his sexual desire. Consequently Grégoire becomes the perfect model of the romantic white lover:

> Grégoire loved women. He liked their nearness, their atmosphere; the tones of their voices and the things they said; their ways of moving and turning about; the brushing of their garments when they passed him by pleased him. He was fleeing now from the pain that a woman had inflicted upon him. . . . The sight of 'Tite Reine's distress now moved him painfully.
>
> (*CW*, 329)

The potential critique of "In Sabine" might have been devastating: instead of the homosocial black/white male struggle over the white female body, Chopin shifts to an all-white male context that refocuses male anxiety over sexuality and power within the terms of a purely white community. But since Reine's final savior is in fact the white Grégoire and not the black Mortimer, Chopin both references and then forecloses a more extended (and dangerous) political discussion of race, masculinity, and desire.

WHITE WOMEN AND METAPHORS OF BLACK (FE)MALE SEXUALITY

In *At Fault*, "A No-Account Creole," and "In Sabine," Chopin references post-Reconstruction fantasies of the black beast and the white female/nation as victim without relinquishing her impulse toward white racial solidarity. In "A Lady of Bayou St. John" (1893) and its companion story "La Belle Zoraïde" (1894), Chopin sustains her commentary on the restrictive linkage between white female bodies and the South, moving to a critique of ideologies of white sexual suppression through an evocation of desire for the black body. Not surprisingly, this evocation is heavily regulated through her use of the mulatto, the ubiquitous figure throughout Western discourse representing interracial sex. What results is a teasing play on miscegenation that excites and therefore challenges white sexual self-repression, without seriously threatening her contemporary white audience's abhorrence for integration.[64]

Chopin's preoccupation with the taboo of female sexual desire, and her critique of double standards on the subject of male sexuality, is of course made abundantly clear in her stories on Southern women during slavery, in the era of Reconstruction, and beyond. Her characterizations in **The Awakening** and **"Désirée's Baby"** are obvious examples. Though set during slavery, **"Désirée's Baby"** critiques white hypocrisy over miscegenation for an audience mindful of racial tensions in the 1890s, and not just of the memories of slavery and the Civil War.[65] However, **"A Lady of Bayou St. John"** and its companion story **"La Belle Zoraïde"** advance a criticism of particular white female stereotypes that were directly sustained by and utilized for promoting the myth of the black rapist, and that by implication justified the widespread use of racial violence allegedly to protect whites from blacks.

Set during the Civil War, **"A Lady of Bayou St. John"** focuses on the appropriately named Madame Delisle, a Southern belle effectively isolated and immobilized on her husband's plantation. Cared for by her black mammy Manna-Loulou, Madame Delisle embodies the stereotype of a male-authored Southern femininity that denies female adulthood and independence to white women. Madame Delisle's inaction is contextualized by the traditional sources of power in the South (the upper-class white patriarchy signified by the plantation), an idealized blackness in submission (the vague reference to her only companions, the slaves), and also the far-off violence of the Civil War, which eventually precipitates a shift in Southern social roles.

But since the story focuses on a world on the verge of transition, an assault on traditional plantation life, traditional forms of white power, and (therefore) traditional forms of white female containment, is indeed the promised end. This end comes not in the form of social "rape" by an emancipated black population, but rather in Madame Delisle's near-seduction via love letters by her white neighbor Sépincourt. Yet, though life with Sépincourt promises more richness and sexual possibility than were hers in her previous existence, Madame Delisle finally fails at the critical moment. Learning of Gustave Delisle's death she rejects Sépincourt and constructs an altar out of her dead husband's portrait: "Can you not see that now my heart, my soul, my thought—my very life, must belong to another?" (**CW,** 301).

Her self-sacrifice reinitiates her into servitude to Southern patriarchy, signifying that, while the Civil War will free

Manna-Loulou and the rest of the Delisle slaves, white women's adherence to old constructions will perpetuate their restriction into the post-Civil War era. In Madame Delisle's embrace of this traditional role, she literally becomes the Old South of plantation fiction lore, a living memorial to a past ideal of white manhood:

> "My husband has never been so living to me as he is now. . . . I hear his familiar voice, his footsteps upon the galleries. We walk once more together beneath the magnolias; and at night in dreams I feel that he is there, there, near me. How could it be different! Ah! I have memories, memories to crowd and fill my life, if I live a hundred years!"
>
> (**CW,** 301)

Consequently this embodiment of the South through the figure of the belle signifies the death of white femininity, not its protection. White supremacist identification of the white woman with the essence of Southern values and sectional identity is in effect a form of annihilation.

"La Belle Zoraïde" has traditionally been read as Chopin's commentary on what Madame Delisle has lost, since she implicitly contrasts her white heroine with the passionate main character of one of Manna-Loulou's bedtime stories. Like Madame Delisle, the octoroon slave Zoraïde is the tempter of male desire: "'La belle Zoraïde had eyes that were so dusky, so beautiful, that any man who gazed too long into their depths was sure to lose his head, and even his heart sometimes'" (**CW,** 304). But whereas white men have the option of losing head and heart, of lusting and even loving, Zoraïde (who is clearly a reference for Madame Delisle) does not.

Zoraïde's dilemma lies in the fact that she must choose between M'sieur Ambroise, a light-skinned body servant favored by her despotic mistress Madame Delarivière, and the black fieldhand Mézor. When Zoraïde takes Mézor as her lover and becomes pregnant, an angry Madame Delarivière arranges for Mézor to be sold and then snatches away the newborn baby. Believing her child to be dead, Zoraïde goes mad, clutching at a bundle of rags in place of her infant. Insanity saves her from marrying M'sieur Ambroise, but it also cuts her off from motherhood, since she refuses the child returned to her by a remorseful Madame Delarivière. At the story's end, Madame Delisle's only reaction is to moan "'La pauv' piti! Mieux li mouri!'" ("The poor little one! Better had she died!") (**CW,** 307), in ambiguous response either to the fate of the child or to that of Zoraïde, with whom she perhaps identifies.

As Anna Shannon Elfenbein writes, Chopin's story suggests that "neither lady nor tragic octoroon can be free, since one is forced to live vicariously through tales of romance, and the other forced to escape the realities of her lot by going mad."[66] Certainly Madame Delisle suggests the tragedy of self-repression for white women, while Zoraïde suggests the tragedy of slavery: both conditions produce a loss of female potential in terms of sexuality and motherhood. But while Zoraïde's fate mirrors that of

Madame Delisle's, their stories are not analogous. Zoraïde instead becomes the final index of female hysteria, the real symbol of excess in female behavior, an excess that is at least hinted at by the fact that Zoraïde is akin to the white supremacist stereotype of the oversexed black who reproduces.

Zoraïde also becomes a referent for the story's subtextual flirtation with miscegenation as a corrupting social practice. At the start of the story Madame Delisle is figured as a lonely picture of dormant white sexual energy lying sensually "in her sumptuous mahogany bed," an energy answered by the ministrations of Manna-Loulou: "The old negress . . . bathed her mistress's pretty white feet and kissed them lovingly, one, then the other. She . . . brushed her mistress's beautiful hair" (*CW,* 303). Borrowing from Sander L. Gilman's analysis of eighteenth- and nineteenth-century visual representation of race and womanhood, where in paintings such as Manet's *Olympia* "the figures of the black servants mark the presence of illicit sexual activity," I would argue that the juxtaposition of Madame Delisle and Manna-Loulou references nineteenth-century white fears of the detrimental connection between masters and slaves, especially since Manna-Loulou's protection of the seemingly helpless Madame Delisle figures as a corruption, her "soothing" bedtime story perhaps inciting the chaste female mind to lust and infidelity.[67] Manna-Loulou even lends a dangerously "Sapphic" air to the scene with her caresses, actions made more riveting by the contrast of the servant's skin, "black as the night" (*CW,* 303) with Delisle's blond paleness.[68] Ultimately the physical separation of black and white is reengaged in the story of Zoraïde herself. With her "'café-au-lait'" skin and a figure envied by "'half the ladies who visited her mistres'" (*CW,* 304), Zoraïde is a fantasy of desirable blackness and desirable black female passion. Thus Chopin seems to defy and confirm the need for Jim Crow laws, which were well established by the time of the story's publication.

The connection between Zoraïde and Madame Delisle is clear: both are petted; both are fair; both are oppressed by similar rules of social behavior. But in contrast to Madame Delisle, who senses Sépincourt's desire in a "glance that penetrated her own" yet refuses to act upon her "awakening," Zoraïde at first reverses the process of female objectification by tapping into her own sensual feelings: "'Poor Zoraïde's heart grew sick in her bosom with love for le beau Mézor from the moment she saw the fierce gleam of his eye'" (*CW,* 299, 304). The octoroon whose body excites white male lust is herself capable of lust; but because of the story's framing, she must become the conduit for frustrated white desire, rather than a subject in her own right. Madame Delisle—and Chopin's white readers—can still fantasize about sex in comfort and safety: the spectacle of Zoraïde's sexual transgression furnishes the reader/listener with a moment of distanced sexual pleasure, and the punishment for that pleasure (insanity and social exclusion) is distanced within the black body. In a sense Chopin rewrites black sexual criminality (Mézor is not the black rapist, but rather the desired lover; Zoraïde is not the

prostitute, but rather the desiring lover) to speak for white sexual lack, without necessarily disrupting the white supremacist linkage of blackness to bodily excess.

Chopin's complicated play on stereotypes of black and white femininity—to gratify Delisle's longing and then absolve her character of that longing—further grapples with patriarchal notions of white desire by underscoring the excitement inspired by the stereotype of black male sexuality. As a possible sign of her rejection of "her white godmother's racist values," Zoraïde spurns the mulatto M'sieur Ambroise, "with his shining whiskers like a white man's, and his small eyes, that were cruel and false as a snake's" (*CW,* 304).[69] In **"A Lady of Bayou St. John"** Sépincourt's appearance is more appealing: darkened by the sun, he has "quicker and hotter blood in his veins" than his white neighbors. Though he has a "slim figure, a little bent" (*CW,* 298-99), he is still more desirable than Gustave Delisle's portrait, near which the dead man's impotent sword hangs.

But all three men are overshadowed by the sexually charged Mézor; if Sépincourt seduces with words, Mézor seduces with the promise of the black phallus: "Mézor was as straight as a cypress-tree and as proud looking as a king. His body, bare to the waist, was like a column of ebony and it glistened like oil" (*CW,* 304). As with the stereotype of the black rapist, in Chopin's and the reader's— and presumably Madame Delisle's—eyes, Mézor is finally the object of white desire instead of white terror. And more than Sépincourt, who wants Madame Delisle but cannot "comprehend that psychological enigma, a woman's heart," Mézor proves to be a compassionate lover, with "kindness" in his eyes and "only gentleness in his voice" (*CW,* 302, 305).

Despite such gentleness, Mézor also excites because of the danger implied by his presence. Zoraïde (and through her, the reader) first catches sight of him in New Orleans' Congo Square performing the Bamboula, one of a number of antebellum slave dances characterized by "a frenzied African beat" that whites found both disturbing and fascinating.[70] According to early white observers, dances like the Bamboula

> mounted from a slow, repetitious, and grimly deliberate opening phase . . . in an increasingly lascivious crescendo to a final frenzy of "fantastic leaps" in which "ecstasy rises to madness," and finally, suddenly, the dancers fell, exhausted and unconscious, "foam on their lips," and were "dragged out of the circle by their arms and legs" as new dancers took their place, the music never ceasing.[71]

As the symbol of racial regression in the story, Mézor functions doubly as the romantic connection to an exotic African past and as a forbidding reference to a "savage" black passion that, according to Chicago physician G. Frank Lydston, accounted for why "the Ashantee warrior knocks down his prospective bride with a club and drags her off into the woods." According to Lydston the primitive sexual feeling that marked the regressive African provided "an excellent prototype illustration of the criminal sexual acts of the negro in the United States."[72] But though he personifies the black phallus, as the potentially violent lover who restricts his animal passion to his dances, Mézor is made safe in Chopin's narrative, always tethered to the earth, under white control, "hoeing sugar-cane, barefooted and half naked" (*CW,* 305), the subdued African body.

Chopin's Mézor resembles the larger-than-life slave, African prince, and sometime dancer of the Bamboula, Bras-Coupé, who appears in George Washington Cable's historical novel set in 1803 New Orleans, *The Grandissimes: A Story of Creole Life* (1880).[73] Revered by the quadroon Palmyre but feared by whites, Bras-Coupé functions in *The Grandissimes* less as a character than as Cable's stereotype of enslaved black masculinity in all its passion and primitive power. A violent figure who showers curses on his master's family but bows down as a tributary before white women, Bras-Coupé is finally mutilated by exasperated slaveholders; and like the lynch victim of post-Civil War American culture, he casts his shadow over Yankees and Southerners struggling to achieve national reunion.

In Mézor, Chopin evacuates altogether the violence that distinguishes Cable's Bras-Coupé, but neither figure has a presence temporally coexistent with the principal white characters; instead they are written out of the national narrative as actors, to remain finally as symbols of white guilt and desire. Consequently Mézor's safeness is precisely what accounts for his usefulness as a device to stage the articulation of Madame Delisle's suppressed lust. Under the burden of the story's framing, Zoraïde is a frustrated octoroon out of control who must stand in for a white woman unable to imagine herself out of control. Mézor, on the other hand, as a black man is always in the narrator's grasp, trapped within the white idealization of the perfect lover, referencing finally white, not black social insurrection.

The criminalization of blackness that enforces distance is also underscored by the mingled discourses of failed maternity, eugenics, and racial regression invested in **"La Belle Zoraïde."** Within the story's late-nineteenth-century context, "[m]iscegenation . . . was a fear not merely of interracial sexuality but of its results, the decline of the population."[74] Zoraïde's black maternity highlights both Madame Delisle's and Madame Delarivière's barrenness: Delisle moves from immaturity to childless widowhood, while Delarivière can only manage a surrogate black daughter instead of a white one.

The play on black fecundity here as a sign of white disempowerment is further emphasized because the birth of Zoraïde's child in the story signifies the octoroon's disobedience to white law. By denying Zoraïde her child, Delarivière deprives her slave of any claim to a domestic identity, and here Chopin seems to be rejecting antebellum

social relations much as she does in *At Fault,* because they allowed such abuses.[75] But though Chopin seems to be engaging in racial disloyalty by validating black female maternal rights, she sets into motion turn-of-the-century discourses about racial inferiority that deny black capacity to exercise those rights.[76] Zoraïde might reproduce, but she is ultimately unfit for parenting even when a regretful Madame Delarivière returns the child.

Nineteenth-century medical discourse would have attributed Zoraïde's madness not only to her grief over the loss of the child, but to her "impure" racial identity: an octoroon rendered inherently unstable by her heritage of racial interbreeding. The eugenicist language of the story casts M'sieur Ambroise as diminutive, imitative of whiteness, but finally deceitful and cruel, the product of racial refinement that does not improve physical or temperamental characteristics. In *The Grandissimes* Cable's quadroons are similarly afflicted: they suffer either from uncontrollable anger or from a failure of will. Thus at the moment of her rejection of white domination, Zoraïde proves herself to be a version of the "tragic mulatto" who goes mad at the restrictions set upon her identity.[77]

But whereas Zoraïde is trapped within madness and slavery because of the unchangeable features of race and blood, Madame Delisle is trapped by Southern tradition and history, conditions about to undergo radical change in the story because of its setting during the Civil War. Thus, Zoraïde finally exemplifies black sexuality but also black powerlessness, if we read Madame Delisle's "La pauv' piti! Mieux li mouri!" as a comment on the slave's hopeless condition. On the other hand, Delisle exemplifies white female empowerment precisely because of her race, and the frustration generated in the narrative by Zoraïde's tragedy as a black slave becomes finally a frustration at Madame Delisle, who does not exercise the choices Chopin implies are hers by virtue of her whiteness.[78]

It is worthwhile to return to Chopin's heroine in *At Fault,* Thérèse Lafirme, as a rewriting of women like Madame Delisle. Rousing herself from the stupor of the antebellum age, refusing to become a memorial for her husband, Thérèse actively inserts herself into Southern economic life and indeed harnesses and flirts with black sexuality. Like Madame Delisle, Thérèse possesses a black "mammy," Tante Marie Louise, who plies her with food and gentle massages, providing a haven of female sensuality for her weary white mistress. Thérèse is on similarly close terms with Joçint's mixed-blood father Morico, taking delight in combing "that exquisite white hair of his" (*CW,* 805). She does not proffer similar intimacies to Joçint, however; and her rejection of Joçint affirms her instinct for racial self-policing, even as she reorders the sinfulness of the black body with Marie Louise and Morico. Thus Thérèse's rebellious attraction to blackness, tempered by her maintenance of firm control over the latter, becomes a measure of her newly found power as Chopin's ideal of New South womanhood.

I have been arguing in this [essay] for a reconsideration of Kate Chopin as neither disengaged from the racial politics of the late nineteenth century nor actively in resistance to white supremacist thought. Rather, Chopin's female characterizations are as much a response to stereotypes of race as they are a reaction to patriarchal domination. While traditional readings cast her as resistant to the gender conventions of her age, I would argue that Chopin's feminism worked in tandem with her investment in turn-of-the-century racist discourses. As such, her fiction offers an added site from which to consider the racialization of gender within turn-of-the-century white women's fiction. Her fiction also helps to decenter monolithic notions of white supremacist discursive patterns. Inasmuch as Chopin contributes to white supremacist thought with works such as **At Fault, "In Sabine,"** and **"La Belle Zoraïde,"** she revises the white supremacist association of the white female body to suggest a more affirming sexualization and a site for white female subjectivity. She does not address the problem of rape as a category of white racial violence against blacks, but she does register a sense of white anxiety with regard to lynching and mob rule, as exemplified in the behavior of characters such as the Santiens.

However troubling may be Chopin's failure to address fully in any politically meaningful way the horror of lynching, she critiques the balance of power within the gender relations prescribed by turn-of-the-century white supremacy in its restriction of female access to economic and sexual freedom. Chopin's work also registers tensions within "white" culture about the nature of whiteness itself and about the boundaries among ethnicity, race, and region in determining American enfranchisement. As a result, Chopin's work reveals the complex entanglement among white supremacist public discourses, "mainstream" white writing on regional and community development, and especially female "nonpolitical" fiction as she subtly evokes a vision of white supremacy that both liberates and confines.

Notes

1. For general studies on white female activism in the nineteenth-century public arena, see Aileen S. Kraditor, *The Ideas of the Woman Suffrage Movement, 1890-1920* (1965; New York: W. W. Norton, 1981); Ellen Carol DuBois, *Feminism and Suffrage: The Emergence of an Independent Women's Movement in America, 1848-1869* (Ithaca, N.Y.: Cornell Univ. Press, 1978); Carroll Smith-Rosenberg, *Disorderly Conduct: Visions of Gender in Victorian America* (New York: Oxford Univ. Press, 1985); Jean Fagan Yellin, *Women and Sisters: The Antislavery Feminists in American Culture* (New Haven, Conn.: Yale Univ. Press, 1989); and Paula Baker, "The Domestication of Politics: Women and American Political Society, 1780-1920," in *Unequal Sisters: A Multicultural Reader in U.S. Women's History,* ed. Ellen Carol DuBois and Vicki L. Ruiz (New York: Routledge, 1990), pp. 66-91.

2. Quoted in Joel Williamson, *The Crucible of Race: Black-White Relations in the American South Since Emancipation* (New York: Oxford Univ. Press, 1984), p. 128. See also John E. Talmadge, *Rebecca Latimer Felton: Nine Stormy Decades* (Athens: Univ. of Georgia Press, 1960), especially chapter 13.

3. Quoted in Ida B. Wells, *Crusade for Justice: The Autobiography of Ida B. Wells,* ed. Alfreda M. Duster (Chicago: Univ. of Chicago Press, 1970), 151-152. For more information on Willard, Wells, and lynching, see Ruth Bordin, *Frances Willard: A Biography* (Chapel Hill: Univ. of North Carolina Press, 1986); and Vron Ware, "'To Make the Facts Known': Racial Terror and the Construction of White Femininity," in *Beyond the Pale: White Women, Racism and History* (London: Verso, 1992), pp. 167-244, especially 198-205.

4. Ware, *Beyond the Pale,* p. 203.

5. Jane Addams, "Respect for Law" [1901], reprinted in *Lynching and Rape: An Exchange of Views,* ed. Bettina Aptheker (New York: American Institute for Marxist Studies, 1977), pp. 24, 25, 26. See also Aptheker's "Introduction," p. 12.

6. Ida B. Wells, "Lynching and the Excuse for It," reprinted in *Lynching and Rape,* pp. 29, 34.

7. Quoted in Angela Y. Davis, "Racism in the Woman Suffrage Movement," in *Women, Race and Class* (New York: Vintage, 1983), p. 72. See especially her chapter "Woman Suffrage at the Turn of the Century: The Rising Influence of Racism", pp. 110-126; and Paula Giddings, *When and Where I Enter: The Impact of Black Women on Race and Sex in America* (New York: Bantam, 1984), chapter 7.

8. Jacquelyn Dowd Hall, "'The Mind That Burns in Each Body': Women, Rape, and Racial Violence," in *Powers of Desire: The Politics of Sexuality,* ed. Ann Snitow, Christine Stansell, and Sharon Thompson (New York: Monthly Review Press, 1983), p. 338. See also Hall's book-length study, *Revolt Against Chivalry: Jessie Daniel Ames and the Women's Campaign Against Lynching* (New York: Columbia Univ. Press, 1974).

Ames's movement did not by any means suggest a national shift in white women's racial alliances. For information on the campaign to increase white female enrollment in the revived Ku Klux Klan during this same period, see Kathleen M. Blee, *Women of the Klan: Racism and Gender in the 1920s* (Berkeley: Univ. of California Press, 1991).

9. In her memoir *The Walls Came Tumbling Down* (New York: Harcourt, Brace, 1947), the white NAACP activist Mary White Ovington includes her riveting short story "The White Brute" (pp. 88-99), in which a black newlywed couple traveling southward encounter trouble in a small town. While they wait for the arrival of their homebound train, two white men (one of whom turns out to be the son of the local sheriff) kidnap the bride for the purpose of

rape, keeping the horrified groom at bay with the threat of lynching. The story was originally published by Max Eastman in *The Masses* in 1916. I am indebted to Steve Gray for bringing the Ovington piece to my attention.

10. Mary Johnston, "Nemesis," in *The Collected Short Stories of Mary Johnston,* ed. Annie Woodbridge and Hensley C. Woodbridge (Troy, N.Y.: Whitston, 1982), p. 61.

11. Vernon Loggins, *The Negro Author: His Development in America to 1900* [1931] (Port Washington, N.Y.: Kennikat, 1964), p. 326.

12. For an important discussion of Northern publishers and their reluctance to engage in radical discussions of race and reform in the aftermath of slavery, see Kenneth W. Warren, *Black and White Strangers: Race and American Literary Realism* (Chicago: Univ. of Chicago Press, 1993), chapter 2.

13. With regard to Chopin and turn-of-the-century racialized discourses on gender, modern white feminist scholarship on Chopin is undergoing a long overdue change. Two recent studies that link the concerns of white feminist critics (that is, a study of Chopin's feminism) with the impact of region and race are Anna Shannon Elfenbein, *Women on the Color Line: Evolving Stereotypes and the Writings of George Washington Cable, Grace King, Kate Chopin* (Charlottesville: Univ. Press of Virginia, 1989), and Helen Taylor, *Gender, Race, and Region in the Writings of Grace King, Ruth McEnery Stuart, and Kate Chopin* (Baton Rouge: Louisiana State Univ. Press, 1989). Neither of these studies has "failed to recognize how Chopin's feminism is mediated through her implicit positions on race and regionalism" (Taylor, p. 139), and I am indebted to them for shaping my own thinking about Chopin's creole stories. See also Wai-chee Dimock, "Rightful Subjectivity," *Yale Journal of Criticism* 4 (1990): 25-51; and Elizabeth Ammons, *Conflicting Stories: American Women Writers at the Turn into the Twentieth Century* (New York: Oxford Univ. Press, 1992). For a consideration of race and sex in *The Awakening,* see Michele A. Birnbaum, "'Alien Hands': Kate Chopin and the Colonization of Race," *American Literature* 66 (June 1994): 301-23.

Notable early exceptions to the dehistoricizing and deracialization of Chopin's work include Robert D. Arner, "Landscape Symbolism in Kate Chopin's 'At Fault'," *Louisiana Studies* 9 (1970): 142-53; Richard H. Potter, "Negroes in the Fiction of Kate Chopin," *Louisiana History* 12 (Winter 1971): 41-58; Joyce Coyne Dyer, "Bright Hued Feathers and Japanese Jars: Objectification of Character in Kate Chopin's *At Fault,*" *Revue de Louisiane/Louisiana Review* 9 (1980): 27-35; Joyce Coyne Dyer and Robert Emmett Monroe, "Texas and Texans in the Fiction of Kate Chopin," *Western American Literature* 20

(1985): 3-15; and Anne Goodwyn Jones, *Tomorrow Is Another Day: The Woman Writer in the South, 1859-1936* (Baton Rouge: Louisiana State Univ. Press, 1981).

Ironically, Cyrille Arnavon's 1953 introduction to the French translation of *The Awakening* (entitled *Edna*) spends more time contextualizing the novel in its historical and regional setting than many American feminist readings of the past two decades. For a translation of the Arnavon introduction, see *A Kate Chopin Miscellany,* ed. Per Seyersted and Emily Toth (Oslo and Natchitoches, La.: Universitetsforlaget and Northwestern State Univ. Press, 1979), pp. 168-88.

14. Jones, *Tomorrow Is Another Day,* p. 149.

15. I am especially guided here by two early articles on the context of Chopin's local color fiction: Donald A. Ringe, "Cane River World: *At Fault* and Related Stories," in *Modern Critical Views: Kate Chopin,* ed. Harold Bloom (New York: Chelsea House, 1987), pp. 25-33; and Patricia Hopkins Lattin, "Kate Chopin's Repeating Characters," *Mississippi Quarterly* 33 (1979-80): 19-37.

16. Taylor, *Gender, Race and Region,* pp. 155, 157.

17. Hazel V. Carby, "The Canon: Civil War and Reconstruction," *Michigan Quarterly Review* 27 (1989): 39.

18. Per Seyersted, *Kate Chopin: A Critical Biography* (Oslo and Natchitoches, La.: Universitetsforlaget and Northwestern State Univ. Press, 1969), p. 14. For information on the O'Flaherty slaves, see Emily Toth, *Kate Chopin* (New York: William Morrow, 1990), p. 57.

19. Toth, *Kate Chopin,* p. 64.

20. Seyersted and Toth, *A Kate Chopin Miscellany,* pp. 115-16. See also a letter written by Kate Chopin's mother Eliza to her Louisiana relatives towards the close of the war, *Miscellany,* 103-4.

21. John W. Blassingame, *Black New Orleans, 1860-1880* (Chicago: Univ. of Chicago Press, 1973), 15-22. See also chapter 7 of Blassingame's book for a discussion of race relations after the war.

22. Ted Tunnell, *Crucible of Reconstruction: War, Radicalism and Race in Louisiana, 1862-1877* (Baton Rouge: Louisiana State Univ. Press, 1984), p. 67.

23. Blassingame, *Black New Orleans,* p. 174.

24. Taylor, *Gender, Race and Region,* p. 145.

25. Toth, *Kate Chopin,* pp. 122-23.

26. Toth, *Kate Chopin,* pp. 134-36. At the time of the Battle of Liberty Place, Kate Chopin was away visiting her family in St. Louis.

27. Allen W. Trelease, *White Terror: The Ku Klux Klan Conspiracy and Southern Reconstruction* [1971]

(Westport, Conn.: Greenwood, 1979), p. 93. According to Trelease, voter intimidation, election fraud, murder, and violence against politically active blacks and white Republicans became the norm in the early years after the war. During the 1868 election year, "[i]t was reported that in the course of a month at least twenty-five or thirty [n]egro bodies floated down the Red River past Shreveport" (130).

28. Trelease, *White Terror,* p. 131.

29. Emily Toth, "Kate Chopin's New Orleans Years," *New Orleans Review* 15 (1988): 58.

30. Herbert Shapiro, *White Violence and Black Response: From Reconstruction to Montgomery* (Amherst: Univ. of Massachusetts Press, 1988), pp. 61-63. Ida B. Wells discusses the incident in her third pamphlet *Mob Rule in New Orleans: Robert Charles and His Fight to the Death* (1900), reprinted in *Selected Works of Ida B. Wells-Barnett,* comp. Trudier Harris (New York: Oxford Univ. Press, 1991).

31. For a startling account of the intense violence during Reconstruction in the Red River area of Louisiana, see especially Ted Tunnell's incredible chapter 9, "Showdown on the Red River," in *Crucible of Reconstruction.* White supremacists viciously attacked blacks as well as white Northerners who came to "reconstruct" these areas.

32. For the full text of Breazeale's memoir, see Seyersted and Toth, *A Kate Chopin Miscellany,* pp. 157-66. Helen Taylor is one of the first critics to consider the importance of this document for providing clues to the social and racial world Chopin inhabited in Natchitoches Parish. See her discussion on racial tensions in *Gender, Race and Region,* pp. 144-45.

33. Seyersted and Toth, *A Kate Chopin Miscellany,* p. 159.

34. See Toth, *Kate Chopin,* pp. 323-4, 177, for information on Chopin's friendship with Breazeale, and for a description of characters like the Santien brothers.

Chopin seems destined to have her name associated with the most violent men in Cloutierville. Toth has suggested that after Oscar's death, Chopin had an affair with her neighbor Albert Sampite. Handsome, charming, and wealthy, Sampite was nevertheless a reincarnation of the Chopin-McAlpin myth, since he was cruel to his black workers and would beat his wife with a leather strap. See Toth, *Kate Chopin,* pp. 165-66, 171. For an earlier reference, see Seyersted's introduction to *The Complete Works of Kate Chopin* (Baton Rouge: Louisiana State Univ. Press, 1969), p. 26.

35. Gwendolyn Midlo Hall, "The Formation of Afro-Creole Culture," in *Creole New Orleans: Race and Americanization,* ed. Arnold R. Hirsch and Joseph Logsdon (Baton Rouge: Louisiana State Univ. Press, 1992), p. 60.

36. L'Isle des Mulâtres was of course the real-life Isle Brevelle in Natchitoches Parish. For the history of the black creole settlement on the island, see Gary B. Mills, *The Forgotten People: Cane River's Creoles of Color* (Baton Rouge: Louisiana State Univ. Press, 1977).

37. *The Complete Works of Kate Chopin,* ed. Per Seyersted (Baton Rouge: Louisiana State Univ. Press, 1969). All references to Chopin's fiction come from this two-volume set, and are indicated in the text by the abbreviation *CW.*

38. Here I am relying especially on Donald A. Ringe's "Cane River World" for an important early discussion of Chopin's possible attitude toward creole violence and the post-Civil War South.

39. I am indebted here to Lattin's "Kate Chopin's Repeating Characters," pp. 21-25, for her discussion of the Santien brothers.

40. Joseph G. Tregle, Jr., "Creoles and Americans," in *Creole New Orleans,* p. 135.

41. "A No-Account Creole" was based on one of Chopin's first short stories. Variously titled in her notes "Euphrasie," "A Maid and Her Lovers," and "Euphrasie's Lovers," the story was eventually pared down and published in its present form in the *Century* in 1894. See Toth, *Kate Chopin,* pp. 177-78.

42. Robert D. Arner identifies some of the same qualities in Joçint but does not contextualize him within the postwar context of racism that provided the background to Chopin's literary production. See Arner, "Landscape Symbolism," p. 152.

43. Ringe, "Cane River World," p. 29.

44. Taylor, *Gender, Race and Region,* p. 170. My reading of *At Fault* is informed by Taylor's perceptive commentary. See her discussion of the novel in *Gender, Race and Region,* pp. 166-70.

45. Taylor, *Gender, Race and Region,* p. 170.

46. Thomas Dixon, Jr., "Booker T. Washington and the Negro," *Saturday Evening Post* (19 August 1905): 2.

47. See also Taylor, *Gender, Race and Region,* pp. 167-69.

48. Wilbur Fisk Tillett, "Southern Womanhood as Affected by the War," *Century Magazine* 43 (November 1891): 12. For an illuminating discussion of white female management during the Civil War, see Drew Gilpin Faust, "'Trying to Do a Man's Business': Slavery, Violence and Gender in the American Civil War," *Gender and History* 4 (Summer 1992): 197-214.

49. Henry W. Grady, *The Race Problem* [1889] (Philadelphia: John D. Morris, 1900), p. 546.

50. Grady, *The Race Problem,* p. 542.

51. Henry W. Grady, *The New South* (New York: Robert Bonner, 1890), p. 146.

52. Place-du-Bois is based on the old Chopin estate, and McFarlane is the renamed Robert McAlpin, the land's previous owner who was allegedly the model for Harriet Beecher Stowe's Simon Legree.

53. See Thomas Nelson Page, *In Ole Virginia: Or, Marse Chan and Other Stories* [1887] (Nashville: J. S. Sanders, 1991), and *Red Rock: A Chronicle of Reconstruction* (New York: Charles Scribner, 1898).

54. This point is made by Donald Ringe, though from a different perspective. See his "Cane River World," pp. 29-30.

55. A similar incident occurs in "In and Out of Old Natchitoches" (1893), when the planter Alphonse Laballière loses his temper and tries to force a young creole school teacher to integrate her classroom.

56. Arnavon, "Introduction" to *Edna* in Seyersted and Toth, *A Kate Chopin Miscellany*, p. 174.

57. Aiken's ethnic identity is especially important, since Chopin is much more generous in her portraits of lower-class whites of French background (the cajun characters). The bumbling but kindhearted Bobinôt in "At the 'Cadian Ball" and "The Storm" and the gallant Telèsphore in "A Night in Acadie" offer examples of romantic portrayals of lower-class cajun chivalry. On the other hand, when Chopin wants to hint at unbridled sexual energy, class and ethnicity come into play with half-Spanish, half-French characters such as Calixta in "At the 'Cadian Ball" and "The Storm" and Mariequita in *The Awakening*.

58. Elfenbein, *Women on the Color Line*, p. 119.

59. Tregle, "Creoles and Americans," p. 173.

60. Tregle, "Creoles and Americans," p. 132. See also Dyer and Monroe, "Texas and Texans in the Fiction of Kate Chopin" for a discussion of cajun or 'Cadian balls (where Grégoire would have met 'Tite Reine), as places frequented by "sensual, 'disreputable' women who threaten domesticity and monogamy" (6). Dyer and Monroe offer an entirely different reading of ethnicity from my own.

61. Thomas Dixon, Jr., *The Leopard's Spots: A Romance of the White Man's Burden—1865-1900* [1902] (Ridgewood, N.J.: Gregg, 1967), p. 372. Ironically, in white supremacist fiction of the period, usually the middle-class white hero embodied an ennobling racial hatred that expressed itself in justifiable and retributive white violence. Any obvious excesses of white brutality were usually construed as the acts of lower-class whites who were invariably thought to make up the undisciplined mobs that wreaked havoc during the numerous race riots of the 1890s and early 1900s. See, for instance, the stereotypes of white violence represented in Dixon's Ku Klux Klan trilogy of *The Leopard's Spots, The Clansman* (1905), and *The Traitor* (1907).

62. Dyer and Monroe, "Texas and Texans," pp. 1, 5-7.

63. Dyer and Monroe, "Texas and Texans," p. 6.

64. See Joyce Coyne Dyer's useful but strangely uncritical description of Chopin's invocation of race to distance and connect her white readers with the sexual desire demonstrated by the black characters in "Techniques of Distancing in the Fiction of Kate Chopin," *Southern Studies* 24 (1985): 69-81. See also Michele A. Birnbaum's reading of the quadroon nursemaid in Chopin's *The Awakening,* in her article "'Alien Hands': Kate Chopin and the Colonization of Race."

65. Cynthia Griffin Wolff makes an excellent point about the historical resonance that "Désirée's Baby" might have had for Southern readers in its subtle references to causes of the Civil War, but she fails to recognize that Southern (and Northern) readers in the 1890s were just as concerned about miscegenation as the story's main character, Armand. See Wolff, "The Fiction of Limits: 'Désirée's Baby'," in *Modern Critical Views: Kate Chopin,* ed. Harold Bloom (New York: Chelsea House, 1987), p. 38.

66. Elfenbein, *Women on the Color Line,* p. 131.

67. Sander L. Gilman, "Black Bodies, White Bodies: Toward an Iconography of Female Sexuality in Late Nineteenth-Century Art, Medicine, and Literature," *Critical Inquiry* 12 (Autumn 1985): p. 209. The specific idea of black corruption of whiteness is not new, of course. Northern white abolitionists had long feared that part of slavery's danger was the potential moral contamination achieved through associations with uncivilized black slaves. See, for example, Ronald G. Walter's extremely useful article "The Erotic South: Civilization and Sexuality in American Abolitionism," *American Quarterly* 25 (1973): 177-201.

68. See Gilman's reading of blackness, female sexuality, and disease in "Black Bodies, White Bodies," especially at p. 237. For a useful discussion of the metaphoric uses of Sappho as an emblem of corrupting lesbian relations in medical discourse, see Nicole Albert, "Sappho Mythified, Sappho Mystified or the Metamorphoses of Sappho in Fin de Siècle France," *Journal of Homosexuality* 25 (1993): 87-104.

69. Elfenbein, *Women on the Color Line,* p. 133.

70. Blassingame, *Black New Orleans,* p. 3. See also Jerah Johnson, "New Orleans's Congo Square: An Urban Setting for Early Afro-American Culture Formation," *Louisiana History* 32 (Spring 1991): 117-57.

71. Johnson, "New Orleans's Congo Square," pp. 143-44.

72. Hunter McGuire and G. Frank Lydston, *Sexual Crimes Among the Southern Negroes* (Louisville: Renz & Henry, 1893), p. 7.

73. George Washington Cable, *The Grandissimes: A Story of Creole Life* [1880] (Athens: Univ. of Georgia Press, 1988).

74. Gilman, "Black Bodies, White Bodies," p. 237. White fears of black and European immigrant overpopulation were of course widespread in the post-Civil War era, and white supremacists anxiously countered reports of the decline in the birthrate among whites with the notion that, without slavery, blacks were heading for extinction by the end of the nineteenth century. For a discussion of the issue of black/white population growth, see George M. Frederickson, *The Black Image in the White Mind: The Debate on Afro-American Character and Destiny, 1817-1914* (Middletown, Conn.: Wesleyan Univ. Press, 1971), chapter 8. For advice given to women to avoid what Theodore Roosevelt termed "race suicide," see Barbara Ehrenreich and Deirdre English, *For Her Own Good: 150 Years of the Experts' Advice to Women* (Garden City, N.Y.: Anchor, 1978), pp. 134-37.

75. The context here, of course, would be Harriet Beecher Stowe's *Uncle Tom's Cabin* (1852).

76. It is important to note that black female claims to equality with white women had been argued in the nineteenth century through the figure of the maternal. See, for instance, Harriet Jacobs in *Incidents in the Life of a Slave Girl* (1861) and, at the very moment of Chopin's stories, the numerous domestic novels by black women that stressed black female capacity for responsible motherhood and racial uplift.

77. For a discussion of blackness and madness in nineteenth-century thought see Gilman, *Difference and Pathology: Stereotypes of Sexuality, Race and Madness* (Ithaca, N.Y.: Cornell Univ. Press, 1985), chapter 5. There was of course a separate discourse on womanhood and madness; and my argument here is that, as a racial hybrid and a woman, Zoraïde bears the burden of a body doubly inscribed as the site of madness.

78. See also Birnbaum's discussion of race and female empowerment in *The Awakening* in "'Alien Hands',", p. 304.

Andrew Delbanco (essay date 1997)

SOURCE: Delbanco, Andrew. "Was Kate Chopin a Feminist?" In *Required Reading: Why Our American Classics Matter Now,* pp. 113-32. New York: Farrar, Straus and Giroux, 1997.

[*In the following essay, Delbanco explains why he believes Chopin's works deserve a place among the classics of American literature.*]

It seems a long time ago that teachers could distribute without embarrassment *The Lifetime Reading Plan* or some such guide to literacy and expect students to measure their progress toward adulthood by the number of checks beside the titles read. There is a certain comfort in the authority of lists. But since we may never again have such lists, the idea of the classic—if it is to be preserved at all—needs to be saved from the idea of the absolute. In a charming rescue operation conducted some years ago, Frank Kermode gave this modest definition of what a classic is: "A classic . . . is a book that is read a long time after it was written."

It is now nearly a century since *The Awakening* was written—a once obscure, now famous, novel of adultery and suicide by Kate Chopin. Born into a well-to-do St. Louis family in 1851, Kate O'Flaherty married at the age of nineteen a prosperous New Orleans merchant named Oscar Chopin, who died twelve years later, leaving her a widow in her early thirties. It was under these conditions that she began to write stories.

The reputation of the one novel Kate Chopin published, *The Awakening,* has fluctuated from scandal when it first appeared in 1899 and was angrily received as an American *Madame Bovary* to near-oblivion during the first half of the twentieth century until Cyrille Arnavon translated it into French and Robert Cantwell and Edmund Wilson began to reclaim it for our own literature. According to my last count, it was in print in sixteen editions competing for the college and high school market.

During its long dormancy, *The Awakening* did manage to survive in scholarly histories as an example of regionalism or "local color." To be designated a work of "regionalism" was, not too long ago, to be dismissed as provincial, but one reason *The Awakening* is now a classroom staple is that "local" has become an honorific term. If it once implied limits and smallness, the word "local" now suggests integrity, purity, and resistance to a malevolent power often referred to in academic circles as the "center." I want briefly to consider this strange new geography of value before turning to the novel itself.

One representative critic, Marjorie Pryse, puts the matter clearly:

> The belief in universals has [too long] held its own in the face of attacks by what we might collectively term regional interests: black studies and the civil rights movement, women's studies and the resurgence of feminism, American studies and a return to grassroots politics, as well as movements for gay rights, Native American heritage, and so on. Therefore, a reevaluation of regional concepts must begin by accounting for the pervasive undermining of "local" concerns and texts by the conviction the majority of citizens in the culture share that there do indeed exist "universals."

Reclaiming the regional tradition amounts, in this view, to an act of solidarity with the excluded, the oppressed, the "marginalized."

It may, however, be worth enlarging the question of why regionalism has lately enjoyed academic revival by looking beyond the sphere of literary study. As recently as thirty years ago in the United States, "the revision of accepted standards of cultural value" (Pryse's phrase) chiefly meant revision of such "universals" as these: race hatred, indifference toward the poor, and tolerance of prevailing conditions in the industrial workplace. Moreover, the revision of these accepted standards was carried out not regionally but from Washington, the nation's center of political power.

In what is surely a conspicuous irony, the language of antagonism toward the "center" has become, in the last twenty years or so, the shared property of the political right and the academic left. One remembers, for instance, that Richard Nixon often invoked the formula that it was "time for power to stop flowing from the people to the capital, and to start flowing from the capital to the people," a kind of talk that became more common in the 1980s and 1990s (even as I write, the responsibility for millions of needy children is being redistributed, through the process of welfare "reform," to "local" authorities) and is the leading language of cultural criticism as well. The leftish academy celebrates regionalism as an assault on what it decries as the pernicious "norms" of American ideology (patriarchy, laissez-faire capitalism, imperial expansion), while the political right invokes the idea of regional autonomy as a way to restore those very norms under new names: "family values," entrepreneurship, national defense. If regionalism is in good odor among both professors and politicians, perhaps we ought to wonder if the gap between the academic left and the political right is as wide as both sides like to claim.

With this question in mind, what does one make of *The Awakening,* whose transformation from a work of local interest into a prestigious novel has been rivaled only by Zora Neale Hurston's *Their Eyes Were Watching God?* This book does not fit within any of the customary ideological categories. Anyone who has discussed it in the classroom knows that it can be read with assent by readers of quite opposite convictions on issues of sexual politics. This story of a frantically unhappy woman sets itself off from the usual regional evocation of the sexually awakened country girl—as Hamlin Garland described her, for example, in his collection of sketches about life in the Midwest, *Main-Travelled Roads* (1891):

> "Girls in love ain't no use in the whole blessed week," she said. "Sundays they're a-lookin' down the road, expectin' he'll *come.* Sunday afternoons they can't think o' nothin' else, 'cause he's *here.* Monday mornin's they're sleepy and kind dreamy and slimpsy, and good f'r nothin' on Tuesday and Wednesday. Thursday they git absent-minded, an' begin to look off toward Sunday agin, an' mope aroun' and let the dishwater git cold, right under their noses. Friday they break dishes, and go off in the best room an' snivel, an' look out o' the winder. Saturday, they have queer spurts o' workin' like all p'sessed, an' spurts o' frizzin' their hair. An' Sunday they begin it all over agin."

This Midwestern Penelope is not yet grown into an adult capable of stratagem, but she is on her way to becoming

the eternally untarnished wife, a human exemplar of the fertile land in which she makes her life, or, more accurately, in which she performs her service. She is what Carrie Meeber would have been if she had stayed in rural Wisconsin and never boarded the train for Chicago.

The tormented wife and mother of *The Awakening,* Edna Pontellier, is entirely different. The daughter of a Kentucky Presbyterian who "atone[s] for his weekday sins with his Sunday devotions," Edna marries into the dying French Catholic culture of New Orleans, where, even at the end of the nineteenth century, women were still living virtually without rights under a version of the Napoleonic legal code. In this static world she becomes a sort of captive ambassador from the frontier country in which she had been born—and an object of flirtatious interest among the quasi-Frenchmen of New Orleans.

These men are of a recognizable sort in turn-of-the-century American fiction. One may think not only of Henry James's ineffectual males ("Young men are very different from what I was," says the elder Mr. Touchett in *The Portrait of a Lady* [1881], "when I cared for a girl—when I was young—I wanted to do more than look at her") but of Dreiser's Hurstwood in *Sister Carrie* descending through shabbiness into despair, or of Stephen Crane's boy-soldier in *The Red Badge of Courage* trying to prove himself on the battlefield, or, a little later, of this complaint from Mrs. Bart in Edith Wharton's *The House of Mirth* (1905): "It had been among that lady's grievances that her husband [whose bankruptcy and death have left the family groping for position] in the early days, before he was too tired, had wasted his evenings in what she vaguely described as 'reading poetry.'" If the literary record can be trusted, America at the turn of the century seems to have been populated by men who could not cope.

Kate Chopin agreed. She witnessed in New Orleans what Wharton saw in New York and what another "regionalist," the New England writer Sarah Orne Jewett, saw in coastal Maine: a once haughty privileged class on the edge of extinction, nominally led by men too shriveled to lead. Edna's first infatuation, Robert Lebrun, brings his "high voice" and "serio-comic" charm each summer to the tony resort at Grand Isle, where he constitutes "himself the devoted attendant of some fair dame or damsel . . . sometimes a young girl, [or] a widow . . . [or] some interesting married woman." He seems best pleased as a kind of humored troubadour sitting at the feet of an unavailable lady. From this posture he recites titillating accounts of his amorous adventures, and is excited in turn by "the lady at the needle [who] kept up a little running, contemptuous comment: *Blagueur—farceur—gros bête, va!*" There is a hint of sexual self-abasement here, but in the end such entertainments on even the hottest Louisiana nights feel more filial than carnal. This man has fallen out of the active world. He has become something between a jester and a gigolo.

So male attenuation is one theme Chopin shared with other regional writers of her time. Jewett populated her *Country of the Pointed Firs* (1896) with men who are either drifting into senility or frozen in boyhood, keeping about them "a remote and juvenile sort of silence." But whereas Jewett gives us a settled psychic condition as a consequence of New England's economic decline (her men languish in a kind of melancholy reverie about the past), Chopin shows us a Southern version of the same problem as social *process*—a process she makes visible by giving us glimpses of Creole men who are mainly devoted to dissipation. Robert, whose voice Edna finds so "musical and true," leaves suddenly for Mexico with no evident itinerary. Alcée Arobin, whose "good figure [and] pleasing face" console her after Robert's departure by "appealing to the animalism that stirred impatiently within her," has no evident vocation—except to be her second conquest.

As Edna ventures further from her husband, she finds herself, sometimes literally, on a border between old and new. "I saw her," reports Dr. Mandelet, ". . . walking along Canal Street"—the dividing line between the French Quarter and the modern city that was outgrowing the historic New Orleans boundaries. Her house, dressed and painted "a dazzling white" to please the scanning eye, is an expression of the old Creole femininity as a self-advertising bauble. Graceful, glad to be owned, its "round, fluted columns support the sloping roof." But it is also Edna's prison. Chopin conveys the sense of confinement from the first sentence of the novel, which presents "a green and yellow parrot . . . hung in a cage," making imitative sounds to the amusement of visitors.

When she gets an occasional furlough, the place where Edna most likes to spend her free moments is the home of Mademoiselle Reisz, whose "apartments up under the roof" are high above the world of noise and barter. "There were plenty of windows in [Mademoiselle Reisz's] little front room. They were for the most part dingy, but as they were nearly always open it did not make so much difference . . . From her windows could be seen the crescent of the river, the masts of ships and the big chimneys of the Mississippi steamers." If Edna's house is all surfaces, the home of Mademoiselle Reisz has an interior genuinely expressive of its owner, but also bravely open to the world.

Much of the novel is concerned with Edna's attempt to learn something from this example. She struggles to open her mind to the meaning of the appurtenances—some chosen, some not—among which she must live out her life. To put it another way, she begins to understand that she can at least modify the scenes of her existence. Rooms, views, streets, furnishings—in the full sense of the word, "decor"—are a realm of experience whose significance had once been lost on her. Now that she begins to distinguish between the life assigned to her and the possibility of fashioning herself anew, she makes her boldest (and most often quoted) declaration: "I would give up the unessential; I would give away my money, I would give my life for my children; but I wouldn't give myself." With this series of renunciations, she has come to sense the existence of a free and irreducible self.

But what constitutes this self? What can be discarded as "unessential"? Edna's first hint of an answer, as she rises out of her appointed role as imported wife, is her discovery that self-awareness begins with the sense of touch:

> Edna, left alone in the little side room, loosened her clothes, removing the greater part of them. She bathed her face, her neck and arms in the basin that stood between the windows. She took off her shoes and stockings and stretched herself in the very center of the high, white bed. How luxurious it felt to rest thus in a strange, quaint bed, with its sweet country odor of laurel lingering about the sheets and mattress! She stretched her strong limbs that ached a little. She ran her fingers through her loosened hair for a while. She looked at her round arms, as she held them straight up and rubbed them one after the other, observing closely, as if it were something she saw for the first time, the fine, firm quality and texture of her flesh. She clasped her hands easily above her head, and it was thus she fell asleep.

Complaining that he meets his wife now only "at breakfast," Mr. Pontellier has no role in his wife's sexual awakening, but neither exactly does the flirtatious Robert, who seems poised to supplant him as her partner: Robert's "face [grows] a little white" when she gives him a glimpse of her aroused sexuality. Even Arobin, though less hesitant to test his capacity to slake her desire, is more voyeur than lover. In thwarted pursuit of partnership, Edna grows more and more lonely. Whenever she hears her friend Mademoiselle Reisz play a certain plaintive piano melody (though she knows that "the name of the piece was something else") she calls it "Solitude," and imagines "the figure of a man standing [naked] beside a desolate rock on the seashore." She is haunted by this image of a single figure interrupting an unpeopled vista. Her situation calls to mind that wicked rejoinder spoken by Marilyn Monroe at the opening of Arthur Miller's screenplay for *The Misfits*: The devastated young husband, just discarded on the courthouse steps after signing the divorce papers, begs her to say why she wants to leave him. "If I have to be alone," she replies, "I'd rather be by myself."

Edna, too, refuses to be part of her husband's bric-a-brac and begins to create an environment of her own invention—a process that begins in earnest with her husband's departure for New York on business. As the day for his leaving draws near, she scurries about the house in a new kind of agitation—guilty, we suspect, not so much over remaining without him as over her premonition of the temptations of independence. "She was solicitous about his health and his welfare. She bustled around, looking after his clothing, thinking about heavy underwear . . ." Nearly twenty-nine, she behaves like a child of sixteen whose conscience acts up in anticipation of a weekend without supervision. But when she is at last left alone, relief conquers guilt, and she tours "her" house with a combination of proprietorship and sensory excitement:

> A feeling that was unfamiliar but very delicious came over her. She walked all through the house, from one room to another, as if inspecting it for the first time.

She tried the various chairs and lounges, as if she had never sat and reclined upon them before. And she perambulated around the outside of the house, investigating, looking to see if windows and shutters were secure and in order. The flowers were like new acquaintances; she approached them in a familiar spirit, and made herself at home among them. The garden walks were damp, and Edna called to the maid to bring out her rubber sandals. And there she stayed, and stooped, digging around the plants, trimming, picking dead, dry leaves. The children's little dog came out, interfering, getting in her way. She scolded him, laughing at him, played with him. The garden smelled so good and looked so pretty in the afternoon sunlight. Edna plucked all the bright flowers she could find, and went into the house with them, she and the little dog.

This is a passage into discovery but not, I suspect, an introduction to self-knowledge. Edna's mood of release at her husband's departure, which begins as involuntary exultation, quickly becomes conscious and strategic, until she takes the first step toward remaking her life. She will, she decides, move out of the big house into a cottage around the block. "Just two steps away," she tells Mademoiselle Reisz, who has challenged her for an explanation. "I'm tired of looking after that big house. It never seemed like mine, anyway—like home." As Mademoiselle Reisz senses, the key word is "mine"; Edna is developing a taste for ownership. She falls into pecuniary explanations:

> Oh! I see there is no deceiving you. Then let me tell you: It is a caprice. I have a little money of my own from my mother's estate, which my father sends to me by driblets. I won a large sum this winter on the races, and I am beginning to sell my sketches.

It is now possible to see why Chopin has used a teasing, ironic sentence to mark the moment when the novel shifts from the open spaces of Grand Isle to the interiors of New Orleans: "The Pontelliers possessed a charming home on Esplanade Street." Strictly speaking, Edna—as distinct from her husband—possesses nothing. As Margaret Culley, one of the modern editors of *The Awakening,* has pointed out about the Louisiana legal code, "all of a wife's 'accumulations' after marriage were the property of her husband, including money she might earn and the clothes she wore." Yet Chopin implies that in a larger sense Edna is becoming an equal partner in the plural subject ("the Pontelliers") of her sentence. She is becoming a possessor. She has begun to escape the condition of being (or at least learning to be) a proper Creole lady. But it is not sufficient to speak of what she is leaving behind. To come fully to terms with this novel, we must follow Edna into the terrible limbo into which she now falls. By the time of her husband's departure, *The Awakening* has become a book about her suspension not merely between Kentucky Presbyterianism and Creole Catholicism, or between halves of the city divided by Canal Street, but between the genders themselves.

This transformation has been hinted from the start. "She was rather handsome than beautiful," we are told early,

and before long she learns to drink "liquor from the glass as a man would have done." This most basic of the novel's suspensions—between femininity and masculinity as forms of social being—takes a predictably large psychic toll. Edna's statement that "I am beginning to sell my sketches," for instance, is a check on her emerging artistic commitment, which is explicitly associated with female dissent from the male world of commodity display and exchange. Surely her moment of highest self-realization comes when she is able—like her friends Madame Ratignolle (with her children) and Mademoiselle Reisz (with her music)—to take pleasure in the intrinsic value of something she has produced. Edna "had reached a stage [with her painting] where she seemed to be no longer feeling her way, working, when in the humor, with sureness and ease. And being devoid of ambition, and striving not toward accomplishment, she drew satisfaction from the work in itself."

In Chopin's world, this experience is unavailable or, more accurately, unaffordable for men. Edna's brush with it is one of those moments when it is useful to think of *The Awakening* in roughly Marxian terms: she has escaped, at least momentarily, from alienation. Even if it is only a fleeting freedom, she conceives, for a moment, of neither her work nor herself as a commodity—which is why "I am beginning to sell my sketches" is double-edged. What in one sense is the beginning of independent professionalism—a feminist victory—is also a lapse into equating the expression of self with marketable goods and services. Edna, who has been bought and sold, is entering the marketplace as a vendor.

Both aspects of this awakening—liberation and constriction—are adumbrated in the brilliant account of her father's visit. Once a proud colonel in the Confederate Army, he sits "before her pencil . . . rigid and unflinching, as he had faced the cannon's mouth in days gone by." This is, if ever there was one, a phallic pencil: an emblem of daughterly usurpation. "Her lack of filial kindness and respect" is not excused by the scrutiny to which she subjects him while making his portrait. When she refuses to attend her sister's wedding, he accuses her of further deficiencies: a "want of sisterly and womanly consideration." As both Mademoiselle Reisz and Madame Ratignolle realize, Edna is replacing her thralldom to men in general and to particular men—father, husband, imagined lovers—with the thrill of partaking in exactly the experience that they had once monopolized: the experience of power.

This exchange of roles creates the conditions for her self-destruction:

> "Take the fan," said Edna, offering it to [Robert].
>
> "Oh, no! Thank you. It does no good; you have to stop fanning some time, and feel all the more uncomfortable afterward."
>
> "That is one of the ridiculous things which men always say. I have never known one to speak otherwise of fanning."

Mocking Robert for the calculus of pain and pleasure that he applies to the most trivial choices, Edna has had enough of computation; enough, when she wants to linger outside in the night, of her husband's "you will take cold out there." To fan or not to fan, she suggests, is a pathetic question. Edna is learning a new language of impulse that is explicitly identified as female, at least within the universe of the novel, and this is precisely why it is so ominous when she falls back, like the caged parrot, into mimicry: "I hardly think we need new fixtures, Léonce," she says to her husband. "Don't let us get anything new: you are too extravagant. I don't believe you ever think of saving or putting by." Such spousal scolding is a fair imitation of her husband's nagging.

Edna's "awakening" never wholly renovates her consciousness. She "never awakens," as Elaine Showalter has pointed out, "to the dimensions of her social world . . . never sees how the labor of the mulatto and black women around her makes her narcissistic existence possible." Because of the servants, she is able to keep the world of her children at a muted distance: "The boys were being put to bed; the patter of their bare, escaping feet could be heard occasionally, as well as the pursuing voice of the quadroon." The children's life upstairs is a bit of background noise. Edna exists in a relation to governess and children not very different from her husband's relation to her, as a remote employer. "If one of the little Pontellier boys took a tumble whilst at play, he was not apt to rush crying to his mother's arms for comfort; he would more likely pick himself up, wipe the water out of his eyes and the sand out of his mouth, and go on playing." Childbirth itself is something she had once barely apprehended through an anesthetic haze. And the numbness lingers not only in memory but as a "stupor which had deadened sensation," and which, despite the novel's title (chosen, we should recall, by the publisher, not the author), closes tighter and tighter around her as her "awakening" proceeds: "She felt no interest in anything about her. The street, the children, the fruit vender, the flowers growing there under her eyes, were all part and parcel of an alien world." Sensory deprivation is another point toward which she converges in company with the men around her. Léonce sits at their dining table pouring "pepper, salt, vinegar, mustard—everything within reach" into his soup, in the hope of giving it some bite. He and Edna are not so much an opposition as a matched pair.

But if Edna and her husband descend together into dull discontent, they differ in how they cope with the death-in-life they share. For him the only release is to carry on his business, to make the pretense that nothing is off-center in his life. For Edna, the resort is to sex:

> She leaned over and kissed [Robert]—a soft, cool, delicate kiss, whose voluptuous sting penetrated his whole being—then she moved away from him. . . . She took his face between her hands and looked into it as if she would never withdraw her eyes more.

Granting to Edna this control over the rhythm of penetration and withdrawal, Chopin takes her still further away from "femininity." Squeamish Robert is appalled. "Foolish boy," Edna calls him, and declares herself "no longer one of Mr. Pontellier's possessions. . . . I give myself where I choose." As Robert declines to receive this gift, *The Awakening* becomes one of those books devoted to exposing the male fear of female sexuality, a fear that runs deep through American culture, from drawing-room magazines such as *Godey's Lady's Book* to the *Playboy* airbrush. Robert cannot abide what F. Scott Fitzgerald was later to call the "ghastly reiterated female sound" of a woman's orgasm.

Arobin is more willing to parry Edna's thrusts. Yet there is no fulfillment in her intimacy with him. Using the language of pathology, Chopin remarks that "the excitement [of Arobin's presence] came back upon her like a remittent fever." She acquaints Edna with desire not only for men but for drink, for gambling, for anything that will heat her blood. It is an appetite of which Edna is aware to the point of fear:

> "Will you go to the races again?" he asked.
>
> "No," she said. "I've had enough of the races. I don't want to lose all the money I've won, and I've got to work when the weather is bright, instead of—"
>
> "Yes; work; to be sure. You promise to show me your work. What morning may I come up to your atelier? To-morrow?"
>
> "No!"
>
> "Day after?"
>
> "No, no."
>
> "Oh, please don't refuse me! I know nothing of such things. I might help you with a stray suggestion or two."
>
> "No. Good night. Why don't you go after you have said good night? I don't like you," she went on in a high, excited pitch, attempting to draw away her hand. She felt that her words lacked dignity and sincerity, and she knew that he felt it.

Arobin has attached himself to her not with anything resembling love, but with an anthropological interest in a woman who has put away her husband, who paints, and who plays the horses like a man. She knows that his patronizing visit to her studio would contaminate her. She does not want to paint for the likes of him, to be beholden to him; and as their confrontation comes to its manifold climax, she pays a high price for her excitement:

> ". . . I can tell what manner of woman you are." His fingers strayed occasionally down to her warm, smooth cheeks and firm chin, which was growing a little full and double.
>
> "Oh, yes! You will tell me that I am adorable; everything that is captivating. Spare yourself the effort."
>
> "No; I shan't tell you anything of the sort, though I shouldn't be lying if I did."

"Do you know Mademoiselle Reisz?" she asked irrelevantly . . .

"I'm told she's extremely disagreeable and unpleasant. Why have you introduced her at a moment when I desired to talk of you?"

Edna has, of course, introduced Mademoiselle Reisz not "irrelevantly" at all, but as a last shield against him. Work and sex are explicitly countervailed at this critical moment—just as they are in a number of Chopin's best stories (**"Wiser Than a God"** [1889], **"Aunt Lympy's Interference"** [1897]) that document a woman's refusal to give up her vocation for a sexual attachment. Arobin, Edna knows, is nothing more than a measure of her desperation to find an antidote to numbness.

He is, however, no fool. He chides her with wicked aptness about her plan to hold a *fête* in honor of her leaving the old house: "What about the dinner," he asked, "the grand event, the *coup d'état*?" His phrasing cannot be improved upon, for it drives home the point that Edna's is to be a revolution in incidentals only. Nothing, Arobin implies, will change except the identity of the ruler, a proposition with which Chopin appears to agree: "There was something in her attitude, in her whole appearance when she leaned her head against the high-backed chair and spread her arms, which suggested the regal woman, the one who rules, who looks on, who stands alone." With Mademoiselle Reisz propped on a cushioned chair as if in proxy for Edna's absent children, the whole affair has an air of unintentional self-mockery. Edna sits alone, presiding at a childless table while her lover undergoes interrogation by the one man present who speaks for the *ancien régime*—Monsieur Ratignolle. This is one of the great sad parties in American literature. It ranks with the Touchetts' tea at Gardencourt (in *The Portrait of a Lady*) and the revels on Gatsby's lawn. After this *coup d'état* (Edna takes possession of her "pigeon house" upon her thirtieth birthday), the rest of the novel is a long coda.

What makes the final pages of *The Awakening* so painful is their accumulating sense that Edna is living with foreknowledge of her doom. She sputters in sentences that start and stall and start again. She tells Dr. Mandelet:

> There are periods of despondency and suffering which take possession of me. But I don't want anything but my own way. That is wanting a good deal, of course, when you have to trample upon the lives, the prejudices of others—but no matter—still, I shouldn't want to trample upon the little lives. Oh! I don't know what I'm saying, Doctor. Good night. Don't blame me for anything.

It was this kind of self-exoneration that offended Chopin's first readers. Edna has lost a battle that, according to the respectable opinion of her time, she should never have begun. She has lost her fight against ennui and, what is worse, she knows it: "There was no one thing in the world that she desired. There was no human being whom she wanted near her except Robert; and she even realized that

the day would come when he, too, and the thought of him would melt out of her existence, leaving her alone." Her walk into the sea delivers her from a limbo that Chopin is at pains to liken to that of the mulatto woman in whose home Edna takes refuge: "'Do you come here often?' Robert asked, in the woman's garden. 'I almost live here,' Edna answered."

This bitter remark tells what sort of book *The Awakening* finally becomes. Edna's flight from her condition as her husband's possession is strikingly akin to what one encounters in many turn-of-the-century novels that take the predicament of the mulatto as their main theme. These books are built on a tragic paradox: that the only hope for the fugitive is to become indistinguishable from those from whom she is in flight.

One well-known example of such a novel is Charles Chesnutt's *The House Behind the Cedars* (1900), a book that attacks the premises of racism (as *The Awakening* does the idea of woman's "proper place") by demonstrating the danger of revealed genealogy. Like *The Awakening,* it is a meditation on how the sex or color of the body with which one is born becomes an ineffaceable sign of one's obligation and worth. "One drop of black blood makes the whole man black," says one of the many bigots in Chesnutt's novel, and we cringe, much as we do when Mr. Pontellier rattles off the time-honored proscriptions that Edna is beginning to defy. Yet the suspense of Chesnutt's novel builds as the white lover stumbles close to the discovery that there is "black blood" in the veins of his beloved. Holding our breath as we follow her efforts to conceal this fact from him, we become complicit in a strategy that amounts to a repudiation of her past. The naming of blackness in such a book becomes a drifting illusion: a woman is black only if someone knows it, only if (in the phrase of an earlier novelist, William Wells Brown) "the melting mezzotinto" in the iris of her eye is noticed. I suspect that this reduction of black identity to an epistemological riddle goes some distance toward explaining why Chesnutt spent the last thirty years of his life in literary silence.

Except for a few stories and reviews, Chopin, too, fell silent before her writing life seemed ready to end. She died in 1904 without producing or even embarking on a work comparable in ambition to *The Awakening.* In her earlier work she had been explicitly concerned with the mulatto theme only rarely, notably in her well-known story **"Désirée's Baby."** Yet surely it is no accident that Edna seeks refuge in a mulatto woman's home. We wish Edna free. We shudder at her confinement and thrill to her release. But her "awakening" leaves her mimicking the social instincts of those who have suppressed her in the first place. Just as the "ex-colored" awaken one day to find themselves irredeemably white, she becomes what she once fled.

In other words, Edna recognizes in her "awakening" a new form of degradation. She swims to her death not, as some readers would like to imagine, in a kind of ecstatic suicide amid the warm Gulf waves, but in despair at not having found a third way between the alternatives of submission and emulation when faced by those who regard power as the ground of all human relations.

Pearl L. Brown (essay date March 1999)

SOURCE: Brown, Pearl L. "Awakened Men in Kate Chopin's Creole Stories." *American Transcendental Quarterly* 13, no. 1 (March 1999): 69-82.

[*In the following essay, Brown discusses Chopin's depiction of men who experience liberation from cultural restrictions in their relationships with women.*]

Much has been written about Kate Chopin's defiant women. Not only Edna Pontellier, the rebellious heroine in *The Awakening,* but also the independent-minded women in her Creole stories have received extensive commentary. However, very little has been written about Chopin's defiant men, some of whom have experiences that parallel those of the women. Just as a woman in an intimate moment with a man awakens to an inner self buried beneath a culturally sanctioned social one, so does a man in an intimate moment with a woman discover a subjective self buried beneath a public persona. Just as women defy social expectations for women in the Creole culture, so do men defy that culture's masculine norms. In fact, in Chopin's Creole stories revolving around an intimate moment between a man and a woman, whether a story is told from a male or a female perspective, the narrative follows a similar pattern of discovery. For both men and women such epiphanies lead to self-knowledge as well as a better understanding of cultural norms and of the ways these norms do not satisfy psychological needs. As a consequence, these stories embody a vision of a society considerably more liberated than the social hegemony of nineteenth-century America in general or that of the old South and French Louisiana in particular.

In Chopin's collections, *Bayou Folk* and *A Night in Acadie,* certain stories come together around common features of plot and characterization and can be grouped accordingly. In one group of stories men and women are already established in a social identity and gender role, the men in the workplace and the women in marriage. In these stories both men and women during moments of sexual intimacy and intense feeling awaken to a buried self and to an understanding that the social identity they have created or have accepted from their culture is not compatible with newly discovered psychological needs. Consequently, even men and women who seem already to have begun rebelling against cultural norms are affected by such moments of intimacy. In a second group of stories, men and women, typically young and unmarried, are unawakened both psychologically and socially. Before their intimate experiences, they neither knew themselves nor had given much thought to the gender expectations of their culture or to

life choices for themselves. Hence, the intimate encounters come at a turning point in their lives when they are presumably still open to alternative life choices. However, regardless of the groupings, stories have one common feature: both men and women are changed by such intimate moments; both awaken to the possibilities of a fuller, richer life. Though readers of these stories have focussed almost exclusively on female awakenings, Chopin insists on the importance of social and psychological awakenings in men as well as in women.

Though readers might agree with Nancy Walker's assessment that Catholic Creoles lived a freer, more sensuous life-style than their Protestant counterparts (95-103), the social structure reflected in Chopin's Creole stories set in New Orleans and rural Louisiana does not allow for much deviation from cultural norms. Helen Taylor is certainly correct in her observation that the stories set in the Cane River region in particular reflect "fixed social relations and ideologies" and depict a culture in which "characters are allowed limited autonomy . . ." (165). That world of the plantation aristocracy during and after the Civil War embodies the values of a conservative culture, values reenforced by both the Catholic Church and the close-knit rural community. It is a culture that measures a woman's worth by her devotion to family, her self-abnegation, and her graciousness and charm in performing her social duties and a man's worth by the degree of authority he exercises over his household. Indeed, even New Orleans Creoles in Chopin's fiction are on the whole isolated in their own cultural enclave with close ties and easy access to their rural origin. In The Awakening urban Creoles like the Lebruns and Ratignolles rarely venture across Canal Street to the American side of the city, and the Pontelliers maintain close ties with Leonce's rural home. It is against such an insular world that the rebellion of Chopin's women has been measured. It is against such a world that her men's rebellion must also be measured.

To explore male norms and departures from them in these stories, Chopin introduces a range of Creole male types from both rural and urban Louisiana and variations on the pattern of a story climaxing with an awakening. She introduces the urban businessman and the professional as well as the independent farmer and the plantation owner. She introduces men who are very conservative in their social and political views, and others who see themselves as socially progressive, even outside the traditional masculine norms of Creole society. Some are in the position of having already made life choices which they come to reevaluate during an intimate experience with a woman. Others seemingly have no such moments or, if they do, have only limited insight into themselves or their culture. Still others are just beginning to plan their lives when they experience such moments. However, regardless of differences in circumstances, lifestyle or ideology, certain men in these stories are presented with epiphanic moments that are potentially as liberating and thus life altering as the moments women experience. Chopin's narrative strategy in a story is to introduce two men who represent contrasting or opposing male types to suggest alternative life styles and the possibility of different life choices. Stories can also be paired as companion studies suggesting variations on the pattern of self-discovery and of insight into cultural norms. In fact, comparing men from stories in the two different groupings, a man already committed to a social role and one just beginning to consider his choices, can also be illuminating in that such a comparison reveals more clearly the consequences of making wrong choices or of denying the subjective self or of acquiescing too unreflectingly to cultural norms.

In the stories in which men and women seem already established in a gender role, Chopin pairs men who are opposites ideologically and socially. On one end of the socio-political spectrum is the unmarried Creole man who shares an intimate moment with a married woman, an experience that inspires a psycho-sexual awakening in both. Introduced as a social rebel, this Creole bachelor has created for himself an unconventional public image which separates him from more conventional Creole men. In fact, his unconventionality serves as a stimulus for the awakening in the woman he encounters. However, he too is awakened by the intimate experience in that he gains self-knowledge that compels him to question the public or social self he has created and the life choices he has made.

On the other end of the socio-political spectrum is the woman's conventional husband, who has accepted his culture's norms for men. Such a patriarchal male figure has as his primary function the embodiment of the conventions of masculine social and public life against which the defiant men rebel. For example, Gouvernail, who becomes a married woman's confidante in two of these Creole stories, **"A Respectable Woman"** and **"Athenaise,"** is a liberal-minded journalist with ties to the bohemian community in New Orleans. He is much less conventional than the husbands of the two women he has encounters with. Both Cazeau, Athenaise's husband, and Gaston Baroda, the husband in **"A Respectable Woman,"** are conservative and conventional in their understanding of the political and social norms that define Creole masculinity. In another story with close parallels to **"A Respectable Woman,"** **"A Lady of Bayou St. John,"** Sepincourt similarly has attempted to distance himself from the socio-political norms for men. Presumably a Creole aristocrat by birth, he has established himself as an outsider to the Creole plantation culture he is a part of even before he meets the married woman who will inspire him to reconsider his life choices. He has rejected the traditional plantation values by refusing to support the Southern cause in the Civil War. Unlike Madame Delisle's husband, Gustave, and presumably other Creole aristocrats, Sepincourt has not joined General Beauregard's military campaign in Virginia. Thus, even before their encounters with women, both Gouvernail and Sepincourt are depicted as having rejected some aspect of the traditional public life of a Creole man. In fact, Gouvernail has rejected even some of the accepted social rituals for men. In **"A Respectable Woman,"** Madame Baroda has been told by her husband, Gaston, that his old

school friend is definitely not the typical Creole bachelor, a "man about town" (333). At home in New Orleans he frequents gatherings in the American quarter rather than attend the Sunday social functions in the Creole section of the city. And his retreat to the country does not include the customary male recreations Gaston Baroda had been looking forward to, fishing and hunting. Gouvernail has no interest in either.

However, though both Gouvernail and Sepincourt are unconventional in their expression of a discontent with the prevailing masculine order, until their intimate moments with the women who come into their lives, both have either ignored or repressed psychological needs. Presumably, Gouvernail has never before acknowledged his feelings of loss, emptiness, and unfulfillment in the life he has chosen until his talk with Mrs. Baroda. This discussion moves him to speak of his past friendship with Gaston when the two meant something to each other and of his past "blind ambition and large intentions." Only then is he able to admit to himself that over the years all he has been left with is a "philosophic acquiescence to the existing order" with "only a desire to be permitted to exist" (335). What the intimacy of the night and the presence of his hostess open him up to is the realization that neither in terms of personal relationships nor in terms of the direction his life has taken does he currently feel fulfilled. Withdrawing to the country to find some solace from an existence to which he can only acquiesce, he discovers that "little whiff of genuine life" (335) which at least momentarily lifts his spirits as he sits on a bench savoring the night and sharing his most private reflections with his hostess.

Sepincourt's response to the war echoes Gouvernail's alienation from "the existing order." He shrugs his shoulders "over this strife between brothers, this quarrel which was none of his" (298). His rejection of the Southern cause certainly represents a departure from the prevailing masculinist social and political views; yet, until his meetings with Madame Delisle, his unconventionality rings hollow. His initial remark to Mrs. Delisle about the war—that "it made life uncomfortable" (298)—certainly does not reveal a deeply felt political ideology. He comes to understand, like Gouvernail, that his discontent has a psychological rather than a social or political origin. Like Gouvernail, he is compelled to acknowledge the existence of a subjective self buried beneath his superficial public persona of the rebel. Ironically, it is a child-like Creole woman, herself unawakened both psychologically and socially, who inspires this sophisticated Creole man to drop his public pose as he begins to respond to the intimacy that permeates their afternoon walks. He begins to relish those moments when they are "unconsciously unfolding themselves to each other" (299). Certainly, his proposal to Mrs. Delisle that they leave Louisiana to live outside Creole social and moral norms reveals a more deeply felt rebelliousness than his earlier protest against the Southern cause. Though the life he envisions with Madame Delisle is not meant to be, he has had his moment of self-knowledge and has had to acknowledge psychological needs not satisfied by a public image as a sophisticate and a political critic.

Both women caught in these intimate encounters are at least momentarily awakened to psychological needs that their culturally defined social roles as Creole wives do not sanction. To depict the society these women are inspired to rebel against, Chopin explicitly delineates the culturally sanctioned separation between the domestic and feminine, on the one hand, and the public and masculine, on the other. In the context of the separate spheres, Chopin reflects on what was a reality about gender roles until very recent times. A man's social or public identity was defined primarily by his work and only secondarily by his marital status, though in the Creole culture a man was expected at some point in his life to assume his proper role as the patriarchal head of a household. A woman's social or public identity was defined exclusively by her preparation for marriage and the marital state itself. In stories such as **"A Respectable Woman"** and **"A Lady from Bayou St. John,"** the male world of purposeful action is carefully demarcated from the isolated, passive world of feminine concerns. In **"A Lady of Bayou St. John,"** the husband's guarded letters from the war front are intended to communicate little of the realities of war to the child-wife he has left behind. Indeed, for Madame Delisle the image of her husband has receded into a misty memory. As she begins to awaken sexually and psychologically, the one activity she remembers sharing with her husband, walks beneath the magnolias, seems unreal and inconsequential compared to her intimate walks with Sepincourt. Her walks with Sepincourt are filled with incessant talking or silences in which neither feels the need to talk.

In **"A Respectable Woman,"** the separate worlds of Creole husband and wife meet in the fulfillment of social obligations demanded by the plantation culture. Gaston encourages his wife in her feminine "work"—the social life of the plantation culture. He accompanies her to New Orleans for the seasonal parties and balls, the "mild dissipations" (333), and he indulges her trips for spring fittings necessary for a fashionable Creole wife. But the world he identifies with as a Creole man is revealed in his anticipation of some hunting and fishing and some male talk when his old college friend Governail comes to visit. Her conversation with Gouvernail introduces her to a world far removed from the social rituals of a Creole wife. Like Madame Delisle's moments with Sepincourt, Mrs. Baroda's encounter with Gouvernail is intimate, deeply felt, and individualized, and thus socially unsanctioned by the culture.

Until their encounters with Sepincourt and Gouvernail, Madame Delisle and Madame Baroda apparently had settled into the conventional roles for Creole women in marriage and in society. The two in fact represent different Creole female types as a kind of parallel to Creole male types in the stories. Madame Delisle has passively accepted her asexual and completely dependent role as the Creole child-woman who is not expected ever to grow up;

and, until her encounter with Gouvernail, Mrs. Baroda has remained sexually unawakened in her role as the charming social hostess for her husband. When Gouvernail is first mentioned to her, Mrs. Baroda can only think in terms of social stereo-types, but she soon discovers he is not the charming conversationalist she had come to expect an unmarried Creole man to be. Instead, she finds him "mute and receptive before her chatty eagerness to make him feel at home" (333), decidedly lacking in the courtliness of the Creole gigolo. It isn't until the night Gouvernail shares with her his intimate reverie that she is aroused out of her smug world of superficial social functions and respectable behavior as the desire to draw close to him and touch him almost overwhelms her. That night she is able to repress these unsanctioned desires, but the story ends ambiguously. When Gouvernail comes again to visit, she may be ready to liberate more completely the suppressed sexual self of the respectable Creole wife.

Likewise, Madame Delisle's afternoon walks and talks with Sepincourt momentarily awaken her to an existence different from that of the passive child-wife absorbed in her own loveliness and Manna-Loulou's bedtime stories. With Sepincourt's declaration of love and his proposal for a new life abroad, she momentarily becomes "a woman capable of love or sacrifice" (299). But her awakening proves to be as brief as it is sudden. When she hears of her husband's death, she reacts to the tragic news by sublimating her awakened passion to a religious ecstasy, a life-long devotion to his memory. Her retreat to the stereotypical role of the grieving, devoted Creole wife and Mrs. Baroda's struggle to check her desires suggest that for Chopin moments of self-awareness do not necessarily mark the beginning of permanent change, but they are nonetheless deeply felt and thus life altering. The moment the two have shared is much more than a "tentative transgression" (Fluck 155). It is Chopin's reminder to her nineteenth-century readers of what the relationship between a man and a woman could be and should be.

"A Respectable Woman" and the other story in which Gouvernail appears, **"Athenaise,"** are companion studies of male and female awakenings with parallel scenes that follow a similar narrative structure. **"A Respectable Woman"** ends with a woman's awakening to an inner self-buried beneath an external self comprising social responsibilities. **"Athenaise"** ends with a man's awakening to an inner self buried beneath an external self, defined by his public image as the liberal-minded professional man. Though Gouvernail's moment of genuine life is important in **"A Respectable Woman,"** the focus of the narrative is much more on Mrs. Baroda and her psycho-sexual awakening. In contrast, in "Athenaise," while the young wife's rebellion against social expectations for women is certainly important, the awakening placed at a climactic moment in the narrative is Gouvernail's. In a scene that parallels Gouvernail's awakening Mrs. Baroda with his reverie, Athenaise awakens Gouvernail with her intimate outpouring that arouses the buried emotional self in this detached, smugly complacent man. And, in contrast to "A

Respectable Woman," it is the unconventionality of a rebellious married woman that inspires an epiphany in a man. It is Athenaise's frank confession of her unhappiness in an oppressive Creole marriage that liberates the subjective in Gouvernail and compels him to reconsider the public image he has created for himself.

When Gouvernail first meets Athenaise and must share the breakfast table with her, he is "annoyed at having his cherished privacy invaded" and is relieved when she leaves (443). The extent to which he has acquiesced to the existing order of things alluded to in **"A Respectable Woman"** becomes clearer in **"Athenaise."** In New Orleans he emerges as a professional man of regular habits and "invariable" customs, described by the narrator as possessing "a quiet, unobtrusive manner that seem[s] to ask that he be let alone" (443-44)—until his encounter with a weeping Athenaise one night. In **"A Respectable Woman,"** it is Gouvernail's discontent with the existing order that awakens Mrs. Baroda out of her superficial social existence, but in **"Athenaise"** it is the young wife's discontent with the existing order of things that awakens Gouvernail out of his orderly predictable life. And Athenaise's intimate moment of reverie is presumably inspired by her finding at last a receptive audience in Gouvernail, just as Mrs. Baroda's awakening was inspired by Gouvernail's reverie.

As Athenaise experiences the emotional freedom to talk about her married life and to ruminate longingly over the sights, sounds, and scents of her family home on Bayou Bon Dieu, Gouvernail feels "a wave of pity and tenderness [sweep] over him" (450), and he is once again in touch with his subjective self as he was when he savored the night and spoke to Mrs. Baroda of that "whiff of genuine life" in **"A Respectable Woman."** And, as Gouvernail reflects on the possibilities of a future with Athenaise, he realizes that the fact of her being already married makes no difference to him: "When the time came that she wanted him—as he hoped and believed it would come—he felt he would have a right to her. So long as she did not want him, he had no right to her—no more than her husband had" (450). Unlike Edna Pontellier's conventional-minded lover in The Awakening who cannot imagine a union outside of social and moral norms, Gouvernail is ready to gamble all for a future with Athenaise. The young wife's reaction to her discovery that she is pregnant and her subsequent decision to return to her husband bring an end to Gouvernail's dreams of a future with the woman who has awakened him.

In **"Athenaise"** Gouvernail is not introduced until section VII of a narrative divided into eleven sections. At that point Athenaise's rebellion from her oppressive Creole marriage to the autocratic Cazeau takes her to New Orleans and her encounter with Gouvernail who has rooms in the same house where she is staying. Chopin's strategy is to prepare for the introduction of a culturally deviant Creole male such as Gouvernail by carefully establishing masculine norms in the depiction of Athenaise's husband. In fact, one variation on the narrative pattern of stories in

this group is that this one is more concerned with the Creole marriage and family and the culture's codification of norms for both husbands and wives than either of the two stories discussed earlier. Athenaise's patriarchal husband serves as a foil to Gouvernail, who has allowed himself to respect marriage but has apparently chosen to disregard his culture's expectations for a Creole man—that he marry and assume his role as head of a household. Cazeau has accepted his role as master over his wife and plantation—until his wife leaves him to return to live with her parents. Self-controlled and controlling, he has expected his wife to accept as uncompromisingly as he does the rules of their society—that he be the authority in their marriage and that she passively submit to him.

When Athenaise leaves her husband the first time and seeks a haven in her family home, even her parents assume that it is Cazeau's right as a husband to discipline their rebellious daughter. For his part, Cazeau refuses to admit that her actions bother him except in his musing that "he would find means to keep her at home hereafter" (428). He is "quite prepared to make the best" (428) of the marriage, accepting as he does his culture's view that it is a lifelong arrangement between a man and a woman. Furthermore, when he acts the role of the patriarchal husband and goes to his in-laws to fetch his wife home, his pride will not permit him even to speak to her or to allow her to voice her grievances.

To expand on her exploration of masculine self-discovery, Chopin has even the rigidly patriarchal Cazeau experience a moment of epiphany as he "drives" his wife home. As he follows her on horseback, an image from the past—of him and his father driving a runaway slave back to the plantation—is superimposed on the scene unfolding before him in the present, as he follows behind his runaway wife on their way home. He suddenly realizes that his relationship to his young wife duplicates that of a master over a slave. So disturbing is that revelation that he quickly rides to catch up with her and escort her home, and, when she leaves him a second time to escape to New Orleans, he resolves to let her go because he does not want to feel again the baseness of a master subduing a slave. This epiphany prepares the way for his acknowledging to himself his deep sense of loss at her second leaving, a significant psychological change in this conservative man whose behavior has established him as a stereotypical patriarchal male. Though the story ends without elaborating on the difference in this marriage after the wife's return to her husband, one can only speculate that the awakenings in both will have a salutary effect on their relationship.

In the second group of stories with common narrative features, men and women have barely begun the process of learning about themselves, but they are at a turning point in their lives, a time when they will soon be expected to take a place in a society that endorses gender specific roles. Unlike socially and publicly established men like Gouvernail and Sepincourt, the men in this second group of stories have just begun or have not yet begun to define themselves in terms of a social identity or public image. In fact, their epiphanies come at particularly decisive moments because they are on the verge of making critical decisions around life choices. If not for such moments, Chopin implies, they may have acquiesced to masculine norms, as have the conventional husbands in the other group of stories, or have created a public image that ignored or repressed psychological needs, as have Gouvernail and Sepincourt. Of course, the women awakened by such intimate experiences are also approaching a decisive period in their lives, a time when they will have to decide on a mate and attempt to assert some influence on the kind of marriage they will have. Similar narrative patterns emerge among the stories in the two groups. For example, in these stories about young uninitiated people, unconventionality again stimulates epiphanies; however, unconventionality in women instinctively rebelling against feminine social norms, rather than unconventionality in men, is at the center of such experiences.

Another common narrative pattern Chopin uses is contrasting male types as a device with which to comment on masculine norms in the Creole culture. In such stories of young adulthood, two men who are rivals for the hand of an unawakened woman are opposites, both temperamentally and socially. In **"A No-Account Creole,"** for example, Placide Santien is in some ways a younger version of Athenaise's autocratic husband, Cazeau. He has never questioned his right as a man in this plantation culture to dominate Euphrasie, the daughter of the manager of his family's plantation and the girl he has loved since childhood. Both he and his community assume she will submit to his will and agree to marry him. And Euphrasie herself has not really questioned that assumption. Unambitious and irresponsible, Placide is the no account Creole of the title of the story and the perfect foil to Euphrasie's other suitor, the ambitious, goal-oriented Wallace Offdean. Indulged by both his community and his family, Placide has yet to assume the responsibility of restoring the family plantation. In contrast, his rival for Euphrasie's hand, the Anglophile, Wallace Offdean, aspires to become an enlightened New Orleans businessman. Before his awakening, he reminds the reader of the repressed Gouvernail in that both are preoccupied with their public image, with a well-ordered life that balances respectability with progressive ideas. Offdean has had the predictable experiences of an intelligent young man of his social class and now, with his inheritance in hand, smugly envisions for himself a well-planned life, one that avoids "the maelstroms of sordid work and senseless pleasure in which the average American business man may be said alternately to exist" (81). His objective is to model himself on the image of the emerging nineteenth-century businessman striving for success, unsullied by the vulgarities of traditional mercantilism. At least that was his life's goal, until he is sent to appraise the Santien plantation and meets Euphrasie.

One variation on the narrative pattern of discovery and self-discovery in this story is that the psycho-sexual awakening necessitates a departure from the gender-specific roles of the Creole culture. During Offdean's first conversation with Euphrasie, he wonders why he is bothering to discuss the property with "a mere girl"; but, after she joins him on his daily excursions to appraise the land, he gains respect for her knowledge of the plantation and for her practical intelligence. Of course, the land inspection is a cover for their awakening passion, though neither is able to acknowledge or express that love until a near violent confrontation between Placide and Offdean over Euphrasie forces the three to make decisions. Euphrasie is compelled to examine what her community approves of, marriage to her old childhood friend, Placide. She comes to understand that marriage to Placide would put an end to what she has come to desire—applying her newly discovered interest and talent in managing land to make the decaying Santien plantation productive again. For his part, Offdean makes the decision to put aside his carefully planned future as an enlightened urban businessman. Instead, he wants to share Euphrasie's life and her dream to rebuild the Santien plantation. Theirs surely will be a nontraditional marriage with Euphrasie actively involved in running the plantation side by side with her husband. Even Placide, like Cazeau in **"Athenaise,"** has an awakening. When Placide relinquishes his claim on Euphrasie, it is because he finds he must reject the Creole man's sense of ownership and entitlement in relation to a woman. Creole male pride must give way to a sense of honor and respect. In this story both men and the woman gain a better understanding of what it is about the gender norms of their culture they cannot accept.

In at least two of these stories focussing on awakenings in young men, an epiphanie moment inspires a rejection of the notions of status and materialism that define masculine success for Creole men like Leonce Pontellier in **The Awakening.** When Telesphore in **"A Night in Acadie"** begins to think about acquiring a wife, he thinks in terms of one who will be the perfect ornament for his home, combining all of the virtues of the stereotypical Creole belle. She will be charming, beautiful and fair-skinned with no hint of racial impurities. She will also bring some wealth to the marriage as well as be an energetic homemaker who will enhance Telesphore's social status in the community. It is no wonder that, before his chance meeting with Zaida, he has been unable to settle on the right woman to be his wife. It is said of Telesphore that he has spent much of his young life trying to be the opposite of his disorderly, lazy, and socially disreputable uncle some had thought the young man resembled. Telesphore, as a consequence, has been cautious and indecisive, preoccupied with external appearance and not at all aware of personal needs. **"A Night in Acadie"** is similar to **"A No-Account Creole"** in that it follows the narrative pattern of two young men who are opposites coming together in a confrontation over a woman. In fact, the drunken, disheveled Andre Pascal probably reminds Telesphore of his uncle. The outcome of the physical confrontation between the two men is that Telesphore recognizes his attraction to Zaida and to the spontaneity and individualism she represents. Here Chopin offers a variation on the theme of the importance of deciding wisely on a mate. **"A No-Account Creole"** ends with the prospects of a marriage that will promote self-fulfillment for both husband and wife because it will be a joint partnership that will transcend the nineteenth-century ideology of the separate spheres. **"A Night in Acadie"** is more concerned with the choice of a mate as marking a departure from the conventional formula for masculine success and respectability in Creole Louisiana.

Parallels with other stories are easy to find. The young Cajun farmer, Telesphore, certainly differs from Offdean, the urban intellectual. Still, in his naive quest for the perfect wife, Telesphore reminds one of Offdean's quest for the perfectly balanced life. Telesphore's plans to establish himself as a successful and respectable farmer and head of a household are as uninformed psychologically as Offdean's career plans before meeting Euphrasie. In addition, Zaida reminds the reader of the rebellious Athenaise. Both defy their culture's social norms for women. Zaida has openly defied her parents by making plans to meet and marry Andre secretly under the pretext of attending a dance. She would seem to be an even more inappropriate choice for Telesphore, given his ambitions, than Euphrasie for Wallace Offdean. Yet, everything about Zaida, her free and easy walk, her excited and excitable nature, her emotional frankness and unconventional behavior, her bold rebellion from parental rule, appeals to Telesphore as he begins to be less inhibited under the influence of his awakened passion for her. As a catalyst for a man's awakening, she has a similar effect on Telesphore that Athenaise has on Gouvernail. In fact, before his awakening, Telesphore seemed destined to have the kind of unreflective life of conventional-minded men in the plantation culture such as Gustave Baroda in **"A Respectable Woman."**

In at least one of these stories grouped around young unawakened men and women, a man's awakening reflects critically not only on cultural norms defining masculinity and the materialistic values of status in the male world of work, but also on the Creole plantation hegemony itself. In **"Azelie,"** before his encounter with Azelie, 'Polyte accepted without question the social and economic hierarchy of the plantation culture. His daily life revolved around the responsibilities of his work—running the plantation store. He never speculated that an impoverished, displaced family like Azelie's may not accept the social and moral codes that support the foundation for the plantation economy. Azelie certainly threatens "the calm orderliness of 'Polyte's existence" (Dyer, "Sleeping Bruties" 72), as Euphrasie has shaken Offdean's identity as an urban businessman and Zaida has shaken Telesphore's as a successful farmer. It is not only 'Polyte's understanding of his social identity as an assistant manager on a plantation that she threatens, but also his smug identification with the hegemony of the plantation culture in general. Azelie's defiance of the plantation culture forces 'Polyte to examine the plantation world he has accepted. From her he learns much about the injustices of the system he has helped to perpetuate and re-examines his own values. His leaving

the plantation to join Azelie and her family on Lile River represents not only an insight into his own personal needs but also an expansion of his social and moral consciousness. Unlike the two respectable men in the story, the morally unconventional Azelie actively rejects traditional principles of justice and morality as well as the values of the patriarchal southern plantation. She pays 'Polyte for services rendered by stoically tolerating his caresses; but, when he asks her to stay behind with him when her family must leave, she chooses an uncertain future with her family over the security and respectability he could give her. 'Polyte's decision to leave the plantation and join Azelie and her family on Lile River represents not only his acceptance of the life of the instincts and passions, but also his rejection of the emptiness of his morally conventional and materially secure world.

Awakenings in men in Chopin's Creole stories inspire them to reflect on their position in this highly patriarchal and hierarchical society, particularly to consider whether they should move toward an acceptance of values more consistent with their own psychic and social vision than those their culture validates. The vision that emerges not only encompasses the liberation of a buried self and a departure from gender norms and conventional social values, but also hints at the wisdom of a more androgynous union between a man and a woman than the nineteenth-century ideology of the separate spheres encouraged. Certainly, some awakened men in these stories become less preoccupied with order, rationality, control, and authority; and awakened women become less dependent, submissive, and self-abnegating. Like her awakened women, Chopin's awakened men cannot always effect a permanent change in their lives; but their moments of self-revelation are, nevertheless, important because they provide a vision not only of a more integrated, fuller life for a man but also of a union between a man and a woman which is freer of the traditional gender roles. Chopin scholarship has understandably concentrated on the awakening of her women, but the awakening of her men also deserves attention. In Chopin's vision of a progressive society, both men and women must strive for autonomy.

Works Cited

Chopin, Kate. *The Complete Works*. Ed. Per Seyersted. Baton Rouge: Louisiana SUP, 1969. Dyer, Joyce. "Kate Chopin's Sleeping Bruties." *The Markham R* 10 (1980 Fall-1981 Winter): 10-15.

Fluck, Winfried. "Tentative Transgressions: Kate Chopin's Fiction as a Mode of Symbolic Action." *SAF* 10.2 (1982): 151-71.

Walker, Nancy. "Feminist or Naturalist: The Social Context of Kate Chopin's *The Awakening*." *SoQ*. 17.2 (1979): 95-103.

Barbara C. Ewell (essay date summer 1999)

SOURCE: Ewell, Barbara C. "Unlinking Race and Gender: *The Awakening* as a Southern Novel." *Southern Quarterly* 37, no. 3-4 (summer 1999): 30-37.

[*In the following essay, Ewell argues that both* The Awakening *and Chopin were heavily shaped by the tradition of Southern American literature.*]

We do not typically think of *The Awakening* as a southern novel, which (set in Louisiana and dealing with many Reconstruction issues, such as the post-war role of women and life in the upper classes) it certainly is. At the same time, we do customarily regard Kate Chopin as a southern writer—despite the fact that she was from St. Louis (albeit in a family of southern sympathizers) and that she only spent the thirteen years of her marriage in the South and that much of her fiction (fully a third) is not specifically southern. But if Kate Chopin is not technically a southerner and *The Awakening* does not always "feel" like a southern novel, both writer and text were shaped by the very specific contexts of southern literature.

Perhaps what has diminished our sense of this famous feminist text as southern is the conflicted character of those contexts themselves. On the one hand, as Susan Donaldson so articulately argues, the canon of southern literature has been determinedly defined as "white, male, and conservative" (493). Donaldson traces what she calls the southern "project of imposing boundaries and exclusions" back from modernists like Allen Tate and John Crowe Ransom to antebellum critics like Henry Timrod and William Gilmore Simms (495). But such careful boundary-keeping—especially against women and African Americans—only exposes the "gender and racial anxieties" they are meant to contain (Donaldson 493). Such practices of exclusion simply reveal how profoundly southern literature resists enclosure any carefully marked perimeters, how fundamental and unstable race and gender are in southern writing.

Naming the crucial links among race, gender, and notions of region has become a familiar practice in southern studies.[1] In numerous texts, writing by African Americans or by white women has been shown to challenge standard contours of southern identity and its explicit reflection of patriarchal values. For example, both the reevaluation of nineteenth-century local color and the attention to the slave narrative as a southern genre have exposed the gaps and fissures that everywhere disturb the serenity of the plantation myth underlying definitions of southern literature.[2] But if inserting an alternative notion of gender or race (or class or sexuality) into a text undeniably troubles its regional identity, the sheer persistence of southernness alone suggests that the ultimate effect is not as destructive as those who abhor racism and sexism or elitism might hope: southern identity might waver a bit, but it does not shatter. Deconstructing southern literature turns out to be no easy feat, not least because of the complexity of the interrelationships on which a notion of region depends. The staggering appeal of southern mythology affirms just how coherently its pieces interlock and how many can be damaged or absent without seriously distorting its recognizability.

At the turn of the century, when Chopin was writing her own text about a southern woman, southernness was being sharply contested—as indeed were notions about women, about race, and even class. The South in 1898 (when Chopin began to write her second novel) was just emerging from the wholesale reconfiguration were not altogether set. The effects of *Plessy v. Fergusson* had legally, but not socially, rigidified the color line; the defeat of southern Populism in the elections of 1896 had practically but not completely dashed hopes for improving the lot of working-class southerners; and the racial compromises of the National American Woman Suffrage Association to attract southern support had not fully resolved the "woman question" in the region.[3] Chopin's own agenda as a writer could not but be shaped by these shifting and unstable contexts in which southern literature, indeed, the national identity itself, was being redefined. Examining just how Chopin negotiated these contexts and with what success is one way of gauging the southernness of her novel. But such an inquiry also exposes how Chopin's proposed interrogation of gender roles implicates a complex web of southern identity, one whose designs on women could not easily—if at all—be detached from notions of race and class. By employing a southern setting for her reconsideration of the ways that social roles limit female selfhood, Chopin also discloses how fiercely the fortresses of southern identity resist any challenge to its interlocking hierarchies.

Chopin was certainly conversant with the texts that had helped to shape southern consciousness. As we know from her notebooks and her biographers, her reading habits as a child were both conventional and wide-ranging. Her best friend, Kitty Garesché, recalled that they particularly enjoyed *Ivanhoe* by Sir Walter Scott—the novelist whose romantic spirit and aristocratic trappings southerners had eagerly incorporated into their fictional self-images. As an avid reader and an active contributor to the burgeoning literature of southern local color in the 1890s, Chopin would have understood, with no small degree of sympathy, the issues of southern identity and social conservatism that the genre encoded. (Her husband had after all been a member of New Orleans's reactionary White League.) She knew the work of Thomas Nelson Page (whose *Red Rock* was a bestseller in 1898) and Joel Chandler Harris (whose *Sister Jane* she reviewed in 1897 [*The Complete Works of Kate Chopin* [hereafter abbreviated as *CW*] 718-19]), as well as that of James Lane Allen (whose "exquisite" short novel "A Kentucky Cardinal" she approvingly mentions in 1894 [(*A Kate Chopin Miscellany*) *Miscellany* 91]), Ruth Stuart (whom she met with great pleasure in 1897 [*CW* 711-12]), and many others, including George Washington Cable and Grace King, with whom she was often compared.

Among the representations most crucial to postwar fiction, and on whom southern regional identity most prominently depended, was of course the antebellum belle. As Anne Goodwyn Jones insists, "the southern lady is at the core of [the] region's self-definition; the identity of the South is contingent in part upon the persistence of its tradition of the lady" (4). As traced by contemporary scholars, the lineage of the belle lies both in the romantic traditions of Sir Walter Scott and in the domestic fiction by women that dominated mid-nineteenth-century canons. From Scott and other sectionalist writers (like Lord Byron and Jane Porter, whose *The Scottish Chiefs* was recalled by Kitty Garesché as one of hers and Katie's childhood favorites [Toth 51-52]), the belle obtained her aristocratic status. Placed on the pedestal of chivalric caste, she was relieved (theoretically at least) from the domestic drudgery assigned to most women of the world. In the South, slavery enabled upper-class (and many middle-class) white women to assume in fact the exceptional status of leisure conventionally reserved for nobility. Pointedly excused from any other specific labor, the belle, as Kathryn Lee Seidel explains, became herself the culture's "object or work of art . . . the projection of her society's attitudes toward woman and sexuality, toward blacks and guilt, toward itself and its weakness and loss" (xv). But as Diane Roberts observes, this elevated "positioning within the political discourse" of southern feudalism also "placed her in the center of pro-slavery rhetoric" (6). Her leisure and refinement provided the chief evidence of aristocratic privilege, and the belle became the focus of any effort to defend or to discredit the South's peculiar institutions. Maintaining the privilege of the white woman became both a literal and figurative justification for slavery before the Civil War and for Jim Crow after it. The Lady was the South; as in other romantic traditions, her status and fate became identified with that of the region. Seidel traces this merging of the rhetorical image of the South as the Great Lady, fallen but still dignified, with the post-war version of the antebellum belle, who begins as spokesperson for the lost cause and gradually becomes its alter ego.[4]

The belle's other ancestry derived from the traditions of domestic fiction, with its powerful ideology of feminine culture. Writers like E. D. E. N. Southworth, Susan Warner, Dinah Mulock Craik, and Harriet Beecher Stowe (all familiar to Chopin) helped to construct an image of women as morally superior, functioning in a domestic sphere of her own, which served both to challenge and to support the public sphere of male power. As virgin, wife, and especially as mother, the Victorian lady epitomized the highest values of her culture. The southern belle was par excellence such a lady, defined by and destined for motherhood. But like her aristocratic status, that destiny made her a crucial site for white southern identity. As Roberts writes, if the body of the belle "provide[d] white heirs to the property[,] her chastity guarantee[d] racial purity" (186); a particular concept of gender thus explicitly maintained the privileges of class and white supremacy.

As in domestic fiction generally, motherhood in plantation ideology also assumed a spiritual cast, though not without significant contradictions. Like the "motherland" itself, the plantation mistress "mothers" all—even those persons who as chattel could be sold or abused. Such cruelty patently violated the regime of care that the idea of women's "domestic space" enshrines, so that, in a bitter irony, the nurturing work of women reinforced the patriarchal structures of a slave society. The ideal of womanhood both valorized the duties of the mother as caregiver and modeled a devout obedience to "higher powers," even when those "higher powers" manifested themselves as the male marketplace—from whose intrusions the home was supposedly a refuge. The sacredness of motherhood could in no way protect a woman's children, whether actual or metaphorical, from the cruel requirements of profit.

If the ethic of care disguised certain demands of the marketplace, it also concealed what Roberts neatly terms the "fissures in sexual decorum" that marked actual plantation life (188). For while motherhood was the special calling of the lady, the passage through sexual experience necessary for individual women to reach that elevated status was systematically effaced in nineteenth-century discourse on womanhood, markedly so in the South. White women were not supposed to be sexual; that physical and implicitly inferior task was imposed on "other," less pure, females: whores and black women (which in southern ideology were indistinguishable). This suppression of sexuality among "ladies" was central to the ideal of nineteenth-century motherhood. An influential tract on *The Functions and Disorders of the Reproductive Organs* (1857) by Sir William Acton intones, for example, that "a modest woman seldom desires any sexual gratification for herself. She submits to her husband, but only to please him; and, but for the desire of maternity, would far rather be relieved from his attentions" (qtd. in Roberts 188). Roberts also observes how "it was a southern gynecologist . . . who recommended that a patient who found intercourse 'painful' have sex while unconscious on chloroform so that she might conceive" and thus achieve her sacred duty of motherhood (189). This erasure of women's sexuality in a rhetoric of maternal worship ensured that no threatening female passion would unsettle the systems of marriage, family, and racial caste that their bodies were required to support. Not only in the antebellum period but even more emphatically after the war, when those institutions were being steadily pressured by large populations of ex-slaves and intensifying economic and political forces, that erasure proved a significant bulwark against unwanted social change.

Much Reconstruction fiction consciously constructed this view of self-sacrificing, asexual motherhood, reinforcing its potency as an ideal by merging female identity with southern regionalism. Since "true women" can exist only in and for their children (and the South can only live for its "true inheritors"), any sexual violation (which damaged the integrity of the racial or property lines insured by her purity) or sexual assertiveness (which manifested a threatening independence), necessarily results in the death of the lady, either figuratively or literally. Yankee ideas, black upstarts, and "outside agitators" all represented mortal, as well as moral, danger to the southern belle. Committed exclusively to the welfare of her children, she manifested an absolute, ahistorical identification with "traditional ways of life," even though those traditions defined away her selfhood almost as radically as it abolished the humanity and independence of the former slaves. Thomas Dixon's *The Clansman* (1905), for example, among the most virulent of the southern apologia, makes explicit this connection among woman, child, and region: the mother so identifies with her raped daughter that she leaps to death with her, indicating, as Roberts suggests, her clear preference for annihilation over the chaotic reality of Reconstruction in which such "violations" of social order have become so commonplace that neither the southern lady nor the traditional values of the motherland can continue to exist (190).

Chopin's first novel, *At Fault* (1890), which exploited many of the conventions of southern fiction, including its North-South romance structure and its focus on the belle, signaled the beginning of her own fictional exploration of female desire within the confining social and institutional contexts of the South. However, throughout her short stories of the next decade, she thoughtfully posed a variety of narrative answers to how women might achieve or maintain selfhood inside and against the rigid roles prescribed for them—not exclusively in southern contexts.[5] In that exploration, Chopin aligned herself with a new generation of women writers, many of whom, like Sarah Jewett, Mary Wilkins Freeman, Mary Catherwood, or Mary Austin, were using the conventions of local color to express their own conflicted responses to the positive, though restrictive, aspects of "domestic culture" and the need to articulate their emerging sense of independent female selfhood. Linda Dowling asserts that the rebellion against Victorian culture and the cult of motherhood was expressed by these writers "chiefly through sexual means—by heightening sexual consciousness, candor, and expression" (qtd. in Showalter 69). Female sexuality, the admissability of passion for women, became the battleground for female selfhood, with motherhood emerging as an equivocal adversary.[6]

For southern women writers, the admission of sexuality into women's experience, even in fiction, was particularly difficult. As numerous Reconstruction novels and tracts insisted, challenging the ideal of the belle challenged sectional loyalty as well.[7] Preserving the southern lady inviolate and impervious either to internal resistance or outside influences confirmed the South's regional fidelity to its old "verities" of caste and race. In posing the dilemma of her heroine explicitly in terms of motherhood (an issue that she had approached in several short stories, notably **"Wiser than a God," "Regret,"** and **"Athénaïse"**), Chopin knew that she was engaging head-on the central issue for many nineteenth-century women writers: how to reclaim women's displaced desire, so that she might, in Cynthia Wolff's terms, re-possess her own libido from her children (8) or, in Edna terms, retain the "essential." As Elizabeth Fox-Genovese suggests, Chopin may well have thought that her explorations of female sexuality were less threatening to the southern social order than exploring women's social

independence. In other words, as Fox-Genovese argues, Chopin may have believed that Edna's struggle—that every woman's struggle—was an individual matter, necessary for personal fulfillment, but only incidental to the larger social structures that constrained her (39): that the lady's release from the pedestal would not undo the society that put her there.

But by setting her novel in south Louisiana, Chopin, whether she meant to or not, was also engaging issues critical to southern identity. Given her resistance to being classified as a regionalist and the drift of her late fiction away from specifically southern settings, it is unlikely that she saw her new novel as part of the contemporary conversation on the fate of the South. She had already been there and done that in *At Fault*. But southern identity implied not simply a useful construction of womanhood, but also its complex interdependence on race and class, not all of which was Chopin equally prepared to challenge. As Margaret Ferguson analogously argues of Aphra Behn's *Oronooko,* Chopin's asymmetrical allegiances to woman's desire and white, upper-class privilege strikingly reveal the intricate interdependence of region upon constructions of race, class, and gender. Not necessarily intending to write a southern novel, but only to make use of its evocative locales, Chopin discloses the dependent relationship between what seems to be an individual woman's desire for "personal fulfillment" and the system of hierarchies that circumscribes any southern identity. The lady simply cannot escape being southern, just as Chopin's parable about seeking freedom from the restraints of gender ultimately cannot separate itself from the suppressions of race and class that its setting presupposes. Nonetheless, writing out of—or into—such contrary allegiances, Chopin successfully exploits those conflicting relationships toward her own ends: creating selfhood for her character and narrative authority for herself.

The creole South in which Chopin sets Edna's search represented a familiar fictional terrain, one whose exotic distances and conventional assumptions helpfully exaggerated the role of women that she wished to explore and critique. Chopin could rely on audiences, northern and southern, to appreciate the importance of being a lady in the upper-class South—and creole society was, thanks to Cable, viewed as notoriously elitist and exclusive. But Chopin uses that elitism not only to underline Edna's difference as an outsider (a "northern" southerner, whose radical ideas are specifically alien to the conservative creoles), but also to provide her with an economic mobility that in fact gives her choices. Edna's very presence on Grande Isle indicates her economic means to escape the heat and disease of New Orleans's summers, a status confirmed by the upper-class occupations she pursues in the city: entertaining the female relatives of Léonce's business associates, attending musical soirees at the Ratignolles or the racetrack with her father and Alcée Arobin, participating in Léonce's decoration and travel plans. Mr. Pontellier's wealth underwrites Edna's leisure, though she begins to resist the constraints imposed by that ladyhood. That Edna wants to be an artist rather than a cultural artifact certainly affirms her agency, but that she can in fact "do it" demonstrates that even her presumed autonomy depends on her position in the same culture whose confinements she resists. When Edna begins to defy her conventional role, she already has what Virginia Woolf knew was essential: a room of her own. As a southern mistress (rather than as, say, a single or lower-class woman), Edna can enlist the whole hierarchy of her household "in the service of art"; children, quadroons, housemaids—all take turns posing in the atelier as material for her self-expression (*CW* 19: 939). The very responsibilities that Edna experiences as encumbrances to her autonomy specifically enable her to explore it.

Edna's freedom assumes racial as well as economic caste. Unlike her contemporaries King and Stuart and most other southern writers, Chopin was not particularly engaged by southern sectionalism and the racist agenda of segregation that most defenders of the South supported. Even so, as Violet Harrington Bryan indicates, *The Awakening* tacitly approves the racial structures of southern society (58). The labor and presence of black people are systematically assumed in the novel. Edna's spiritual journey is directly supported by the nameless black servants who care for her children and cook her meals and drive her carriages while she tries to figure out how to be a lady and still have a self. As Pamela Menke argues, Chopin's focus (not unlike Behn's) simply did not permit her to see the ways that the chafing suppression of her own "dark desires" depends upon the control of the same "dark people" who make possible her individual enfranchisement.

If the notion of female autonomy is not separate from southern contexts but in fact dependent upon them, even Chopin's focal issue—detaching "womanhood" from synonymity with selflessness—is complicated by southernness. Edna protests to Adèle that she simply wants to preserve what is "essential" about her being. She would readily sacrifice the external and physical "self" that motherhood demands ("Nobody has any right—except children perhaps. . . . Still, I shouldn't want to trample upon the little lives" [38: 995-96]), but she does not want to allow that sacrifice to exhaust her entire identity as a human being. But while Edna perceives sexual desire as the touchstone of a deeper selfhood, the *sine qua non* of existence, the novel itself retains alternative space for more conventional options. Though Edna pities the Ratignolles' life of "domestic harmony" as "appalling and hopeless ennui," Chopin clearly reserves more irony for Edna's vague longing for "life's delirium" than for Adèle's apparently rich and sexually satisfied life (18: 938). Conspicuous in her fertility as well as in her marital content, Adèle counters Edna's restless desire with an affirmation of the mother-woman that does not, in fact, exclude a satisfying female sexuality. If "[t]here are no words to describe [Madame Ratignolle] save the old ones" reserved for "the bygone heroine of romance and the fair lady of our dreams" (4: 888), those words only half-conceal their sexual charge: "the spun-gold hair that comb nor confining pin could restrain . . . two lips that pouted, that were so red one could

only think of cherries or some other delicious crimson fruit" (4: 888). The perfect southern mistress perfectly congruent and even happy with her assigned place in creole society, Adèle astutely recognizes Edna's own alienation and warns Robert, "She is not one of us; she is not like us" (8: 900). If Edna's difference does indeed challenge the sufficiency of motherhood in meeting the needs of a fully human self, it nonetheless fails to discount the adequacy of that role for at least some women within the limited terms of creole society. The presence of Adèle, desiring and desirable, as well as a source of unfailing good sense and sound advice, unsettles Chopin's own critique of conventional mother-womanhood.[8] When stretched across the narrow grid of region—or any other cultural space—the selflessness of women appears a perfectly comprehensible, even admirable, description of selfhood.

While Edna's central insistence on her "own way" exposes intolerable constrictions on southern places for women, it still cannot entirely deconstruct southern womanhood. The radical ambivalence of her suicide, together with the contradictory affirmations of southern hierarchy that the text incorporates, ultimately minimizes the effectiveness of Edna's revolt. Even her most dramatic attempt to move out of the social place assigned to her (like the novel's singular focus on gender) results in an ironic reaffirmation of the larger systems that define female status. The pigeon house is, after all, purchased with Edna's father's money and staffed by a black servant, and though Edna can invite Robert to resist a conventional relationship there, she cannot finally rescind his gentlemanly allegiance to patriarchal propriety—or stop him from leaving.

In posing her heroine's dilemma as essentially gendered, Chopin succeeded in undermining one version of the southern belle: the nurturing, selfless, undesiring female. But to construct her alternative in a specifically southern setting, Chopin also had to leave in place the economic and racial hierarchies that had made the belle central to southern ideology. Differences of race and class were critical to the exaggerated female identity that Chopin sought to challenge. Yet Edna's own difference from southern society remains equivocal. Her (admittedly incipient) version of autonomous selfhood still depends on the same hierarchies of class and race that support the conventional belle. By framing Edna's repression solely in terms of feminine desire and not also in terms of the racist hierarchies the belle is meant to protect, Chopin corroborates a modern critique of the South, one that insists on the interdependence of race and gender and class in defining regional identity—or any enclosed system. In its partiality, Edna's problem and her solution remain personal and unique—and thus safely marginal. At the end, Edna may seem to slough off the stifling roles that constrict her dream of an essential self, but her birth remains an act of individualism, itself enveloped by figures of the South she has supposedly rejected. The voices of the sea are those that recall her to a very southern place of fathers and families, sycamores and cavalry officers, humming bees and musky pinks (*CW* 39: 1000).

Partiality inevitably limits the effectiveness of Chopin's interrogation, but it also enables her critique. For if Edna is not wholly outside the paradigms of southern culture, neither is she contained by them. Chopin's calculated use of southern womanhood does heighten Edna's dilemma, and the novel's insistence on the ownership of sexual desire as critical to human wholeness does conspicuously broaden the fictional territory of female identity. At the same time, Chopin's deployment of a southern locale in the interests of a problem she clearly understood to be "universal" reflects a notion of region as a far more significant space than its contemporary relegation to "mere local color" would admit.

Unfortunately for Chopin's own authority as a writer, neither of these achievements were much appreciated by her early readers. Precisely because Edna was a southerner, her concerns (like all regional matters) could be all the more easily dismissed by literary history as merely the plight of another aberrant southern "other"—certainly "not one of us." And even when the importance of the South as a site for examining issues of national concern was acknowledged, it was race, not gender that engaged modern attentions. Indeed, southern writing has remained markedly resistant to images of female autonomy even though it has not infrequently challenged the erasure of black people's individuality. If southern writers considered the problem at all, they continued to isolate and privatize women's resistance to oppressive social roles, failing to perceive their function in supporting white supremacy or sectional loyalty, matters which even many southern white women continued to sympathize with or defend. If Chopin could not see the systemic links between racism and sexism, she was hardly alone. But she was unique in appreciating how damaging to white women were the narrow role of the southern belle and the loss of sexuality to female identity. By writing about that dilemma as applicable to "all" (white upper-class) women, Chopin thus not only profoundly revised the place of female desire, but she also expanded regional writing beyond sectionalism, opening the way for the next century's renderings of women as autonomous subjects and the South as the site of this nation's most searing self-examinations. Neither the southern novel nor the southern woman could ever be the same.

Notes

1. The best recent contribution to this discussion is Jones and Donaldson's *Haunted Bodies*. See especially their introduction, "Rethinking the South through Gender" (1-19.) See also the essays in Humphries.

2. On reassessing southern local color, see Taylor and Ewell.

3. See Ayers for fuller explication of these issues.

4. Seidel shows how the belle merely articulates the southern perspective in early works like William De-Forest's *Miss Ravenel's Conversion* (1867), but functions more and more allegorically in novels like De-

Forest's *The Bloody Chasm* (1881), or Page's very popular *Red Rock* (1897), or Cary Eggleston's rather obvious *Dorothy South* (1902); Seidel, 23ff.

5. See "Mrs. Mobry's Reason," "A Shameful Affair," "Lilacs," "Her Letters," "The Kiss," "Fedora," and "An Egyptian Cigarette," among others.

6. Earlier in the century, the role of motherhood had been, in Harriet Stowe's words, "the 'Woman Question' of the day" (Showalter 14). But instead of trying to bring maternal virtue to the "public sphere," the new women writers of the 1890s were asking if motherhood itself were not an obstacle to creativity and personal fulfillment.

7. Thomas Nelson Page's nostalgic anatomization in *The Old Dominion: Her Making and Manners* (1908) is one of the most explicit versions of this identification (see Roberts 8-9).

8. Certainly Chopin's affirmation of motherhood in numerous short stories, like "Athénaïse," "Regret," or "A Matter of Prejudice," together with her own evident personal satisfactions in the role, reinforce the ambiguity in Edna's desire for autonomy. See Chopin's comments about her own first experience of motherhood (*Miscellany* 92).

Works Cited

Ayers, Edward L. *The Promise of the New South: Life after Reconstruction.* New York: Oxford UP, 1992.

Bryan, Violet Harrington. *The Myth of New Orleans in Literature: Dialogues of Race and Gender.* Knoxville: UP of Tennessee, 1991.

Chopin, Kate. *The Complete Works.* Ed. Per Seyersted. Baton Rouge: Louisiana State UP, 1969.

———. *A Kate Chopin Miscellany.* Ed. Per Seyersted and Emily Toth. Natchitoches: Northwestern Louisiana State UP, 1979.

Donaldson, Susan V. "Gender, Race, and Allen Tate's Profession of Letters in the South." In Jones and Donaldson. 492-518.

Ewell, Barbara C. "Changing Places: Women and the Old South; or What Happens When Local Color Becomes Regionalism." *Amerikastüdien/American Studies* 42.2 (1997): 157-79.

Ferguson, Margaret W. "Juggling the Categories of Race, Class and Gender: Aphra Behn's *Oronooko.*" *Women's Studies* 19 (1991): 159-81.

Fox-Genovese, Elizabeth. "*The Awakening* in the Context of the Experience, Culture, and Values of Southern Women." *Approaches to Teaching Chopin's "The Awakening."* Ed. Bernard Koloski. New York: MLA, 1988. 34-39.

Humphries, Jefferson, ed. *Southern Literature and Literary Theory.* Athens: U of Georgia P, 1990.

Jones, Anne Goodwyn. *Tomorrow Is Another Day: The Woman Writer in the South, 1859-1936.* Baton Rouge: Louisiana State UP, 1981.

Jones, Anne Goodwyn, and Susan Donaldson, eds. *Haunted Bodies: Gender and Southern Texts.* Charlottesville: UP of Virginia, 1998.

Menke, Pamela. "The Catalyst of Color and Women's Regional Writing: *At Fault, Pembroke,* and *The Awakening.*" *Southern Quarterly* 37.3-4 (1999): 9-20.

Roberts, Diane. *Faulkner and Southern Womanhood.* Athens: U of Georgia P, 1994.

Seidel, Kathryn Lee. *The Southern Belle in the American Novel.* Tampa: U of South Florida P, 1985.

Showalter, Elaine. *Sister's Choice: Tradition and Change in American Women's Writing.* Oxford: Clarendon, 1991.

Taylor, Helen. *Gender, Race, and Region in the Writings of Grace King, Ruth McEnery Stuart, and Kate Chopin.* Baton Rouge: Louisiana State UP, 1989.

Toth, Emily. *Kate Chopin.* New York: Morrow, 1990.

Wolff, Cynthia Griffin. "Un-utterable Longing: The Discourse of Feminine Sexuality in *The Awakening.*" *Studies in American Fiction* 24 (1996): 3-22.

William Nelles (essay date fall 1999)

SOURCE: Nelles, William. "Edna Pontellier's Revolt against Nature." *American Literary Realism* 32, no. 1 (fall 1999): 43-50.

[*In the following essay, Nelles argues that Edna's suicide at the conclusion of* The Awakening *is the result of her realization that she is pregnant.*]

Virtually every critic (and certainly every classroom teacher) of **The Awakening** has felt compelled to address the problematic ending of the novel. The ending appears to be ambiguous in the strict sense, leaving the reader with only two opposed and mutually incompatible interpretive options. In Patricia Hopkins Lattin's formulation, "As she swims into deeper water, Edna is herself torn between the two possibilities of triumph and defeat, and the scrupulously objective narrator provides no solution to the ambiguity facing the reader."[1] Such a fundamental interpretive challenge has, of course, contributed to the narrative's aesthetic (and pedagogical) lure in provoking a range of illuminating symbolic, thematic, and historical explanations of the ending. Oddly enough, none of these readings has yet marshaled a critical consensus about what would usually be the simplest levels of analysis. As Manfred Malzahn remarks in his recent survey of this problem, "it all may look meaningful enough from a critic's point of view; however, that does not mean that the internal narrative logic of the story is explained. Why did she do it? Remains the question that still demands a satisfactory an-swer."[2] Chopin simply does not provide, at the literal level, any clear or compelling reason why Edna commits suicide.[3]

Malzahn himself offers two suggestions. The first, "that Edna is just cracking up," is merely circular, explaining irrational behavior by an appeal to the character's irrationality, and he seems to be offering it only to reject it himself.[4] After noting the potentially significant proximity of Adèle Ratignolle's childbirth scene to that of Edna's death, he broaches the second line of analysis, that

> She has been sleeping with Arobin, and there is at least the possibility that this has resulted in pregnancy. Before dismissing this as a far-fetched interpretation, one should consider that it would ultimately make sense of the ending: Edna revolts against Nature itself by destroying herself as a means of procreation, but ironically by following another natural impulse that is directed at self-destruction, the impulse that drives a lemming, or, in the vision of Edna herself, "humanity like worms struggling blindly towards inevitable annihilation."[5]

Malzahn limits his reading to these two sentences, perhaps because of his fear that it will indeed be dismissed as farfetched. But I have heard this interpretation before (offered by students in a sophomore Introduction to the Novel course, to be specific) as, I suspect, other teachers have, and found it quite persuasive.[6] In any event, the evidence and argument for the reading should be presented more fully than in Malzahn's version before being submitted to dismissal or approval.

The essentials of such a reading may readily be sketched. That Edna is having physical sexual relations with Arobin seems to be universally granted, though the precise point at which that begins might be located within either of two passages. Here, as so often in this novel, Chopin's daring subject matter can only be presented indirectly. The standard reading locates their initial intercourse in the gap between the last sentence of chapter 27—"It was a flaming touch that kindled desire"—and the first sentence of chapter 28—"Edna cried a little that night after Arobin left her" (139).[7] It may be, however, that they have already become lovers in chapter 26: "They became intimate and friendly by imperceptible degrees and then by leaps. He sometimes talked in a way that astonished her at first and brought the crimson into her face; in a way that pleased her at last, appealing to the animalism that stirred impatiently within her" (133). In this latter reading, her sexual activity may be seen as the otherwise absent precipitating motive for Edna's moving out of her husband's house. When Mademoiselle Reisz (along with the reader) learns of this momentous decision, her response underscores the need for an explanation: "Your reason is not yet clear to me"; Chopin adds, "Neither was it quite clear to Edna herself . . ." (135). If an extramarital sexual relationship is the reason, Chopin's repeated insistence that no explanation can be given might be as clear a signal as contemporary mores allowed.

The penultimate sentence of chapter 26—"It was the first kiss of her life to which her nature had really responded" (139)—might seem to flag the later point as the first intercourse. But Chopin's narrative idiom operates differently. In the most frequently adduced *Awakening* intertext, Chopin's own **"Athénaïse,"** the parallel phrase, "He felt her lips for the first time respond to the passion of his own" (261), is an index not of an initial sexual encounter, but of the onset of pregnancy.[8] Only when Athénaïse was already pregnant had "the first purely sensuous tremor of her life swept over her" (258). Indeed, one collateral argument for this reading is the degree to which it strengthens the already striking parallels between the novel and the short story. A number of critics have noted these parallels in language that seems to all but demand that Edna be pregnant. Bernard Koloski notes that **"Athénaïse"** "shares . . . with *The Awakening* its structure shaped by a pregnancy," without remarking that many of the examples he offers are truly parallels only if Edna is the one who becomes pregnant in the novel.[9] Similarly, after listing numerous significant connections between the two works, Lattin acknowledges that "The most significant contrast relates to childbirth and motherhood. . . . Athénaïse's 'awakening' comes in a flash as soon as she realizes she is pregnant. . . . In *The Awakening* . . . the pattern is complex and includes no simple cause and effect."[10] Obviously, I am not disagreeing with Koloski and Lattin; both of their readings seem, rather, to call for this extension of their insights. Edna's final awakening comes at precisely the same moment as Athénaïse's, with the realization that she is pregnant; the key contrast lies in their opposite reactions to this knowledge, which does provide the realistic "cause and effect" that so many readers miss in the novel.

The **"Athénaïse"** intertext also suggests the parameters of an approach to the chronology of Edna's pregnancy. Does the novel allow enough time for her to have become aware of her situation? Athénaïse only learns of her own condition as "The fourth week of Athénaïse's stay in the city was drawing to a close," by which time unspecified symptoms—"she was not well; she was not herself . . ." (257)—lead the naive young woman to consult with her more sophisticated landlady, Sylvie, who quickly enlightens her. While "Athénaïse was very ignorant" of such matters (257), Edna herself has already had two children, and would need only the passage of time, not outside advice. The chronology—specifically, the duration—of *The Awakening* is often imprecise due to the frequent use of the iterative mode. In chapter 33, for example, between the beginning of sexual relations with Arobin and the discovery of her pregnancy, we are told that "It happened *sometimes* when Edna went to see Mademoiselle Reisz . . ." and that "Edna had neglected her much of *late*" (152, 153; my italics). Such unspecified passages of time, quite common in the book, would seem to automatically allow for the time needed to learn of her pregnancy. Even setting all of these iterative passages aside (though remembering that Chopin may well have included them for this very purpose), those parts of the chronology that are specified would still fit the timetable. The latest plausible terminus a

quo for the initiation of sexual relations with Arobin is between chapters 27 and 28. The next day she tells Arobin that the dinner party will be "Day after to-morrow" (141); then, "After a little while, a few days, in fact," Edna "spent a week with her children in Iberville" (151). Following a number of iterative passages suggesting the lapse of an unspecified length of time, she meets Robert again, then does not see him the next day, nor "the following day, nor the next"; after still more iterative passages, she then spends another night with Arobin (163) before meeting Robert again. The minimum possible span of time covered here is about three weeks, and a somewhat longer span is suggested by the iterative passages. Recalling that Athénaïse, despite the "bewildering" "extent of her ignorance" (257), figures it out in something less than four weeks, one can safely conclude that Chopin has been careful to allow Edna enough time—but, significantly, only enough—to come to the same realization.

Of course, Chopin, who invented the pregnancies, is aware of them before either of the two women realistically could be, and provides the reader with clues to that knowledge well before the characters realize it for themselves. Running parallel to this realistic level of chronology and biology we have been scanning is a symbolic level along which Chopin strews signs of Edna's condition, most in the form of cultural clichés of pregnancy. If Edna and Arobin have indeed begun sexual relations during chapter 26, then the first clue may be the otherwise odd observation that her chin "was growing a little full and double" (138). Immediately after the "first kiss of her life to which her nature had really responded," a phrase which serves as a marker of pregnancy in "Athénaïse," the experience is described as "this cup of *life,*" (139; my emphasis) which may be read as both a euphemism for sexual excitement and as a reminder of one consequence of sex. The next day Arobin finds her "upon a high step-ladder" (140), a stereotypical site of danger for pregnant women, and immediately gets her to come down. She is on the ladder, of course, because she is making preparations to move into the "pigeon house" (140); Mademoiselle Reisz has just called Edna a "bird" and checked her wings (138), calling forth the cultural cliché "nesting." At the dinner she even exhibits the stereotypical "glow" of pregnant women, "the glow, the myriad living tints that one may sometimes discover in living flesh," a description followed by Edna's first, still unconscious, premonition of her condition, "something which announced itself; a chill breath that seemed to issue from some vast cavern wherein discords wailed" (145). The uterine imagery, together with breath and wailing, as well as the concomitant discord, certainly fit and extend this analysis. By chapter 31 Edna "seated herself with every appearance of discomfort," prompting Arobin to ask if she was tired, to which she replied that she felt as if "something inside me had snapped" (149). Mr. Pontellier's orders to add "an addition—a small snuggery" (150) to the house, presumably, in the terms of his "cover story," for a new baby, may also be a (dramatically ironic) strand of this same pattern. Again, let me emphasize that these are semiotic markers provided by the author for the reader, not mimetic indications that should alert any of the characters to Edna's pregnancy. While realistically Edna would not yet be putting on weight or glowing, these indexes function as symbolic foreshadowing.[11] Recall that all of the patterns gathered here would normally work in conjunction with explicit narrative exposition and character development. Because of Chopin's risky subject matter, however, indirection and connotation must tell the entire story of the pregnancy; given this rigorous constraint, it is perhaps not surprising that so many readers have recognized that the novel never really explains Edna's literal motive for suicide.

Edna's own realization of her condition may only come as she is brought literally face to face with it during the scene of Adèle's delivery. In any event, she has her own pregnancy on her mind during the conversation she has immediately afterward while walking home with Dr. Mandelet.[12] Chopin has carefully established Mandelet's sensitivity to the stages of Edna's awakening and the accuracy of his assessment of these stages in two previous scenes.[13] In the first, Mandelet learns from Pontellier that he and Edna have suspended sexual relations—"you understand—we meet in the morning at the breakfast table" (118).[14] While Mandelet adopts a self-deprecating stance during their conversation—"ordinary fellows like you and me . . . needn't try to fathom" Edna's changed behavior (119)—the narrator allows the reader enough access to his unspoken thoughts to establish that he is in fact far more acute than Pontellier: "The Doctor would have liked during the course of conversation to ask, 'is there any man in the case?'" (120). In this economical scene Chopin shows the reader that the Doctor is not only perspicacious, but circumspect; the reader can trust his conclusions, while both Pontellier and Edna can trust his ability to keep his mouth shut. Both points are reemphasized in the subsequent dinner scene, which allows Mandelet to observe Edna first hand. When we are told that "She reminded him of some beautiful, sleek animal *waking* up in the sun" (123, my emphasis), the echo of the very title of the book lends him an echo of authorial reliability. The privilege accorded his observations is nailed down securely by his final thought of the evening, "I hope it isn't Arobin" (124), which demonstrates knowledge well in advance of the reader's (or at least narratee's) at this point. Despite his evident certainty that Edna is embarking on an affair, his advice that Pontellier let her do as she likes remains unchanged, and he continues, if reluctantly, to keep "the secrets of other lives" (124).

In the first of these two scenes, Mandelet's relation to Edna's story is through hearsay from Pontellier; in the second, he "observed his hostess closely" at first hand (123); Chopin then completes the progression with the third scene, in which the two finally converse directly. The placement of the scene could hardly be more crucial for the narrative: their conversation is the only event between Adèle's childbirth scene and Robert's farewell note. Most readings take one (or sometimes both) of these scenes as the key to Edna's motive for suicide, but both are subordinate to Edna's pregnancy, which is the true catalyst for her actions. Adèle's scene has its power for Edna precisely because she now realizes that she will have to go through that "torture" herself (170). Robert's scene carries the attack from biology to society when his cowardly flight before the prospect of her independence allows us to extrapolate how much more she will have to face when he (and everyone else) learns the truth about her pregnancy. The final scene with Mandelet, then, links and explains the Adèle and Robert passages. Indeed, any interpretation that fails to tie this scene to the obviously crucial ones that precede and follow it must raise perplexing questions about Chopin's artistic competence: why insert a pointless interruption at the very climax of the narrative?

Given that Edna is pregnant, their conversation becomes so rich in interpretive consequences that it is tempting to simply quote it in full. A few highlighted passages, however, might suffice for purposes of exemplification: "'I want to be let alone. Nobody has any right—except children, perhaps—and even then, it seems to me—or it did seem—' She felt that her speech was voicing the incoherency of her thoughts, and stopped abruptly" (171). The Doctor, "grasping her meaning intuitively," offers her the odd assurance that "Nature takes no account of moral consequences." He then tells her that "you seem to me to be *in trouble*. I am not going to ask you for your confidence. I will only say that if ever you feel moved to give it to me, perhaps I might help you. I know I would understand, and I tell you there are not many who would—not many, my dear" (my emphasis; the expression "in trouble" was already established as a euphemism for a pregnancy outside wedlock—the *OED* citations with this meaning are both dated 1891). She finishes her next "incoherent" speech with "still, I shouldn't want to trample upon the little lives. Oh! I don't know what I'm saying, Doctor. Good night. Don't blame me for anything," and he responds, "Yes, I will blame you if you don't come and see me soon. We will talk of things you never have dreamt of talking about before" (171-72).

Mandelet is offering not to listen to a confession of adultery, but to perform an abortion. The risqué book that circulates over the summer establishes early in the novel that sex is not a thing that people "never have dreamt of talking about," but rather a topic "openly criticised and freely discussed" in this society, and we know that Edna quickly "gave over being astonished" by such matters (53). Chopin is careful to overdetermine this point of characterization, putting Edna through a parallel initiation with Arobin, whose racy talk "astonished her at first" but "pleased her at last" (133). But abortion, especially in this Catholic milieu, would constitute the one taboo topic even for an Arobin. Chopin's portrayal of Mandelet as a shrewd judge of human nature, particularly of "that inner life which so seldom unfolds itself to unanointed eyes" (124), and as the confidant of its secrets, is derived from Maupassant, her avowed literary mentor, who presents precisely this figure of the physician in story after story.

As Angela Moger has remarked, Maupassant's frequent inclusion of a physician in his tales is a "logical choice" in part because his professional identity marks him as "someone who accepts everything and does not make moral judgments (moral judgment is here replaced, in fact, by the doctor's apparent detachment)."[15] Maupassant's disciple and translator, Chopin, relies on Mandelet not only because he is the only person who could talk to Edna about an abortion, but for the further excellent reason that he is the only one who could perform one. In a final attempt to underscore the doctor's role and to focus our attention on their necessarily veiled conversation, Chopin has Edna's final articulate thought before drowning return to Mandelet: "Perhaps Doctor Mandelet would have understood if she had seen him—but it was too late; the shore was far behind her, and her strength was gone" (176).

Mandelet serves throughout to guide the reader's perceptions and judgments, not only with cues to infer the taboo subject, but also with his advice to suspend traditional moral strictures and to forgive her behavior, advice ostensibly given to Edna but also (perhaps primarily) meant for the reader. The failure of her contemporary readers, especially book reviewers, to heed this advice has, of course, become part of the Chopin legend.

Notes

1. Patricia Hopkins Lattin, "Childbirth and Motherhood in *The Awakening* and in 'Athénaïse,'" *Approaches to Teaching Chopin's The Awakening,* ed. Bernard Koloski (New York: MLA, 1988), p. 44.

2. Manfred Malzahn, "The Strange Demise of Edna Pontellier," *The Southern Literary Journal,* 232 (Spring 1991), 36.

3. Sandra M. Gilbert has asked, I'm not sure how seriously, "And how, after all, do we know that she ever dies? What critics have called her 'suicide' may be simply our interpretation of her motion, our realistic idea about the direction in which she is swimming" ("Introduction: The Second Coming of Aphrodite," *The Awakening and Selected Stories* [New York: Penguin, 1986], p. 32). Granting Gilbert's emphasis on a subtext of mythic patterning does not, however, seem to get the reader off the "realistic" hook here; for other points she discusses in the novel, her reading requires explanation at *both* "realistic" and mythic levels. Gilbert herself doubts whether Chopin "consciously intended" the mythic parallels (32), which would seem to underscore the call for a realistic explanation whether or not the mythic parallels are convincing.

4. Malzahn, p. 36.

5. Malzahn, p. 38.

6. Lisa Starr, a student in my sophomore Introduction to the Novel class in spring 1997, suggested this reading in the course of a class discussion, and also wrote her term paper on the topic That was the first time I had ever heard the idea, and while her paper and mine share little beyond the thesis, I want to take this opportunity to give her, along with the other students in that class, full credit for setting me on this problem. I only encountered Malzahn's comments later.

7. This quotation and all subsequent quotations from *The Awakening* are taken from *The Awakening and Selected Stories* (New York: Penguin, 1986).

8. This quotation and all subsequent quotations from "Athénaïse" are taken from *The Awakening and Selected Stories* (New York: Penguin, 1986).

9. Bernard Koloski, *Kate Chopin: A Study of the Short Fiction* (New York: Twayne, 1996), p. 36.

10. Lattin, p. 41.

11. Michael Riffaterre's concept of the hypogram provides a theoretical framework for this type of reading, in which a central descriptive system generates semiotic rather than strictly referential meaning: "a transformation of a minimal sentence, the cliché . . . is given in reference to time. Not to real time, however, but to certain, already established, familiar signifiers of the signified 'time'" (*Text Production,* trans. Terese Lyons [New York: Columbia Univ. Press, 1983], p. 45).

12. An earlier possibility for this epiphany comes at the end of chapter 35, when Arobin has detected "the latent sensuality, which unfolded under his delicate sense of her nature's requirements like a torpid, torrid, sensitive blossom" (163). Such sensuality, as noted above, is a marker of pregnancy in Athénaïse, and this loaded description of Edna's blossoming is immediately followed by the phrase "nor was there hope when she awoke in the morning": an allusion to the continued suspension of her menstrual cycle? The cultural requirement that Chopin work by indirection in exploring such unspeakable subjects justifies looking between the lines. One thing Chopin could not possibly do was to say anything openly about pregnancy or menstruation.

13. Mandelet is often dismissed as just another Léonce, the obtuse spokesman for what Cynthia Griffin Wolff calls the "confident weight of received opinion," a "fettering force" ("Un-Utterable Longing: The Discourse of Feminine Sexuality in *The Awakening*," *Studies in American Fiction,* 24 [Spring 1996], p. 14). My own take on Mandelet aligns him with Edna and Mademoiselle Reisz (and, in Wolff's analysis, Arobin) as one of the free-thinking characters not ruled by received opinion, who "hold out the possibility that Edna might resolve her dilemma" (Wolff, p. 15).

14. This key piece of information also establishes Arobin as the father and eliminates a possible "realistic" plot

option for Edna, who could otherwise solve at least part of her problem by presenting the child as Pontellier's.

15. Angela S. Moger, "Narrative Structure in Maupassant: Frames of Desire," *PMLA,* 100 (May 1985), 322.

Martha J. Cutter (essay date 1999)

SOURCE: Cutter, Martha J. "The Search for a Feminine Voice in the Works of Kate Chopin." In *Unruly Tongue: Identity and Voice in American Women's Writing, 1850-1930,* pp. 87-109. Mississippi: University Press of Mississippi, 1999.

[*In the following essay, Cutter explores the differences in Chopin's portrayal of women in her short stories from that in* The Awakening.]

When Kate Chopin's novel *The Awakening* was published in 1899, it was condemned as vulgar, morbid, and unwholesome. The book was allegedly banned from some libraries, and Chopin was ousted from social clubs. She eventually lost the contract for her next collection of fiction, *A Vocation and a Voice,* and it was not published until almost a hundred years later. About the whole furor, Chopin commented ironically: "I never dreamt of Mrs. Pontellier making such a mess of things and working out her own damnation as she did. If I had had the slightest intimation of such a thing I would have excluded her from the company. But when I found out what she was up to, the play was half over and it was then too late" (**"Aims and Autographs"** 612). Despite the flippancy of these remarks, according to Per Seyersted the scandal "hurt her to the core of her being" ("Kate Chopin's Wound" 73). After publication of *The Awakening* Chopin faded almost into oblivion; as Seyersted explains: "At her death in 1904 she was nearly forgotten, and a book published in 1905 on Southern Writers does not even include her name" ("Kate Chopin" 153).

Why did *The Awakening* present such a radical challenge to Chopin's society? Neither Freeman nor Cooper were rejected when, like Chopin, they demonstrated that women's language has the potential to unhinge patriarchal discourse. Unlike Freeman and Cooper, however, Chopin suggests that feminine desire is an aspect of women's search for voice; Edna Pontellier drowns herself partially because she can find no one who understands the new sexual and social identity she is attempting to articulate. Like the New Women described in chapter 1, Edna connects an unruly feminine language of self-assertion to the enunciation of a self-defined desire. That Chopin's text speaks this new sexual and social identity made it shocking and also connects her to later writers like Cather and Fauset, who too insist that feminine desire plays a crucial role in women's struggles for identity, voice, and art.

The protagonist of *The Awakening* understands that the cult of domesticity offers her no viable mechanism for a self-defined subjectivity or voice, and she reaches beyond it toward a new theory of language and identity. But Edna seeks a feminine, maternal language that is represented as existing outside of patriarchy; therefore she never finds a voice that functions in the everyday world she inhabits. In her short fiction, however, Chopin mediates the conflict between feminine discourse and patriarchal language through assertion of a covert voice that attempts to undermine patriarchal discourse through mimicry and through hollowing out patriarchy from within its own structures. Thus while some of Chopin's characters still seek a purely "feminine" voice beyond patriarchal discourse, others have found a metalinguistic one that traverses and deconstructs patriarchal language, a voice that can be heard through the widening cracks of hegemonic discourse. This metalinguistic voice is, finally, one that Chopin (unlike mid-nineteenth-century writers) refuses to silence, repress, or erase.

In 1896, Kate Chopin wrote a short poem that was first titled **"To a Lady at the Piano—Mrs. R—n."** It goes as follows:

> I do not know you out upon the street
> Where people meet.
> We talk as women talk; shall I confess?
> I know you less.
> I hear you play, and touched by the wondrous spell—
> I know you well—
>
> (731)

This poem implies that the commercial spheres of a patriarchal world ("the street") inscribe women within constricting roles, roles that mean that they cannot know each other well. Moreover, when women talk in a conventional, patriarchal mode ("we talk as women talk"), their conversation only means they "know" each other "less." Yet music creates a nonpatriarchal language that allows them to move beyond cultural and linguistic inscriptions: "I hear you play, and touched by the wondrous spell / I know you well."

Throughout *The Awakening,* the protagonist searches for a realm like that created in this poem by women's music—one beyond patriarchal stereotypes of femininity, beyond the realm of the symbolic (the established order of patriarchal language and culture). Edna attempts to undo her inscription within patriarchal language by returning to a maternal, pre-symbolic discourse. In the voice of the sea, in Mademoiselle Reisz's piano playing, and in her own art, Edna seeks what Julia Kristeva has called a poetic or semiotic language. The poetic language that Edna seeks is disruptive, but because it is figured as existing outside of culture, its subversive quality cannot be maintained. *The Awakening* thus dramatizes, but finally rejects, the dream of a maternal, feminine, poetic discourse that is not already inscribed within hegemonic language.

Edna's search for a semiotic voice and the text's final rejection of this concept have not received extended critical analysis. Of course, in the last fifteen years, the protagonist's struggle for language has been a central topic. In a linguistic analysis of the text, for instance, Paula Treichler states that "*The Awakening* charts Edna Pontellier's growing mastery of the first person singular, and . . . when 'I' has been created, the book has successfully completed its mission and comes to an end" (239-40). Using a Bakhtinian approach, Dale Bauer argues that Edna struggles "to make her internally persuasive voice—her impulses and desires—heard against the overpowering authoritative voices of her culture, her religion, her husband's Creole ideology" (141). Patricia Yaeger reads Edna's struggle for voice through a variety of poststructuralist lenses, but is less certain her resistance is successful: "Edna Pontellier has no language to help her integrate and interrogate the diversity of her feelings; she experiences neither world nor signifying system capacious enough to accommodate her desires" (219). Yet while Yaeger, as well as Mylène Dresser and Deborah Barker, employ psychoanalytical concepts, none of these critics apply Kristeva's concept of the semiotic to Edna's search for voice. Using Kristeva's concept of the semiotic, as well as Judith Butler's critique of this concept, clarifies not only what Edna seeks in language and where she situates her moments of voice but, most important, why her search is finally unsuccessful.

Although the novel primarily investigates the theoretical basis of Edna's linguistic oppression, Chopin does not divorce this subject from a historical context. As Frances Harper will do, Chopin situates her character on the cusp between two historical stereotypes of femininity. The novel begins in 1892, when the controversy over the New Woman had not yet exploded in the *North American Review,* or in novels by Sarah Grand, Grant Allen, and George Egerton. Edna is caught precisely at the moment when the True Woman had become outmoded but the new image had not yet reached popular consciousness. As Edna admits to Arobin: "One of these days . . . I'm going to pull myself together for a while and think—try to determine what character of a woman I am; for candidly, I don't know. By all the codes which I am acquainted with, I am a devilishly wicked specimen of the sex. But some way I can't convince myself that I am" (966). The codes surrounding Edna construct her as "wicked," but she finds no alternative "code" that can help her understand who she is. Harper's characters uses a liminal space between the True Woman and the New Woman to remake these ideologies, but for Edna this liminal space is less empowering.

Clearly, Edna is not a domestic saint, as the text explains: "In short, Mrs. Pontellier was not a mother-woman" (888). Edna is willing to give up her physical self for her children, but not her identity, as she says: "I would give up the unessential; I would give my money, I would give my life for my children; but I wouldn't give myself" (929). This statement shows how far Edna has come from the model of selfless domesticity embodied by characters such as Fern's Ruth Hall or even Alcott's Jo March. Edna realizes that she has a self separate from others and desires she will not relinquish for others. Yet when Edna kills herself,

it becomes apparent that she has not entirely forsaken her orientation to domesticity. As she walks on the beach before her suicidal swim, she repeats to herself, over and over: "To-day it is Arobin; to-morrow it will be some one else. It makes no difference to me, it doesn't matter about Léonce Pontellier—but Raoul and Etienne!" (999). Edna feels responsible for her children, and this is one of the reasons she kills herself. Of course, in the act of killing herself, Edna does try to preserve the essential part of her personality that will not be subservient to others. Edna is striving, as Chopin explains, to "becom[e] herself and . . . cast aside the fictitious self which we assume like a garment with which to appear before the world" (939). But her success in "becoming herself" is only partial, for she can formulate no concept of identity that allows her to move beyond the codes of her time period, codes that construct her as "wicked."

To dramatize Edna's incomplete process of casting aside her fictitious self and finding a new identity, Chopin uses ambivalent symbolism. At novel's end Edna stands naked before the ocean, "like some new-born creature, opening its eyes in a familiar world that it had never known" (1000). This imagery suggests a rebirth of self for Edna that is "strange and awful" but also "delicious" (1000). Yet this positive language is contradicted by the novel's last few lines: "She heard her father's voice and her sister Margaret's. . . . The spurs of the cavalry officer clanged as he walked across the porch. There was the hum of bees, and the musky odor of pinks filled the air" (1000). Edna's father, the spurs of the calvary officer, and Edna's harsh sister Margaret are all reminders of patriarchal forces that have entrapped Edna throughout her life. Furthermore, the hum of bees and the smell of flowers suggest the forces that would drag Edna down, into the soul's slavery: her children and her sensuality. The imagery suggests rebirth into a new world but also that even in death, Edna has not formulated an identity that escapes the old world of patriarchal inscription.

Therefore, although Edna reaches beyond the selflessness of the domestic saint, she never quite replaces the "fictitious self" she has been wearing. At stake here for Chopin, also, is Edna's inability to find a voice that articulates her new identity. For Chopin, self-possession and self-expression are crucially interlinked. Edna never formulates a theory of voice viable in the world she inhabits; therefore her sense of self is constantly being eroded by the languages of the world around her. Furthermore, Chopin is critical of Edna's new theory of language because it locates the subversive potential of the "feminine" voice outside Edna's society. Finally, Edna speaks "a language which nobody understood"—a language that has no community of listeners.

The novel is structured around a gestation and birth (it begins in June, when Adèle Ratignolle is just beginning to feel her "condition," and ends nine months later, when she gives birth). Here form and content mesh, since the novel is centrally concerned with Edna's attempt to birth herself into an alternative, feminine, maternal discourse. As Chopin explains at the novel's start, Edna is attempting to create herself anew: "But the beginning of things, of a world especially, is necessarily vague, tangled, chaotic, and exceedingly disturbing. How few of us ever emerge from such beginning! How many souls perish in its tumult!" (893). Language is central to Edna's struggle for subjectivity, as the next few sentences of this passage demonstrate:

> The voice of the sea is seductive; never ceasing, whispering, clamoring, murmuring, inviting the soul to wander for a spell in abysses of solitude; to lose itself in mazes of inward contemplation.
>
> The voice of the sea speaks to the soul. The touch of the sea is sensuous, enfolding the body in its soft, close embrace.
>
> (893)

The ocean represents a maternal realm of language as it might exist in the presymbolic, libidinal world of the mother and child. Chopin's novel returns to the earliest stages of women's inscription within language, asking whether there is some other process of being birthed into language than the oedipal one, some way of achieving subjectivity and voice that does not involve total submission to the Law of the Father, total silencing of the unruly feminine self and the unruly feminine tongue. As Yaeger states, the voice of the sea frames and articulates "Edna's incessant need for some other register of language, for a mode of speech that will express her unspoken, but not unspeakable needs" (219). In the ocean, Edna seeks a maternal voice that avoids the repression of patriarchal language, its erasure of feminine identity and desire.

Such a voice is needed because of the way language functions in a patriarchal world, and in the realm of the symbolic. According to Lacanian theory, an individual enters the symbolic by repressing primary libidinal impulses (including the dependency of the child on the maternal body) and adopting a language structured by the Law of the Father. For women, there are several problems with adopting this language. First, symbolic language suppresses multiple meanings—which recall the libidinal multiplicity of the pre-symbolic realm—installing unambiguous and discrete meanings in their place (Butler, *Gender Trouble* 79). So entering the symbolic entails giving up the body of the mother as well as the multiplicity of discourse and identity that might be associated with this pre-symbolic realm. As Kristeva states: "Language as Symbolic function constitutes itself at the cost of repressing instinctual drive and continuous relation to the mother" (*Desire in Language* 136). Second, this process actually reserves the "I" position for men: "Women, by gender lacking the phallus, the positive symbol of gender, self-possession, and worldly authority around which language is organized, occupy a negative position in language" (Jones 83). Inscription into symbolic language is thus extremely problematic for women; as Ann Rosalind Jones explains, "in a psycholinguistic world structured by father-

son resemblance and rivalry and by the primacy of masculine logic, woman is a gap or a silence, the invisible and unheard sex" (83). The acquisition of symbolic language, then, suppresses women's relationship to the maternal, solidifies identity and discourse, and forces women to occupy a negative position in language.

Chopin depicts this becoming "the invisible and unheard sex"—a sex without desire and language—through her characterization of Edna. Rather than being seen as a subject in her own right, Edna is seen as a possession to be traded back and forth between men. Edna's husband views her as an "object" (885) or a "valuable piece of personal property" (884), and she is also called the invention (971) of her father. Edna is also the object of male discourse; she is most often spoken to and of, rather than speaking herself. When Mr. Pontellier reproaches Edna for her "neglect" of the children, for example, he talks in "a monotonous, insistent way" (885), while Edna is silent: "She said nothing, and refused to answer her husband when he questioned her" (885-86). Edna's silence, here, is that of one who does not possess words: "She could not have told why she was crying. . . . An indescribable oppression, which seemed to generate in some unfamiliar part of her consciousness, filled her whole being with a vague anguish" (886). At this stage in the novel, Edna obeys her husband mechanically and silently, and this demonstrates her inscription within symbolic language, within a discourse that renders her voiceless and powerless. This inscription within the symbolic also involves a suppression of Edna's instincts and drives, a suppression that leaves her without any passion: "Edna found herself face to face with the realities. She grew fond of her husband, realizing with some unaccountable satisfaction that no trace of passion or excessive and fictitious warmth colored her affection" (898). Dr. Mandelet knows Edna as a repressed, "listless woman," and he is surprised later in the novel to see her transformed into a being "palpitant with the forces of life" (952). In the early stages of the book, then, Edna is inscribed within a symbolic language that renders her silent, passive, and passionless.

Yet the voice of the sea continually hovering in the background of these early scenes suggests there must be something more: "the everlasting voice of the sea . . . broke like a mournful lullaby upon the night" (886). The ocean (*mer*)/mother (*mère*) sings a crooning cradle song to Edna that suggests another relationship to language. As argued in the discussion of Alcott's "A Whisper in the Dark," Kristeva posits that the poetic or semiotic dimension of language is never completely destroyed by inscription into the symbolic. The semiotic therefore has the potential to disrupt patriarchal discourse. In Chopin's text, the ocean represents this semiotic, disruptive potential of language, a recovery of the maternal body that Edna believes will allow her to dislodge her inscription within patriarchal discourse.

Edna also seeks other physical and intellectual realms that might allow the recovery of a maternal, poetic voice.

Chopin uses the image of the meadow in Kentucky, for example, to suggest that Edna was not always inscribed within the symbolic, within the Law of the Father. Edna recalls that as a young girl, she had a sense of limitless possibilities while traversing this meadow: "I was just walking diagonally across a big field . . . I could see only the stretch of green before me, and I felt as if I must walk on forever without coming to the end of it. I don't remember whether I was frightened or pleased. I must have been entertained" (896). This meadow represents a pre-symbolic realm in which Edna experiences a sense of freedom, instinctual drives, openness, and passion. When asked why she was traversing the meadow, Edna comments that "Likely as not it was Sunday . . . and I was running away from prayers, from the Presbyterian service, read in a spirit of gloom by my father that chills me yet to think of" (896). Edna is running away from the Law of the Father, from the father's harsh and repressive voice, a voice that still has the power to chill her. At this early phase in her life, Edna can still escape to the realm of the meadow, to the realm of impulses and drives: "I was a little unthinking child in those days, just following a misleading impulse without question" (896). This phase of Edna's life is also characterized by passion, by desire: "At a very early age—perhaps it was when she traversed the ocean of waving grass—she remembered that she had been passionately enamored of a dignified and sad-eyed cavalry officer who visited her father in Kentucky" (897). Edna had impulses, drives, passions that had not yet been repressed by the Law of the Father, and these impulses and passions are captured by the image of the meadow.

At Grand Isle, Edna once again feels as if she is in this pre-symbolic world of the mother: "sometimes I feel this summer as if I was walking through the green meadow again; idly, aimlessly, unthinking and unguided" (897). Edna also feels "flushed and intoxicated with the sound of her own voice and the unaccustomed taste of candor. It muddled her like wine, or like a first breath of freedom" (899). Grand Isle functions as a retrieval of the maternal realm, and a retrieval of a subversive maternal voice that exists before patriarchal discourse has repressed the semiotic, poetic dimension of language. The resort area is dominated by mother figures like Adèle Ratignolle, Madame LeBrun, and the storyteller Madame Antoine; it is a place where men come to stay for the weekend but are, at best, visitors, interlopers, not part of the central social structure of mothers and their children. The men permitted to function in this realm—such as Victor and Robert LeBrun—do so by becoming attached to some maternal woman (Robert) or by remaining in a perpetual state of childhood (Victor).

Perhaps this is why Edna and Robert can talk freely at Grand Isle: while there Robert seems to have not yet completely internalized the Law of the Father or taken his place within the patriarchal world. Mr. Pontellier commands his wife or is bored by her "nonsense" (882), but Robert participates with Edna in conversation: "They chatted incessantly: about the things around them; their amusing adventure out in the water . . . about the wind, the trees, the people who had gone to the *Chênière*" (884). Robert and Edna are on terms of discursive equality, and this certainly has something to do with Robert's placement within a maternal sphere. In fact, Robert rejects the patriarchal realm of the Father in favor of this maternal space and discourse. When Mr. Pontellier tries to convince Robert to go to Klein's—a club for men—Robert admits "quite frankly that he preferred to stay where he was and talk to Mrs. Pontellier" (882). For Edna (and possibly for Robert, too) Grand Isle figures as a maternal space that recalls a time when the social and sexual divisions of patriarchal discourse, of the Law of the Father, had not yet been introduced.

Chopin's novel investigates whether there is a way of entering language that allows this maternal world not to be entirely erased. Specifically, Chopin's text explores whether a maternal, semiotic dimension of language can be preserved through women's art—whether art can become a poetic language that disrupts symbolic language. Edna's awakening begins the night she first responds to Mademoiselle Reisz's playing: "The very first chords which Mademoiselle Reisz struck upon the piano sent a keen tremor down Mrs. Pontellier's spinal column. . . . [T]he very passions themselves were aroused within her soul, swaying it, lashing it, as the waves daily beat upon her splendid body. She trembled, she was choking, and the tears blinded her" (906). This passage suggests a kinship between Mademoiselle Reisz's music and the ocean: both are characterized by libidinal passions, instincts, and drives characteristic of the pre-symbolic realm. Chopin's description of Edna's response to this music is certainly sexual, and we might be tempted to read this passage as an awakening to what Lacan might call *jouissance* (if he accepted that women have a knowable *jouissance*). And later that evening, when Edna first swims in the ocean (under the maternal moon), she seems to be "reaching out for the unlimited in which to lose herself" (908)—to be experiencing a loss of self that we might associate with a sexual awakening, with a "little death." But what Edna awakens to through Mademoiselle Reisz's playing is not a specific sexual desire, directed to or at someone or something, but rather an understanding of how much of her desire has been repressed by her inscription into symbolic language. The music allows Edna to immerse herself in the realm of the maternal and to begin the recovery of the multiplicity of desire and discourse her inscription within symbolic language repressed. And this immersion enables her to find a subversive voice that disrupts patriarchal discourse through a reinstating of feminine desire, feminine wants. Later that evening when Léonce commands Edna to come inside, she responds: "Léonce, go to bed. . . . I mean to stay out here. I don't wish to go in, and I don't intend to. Don't speak to me like that again; I shall not answer you" (912). In the past, when her husband commanded she submitted, but now her "will had blazed up, stubborn and resistant" (912). Edna combats her husband's verbal harassment with a voice that calls upon her own desires: "I don't wish to go in, and I don't intend to." Mademoiselle Reisz's music awakens "strange, new voices" in Edna (946), voices that Edna uses to combat the silencing and erasures of symbolic language.

Of course, Léonce is adept at coopting such resistance, and when Edna refuses to go in, he simply sits outside with her until she gives up. Edna feels "like one who awakens gradually out of a dream, a delicious, grotesque, impossible dream, to feel again the realities pressing upon her soul" (912). She awakens from her dream of a maternal language of desire that subverts patriarchal discourse and finds herself caught in the everyday world. Edna returns to the domestic discourse that she had used earlier in the novel, a discourse that focuses solely on others, asking her husband, "Are you coming in, Léonce?" (913). Certainly, the novel charts the growth of Edna's voice and her self-defined subjectivity and sexuality. By the end of the novel, Edna claims that she has gotten into the extremely "unwomanly" (990) habit of expressing herself and that she has resolved never again to belong to anyone (963). But as the above scene with Léonce demonstrates, Edna's voice continually falters. In the novel's penultimate chapter, when Dr. Mandelet asks whether Edna plans to go abroad with her husband, she cannot respond clearly: "Perhaps—no, I am not going. I'm not going to be forced into doing things. I don't want to go abroad. I want to be let alone. Nobody has any right—except children, perhaps—and even then, it seems to me—or it did seem—" (995). She finds herself "voicing the incoherence of her thoughts" (995), and she says: "Oh! I don't know what I'm saying" (996). By the end of the novel, Edna's voice of resistance has been eroded, and even her sense of subjectivity seems to be under attack.

Edna also seeks voice in her painting, only to have this voice undermined. Noting that "there are no words to describe [Adèle] save the old ones that have served so often to picture the bygone heroine of romance and the fair lady of our dreams" (888), Edna tries to capture her friend. Yet while old, patriarchal words do not capture Adèle, Edna is no more successful at portraying her on canvass: "The picture completed bore no resemblance to Madame Ratignolle. [Edna] was greatly disappointed" (891). Later in the novel, Edna comments to her friend: "Perhaps I shall be able to paint your picture some day" (937), but that day never arrives. Edna's art frequently focuses on women and is frequently sensual. It is possible that in her art Edna seeks a language unlike the "old" words of symbolic language, one that articulates, rather than erases, feminine desire. However, although Edna's teacher says her work grows "in force and individuality" (963), Edna herself remains dissatisfied with her painting and claims that she is not an artist (939). When Mademoiselle Reisz tells her that "the bird that would soar above the level plain of tradition and prejudice must have strong wings" (967), Edna remarks blandly, "I'm not thinking of any extraordinary flights" (966). And when Edna kills herself, it becomes clear that her art has not provided her with a voice of the sea that could break apart symbolic language or speak feminine desires. As Edna walks into the ocean, Chopin

tells us that "All along the white beach, up and down, there was no living thing in sight. A bird with a broken wing was beating the air above, reeling, fluttering, circling disabled down, down to the water" (999). This image emphasizes Edna's isolation ("there was no living thing in sight") as well as her inability to find a new theory of voice that transcends patriarchal language. Rather than being the poetic artist who soars above patriarchal discourse, she is the woman who is silenced, alienated, and disabled by symbolic language—a reeling, fluttering, broken creature, rather than a triumphant creator.

Why does Edna's attempt to formulate a viable new theory of language fail? Edna seeks a voice that can disrupt patriarchy but also one that is apart from, or underneath, or before the symbolic—the voice of the ocean, of the presymbolic realm of the meadow, of Mademoiselle Reisz's semiotic music, of her own painting. But because this voice is constituted as being *outside* of patriarchy, its subversions cannot be maintained. Butler's critique of Kristeva can be applied to Edna's struggle for voice. Because Kristeva situates the semiotic outside of cultural practices, she limits its potential for cultural subversion: "Poetic language and the pleasures of maternity constitute local displacements of the paternal law, temporary subversion which finally submit to that against which they initially rebel. By relegating the source of subversion to a site outside of culture itself, Kristeva appears to foreclose the possibility of subversion as an effective or realizable cultural practice" (*Gender Trouble* 88). Edna sometimes finds a voice of resistance, but because it is located outside all her cultural and linguistic matrices, its subversions are only temporary. She is finally silenced by her own inability to find a theory of language that does not put her outside all existing speech communities.

Like the parrot who introduces the novel, then, Edna finally speaks "a language which nobody understood" (881). Or as Treichler puts it, "at the point of her final movement, [Edna] speaks and embodies a language which cannot be spoken. Only in solitude can the true self speak and be heard" (254). When Edna tries to explain her newfound sense of selfhood to Madame Ratignolle, the two women "did not appear to understand each other or to be talking the same language" (929). And when Robert returns from Mexico, he seems to have lost his earlier ability to "chat" with Edna. Robert has become caught within a patriarchal logic and discourse that sees women as possessions to be traded between men, possessions that lack subjectivity and voice. No wonder, then, that he does not understand Edna:

> "You have been a very, very foolish boy, wasting your time dreaming of impossible things when you speak of Mr. Pontellier setting me free! I am no longer one of Mr. Pontellier's possessions to dispose of or not. I give myself where I choose. If he were to say, 'Here, Robert, take her and be happy; she is yours,' I should laugh at you both."
>
> His face grew a little white. "What do you mean?" he asked.

(992)

Robert blanches before Edna's assertion of personal and linguistic freedom. Edna has found an unruly voice that puts her outside of his comprehension, and, indeed, outside the comprehension of her culture as a whole. Edna truly becomes, then, what Chopin's original title for the novel ("A Solitary Soul") implied; she becomes a solitary soul, with a solitary voice that only she (and perhaps not even she) can understand. Finally, neither the voice of the sea nor Mademoiselle Reisz's music nor her own art or language provides Edna with a maternal discourse that can disrupt patriarchal language. These maternal discourses cannot be translated by Edna into a language that can be spoken to a listener.

In discussing the notion of a female body that exists beyond the Law of the Father, Butler comments: "If subversion is possible, it will be a subversion from within the terms of the law, through the possibilities that emerge when the law turns against itself and spawns unexpected permutations of itself. The culturally constructed body will then be liberated, neither to its 'natural' past, nor to is original pleasures, but to an open future of cultural possibilities" (*Gender Trouble* 93). Applying this idea to Edna's search for language, we might say that Edna dreams of a return to a maternal language that is outside symbolic language, that gives voice to her newfound subjectivity and sexuality. However, she learns that because this language is outside of patriarchy, it cannot subvert patriarchy. Edna discovers that "if subversion is possible, it will be a subversion from within the terms of the law," a subversion from within the terms of patriarchal discourse itself. Dale Bauer argues that Chopin;'s novel is dangerous because it suggests the possibility, however imprecise, "of a world beyond: the world of the body, perhaps the world under threat of erasure by a moving, returning ocean that sweeps [Edna] back to the beginnings and beyond" (154). Yet finally, the novel rejects this dream of a world beyond, of a retreat to a language that exists in the beginning, before the Law of the Father has been imposed. When Edna drowns herself, "the voice of the sea is seductive, never ceasing, whispering, clamoring, murmuring, inviting the soul to wander in abysses of solitude" (999). Chopin repeats the lines she had used earlier to suggest that the voice of the sea functions as a maternal realm *outside* culture, a solitary world beyond patriarchal discourse that cannot exist within the culture Edna knows. The voice of the sea does not provide Edna with a viable theory of feminine voice, and Chopin finally rejects the idea that music, or art, or anything but language itself can subvert language. In the end, Chopin suggests that if we wish to be comprehended, we cannot speak "a language which nobody understood" but rather must talk "as women talk," waging our linguistic struggles in the here and now, in the interstices and gaps of patriarchal discourse.

Despite the liberation engendered by the decline of domesticity, not all fictional characters can find a viable theory of feminine voice, as Edna Pontellier's struggle demonstrates. Indeed, as Yaeger argues, the novel describes "a frightening antagonism between a feminine subject and the objectifying world of discourse she inhabits" (211). This frightening world is also present in Chopin's short fiction, and yet a comparison of her early and later short works shows her moving toward a clearer understanding of how women can most effectively resist the Law of the Father. In her earlier works, Chopin frequently depicts silent, passive women—women who seem incapable of expressing themselves or their desires. Chopin also depicts Anglo American and African American women who attempt to enunciate their desires and experiences through a voice of overt resistance that is quickly labeled meaningless or "insane." Early works such as **"At the 'Cadian Ball," "La Belle Zoraïde," "Désirée's Baby," "Wiser than a God,"** and particularly **"Mrs. Mobry's Reason"** depict a voice of pure resistance that attempts to locate itself *outside* of patriarchal discourse and culture. Like Edna's maternal voice, these resistant voices are quickly erased, negated, or labeled "insane" by patriarchal structures. In some of Chopin's later short works, however—particularly those written during or after 1894—she moves toward depicting women who are more active and more vocal. Moreover, these stories' strategies of resistance often entail a covert, metalinguistic voice. Works such as **"Her Letters"** and **"Elizabeth Stock's One Story"** depict a discourse of insubordination that attempts to bridge the gap between women who speak, like Edna, "a language which nobody understood," and women who are silenced by patriarchal discourse. These later works therefore reject a feminine voice existing outside of patriarchal discourse, and instead find a metalinguistic voice that forces patriarchal discourse into a subversive dialogue, a dialogue that shows its categories to be nonabsolute.

Chopin's short fiction does not reflect a linear movement from silence to voice; rather, as her career progressed Chopin continued to test the ways women could—and could not—achieve articulation. Given her own experiences as a writer, Chopin's development of a covert, metalinguistic voice seems logical. Early in her career, when she wrote charming Creole stories with happy endings, she had little difficulty finding publishers. And when she depicted women who were silent and submissive, the reading public readily accepted her works. But, as Emily Toth shows, after 1894 Chopin attempted to be more daring in her short fiction; concurrently she had more difficulty finding publishers (224; 232-33). Moreover, her most subversive works—stories that often involved female heroines with strong desires and voices—were repeatedly refused by publishers, and, of course, the public and literary critics alike condemned the unconventional Edna Pontellier. Toward the end of the short decade during which Chopin wrote, she did not even attempt to publish works that posited a direct challenge to the literary and moral standards of her time. Yet she did not give up on challenging these standards. Rather, her challenge went "underground": it became less open and direct, more covert and inscribed. These covert strategies of resistance were Chopin's most effective weapon, because they allowed her to slip subversive messages past the censoring dictates of her own society.

Early in her career, Chopin tends to depict women who are silent, women who seek but do not find a voice, or women who find a voice only to have it labeled insane or meaningless. In an early story such as **"A No-Account Creole"** (1888, 1891), for instance, Euphrasie becomes engaged to Placide Santien even though she does not love him. When Euphrasie realizes she loves another man, Wallace Offdean, she takes no steps to end her engagement. Even when Offdean declares his love for Euphrasie, she still cannot enunciate her desire: "She could not speak. She only looked at him with frightened eyes" (98). Throughout the story Euphrasie remains incapable of expressing her marital preferences and embarrassed about her sexual attraction to Offdean. Similarly, in another early story, **"Love on the Bon Dieu"** (1891), Lalie's silence causes her great harm: "Because she had been silent—had not lifted her voice in complaint—[the village people] believed she suffered no more than she could bear" (162). For Lalie, speech is a great effort: "Lalie had spoken low and in jerks, as if every word gave her pain" (160). And like Euphrasie, Lalie seems incapable of articulating her desire; she almost dies with her secret—her love for Azenor—completely unspoken.

These female characters are relatively passive, so perhaps it is no surprise their voices seem ineffective. Yet even more aggressive women, such as Calixta and Clarisse of **"At the 'Cadian Ball"** (1892), have difficulty. In this story, Calixta exhibits verbal dexterity, swearing "roundly in fine 'Cadian French and with true Spanish spirit" (219) and wittily chiding Bobinôt for standing "*planté là* like ole Ma'ame Tina's cow in the bog" (224). Yet Calixta's society dislikes her linguistic proficiency, as the crowd's reaction to this sally demonstrates: "Madame Suzonne, sitting in a corner, whispered to her neighbor that if Ozéina were to conduct herself in a like manner, she should immediately be taken out to the mule-cart and driven home. The women did not always approve of Calixta" (224). Apart from her linguistic forwardness, Calixta also behaves aggressively, slapping her friend Fronie's face when insulted, and eventually forcing Bobinôt to marry her.

Clarisse, too, is aggressive. She rides out alone in the middle of the night to "rescue" Alcée from Calixta, and forces him away from her rival. Yet Clarisse plays the role of the soft-spoken, pure woman; she is shocked, for example, by the "hot, blistering love-words" (220) Alcée pants in her face one day. Eventually, Clarisse admits she loves Alcée, but Chopin switches to indirect discourse and narrates this moment through the eyes of Alcée: "He began to wonder if this meant love. But she had to tell him so, before he believed it. And when she told him, he thought the face of the Universe was changed. . . . The one, only, great reality in the world was Clarisse standing before him, telling him that she loved him" (227). For the delicate Clarisse to enunciate her desire for Alcée would break the narrative parameters established for her character—as well as for the series of women Chopin portrays in these early works. And as we know from **"The Storm"** (1898) (the sequel to **"At the 'Cadian Ball"**), more ag-

gressively verbal women such as Calixta end up with boring men like Bobinôt, and have to wait five years for the consummation of their desires.

Like Alcott's writing, then, Chopin's earliest fictions sometimes reward women who accept their inscription into symbolic language and punish women who assert an unrully voice. Even as late as 1896, Chopin sometimes censors the unruly tongues of her female characters. **"A Night in Acadie"** depicts Zaïda Trodon, a woman who has "an absence of reserve in her manner" and "the air of a young person accustomed to decide for herself and for those about her" (487). Yet after Zaïda realizes her would-be fiancé is a drunkard, after she must be rescued by another man, she loses her self-control and even her voice: "Her will, which had been overmastering and aggressive, seemed to have grown numb under the disturbing spell of the past few hours. . . . The girl was quiet and silent" (498-99). The last phrase—that the girl is both "quiet and silent"—seems repetitive for the usually concise Chopin, yet it marks her double attempt to appease her editors, who complained about the story's first ending in which Zaïda forces another suitor to marry her. According to Toth, this ending offended Chopin's publishers, and she bent to the literary tastes of her time, silencing Zaïda.

Zaïda is described as having the free carriage of "a negress" (487), but racialized women in Chopin's early fiction also have their voices censored. In **"La Belle Zoraïde"** (1893), Zoraïde (a light-skinned slave) wishes to marry the man who attracts her rather than the one her mistress (Madame Delarivière) has picked. Zoraïde tries to express her desire and to reason logically with Madame Delarivière: "Doctor Langlé gives me his slave to marry, but he would not give me his son. Then, since I am not white, let me have from out of my own race the one whom my heart has chosen" (305). But like Robert in *The Awakening,* Madame Delarivière simply ignores expressions of subjectivity and language contradicting her understanding of the world. When Zoraïde becomes pregnant by her forbidden lover, Madame Delarivière has him sold and later tells Zoraïde her baby has died. Zoraïde goes insane, believing a dead bundle of rags is her living child, even refusing to accept her real infant. She also loses the ability to speak rationally, becoming inscribed under a label of insanity as "Zoraïde la folle" (307). This story seems to indicate that for African American women there is no middle ground between sexist and racist repression of speech and a discourse that goes unheard because it is labeled "insane." And this pattern is replicated in the story's frame. Manna-Loulou, an African American servant, tells this tale to her mistress, Madame Delisle. But Madame Delisle misses the point of the story, sympathizing with the abandoned child rather than the silenced mother (307).

Resistant feminine voices of racialized characters, then, simply go unheard. Eventually such voices are erased by madness or suicide, as **"Désirée's Baby"** (1892) depicts. An orphan, Désirée marries a man who claims not to care about her obscure origins: "He was reminded that she was nameless. What did it matter about a name when he could give her one of the oldest and proudest in Louisiana?" (241). Désirée's husband, Armand, will inscribe his wife under his own social and linguistic identity, under his linguistic law. But when Désirée bears a child that shows signs of being African American, Armand takes this social and linguistic protection away, telling her to go. Armand also refuses to hear Désirée's language once he knows of her racial status. "I am white! Look at my hair, it is brown; and my eyes are gray, Armand . . . And my skin is fair . . . whiter than yours, Armand" (243), Désirée says to her husband, but Armand ignores her arguments. Soon Désirée becomes silent: "She tried to speak to the little quadroon boy; but no sound would come"; "She was like a stone image: silent, white, motionless" (243). As Ellen Peel has pointed out, Désirée appears to be a blank screen onto which others project their desires, a screen with no identity of its own. And no language, I would add, once patriarchal protection, the Name of the Father, has been removed. The story clearly depicts a repressive structure in which phallicism sustains itself through an erasure of the voices of feminine and racialized "others," but it presents no way of challenging this structure.

In Chopin's early fiction, Anglo American women are more likely to retain their identity than their African American counterparts, but not necessarily their voices. Discourses spoken by Anglo American women can easily be labeled as "insane" as Zoraïde's, particularly when they do not enunciate socially acceptable codes, as Paula Von Stoltz of **"Wiser than a God"** (1889) learns. Paula's suitor, George Brainard, talks fluently, utilizing the language of romantic passion, while Paula (a musician) is silent: "Say if you love me, Paula. I believe you do. . . . Why are you speechless? Why don't you say something to me!" (46). Paula does finally attempt to explain her emotions to George: "'What do you know of my life,' [Paula] exclaimed passionately. 'What can you guess of it? Is music anything more to you than the pleasing distraction of an idle moment? Can't you feel that with me, it courses with the blood through my veins? That it's something dearer than life, than riches, even than love?'" (46). Paula's speech calls upon codes other than those of romantic love and articulates the view that to an artist—even a female artist—art is life. None of this is understood by George, who only exclaims: "Paula listen to me; don't speak like a mad woman" (46). Paula flees from George and pursues her art, eventually becoming a successful pianist. But Paula continually finds that her language is not understood; even her mother tells her not to "chatter" (40).

"Mrs. Mobry's Reason" (1891) also depicts Anglo American women trapped between patriarchal silence and a discourse labeled meaningless or insane. The story concerns a generational struggle for voice in which the mother, Editha Mobry, acquiesces and is silenced, while the daughter, Naomi, resists and becomes insane. Editha is reluctant to marry John Mobry, but he is "of that class of men who, when they want something, usually keep on wanting it and striving for it so long as there is possibility of attainment

in view" (71). Editha cannot resist such a superior force of "wanting," despite her own obvious lack of enthusiasm for the marriage: "Her tired face wore the look of the conquered who has made a brave fight and would rest. 'Well, John, if you want it,' she said, placing her hand in his" (71). Editha therefore enters the symbolic order of language only by internalizing male desire; she phrases her wishes in terms of the male's—"Well, John, if you want it"—even enclosing her body, her hand, within the masculine sphere of desire. Because Editha enters the symbolic through the masculine gaze she silences herself, making herself part of the "invisible and unheard sex."

Editha also tries to make her daughter part of this invisible and unheard sex. Mrs. Mobry is a firm believer in the late-nineteenth-century view that women should not develop their intellect and mind; she believes that "ologies and isms and all that for women" (72) are useless and possibly injurious to women's mental stability. She will not allow her daughter to engage in intellectual pursuits that might lead to a mastery of language or knowledge. However, Mrs. Mobry has a secret reason for her behavior. Her lineage contains a hereditary strain of insanity, and her reluctance to marry stems from fear of passing on this taint. She also tries to prevent the spread of insanity by keeping her daughter unmarried. Mrs. Mobry therefore attempts to shield her daughter from both sexual and intellectual knowledge, from learning and love.

Yet she is unsuccessful. Naomi falls in love with her cousin Sigmund, and caught between her desire for Sigmund and her desire for her mother's approbation, she loses her mind. Moreover, when Naomi loses mental self-possession, she begins to speak a language not grounded in any normative conception of meaning. She believes she has mastered all discourse and can even understand what nature is saying: "I know everything now. I know what the birds are saying up in the trees . . . I can tell you everything that the fishes say in the water. They were talking under the boat when you called me—" (78). Naomi's unrepressed language is also tied to a sexual liberation: "'Sigmund,' she whispered, and drawing nearer to him twined her arms around his neck. 'I want you to kiss me, Sigmund'" (78). But Naomi speaks "a language which nobody understood"—a language that is so contradictory and illogical it can only be considered insane. Sigmund, for example, reads Naomi as a blank; looking into her eyes, he finds that "there was no more light in them" (78). Furthermore, by the end of the story, Naomi has become silent: "Naomi sat upon a lounge. She was playing like a little child, with scraps of paper that she was tearing and placing in rows upon the cushion beside her" (79). Naomi can finally only escape from patriarchal dictates by regressing to childhood and silence.

The discourse Naomi achieves in **"Mrs. Mobry's Reason"** is thus a form of escape from patriarchal repression that renders the escapeé insane and seems to erase her personality. Between the silent mother and the daughter's insane babble, there must be an alternative discourse. This is the discourse not of overt resistance but of covert subversion. As in *The Awakening,* in her short fiction Chopin finally rejects a discourse located outside patriarchal culture, realizing that linguistic struggles must be waged in the here and now, in the daily "chatter" of women. For as Bauer explains, "The feminist struggle is not one between a conscious 'awakened' or natural voice *and* the voice of patriarchy 'out there.' Rather, precisely because we all internalize the authoritative voice of patriarchy, we must struggle to refashion inherited social discourses into words which rearticulate intentions (here feminist ones) other than normative or disciplinary ones" (2). Chopin's later texts continue the struggle through a covert, dialogic theory of voice that refashions inherited discourses, rather than through a feminine language outside society or outside the Law of the Father.

These covert, dialogic voices are depicted most clearly in Chopin's portrayals of women who write. **"Her Letters"** (1894) tells of a dying woman unable to destroy her adulterous love letters. Upon her death, she compels her husband to destroy the letters unread. The husband does so but then finds himself consumed by curiosity about their contents. Unable to pierce the mystery, he eventually follows the letters to their watery grave, drowning himself. The unnamed woman's letters are therefore subversive of male control in the most literal sense: they drive a husband to question his perception of his wife and to kill himself.

However, these letters are also subversive in a discursive sense, both for the woman and for her husband. This forbidden discourse—not her husband's presence or counsel—has nourished the woman for the last four years of her illness: "they had sustained her, she believed, and kept her spirit from perishing utterly" (398). Moreover, the letters—not her husband, or even her lover—provide the story's one moment of erotic pleasure: "But what if that other most precious and most imprudent one were missing! in which every word of untempered passion had long ago eaten its way into her brain; and which stirred her still today, as it had done a hundred times before when she thought of it. She crushed it between her palms when she found it. She kissed it again and again. With her sharp white teeth she tore the far corner from the letter, where the name was written; she bit the torn scrap and tasted it between her lips and upon her tongue like some godgiven morsel" (399). In this subversive revision of the Eucharist, the word becomes wholly sensual, yet wholly disembodied. It is not her lover's presence the woman relishes but the tokens of their mutual esteem, the words making up their dialogic intercourse. Discourse becomes a subversive replacement for the bodies of men.

For the husband, the letters function differently, forcing him into a subversive dialogue that completely undermines his sense of knowledge and subjectivity. His wife's secret letters irrevocably change his world, for he realizes their probable contents. Although he can find no other written evidence documenting that "his wife had not been the true

and loyal woman he had always believed her to be" (403), the letters seem to prove his wife had a hidden personality he could not discover while she was alive, and cannot fathom after her death. These covert texts, these unfathomable letters, force the husband to question his monolithic perception of his wife. He continues this dialogue with other men who have known her but finds only that his friends also misperceive her: "Foremost he learned she had been unsympathetic because of her coldness of manner. One had admired her intellect; another her accomplishments; a third had thought her beautiful before disease claimed her, regretting, however, that her beauty had lacked warmth of color and expression. . . . Oh, it was useless to try to discover anything from men!" (404). Other men believe his wife to be cold and asexual, but the letters seem to tell another story. The husband thus finds that the letters enact a subversive dialogue undermining his perceptions of the woman he thought he knew so well.

The letters, besides creating a dialogic problem, also create a linguistic problem, causing the husband to question his own understanding of how words function. Previously, when his friends claimed to have seduced women, he has "heard the empty boast . . . and had always met it with good-humored contempt" (403). Now, however, he distrusts his perception that these words are empty: "to-night every flagrant, inane utterance was charged with a new meaning, revealing possibilities that he had hitherto never taken into account" (403). The letters alert the husband to levels of covert meaning in language he has previously believed he could fathom but now finds he cannot: "He was remembering how she had conducted herself toward this one and that one; striving to recall conversations, subtleties of facial expression that might have meant what he did not suspect at the moment, *shades of meaning in words that had seemed the ordinary interchange* of social amenities" (403; my emphasis). The husband seems to have an awakening into the unreliable and potential disruptive possibilities of language—an awakening that profoundly destabilizes his whole universe.

Ultimately, the husband's identity and sense of language are so destabilized he kills himself. If subjectivity is irremediably founded on the oppression of the Other, then endowing this Other with some unfathomable but private sense of self—as Chopin's covert letters do—seems to undermine the construction of male subjectivity. As Luce Irigaray explains: "If there is no more 'earth' to press down/repress, to work, to represent, but also and always to desire (for one's own), no opaque matter which in theory does not know herself, then what pedestal remains for the ex-sistence of the 'subject'?" (133). Covert texts such as these letters take away the pedestal for the existence of the subject by suggesting men do not really know the women they marry, live with, and believe they construct. The wife dies, but her letters affirm the presence of an unruly discourse and an unruly feminine subject. And unlike earlier writers, Chopin refuses to contain this discourse, to repress it under the Law of the Father; ultimately, it is a force that cannot be denied.

Texts, it seems, have a life of their own, a life that begins to undo some of the silences of the patriarchal masterplot. This theme is articulated most clearly in **"Elizabeth Stock's One Story,"** a complicated text that needs to be examined in detail to hear Chopin's subversive, covert message. Like the wife in **"Her Letters,"** the title character of **"Elizabeth Stock's One Story"** dies, but she leaves behind a text that undermines patriarchal control of discourse by giving voice to her subjectivity. Elizabeth is an independent woman who supports herself through her job as postmistress in the small village of Stonelift. Within the society Chopin depicts, however, an independent woman cannot be tolerated for long. When Elizabeth reads and delivers an urgent postcard that arrives late, officials dismiss her for "reading postal cards and permitting people to help themselves to their own mail" (590). Read on the level of discourse, she must be dismissed by an "official" text for her transgressive, unofficial textual practices, as she explains: "One morning, just like lightning out of a clear sky, here comes an official document from Washington, discharging me from my position as postmistress of Stonelift" (590). After her dismissal from her job she becomes ill and dies. Official texts turn upon her, depriving Elizabeth of her livelihood and her life. Males retake the mail.

According to the narrator who introduces Elizabeth's story, the physicians at the hospital where Elizabeth is sent to recuperate "say she showed hope of rallying till placed in the incurable ward, when all courage seemed to leave her, and she relapsed into a silence that remained unbroken till the end" (586). Yet Elizabeth's silence is not "unbroken to the end"; her silence is only the final battle in a long war for self-expression she has waged. She is not content with the limits a patriarchal society has placed on her access to texts. There is a certain "Bartlebyesque" kind of irony in her job as a postmistress: she is responsible for the care and sorting of *letters,* yet she is not supposed to read these letters. But, as she explains, it is human nature—especially feminine nature—to want to possess knowledge: "I leave it to any one—to any woman especially, if it ain't human nature in a little place where everybody knows ever one else, for the postmistress to glance at a postal card once in a while. She could hardly help it" (587). Elizabeth desires to do more than just read texts, however. She also desires to author them, as the narrator informs the readers: "In Stonelift, the village where Elizabeth Stock was born and raised . . . they say she was much given over to scribbling" (586). But again, patriarchal forces must attempt to control and limit women's voice; Elizabeth's writing, like her body, must be deemed hopeless and incurable. The narrator finds the story—Elizabeth's one and only story—in her desk, "which was quite filled with scraps and bits of writing in bad prose and impossible verse." Out of "the whole conglomerate mass" the narrator can discover only one item which "bore any semblance to a connected or consecutive narration" (586). Elizabeth's one story, then, is a found narrative, and after this belittling introduction, the narrator disappears, letting the story speak for itself.

Perhaps influenced by certain masculine notions of literature current in the 1880s and 1890s, the narrator faults Elizabeth's writing for lacking a coherent, linear style. Elizabeth's Uncle William, on the other hand, derides her stories because they lack a unique and adventurous plot, as she explains: "Once I wrote about old Si' Shepard that got lost in the woods and never came back, and when I showed it to Uncle William he said: 'Why, Elizabeth, I reckon you better stick to your dress making: this here ain't no story; everybody knows about old Si' Shepard'" (586). Like the narrator, Uncle William believes Elizabeth's writing is "incurable," and he sends her back to more feminine pursuits like "dress making." Elizabeth's society extols masculine, heroic narratives that she finds herself incapable of producing: "I tried to think of a railroad story with a wreck, but couldn't. No more could I make a tale out of murder, or money getting stolen, or even mistaken identity; for the story had to be original, entertaining, full of action and Goodness knows what all. It was no use. I gave it up" (586-87). Elizabeth cannot come up with any original, action-packed, muscular design for a plot. Yet she still wants to write: "But now that I got my pen in my hand . . . I feel as I'd like to tell how I lost my position, mostly through my own negligence, I'll admit that" (587). Admitting the negligence of the story, itself, *as a story,* Elizabeth's tale nonetheless asserts its right to textual existence. If Elizabeth cannot tell the tale of an American Adam, she may be able to tell the tale of an American Eve—the tale of a woman who tastes of forbidden knowledge, forbidden discourse, and thereby loses a privileged status.

Elizabeth's content, then, violates patriarchal norms, as do her style and structure. Her story is fragmentary and non-linear, moving far back into Elizabeth's childhood, plunging forward into the present, receding to the past events of Elizabeth losing her job. It vacillates, waffles, wavers, digresses, gives details unrelated to the "plot" of Elizabeth losing her job, and frequently draws attention to its own flaws. Furthermore, the style is personal, subjective, colloquial: "Often seems like the village was most too small"; "Anyway, the train was late that day. It was the breaking up of winter, or the beginning of spring; kind of betwixt and between; along in March" (587). Most important, at the heart of the story there is a mystery: was Elizabeth the victim of a plot to oust her from her position as postmistress? And is she aware of the details supporting such a reading of events? On this crucial point the text is silent; it remains a riddle, a structure that resists closure by asserting its own mysteriousness.

According to Ewell, Elizabeth's voice is "colloquial and elliptical"; furthermore, "the one story Elizabeth Stock finally tells . . . has no conventional plot" (166). Elizabeth's story emphasizes its difference from patriarchal forms of writing through its cumulative rather than linear structure, its multiple narrative viewpoints, and its open ending: "But indeed, indeed, I don't know what to do . . . After all, what I got to do is leave everything in the hands of Providence, and trust to luck" (591). Elizabeth also allies her writing not with masculine novelty and heroism but with the repetitive, nonlinear structures of piecing and quilting: "I laid awake most a whole week; and walked about days in a kind of dream, turning and twisting things in my mind just like I often saw old ladies twisting quilt patches around to compose a design" (586-87). So while Elizabeth's other scraps and bits of writing have been read as babble and discarded, the tale itself endures, pieced, patched, and puzzling, but uniquely expressive of her own voice. Thus Elizabeth's silence is not "unbroken to the end," as the narrator and critics such as Heather Kirk Thomas (26) have claimed. Sometime *after* losing her job, but *before* she dies, she describes her experiences in her own, unique way.

In so doing, she finds a voice that is her own but that also hollows out patriarchal discourse from within its own parameters. In earlier depictions of women writers such as **"Miss Witherwell's Mistake"** (1889), Chopin shows women content to write about domestic topics such as "'Security against the Moth.'" But Elizabeth refuses to force her writing into the mode of domestic discourse. Her writing is also not totally outside the realm of patriarchal understanding, like the "scraps and bits of writing" the narrator finds in Elizabeth's desk and discards, like Naomi Mobry's mad voice, or like Edna Pontellier's "feminine" language. The unknown narrator does not see this one particular tale as insane scribbling; believing it to tell a connected, consecutive narrative, the narrator admits it to the sanctified halls of discourse. But Elizabeth's tale exists in a middle ground: it is neither a linear, masculine, patriarchal plot, nor an insane, illogical, fragmented feminine discourse.

In short, Elizabeth finds a covert voice that allows her self-expression but that is not entirely repressed by patriarchy. Elizabeth disarms her readers with her forthright, simple tone; in other words, she plays the fool. But she is no fool. She remembers the name on the postcard—Collins—well enough to repeat it to her readers three times (588) but apparently does not make the connection that the postman hired to replace her after her "negligence" is also named Collins. She blithely informs the reader that one reason for her dismissal was that she allowed people to help themselves to their own mail, while apparently forgetting that the only one who ever actually helped himself to his mail was Nathan Brightman. Nathan Brightman is also the only person who had other concrete evidence for her dismissal, and the only person in town who knew the Collins family. Does Elizabeth know that Nathan Brightman had her fired so his friend Collins could get the job of postmaster? She does not say. Instead, Elizabeth presents the reader with 2 + 2 but does not add them up to 4. She plays the fool, creating a subversive dialogue between the reader and the text, a dialogue in which we are left to ponder just how much Elizabeth actually knew. If, as Bauer argues, a fool represents "a resisting reader *within* the text" who provides "the means of unmasking dominant codes" (11), then Elizabeth fits this paradigm perfectly.

Moreover, Elizabeth's text, while seeming to conform to patriarchal dictates (at least in terms of being nonoffensive or noninflammatory) still asserts its difference. Though pressure is exerted on the tale externally, by a hostile narrator, and internally, by an unsympathetic interpretive community, the text does not succumb. Elizabeth refashions patriarchal discourse, making it take account of her own specific experiences, her own subjectivity. Elizabeth's greatest creation, finally, is her own voice, her own self, which, as Ewell argues, rises "well above any conventional characters she might invent" (167). **"Elizabeth Stock's One Story"** depicts its own exclusion from "proper" discourse, but in so doing nevertheless subverts male control of texts, and perversely insists upon women's right to write/right their own stories. And once again, Chopin refuses to contain her character's unruly voice: Elizabeth's story lives on after her death, enunciating the subversive messages patriarchal society and discourse seek to repress.

Elizabeth's subversive message is that women are excluded from language—from reading and writing—and denied self-determination. Her story enunciates the theoretical mechanisms whereby patriarchal forces create speaking masculine subjects through a silencing of a feminine "other." But her story also presents another theory of language in which women become speaking subjects through the use of covert, dialogic methods. Elizabeth did not end her quest for a form of resistance to patriarchal norms; she only made it less overt. And neither did Chopin. Despite the "failure" of *The Awakening,* she is still looking for ways to subvert patriarchal control of women's subjectivity and voice.

Although Chopin sought a publisher for **"Elizabeth Stock's One Story"** she was not successful, and after the furor over *The Awakening* its publication in *A Vocation and a Voice* was delayed for almost one hundred years. Toward the end of her career, Chopin did not even attempt to publish some of her most daring works, such as **"The Storm."** Chopin's fiction as a whole thus depicts a distinct pattern of repression of women's voices—a pattern reflected within the lives of the characters she creates as well as within her own career as a writer. A patriarchal society denies women's right to control their destinies, their desires, and their discourses, and censors or erases unruly female voices that do not conform to its dictates. And yet authors like Chopin realize that to conform to patriarchal dictates is to be silent as women; as Xavière Gauthier has explained: "As long as women remain silent, they will be outside the historical process. But, if they begin to speak and write *as men do,* they will enter history subdued and alienated; it is a history that, logically speaking, their speech should disrupt" (162-63). How to speak in a voice that disrupts patriarchal discourse, without being censored by patriarchal structures? Throughout her career, Chopin confronts this problem, trying various strategies for creating a voice of insubordination: characters who are mostly silent, characters who use overtly resistant feminine voices that go unheard, characters who find a covert discourse. Like earlier writers, Chopin sometimes destroys the unruly voice of her female characters. However, the overall focus of her fiction is an investigation of the way patriarchal theories of subjectivity and voice silence women, and a resistance to this silencing that involves a release and a validation, rather than a repression, of a subversive feminine voice.

Clearly, for Chopin, certain voices (like Naomi Mobry's) sacrifice the self for a momentary eruption of language no one can understand. There is no subversion that can occur from "outside" the confines of dominant discourses; as Edna Pontellier learns, there is no feminine voice "out there" that can be used to disrupt the voice of patriarchy that is "in here." But some forms of discourse walk the delicate tightrope between "a language which nobody understood" and the silence that is patriarchal repression of women's speech. Some forms of voice successfully challenge patriarchal language through a covert, metalinguistic interrogation of its very premises. So stories like **"Her Letters"** and **"Elizabeth Stock's One Story"** may be paradigmatic texts for women's experiences with patriarchal language and their development of an unruly voice. In *Julius Caesar* Mark Antony states that "the evil that men do lives after them." But texts, too, have a life of their own, a life that may exceed the author's and one day *undo* the evil men do. Like Elizabeth Stock's one story and the messages of the wife in **"Her Letters,"** Chopin's texts live on after her, graphically depicting the way women were silenced and effaced but also speaking the subversive message that women desire—and sometimes find—a subjectivity and voice that exceeds that granted to them by the Law of the Father. I think Kate Chopin would be pleased to know that today, her most daring works— works like *The Awakening*, **"Elizabeth Stock's One Story,"** and **"The Storm"**—are widely anthologized, admired, and read. In the end, Chopin had the last laugh. She may have lost the battle for feminine self-expression, but she won the war.

Kate McCullough (essay date 1999)

SOURCE: McCullough, Kate. "Kate Chopin and (Stretching) the Limits of Local Color Fiction." In *Regions of Identity: The Construction of America in Women's Fiction, 1885-1914*, pp. 185-226. Palo Alto: Stanford University Press, 1999.

[In the following essay, McCullough attempts to show how Chopin both challenged and reinforced the status quo of Southern regional writing.]

> Realism is nothing more and nothing less than the truthful treatment of material . . . let fiction cease to lie about life; let it portray men and women as they are . . . let it show the different interests in their true proportions . . . let it not put on fine literary airs; let it speak the dialect, the language, that most Americans know—the language of unaffected people everywhere.
>
> —William Dean Howells, *Criticism and Fiction* (1891)

LOCAL COLOR, SOUTHERN FEMININITY, AND THE POLITICS OF CANONIZATION

In May of 1899, a month after Kate Chopin (1851-1904) published *The Awakening* and at the time when its negative reviews had begun to appear, Chopin responded to her critics:

> Having a group of people at my disposal, I thought it might be entertaining (to myself) to throw them together and see what would happen. I never dreamed of Mrs. Pontellier making such a mess of things and working out her own damnation as she did. If I had had the slightest intimation of such a thing I would have excluded her from the company. But when I found out what she was up to, the play was half over and it was then too late.
>
> (quoted in Toth 344)[1]

Such a disclaimer is as disingenuous as it is ironic, but even if Chopin knew full well that Edna Pontellier was going to make "a mess" of her life in exploring her self and her erotic desires, one might argue that she could not have anticipated the critical abuse that this most famous of her works was to receive, since she had, in fact, previously published material which, although every bit as outrageous, had not been attacked by the press. On the other hand, given that Chopin was, as Emily Toth has shown, a savvy businesswoman who knew the currents of the publishing industry, she might have expected the negative critical response to *The Awakening*, since it was in this novel that Chopin finally abandoned the cover of Local Color fiction to depict an upper-class white woman's discovery of her subjectivity and the role sexuality played in that subjectivity.

Unlike Ruiz de Burton, Chopin is now an accepted member of the American literary canon, largely on the basis of *The Awakening*. Her membership in this club, however, is fairly recent: in contrast to Jewett, say, who has always been allowed a space (if a diminutive one), Chopin was largely ignored for the first half of the century, then recovered first by the work of Per Seyersted and later, more forcefully, by feminist literary critics of the 1970s and 80s.[2] These critics celebrated *The Awakening* for its depiction of its upper-class, white female heroine's erotic desire and for its refusal of motherhood as an all-consuming identity category; by now *The Awakening* is a text likely to appear in any recent discussion of literary treatments of the female body and female sexuality, not to mention many American literature survey courses. But while feminist literary critics succeeded in bringing Chopin into the canon, the grounds on which they did so, ironically, more faithfully reflect issues central to second-wave (largely white, bourgeois) feminism than to Chopin's work as a whole. As a result her canonical status, I would argue, really only applies to *The Awakening*. Her earlier work—her first novel, *At Fault* (1890), her two collections of short stories, *Bayou Folk* (1894) and *A Night in Acadie* (1897), and numerous short stories published in national magazines—remains underread and is often seen as simply the apprenticeship leading up to the more "universal" text of *The Awakening*. But this narrative misrepresents Chopin and her work, for *The Awakening* is neither fully representative, nor is it the culmination, of Chopin's fiction as a whole. While her short fiction does display an interest in female erotic and maternal desire, it does so in explicitly regionally, racially, and ethnically marked ways. It directly engages—challenging, complicating, and replicating—dominant notions of Southern womanhood in order to offer not a transcendent vision of an emerging female identity (such as Edna Pontellier's) but rather multiple representations of locally grounded Louisiana Creole and Cajun women (among others), representations that both reflect and disrupt Chopin's own positioning as a "local color writer" in a national discourse of American letters.

The discrepancy between the critical reception of *The Awakening* and the critical reception of Chopin's short stories (in her own day, and, less directly, in ours) locates her work at the center of turn-of-the-century debates over regionalism both as an American literary form and as a part of the broader cultural discourse on national identity. Perhaps more than any other author under discussion here, Chopin consciously entered these debates through both her essays and her fiction; consequently, her work provides an illustrative instance both of the way regionalism, as Richard Brodhead points out, "was so structured as to extend opportunity above all to groups traditionally distanced from literary lives" and of the way it "made places for authors but made them *in a certain position.* By virtue of its historical situation, when writers came into authorship through this genre they were placed in inevitable relation with the field of forces that structured its social place" (116, 137). In Chopin's positioning as (not) a Local Color writer, the complexities of her relation to regionalism begin to emerge, both in terms of the ways critics—then and now—understood and defined her work and in terms of her resistance to being positioned by this "field of forces." This resistance can be seen in Chopin's efforts to locate herself by exploiting regionalism as a literary category while simultaneously insisting, on the level of plot, on an American culture made up of internally fractured and marked regions.[3] That is, although Chopin had publicly positioned herself as a writer in relation to both Local Color and Realism, disclaiming the former and celebrating the latter, in her early work she concurrently exploited Local Color, using it to subvert the terms of middle-class models of womanhood, dismantling a monolithic image of America and American True Womanhood by representing various "American" women whose identities are marked by a variety of ethnic, racial, regional, religious, and class identifications. Her work and its reception thus illustrate the force of expectation in the reception of Local Color fiction and speak to the genre's power to contain and diffuse the power of women's writing. This same body of work, however, also shows how those same expectations and categorical assumptions can be used against a genre by a self-conscious writer, and how they can be used to produce a body of work that reflects American racial, regional, and ethnic relations through a gendered lens.

The literary context of Chopin's self-positioning might best be exemplified by recourse to William Dean Howells. As editor first of the *Atlantic Monthly* and later of *Harpers'*, Howells was, of course, one of the most important editors in postbellum America: for roughly twenty-five years he championed Realism and in the process helped both to define its American form and to label that form as particularly American. In his enormously influential work, *Criticism and Fiction,* Howells defines Realism as implying a mimetic fidelity to "life," but a fidelity that he demands be "proportional." He both calls for mimesis and dictates its contents, arguing that what he calls an American literary "tradition of decency" is "truer to life" than a French "tradition of indecency" and that "the study of erotic shivers and fervors," for instance, is not true realism because it is not proportional to life (72). Finally, Howells dictates the very form of this "proportional" and "decent" Realism, calling for the use of dialect and the continued development of the short story form, a form he saw as a particularly American genre (64). A content that chronicles American life is thus, for Howells, happily wedded to a particularly American form.

Howells's argument is worth tracing because it throws into relief the generic hierarchies that subsequently emerged from it. As Howells charts American literature, Local Color is not merely related to Realism, it represents its apogee. By the end of the century, however, this hierarchy had been inverted, so that Local Color had become a minor subgenre of the privileged Realism. This hierarchy is still enacted by contemporary literary critics such as James Cox, for instance, who calls regionalism "a small-scale representation of the larger reality of national literature" (767). The shift in the valence of regionalism/Local Color occurred as a hierarchy of gendered and geographic literary value emerged in antebellum America. That Local Color became a marginalized literary form on the basis of (racially inflected) gender and that as a marginalized form it has been used to contain and dismiss women writers is by now fairly clear. Although both men and women wrote Local Color fiction, white women make up the majority of Local Color writers, and the authors most celebrated as exemplary Local Color writers then and now have been white women: Chopin, Sarah Orne Jewett, Mary Wilkins Freeman, Mary Noailles Murfree, Mary Austin, and Grace King, to name only a few. As a literary category, this "woman's" subgenre has been represented as a diminished version of canonical Realism: though both attempt to represent lived reality with an attention to detail and common life, Local Color has been dismissed as a quaint, backward-looking, and diminutive form (often short stories) written by women writing on a small scale, a form dismissed as nostalgic and concerned with loss and the rural. Canonical Realism and its heir, Naturalism, in contrast, have been valued for centering on the urban industrialized present/future.[4] This contrast has often been represented in terms of form as an opposition between the short story and the novel.

Informed by these nineteenth- and twentieth-century gender hierarchies, Local Color is also deeply imbricated in broader national discourses of region and race. Centered in Boston and New York, the postbellum publishing industry (conveniently bodied forth by Howells) contributed to the ideological work of national reconciliation while also confirming the Northeast as America's literary center, in keeping with the North's position as victor of the Civil War. Amy Kaplan, in "Nation, Region, and Empire" goes so far as to read the Civil War as *the* structuring paradigm for American literature from the war until the turn of the century, calling national reunification "the cultural project that would inform a diversity of American fiction for the following three decades" (240). While this claim needs to be complicated in the case of Western fiction like Ruiz de Burton's, it is certainly tenable for Southern fiction. The Northeast (New England/New York) claim to the cultural primacy of center (de facto defining all other areas as outlying regions) produced a dichotomy that, in the case of the postbellum South, took on other meanings as well: North/South became urban/rural, future/past, masculine/feminine, and victor/vanquished.[5] Thus, Northern publishers publishing "regional" writers both displayed the North's cultural monopoly and celebrated the complexity of America without any fear of the bitter sectarianism of the Civil War, demonstrating that the South as region had become entertaining rather than threatening. As Helen Taylor has noted, by "the late 1870s the northern magazines were very keen to foster a fresh sense of nationalism, and the major publications adopted a policy of reconciliation that meant deliberately seeking copy from regions hitherto little known or courted for their literary output" (18-19). Simultaneously, this regional discourse intersects with the racial discourse of the period, since part of Local Color's ideological work of postbellum reconciliation, of course, was to play down racial dissent by offering happy portraits of Southern racial harmony at a time when virulent racism was evident everywhere from the rise of lynching to the NWSA's white suffragists' abandonment of African-American women. To this end, as Taylor points out, "the invention through a dialect of a tamed, quaint black folk-hero contributed in large measure to popular complacency about the condition of southern blacks in postbellum America" (20). If Southern Local Color fiction was in the process of being marginalized within literary canons, then, it remained at the center of struggles over representations of national identity.

This marginalizing of the South both in broader cultural terms and in the more narrow terms of its fiction speaks to Chopin's position as a "Southern" writer,[6] for on the graph of specifically Southern Local Color fiction, gender and geography run on more than parallel lines; their lines intersect in ways that confirm nineteenth-century Southern literature's status as "minor." Twentieth-century literary history's vision of Local Color fiction as a "female" genre has its analogy in a more generalized feminization of Southern fiction and culture. Anne Goodwyn Jones has shown that the ideal of the Southern Lady, the white, privileged, regional complement to the American Ideal of True Womanhood, operated in nineteenth-century America as the figure for the South itself, embodying "the values by

which southerners have defined the region's character through Civil War and Reconstruction, New South and Modernism" (8).[7] Add to this the fact that the South was emasculated both literally and figuratively by the Civil War: in literal terms, as Taylor notes, by 1890 "there were around sixty thousand Confederate widows in the South; in every state women outnumbered men in all age groups" (6); in figurative terms the South became the powerless, passive captive by its loss. Southern Local Color, then, provided the literary enactment of a larger cultural alignment between the South and femininity, an alignment metaphorized in the postwar fictional plots that showed a war-torn nation reunited by the marriage of the Southern belle to the Northern hero. Through Local Color the South acquired its literary status as one of "America'"s (read the North's) Others: the exotic and often eroticized stranger onto whom was displaced the qualities of violence, passion, and a not-quite-civilized rural world of the past.

Postwar Southern letters in the form of Local Color fiction was thus written out of "real men's" literature, aligned with the losers and the women, providing a space for fiction that was popular but rarely taken seriously. That Southern Local Color fiction came to be gendered female is hardly surprising given the accumulated links between the South and images of femininity, but Chopin's Southern Local Color fiction has a far more important, though less evident, link to gender. Cecilia Tichi argues that "the [American] new-woman writers . . . rejected the camouflage of domesticity but gained acceptance, many of them, under another rubric—regionalism" (597). But what in Tichi sounds coincidental was, in fact, no accident at all: Chopin was quite aware of the politics of Local Color— both the benefits and costs of being associated with it— and so chose to identify with Realism as a political strategy of self-authorization in the face of the threat of marginalization. At the same time, however, Chopin used both the conventions and the marginalized status of Local Color fiction as a cover: as a marginalized form it allowed Chopin to experiment with representations of American womanhood, rejecting a kind of Northeastern Puritan tradition of non-representation of female sexuality and following Realism's move toward mimesis so as to dismantle models of True Womanhood as well as those of the Southern Lady. In a complex set of multiple positionings, Chopin, the upper-class, white, St. Louis-born, widowed mother of six children, translated her knowledge of Creole and Cajun culture into nationally published fiction. And just as regionalism didn't exclude the exotic but rather translated it into something quaint and safe, Chopin herself, like her subject matter, was regional enough to be taken by Northern audiences as an authentic voice while central enough (by virtue of her race and class positioning and her schooling in high culture) to be perceived as a safe translator by her audience. Within her early work Chopin is constantly in conversation with the conventions of Local Color fiction, both challenging its gender norms and often reinscribing its racial and ethnic stereotypes as she attempts to push at Realism's representational limits. Offering heroines who disrupted a monolithic representation of American womanhood in the multiplicity of their ethnic, racial, class, religious, and regional positioning, Chopin complicates dominant definitions of both what gets to count as Southern and what gets to count as American.

CELEBRATING REALISM, DEPLOYING LOCAL COLOR

Chopin was clearly aware of the hierarchy of genres operating in American literature, and in her essays and critical writing she carefully positioned herself accordingly in relation to Realism and regionalism, as well as to European letters. Of French and Irish family, Kate O'Flaherty Chopin was raised within her mother's extended French family and was widely read in French literature, a national/cultural association that proved influential, as I will discuss, in her marriage and also in the worlds she would portray in her stories. In terms of her literary alignments, this background was influential in that it grounded her in a tradition of French, as well as American, literature.[8] The only literary influence she ever acknowledged as an adult was Maupassant, traces of whose form and content both can be seen in her short stories. Although she did not like Zola ("his constructive methods," she complained in a review called **"Emile Zola's 'Lourdes',"** are too "glaringly revealed" [697]), she praised Maupassant in an 1896 essay entitled **"Confidences,"** for being realistic in form:

> I read his stories and marvelled at them. Here was life, not fiction; for where were the plots, the old fashioned mechanism and stage trappings in that vague, unthinking way I had fancied were essential to the art of story making. Here was a man who had escaped from tradition and authority, who had entered into himself and looked out upon life through his own being and with his own eyes; and who, in a direct and simple way, told us what he saw. When a man does this, he gives us the best that he can; something valuable for it is genuine and spontaneous.

(700-701)

For Chopin, Maupassant's value lies in his fiction's proximity to "life" and its distance from "tradition," "authority," and "old fashioned" narrative machinery. In contrast, in **"As You Like It,"** an 1897 essay on *Jude the Obscure*, she condemns Hardy's novel as humorless, unconvincing, and not lifelike, complaining that its "brutality is an obvious and unhappy imitation of the great French realism" (714), implying that it is the unskilled handling of "brutality," not the brutality itself, that is objectionable. She concludes that the novel "is detestably bad; it is unpardonably dull; and immoral, chiefly because it is not true" (714). Unlike many of her contemporaries, Chopin objects to what she sees as a nonmimetic content (its lack of "truth" or adequately "real" realism) rather than an immoral one.

In her stories Chopin also ridiculed generic plots that fell back on conventions at the cost of Realism. In **"Miss Witherwell's Mistake"** (1889, 1891),[9] for instance, Chopin rehearses the comic plot of the eventual uniting of thwarted lovers, but in doing so she also parodies it, mak-

ing the "old fashioned mechanism and stage trappings" the butt of her joke. Miss Witherwell's niece Mildred, sent to her aunt to recover from the love her parents have forbidden, fictionalizes her own plight to her aunt, representing it as "a little story" that she is writing. Mildred, under the cover of this fiction, asks her writer aunt's advice on how to resolve the action, claiming that she is stalled at the point where the crossed lovers, deeply in love, have been brought together again by fate. When Miss Witherwell explains that the hero "must now perform some act to ingratiate himself with the obdurate parent," and recommends having him save the father from a train crash or shipwreck or "avert a business catastrophe," Mildred objects:

> "No, no, aunt! I can't force situations. You'll find I'm extremely realistic. The only point for consideration is, to marry or not to marry; that is the question."
>
> Miss Witherwell looked at her niece, aghast. "The poison of the realistic school has certainly tainted and withered your fancy in the bud, my dear, if you hesitate a moment. Marry them, most certainly, or let them die."

(65)

Mildred's realism—she secretly marries her suitor then brings him home and reconciles the family to him—is one of life imitating an art that is really a disguised version of life, a narrative move that suggests Chopin's support of "the realistic school," as opposed to the "mistake" of Miss Witherwell's school of romantic and rhetorical excess.

Chopin's championing of Realism takes the form not only of an attack on conventional narrative "machinery," but also of an attack on regionalism, which she characterizes as naïve and unrealistic. And while her defense of Realism includes European fiction (indeed, often citing French literature as the model), her critique of regionalism is specifically focused on American letters. In an extraordinary piece she wrote for the *Critic* after attending her first literary conference, the 1894 annual meeting of the Western Association of Writers, for instance, Chopin equates regionalism with an American provincialism of the worst kind, despite her opening disclaimer:

> Provincialism in the best sense of the word stamps the character of this association of writers, who gather chiefly from the State of Indiana and meet annually at Spring Fountain Park. It is an ideally beautiful spot, a veritable garden of Eden in which the disturbing fruit of the tree of knowledge still hangs unplucked. The cry of the dying century has not reached this body of workers, or else it has not yet been comprehended. There is no doubt in their souls, no unrest: apparently an abiding faith in God as he manifests himself through the sectional church, and an overmastering love of their soil and institutions.

(691)

Her snideness here is striking, as is her disapproval of what she clearly views as a naïve and narrow-minded approach to life and literature. She notes that these writers show "a clinging to past and conventional standards," then goes on to proclaim that there is "a very, very big world lying not wholly in northern Indiana, nor does it lie at the antipodes, either. It is human existence in its subtle, complex, true meaning, stripped of the veil with which ethical and conventional standards have draped it" (691). Rejecting the regional as limited and censored by "ethical and conventional standards" and, like Miss Witherwell, as "too often sentimental" (691), she aligns herself with the Realists, an alignment that clearly implies for her a freedom of representational choice as well as a move toward narrative authority and away from the marginalized status of the regional.

In the same year Chopin more directly acknowledged the geographical politics of American regionalism. In an article entitled **"'Crumbling Idols' by Hamlin Garland"** she responds to Garland's critique of the East as a literary center by viewing his attitude as one "to be deplored." She goes on to comment,

> The fact remains that Chicago is not yet a literary center, nor is St. Louis (!), nor San Francisco, nor Denver, nor any of those towns in whose behalf he drops into prophesy. There can come no good of abusing Boston and New York. On the contrary, as "literary centers" they have rendered incalculable service to the reading world by bringing to light whatever there has been produced of force and originality in the West and South since the war.
>
> (694)

As a native of St. Louis who lived in and wrote about Louisiana and was published by Northern publishers for a largely Northern audience, Chopin clearly had experience of the regionally inflected power structures that organized the publishing world. Her response to Garland reflects this; it is no accident that as a regional woman writer Chopin chooses here to represent Northern publishing of Western and Southern fiction as an "incalculable service" to the public rather than as an act of appropriation or postwar reconciliation. This sort of response was typical of Chopin, indicating a caginess toward the industry that she was to exhibit throughout her career and that suggests a region's strategic response to a center's condescension.

However, if Chopin defended publishing powers and aligned herself with Realism, ridiculing both provincial writers and generic plots as limited and partial, and calling instead for a mimetic depiction of life, she also exploited the "provincial" form of Local Color fiction to get published. Consider, for instance, her choice of *Bayou Folk* as the title of her first collection of short stories. And certainly, notwithstanding whatever allegiances Chopin herself claimed, critics had identified her with Local Color as early as 1890 in reviews of her first novel, *At Fault*. The *St. Louis Republic* called *At Fault* "a clever romance of Louisiana life" (quoted in Toth 190); the *New Orleans Daily Picayune* identified it as a "life of a handsome Creole widow" (quoted in Toth 192); and a St. Louis magazine called *Fashion and Fancy* linked Chopin to "that

bright galaxy of Southern and Western writers who hold today the foremost rank of America's authors" (quoted in Toth 192). But if these Southern reviews celebrated Chopin as a Local Color author and promoted her depiction of their region, national reviews of *Bayou Folk* shifted the tenor of that label, establishing Chopin as an important Local Color writer but making it clear that Local Color was Realism's poor country cousin. *The Review of Reviews* called *Bayou Folk* "realistic" and "direct" and identified the influence of Maupassant (quoted in Toth 625), but reviews such as *The New York Times*'s and *The Critic*'s, among others, not only identified Chopin's work as Local Color but also helped to delineate the genre more clearly for their audience. Taking great pains to set the scene, these reviews explain the "exotic" bayou to the reader as if Louisiana were a foreign country. The *Times* review, entitled "Living Tales from Acadian Life," goes on to establish the inhabitants as anachronistic "Frenchmen of the seventeenth century" who are "barbarians softened by Catholicism . . . showing a pagan primitiveness" (23). For all this, however, the reviewer smugly claims that theirs is "a world easily understood, because it is not in the least affected" (23).[10] Louisiana thus in one sweep becomes a regional Other and inferior to New York while also representing the non-"American" national and religious identity of the French Catholic. As in reviews of Sui Sin Far's representations of Chinese-American communities of the West Coast, a national/ethnic Other is conflated with a regional Other. The regional hierarchy being established here is obvious, but reviewers like *The Critic*'s also conflate this with a genre hierarchy. Calling *Bayou Folk* an "unpretentious, unheralded little book," the reviewer remarks upon the book's "queer *patois* people" and then characterizes both the stories and their contents as diminutive, calling them

> simple tales, whose very simplicity increases their verisimilitude and makes in some cases a powerful impression on the imagination. She takes Middle-Upper Louisiana . . . as the scene of her little dramas and reproduces for us, often very realistically and pathetically, the oddities in life and character which she has observed there. In her sheaf of twenty-three sketches some are like rude cartoons whose very rudeness brings out a more vivid effect. . . . These are admirable little bits.
>
> (300)

While the reviewer recognizes and praises Chopin's "photographic realism," such praise operates as a throwaway line in the face of the reviewer's patronizing categorization of both the region and the stories as "little bits." Toth shows that "*charming* was a recurring word in later reviews of *Bayou Folk*" (226): it is a word that aptly indicates a general attitude toward Kate Chopin's short stories, a word gender-coded female and implying a patronizing praise of a marginalized form.[11]

In addition to establishing Chopin as the author of charming female Southern stories, these reviews also make clear that the exotic nature of her fiction is located not simply in a representation of Southern life, but of a specific form of Southern life and a form specified in ethnic rather than simply geographical terms. That is, although Chopin created a wide variety of heroines—urban, rural, Northern, Southern, African-American, Anglo-American, Native American—she rarely wrote about and was almost never understood as writing about a generic Southerner. In fact, critics generally understood her to be representing Creole or Cajun heroines and cultures, with all the ethnic and racial complexity carried by these terms in the context of nineteenth-century Louisiana. As a term, *Cajun* is derived from *Acadian,* a reference to this population's origin in Nova Scotia's Acadian population. In the mid-eighteenth century this population dispersed, with a part of it settling in Louisiana's bayou country. Ethnically French, the settlers brought French language and culture to rural Louisiana. Although they were a complicated and multiply-classed society, by the end of the nineteenth century they had come to be viewed by outsiders, as Carl Brasseaux puts it, "as a monolithic group of honest but ignorant and desperately poor fishermen and trappers, clinging tenaciously to an ancient way of life in the isolation of Louisiana's swamps and coastal marshes" (3).[12] Because they maintained linguistic, religious (Catholicism), and other cultural markers of their French heritage, Cajuns were also seen as un-American. Significantly, they were criticized by both Northerners and other Southerners in terms that replicated the broader stereotypes about the South in the postwar period: Brasseaux notes the terms of the complaints as "laziness, lack of ambition, ignorance, backwardness, and an unrelenting refusal to assimilate" (103). By Chopin's day, then, Cajuns were seen as white ethnics who were regionally specific, always inferior, always of French descent, and always of lower-class standing.

Moreover, by the postbellum period, outsiders often conflated Cajuns with Creoles, a term complicated enough in its own right. Albert Rhodes, in an 1873 article titled "The Louisiana Creoles," for instance, calls the Cajuns "a small portion of the Creole population" and asserts that they are "the least intelligent of the Creole population, and occupy small patches of land along bayous and the coast, which are just sufficient in extent to satisfy the wants of their simple lives" (254). In fact, the two groups are, in derivation and later identification, distinct. As I discuss in Chapter 2 [of *Regions of Identity*], the Louisiana usage of "Creole," while originally signifying the first-generation, American-born offspring of European parents, swiftly became a complicated and contested term. Not originally racially inflected, by the 1830s "Creole" was, as Virginia Domínguez notes, taken to mean a descendent of French settlers although not necessarily white (121). In the postbellum period, however, in part because Louisiana shifted from its original French tripartite legal categorization of race to an American binary system, racial lines became more at issue and two competing definitions came into circulation. As Domínguez explains it, for white Creoles, "Creole" came to mean white "blood" only, of French or Spanish descent, and generally of class privilege, while "Cajun" meant the white descendant of the Acadians; for

Creoles of color, however, "Creole" came to mean of racially mixed blood, not necessarily of French or Spanish descent, while "Cajun" meant of Acadian ancestry but not necessarily white (149, 150). Moreover, in addition to these two groups and sometimes overlapping with them, the Louisiana population contained the descendants of what had been known in the antebellum period as the *gens de couleur libre* (free people of color) as well as in some areas a population known as Redbones, defined by Marcia Gaudet as "people of part-Indian ancestry" (45). Michael Omi and Howard Winant remind us that "the categories employed to differentiate among human groups along racial lines reveal themselves, upon serious consideration, to be at best imprecise, and at worst completely arbitrary" (55); both in the Louisiana of Chopin's day and in her work, these long-complicated categories were deeply intertwined with categories of ethnicity and class and were often contingent on an urban/rural dichotomy that identified New Orleans's "founding families" as Creole while locating Cajuns as specifically rural, sometimes accompanied by Creoles of color.

Chopin's stories reflect this complicated landscape and also reflect her own complicated positioning in relation both to these margins and to cultural centers. Like many of the writers we now view as regionalists, Chopin was not really an "authentic" voice of the communities she depicted—either Cajun or Creole Louisiana—although she had ties to both of them.[13] She was, first of all, not from Louisiana at all, but from St. Louis, Missouri, a city that although in a free state had had many supporters of the Confederacy during the Civil War, including Chopin's own upper-middle-class slave-owning family. As "the gateway to the West" St. Louis was seen variously as a Western city and as a Northern city, a blurring Chopin reflects in *At Fault* in her positioning of the protagonist David Hosmer. The narrator reports that Thérèse Lafirme, the Creole widow heroine, "had guessed he was no Southerner," but just what he is proves harder to identify (744). When he meets Thérèse, Hosmer "introduced himself vaguely as from the West; then perceiving the need of being more specific as from St. Louis" (744), but the flexibility of St. Louis's regional affiliation becomes clear when, in response to the fact that none of the servants on the Lafirme plantation will work for Hosmer's sister Melicent, Thérèse explains that "the negroes were very averse to working for Northern people whose speech, manners, and attitude toward themselves were unfamiliar" (753). Whether viewed as Northern or Western, St. Louis was definitely not Southern.[14]

At the same time, however, Chopin, while the daughter of an Irish immigrant father, was also French on her mother's side and was raised largely in that context, so that she was both Catholic and bilingual.[15] As a result, when she married into the French Creole family of Oscar Chopin she was geographically an outsider but not entirely culturally foreign to his world. After spending the first nine years of their married life in New Orleans, Kate and Oscar Chopin moved with their young family to Oscar Chopin's family plantation in Cloutierville, Natchitoches Parish, Louisiana, where they lived for five years until Oscar Chopin died in 1882. Kate Chopin remained there until 1884, when she returned to St. Louis to live for the rest of her life. Chopin thus might be said to have been neither quite an insider nor an outsider to Louisiana culture. As Roxana Robinson so aptly states, Chopin was "an outsider with inside information" (xi), linked to Louisiana Creole and Cajun culture by language, religion, marriage, and nearly fifteen years residence; separated by a St. Louis origin and upbringing.

Situating Chopin's work in this context allows us to realign both the work and Chopin's attitude toward it. Taking as a starting point that the valence of Local Color was never neutral and that Chopin was well aware of this, one can read her stories as responses to this politics of marginalization. They are manipulations of the very form meant to contain them, a strategy exemplified by **"A Gentleman of the Bayou Têche,"** a story from Chopin's 1894 collection, *Bayou Folk.* In the story Mr. Sublet, an artist visiting the Bayou Têche plantation of his friend, sees the Cajun Evariste and wants to draw his picture, for Evariste is, the narrator notes, "rather a picturesque subject in his way, and a tempting one to an artist looking for bits of 'local color' along the Têche" (319). Sublet pays the man two dollars in advance, but when Evariste's daughter, Martinette, tells her neighbor, "Aunt Dicey," the news, the woman interprets the artist's intentions as indicative of patronizing appropriation, claiming that the artist will label the picture "Dis heah is one dem low-down 'Cajuns o' Bayeh Têche!" (320). Hearing this, Martinette convinces her father that to allow his picture to be drawn would be humiliating and then goes in his place to return the money. As she does, her father rescues Sublet's child from a boating accident, a rescue that prompts the artist again to want to draw Evariste and label him "a hero of Bayou Têche," a label that only further embarrasses Evariste. Finally, in the story's resolution Evariste himself names his portrait, calling for it to be titled, "Dis is one picture of Mista Evariste Anatole Bonamour, a gent'man of de Bayou Têche" (324). Through the battle over the picture's caption, Chopin delineates the artist's appropriation of "local color" and the patronizing condescension at the root of it. Read as a metaphor for the North's consumption of Southern Local Color fiction, it becomes a pointedly political tale that reveals that a romantic objectification of the Cajun (or the Cajun as stereotype of the Southerner in general) strips him of his dignity, his power to name himself, and even, Chopin implies, some of his humanity.

When Sublet first approaches Evariste with his request, Evariste agrees and promises to make himself "fine" for the event. But as Evariste recounts to his daughter Martinette, Sublet "say', 'No, no,' like he ent please'. He want' me like I come out de swamp. So much betta if my pant'loon' an' coat is tore, he say, an' color' like de mud" (319-20). Mud-covered and emerging from the swamp, Evariste embodies Sublet's vision of the stereotypical Cajun: more animal than human. But while Evariste is puzzled by this, it takes Aunt Dicey to explain the "eccen-

tric wishes on the part of the strange gentleman" (320) as a covert insult. She does so by means of a story she tells Martinette, the story of how the artist's child tries to photograph Aunt Dicey as she stands at her ironing board:

> "Dat li'le imp he come a hoppin' in heah yistiddy wid a kine o' box on'neaf his arm. He say' 'Good mo'nin', madam. Will you be so kine an' stan' jus like you is dah at yo' i'onin', an' lef me take yo' picture?' I 'lowed I gwine make a picture outen him wid dis heah flati'on, ef he don' cl'ar hisse'f quick. An' he say he baig my pardon fo' his intrudement. All dat kine o' talk to a ole nigga 'oman! Dat plainly sho' he don' know his place."
>
> "W'at you want 'im to say, Aunt Dice?" asked Martinette, with an effort to conceal her distress.
>
> "I wants 'im to come in heah an' say: 'Howdy, Aunt Dicey! will you be so kine and go put on yo' noo calker dress an' yo' bonnit w'at you w'ars to meetin', an' stan' 'side f'om dat i'onin'-boa'd w'ilse I gwine take yo' photygraph.' Dat de way fo' a boy to talk w'at had good raisin'."
>
> (321)

The boy's request offends Aunt Dicey for two reasons. She is offended first by the kind of representation the boy wants to record: his image of her, which reduces her to a laborer (and might be read as echoing images of house slaves at work). Against this she posits her own image of herself, presented in her best clothes, representing Sunday leisure. The belittling of Aunt Dicey implicit in the boy's image is echoed in the form of his request, where his formal and polite language is read by Aunt Dicey as a disrespectful ridiculing of her. Her comment that the boy does not know his place suggests this, contravening the common usage of knowing one's place, where the phrase carries the connotation of lower status: that is, it is usually people aspiring "above" their place who are accused of not knowing it. While Aunt Dicey's statement might imply this meaning because of the boy's inferior position relative to an adult, in fact, this white boy's "place," because of race and gender hierarchies, is above hers as a black woman, a hierarchy that leads Aunt Dicey to suspect she is being ridiculed. This incident stands as a metaphor of the story as a whole, foregrounding as it does the question of who controls representation and whose purposes it serves.

In the end, the story hinges not on whether a given representation is positive or negative: Evariste is as distressed at the possibility of being labeled a hero as a "low-down 'Cajun." Rather, the issue here focuses on who controls the representation. Calling attention to this, Chopin inverts a more conventional plot (a father protecting his daughter's honor) by having Martinette defend her father's dignity, and gives the power of naming to the subject of the portrait. In addition, she gives the power of interpretation, ultimately, to Aunt Dicey, a pointed reminder that the charming and exotic Other both recognizes and resents his/her appropriation. In doing so Chopin offers a critique of the outsider's (Sublet's/the North's) appropriation of the South and the accompanying demand that the South embody Northern stereotypes of backward poverty—the swamp man, the ironing woman. Significantly, this particular plot—especially the incident between Aunt Dicey and Sublet's son—underscores the analogies and intersections among racial, regional, and gender hierarchies. In doing so it simultaneously insists on a recognition of the multiple levels of Louisiana culture that these hierarchies produce, from the plantation owner, to the racially unmarked Cajun, to the African American. Chopin can thus here be read as reappropriating Local Color for her own ends, contesting the image of the South, specifically the Cajuns, as exotic, quaint primitives, and locating them instead in a complex social system composed of various class, race, and gender stratifications.[16]

At the same time, however, Chopin might be read as offering an ironic self comment on the position of the Local Color artist: was she, a non-Cajun writing bayou stories in local dialect, any less guilty of appropriation than her character Sublet? Chopin clearly benefited from being seen as an inside chronicler of Louisiana life; certainly, many people read her as just another quaint Local Color writer playing into generic stereotypes and thus saw her early work as part of that "charming" Local Color tradition (and so saw *The Awakening* as a shocking break from it).[17] But this reading does not do justice to the complexity of Chopin's early work. While her depictions of race and gender relations in a class-stratified Louisiana are often deeply or irreparably flawed by the use of racist discourse (to some extent substantiating accusations that Local Color offers quaint, charming images of a primitive people), Chopin also frequently offers more radical interventions into dominant national discourses of region and gender, sometimes deploying both reactionary and progressive discourses in the same story.

If her early work escaped the censure attached to *The Awakening,* I would argue that it did so specifically because of the cover of Local Color and the strategies of displacement it afforded Chopin. Critics and readers didn't see Chopin's stories as shocking partly because of their form and the force of expectation: Local Color, as a genre, was seen as quaint and conservative of old values, not suggestive of complicated or new ones. Additionally, however, Chopin's choice of heroines in her short stories also diffused a potentially hostile response to her stories. In choosing for the most part to depict the "exotic" heroines of Local Color fiction—characters who were Cajuns, African Americans, or poor Creoles—rather than simply focusing on white upper-class Anglo Americans (or even, at a stretch, upper-class, white Creoles), Chopin was choosing characters who were already, in the terms of dominant cultural and literary codes, not eligible for the white, middle-class category of the True Womanhood. Moreover, Chopin not only chose to focus on such characters, she also frequently employed a conventionally racist discourse to represent them. Hence, while Chopin was able in her fiction to disrupt certain dominant norms of femininity, she often did so only at the cost of offering images that re-

inscribed others and thus would have reassured her largely white audience.

Within the context of Local Color fiction, then, one might read Chopin, as Judith Fetterley and Marjorie Pryse do, as a sympathetic insider chronicling Louisiana life, or as just another Sublet: an outsider artist looking for a bit of local color to put into stories about Cajuns, free people of color, New Orleans Creoles, and Cane River Creoles. Alternatively, one might abandon this dichotomy altogether to consider the fact that Chopin also wrote stories featuring Missouri farms and Northern heroines, as well as stories set in St. Louis, and that in most of her fiction, regardless of its setting, her heroines are ethnically, racially, religiously, and class marked, frequently Other, not only to some amorphous Northern readership but, within the world of the fiction, to each other as well. Paradoxically, Chopin's short fiction ultimately broadens certain representations of American identity at the same time as it often replicates easy stereotypes of Southern Local Color fiction. Moreover, these representations are not simply the products of the immature writer who would grow up to write *The Awakening* as the masterpiece of her late career. Rather, her representations of regional identities are intricately bound up with her representation of female identity (and often, specifically, female desire) in ways that allow us to see *The Awakening* as thematically overlapping with Chopin's early fiction though in some ways quite distinct from it.

Fetterley and Pryse, in their introductory comments on Chopin in *American Women Regionalists 1850-1910,* suggest a link between these two concerns by arguing that "regionalist fiction opened up possibilities [for Chopin] that were not publishable—the 'region' of women's sexuality" (411), a link that I have suggested that Chopin made by using Local Color as a strategic cover. In this sense the marginalized form serves as a vehicle for a discussion of female sexuality; the protection afforded by marginalization allows the author to push the envelope of what can be represented in fiction. At the same time, however, just as the regional enabled Chopin's representations of female sexuality, her representations of female sexuality serve as the vehicle for an articulation of regional and national identity. In the remainder of this chapter I will examine the ways gender and regionalism intersect in Chopin's short stories, focusing this broad examination on the ways Chopin's reworking of two central components of American Womanhood—passion(lessness) and maternity—recast these often essentialized areas as still important but always in conversation with other equally important identity categories of ethnicity, region, and race. Drawing on the narrative values of Realism, Chopin offered unusually explicit representations of female desire under the cover of Local Color fiction, but her attempts to open a narrative space for the representation of a new sort of heroine ultimately foundered on the racist and sexist discourses underpinning Local Color fiction.

Passionate True White Womanhood

Working within the dominant culture's terms, Chopin's fiction frequently contests the notion of the proper (white) American woman as passionless. She does this in stories that frame white female erotic desire in terms of class while concurrently marking it as regionally inflected.[18] That these stories are also structured in racialized/ethnic terms is often less explicitly marked in the texts, but such structuring is nonetheless central to them, for a combination of racial and ethnic marking becomes the necessary ground for Chopin's representation of white erotic desire. I will look here at only two such stories, **"A Shameful Affair"** (1891, 1893) and **"A Night in Acadie"** (1896, 1897), as a way of exploring various of Chopin's versions of white womanhood inflected by erotic desire.

In Mildred Orme, the protagonist of **"A Shameful Affair,"** Chopin ironically embodies the Northeast as cultural center of the U.S.: Mildred is a white and privileged New England woman whose snobbery is intellectual as well as class-based. Her story interweaves class and gender identities and locates desire on the ground of exoticized ethnicity.[19] The "affair" in question involves Mildred and a nameless worker on the German Missouri farm where Mildred has chosen to vacation. Mildred's patronizing yet clearly erotic interest in the farmhand leads her to seek him out in a confrontation that results in a sudden, passionate embrace and kiss. The nature of Mildred's response—a shamed panic—operates as the core of the story, revealing a class-determined erotic desire as a component part of white female identity.

That Chopin locates this story on the Kraummer farm is not incidental, for this specifically German site, in combination with Mildred's class privilege and extreme class-consciousness (both of which Chopin satirizes), positions Mildred in the space of the patronizing outside observer of local color. Mildred sits on the porch of the farmhouse, reading Ibsen or Browning and watching, for her amusement, the work of the farm going on around her. Rhetorically erasing the actual work of the farm, Mildred views it as simply a backdrop for herself, describing herself, as the narrator reports, as "Mildred Orme, who really ought to have been with the rest of the family at Narragansett—who had come to seek in this retired spot the repose that would enable her to follow exalted lines of thought" (133). The story emphasizes that Mildred's is not a curiosity based simply on rural or class difference but also on the ethnic "difference" of the farm; Chopin includes conversations between Mildred and Mrs. Kraummer that underscore both Mrs. Kraummer as Other and Mildred as outsider, as, for instance, when Mildred asks Mrs. Kraummer about her farmhands:

> "Who are these men, Mrs. Kraummer, that work for you? Where do you pick them up?"
>
> "Oh, ve picks 'em up everyvere. Some is neighbors, some is tramps, and so."
>
> "And that broad-shouldered young fellow—is he a neighbor? . . ."

> "Gott, no! You might yust as well say he vas a tramp. Aber he works like a steam ingine."

> (132)

The use of dialect for Mrs. Kraummer's speech marks her as the "exotic other," her local color ethnic rather than regional or racial. And it is precisely in this space of the Other that Mildred first experiences desire, in a scene that also underscores her status as outside observer. The narrator tells us that Mildred never looked at the workers because "farmhands are not so very nice to look at, and she was nothing of an anthropologist" (131), then goes on to offer the following:

> But once when the half dozen men came along, a paper which she had laid carelessly upon the railing was blown across their path. One of them picked it up, and when he had mounted the steps restored it to her. He was young, and brown, of course, as the sun had made him. He had nice blue eyes. His fair hair was dishevelled. His shoulders were broad and square and his limbs strong and clean. A not unpicturesque figure in the rough attire that bared his throat to view and gave perfect freedom to his every motion.

> (131)

Mildred's position, as the leisured and privileged outsider observing the "not unpicturesque" local worker, recalls that of Sublet as he goes looking for "bits of 'local color' along the Têche" (319). It also recalls Richard Brodhead's claim that "the late nineteenth-century American elite, self-defined through its care for high art, was also identified by its other distinctive leisure practices . . . particularly its arts of leisure travel" as well as its "habit of mental acquisitiveness" (125, 133), but the privileged tourist's voyeuristic acquisitiveness here is specifically marked as erotic, charged with a desire the story suggests is only accessible to the proper lady in the context of an ethnically and class-marked margin. From her seat of repose Mildred plans to offer the laboring farmhand a "condescending little smile" (132) and is offended when he refuses to drive her to church. Played out in gendered terms—the man's refusal to perform social courtesies for the woman—this snub operates as a class-based insult as well. As a woman whose family summers in the moneyed classes' seaside resort of Narragansett, and who clearly has literary pretensions, Mildred may summer with the "farmhands" but only as the lady who expects to be served.

The depictions of Mildred's direct interactions with the man are similarly structured by a combination of class and gender codes in which she casts him as the lower-class Other. In a scene where Mildred engineers a confrontation with him, the narrative establishes her motives grounded both in erotic desire and in a desire to reassert class superiority. While she speaks "politely and with kindly dignity, which she supposed would define her position toward him" (133), the narrator points out that at the same time Mildred's hat has "slipped disreputably to one side" (133) and her eyes "gleamed for an instant unconscious things into his own" (134). Her response to his embrace and kiss is equally shaped by her class positioning, her immediate reaction purely conventional shame, articulated in conventional middle-class language: "her chaste lips had been rifled of their innocence" (134). The shame of violation later gives way, however, to the shame of an admission of a pleasure forbidden to the proper lady, as she admits that his kiss was the "most delicious thing she had known in her twenty years of life" (135). Class, both in terms of the power hierarchies it establishes and in terms of the behavior and interpretations it dictates, permeates this erotic encounter.

In a rapid denouement Mildred learns that the man is not an ordinary farmhand but rather one Fred Evelyn, a man of her own class, a "crank" who "likes to live more lives than one kind" (135) and so is spending the summer living life as a farmhand in his own particular version of the privileged tourist in search of local color. But the revelation of this identity is followed by a more salient plot twist, as Mildred realizes that the class status of her object of desire, ultimately, is not the problem: her shame lies more in her own desire than in his class background. Even the knowledge of his class status cannot "take somewhat of the sting from the shame that tortured her" (135). Ultimately, the story suggests that whether Mildred desires an eccentric gentleman or a sexually aggressive lower-class stereotype is irrelevant in the face of her transgression of middle-class female ideals in desiring at all.[20] Chopin's representation of the unmarked American lady, the white, class-privileged New England "passionless" woman, thus foregrounds class as the structuring determinant of that woman's (lack of) desire. Moreover, while the story works to call into question the passionlessness of its proper lady, it does so only by drawing on the inverse of that model, which links desire to the cultural Other. That is, to ascribe erotic desire to Mildred, the story must borrow it, as it were, from the space of the exotic Local Color setting that is marked as class and ethnically Other. The story thus calls into question one stereotypical representation only by reinforcing another.

In contrast to this representation of the Northern white lady, Zaïda Trodon, the protagonist of **"A Night in Acadie,"** provides a portrait of a white Cajun woman, a country girl from Avoyelles Parish, the setting of most of Chopin's Cajun stories.[21] The story's plot traces Zaïda's secret plan to marry one André Pascal, as seen through the point of view of her new suitor, Telèsphore Baquette. Unlike Mildred, Zaïda is explicitly ethnically marked, both by her name and her language—a mixture of English and Cajun French—as well as by her affect. That is, Chopin attributes Zaïda's independence, spirit, and sensuality to her Cajun identity, using this ethnic/regional tag to define the character as a special category of American Womanhood—"American" but not precisely embodying the values of the proper lady. In other words, Chopin simultaneously rehearses conventional images of Cajun/French character and insists on the regional specificity and distinctiveness of that character. Telèsphore's initial encounter with the young woman on a train establishes this: "he

wondered if she would speak to him. He feared she might have mistaken him for a Western drummer, in which event he knew that she would not; for the women of the country caution their daughters against speaking to strangers on the trains. But the girl was not one to mistake an Acadian farmer for a Western traveling man. She was not born in Avoyelles parish for nothing" (486). Zaïda here embodies the dominant culture's conventional female traits of modesty and discretion in public, but at the same time she emerges as Cajun specifically because of her quick-witted discernment and her ability to identify those of her own community. This community further serves to dismantle a homogenized version of regional others and to replace that with a version of multiple regions that are in relation to each other rather than in relation to the center. Although Acadian community would function for a Northern readership as implicitly set against the North and as easily conflatable with or representative of the South as a whole, Chopin explicitly sets it here against the wildness of the "West" (a space generalized here but marked more specifically in many of Chopin's stories by Texas). This narrative move insists on the differentiation of various regions and puts Avoyelles Parish in relation to, say, Sabine Parish (to the west, near Texas) or Nachitoches Parish (to the north), marking this intraregional differentiation through the characterization of Acadian women, specifically Zaïda.

The protagonist's character is revealed through her conceiving and enacting a plan to marry the lover forbidden her by her family: she slips out of a Cajun ball at midnight and, accompanied by the hapless Telèsphore, drives through a dark countryside to meet her lover, whom she then rejects because he turns up late and drunk. Zaïda's power and agency in choosing the object of her desire are coded by the narrative as Cajun and as positive, but they remain grounded in the body, a conventional source of female power, and grounded in the specifically ethnically marked body. As a result, like Mildred Orme's, Zaïda's desire ultimately reinforces racist, dominant cultural alignments of racially/ethnically Othered women with the sensual and the erotic even as it claims that same erotic for the white (ethnic) woman. The clearest instance of this is the fact that the narrator signals the heroine's combination of self-assurance and sensuality by noting that she "carried herself boldly and stepped out freely and easily, like a negress. There was an absence of reserve in her manner; yet there was no lack of womanliness. She had the air of a young person accustomed to decide for herself and for those about her" (487). Martha Cutter argues that this description associates freedom with blackness (20); I would more directly point out that "negress" here functions as a racist shorthand, evoking, through its alignment with "boldly," "freely" and "easily," the stereotype of the eroticized African-American woman. Michele A. Birnbaum, in a perceptive study of the role of race in *The Awakening,* contends that Edna "first discovers the erotic frontiers of the self by exploiting the less visible constructions of sexual difference associated with the blacks, quadroons, and Acadians in the novel" and that she "employs as well their tropological potential, their associations with the marginal, and ultimately, with the erotic" (321, 324): Chopin's representation of Zaïda, I would suggest, performs the same movement. Ironically, then, at the very moment when Chopin posits an alternative to the model of proper white femininity that denies female sensuality or desire, she falls back on the inverse of this image: the stereotype that assigns all sensuality and desire to African-American womanhood. Although it is clear that this description is meant to function as positive, just as Zaïda's courage and spirit function as positive within the context of the story as a whole, as Birnbaum points out, "white women's desire for sexual expression . . . may lead to a sympathetic admiration nevertheless predicated upon racialist notions of sexuality" (332). Simply put, Chopin here stakes a claim to white female erotic desire only by way of reinscribing a racist eroticizing of black women.

The ending of the story, however, complicates this set of alignments somewhat. In the original version of the story, as Toth points out, after Zaïda watches Telèsphore and André fight, "the original Zaïda, her will as strong as ever, had demanded that Telèsphore marry her on the spot" (283), a demand that leaves Zaïda with her desires unpunished and with control over her life. (Control, of course, is here limited: in the original ending Zaïda remains within the structure of the heterosexual marriage, where control translates to the choice of a husband.) But this ending was unacceptable to *Century*'s editor Richard Watson Gilder, to whom Chopin submitted the story, so she produced a revised ending that, significantly, reworked her heroine into a far more conventional "good" American girl. In this version Zaïda's experience with her drunken fiancee André serves as a cautionary lesson, so that, as Chopin wrote to Gilder, "the girl's character [is] softened and tempered by her rude experience" (quoted in Toth 283). The story then follows a more conventional plot line, as an overly exuberant girl is taught to dampen her spirits, to become passive and to rely on men for her rescue and direction. By the story's close the revised Zaïda is described as submissive, and the narrator notes that her "will, which had been overmastering and aggressive, seemed to have grown numb under the disturbing spell of the past few hours" (498). Numbness gives way to a proper female passivity, so that in the story's closing lines, when Telèsphore announces that he is taking her home, "she was like a little child and followed whither he led in all confidence" (499).

However, because desire and agency in this story function as part of the definition of the Cajun woman, when Chopin writes them out, the protagonist becomes unconvincing: by the story's end Zaïda reads less like a Cajun girl than like an imitation of a Northern-magazine-story, white heroine dressed unconvincingly in Cajun trappings.[22] Roxana Robinson contends that Chopin's Cajun women are wilder, more dramatic, and less conventional than her Creole women (xiii), and that within the collection of stories Robinson edits, "social status is inversely related to female power: Chopin's black women are more powerful than the whites, and Cajun women more powerful than Creoles" (xx). While this is not true in terms of social, economic, or class power, in terms of emotional and erotic force and/or agency, it is certainly true of Chopin's Cajun and Creole women at least. (The argument is more complicated with respect to Chopin's African-American female characters.) Rather than linking female power to social status, however, I would reformulate Robinson's claim to read "female erotic power is inversely related to ethnic/regional status": that is, the degree of erotic agency and power Chopin grants her female Creole and Cajun characters is directly related to their ethnic/regional identities. In inverse proportion to their proximity to the category of unmarked but implicitly Northern, class-privileged, white womanhood, this power thus replicates conventional racialized thinking of the period, locating erotic desire in the Othered woman and offering the white ethnic woman access to this desire via her status as ethnic. The category Cajun thus does double labor in Zaïda's story: it signals white and also ethnic, the latter a category that can slide from safe, entertaining difference to cultural Other. And just as Chopin played this doubled valence as it applied to Local Color fiction, she plays it here as well, for one might read the rewriting of Zaïda as a process of moving from one aspect of Cajun to the other: the original version of the story emphasizes traits that Chopin ascribes to Zaïda's ethnicity, while the final version with its revised ending emphasizes traits associated with whiteness as the category of conventional femininity. Thus, when Chopin rewrote Zaïda as less powerful and more conventional—closer to dominant norms of white femininity—she also made her, in the logic of the story, less ethnic and more "white." Because Chopin left the character's regional and ethnic marking intact, however, she ended up with a heroine who is internally inconsistent on the plot level and yet still unqualified for True Womanhood. Ultimately, what both Zaïda's and Mildred Orme's stories show, then, is that both the dominant American ideals of femininity and Chopin's challenge to them are compromised by the terms of the racial discourse out of which they emerge and are defined not simply by behavior and race, but also by regional identity, class, and ethnicity.

VERSIONS OF A REGIONAL MATERNAL

Just as representations of female agency and erotic desire in Chopin's short fiction emerge from a complicated matrix of racial, gender, and ethnic discourses and so intervene in both radical and reactionary ways in dominant discourse on women, Chopin's representations of the maternal both draw on and discredit conventional universalized models of motherhood. While using certain elements of the maternal to link her Southern heroines to Northern ideals, Chopin simultaneously uses the category as a means of differentiating among various Southern heroines and among various enactments of the maternal. In doing so she disrupts monolithic representations of Southern womanhood by disrupting the absolute meaning of maternity and emphasizing the wide variety of forms motherhood can take. In Chopin's stories the space of the maternal takes on wildly varying meanings according to who occupies it where and when. There is here no idealized type for the American mother or even the Southern mother; instead, there are *mothers*: a range of identities that make it impossible, ultimately, to essentialize maternity. One result of this recasting of the maternal is that white, class-privileged motherhood is no longer celebrated as innate and natural but rather revealed to be socially constructed within a discourse of power, contextual, and contingent on other aspects of female identity—race, region, and class, primarily. A second result of this deessentializing of the maternal is that Chopin's stories foreground and to some extent challenge the strategies by which slavery attempted to strip enslaved black women of access to the category of the maternal. Taken as a group, the stories that focus on maternity make visible the fact that motherhood, like erotic desire, is neither "natural" nor unmarked but rather ultimately determined by factors such as region, race, ethnicity, and class. In what follows I will attempt to trace the ways and places in which these discourses interrupt each other, tracking the intersection of a racist and reactionary racial discourse with more progressive gender and regional discourses, as well as the degree to which a focus on ethnicity allows Chopin to sidestep a direct confrontation with race.

In **"La Belle Zoraïde"** (1893, 1894) the representation of maternity is specifically inflected by race and racial discourse's relations to a maternal that might arguably be seen as regional, that is, Southern. The story focuses on slavery's structuring impact on the maternity and erotic desire of both the African-American and the white Creole women in the story, establishing that the maternal is a highly contingent rather than natural category.[23] As my discussion of Hopkins in Chapter 3 indicates, maternity and erotic desire were, of course, already imbricated in a racial discourse by Chopin's day. The category of the Southern lady constituted her as always chaste and white, but moreover the category also always demanded that her sexual excess be projected onto her racial Other, the African-American woman. At the same time, maternal instinct was attributed to the Southern lady but denied to all Others, particularly the enslaved (and even at times the free) African-American woman. Thus, maternal and erotic desire functioned as mutually exclusive. As Anna Shannon Elfenbein cogently notes in her article on *The Awakening*, "for much of Chopin's audience the troublesome issue of female desire was resolved through a racist conception of passion and purity according to which passion was projected onto 'dark' women while purity was reserved exclusively for 'white' women" (304). In setting **"La Belle Zoraïde"** in the antebellum South, Chopin participates in this American cultural discourse, which occurred at the crossroads of racial, regional, and gender discourses. While such a story contributes to postwar regional reconciliation by offering images of racial conflict safely located in the antebellum past, it simultaneously complicates the terms of the racialized discourse on femininity, revealing it as regionally inflected and never fixed.

The story reworks the plot of the slave woman parted from her lover by her "owner":[24] Zoraïde is the beautiful and privileged mulatto slave of Madame Delarivière. She is well-treated until she defies Madame by falling in love with the handsome black slave Mézor rather than the mulatto M. Ambroise, whom Madame has chosen for her. When Zoraïde becomes pregnant by Mézor, Madame, first angry and then pained, has him sold by his "owner," her own suitor, then lies to Zoraïde at the child's birth, telling her that the child is dead. Zoraïde grows demented in response, so much so that when Madame finally returns the child to her in an attempt to cure the madness, Zoraïde does not recognize the child and clings instead to the bundle of rags she has substituted for her baby. Hence, she dies an old, mad, unmarried woman, known as "Zoraïde La Folle" instead of **"La Belle Zoraïde."** Her story is presented within a frame in which Manna-Loulou ministers to her mistress Madame Delisle, ministerings that include the telling of the bedtime story of La Belle Zoraïde. The frame story insists that Zoraïde's story is fact, for Madame Delisle, Chopin notes, "would hear none but those [stories] which were true" (304). Set in the antebellum south, Zoraïde's tale thus works in tandem with the frame tale to produce the story's effect.

Zoraïde's history, as told by Manna-Loulou, emphasizes slavery's impact on both female erotic desire and maternal "instinct." Because she is a slave, Zoraïde is not attributed the maternal "instinct" that is culturally assigned to white women, and her "owner" views neither Zoraïde's desire nor her reproductive potential as her own; both are, rather, commodities belonging to her "owner." Manna-Loulou's version of Zoraïde's story, however, offers a counternarrative to this one. Manna-Loulou represents Zoraïde as bearing an erotic desire that is linked to romantic love, racially inflected, and self-directed. She also attributes to Zoraïde a form of maternal "instinct" that is in keeping with idealized models of white womanhood but is forcibly redirected by slavery. These competing versions of the enslaved African-American woman's relation to erotic and maternal desire stand alongside the story's representation of Madame Delarivière, who, as an upper-class white woman, is assumed to have maternal "instinct"—enacting it metaphorically with her non-offspring, the enslaved young woman—and to lack overt erotic desire. Manna-Loulou's narrative also counters this particular, racially inflected version of womanhood, revealing that the white slaveholding woman's maternal sense is simply another form of ownership, and her passionlessness is accompanied by the knowledge of her erotic power. Chopin's choice of an enslaved woman as narrator thus provides a space for a complicating of both black and white racialized narratives of American womanhood, although ultimately this counterdiscourse is contained both by the fate of Zoraïde (madness) and by Chopin's safely locating the story in the antebellum past.

Racial location structures the face of maternity and desire in the Creole white woman, Madame Delarivière. In a combination of class and racialized gender expectations—a combination of a sort of *noblesse oblige* and maternal "instinct"—she initially poses as a surrogate mother for Zoraïde. As the "privileged" slave, Zoraïde is raised in comfort by her mistress, who is also her godmother; her "fingers," Manna-Loulou recounts, "had never done rougher work than sewing a fine muslin seam" (304). But while Zoraïde's "mother" makes plans to have Zoraïde married in the prestigious New Orleans Cathedral and promises to provide her with a fine wedding gown and *corbeille,* the maternal role is merely a fiction, a cover for what is in fact a relationship grounded in power and economics: Madame's power over Zoraïde comes not from a "natural" mother-child bond but from a legal master-slave bond. When Zoraïde refuses to marry the man Madame has chosen for her, Madame drops the fiction of maternal love and exposes her power as a white woman and slaveholder. Trading on her own position as desirable white woman and revealing it as an economic/social location, she induces Mézor's owner, who is in love with her, to sell Mézor (Manna-Loulou explains that Mézor's owner "had long wanted to marry Madame Delarivière, and he would willingly have walked on all fours at noon through the Place d'Armes if she wanted him to. Naturally he lost no time in disposing of le beau Mézor" [306]). She then manipulates Zoraïde for her own convenience by lying, telling Zoraïde that her newly born child is dead. This is the action of the irritated slave owner, not the concerned mother: Manna-Loulou explains that "Madame had hoped, in thus depriving Zoraïde of her child, to have her young waiting-maid again at her side free, happy, and beautiful as of old" (306). This comment at once divests Madame of her maternal role and locates her as part of the racist dominant culture that denies the enslaved woman an affectional bond to her child. Continuing to think of the off-spring of a slave mother as chattel rather than child, Madame cannot understand why Zoraïde becomes "demented" at the loss of her child; mystifying the cause of this dementia, Madame thinks of it as "this terrible affliction that had befallen her dear Zoraïde" (307). Manna-Loulou's tracking of Madame's coercion and controlling of Zoraïde's sexuality—her denial of both Zoraïde's choice of erotic object and her status as mother—makes it obvious that Madame Delarivière's behavior mirrors the actions of white male slaveowners toward their female slaves rather than those of a mother toward her child.[25] Manna-Loulou's narrative thus exposes this white woman's maternal instinct as neither instinctual nor even real. At the same time, this narrative reworks dominant images of white female passionlessness, acknowledging white female erotic power but detaching it from the innate or bodily realm and relocating it as a social power relation.

In contrast, Manna-Loulou's narrative attributes to Zoraïde a kind of innate maternal love while also claiming erotic desire for her. Zoraïde's love for Mézor offers the first instance of this particular racial counter-narrative, both in Zoraïde's object choice and in her story's complicated relation to stereotypes of African-American female desire. The description of Zoraïde falling in love, for instance, locates this love within a discourse of race:

> Zoraïde had seen le beau Mézor dance the Bamboula in Congo Square. That was a sight to hold one rooted to the ground. Mézor was as straight as a cypress-tree

and as proud looking as a king. His body, bare to the waist, was like a column of ebony and it glistened like oil.

> Poor Zoraïde's heart grew sick in her bosom with love for le beau Mézor from the moment she saw the fierce gleam of his eye, lighted by the inspiring strains of the Bamboula, and beheld the stately movements of his splendid body swaying and quivering through the figures of the dance.

(304)

This description represents Zoraïde's love as both erotic and romantic and as specifically racially inflected: Zoraïde loves the "ebony" Mézor, whose body here signifies pride, grace, and stately power. This power is directly linked to his race; significantly, Zoraïde first sees Mézor dancing in Congo Square, a New Orleans gathering place where slaves celebrated their traditional cultural identities through dance and ritual. In contrast to and underscoring this point, Manna-Loulou describes Monsieur Ambroise, the man Zoraïde's owner wants her to marry, as a "little mulatto, with his shining whiskers like a white man's and his small eyes, that were cruel and false as a snake's" (304). As Elfenbein points out in *Women on the Color Line,* the fact that the object of Zoraïde's desire is the blacker of the two men itself inverts a conventional fictional representation of a hierarchy of racial value.[26] Yet the fact that Chopin ascribes erotic desire to Zoraïde and that she focuses in the passage above on the eroticized body of the black man also opens the possibility that Chopin is simply rehearsing stereotypes of the hypereroticized African American or of a primitivized "savage" who is closer to natural rhythms. Although these stereotypes lurk in the margins of this story, I would argue that the representation of Zoraïde's desire complicates, if not disrupts, that racialized discourse in several ways: by involving "true love"; by aiming that love at the African man; and by being self-directed—Zoraïde actively chooses Mézor over Ambroise.

Through Zoraïde, Chopin explicitly marks race as determining the cultural meaning of romantic or erotic agency: race is the structuring axis of the slave system, and because Zoraïde is a mulatta slave rather than a white lady, she does not have ownership of her own desire. At the same time, however, the story charts Zoraïde's resistance to this equation, as when, after confessing her love of Mézor, she rhetorically asks Madame if she is white and answers her own question: "'I am not white,' persisted Zoraïde, respectfully and gently. 'Doctor Langlé gives me his slave to marry, but he would not give me his son. Then, since I am not white, let me have from out of my own race the one whom my heart has chosen'" (305). This momentary rhetorical doubt over Zoraïde's race (like the uncertainty over whether the heroine of **"Désirée's Baby"** is a white aristocrat, or a tragic mulatto) produces a moment in which Chopin subversively uses one woman to represent the possibility of both the black woman's and the white woman's desire. Ultimately, however, regardless of the privileges her owner might bestow on her, Zoraïde recognizes that in occupying the place of "mulatto slave" she by definition has only limited rights and has access to privilege only at the discretion of a white patron. In an act that is doubly transgressive, however, Zoraïde opts for autonomous choice, a choice within her "own race," telling Madame, "I have chosen a husband, but it is not M'sieur Ambroise; it is le beau Mézor that I want and no other" (305).

Just as Chopin represents Zoraïde's desire as both constrained by and in resistance to slavery, the enslaved woman's occupation of the space of the maternal here takes on meaning both through its erasure within slavery and through Zoraïde's ironic deployment of it at the story's end. Zoraïde's rejection of her child once Madame relents and brings the little girl back to Zoraïde, her "sullen suspicion," and her reading of the strategy as "a plot to deprive her of" her rag bundle surrogate child—all these signal Zoraïde's awareness that Madame would control and redirect Zoraïde's maternal desire just as she has attempted to do with Zoraïde's erotic desire (307). Further, through the rag bundle fantasy child, Zoraïde not only reclaims the maternal, she also evades a forced marriage to M. Ambroise. In a key moment near the end of the story, we learn that despite the "death" of the child and Zoraïde's paralyzing grief in the face of it, M. Ambroise continues to want to marry Zoraïde, information Manna-Loulou glosses by noting, "and she seemed to consent, or rather submit, to the approaching marriage as though nothing mattered any longer in this world" (306-7). But immediately after this, Manna-Loulou presents Zoraïde in her dementia, sitting with "a look of strange and vacuous happiness" next to the rag baby (307). This juxtaposition, along with Manna-Loulou's comment that Zoraïde was known ever afterward as "Zoraïde la folle, whom no one ever wanted to marry—not even M'sieur Ambroise" (307), points to several conclusions at once. It first stakes a claim to an innate maternal on behalf of Zoraïde, suggesting that the African-American woman has, just as the white woman is assumed to have, a mother's love that she cannot be forced to surrender. Secondly, this scenario forces the recognition that slavery has reformed and deformed the maternal for the enslaved woman, as represented here by Zoraïde's being forced to rechannel her maternal love from her child to the surrogate rag doll child. Finally, Manna-Loulou's telling of the story suggests an ironic or canny deployment of the maternal on Zoraïde's part, a claiming of a "demented" version of it in order not only to defend her right to the maternal but also to defend her right to erotic agency against the controlling of her desire through a forced marriage to M. Ambroise. By linking these two rights, this claim also challenges dominant notions of erotic and maternal desire as mutually exclusive.

As a foil to this image of the slave woman nursing a fantasy child, the story framing Zoraïde's presents another form of a rechanneled maternal allowed to black women under slavery: the role of surrogate mother to the white child. The opening of the story establishes Manna-Loulou's relation to Madame Delisle as one of intimacy structured by a racial power hierarchy, for Manna-Loulou is pre-sented as a "Mammy" figure to her infantilized white owner. At the opening of the story Manna-Loulou, "herself black as night," has already, we are told, bathed and kissed her mistress's feet, and she has "brushed her mistress's beautiful hair, that was as soft and shining as satin, and was the color of Madame's wedding ring" (303). The alignment of whiteness with economic privilege signaled by the gold of Madame's hair and ring stands in contrast to the "black" Manna-Loulou's position of servitude, as she actively waits on the passive, infantilized Madame, "who lay in her sumptuous mahogany bed, waiting to be fanned and put to sleep to the sound of one of Manna-Loulou's stories" (303). This image of white power over the faithful black slave demonstrates Chopin's rehearsal of nostalgic racism, gesturing toward post-Civil War fantasies on the part of the white South to the pre-war slave order.

However, this image might also be read as one of passive white dependence on black agency, a reading that is mirrored on a certain narrative level. For while Manna-Loulou is the servant, she also has control of the narrative, which grants her a kind of authority, particularly when compared with Madame Delisle's obvious misinterpretation of the tale, her listening to "the sound of one of Manna-Loulou's stories" rather than understanding the meaning of it. Manna-Loulou's interpretive authority gets enacted initially over the issue of Zoraïde's desire, as Manna-Loulou locates Zoraïde's actions within a plot of "true love": the comic plot of the two lovers overcoming obstacles in order to be together. Following this, once Chopin has opened the story with the introduction of Manna-Loulou and Madame Delisle, these characters interrupt Zoraïde's story only once before their reappearance at the story's close. Significantly, Manna-Loulou interrupts just after Zoraïde asks to choose her own husband. In an important and complicated passage, Manna-Loulou tells Madame Delisle,

> "However, you may well believe that Madame would not hear to that. Zoraïde was forbidden to speak to Mézor, and Mézor was cautioned against seeing Zoraïde again. But you know how the negroes are, Ma'zelle Titite," added Manna-Loulou, smiling a little sadly, "There is no mistress, no master, no king nor priest who can hinder them from loving when they will. And these two found ways and means."
>
> (305)

Elfenbein reads this interjection as Manna-Loulou's implication that "whites envy [black] passion forbidden them and would control it or appropriate it if they could (132):[27] one might also read this as Manna-Loulou's support of the "negroes'" resistance to white authority's attempt to coerce their desire, as well as her recognition (signaled by her sad smile) of the costs of such resistance. At the same time, however, extratextually, of course, Manna-Loulou's interpretive authority is still in the hands of the white woman writer, and so this passage must also be read reinscribing the stereotype of "natural" African-American female erotic desire uncontrollable by church or state. Moreover, this alignment of Zoraïde and sexuality is echoed in the terms of Manna-Loulou's relationship to Madame:

Birnbaum rightly argues that women of color tend to serve as "sexual coaches" for white women in Chopin's work, that "the experienced women is always of a lower racial or ethnic status than her novitiate; if the heroine is white Creole, her mentor may be Acadian; if she is Acadian, her guide may be 'black'." She points to Manna-Loulou as an example of this (327).

Yet Manna-Loulou's understanding of Zoraïde's story also offers a foil to Madame Delisle's self-protective and equally racist misreading of it. That is, both Manna-Loulou's and Madame Delisle's versions of Zoraïde's story are written in the terms of the dominant racial discourse, and although Chopin ultimately critiques Madame's version, she does so only by means of the version to which Manna-Loulou gives voice. At the story's close Madame Delisle comments, ". . . Ah, the poor little one, Man Loulou, the poor little one! better had she died!" (307). By shifting the focus of the story from Zoraïde to her child, Madame Delisle reveals that she has missed the point entirely, but such a misreading works in her favor. For by turning Zoraïde's story into the story of a poor orphaned baby, Madame Delisle erases Zoraïde, sidesteps the issue of a white woman's power over a slave woman's life, and thus avoids identifying with Madame Delarivière. Ironically, however, this comment also aligns Madame Delisle with Madame Delarivière in that it positions Madame Delisle in the same space of false maternal solicitude that Zoraïde's "owner" occupies. The narrative itself further produces this identification by the imposition of one last narrative level to frame the frame.

After recounting Manna-Loulou and Madame Delisle's final conversation, the story closes by re-presenting it in Creole patois, prefaced by the statement that "this is the way Madame Delisle and Manna-Loulou really talked to each other" (308). Recalling Converse's claim to be translating her characters' French, this narrative strategy is a model of efficiency, operating both without and within the story to structure an understanding of that story. Exterior to the narrative, the patois positions the story as a deferential yet exotic Local Color tale. Comforting to a Northern reader, this strategy produces maternity as an issue in the South and in the past, an issue familiar to the Northern reader yet rendered safe by distance. At the same time, however, this strategy also insists on a recognition of regional difference: the patois forces an understanding of the story and its representation of the maternal as regionally specific because of the conditions of slavery, while that same patois distances the non-patois speaking reader from an identification with the story's characters. It is, after all, on the reader's behalf that Chopin has ostensibly served as translator, rendering the story in English. At the same time, however, the patois breaks down the monolithic image of the "South," showing that even within the South there are a variety of regions and, moreover, that even within a given region, there are a variety of both identifications and splits. That is, internal to the story the patois links both Manna-Loulou and Madame Delisle to Zoraïde and her mistress (who, the reader might assume, would

also speak patois), thus indicting Madame Delisle for her refusal to identify with Madame Delarivière's structural position of power. The use of patois also represents a regional identification across racial and class lines between Manna-Loulou and Madame Delisle, indicating both their difference from the reader and their similarity to each other. The patois, then, both differentiates among and links the characters, underscoring the regional and racial specificity of this version of maternity within the larger context of white-black power hierarchies in the postbellum South. As it does in both Pauline Hopkins's and Sui Sin Far's works, motherhood emerges here as not "natural" to white women; as not alien to Othered women; as not necessarily a source of joy; and as not mutually exclusive of erotic desire. What it does emerge as is contingent, visibly reworked by slavery and race, and no less determined by the less explicitly violent factors of regional and class location.

As in **"La Belle Zoraïde,"** the impact of racial positioning on the maternal is also at stake in **"Désirée's Baby"** (1892, 1893), but **"Désirée's Baby"** also foregrounds class status (as influenced by race) as a determinant of the maternal. Where Zoraïde's final deployment of a fantasy maternal saves her from a coerced marriage, Désirée's accession to the place of the maternal destroys her marriage, reassigns her racial status, and indicates just how fragile and contingent both racially and class-privileged identities are. As Pauline Hopkins would go on to do in a more optimistic vein, Chopin in this story reworks the "tragic mulatto" plot to foreground the doubled powerlessness of a "black" woman while also commenting on the dangerous force of the maternal.[28] Désirée, found as an abandoned child by the Valmondés at their plantation gate, provides Madame Valmondé with the opportunity of figurative motherhood: Madame believes that Désirée "had been sent to her by a beneficent Providence to be the child of her affection, seeing that she was without child of the flesh" (240). Once grown, Désirée marries the proud and wealthy Armand Aubigny but finds her idyllic life destroyed by the birth of her son, who is visibly of mixed "blood." Aubigny casts off his wife, who disappears into the bayou rather than heeding her mother's plea to "come home to Valmondé; back to your mother who loves you. Come with your child" (243). The story ends by establishing that Aubigny himself is the offspring of a white man and a mulatto mother, but Désirée's parentage is never clearly established.

As Anna Shannon Elfenbein has so skillfully demonstrated in *Women on the Color Line,* the "white" man's is the only real position of power here: even as the apotheosis of white womanhood, Désirée, as her name implies, has only a tenuous power, one that is dependent on her being desired (127) and, I would add, on an always unstable myth of purity of blood.[29] Even maternity serves only to reveal just how tenuous even the privileged white Southern woman's power is: both Désirée's desirability and her blood's "purity" are called into question by the birth of her son. **"Désirée's Baby"**'s thematizing of issues of "blood" and maternity echoes antebellum narratives (Stowe's *Uncle Tom's Cabin* or Harriet Jacobs's *Incidents in the Life of a Slave Girl,* for example), which protested against slavery on the basis of its disruption of a "natural" mother-child bond. Motherhood in these texts is depicted as far more dangerous for the slave woman than for the free woman, both because the slave woman's child was not legally her own and because it was often born of white man's rape,[30] Chopin frames the issue slightly differently; maternity in intersection with race in **"Désirée's Baby"** becomes the site of danger for both mother and child both because Désirée's becoming a mother puts her into the space of the "black" woman, figuratively if not literally enslaved, and because her becoming a mother shows just how uncertain racial identity can be. Maternity, that is, here destabilizes not only the child's but also the mother's racial identity: it is the birth of the son that calls Désirée's racial "purity" into question. Nevertheless, the danger here is posited as a threat only to the privileged white woman, revealing racial logic that here as elsewhere limits Chopin's achievement; as Ellen Peel points out, the story "directs sympathy less toward black characters than toward characters on the margin between black and white," and it "invites sympathy for Désirée partly on the sexist grounds that feminine women are weak and on the racist grounds that white members of the master class do not deserve to be treated like slaves" (64, 66).[31] Hence, while **"Désirée's Baby,"** like **"La Belle Zoraïde,"** denaturalizes an idealized version of the maternal in which maternity is the highest fulfillment of a woman's life (for Désirée, maternity proves to be not her fulfillment but her ruin), it does not challenge the conventional hierarchies of the racial discourse out of which it emerges.

Further, the image of unconditional maternal love in this story is white, embodied in the figure of Madame Valmondé. But in contrast to Armand Aubigny's love, a love that is dependent on racial "purity," Désirée's adoptive mother's love is not only loyal, it is also independent, in two senses, of fictions of "blood." Whereas Désirée's mother's love is not dependent on Désirée's having "white" blood, it is also independent of literal mother-child bloodlines: that Désirée is "the child of her affection" rather than "the child of the flesh" has no impact on Madame Valmondé's love. Chopin thus implicitly retains dominant racial hierarchies while she links maternity to questions of shifting racial identity and prizes it apart from essentialized claims of blood ties, locating it in the realm of social power relations rather than in an apolitical, universalized bodily space.

"Athénaïse" (1895, 1896) similarly foregrounds the maternal as a sphere of social power, linking it, as does **"La Belle Zoraïde,"** to erotic desire, and coding it, as does **"Désirée's Baby,"** as determined by class and race. Unlike in **"Désirée's Baby,"** however, where the maternal reveals the tenuousness of even the privileged white Southern lady's class positioning, in **"Athénaïse"**'s story of the white Creole woman, the protagonist's move into the space of the maternal both produces her erotic desire and secures her class position. The story traces a fairly conventional plot: the move of the unhappy newlyweds to a state of marital accord as a result of the wife's discovery of her pregnancy, a discovery that produces a sense of family unity and, less predictably, the wife's erotic response to her husband. Through focusing most of the story on Athénaïse's unhappiness in and rebellion against her marriage, Chopin offers a critique of that institution that anticipates that of **The Awakening,** but by giving **"Athénaïse"** the particular happy, if abrupt, ending that she does, Chopin not only mitigates the threat of her critique, but also implicates maternity in the construction of female erotic desire and depicts maternity as the site of the solidifying of class and racial privilege.

The story opens with Athénaïse's fleeing from her marital home and husband Cazeau to return to her family, then charts her eventual return to the place of wife. It concurrently traces her move from child to woman, innocent to self-conscious (including an awareness of her own erotic desire) adult. Near the opening of the story the narrator notes that "people often said that Athénaïse would know her own mind some day, which was equivalent to saying that she was at present unacquainted with it" (433). By the narrative's close, however, this narrator notes that "no one could have said now that she did not know her own mind" (452). Knowing her own mind, it turns out, means locating herself in the social/economic/racial context of the Creole planter world, a process that occurs through Athénaïse's realization that she is pregnant and her consequent recognition of erotic desire for her husband.

Initially, Athénaïse is represented as unhappy despite the social and economic benefits her marriage brings her, and the story suggests that she has traded her sense of autonomy, privacy, and independence for the class comfort and protection her husband embodies. Cazeau comes from a white, privileged, slave-owning family, so that marriage to him signals for Athénaïse a move up from the social position of her family, who are "running" the "old Gotrain place" for an absentee owner (428). But Athénaïse is unhappy, offering complaints that form a critique of marriage as an institution that confines and limits women. Employing the image of wife as slave, Chopin draws on a problematic parallel frequently evoked in nineteenth-century white women's texts and simultaneously marks her story as specifically Southern: Cazeau, bringing Athénaïse back from her parents' home, is reminded of his father's driving a captured runaway slave home. But indicating his status as ultimately a good husband, when Athénaïse runs away a second time, he decides that although he has the legal right to do so, he will not again "compel her to return to the shelter of his roof, compel her cold and unwilling submission to his love and passionate transports" (438), and so he waits instead for her voluntary return.

As this reference to the wife's "unwilling submission" to her husband implies, what Cazeau recognizes as Athénaïse's "growing aversion" (427) and her brother Monteclin calls her "constitutional disinclination for marriage" (431) is based on physical distaste as much as psychological confinement. For Cazeau, by Athénaïse's own admission, has never mistreated her: his "chief offense seemed to be that he loved her" (434), a love, clearly, that is meant to be understood as physical as well as emotional. Speculating about an acquaintance's romantic history, for instance, Athénaïse, we are told, "could not fancy him loving any one passionately, rudely, offensively, as Cazeau loved her. Once she was so naïve as to ask him outright if he had ever been in love, and he assured her promptly that he had not. She thought it an admirable trait in his character, and esteemed him greatly therefor" (449), while she assesses her marriage by stating,

> "No, I don't hate him," she returned reflectively; adding with a sudden impulse, "It's jus' being married that I detes' and despise. I hate being Mrs. Cazeau, an' would want to be Athénaïse Miché again. I can't stan' to live with a man; to have him always there; his coats an' pantaloons hanging in my room; his ugly bare feet—washing them in my tub, befo' my very eyes, ugh!" She shuddered with recollections, and resumed, with a sigh that was almost a sob: "Mon Dieu, mon Dieu! Sister Marie Angélique knew w'at she was saying; she knew me better than myse'f w'en she said God had sent me a vocation an' I was turning deaf ears. W'en I think of a blessed life in the convent, at peace! Oh, w'at was I dreaming of!" and then the tears came.
>
> (431)

That Athénaïse's complaint against marriage is grounded in Cazeau's physical presence in her room (especially when read against the contrast of the "blessed convent") suggests that part of the process traced by the story—the process of Athénaïse "knowing her own mind"—involves Athénaïse's coming to terms with the physical, heterosexual relationship implicit in marriage, a shift here figured not simply as the passive acceptance of her husband's desires but also as a recognition of her own: Athénaïse moves from feeling repugnance at her husband, synecdochically represented by his feet, to a moment of desire for him; at the story's end the narrator notes that as Cazeau "clasped her in his arms, he felt the yielding of her whole body against him. He felt her lips for the first time respond to the passion of his own" (454).

This potentially radical claim to erotic desire on the part of the white lady is made further disruptive by Chopin's identifying it with maternal desire. For it is on learning that she is pregnant that Athénaïse first thinks of Cazeau with a newfound sense of desire:

> One mood quickly followed another, in this new turmoil of her senses . . . Cazeau must know. As she thought of him, the first purely sensuous tremor of her life swept over her. She half whispered his name, and the sound of it brought red blotches into her cheeks. She spoke it over and over, as if it were some new, sweet sound born out of darkness and confusion, and reaching her for the first time. She was impatient to be with him. Her whole passionate nature was aroused as if by a miracle.
>
> (451)

But in fact the language of the story represents this transformation not as an inexplicable "miracle," but specifically as the result of pregnancy and the new knowledge and maturity it implies. Chopin first employs the abstract language of the passage above in describing Athénaïse's response not to Cazeau, but to the news of her pregnancy itself, which is figured as a fall into knowledge as well as a sensuous experience in its own right. The narrator comments that in the conversation where Athénaïse learns she is pregnant, the "extent of her ignorance and the depth of her subsequent enlightenment were bewildering," and describes her as "stunned" and "still" in response, as "her whole being was steeped in a wave of ecstasy" (451). Interestingly, after Athénaïse's realization of both her pregnancy and her desire for her husband, the narrator describes her as "silent and embarrassed as Eve after losing her ignorance" (453). That Chopin retreats to metaphoric and abstract language to describe the topics of pregnancy and erotic desire is not especially surprising given the literary codes of her day, but the fact that she uses the same sort of language to describe the two is significant, for the effect of this shared rhetoric is to link erotic desire/knowledge with the maternal, a link rarely made in Chopin's day.

The disruptiveness of this representation of the erotic and maternal and of their conjunction, however, is ultimately compromised by the story. The claim to essentialized erotic desire is mitigated in part through that desire's being legitimated by being aimed at a husband and in part through Athénaïse's status as Creole; as the use of dialect in her speech signals, Athénaïse, like Chopin's Cajun women, is ethnically marked and so more easily conflatable by a white audience with the eroticized female Other. Further, the fact that it is her "quadroon" landlady Sylvie—whom, we are told, "was very wise" while Athénaïse "was very ignorant" (451)—who reveals Athénaïse's pregnancy to her both supports Birnbaum's claim that Chopin's women of color do the work of "teaching" white women about their sexuality and helps to further code the erotic as the province of the racially/ethnically marked woman.

This intersection of racial and gender discourses is further complicated by the introduction of a discourse of class: the story dilutes the Othering effects of Athénaïse's alignment with erotic/maternal desire by framing that desire in an economic context as well, a context that partly determines the desire and simultaneously locates Athénaïse in the space of the privileged white lady. The connection between economic desire and erotic desire is raised early in the story, when the unhappy Athénaïse tries to explain why she married Cazeau. The narrator comments:

> Why indeed? It was difficult now for her to understand why, unless because she supposed it was customary for girls to marry when the right opportunity came. Cazeau, she knew, would make life more comfortable for her; and again, she had liked him, and had even been rather flustered when he pressed her hands and kissed them, and kissed her lips and cheeks and eyes, when she accepted him.
>
> (430)

Athénaïse responds dually, being physically "flustered" and economically reassured. The story's conclusion reiterates this yoking of determinants. While hiding in New Orleans, Athénaïse cannot find a means of support "with the exception of two little girls who had promised to take piano lessons at a price that would be embarrassing to mention" (451); but the return to Cazeau made possible by her discovery of her pregnancy and her erotic desire implies an insertion into not only the position of the maternal, but also that of the white plantation mistress; like the conclusion of Zaïda's story, the ending of "Athénaïse" emphasizes that she occupies the cultural space of class and racial privilege. Following the description above of Athénaïse's passionate reunion with Cazeau, the story closes by grounding this passion in local circumstance:

> The country night was dark and warm and still, save for the distant notes of an accordion which some one was playing in a cabin away off. A little negro baby was crying somewhere. As Athénaïse withdrew from her husband's embrace, the sound arrested her.
>
> "Listen, Cazeau! How Juliette's baby is crying! Pauvre ti chou, I wonder w'at is the matter with it?"
>
> (454)

The story's end thus conflates Athénaïse's erotic desire with her identification with the maternal and a concurrent *noblesse oblige* that signals her status as the white lady who stands, like Madame Delarivière, in the position of pseudo-mother toward her "dependents." As the use of dialect in Athénaïse's comment suggests, however, this story allows its heroine ethnic specificity as well as the status of white and class-privileged; or perhaps Chopin can afford to allow Athénaïse her ethnicity *because* of that privileged racial and class status. Athénaïse's identification with the cultural place held by the maternal ultimately secures her racial and class locations, locations that shore up each other and enable her erotic desire. Michael Omi and Howard Winant remind us that "racial dynamics must be understood as determinants of class relationships and indeed class identities, not as mere consequences of these relationships" (34): **"Athénaïse"** demonstrates the intertwined, determining effects of both racial and class discourses on femininity.

The use of the maternal as the vehicle for the enactment of regionally specific, class-privileged, white female identity occurs as well in **"A Matter of Prejudice"** (1893, 1895), a story that, like **"Athénaïse,"** focuses on Creole womanhood but in this case on its urban version: the upper-class New Orleans Creole woman. The maternal here serves to foreground white ethnic difference within New Orleans culture while providing the means for family reunification in the face of the ethnic prejudice that has divided it. As Florence Converse does with her portrait of the Dumarais family, Chopin, in Madame Carambeau, depicts the old-guard French Creole privileged class of New Orleans:

> Old Madame Carambeau was a woman of many prejudices—so many, in fact, that it would be difficult to name them all. She detested dogs, cats, organ-grinders,

white servants and children's noises. She despised Americans, Germans and all people of a different faith from her own. Anything not French had, in her opinion, little right to existence.

> She had not spoken to her son Henri for ten years because he had married an American from Prytania street.
>
> (282)[32]

The story traces the transformation of Madame Carambeau's "prejudice"—a combination of elitism, racism, nativism, and assorted other biases—into a willingness to accept her son and his family, a transformation that occurs through an "American" child's triggering of Madame's maternal feeling. A skilled nurse, Madame Carambeau transcends her prejudice in the exercise of this talent; the narrator notes dryly that Madame "would have treated an organ-grinder with tender consideration if one had presented himself in the character of an invalid" (283), so that when faced with a small, sick "American" child, she nurses her back to health.

Similar to Florence Converse's representation of Roma Campion, Chopin's depiction of Madame Carambeau and her interaction with the child provides the opportunity to display some of New Orleans's ethnic/cultural diversity to a Northern readership. At the same time, Chopin traces the impact of Madame Carambeau's maternal feeling on her ethnic prejudices. The child does not understand French, and "prattle[s]" in what the narrator describes as "that language which madame thought hideous" (284), an identifying tag that leads Madame to identify the little girl as "American" and to complain that "Americans" do not deserve children because they are unable to care for them properly. Predictably, however, the child is "a sweet child, gentle and affectionate" (285), and so undermines Madame's biases:

> Madame . . . had never before nursed so objectionable a character as an American child. But . . . after the little one went away, she could think of nothing really objectionable against her except the accident of her birth, which was, after all, her misfortune; and her ignorance of the French language, which was not her fault.
>
> But the touch of the caressing baby arms; the pressure of the soft little body in the night; the tones of the voice, and the feeling of the hot lips when the child kissed her, believing herself to be with her mother, were impressions that had sunk through the crust of madame's prejudice and reached her heart.
>
> (285)

As a result of this experience Madame crosses into the Garden district, the "American" quarter of the city, to visit her son, his wife, and her granddaughter, who turns out to be the little "American" girl she has nursed. The story ends with an image of family reconciliation that might also stand as a metaphor for the unification of diverse white ethnic American traditions: Madame Carambeau says of her granddaughter, "her grandmother will teach her

French; and she will teach her grandmother English" (288). This happy image of a polyglot American family achieved through maternal love reflects a nativist national rhetoric of white ethnic assimilation, a sort of "melting pot" version of U.S. society. At the same time, Chopin uses this implicitly racist model to participate in American discourses of region and gender. For this plot device also allows Chopin to have the maternal, as it were, both ways: Madame Carambeau's nursing of what turns out to be her own granddaughter can be read as the innate enactment of maternal love and recognition of kinship, or it might be read as the embodiment of a French Creole sense of *noblesse oblige,* a regionally and class-specific form of social power relations that resists a homogenizing national pressure to identify "American" as Northern and Anglo.

Ultimately, understanding Chopin's representations of both erotic and maternal desire as contingent can help us reassess her work and its importance. Viewing femininity not as the central focus of Chopin's fiction—as critics of **The Awakening** have been wont to do—but rather as a site of the convergence of a number of different vectors enables a fuller appreciation of both the complexity and the importance of her early work. Using Local Color as a cover to write about female identity and sexuality, Chopin also exploited the form and many of its racist conventions to publish. Simultaneously, she used female identity and sexuality to write about regional identity and, implicitly, national identity. Taking the short stories as a group, it become clear that Chopin both challenged and rehearsed regional stereotypes in her representations of Southern women. Implicitly dismantling certain norms of white American femininity by revealing their regional, class, and religious inflections, Chopin's short fiction offers female characters who are specifically not New Englanders, also not generic Southerners, generally not Protestants, and not even unmarked Anglo-Americans, but who, instead, are explicitly racially, ethnically, regionally, religiously, and class marked, and who rewrite narratives of female purity and passionlessness. At the same time, however, these revisions of white femininity are grounded in the rehearsal of racist alignments of women of color and eroticism. As a result, while Chopin's use of realist literary strategies in her depiction of regionally marked heroines does allow for more narrative space for the representation of white female erotic desire and (at points) both black and white maternal desire, her manipulation of Local Color leads her to draw on a racist discourse of sexuality in her search for a language and form to represent such desires. Ultimately trapped within the literary conventions that she in some ways set out to overthrow, Chopin demonstrates the limits of any literary endeavor grounded in the racial, regional, and sexual discourses of her day.

Notes

1. Publication information is taken from Emily Toth's recent biography (412). Toth's biography supersedes both Daniel S. Rankin's *Kate Chopin and Her Creole Stories* (Philadelphia: University of Pennsylvania Press, 1932) and Per Seyersted's *Kate Chopin: A Critical Biography* (Baton Rouge: Louisiana State University Press, 1969). Toth provides much needed information on the class and, to a lesser extent, race relations that shaped Chopin's life.

2. Daniel S. Rankin did publish his *Kate Chopin and Her Creole Stories* prior to Seyersted, but his framing of Chopin's work simply reinforced her earlier dismissal as a Local Color writer. He describes her collection *Bayou Folk,* for instance, as depicting "a little world, it is true, but full of fresh life and interest," as chronicling "the quaint and picturesque life among the Creole and Acadian folk of the Louisiana bayou" (136; 136-37). He goes on to contend that Chopin "seems to have gone straight to the heart of the Nachitoches folk. She has heard their little confidences of joy and grief" in these ". . . simple stories simply told" (139). See *Kate Chopin and Her Creole Stories* (Philadelphia: University of Pennsylvania Press).

3. There was and still is some confusion over the distinction between Local Color and regionalism as literary categories. Chopin's contemporaries often used the two terms synonymously to describe fiction focused on a particular region and community within it. Twentieth-centur critics, however, have differentiated the two categories on the basis of point of view. Judith Fetterley and Marjorie Pryse have been the driving forces behind this differentiation process, through their Norton Anthology, *American Women Regionalists 1850-1910* (New York: Norton, 1992). There they define local color as satirical or dismissive of the community it portrays, written by outsiders who make fun of the community for an audience of outsiders. Regionalism, in contrast, they see as emerging from within the community, written by insiders from a sympathetic point of view. They also argue that regionalism, defined in these terms, was a particularly female genre. Fetterley and Pryse explicitly note that they are establishing these categories, acknowledging that the writers themselves probably did not draw these distinctions. I will use the term Local Color to refer to the literary category known variously as Local Color and regionalism, in part because most of the references to it by Chopin and her critics use this term. In addition I use Local Color to describe the specifically literary category, because by regionalism I want to suggest a broader usage of the term that carries the sense of cultural (rather than exclusively literary) categories loosely based on geographic regions.

4. Thus, even women writers writing of the privileged geographic area, New England, could be dismissed by twentieth-century critics as non-canonical. Sarah Orne Jewett, as I discuss in Chapter 1, despite writing of New England, became known as a Local Color nostalgic writer. For more on what Michael Davitt Bell calls the "heavily gendered assumptions at the heart of American realist thinking" (66), see his

"Gender and American Realism in *The Country of the Pointed Firs*; see also Brodhead.

5. Helen Taylor provides a very helpful discussion of regionalism and Northern publishing practices. Cox also offers useful information but ultimately replicates a nineteenth-century hierarchy of value, locating America's "essence" in New England. My thinking here has also been shaped by Raymond William's *The Country and the City* (London: Chatto & Windus, 1973).

6. This description, it is important to note, is one that is relevant to the content of her stories rather than to her own geographic origins, as I will discuss below.

7. This figure was one that Chopin herself employed. See, for example, *Bayou Folk*'s "Ma'ame Pelagie," whose title character stands as a memorial not just to Southern womanhood but also to the antebellum South itself. Jones further argues that the ideal of Southern manhood—the planter gentleman—itself involved feminized values: the image invoked a man who was "gentle and genteel, leisurely and cultivated, a lover of beauty, goodness and grace" (41).

8. Or as Howells might have put it—and as critics did in objecting to *The Awakening* as showing French influences—Chopin was schooled in both a tradition of indecency and a tradition of decency.

9. Although much of Chopin's work is now available in a variety of editions, for consistency's sake I take all of my citations from Per Seyersted's two-volume edition of *The Complete Works of Kate Chopin*. Cited dates are the year the story was written, followed by the year of its first publication or, if the two are the same, the single year.

10. For a more in-depth reading of the reviews, see Toth. She points out that the *New York Times* review makes a number of factual mistakes in the long description of Acadian Louisiana, not the least of which is the misspelling of "Cajun."

11. Reviews of Chopin's second collection, *A Night in Acadie,* only confirmed both her categorization as a Local Color writer and the generic marginalization that it implied. *The Critic*'s review, for instance, described the volume as centered on "the simple childlike Southern people" (266).

12. My redaction of Cajun and Creole positioning in Louisiana is taken largely from Brasseaux and Domínguez, both of whom offer extremely clear and helpful discussions of these complicated categories.

13. While most of the New England writers (Sarah Orne Jewett, Rose Terry Cooke, and Mary Wilkins Freeman, for instance) considered regionalists were, in fact, generally born and raised in New England, other writers considered regionalists were outsiders to the regional community about which they wrote, either because of class (Mary Noailles Murfree, for instance), or because of some combination of geographic origins, ethnicity, or race (Chopin, Mary Austin, Alice Dunbar-Nelson, Sui Sin Far, Zitkala-Sä). The question of being an authentic voice of the community in geographic terms also dovetails for many of these writers with the question of authenticity in ethnic or racial terms, particularly for women of "mixed" racial or ethnic identity (Alice Callahan, Dunbar-Nelson, Sui Sin Far, or Zitkala-Sä, for example).

14. This shifting positioning of St. Louis testifies to the fact that it is not only the center that is able to collapse its "Others": here, the South collapses other regions into what is, essentially, the not-South.

15. Biographical information on Chopin is readily available; the most complete source, however, is Toth's biography.

16. Taylor makes a similar point in claiming that New South writers used Local Color "as a means of setting straight a record which, it was felt, had been left to the north to write" (18). She reads this revision as a nostalgic recreation of the "good old days" before the Civil War. While Chopin participates in such racist nostalgia, I am more interested here in her representations of her contemporary South and the ramifications of the intersection of racist discourse with more radical discourses of gender and region in these representations.

17. Given that critics insisted on viewing Chopin as a recorder of quaint, charming primitive people, it is not surprising that they were so offended by *The Awakening,* for not only does this novel fail to conform to Local Color standards, it also presents an upper-class white heroine whose identity is constituted at least in part by her various levels of desire.

In this overt representation *The Awakening* resembles its contemporary British New Woman fiction far more than Chopin's contemporary American women's fiction. Certainly, the rhetoric of *The Awakening*'s reviews bears out this identification: reviewers describe it in the same terms as critics used for New Woman fiction. The *Globe Democrat* describes *The Awakening* as "not a healthy book" (quoted in Toth 341); the *Chicago Times-Herald* states that with this novel Chopin "enter[s] the overworked field of sex fiction" (quoted in Toth 347); the *Providence Sunday Journal* calls Chopin "another clever woman writer" and claims that *The Awakening* "fairly out Zolas Zola" (quoted in Toth 347). It is the *Los Angeles Times*'s review, however, that most plainly signals *The Awakening*'s affinity to New Woman fiction, for the reviewer likens the novel to "one of Aubrey Beardsley's hideous but haunting pictures with their disfiguring leer of sensuality, but yet carrying a distinguishing strength and grace and individuality . . . it is unhealthily introspective and morbid in feeling, as the story of that sort of woman must inevitably be" (quoted in Toth 349). This is the language of British reviewers of New Woman fiction, from its invocation of Beardsley to its accusation of sensuality, morbidity, and illness. Thus, I would suggest, *The Awakening* fits far better into the New Woman novel genre than American Local Color fiction, and had it appeared in England, would not have caused such a stir, for critics would have been able to read it as part of a generic scandal. That is, rather than being an isolated and seemingly anomalous threat, it would have been labeled (and, at least partly, so contained) as a New Woman novel.

Taylor makes an analogous point in identifying Chopin with her French influences over her American ones, claiming that "St. Louis newspaper editors were happy to publish Maupassant and other European writers, but found Edna Pontellier too hot to handle; this heroine was, after all, an *American woman*" (151). While I would link *The Awakening* more closely to British New Woman fiction than French fiction, I would certainly agree with Taylor's point that Mrs. Pontellier's behavior was seen by American critics as appalling particularly *because* of her nationality.

18. For a particularly cutting depiction of the class privilege on which the model of proper "American" Womanhood rests, see Chopin's "Miss McEnders" (1892, 1897).

19. Although the story does not identify Mildred's origins explicitly, the fact that her family summers in Narragansett, Rhode Island, suggests that she is from New England or at least the (North) East Coast.

20. "At the 'Cadian Ball" (1892) offers a useful comparison here: the privileged Creole heroine of this story, Clarisse, responds as a proper lady to Alcée Laballière's declaration of love. Regardless of the fact that he is a Creole plantation owner, and so her social equal, when he "panted a volley of hot, blistering love-words into her face" (220), she responds with a disdainful dismissal.

21. Chopin generally codes her Cajun characters as white, usually by leaving them racially unmarked while marking other characters in the story. Thus, in "A Gentleman of the Bayou Têche," the Cajun Evariste and his daughter Martinette are left racially unmarked, while Aunt Dicey is identified as black; similarly, in "A Night in Acadie," Zaïda is unmarked while Douté, the cook, is marked as black.

22. Interestingly, in this case, in the face of Northern editorial opposition, even the marginalized shelter of Local Color could not provide a space for Chopin's original representation.

23. Almost completely ignored by early Chopin criticism, the issue of race in Chopin's work has recently come under scrutiny in a number of important studies. These works assess her representations of race and sometimes subsequently evaluate her character accordingly. Toth, for instance, reads Chopin's representations of race as "liberal in her day" compared to those of her contemporaries, whom Toth claims were "far more committed to the 'happy darky' stereotype" (269). Helen Taylor, on the other hand, argues that "Chopin's racism is a central element in her writing and cannot be ignored or simply excused . . . her inability or refusal to confront it created critical problems and severely limited her achievement" (156). As should be evident, I concur with Taylor and am indebted to her work.

Chopin's racial politics are hardly surprising, given her background. As Taylor usefully points out, Chopin was in New Orleans for the last seven years of Reconstruction, and there and in Natchitoches she witnessed racial tensions and the rise of white supremacy groups. Indeed, both her husband and her brother-in-law Phanor Breazeale were members of such a group—the White League—and at least briefly supported a rebellion against the government in 1877. Whether or not Chopin herself supported the White League is unknown: unfortunately, she left almost no documentation in her papers or her work of her explicit position on political and, more specifically, racial issues. She did, however, produce a number of "loyal slave" stories that articulate a romanticized version of conventionally racist attitudes, among which "For Marse Chouchoutte" (1891), "The Bênitous' Slave" (1892), and "Tante Cat'rinette" (1894) stand out as perhaps the most obvious examples. She also offered slightly more complicated, though ultimately equally conciliatory, versions of interracial relations in stories such as "Ozème's Holiday" (1894, 1896), "A Dresden Lady in Dixie" (1894, 1895), and "Odalie Misses Mass" (1895). Toth's biography provides important background information on race relations in Chopin's New Orleans and Nachitoches. For contextualized information combined with literary analysis, two recent books are particularly nuanced in their readings: Taylor's *Gender, Race and Region in the Writing of Grace King, Ruth McEnery Stuart and Kate Chopin* and Anna Shannon Elfenbein's *Women on the Color Line: Evolving Stereotypes and the Writings of George Washington Cable, Grace King, and Kate Chopin.* Elfenbein traces with exceptional clarity the complicated history of New Orleans's racial mixture. See also Birnbaum's excellent article and Sandra Gunning, *Race, Rape and Lynching: The Red Record of American Literature* (New York: Oxford University Press, 1996).

24. I have enclosed *owner* in quotation marks in this section to underscore not only the story's discussion of the impossibility of owning someone else's desire, but also the more fundamental paradox on which it is based: the idea of one human being's "owning" another.

25. Moreover, Madame's coercive actions, especially over Zoraïde's marriage partner, also mirror aristocratic actions conventionally attacked by the middle classes.

26. Chapter 4 of Elfenbein's book focuses on Chopin and provides what may well be the definitive reading of "Désirée's Baby" as well as an extremely nuanced reading reading of "La Belle Zoraïde."

27. Elfenbein's reading here becomes more convincing when "La Belle Zoraïde" is read against Chopin's "A Lady of Bayou St. John," where Madame Delisle is shown renouncing the present and its promise of love and passion to focus upon her past and her dead husband.

28. Paradoxically, in this story Chopin both exploits the stereotype of the "exotic," "erotic" mulatta—naming her heroine Désirée, for instance—and undermines both the "purity" of categories of racial identity and the stability of the racist alignment of "erotic" and "African American."

29. Further, the story suggests that even the woman whose racial purity has not been called into question—Madame Valmondé—is powerless to save Désirée in the face of the white man's power.

30. The painful and vexed relation of slave women to maternity, as well as the legacy of that relation, remains at issue for many contemporary African-American women writers. See, for instance, Gayl Jones's *Corregidora,* Toni Morrison's *Beloved,* or Sherley Anne Williams's *Dessa Rose.*

31. And significantly, maternity here calls into question the racial "purity" of the "white" lady but not that of the "black" slave: if "La Blanche," the mulatto slave, is expected to have "little quadroon boys" (242) following Aubigny's visits to her cabin, Désirée is not.

32. Toth claims that Chopin was drawing on her father-in-law, Jean Baptiste Chopin, in this portrait (122). In more general terms one might see this characterization as the St. Louis outsider Chopin's sarcastic depiction of the New Orleans Creole culture for which she could never quite qualify.

Lawrence L. Berkove (essay date winter 2000)

SOURCE: Berkove, Lawrence L. "Fatal Self-Assertion in Kate Chopin's 'The Story of an Hour.'" *American Literary Realism* 32, no. 2 (winter 2000): 152-58.

[*In the following essay, Berkove contends that Chopin's narration of "The Story of an Hour" is ironic rather than straightforward.*]

Kate Chopin's thousand-word short story, **"The Story of an Hour,"** has understandably become a favorite selection for collections of short stories as well as for anthologies of American literature. Few other stories say so much in so few words. There has been, moreover, virtual critical agreement on what the story says: its heroine dies, ironically and tragically, just as she has been freed from a constricting marriage and has realized self-assertion as the deepest element of her being. Confidence in this interpretation, however, may be misplaced, for using the standard proposed for the story by Toth and Seyersted—"every detail contributes to the emotional impact"[1]—there is evidence of a deeper level of irony in the story which does not regard Louise Mallard as a heroine but as an immature egotist and a victim of her own extreme self-assertion. This self-assertion is achieved not by reflection but, on the contrary, by "a suspension of intelligent thought" masked as "illumination." As a result, a pattern of basic contradictions and abnormal attitudes emerges which gives structure to the story and forecasts its conclusion. The key to recognizing this deeper, ironic level is to carefully distinguish between the story's narrator, author, and unreliable protagonist.

Seyersted's early biography of Chopin describes the story neutrally as "an extreme example of the theme of self-assertion."[2] More recent interpretation has largely followed a strong, and at times an extreme, feminist bent. Representative of this in both approach and language is Emily Toth's well-known characterization of the story as one of Chopin's "most radical . . . an attack on marriage, on one person's dominance over another."[3] Toth further elaborates this position in a later article in which she comments that "[a]lthough Louise's death is an occasion for deep irony directed at patriarchal blindness about women's thoughts, Louise dies in the world of her family where she has always sacrificed for others."[4] Ewell similarly sees in the story's "surfaces" Louise's struggle for selfhood against "society's decree" for female "selflessness, being for others."[5]

But in the text of this very short story there is no hard evidence whatsoever of patriarchal blindness or suppression, constant or selfless sacrifice by Louise, or an ongoing struggle for selfhood. These positions are all read into the story from non-textual assumptions.[6] The simple truth is that this story is not about society or marriage, but about Louise Mallard. The single possible reference in the text to difficulties in her life is a sentence, which says that the lines of her face "bespoke repression and a certain strength."[7] It is not at all clear, however, what the cause of that "repression" was; whether, for instance, it might have been external, in society or in her marriage, or whether it was internal, a recognition that it takes strength to control one's feelings or whims. Such few hints as the story supplies incline toward the latter position. While the text enables us to make certain inferences about Louise, it does not supply us with any information about the truth of her life except her perceptions, and these, as I intend to show, are unreliable and, insofar as they are taken as the statements of the story's omniscient narrator, misleading and contradicted by other textual evidence.

Support for this position is spread throughout the story but the most dramatic elements appear in the following three paragraphs:

> There would be no one to live for her during those coming years; she would live for herself. There would be no powerful will bending her in that blind persistence with which men and women believe they have a right to impose a private will upon a fellow creature. A kind intention or a cruel intention made the act seem no less a crime as she looked upon it in that brief moment of illumination.

> And yet she had loved him—sometimes. Often she had not. What did it matter! What could love, the unsolved mystery, count for in face of this possession of self-assertion which she suddenly recognized as the strongest impulse of her being!

> "Free! Body and soul free!" she kept whispering.

In these paragraphs, the story's omniscient narrator takes us into Louise's mind. However, while the attitudes expressed are definitely Louise's there is no textual justification for also ascribing them to the narrator. Further, it would be a mistake to project them onto Chopin, for that would confuse narrator with author, a move that denies Chopin the full range of literary technique, and that would reduce this brilliant and subtle work of fiction to behind-the-scenes sermonizing.

It is significant, in the quotation's first line, that Louise wishes to "live for herself." This has been generally understood to imply that she had hitherto sacrificed herself for her husband; however, there is no evidence for this in the text. Nor is there any evidence that her husband had done her living "for her," whatever that might mean. It is an ipse dixit comment, arbitrary, without support, one of several she makes.

In the quotation's second paragraph, Louise discounts love as secondary to self-assertion. While this is undoubtedly her position, there is no textual reason to assume it is also Chopin's. Louise also recognizes self-assertion "as the strongest impulse of her being." This is a peculiar value for a married person and is indeed incompatible with marriage, where an emphasis upon shared goals and mutual commitment is the opposite of self-assertion. The unreasoning self-centeredness of Louise partly explains the first two sentences of the quotation's second paragraph, and they tell us more about her than about her husband. Of course, even married people who sincerely love each other have occasional disagreements and may not feel much love for the other at particular times. For most lovers this is not so much a contradiction as a paradox; the moments of hate occur within the larger context of love. But the warmest sentiment that Louise can express after being married to a man whose benevolence the previous paragraph explicitly affirms with its description of his "kind, tender hands" and his face "that had never looked save with love upon her" is the niggardly concession that she had loved him "sometimes."

It is obvious that there is quite a discrepancy between the way Louise and Brently Mallard feel about each other, but all the mystery of the difference is on Louise's side.

Whatever her original reason had been for marrying Brently, it is clear now that feeling the way she does about him she would be better off not being married. Her love for herself—"she would live only for herself"—does not leave room for anyone else. How, then, would she live?

Her justification for preferring to live for herself, the second and third sentences of the quotation's first paragraph, are extravagant, unrealistic statements, each segment of which is controversial. She views her husband's constant love as a "powerful will bending hers in [a] blind persistence." Blind? Why is it blind? Inasmuch as Louise has apparently repressed her true feelings about her husband and marriage, if his love for her is blind it is because she has blinded him. In the absence of open communication about her feelings, how would he know what she wants, or what to do or say? In that circumstance, his persistence, which clearly annoys her, may only be a natural attempt on his part to please her and to convince her of his love. The failure of Brently's persistence is due at least in part to Louise's strange view of love—and the wording of the second sentence includes her as well as her husband—as a "crime," a powerful will that "bends" the other person. This is a distorted view of love, which typically delights in pleasing and giving to the other. Believing love a "crime" cannot be considered a normal attitude, much less an emotionally healthy one.

But even if we grant this point of view, where can we go where the presence of other people does not "impose" some conditions upon us that limit our freedom? There are only two places on earth that meet this specification: an uninhabited spot or the grave. If we have friends, it is assumed that we hold values that are in concord with theirs, and that we do not act in such a way as to violate friends or their principles. Even if we do not have friends but just live in society, there are laws and mores which, out of mere civility, we follow as a condition of being acceptable members of society. And this works equally in reverse. Does Louise not expect that friends will somehow fulfill and continue to meet her personal standards and thereby be more desirable for a closer relationship with her than would strangers? Is this "imposition"? Is she not by her contentions denying herself both friends and society, unless she has no expectations that fellow creatures will observe certain basic laws and mores? If this is true for friends and fellow members of society, how much more is this so for people in love, and especially those who are married! How can the extreme sort of freedom that Louise contemplates, in which there are no expectations or obligations upon anyone, co-exist with living with other human beings?

Marriage of course restricts freedom. Whoever marries, or even loves, gives up large areas of freedom—usually willingly. It is aberrant, therefore, to reduce love merely to an "imposition" of a "private will upon a fellow creature." Inasmuch as Brently loves her "tenderly," her attitude about imposition reveals that she is only irritated by a display of affection and equates it with a loss of freedom. One paragraph later, Louise first characterizes love as an "unsolved mystery," and then immediately dismisses what she admittedly does not understand in preference for the "impulse" of self-assertion, which she, ironically, also appears not to understand either in its form of self-love or in its consequence of radical loneliness.

Even more astonishingly, why is no distinction to be made between a kind and a cruel intention? Here is yet another product of her "suspension of intelligent thought" another arbitrary and whimsical dictum that would incriminate both friend and spouse. But the proposition is contradicted by actions in the story. At the beginning of the story, for example, her husband's friend Richards hastens to tell Louise himself the news of her husband's death, "to forestall any less careful, less tender friend in bearing the sad message." At the end, Richards attempts vainly to screen Brently from the view of his wife. Are these loving acts of kind intentions crimes? Even more to the point, Louise's whims imperiously put her husband into a no-win situation where *anything* he does is not only wrong, but also a crime against her absolute freedom. These conceits go beyond being merely strange and impossible views for any social relations, let alone a marriage. What Louise regards as "illumination" are dark and twisted fantasies that reflect a confused and unhealthy mind.

In truth, Louise is sick, emotionally as well as physically. The story's first line tells us that "Mrs. Mallard was afflicted with a heart trouble." The phraseology is vague; however, the rest of the story gradually makes clear the nature of the heart trouble. Alone in her room, when she "abandoned" herself, a whispered word "escaped" her lips: "Free!" The conjunction first of abandonment and then of something escaping her is significant. What was then in her heart is made clear by the two lines of the next paragraph: "She did not stop to ask if it were or were not a monstrous joy that held her. A clear and exalted perception enabled her to dismiss the suggestion as trivial." Again, Chopin's omniscient narrator makes a subtle but very significant shift from reporting "objectively" in the first line what Louise is thinking to letting us, in the second line, know Louise's opinion about her thinking process. First, she believes that she is enjoying a "clear and exalted perception." Two paragraphs later she exalts this self-congratulatory perception to an "illumination" when she concludes that love is a crime. Here again, while these extravagant value judgments are certainly Louise's, they cannot be confidently ascribed to either the narrator or Chopin.

Next, Louise dismisses as "trivial" the suggestion of doubt as to whether or not her joy was "monstrous." But the question most certainly is not trivial. It is a natural question, an important and a healthy one, an intelligent check on unreflected impulse, and the fact that Louise does not

address it is ominous. She does not give the question a chance; she does not even face it; she dismisses it out of hand. What Chopin is doing, very subtly, is depicting Louise in the early stages of the delusion that is perturbing her precariously unstable health by aggravating her pathological heart condition. The "monstrous" surge of joy she experiences is both the cause and first sign of a fatal overload to her feeble heart.

In the next paragraph Louise contemplates "a long procession of years . . . that would belong to her absolutely." "Absolutely" is a loaded word, further evidence of her extreme and unrealistic egotism in preferring her own company exclusively. In light of Aristotle's statement that "whosoever is delighted in solitude, is either a wild beast or a god,"[8] the joy that Louise takes in the thought of absolute possession of future years may indeed qualify as "monstrous." And for someone afflicted with heart trouble, the anticipation that those future years will be a long procession is also presumptuous. Louise is not thinking clearly. Insofar as her anticipation reflects growing mental confusion and raises unrealistic hopes, it is also perilous.

After she puts off her sister Josephine, who "implores" admission to the room out of fear that Louise will make herself ill (another case of a "crime" of a powerful will attempting to bend her by imposing a kind intention?), we are told in the next paragraph that "[h]er fancy was running riot." "Fancy," with its connotations of fantastic and capricious imaginings, is another signal that Louise is not thinking clearly, and the narrator's observation that it is "running riot" is an additional indication that she is well on the way to losing control of her mind.

This prospect is enhanced by a sentence in the next paragraph: "There was a feverish triumph in her eyes, and she carried herself unwittingly like a goddess of Victory." Here Chopin displays her remarkable ability to compress layers of complexity and irony into a single line. "Feverish" is the key word that diagnoses Louise's pathological condition, and the phrase in which it occurs ironically suggests that the fever has already progressed to the point where it is fatally triumphant over her. The rest of the short sentence rapidly but elegantly elaborates on the situation. "Unwittingly," with its connotation of the absence of reason, reinforces the idea that Louise's fever has triumphed, and her assumption of the posture of the "goddess of Victory" is a double delusion: she is no goddess and she has achieved no victory.

Her husband's unexpected reappearance ends the delusion based on "a monstrous joy." It has long been recognized that the story's last line is ironic, but it is even more ironic than has previously been surmised. The doctors were technically correct: she did die "of joy that kills." Louise was indeed doubly afflicted with heart trouble. Physically, her heart was weak, and emotionally, it had no room for anyone else.

We can infer from both the way the description of Louise unfolds and from the absurd nature of Louise's ideal that

Kate Chopin was not a romantic. On the one hand, Chopin did not regard marriage as a state of pure and unbroken bliss, but on the other, she could not intelligently believe that it was desirable, healthy, or even possible for anyone to live as Louise, in the grip of her feverish delusion, wishes: to be *absolutely* free and to live totally and solely for oneself. Absolute freedom is possible only for a divinity, and Louise demonstrates by her death as well as her life that she is not divine. Although earthly love is not ideally perfect, it may at least be the closest thing to the ideal that we can know. Louise's "self-assertion," really in her case a manifestation of an extreme of self-love, is exposed in this story as an emotional affliction of her heart that has physical consequences. What she wants is, literally, not obtainable in this life. It is a fantasy, a dream, and **"A Story of an Hour"** was indeed first published in *Vogue* magazine in 1894 under the more revealing title of **"The Dream of an Hour."**[9]

Given her dissatisfaction with the best that life has to offer her and her unrealistic expectations of absolute freedom, therefore, there is no other option for Louise except death. The conclusion of the story follows logically upon Louise's specifications of her deepest wishes. Chopin's exposé of the fanciful dream of Louise is richly subtle, and is an exquisite example of her remarkable ability to present an untenable view in a seemingly sympathetic way.[10] In **"The Story of an Hour"** Chopin projects with delicately incisive irony what would happen if an immature and shallow egotist were to face the earthly consequence of an impossible dream of her afflicted heart.

Notes

1. Emily Toth and Per Seyersted, eds., *Kate Chopin's Private Papers* (Bloomington: Indiana Univ. Press, 1998), p. 245.

2. Per Seyersted, *Kate Chopin: A Critical Biography* (Baton Rouge: Louisiana State Univ. Press, 1969), p. 58.

3. Emily Toth, *Kate Chopin* (New York: William Morrow, 1990), pp. 252-53. Similarly, the story's emphasis upon a woman was equated in a subsequent article by another critic with an attack on the institution of marriage, which is treated as the "culprit" of the story because by its means "[p]atriarchy's social conditioning creates codes of social behavior to ensure the suppression of feminine desires." Angelyn Mitchell, "Feminine Double Consciousness in Kate Chopin," *CEA Magazine*, 3 (Fall 1993), 59-64.

4. Emily Toth, "Kate Chopin Thinks Back Through Her Mothers: Three Stories by Kate Chopin," *Kate Chopin Reconsidered*, ed. Lynda S. Boren and Sara deSaussure Davis (Baton Rouge: Louisiana State Univ. Press, 1992), p. 24.

5. Barbara C. Ewell, "Chopin and the Dream of Female Selfhood," *Kate Chopin Reconsidered*, pp. 160, 162.

6. The film, "Five Stories of an Hour" (Films for the Humanities, Inc., 1991), widely available and used in educational settings, is a testimony as to how the sparseness of the text invites explanations which require additional text and details. Although the skits which comprise this film complement the story's fictile possibilities by means of creative reader responses, in modifying and going beyond the text those skits do not and cannot explain the text itself.

7. Kate Chopin, *The Complete Works of Kate Chopin*, ed. Per Seyersted (Baton Rouge: Louisiana State Univ. Press, 1969), pp. 52-54. The entire story occupies only three pages, so page numbers are not used.

8. Aristotle, *Politics* I, qtd. in Francis Bacon, "Of Friendship."

9. Toth, "Kate Chopin Thinks Back," pp. 22-23.

10. For an example of how this phenomenon appears in other of her stories, see my article, "'Acting Like Fools': The Ill-Fated Romances of 'At the 'Cadian Ball' and 'The Storm,'" *Critical Essays on Kate Chopin*, ed. Alice Hall Petry (New York: G. K. Hall, 1996), pp. 184-96.

FURTHER READING

Bibliography

Green, Suzanne Disheroon, and Caudle, David J., eds. *Kate Chopin: An Annotated Bibliography of Critical Works.* Westport, Conn.: Greenwood Press, 274 p.

Comprehensive survey of criticism on Chopin published between 1976 and 1998, including annotated entries for books, essays, dissertations, biographical studies, and bibliographical works.

Biography

Toth, Emily. *Kate Chopin.* New York: William Morrow and Company, Inc., 1990, 528 p.

Biography that questions long-held views on Chopin's life and writing; includes appendices, photographs, and a select bibliography.

Criticism

Black, Martha Fodaski. "The Quintessence of Chopinism." In *Kate Chopin Reconsidered: Beyond the Bayou*, edited by Lynda S. Boren and Sara deSaussure Davis, pp. 95-113. Louisiana: Louisiana State University Press, 1992.

Black discusses political and cultural influences on Chopin's feminism in her writing.

Bloom, Harold, ed. *Modern Critical Views: Kate Chopin.* New York: Chelsea House, 1987, 138 p.

Reprints seminal writings on Chopin's works from early commentary to more recent critical views.

Ewell, Barbara C. "Kate Chopin and the Dream of Female Selfhood." In *Kate Chopin Reconsidered: Beyond the Bayou,* edited by Lynda S. Boren and Sara deSaussure Davis, pp. 157-65. Louisiana: Louisiana State University Press, 1992.

Ewell examines the notion of American individualism in Chopin's works.

Jones, Suzanne W. "Place, Perception and Identity in *The Awakening.*" *Southern Quarterly* 25, no. 2 (winter 1987): 108-19.

Views the two locales in which *The Awakening* is set, New Orleans and Grand Isle, as enabling "Chopin to expose not only the confusion that arises when a woman experiences a new place, but also the way in which a social setting controls thought and determines identity."

Koloski, Bernard. *Kate Chopin: A Study of the Short Fiction.* New York: Twayne Publishers, 1996, 165 p.

Surveys Chopin's short stories and reprints reviews and essays on Chopin's life and work as a short story writer.

Petry, Alice Hall, ed. *Critical Essays on Kate Chopin.* New York: G. K. Hall, 1996, 257 p.

Reprints early reviews and later essays devoted to Chopin's works as well as including original essays examining *The Awakening* and several of Chopin's short stories.

Schweitzer, Ivy. "Maternal Discourse and the Romance of Self-Possession in Kate Chopin's *The Awakening.*" In *Gendered Agents: Women and Institutional Knowledge,* edited by Silvestra Mariniello and Paul Bové, pp. 161-91. Durham: Duke University Press, 1998.

Contrasts the protagonists of Nathaniel Hawthorne's *The Scarlet Letter* with Chopin's *The Awakening* based on the fact that Edna Pontellier had the experience of motherhood while Hester Prynne did not.

Wershoven, C. J. "*The Awakening* and *The House of Mirth*: Studies in Arrested Development." *American Literary Realism* 19, no. 3 (spring 1987); 27-41.

Contends that Chopin's *The Awakening* and Edith Wharton's *House of Mirth,* while evidencing numerous dissimilarities, are in fact "related in patterns of conflict, grouping of characters, development of protagonists and, more subtly, in a cluster of images that reflect desperate and dangerous polarities."

Wolff, Cynthia Griffin. "Un-Utterable Longing: The Discourse of Feminine Sexuality in Kate Chopin's *The Awakening.*" In *The Calvinist Roots of the Modern Era,* edited by Aliki Barnstone, Michael Tomasek, and Carol J. Singley, pp. 181-97. Hanover, New Hampshire: The University Press of New England, 1997.

Considers elements of modernist and minimalist techniques in *The Awakening* and "the relationship of between these elements and Edna Pontellier's personal tragedy."

Additional coverage of Chopin's life and career is contained in the following sources published by the Gale Group: *American Writers Supplement,* Vol. 1; *Authors and Artists for Young Adults,* Vol. 33; *Concise Dictionary of American Literary Biography,* 1865-1917; *Contemporary Authors,* Vols. 104, 122; *Dictionary of Literary Biography,* Vols. 12, 78; *DISCovering Authors; DISCovering Authors Modules: Most-studied Authors* and *Novelists; DISCovering Authors: British; Exploring Novels; Exploring Short Stories; Feminist Writers; Literature and Its Times,* Vol. 3; *Literature Resource Center; Modern American Women Writers; Novels for Students,* Vol. 3; *Reference Guide to American Literature,* Ed. 4; *Reference Guide to Short Fiction,* Ed. 2; *Short Story Criticism,* Vol. 8; *Short Stories for Students,* Vols. 2, 13; *Twentieth-Century Literary Criticism,* Vols. 5, 14; **and** *World Literature Criticism Supplement.*

John Collier
1901-1980

English novelist, short story writer, poet, and screenwriter.

INTRODUCTION

A versatile writer who is best remembered for his fantastic plots, Collier is almost equally famous in the mystery genre. His short story collection *Fancies and Goodnights* (1951) was selected for the "Queen's Quorum," Ellery Queen's list of outstanding mystery collections. The wit, irony, and imagination in Collier's novels and stories is often compared to that of such writers as Saki, Ambrose Bierce, and Roald Dahl.

BIOGRAPHICAL INFORMATION

Collier was born in London in 1901 to John George and Emily Noyes Collier. After kindergarten, Collier was educated privately. He began his writing career as a poet and was first published in 1920 at the age of nineteen. His focus later shifted to writing novels and short stories. His earliest novel, *His Monkey Wife; or, Married to a Chimp,* was published in 1930, followed a year later by his short story collection *Epistle to a Friend.* During the early 1930s Collier's fiction earned him a reputation for whimsy and caustic wit that carried across the Atlantic and helped land him a contract, in 1935, to write screenplays for RKO Pictures. His most famous Hollywood accomplishment was writing the storyline for the classic film *The African Queen,* starring Katherine Hepburn and Humphrey Bogart. During the next thirty years Collier continued writing novels and short stories, developed many screenplays, and was active in television. He died of a stroke in Pacific Palisades, California, in 1980.

MAJOR WORKS

Collier's first novel, *His Monkey Wife; or, Married to a Chimp,* depicts a man who visits Africa, returns with a chimpanzee named Emily, and falls in love with her, eventually marrying her and moving back to Africa. While some readers and critics were shocked by Collier's portrayal of the interspecies love affair, others recognized in it Collier's talents for social criticism and satire, and the novel experienced great success. Collier's subsequent novels, *Tom's A-Cold* (1933) and *Defy the Foul Fiend; or, The Misadventures of a Heart* (1934), were less successful. While Collier's writing was always considered nearly per-

fect, critics found that this, combined with his wit and satire, were not enough to sustain novel-length fiction. Collier's short fiction, however, was consistently well received. His fantasy stories contain wit, irony, and creative plots that provide insight into human nature. One example, "Evening Primrose," is the story of a young poet who seeks sanctuary from the harshness of society. He plans to live in a large department store in seclusion but discovers that at night, after the doors close, the mannequins come to life. He finds their society as repressive, materialistic, and uncompromising as that of the real world. In another tale, "Thus I Refute Beelzy," a boy's imaginary friend comes to life to exact revenge on the boy's cruel and overbearing father. Collier's mysteries contain sophisticated characters who are often undone by their own wrongdoings and clever plots with ironic and abrupt endings. In "Another American Tragedy" a young man plans to murder and then impersonate his wealthy uncle in order to change the old man's will in his favor. As part of the scheme he has his teeth removed, but his real hardship begins for him when the family physician, who is currently the old man's heir, arrives on the scene with secret knowledge of the nephew's intent. Hints of misogyny also appear throughout Collier's work, particularly in his mysteries. His tales of murder often portray troubled marriages in which husbands are motivated to kill their nagging or unfaithful wives and then hide the bodies in the basement. "De Mortuis," one of Collier's most famous and frequently anthologized stories from *Fancies and Goodnights,* features a New York doctor married to a woman whom his friends know to be unfaithful. When they see the doctor patching his basement floor they assume that he has buried her. They pledge their loyalty to him and then share tales of the wife's escapades while, unbeknownst to them, the wife is actually returning home. In 1973 Collier published *Milton's Paradise Lost: Screenplay for Cinema of the Mind,* in which he recast and updated John Milton's famous epic poem into a screenplay format. Whether or not Collier intended the work to ever be filmed remains unknown. Critics praised Collier's efforts, although some noted that Milton's original depiction of his Genesis characters was lost amid Collier's attempts to further romanticize the story.

CRITICAL RECEPTION

Collier was very popular in the United States, where his most memorable literary pieces were collected in *The John Collier Reader* in 1972. Like many writers of fantastic fiction, Collier was largely ignored by scholars but received high praise from the public. Critics often noted that Collier had a rare talent for writing perfectly crafted, highly stylized sentences. Marjorie Farber wrote in a review of *The Touch of Nutmeg,* (1943) "Collier handles clichés with the deft conviction of a poet." Many of his stories adapted for film and television—in some cases by accomplished directors such as Orson Wells and Alfred Hitchcock—are also celebrated by viewing audiences. Commenting on Collier, Anthony Burgess stated, "Though not a writer of the very first rank, he possessed considerable literary skill and a rare capacity to entertain. . . . He needs to be rediscovered."

PRINCIPAL WORKS

His Monkey Wife; or, Married to a Chimp (novel) 1930
Epistle to a Friend (short stories) 1931
Gemini: Poems (poetry) 1931
No Traveller Returns (short stories) 1931
The Scandal and Credulities of John Aubrey (nonfiction) 1931
Green Thoughts (short stories) 1932
Just the Other Day: An Informal History of Great Britain Since the War (history) 1932
Tom's A-Cold (novel) 1933; also published as *Full Circle: A Tale,* 1933
Defy the Foul Fiend; or, The Misadventures of a Heart (novel) 1934
The Devil and All (short stories) 1934
Variation on a Theme (short stories) 1935
Witch's Money (short stories) 1940
Presenting Moonshine: Stories (short stories) 1941
The Touch of Nutmeg, and More Unlikely Stories (short stories) 1943
Fancies and Goodnights (short stories) 1951
Pictures in the Fire (short stories) 1958
The John Collier Reader (short stories and novels) 1972
Milton's Paradise Lost: Screenplay for Cinema of the Mind (screenplay) 1973

CRITICISM

Josiah Titzell (review date 5 April 1931)

SOURCE: Titzell, Josiah. "An Exciting First Novel." *New York Herald Tribune Books* (5 April 1931): 6.

[*In the following review, Titzell notes that* His Monkey Wife *is "original" and "extraordinary."*]

His Monkey Wife is a book with which to choose your friends. Either they will like it tremendously or they will not be able to see it at all, but in either case they will feel strongly and you can accept or reject them depending on whether or not their reactions square with yours. I shall choose mine among those who share my excitement for this extraordinary first novel.

It is a dangerous business if you want people to like this book to try to tell them what it is about. Described it can seem to have a quantity of things in it that are not actually there, and similarly it is impossible to convey the subtle wit which makes you laugh aloud, the beauty and the penetrating satire which blend so perfectly into its brilliance.

It is the story of Emily, a chimpanzee, who has been adopted into the house of Mr. Alfred fatigay in Boboma, the Upper Congo. Mr. Fatigay is a mildly idealistic schoolteacher whose duty it is to teach the pickaninnies, and since Emily has already begun to show that devotion which springs from her primitive emotions, she sits quietly in the back of the classroom, closely following every word of her lord and master. In a short time she has, through her unostentatious concentration, learned to read, but being physically incapable of learning human speech her accomplishment is unknown to any one. And there Emily's story begins. She has developed an intelligence which is soon to ripen into an intellect.

Had Mr. Fatigay's choice of books and his ideas of feminine conduct been less Victorian, the chimp's story would have been quite different and Mr. Collier's novel would have been deprived of its particular keen satire. The conflict, when the scene has changed to England, between Mr. Fatigay, Emily and Mr. Fatigay's fiancee, Miss Amy Flint, might have been literally quite another story. But there were the books and there was Emily. "Beneath that rather Charlotte Brontë surface there was actually, a Charlotte Brontë interior, full of meek pride, hopeless hope, and timid determination."

Mr. Collier, whose talents are many and varied, has not stinted himself in this most original novel. There is a tenderness which is only heightened by the beauty of his writing in the scene where Emily, in a thin stuff dress, is sent out into the blackthorn winter to gather primroses. There is a robust humor in the description of the ceremonies—particularly the Masque—performed for Mr. Fatigay on his departure from Boboma and Emily's journeys to the British Museum in Amy's boots and a rather simple dress, with a Japanese parasol held well down over her face. There is a wealth of terribly wise and terribly revealing emotional psychology in his malicious observations on the conduct of his characters, as well as the already mentioned satire, pointed by the ironic twists of the intellect which directs it. And for this highly exciting display of a crisp, creative mind the author has been blessed with a prose style which is no less brilliant than its content.

His Monkey Wife is one of the best books of the year and one of the most amusing books in many years.

Dudley Carew (review date 5 May 1931)

SOURCE: Carew, Dudley. "New Novels." *Times Literary Supplement,* no. 1514 (5 May 1931): 96.

[*In the following review, Carew praises Collier's wit and satire in* His Monkey Wife, *but notes that the novel will be intensely disliked by some readers.*]

The title of Mr. John Collier's first novel, *His Monkey Wife or Married to a Chimp,* suggests a somewhat un-pleasing variation on a zoological theme made popular by Mr. David Garnett in his "Lady into Fox." Actually, how-ever, the relationship between the two books is slight to the point of disappearance, for the fact that Emily hap-pened to be a chimpanzee was the least important thing about that noble and intellectual character. Emily was, of course, a chimp (Mr. Collier insists throughout on the abbreviation) in a million, but it was not so much her abil-ity to read as her steadfastness in love and her unlimited capacity for self-sacrifice that marked her off from the rest of her tribe. Emily loved Mr. Fatigay, a simple-hearted En-glishman who spent his days teaching native children in the wilds of Boboma, but she concealed that fact from him just as she concealed her reading. Mr. Fatigay was, as it happened, engaged to a woman in England called Amy, whose letters to Mr. Fatigay caused Emily, who, with the pardonable curiosity of her sex, had read them, grave con-cern. They seemed to her the expression of a nature at once shallow and hard and, when she and Mr. Fatigay eventually land in England, her worst fears are realized. Amy talked in the *clichés* of Bloomsbury—revolting to Emily's sensitive intelligence—and her heart was as empty of love for Mr. Fatigay as her head was of any idea that was not smartly second-rate. Poor Emily, who is made Amy's servant, suffered agonies of torment, not for herself but for Mr. Fatigay, who would assuredly be committing himself to a life of misery should the monstrous marriage ever take place; and, eventually, by a trick, she takes Amy's place at the altar and is married. Her troubles are by no means over, however; for Mr. Fatigay is not unnatu-rally furious, and Emily is ordered to return to Africa and solitude, but such devotion as hers cannot but fail to earn its reward. Emily, who goes on the stage and becomes im-mensely rich, is allowed by fate first to become the minis-tering angel to a Mr. Fatigay reduced to starvation and poverty, and, finally, back in Africa, to be his own true love as well as his legal wife.

This is by no means a book for everybody, and those who do not like it inordinately may dislike it immensely. Mr. Collier is obviously entirely indifferent to the feelings of his readers, and it is not only the squeamish who will ob-ject to certain passages; but, to set against them, there is the brilliance of Mr. Collier's wit, the point and subtlety of his satire and the rich, close-woven texture of his prose. Besides, those who do not like fantasy and object to chimp heroines can read it as a bitter and effective anti-feminist tract.

Herschel Brickell (review date 1931)

SOURCE: Brickell, Herschel. "A Variety of Fiction." *The North American Review* 231 (1931): 574.

[*In the following review, Brickell comments on Collier's satire and humor in* His Monkey Wife.]

One of the most engaging of recent novels is an English satire by John Collier and called *His Monkey Wife or Married to a Chimp.* In brief, it is the story of the return from Africa to England of a young Englishman. His com-panion is a lady chimpanzee named Emily. Once at home, he falls in love with a pretty girl, but after many difficul-ties decides to marry Emily and return to Africa. This is a highly entertaining piece of fiction, and also a sharp and amusing comment upon civilization. It is no small feat to hold the interest of the reader in a book of this kind and to give its impossible story plausibility, but Mr. Collier has succeeded in both and heartily deserves a hearing. Brainerd Beckwith's *Galloping Down* is a fine stirring story of Irish-men and horses, which begins in Ireland and finishes in Canada, a book that is sure to delight any one who has ever loved horses. There is a good love story, while the tale is not without its melodramatic touches, it holds the interest to the very end, its especial strength lying in the well-portrayed conflict between a wild father and his son. This is Mr. Beckwith's second novel, and it reveals a sound talent, one that is well worth watching. It is refreshing to find a novelist in these days who has real enthusiasm for his subject, and this Mr. Beckwith has—he can set the pulses stirring—provided again one has ever loved horses—by the mere mention of the beasts. It is probably not necessary to explain that the Landscaper pretty well grew up on horseback, and that one of his deepest sorrows is the replacement in his own part of the country of good saddle horses with Fords.

Basil Bunting (review date August 1932)

SOURCE: Bunting, Basil. "Valentine and Orson." *Poetry* 40, no. 5 (August 1932): 293-95.

[*In the following review, Bunting regards* Gemini *as a "sizeable achievement" despite its affectations.*]

Edith Sitwell says: "A writer to whom the gentle and in-sipid word 'talent' cannot be applied, but a greater word of whose use we are, as a rule, afraid." In case you inquire for Miss Sitwell's credentials, here they are: "The only modern poet who is completely successful in verse seems to me to be Miss Edith Sitwell": by John Collier, preface to *Gemini.* These poems have also been awarded two valu-able prizes, so they come well recommended. Finally, they are, it seems, a sort of hail and farewell to verse; the poet stepping into the arena for half a mo', then right out again before the critical wild beasts have time to tear him.

After all these prefatory safeguards, this suspiciously heavy insurance of a not very extensive property (33 pages), and the circumspect disclaimers of the *Apology* prefixed, the reader is sure to expect a mouse to come out of the mountain, and he will, as was probably calculated, be pleasantly surprised to behold instead quite a moderate-sized rat, maybe something even a size larger. But oh, the affectations of the animal!

Valentine and Orson, Mr. Collier calls himself; Orson the author of *Three Men in One Room,* Valentine responsible for the shorter poems. Take Orson first. His gait, heroic couplets, ill-suited to his build, stumping dancing-bear-wise around the subject. The subject divided against itself: half moralizings in eighteenth-century pastiche on sordid old-age; half, deeply felt, the misery of thwarted but unrenouncing love, tricked out, certainly, in similar semi-antique cast-offs but not disguised by them. Indeed, the threadbare flutter of antitheses and inversions lends these five pages the awkward pathos of misery that must stammer because it does not know its own cause well enough to cry out sharply. Maybe it was because he saw this that Mr. Collier forebore to rewrite the poem; for in the second half of *Three Men in One Room* he has stuff for a very fine poem, in a less hampering metre. The satire of strong passions known intimately has always a headlong momentum: Mr. Collier knows it, and specifically recognizes that his poem is "at war with the medium"; but he takes the medium to be verse itself, not merely the wrong sort of verse. Quotation is useless, the poem is too through-and-through crippled; and the satire is sometimes forced, sometimes frivolous. Curse the habit of taking attitudes, it has robbed us of something moving and memorable.

Valentine is warier. He watches his step. He does not fall into the toils of great emotions and he chooses his metre sapiently. A man moving in the half-light, speaking in the half-tones of culture, always in the absence, in the poignant—maybe—memory of emotion:

> Lost past! for even gaining a more clear
> Image, a photograph, one finds at most
> (As floats in a dim green bath a single coarse hair)
> Alien impertinence, a ghost
> Claiming relation. . . .

Never in contact with the actual:

> More voices in waves than streets
> More tongues in trees than men,
> And no ear in which to name his grief
> Anew, to form it and bind it again.

In such a mood or its aftermath one hopes to see at last

> the frail flowering of the heart, its lonely
> Fugitive poem heard in the quiet when words die—
> This only is I. . . .

But it evades us, for in reality the flowering of the heart takes place in the storm mishandled by Orson a few pages back.

It is not supposable that Orson would always flounder in metres ill-chosen. If Mr. Collier really has abandoned verse we have lost a fine poet. We cannot regard *His Monkey Wife, or Married to a Chimp* as a fair swop for the poems the coalescence of Valentine and Orson should produce. The affectations are, after all, superficial, and even in this small volume we have, for this age, quite a sizeable achievement.

Rolfe Scott-Thomas (review date 20 October 1932)

SOURCE: Scott-Thomas, Rolfe. "Informal History." *Times Literary Supplement,* no. 1603 (20 October 1932): 760.

[*In the following review, Scott-Thomas finds* Just the Other Day *to be lacking in the appropriate gravity and perspective.*]

Mr. John Collier and Mr. Iain Lang, the authors of *Just the Other Day*—an "Informal History of Great Britain Since the War," as the sub-title runs—acknowledge their indebtedness for their main idea to Mr. F. L. Allen, who treated the post-War years in America in his book *Only Yesterday.* But an earlier and better example of this kind of writing is to be found in Mr. R. H. Gretton's *Modern History of the English People,* which ends at the year 1922. Mr. Gretton reviewed all aspects of the national life, serious and light, with equal breadth, versatility and vivacity, but with more essential gravity.

Gravity the present book undoubtedly lacks, and that implies the absence of a sense of proportion distinguishing what is fundamental from what is superficial. The authors find it difficult to refrain from a quizzical attitude to anything and everything that they touch, so that the scale of values is reduced to a least common denominator which is wholly negative. This suspicion of pertness in the treatment of all national questions, from the fall of a Government to a raid on a night club, weakens the reader's confidence in the authors' statement of facts and opinions. This is a pity, for they have been very careful in ascertaining the truth about public events which have often been misrepresented, and the narrative is on the whole reliable; and their passing judgments on social, literary, and artistic movements are free from many of the follies of contemporary prejudice. Their book deserved something better than the trivial jacket in which it is displayed.

In such a survey the mistakes of the past loom large before us. The book starts in that post-Armistice year when the talk was of "hanging the Kaiser," "making Germany pay" and "reconstruction"; when the "task" was defined as that of making "Britain a fit country for heroes to live in" (the authors avoid the mistake so often made in quoting those words). In regard to German reparations, we are confronted with an astonishing extract from so sober a journal as the *Economist.*

> As for collecting the bill without damaging our industries, this should not be a very difficult matter. . . . In normal times, when it is allowed to do business on

business methods, Lombard Street has little difficulty in transferring any amount of money between nations that are in economic communication.

From "flag-waving" and peace-making the authors turn to post-War housing, industrial unrest, strikes; and from these subjects to Mr. Vale Owen, night clubs and Dora, Mr. Wells's *Outline of History* and so to the Irish Civil War, the Black and Tans and the Irish Treaty. In dealing with the Irish war the authors reveal less than their usual fairness in apportioning praise and blame, and present a wholly inadequate account of the final settlement. They conclude this section with the remark: "The Irish showed a lack of historical tact . . . in not staging their revolution half a century earlier."

In quick succession they review the events of the years of "Tranquillity," the General Strike, the second Labour Government and the National Government, and the topics that from time to time have been the talk of the moment—Mlle. Lenglen, Mr. Baldwin's pipe, greyhound racing, the boom of the "sports girls," cricket matches, neo-Georgian poetry and the "Bloomsbury circle." All of these have belonged to the social life of the last fourteen years, and enter into the authors' conception of history, which, they say—adapting the words of Emerson—is "the lengthened shadow of Mr. Everyman."

New Statesman and Nation (review date 12 November 1932)

SOURCE: "Since the War." *New Statesman and Nation* 4, no. 90 (12 November 1932): 599-600.

[*In the following review, the critic finds* Just the Other Day *to be well written and conceived but overly didactic in its social commentary.*]

There is a peculiarly revolting passage in the adventures of Gulliver in Brobdingnag where Swift describes the impression conveyed to his hero by a sojourn in the private apartments of some ladies of the court. Magnified out of all friendly perspective these ladies, engaged on their toilets, are revealed as loathsome, hideous monsters. Allowing for twentieth century restraint, Gulliver's point of view on this occasion is that adopted by Messrs. John Collier and Iain Lang in their "informal history of Britain since the war." To them history, informal, is on the whole the lengthened shadow of a moron. As a compilation their book is admirably complete. Each flying folly of the past twelve years is gravely, dispassionately presented; each nine-days'-wonder made to gleam anew in a colder, steadier light. We have chapters on the Bright Young People, Brighter London, Sport and Spectacle, Murder and Morals in the Making, besides the less amusing but not less important topics of Labour's Rise and Fall, the Economic Aspect and the Crisis. All are treated in the same strain of ironical pseudo-detachment—enough facts to relieve the text from an appearance of persiflage, enough

gentle comment to provide almost consistently lively reading as one is led through labyrinths of thought and feeling which seem only half familiar. The perspective adopted is largely a reflection of the amount of space devoted to the events as they occurred by the daily and Sunday press, and the result is, as may be expected, an unflattering comment on the world we live in.

Sometimes the implied generalisations are a little glib, the retouching of the faded scenery a little crude. Commenting on the country's reception of the German Navy's last gesture at Seapa Flow, for instance, the authors will not allow us even a sense of humour:

> Von Reuter was sent to Park Hall internment camp at Oswestry, where, a week after the scuttling of the Fleet, he was attacked by a crowd and struck in the face with a rotten egg. With this expression of indignation and frustrated triumph the nation had to rest content.

Even in such an orgy of victory the egg, one feels, is an over-simplified symbol of the nation's mixed emotions on the occasion. Mr. and Mrs. Everyman, whose views are frequently quoted, are at times endowed with a reflective, introspective intelligence which one feels regretfully to be far beyond their limited capacities. "Man felt," say Messrs. Collier and Lang, "that he had lost his place in the historic procession, and he was eagerly grateful to any guide who offered to help him find it." To which one is tempted to retort that fully eighty per cent of the population have never had any conception of a historical procession, and is therefore unlikely to worry unduly about its place therein until the uneasiness of the intelligentsia filters down through the brains of popular novelists and journalists, and is reinforced by harsh personal application. A similar criticism might be made of the very amusing chapter on changes in morality. For all the publicity which has been given them, these phenomena have still to penetrate the tough shells of tradition in which most of His Majesty's subjects contrive to live more or less contented lives.

In truth, this volume, for all its apparent, if limited, validity as a social document, tends to prove too much. It is not so much an impression of what has passed through the minds of Mr. and Mrs. Everyman since the war as a record of what a handful of weary sub-editors, night by night, thought would interest them. Politicians have every reason to know that newspapers are painfully untrustworthy indices of popular opinion, even when prejudices are dressed up to look like news at the instance of swollen-headed proprietors. And what is true of politics is even truer of more general interests. The newspaper-for-the-many is a mental relaxation, not a stimulus, to be skimmed by half-awake husbands on their way to work and dozed over by tired wives before going to bed. The sub-editor's eccentric hours of work render him peculiarly subject to "occupational parochialism." He is never in a position to tell what ordinary people are thinking, and one feels that his unhappy guesses are the main source of Messrs. Collier and Lang's material. Nevertheless, as stimulating commentary on the cheaper side of the human shop-window, *Just the Other Day* was well worth writing and has been written very well.

The Spectator (review date 18 November 1932)

SOURCE: "Outmoded Cavalcade." *The Spectator* 149, no. 5447 (18 November 1932): 714.

[*In the following review, the critic finds* Just the Other Day *overly casual in places but overall informative and enjoyable.*]

The authors of *Just the Other Day* have based their work upon Mr. F. L. Allen's survey of the post-War years in America entitled *Only Yesterday*. It was a happy idea to apply a similar technique to recent English history, and the collaboration of Mr. Collier and Mr. Lang has been exceedingly fortunate. The material cannot have been easy to select and compress, but they have done wonders. Dealing first of all with the immediate aftermath of the War, the "hang the Kaiser" campaign, Amritsar, and the visit of "Pussyfoot" Johnson, the authors pass *via* Brighter London, including in their survey the "Mr. A." case and the exploits of Brilliant Chang, Mrs. Meyrick and Sergeant Goddard, to Labour troubles and the Irish War. One wishes that what they have to say about the Black and Tans could be made compulsory reading for those vast masses of the English people who remain ignorant of this very dirty page of our national history. Next they survey the development of sport and spectacle, gambol among politics and the Bright Young People, to come up against the uncompromising reality of the General Strike, of which they give an admirable account. Chapter nine is headed "Morals in the Melting Pot," and discusses among other topics the censorship, *The Well of Loneliness*, D. H. Lawrence's pictures, and the case of "Colonel" Barker. Further chapters survey notorious murder cases, the development of outstanding figures in literature and art, the careers of Bottomley, Bevan, Hatry and others, and the book concludes with an economic survey in a chapter entitled "England's Crisis."

The text throughout the book is exceedingly lively, and the authors' comments vigorous and pointed. Sometimes, as is natural, the effort to keep up its spirit leads to strain, and one wishes for fewer epigrams and a more sober style of narrative: but the authors are always serious when seriousness is called for. The book abounds in anecdote of every kind, and it is salutary to be reminded of incidents which most of us would perhaps like to forget, such as certain of the incidents following the Crumbles murder.

We have found the book of absorbing interest throughout, and can complain of few omissions and no misrepresentation. It might have been possible to add a section upon the spiritual development of recent years, which has not after all been confined to the utterances of the Rev. Vale Owen

and others: we might have expected, for instance, that the cult of Buchmanism would afford the authors scope for characteristic comment. Prize-fighting, too, seems to merit a fuller treatment than it has received—but, after all, small holes can be picked in any survey, and Messrs. Collier and Lang's is so well and so lightly done that any such proceeding is not only ungenerous, but ungrateful.

The authors of *Our Mothers,* which is likewise a collaboration, cover a longer period, and set about their task as orthodox historians. By comparison with *Just the Other Day* their narrative is sober and severely practical. It is by no means lacking in liveliness, but, with so much ground to cover, Mr. Bott and Miss Clephane have wisely been content to rely for humour chiefly upon the unconscious humour of the pictures. Of these there are an enormous number, illustrating as fully as can be imagined the life of woman during the last thirty years of the nineteenth century. The following quotation will give a fair idea of the authors' careful style:

> "Cooking was done on immense kitchen ranges which swallowed coal by the bucket (a fact of less moment in those days than it would be to-day, since coal averaged less than £1 a ton). These domestic engines were often temperamental; if the wind set in a particular direction, the fire would not draw or the oven would not heat. They were agreeable enough kitchen companions in the winter, but in summer they made cooking a torture. Jams, preserves, and pickles were made at home, in the stillroom if the house boasted one, in the kitchen if not. In winter, much coal carrying was involved by the open fires in all the living-rooms, which had to be laid, lighted, and replenished during the day. Fortunately for the domestic staff, fires in the bedroom were a luxury allowed only during illness except in rich households."

Our Mothers is both valuable and entertaining, and is a notable piece of book production at the low price of 8s. 6d.

David Garnett (review date 8 April 1933)

SOURCE: Garnett, David. "Current Literature." *New Statesman and Nation* 50, no. III (8 April 1933): 448.

[*In the following review, Garnett considers* Tom's A-Cold *a disappointing follow-up to Collier's earlier works.*]

When I had read a few pages of *Tom's A-Cold,* by John Collier, I thought that the author of that highly original book *His Monkey Wife* had given us another *After London*. For Mr. Collier has taken the alarmists, who predict the collapse of civilisation, at their word and has drawn England in the nineteen nineties when, after wars, plagues, and famines have done their worst, what is left is almost exactly like what Jefferies described in the Relapse into Barbarism, the first part of *After London*. The towns are in ruins, the rivers have been choked up in swamps, the forests have extended to twenty times their size; the cats have reverted to the grey brindled wild cat; dogs, horses and cattle are all wild. There is a talk of wolves, which shows that Whipsnade has been working well, and man himself has become a savage beast. But where Jefferies presented us with a sentimentalised feudalism, Mr. Collier shows us verminous and lonely groups of outlaws, who subsist on rabbits, and when undisturbed are able to grow a few potatoes. The more sordid and hopeless the surroundings, the more necessary it seems to give the reader a really heroic hero. Here we are given a magnificent young aspirant to the chiefdom who is coached by the oldest member of the clan—who, it is odd to reflect, must be living amongst us somewhere and just beginning to study Greek.

Mr. Collier says in an Introduction:

> To describe emotions and events totally incompatible with present-day life here it was absolutely necessary to choose some other scene: the question was—When or where?

He looked about—to Neolithic times and to savage islands, but these had their drawbacks, so he chose the setting of this tale. Thus the book is not written out of a deep emotion of hatred as Jefferies wrote, nor out of a deep conviction such as H. G. Wells would have brought to it. This is fatal. The clan has a tradition of the finer things of life, represented by the memories and the knowledge of the classics, of the old man. Unfortunately when it comes to a test, the finer things of life come to mean no more than the ability to murder a sick man under the pretence of healing him, and primitive contraptions for staging a terrific massacre of the Swindon folk which would have looked well in a book by Rider Haggard, but which is out of place here. The entire absence of nobility nullifies the sympathy we are expected to feel for the father. The descendants of a curate and a girl-guide would have been worth all this ignoble clan and we might have wept on seeing them kneeling on the rabbit-bitten turf. It was a mistake to leave out religion and morality; they were necessary, and the conditions would have produced them. It was also a mistake to let the second generation revert to the Intelligentsia and begin to discuss each other's motives as though they were hikers who had been reading Shaw. *Tom's A-Cold* is therefore a disappointing book from the author of that beautiful and brilliantly comic story, *In a Green Shade* (Joiner and Steele). The description of the Swindon girl, Rose, and the attack on the tower, is very good indeed. But if Mr. Collier was a cat this is not what he would have drawn.

Iris Barry (review date 7 May 1933)

SOURCE: Barry, Iris. "A Tomorrow Grown out of Today's Fears." *New York Herald Tribune Books* (7 May 1933): 6.

[*In the following review, Barry considers* Full Circle *to be a provocative book.*]

This is no novel about the future, in the ordinary sense of that phrase. It is not compounded of Wellsian characters or situations, but of men like our neighbors, like Francis Bacon or General Marbot, in situations such as men have faced before. Suppose all is lost, since the economic pundits tell us all may so easily be lost, and civilization as we know it shattered to chaos, to the dark ages and worse again, to beyond the bronze age if you will—what then? Annihilate cities, tear down communication, destroy all material amenities: then let us look at these people of Mr. Collier's, a group of men and women roughly dressed in skins, furnished with a little metal and normal wits, entrenched in a stronghold on the Hampshire hills. These again are not men of the future in the accepted sense, but men of today living in a tomorrow grown out of our today's fears. It is a world of Hoovervilles: and Hooverville is not of the future.

Because this is an important and lovely novel which I like to think will be read and enjoyed widely, I have begun by stressing the fact that *Full Circle* is not a fantasy: unless one were to call *Candide* fantastic. Also, leaving aside its basic implications, it happens to be a first-rate narrative. It is packed with adventure—bloodshed and craft, romance and tragedy, crime. There are rich, unforgettable characters in it whose desires and actions alike convince and surprise one. There is brilliant observation throughout, dazzling intensity so that one remembers every tiny detail, the very look and mood of the dawn-hour when Swindon stronghold wakes to rapine, or when the wild mare runs over the downs, or Harry after the counter-attack carries Rose through the frosty night. It is written in gracious and lively prose, not mannered but agreeable to the inner ear because it is personal to the author while betraying what good company he has appreciatively kept among his forerunners in literature.

In the savage stronghold there are old men who remember the vanished world, the one we know. One recalls most keenly an autumn day's shooting in the 1930's. Another reveres not merely learning itself but the undying ghost of all art, all statecraft: a tie between mankind and its deepest vision. So tradition lingers on. One comes with a sharp sting of emotion, so actual does the story seem, on a tattered Carraci over the fireplace of the great dining-hall, on hearing young men speak of the sea they have never seen and of the dead men whose eyes turn to pearls in that strange tumble of multicolored water. So it would, so it should be, one feels. Equally right is the growing up of another tradition, new for the new world, which is discernible in the reactions and behavior of the younger men. There is no diminution of passion or ambition or humanity here, despite the squalor. There is no lack of greatness or great vileness. There are virtuous men whom some praise and all follow when the virtue burns, who when they themselves falter into darkness can still compel others to follow or force them towards the light.

The story itself centers round a raid made on a distant settlement for the purpose of obtaining more women: the group with which the story is concerned has definite ideas about improving and controlling the "family." Harry, leader of the raid, captures a woman unlike the women of his own group and one whom he had seen previously under circumstances that fired his imagination. His chief is wounded, and under not entirely natural circumstances dies, leaving Harry as his obvious successor. Leadership and personal tragedy go hand in hand for him. Events culminate in the flight of the captured Rose, an attack on the stronghold by her group, the death of Harry's close friend, Crab the philosopher, and the final choice on the part of Harry to accept the evil in the world—he had not recognized it before—and to do good. All these main incidents are built up carefully and cleverly of delicate moods, moments, scenes, conversations, so that a very strong illusion is created of participating, even more vividly than in much of life, in the events of the narrative. Mr. Collier's appeal to the visual sense is really remarkable; outside of poetry I do not know what other writer can so conjure up color and movement, sound and scent. And what surprising knowledge he has of human nature!

Full Circle is even better than his first novel, **His Monkey Wife.** Very much of the moment, this author is not so much unafraid of sentiments and passions as unaware that one could or need be afraid of them. He would speak, one feels, as his elders would not dare of the beautiful, the true and the good. After so much desiccated intelligence conscientiously devoid of feeling as we have had from "young" writers this is almost touchingly delightful. Mr. Collier, armed with a fine intelligence springing from the heart, with erudition and breadth of fancy excitingly mingled, and a singular mastery of his craft has remained utterly unaffected by influence that made many lesser postwar writers a nightmare for the old and a pitfall for the growing. He plainly wants to move his readers. Few living novelists carry forward the tradition of letters as bravely, or display a more pleasing narrative gift. Also he has something very definite to say.

From living today as man does in material and spiritual insecurity, harassed, however secretly within himself, by fears of international catastrophe and domestic crisis, each individual may well now and then anticipate a tomorrow of after-calamity such as this book describes. We speak of civilization. Some say it is cracking up. What then if it cracks? What can we look to save, what endures? The pleasures of appreciation in strain of music, phrase of verse, line or composition in the visual arts—all gone for ever and the brave spirit and desire too that made and enjoyed them? Gone Charlemagne and Loyola and Bentham, the weary beauty of last year's Marathon winner, Machiavelli and Chaplin, the great villains and happy servants, all of them, never to be re-echoed or repeated again? If the cities, the communication and the comfort go is there to be nothing but a herd of yellowish-pink monkeys grubbing and shivering in the undergrowth?

We have to ask ourselves this: it is one of the functions of art continually to make us ask such questions, and another to suggest—not give—the answer. It must be a clear and pregnant, a provocative answer, like the note from a distant bell. Such Mr. Collier gives here. Few who read *Full Circle* will fail to hear it, or fail to be grateful to its author, or a little richer in spirit.

John Cournos (review date 28 June 1933)

SOURCE: Cournos, John. "An Old, Old Story." *The Nation* 136, no. 3547 (28 June 1933): 732-33.

[*In the following review, Cournos regrets that Collier has wasted his talents writing* Full Circle.]

It will be remembered that in the last two pages of *Penguin Island* Anatole France furnishes us with a sketchy picture of the day when civilization will have run its course, and men, "barbarians" once more, will have begun to build a new civilization not so different from the old. John Collier takes up the theme in this his second novel and elaborates it in nearly three hundred pages. Only it is not France but England which is the author's focal point— England in 1995, a generation or two after it has been devastated by terrific wars and left a vast ruin inhabited by mutually hostile tribes indulging in atavistic adventures.

In a brief introduction [to *Full Circle*] Mr. Collier asserts that he has written a "tale" pure and simple and that there has been no intention on his part to supply any sociological interest, which, he supposes, is expected in novels dealing with the future. As a tale, then, his book is to be judged. Naturally one does not expect truth but an aspect of truth, which in a work of fiction might be called verisimilitude. Broadly speaking, one gets it, but not without some glaring faults in detail. The hero of the tale, Harry, rival of the chief of his tiny community and leader of a marauding party making an assault on a neighboring village to acquire the necessary supply of women, may legitimately grow lyrical about nature or the divine girl in yellow who gives zest to his adventure, but it is really questionable if, being the sort of man he is, in a community so primitive, he would be apt to show himself such an adept in elegant abstractions. Some of his speeches addressed to his bosom friend, Crab, sound very unreal indeed, though they would be unobjectionable enough if dissociated from their background.

Apart from the setting, Harry's problem is not so very different from our own; it belongs to human nature. Friendship, love, treachery, and all that sort of thing are involved.

> He was caught in an abominable circle. At this point he observed, in a sort of stealthy flash (but did not heed much), that though all that hurt him lay inside the circle, what broke his spirit was the disparity between his life, inside, and the rest of the life, without.

Mr. Collier can write well; I find myself wishing he had applied his skill to a theme less full of pitfalls than this.

Wyndham Lewis (review date 8 June 1934)

SOURCE: Lewis, Wyndham. "Demos Defied." *The Spectator* 152, no. 5528 (8 June 1934): 892.

[*In the following review, Lewis finds that* Defy the Foul Fiend *begins on a weak note but soon becomes an accomplished work.*]

The diabolical presence who is *defied* in this book is the demon called Demos. Democracy—as is today on all hands and increasingly the case—is compelled to assume the horn and hoof. And the colours that are sported by this newest hero are the "Tory" colours—though that, I venture to believe, is a mistaken tag, as his politics, as they are revealed to us in partly humorous, partly impassioned scenes, of very great vivacity, are much less artificial than such a term would suggest.

Mr. Collier's narrative opens as the very much stylized history of a fool. You imagine yourself at first to be in the presence of one of those creatures of whom the heroic exemplars are Don Quixote or the Idiot. "Our hero," as Willoughby Corbo is called, is the by-blow of an impossible decayed nobleman. He is ushered into the book by a mock-melodramatic company, from whose unreality he never quite escapes, nor from the slight confusion ensuing from the doubt as to his status—whether full fool or not. It is in conversation with an individual named Baiye that he first becomes thoroughly real, and also divested of "idiocy." That is perhaps where this book should have opened—for it turns out that he is no fool but the reverse.

What a very serious and impressive contribution to contemporary fiction *Defy the Foul Fiend* is will be most apparent to the reader when he reaches those chapters where the relentless Willoughby is engaged in destroying the cherished Marxist dope of the old "wrapper-scrapper," who eventually, all his proletarian illusions ground to dust, takes his life at a seaside resort to which "our hero" has sent him to recuperate after two weeks of gruelling political argument.

This homeric political debate is the climax of the book—that and the doctrinaire idealism of the love-making that precedes it. The young enthusiast even succeeds in convincing this hardened old Kropotkinite that there is such a thing as *honour*: for he goes at it hammer and tongs, morning and night. "He had never done anything so seriously in his life before: he spoke with an almost un-English seriousness." (It is this "un-English seriousness" which is so "modern"—a passion beneath these *pastiche* literary trappings that no eighteenth-century worthy could have understood at all, and which belongs much more to "extremist" politics of today, of course, than to anything than can distantly be described as "Tory.") "I have a vague feeling that the old notions of virtue may be salutary," exclaims this paradoxical young prophet. "One becomes *real* by practising them. . . . I was always a little inclined to the *sentiment of honour,* for example. I shall now perhaps practise

it on more conventional lines: never tell a lie, or overlook an affront—all that. It will keep me morally fit."

His aged companion is profoundly scandalized when the word first falls upon his ears—this word "honour" is the most disquieting thing of all—a word so long taboo among all classes that it is even indelicate so much as to use it. "That word," the old man objects, "has *an aristocratical sound!*"

But he succumbs nevertheless, in the end. "In the end he was scarcely an optimist at all. 'It is all very well,' he said, 'but I have had a dream . . . you ask me to give it up' . . . our good Willoughby, with that destructive fury that rages in all who are bit by a certain kind of fly, took care to undermine his belief in the leaders of socialism and science." There was then little more to be done Again, in some of the most beautiful love-passages in recent fiction we are shown Willoughby converting the kind and virtuous Lucy Langton to emancipated and revolutionary ways of thinking. His work is as effective as it is later on, but the other way round, in the case of his elderly socialist victim. Lucy becomes a doctrinaire libertine (he is appalled at the *number* of her lapses, when she informs him some years afterwards). When he attempts to reconstruct the *unspoilt* Lucy, however, upon the ruins of his own making, his efforts are not attended with success. And on the last page we leave him doggedly immured for life upon a seven-hundred-acre estate.

"Such things as beauty, bravery, honour" are then this writer's strange stock-in-trade—just as much as Mr. Lytton Strachey's stock-in-trade, for instance, was the reverse. And "go out into the streets," says he, and observe Mr. and Mrs. Everyman. "Read their wit in the evening papers, or hear it in a saloon bar." There is little enough beauty: "their songs do *not* improve. . . . They are brave in herds in their blind wars: that salesman was probably brave then, but when they are alone they are not so very bold. As for honour, everyone is a hireling these days, and it is almost impossible for a hireling to be honourable."

But what comes next is so significant that I will select it for quotation, to conclude this review. It is a passage that does Mr. Collier singular credit, for this is what he says: "It used to give me pleasure to contemplate these little deficiencies," in Mr. and Mrs. Everyman, namely. "It made me feel superior. Now I perceive that I am contemplating myself. I identify the hateful elements in man by looking into my own greedy, treacherous, sentimental, hypocritical heart." In other words, *he* is—you and I are—responsible for the Mr. and Mrs. Everyman we encounter. Every man gets the Mr. and Mrs. Everyman he deserves! But, in the world of literature as we find it today, it is truly magnificent to have arrived, as Mr. Collier has done, at this understanding—to have turned round upon himself—for a man in fine to have blamed *himself*—where most are content to blame Fate—or their Victorian grandparents—for the pass in which we all find ourselves, without distinction.

William Rose Benét (review date 4 August 1934)

SOURCE: Benét, William Rose. "The Misadventures of Young Lovers." *Saturday Review of Literature* 11, no. 3 (4 August 1934): 33.

[*In the following review, Benét finds* Defy the Foul Fiend *a disappointment after the success of* His Monkey Wife.]

There are two books for which everyone should evermore praise John Collier. One is the novel, **His Monkey Wife,** which appeared a few years ago, and the second his editing of what he has called **The Scandal and Credulities of John Aubrey.** In their several ways I do not know which I like better; but I do know that I like both passing well.

Therefore when I opened a new novel by him with such a grand title as **Defy the Foul Fiend,** and such an appealing introductory quotation from Shakespeare as "Keep thy foot out of brothels, thy hand out of plackets, thy pen from lenders' books, and defy the foul fiend," I thought that my soul must rejoice in the contents thereof. Well, my soul has not precisely rejoiced. A trivial circumstance that has nothing to do with the merit or demerit of Mr. Collier's writing first contributed to this feeling. I was compelled to skip from pages 13 to 41, with no knowledge of what had gone between, because by accident I was sent a defective copy of the book for review. Therefore I shall never know just what occurred to Willoughby during a certain brief period of his youth—for I do not think I shall reread the book. That is really the crux of my criticism. I *shall* reread **His Monkey Wife** and the **Credulities,** I hope till I am evilly old and grey. But in **Defy the Foul Fiend** I had a deathly feeling at first that Mr. Collier had decided to go "smart young Englishman" on his devoted audience. True, this fear was soon dissipated, save that from a page or so a very occasional aroma would rise like a quick whiff of coal-gas; but when the author hit his stride, he was clean of wind and limb, and, moreover kept his story going at a brisk pace. The only trouble is that, from the days of H. G. Wells, there have been a large number of quite passable young-love stories written; and suave and intelligent as is Mr. Collier, and amusing as he can be, albeit upon too rare occasions in this book, all that does not seem enough.

Perhaps it lies with the jaded reviewer. I know that this novel is a more sapient and accomplished novel than a great many you will be reading, Dear Average Reader. Mr. Collier says certain things that delight me, such as:

> Revolt was in the air in those years. Customs to which no cultivated person had ever adhered, books none such had ever read, pictures never looked at except by short-lived duty, poor old men at whom even their contemporaries had laughed, even the wretched aspidistra, were dragged up to be rebelled against.

And the spirited conversation Willoughby addresses to the Black Stock person in the Whistlerian house in Chelsea, is prime. But where did Mr. Collier pick up his peculiar version of Swinburne, "The hounds of Spring are free of the leashes," and why did he write on and on in this book, and so very, very much of it? The fine and fornicating Frances toward the end is scarcely worth so much space, beautiful as she may have been. There is a great deal of the story that one takes with a hop-skip-and-jump, positive that nothing serious can have happened that it would be a pity to miss. And when one returns, shamefacedly to see whether one's prognostication was true, one is amazed to find how true it was!

No, this is a novel that the writer enjoyed as he enjoys settling himself in an easy armchair; and easy writing proverbially makes hard reading. Mr. Collier is never slovenly. His English is always impeccable, his sly witticisms occasionally glint like diamonds, he is always an authoritative gentleman-of-letters; but in this book he evinces very little sense of drama, and tries hardly at all to keep the reader interested. Because of an atmosphere deeply relished and fully conveyed, the scenes at Willoughby's uncle's in the country—and Willoughby, upon the death of his uncle, quite sensibly, ends up in the country, with Lucy—are the best. We have had so much of London in novels, and of down-at-heel London too, that even the appealing character of the old man who addressed envelopes no longer prevails upon us. This book is a queer mixture of simple, delightful, almost naïve pleasure in life, in really pretty and adorable girls, fine weather, and fresh air; and a sophistication that almost breaks into a giggle whenever it touches upon the unmysterious mysteries of sex,—a desire to titillate.

As for Willoughby, he was an illegitimate child who had to learn everything for himself. Fundamentally a very decent sort, he encounters life with some hilarity and a great deal of innocent surprise. His misadventures would constitute a good novel by anyone else; but unfortunately for Mr. Collier we have learned to expect from him nothing less than a *nonpareil*!

***The Nation* (review date 8 August 1934)**

SOURCE: "Shorter Notices." *The Nation* 139, No. 3605 (8 August 1934): 168.

[*In the following review, the critic declares that* Defy the Foul Fiend *will fail to gain a wide readership despite its attributes.*]

These two novels, [**Defy the Foul Fiend,** and *Brian Guy,* by Benjamin Appel] so completely different in temper and style, are in many respects the same story. They each describe a gifted young man who would rather do anything than earn what is described by old-fashioned persons as an honest living; the two heroes are both agreeable wastrels, in short, with no regard for their elders and betters and with an irresistible attraction for charming young ladies— the one for amateur, the other for professional whores. But not to pursue the comparison too far, it should be said hastily that Mr. Collier's novel is urbane, intelligent, and a delight to the ear; and beneath its witty and cruel casualness is a deep foundation of tradition and sober virtue, along with an ability to render the English countryside in terms that make it tender and real. Mr. Appel's novel, on the other hand, is one of the more unfortunate examples of the tough-baby, put-'em-on-the-spot, but-I'll-always-be-true-to-my-little-girl type of modern fiction. There is every reason to expect that *Brain Guy*, however, will have the same sort of success, although it is not so direct or so sharp, as *The Postman Always Rings Twice*. While *Defy the Foul Fiend*, it is to be feared will be read only by that comparatively small group of persons who appreciate excellence, particularly when it is combined with wit. If advice from a reviewer is pertinent at this point, it might be wise to borrow *Brain Guy* from an obliging friend, and to spend the required sum to make *Defy the Foul Fiend* one's own.

Fanny Butcher (review date 22 September 1934)

SOURCE: Butcher, Fanny. "Collier Writes with Brilliance in New Novel." *Chicago Daily Tribune* XCIII, no. 228 (22 September 1934): 15.

[*In the following review, Butcher offers high praise for* Defy the Foul Fiend *despite Collier's lack of development of his protagonist.*]

John Collier, whose *His Monkey Wife* was one of those lodes of pure brilliance which is rarely found in the good mines of English literature, and upon whom the eyes of those who would like to feel themselves his peers have been turned with eagerness, recently offered us *Defy the Foul Fiend*, which proves—to this reviewer, at least—one of the most difficult of books to judge.

First of all, and probably more obviously than anything else about it, the style in which Mr. Collier writes is so dazzling, so blindingly brilliant, that it is hard to see the stars for the fireworks. The reader who likes pyrotechnics of style revels in sentence, paragraph, page, chapter, in the startling use of words which gives them a new significance, a new life. Mr. Collier's gift of style is a real one, without affectation.

But about the use to which Mr. Collier puts that natural gift one cannot say as much. The affectation of striving for bizarre effect, of twisting situations into unreal contortions, Mr. Collier does with a sort of satanic glee.

Willoughby, the hero of his *Misadventures of a Heart,* is the son of a Lord Ollebeare, a rake of the old school, and his cook, who was "so exceedingly honest . . . that when she ran away with a lawyer's clerk . . . she could not bring herself to take the principal gift of Lord Ollebeare's bestowing, but left it in his bed awaiting him, that he might sleep the warmer for it, if not perhaps as dry."

Willoughby was supported unwillingly by his uncle, who rarely saw him, but oftener than he cared about the sight. The boy was reared by his uncle's butler and his uncle's rather exotic library, and when at 20 he was hurtled into the world as secretary to a stuffed owl with a pretty and amorous wife Willoughby's equipment for life was by no means adequate.

Mr. Collier takes his hero through every phase of London life, including one which is so deliciously funny that the reader wonders why it has not been exploited in just this ribald fashion before. Willoughby, in revolt against pharisaism, takes up the cult of Dostoievsky, and his adventures in self and human immolation are funny beyond words. Mr. Collier can do supreme irony when he will. But somehow always Willoughby remains a lay figure upon which Mr. Collier can drape superb sentences and bizarre ideas. He never emerges as a human being who has an existence (as the heroes and heroines of all great novels have) within himself.

The really fine characters of literature (fine in the sense of being works of art on the part of the author, whether hero or villain) achieve a reality greater than one's next door neighbor. They live. The neighbor dies and is forgotten. Willoughby never lived.

And it's too bad, because Mr. Collier's gift of making words sing and dance, and gambol, and glow with sunshine, and drip with dew, is a major one.

C. J. Eustace (review date September 1934)

SOURCE: Eustace, C. J. "Philanderer's Progress." *Canadian Forum* 14, no. 168 (September 1934): 488.

[*In the following review, Eustace offers a negative assessment of* Defy the Foul Fiend *but admits that Collier's writing evidences genius.*]

The writer must confess his abysmal ignorance! Before this book he had never heard of Mr. John Collier. Apparently Mr. Collier has published two other books, both of them highly praised by the reviewers in England. The names of these novels are *His Monkey Wife* and *Tom's A-Cold.* We are assured, by the reviewers of both these works, that the writer of them is a man of genius. And yet!

In *Defy the Foul Fiend* we are allowed a glimpse into the mind of a young man whose amorous adventures are paraded on the housetops for our edification. The mind of the young man is peculiarly degenerate, and as his sponsor into the realms of the written word has not seen fit to make him the victim of pragmatic illusions (in which case we could have sympathized with him, as we did with the protagonist of Joyce's *Ulysses*), and as his horrid little antics do not seem to be motivated by any higher complex than the complete indulgence of his Freudian urges, we must admit that we did not enjoy him.

Literature being selective as well as eclectic, we would seem justified in stating that the true Rabelaisian was the product of his age. He was a ripe, honest, if somewhat gross and lusty individual whose bawdiness did not offend because much of it came from high-blood pressure. There seems very little excuse for his progressive philandering.

But—it must be said at once—Mr. John Collier can write. His wit is piercing, even if it brings with it, occasionally, the aroma of the latrine. His style is so artificial, and his situations so removed from life, that at times one is tempted to dismiss him lightly. But he makes us think. He is unpleasantly direct. In his way he *is* a genius, and his book will probably achieve a wide sale in the lending-libraries. This, too, is but further evidence of his wisdom.

Geoffrey West (review date 12 December 1934)

SOURCE: West, Geoffrey. "New Novels." *Times Literary Supplement* no. 1717 (12 December 1934): 920.

[*In the following review, West finds the stories in* The Devil and All *to be well written but shallow.*]

Mr. John Collier's **The Devil and All** reveals him as master of the art of saying, with consummate skill, almost exactly nothing at all. These six short stories are a demonstration of accomplishment and dexterity to be compared to the performances of a champion trick skater. His prose glides and turns, pauses and pirouettes, leaps and wheels, and in general does the nicest tricks with unfailing coolness and precision. Seldom is even a comma misplaced, and the screech of an unnecessary emphasis (as the italicization of "human" on p. 31) is so rare as to remain a blemish upon the prevailing perfection. And, like many of the best performers, Mr. Collier prefers a strictly artificial rink; if thin ice cannot be altogether avoided, at least he will run no risk of tumbling through it into authentic depths. He chooses to write of the Devil, it is plain, not because he believes but because he does not believe in him. It amuses him (Mr. Collier) to outfit Hell with every modern inconvenience because he is quite certain he will never go there.

The individual tales touch varying depths of hellishness. In one we encounter nothing worse than a nice young modernist poet. In a couple more two would-be suicides score off, in one case the Proprietor himself, in the other a distinctly peevish subordinate. In a fourth an infernal hobbledehoy takes a very long while netting his game—or, more appropriately, as the reader will learn, his ball; the moral of this story might be that patience is a virtue even in devils. The next also shows, but more usually, Virtue Triumphant in Hell's newest suburb. Paradox enters again into the sixth, which tells how an angel may win, even though a little lower than the devils! Heaven, it appears on balance, can still hold its own. But Mr. Collier might just as well have made it the other way, had the whim taken

him. As the Devil himself retorted when asked why the damned should spend eternity in a dance lounge, "Why not?"—the more so in view of the revelation that the universe is, anyway, no more than a pint of beer. That is the humour of these admirably printed but rather too ornately bound stories; it is also their limitation.

Ben Ray Redman (review date 1 February 1941)

SOURCE: Redman, Ben Ray. "Imagination at Large." *Saturday Review of Literature* 23, no. 15 (1 February 1941): 5.

[*In the following review, Redman praises Collier's imaginative plots in the stories in* Presenting Moonshine.]

This latest presentation of John Collier's own, particular, and inimitable brand of literary moonshine contains the story, **"Thus I Refute Beelzy,"** which recently disturbed and baffled the less imaginative readers of *The Atlantic*. It contains other tales, among its twenty-four, that would not only baffle and disturb but horrify them. By these same tales, more imaginative readers will be delighted, for almost every one of the double-dozen can be labeled accurately: *Collier—Grade A*. And that is a respectable label.

Moving among occult phenomena with the familiarity of a Machen or a Blackwood, Mr. Collier moves without their solemnity. In the presence of the supernatural and magical, he is gay and impudent. He is a collector of demons, a connoisseur of jinn, and an old acquaintance of the Devil himself, who has more than once provided him with admirable copy; and it is obvious that fiends, large and small both, clutter the world in which he lives.

But neither they nor Hell hold any terrors for him: he is as much at ease with them, or there, as with his tobacconist or in his tub. When writing of matters eerie, awesome, terrifying, macabre, or horrible, his manner is candid and calm; while humor, like a playful imp, disports itself in even his most fearsome stories. Luscious ladies, no less than fiends, engross him, and with sex he deals slyly but without smirking.

Impossibility is the foundation on which Mr. Collier prefers to build: the more outrageous his yarn, the more plausible his spinning. Grant him an ell and he will lead you, unquestioning and entertained, for a mile. His brevity is a model to be studied by those who would make small words do big jobs. He achieves his strongest effects by underwriting. He is master of the double and triple twist.

The plots? I shall not pare them to synopses, for fantasy strips badly. Readers unfamiliar with Mr. Collier's work should at once correct their unhappy state by way of **Presenting Moonshine.** Those who do know his work will not wait upon reviews. Relaxation is good for even the most serious-minded persons, even in times that try men's souls. Relaxation and refreshment are provided in abundance by John Collier's unpredictable imagination.

Otis Ferguson (review date 3 February 1941)

SOURCE: Ferguson, Otis. "Collected Waxworks." *New Republic* 104, no. 1366 (3 February 1941): 155.

[*In the following review, Ferguson finds the stories in* Presenting Moonshine *enjoyable but superficial.*]

John Collier in his short stories has opened up a vein of fiction that comes strangely in this time. All his pieces [in **Presenting Moonshine**] are in this same manner—which is not, incidentally, the more humane and engaging manner of the two novels: **His Monkey Wife** and **Defy the Foul Fiend.** They are matter-of-fact in tone, smoothly joined in the writing, and deal in one way or another with the supernatural. I don't like them. They are clever and at times brilliant; they start where Poe leaves off, without ever quite achieving the memorable effect of the occasional Poe success. It is perhaps wrong to speak of them as being in any vein, for there is no blood in them; they are about everyday things in New York or London and as far away as Jules LaForgue or Patagonia. Their restraint and humor and well breeding in the presence of the clammy grotesque must inevitably suggest an exercise, controlled and deliberate; and I don't like them.

There is a fascination, though, as of rare deep-sea creatures and the life under a damp flagstone, and this sort of life beneath life is exquisitely cultivated. There is the case of the man-eating orchid which assimilated a household; there are the night shapes of life after death in the society of department stores, with the ghost-eating Black Men from the night life of undertaking parlors; there is the dim clerk who died for love of a store-window dummy; there are old men with magic bottles and a best-selling gorilla; there are even some complicated heterosexuals, though oh so faintly. There are a few stories where death or worse is neither present nor foreshadowed—one a good satire on the phony exquisite as writer, one a pretty threadbare exercise in smug innocence betrayed, etc. The devil appears and also justice, especially in the case of the man who became known in the East as the man who laughed at the Indian rope trick. Every young woman for whom the young man of the story would sign away his life is exactly as ravishing in every catalogued proportion, and as completely a blank, as the young ladies of P. G. Wodehouse; and in fact I can think of no character that can be remembered except by what happened to him.

This is all cabinetwork of fertile imagination, a craftsman's skill, and delicate and costly woods. As such you may enjoy it thoroughly, though, as I said, it has not that extra power of the grotesque in literature which can make sleep hazardous and eating a debatable proposition. The truly striking thing about it is its urbane presence in this time, its end unto itself and apparent success with a fairly wide magazine audience. This is the man from the other side of a century or the man from the moon, but perfectly among us and easy in a dinner jacket.

Paul Theroux (essay date 26 November 1972)

SOURCE: Theroux, Paul. "Very Wayward Miniatures." *Washington Post Book World* (26 November 1972): 4.

[*In the following essay, Theroux discusses Collier's place in literary tradition.*]

The critical reaction was mixed in 1931 when John Collier's first novel, **His Monkey Wife; or, Married to a Chimp,** was published by Appleton. *Books* called it "an extraordinary first novel" and *The Boston Evening Transcript* said it was "unique and thoroughly entertaining satire." *The Nation* regretted that it was not so deft as David Garnett's *Lady Into Fox*; *The New Republic* said there was in it "less humor than artifice" and *The Spectator* concluded that it was "a good dish spoiled in the cooking." There was, even in the reviewers' praise, a great deal of shy euphemism. But that is understandable—after all, it is the story of a man who copulates with a chimpanzee, and monkeyshines of this sort still have the power to shock.

In his appreciative introduction to this Collier anthology, Anthony Burgess stresses the kind of embarrassment "serious" readers and scholars feel in the presence of a writer whose fantasies are almost plausible; who bears a passing resemblance to Saki and Mervyn Peake, but who otherwise belongs to no literary tradition; who was a marvelous scriptwriter (Collier wrote the scenario to *The African Queen*), the author of privately printed books containing the publicly unprintable; who had Osbert Sitwell as a supporter and the experience of what was most strange in two countries, England and America, to draw upon; a creator, Burgess says, "of very wayward miniatures."

Collier described himself (on the dust-jacket of **Full Circle,** 1933) as "indistinguishable in appearance and pursuits from any other country bumpkin." The available facts of his life are few. He was born in London in 1901; he wrote poetry and published it, was interested in John Aubrey, and apart from the two novels already mentioned and **Defy the Foul Fiend,** published four collections of short stories: **Presenting Moonshine, Fancies and Goodnights, The Devil and All,** and **The Touch of Nutmeg.** At some point, perhaps in the late forties, he went to Hollywood and worked in films. He is still very much alive, and if Burgess is right in saying that he "eschews fame and has a horror of publicity" it is easy to predict that Collier will be horrified before long, for this reprint will undoubtedly be regarded as one of the happiest literary events of this year.

The persuasive part of the otherwise extremely bizarre **His Monkey Wife**—the eternal triangle with a chimpanzee as its hypotenuse—is the character of Emily, the monkey.

She is sensitive, witty, resourceful and fairly glows with personality. The humans in the book look rather pale beside her, and if the book has a message it might be that, observed by a chimp, the jaded twenties types are the true apes of God who need a simian redeemer. Emily arrives from Africa as Alfred Fatigay's gift to his fiancée. Fatigay's name deserves no further comment. As Emily is taken through the chartered streets of London she is "struck by the appearance of abject misery which was apparent in all the passersby, especially in their sickly complexions, their peevish or anxious looks, their slave's gait, and, most of all, in their rare and rickety smiles." Emily longs to be married to Alfred, but Alfred is engaged to the empty-headed social climber Amy for whom Emily works as a domestic. To complicate matters further, Amy gives a party and invites all her artistic friends, and as Emily serves drinks (and is nearly seduced by a guest), Amy finds herself a second admirer. Meanwhile, Alfred is accosted by a female who is charmed by his "too thrilling Conrad-sort of background."

But the marriage between Amy and Alfred goes on. Emily, however, is named as bridesmaid, and in a series of tricky maneuvers which includes an edition of Poe open to "Murders in the Rue Morgue" Emily shows up heavily veiled in the bride's dress. Without anyone guessing—for the monkey has a physical similarity to Amy—Alfred is married to his lovestruck pet. Recriminations follow. The monkey finds all of it tedious and soon both she and Alfred are wandering the streets of London, left to their separate fates. Some time later, and after Alfred has a vision of the Congo in Picadilly Circus, he spots Emily at the Ritz and they compare tales. Emily has risen in the world, Alfred has fallen; they live together for a while and finally decide to return to Africa. It is there, in Boboma, where we first saw the pair, that their love is consummated in the last remarkable paragraph of the novel. Alfred cries, "My love!"

> Under her long and scanty hair, he caught glimpses of a plum-blue skin. Into the depths of those all-dark lustrous eyes, his spirit slid with no sound of splash. She uttered a few low words, rapidly, in her native tongue. The candle, guttering beside the bed, was strangled in the grasp of a prehensile foot, and darkness received, like a ripple of velvet, the final happy sigh.

There is not a little misogyny in the tale, but it is such a wickedly cheerful kind it is irresistible. "Behind every great man there may indeed be a woman," says Alfred to the newsmen covering his departure, "and beneath every performing flea a hot plate, but beside the only happy man I know of—there is a chimp."

Collier's next novel, not included or even mentioned in this anthology, was *Full Circle,* a futuristic look at a tribally divided England in the year 1995. It is as savage and gloomy as *His Monkey Wife* is witty and fantastical, and concerns an expedition to capture women from a neighboring settlement. On its publication it must have had the effect of scaring the daylights out of readers who had laughed so hard at the farcical coupling of Emily and Alfred. Still, *The John Collier Reader* is a hefty volume and contains over 50 stories, from the Saki-like tales featuring Willoughby, to the stories of explicit horror which have been identified with Collier's name. There are many murders, many devils—even the Devil himself—and there is a joyful balance about the stories that is uncommon in the macabre. A nagging wife is eaten by a megatherium ("**Incident on a Lake**"), a man is entombed in a bottle ("**Bottle Party**"), a cheery neighbor is made into a murder suspect ("**Wet Saturday**"), a refugee in a department store is sadistically transformed into a window dummy ("**Evening Primrose**"). Some of the most horrible of his stories have what you might call happy endings, and all have perfectly direct openings which seize the reader's attention. "**The Devil George and Rosie**" begins, "There was a young man who was invariably spurned by the girls, not because he smelt at all bad, but because he happened to be ugly as a monkey." That is a Faustian story, and in fact many of the stories have as their pivot the Faustian bargain.

Literary scholars have largely ignored the horror story as an art form, and this might account for the profusion and diversity of the macabre tale. Think about it and you come up with W. W. Jacobs, Elizabeth Bowen, all of Shirley Jackson and some L. P. Hartley, James's "The Turn of the Screw," Stevenson's "The Bodysnatchers," Saki's little frights and of course John Collier's comedians doing evil things. What do such writers have in common? Very little, one would think, apart from their fascination with the hard-to-prove and their command over readers' feelings. It seems to me that the writer of nightmares, caring little about his place in literary history, seeks only the sympathy of an imaginative reader, whom he will ply with horribly pleasurable detail. It is art deliberately acting upon a person's emotions and stopping just this side of outrage. John Collier is a master of this art, and he has the added advantage of being very funny, the author of ironies "so perfectly balanced," the late Basil Davenport said, "that his horror is hardly ever quite free of humor, nor his humor of horror."

New Republic (review date 9 December 1972)

SOURCE: "In Brief." *New Republic* 167, no. 22 (9 December 1972): 33-34.

[*In the following review, the critic examines the works included in* The John Collier Reader, *concluding that much of Collier's canon is charming but light reading.*]

We may still believe in God—our money and our pledge of allegiance say we do—but few nowadays believe in Satan. True, we can muster up a pharisaical contempt for antisocial behavior; we can generate a proper Republican shudder at breaches of law'n'order; and of course any sexual naughtiness still provides a spasm of titillation or moral indignation (which T. S. Eliot said is "the favorite emotion of the middle class"). But despite the current bumper crop of public and private evil, no one could make even an election issue of it, recently.

This is regrettable—not merely for moral or political reasons, but for esthetic ones. "The death of Satan was a tragedy," Wallace Stevens observed, "for the imagination." True indeed. Evil in art, which had always been primarily human, became merely human and then became mere error, maladjustment, environmental deprivation . . . or it was sentimentalized and glorified by such as Genêt. Perhaps only in the writings of Nabokov, now, is evil occasionally to be found pure. John Collier has glimpsed it, however; evil flickers in and out of his best stories.

His latest collection [*The John Collier Reader*] is distinguished by the inclusion of the fine novel *His Monkey Wife*—which is about precisely that—as well as 47 of his short stories. Their basic style might be described as that of a perceptive, educated and witty Wodehouse:

> Edward deposited his bags in Mergler's Hotel, which stands opposite the funeral parlor. After a minute or two, he stepped outside and checked up on the signs.

> "Why, you low-down, snooping bastard," she began, and the conversation continued with the utmost vivacity.

His material is obscured too often by obsolescent theological equipment—angels, devils, meaningful coincidence, the supernatural, etc.; but at his best Collier deals in sharply observed psychological evil, the evil that men intend toward one another . . . or, more often, that men and women intend toward each other. His treatment of the subject is characteristically brief, elegantly stylized and comic; he persuades us not of the reality of his tale, but of the probability that real men and women might feel and do such evil things. When read in heaps, the stories tend to display their machinery rather immodestly, but as a Christmas gift, a bedside book, this book is fine; and *His Monkey Wife* is a wonderfully sustained feat of imagination.

Jay Martin (review date 23 June 1973)

SOURCE: Martin, Jay. "Praise for the Blighted and Blasted." *New Republic* 168, no. 25 (23 June 1973): 28-29.

[*In the following review, Martin finds* Milton's Paradise Lost *predictable and unsatisfying.*]

Although John Collier has titled his new book *Milton's Paradise Lost* and announces that he intends to reproduce "Milton's concept" in a screenplay, in almost every respect this work is unlike Milton's; and only in appearance is it a screenplay. It is all John Collier and entirely romance.

For a starter Collier replaces Milton's Ptolemaic System with a physically correct galactic universe through which

Satan plummets like a stricken astronaut. Then he substitutes for the sword of God "an electronic barrier" which sweeps the gateway of Eden. But these are incidental to his real intention, which is not to revise but to reverse Milton's poem. Collier rejects the two beliefs central to Milton's work: that the divine design was perfect, and that a poem in praise of that design should strive for perfection. Collier, to the contrary, is interested in the blighted and blasted, the defective and changeable.

He is not the first of Milton's readers, of course, to show dissatisfaction with the notion that a perfect God was the poem's hero. Many 19th- and 20th-century readers have had difficulty in discerning anything but boredom in perfection. How could an omnipotent, omniscient Being be interesting when by definition he could have no conflicts, feel no tensions, suffer no existential pathos? William Blake began the search for alternate heroes by suggesting that quite in opposition to Milton's intentions Satan, who at least is interesting in his ruin, was the central figure of the poem.

Collier goes much further, but at first it does appear as if Satan is the hero. The opening scenes show him to be magnificent in his defiance of God, especially so in his ability to restore himself after his total defeat. The fall of the angels, their torment in the burning lake whence Satan leads them, their creation of Pandemonium, Satan's struggle with Death and Sin—in all these scenes Collier emphasizes alteration, transformation and renewal. Not endurance but change is the central power of the universe. Late in the book Satan exults to Gabriel: "All our glory is change. Poor imperfection *must* change. . . . And poor Perfection cannot. A stagnant glory!" Satan, too, is given heroic qualities as a guerrilla leader and speculative philosopher. God is stagnant the archangels are plain soldiers, stereotyped in goodness; while the archfiends are malicious imps (though 40 feet tall), stereotyped in evil. As for the humans in the action, God made "two imperfect things. Of these—one snores." So much for Adam. As for the other, when Raphael arrives in the garden he utterly ignores Eve except to remark that she is "a creature incomplete, and most imperfect." So much, it appears, for her.

But it is just in Raphael's characterization that we have the first hint of who the real hero is. While Adam hungers to imitate God's crystalline perfection, Eve never even begins to delude herself. She discovers and eventually learns to celebrate human incompleteness and imperfection, and, above all, the labyrinthine dynamism of her changing mind. What she discovers in Satan is really her own being, while Adam had never arrived at the threshold of his humanity while bent on becoming a god. It is Eve, then, who becomes the moving center of the universe. Satan is her discovery, the cinema of her mind: his fall has been merely a stage in the progress of humanity toward the Fall of Man.

Satan even acknowledges Eve's superior vision of change when he comes to see the world through her eyes:

Sin and Death Seen by Eve

It is the hitherto unseen side of each that is visible to Eve. With her, we see two figures of great beauty. Sin cradles something in her arms, the nature of which becomes clear only when Eve speaks of it.

Eve
But she is beautiful.
What's that she has at her breast?
I know their names.
Those are *Love* and *Birth*.

Shaken to the roots of his being, Satan looks at Eve in rapture, like one awakened to a new and thrilling view of things.

Early in the book, Satan had made much of the invincibility of mind and of the notion that the whole drama was being enacted in the infinite space of his brain. But at last it is clear that the drama is instead Eve's human comedy, with God, the angels, Satan, heaven and hell as the figures of her creative dreaming. When Adam wakes up from his snoring, he joins in her dream. He is her last creation—the most imperfect and therefore the best of Eve's creatures.

In form Collier's "cinema of the mind" is the reverse of Milton's epic. His work is designed to be incomplete, open-ended, and thus to push the reader away from it into his own creations rather than enclosing him in the totality of the perfect work. What Collier wants is not Milton's divine words, but the "weaker words" of defective humanity—incomplete images, half thoughts, partial pictures. In his "Apology" Collier writes: "Many of Milton's jewels are rough at the edges in this version, having been rudely ripped from their rich setting. I like them rough at the edge."

Milton originally intended to write his great work on King Arthur, and to take up the theme of the Fall of Man later. Collier began by wishing to rewrite Milton's epic and ended by writing the romance which Milton abandoned. His interest in magic and in human imperfection, and his idealization of woman all have strong affinities with the romances of Chrètien de Troyes or Marie de France, and with Arthurian themes. Furthermore his Satan is chivalrous. Though unwilling to be ruled by his Liege-Lord, he proposes to make Eve the "Empress of Hell" and to be ruled by this lady. Milton could never have entertained that proposal, and even the lesser devils are shocked by it. But we modern humans have seen much; Collier's audience is likely to find his romantic conclusion to Satan's Complaint quite predictable and only mildly amusing.

John Updike (essay date 20 August 1973)

SOURCE: Updike, John. "Milton Adapts Genesis; Collier Adapts Milton." *New Yorker* 49, no. 26 (20 August 1973): 84-86, 89.

[*In the following essay, Updike explores Collier's interpretation of Milton's "Paradise Lost."*]

No clue is offered, on the jacket flap or in the author's rather testy "Apology," as to what possessed John Collier to turn John Milton's "Paradise Lost" into a screenplay. Was this a commercial, practical project—after all, Cecil B. De Mille mined Exodus and Judges for a pretty penny—from whose shipwreck the writer salvaged his script? Or was it always to be a curiosity purely literary—a "Screenplay for Cinema of the Mind," as the title page advertises? ***Milton's Paradise Lost: Screenplay for Cinema of the Mind*** (sumptuously produced by Knopf in a kind of Loew's Orpheum Art Deco) begins as space opera, "2001"-plus: "We are moving upward into a region where the blue is lighter and clearer;" a distant star becomes a comet; the comet's tail becomes a torrent, a waterfall whose mist is bubbles, and each bubble "is made of six or eight living creatures. These are gigantic and glorious beings with beautiful, stricken faces and flying hair. They wear minimal golden armour, such as we are accustomed to associate with demigods or angels." They *are* angels, dressed like Barbarella, millions of them, and then we see them charred and writhing in a lake of lava, and Satan himself, "burned to incandescence, like a log that is red all the way through, ready to fall to pieces." But he does not fall to pieces; instead, inventing magic on the spot (one of Collier's anthropological updatings of Milton's version), he pulls himself together and then invents oratory, announcing to the lake of the tormented, "All is not lost. The unconquerable will, and study of revenge, immortal hate, and courage never to submit nor yield." These three lines from Milton are the only ones Collier quotes entire; elsewhere he resists the delicious thunder of Milton's pentameters and for cinematic speed substitutes his own tinny *vers libre.* Satan's rhetorical question in Milton

". . . But first whom shall we send
In search of this new world, whom
    shall we find
Sufficient? who shall tempt with
    wand'ring feet
The dark unbottom'd infinite Abyss
And through the palpable obscure
    find out
His uncouth way, or spread his
    aery flight
Upborne with indefatigable wings
Over the vast abrupt, ere he ar-
    rive . . ."

becomes in Collier's script

"Who'll fly through night, and
chaos and the endless void?
And find this race called Man?
Who'll dare?
Who'll go?"

The loss in magnificence is well-nigh total, but Milton is already on record, and Collier is attempting a new thing.

His description of the Burning Lake and charred angels evokes Dresden, Hiroshima, and napalming; the conclave of the damned in Pandemonium draws imagery from Fascist rallies, even to a clenched-fist salute. Space flight—the fact and technics of it—infuses the heavy epic with easy momentum. In Milton, Satan's passage from Hell to earth is a sloggy business, a piece of Renaissance exploration: "the fiend / O'er bog or steep, through strait, rough, dense, or rare / With head, hands, wings, or feet pursues his way, / And swims or sinks, or wades, or creeps, or flies. . . ." In Collier, he generates speed as smoothly as an equation, and travels as a "dark ripple in space." We ride "that wave of darkness, which is Satan in flight," and, as under the eyes of our astronauts, the huge, curved horizons of earth and sun float into view. Milton, after Gabriel confronts Satan in Paradise, has Satan hide by circling the earth on the side of darkness; though the possibility fits with Newtonian astronomy, it seems far-fetched and uncomfortable in the verse, mixed with antique imagery:

> . . . thrice the Equioctial Line
> He circl'd, four times cross'd the
>   Car of Night
> From Pole to Pole, traversing each
>   Colure. . . .

For Collier, such an orbiting is a familiar stunt; Satan hangs in darkness "like a surfer awaiting the wave" and exultantly teases both sunset and sunrise in the course of his confident free fall. "Free Fall," for that matter, would be a pretty good title for this movie, were it ever made.

When Satan arrives in Paradise, we arrive at hackneyed territory. Mr. Collier refreshes the fable with a lot of delightfully precise botany, some clever lighting, and an attentiveness to Eve's dreams worthy of a psychoanalyst. But his retelling founders where most modern retellings do: he does not believe in God, and God is the most interesting character in the story. He has a plan and a hope; He experiences love and regret. Satan is just a successful saboteur by comparison, and Adam and Eve are a pair of gullible yokels. The God of Genesis brims with surprises; his question of Adam, "Who told you that you were naked?," has all the cunning innocence of do-your-own-guilt paternalism since the world began. How affably, without a blink, the blame having passed from Adam to Eve to the serpent, does He curse the serpent first and how obligingly, having delivered the curses to all three, does He squat down like a tailor and make for His two errant children, grown out of nudity, "garments of skins." Adam and Eve are banished from Paradise not spitefully, as punishment for what cannot be undone, but as a simple Self-protective measure, to prevent the created pair, who have already eaten from the tree of the knowledge of good and evil and become "like one of us," from eating now also from the tree of life and living forever; the cherubim and the flaming sword guard not the gates of Paradise but the path to the tree of life—not the way back but the way out. This pleasant plantation owner, safeguarding His prerogatives against a slave uprising, is a remote rustic ancestor of Milton's God, a defensive monarch always ready to argue the legalities of his own decisions. To "justify the ways of God to men" was Milton's announced purpose, and the thorny conundrums of Justice and Mercy, Free Will and Divine Foresight, Liberty and Order frame the Biblical events in a continual dialectic of serious political argument. Foreseeing Man's Fall, God sends Raphael to Adam to

> ". . . advise him of his happy state,
> Happiness in his power left free to
>   will,
> Left to his own free Will, his Will
>   though free,
> Yet mutable; whence warn him to
>   beware
> He swerve not too secure: tell him
>   withal
> His danger. . . ."

Milton then assures us, "So spake th' Eternal Father, and fulfill'd / All Justice." And Adam, when Eve complains that his failure to command "absolutely" permitted her to sin, answers in echo of God:

> "I warn'd thee, I admonish'd thee,
>   foretold
> The danger, and the lurking Enemy
> That lay in wait; beyond this had been
>   force,
> And force upon free Will hath here no
>   place."

Mr. Collier is a modern atheist, and will have none of this. The long middle of Milton's poem—Raphael's exposition to Adam of the Christocentric universe—he almost entirely omits. The theological reasoning that Satan was permitted to perpetrate evil "but to bring forth / Infinite goodness, grace, and mercy" elicits from Collier the scornful paraphrase "In other words, the prisoner was paroled in order that he might commit fresh crimes and incur a yet heavier sentence. Man, at the cost of death to all and damnation to many, was to serve as bait in this outrageous trap." Mr. Collier then goes on to praise Satan as morally superior to God (". . . he is the rebel against the Establishment, the defeated, the exile, the endungeoned, the resurgent, and the guerrilla. . . . We watch in vain for some example of his wickedness. . . . He inflicts no tortures"). Mr. Collier is of course entitled to his humanist pieties and left-wing wrath, but he has no artistic right to pump the Voice of God into the end of his scenario. The Voice has been labelled hollow. The plot that turns on the strictures of such a moral nonentity as Mr. Collier's God falls to nonsense. You can have a sentimental Satan, and an adorable Jungian Adam and Eve, and an apple that is all vitamins and eroticism, but you cannot have these and Jahweh too. By the time this script reaches its last shot (Satan smiling out of the screen at us, just like Walter Huston in that old Hollywood make of *The Devil and Daniel Webster*), the corniness betrays an inner chaos. The God of Genesis walking in His garden in the cool of the day had a blunt corporeal reality. The God of Milton derives actuality from the believer's tortured strenuousness. Collier's God is just a black hole in a funny old story that must ("*Must!* That's the word now," Adam says) have something profound about it.

What did attract this excellent British fantasist to "Para-dise Lost"? Possibly its superficial shimmer of the fantas-tic, of the hallucinatory. The conceit of making it into cin-ema recalls an image Santayana uses, of Dante, in "Three Philosophical Poets": after pages of praise for the medi-eval poet, Santayana adds the devastating demur ". . . he has no true idea either of the path to happiness or of its real conditions. His notion of nature is an inverted image of the moral world, cast like a gigantic shadow upon the sky. It is a mirage." It may be that some such mirage-sense of Milton's poem is at the root of the curious meta-morphosis Collier has wrought. Of the assembly in Pande-monium his scenario says, "Perhaps this vast, dark sphere is Satan's brain, and the luminous seraphs are the brain cells, glowing or flashing or dimming according to the electrical impulses that pass through them." A frequent (and, I would think, technically implausible) feature of his script is the specification of elaborate trompe-l'oeil effects:

> . . . a reddish flush emanating from the maddened ser-aphs hangs like a luminous cloud in the centre of the vast, dark sphere. Soon it coalesces into a tangle of fuzzy, incandescent lines which form a fiery tracery, semi-abstract, showing an imagined assault on the battlements of Heaven.

Satan ruffles a tree of dark leaves with light undersides so that from a hundred yards it exactly resembles Eve; Mul-ciber's body goes transparent and becomes his palace; a vast horde of devils so disperses itself as to shadow forth the forms of Adam and Eve, like a marching band at half-time. What does Collier intend by such illusions except to transfer the entire cosmic epic to the realm of dream and subjective psychology? A movie screen has no substance; it exists only for our eyes, which in turn—physiologists tell us—are specialized segments of the brain, the only ones that have surfaced.

But would these grandiose tricks—mist into angels, angels into "semi-abstract" tracery—work? Much is possible to the movie camera, but it remains a camera, a mirror of the external world's texture and accidents. Though there is immense visual ambition in Mr. Collier's directives to his hypothetical technicians, there is little that is effortlessly concrete. Phantasmagoria eclipses the luminously mun-dane. The human protagonists, for instance, are presum-ably naked until their fig leaves descend, but the script never brings Eve's body to our awareness like these lines of Milton:

>   . . . but Eve
> Undeckt, save with herself more lovely
>   fair
> Than Wood-Nymph, or the fairest
>   Goddess feign'd
> Of three that in Mount Ida naked strove,
> Stood to entertain her guest from
>   Heav'n. . . .

Collier's "Apology" announces that his hero is Eve, yet she seems more the subject of speculation than an object of vivifying love. This kind of love Milton shows her when he has Adam say:

> "Neither her out-side form'd so fair, nor
>   aught
> In procreation common to all kinds . . .
> So much delights me, as these graceful
>   acts,
> Those thousand decencies that daily
>   flow
> From all her words and actions. . . ."

Collier's Adam says:

>   ". . . she grew so lovely that
> all she does and says seems
> wisest and most virtuous and best."

Which is indeed bleak praise, if not blank verse. Milton has not been generally prized for the virtues of psycho-logical tenderness or lively sensuality; Mr. Collier's script leads us to realize how much of those virtues Milton pos-sessed. And it leads us to suspect that in a fictional uni-verse there is no borrowed gravity; unless an author is writing for his life, images become mere "effects" and fly into space. Precision is a function of attention, and atten-tion is a function of concern. Too diffidently Mr. Collier tells us, of the poem's Christian content, "I do not share these beliefs, and I have substituted other ideas, also not profound in themselves, but which are more in accord with those commonly held today." There are ideas here, but no possessing *idea*. Milton's God may be a tedious old bluffer, but he fascinated Milton, and aligned the poet's in-spirations in one magnetic field. A phrase like "those thou-sand decencies that daily flow" holds a piece of felt reality up to a moral light, and transfigures all women, all wives. Mr. Collier's Eve, on the other hand, is conceived un-steadily: eating the apple on her knees like a drugged porn queen, voting for life like some vociferous Shavian hero-ine, snivelling like a groupie when the angelic fuzz ar-rives, jerked through a series of attitudes by the dead strings of Genesis 3. The script ends—for this viewer, at least—as a flicker of unweighted significances and sym-bols. The projector throws not a beam of light but a tatter of brilliancies.

Anthony Burgess (essay date 1973)

SOURCE: Burgess, Anthony. "Introduction." In *The John Collier Reader*, pp. xi-xv. New York: Alfred A. Knopf, 1973.

[*In the following essay, Burgess surveys Collier's literary career.*]

Ask the average Englishman about Milton, and he will say it is the name of a patent antiseptic. This is true, though not exclusively. Ask him about John Collier, and he will say that it is the name of a chain men's outfitters, probably adding the television jingle "John Collier, John Collier, the window to watch." There is a nice irony about the fact that the real or immortal John Collier—writer, not tai-lor—is the last man in the world whose window is to be watched. He eschews fame and has a horror of publicity. He is probably happy enough to know that people regard *The African Queen* as a film with a great script, without being particularly interested in who wrote it, and that the novel **His Monkey Wife** keeps finding a new batch of delighted readers every decade or so, readers too intrigued by the theme and the style to be curious about the author. The situation in America as regards Collier is much the same as in Britain, except that here he cannot be confused with a tailoring firm. Some of his stories must worry Americans who chance upon them. They show a large familiarity with America and even use with ease various kinds of American spoken idiom; yet they seem to be written by a very English Englishman, quaint, precise, bookish, fantastic—the sort of man who might keep to his country estate or college rooms and shudder at the prospect of engaging the New World. And yet John Collier has spent a long time working for that newest sector of the New World, Hollywood, and is a master of the script-writer's craft. Read his short stories and you will see all the script-writer's virtues—intense economy, characterization through speech, the sharp camera-eye of observation. You will also find literature, grace, allusiveness, erudition, the artist as well as the craftsman.

People who read Irving Wallace and Irving Stone and the other Irvings may not be expected to read Collier, but scholars who write about Edith Wharton and E. M. Forster may also be expected to neglect him. Take it further: histories of Anglo-American fiction rarely, even at their most comprehensive, find room for him, but the same may be said of other imaginative writers who share some of his qualities—Saki, for instance, and Mervyn Peake, and the royal physician who wrote the anonymous comic masterpiece *Augustus Carp Esq.* (what a treat is coming to Americans when some publisher decides to reprint it). To write tales about hell under the floorboards, the devil as a film producer, men kept in bottles, a man who marries a chimpanzee is a sure way to miss the attentions of the "serious" chronicler of fiction. The puritanism of the scholarly tradition leads Oxford dons to produce detective stories pseudonymously but to refuse to write "seriously" about the form (T. S. Eliot always promised to produce a considered thesis on the *genre,* but—because of shame or decorum or lack of time or something—the promise was not fulfilled). It also exhibits *pudeur* in the presence of fantasy, especially when it has no evident didactic purpose. *Gulliver's Travels* is all right, but the works of Carroll and Lear are for the depth psychologist rather than the literary historian.

John Collier is essentially a fantasist, but not of the romantic order that purveys Gothick, both paleo- and neo-, and science fiction. He makes literature out of the intrusion of fantasy, or quiet horror, into a real world closely observed, not out of the creation of a parallel world (windy, bosky, and machicolated; steely and computerized; hobbitish). In **His Monkey Wife** it is the world of the 1920's, whose properties shine through a classical and allusive prose that belongs to a more elegant age:

> *The snow's a lady* . . . and, like the rest of her sex, though delightful in her fall (to those who enjoy her), once she has fallen her effect is depressing, particularly in Piccadilly. A heavy blizzard had begun at noon, and continued for a couple of hours, during which time it was whisked and beaten by wheels and feet and sweepers into a kind of stale and ghastly sundae, edging, like Stygian spume, the banks of the stream of black and glassy traffic, which creaked along as slowly and uncouthly as a river of broken ice.

Though we may be said to have sundaes still with us (though not, since the passing of a highly moral Act of Parliament, fallen ladies in Piccadilly), we no longer have the referent of the following "metaphysical" image:

> For the heart is, in a sense, like the Prince of Wales; we would not have it cut in stone, yet how pathetic it is, when, as at Wembley, we see it modeled in butter.

This refers to the British Empire Exhibition of 1924, at which the then Prince of Wales, late the Duke of Windsor, was indeed sculpted fullsize in butter by New Zealand dairy exhibitors. Reading **His Monkey Wife** in the 1970's, we experience the agreeable literary piquancy of seeming to be in three historical periods at the same time—that of the prose, that of the imagery, that of a story which is as potent now as when it was first written, for it is pure myth.

Why write a full-length novel about a chimpanzee that falls in love with, and eventually marries, an undistinguished colonial schoolmaster? Osbert Sitwell enthused many years ago—on the occasion of a reprint—about the deep symbolism: man needs to face his atavistic self, to be refreshed (the hero's name is Fatigay) through contact with the animal world, and so on. This will do well enough; indeed, anything will do, from cartoon charm to Swiftian satire, but we always end up with a chimp falling in love with a man. And we literally end up with this:

> Under her long and scanty hair, he caught glimpses of a plum-blue skin. Into the depths of those all-dark lustrous eyes, his spirit slid with no sound of splash. She uttered a few low words, rapidly, in her native tongue. The candle, guttering beside the bed, was strangled in the grasp of a prehensile foot, and darkness received, like a ripple in velvet, the final happy sigh.

Though Sir Osbert saw here (and who will not say legitimately?) man's soul returning to the anarchic night whence it came, there is something else, forbidden by the eyeshades of decorum—a man copulating with a monkey. There is what is sometimes called *wickedness* in Collier—a quality different from salacity. There is also the logic of the metaphysical conceit (there are enough references to Donne in the book, beginning with the very first sentence, to prepare us for this), which does not balk, as the cartoon fantasy does, at the inescapable conclusion, though it leaves everything to the imagination. The Collierian melodic line deliberately seduces us into accepting reality through the agency of a "double take." It happens, for instance, at the end of the story called **"Bottle Party,"** where the hero is glassed and corked and put on sale:

In the end, some sailors happened to drift into the shop, and, hearing this bottle contained the most beautiful girl in the world, they bought it up by general subscription of the fo'c'sle. When they unstoppered him at sea, and found it was only poor Frank, their disappointment knew no bounds, and they used him with the utmost barbarity.

That final word covers a great deal, but Collier the scriptman, the visual conceptor, undoubtedly has a number of specific images in mind. Or just one.

An appreciation of many of Collier's effects depends on one's own erudition. In *His Monkey Wife,* Emily the chimp visits the London Zoo, where she encounters an old acquaintance of the jungle, another chimp called Henry:

> "Well, Emily!" he muttered. "Have you too come to haunt me? I know I was wrong to throw that banana skin, and, it's true enough, I meant to do worse still. I determined that, if I could get you on the rebound, so to speak, that day you ran away from the schoolmaster, I'd take it out of you for daring to love anyone but me. But I was punished, Emily, and I'm being punished still. When I was in the very act of making up to you, a leopard sprang on me—no doubt you saw it—and I felt his red-hot teeth and claws, and then all was dark, and I awoke to find myself in the hands of friends, who bore me here—to Hell! Sweet Em, what shall become of Henry, being in Hell forever?"

It is probable that, apart from being able to recognize the *Doctor Faustus* quotation at the end, one needs to be equipped with a knowledge of the history of English fictional dialogue to enjoy this fully. Collier seems to echo, in rhythm as well as idiom, a tradition of speech that could be courtly, melodramatic, colloquial, biblical. His animals know it best. But when his human characters in the short stories seem to speak a respectable enough American, there is always somehow a touch of the bookish, as though Collier is deliberately echoing a *Punch* joke about Americans from the 1850's:

> "I'd have given her the world," said he. "And I would yet. But she's gotta see reason. I'll make her listen to me somehow. Let me get her within reach of my arms, that's all! Landlord, I'll have a bottle of this hooch up in my room, I reckon. I gotta do a bit of thinking. Good night, pal. I'm no company. She's roused up the old caveman in me, that's how it is. I'm not claiming to be any sort of sheik, but this little Irish wonder lady's gotta learn she can't make a monkey of a straightforward American businessman. Good night!"

The inversion ("said he") reinforces the slight but flavorsome archaism.

Collier ransacks traditions, but he does not himself seem to belong to any tradition (any more than does Mervyn Peake). *His Monkey Wife* and *Defy the Foul Fiend* do not exemplify any direction in the course of the novel form, and the short stories suggest fable, or grand guignol, more than the naturalistic irony of the *conte*. All this means

that he does not play a part in the development of a literature, although he is himself very "literary." It has been regarded by some critics as a sure sign of slightness, the badge of the inconsiderable, for a writer to make some of his effects out of his reading (like the school of essayists that followed Lamb). Add to this an almost exclusive concern with horror and fantasy, and you seem to have a double cause for overlooking Collier. But the interests of the literary critic-historian and of the cultivated fancier of good writing so often fail to meet. One could pursue somewhere, not here, the theory that the books that mean most in the average literature lifetime are not the collected works of Scott, George Eliot, Balzac, Trollope, Zola, Hardy, and other "makers" of the novel, but the unclassifiable "sports"—*Gargantua, Vathek, The Marriage of Heaven and Hell, Les Illuminations, Alice, Mrs. Caudle's Curtain Lectures, Diary of a Nobody, Cardinal Pirelli, The Unquiet Grave, Titus Groan,* **His Monkey Wife.** If Collier had produced many more full-length works of fiction, then critic-historians would be able to look for patterns and find him a legitimate scholarly niche. As it is, he is chiefly a creator of very wayward miniatures, and all that can be done with these is to enjoy them. In this volume you have most of his stories, as also a part of *Defy the Foul Fiend,* which stands easily on its own, and of course **His Monkey Wife.** Whatever this volume has cost or is going to cost you, it is, believe me, a great bargain.

Tom Milne (essay date spring 1976)

SOURCE: Milne, Tom. "The Elusive John Collier." *Sight and Sound* 45, no. 2 (spring 1976): 104-8.

[*In the following essay, Milne explores Collier's writing and films based on his stories.*]

> 'If thou be'st born to strange sights *and if you don't mind picking your way through the untidy tropics of this, the globe, and this, the heart, in order to behold them, come with me into the highly coloured Bargain Basement Toy Bazaar of the Upper Congo. You shall return to England shortly.'*
>
> —John Collier, **His Monkey Wife**

After languishing in limbo since its appearance at the London Festival three years ago, James B. Harris' *Some Call It Loving* has just re-emerged as the other half of a London sexploitation double bill: a strange but perhaps not entirely inappropriate apotheosis for a film that assumes the persona of the Dream Factory to demonstrate the innocence of corruption as well as the corruptibility of innocence.

At the end of the film, determined to preserve the Sleeping Beauty he has rescued from a carnival and fallen chastely in love with from being contaminated by his own world-weary depravity, the hero salvages her purity—thereby restoring it, however, to the defilement of the sideshow, where admirers may try to wake her for a dollar a kiss—by re-administering the drug that kept her asleep. The John Collier story on which the film is based reaches a similar conclusion, but for simpler, sharper and altogether less metaphysical reasons.

Waiting patiently for his ideal to awaken after he has rescued her from captivity, the hero, an Englishman of means adequate to his simple but exquisitely cultivated tastes who has brought back this prize from a trip to America, at last sees his fragile beauty stir, bringing instant disillusion. "'How do you do?" said Edward. "At least . . . I mean to say . . . I expect you wonder where you are." "Where I am, and how I goddam well got here," said his lovely guest, sitting up on the bed. She rubbed her brow, obviously trying hard to remember. "I must have passed right out," she said. And then, pointing at him accusingly: "And you look like a son of a bitch who'd take advantage of me.'"

Time was, if you remember, when Borges was not yet a cult writer, celebrated by mysterious references in films like *Paris Nous Appartient* and *Les Carabiniers,* largely ignored until, around the time of *Performance,* Borges was published or republished and at last read. So too, in a rather different way, with John Collier, whose sizeable body of novels and short stories remained out of print and forgotten but whose name was kept tantalisingly alive by a series of distinguished adaptors. Hitchcock included two of his stories, **'Back for Christmas'** and **'Wet Saturday'**, both personally directed, in his TV series *Alfred Hitchcock Presents.* Orson Welles, also for TV, adapted the story **'Youth from Vienna'** as *Fountain of Youth* (see Joseph McBride's article in *Sight and Sound,* Winter 1971/72). Sandy Wilson made a charming musical out of Collier's equally charming first novel, **His Monkey Wife** (published in 1930). Stephen Sondheim, no less, did the music for a TV version of 'Evening Primrose', a pleasing fancy about a wraith-like tribe living in voluntary seclusion from the pressures of life in a New York department store, not unlike Giraudoux' *Madwoman of Chaillot* but given a note of chill horror by the presence of the Dark Men, a similar but unmentionably sinister (cannibalistic?) tribe who have chosen to live in a funeral parlour and who are called in to deal with interlopers. And of course, in relatively recent cinema history, there was Collier's name among the credits for Franklin Schaffner's *The War Lord,* presumably accounting for the weird aura of magic and myth that infused a Hollywood historical romance.

Recently, a small oasis in the literary desert has appeared with the publication of **The John Collier Reader**,[1] an anthology containing forty-seven short stories, the whole of **His Monkey Wife** and, disappointingly, only two chapters of **Defy the Foul Fiend** (to my mind Collier's best novel, published in 1934 and certainly something of a key to him as both man and writer). Received with general enthusiasm only slightly tempered by the doubts normally reserved by reviewers for writers devoted to fantasy, this anthology has focused due attention on a writer described by Eric Korn in the *Times Literary Supplement* as 'a phenom-

enon, perhaps a cult, on his way to becoming an industry.' Published with no bibliographical information whatsoever, and with an introduction by Anthony Burgess that is critically perceptive but of little help informationally (and indeed introduces a new mystery by recalling that of Collier's connection with *The African Queen*), this volume has left most reviewers enthusing over John Collier (b. 1901, poet, novelist, short story writer and scriptwriter) but echoing *New Yorker* editor Harold Ross' celebrated 'Who he?'

> JOHN COLLIER: 'I started off as a poet, kept going by a small allowance from my father, who was extremely poor. I helped keep him that way for nearly ten years, and finally managed to write a novel, *His Monkey Wife,* which was kindly received, and it led to my writing a good many short stories for the *New Yorker.*
>
> 'I went to live in Cassis, a delightful little seaport near Marseilles. While there I fell in love with a sturdy fishing boat which was up for sale. At a low price, too, but more than I could beg or borrow. So I was walking around the port, casting languishing glances in that direction, when a nice little girl rode up on a bicycle and gave me a telegram. It was from my agent. Would I go to Hollywood on a two month writing job for wages that seemed to me princely, and which would buy the boat. I was off like a shot.
>
> 'That was for *Sylvia Scarlett* . . . to join a couple of other writers on the screenplay. Unfortunately it didn't turn out as well as was hoped. It had all the elements of a really good film. Based on a lively book, a first-rate cast, and in Cukor an outstandingly brilliant director. Unfortunately, again, not a good script. In the main, my fault. It happened that I was abysmally ignorant of the cinema; I'd seen scarcely a dozen films in my life. I couldn't have had a better guide than Cukor, but I wasn't in the mood to learn. Frivolous and pigheaded at the same time: a combination not unknown among the lesser literary lights in England in the Thirties. What must have made it all the sadder for Cukor is that he'd asked for Evelyn Waugh. And I turned up instead . . . some confusion in the front office. . . .'

Sylvia Scarlett (1935), though a flop at the time, is now of course something of a cult classic. In *On Cukor,* Gavin Lambert and Cukor discuss the film rather at cross purposes, with the interviewer wondering why 'there was such a terrific controversy over something very charming and very lightweight . . . a simple, mildly eccentric tale of a girl who disguises herself as a boy to help out her dear old father, who's a thief and a con man, and both men and women fall in love with him/her,' while Cukor isn't too sure whether or not he had thought it daring at the time. 'But then we got John Collier for the script, and he was a daring kind of writer, so I suppose I *must* have been thinking in that way.'

The common ground that Cukor and Lambert never quite reach is that Collier at his most characteristic is simultaneously disarming and daring, producing the effect that Anthony Burgess calls his *wickedness,* illustrating the point by quoting the closing lines of **His Monkey Wife**: a lyric celebration of romance finally consummated in which Col-

lier delicately resurrects the fact, long buried under a fili-
gree of emotional arabesques, that the happy Isolde melting into her Tristan's arms is, nevertheless, a chimpanzee.
'Under her long and scanty hair, he caught glimpses of a
plum-blue skin. Into the depths of those all-dark lustrous
eyes, his spirit slid with no sound of a splash. She uttered
a few low words, rapidly, in her native tongue. The candle,
guttering beside the bed, was strangled in the grasp of a
prehensile foot, and darkness received, like a ripple in velvet, the final happy sigh.'

Wryly commenting on the experience of *Sylvia Scarlett,*
Cukor notes that 'the picture did something to me. It
slowed me up. I wasn't going to be so goddamned daring
after that.' Collier, like so many writers who tangled with
the Hollywood machine, from Fitzgerald to Nathanael
West, found the experience a rich source for satire. His
most barbed story is **'Pictures in the Fire'**, a morality
brilliantly worked out in strict movie terms, in which a
writer who sells his soul to the Devil (in town to become a
movie mogul and revolutionise Hollywood) for a tempting
contract, wins it back by encouraging the latter's casting-
couch sweetie to play the ever more outrageously demanding star. Everything is dipped in vintage Hollywood vit-
riol, from artistic humiliation ('But,' said she, 'do you
think I ought to be seen about with a writer?') to private
revenge in the scriptwriter's rewrite of *Romeo and Juliet*:
'O.K. We'll modernise it. The Capulet apartment is in a
New York skyscraper. Romeo's a young G-Man, from
Harvard, but disguised as a Yale man in order to outwit
the gangsters. Capulet's Harvard, you see. It builds for a
reconciliation, a happy ending. Romeo's keen on mountain
climbing; that builds up for the balcony scene. On a skyscraper, you see. Only his name's not Romeo. It's Don.'

Nevertheless, Collier remained in Hollywood, receiving
screen credit for a very mixed bag of films and obviously
developing a kind of quizzical affection for the place. His
attitude is reflected, probably much more accurately than
in **'Pictures in the Fire'**, by the brilliantly funny but
oddly affecting story **'Gavin O'Leary'**, about a flea who
becomes smitten with the charms of movie queen Blynda
Blythe after sampling the blood of a star-struck poet in a
cinema. Itch-hiking the three thousand miles from Ver-
mont to Hollywood, he negotiates the delicate problem of
making his heroine's acquaintance by becoming her co-
star in a doss-house sequence where the actress is to be
subjected to total naturalism and real fleas. From there, becoming a star himself and taking up residence in mutual
admiration with a narcissistic leading man, Gavin's story
(leading to his final regeneration) is an hallucinating tangle
of realism and fantasy viewed through the extravagant distorting mirrors of the Dream Factory: 'It was not long before ugly rumours were in circulation concerning the flea
star. People whispered of his fantastic costumes, his violet
evening suits, his epicene underwear, his scent-spray
shower-bath, and of strange parties at his bijou house in
Bel Air. A trade paper, naming no names, pointed out that
if individuals of a certain stripe were considered bad security risks by the State Department, they must be even

more of a danger in the most influential of all American
industries. It seemed only a matter of time before Gavin
would be the centre of an open scandal, and his pictures
picketed by the guardians of our morals.'

'I was extremely lucky in the friends I made and in
some of the jobs I was given. Not all of them, of course.
Maybe half were impossible. There's a deplorable propensity in the film industry there, here and everywhere,
to latch on to basic material which has an inbuilt hopelessness. It's up to a writer to have nothing to do with
such stuff. There were times when I was too timid or
too greedy to turn my back on an offer, and I very
justly got stuck. Some of the other jobs were as good
as I could make them. When at last I learned a bit.

'I was given an excellent chance after *Sylvia Scarlett.*
Charles Laughton, then at his peak with Captain Bligh,
had a great desire to play a London bobby. Thalberg
hired me to write an original story and screenplay. It
was one of the great plums, fallen into my mouth. But
it happened that while I was still fumbling with the
first draft, Laughton left for England to do *Rembrandt*
for Korda. And at the same time Korda offered me *Elephant Boy* with Flaherty directing. Thalberg, who
could be magnificently kind, allowed me to take a leave
of absence. But, while I was still in England, poor
Thalberg died. And, as with earlier potentates, his
slaves were given the job of escorting him to the next
world, on a one-way ticket. In my case, the next world
was India.

'I had presented myself at the studio for *Elephant Boy*
and was politely asked to wait a little. Bob Flaherty
had been in India for eighteen months past, and would
soon be coming home. He had been delayed a while
owing to the fact that they'd sent him off to India to
make a film on the Kipling story without giving him a
script. After all, a script has an end, often the best part
of it. Without a script, Flaherty could not reach that
end. He therefore continued to make the most superb
photographs of India, of the most ravishing temples,
the most heavenly skies and particularly the most el-
ephantine elephants, some of which were going to the
right; others to the left; others seeming to charge directly at the audience. It was said that there were three
hundred thousand feet of these superb photographs,
and Alexander Korda cried out in mortal pain.

'I diffidently suggested that it might more or less save
the situation if we got the child Sabu over from India
and if we devised some brief and simple scenes, in
which he might utter a few words, and perhaps be intercut against an advancing elephant bent on destruction and, holding up his hand like a juvenile traffic cop,
soon be connected with one of the shots of a hinder
view—there were a great many to choose from—and
he would thus appear to have saved the village. "Mr.
Collier, you ask twenty-nine impossibilities."

'So we went off to the Hungaria Restaurant, and
scribbles were made on the interior parts of Player's
cigarette packets. I think the exteriors carried no sort of
warning. Anyway, a sort of jury-script was tacked together, much in the way that shipwrecked sailors rig
out their rafts with whatever petticoats and spars may
be bobbing around. Sabu was sent for, and arrived. In

the interval the engaging little imp had exercised his constitutional right to grow into a plump and amiable lubber at least twenty pounds heavier and twelve inches taller than the diminutive pixie he had been when Flaherty first photographed him with his gigantic charge, Kala Nag. In the whole eighteen months the slow-living pachyderm had not grown an inch. There was a scene where he had to lift Sabu high in the air with his trunk. I dreaded a visit from an inspector of the R.S.P.C.A.

'My long education as a scriptwriter may have begun to pay off, I think, about ten years later when I read C. S. Forrester's *The African Queen.* I wrote an enthusiastic note to Jack Warner, and persuaded him to buy the novel and to let me write the screenplay. All that was necessary was to transpose the book into the conventional script form. But when I had done the first draft, Warner, who had neglected to read the book, was told that it was concerned with two people all alone on a little riverboat, and that it would cost nearly three million dollars to make. Some ill-disposed person whispered to him that the script had been written with Bette Davis in mind, and that she was disposed to play the part. I'm told that he was reminded also that Miss Davis had the right to pre-empt the feminine lead in any property produced by the studio. Choler prompted him to get rid of me, an impulse he responded to with such alacrity that Reason had not the time to get a word in edgeways. When at last its small still voice could make itself heard, it advised him to get rid of the script also, lest Miss Davis exercise her right. So he sold it to me for a song, and I sold it to Sam Spiegel for the equivalent of a grand opera, and he passed it on to John Huston, who made an immensely popular film out of it.

'I did only the first draft, but the end was different. Since you ask, my version did not contain the marriage scene. You'll remember that Allnut and Rose have lashed two cylinders full of explosive to the bows of the Queen, thus transforming her into a super torpedo. They lie hidden in the reeds until the German gunboat comes along in the gathering darkness. Then they set out to ram her and blow her and the Queen and themselves out of the water. But a wind has sprung up and the open lake has waves on it, and they ship so much water that before they reach the gunboat the poor old Queen sinks by the stern, leaving them floundering in three feet of water. The makeshift torpedoes are sticking up just level with the surface. Rose and Allnut attract the German's attention with shouts in English. The gunboat trains a searchlight on them and steams inshore in pursuit, lured on to a course which is going to bring it right down upon the waiting torpedoes. Rose and Allnut renew their shouts to keep it following. A machine gun opens up. They are likely to be cut to pieces. At that moment the gunboat goes up in a sheet of flame and the lake is clear for the British.

'Rose and Allnut struggle to the beach and fall on the warm soil, dead beat. When they wake, the sun is just rising. For mile after mile to the south, the lake shore is scalloped with beaches leading down to the open country now held by the British. They walk on down and the shore birds rise in front of them as they go. A happy end? Bet your life it was. I had a very comfortable percentage, and, believe it or not, I was paid every penny that was due to me.'

Of his own screenwriting efforts, at least up to the aborted *African Queen,* Collier has little that is complimentary to say: 'I suspect that what I wrote was far too wordy and far too literary; and most of those highly polished MGM pictures were too full of glossy magazine thinking.' One might perhaps cite as an example the line in *Deception*—pianist Bette Davis torn between composer Hollenius (Claude Rains) and cellist Novak (Paul Henreid)—pounced upon by Charles Higham and Joel Greenberg (writing in *Hollywood in the Forties*) to support a description of Collier's script as 'very pretentious'. The cellist, asked in an interview which living composers should be admired, replies: 'Let's see. Stravinsky when I think of the present. Richard Strauss when I think of the past. And of course Hollenius, who combines the rhythm of today with the melody of yesterday.' In point of fact, the only thing wrong with the line is that it is used within the context of a glossy magazine, romantic tosh view of art and artists.

As a writer, Collier has a quality all his own. At its root is a certain gentlemanly, world-weary cynicism, allied to an eighteenth century elegance of wit and a metaphysical's fondness for whimsical conceits: 'Lord Ollebeare had a face like a coat of arms. His nose might have been a fist, clenched and mailed, gules. In fact, he was one of those men you sometimes see in the street. His moustaches were two dolphins argent, his eyes two étoiles azur. He had also an inalienable two hundred a year, paid weekly, a top bed-sitting-room with a good toasting fire to it, six Norman names, a ruined house, a wild park, and one large and barren farm. . . . Twenty-odd years ago, for we must hark back a little, he had had less nose, more money, much credit, and the best suite in Albany. There he had a charming cook, on whom, in the most careless fashion imaginable, he begot the hero of this story.'

What follows (this is the beginning of **Defy the Foul Fiend**), combining the manner of Sterne with that of Diderot, is the sentimental education of the well-born byblow in the ways of a world teetering on the verge of vulgar modernity. Like the hero of Ford Madox Ford's Tietjens tetralogy, young Willoughby Ollebeare is a Tory so pure that he is also the perfect radical; and when his heart is doubly broken by the pretty girl and the native land he simultaneously falls in love with, the twin reconciliations are a Pyrrhic victory in which Willoughby is left to face solitude as the last English country squire: 'Taking two people, of equal generosity of spirit, each of a courageous and sincere intelligence, each of that order which ardently desires to live, and is scornful of living without a faith, it is more likely than not that the woman will be a Liberal, and it is quite certain that she will be all the more so, if the man happens to be a Tory. He on his part will view all progressive notions with increasing distrust, as his reactionary programme forces his wife to raise them as the standard of her independence.'

'Well, I was certainly influenced by Sterne, and by Smollett and Fielding, who were my greatest pleasure as a boy. Later, as I became more and more involved in field sports and taproom company, I found that the racy, slangy style of Surtees provided me with all the lingo I needed to express the narrowness of my views and the intensity of my pleasures. After half a lifetime, I still blush when I remember the enjoyment I felt in slaughtering harmless beasts and birds. How one could have lived so stupidly and yet in a perpetual intoxication with the most vivid beauty is something I shall everlastingly wonder at. I might wonder even more at some of the opinions I held in those days, but of those the less said the better.'

Around that time (1933, in fact), Collier wrote a sort of declaration of faith: 'I cannot see much good in the world or much likelihood of good. There seems to me a definite bias in human nature towards ill, towards the immediate convenience, the ugly, the cheap . . . I rub my hands and say "Hurry up, you foulers of a good world, and destroy yourselves faster."' The cynical disenchantment expressed here informs most of Collier's writing, but governs only the more conventional short stories, including the two selected by Hitchcock: diabolical murder plots conceived by resentful husbands and spiteful wives who observe the utmost social aplomb in the niceties of their strategy, and who are suavely brought to book by neat O. Henry twists, whether internal (both husband and wife execute the same successful plan simultaneously in **'Over Insurance'**) or external (the dead and buried wife in **'Back for Christmas'** had previously arranged repairs to the cellar as a surprise for her husband). Mildred Natwick, blithely chirruping 'What seems to be the trouble, Captain?' as she stumbles upon Edmund Gwenn dragging a corpse about by the heels in *The Trouble with Harry,* is so quintessentially a Collier character that it is surprising as well as sad that Hitchcock—not to say Hollywood—never made more use of Collier as scriptwriter or source.

But Collier, of course, could be much subtler and more disorientating. The magnificent **'Are You Too Late or Was I Too Early?'**, conceived entirely as a subjective narrative, is the haunting love story of a man for the mysterious ghostly woman who appears, tantalisingly, in his flat as a Crusoe footprint, a breath dimming the mirror, a scented breeze in passing, until an overheard telephone conversation takes us through another looking-glass: 'I heard, in a full opening of the sense, the delicate intake of her breath, the very sound of the parting of her lips. She was about to speak again. Each syllable was as clear as a bell. She said, "Oh, it's perfect. It's so quiet for Harry's work. Guess how we were lucky enough to get it! The previous tenant was found dead in his chair, and they actually say it's haunted."'

The nightmares of the imagination discovered by Poe are never very far away in Collier's stories, where a sculptor seeking success as a ventriloquist creates a dummy so lifelike that it assumes his life (**'Spring Fever'**); a lovelorn young man conceives the notion of having himself stuffed and placed in his beloved's presence as an eternal reproach (**'Squirrels Have Bright Eyes'**); a stuffy father ordering his small son to banish an imaginary playmate called Mr. Beelzy is himself mysteriously consumed

(**'Thus I Refute Beelzy'**). In these stories, however, Collier invariably sets out from reality: from the psychological inadequacies and emotional disturbances that lead to strange fancies. The Devil, for instance, might be said to have taken a hand at the end of **'Thus I Refute Beelzy'**; more particularly, however, the child has simply turned at last on the father determined to mould him into a replica of his pedestrian self. While the sculptor-ventriloquist is merely the victim of the *reductio ad absurdum* outcome of his self-imposed, stubbornly blinkered and Sisyphean task of persuading a society fed on Brancusi, Lipchitz and Brzeska that representation is the only purpose and justification of art.

Despite the profusion of devils in his work, Hell, for Collier, is essentially of our own making. Yet even as he excoriates the world for its follies, Collier is clearly increasingly preoccupied by—and sympathetic to—the human predicament expressed by his collection of lonely castaways yearning for a little romance, a little tenderness and a little understanding. Oddly, but again not inappropriately, the man who hungered for the world to destroy itself more rapidly, and spent his days killing harmless beasts and birds, covertly expresses his new concern by way of the amazing collection of animals who proliferate in his stories, sometimes as mute (or not so mute) witnesses to human destructiveness, but more often as surrogates for the unrealised aspirations.

One of his most haunting stories is **'The Steel Cat'**, about a man who evolves an idea for a Heath Robinson mousetrap after saving a mouse from drowning in his bath. Proudly aided by the rescued mouse, now his friend and still unable to swim, the inventor demonstrates his invention to a tycoon in the hope of a lucrative contract. His interest taken less by the Steel Cat than by the demonstration mouse, the tycoon nibbles and insists on signing an immediate contract; meanwhile, as the distraught inventor hesitates to risk a fortune by interrupting the busy tycoon's tight schedule, his friend slowly drowns. And somehow this death of a mouse reverberates with the clear bellnotes of tragedy. The richer and riper Collier revealed in such stories spent most of Hollywood's blacklist years in Mexico City: not exactly blacklisted, more a voluntary exile in a place he loved from what he calls 'a sort of greylisting'.

> 'There were reasons for this greylisting. Some were comic reasons. One is that I had a distinguished namesake in John Collier, the Commissioner for Indian Affairs, and he made several speeches at an organisation which Roosevelt had asked should be set up to get writers to do things for the war effort in 1944-45, and which continued afterwards with some strong political coloration. Whatever he did, I got the credit or debit for, and I expect he got some from me. I went to dine with Henry Wallace when he was running for President. Also, I was strongly on the side of the 'Communists' who were attacked, the first ones to be singled out. Several of them were personal friends. I was a sympathiser, let's say, with nine-tenths of their ideas, but I wasn't very much involved until the perse-

cutions began, which made me rather hot under the collar, and I was concerned with getting some facts out to papers round the world.'

It was Henry Cornelius, ignoring the blacklist, who brought Collier back to England to script *I Am a Camera,* a film which Collier now agrees would have been much better had he approached Isherwood's stories from the narrative standpoint adopted by Welles in *Fountain of Youth,* and which he had himself envisaged at around the same time for an abortive TV project: a collection of his own stories to be presented by Robert Morley as dreams of his in which he would be interlocutor, sometimes star, and sometimes an obscure character. Since then Collier has written two scripts, one realised and one not.

'I certainly wasn't responsible for everything in *The War Lord,* but it was I who tried to introduce what you call the magical-Druidical element. Leslie Stevens' play was set much later, in the thirteenth century, I think. I put it back to the eleventh century. The invasion of the Low Countries by the Catholic Church was late, and at that time the inhabitants were still following, more or less, the old neolithic, animistic religion. What interested me was the effect on the invader of this primitive element. In those days, of course, one was thinking of the fate of the little lieutenant in Indo-China, a Frenchman stuck up in North Vietnam with his platoon, holding a losing outpost. I thought it might be interesting to make a parallel.

'I admit that I felt very bothered when I found that the script had been changed into someone's quite extraordinary idea of what a successful costume picture should be. Another unfortunate writer became involved, quite a respectable one, Millard Kaufman. It seems that someone else put in all sorts of atrocities like "I hate your knightly guts" etc. At the time, I felt somewhat aggrieved at Charlton Heston for having failed to prevent the spoilage, but later I realised that it was exactly the sort of thing I should have expected.'

Collier's other script, published in 1973 as *Milton's Paradise Lost: A Screenplay for the Cinema of the Mind,* is a vast and visionary attempt not simply to stage Milton, but to interpret his account of the fall of Lucifer in subversive terms that delve further into the nebulous zones explored in *The War Lord.* In the preface to the script, for instance, Collier notes the anomaly whereby Satan and his followers are doomed to torture without end, yet soon contrive to extricate themselves, restored to their former personal glory and purpose, from the lake of hellfire. 'Luckily Milton, after setting down this explanation [the prisoner was paroled in order that he might commit fresh crimes and incur a yet heavier sentence], shows us, without naming it, a more likely and a more tolerable one. He shows us the effects of a force that originated in Hell and that has been used on earth, in Heaven's despite, throughout the ages. Frazer could have named it; it is magic. See how Pandemonium, that fairy palace, rose out of the sulphurous, burned-out soil: *It rose like an exhalation, with the sound of dulcet symphonies, and voices sweet.* What better demonstration could we have of the operation of the magic

power? And what better formula than Satan's other great dictum, more profound than the first: *The mind is its own place, and in itself / Can make a Heaven of Hell, a Hell of Heaven.*'

Opening new perspectives and inviting new techniques by its deployment of this Luciferian formula, Collier's *Paradise Lost* screenplay still awaits a director.

'No, the *Paradise Lost* screenplay wasn't exactly a commission. I had the idea of doing it, scribbled a few pages saying how I saw it, and sent them off to Howard Houseman, who is a great agent and a great arranger. He at once interested a producer, Martin Poll, who sent me a letter full of promises, some of which were kept. I got an advance of some sort and got busy. When it was finished, the producer was unable to raise the backing that he had hoped for. I got it back from him after a while, and now I have it.

'All sorts of enthusiastic people have advanced it in various quarters. At one time I thought that Fellini had agreed to do it; United Artists were willing to make the picture if he would do it. But although I believe, from the reports I got at second hand, he liked the general theme very much, he found there was a difficulty with the English language. Also, he was apparently in love with a Casanova project he had on hand. Since then I've not been able to find the sort of director whom I'd hoped would do it. It's been shown to four or five who might have handled it very well, but none of them were quite willing to go out on a limb for it. Why should they? Usually the ten million dollars has been the obstacle, though laboratory technicians assure me that electronic advances mean that there is no real need for such a vast budget.

'Recently, things have been thickening up concerning a possible production as a theatre piece. Extraordinary things can be done in theatres without immense cost, as long as one doesn't try to have real water in the canals or real fire in Hell. Old-fashioned classical realism and high polish would ruin the thing anyway. I think that the theme of *Paradise Lost* is singularly suited to attract the wide audience, and especially the young audience, of today. It is quasi-religious, quasi-scientific, and deeply humanistic, being the thrilling story, with which we can all identify, of how innocent, vegetarian, Proconsul or Pithecanthropus was caught up in the guerrilla war waged by Satan against the authoritarian dictatorship which orders the universe, and how he emerged as moral and immoral, curious, inspired, murderous and suffering Man.

'What I should like to offer them is a big, rough, ostensibly slapdash production, dazzling with light effects, deafening with sound and sometimes enchanting with music, and above all bursting with energy so that it breaks out of the conventional frame of proscenium and footlights and often out of the frame of conventional dramatic form. Imagination rather than money is the solvent to my problem. But so few people have enough of either.'

Note

1. Souvenir Press, 1975. £5.00.

FURTHER READING

Bibliographies

Arrowsmith, J. E. S. "Fiction—I." *London Mercury* 28, no. 164 (June 1933): 169-71.

Arrowsmith laments that Collier failed to put "more of himself" into *Tom's A-cold*.

Moran, Helen. "Fiction II." *London Mercury* 30, no. 177 (July 1934): 277-79.

Moran finds the inconsistent tone and mood of *Defy the Foul Fiend* to be disorienting to the reader.

Additional coverage of Collier's life and career is contained in the following sources published by the Gale Group: *Contemporary Authors,* **Vols. 65-68, 97-100;** *Contemporary Authors New Revision Series,* **Vol. 10;** *Dictionary of Literary Biography,* **Vols. 77, 255;** *Literature Resource Center;* *Short Story Criticism,* **Vol. 19;** *St. James Guide to Fantasy Writers;* **and** *Supernatural Fiction Writers.*

Eduardo de Filippo
1900-1984

Italian playwright, screenwriter, poet, and director.

INTRODUCTION

De Filippo was among Italy's most distinguished contemporary playwrights. Strongly influenced by the social milieu of his native Naples, de Filippo continues to be highly respected in Europe for his farces, in which reality is often treated as shifting and transitory.

BIOGRAPHICAL INFORMATION

De Filippo was born in Naples, Italy, in 1900, to Eduardo Scarpetta and Luisa de Filippo. He entered the theater while still an adolescent, performing with siblings in his father's acting troupe, then moving to comedic and musical companies. By 1930 de Filippo had collaborated—frequently under pseudonyms—on numerous skits and one-act farces. Around this time he reteamed with family members and began performing his own works in Naples. He also commenced his film career, appearing in the 1932 production *Tre uomini in frak.* Five years later he made his screenwriting debut with *Sono stato io!* (1937). During World War II de Filippo worked only sporadically, but once peace was restored he resumed his varied careers, and throughout the remainder of the 1940s he produced what are usually considered his greatest works. De Filippo continued to write plays and later screenplays through the 1950s, 1960s, and 1970s, and in the early 1980s he was a lecturer at the University of Rome. He also maintained a very successful acting career, both on stage and in films. He died in 1984.

MAJOR WORKS

Among de Filippo's most important works is *Napoli Milionaria* (1945; *Naples Millionaire*), a realistic drama about a family's involvement in the Italian black market. He followed this work with *Questi fantasmi!* (1946; *Neapolitan Ghosts*), a comedy in which a husband mistakes his wife's ever-present lover for a ghost. In 1946 de Filippo also wrote *Filumena marturano* (*Filumena*), in which a former prostitute obtains financial stability for her three offspring by successfully conning her lover—who is already engaged to a younger woman—into marriage. De Filippo continued his success in Italy with *Le voci di dentro* (1948; *Inner Voices*), in which a man mistakes for reality his

dream in which a friend is murdered by neighbors. After learning of his folly, the dreamer is visited by the falsely accused neighbors, who accuse each other of plotting the crime. Shifting reality is also the premise of *La grande magica* (1949; *Grand Magic*), de Filippo's complex comedy about infidelity and faith. In this play an adulteress cuckolds her husband after vanishing as part of a magic show. When she fails to return, her husband is given a small box from which she can be produced if he trusts in her fidelity. Four years pass before the untrusting husband, convinced by the magician that only a few minutes have elapsed, decides to open the box. But before he has opened it, his wife reappears. The husband, however, prefers to believe that she is still inside the box.

It is probably as a screenwriter that de Filippo received his greatest recognition in the United States. Italian sex comedies were particularly prevalent among foreign films shown in America during the 1960s. Among de Filippo's contributions to this genre included such films as *Matrimonio all'italiana* (1964; *Marriage Italian Style*), featuring Sophia Loren and Marcello Mastroianni—adapted from de Filippo's *Filumena,*—and, *Shoot Loud, Louder . . . I Don't Understand* (1967), adapted from *Le voci di dentro* and pairing Raquel Welch with Mastroianni. With English-speaking audiences, de Filippo enjoyed perhaps his greatest theatrical success in the 1970s with *Saturday, Sunday, Monday,* a translated production of his play *Sabato, Demenica e Lunedi* (1959).

CRITICAL RECEPTION

Largely because his language and themes do not translate well, de Filippo is not generally known in the United States. However he still enjoys immense status in his native Italy, with some critics ranking him second only to Luigi Pirandello, with whom de Filippo once worked. Some critics have also seen de Filippo's influence in the works of later Italian playwrights, notably Dario Fo. He developed such a following as an actor of both stage and screen that he is readily identified by just his first name in Italy.

PRINCIPAL WORKS

Farmacia de turno (play) 1920
Ditegli sempre: si (play) 1931
Natale in casa Cupiello (play) 1931
Chi è chiù felice 'e me! (play) 1932
Ditegli sempre si (play) 1932
Gennariello (play) 1932
Quei figuri di trent'anni fa (play) 1932
Sik-Sik, l'artefice magico (play) 1932
Uomo e galantuomo (play) 1933
La speranza ha trovato un alloggio [with G. Riva] (play) 1936
Sono stato io! (screenplay) 1937
Pericolosamente (play) 1938
Uno coi capelli bianchi (play) 1938
La parte di Amleto (play) 1940
Non ti pago! (play) 1941
Io, l'erede (play) 1942
Napoli Milionaria [*Naples Millionaire*] (play) 1945
Filumena marturano [*Filumena*] (play) 1946
Questi fantasmi! [*Neapolitan Ghosts*] (play) 1946
San Carlino 1947 (play) 1947
Le bugie con le gambe lunghe [*Lies With Long Legs*] (play) 1948
Le voci di dentro [*Inner Voices*] (play) 1948
La grande magica [*Grand Magic*] (play) 1949
La paura numero uno (play) 1950
Il paese di Pulcinella (poetry) 1951
Amicizia (play) 1952
Il morti non fanno paura (play) 1952
Il successo del giorno (play) 1952
Bene mio e core mio (play) 1955
Mia famiglia (play) 1955

Cantata dei giorni pari (plays) 1959
Sabato, Demenica e Lunedi [*Saturday, Sunday, Monday*] (play) 1959
Il sindaco del Rione Sanita (play) 1960
De pretore Vincenzo (play) 1961
Ieri, oggi e domani [*Yesterday, Today, and Tomorrow*] [with Alberto Moravia and Cesare Zavattini] (screenplay) 1963
Matrimonio all'italiana [*Marriage Italian Style*] [adaptor; from the play *Filumena marturano* with Renato Castellani, Antonio Guerra, Leo Benvenuto, and Piero de Barnar] (screenplay) 1964
Shoot Loud, Louder . . . I Don't Understand [director and adaptor; from the play *Le voci di dentro*] (screenplay) 1967
Il contratto (play) 1971
Il monumento (play) 1971
Ogni ano punto e da capo (play) 1971
Gli esami non finiscono mai (play) 1973
La poesie di Eduardo (poetry) 1975
Three Plays (plays) 1976
†*Four Plays* (plays) 1992

*This work contains translations of *Il sindaco del Rione Sanita, La grande magica,* and *Filumena marturano.*

†This work contains *The Local Authority, Grand Magic,* and translations of *Filumena marturano* and *Napoli Milionaria.*

CRITICISM

Eric Bentley (essay date winter 1951)

SOURCE: Bentley, Eric. "Eduardo de Filippo and the Neapolitan Theatre." *Kenyon Review* 13 (winter 1951): 111-26.

[*In the following essay, Bentley surveys de Filippo's themes in his major plays and discusses the influence of his life in Naples on de Filippo's work.*]

Both in technique and philosophy, Eduardo de Filippo is traditional. At the same time he strikes me as one of the three or four original figures in the theatre today. Let me tell something about his plays, beginning with the two latest: **La Grande Magia** (**The Big Magic**) and **La Paura Numero Uno** (**Fear Number One**).

Calogero di Spelta is so jealous he will hardly let his wife Marta out of his sight. Her friend Mariano has to resort to strategem to be alone with her. He bribes a visiting conjurer to use Marta in a disappearing act. The conjurer thus brings her where Mariano is—but instead of returning after fifteen minutes, as arranged, the young couple run off to Venice. Meanwhile the conjurer must save face before his audience. He tells Calogero that his wife can be produced out of a small box—which he shows the company—*if* he, the husband, has complete faith in her, that is, is sure she is "faithful" to him.

Otto the conjurer saves the occasion. But days pass, and weeks, and months, and the waiting husband is not to be appeased by the improvisation of a moment. He has to be convinced of the truth of the whole magical philosophy of life: what seems real is only illusion. Thus, while Calogero has the illusion of time passing, he yet, under Otto's influence, has faith that no time has passed: all this is but a dream transpiring in the moment before Marta's reappearance at Otto's performance.

The idea grows on Calogero. It is a game, which he is more and more determined to play out to the end. He is so eager to agree to the basic premise (time is not passing) that he tries to do without eating and excreting. Otto, who had practised conscious deceit from the start, takes pity on him and urges him to open the box and finish a losing game. Calogero, however, is determined to win. He will open the box only when his faith is complete. He is just reaching this point and is bracing himself to open the box, "one, two . . ." when Otto cries ". . . and three!"—Marta has returned, after four years. But it is a moment too soon. The box is still closed, and Calogero's faith still untested. He cannot accept Marta on these terms. He clings to the box, and does not open it.

When this story was first placed before an audience, in Rome last February, everyone cried "Pirandello!" Like the Sicilian master, Eduardo had insisted that illusions were needed because the truth was more than we could stand. Like Pirandello in *Il piacere dell'onestà* (*The Pleasure of Honesty*) and *Ma non è una cosa seria* (*But it isn't a serious matter*), Eduardo had shown an idea beginning as fiction, an escape from life, and later incorporated into life. There are even more specific resemblances to *Enrico IV*. At the beginning of each play a man retires from the bitter reality—of sexual rivalry into a deliberate unreality in which time is supposed to stand still (though its not doing so is in both cases indicated by the protagonist's greying hair). At the end of each play reality irrupts into the illusion in a way calculated to shatter it; but the result is the opposite; the illusion is accepted by the protagonist in perpetuity.

Whether Eduardo was influenced by Pirandello or was simply nourished from the same sources and interested in the same problems was not discussed. Worse still: the word "Pirandello," as such words will, prevented people from seeing things that would otherwise have been evident. For all the superficial "Pirandellism" of *La Grande Magia,* the play is really a much simpler, more commonsensical affair. Pirandello, if I am not mistaken, manufactures out of his despair a nihilistic relativism. The veiled lady at the end of *Così è (se vi pare)* is one person or another as you choose; in which proposition the law of contradiction itself (that a thing cannot both be and not be) is denied. In Eduardo, on the other hand, no such nonsense

is thrust upon the universe. If one man has an illusion, another sees it as such. The apparent magic in even his spookiest play *Questi Fantasmi* (*These Phantoms*) is all explained away as the chicanery of a servant or the secret generosity of a friend. So in *La Grande Magia,* Otto's "little magic" is rather brutally exposed from the beginning as mere charlatanism. The "big magic"—the magic not of the parlor but of life itself—is magic only honorifically. The word "magic" is a figure of speech. Illusions, mad ideas (we are given to understand), may be instrumental in a man's moral development. Thus Calogero's sin had been jealousy, lack of faith in a woman. Once he has entered upon the great moral game of life, he must not be deflected from it until he has ceased to be jealous, until he has found faith. Otto's assumption that it would be enough to produce Marta—as out of a hat—shows to what a degree his understanding is limited to the realm of the little magic. His actually producing her is the completest betrayal of the greater game. Now Calogero will never open the box: his faith is locked in it.

La Grande Magia, then, is not about the nature of reality, it is about faith in one's wife. Eduardo likes to use some big, much-discussed subject as a kind of come-hither. It turns out to be incidental. He may almost be said to have tried this once too often with *La Paura Numero Uno* where the big, much-discussed subject is right now so bothersome that, once mentioned, it is not easily shaken off. This subject—our "fear number one"—is the third world war. Eduardo deals so cleverly with it in his first act, and even his second, that the third, in which it is definitely pushed into the background, seemed pretty much of an anti-climax to the audience that gathered to see the play at the Venice Festival in July. We should have to be as free of "fear number one" as Eduardo wishes us to be to recognize all at once that the subject of his play is parenthood.

Eduardo shows us a father and a mother. Matteo Generoso, paterfamilias, is so possessed with fear of the third world war that all business on hand, and notably his daughter's wedding, keeps being postponed. The young people decide to put his soul at rest by faking a radio announcement that war has actually broken out. . . . The mother of the play is the bridegroom's mother, Luisa Conforto. She also is an obstacle in the young couple's way since she resists the loss of her son. She has lost his only brother already and his father. In the fanaticism of her maternal love she contrives to postpone the marriage for eleven days by walling her son up in a little room where she feeds him all his favorite dishes.

In the end the marriage is celebrated, and war has not broken out; the play is a comedy. What of the delusions and distortions in the minds of the two parents? The conclusion enforced by the action of the play is that the father's case, though "normal," is more deplorable because it disqualifies him from being a father. The mother's case, though a psychiatrist would take a stern view of it, is found excusable, a case of virtue driven into a corner. One recalls the conjurer's accurate description of Calogero in

La Grande Magia. "[He] is not mad. He is a man who knows he has been stricken and reaches after the absurdest things in order not to confess it even to himself." Calogero will continue his fight for faith if he has to "reach after the absurdest things" in the process. Luisa Conforto will continue to be a mother even if she too does the absurdest things in the process.

In calling Eduardo traditional, I had in mind, among other matters, that drama has so often and over so long a period been a defense of family piety. In Greek tragedy it is the desecration of this piety that horrifies us. In the comedy of Molière it is the desecration of this piety that we find ridiculous. Then in modern times there has been that enormous assault upon all our intimate relations which Balzac described through all the volumes of his great comedy and which Marx and Engels announced in their tragic rhapsody of a manifesto.

Italy has written its own sad chapter in this story. After the heroism of Garibaldi and his thousand, the indignity of the millions. The fascist era was but the lowest point of a steep descent, and whether the long climb up again has really got under way since 1945 seems doubtful. Abroad, people know about the brutalities of fascism, far more indeed than the citizens of fascist countries. What they know less about is something evident in every institution and every social group where fascism has secured a foothold—the corruption, the petty knavery, the bottomless indignity, the dishonor.

There is no politics in Eduardo but in play after play he has put his finger on the black moral spot. Perhaps *Le Voci di Dentro (The Voices from Within)*, famously written in 17 hours, is its most devastating diagnosis. A man accuses a whole family of mudering a friend of his. Later he realizes that he dreamt it all, perhaps not even dreamt it. The friend is alive. But the accuser is not mad. He had sound intuitions ("voices from within") and they crystallized into a single clear hallucination. Eduardo's main point is in the subsequent behavior of the family. They accept the charge because each thinks it quite possible that one of them *has* committed the murder. As their accuser cries:

> I accused you and you didn't rebel although you were all innocent. You thought it—possible—normal—you have written Murder in the list of daily events, you have put Crime in the family book of accounts. Respect, mutual respect, that puts us on good terms with ourselves, with our conscience . . . what shall we do to live, to look ourselves in the face?

In *Questi Fantasmi,* it is the petit bourgeois protagonist who has lost self-respect:

> If you knew how humiliating it is, and sad, for a man to have to hide his poverty and pretend to be playful with a joke and a laugh. . . . Honest work is painful and miserable . . . and not always to be found. . . . Without money we become fearful, shy, with a shyness that is embarrassing, bad. [To his rich rival:] With you

I don't feel envy, pride, superiority, deceit, egoism. Talking with you I feel near God, I feel little, tiny . . . I seem to be nothing. And I *like* destroying myself, seeming nothing . . . in this way I can free myself from the weight of my own being which oppresses me so.

In *Napoli Millionaria (Millionaire Naples)*, Eduardo shows how common folk are de-humanized, how a family is ruined and divided—mother from father—by blackmarketeering In *Natale in Casa Cupiello (Christmas with the Cupiellos)*, he portrays a father who lacks paternal maturity and we realize to what a large extent the childishness of the "little man" may contribute to catastrophe.

> Luca Cupiello, your father, was a big baby. He took the world for an enormous toy. When he saw it was a toy you couldn't play with as a child any more but only as a man . . . he couldn't make it.

The special relevance of Eduardo's defence of the pieties may now be clearer. They are the bedrock above which everything else, even sanity perhaps, has been shot away. The sane are only hypocritical parties to the general offence. Humanity has taken refuge in the crazy and infirm. Uncle Nicolo in *Le Voci di Dentro* has vowed himself to silence because he holds that mankind is deaf. From time to time he spits. Old Luisa Conforto in *La Paura Numero Uno* needs no convincing that war has broken out because she holds that it is in full swing already! Deprived of both her sons, she now has nothing much to call her own save her jams and conserves. How these can mean so much is perhaps explained by a longish quotation. The passage is worth exhibiting also because, however simple, it could be by no playwright but Eduardo.

MATTEO:

> Now, I swear, if twelve wars broke out one after the other, they'd make no impression on me. But you never believed in this "outbreak of war." You've been convinced all the time that we're at war! And I don't know what I'd do. . . .

LUISA:

> Don Mattè, you're a darling! I'm old now as you see . . . you are much younger than I am—but I assure you I wouldn't change my brain for yours!

MATTEO:

> Why not?

LUISA:

> Why, because you believe a thing when the radio says it. I mean: to you the radio is more important than your own thoughts. You want to convince me there isn't a war on while you yourself talk of it—as a "tragic problem that makes you sick of life itself": you complain of the chauffeur who forces you into selling your car so as to be rid of a nuisance, of the maid who doesn't take a liking to you and robs you, of your struggle with the tenants, of the tailor who drives you into the poor-

house, of the frauds, extortions, betrayals of friends. . . . Come here. (She goes towards the cupboard where the conserves are. Matteo follows her automatically.) Do *you* like jam?

MATTEO:

Yes. I'm not mad about it, but a little once in a while. . . .

LUISA:

(opening the cupboard doors and showing Matteo the little jars). These I made for you.

MATTEO:

And what exactitude! (Reading some of the labels:) Amarena, strawberry, apricot. How nice to keep all these things at home. (Fastening his attention on a jar of cherries preserved in spirits.) Oh, those! I'm crazy about them! In winter they're a real comfort. (Reading:) "Cherries in spirits."

LUISA:

I've taken to these jams. I love them. As if they were my children. When I'm alone and a longing for a bit of amarena comes over me, for example, I talk to it as to a living soul.—"How good you are. How tasty you are. *I* made you with my own hands. How happy I am you've turned out well."—And they answer—with their bit of sweetness. The only sweetness a poor woman like me can expect in life. And I understand . . . I understand why my good soul of a mother did the same and turned the house upside down if someone in the family helped themselves without asking her permission.

MATTEO:

Oh yes. Says she: "That's mine!"

LUISA:

Surely. But it's hard. The jam is really mine and nobody can take it away from me. The same with the flowers. You see this balcony. . . . They're all plants I made grow with my own hands. (Pointing to a plant:) That one, I don't know, I don't recall how many years I've had it. Just think, I was a young lady. Many's the move I've seen. Like that piece. (She points to the writing table.) It was my grandmother's, then my mother's . . . when we lived at Foria . . . then at Riviera . . . then near the Church of the Conception . . . I can't tell you how many different houses that table has lived in. (In a good-natured tone, thoughtful:) Not long ago your wife said: "Blessed be you that can take life so easy!"

Don Mattè, I never let my sons breathe. From the time they began to use their reason I'd interfere with any of their pleasures rather than lose their company even for a moment. If ever they came home a half hour later than they were expected, I was thinking of a disaster right away. I used to think out ways of keeping them in the house. No good, I couldn't curb them. And sometimes they openly let me know my presence annoyed them. They ran out. They went away. They found excuses, pretexts. They told me a pack of lies to get away, to leave me, to live their own life, which was to be no concern of mine. . . . Don Mattè, I shut Mariano up! You see now? With a wall of brick and cement . . . he couldn't get out! And if one of you had gone and reported it, wouldn't the authorities have shut me up in the madhouse? "Crazy!" "See her, she's crazy!" "You know what she's done? She shut her son up in a room and built a wall in front of the door!" "And why?"—Because I wanted to have him near me, because I didn't want to lose him! . . . You yourself, in the family circle, haven't you said almost these very things? (At this point she can't control her feelings. Her voice becomes thick. But a quick succession of sobs, at once repressed, puts her to rights.) Don Mattè, before God you must believe me. If what I say is a lie may I never see tomorrow's light I am not sorry for what I did. For fifteen days I felt him to be once more—my son. Like when I had him here. (With both hands open she strikes her stomach.) Don Mattè, take good note: here! (She repeats the gesture.) Like during the nine months of pregnancy when I found a way of being alone with him, lying on a couch with my hands like they are now, to talk to him. And he moved inside me and answered. As the jam answers me today. And I ate . . . I ate more than I wanted, so he'd be born strong and healthy . . . For fifteen days I slept peacefully—as I'd never managed to sleep since he came into the world. So many things to keep me busy, thoughts, responsibilities. . . . Ever since he started to walk. "If he falls. . . . If he hurts himself badly. . . ." And the vaccinations, the fevers, the illnesses. . . . And then the war. . . . You remember hearing the German's giving instructions over the radio? . . . "Those men who do not present themselves at German Headquarters will be punished with death". . . . "Parents hiding their sons will be shot at sight. . . ." For fifteen days he was my son again. Shut in! And in bed with my hands here (repeating the gesture) I went to sleep happy because I felt him inside me once more. . . ."

II

It is sometimes debated how far we need to know an author's background in order to judge his work. I should think we need to know it whenever we should otherwise be in danger of taking something as his personal contribution when it is a representative product of his time and place. Thus some of Eduardo's attitudes, as I have described them, may seem forced when we take them an assertion of his will, whereas as an expression of a social tradition we might let them pass. I have in mind the impression probably produced by the foregoing pages that what Eduardo principally does in a play is to put his own special ideas across—the impression in short that he writes laborious *drames à thèse*.

The extreme individualism of Matteo's final attitude to war—"if twelve wars broke out one after the other they'd make no impression on me"—may be open to criticism but, in context, is an expression of a traditional group feeling and not a pet idea of the author's. It belongs to Naples where the State is regarded as an enemy—and whose regionalism the fascist State did in fact try to suppress. To tell people to forget the newspapers and get on with their private lives, valid or not as a piece of advice to us all, has somewhat different meaning in a city which for so long has had to consider how to survive under different masters and amid recurrent conflagrations. Eduardo is true to this situation when he shows people, such as Luisa, achieving dignity in their apartness. When he longs for dignity, moreover, he is not an aristocrat or would-be aristocrat bemoaning the inundation of aristocratic culture by plebeian hordes. On the contrary it is the dignity of the plebs he is championing, the *urbanità* of the poor who throng the alleys and docksides of Naples while the aristocrats and their wars come and go.

Not that Eduardo sees the life of "the other half" as uniformly dignified. The lower depths of Naples form as fantastic a society of adventurers and desperadoes as can well be imagined. Living by the skin of their teeth, a dreary past behind and a blank future ahead, they accept the present with peculiar vehemence. Familiar with death, they do not take life too seriously. They are willing to see it as a joke, a paradox, a fantasy, a show, a game. As absurd, the existentialists would say. There is something existentialist, in one of the popular meanings of the word, about *La Grande Magia*: the world is lawless, ethics are at best improvised, yet the imperative remains to improvize them. Perhaps it was occupation by the Germans that precipitated the anguish of the French writers and of this Italian. To Eduardo's credit it must be said that he gives also the sense of emerging from under the incubus and looking about him. A recurrent character in his plays is coming to be the man in midpassage through life, tortured, perplexed, deflected from normal paths, but undefeated, questing. But Eduardo has never stuck in the quagmire of "Teutonic" lugubriousness. Here again plebeian Naples came to his aid. There is a philosophy of the absurd, after all, in plebeian humor in general: your life is hopeless but you laugh, you are cheerful, and morally positive, against all reason. Thus, while *La Grande Magia* is one of Eduardo's most somber pieces, it is also his most ambitious projection of the idea that life is a game. And it is when we feel that fairy-tale quality of the story that we get it right—when, that is to say, we talk less of *pirandellismo* and more of Naples.

Naples is the reservoir on which, consciously and unconsciously, Eduardo draws. Not only the city as a whole but the Neapolitan theatre in particular. It is a popular as against an art theatre. This means, to begin with, that it is a dialect theatre and not an "Italian" one. It uses a popularly spoken language and not an official, national, bourgeois language—in this respect resembling Synge and O'Casey rather than Pinero and Galsworthy. The lack of a national theatrical repertoire in Italy may be deplorable but the quality of the defect is—the regional repertoire.

The next most salient feature of Neapolitan popular theatre as I have seen it is the style of acting. In Paris today you hear much about *commedia dell'arte*. What they show you is Jean-Louis Barrault and the Piccolo Teatro di Milano (the latter being more the rage in Paris than in Milan).

These things are very fine but they are art theatre, and the *commedia dell'arte* was nothing if not popular theatre. You would find a much more authentic version of its famous artificial clowning in the Neapolitan comedian Totô. And for another side of the tradition—not famous at all unfortunately—you must go to Eduardo.

It is no slur on his playwriting to say that he is first and foremost an actor, perhaps the finest actor in Italy today, the son of a fine actor, the brother of a fine actor and an even finer actress. For anyone who comes to Italy with normal preconceptions, for anyone who has seen any of the great Italian stars of recent times or who today catches the last echo of D'Annunzio's generation in the voice of the aged Ruggeri, Eduardo on the stage is an astonishment. For five minutes or so he may be a complete letdown. This is not acting at all, we cry, above all it is not Italian acting! Voice and body are so quiet. Pianissimo. No glamor, no effusion of brilliance. No attempt to lift the role off the ground by oratory and stylization, no attempt to thrust it at us by force of personality. Not even the sustained mesmerism of big Ibsen performances. Rather, a series of statements, vocal and corporeal. When the feeling of anti-climax has passed we realize that these statements are beautiful in themselves—beautiful in their clean economy, their precise rightness—and beautiful in relation to each other and to the whole: there are differentiations, sharp or shifting, between one speech and the next: there is a carefully gauged relationship between beginning, middle, and end.

My point here is not so much to praise Eduardo as to observe that here is an actor more likely—for demonstrable historical and geographic reasons—to be the heir of *commedia dell'arte* than any other important performer now living and that his style is distinctly different from anything one expected. It is a realistic style. It makes few large departures from life. No oratory, no stylization. Both in speech and in gesture, rhythm, accent, and tempo are an imitation of life. The "art" consists in the skill of the imitation, the careful registering of detail and nuance, and a considered underlining of the effects—the outline is firmer, the shape more sure. The assumption is that there is more drama in real speech and gesture—for these are arts and not raw material like a sculptor's clay—than in invented speech and gesture. That this realism is not just Eduardo's personal style or due—God save the mark!—to the influence of Stanislavsky you may prove by visiting the grubby popular theatres of Naples, notably the Apollo and the Margherita, any day of the week.

One of the persistent heresies about *commedia dell'arte,* often as Italian scholars denounce it as such, is the idea that the actors made up their lines as they went along. The nearest they ever got to this is probably that they sometimes wrote their lines, the script being the fruit of a collaboration between various members of the cast. At any rate Eduardo de Filippo began his career as an actor doing this sort of writing. From reports I gather the impression that the plays he acted in must have been rather like Chaplin shorts. There would often be several to an evening, and they would represent incidents in the life of the little man, the *povero diavolo*. A play like *La Grande Magia* is of course as far from a one-act farce or melodrama in a popular Neapolitan theatre as *Monsieur Verdoux* is from a Keystone Comedy. In each case, however, the later work is made up to a surprising extent of elements from the earlier. And it is these elements which save both film and play from polemical aridity, which give them a tang and an identity, which make them dramatic art.

They would not do so if they operated as mere comic relief or melodramatic seasoning; their function is to lend definition to the author's subject. Thus in *La Grande Magia,* the idea of life as a game, the world as a show, is given body and form by, among other things, the brilliant theatre of Otto's conjuring, in which we get a back-stage glimpse of all the mechanism of magic. To be told, as my reader has been, that Otto had to convince Calogero of the reality of magic is very little compared to actually seeing Otto play his phonograph record of applause and persuade Calogero it is the sea. To be told, as my reader has been, that Matteo in *La Paura Numero Uno* is tricked into believing war has broken out is very little compared to actually seeing the enactment of the ruse with the microphone and the comic sequences that follow. Matteo talks at cross-purposes with the other tenants: he thinks they are talking about the war, they think he is talking about the house. Another sequence ends with Matteo's mistaking a multinational group of pilgrims for an invading army. These two sequences lead up to a climax of laughable absurdity at the conclusion of acts one and two respectively.

For, although Eduardo's plays are chock full of amusing and imaginative details—minor characters, bits of business, meditations as of an unsophisticated Giraudoux—they have a solid over-all structure, usually in three clearly marked phases or acts. If the sequences within the acts often derive from popular farce, the act-structure is even more often that of popular melodrama. Eduardo likes to bring the curtain down, especially the curtain of act two, on a terrific moment—which means "at the psychological moment," a moment when two lines of narrative suddenly intersect by amazing coincidence. Thus in *Natale in Casa Cupiello,* the ugly rivalry of husband and lover reaches boiling point just as Luca Cupiello's idyll, the adoration of the magi, comes to actual performance—a big curtain for act two! In *La Grande Magia,* it is the denouement in act three where the arm of coincidence is longest and most active: it just happens that Marta, absent for four years, reappears one second before Calogero is to open the box. Eduardo is saying not only "such is the wonder of fairy land" but also "such is the perverseness of reality." He has not surrendered to melodrama; he has exploited it. For him it is not a jazzing-up of otherwise inert and tiresome elements. It is a legitimate accentuation of the fantastic character of life.

This purposeful manipulation of fable is nowhere more striking than in Eduardo's most popular play, *Filumena*

Marturano. Since this play is also one of his most realistic works, the reader may be interested to see in more detail how the apparently curious mixture of realism and its opposite actually works out. Since moreover the play is Eduardo's most powerful tribute to mother love, a note on it may serve to bind together the first and second parts of this essay and leave us with a rounded if not complete impression of Eduardo's playwriting.

The story is the unprepossessing one of the man who makes an honest woman of a prostitute. What stands out in Eduardo's play is the prostitute herself, a heroic plebeian, a tigress of a mother. The portrait derives half its life from the language—which, in translation, can scarcely be shown. But, as already intimated, the mode of the narrative is a contributory factor.

Filumena comes from the lower depths of Naples. She is rescued from poverty by a prolonged liaison with a rich man, Domenico Soriano. When they are both getting along in years, and he wants to marry a younger, more beautiful, and more respectable girl, Filumena pretends to be dying and arranges a death-bed marriage. The ceremony over, she jumps lightheartedly out of bed, and Domenico realizes he has been had. It is at this point that Eduardo raises the curtain on his first act! The stormy exposition is followed by a revelation. Filumena has not been acting selfishly. Unknown to Domenico she has three grown-up sons: they are now legitimized!

The first act ends with Domenico rushing off for a lawyer to rescind a marriage held under false pretences. In the second, it seems that he will have his way, and Filumena, crushed for the moment, accepts the hospitality of her son Michele. As a parting shot, however, she tells Don Domenico that he is the father of one of the three sons. Another melodramatic revelation! Further: with a secrecy at once melodramatic and realistic, she will not tell him which one, because she wants no discrimination against the other two. End of the second act.

Act three is a happy epilogue. In the time between the acts, Domenico has come around. The old marriage has been rescinded, but a new one is now being celebrated. He gladly accepts Filumena as wife and all three young men as sons. "I am 52, you are 48. We are two mature souls in duty bound to understand what they are about—ruthlessly and to the depths. We have to face it. And assume full responsibility."

This sententiousness is naive but the language, sunny and bland in the original, implies some unworried awareness of the fact. There is an irony about this happy ending (as there is about many others). What stays with us is the conclusion arrived at and, far more, the sense of danger and

Ferdinando D. Maurino (essay date February 1961)

SOURCE: Maurino, Ferdinando D. "The Drama of de Filippo." *Modern Drama* 3, no. 4 (February 1961): 348-56.

[*In the following essay, Maurino presents an overview of de Filippo's plays, focusing on their Neapolitan themes.*]

At the end of World War II the plays of Eduardo De Filippo, a Neapolitan writer, began to attract not only the audiences and readers in Italy but also those abroad. Eric Bentley[1] and Lander MacClintock[2] wrote briefly on him; and a few years ago Thornton Wilder[3] stated that De Filippo was his favorite contemporary dramatic author.

Previously De Filippo had been known mainly as a comic actor whose plays were considered as vehicles for his acting. In fact, when in 1955 *Theatre Arts* devoted an issue to the Italian theater, he was treated chiefly as an actor.[4] This is, however, no longer the case. After reading and studying his drama, one may well believe that a new voice and a great playwright has arisen. The *maschera* of a new Pulcinella has fallen, and the humor has turned to grave considerations of the problems of life, not only in Naples but also in the universe. As Pirandello forsook his Sicilian characterisics in favor of universal concepts, and as Di Giacomo left the Neapolitan environment for a wider world,[5] so De Filippo progressed from presentations of local Neapolitan foibles to profound reflections on man's problems.

Like many contemporary writers, he has at times dealt with realistic topics of Naples during the occupation, and he has injected into his work a pathos seldom felt in other contemporary dramatic works. One thinks principally of his *Napoli milionaria* (*Naples Full of Millions*), and of some of the poetry from his *Il paese di Pulcinella* (*The Land of Pulcinella*). Through these works he made his contribution to post-war realism with a bitter, at times sarcastic, and always pathetic, humor. But what begins as realism becomes towards the end of the play a double reality, an illusion, or an untruth. Thus, a father who inveighs against the disrespectful behavior of today's youths, including his own son, suddenly loses his power of speech; but he only simulates his loss as a hopeless protest against modern society.[6] Unlike the realism of Moravia, Vittorini, Marotta, Levi, Pavese, Pratolini, and other contemporary Italian authors known in America, De Filippo's realism is like that of Pirandello's: an excuse to evade realism itself. In fact, the truer De Filippo, both by natural propensity and by training, has always leaned toward the abstract, the illusional, and the metaphysical, as is evident from his short plays before World War II when his mind was being formed in the school of Pirandello in whose troupe he was an actor, and from his recent works in which he has attained a far greater artistic skill.

This revival of Pirandellian influence on the Italian stage is duplicated in other countries, especially in France where the shadow of that modern master can be discerned to the extent that Lerminier recently wrote, "Pirandello est présent partout."[7] His influence has been felt by such writers as Salacrou, Neveux, and even Camus. Among the Spaniards, at least two have imitated him: Alejandro Casona and Victor Iriarte.[8]

Italian critics have, of course, reminded De Filippo of that influence—an influence the Neapolitan playwright is reluctant to admit.[9] When, in the summer of 1958, I told him that I saw Pirandellian traces in certain abstract, fantastic, and illusive situations, he seemed slightly annoyed. With a typical Neapolitan gesture of his hand, he called to my attention that such interpretations of the subjectivity of reality "are as old as Plato." Thus, he did not deny the similarity of themes or situations, but he denied that he imitates Pirandello. His is the same argument given by Casona[10] when Casona was criticized for lack of originality in his plots and style. De Filippo is sincere and, moreover, correct in his assertion, as is Casona; otherwise we would have to accuse Pirandello, too, of having somewhat imitated writers like Sophocles, Cervantes, Calderón, and perhaps (although this may be difficult to see at first) the imaginative Ariosto. With such thoughts in mind I told the affable but pensive De Filippo that I considered that influence and similarity to be principally due to a natural affinity rather than a conscious imitation. He did not answer me, but was visibly pleased.

This Neapolitan writer has, then, treated subjects both of the realistic school and of the school of the subconscious. Realism in his case means what is commonly known to be Neapolitan in language and content. Some critics have even seen in him the traditional Neapolitan school; unfortunately, some of his clichés with farcical expressions and situations are indeed typical of dialectal *macchiette* and literature, but he is not the successor of Petito, the last of Pulcinellas.[11] In De Filippo's *Filumena Marturano*, Filumena is a prostitute who becomes a real woman because she also becomes a mother. But she is not the fragile Assunta Spina of Di Giacomo, nor an echo of other Neapolitan writers. If she is realistic, she is a realistic heroine in the sense of the French naturalistic or the Italian veristic school. Yet some writers and producers have interpreted the play as mirroring Neapolitan life.[12] Without denying the verity of some scenes of local color, one can assert that there is, however, little that is truly traditional or typically Neapolitan in this piece.

The play has been considered to be his masterpiece to date and a well-nigh perfect work. However, *Questi fantasmi, Napoli milionaria,* and *La grande magia* exhibit deeper sadness, emotion, and despair respectively. Filumena lacks true passion; she has no tragic or suffering moments. She has experienced hunger, humiliation, and prostitution, but it was all long before the play begins. Now she is bent on avenging her former life. She is entitled to such a revenge, but that fact itself and the fact that she is a strong-minded person, sure of the final outcome, tends to reduce the dramatic action of the play. Weak Amalia of *Napoli milionaria* is a more tragic, and, consequently, a more dramatic character. Only in Filumena's long speeches,[13] resembling soliloquies because she is speaking mainly to herself as she recalls her youth and her later life, does one find a deep and human compassion which truly becomes art despite the sensational scene of the first act. This scene of simulated agony is similar to Gennaro's "death" in *Napoli milionaria,* and both are reminiscent of some traditional, farcical plays and *macchiette*. These scenes detract from De Filippo's art.

In *Filumena Marturano* one sees also, but only to a minor extent, the elusive, the unexpected, the unreal: Filumena's feigned moribund state just mentioned and her disclosure, after many years, that she is the mother of three children and that one of them is the son of Domenico, her lover and later her husband. Which one of the children is the husband's own? The mother refuses to let Domenico know, and the result is that if he is to be sure that he cherishes his own child he must cherish them all. But two out of three times he will be mistaken.

The originality of the plot as a whole must be recognized at this point as equaling the fertile imagination found in *Questi fantasmi* and *Napoli milionaria* which are De Filippo's most original plays.[14]

A true Neapolitan element in De Filippo of course exists, but it does not follow the traditional pattern; it is the every day happenings that he sees in his Naples during and after the war and it bears the unique stamp of the author. *Napoli milionaria* is a sarcastic title for a tragic plot which ends bitterly. Gennaro has become lost during a bombing raid by American planes and has wandered for a year. When he returns home he discovers that his wife has been unfaithful, his daughter is pregnant, and his son a thief; and all enriched through the black market. Gennaro, realizing that war destroys men and women even after the last shot has been fired, pitifully tells his repentant wife that the war is to blame for everything. Then he forgives all and offers his wife a cup of coffee. What a price to pay for the millions of *lire* his family had acquired during his absence! Hence, the bitter title: *Naples Full of Millions*. Gennaro, the real victim, forgives; and herein lies the tragedy, because war remains forever victorious, and humanity remains defeated and in a state of impotent resignation for unexpiated sins.

Many recent Italian writers have dealt remarkably well with war topics, including Moravia in his latest *La Ciociara* (*Two Women*); but *Napoli milionaria* possibly remains the post-war human epic of Italian literature: it is unsurpassed for its poignant and striking pathos which creates an unparalleled mood of powerlessness and human pity as exemplified by the last scene. It must have made many Neapolitans and non-Neapolitans alike weep silently with guilty eyes amidst the many "ruins" of war.

It can be seen that we encounter here a dramatist who for once is devoid of paradoxical, or neurasthenic situations. His Naples is a pitiful city, a Naples which was defeated twice, once by the enemy and once by her own people. Here the Neapolitan playwright shows his love for his city, not with a hyperbolic, melodious Neapolitan song but with ironic and subdued bitterness. He has noticed everything and has wept in the penumbra of a Naples that was: the *Napoli nobilissima,* the Siren of the Tyrrhenian Sea, the Capital of the Kingdom of the Two Sicilies, the Capital of the World of Songs, and the Naples Full of Millions.[15]

The greater part of De Filippo's theater is given, as has been stated, to mental and abstract themes reminiscent of Pirandello but blended with the author's unmistakable, personal style and more genuine humor. The works in which the author ventures deepest into the abyss of the subconscious and the metaphysical are the plays, *Questi fantasmi* (*These Ghosts*), *La grande magia* (*The Magic Performance*), *Le voci di dentro* (*The Voices from Within*), and the poem *Vincenzo De Pretore.* All have been written since the end of the war but the war is conspicuously absent.

In *La grande magia* Calogero finds refuge in an illusion, as it were, in the emergence of his subconscious. A magician makes his wife disappear, and in front of all the people watching the performance he gives the husband a little box which he is told contains his wife. His wife aided by the magician during the act has run away with her lover. Calogero believes or forces himself to believe that she is in that box which, however, he does not dare to open. The alternative to this belief or faith is to realize the truth and to react brutally as did Othello and Don Gutierre.[16] One may perish in the anguish that reality brings; for reality must be confronted or changed. Othello, for example, met it; Calogero following the traces of Enrico IV changes it. This is a modern solution.

Actually, illusion and reality do not contradict each other as is commonly believed; rather, they fuse to form that dual reality which saves some people from utter destruction. That is why the box is not really empty: it contains a reality, a faith. If the little box does not, nor could not, contain Calogero's wife, nevertheless it holds his firm hope and a real illusion which destroys the hard facts of life. Like Ponza in *Cosi' e'* (*se vi pare*), and like Enrico in *Enrico IV*, Calogero is not insane; he pretends, as one must pretend and at the same time believe. That box, then, has taken the place of someone, something in his pathological and painful state of mind, and is his *summa ratio* for forcibly believing.

Don Quijote also believed in an illusion, but when it ceased to be a fantasy and he realized the truth, he died. Enrico IV also realizes at a certain moment his true situation, but unlike Don Quijote he chooses to go back to that variable reality as a lasting though painful escape. Calogero likewise remains steadfast in his illusion as did Enrico IV and also Ponza. With Pirandello and De Filippo, reality venishes into simulation.

The play takes on quite often classical and universal overtones. In it the world of the characters encompasses the illimitable cosmos of the mind, and the author soars on the wings of metaphysics to a battleground where the mind and the heart conflict. The mind must believe what is not true because it fears that otherwise reality will break the heart. If the heart knows, it feels . . . and dies. Therefore, the mind attempts to deceive the heart which pretends to believe. Naturally, it merely pretends because, as the proverb says, and as the Neapolitans know it most particularly, *the heart is never mistaken and cannot be deceived* (*Il cuore non si inganna mai*). The mind, on the other hand, is finally convinced by its own illusion, and is convinced that the heart does not know. Only by following such a course can the mind save itself from total disintegration. The heart and the mind form then a state of semi-consciousness in which the heart secretly and softly weeps while the bombastic mind pitifully boasts.

Thus Calogero in the last scene refuses to recognize his returning, wayward wife; and when she openly admits her betrayal so that he can leave his "mad illusion," he exclaims: "What have you done?" betraying his "madness" if only for a second. But it is exactly here that we encounter the art which makes the play also human and heartfelt, not mental and evanescent. There is veiled in the background a heart pulsating with reality that makes illusion truly painful because the illusion is based on something true: it is sensitive to a subconscious reality that hurts. The mind becomes a true actor on the stage while the human soul or heart remains backstage. Therefore, the illusion is sincere but not totally beguiling; and pain and sorrow remain somewhat distant and ecstatic as if in a trance, yet ever present in that very unreality. This is De Filippo's art.

La grande magia, the play that reflects Pirandellian influence more than any other of De Filippo's works, also shows the defects found in Pirandello. There is artificiality in some of the situations and in the style itself. The dialogue is forced and lacks spontaneity, but the play remains an impressive work nonetheless.

I consider *Questi fantasmi* De Filippo's best play and am supported in this conclusion by the author himself. When I asked him point blank which play he considered his greatest work, I had expected some hesitation. But Eduardo, as he is affectionately called in Italy, promptly answered, *"Questi fantasmi."*[17]

In this pathetic and, at times, humorous play we have the naïve situation of a man who believes in ghosts. It seems like a medieval legend, but it takes place today in Naples. Like Calogero, Pasquale of *Questi fantasmi* saves himself from actual tragedy because he can think that his wife's lover is a ghost who haunts his house and benevolently leaves him money. The height of the irony occurs when Pasquale welcomes the ghost into his home and when he accepts the ghost's money in order to be able to buy little things for his wife, Maria, whom he loves.

Pasquale is not as dramatic a personality as Calogero armed with a little, "empty" box is; he is a man who is happy in his own fashion because he is able to delude himself. Neither is he the epic Gennaro who painfully but resignedly accepts dishonor. Pasquale will never know the truth, and his young wife thinking that he ignores her lover for the sake of money considers him to be a coward and detests him all the more.[18] *We* know the truth and *it is we* who suffer. Thus, once again we have a prismatic reality; for if Pasquale does not attain to a metaphysical make-believe, he nevertheless believes, like Calogero, in something that is not. He, too, is surrounded by a world of

fiction, or perhaps even of fairytale. In this sense De Filippo solves the problems posed by reality in an innocent and novel way: he enables Pasquale to believe in ghosts. This is an original device totally free of Pirandello's artistry.

Pirandellian influence is discernible only in the scene where Armida, the abandoned wife of Maria's lover, appears with her children who, having been badly taken care of, truly resemble ghosts. Here it is apparent that the source for this scene is *Six Characters in Search of an Author;* and the language used lends definite credence to this opinion. The scene itself, however, has a different significance with a tenderness and grief not found in the play of the Sicilian writer. The poor and unfortunate Armida is in a nervous frenzy and one of her children has a terrible, ugly tic which his neurotic mother cannot bear. Is any one of them to blame? Interrupting her neurasthenic speech, the mother orders the child to stop, but the child cannot and repeats the automatic action. The mother gives the child a resounding slap in the face. The child staggers . . . and we with him.

Pasquale is a major creation whose soul is like that of a child. When he talks to his wife he is convinced that what he does is right, and that "he knows his business." These words acquire a different meaning in the poisoned mind of Maria. The result is a double talk that hurts the reader who knows the truth while she continues to scorn her husband. Pasquale, too, becomes epic and classical like Gennaro and Calogero but in a different sense. He does not even suspect that he might be a hero; he is indeed not that kind of protagonist. He is a person who defies time and does not grow old. He is a poet with an innocent, pure imagination whom Vico would have appreciated. In this drama the double side of reality has taken a holiday (except for the reader).

Finally, in the play none of the characters knows the truth, except towards the very end when the "ghost" alone realizes what has happened and leaves forever. Because of this situation we have a different type of tragic play. Pasquale remains a satisfied, rather happy person. He even hopes the "ghost" will come back at some other time to bring him more money. Maria is not repentant or grief-stricken like Amalia because she continues to believe her husband is a coward; consequently, she still feels she is justified in her betrayal. Thus, the truly tragic element does not exist for the characters: not for a cynical Maria, not for an ignorant Pasquale. Yet the tragedy of the drama does exist; it exists among the spectators in the theater or within the readers in their own rooms. The author has placed all of us in the play, but after the last curtain falls—a most disturbing and poignant role. But we know the truth; and it is not easy for us to pretend, nor can we believe in spirits. Tragedy, then, is transferred to the spectator or to the reader as Pasquale happily ends the play pocketing the ghost's money. Then the playwright himself seems to appear on the stage or in our room with an ambiguous smile to tell us: "Choose now: Calogero or Gennaro?"

Once again then, this is not the characterisic Naples of Viviani, F. Russo, Bovio, Serao, or even of Di Giacomo or Bracco.[19] It is not the veristic Naples of the *camorristi* (gangsters), or the lyrical city of the famous "'O sole mio." This is an intellectual, fantastic Naples with no local color. It is a city steeped now in universal, tragic, and human concepts; a Naples with artistic, dramatic qualities that joins the new Neapolitan world of Salvatore Di Giacomo with its highly poetical horizon.

De Filippo realizes all this when he states in his poetry[20] that what he writes is not comical—an adjective stamped on things Neapolitan since the *gliommeri*[21] and the *farse cavaiole* of the late Renaissance period. Indeed, with the first poem in **Il paese di Pulcinella** he introduces his reader to his poetry sullenly remarking that people have not understood him. People laugh when they meet him remembering his "funny" plays; but he asks, "Is it a laughing matter when I portray comical situations arising from everyday life?" Then answering his own question: "I don't think so." In another poem the poet again takes his reader to task, counseling him not to look at the calendar to tell one's age. Regardless of what the calendar says, life lasts but one year; after that year all that remains is superfluous. "And suddenly it is night" (*Ed e' subito sera*), as Quasimodo says.

De Filippo's Neapolitan language reflects the mood or tone of the content or plot. It is the true dialect when Naples and its people are the protagonists, becoming soft, mellow, and humorous; it becomes Italian or very close to it when the subject matter calls for a loftier expression, as in the plays dealing with unreality. It is not Olympian or classical as in Pirandello, but warmer and mellower. Very often, it is a fresh, natural, and melodious Italian with Neapolitan constructions and nuances. When I asked De Filippo why he so often employed standard Italian rather than dialect he replied that because of the radio, the movies, and television the Neapolitans are increasingly speaking the standard language. But can it be that the author is conscious of his themes and motives and wants to be sure he will reach the whole Italian people at a higher level?

Thus, De Filippo has left his beautiful Naples which he nevertheless truly loves; his dramatic art involves him now in deeper, wider problems in the realm of the mind and conscience. He is concerned with the problems which have occupied the minds and the hearts of great dramatists who have tried to portray the agonizing souls of characters searching for a solution to alleviate their sorrows— Sophocles was concerned with the agony of immovable Fate; Shakespeare with the grief of man or kings. The solution at times is a world of illusion as in Cervantes who created a poetical mirage as an escape; as in Calderón de la Barca who fused life with dream, or as in Pirandello who interpreted life with a bitter compassion, so painful that it must flee to the realm of the intellect. Man has often felt the vacuum that stark reality produces, and through such writers as the foregoing he has attempted to penetrate the mystery of the mind and of the heart. Such an attempt can fuse, not confuse, dream with reality.

Eduardo De Filippo has joined in his own manner this lofty company, and he is still writing.

Notes

1. *In Search of Theatre* (New York, 1953), pp. 281-95.

2. *The Age of Pirandello* (Bloomington, 1951), pp. 124-27.

3. In *College English,* Vol. XVII (Nov., 1955), 119. See moreover same (Dec., 1955), 164, Wilder's statement concerning the difficulty of translating De Filippo.

4. (May, 1955).

5. See my *S. Di Giacomo and Neapolitan Dialectal Literature* (New York, 1951), p. 133 ff.

6. *Mia famiglia* (1955) which was praised by Vito Pandolfi, "Un umorismo doloroso," in *Sipario* (March, 1956), 3.

7. *Pensée française* (March, 1958), 59-61.

8. See A. Valbuena Prat, *Historia de la literatura española,* 4th Edition (Barcelona, 1953), Vol. III, p. 803.

9. See especially Corrado Alvaro, "Eduardo" in *Sipario* (March, 1956), 2; and Bentley, *In Search of Theatre,* p. 288. De Filippo told me personally that he agreed with Bentley's interpretation that such an influence "was simply nourished from the same sources, and interested in the same problems. . . ."

10. From his "Nota preliminar" in *La barca sin pescador* (Buenos Aires, 1951), p. 9. On this same topic see also Anatole France (*La Vie littéraire*), and more recently Giraudoux on the plot of his *Amphitryon.*

11. For the background of this tradition see MacClintock, *The Contemporary Drama of Italy* (Boston, 1920), pp. 201-05; for a very recent critical comment on the whole Neapolitan theater tradition in De Filippo, see Federico Frascani, *La Napoli amara di Eduardo De Filippo* (Firenze, 1958), pp. 13, 22-23, and *passim.* As this study goes to press two new books on De Filippo have appeared in 1959 and 1960 respectively: Gennaro Magliulo's, and G. B. De Sanctis'. This latest information comes from a well-known scholar: Joseph G. Fucilla.

12. This play has been given all over Europe including Russia, and in South America; it was also given in New York City on October 26, 1956, at Lyceum Theater under the title *The Best House in Naples* and ended in a complete fiasco after a little more than a week. The actors spoke English with a strong foreign accent and they could not be understood; the translation by F. Hugh Herbert was really a free adaptation. Notice the title; the connection is obscure. For reviews and criticism: *New Yorker,* Nov. 3, 1956, 73-4; *Theatre Arts,* Jan., 1957, 20. For De Filippo's own comment see again Frascani, p. 130. The author,

moreover, told me in Naples that Herbert's version had nothing of his own work; he approved it through a misunderstanding.

13. Those found toward the end of Act I and Act II.

14. As far as I know, no due credit has been given the author for this originality.

15. This is not the Naples of Neapolitan "popular tradition" to which Bentley, Frascani, and Pandolfi (*Il dramma* [May, 1948], 8) refer, which in the end becomes literary tradition. These critics perhaps confuse the actor and his Neapolitan mime with the playwright and his genius. This is a new, contemporary Naples.

16. See *El médico de su honra* by Calderón, and notice the similarity of its plot with *Othello*.

17. Silvio D'Amico had already highly praised both De Filippo and this particular play, and MacClintock (*The Age . . .* p. 124) reports that that foremost drama critic considered this play the best in Italy since 1920.

18. It is to be noted that Pasquale is not Ciampa of Pirandello's *Il berretto a sonagli* who rebels against his wife's infidelity only when he knows that others too have learned of her conduct. A touch of this behavior can be found elsewhere in De Filippo: in Libero of *Le bugie con le gambe lunghe* when Graziella suggests that they get married (Act I).

19. For these writers see F. Flora, "Poeti napoletani," in *Pegaso* (Dec., 1929), 339-49; A. Tilgher, *La poesia dialettale napoletana* (Roma, 1920); or Maurino, pp. 157-72.

20. See his *Il paese di Pulcinella* (Naples, 1951). For a rapid, critical view of Neopolitan poets since World War II, including De Filippo's poetry, see my article, "Neapolitan Poetry," in *Books Abroad* (Fall, 1955).

21. Even the great Sannazaro wrote *gliommeri* in the Neapolitan dialect.

Mimi D'Aponte (essay date December 1973)

SOURCE: D'Aponte, Mimi. "Encounters with Eduardo de Filippo." *Modern Drama* 16 (December 1973): 347-53.

[*In the following essay, D'Aponte recounts discussions she has had with de Filippo.*]

JANUARY 4, 10:00 P.M. TEATRO ELISEO, ROME

"People do become monuments." Eduardo De Filippo is sitting alone in his dressing room, smoking. I come in without an introduction (having made my way backstage between Acts 2 and 3 of *Il Monumento* by looking stranded and murmuring something about an American study of Neapolitan theatre), and he immediately gets up

and shakes my hand. He invites me to sit down, returns to his chair, and continues smoking. I explain my real wishes in nervous Italian (may I speak with him about his work when he returns to Naples in the spring?) and his answer is honest and to the point: "I won't remember your name. Tell my secretary you spoke with me in Rome." I compliment him on the first two acts of his new play. De Filippo is dedicated to *Il Monumento*'s philosophy,[1] and words begin to pour out of him as he launches into a discussion of Ascanio Penna's character—his character.[2] He speaks of Penna's entombment, both physically and psychologically, within his ideals. We sense someone standing at the door, and turn together to see my husband who has come to learn if I have found Eduardo. De Filippo greets him as warmly and openly as he had me, and picks up his thread of thought regarding the play. "People do become monuments because . . ." The stage manager knocks and calls out, "It is time, *Maestro,*" and the philosopher turns actor and is ready for his cue. He thanks us for coming and urges me to call him in Naples. He is off.

We have not learned why people become monuments, but we have learned something of the energy and intensity and immediacy of De Filippo. Eduardo is old if one counts by years (born May 14, 1900),[3] but it is difficult to think of age in his presence. The gaunt face and body are set in motion by strong and quick movements which suggest youth. His immediate and open friendliness have escaped that aging which comes of "being someone" for too long. His passionate interest in discussing the philosophy which motivates his character reveals a mind continually searching, re-examining, building. Notions suggested by other people about Eduardo—"he is remote," "he has become a recluse"—during my three-month stay in Italy fall by the wayside. I will see him in Naples in March. . . .

MARCH 16, 11:00 A.M. HOTEL ROYAL, NAPLES

Signora Quarantotto is Eduardo's secretary. She is charming, attractive, and perfectly bilingual. "Eduardo will be down in several minutes; he has been working this morning." I begin to ask her opinion of some questions I have prepared, but almost immediately *Il maestro* appears and takes over. And, happily, organized questions are forgotten as his words begin to flow again.

De Filippo is a writer during the summer, an actor-director during the rest of the year. As writer he must work early in the morning; as actor and director he can function only in the late afternoon. His approach to directing calls for intense preparation (a startling contrast to the seemingly improvised results): he will rehearse his actors in a new play around a table continuously until lines are learned, then set them on stage and provide gestures and movements to fit their words. After twenty to thirty rehearsals the play will be ready for performance. In his writing, whatever preparation takes place is mental. If, as he is writing, he cannot envision the staging easily, he simply stops and ponders the problem until it has smoothed itself out. He uses no notes, and although he may have stored the conception and plot of a play in his head for ten years, he will begin to write it only when the right moment comes; that is, when he has found the right actors for his imagined characters. Two examples. He has revived his interest in a play thought out years ago. He had planned to use his sister, Titania, in the lead role, but she became ill. He is about to begin writing it now because he has finally found the right actress for this part. And he wants to write another play about love again because he has found the right actors for the lovers' parts.

His approach as actor? He mentions working out a characterization before a mirror. He refers to his essay written for *Actors on Acting* "at Toby Cole's repeated request,"[4] in which he states that an actor's art evolves continually, and that the real study of that art begins upon contact with an audience.[5] He speaks of knowing one's character so thoroughly that this knowledge may often be reflected in ways unknown to the actor himself. And he remembers that when asked by a young actor many years ago how he developed his characterizations, he had to answer that he did not know.

He does know, however, and most clearly, how his actors are trained (perhaps "planted" might be a better word). After a new member of his company has been selected, De Filippo as *maestro* demands three things: time, then patience, then impatience. The new actor is hired for a period of either two or three years. During the first year or so, he is instructed to observe—"nothing else!" He is paid to watch his would-be colleagues perform their craft. When, despite his desire to succeed, the actor is ready to quit out of sheer boredom, he is then given a part—a small part. For now, says Eduardo, he has learned as much as possible from observation. And now it is Eduardo's turn to offer time, patience and impatience.

"The theatre is made up of great actors and good actors, of big actors and small actors. All are necessary to the health of the theatre." These remarks are made with direct reference to an actor in the company whose work Eduardo thinks is going well; he is satisfied with the progress shown. And even as he speaks of giving the actor time to develop and of having patience in discovering the scope of his individual art, I am aware of listening to the voice of a rigorous taskmaster—one whose actors must strive mightily to please, perhaps as much for the sake of his satisfaction as for the aske of their own survival.

We speak of philosophical matters. Eduardo has an intense interest in the multiplicity of things which happen simultaneously. We are speaking happily away about theatre, and at the same time all sorts of terrible things are taking place. The juxtaposition of simultaneous events is one of life's most poignant ironies, Eduardo feels, and a favorite in the dramatic worlds of his creation. In the two De Filippo plays performed at the San Ferdinando theatre in Naples this year, for example, such juxtaposition creates the central conflicts.[6] I ask Eduardo whether he thinks the force of human good greater than that of human evil. I ex-

pect a negative answer based upon my understanding of that comic pessimism which pervades his writing and often causes a seemingly pure comedy to twist tragically with shocking abruptness. But such an answer is not forthcoming. "There is a balance between the good and bad in man. We never know whether human action has worked out to help the good or the bad. What is evil can have good effects." And Eduardo goes on to defend, with marvelous intimacy, the actions of Geronta Sebezio—as if that character were among his dearest friends. Geronta Sebezio is the central figure in *Il Contratto*[7] who, after having been established as a comic, quasi-divine hero, is discovered to have been manipulating in the most fraudulent manner the poor and ignorant peasantry.

We return to a more conventional subject—what is happening in contemporary European and American theatre. Eduardo states that, while he approves of experimentation, he does not believe in instant theatre, nor does he believe in coercing audience participation. He believes in the seeming improvisation of gifted and disciplined actors, rather than the improvisation of non-actors. He accepts as theatre new forms of presentation which evolve, but does not think that presentations which change radically from one performance to another can be called theatre. Audience participation comes of wooing, of ensnaring with laughter perhaps—but not of forcing or demanding. "In my theatre, the audience is not in the theatre, but where the play takes place. When the play is over, the audience should wake up in the theatre, as if it has been asleep, dreaming." As for the development of his own theatre: "It grew because it was left alone. Nobody disturbed it for thirty years. ('Oh, it's dialect theatre—it will pass.') And so, with time and the opportunity to grow naturally, a theatre developed. You can't learn to act in a year, or build a theatre in a year."

Throughout this conversation I am continually struck by the independence of this seventy-one year old man. He does not go out of his way to be diplomatic (must we not all espouse the doings of the theatre of the moment for fear of being outdated ourselves?), nor is he particularly gentle ("I would kill my mother in order to get something done on stage in the way I think it must be done!"). He is forthright and intense and very much his own man. Eduardo is that rarity in the world today—a free artist in the theatre. As an actor he need submit only to his author self. He is free—because of his genius perhaps, because he has achieved worldly success, or because he has cultivated a lifetime habit of going his own way.

APRIL 5, 6:00 P.M. TEATRO SAN FERDINANDO, NAPLES

Neapolitan traffic on Mondays is unbelievably ghastly, and we arrive at the theatre in a foul humour—late for a rehearsal I had asked a month ago to see. Act 2 of *Napoli Milionaria* has just begun: a single brush-up rehearsal before the revival, which has been playing in Rome, opens in Naples for a two-month run. Eduardo is simply putting the pieces back just so—to where they were before the troupe left Naples, or to where they were in 1945 perhaps?

Eduardo, three giggly female fans of a young actor and ourselves are the only occupants in the darkened theatre. My husband is having a difficult time controlling his laughter, and, while cursing him inwardly for understanding all the dialect jokes, I am delighted that the dialogue is so quickly alleviating his driver's headache. The laughs are flowing steadily when suddenly Eduardo stops everything. A chair has been moved to the wrong position. The second interruption occurs after another twenty lines or so—this time over the unnecessary addition of the monosyllable "eh" following the line *Sono zitella?* ("Am I a virgin?" by a female character whose husband departed for the battle-front immediately following their wedding night spent in a crowded air raid shelter.) Another, longer "ehhhhh!" brings about the next correction: its pitch must rise as its volume becomes crescendo. All the actors laugh as Eduardo demonstrates, and my husband laughs as the actress gets it right this time. The would-be lover of the central female character is criticized for seeming *antipatico* when he suggests casually that perhaps her soldier husband is already dead—the line must be read with concern. The central character is reminded that she has substituted *tornati* for *arrivati*. Eduardo is not directing from a script.

Eduardo's transition from director to actor is so deceptively simple that it is all but unrecognizable. At the beginning of Act 3 he walks casually up the stairs which separate stage from house, as he has done several times during Act 2, and proceeds to speak softly. I suddenly realize that he is neither demonstrating nor explaining. He is speaking for himself—in this instance Gennaro Jovine, soldier-come-home and father of a dangerously ill little girl. De Filippo is so polished; his acting is as polished as his directing, or is it the other way around? The word which comes to mind is showman: Eduardo is an impeccable showman.

What remains to be spoken of regarding this look into Eduardo's rehearsal life is that exhausted subject in American theatre, the director-actor relationship. As with so many overly discussed American relationships what is needed, perhaps, is a bit of Italian despotism. Eduardo appears, so Signora Quarantotto tells me, half an hour early at each and every rehearsal. Can minutiae of this sort explain the reverence with which these actors absorb their master's every word? Italian good manners perhaps. (But whenever did so many Italians listen so attentively to one of their number?) Is it crass to mention that Eduardo pays everyone's salary and possesses the ultimate power of hiring and firing? Or is it perhaps that, for these actors, as for most, the embodiment of discipline and devotion and success is hard to come by—and Eduardo represents these qualities to his company. Then there is the way in which Eduardo expresses himself as critic: the actor's smallest action and least sound are worth his highest attention and a trip up onto the stage. Traditional directing perhaps? Or simply good directing? There is not a moment wasted. It is a serious business and very hard work, this creation of laughs.

MAY 21, 11:00 P.M. S. AGNELLO, SORRENTO

A chronological reading of De Filippo's plays reveals the initial predominance of dialect writing and its gradual abandonment in favor of formal Italian after the Second World War. I mentioned to Eduardo during our meeting in March that, in this respect, his plays had become increasingly easy for me to read. I wondered in what way this linguistic transformation might correspond to a recent statement of his: "The effort of my life has been to release the dialect theatre, bringing it toward a national theatre."[8] Eduardo's answer was to refer me immediately to a newspaper article he had written in 1938.[9] This rebuts the well-known critic, Gherardo Gherardi, who had accused him of helping the Italian theatre to remain a backward and nomadic organization, when he might better have been aiding and abetting its growth and development. The reply which De Filippo offered the readers of *Il Giornale d'Italia* is inspiring, and doubly so when read thirty-three years later with the results of that inspiration at hand. The dialect actors of Italy are good Italians, asserts De Filippo, and they do not resign themselves to remaining enclosed in regional circles. The methods of dialect companies might well be recommended to all aspiring Italian actors, for these demand discipline and sacrifice and love of the art of theatre. And Eduardo offers Gherardi advice if he is truly interested in the future of Italian theatre: (1) constitute small, but excellent companies; (2) give the actors the security of from three to five years' work so that they may study and work together in tranquillity of spirit; (3) give them strong direction; (4) give the company a free choice of repertory—and look forward to a healthy national theatre! Eduardo has been acting since 1910 and writing plays since 1920 (nearly fifty of these have been produced). It is extravagant, but satisfying nonetheless, to suggest that at the time of writing there is no Neapolitan who is not proud of his fellow, Eduardo De Filippo, and no theatre-conscious Italian who does not claim Eduardo's work as part of his own national theatre.

Perhaps a key to Eduardo's genius is his time sense: in comic dialogue, in comedy-tragedy reversal, in those carefully choreographed, seemingly improvised stage movements which are the trademark (or should one say birthright?) of his actors, in that slow nutritive process of directing and teaching and liberating actors so that their individual techniques become strong, in his staging of the lives of strong acting companies. Eduardo the tightly-coiled philosopher of theatre aesthetics, Eduardo the patiently demanding director, Eduardo the most outwardly relaxed of actors. The *when* of the theatre is Eduardo's secret, and there are few who understand it as well as he.

Eduardo owns an island—Ischa (not Ischia!), which is directly off the coast of Nerano, and indirectly off that of Positano. He goes there—in summertime only—to take up his morning writer's existence. The parish priest of Positano, Father Raffaele Talamo, tells the story of the young Positanese boy whom Eduardo chose to appear in a television drama of his some years ago. This handsome *giovanotto* is not an actor today, but a naval officer (for his mother was put down by the other mammas in town for having exhibited excessive pride in the TV performances of her man-child). Perhaps many will heave a sigh of relief to learn that this young man has escaped the grip of the theatre (with money in the bank from the television series), but I would disagree. For the boy at ten, like Eduardo when he was ten, was learning to act under Eduardo's tutelage in that timeless way which produces true actors. The plentiful years of learning without rush—the apprenticeship. An unpopular concept today, for now it is instant theatre, commercial splash, do-it-yourself. But if we are to speak of the theatre of Eduardo De Filippo, then we must speak of a more complete time sense.[10]

Notes

1. *Il Monumento,* Torino, 1970. The play proposes De Filippo's social theory once again: the underdog is "the good guy." This "good guy" is not perfect, but he at least retains his humanity—as men in positions of authority do not. De Filippo's concept of humanity might be illustrated by paraphrasing a sentence from his preface to the play: the belief in love—love between man and woman, man and children, man and country.

2. The play permits Eduardo to function easily both as director and, philosophically speaking, as central character. Its action develops from what Penna thinks now and did long ago, and from what he, therefore, does not do now. His non-doing causes the other characters to do everything around him, thereby permitting the actor of Penna to function as director of those other characters' actions. Penna's/Eduardo's primary function in the play is to listen; his secondary function is to die.

3. He has written himself a part in *Il Monumento* in which his wife demands that he dye his hair—hair which is put on nightly.

4. Eduardo does not believe that the writing of acting theories helps to create better theatre; the end result is usually argument and misinterpretation.

5. Eduardo De Filippo, "The Intimacy of Character and Actor," trans. by Vivian Leone, *Actors on Acting,* ed. by Helen Krish Chinoy and Toby Cole, New York, 1970, pp. 470-72.

6. In *Il Monumento,* Ascanio Penna lives underground, withdrawn from the world above him, which cast away twenty years ago the ideals to which he still clings so tenaciously. In *Napoli Milionaria* (Torino, 1945), Gennaro Jovine fights a war while his wife becomes rich on the blackmarket and his son becomes a car thief. And when he begins to speak compulsively of war's sufferings on his return, his family

and friends refuse to listen and proceed to celebrate—something he is no longer capable of doing.

7. Besides *Il Contratto* (Torina, 1967), the following plays contain the comic-tragic twist mentioned above. In *Natale in Casa Cupiello* (Torino, 1931), the family looks on as Luca dies blessing his daughter and her lover, whom he takes to be his son-in-law—who is also observing the scene! In *La Parte di Amleto* (Torino, 1940), an old actor is cruelly tricked into believing that he will play Hamlet for the tardy leading man. In *Le Voci di Dentro* (Torino, 1948), Zio Nicola, the hilarious figure who addresses remarks to the rest of mankind exclusively through the medium of firecrackers, is found dead in his self-devised aerial shelter. In *Il Cilindro* (Torino, 1965), the central characters seem to have happily escaped their problems only to find that one of them has learned too much of the selfishness of the other three to continue with their family life. Except for the most recent *Il Contratto* and *Il Monumento,* all of Eduardo's works may be found in *Cantata dei Giorni Pari* (5th rev. ed.), and *Cantata dei Giorni Dispari* (7th rev. ed.) (Torino: Einaudi, 1966).

8. See Chinoy and Cole, *Actors on Acting,* pp. 470-72. This statement, translated above from Eduardo's original Italian manuscript, seems to have been deleted from the current edition.

9. Eduardo De Filippo, "Edùardo De Filippo difende il suo teatro," *Il Giornale d'Italia,* Roma: 15 dic. 1938.

10. Throughout this article, quotations have been translated by the author.

Mario B. Mignone (essay date 1984)

SOURCE: Mignone, Mario B. "De Filippo's Inspiration and Creative Process." In *Eduardo De Filippo,* pp. 20-36. Boston: Twayne Publishers, 1984.

[*In the following excerpt, Mignone examines the role of the city of Naples in shaping de Filippo's art.*]

NAPLES: DE FILIPPO'S MAJOR INSPIRATION

Eric Bentley has put well the need for examining De Filippo's art in the context of his city: "It is sometimes debated how far we need to know an author's background in order to judge his work. I should think we need to know it whenever we would otherwise be in danger of taking something as his personal contribution when it is a representative product of his time and place. Thus some of Eduardo's attitudes . . . may seem forced when we take them as an assertion of his will, whereas as an expression of a social tradition we might let them pass"[1]. To the mind of a foreign spectator, the attitude of Gennaro in *Millionaires' Naples!*—the husband who disapproves of, yet cooperates in his wife's illegal business—may appear inconsistent.

However, his actions, like those of other De Filippo characters, are consistent with the world view of the people of Naples. To Eduardo's people, the state is the enemy. The Fascist suppression of Neapolitan regionalism was only the most recent episode in their long history of oppression. When Matteo Generoso, the protagonist of **Fear Number One,** says, "If twelve wars broke out one after the other, they'd make no impression on me," this is not some absurd idea of the author's, but rather an expression of a fundamental Neapolitan attitude. Getting on with the business of day-to-day living, regardless of what happens in the newspapers, is the people's concern.

Naples is a city of paradoxes: poor in industries, rich in the sun, suffering, and song. It is a city that venerates the innocent charm of children and a city where children lose their innocence very early. Naples reflects the practice of *dolce far niente* ("sweet idleness") and hums day and night with the kinetic energy of human beings working, selling, arguing, singing, cursing. Neapolitans can cry and laugh at the same time. They are gay, ruthless, life-loving, cynical, superstitious, kindly, and extremely patient. For them life is lived from day to day; luck in the next lottery may be just across the piazza.

De Filippo's Naples is not the stereotyped tourist panorama of Vesuvius and the bay, as it is idealized on postcards, but a complex, volcanic city, full of contradictions, absurdities, and extravagance, reflecting the full spectrum of the human condition. It is the Naples that Thornton Wilder characterized as an "anthill of vitality—cynical yet religious—religious yet superstitious—shadowed by the volcano and the thought of death—always aboil with one passion or another, yet abounding in courtesy and charm. Above all, profoundly knit by the ties of the family, parent and child"[2]. De Filippo's attention is focused above all on the masses and lower middle class of Naples, on that part of the population for whom the tests of life are harder but not necessarily more tragic than for those "better off," because they have an innate flair for life. In lower-class Naples the duality of social relations is very evident. People are close to one another, aware of one another, ready to defend one another; but this same closeness provides opportunities for exploitation as well as protection and aid. In short, as Bentley notes, "the lower depths of Naples form as fantastic a society of adventurers and desperadoes as can well be imagined. Living by the skin of their teeth, a dreary past behind and a blank future ahead, they accept the present with peculiar vehemence. Familiar with death, they do not take life too seriously. They are willing to see it as a joke, a paradox, a fantasy, a show, a game"[3]. Neapolitans of the lower classes run the gamut of human life:

> It is because of their capacity for community and individuality at once that the Neapolitan situation is tragic and not merely pathetic. For they are a people who have perfected the art of *communitas* while at the same time celebrating the human personality for the riches it contains. Could they fashion a utopia of their own, I am certain it would be anti-platonic—a social organiza-

tion for diversity and maximal self-expression. Just as Plato would have cast out actors and playwrights as subversives, the Neapolitans would give these a central role, for they represent the full range of human feelings and catch all the rays that shine from the prism that is man.[4]

For De Filippo, Naples is not just a city or his city, but a magnifying glass through which he contemplates humanity in its myriad manifestations.

Even the less keen and sensitive observers are struck by the pulsation of life in this city. And life is an event to be celebrated because existence is a movable, continuing feast. Its living soul is as Belmonte observes:

> . . . resolute and passionate, but it is also unconscious, and insensate to the prod of awareness and reason. As such it can emerge, or it becomes hypnotic. The movement in Naples—the traffic jams, the pushy, shoving crowds, the absence of lines forming for anything, the endless barrage of shouts falling like arrows on ears, the simultaneous clash of a million destinations and petty opposed intentions—combine into a devastating assault on the senses. Or else the entire scene retreats, slowing and settling finally into a brilliantly colored frieze depicting a grand, if raucous, *commedia*.[5]

In Naples, behavior is charged with a meaning that may either reveal the truth or mask it, and spontaneity and artifice blend into one another like the tints of a watercolor. Much of Neapolitan life, especially its more passionate side, has a basic and undeniable theatricality. It is not accidental that one of the greatest moments in Naples's theater history is its improvisational *commedia dell'arte,* with its emphasis on spontaneity, immediacy, and broad physical actions. Anyone who watches Neapolitans in conversation soon realizes that the hands, and indeed the entire body, often communicate as much as the accompanying words. The outsider can easily mistake a simple conversation for a heated argument, since many Neapolitans converse with a commitment and excitement that is often not commensurate with the importance of the subject matter under discussion. This gesticulation and the spirit it expresses are theatrical, if not operatic, suggesting a performance even when none is intended.

Indeed, in the poor quarters of Naples even the most banal events can be elevated to the level of drama. Action is a vehicle of communication, and "in the language of symbolic action, a rage might be a plea, a kiss an economic stratagem." The tonalities are theatrical. In the poor quarters of Naples every person becomes a playwright and an actor, seeking to determine and organize the reactions of an audience—but a critic too, more than ready to demolish the transparent devices and weaker props of his fellows. In the words of Thomas Belmonte, "if drama was originally invented as a metaphor for life, in Naples the metaphor has overwhelmed the referent, and society presents itself as a series of plays within plays."[6]

To love and understand De Filippo's theater one has to love and understand the theater performed on the vast stage of Naples. Because he could capture it in its fullness, De Filippo achieved a high degree of drama and theatricality even in dealing with seemingly cerebral themes. For example, the philosophy of the absurd, very evident in his plays, is not so much the subject matter of his characters' discussions as the Neapolitan way of living. As Bentley says, "There is a philosophy of the absurd, after all, in plebeian humor in general: your life is hopeless but you laugh, you are cheerful and morally positive, against all reason'"[7]. But Neapolitans are believers. In spite of their cynicism about most aspects of life, they give themselves to religion with unconditional fervor. They preserve a facade of Catholic ritual, but prefer their Madonna-goddesses to Christ and maintain an active belief in a myriad local house-spirits, reminiscent of the pre-Christian epoch. Similarly, De Filippo's characters are Christian-pagans for whom God, Christ, the Madonna, and all the saints are little more than agencies on hand for the purpose of healing and punishing, as they are, for example, in *I Won't Pay You, Filumena Marturano,* and many other plays.

Among the manifold components of this Neapolitan life, De Filippo focuses his attention very often on the family. Pushing aside the mythology of sentimental "familism" that pervades Italian culture, he shows the contradictions of family life, the violent clash of motives, and the tangled web of longings, jealousies, and long-nurtured resentments that form the substrata of so much family interaction. He commonly notes that the individual behaves differently within the family circle than in other social arenas. The home is not a stage for presenting hypocritical spectacles to others. Whatever a person may appear to be elsewhere, the family knows better. The secret weaknesses of the individual, the shame of sins long hidden from the world, the family assimilates and keeps to itself. If the honesty of the family is often cruel, it may also be redemptive and sometimes therapeutic, as in *Millionaires' Naples!* and *My Family!* The Neapolitan family remains at the core of De Filippo's art, and he is a keen observer of its minute particularities. Indeed, it is extraordinary what subtle variations he can play on this perennial theme—in *Christmas at the Cupiello's, Filumena Marturano, My Love and My Heart, Saturday, Sunday, and Monday,* and many others.

In portraying Naples, De Filippo writes of the very society from which Pulcinella grew and to which Pulcinella has most meaning. Like him, De Filippo's characters move rather hopelessly around the fringe of life; like him, they possess an indomitable will to live in spite of everything[8]. However, in contrast to the Pulcinella of the *commedia dell'arte,* De Filippo's protagonist possesses an activated social conscience. As Mario Stefanile has said:

> De Filippo's Pulcinella is made up of Molière and Goldoni, a bit of Shakespeare and a lot of Viviani, almost all of Scarpetta, and most of Petrolini, and even certain formulas of the mature Jouvet. This is because, through Pulcinella, what is expressed is the morality of Naples, the desire typical of the Parthenopean, to correct the social aspects of life in his own favor and to

reduce everything to his own image and likeness—splendor and misery, nobility and indignity, racketeers and honest men, the rich and the poor, men and women.[9]

De Filippo's characters are neither heroes nor clowns. They are men—more often than not part hero and part clown, each one having his own personality, his own nature, and stamped with the character of the land in which he was born and lives. They live in a world that man still values. In it they can continue to live, struggle, hope; they continue to cheat and love each other, to despise and pity one another. And, above all, in spite of everything, they continue to delude themselves in the search for truth. Theirs is not a confused search for abstract truth, but a search based on total suspicion and mistrust—yet tempered with a constant, naive hope for something better, with the same hope that animates the lower-middle-class Neapolitans to live and survive day by day. Illusion and reality are fused, as if man needed to create an unreal world which is all his own, while at the same time keeping close watch on reality. Perhaps some day things will change, but meanwhile life has to go on: "Eventually the night has to pass . . . ," says the protagonist in the closing line of *Millionaires' Naples!*

In the plays De Filippo wrote during and immediately after World War II, Naples represents both the human and the economic destruction of a particular city and the fate of the many countries that had experienced the same devastation, the same anguish and existential boredom that dominated the life of those years. In the plays written in the 1960s and 1970s Naples is a city at the mercy of the selfishness, hypocrisy, corruption, and violence of the materialistic society which evolved in those years. Eduardo's attachment to Naples, then, is not merely sentimental. Although his suppositions seem to be those of an earlier breed of popular Neapolitan playwrights with old-fashioned notions, it must not be supposed that Eduardo is a producer of locally acceptable social drama, on a different wavelength from the avant-garde and from modern European comedy in general. On the contrary, while nourishing himself on the rich humus of Neapolitan life and theater, he shows himself perfectly familiar with the comedy of European intellectuals, for the most part born of mistrust, its ethos repeatedly one of meaninglessness and isolation in an absurd world, in which language has ceased to convey meaning and the structures of society are mocked. Yet De Filippo only partially accepts this legacy of Pirandello, Jarry, and their successors, with its special kind of liberating irony which allows the spectator to dismiss, for the duration of a play, the demands of everyday life. The world of these playwrights—socially hollow, reeling, having no center of traditional bourgeois gravity, where one has to be off-center if he is to escape the void, where the heroes are individualists, nonconformists, eccentric, and way-out—De Filippo can accept only for the crisis it presents, not for its nihilistic content.

For De Filippo the world is not hollow. Life has a meaning; when things go wrong it matters; and that meaning and matter may be adequately conveyed by language. However, elements of relativistic and existentialist thinking as well as the idea of a disintegrating world are recurring themes in his plays, explicitly so in ***Millionaires' Naples!, Those Ghosts, My Family!, The Voices Within,*** and ***The Local Authority.*** These plays are the products not only of a postwar setting but also of a relativistic age, of a world falling apart both physically and metaphysically. The children in ***My Family!*** strive for existential freedom no less than the characters of Sartre, and the dialogue echoes, more intimately, less portentously, the same dilemmas faced by the French philosopher. The Cimmaruta family in ***The Voices Within*** is fragmented by conflicting versions of nonexistent truth; truth is chimerical in ***Those Ghosts!*** and ***The Big Magic.*** De Filippo's sophistication extends to a canny understanding of voguish attitudes, and he finds the voguish attitudes wanting.

DE FILIPPO'S ENCOUNTER WITH PIRANDELLO

Many critics have long assumed that Luigi Pirandello served as a key literary influence on Eduardo De Filippo. Eduardo was very young and still unknown when he began to experience the fascination of Pirandello's art and thought. The Pirandellian quality of some plays of De Filippo could be, therefore, a consequence of a youthful infatuation.

De Filippo first saw Pirandello's *Six Characters in Search of an Author* in 1921. Two years later he had read everything Pirandello had written, and he remained very impressed with his art. In 1933, when De Filippo had reached a certain degree of popularity, he met the older playwright who asked him to produce *Liolà*[10]. After twenty-five rehearsals, all of which Pirandello attended, *Liolà* opened at the Teatro Odeon in Milan, with Peppino De Filippo in the title role. The performance received twenty-two curtain calls. Sometime later they met again in Naples, and Pirandello asked De Filippo about the possibility of adapting his short story *L'abito nuovo* (The new suit) for the stage, overwhelming him with the suggestion that they write the play together. For fifteen days during December 1935, from 5 to 8 P.M., the two playwrights worked together in Rome, where De Filippo's company was performing. Pirandello wrote a prose outline of ideas and action. From time to time he would hand sheets of paper to De Filippo, seated at a desk next to him, who would write the dialogue. During one of the last evenings Pirandello asked De Filippo to adapt his *Cap and Bells.* Only a month later this play opened in Naples at the Fiorentini Theater, with Eduardo in the leading role, and played twenty-two sold-out performances.

While performing this comedy in Milan, De Filippo received a telegram from Pirandello asking him to produce *The New Suit.* He answered that the production of *Cap and Bells* had exhausted him and that he would prefer to wait a year before staging the work. Pirandello was hurt and did not reply. About four months later Eduardo saw Pirandello during an intermission of *Cap and Bells,* which

he was performing at the Quirino Theater in Rome. To Eduardo, the old and famous playwright resembled a young author eager for his first production, and Eduardo told him so. Pirandello replied, "But you, my dear Eduardo, can afford to wait; I cannot!" A month later, rehearsals started, but Pirandello was dead of pneumonia before the play opened.

This very close contact with Pirandello and his theater inevitably left an imprint on De Filippo which is evident in his view of life and the way he gives it theatrical expression. Corrado Alvaro points out the influence in negative terms: "Eduardo De Filippo, believing himself to be far removed from modern life and the life common to all, tries to exceed his limits by attempting the style of Pirandello, the form least suited to Eduardo and which Pirandello himself finally dropped uneasily"[11]. But Eduardo has been less ready to admit that he has been significantly influenced by Pirandello. When asked about it, he replied:

> When I began to write my plays, I did not know of Pirandello. In 1928 I wrote ***Chi è chiù felice 'e me!*** [***Who is happier than I!***] and made my debut with this play in 1931. Thus I began to write before I began to associate with him. . . . The conclusions about life which I have come to are not, in fact, Pirandello-like conclusions. We are close in our mentality: Neapolitans are sophisticated in the same way Sicilians are. The characters of ***Non ti pago*** [***I won't pay you***] win out at all costs and actually conquer by their will power, by their stubbornness which is similar to that of the Sicilians.[12]

Eric Bentley has also maintained that, except in ***The Big Magic,*** Pirandello's influence on De Filippo is only superficial. Certainly, many affinities with Pirandello's theater can be found: in the way De Filippo celebrates maternal love, in his metaphysical speculation on the nature of reality and illusion, in his emphasis on the drama of fear and compassion. However, as Bentley points out, while Pirandello deals with abstract concepts, never revealing the truth on any given matter because truth is relative and definite judgment is impossible, De Filippo concerns himself with specific personal traumas. In many plays he deals with the Pirandellian theme that illusions are needed because life is more than we can stand; in some cases the conclusions of the plays recall those of the great master in that the intrusion of reality, which had threatened to shatter the illusion, instead ironically reinforces it and makes it permanent. At times, too, their characters show similarities. It is difficult to establish to what degree these affinities are due to influence because, as De Filippo himself has said, at the base of their art there is a common denominator: the Southern Italian outlook on life. Long traditions bind together the mainland and the island Kingdom of the Two Sicilies. Unable to live freely under centuries of Spanish domination, the people of Sicily and those of Naples learned to cope in the same manner, by meditating and philosophizing. But for the dialectical Sicilian fury of Pirandello, De Filippo substitutes Neapolitan cynicism. Even the pessimism of De Filippo's characters, which makes one think of the nihilism of Pirandello's, is a mocking negativism which, while it has the flavor of paradox, has its origin in the traditional popular attitude of "goldbricking."

Moreover, alike as their plays might appear, they differ greatly in tone. Pirandello's bleak, pessimistic outlook becomes less dreary with De Filippo. No matter how much De Filippo's characters suffer in the play, the endings are often resolved happily. Furthermore, the truth is discoverable to those who wish to find it. Illusions are never allowed to remain ambiguous; if one man has an illusion, others recognize it as such.

De Filippo's plays are not drama in the Pirandellian sense, nor comedies in the sense that English-speaking audiences—and especially the Broadway audience—understand the term. As Bentley observes:

> Naples is a different place, and Neapolitan folk drama is a different art; one enjoys it not least for its difference. . . . One enjoys, above all, the fine blend of comedy and drama, the naive pathos, the almost noble seriousness of what might easily become ludicrous. Some non-Italians are surprised, even displeased, by this last feature. "Why don't they play comedy as comedy?" Fully to answer the question would be to explain and justify a simpler, but also more delicate, realism than our own stage at present has to show.[13]

There is a wide spectrum of humor in a De Filippo play. The laughter he elicits ranges from chuckles to belly laughs. But there is also a central fiber, a sense of the tragedy of life. For his propensity for the tragicomic, De Filippo could be called the Italian Gogol. This blend of comedy and pathos also recalls some moments in Chaplin's works.

It is the blend of comedy and pathos that lends the work of De Filippo its special tone. His plays may be both realistic and fantastic, both comic and moralistic, both sentimental and grotesque. It is a blend that De Filippo achieves through his examination of the bittersweet plebeian life of Naples.

THE PLAYWRIGHT IN HIS CREATIVE PROCESS

De Filippo has occasionally spoken about the content and form of his art. In a 1956 interview he said: "The theater is neither a book nor a literary work: it must always be lively, and thus for one-and-a-half to two hours it must always have elements of surprise. That's why the public comes to see my plays, because it enjoys itself and takes something home as well"[14]. In December 1972, upon receiving the Feltrinelli International Prize for the Theater, he pointed out the elements that contribute to the creation of his plays. Except for a few works written in his youth, at the base of his art "lies always the conflict between individual and society."

> In general, if an idea does not have social meaning or social application, I'm not interested in developing it. It's clear that I'm aware that what is true for me might

not be true for others, but I'm here to speak to you about myself, and since pity, indignation, love, and emotions in general, are felt in the heart, this much I can affirm—that ideas spring first from my heart and then from my brain.[15]

De Filippo points out that it is easy for him to have an idea, difficult, on the other hand, to give it form and communicate it. He has been successful mainly because, as he says, "I was able to absorb avidly and with pity the life of so many people, and I have been able to create a language which, although theatrically elaborate, becomes the means of expression of the various characters and not of their author"[16]. He explains:

> In most cases, the creative process is long. The germinal idea undergoes the seasoning of time to test the degree of its validity: after having had the idea and given it a sketchy form, there begins the long and laborious period during which, for months and more often for years, I keep the idea enclosed in me. . . . If an idea is not valid, little by little it fades away, disappears, and does not obsess the mind any longer; but if it is valid, with time it ripens and improves and consequently the comedy develops both as text and as theater, as a complete show, staged and acted down to the smallest detail, exactly the way I wanted it seen and felt. In a way this is unfortunate, as I will never feel it again once it has become a theatrical reality.[17]

Then the play staged in his mind and carried with him for so long is fixed in the pages of the script: "Only when the beginning and the end of the 'action' are clear to me and I know to perfection the life, death and miracles of every character, even the secondary ones, do I begin to write"[18]. He writes the play, staging it in his mind's eye as he goes along. True, this is the practice of every playwright; but De Filippo does it by fusing the writing process to the acting and directing experiences. Such fusion is evident not only in the fluidity, spontaneity, and naturalness of the dialogue, but also in the numerous and often detailed stage directions.

Early in his artistic career De Filippo made a statement that has remained true up to the present:

> Our purpose in coming forward on the stage has never been to hold conferences, to conduct discussions about grave problems, or to teach courses in philosophy. We are truly people of the theater, free from every bond and bias, and we are theater people in the sense of being both actors and audience; that is why we concern ourselves with reproducing in our plays life as people see it and feel it, with its elements of comedy and sentiment, poetry and the grotesque, with its contrasts of suffering and buffoonery, and nothing more. To sum up, every day we are more strongly convinced that this is exactly what the public seeks from us, and for this they applaud us generously as actors and as authors.[19]

De Filippo writes a play basing it not on the presentation of lofty philosophical abstractions, but as a part of life, to make it live in its own right as a work of drama. Every character, like every life, however minor, always has something to say, comic or serious, emotionally or intellectually, and De Filippo aims to create characters who reflect in varying degrees sentiments and ideas possessed of a certain universality.

When the curtain rises on an Eduardo De Filippo play, the audience is not apt to receive a scenic surprise. For over fifty years, the settings of his comedies have been remarkably consistent. One sees the interior of a lower-middle-class apartment. Seldom does Eduardo write a play which, like **De Pretore Vincenzo** or **Tommaso D'Amalfi,** moves out into the streets and alleys of Naples. The playwright's choice of the interior setting shows his interest in exploring the motives, values, and plight of the poor and the struggling. Although the strain of naturalism in De Filippo is not of Strind-bergian intensity, it is strong enough in this essentially realistic playwright to cause him to examine people in the environment where they are most likely to be themselves. For Eduardo is committed to exposing the hypocrisy of human beings, and their financial, physical, or spiritual destitution:

> Except for a few works I wrote when I was young, . . . at the base of my theater there is always the conflict between the individual and society. I mean to say that everything always starts from an emotive stimulus: reaction to an injustice, scorn for hypocrisy, mine and others', solidarity with and human sympathy for a person or a group of people, rebellion against outdated and anachronistic laws, fear in the face of events, such as wars, which disrupt the life of the people.[20]

De Filippo finds drama particularly in the life and language of those living in poverty and suffering social injustice. From the early works—light farces, yet already sensitive to human value—to the great neorealist plays of the immediate postwar period, which explore the drama of humanity ravaged by war, to the most recent works cast in the form of "parables" and some strongly critical of our present-day society. De Filippo shows a continuous effort to reach his audience with his commitment to mitigating the absurdities and incongruities of life through the correction of social ills. By his own admission, he writes in reaction to the injustices perpetrated against the weak in society: the illegitimate, the unhappily married, the poor, the oppressed. From his passionate identification with the socially deprived arises the plays' moral protest, which attempts to produce awareness of the human predicament and to compel reflection. Yet his theater is not political propaganda. De Filippo himself rejected this label: "I am not Brecht, and for that matter I would not like to be him. I do not approve of political speeches in the theater. However, I certainly am in favor of pointing out [social] wounds"[21].

Neither can his theater be labeled "social theater," since it does not, for instance, concern itself so much with the class struggle or with the social and economic condition of the deprived classes, as with moral failure and its social consequences. He focuses his attention on such themes as hypocrisy, evil masquerading as good, egoism disguised as charity, the alienating influence on the individual of a demoralized society, the oppressive condition arising from lack of tolerance and respect for human dignity, the arbitrariness of society, the absurdities and inadequacies of the judicial system. Only a very few plays fail because of De Filippo's commitment to social betterment. Usually, this very commitment accounts for the depth of inspiration, the thematic richness, the authenticity in character and dialogue, the balance of irony and humor, and thus the sense of perspective in his dramatization of social issues. He writes play after play exposing one wrong after another, spurred on by the conviction that the only way to remedy the ills of society is to prompt public reaction to them. He is not always successful in arousing this reaction and often overstates his point, but he is always faithful to his vision of the playwright as society's moral guide. Over the years he has maintained this interest and has increasingly confirmed the importance that he attaches to the involvement of the public, for it is this public that must fulfill the moral function of his work.

LANGUAGE

Part of De Filippo's artistic achievement is undoubtedly due to his successful working solution to the problems of finding, or inventing, a form of spoken Italian suitable for use on the stage. This is an accomplishment because literary Italian, and above all stage Italian, is essentially an artificial language. While standard English, standard French, or standard American is spoken, if not by the whole population at least by important sections of it, standard Italian only exists on paper. In ordinary life even the most educated Italians have their clearly defined regional accent and vocabulary. It is therefore far more difficult in Italian to write dramatic dialogue which sounds like real speech, yet free from local overtones and the limitations on intelligibility imposed by the use of a dialect. Only during the 1960s, for a variety of reasons—mass communications, the urbanization of large numbers of former agricultural workers and their families, geographical migration, travel for pleasure—did a generalized form of spoken Italian start to assert itself on a wider scale. Theater has mostly used the Italian literary language, an abstraction usually bombastic or stilted, incomprehensible to the majority of Italians, and therefore necessarily restricted both socially and in its range of expressive possibilities. As Pier Paolo Pasolini commented, "traditional theater has accepted . . . an Italian which does not exist. Upon such a convention—that is, upon nothing, upon what is nonexistent, dead—it has based the conventionality of diction. The result is repugnant"[22]. Side by side with literary theater exists a tradition of regional theater, richer in expressiveness, but very limited, by reason of the mutual incomprehensibility of Italy's many dialects, in its potential for reaching people beyond the local area. De Filippo is the one playwright who has resolved the division between these two kinds of theatrical language. To overcome the linguistic conventionality of bourgeois theater, he invented a new vehicle of oral expression which has the spontaneity and immediacy of popular dialect while still retaining that minimum of conventional abstraction necessary to reach a wide audience.

In his early works De Filippo used almost exclusively a pure Neapolitan dialect, which was not only appropriate for his characters, who had affinities with those of the cabaret theater and the *avanspettacolo,* but also reflected with almost obsessive rigor the life of the Neapolitan masses and lower middle class. At the beginning of their careers, the use of the dialect was also unavoidable for Eduardo and his brother and sister, since they saw themselves as continuing the tradition inherited from Scarpetta. But as De Filippo's repertory changed, due to his desire to appeal to an audience all over the peninsula, his means of expression changed too. The Neapolitan vernacular went through a process of Italianization, following the lead of the "half-Neapolitan" already spoken by middle-class Neapolitans and becoming more understandable to other Italians. Since the war, De Filippo has developed a dramatic dialogue that comes very close to the everyday spoken vernacular employed throughout southern Italy, but with the particular inflection and cadence characteristic of Naples. It is, moreover, a language which has a "common denominator" with spoken Italian and is readily understood in other regions.

De Filippo's texts reproduce the rhythm and flow of ordinary conversational Italian as faithfully as possible. They are characterized by run-on sentences, with pauses in the form of dots (. . .) dividing each clause, instead of carefully constructed, grammatically self-contained periodic sentences. Although in the later works dialect expressions appear only rarely, his scripts are colored with expressive idioms, popular slang, and frequent, sometimes outlandish puns. Sometimes the author inserts a few words in Neapolitan dialect at the end of a punchline, to enrich the local "flavor" and maintain the immediacy of geographical setting. However, dialect never serves merely to add charm or mere local color to his characters' speech, or to give an air of "scholarly" authenticity, as an aesthetic device for its own sake. Rather, it serves to heighten either their plight or their overflowing excitement. With most of the characters, De Filippo mingles dialect with Italian, alternating the pungency of the one with the suavity of the other and extracting all the flavor and fun he can from the rich tonality of their utterance.

The result is a collection of plays free of intellectual abstractions, rhetorical figures, and learned metaphors. It is unfailingly expressive, rich in comic elements, and full of the spontaneous, colorful epithets of "street language." Thornton Wilder made a particular point of admiring Eduardo's language: "To know and love his plays one must have a relish for dialect and regional speech, for that color and immediacy of the language, used for a longtime by a portion of the society little touched by the oversophisticated and cultivated 'polite' world"[23]. For this same reason Bentley hails Eduardo's theater as "popular": "It is a popular theater as against an art theater. This means . . .

that it is a dialect theater and not an 'Italian' one. It uses a popularly spoken language and not an official, national, bourgeois language—in this respect resembling Synge and O'Casey rather than Pinero and Galsworthy. The lack of a national theatrical repertoire in Italy may be deplorable, but the quality of the defect is—the regional theater"[24]. Indeed, with De Filippo as with the Irishman John Millington Synge, half of the effect of the play lies in the dialect. The language of *The Playboy of the Western World* serves to turn a potentially tragic situation into a richly comic one. Similarly, **Filumena Marturano**'s Neapolitan dialect dispels any lugubrious potentialities of the plot—the old story of the prostitute with the heart of gold—and makes her a truly heroic plebeian. Just as a Synge play would lose much of its value if it were rewritten in American English, so do the Neapolitan comedies of De Filippo seem essentially untranslatable[25].

Moreover, in addition to the language, his comedies depend for much of their effect upon the gestures used by the characters. Although the Italian stage does not have an Oriental "gesturology," different regions, and Naples in particular, have virtually a system of gestures with accepted meanings. The side of one's hand repeatedly jabbed at one's ribs indicates hunger; pulling the lower eyelid down with one finger is the nonverbal way to describe shrewdness in another person. One must, indeed, study beforehand the meaning of Neapolitan gestures to derive the full flavor from a De Filippo performance[26]. With gestures and dialect both lost in foreign performances, Eduardo's plays in translation hardly approximate the original works.

Notes

1. Eric Bentley, *Kenyon Review,* p. 119.

2. Letter from Thornton Wilder to the author dated 9 October 1971.

3. Eric Bentley, *In Search of Theatre* (New York: Knopf, 1953), p. 289.

4. Thomas Belmonte, *The Broken Fountain* (New York: Columbia University Press, 1979), p. 29.

5. Ibid., p. 7.

6. Ibid., p. 30.

7. Bentley, *In Search of Theatre,* p. 290.

8. Robert G. Bander, "A Critical Estimate of Eduardo De Filippo," *Italian Quarterly* 11, 43 (1967):44.

9. Mario Stefanile, *Labirinto napoletano* (Naples: E.S.I., 1958), p. 115.

10. De Filippo recounted his encounters with Pirandello in a symbolic letter, "Open letter to Pirandello," *Il dramma,* Dec. 1936. It was written just a few days after Pirandello's death (10 December 1936).

11. Corrado Alvaro, "Eduardo," *Sipario* 11 (March 1956):6.

12. Vito Pandolfi, "Intervista a quatr'occhi con Eduardo De Filippo," *Sipario* 11 (March 1956):5.

13. Eric Bentley, *What is Theatre?* (Boston: Beacon Press, 1956), p. 200.

14. Pandolfi, "Intervista," p. 5.

15. "Prefazione," *I capolavori di Eduardo* (Turin: Einaudi, 1967), p. vii.

16. Ibid., p. viii.

17. Ibid., pp. viii-xi.

18. Ibid., p. ix.

19. Cf. Corsi, *Chi è di scena*, p. 49.

20. *I capolavori di Eduardo,* p. vii.

21. S. Lori, "Intervista con il grande autore-attore napoletano," *Roma,* 7 May 1969.

22. Pier Paolo Pasolini, "Manifesto per un nuovo teatro," *Nuovi argomenti* 9 (Jan.-March 1968):13.

23. Thornton Wilder, from the letter cited in Chapter 1, note 1.

24. Bentley, *In Search of Theatre,* p. 290.

25. Indeed, the translation into standard Italian of *Filumena Marturano* (a dubious enterprise from the start) was not successful and has never been restaged.

26. Desmond Morris et al., *Gestures* (Briarcliff Manor, N.Y.: Stein & Day, 1979) gives an excellent account of Neapolitan gestures.

Mario B. Mignone (essay date 1984)

SOURCE: Mignone, Mario B. "Early Works: Range and Versatility." In *Eduardo De Filippo,* pp. 37-66. Boston: Twayne Publishers, 1984.

[*In the following excerpt, Mignone explores the development of de Filippo's major themes as they appeared in his early, often critically neglected plays.*]

FROM FARCE TO SATIRE

De Filippo's theatrical works of the first phase, written before World War II and collected under the title *Cantata dei giorni pari* (*Cantata for even days*), are usually neglected by critics. In 1945 De Filippo himself characterized them as "plays of the old theater":

> In those plays I wanted to show the world of plot and intrigue and interest: the adulterers, the gambler, the superstitious, the slothful, the fraudulent. All part of a recognizable, definable Neapolitan way of life, but a way of life belonging to the nineteenth century. In those plays I kept alive a Naples which was already dead in part, and in part was covered up and hidden by the "paternalistic" care of the Fascist regime, and which, if it should revive today, would be seen in a different way, under a different aspect.[1]

But De Filippo's judgment on his work is too severe, for many of these plays have been restaged since 1945 with great success because of their relevancy and their theatricality.

The early works cannot be discarded, not only because they have documentary value, but also because, despite the influence of earlier Neapolitan playwrights, they introduce some of the themes that will become characteristic of him. Focused on the problems of contemporary Neapolitan society, these plays have a satirical bite, a tinge of irony. They reflect "even days" in appearance only; fascism wanted to project Italy as a country with its dreams fulfilled, but even the farces convey the desolate condition of the masses and lower middle class in the 1920s and 1930s.

While apparently simple, though obviously put together by a skilled actor, these first works are not pure experiment, sketches, or "pretexts" for acting. In their preference for jest and movement over words, in the lively action, the comical situation full of surprises and misunderstandings, in the quick lines studied to seem natural and full of the spirit of the spoken language, they echo the pulcinellata[2]; however, they already manifest a humor which verges on the grotesque, a dramatic tension at times approaching the tragic, a tendency to psychological intimacy, and a moral sensitivity to social conditions. The vivacity of the action is sustained by the many minor characters, at times mere caricatures, who carry with them an inexhaustible mimic potential. Seldom are they solidly fitted into the overall structure; rather, they remain accessories, tending to predictability because they have the fixed, generic characteristics of types. They appear, then just as suddenly disappear, the laughter of the audience trailing after them. The farcical situations do not, however, arise from accident and chance, as in the *commedia dell'arte* and traditional Neapolitan dialect theater, but from a human condition that is basically dramatic; and the *lazzi,* or comic business, while they make us laugh, at the same time exteriorize the pain of that state, rendering it sensible, immediate, and visible. At the center of this world is the main character, part of everyday reality, whose vitality stems from the absurdity of humble life observed from a new angle.

The theatrical strength of these characters lies not merely in their mimicry, but also in their language. The dialogue, at times rudimentary, at times abrupt and excited, never becomes monotonous or colorless, but always maintains its spontaneity and the fluidity necessary to remain theatrical. Although the Neapolitan linguistic texture gradually absorbs Italian forms, colored so as to indicate the characters' social levels, De Filippo sustains his artistic preference for dialect even when complying with the prohibition of dialects during the last years of Fascism. And at the base of the farcical situations and the language, there is always Naples itself, with its tragicomic, its humble and desolate reality, its scarcity of sustenance and human resources.

The one-act *Farmacia di turno* (*Pharmacy on duty*), the first work in *Cantata for Even Days,* was written in 1920 for Peppino Villani's company, but never staged. While an actor in the company, De Filippo had begun writing his own monologue. But this play is no product of a tyro's enthusiasm and ebullience. Though only twenty, De Filippo had sixteen years of acting experience behind him, and the play bears the mark of a skilled actor who knows the language of mimicry, movement, pauses, and nuances. Little more than a sketch, it nonetheless contains early versions of later themes: the isolation of the individual, the injustice of the law, the plight of the poor. Moreover, it shows De Filippo's dissatisfaction with the condescension implicit in "picturesque" representation and local caricature. Approaching writing from both his stage experience and his experience in living, he invests familiar comic types with a bitter humanity.

This first work is certainly naive in its use of theatrical conventions and stock types, but the earthiness and spontaneity of the dialogue are arresting. The scenes show no divergence between study and invention, theory and practice. The Neapolitan dialect theater, direct descendant of the *commedia dell'arte,* acquires a new complexion when filtered through De Filippo's sensibility. The result is a realistic world, with its own characters, and a credible plot which in its comicalness evinces suffering. The work is characteristic of De Filippo's early theater in its focus on characterization. Each character, however sketchy, has some personal story to tell.

The play centers on the pharmacist Don Saverio, a proud man who despite his rational approach to life, is compelled to endure an evil fate. He had approached marriage pragmatically, first making sure that his business was a success. But his wife in the meantime has left him for a richer man, and now he is alone, ridiculed by the neighbors; his inward pain at lacking a family is reflected in his refusal to assent to an annulment on the grounds of childlessness. So, at once resigned and humiliated, he spends his day serving the poor customers of his area, often in the company of his doctor and friend Don Teodoro, who comes in to chat, to take a nap in the cozy armchair, or to ask advice on the best way to get rid of the mice in his house. The play begins realistically, but the plot twists soon recall the *pulcinellata.* One of the first customers is Carmela, maid to Don Saverio's ex-wife, who comes in to buy some aspirin for her mistress; distracted by the unexpected appearance of her suitor Enrico, she leaves instead with an envelope containing Don Teodoro's rat poison. A wretched couple arrives looking for the doctor. The wife is clearly suffering from malnutrition, but no one would dare diagnose it as such because to do so would reflect on their economic status and deal a severe blow to their pride. Don Teodoro's diagnosis is no different from earlier doctors', and the couple cannot pay for the consultation. Finally, the doorman Gregorio arrives, his face swollen, and Don Saverio is happy to be able to show off his skill in extracting a tooth. But his satisfaction is short-lived: the next visitor is the policeman who has come to arrest him for attempting to poison his ex-wife. Don Saverio is led away with such despatch that the drugstore is locked with the door-

man inside. Gregorio's plight, however, is a temporary inconvenience and, coming upon the heels of Don Saverio's arrest, it provides dramatic relief, minimizing the seriousness of the pharmacist's predicament.

Pharmacy on Duty alternates between the bitter reality of poverty borne with pride and the farce of the *pulcinellata,* over all of which hovers the author's own sense of irony. De Filippo's fatalistic vision of the irony present in everyday life will not allow any of the characters to triumph. Saverio's ex-wife is herself a victim, fatally ill, while Gregorio's temporary imprisonment provides a physical symbol of the common state of the characters, each imprisoned in his private situation and powerless to change it. From his first appearance as an author, without over-insistence, De Filippo shows the moralistic intentions that characterize his most famous plays. Nonetheless, watching this play, one has the impression of being still in the mainstream of the San Carlino theater tradition. The stuff of farce, for example, is the doctor's haste in changing chairs when the pharmacist tells him that his father died sitting in that very chair, Enrico's flirting with Carmela in the presence of Don Saverio, who has no choice but to go along with the love affair, the accidental substitution of rat poison for medicine.

The *vis comica* is the result not just of unexpected situations, but also of the unexpected and naively witty punchlines, as for example when Vincenzo brings in his young wife Rafilina who has reluctantly consented to be examined by Don Teodoro, the doctor:

TEODORO:

Sit down, please. (Rafilina sits down and starts to take off her shoes.) Wait a minute! . . . Wait a minute! . . . Leave your shoes alone! . . . Just undo your blouse a bit.

RAFILINA:

[To her husband Vincenzo] And you made me change my stockings!

TEODORO:

You thought you were taking her out to buy a pair of shoes?

VINCENZO:

O.K., forget it . . . When we go home you can put the ones with holes back on.

TEODORO:

Well, now, how do you feel, young woman?

RAFILINA:

How do I feel?! Oh! Nobody knows how I feel!

TEODORO:

But I'm the doctor. I have to know![3]

Here the whole situation is comical, building to an explosion of laughter as the meaning of the expression "Nobody knows how I feel!" ("'O saccio sul' io"), a common Neapolitan exclamation, is transferred from the idiomatic to the literal level. No less comic are Vincenzo and Enrico's gimmicks, which nonetheless at the same time evince their suffering. As soon as the spectator stops laughing, he feels the bitterness of the situation.

Dominated by a crepuscular, Chekhovian atmosphere, the play seems only a moment in a faded, melancholic life. De Filippo's way of making the characters speak and move in chiaroscuro goes back to the Neapolitan playwright Lìbero Bòvio. But as Robert G. Bander writes,

> The melancholy strain which Eduardo has introduced into the farcical tradition of Italian dialect theater is a measure of his difference from Ruzzante, Goldoni, and Gallina; his comic inventiveness sharply differentiates him from Di Giàcomo, Bracco, Russo, Mùrolo, and most of the other Neapolitan vernacular dramatists of an earlier period. De Filippo's sense of spiritual unrest, and his ability to dramatize it in a colloquial manner with which his audience can empathize, is his mark of individuality as a playwright.[4]

Most important, even at this early point in his artistic career, De Filippo had already begun to create a mythic, universal character. At the very outset he struck a rich vein of comedy, a vein that led deep into humanity and could therefore be appreciated and understood by all. Incidents in the life of poor Neapolitans come to represent the comic-pathetic condition of the universal "little man."

The problems of the "little man" are chiefly economic in the one-act *Filosoficamente* (*Philosophically,* 1928). Gaetano Piscopo seems at first to be a stereotypical Neapolitan, believing passionately in the power of dreams to give him winning numbers in the weekly lottery and refusing to take responsibility for his obsession, preferring to blame his dead wife. But beneath the humor is real pain. Gaetano's primary worry is not his gambling, or even his perennial losses, but his two unmarried daughters, Maria and Margherita. The first part of the act shows the family trying to scrape together the money to buy pizzas and fruit for one of the modest parties that are Gaetano's way of introducing his daughters to well-intentioned young men. They are under threat of eviction, and to throw the party they have to go hungry for a few days. Gaetano's efforts to keep up appearances despite his poverty show the superficiality, but also the endurance, of the Neapolitan lower bourgeoisie. The party is a failure. Despite the jokes, the conversation between the old and the young comes to nothing, and even in the young people's conversation there is a certain rancor and envy. The characters are united in a lifeless, pathetic attitude, and everything seems placed on the same plane, portrayed with analytical objectivity.

Evident in these early works is De Filippo's ability to turn traditional farce in whatever direction he wants—toward pathos or toward social criticism. Nonetheless, most are dominated by humor for the pure enjoyment of it. The complicated three-act *Uomo e galantuomo* (*Men and gentlemen,* 1922), about the interactions of traveling actors with provincial nobility, shows De Filippo's total assimilation of the comic effects of the Neapolitan popular theater. The influence of the *pulcinellata* shows in the vivacity, freshness, and wit of the spoken language, the fanciful, exuberant dialogue, and the *lazzi pulcinelleschi* or comic "bits." The pompous exuberance comes from the plays of Pasquale Altavilla, while from Scarpetta comes the overall scheme, the types, the inner movement of the action, the comical expedients, and the use of social background. The essential elements of De Filippo's comedy— the traditional chase of love and treachery, the slapstick, the craziness and tricks, mistaken identity and misunderstandings, gossip and buffoonery—as well as his skills at interweaving plots and using dialect realistically are all here in this one play.

Quei figuri di trent'anni fa (*The old gang of thirty years ago,* 1929) is a comic farce; at the same time, however, it criticizes the Italy of the "golden times" of Fascism, showing the misery beneath its alleged heroic grandeur. In this play De Filippo leaves the familiar lower-middle-class setting and turns to another corner of Neapolitan life, to a clandestine gambling house operated by a certain Gennaro Ferri. Gennaro hires Luigi as a shill in a gambling game; and as Luigi is schooled in the secrets of the trade, he shows comic slowness in understanding just what trade he is learning, what is expected of him, and consequently what will be the outcome of his involvement. Luigi's ingenuousness is the source of all the jokes in this play, so obviously rooted in the *pulcinellata* of Scarpetta and the *commedia.* As in *Men and Gentlemen,* here there is none of the pity and desperation expressed in *Pharmacy on Duty* and especially in *Philosophically.* The dialogue and funny situations keep the spectators detached from the stage action, so they can better understand De Filippo's implicit criticism of Fascism. In fact, the intent of the play did not escape the censor, Leopoldo Zurlo, who made De Filippo change the title, originally *Le bische* (*The gambling-house*), and forced him to set it thirty years earlier, prior to the coming of Fascism, under the pretense that the regime had abolished such illicit practices. Under Fascism there could be no aberrations, only "even days."

No such political implications are apparent in *Pericolosamente* (*Dangerously,* 1938), a modernized *pulcinellata* on the theme of the taming of the shrew. In the San Carlino theater, as in the Punch-and-Judy show, Pulcinella, a coward outside the house, always used a stick when teaching wisdom to his wife. The twentieth-century Pulcinella uses a gun loaded with blanks, which, like the cardboard slapstick, makes a lot of noise but does no harm.

In most of De Filippo's early works farce serves to veil the wretchedness of the characters as they resort to precarious stratagems in order to save face or to survive. At times, the grotesque situations become pathetic because of the protagonist's inability to establish communications with the surrounding world. From such a world of misery and loneliness emerges Sik-Sik, De Filippo's first major character, who exhibits a hopeless will to survive even as he sorrowfully resigns himself to the squalor around him— the same squalor that will face the protagonists in many of the postwar plays. *Sik-Sik, l'artefice magico* (***Sik-Sik, the Incomparable Magician,*** 1929), written for Mario Mangini's *Pulcinella principe in sogno* and interpreted by the three De Filippos, was the first work in which Eduardo wrote a part for himself; his first big success, it became a hallmark of his style of humor and the first clear sign of his future greatness. The stage directions describe the magician as follows:

> Sik-Sik is a man of about 40, with a thick black moustache. He is wearing a light-colored jacket that is none too clean; his black pants belong with the tail-coat he will put on during his performance. He wears a soft hat. In one hand he carries a small suitcase and in the other a cage containing two identical pigeons. He has a cigar stump between his teeth. Sik-Sik is the typical traditional strolling actor: poor, tormented, and . . . a philosopher. Giorgetta, his wife, follows him. She wears no hat and has a threadbare coat over her shoulders. Her untidy dress clearly shows her to be pregnant. Like her husband, she looks tired and discouraged.

[p. 121]

The protagonist might almost be the author himself as he was at the time of his association with the Kokasse company: so thin as to be almost emaciated, *sicco sicco* in Neapolitan. Sik-Sik and Giorgetta are presented as somewhat lacking in talent, very poor, discouraged to the point of futility, but nonetheless dedicated to their profession. Their magic act reveals their destitution in terms of the magician-actor's belief in his art, in terms of the hunger that forces him to use his pregnant wife in the act, even down to locking her in a trunk, and in terms of the stage on which what amounts to a real contest takes place between him and the audience.

Arriving late one evening Sik-Sik misses his regular assistant Nicola. After scolding his wife, he desperately latches onto Rafele, a "shabby and wretched man" who asks him for a light and whom he asks to be his partner in the act. There follows a dialogue reminiscent of Abbott and Costello's "Who's on first?":

Sɪᴋ-Sɪᴋ:

> I'll do very easy tricks tonight because you are new at the job . . . O.K.,; the curtain rises. You'll know the minute I'm supposed to come on, because the music will go like this: Pe . . . pepe, pe . . . pepe, pe . . . pepe, pe . . . pepe. Got it? (The tune Sik-Sik hums is the trumpet motif from *Mephistophele.*)

Rᴀғᴇʟᴇ:

> And he makes his entrance.

Sɪᴋ-Sɪᴋ:

> Who makes his entrance?

Rᴀғᴇʟᴇ:

> Peppe.

Sɪᴋ-Sɪᴋ:

> Who's Peppe?

Rᴀғᴇʟᴇ:

> The fellow you just told me about.

Sɪᴋ-Sɪᴋ:

> No. Pepe is the trumpet.

Rᴀғᴇʟᴇ:

> Oh, the trumpeter is called Peppe.

Sɪᴋ-Sɪᴋ:

> No, no, no, no, no. That's the noise the trumpet makes. Don't confuse the issue. Then, after the blare of the trumpet, I make my entrance. You'll recognize me at once. I'll be wearing a genuine Chinese kimono, you know, so I look more important. When you see me enter, you say: This guy really looks Chinese. The audience will already be impressed because, as you know, the Chinese are past masters of this kind of show. Their skill and patience are endless. You ought to see how patient the Chinese are.

[pp. 123-24]

Robert Corrigan's statement that "Eduardo De Filippo . . . is unquestionably the fullest contemporary embodiment of the *commedia* spirit" finds justification especially in plays like this, where *commedia* elements are easily identifiable in the linguistic devices, line exchanges, and slapstick visual comedy[5]. Sik-Sik suggests a combination of Pulcinella and Bragadoccio, Giorgetta a combination of Columbina and Speraldina, Rafele the *zanni* (*commedia* clowns), but with a twentieth-century twist. Rafele makes the audience laugh, but he also increases Sik-Sik's desperation to an almost tragic intensity as he gives away the secrets of the three basic tricks that make up the show: the water-drinking trick, the trunk escape, and the trick of the disappearing dove.

At the last moment before the performance, Sik-Sik's usual assistant Nicola arrives and wants his part back. Rafele is aware of his own limitations, but he needs the money and, besides, he needs to prove himself superior to the equally foolish Nicola. In the ensuing scuffle Rafele loses the fake padlock used for the trunk escape, as well as his pigeon, which, however, he is able to replace with a chicken. When during the performance Sik-Sik asks for a volunteer from the audience, he is faced with two. Predictably, the three tricks are disasters. But Sik-Sik's resourcefulness is limitless. When each of the partners testifies that the water went down his gullet, Sik-Sik announces that he has materialized half of the glassful for each of them. There is no padlock for either partner to substitute; to free his wife Sik-Sik has to break the good one. When, finally, a chicken comes out of Rafele's hat instead of a pigeon, Sik-Sik concludes triumphantly that not only has he translated the pigeon from the cage to the hat, but also changed it into a chicken. Though the spectator can laugh at the failure of the tricks, nonetheless he cannot laugh at Sik-Sik and his wife, victims of events over which they have no control. Mechanically, the orchestra breaks into a fanfare, ironically emphasizing the failure of Sik-Sik's act; "the curtain, however, is more compassionate, and it falls to end the play."

Sik-Sik, the Incomparable Magician might seem no more than the dodges of a second-rate magician capable of extraordinary mimicry, juxtaposed with the pulcinellesque improvisations of a very stupid foil. But it is also the drama of a wretched man forced to make ends meet. Sik-Sik is a character on the edges of society, clinging to life by means of his poor tricks; to convince himself of their adequacy, he often repeats to Rafele that when he comes on stage and performs, "it will bring the house down." His thirst for applause almost equals the hunger of his stomach; and if his illusion, that he can impose himself on the audience by his appearance alone, crumbles bit by bit when he is actually on stage, nonetheless he resists and finds a way to save at least the illusion of not being wholly beaten.

In De Filippo's work tragic humor is defined by the destruction of illusions, the collapse of ideals, the irony of fate, and, sometimes, the ability to bear it all. One notes a foretaste of the attitude of the characters of the mature dramas—Pasquale Lojacono of *Those Ghosts!*, Calogero Di Spelta of *The Big Magic*, Pasquale Cimmaruta of *The Voices Within*—as Sik-Sik tenaciously refuses to recognize his failure in order to preserve the authenticity of his art, as he stubbornly fights to remain "the incomparable magician" by enclosing himself in illusions. In fact, when Defilippian characters cannot otherwise escape the sad reality that traps them, they often flee into dreams or magic. The difference being that, good or deceitful, dreams come from outside, as a supernatural intervention, supplying, let's say, a winning number in the lottery (*Philosophically, I Won't Pay You*), or revealing a distressing situation (*The Voices Within*). Magic, on the other hand, is entirely in the hands of man, who must succeed by his own resourcefulness (*The Big Magic, The Top Hat*). Gennaro Magliulo put it quite well when he observed that in this short drama we find both "the Defilippian intuition of an oppressing human and social condition and also the intuition of the attitude which the *homo Neapolitanus* is accustomed to assume in facing that condition"[6]. The knockabout comedy is qualified by a subtle, painful humor, the "sorrowful humor" that Pandolfi observes as the dominant note of De Filippo's mature plays[7].

Much of the serious note is conveyed in the stage directions, which, kept to a minimum up to this work, now increase in number and elaborateness. De Filippo describes in great detail not only the scene but the prelude to it, defining an emotional atmosphere that assures identification with the character:

Once again he draws back the curtain, but the trunk remains inexorably closed. What will the audience say? What will they do? But the magician is thinking of his wife Giorgetta, about to become a mother, and locked inside! The trick, the theater, the audience, everything else vanishes from Sik-Sik's mind. He has an idea, the only way he can help her. He goes off into the wings and comes back with a hammer. He slips behind the curtain, and soon we hear muffled desperate strokes of the hammer, with Sik-Sik's panting voice counting aloud above the hammering: "And a one! and a two!"

[p. 136]

Clearly, the author has also assumed a narrative distance from his creation. His stage directions are no longer merely instructions to the actors. Instead, they articulate the vision of a man who wants to go beyond the limits of theatrical language and comment on suffering humanity. Sik-Sik is enmeshed in a situation which an ambiguous Pirandellian humor addresses with laughter though aware of the tragic undertones of the situation. By this direct intervention De Filippo wants to make us feel the complete, inexpressible drama of Sik-Sik in this moment of surprise, strain, discouragement, and dejection, all of which must be interpreted by an actor in a gesture, in intense and prolonged mimicry. The stage directions are thus like musical cadences, hinted at but not fixed in a definite way and therefore capable of later development and new interpretations, according to the ability of the actor and the receptiveness of the audience. Words thus express only one, partial aspect of De Filippo's artistic personality; along with his linguistic ability goes his acting and directing sense. As the years pass, the significance of the stage directions increases, and in the postwar plays they often are concerned with portraying custom and reiterating satirical social criticism.

Though not added to the text until about 1934-35, the first stage direction of the play nonetheless sheds light on De Filippo's growing consciousness of himself as an artist and commentator on his own works:

It is nine-thirty.

The public is gathering in front of the ticket office. In fifteen minutes the show will start. This is the moment when I am most aware of the awesome responsibility facing me: the crowd is anonymous, all strangers; one enormous question mark. Never more than at this moment am I so completely outside the fiction of my role. I'm not yet convinced of the character I shall become in a few minutes, on the stage. I feel that I'm part of the crowd; it's as if I was going to go up to the ticket office and ask for an orchestra seat to see the show too. Not until the moment when the spotlights blind me with their stars of light and the curtain rises on the dark theater pit, can I possibly take up my part in the fiction. The minutes pursue me inexorably. They sweep me on in their rush, they overwhelm me, they push me toward the little stage door, which closes ominously, with a hollow sound, behind me.

[p. 121]

It is clear that here we are in the presence not merely of stage directions, but of a man addressing his own methods of expression. De Filippo wants to maintain not only the "fictitious character of the stage, but also that degree of freedom of the imagination, that unforeseeable suggestion of the stage—the engulfing stage with its blinding lights," the extraordinary rapport with the audience which he must constantly enliven and renew, and the deep desire to understand, to interpret, to give a significance to every encounter[8]. The conception of the nature of theater first suggested in *Sik-Sik* marks the beginning of De Filippo's interest in the theoretical aspects of the theater, an interest which finds its fullest expression in *The Art of Comedy* and *The Top Hat*.

De Filippo's first six plays demonstrate his debt to *commedia dell'arte* and to the Neapolitan theatrical tradition. And, albeit in germinal form, they establish those features that will later come to characterize his theater: the importance of acceptance by the audience, the emphasis on characterization, the mixture of humor and pathos, the development of a recognizably Defilippian protagonist, and the necessity to theorize on human nature, the dramatic situation, and, of course, the role and status of the theater.

INTERIOR VACILLATION AND INTIMATE DRAMA

The combination of pain and humor evident in De Filippo's early works is conveyed less in action, more in mood, in some of the plays that follow. Of significance to De Filippo is what is sensed and fleeting, transmitted indirectly through glances, sighs, and subtle crises: a panoply of feelings, from remorse to hatred. The plays' expressive realism reflects the influence of Neapolitan playwrights like Rocco Galdieri, Libero Bovio, Enzo Mùrolo, and Eduardo Nicolardi, and, from outside Italy, Anton Chekhov, whose plays were very popular in Italy during the late 1920s and the 1930s.

It seems logical and perhaps inevitable that De Filippo should follow this course, for he treats characters who live according to outmoded ideals, once cherished, but potentially destructive in a world that no longer honors them. Some people are so sentimentally attached to their ideals that they become blind to reality and to the needs of those around them, even to the extent of destroying their families. Their happiness proves to be naive; and when it crumbles, it leaves a malancholy sense of loss. All in all, the plays are informed with irony, humor, and the playwright's growing pessimism.

In the two-act *Chi è chiù felice 'e me!* . . . (*Who is happier than I!* . . . , 1928), the protagonist Vincenzo is a sensible, prudent, discreet man who avoids everything that might disrupt his quiet life. He lives on a small monthly income which is enough to ensure his contentment despite the little sacrifices he must make to afford an occasional luxury: a more expensive pipe tobacco, for instance, means fewer cartridges for his biweekly hunting trips. Happiness means order; there can be no risks, no unknown factors.

His day includes at least one meal, an afternoon walk, and a card game with friends; he retires every night at twelve o'clock sharp. With his beautiful young wife, Margherita, and a carefully circumscribed life, Vincenzo thinks himself the happiest man in the world. But one day a local dandy, who has killed in self-defense, takes refuge in Vincenzo's home, as if to warn him that his happiness is precarious and that any external intervention could destroy it. Riccardo, the young man, falls in love with Margherita, who, feeling her femininity reawakening after years of boring "happiness," accepts his attentions. But the neighbors' gossip cannot disturb Vincenzo's peace or compromise his idealism. Realizing that his wife no longer treats him as she used to, he tries to reaffirm his happiness and prove his wife's fidelity to himself and his neighbors by calling them to witness as she begs Riccardo to leave, declaring that she will never give herself to him. Vincenzo is thrilled at these words, then disheartened when Margherita gives Riccardo a passionate good-bye embrace that shows how much she loves him.

In this play the traditional themes of farce—conjugal misfortune, the betrayed and unaware husband—are invested with a new spirit, to become intimate drama. The strength of the play is in its caricatured types set in the realistic context of Neapolitan customs. The betrayed husband appears both comical and humiliated; and events are treated with a bitter sarcasm. Behind the comedy of character, behind the caricatures, the lively dialogue, the sarcasm and farcical episodes, lies a middle-class psychological drama on the theme of conjugal happiness which will be developed more subtly in *Those Ghosts!*

Vincenzo is something of a negative character. By being content with what he has, he becomes in fact "a priest of the isolated happiness, stubbornly pursuing it with a faith which leaves no room for even modest uncertainties!"[9]. He is a deserter in the struggle of life, and from his suffering stems an ambivalent tension between tragedy and comedy. On the other hand, Margherita is the first of many positive women in De Filippo's plays. Though she tries to go along with her husband's kind of forced happiness, she can find no lasting personal satisfaction. She is unable to repress her feeling for Riccardo despite her will to remain faithful and preserve the family honor. She thus unconsciously rebels against those conventional attitudes that often define the housewife's domesticity as merely a form of resignation. In this respect she is the first in a long line of De Filippo's women who take an active role in determining their destinies. As its ironic title indicates, with this play De Filippo begins developing paradoxes of the Pirandellian sort. To the unreflecting illusions of the blinkered optimist, he juxtaposes the vulnerability of human certitude in the face of chance, which so easily dissolves conventional beliefs and promises; what dominates, more or less vainly opposed by laws and moral norms, is the sweeping force of passion and carnal desire. The situations thus are more complex and dramatic than in the previous works.

In his concern for characterization De Filippo does not wholly abandon social criticism. In Vincenzo one may easily see the typical attitude of the middle-class Italian of those years: passive submission to the comfortable socio-economic ambiance provided by a political system—Fascism—which frees the individual from every responsibility while lulling him into self-satisfied optimistic apathy. Moreover, as Scornavacca notes, one may easily see in the treatment of the minor characters an anticipation of De Filippo's later satire of manners:

> The hypocritical maneuvers and the fictitious ingenuousness with which Vincenzo's neighbors and so-called friends proceed to stir up suspicion in his brain, instilling it drop by drop, with minced phrases, treating him with malicious compassion, underline the love for the satire of manners which has remained a characteristic of Eduardo's theater.[10]

The satire of the earlier plays here is more refined, underlying not merely an action or scene, but the whole play.

In most of the plays to this point the main character has consistent features: a weak will and the inability to separate reality from fantasy. In the plays that follow the protagonists often ruin their lives because they are unable to assert their "selves." Ironically, they are anti-heroes in the supposedly heroic era of Fascism. They do not transcend themselves, though at least they overcome their immaturity. At this point, the drama functions to criticize Fascism implicitly, the middle class explicitly. Later, with the fall of the regime, this kind of protagonist is criticized in order to emancipate him from the past, its moral codes, its doctrines, its atavistic ways of thinking.

Gennariniello (1932) is another variation on the situation of the characters trapped because one of them is unable to face reality. Gennaro, the head of the family, though his authority is somewhat undermined by the double diminutive on the end of his name, is incapable of a decisive, serious act of will; that is, though he can act decisively, he cannot will seriously. Instead of worrying about his son's stupidity, he worries that he does not pursue girls; instead of worrying about his spinster sister's psychological problems, he worries about marrying her off. He makes his living creating and selling foolish inventions and dreaming of others that will make him rich. Deeply discontented with his modest lot in life, he aspires to a higher social station. An attractive neighbor comes to symbolize for Gennaro a life beyond his reach; but when he makes advances to her, she responds by teasing him in front of everyone, causing serious domestic quarrels and finally exposing him to the silent pity of his family, neighbors, and onlookers. This character exhibits the senile sensuality of the poor man who inevitably must make a bitter, grotesque return to the truth and to his gray and advanced autumn. The play presents a picture, at once pathetic and funny, of Neapolitan life as well as a portrait of a human type very dear to De Filippo: the man who seems generally ignorant of the wretchedness around him, and who aspires to a dignity that because of his very ignorance is unbecoming to him.

As in all the prewar plays with similar situations, De Filippo never shows how the character will deal with the discovery that he has been living a lie. The playwright suggests, however, that in those years of strong Fascist control the masses and the lower middle class, exemplified in Gennariniello, had no chance. Implicit criticism of Fascism may be seen in Gennariniello's *gallismo*—his boasting of his sexual prowess, typical of the current *machismo*. *Gallismo* was encouraged by the Fascist regime as an expression of strength and defiance, and Gennariniello's unconscious acceptance of it shows the Italian inability to rebel against anachronistic ideas. Ranged against the male character's empty illusions is the practical world of the female character, Concetta, who plods through the day working as a housemaid to make a few lire and save the family from starvation. She fills the void left by her husband; and though she whines somewhat when he is off in his dream world, she comes to his defense in moments of crisis. Add to these two characters the only son, an adolescent coddled by his parents, yet ready to give them his affection in their worst moments, and the husband's sentimental spinster sister, in other plays often replaced by a bachelor brother, and we see the pattern for the Neapolitan family of many of De Filippo's later works. From the family life portrayed here flows an intimacy strong to the point of sentimentality, but corrected with the same kind of grotesque twist at which De Filippo aims in Sik-Sik[11].

More and more, De Filippo seems attracted to a protagonist who lacks any heroic potential, who drifts wherever he is led by his failure to take life seriously. He is a tragic-comic character: whereas heroes insist on the truth, he avoids it, and instead of being the protagonist in a conflict between truth and illusion, he, often unwittingly, exposes the conflict between truth and self-deception. His dreams frequently help him evade the future and regress permanently. All this usually occurs against the backdrop of the family, which the protagonist often needs to idealize despite its actual state of degeneration. Nowhere is this situation more evident than in *Natale in casa Cupiello* (*Christmas at the Cupiellos'*, 1931), which De Filippo himself has called one of his most significant works. The high point of his first creative phase and, for many reasons, a key work in his artistic development, it still enjoys success with audiences and critics; in 1966 it was produced at the Malyj Theater in Moscow, directed by Leonid Varpokhovsky, and for Russian television in 1973, again under his direction, with the well-known Vladimir Doronin in the lead.

The action swings between farce and drama, between naturalistic realism and spiritual investigation, between comedy and irony, all given a balance exceptional for De Filippo in this period. The opening scene is a normal one in the everyday life of the Neapolitan lower middle class. Concetta, patient, calm, a cup in her hand, tries to wake her husband, the monotony of her voice reflecting her resignation:

CONCETTA:

(With the monotonous tone of someone who knows beforehand that she will have to call many times before being heard) Luca . . . Luca . . . Wake up, it's nine o'clock.

Pause. Luca continues to sleep.

(As before, but a little louder) Luca . . . Luca . . . Wake up, it's nine o'clock.

Luca grunts under the blankets as he turns over. Pause.

(As before, in the same tone) . . . Luca . . . Wake up, it's nine o'clock. Here's your coffee.

LUCA:

(Without understanding, still half asleep) Oh? . . . The coffee? (Murmuring something incoherent, he sticks his head out, completely swathed in a woolen shawl, then he sits up in bed, stretches out an arm as if he were about to take the cup of coffee, but then slowly lets his arm fall down again; his head sinks back and he falls asleep again. All of this is done with his eyes closed.)

[pp. 221-22]

De Fillippo's scenes and stage directions deserve accurate reconstruction, since he presents his characters not only through dialogue but also suggestive visual details. The opening action really tells us nothing that could not be deduced from the words, but it does emphasize the eternal lethargy of the characters and the fact that they live worlds apart from one another. It presents them visually and therefore more cogently than words can, particularly when words must create the illusion of everyday speech. And it becomes particularly revealing when the protagonist does not speak much. In the scene there is a perfect harmony between the atmosphere created by the stage business and that created by the words and tone of voice; indeed, in this expressive Defilippian language, there is meaning even in the pauses, rich in their interior tonalities.

Luca Cupiello wants to keep alive the joy of earlier years, when the children were small and the family was all united. In a glow of nostalgia he builds the traditional Nativity scene, oblivious to his children's cynicism and his family's struggle against poverty and the threat of dissolution[12]. Only when the family conflict reaches a climax, at the end of act 2, does Luca peep out from behind his paper toys. Ninuccia, his daughter, is surprised by her husband in the arms of another man. Insults are hurled, the rivals rush outside to fight, mother and daughter are left fainting and hysterical. This is the moment Luca chooses for his entrance as one of the three Wise Men of the Nativity story, a long rug draped over his shoulder, a gold paper crown on his head, a sparkler in one hand and an umbrella in the other as a Christmas present for his wife. With his son and brother behind him, dressed in similar fashion, he kneels before his appalled wife and sings a carol as the curtain falls. Three days later, with the opening of act 3, he lies in bed again, paralyzed by his encounter with reality; and in the end he dies, unable to come to

grips with the grown-up world. His eyes are filled with the vision of a vast, world-sized manger in which a giant newborn baby Jesus howls; as he breathes his last, he cries, "What a beautiful crèche!" and, as an added touch of irony, he asks forgiveness for his daughter as he joins her hand with her lover's, mistaking him for her husband.

In the very setting of the first act, the Cupiellos' master bedroom, we are faced with abject poverty. Luca, his wife, and their son Nennillo must all share the one bedroom. The house is obviously unheated: Concetta wears a shawl about her shoulders. Luca's head is wrapped in a woolen scarf, and Nennillo is buried under the bedcovers. A similar setting will be seen in *Millionaires' Naples!* and *Filumena Marturano.* The protagonist, despite his advanced age, personifies innate simplicity, purity, and traditional values as he insists on using his Christmas manger to communicate his world to others. Luca is hardly a new character for De Filippo; there were glimpses of him in Vincenzo of *Who Is Happier than I!*, who pursued happiness, if not as naively as Luca, just as unrealistically. There is, however, a marked difference. More than merely a simple, naive person who does not want to grow, Luca also wants to keep the world around him the way it was. With his manger he pays homage to a very old and not exclusively Neapolitan tradition, motivated by the childlike residue of uncorrupted goodness lying more or less hidden in every man. Convinced of Christ's benevolence, he would like to find that same genuine love among men. But it is a vain desire. He and his manger are rejected by all; and in that rejection is the rejection of the spirit of Christmas—its joy, hope, love, and family unity—and all humanity's rejection of the mystery of love expressed in Christ's incarnation. The manger is on stage for the audience too. More than a way of telling us what is going on in the characters' minds, it forces us to reflect on the contrast between apparent joy and actual misery. In a materialistic world—De Filippo seems to suggest—only innocent and perhaps naive people like Luca are capable of such love.

However, Luca's stubbornness in building the Nativity scene also demonstrates his immaturity and irresponsibility; it is a way of fleeing into a world of illusion. He does not exercise the necessary paternal authority and guidance, either by helping his lazy son make a life for himself or by persuading his libertine daughter to remain faithful to her husband; his family goes to pieces, and he must suffer for his unconscious escapism. Through the attending physician, De Filippo comments bitterly and sadly: "Luca Cupiello has always been a big child who thought of the world as an enormous toy . . . when he realized that the toy should be played with, not as a child, but as a big man . . . he couldn't do it. The man in Luca Cupiello is missing." "Luca dies and must die, even if he arouses pity," De Filippo told me in an interview. "He is a victim of his own addiction to the game of childish illusions. The manger he builds is a kind of drug which paralyzes his imagination and distracts him from daily living." In fact, Eduardo concluded that "the manger also symbolizes anything which does not have any relation to the real problems of a man or a class of people, anything which is encouraged by the authorities." It is a kind of Homeric lotus, a soporific, like soccer, television, or whatever else is used to put the conscience to sleep.

This implicit social criticism, so characteristic of De Filippo's postwar theater, comes through most clearly in the structural elements which will become basic in those later plays. In the majority of the mature works the action centers around a tormented, disillusioned character who suffers from alienation and lack of communication with the surrounding world, particularly the family. On stage, Luca is always shown somewhat isolated from others, often in confrontation with them. But the others do not constitute a solid opposition. They have differing opinions, but, in their own way, they too lack any balanced, realistic approach to life, living their lives in absurd pettiness, busy with concerns important for appearances only. In them one sees the historical condition of Italian society in that period, and one recognizes in particular the spirit of the Neapolitan lower middle class—their desires, resourcefulness, ardor and extravagance, goodness and impulsiveness, misery and will to live—and at the same time their unawareness of their social and political plight. Luca, his neighbors, and their whole class lack the courage to look beyond Fascism's facades and discover the reality; they represent an irresponsible society which, by continuing to play with toys, indirectly indulges the wishes of the political power. In the postwar plays De Filippo tries to show how his characters can deal with a crumbling world by achieving solidarity as a family (witness the Jovine family in *Millionaires' Naples!*). However, this solidarity is as frequently betrayed within the family as in the society it reflects. This betrayal is developed most poignantly in De Filippo's treatment of World War II, and it is visible in less blatant injustices like the exploitation of the poor and the oppression of the weak through regressive, suffocating social institutions and the indifference of society as a whole.

But even when dealing with such complex themes, De Filippo does not abandon his comic vein. *Christmas at the Cupiellos'* gets its humanity from its Neapolitan atmosphere and its vivacious comedy from its structure, a series of blunders reminiscent of the *pulcinellata*. The unsuspecting Luca first delivers to his son-in-law his daughter's confession that she is running away with her lover, then insists that the lover stay for Christmas dinner. But in his Pulcinellesque mistake of uniting the lovers at his deathbed, he imparts a lesson on the importance of love, be it extramarital or not. Like every Pulcinella, he is unaware that he pronounces truths that society would prefer to ignore. And so it is that the farcical elements have a serious side. There are reminiscences of the *lazzi* of the *commedia* in the confrontation between the weak father and his stubborn son, in the uncle who is always being robbed and mocked by his nephew, in the boy's persistence in finding the manger ugly. Nennillo and his uncle are still tied to the fixed types of the tradition, but they

point toward more individualized characters later on. The one serious character is again a woman. While her husband builds the manger, Concetta must take care of the details of everyday life and even prepare the glue and provide the nails for his project. Like the wife in *Gennariniello,* she must bear the family responsibility alone and, like her too, she genuinely loves her husband.

TOWARD THE THEATER OF THE GROTESQUE

In an era that Pirandello characterized as grandiose in the worst sense—"Italians all living the life of the senses, intoxicated by sun, light, color, exulting in song, each one playing some easy musical instrument . . . fanciful men of letters speaking a grandiloquent tongue, magnificient adorners, and evokers of past glories"—De Filippo portrayed the humble and even the degenerated aspects of life. Inherent in his writing is an essentially ethical purpose: to castigate the moral failure of the men of his times and to condemn dissolute or immoral customs, evil masquerading as good, egoism in the guise of charity. Although his ethical position has a social basis, his interest in social issues is less urgent than his concern for moral or existential issues. With moral themes, his sarcasm and irony are accentuated. However, the reduction of men to puppets elicits pity as well. While openly attacking the games of pretense which convention compels people to play, while demolishing the facade of bourgeois respectability, De Filippo nonetheless takes a sympathetic attitude toward the individual victim, showing genuine feelings crumbling under the pressure of an inflexible code of conduct.

De Filippo brings to these themes his own understanding of the popular theater and the theater of the grotesque. Luigi Ferrante remarks that De Filippo's "grotesque is expressed by means of an irony of popular origin which operates in his plays as a means of demystifying hypocrisies and clichés"[13]. By ironically decomposing reality, De Filippo reveals the factitious nature of what is taken for reality, displaying in his characters the behavior of man in a post-heroic age. Irony also derives from the playwright's awareness that the values of that period, the age of Fascism, have themselves been shown to be fragile and hollow. The result is a drama of emptiness, of people who have no future.

In the two-act *Ditegli sempre di sì (Always say yes!,* 1932) the hero Michele is the victim of a conflict between an "idiotic" self-effacement and the practical need for self-assertion. The dominant signifiers here are the "fool" and the "wise man" juxtaposed humorously to suggest that wisdom and madness are not always distinguishable. "Foolish," like "crazy," is a label other people impose on someone who threatens their conventional, rigidly prescribed view of reality, and Michele earns both qualifiers as he returns from "a long business trip"—actually a period in a mental asylum—and starts naively revealing everyone's secrets. Out of the "madness" of social relationships—so De Filippo paradoxically suggests—arises the protagonist's personal history. His is the kind of madness described by Roland Barthes in a review of Foucault, a madness which no longer demands a substantive definition as a disease, or a functional definition as antisocial behavior, but a structural definition as the discourse of reason about nonsense. The madman's derangement derives from his belief that others perceive the same reality as he does, and from his failure to recognize that each person must find the truth for himself. Michele speaks with the voice of madness as he rebels against conventional roles and behavior. But his madness is no mere comic resolution to a funny situation, as it was in **Men and Gentlemen**; rather, it is a paradoxical twisting of social reality by a man who takes euphemisms and clichés seriously and thus judges the "wise" speakers insane. His position therefore is not farcical, but grotesque. In renewing the old theme of the "madman" who reveals the craziness of sane people, De Filippo relates himself to Pirandello, Dostoievski, and the literature of Decadence in general, but with a Neapolitan spirit.

In these works written during De Filippo's association with Pirandello, the master's evident influence never distorts the essentially popular nature of De Filippo's theater; the solid realism at their base saves them from the dry intellectualism and abstraction that often plague the grotesque theater. *Uno coi capelli bianchi* (*A fellow with white hair,* 1935) fails for a different reason: the dialectic of being and appearance, face and mask, and the relativity of truth, is never adequately connected to the other motifs, in particular the conflict between the older generation and the younger. This conflict was of great contemporary concern, however, because of the Fascist regime's reactionary doctrine and praxis, and the play was well received by the Fascist public despite its faults.

With this three-act play De Filippo sets aside the lower-middle-class milieu for the arrogant, well-to-do upper middle class. His growing polemical tendency manifests itself as he turns the grotesque to the task of denouncing a specific bourgeois type, the man of privilege who thinks he has the right to impose his views on others and judge them with an air of superiority. Thus, he creates his first wholly negative character—one who nevertheless deserves our pity. The title of the play is a phrase used to describe an older person who acts in a manner unbefitting his age. Old Battista Grossi should be disinterested, serene, indulgent, and trustworthy. Instead, he is hypocritical, impulsive, and irresponsible. He feigns modesty, but is deeply self-centered. He pretends support for youth, but would be the first to blame them. Simulating innocence, he is flagrantly culpable of inadequacy as a human being.

Battista is obviously a caricature; and, as Freud observes, caricature is a means of rejecting those who stand for "authority and respect and who are exalted in some sense"[14]. Nonetheless, De Filippo does not make Battista a pathological case. The character does not act wholly out of malice, but because, after so many years of hard work, he refuses to accept being replaced by his son-in-law as head of the family business. Because everyone respects the wisdom of someone with white hair, Battista can involve himself again in the life around him; but he does so by creating intrigues, suspicion, and discord, perhaps feeling that only in this way can he regain a measure of power and keep up the illusion of youth. Unfortunately, the more he wants to be part of the family and feel important, the more he forces himself on them and the more he is isolated. Through a protagonist like Battista, living an existential drama in a hostile world, the grotesque situation becomes Pirandellian tragicomedy. The protagonist is a victim, his oppressor Time; and, as always, Time wins. What seems at first a private tragedy thus becomes a profoundly human drama of universal importance.

Battista suggests a more deeply explored Luca Cupiello. However, he lacks Luca's poetry, remaining an aged child, one who does not understand the cycle of life. In him there is the hypocrisy of Molière's Tartuffe and the slander of Don Marcio in Goldoni's *La bottega del caffè*. De Filippo has suggested that Battista is a product of capitalism: his father and grandfather created wealth, but he himself has accomplished little, living on what others have done and envying whoever replaces him in the world of work. But, however well drawn, he cannot guarantee a good play, and this one lacks the theatricality that one expects from De Filippo and the cohesion needed for it to live on stage. The contrast between life and form—obviously Pirandellian—is not given an adequate problematic suspense, and the play ends up confused in tone, satirical and documentary at the same time.

A Pirandello short story that De Filippo and Pirandello dramatized together, "L'abito nuovo" (The new suit, 1936) rewards attention by showing how De Filippo could bring his theatrical and thematic abilities to bear on a structure not his own[15]. As with other Pirandello short stories, the world of this story is permeated by a bitter sadness that expresses itself in the grotesque deformation of a man's life. The down-at-heel Michele Crispucci has had to suffer the shame of his wife's desertion and now, on top of that, the indignity of the wealth, of suspicious origin, he has inherited at her death. His colleagues, who mocked him as the betrayed husband, envy his newfound wealth. Michele would like nothing more than to give it away to them, but his mother and daughter are opposed to his wish. It is emblematic of his decision to accept the legacy when he comes home wearing a new suit. More than simply a sketch awaiting broader development, the story is perfect in itself, with its own life. In sharp, concentrated language, Pirandello had created a dramatic work which could easily have been expanded as it was and divided into highly effective theatrical scenes.

But when De Filippo transformed it into a play, he did not merely adapt it; the final three-act work is quite different from the original. While the short story concentrates exclusively on the central character and "the difficulty and the pain of lifting his voice out of that abyss of silence in which his soul had been submerged for so long," the play fuses realistic, grotesque, and absurd elements to develop a wider significance and a new spirit. The themes remain Pirandellian: an honest man succumbs because he cannot bear to continue wearing the mask that society imposes on him, or perhaps because he realizes that he is not the person others see in him. But De Filippo continues to develop his own drama, the drama of the man attached to a fictitious reality which he has made for himself and which he does not want to see destroyed by others, but who nonetheless—like Luca, Battista, or Vincenzo—is finally defeated. The abstractly allusive surrealistic tone of the short story is not to De Filippo's taste; accordingly he fills the play with characters of a Neapolitan cast and color.

The New Suit is a satire on the bourgeois mentality which values only money and appearances. It is a bitter play, intended to convey a certain warning to a world in which men of moral scruples like Crispucci are getting fewer, while people like Concettino and the greedy neighbors multiply, infinitely multiplying offenses to conscience. The characters are thus larger in the play than in the story, especially the ex-wife, who from a modest prostitute becomes a new Aphrodite and a symbol of lust. The strongest effects—dramatic, ironic, harsh, and irritating—come from the theater of the grotesque, the vivacity comes from the popular theater. The protagonist is obviously Pirandellian, but his existential suffering is typically Defilippian, a suffering that will become more pronounced in postwar plays like *Those Ghosts!* and *The Big Magic.*

In *Non ti pago* (*I won't pay you,* 1940), as in *The New Suit,* De Filippo casts Neapolitan milieu and elements from the popular theater in a Pirandellian mold. Again, the focus is on the paradoxes of everyday life, expressed in a protagonist whose innate stubbornness recalls Pirandello, but whose characteristic habits are Neapolitan: the ancient passion for the lottery, the superstitious belief in the power of dreams, and the dependence on a palliative religion—all illusory antidotes for an incurable poverty. As Carlo Filosa has pointed out, in *I Won't Pay You* De Filippo makes perfect use of two essential methods of Pirandello's theater: the initial static one of giving the basic paradox a striking but apparently realistic context; and the second dynamic one of demonstrating the paradox through an insistent and ultimately sophistic dialectic[16]. However, here the similarity ends, for De Filippo is most interested in the moral implications of the situation, and he reserves his most powerful condemnation for ignorance, superstition, and the unscrupulous clergymen who exploit them.

The play centers on Ferdinando Quagliulo, the manager of a *lotto* office, and his paradoxical refusal to pay off on a four-million lire jackpot. He contends that the winner, his dependent and his daughter's fiancé Mario Bertolini, accidentally intercepted numbers that Ferdinando's dead father had intended to reveal to Ferdinando himself. Unbeknown to his father, Ferdinando had changed addresses, and Mario instead was on hand to dream the prophetic dream! After many quarrels, Ferdinando finally pays; but he calls on the realm of the dead to burden Mario with a problem for every lira. And, indeed, Mario faces so many troubles that he is in the end compelled to renounce the money to free himself from the curse.

Ferdinando's strange refusal to honor a legitimate winning ticket reflects lower- and middle-class Neapolitans' belief in dreams and their connection to the numbers game of *lotto,* a belief so strong that the Book of Dreams, which assigns numbers to dream objects and events, becomes almost a new Gospel, and superstition becomes a faith inseparably fused with religion. Mario's actions too are reactions to a reality created wholly out of his credulity. Thus, in a Pirandellian way, illusions, desires, and fact become one indivisible reality. However, unlike Pirandello, De Filippo indirectly shows the social nature of the illusions. In his view, superstition is a bow to the fearful and inexorable power that the poor people unconsciously feel lies behind the misfortunes of life. Behind the comedy is thus a bitter reality which justifies De Filippo's sarcastic tone when Ferdinando confronts the priest, the one wanting to know about the life beyond and the reason for his father's mistake, the other defining everything as a "mystery" because he is comfortable with other people's superstition. But De Filippo anticipates the solutions devised by the protagonists of his mature plays, especially *Those Ghosts!* and *The Big Magic,* in making Ferdinando—still victimized, still trapped by superstition—defend himself by a bold, realistic-fantastic stratagem. Thus, as much as certain situations or attitudes may suggest Pirandello, the influence is on again, off again, often external—sometimes a matter of plot only. Don Ferdinando's "proofs" for his contention, which tend toward the absurd and surreal, never detract in the slightest from the joyful involvement of the spectator; they are staged with rare comicalness, rendered with an able, relaxed attention to dialogue, and moved by a spirit of excitement.

I Won't Pay You marks the climax of the first phase of De Filippo's career as a playwright and, in its portrayal of the central character, a major step in his artistic development. In this play his special brand of paradoxical fantasy is at its freshest. His unbreakable attachment to the San Carlino theater—its types, manners, and traditional subjects—is evident in the swift pace of the scenes, constantly governed by a logic which makes fantasy and reality work naturally together, and in the lively speech, its style ironic but glib and easy. Nonetheless, the deep seriousness of his comedy shows unequivocally that he entertains a more profound purpose and draws his motives from feeling. The play thus has the playfulness of a joke, but is enriched by human excitement and satirical jabs. Italian audiences responded heartily to Eduardo's ironic messages, chief of which was that to gain a little one must work hard, but to gain a great deal one need do nothing at all.

In the postwar plays corruption, misery, and existential desperation are clearly connected to their social causes, and De Filippo often gives his central character a subsidiary function as his spokesman in condemning social evils. In the early 1940s such criticism, however peripheral, had to be disguised because of the Fascist censorship. Nonetheless, *Io, l'erede* (*I'm the heir,* 1942), the last of the early works, points toward things to come. Through yet another Pirandellian plot, De Filippo shows how philanthropy can at times be destructive to both giver and receiver. Once again he exploits a situation dear to the popular Neapolitan theater: Ludovico, a sly sponger, manages to trick his way into a household and live without working. Characteristically, the old theme acquires a new value as a vehicle for criticizing the middle class for its unscrupulous charities and—recalling Brecht's *Rise and Fall of the City of Mahagonny*—commenting on the generally negative effect that philanthropy has had on social progress. A great success abroad, especially in London and Russia, it was revived in April 1968 at the Valle theater in Rome under the title *The Heir* and was more successful than it had been a quarter century earlier.

Through the protagonist, Prospero Ribera, De Filippo expresses his contempt for the hypocritical gestures of wealthy landowners who attempt to consolidate their power under the guise of charity. Ludovico would like to live according to a human code, and he therefore proposes a new article to be added to the Code of Civil Law:

> Any person who, in order to sleep in peace at night and to reserve a place for himself in Paradise, commits an abnormal act of kindness against a fellow citizen, thereby removing from circulation and rendering unproductive a portion of our human capital, and who, to justify this same act of egotistical profiteering, attributes it to Christian charity, shall be punished by so many years imprisonment.
>
> [p. 527]

Ludovico is no simple sponger, but, rather, a living reproach to the world which had made his wronged father its dependent; and he submits to it only in order to take his revenge on it. This society cannot take hold of its conscience by itself; he must shake it loose from ingrained customs by exaggerated, absurd behavior. In De Filippo's mature plays the main character develops beyond Ludovico's kind of self-critical reaction against the system; in demonstrating his thesis, Ludovico does not really succeed as a human character, though he does manage to bring a certain dramatic force to a situation initially stagnant.

In these last plays De Filippo presents a main character who attempts to free himself from a suffocating existence. However, he gives such painstaking attention to the comic-grotesque chorus, in order to portray the moral and social misfortunes of the lower classes, that the humor becomes painful, the irony too biting, the dialogue sometimes too stylized and even pedantic. But, notwithstanding these defects, De Filippo shows a new sureness of structure. The scenes are always functional, ending neatly either with a cap line or with a dramatic turn of events that gives the action new development. The main characters, in the early works mere sketches, maintain the vivacity of their theatrical antecedents and receive more attention, have more purpose. The early works depend on clownish gimmicks, slap-

stick, surprise, misunderstandings, double entendre, and comic lines that indirectly underline the main character's interior drama. In the last works the comedy is a higher comedy which usually stems not from the lines themselves, but from the more studied situations in which the main character is put. The secondary characters are almost free of the limitations of type; often they function to increase the main character's desperation or to create an atmosphere that contrasts with that desperation and lets us feel it more.

Notes

1. As quoted by R. Iacobbi, "Napoli milionaria!," *Il cosmopolita,* 1945; reprinted in English in a pamphlet distributed to the spectator of *Millionaires' Naples!* at the Aldwych Theatre, London, 1972. De Filippo's collected plays are published in two series: plays from 1920 through 1942 in one volume, entitled *Cantata dei giorni pari* (Cantata for even days); those produced between 1945 and 1965—with the addition of *Non ti pago,* which is dated 1940—in three volumes, entitled *Cantata dei giorni dispari* (Cantata for odd days). The latter group contains his most celebrated successes. Thus stated, however, the order is deceptive, since the first volume to appear was actually the initial volume of the second series, *Cantata dei giorni dispari,* which came out in 1951 without the indication that it was Volume 1 of a series and without the original dates of the plays. A second edition of the same volume, with play dates ranging from 1945 to 1948, bears the copyright date 1957, by which time the project of publishing his entire works appears to have taken shape. Volume 2 of *Cantata dei giorni dispari,* containing, in addition to two earlier works, the plays written between 1950 and 1957, came out in 1958. Volume 3, plays produced between 1957 and 1965, did not appear until 1966. The success of the first volumes of *Cantata dei giorni dispari* led to the publication of the collected early works, in 1959, under the derivative title of *Cantata dei giorni pari.* The titles—which have been criticized as being not especially descriptive and somewhat pretentious—are in any case ambiguous. The phrase "giorni dispari" can mean either the odd-numbered days of the month or the odd days of the week, considered in Italy to begin on Monday. Perhaps the distinction is unimportant, however, since, in either case, the implication is that the "odd days" are the unlucky ones (cf. our own Friday the 13th). The title *Cantata of Odd Days,* given in 1951 to the plays dating from the immediate postwar period, referred to the misfortunes of Italy in that time. The "even days" of the title later attributed to the plays of the prewar Fascist period are an ironical adaptation of the former title and presumably should be interpreted to mean "the days when everything *seemed* to be going well."

2. Anton Giulio Bragaglia in *Pulcinella* (Rome: Casini, 1953) affirms that in the *pulcinellata* there is a pre-

ponderance of jest and movement over word: "it is a theater free of any rigidly schematic form and the major techniques employed were those of repetitions of situations and the use of double meanings attached to situations, words and events."

3. *Cantata dei giorni pari* (Turin, 1967), p. 20. Hereafter page numbers in brackets in the text in this chapter refer to this edition. Translations are mine unless otherwise noted.

4. Bander, "Critical Estimate," p. 9.

5. Robert W. Corrigan, *Masterpieces of the Modern Italian Theatre* (New York: Collier Books, 1967), p. 8.

6. Gennaro Magliulo, *Eduardo De Filippo* (Bologna, 1959), p. 35.

7. Vito Pandolfi, *I contemporanei,* vol. 3 (Milan: Marzorati, 1970), p. 363.

8. Luigi Ferranti, *Teatro italiano grottesco* (Bologna: Cappelli, 1964), p. 57.

9. Sergio Torresani, *Il teatro italiano negli ultimi vent'anni (1945-1965)* (Cremona, 1969), p. 242.

10. Simonetta Scornavacca, "La storia della 'Gente' attraverso l'opera di Eduardo." Unpublished thesis written at the University of Rome, 1970, p. 27.

11. In two other early one-acts—*Quinto piano ti saluto* (Farewell to the fifth floor, 1934) and *Il dono di Natale* (The Christmas gift, 1932)—De Filippo shows ability to give this intimate note a semimelodramatic cadence, more fully developed in mature works like *Filumena Marturano.*

12. The "presepio" or crèche, an elaborate recreation of the scene of Christ's Nativity, is a feature particularly characteristic of the churches and homes of Naples at Christmas time.

13. Luigi Ferrante, *Teatro italiano grottesco* (Bologna: Cappelli, 1964), p. 31.

14. Sigmund Freud, *The Basic Writings* (New York: A. A. Brill, 1938), p. 77.

15. For the Pirandello story in English, see Luigi Pirandello, *Short Stories,* trans. by Lily Duplaix.

16. Carlo Filosa, *Eduardo De Filippo: Poeta comico del 'tragico quotidiano'* (Frosinone, 1978), p. 132.

FURTHER READING

Criticism

Acton, Harold. "Eduardo de Filippo." In *The Genius of the Italian Theater,* edited by Eric Bentley, pp. 551-63. New York: The New American Library, 1964.
    Acton notes the difficulty of translating into English de Filippo's poetic Naples dialect in his work.

Additional coverage of de Filippo's life and career is contained in the following sources published by the Gale Group: *Contemporary Authors,* Vols. 114, 132; *Literature Resource Center; Major 20th-Century Writers,* Ed. 1; and *Reference Guide to World Literature,* Ed. 2.

G. W. Pabst
1885-1967

(Full name Georg Wilhelm Pabst) Austrian director and screenwriter.

INTRODUCTION

Pabst is known for chronicling in his films the turbulence and neuroses of Europe during and after the two World Wars. His particular interest in exploring the psyches of the women of his time led to his legendary associations with actresses such as Brigitte Helm and Louise Brooks and set him apart from most of his contemporaries in cinema.

BIOGRAPHICAL INFORMATION

Pabst was born in Raudnitz, Bohemia, in 1885. He received his education in engineering at a technical school and at the Academy of Decorative Arts, both in Vienna, from 1904 to 1906. Beginning in 1906, Pabst worked as an actor, traveling to the United States with a German language troupe in 1910. He returned to Europe and entered the military where he was captured and placed in a prisoner-of-war camp from 1914 to 1918. At the end of the war, he moved to Prague, where he directed a season of expressionist theater in 1919. The following year he joined Carl Froelich's film production company. He directed his first film, *Der Schatz* (*The Treasure*), in 1923. In 1928 he formed with Heinrich Mann, Erwin Piscator, and Karl Freund the Popular Association for Film Arts. A year later he traveled to London to study sound film techniques, and in 1933 he moved to Hollywood. Pabst returned to France in 1935. He planned to emigrate to the United States with his wife and son at the outbreak of World War II, but illness forced him to remain in Austria. During World War II Pabst was compelled to make films for the Nazi regime, for which he has been harshly criticized. Most commentators agree, however, that Pabst did not sympathize with Nazi ideology, and the tone and subject matter of much of his film canon supports this. After the war, in 1948, he was awarded the Best Director prize at the Venice Festival for *Der Prozess* (1947; *The Trial*) and in 1949 he formed Pabst-Kiba Filmproduktion. Pabst worked in Italy from 1950 to 1953. He died in Vienna in 1967.

MAJOR WORKS

Pabst's films were deeply informed by both the socio-political events of his lifetime and his personal interest in

Freudian psychoanalysis. Like other German directors, Pabst drifted to the cinema through acting and scripting. His first film, *The Treasure*, explores a search for hidden treasure and the passions it arouses. Expressionist in feeling and design, the film echoed the trend then in vogue in German films, but in *Die freudlose Gasse* (1925; *The Joyless Street*) Pabst brought clinical observation to the tragedy of his hungry postwar Europe. In directing the young Greta Garbo and the more experienced Asta Nielsen, Pabst was beginning his gallery of portraits of women, to whom he would add Brigitte Helm, Louise Brooks, and Henny Porten. In *Geheimnisse einer Seele* (1926; *Secrets of a Soul*) Pabst explored his interest in the subconscious, dealing with the Freudian subject of the dream and using all the potential virtues of the camera to illuminate the problems of his central character, played by Werner Krauss. *Die Liebe der Jeanne Ney* (1927; *The Love of Jeanne Ney*), based on a melodramatic story by Ilya Ehrenberg, reflected the upheavals and revolutionary ideas of the day. Two of Pabst's films have a special significance. *Die Büchse der Pandora* (1928; *Pandora's Box*) and *Das Tagebuch einer Verlorenen* (1929; *Diary of a Lost Girl*) featured the American actress Louise Brooks, in whom Pabst found an ideal interpreter for his analysis of feminine sensuality. Lesser-known films of Pabst's career include *Gräfin Donelli* (1924; *Countess Donelli*), which brought more credit to its star, Henny Porten, than to Pabst; *Man spielt nicht mit der Liebe* (1926; *One Does Not Play with Love*) featured Krauss and Lily Damita in a youth-and-age romance; and, *Abwege (Begierde)* (1928; *Crisis [Desire]*), a more congenial picture that took as its subject a sexually frustrated woman. Pabst's other noted films include *Westfront 1918* (1930), an uncompromising anti-war movie; *Die Dreigroschenoper* (1931; *The Threepenny Opera*), an adaptation of the play by Bertolt Brecht, is a satire on the pretensions of capitalist society; *Kameradschaft* (1931; *Comradeship*), a moving plea for international cooperation; *The Trial*, which deals with Jewish pogroms in nineteenth-century Hungary; and *Der Letzte Akt* (1955; *The Last Ten Days*), about the last days of Adolph Hitler.

CRITICAL RECEPTION

Pabst's films are known to be both technologically advanced and narratively intimate. Pabst achieved this by using film techniques that blended both expressionistic and realistic elements in his films. Critics note the success of these two elements in such films as *Joyless Street* and *Secrets of a Soul*. As Jean Renoir said of him in 1963: "He knows how to create a strange world, whose elements are borrowed from daily life. Beyond this precious gift, he knows how, better than anyone else, to direct actors. His characters emerge like his own children, created from fragments of his own heart and mind." Critic Linda Schulte-Sasse also notes Pabst's uniqueness among the Nazi genius films for "allowing a woman to forge historical progress" in *Komödianten* (1941). However, critic Eric Rentschler characterizes Pabst's films as "problematic" because they tend to involve vacillation and uncertainty.

PRINCIPAL WORKS

Der Schatz [*The Treasure*] [screenwriter and director] (film) 1923

Gräfin Donelli [*Countess Donelli*] [director] (film) 1924

Die freudlose Gasse [*The Joyless Street*] [director] (film) 1925

Geheimnisse einer Seele [*Secrets of a Soul*] [director] (film) 1926

Man spielt nicht mit der Liebe [*One Does Not Play with Love*] [director] (film) 1926

Die Liebe der Jeanne Ney [*The Love of Jeanne Ney*] [director] (film) 1927

Abwege (Begierde) [*Crisis (Desire)*] [director] (film) 1928

Die Büchse der Pandora [*Pandora's Box*] [director] (film) 1928

Das Tagebuch einer Verlorenen [*Diary of a Lost Girl*] [producer and director] (film) 1929

Die weisse Hölle vom Pitz-Palu [*The White Hell of Pitz-Palu*] [director] (film) 1929

Skandal um Eva [*Scandalous Eva*] [director] (film) 1930

Westfront 1918 [director] (film) 1930

Die Dreigroschenoper [*The Threepenny Opera*] [director] (film) 1931

Kameradschaft [*Comradeship*] [director] (film) 1931

L'Atlantide [*Die Herrin von Atlantis*] [director] (film) 1932

Don Quichotte [director] (film) 1933

Du haut en bas [*High and Low*] [director] (film) 1933

A Modern Hero [director] (film) 1934

Mademoiselle Docteur [*Salonique, nid d'espions*] [director] (film) 1936

Le Drame de Shanghai [director] (film) 1938

Jeunes Filles en détresse [director] (film) 1939

Komödianten [screenwriter and director] (film) 1941

Paracelsus [screenwriter and director] (film) 1943

Der Prozess [*The Trial*] [director] (film) 1947

Geheimnisvolle Tiefen [producer and director] (film) 1949

La Voce del silenzio [director] (film) 1952

Cose da pazzi [director] (film) 1953

Das Bekenntnis der Ina Kahr [director] (film) 1954

Der Letzte Akt [*The Last Ten Days*] [director] (film) 1955

Es geschah am 20 Juli [*Jackboot Mutiny*] [director] (film) 1955

Durch die Walder, durch die Auen [director] (film) 1956

Rosen für Bettina [director] (film) 1956

CRITICISM

Thomas Elsaesser (essay date July 1983)

SOURCE: Elsaesser, Thomas. "Lulu and the Meter Man: Louise Brooks, Pabst, and '*Pandora's Box*'." *Screen* 24, no. 4 (July 1983): 4-36.

[*In the following essay, Elsaesser explores Weimar culture's response to* Pandora's Box *and to the American actress Louise Brooks starring in the film.*]

I

For several decades, G. W. Pabst's film, *Die Büchse der Pandora/Pandora's Box* (1928-29) was practically unavailable, except as one of the very special treasures of Henri Langlois' Cinemathèque in Paris. The star of the film, Louise Brooks, an actress from Wichita, Kansas, was to have one of the most enigmatic careers in film history. After the release of the two films she made with Pabst (the other one is *Tagebuch einer Verlorenen/The Diary of a Lost Girl*, 1929) she became a Paris cult figure in 1930, but on returning to Hollywood she virtually ceased appearing in films, and literally became a 'lost one'. Langlois' infatuation with Louise Brooks made him feature a huge blow-up of her face—by then barely recognised by anyone—at the entrance of his 1955 'Sixty Years of Cinema' exhibition:

Those who have seen her can never forget her. She is the modern actress par excellence because, like the statues of antiquity, she is outside of time . . . She is the intelligence of the cinematographic process, she is the most perfect incarnation of photogenie; she embodies in herself all that the cinema rediscovered in its last years of silence: complete naturalness and complete simplicity.[1]

Among those who could never forget Louise Brooks after Langlois' screenings of her films were Jean-Luc Godard (paying homage to Lulu in *Vivre Sa Vie,* 1962[2]), and James Card, curator of Film at the George Eastman House, Rochester. He went in search of Louise Brooks in New York, found her in almost squalid circumstances, and brought her to live in Rochester, on a small Eastman House stipend. While he encouraged her to write and take an interest in her own past, he also tracked down and restored *Pandora's Box,* so that we now possess the image of Louise Brooks in this film as it had been seen by her first audience.

Pandora's Box was not a commercial success, and in the United States, for instance, only a cut and censored version[3] was briefly in circulation, at a time when the new phenomenon of the talkies eclipsed and consigned to oblivion many of the more outstandingly modern films of the last silent period. In Germany, the film was widely shown and discussed, but Pabst was attacked on several fronts. Even his most consistent supporter, Harry M Potamkin, was disappointed and found the film 'atmosphere without content'[4]. About Louise Brook's performance a Berlin critic wrote: 'Louise Brooks cannot act. She does not suffer, she does nothing.'[5]

A good deal of criticism tried to prove Pabst's shortcomings as an adaptor of Wedekind's plays, and complained about the film industry's general temerity of turning a literary classic into a silent film with nothing but laconic intertitles.

Lulu is inconceivable without the words that Wedekind makes her speak. These eternally passion-laden, eruptive, indiscriminating, hard, sentimental and unaffected words stand out clearly against her figure. . . . The film is unable to reproduce the discrepancy between Lulu's outward appearance, and her utterance.[6]

This assessment is contradicted by Siegfried Kracauer, who writes in his book *From Caligari to Hitler*:

A failure it was, but not for the reason most critics advanced. . . . The film's weakness resulted not so much from the impossibility of translating (the) dialogue into cinematic terms, as from the abstract nature of the whole Wedekind play. . . . Pabst blundered in choosing a play that because of its expressive mood belonged to the fantastic postwar era rather than to the realistic stabilising period.[7]

The almost unanimously unfavourable response to the film is interesting in several respects. Even if we can assume special pleading on the part of the literary establishment,

busy safeguarding its own territory[8], the various complaints outline an ideologically and aesthetically coherent position. It goes right to the heart of the film's special interest within Weimar attitudes to sexuality, class and the representation of women in literature and the visual arts. For the passages quoted are indicative of a resistance that, on the one hand, has to do with the difference between literary language and body language ('utterance'/ 'appearance')—reminiscent of more recent discussions in the area of sexual difference between speaking and being spoken as a subject in language. On the other hand, there is an evident irritation that Louise Brooks is neither active ('she does nothing'), nor actively passive ('she does not suffer') which contrasts unfavourably one kind of body— that of cinematic representation—with another, the expressive body of the theatre performance. Compare this to Langlois' '(her) art is so pure that it becomes invisible': praise that implies a diametrically opposite visual (and literary) aesthetic.

Pabst's choice of an American actress for the part caused consternation among German film-stars. It gives the issue a further dimension if one considers it within the large-scale emigration of German film-makers to Hollywood, the economic difficulties of the German film industry after the 1927 crash and especially UFA and Nero's bid to break into the American market. But ideological attitudes towards America also played their part. Louise Brooks recalls a telling incident:

As we left the theatre (at the opening of an UFA film, at the Gloria Palast, and Pabst) hurried me through a crowd of hostile moviegoers, I heard a girl saying something loud and nasty. In the cab, I began pounding his knee, insisting, 'What did she say? What did she say?' Finally, he translated: 'That is the American girl who is playing our German Lulu'.[9]

Kracauer's comments rather simplify this whole ideological and aesthetic complex, with his implied juxtaposition of Expressionism and the *Neue Sachlichkeit* ('New Objectivity'), but as so often, he has recognised a crucial tension in the film—even if, calling Pabst's choice of subject a blunder, he overlooks the extent to which the film actually reinterprets the inner relationship between Expressionism and *Neue Sachlichkeit,* since this 'American' Lulu gives Pabst a vantage point on *both* Expressionism *and* the *Neue Sachlichkeit,* as well as on the fundamental shift that the cinema (compared to the theatre) has brought to the representation of sex and class, libidinal and political economy.

II

When one wants to understand the place of the cinema in Weimar society and culture, Kracauer's work is still essential reading, even though it appears different now from the book it was when first published in 1946. Historians of Weimar culture consider the cinema as part of what makes Weimar Weimar, but they are certainly far from giving it the privileged status that Kracauer allows it, that of unlocking the *Zeitgeist,* the ever-elusive essence of an epoch. John Willett gives an apt summary in *The New Sobriety*:

> There are existing studies that deal with the culture of the Weimar Republic between 1918-1933 much more broadly. 'When we think of Weimar', writes Peter Gay in the preface to his *Weimar Culture,* 'we think of the **Three-penny Opera,** *The Cabinet of Dr Caligari, The Magic Mountain,* the Bauhaus, Marlene Dietrich.' More recently, that other eminent historian Walter Laqueur has defined its Zeitgeist in very similar terms as 'the Bauhaus, The Magic Mountain, Professor Heidegger and Dr Caligari'.[10]

Laqueur, however, had added a proviso:

> The fact that Marlene Dietrich has not been forgotten in 1974, while many of her contemporaries have faded from memory, need not necessarily mean that future historians of the cinema will have to share the preferences and prejudices of our time.[11]

I take this as an invitation to talk about Lulu, rather than Lola Lola.

The cinema is part of the colourful mosaic of the Zeitgeist, providing an easily recognisable iconography, the period flavour, or—again in John Willett's words—important mainly for its 'atmospheric, essentially nostalgic relevance'[12]. Such is the general view, and it implies an idea of cultural diametrically opposed to that of Kracauer, for whom the cinema was not an addition, among the many forms of entertainment that flourished (Laqueur's account of Weimar cinema is the last part of a chapter called 'Berlin s'amuse') but its hidden centre. A period thinks, compul-represents and interprets itself—and its contradictions—in all the products of its social life, and among the means of self-representation, the cinema had for Kracauer an absolutely preeminent function. In this respect, Kracauer had already applied the lessons of structural analysis and social anthropology, and as Adorno put it: 'his way of considering the cinema (as a cipher of social tendencies) has long since become common property, so much so that it is practically an unquestioned assumption underlying any serious reflection on the medium in general.'[13]

No fundamentally new or different history of the Weimar cinema has thus appeared since Kracauer's sociopsychological study of the 'secret history involving the inner dispositions of the German people'[14]. And this despite the fact that in the field of economic film history particularly, and also textual criticism, many new perspectives have been opened up. The general impact has been that in the intervening time, scholars have become more careful in specifying who—that is, what class, what group—represented itself or was addressed, when 'going to the movies' became a regular habit. A somewhat different understanding of the nature and origin of German fascism has also made it less urgent to read '(the) disclosure of these dispositions through the medium of the German screen' primarily as a 'help in the understanding of Hitler's ascent and ascendancy'.[15]

Today, Kracauer is the historian of the social and sexual imaginary—the structures of anxiety, desire and denegation—that constituted the identity of the German lower middle class. They made up the bulk of the cinema-goers at the Gloria Palast and all the other high-street movie-palaces in Berlin and other German cities. What his book attempts, in a language that borrows some of its key analytical terms from Freudian and Adlerian psychoanalysis—regression, hysteria, impotence, compulsion, sublimation, instinct—is a metaphoric description of a dominant personality-type, whose characteristics are that he is male, paranoiac and masochistic, with repressed homosexual objects of identification. He experiences class barriers as insurmountable, and upward mobility a desire tantamount to parricide, punishable by social *déclassement,* a fate that, like the sword of Damocles, hangs over his head in any case. Kracauer offers a number of reasons why this class and its dominant character-type is representative for 'the German people' generally, and why it is reasonable to assume this to be the target audience of the films:

> In a study published in 1930 (*Die Angestellten*) I pointed out the pronounced 'white collar' pretensions of the bulk of German employees, whose economic and social status in reality bordered on that of the workers, or was even inferior to it. Although these lower middle-class people could no longer hope for bourgeois security, they scorned all doctrines and ideals more in harmony with their plight, maintaining attitudes that had lost any basis in reality.[16]

Kracauer's emphasis on personality-structure and psychoanalysis implies a double thesis: firstly, that political and economic life have a shaping effect on the 'logic' of psychic development, and secondly, that cinematic fictional narrative is a particularly efficient way of crystallising dispositions into attitudes. The two theses have a separate theoretical status, as recent debates make only too clear.[17] Or, one can interpret the implications as a feminist as done:

> *From Caligari to Hitler* consistently and repetitiously depicts . . . a national, middle-class, Oedipal/familial failure peculiar to Germany and its cinema. . . . Beneath its sociological pretense is a perverse discourse on sexuality. . . . (The) argument places the blame on the domestic family, or historically, patriarchy . . . , a massive failure of the family to properly inscribe males into the symbolic of paternal order.[18]

That definitions of masculinity and male identity were in crisis during the Weimar years is not especially new: Peter Gay more or less built the thesis of his book around the father-son conflicts of Expressionist literature and drama. When Walter Laqueur says the opposite about the cinema ('one looks in vain, among German films, for the father-son conflict so prominent on the stage') he indicates either a very literal understanding of the motif, or that he has not looked very far, even in Kracauer. Current studies about 'male fantasies' in the literary and semi-literary products of the time, have continued to explore the manifestations of male paranoia and repressed homosexuality.[19]

But what Kracauer also argues is that the depictions of Oedipal conflicts and their modes of narrative resolution in the films are so paranoid and perverse because they are a 'screen', a field of projection and a compensation for objectively insoluble political contradictions and immovable class barriers. Sexuality—always an overdetermined cultural code—becomes the site for the representation of highly ambiguous fears (ambiguous, because libidinally charged) about any social existence outside the bourgeois order, outside the law, outside the hierarchical markers of identity and difference recognised by the middle class. This is not to say that the representation of sexual conflict, or the many family tragedies in the Weimar cinema simply substitute themselves for the 'real' tragedy of class conflict and economic ruin. Such a view would imply an almost trivial understanding of the Freudian notion of the unconscious, and a serious confusion of levels. The bourgeois film of the Weimar period does indeed have a narrative structure whose symbolic code remains remarkably constant throughout the '20s: it is Kracauer's achievement to have pointed this out. But it does not follow from this that the class conflicts of the period are structured in strict analogy to the stages of the Oedipal conflict. If the various revolutions on the Left failed, it is not because its militants were held back by castration anxiety. However, it is quite another matter if in the fictional and ideological discourses of the period, sexuality and the family become symbolic sites for the construction of political ideology.

To give a historical example. In 1925 the Austrian newspaper editor and writer, Hugo Bettauer, author of *Die Freudlose Gasse* (*The Street of Sorrow,* adapted by GW Pabst, and filmed the same year) was assassinated in Vienna. He had been the popular editor of *Bettauers Wochenschrift,* a journal of progressive social views advocating free love. He was also a Jew. His assassin, a 20-year-old, unemployed, first-generation immigrant from Czechoslovakia, had proven connections with the Austrian Nazi Party and was an avid reader of millenarian political tracts. The trial, which incidentally acquitted him, was entirely preoccupied with the question of whether Bettauer's journal was pornographic and morally corrupting. The young man claimed that it was, and that he had acted spontaneously, out of moral outrage. The jury essentially accepted his plea. What seems interesting in the case is that in a social climate rife with class, ethnic, and party-political conflict and close to civil war, sexuality is the preferred field on which ideological conflict and difference can legitimate itself, to the point of justifying politically and ethnically motivated assassination. Otto Rothstock did not kill in Bettauer the symbolic father, but he did find in sexual outrage a subject position that sufficiently unified the contradictions of his social existence (non-integrated minority, unemployment, ambitions towards gentility) in order for him to act in what seemed to him a politically meaningful way. On his side, Hugo Bettauer, a sex-and-crime formula novelist, found in the sexological articles he published a lucrative market among the semi-literary bourgeoisie for his socially progressive views. For him, too, sexuality implied a political and moral position. The assassin sup-

ported his confused political aspirations by modelling himself on particularly rigid conceptions of sexuality and sexual difference. The victim, on the other hand, supported different though perhaps also vague and indeterminate political goals and views with an inverse, open, 'free' conception of sexuality and individual identity.

To what extent then, one might want to ask, did the very existence of Freudian psychoanalysis and the many sexological investigations that emerged in its shadow and vicinity give the question of sexuality a different social space? Did they reinforce, or on the contrary, limit the kind of metaphoric haemorrhage that makes the period's ideologies of race, of power and authority, of State and the Law, of the Soul and the Will, seem to us so many versions of the same 'perverse discourse on sexuality? An intense curiosity focused on Woman is undeniable, but it antedates the Weimar period. Freud's hesitations, and his cautious remarks about the 'dark continent' of female sexuality were not always heeded by his followers: definitions of the 'nature' of Woman proliferated, precisely because in search of an elusive essence, femininity was so often construed in the negative or oppositional image of a masculinity in crisis. Structurally related to the endless father-son conflicts, where male sexuality appears in its most classically Oedipal fixations, and where women are either terrified bystanders or non-existent, one finds in Weimar culture also the sexually predatory and aggressive woman—phallic mothers, on whom the male subject projects both castration anxieties and masochistic fantasies. But there is a third possibility—and this one seems to me relevant for ***Pandora's Box***—rarely in evidence in either the avant-garde or the 'serious literature' of the time and nonetheless perhaps the single most striking characteristic of its popular culture: sexual ambiguity, androgyny, the play with sexual roles and the fascination attached to the realm between male and female—Isherwood's Berlin, if you like, but also Magnus Hirschfeld's research institute. Yet it documents itself most vividly in the cabarets and the variety-shows, the fashion pages or the photography and drawings in quality magazines for a popular audience, like *Die Dame.* Pabst's Lulu—this is the question—is she the demonic female or a Weimar flapper?

III

The figure of Lulu that Wedekind portrays in *Erdgeist* and ***Die Büchse der Pandora***[20] superficially belongs to the tradition of the femme fatale, the sexually alluring but remote woman, through whom men experience the irrational, obsessional and ultimately destructive force of female sexuality. The social and historical dimension of the figure is too complex to be discussed here, but many of the literary or visual embodiments, especially in the late nineteenth century, project onto the desired woman an aggressiveness and destructiveness whose subjective correlative is guilt and self-punishment: for transgression, for violation, perhaps for desire itself. In Baudelaire, Huysmans, Gustave Moreau this figure is a stylisation and a character often from mythology (Salomé, Judith, the feminised

Sphinx) whose location in the Orient and among the spoils of colonial wars or conquests gives a glimpse of a specifically political source of desire and guilt. In Strindberg, Munch or Klimt the figure is more a reminder of the violations of nature and instinctual life by the ascending bourgeois society and its consolidation of the family. With Wedekind, a specific social milieu, marked by class division, comes into view.

More explicitly than anyone else, he locates the question of sexuality within an ideological field. The repression of almost all manifestations of female sexuality entails an intense eroticism suffusing everything that is a-social, primitive, instinctual, according to a topos that sees nature as devouring whenever its nurturing function has been perverted. At the same time, Wedekind saw very precisely the relationship between social productivity and sexual productivity that the bourgeoisie had fought so hard to establish, and which lay at the heart of its 'sexual repression': it was the energy that had to be subjected to the labour-process, regulated and accounted for. The bourgeois subject, for whom sexual passion is nothing but the reverse of all the frustrations that make up his social and moral existence, is contrasted with the members of the lumpenproletariat—those outside, unassimilable or scornful when it comes to the bourgeois' dialectic of renunciation and productivity.

By locating a deviant, instinctual and liberating social behaviour among circus people, artistes, petty criminals, and calling it sexual passion, Wedekind builds a fragile bridge with another class that also felt itself outside the bourgeois order, the declining aristocracy against whose notions of libertinage, of productivity and non-production, of waste and display, the codes of the bourgeoisie once developed themselves. A non-repressive sexuality thus becomes the utopia where the lumpen-class and the aristocracy meet in mutual tolerance and indulgence: the cliché situation of so many Viennese operettas and popular literature fantasies, the ones that served film directors from Stroheim to Ophuls.

This kind of identification cannot maintain itself other than as a projection that also invests the 'other' with the attributes that the self lacks. The attraction of the *bourgeois* for the lumpenproletariat, however, arises not from the similarity of position *vis-à-vis* a common antagonist, but out of an opposition. Wedekind's Lulu is without family ties, without social obligations, without education or culture. Her psychological existence is free of guilt and conscience, her physical existence the very image of beauty, youth and health. Being outside the social order, she belongs to 'nature'—the only non-social realm that the plays can envisage. Sexuality therefore constructs itself primarily through negative categories, where non-family equals amorality, and the non-social becomes the 'wild' on the animal level, or the tropical plant in the vegetal realm. Several layers of self-projection are superimposed, yet it is the sympathy of the aristocrat for the *lumpen* (one outcast for another) that provides the basis for the glamourisation of these negative, somewhat demonic categories.

To leave it at this, is to suggest a very schematic reading of the plays. Wedekind's Lulu is in a sense not only a more radical critique of bourgeois notions of sexuality, but also of the myth of the femme fatale itself. By critique I do not mean a denunciation or a persuasively argued case for or against. For Wedekind, Lulu is a construct, not a sociological portrait: she represents in all her manipulative deviousness the only constant value, set against the relativity and dissolution of the so-called absolute and transcendental values. This, one suspects, is also because Wedekind endows her with a kind of articulacy and energy that makes her the next-of-kin of another outcast altogether: the artist, traitor to his class—whether aristocratic or bourgeois. She voices not only the artist's disgust with the members of all classes, but with himself, which is why her predatory lust is allowed to vent itself against members of all constituted classes and convictions.[21] Wedekind's notion of female sexuality is thus even more abstract and conceptual than that of the French decadents. As the guise that the artist gives himself, she is distant and alluring, devouring and irresistible. As a woman, she remains *terra incognita*. For Wedekind, the conflict between class and productivity, between class and sexuality resolves itself only through the intermediary of art, and of an art that understood its own productivity as a form of elemental, natural expressivity. Lulu is characterised by her *ex*pressivity, because she is conceived in response to a societal *re*pressivity.[22]

The space where such an expressivity could articulate itself is the theatre. Voice and gesture, thought and body could be unified in the performance and thus represent what one might call an image of non-alienated existence, the enactment of 'destiny as pure present',[23] even if Wedekind is careful to relativise the tragic pathos of his figure by such 'epic' devices as the prologue, the ringmaster and the animal imagery of the circus, as well as stating in the preface that Geschwitz, not Lulu, is the tragic figure.[24]

IV

The cinema, however, is still silent. Its expressivity, the way it speaks to the mind and the senses is different, and different affective values attach themselves to gesture, decor or face. With it, the relation of expression to repression changes; conflict and contrast, antinomies and argument are suggested, and perceived by an audience, in forms specific to the cinema.

When Leopold Jessner staged **Die Büchse der Pandora** in 1911, he had written:

> Lulu is honest, because she is woman, *only* woman, who however, has succumbed to the pleasure of the *senses,* in an elementary form (*Urwüchsigkeit*) that cannot but bring disaster to us civilised beings, removed as we are from animal instincts.[25]

In 1923 he made a film called *Loulou,* with Asta Nielsen in the title role. Louise Brooks, who saw the film, describes Jessner's conception and Asta Nielsen's performance as follows:

> There was no lesbianism in it, no incest. Loulou, the man-eater devoured her sex-victims—Dr Goll, Schwarz, Schoen—and then dropped dead in an acute attack of indigestion.[26]

To Louise Brooks *Loulou* is pure camp, because the relationship between theatrical and cinematic body-language is so different; Jessner's conception of cinema is clearly felt to be inadequate, even though his conception of the figure ('Lulu is honest') would be completely endorsed by Louise Brooks. The cinema itself, and not least the American cinema, had drastically changed what was to be accepted as 'honest' in the visual representation of sexuality and affect. Fritz Rasp, also a favourite actor of Pabst's (**Diary of a Lost Girl, Love of Jeanne Ney, Threepenny Opera**) recognised this very well:

> The first law of film acting has been for me, right from the start, to be very reticent with my gestures. When I came from theatre to the stage, I realised that acting for the living image meant a complete break with the theatre, and that the strongest visual effects are . . . achieved solely through the complete internalisation of a role, for which one is the right physical type. That is why I prefer working for directors who have . . . recognised my physical appearance . . . so that acting in film, although this may seem paradoxical, is for me today not 'acting' at all, but—'being'.[27]

Another aspect needs to be remembered, one that points to a sociological difference between theatre and cinema, in respect of audiences—that is to say, in respect of the kinds of visual pleasure, curiosity and emotion that might bind an audience to the cinema. Wedekind's plays engage an audience's curiosity on a double level: the interest in the representation and dramatisation of raw sexual desire is coupled with the gratification of a social curiosity that allows glimpses at the private pleasures and vices of the ruling classes. In Berlin of the late '20s, by contrast, as Louise Brooks remarks:

> the ruling class publicly flaunted its pleasures as a symbol of wealth and power.[28]

Not only could the film not expect to shock with revelations, the curiosity and fascination which Pabst's **Büchse der Pandora** wanted to arouse had to be of a quite different nature. Again, Louise Brooks:

> At the Eden Hotel, where I lived in Berlin, the café bar was lined with the higher-priced trollops. The economy girls walked the street outside. On the corner stood the girls in boots, advertising flagellation. Actors' agents pimped for the ladies in luxury apartments in the Bavarian Quarter. Race-track touts at the Hoppegarten arranged orgies for groups of sportsmen. The nightclub Eldorado displayed an enticing line of homosexuals dressed as women. At the Maly, there was a choice of feminine or collar-and-tie lesbians. Collective lust roared unashamed at the theatre. In the revue *Chocolate Kiddies,* . . . Josephine Baker appeared naked except for a girdle of bananas. . . .[29]

Louise Brooks' description of 'collective lust' not only highlights the sexually explicit, but also the sexually ambiguous aspect of Berlin high- and low-life. In this respect, the world of entertainment is clearly also part of what defines sexuality and sexual difference for society as a whole.

But once it is no longer prescribed in biological categories (and roles do not divide strictly along the lines of gender), sexuality becomes itself more than a social product: a symbolic structure that can articulate other values, distinctions and categories. In Pabst's film, for instance, Lulu's sexual attraction is invariably portrayed in the context of sexually ambiguous attributes. Throughout the relationship with Dr Schoen, it is her androgynous body that is emphasised. With Alwa Schoen, an incestuous and homosexual element is always present. At her wedding, Pabst makes her dance most sensuously with the lesbian Countess Geschwitz, and on the gambling boat, she lets herself be seduced by a young sailor, in order to exchange clothes with him. Following on directly from this reversibility of attributes seems to be the principal ambiguity that preoccupied critics of Lulu, both in the plays and the film—whether she is a victim or an agent, whether she has a passive or an active role in the events of which she is the centre. Wedekind himself writes:

> Lulu is not a real character, but the personification of primitive sexuality who inspires evil unaware. She plays a purely passive role.[30]

Yet this conception of Lulu as a catalyst of the obsessions and neuroses, of the restless searching for meaning and value among the men she encounters, is rendered ambiguous precisely because she is a 'personification'. As such she has a positive presence, because for Wedekind 'primitive sexuality' does constitute an expressive potential as well as a creativity that is close to an absolute, the presumed 'essence' of woman.[31] Critics did not always see Lulu as 'purely passive'. An English reviewer wrote:

> Wedekind reacted against German Naturalism and his plays are as full-blown and direct as anything the Elizabethans could produce; indeed, the nearest parallel to his Lulu cycle is *The Duchess of Malfi,* except that in the former case the woman is the active principle of evil.[32]

Agency is a crucial question because in our society moral evaluation of guilt or innocence, evil or virtue attaches itself to intentionality and agency. Given the traditional division of sex and gender in terms of active and passive, Lulu's behaviour would find itself interpreted accordingly, and thus her function as a figure of projection for fantasies of power and control is also at stake.

Pabst, it seems to me, resituates all these questions, firstly by a script that drastically reduces the number of protagonists and simplifies their narrative functions, and secondly, by his choice of actress. The narrative, apart from stressing sexual ambiguity, involves the male protagonists (except Schigolch) in a perpetually brooding, scheming, angry and frustrated state, the very parody of inwardness in search of expression and self-realisation. Against this world, obsessed with intentionality, goals and motives, Lulu appears exacerbating and provocative, ie seductively sexual—because she is a being of externality, animated but without inwardness; attentive, but without memory; persistent, but without willpower or discipline; intelligent but without self-reflexiveness; intense but without pathos. Her superiority resides in the fact that these effects-without-causes are experienced by the men as both fascinating and a threat.

As to the choice of actress, the cameraman Paul Falkenberg reported:

> Preparation for *Pandora's Box* was quite a saga, because Pabst couldn't find a Lulu. He wasn't satisfied with any actress at hand, and for months everybody connected with the production went around looking for a Lulu. I talked to girls on the street, on the subway, in railway stations . . .[33]

Louise Brooks had her own conception of the role. She, too, seems inclined to see Lulu as a victim, although elsewhere she says that at the end, Lulu 'receive(s) the gift that has been her dream since childhood. Death by a sexual maniac'.[34] Here is why she thought the film controversial:

> (Besides) daring to show the prostitute as victim, Mr Pabst went on to the final damning immorality of making his Lulu as 'sweetly innocent' as the flowers that adorned her costumes and filled the scenes of the play. . . . How Pabst determined that I was his unaffected Lulu, with the childish simpleness of vice, was part of the mysterious alliance that seemed to exist between us. . . . When *Pandora's Box* was released in 1929, film critics objected because Lulu did not suffer after the manner of Sarah Bernhardt in *Camille*. Publicity photographs before the filming of *Pandora's Box* show Pabst watching me with scientific intensity. . . . (He) let me play Lulu naturally . . . And that was perhaps his most brilliant directorial achievement—getting a group of actors to play unsympathetic characters, whose only motivation was sexual gratification. Fritz Kortner, as Schön, wanted to be the victim. Franz Lederer, as the incestuous son Alva Schön, wanted to be adorable. Carl Goetz wanted to get laughs playing the old pimp Schigolch. Alice Roberts, the Belgian actress who played the screen's first lesbian, the Countess Geschwitz, was prepared to go no further than repression in mannish suits.[35]

It is quite possible to see the film in the terms that Louise Brooks suggests: Lulu is a child-like creature, and her attraction resides in the incorruptibility, the lack of guile, menace, calculation, the simple pleasures she enjoys, among which are sex, but it could be the bulging biceps of a trapeze artist, the sight of old Schigolch in the doorway, the fashion page in an illustrated journal, or mistletoe at Christmas-time. But Lulu is not one of those obsessional figures of the Victorians—a child bride or Browning's 'Last Duchess'. Her sexual ambiguity and indeterminacy

has nothing to do with puberty. Just as Pabst seems concerned to redefine active and passive, so he is at pains not to take up Wedekind's paradigm of the anti-social as identifiable with animal nature or tropical vegetation (it is Dr Schoen who keeps a particularly wild and luxuriant plant in his office). She is modern, in a manner that at the time would have been labelled 'American', even without the choice of a Hollywood actress for the part and the ballyhoo this created. But the film does not make 'Americanism' an issue as did Pabst's *Joyless Street.* On the contrary, it gives us a Lulu practically without origin, or particular cultural associations. No doubt, because it allows for a much more 'symbolic' configuration: Pabst's Lulu in her relations with Schoen father and son, as well as on the gambling boat, acts as a stake for male/male power play, and her role is circumscribed by a male double fantasy: she is the woman that father and son both want to possess; she is also the phallic mother whom they want to destroy, the father by demanding that she kill herself, the son by wishing her to act out his own parricidal desire, so that his guilt feelings become her crime. In this respect, the film takes up in elegantly condensed figurations some of the main themes and motifs of Kracauer's (male, paranoiac) German soul. But the very elegance and sophistication of Pabst's narrative and visual solutions indicates that *Pandora's Box* is not primarily about the secrets of this (German) soul: more a knowing allusion to homosexual latency, and a deconstruction of the pathos of repression/ expression. A central complex of German Expressionism is inspected with serene indifference, an indifference to which Lulu gives a (provisionally) female form.

V

Pabst's particular strategy can perhaps be best demonstrated by a look at the opening scene. A man's back is turned to us. He seems to be noting something in a book. It is the meter man, reading the electricity in Lulu's apartment. We first see her, as she comes from the living room into the hall, in order to give the man a small fee and offer him a glass of liqueur. Torn between looking at the bottle and looking at Lulu's revealing dress, the man drops some coins, but before he can pick them up, the bell rings, and grandly, he volunteers to answer the door for her. Outside is a shabby old man, holding his bowler hat with self-deprecating humility. With another grand gesture, the meter man takes a few coins from his waistcoat pocket, to give to the old man and be rid of him. But Lulu, peering past his back, recognises the visitor, rushes out, and flings her arms around the old man; she pulls him into the apartment and past the meter man into the living room, shutting the door. The meter man, not hiding his surprise and disappointment, stoops to gather up the lost coins, goes over to the chair and picks up his peaked cap and battered briefcase. He gives the closed door an indignant look and exits by the front door.

The scene plays on a number of ambiguities. As I hope the description conveys, the meter man (whom the spectator only gradually perceives as such: without his official uniform cap and his back turned, he merely looks the kindly old gentleman) is caught in both a class- and a sex-fantasy, which allows him, even if only for an instant, to place himself in the position of owner of the apartment, and desirable suitor. He becomes Schoen, the master, by the very appearance of someone socially inferior to himself, whom he can patronise by giving him alms. Mirroring himself in the smile of a ravishing young woman he becomes young and handsome himself, and the fact that his attention is further divided between sexual allure and alcohol, allows him the illusory choice between two kinds of transgressions, of which the one he chooses, namely alcohol, may well be the consolation he seeks for the unattainability of the other.

In this brief episode, remarkable for giving us virtually no plot information, the normal social relations implied by master and servant (or mistress and servant), of favours rendered and money received, of alms, fees and gratuities—in short, the conditions of exchange and value—are comically suspended. But it is not only the meter man's illusions that are shattered, when the mistress of the house and the beggarly tramp fall into each other's arms. The spectator, too, plunged *in medias res,* has no time to get her/his visual bearings, for the scene is staged and edited in a very complex succession of camera-movements, glance-glance shots and glance-object shots, whose function it is to create a very mobile point-of-view structure. It establishes hierarchies and relations between the characters, only then to undo them again. There is, for instance, a very noticeably false continuity-match—Lulu is looking off-screen right, when the logic of the glance-glance cut demands her looking off-screen left—which increases the sense of an imaginary space, not quite destroying but also not quite confirming the realistic space of the hallway and entrance lobby. The two doors, front door and apartment door, suggest a rather theatrical proscenium space, but it is the effect of editing and the dynamic of the point of view shots which establishes the illusion of a real space, while at the same time, undercutting it, making it imaginary. Juxtaposed to this imaginary space, and counteracting the spectator's disorientation (which he shares with the meter man), is the image of Lulu, framed by the door and offering the spectator, too, a radiant smile and the imaginary existence of pleasure and plentitude. The disorientation increases the fascination, the dependence on the image, yet the very excess of the smile (excessive because not registering or responding to the meter man's lowly social status, Schigolch's shabby clothes) breaks the strictly narrative function of her presence within the frame, and makes her a figure of desire in and for the spectator's imaginary.

The scene is a kind of emblem of the film itself: first, in its view of social relations, since Lulu, at the end, when back in the world of Schigolch and past all sense of bourgeois decorum, flings herself into the arms of another outcast, Jack the Ripper, with the same unbounded smile. Secondly, it is also a scene that initiates cinematic identification, by placing the spectator in the fiction, via the meter man, whose lack of plot function turns the episode into a

parable of movie watching as a paid-for pleasure. With his exit, the petit-bourgeoisie, Kracauer's *Angestellten,* exit from the fictional space of the film, and yet, they are the historical audience that the film addresses. They may take pleasure in seeing themselves portrayed on the screen, but—according to Kracauer—they take even more pleasure (and thus open themselves up to the play of pleasure and anxiety) in identifying with their 'betters'. The meter man waiting in the hall of Lulu's apartment, is in some sense also the officeworker waiting in line at the entrance lobby of the Gloria Palast, for the star to appear or the show to begin. The prologue points out, lightly, how fragile his class-identity is, and the play on the man's uniform and status recalls Murnau's *Last Laugh,* of which it is in a sense a parody: the presence of Lulu makes it impossible for sexuality to be the repressed signified of the scene, as it is throughout Murnau's film. Lulu's total indifference to class and status renders the predominant anxiety of the early Weimar cinema—*déclassement* and proletarianisation—a comic rather than a tragic motif. The meter man's humiliation or disappointment derives from the total reversal and reversibility of the social and sexual positions, as Lulu demonstrates.

VI

The opening scene leads me to formulate a cautious hypothesis about sexuality in the film and its power of attraction: sexual desire constitutes itself for Pabst in the hesitation between two roles, between two glances. Lulu's 'essence'—or that of femininity in the realm of the sexual—is nowhere except in these moments of choice and division, in the reversibility of the order of exchange. Lulu is an object of desire in the imaginary of men and women, old and young; but her symbolic position is never fixed, it criss-crosses both class and gender, both the Law and moral authority.

In fact, Lulu is desirable whenever her appearance is caught in the crossfire of someone else desiring her as well, and her sexual attractiveness constructs itself always in relation to someone experiencing a crisis in their own sexual identity. An example is the encounter between Dr Schoen and his son Alwa, when the father, after having decided to give up Lulu as his mistress, realises that his son is sexually interested in her: suddenly his passion is once more inflamed by anger, hatred and jealousy. But the son, too, experiences desire via someone else. He falls in love with her only after having seen the jealous and passionate glances that Countess Geschwitz casts at Lulu in his studio.

Such a triadic structuration strongly suggests a psychoanalytic reading along the lines sketched above: Lulu's murder by Jack the Ripper merely completes the homosexual fantasy that is centred on Alwa. After the father has died in the son's arms, killed by the mother, on whom the son has projected the guilt for his incestuous desire, Alwa appears to have freed himself from his obsession. But Lulu's escape, thanks to Countess Geschwitz, and the appearance of Casti-Piani on the train, trap Alwa once more in a masochistic, self-punishing role, powerless against the father-figures, and displacing his masochism onto Lulu, with whom he identifies. In the London scenes, the regressive—oral and anal—aspects are heavily underscored: the three live in filth, and their abode is penetrated by wind, rain, fog and cold; the skylight window, pictured as a black hole, is constantly torn open. All three of them are exclusively preoccupied with oral gratification, Alwa greedily devouring the piece of bread that Lulu breaks off for him in disgust, and Schigolch sucking his brandy bottle like a baby. He finally settles down to Guinness and a big Christmas pudding—a return to the beginning, where both he and the meter man preferred oral pleasures to sex. Alwa's infantilism—he is in turn enraged and petulant—represents the sado-masochistic stalemate of his unresolved Oedipal dilemma. Emerging from the fog is Jack the Ripper who is also Alwa's double: for in the encounter between him and Lulu the two sides of Alwa's personality are fully played out—the tender, yielding and seductive side, and the punishing, castrating, destructive side. It is a scene filmed without violence and struggle, hence disturbingly archaic, where the very tenderness indicates a fantasmatic and also regressive quality. As the Ripper leaves and meets Alwa at the front door, a sign of recognition seems to pass between the men that sets Alwa free and allows him, too, to disappear into the fog, having found his sexual salvation from ambivalence.

The film is centred on Alwa in such a reading—problematic in terms of plot, but suggestive of a possible male spectator position. Conversely, a feminist reading might argue that Lulu, after challenging Oedipal and patriarchal logic by placing herself outside it, had succumbed to it the very instant she herself manifests sexual desire, as she clearly does for the Ripper. In this sense, her death inscribes itself in a hysterical reassertion of patriarchy: the woman is sacrificed, so that the order of men can continue, cemented by a perpetually displaced homosexuality and a desexualisation of women as represented by the female Salvation Army that accompanies the entire episode.[36] Yet it seems doubtful whether this reading is wholly satisfactory either: however poignant the tenderness, it is without pathos or the element of horror one might associate with such a scene. The tenderness stays, but a cool irony ensures that the end is anticlimactic, a dream that is already faint, and fading, as it occurs, into the darkness that envelops all.

I would prefer to see in the ending another way that Pabst distances himself from the socio-sexual imaginary that Kracauer describes, by showing the events as if he was citing them, and thus holding up for inspection a certain form of patriarchy, or more precisely, a particular vision of sexuality—at once ecstatic and apocalyptic—as it might be said to characterise Wedekind's plays and Expressionism, Kokoschka's *Murder Hope of Women,* or Brecht's *Baal.*

For the dynamism of the film, its vivaciousness—and to this extent, its fundamentally different eroticism—comes in large measure from the stark, but always modulated, and often subtly shaded contrast between Lulu's agility, the diaphanous and transparent quality of her body in motion, and the solidity, the heavy black bulk of the men, blocking her way. Lulu's body is in motion even when she stands still, because motion might carry her away at any instant, unmotivated, mercurial and unpredictable. Just as Lulu smiles, and one hesitates to say why, or at whom, and from what inner vision, so her body moves without necessarily inflecting her gestures with intentionality, whereas about the men, every move, every finger and eyebrow is heavy with significance. Of Fritz Kortner, as Dr Schoen, we mainly see his back. His acting style, and Pabst's use of him to fill the frame, stress the bull-necked, looming and cowering nature of his physiognomy. Such a body conveys to perfection (in that it translates into kinetic-gravitational force) the complex interplay of willpower and instinctual drive, of anger and repression, of frustrated, barely-controlled, finally flaring aggression and masochistic, self-tormenting, suicidal despair, which makes Dr Schoen the quintessential contrast of Lulu, and one that becomes paradigmatic for all the men in the film. After Schoen's death, Alwa, Rodrigo, or Count Casti-Piani merely have to affect a scowl, a frown, to bend a shoulder or raise an arm, and one associates the body of Dr Schoen, what he stands for in terms of ruthless plenitude (despite the contradictions) against Lulu's fluidity and lightning changes of place. As the opening scene shows, Fritz Kortner's back is not even the first in the film, among the long line of backs that finally, in the London scenes, spread blackness everywhere.

Countess Geschwitz, in her sexually ambiguous role, is a good example of how what is male and what is female is defined by its physical and gestural support, the always changing contrast between two kinds of bodies, two kinds of body-languages, two ways of filling and traversing the screen. She, Alwa and Schigolch can appear as one or the other, depending on how the dynamics of the visual composition define and redefine their symbolic positions in the narrative. And while it is comparatively easy to describe the kind of masculinity that manifests itself in Dr Schoen, then transmits itself to Alwa and Rodrigo, and finally, in a less unified, more vacillating form, reappears in the Ripper, it is much more difficult to assign to Lulu—and Louise Brooks' acting—a similarly consistent (in both senses of the word) psychological essence. Dr Schoen's back and its doubles are the very image of motive, design, intentionality, the world of cause and effect, of self-realisation as self-imposition, to which correspond self-abandonment and self-pity as their negative mirrors.

Lulu, by contrast, is always in-between: between the meter man and Schigolch, between Schigolch and Dr Schoen, between Rodrigo and Schigolch, between Alwa and Countess Geschwitz, between Alwa and Dr Schoen, between Rodrigo and Alwa, between the stage-manager and Dr Schoen, between the State prosecutor and Countess Geschwitz, between Casti-Piani and Alwa, between Casti-Piani and the Egyptian. . . . If it was simply a matter of sexual desire, the sexual would indeed emerge as the elemental, irrational, a-social force that it is in Wedekind. Yet almost invariably an economic motif appears to disturb the symmetry. It accompanies the sexual link between the characters, but it also crosses it in the opposite direction. This may be a banal observation if one sees Lulu as a prostitute, who trades sex for money. In actual fact, sex and money stand in a much more complex relation to each other in the film. Certainly, she appears as a kept woman, but it is nonetheless Lulu who gives money—to the meter man and then to Schigolch. Dr Schoen finances Alwa's theatre revue, as a way to stop Lulu getting involved with his son. Schigolch introduces her to Rodrigo, because 'men like Schoen won't always pay the rent', but Rodrigo has no sexual interest in her. Countess Geschwitz supports Lulu financially, because she is in love with her, but the favour is not returned. Casti-Piani blackmails Alwa, but he is not interested in Lulu sexually. On the boat, Rodrigo tries to blackmail her, and it is only with a complicated sexual ploy that she can get rid of him. By this time, Alwa is no longer interested in her sexually, yet constantly demands money from her. The police are offering a reward for her arrest, and the Egyptian is quoting a price for her body: Casti-Piani simply calculates which is the better deal. In the London scenes, where Lulu is most explicitly shown as a prostitute, we never see her with clients or in a financial transaction, and she gives herself to Jack the Ripper precisely because he has no money.

Sexual desire is thus part of a more generalised structure of exchange, and in the case of the men, it seems wholly bound up, but not identical with, money and finance. Male desire, in other words, has a precise exchange value, for which either money or sex serve as accepted currency: Lulu is that which allows both desire and money to circulate. The reward offered in the name of the law, for instance, opens up an unbroken chain between police, Alwa, Casti-Piani, the Egyptian slave-trader, Rodrigo and Geschwitz: it is as if the law fixes Lulu's price, and everyone else enters into an exchange, in order to trade most favourably with the same stock.

The scenes on the gambling ship make the relations explicit: while gambling with cards goes on at the tables, Casti-Piani and the slave-trader bargain over Lulu, and a sexual gamble between Rodrigo and Countess Geschwitz is started by Schigolch: all three of them finally decide Lulu's fate, but they do so negatively. It is the sexual role-change that saves her life. What on the level of the plot appears as the suspense logic of melodramatic complication, is in effect an attempt to dramatise 'the relativity of values' in a given society. (The gaming tables, and the mad rush for the stakes, when Alwa has been caught cheating, inevitably recall the stock exchange and gambling imagery of Lang's *Dr Mabuse the Gambler,* 1922). In this instance, however, as in Wedekind's play, this is accomplished without constructing sexuality as an absolute. On the contrary, in Pabst's film a new kind of equivalence, under the sign of interminable exchangeability, is shown to exist between desire, sex and money, an endless

chain, which is both the motive force behind the men's anger and frustration, and the reason why they are—despite the different Oedipal/class configurations—mere substitutes for each other.

The London episode is here doubly ironic. It takes us back to the world of the lumpenproletariat, a world outside bourgeois society where the nexus capital-productivity (of which the gaming tables are both parody and apotheosis), sex and money does not apply, and the whole libidinal economy of exchange is meaningless: Jack the Ripper and Lulu are not endowed with the kind of super-sexuality which the Lulu plays project onto the lumpenproletariat. Instead, she is at her most maternal and child-like, and he is clearly impotent. At the same time, they meet at Christmas, amidst the dispensations of the Salvation Army. In other words, Pabst takes them outside all constituted forms of exchange into limit-cases and utopian forms of exchange—those of the gift, of grace and salvation. Directed against both Wedekind's social romanticism, and against the emergent capitalist logic of exchange, as well as criticising the institutionalised otherworldliness of religion, the ending is so anticlimactic because it's built as a series of mutually undercutting ironies.

VII

If the gambling ship is in a sense the fictional metaphor for the economic chaos of the Weimar Republic, demonstrating the mechanics of inflation, de- and revaluation as it inflects and transforms sexual difference, and with it the symbolic position of women within a patriarchal society, Pabst also has in mind another emergent institution that is radically transforming society: the symbolic logic that ties together subjectivity and representation, sexuality and the image. This institution might be called the order of the spectacle, and it appears in *Pandora's Box* as the critique of theatre in the spirit of the cinema, this time not focused on acting but on *mise-en-scène*.

At the centre of the first part and as its climax, Pabst has placed a scene in the theatre—in terms of the narrative, it is the point where all the threads so far introduced are tied into the proverbial Gordian knot, which Lulu undoes at a stroke. It is the opening night of Alwa's revue. Lulu suddenly refuses to go on stage, because she has seen Dr Schoen enter, accompanied by his official fiancée, the daughter of the Prime Minister. Despite everyone's protestations and entreaties, Lulu remains adamant. The tension mounts, the stage-manager is frantic. Eventually, Schoen agrees to see Lulu in her dressing-room. But no amount of aggression, verbal or physical, appears to move Lulu to a change of mind. Dr Schoen, eyes blazing with hatred, cannot resist the seductive force of her negativity. Sexually aroused, he embraces her at just the moment when Alwa, frantic, and Schoen's fiancée, worried about his absence, enter the dressing-room. Profound consternation all round, except for the theatre-manager and Lulu, who, triumphant, sweeps past the shocked assembly and leaves the dressing-room in the direction of the stage. The scene ends with a brief exchange between father and son (symmetrical to the one where the two struck the bargain over Lulu's appearance in the revue), to the effect that Schoen will marry Lulu, even though (because?) it will be his ruin.

What gives the scene its force is primarily the editing, as it cross-cuts between the effervescence and mounting chaos on- and back-stage, and the more and more single-minded determination of Lulu to provoke a show-down, once and for all. But determination is perhaps the wrong word, because it makes her seem too active, when in fact it is the strength of her refusal, her negativity, the control she keeps on her absence that makes the events take shape in her favour. Pabst here recasts and reformulates the central 'moral' issue of the play: is Lulu active or passive, evil or innocent? The answer that the film gives is that she is neither, that it is a false dichotomy. Instead, it becomes a matter of presence or absence, of spectacle, of image and *mise-en-scène*: Lulu puts on a show of her own disappearance—and reappearance. The spectacle of her person, about which she controls nothing but the cadence and discontinuity of presence, is what gives rise to desire and fascination. Lotte Eisner, trying to describe the magic of Louise Brooks' acting, after a visit to the set in 1929, circles around the same phenomenon:

> And this Louise Brooks, whom I had scarcely heard speak, fascinated me constantly through a curious mixture of passivity and *presence* which she projected throughout the shooting. . . . (She) exists with an overwhelming insistence; she makes her way through these two films (ie *Pandora's Box* and *The Diary of a Lost Girl*) always enigmatically impassive. (Is she a great artist or only a dazzling creature whose beauty traps the viewer into attributing complexities to her of which she is unaware?)[37]

What Lotte Eisner does not discuss, is the role of Pabst's editing technique in achieving the effect of enigmatically impassive presence. Film history usually credits him with a particular type of montage or editing-style that makes the transitions from shot especially smooth, dynamic and impercpetible, the so-called 'cut on movement':

> At the moment of one cut somebody is moving, at the beginning of the adjoining one the movement is continued. The eye is thus so occupied in following these movements that it misses the cuts.[38]

In observing, say, on an editing table, the way that Pabst breaks down a scene into smaller and smaller units, to reassemble, intercut and build up the fragments into a complex crescendo of frantic motion, one can clearly see the above principle at work in giving the impression of speed, dynamism and simultaneity—the aesthetic juncture between futurism and classic Hollywood narrative cinema. But the more crucial effect in the theatre scene is derived from another logic altogether, that of the point-of-view shot, which is to say, the *mise-en-scène* of glances and the organisation of the look. It essentially reconstructs the action in terms of seeing and being seen, of who looks at whom, across which intercut piece of business, dramatic

fragment or decor space. Lulu disappears from the stage, because, as the intertitle says, she 'will dance for the whole world, but not in front of that woman', meaning Schoen's fiancée. But it is for Schoen's fiancée and son that her tantrum in the dressing-room is staged. When they see her and Schoen in each other's arms, the show is over. Not to appear in public means to re-stage a private, Oedipal, sexual drama in a space ambiguously poised between private and public, thus exacerbating the inherently voyeuristic-exhibitionist relationship between audience and performer.

With it, the battle of the sexes, the question of possession, of who belongs to whom and who controls whom, becomes a battle for the right to the look and the image, the positionality of the subject as seeing or seen. Dr Schoen's undoing, in the film's terms, is precisely that he, supreme possessor of the right to look, emphasised by his glittering monocle and his scowling, piercing eyes, becomes himself the object of the gaze: in other words, an image, which in terms of classical narrative is to say, feminised. Such is the logic of the visible that underpins the general position of women in our society, encouraged to objectify their narcissistic self-image as that which regulates their lives: in order to be and to assure themselves of their existence, they seek a gaze in which to mirror themselves. The star, especially the female star—itself a historical phenomenon—develops the implications of this specularity to its limits. Lulu has no gaze, hence the fascination of her smile. It is so open as to appear empty, unfocused, mirror-like. The few times she frowns or looks puzzled, Pabst neutralises her gaze by inserting a cut that disperses, disorients the direction, as in the deliberate mis-match of the opening scene. Some of the difficulties of finding the right actress, as well as Louise Brooks' detailed account of the shooting, confirm the importance that Pabst attached to the look that poses no threat. At one stage he considered Marlene Dietrich for the part, but is reported to have said:

> Dietrich was too old and too obvious—one sexy look and the picture would have become a burlesque.[39]

In the theatre scene, the private Oedipal family spectacle is set within the public, exhibitionist revue. One seems to be the reason for the other, a kind of exchange seems to exist between them. Superficially, the contrast takes up a division already evident in Wedekind: that between the various bourgeois family dramas where Lulu makes her destructive presence felt, and the circus ring, in which she is exhibited among the wild and beautiful animals. But if Pabst similarly places his representation in a double perspective, it is not Wedekind's of family vs circus, social vs animal. Instead, we have two kinds of theatricalisation, two kinds of public spectacle, two kinds of visualisation (which effectively put both family and spectacle outside anthropological or biological associations). One might say that the film contrasts the world on-stage with the world back-stage, and the ironies, the dramatic interest, derive from the comic clash of two related, but dissimilar realms. However, Pabst's concept seems at once more complex and more reductive: the comic divisions between back-stage and on-stage in the film are actually dismembered and reassembled by Pabst into a single, continuous, but at the same time imaginary space—and this space represents the theatre as a machinery, the interaction of separate but interdependent parts.

In the traditional theatre, the area back-stage is that which is hidden from view, the 'repressed' part of the performance, so that a representation of the disjuncture between back-stage and on-stage invariably draws its comic and dramatic effects from the disjuncture expression/repression, the hidden and the revealed. This disjuncture, as I have been trying to point out, is precisely what Pabst sees as typical of Wedekind's contradictory and patriarchal conception of sexuality and social class, a conception that the film systematically scrutinises. Against 'Loulou the man-eater' he puts Lulu, the bright-eyed American starlet, and sets a modernist-constructivist view of spectacle and visual pleasure against the classical theatre's view of stage, ramp, proscenium, curtain, and the illusion of a self-generated enactment of reality. Less than two years before Pabst made ***Pandora's Box,*** the Bauhaus published in its house-journal the text and picture of what a recent exhibition catalogue lists as a 'kinetic object-box', Heinz Loew's Mechanical Stage-Model, intended as a manifesto 'about stage-mechanics in general':

> Guided by a mistaken feeling, today everyone anxiously tries to hide from view on stage any kind of technical process. Which is why for a modern audience ('den modernen Menschen') back-stage is often the most interesting spectacle, since we live in the age of technology and the machine.[40]

This seems precisely the spirit in which Pabst conceived the scenes at the revue as a deconstruction of theatre by a constructivist cinema. Unlike the theatre, which represses and displaces the split between the spectacle and that which produces it, between the fantasies that lie behind the realism of its illusion, the cinema—although in one sense the realistic medium par excellence and dedicated to the creation of illusions—is, as the phrase has it, a dream *factory.* Pabst's ***Pandora's Box*** situates itself in this very split between back-stage and on-stage, between repression, displacement and the concealed, by showing the mechanics of repression and concealment, the mechanisms of presence and absence, of the imaginary within realism, and fascination within perception.

In Pabst's theatre, activity is a ceaseless, but syncopated succession of instances caught in motion. Animation and commotion constantly fill the frame, which seems incapable of containing the elements that traverse it. People and objects enter and exit, from left to right, but also vertically: the stage-manager is suddenly hoisted into the flies, part of the set that is being moved about blots out the main protagonist, decorations and pieces of costume disappear off-frame as if through an imagined trap door. The very instability of the composition, and the constant changes of view-point and angle, make it impossible to conceive as real, solid, existent the space extending be-

yond and outside the frame, as the illusion of realism demands. At the same time, everyone in frame is both actor and spectator, participant and audience. The performers crowd around when Lulu and Dr Schoen have their argument, and from the moment Schoen and his fiancée become visible, they are performers, in their own, but also more and more public drama. The only spectators that are absent, because never shown, are the members of the first-night audience in the theatre. Why does it not appear? Because it would anchor the fictional space in a realist-illusionist dimension, would allow the cinema-spectator to decide and define his/her own specular position unambiguously, by situating the fragments and partial views within an extra-filmic continuity—that of the staged performance and its location in narrative time and space. This position of knowledge the film withholds, and by refusing to provide the sequence with its master-shot, Pabst indicates the extent to which he shared the concerns and outlook of the constructivists. The cinema here defines itself *through* the theatre *against* the theatre, and through expressionist psychodrama against its concept of repression and Oedipalisation. Faced with an aesthetic problem not unlike that of Brecht, Pabst did not choose opera or the Japanese Noh plays for his *Verfremdungseffekt,* but American film-acting—neutral, minimal, pure surface and exteriority—the interface of sexuality and technology as it was present in Louise Brooks, not least thanks to her training as a dancer in the Ziegfeld Follies.

VIII

Lulu is forever image: framed in the doorway or by Rodrigo's biceps, dancing in front of Schigolch or in a Pierrot costume hanging from the wall. In the jealous encounter between Geschwitz and Alwa she is present as the costume sketches that the Countess has drawn, and with an emphatic finger Schoen stabs at the same sketches when he tells Alwa that one does not marry women like Lulu. In court she is on display in the witness-box—the very image that Count Casti-Piani recognises in the newspaper when her face appears from behind the compartment door on the train. Finally, the Egyptian settles on a price after he has shuffled through a pack of photos, which catch the spectator in a significant hesitation about how to read the image: as 'real' (within the fiction), when in fact it is 'merely' a photo (within the fiction).

The nature and function of the look thus appears to be subject to the same divisions and ambiguities that structure the signifying materials of the fiction: class, gender, body, motion, frame. In strictly cinematic terms, an analysis of the relation of the close-up shots head-on into the camera, and other types of point-of-view shots, or the relation of off-screen space to on-screen space, would probably confirm the systematic use of these markers of difference in order to keep the narrative in the register of hesitation and ambivalence. What interests me here, however, is something else: it is tempting to identify a typically male look, the look of patriarchy, of which Schoen's is evidently the paradigm. It is the look of and through the monocle, a withering look that hits Lulu, Schigolch, Alwa, Geschwitz. We might call it the look of the Father, the Law, and its force is never broken or subdued; after Dr Schoen's death, it is merely passed on—to the State Prosecutor's monocle, to Alwa's scowl and Rodrigo's frown. Of all the sexualised men in the film, only Jack the Ripper's eyes are as unfocused as Lulu's. The film therefore establishes sexuality through the disavowed and hidden power of this look. For the spell to be broken one would have to imagine Lulu return the look in defiance, rather than acknowledge its force by constituting herself as picture and image. One would have to imagine Lulu turning round and sticking out her tongue at Dr Schoen—the way that for instance the heroine of Bunuel's *Un Chien Andalou* mocks a similarly castrating stare—in order to realise how this would change the film, break the fascination, because it would upset the delicate and invisible balance that has displaced the opposition between active and passive: 'one sexy look and the picture would have become a burlesque'. The peculiar ambivalence that surrounds the encounter between Jack and Lulu resides not least in the fact that here, both characters transgress the logic of the look specific to their symbolic role in the fiction. This logic gone, the paradigm of fascination on which the narrative was built is broken.

Again, it would seem that only one reading is possible: the moment Lulu, representative of 'the woman', manifests desire and appropriates the look defined by the film as 'male', she suffers death at the hand of a severely psychotic male, tormented by evident castration anxieties. But the direction of what I have been trying to outline, the systematic difficulty of making units of the represented (in this case, men and women; the one who looks, the one who is being looked at) coincide with the act of representation (briefly, the editing, the point-of-view shot, the framing) suggests that it would be rash to reduce the fiction to a fable where characters act out ideological types or gender-specific positions. Could one not see the ending as a 'disenchantment', the breaking of a spell, and seek from there an answer to the question: what is desire, sexuality and fascination in the film?

The distinction I am trying to draw seems particularly important, since it is logical to ask whether there is opposed to the characters' look in the fiction, an inscribed gaze of the spectator, who after all, looks at all the characters and is free to draw his or her conclusion and assume the proper distance. Is the spectator's look identical with the act of representation? Can one juxtapose to the 'castrating look' the pleasurable look of the voyeur? In aligning these different types of look, it seems possible to see Lulu as the intermediary, the figure that allows for the commutation and exchange of different specular positions. For her response to the look of the Father is not to return the look with a suitably aggressive gesture, but to constitute herself as image and spectacle for the same or another subject's visual pleasure. An obvious because banal example is on the train, when, in response to Alwa's sullen frown, Lulu, as if by chance, attracts the interested and pleased eye of

Count Casti-Piani. Similar reversals structure the entire court-room scene, where Countess Geschwitz, in order to divert attention from Lulu, makes a spectacle (an angry, rather than a pleasing one) of herself, which leads directly into the business of the staged fire-alarm and Lulu's escape.

This division, however, cannot be shown to work throughout. On the contrary, Pabst's use of the point-of-view shot and his editing establish a constant transfer or slippage between the various characters' point of view and that of the camera; since for the spectator characters are stand-ins, markers of position, in the field of signification, whose function it is to split, systematically, and in constantly changing dramatic contexts, the attention of the viewer, Pabst's textual system here introduces subtle but significant variations on the 'norm' of classic realism. A brief reminder of the role played by the meter man in the opening scene: the spectator participates in his point of view, 'moral' as well as physical. Yet, although he is on the screen for no more than a minute or so, his gaze, his back and his preference for liqueur are all 'preserved' for the fiction, as his semantic attributes are split between Schigolch, Schoen and the mobile, hovering, alternating point of view—making hesitation and indeterminacy part of the very definition of spectatorship and its pleasure in this film. Pabst's insistence on Lulu as image, framed picture for the characters in the fiction as well as for the spectator, renders even more ambiguous any distinction between the characters' look and that of the spectator. By far the most disturbing, because virtually unreadable scene—unreadable not in its narrative logic, but in the logic of glance-glance, facial expression, space and gesture—is the death of Dr Schoen. Schoen presses Lulu to kill herself, after he has surprised her in the conjugal bedroom with Alwa's head cradled in her lap. Pabst stages the scene in a series of medium shots, with Lulu and Schoen cut off at the waist. As Schoen tries to force the gun into Lulu's hand, both of them appear in the bedroom mirror. From then on, it is impossible for the spectator to decide whether he sees Schoen or his mirror-image, whether Schoen looks at Lulu, the camera or himself. On their faces, as they struggle, the expressions subtly and continuously change; from surprise, anger, anxiety they modulate until the emotive quality or intentionality of their looks become indecipherable. Finally, a faint column of smoke rises between their faces, Schoen looks pleased, Lulu surprised, but then Schoen's features become rigid, as his body begins to slide out of frame, and blood trickles from his mouth. Lulu's face glazes over, but also shows intent curiosity as the camera pulls back to reveal her holding the smoking gun. As she turns from the mirror, her body is broken up, by a rapid succession of close-ups, before it is virtually smothered by Schoen's slumped body. The scene ends with Alwa re-entering the room, looking fascinated and horrified at his father's dying face.

The very discrepancy between the highly dramatic, but nonetheless coherent narrative situation and the elaborate manner of its staging splits the spectator's perception and points of view in ways that subvert actantial (who does what to whom) and gender identification, in favour of a sliding, reversible, difficult identification of face and gesture. Its effect is to make the scene imaginary, which is to say, it allows us to talk about the scene as a fantasy, be it a primal scene fantasy or Alwa's own wish-fulfilling fantasy. What is important is that such a reading is not a metaphoric interpretation of a diegetically realistic scene. It is a specifically filmic elaboration of the signifying elements which renders the scene imaginary.

One might, however, just as convincingly, construct the scene as 'narrated' from Dr Schoen's point of view. In which case, it could represent his struggle, and ultimate failure, to 'possess' Lulu, to fix, limit and define her—if necessary by the act of marriage—in order to impose on her the negative identity of his obsessions. Schoen at the wedding is depicted as a man whose life is suddenly and dramatically getting out of control, and in the end only a pistol shot can put an end to the chaos. Since the wedding is in some important aspects a repetition of the chaos at the theatre, the notion suggests itself that the way he put a stop to the first one, namely by the proposal of marriage to Lulu, and the second one, the proposal that Lulu commit suicide, are structurally identical: a caustic comment on the bourgeois institution of marriage.

The problem with this reading, however, is that in the light of my earlier observations, it is impossible to ignore that the filmic narration in the scene is considerably more complex, making it unlikely that the narrative point of view is that of Dr Schoen. What the systematic ambiguity of the point-of-view structure does allow one to do is to speculate on the conditions of cinematic perception and fascination. In the staging of Dr Schoen's death, the act of viewing itself becomes an activity of the imaginary: presented as a series of views of 'real' or identifiable objects or part-objects (hands, faces, backs, etc), their sequence is, however, organised in such a way that they constantly imply what we do not see, or evoke a space where we are not. The cinema here is never what is shown: it is always also what the shown implies or demands in the way of the not-shown and not-seen. The many different systems that Pabst develops in this film for splitting perception, in order to create hesitation, indeterminacy or ambiguity are ultimately in the service of producing out of real perceptions imaginary sights. Pabst, one is tempted to say, wanted a *mise-en-scène* that would make Lulu a phantom, and the hyperreal magic of her sexual presence is the indeterminacy, at all these levels, of her sexual identity. Being an object of desire for everyone in the film, she preserves herself by being nothing and everything, a perpetual oscillation in the dramaturgy of conflict and aggression. The fact that Schoen cannot possess her and dies in the attempt to do so, gives an indication of Pabst's concept of the Lulu figure: to create a presence without an essence, a presence that is heightened to the point of hallucinatory clarity solely by the play of difference and ambiguity. He transforms the cinema into an institution that turns the desire for possession into an obsession with the image, and

the obsession with the image into a mirror-maze of divided discontinuous, partial views, whose identification and interpretation always entail a fine and final doubt—for me indicated by the different readings of the symbolic structure I have given, none of which 'settles' the issue.

IX

I said earlier that the meter man never returns. I would now like to revise this statement. We see him first studying a book. He turns round and sees Lulu, *as* the spectator sees her and *when* he sees her. The meter man is thus the first spectator, turning from writing/reading to looking. In a different guise, he returns as the last spectator. After Jack the Ripper kills Lulu, he steps out of a doorway, glances at Alwa, tightens his raincoat and walks off into the night fog. After a brief hesitation, Alwa, too, begins to walk off, disappearing into the night. They look like men leaving the cinema—not the Gloria Palast, but the sort of cinema that caters for men in raincoats. Both look disappointed, disenchanted, as if the spectacle had finally revealed its emptiness, its nothingness, had proven to be 'a masquerade that shows that there is nothing there'. Jack the Ripper, as long as he looks into Lulu's eyes, is held by her image, the smile that fascinates with its radiant openness and indeterminacy. It is only when, in the embrace, he looks *past* Lulu, that the knife appears—the object of his own obsessions, like the 'knife phobia' of the protagonist in Pabst's *Geheimnisse einer Seele/Secrets of a Soul,* 1926. Past the image, past the smile, he encounters once more only himself, only his own anxieties. Jack the Ripper, as a stand-in for the spectator, wanting to grasp the presence that is Lulu, finds that he is distracted/attracted by the flickering candle and the glittering object: oscillating between the source of light and its reflection, his gaze traverses the woman, making her an image, a phantom, a fading sight.

This, once again, suggests a psychoanalytic reading. It suggests that, yes, indeed, the pleasures of spectatorship are of a voyeuristic nature, and that they enact a fetish fixation. And yet, what analysis shows is that the point-of-view structure and the manifold divisions of the film's textual system depend only in some respects on the ambiguities focused on the representation of the woman's body. Sexuality in the cinema, as it emerges from Pabst's film, is not a matter of censorship and innuendo, of frank portrayal and realistic scenes, or any of the other terms one usually finds in public debates about 'pornography'—nor is it a question of degrading acts committed on women: all these positions, moral and ideological, Pabst seems to have anticipated and significantly restated. Sexuality in the cinema, in *Pandora's Box* at any rate, is the infinitely deferred moment of, the constantly renewed movement away from, identity—and the film sustains this movement by the creation of a specifically cinematic imaginary that has no equivalence in either literature or the theatre. Pabst called his film not *Earth-Spirit,* but *Pandora's Box*: Pandora's Box is the cinema-machine, the machinery of filmic *mise-en-scène*. The achievement of Pabst's film, in other words, is to have presented sexuality *in* the cinema as the sexuality *of* the cinema, and to have merely used as his starting point the crisis in the self-understanding of male and female sexuality that characterised his own period. Yet Pabst is far from implying an ontology of cinema, or to posit an essence of film, any more than he believes in an essence of sexual identity. The very play on 'Büchse'/'Box', on the level of the signifier—can of film, camera, Freudian 'symbol' of the female sex—disperses any notion of the fixity of the signified, be it sex or the cinema.

This is why, in some respects, the Louise Brooks of *Pandora's Box,* can be compared with the Maria of Fritz Lang's *Metropolis*—the man-created robot-woman. Significantly enough, the figure of Lulu cannot be conceived as a mother, her eroticism is constructed on the paradigmatic opposition to all the traditionally female roles, and yet, while the same is true of the femme fatale, with the latter, it is a sociological and biological paradigm to which she is contrasted, rather than the technological-constructivism that seems to me to underlie Pabst's conception of Lulu. In Pabst's other film with Louise Brooks, *Diary of a Lost Girl,* the heroine does have a child—illegitimate, and taken away from her—and this fact fundamentally changes the character, making the film more of a melodrama and pathos-laden, the woman becoming the victim and the film a sociological *pièce à thèse*. With the introduction of the biological function of women, we immediately have sociology and morality, whereas in Lulu, it is precisely the absence of these motifs that makes the erotic shine so brilliantly but also so coldly. Indeed, Lulu's hint of a maternal function for Jack the Ripper is precisely that which makes her fallible and vulnerable. The film thus becomes a parable of the new woman, created by man, whose fatal weakness is her maternal 'memories'.

The eroticism of Lulu is paradoxically that of the creature that comes to life, the auto-eroticism of the creator and the narcissism of the creature—a relationship only too familiar from the Sternberg-Dietrich myth, which Pabst very nearly anticipated with Louise Brooks three years earlier. This eroticism is one that plays, however, on a concomitant anxiety—that of the creature which emancipates itself from the creator, the sorcerer's apprentice—a motif which, with some justice, might be called the key motif of the German cinema since *The Cabinet of Dr Caligari* itself, in a tradition where the robot of *Metropolis* constitutes the decisive transformation, from 'medium' or Golem to vamp and woman. It is this genealogy that might give one a clue to the mysteriously truncated subsequent career of Louise Brooks. In her essay on Pabst, she reports that, at the end of her work with him, he took her aside:

> 'Your life is exactly like Lulu's' he said, 'and you will end the same way.' At that time, knowing so little of what he meant by 'Lulu', I just sat sullenly glaring at him, trying not to listen. Fifteen years later, in Hollywood, with all his predictions closing in on me, I heard his words again—hissing back to me.[41]

What Pabst meant by 'Lulu' is perhaps precisely this: a woman, an American actress, created by the film industry into a star, becomes an object among objects, alive only in front of the camera. Louise Brooks' struggle with the film industry, as documented in her autobiographical essays, bore out exactly what it meant for an intelligent articulate woman to be a thing among things. It is as if, at the very threshold of becoming a star, Louise Brooks made a film which had as its subject the psychopathology of this very star system, against the background—not of Hollywood, or an ideological critique, but in terms of a very specifically German argument about expressionism, theatre, modernism and cinema. In this respect, the film is indeed the 'tissue of arguments' it was disparagingly called by Kracauer, testifying to the degree of 'abstraction' that the German cinema, in its commercial output, was capable of. The enigma of Louise Brooks is thus in part the enigma of Hollywood film-making, and the very film that might have made her a star allowed her to see what being a star entailed, in the mirror of a film that dramatised and contrasted the liberating pure externality of the 'American' character—the hope of Modernism for most of the '20s—with the contorted inwardness of the German psyche. Against its obsessiveness, but also its moral essentialism, her externality is seen to be not objectivity, and certainly not New Objectivity, but the object-status and objectification of a subjectivity and sexuality—that of women—that still had no name and no place. It was as if in the debate between patriarchy on the one side, and technological modernism on the other, Louise Brooks had glimpsed, albeit at first unconsciously in her defeats with Hollywood but later with full lucidity, the blank that both left for women as a site of representation and being.

X

Pandora's Box, then, is constructed in terms of indecision, hesitation, reversibility, ambivalence and ambiguity. All of these are characteristics of the imaginary, of the unconscious, and in the cinema they define fascination, pleasure and the desire awakened by the image. Out of the homogeneity of photographically reproduced reality, the cinematic process creates its own specific ambiguities, upon which it constructs systems of difference and differentiation that make up the cinema's particular mode of signification, its semiotic status.

The central thematic and fictional support of ambivalence in Pabst's film is sexual desire. Male obsessions—repressed homosexuality, sadomasochism, an urge to possess, capture, limit and fix—confront feminine androgyny and feminine identity in a play of presence and absence, masks and appearances, in a display of spectacle and image as the expression of a freedom from all teleology and essentialism. But, conversely, this androgyny, this ambiguity on the level of sexual definition and identity is only the support, the metaphoric matrix, if you like, that points in the direction of a whole series of other, abstract and conceptual registers of ambiguity—in this case, those that have to do with cultural and ideological stereotypes of active and passive, subject and object, but also with the cogency of Oedipal narratives and the symbolic roles they assign to male and female subjects, on the basis of which the spectators construct their individual subject-positions, structures of identification and visual pleasure.

The source of all these ambiguities, and that which articulates them as differentiation, structure and semiotic system, is the cinema itself, with its infinite capacity of divisions—based as it is on the total divisibility of its materials (the visible world) and the intermittence of its *physical* material, the individual frames of the celluloid strip, and its *optical* material, the beam of light. Lulu, the 'free woman', living without memory or regret, without guilt or volition, is a pure invention of the cinema. That she seems so modern and so real, is a sign of how much modern reality and the cinema have become interchangeable.

Pabst perceived this perhaps more clearly than most of his contemporaries. His emphasis on the cinema creating its own time—that of the motion of the camera whose signifiers the characters become and to which they lend their gestures, faces and expressivity—and its own space—that of editing and lighting, of the cut on movement or the cut according to the dynamics of the gaze (glance-glance, glance-object)—makes Louise Brooks embody the principle of the cinema itself, in its distinctiveness from literature, the theatre and the other arts. But in this very principle lies an objectification of human beings and a humanisation of technology such as the cinema has developed for itself and—through its institutions—has rendered autonomous, which makes Langlois' praise of Louise Brooks that I quoted at the beginning—'she is the intelligence of the cinematic process'—so apt and so ambiguous. For this intelligence is the principle of divisibility and division itself, of exchange and substitution, as it can be observed in the symbolic logic of Western culture and society. By contrast, it is a sign of Louise Brooks' intelligence that she decided not to become the objectified commodity which the logic of this process demanded of her. What Pabst could not prevent, in any case, was the momentous shift, whereby the film industry, seizing on the woman's body, and focusing gratification so much on the voyeuristic look, turned the cinema into an obsessional, fetishistic instrument, and thus betrayed in some sense its Modernist promise, by making this modernism instrumental and subservient to the logic of capital and the commodity.

Notes

1. Quoted in James Card, 'The Intense Isolation of Louise Brooks', *Sight and Sound,* Summer 1958, p. 241.

2. Godard's references for this film were Renoir's *Nana,* Dreyer's *La Passion de Jeanne d'Arc* and Pabst's *Lulu.* Pabst himself has been quoted as being inspired by Dreyer's film.

3. According to contemporary sources, all reference to an incestuous relation between Alwa and Lulu, a homosexual relation between father and son, a lesbian

relation between Lulu and Countess Geschwitz were removed by appropriate cuts and a change of intertitles.

4. H M Potamkin, 'Pabst and the Social Film', *Hound and Horn,* January-March 1933.

5. Louise Brooks, *Lulu in Hollywood,* Praeger, New York 1982, p. 95.

6. A Kraszna Krausz, 'G W Pabst's Lulu', *Close Up,* April 1929, p. 27.

7. S Kracauer, *From Caligari to Hitler,* Princeton University Press, Princeton 1947, p 178-9.

8. An inverse judgement can be found in Kenneth Tynan's profile of Louise Brooks: '*Pandora's Box* belongs among the few films that have succeeded in improving on a theatrical chef-d'oeuvre', in 'Dream Woman of the Cinema', *Observer Magazine,* November 11, 1979, p. 38.

9. Louise Brooks op cit, p. 95.

10. John Willett, *The New Sobriety,* Thames and Hudson, London 1978 p. 10.

11. Walter Laqueur, *Weimar: A Cultural History* (I am using the German edition, Ullstein, 1977, p 10, which carries the famous Blue Angel still as its cover).

12. John Willett op cit, p. 10.

13. T W Adorno, 'Siegfried Kracauer tot', in *Frankfurter Allgemeine Zeitung,* December 1, 1966, quoted in K Witte (ed), *Siegfried Kraucauer Kino,* Suhrkamp, Frankfurt, 1974, p 265.

14. S Kracauer, op cit, p 11.

15. ibid.

16. ibid.

17. See, for instance, Frederic Jameson, *The Political Unconscious,* Cornell University Press, Ithaca 1981.

18. Patricia Mellencamp, 'Oedipus and the Robot', in *Enclitic,* vol 5 no 1, p 25.

19. cf Klaus Theweleit, *Männerphantasien,* Rowohlt Reinbek, 1980.

20. *Erdgeist* was published in 1895, *Die Büchse der Pandora* in 1904. For a brief sociological analysis of Wedekind's Lulu, see Frank Galassi, 'The Lumpen Drama of Frank Wedekind', in *Praxis,* Spring 1975, p 84-87.

21. In the play, Alwa Schoen makes the following observation: '. . . the curse on our literature today is that it is much too literary. We know of no other questions and problems than those that crop up among writers and intellectuals. We see no further in our art than the limits of our interests as a class. To find back to great and powerful art, we would have to move much more among people who have never read

a book in their lives, and for whom the simplest animal instincts serve as a guide to their actions. I have tried to work along these lines in my play "Earth-Spirit"', *Die Büchse der Pandora,* Act I (my translation).

22. 'When writing the part of Lulu, the main problem was to depict the body of a woman through the words she speaks. With every line of hers I asked myself, does it make her young and beautiful? . . .', Wedekind, quoted in Artur Kutscher, *Wedekind Leben und Werk,* Paul List, Munich 1964, p 128.

23. Georg Lukacs, 'Thoughts on an Aesthetic for the Cinema' (1913), translated and reprinted in *Framework,* no 14, 1981, p 3.

24. According to Kutscher, op cit, p 127, Wedekind told him that he had declared Geschwitz the tragic figure in the preface, because he hoped to deflect the legal objections to his play, raised at three successive trials in Berlin, Leipzig and again Berlin. However, very important is his conception of Geschwitz as 'non-nature', ie outside the binary opposition of social/natural and of gender-based sexual difference: 'What the courts did not object to was that I had made the terrible fate of being outside nature (Unnatürlichkeit) which this human being has to bear, the object of serious drama. . . . Figures like her belong to the race of Tantalus. . . . I was driven by the desire to snatch from public ridicule the enormous human tragedy of exceptionally intense and quite fruitless inner struggles . . .', *Die Büchse der Pandora,* Foreword (my translation).

25. L Jessner, *Schriften,* Hugho Fetting (ed), Berlin (DDR), 1979, p. 213.

26. Louise Brooks, op cit, p 94.

27. Fritz Rasp, 'Die Sparsamkeit der Geste', in *Film-Kurier,* June 1, 1929.

28. ibid.

29. Louise Brooks, op cit, p 97.

30. quoted in ibid, p 94.

31. Artur Kutscher is very good on this point: 'The inner pivot of Lulu is also determined by Wedekind's attitude to the women's question. . . . The nineteenth century and its movements of emancipation has "masculinized" Woman, and literature from . . . Hebbel . . . to Strindberg gave more and more scope and significance to her struggle. Wedekind is an opponent of this movement, he wants to turn this "culture" back to nature, and tries to emancipate, with a certain one-sided virulence, the female of the species ("das Weib") from woman ("Frau"), by stressing animal instincts. It is, however, obvious from the whole conception of the character that he passionately endorses, influenced by Nietzsche, the values of suppleness and vitality.' Kutscher, op cit, p 121.

32. National Film Theatre programme note, no date, no citation or source.

33. quoted in Louise Brooks, op cit, p 95.

34. ibid, p 98.

35. ibid, p 98-99.

36. This reading owes a great deal to a discussion with Mary Ann Doane and a seminar paper she gave at the University of Iowa, in Spring 1979, on *Pandora's Box.*

37. Lotte Eisner, 'A Witness Speaks', quoted in Louise Brooks op cit, p 107.

38. MacPherson, 'Die Liebe der Jeanne Ney', *Close Up,* December 1927, p 26, quoted in S Kracauer, op cit, p 178.

39. quoted in Louise Brooks, op cit, p 96.

40. reproduced in *Film als Film,* catalogue Kölnischer Kunstverein, 1977, p 88.

41. Louise Brooks, op cit, p. 105-6.

Linda Schulte-Sasse (essay date spring 1990)

SOURCE: Schulte-Sasse, Linda. "A Nazi Herstory: The Paradox of Female 'Genius' in Pabst's Neuberin Film *Komödianten* (1941)." *New German Critique* 50 (spring 1990): 57-84.

[*In the following essay, Schulte-Sasse examines the unique place of* Komödianten *as a movie featuring a woman in the genre of Nazi "genius" films.*]

> Ob Männer oder Frauen, ist ganz wurscht:
> Eingesetzt muß alles werden
>
> —Hitler, March 1945

G. W. Pabst's film biography of Caroline Neuber, ***Komödianten*** (1941), follows in most respects the paradigm of the "genius" films that pervaded Nazi cinema in the early forties. These films extol artists like Schiller, Mozart, Andreas Schlüter, or Rembrandt, scientists, inventors, and politicians as rebels combatting an ossified world. Consistent with this master narrative, ***Komödianten*** celebrates Caroline Neuber's efforts to free the German theater from the buffoon tradition of Hanswurst and to institutionalize theater as a serious medium. In this film as well the artist reigns supreme as a chosen being who transcends the ordinary, but whose path is one of "suffering." Neuber, too, is "the way I *have* to be"; she is a visionary who prevails both against a hostile environment and against inner temptation. Like Herbert Maisch's film *Friedrich Schiller* (1940), ***Komödianten*** aligns itself with a late 18th-century aesthetic of the "heart" (taking considerable liberties with historical chronology in the process), and blends biographic events with motifs from 18th-century literature, particularly from the works of G. E. Lessing, who is also integrated into the film's plot. In short, *Komödianten* typifies the genius film in its nostalgic evocation of aesthetic euphoria, in its concoction of an imaginary collective history molded by the struggle of an individual for artistic autonomy, for the uniquely "German." Like other protagonists of the genre, Neuber acts as a fill-in (in Lacan's sense) who reconciles social ruptures in the aesthetic realm. Yet for all of these likenesses, Pabst's film is unique among Nazi genius films in allowing a woman to forge historical progress. I intend to examine this gender perspective in *Komödianten* with the underlying questions in mind: How, given the male orientation of National Socialism, is it possible for a genius film to focus on a woman? Does *Komödianten* suggest that the functionalization of gender in Nazi cinema involves more than a subsumption of all texts under the notion of woman's colonization? Finally, how does the inscription of gender in *Komödianten* relate to the film's apparent valorization of late 18th-century aesthetics?

The fact that woman is relegated to the role of subordinate partner, nurturer, and reproducer of race in Nazi culture and cinema hardly needs reiteration. A glance at the personae embodied by "darlings" of the Third Reich such as "Reich Water Corpse" Kristina Söderbaum or Marika Rökk bears this impression out, as do a number of recent studies such as Anke Gleber's analysis of the subjugation of the female in *Miss von Barnhelm* (Hans Schweikart, 1940), Verena Leuken's reading of *Heimat* (Carl Froelich, 1938), or Karsten Witte's analysis of female guilt in *The Great Love* (Rolf Hansen, 1942).[1] The latter two films illustrate how often even a film personality like Zarah Leander, whose independence and eroticism appear to challenge the patriarchal structure, is redomesticated within the narrative trajectory of her films, led back to her "place" behind or beside man and family.[2]

Conversely, the combination of women and political power in Nazi cinema is catastrophic, as Johannes Meyer's *Fridericus* (1936) illustrates. The film shows Frederick the Great encircled by a bitchy triumvirate: a pouty Maria Theresa, a conniving Madame Pompadour, and an abrasive Elizabeth of Russia. While the Leander vehicle *The Queen's Heart* (Carl Froelich, 1940) portrays Mary Queen of Scots sympathetically, even the film's title suggests its concentration on Mary as a woman tragically doomed by her beauty. The only female whose mythification in Nazi cinema rivals Frederick's is the Queen Luise of Veit Harlan's *Kolberg* (1945). However, Luise was not a ruling head of state, and her idolization as Germany's *Landesmutter* by no means undermines a patriarchal order, as a remark from Heinrich von Treitschke amply illustrates: "it is a touchstone of [Luise's] greatness that one can say so little of her deeds."[3]

As this gender constellation indicates, women are deprived of an independent function in the genius film, generally serving to aid the male protagonist, suffer for him, or impede his mission. In *Friedrich Schiller,* for example, Laura

and Franziska are intuitive comprehenders of male genius who voluntarily surrender Schiller to his art and, ultimately, to history. The women in *Friedemann Bach* (Traugott Müller, 1941) typify the male projections Silvia Bovenschen describes as "imagined femininity": they act as conventional positive (Antonia) and negative (Fiorini) catalysts, representing the polar opposites of "heart" vs. eroticism, community vs. egocentrism, art vs. exchange value within the male protagonist.[4] Many genius films render women even more peripheral, as does *Paracelsus* (1943), the other film Pabst completed in the Third Reich, or *Robert Koch* (Hans Steinhoff, 1939), in which the scientist Robert Koch's obsession with curing tuberculosis nearly drives his wife to despair.

Komödianten reverses this paradigm, "breaks the rules" of gender coding in Nazi film by featuring a woman as its exemplary historical agent. Neuber's diegetic role parallels precisely that of male protagonists in the genre, although, significantly, nowhere in the film is the title "genius" applied to her. I will argue that while *Komödianten* illuminates women's ambivalent social role under National Socialism in the forties, it does not radically reassess the feminine (either as body or as abstract principle) in the Nazi weltanschauung. While the film demonstrates that woman can act as a leader, that she can trespass beyond the boundaries of the private sphere in the name of a "higher cause," it simultaneously restricts woman's historical agency to an essentialist concept of the feminine, and renders woman subordinate to and dependent upon male genius. My analysis will examine how two triadic character groups inhabit the film text: a (more or less fictional) all-female triad in which gender is ultimately displaced as the film's thematic focal point; and the (historical) male-female triad in which gender is restored as a principle of stratification. While the latter valorizes the feminine as crucial to German cultural history, it maintains a hierarchy of leadership in which the masculine ultimately dominates. Moreover, in fictionalizing history while feigning authenticity, it supports Nazism's aestheticization of politics. I will explore this subject further in the second part of my essay.

Komödianten begins with a dispute between Caroline Neuber and Hanswurst after the latter disrupts her theater performance of *Medea* with his vulgar jokes, which, however, are popular with the public. Neuber declares her intention to create "decent German theater." Her theater troupe travels to Leipzig, where they perform Gottsched's *Sterbender Cato,* but after an argument with Gottsched on the direction theater should take, Neuber and her troupe leave. On the way to Leipzig the traveling troupe has picked up a young orphan, Philine Schröder, who has run away after her guardian tried to force her into an affair with Privy Councilor Klupsch in exchange for business favors. The playboy and theater buff Baron Armin Perckhammer falls in love with Philine and wants to marry her against the wishes of his aunt, Duchess Amalia of Weissenfels. Philine is separated from Armin through the intrigue of his relatives, and Neuber's troupe loses the support of the

Duchess following an argument between the two women. Neuber is attracted to the Duke of Courland (Ernst Biron, 'secret ruler' of Russia), who invites her to make a guest appearance in St. Petersburg. The troupe becomes involved in an orgy in St. Petersburg and Neuber realizes that she must return to Germany. Here she burns Hanswurst in effigy, but Hanswurst and his supporters burn her stage and costumes in revenge. When the troupe runs out of money, Neuber's actors abandon her. The Duchess is distressed when Philine informs her of Neuber's plight; moreover, she finally recognizes the sincerity of Philine's love for Armin. Neuber dies in a remote forest, whereupon the Duchess builds a German National Theater in her honor.

I

THREE WOMEN

"An der ist ein Mann verloren gegangen": Neuber

In synthesizing male and female characteristics, Führer and mother, Caroline Neuber (Käthe Dorsch) represents the greatest anomaly among ***Komödianten***'s three "strong" women. The most important "masculine" behavior Neuber adopts is her renunciation of the private sphere for a life in the public domain (parallel to virtually all of Nazi cinema's genius figures), her exclusive devotion to her cause of furthering the theater, which is captured in her recurring command "further! further!" She repeatedly disparages women for their dependency on men, insisting: ". . . if I had ever had to, I would always have chosen art over love." Her subjugation of the private to the public is manifested in Neuber's relationship to her husband Johannes: reversing a common constellation of Nazi cinema, Johannes *is* the wife, the loyal one who waits, who sacrifices personal needs for Neuber's "higher" cause.[5] Yet far from naturalizing this reversal, the film suggests that male subjugation is an aberration. While Neuber crosses gender boundaries with relative ease, the reverse remains a source of discomfort; the spectator's sympathy for Johannes is problematized by a sense of embarrassment at seeing traditionally defined boundaries of masculinity transgressed, as when Johannes renders himself a literal buffoon by donning Hanswurst's clown costume.[6]

While Johannes's feminization provides a narrative counterpoint that facilitates Neuber's status as *Mannsweib,* her other partner, the Duke of Courland, threatens to drive Neuber back to her "natural" place in the private sphere. The interlude with the Duke again violates stereotypic gender distinctions by permitting a male to act as the negative catalyst nearly provoking a woman's downfall. The Duke—played by Gustav Diessl, who often personified dark, exotic men—is a male counterpart to threatening, eroticized women in the popular narrative tradition.[7] The Duke's desire to drive Neuber back into the limited feminine sphere is suggested by his enjoyment of her as spectacle during their first encounter. The spectacle consists not only of Neuber's gala theater performance, but of the "performance" she delivers arguing with the Duchess of Weissenfels over the social status of actors. Yet the pairing of the Duke and Neuber also has an allegorical dimension. The Duke represents the eroticization of the arts (as *divertissement*) as it functioned historically in courtly culture. The opposition between the Duke and Neuber thus represents the opposition between an art subjected to external interests and an art which functions autonomously. ***Komödianten*** champions autonomous art by linking the Duke's notion of art as power with the courtly, the political, the erotic, and the alien: "You evoke passions, I tame them; you free feelings, I use them. Art and politics are related; both want to rule man."[8] Indeed, Neuber's affair with the Duke can be read allegorically as representing the obstacles which prevent the historical development of a powerful (autonomous) artistic culture in Germany. As a woman, Neuber represents the beginning of that process, which is temporarily threatened by the power-obsessed representative of the East who sweeps her away in a flood of eastern eroticism.

Xenophobia of course pervades the semioticization of geography inherent in the Duke's nationality and in Neuber's temporary displacement to the East. The alien Duke lures Neuber away from her place in the *Heimat.* The East with its "subhuman" inhabitants is linked here with the abandonment of boundaries and the pursuit of unlimited (sexual) pleasure, as well as with the amoral value system of courtly culture, standing since the 18th century in opposition to bourgeois "virtue." Much like National Socialism's fantasy of the "Jew," ***Komödianten***'s xenophobic portrayal of the East as the site of perilous dissolution is structurally necessary as a negative social fantasy, which is complemented by the organic unity of the German People as its *positive* form.[9] In other words, the opposition of negative East/positive Volk fills a void in Nazi ideology and thus masks the impossibility of National Socialism's corporatist social vision. As a social fantasy, the East also serves as a negative counterpart to autonomous art, which is portrayed as a domain of self-restitution, of pleasurable decentering within a contained realm. Moreover, by linking the Duke with courtly art as the sphere of the erotic, excessive, and dissolute, the narrative displaces the historical opposition between the courtly and the bourgeois institutions of art onto an *ahistorical* opposition between power and creativity, between "lust" and "virtue," in which lust is a degenerate force that erodes biological and spiritual strength. The film implies that both art and the erotic must be contained as threats to the genius-leader's internal autonomy; it regards the spheres of the self and of art as homologous (hence the Duke's double function as an erotic and artistic threat).

Neuber's trip to St. Petersburg illustrates how the abandonment of *Heimat* is equatable with loss of self; the genius or leader needs a biological foundation in the People in order to function as genius or leader. The episode affords Nazi cinema one more occasion to visualize eastern unculture laced with threatening eroticism—almost as a mise-en-scène of Spengler's theory of the depravity of the East. Like other depictions of Russian courts (cf. *Fridericus,* Karl Ritter's *Cadettes* [1941]), this one embodies Dionysian abandonment and disorder. The monumentality of the mainly interior sets in the St. Petersburg sequence underscores the overpowering effect of this "wild and alien" (Neuber) environment on the characters.[10] Neuber's intoxication with the Duke's eroticism culminates in a room dominated by a massive fireplace that dwarfs (i.e., disempowers) the figures near it, while the fire itself—its flickering shadow reflected on the floor—acts as a metaphoric extension of the "fire" within the figures; Neuber refers to her feelings for the Duke as a "flame." In his insistence that she abandon everything and "finally become a woman," the Duke threatens the equilibrium Neuber has heretofore maintained between her private "family" life with her troupe and the public sphere. Passion demands submission—and submission is the destruction of the artist; hence Neuber fears "what is in [her] heart" much more than she fears Russia. The Duke again verbalizes the "fire" motif as he tells Neuber "burn your life!" and she responds "I'm burning, I'm dissolving. . . ." This is the closest she comes to dissolution (*Entgrenzung*), to losing the boundaries which must be maintained to ensure the containment of her artistic self.

The St. Petersburg sequence similarly underscores the symbiotic relationship Nazi cinema posits between leader and the led; Neuber's own loss of identity contaminates her troupe, which behaves as a "mass" in the sense in which Gustave LeBon used the term, engaging in indiscriminate lovemaking and debauchery. Neuber discovers the actors engaged in an orgy, an enactment of her own internal chaos. She descends a long spiral staircase, a motif which Freud associated with orgasm, and which visually underscores the figures' earlier joking analogy of Russia with "hell." The circular and downward movement of the staircase signals the abyss into which the group has fallen, as do the circular Cossack (*non*-German, i.e., alien) dance movements and shrieks of those indulging in the bacchanal. As in Freud's conception of dream work, the visual manifestation of her own loss of self ("I died inside") functions as a catalyst for Neuber's own self-retrieval, allowing her to restore herself as leader, and return to her work and to her un-erotic relationship with her husband. This again reinforces the dependency of art and genius on maintaining personal boundaries, on taming the desire for dissolution or merging with an Other. Yet once freed from the "fire of passion," Neuber faces a literal fire when Hanswurst and his allies burn the troupe's set and costumes. As a carnivalesque aesthetic principle that ruptures aesthetic boundaries, Hanswurst (significantly characterized by Neuber as one who lacks "yearning," [*Sehnsucht*]) also has to be contained, a triumph achieved only after Neuber dies in abject poverty.

As in other genius films, Neuber's act of fortifying the inner self is as important an achievement as her historical feat itself; indeed, the former is the prerequisite for the latter. In order to be constituted as a historical "personality," the hero must ward off the erotic and become impenetrable, a self contained by what Klaus Theweleit calls "body armor."[11] Theweleit has demonstrated how the fascist male

character creates an external self impervious to weakness. At the expense of an intact ego, the "soldierly" man's ersatz-ego is literally beaten into him through militaristic socialization from an early age, and is manifested in his erect stance, slick hair, and steely gaze, in his uniform, and the things with which he surrounds himself, particularly the "men." Above all he must reject the female Other as a symbol of dissolution that threatens his armored self the moment it transgresses the private sphere (i.e., as a female that is not mother or wife). Like art, the feminine, whether in the form of a female body (the actual, social existence of woman) or in the form of an image (the role of the feminine, the erotic in art), needs to be contained, primarily through the family structure.

Paradoxically, this process applies to a female protagonist like Caroline Neuber as well once she enters the public sphere. Retrieval of self for Neuber likewise means surmounting her own female Otherness, particularly her female sexuality. While hardly a soldierly male, Neuber must likewise undergo a process of transcending "feminine" weakness. The Russian episode is the only one in the film in which Neuber's unfeminine behavior breaks down and she becomes "all woman," and hence nearly abandons her historic mission. The episode is the crucial test that helps to fortify her inner self against alien influence, eroticism, and physicality (a necessary step reflecting the film's subtext of the war, which inaugurates a breakdown of the public-private division). Significantly, in her two scenes with the Duke, Neuber not only appears in lavish dresses emphasizing her womanly figure, but is stylized through framing and lighting as an object of desire. This contrasts with the less "feminine"—even slightly military—design of the clothing she wears in other scenes, such as her travel suit with buttons that recall an officer's jacket, or her rehearsal dress, which has a criss-cross pattern reminiscent of a soldier draped with an ammunition belt.

Like Nazi cinema's male geniuses, Neuber forgoes dissolution with an individual, private Other in favor of a fusion with the collective that is so essential to the National Socialist project. Through their art, which is in Lacanian terminology a contained *objet a,* individuals like Neuber and Schiller become historical figures who compensate or stand in for the People's lack, acting as the People's *objet a.* Yet Neuber's susceptibility to the temptation of dissolution is gender specific, again naturalized by the film as a woman's need—evoking in the spectator a response of relief and disappointment at Neuber's self-retrieval. In this sense, then, the film disavows the leader role it ascribes to Neuber, who, unlike male geniuses, must sort out competing voices within herself. As I will elaborate in the following section, Philine is a transitional figure who eases both the film's allegorical transference of woman from private to public, and the tension between the still privatized female spectator and the public woman.

Another gender-specific characteristic that separates Neuber from male artists is her coding as mother (although to be sure a number of older geniuses such as Paracelsus are father figures). Neuber, portrayed as fortyish and slightly buxom, serves throughout the film as a spiritual mother to her "family" of actors, who are repeatedly described as "a herd" in need of "a shepherd," and develops a particular mother-daughter bond with the orphan Philine.[12] The non-diegetic text opening the film already establishes Neuber's role as mother/teacher:

> Caroline Neuber liberated the theater from the cheap obscenities [*Zoten*] of Hanswurst. Through hard labor she raised/educated [*erzog*] actors and spectators. Without Neuber our classic writers like Lessing, Schiller, and Goethe would have had found no theater to provide a worthy forum for their works.

As demonstrated by figures like Dorothea in *Jew Süss,* Franziska in *Good-Bye, Franziska* (Käutner, 1941), or Maria in *Kolberg,* woman is frequently a metaphor in Nazi cinema for *Heimat,* for roots and nurturance, which are set in narrative opposition to the alienation of aimless wandering. They assume this role because they are still confined to the private sphere and hence function as *objet a* for men constrained by the public sphere. Neuber adopts precisely this female role, only within the public (i.e., male) framework of the theater.

By suffering the exhaustion and humiliation of a vagabond life, she eventually legitimizes theater and provides both her actors and Germany's evolving (male) drama culture with a *Heimat.* Neuber's death scene visually underscores this nurturing role: she dies while leaning against the wheel of a cart in which she is forced to travel (forced to leave the private sphere), unaware of the historical legacy she will leave behind. At the moment of her death the camera travels down to focus on Johannes's brightly illuminated hand grasping hers; this scene then dissolves to a long shot of the newly founded German Theater. The chiaroscuro effects of the shot highlight Neuber's matronly bosom, and the subsequent dissolve virtually allows the building to evolve from her womb as her consummate child, with the windows of the building radiating the same bright light as her breast (i.e., "heart"). At the same time, the shot of her death is centered by the clasping hands, suggesting that a historical mission requires not only leadership, but the relentless fidelity of the follower (in this case Johannes, but by analogy, the People). Philine's final words dedicating the theater again encapsulate the themes of wandering vs. roots: "Caroline Neuberin! You were homeless [*heimatlos*], here is your home. You were without peace; here your bold spirit can rest. You never saw what you longed for, but in everything we create your restless longing shall be alive." In suffering for the collective, Neuber fills in for the female spectator of the Third Reich who was slowly being forced out of the private sphere in early forties.

PHILINE AND THE RECONCILIATION OF PRIVATE AND PUBLIC

Neuber's co-protagonist, Philine (Hilde Krahl), stands in blatant contrast to Neuber by playing a much more tradi-

tional feminine role. The subplot involving Philine and the aristocrat Armin von Perckhammer reiterates the male-female (public-private) constellation of the bourgeois tragedy to which the film alludes constantly. Like the heroines of numerous 18th-century dramas, Philine is an object of desire for a variety of aristocratic males. For most of the film, she remains confined to the private sphere and the quest for "true love," which, as in the bourgeois tragedy, is a paradigm for bourgeois, i.e., "human" virtue. In her beauty and "virtue" Philine recalls Lessing's Emilia Galotti or Goethe's Gretchen, as when a maid addresses her as "noble miss" (*gnädiges Fräulein*) and she responds that she is not of nobility (*gnädig*).

Yet while the story continuously thematizes Philine's innocence, the camera titillates the viewer by cinematically exhibiting her eroticism. Her passivity is suggested by the frequency with which she is viewed sitting, allowing the camera to "leer" down at her décolleté and voluptuous bosom. The film uses strategies typical of classical cinema, in which the heroine serves as erotic object for both the fictional characters and the spectator. Indeed, it puts the spectator in the ambiguous position of sympathizing with Philine as victim, yet enjoying both her suffering and especially the pleasure of seeing her softly illuminated body displayed and hearing her sensuous voice. While Neuber fills in for women emerging from the private sphere, Philine fills in both for men, in the traditional mode of dominant cinema (as object of desire), and for women in the sense proposed by Teresa de Lauretis. De Lauretis sees the female spectator caught in a double identification: with the masterful gaze of the male and with the object being looked at.[13] Here a figure *within* the narrative, Philine takes on the dual position de Lauretis ascribes to the female spectator.

When Armin first encounters Philine, she provides a striking contrast to the promiscuous actress Viktorine, who disrobes in his presence. The first shot of Philine in the scene is preceded by her shocked off-screen voice ("Viktorine!"), which permits the spectator to "see" her with Armin as she sews—a domestic activity reminiscent of Gretchen's spinning.[14] Corresponding to Laura Mulvey's original paradigm, in which "the gaze of the spectator and that of the male characters in the film are neatly combined without breaking narrative verisimilitude," over-the-shoulder shots enable the spectator to share Armin's look.[15] These shots alternate with "objective," unclaimed shots of both Armin and Philine. Nowhere at this point is Philine granted a subjectivity of her own from a cinematic perspective; only Armin possesses authoritative vision. When Philine makes her debut on Neuber's stage (and simultaneously her debut as spectacle for Armin in the subsequent scene), G. E. Lessing, a student and friend of Armin, raves about Neuber's artistic greatness, while Armin can only think of Philine's legs, exposed by her page costume. Their comments not only articulate the difference between the two men, but capture the contrast with which both camera and narrative will treat the two women. The words also link the artists Lessing and Neuber as transcending the physical, with Lessing always the observer of—never the participant in—human interaction.

Virtually every Nazi film set in the 18th century exploits the connotative appeal of the bourgeois tragedy and imitates the class coding of the genre, in which the aristocracy stands for egotism, intrigue, and exchange value, while the middle class stands for virtue, trust, and "love." The genre is so useful to Nazism since its exclusion of an Other (the aristocracy and its concomitant value system) in the People's own history is a precondition for National Socialism's hypostatized unity of the People. However, Nazism redefines the gesture of exclusion in the bourgeois tragedy as an exclusion of a *national* (usually French) Other. This shift constitutes a fundamental reinterpretation of the bourgeois tragedy, since it transforms the latter's attempt to eliminate difference in favor of the universally human into a quest for homogeneity within the parameters of a defined order. In other words, although both the bourgeois tragedy and its Nazified versions represent a quest for "community," in the latter, difference (class, political, racial) is eliminated only *within* the sphere of the "German" in order to fortify it against external elements (*Überfremdung*) or against racial pollution. While 18th-century bourgeois literature was international, the Nazi narrative remains firmly national. Moreover, the 18th-century notion of the universally human was oriented toward a distant future, while Nazism's social fantasy of a People is oriented toward the past (hence the tireless invocation of history). I have demonstrated elsewhere how Veit Harlan's *Jew Süss* (1940) strikingly refunctionalizes the bourgeois tragedy for antisemitic purposes, but the same point can be made for less "overtly" political films like *Komödianten*.[16]

A central element of the bourgeois tragedy exploited by the Philine-Armin story is the "high" Enlightenment motif of the heart's triumph over class division. The use of this motif permits gender difference to replace class difference: in the name of the universally human (*das Allgemeinmenschliche*), class difference is elided, but the woman continues to represent the private sphere, compensating for the alienation of public (male-centered) life. As in Schiller's *Kabale und Liebe,* contradictory forces hinder this transcendence of class division, typically in the form of aristocrats wielding money as a force of persuasion (reliably rejected by the heroes of the anticapitalist narrative) and resorting to intrigue when money fails. In *Komödianten,* a variety of concrete visual barriers suggest class division, such as the gate (marked by a conspicuous "X" design) to the prison where Philine is held, a victim of aristocratic intrigue; the gate which confines the "homely" cousin whom Armin refuses to marry in her aristocratic "prison"; and the massive gate to the Russian court. The first narrative obstacle to a union of the "heart" is Armin himself, whose social class determines his cocky, patronizing attitude toward women, at least toward those of a lower class.[17] Like Mellefont in Lessing's *Miss Sara Sampson,* Armin acquires bourgeois virtue in the course of the narrative, discovering his "true" love for Philine and

abandoning his lust for *divertissement.* He becomes an "aristocrat of the heart." As in the bourgeois tragedy, there need be no explanation for his conversion to virtue beyond the claim that he is merely persuaded by the force of the "heart."

In its quest for "community" *Komödianten* thus appears to valorize feeling, the *cognitio intuitiva* in Sentimentality, which is associated with the feminine and placed in narrative opposition to the dry rationalism of Gottsched and the vulgarity of Hanswurst. Neuber is the public spokeswoman for the "heart"; in the private sphere, Philine adopts this role. Philine's understanding through the "heart" transcends the discursive language of rationality, as Armin articulates when he says: "You have a fine ear; you hear things that one has not even said," or: "Heaven made you more courageous than me and made your heart clearer than my understanding." Philine is ultimately able to triumph over the aristocracy for whom "love is a business" because her "heart" accepts only "yes or no." Furthermore, in keeping with the role accorded to both woman and art since the mid-18th century of compensating for the alienation of a rationalized existence, Philine seems to possess an intuitive reverence for genius. Despite her unfamiliarity with theater and art, Philine not only "feels" that Neuber "serves a great cause," but she seems likewise to sense Lessing's greatness. When Armin introduces Lessing to the troupe as a budding writer, Philine alone is privileged with a close-up shot as she, characteristically captured by a high-angle shot and veritably glowing due to lighting effects, bursts out in awe: "Oh, you want to be a poet!" The use of the word poet (*Dichter*) is significant in that the film constantly contrasts terms suggesting the low contemporary status of theater art with terms valorizing "high," autonomous art.

The film goes so far as to directly integrate famous Lessing phrases into the fiction. When Armin believes himself abandoned by Philine, he declares that he will participate in a military campaign "down in Turkey," thus repeating Werner's phrase in *Minna von Barnhelm.* The motif of "calmness" (*Ruhe, ruhig*) so central to *Emilia Galotti* appears in *Komödianten* as well when, for instance, Neuber remarks to Philine that she is "so unnaturally calm." Philine's response recalls the various stages with which Emilia achieves maturity: "You call this being calm, . . . suffering what one should not suffer, bearing what one should not have to bear. . . ." Most significant is Philine's quotation of the line "Pearls mean tears," with which Emilia expresses intuitive fears about the future of the "community of the heart" she and Appiani have achieved. Several close-ups of Philine fondling a string of pearls visually underscore this motif. The Duchess attempts to bribe Philine with the pearls to leave Armin; hence pearls act as a direct vehicle for aristocratic efforts to uphold class division. The same pearls take on a different function at the end of the film, however, when Philine uses them to convince the Duchess of her sincere feelings for Armin, thus gaining a utopian perspective that is absent in Lessing's *Emilia Galotti.* Here the film merges allusions to Lessing with the political optimism of the early Schiller. Analogous to *Friedrich Schiller*'s reliance on early Schiller drama, *Komödianten* thus blends "life" and canonized fiction to create a nostalgic pleasure in recognizing a history that never was. It thus again augments a mythified image of collective history in which spectators can mirror themselves and feel at least momentarily compensated for "real" life through the aesthetic or through a great collective past.

In addition, the film's exploitation of literary allusions reflects the "achieved" establishment or containment of the aesthetic as a quasi-autonomous sphere in modern societies, which compensates for the agonistic struggles and alienation of everyday life.[18] This compensatory function is disguised, however, since the film (and Western culture in general) mythifies autonomous art as value. As the Other of the modern experience, it connotes the feminine and provides a site for decentering experiences. Yet as such, autonomous art has to be contained because a victory of this (feminine) principle in society would undermine the balance between real-life delimitations and imaginary dissolution on which modern societies rely. Philine comes to symbolize the establishment of a contained realm of autonomous art toward the end of the film when she begins to adopt the non-feminine attitudes of her surrogate mother, Neuber. After the Duchess is finally reconciled to the union of Armin and Philine, i.e., after the class obstacle has been surmounted, Philine declares, as Neuber had earlier, that she must choose her art over love. She thus becomes in effect Neuber's functional double. Like Neuber, Philine transcends both social class and the private sphere through art, emerging as both wife and coalition partner: Armin becomes administrative director; Philine, artistic director of the theater that realizes Neuber's dream. Reflecting the film's subtext of 1941, the domesticated woman undergoes a transition from private to public, from Philine to Neuber. Philine's transition is the condition for the film's imaginary reconciliation not only between the bourgeoisie and the aristocracy, the private and the public, but between the feminine principle contained in art and the masculine principle of rational delimitation—taken together a coalition that provides the basis for the organization of society. Lessing best characterizes Philine's narrative evolution when he chastizes Armin: "You think you have to condescend to Philine. You don't see that she stands beside you, ennobled by her art." I will return to Philine's *Bildungsroman*-style transformation later.

DUCHESS AMALIA AS ARMORED WOMAN

The film's third "unfeminine" woman is Duchess Amalia of Weissenfels (Henny Porten), Armin's aunt and Neuber's Maecenas. She is the central force to insist on the domination of class over heart, speaking of marriage as an institution of *Staatsraison* rather than of love: "Persons of standing are not asked whether they *like* their marriage partner." She demands that the artists performing at her court stay within their "boundaries" and resists Neuber's claim to be the equal of any aristocrat through her art. Before the Duchess appears, a large painting of her in Armin's palace announces her imposing presence. Her own chambers are surrounded by large portraits of Weissenfels ancestors which provide a formidable backdrop against which figures like Neuber and Philine fight for recognition. When, for example, Philine finally confronts the Duchess personally, she is positioned directly between two aristocratic portraits which again visually reproduce the notion of class barrier.

What distinguishes the Duchess most fully from other comparable female figures is her extremely masculine physical coding. In a sense, the Duchess as a political leader displays the most "unfeminine" behavior possible. She wears an ensemble clearly emulating the style of a military jacket (Armin is a lieutenant in her retinue), pinches snuff, and her demeanor is characterized by "decisive" male gestures, much like a stereotypic Prussian officer. The significance of military allusions within Nazi ideology can scarcely be overemphasized, yet it is equally obvious that the military is a male domain.[19] Hence the film reveals the Duchess's extreme masculinity to be a facade, a body-armor erected to repress her "natural" female characteristics. Underneath the body-armor suggested in her "uniform" look, she, like Armin, is an "aristocrat of the heart." Just as Armin's transformation from "playboy" to "aristocrat of the heart" needs no rational explanation within the film's value system, neither does the change in the Duchess. She merely "hears" truth when she meets Philine, whose words provoke the Duchess to utter a series of uncharacteristic Sentimental (*empfindsame*) evaluations: "In your words a pure heart beats. You speak the truth."

The encounter between Philine and the Duchess toward the end of the film articulates the new leader status assumed by women. This scene unites and reconciles the three strong women through the presence of the Duchess and Philine and the absence of the (mythic) Caroline Neuber:

PHILINE:

> [refering to Neuber] A great woman, who had the stuff to be a great man!

DUCHESS:

> Stop! Neuber should remain a woman [*Weibsbild*] and prove what we women are capable of!

Ironically, it is in this scene, when the Duchess articulates the potential of women, that she first wears a strikingly low-cut dress herself, underscoring her own femininity and contrasting sharply with the military ensemble of her first appearance. Yet, the dress accords with her turn to Sentimentality, and thus complements the scene's verbal content. Philine, on the other hand, appears in a very "professional" ensemble with a black jacket and a lace *jabot,* not unlike men's clothing at the time and clearly in contrast to the décolleté of her earlier clothing. In another reversal of classical cinema's predilection for objectifying woman as framed icon, Philine briefly fondles a miniature portrait of Armin she finds while waiting in the Duchess's palace. Philine's transformed appearance prepares her narrative transformation; she informs Armin in this scene that she has chosen the stage over marriage to him. With her declaration, "I have already chosen the stage and must remain faithful to it," she echoes Neuber's frequent comparison of the theater to the lover. Armin, injured by a "Turkish bullet," appears in this scene, with his arm in a sling, as a castrated man forced to forfeit his earlier power over Philine. Through marriage, which Laura Mulvey has discussed as an important aspect of narrative closure that ensures the characters' social integration, both Philine and Armin find their societal niche, and Armin relinquishes his "narcissistic omnipotence."[20] Yet unlike the classical narrative model, Philine does not retreat into the oblivion of married property, but emerges as dominant in the closing dialogue and frames, which position her in the center of the image from an authoritative low angle as she appropriates Neuber's motto "further! further!" Armin stands decidedly at the periphery of the frame, in soft focus, and Johannes is absent in the film's last scene.

In the final shots Philine in effect becomes Caroline Neuber, while Neuber herself achieves the status of myth; she has been disembodied and transformed into an icon. As Philine dedicates the theater to Neuber, her back faces the camera with an engraved relief of Neuber's head visible in the distance. Like the relief, Philine's figure is framed by a door. The frames surrounding both figures suggest not confinement, but the historical inscription of their achievements. The composition renders Philine, who appears quasi-transcendent in a scintillating white gown, a metonymic extension of the canonized Neuber, while permitting the spectator to share her reverent gaze. The shot thus accords to Philine the authoritative look heretofore denied her. The film thereby completes the transition in which the female spectator can vicariously participate. The scene's aura of religious veneration, augmented by organ music, intensifies as Philine proceeds to the interior of the theater, where she again acts as surrogate viewer for the spectator. Philine continues speaking to Neuber, who has become the theater in the sense that it, in the Duchess's words, is "pervaded by Neuberin's creative breath." A long shot of the theater, with Philine glowing from a balcony that elevates her as if on a pedestal, represents Neuber's posthumous affirmation of her spiritual successor. The scene recalls Schiller's triumph at the Mannheim theater in *Friedrich Schiller.* In both scenes, theater serves as a receptacle, a "womb" that nurtures a German culture in which the spectator, here occupying the space of an absent public, can revel in his or her cultural identity. By this point in *Komödianten*'s narrative, a leader/mass distinction in which either gender is capable of assuming the leadership role has overshadowed the gender distinction. Gender has not been replaced but displaced, a displacement made possible specifically by the immediate demands of war, and more generally by modernity's institutionalization of the aesthetic as a stand-in for lack. Here the film slips structurally between the traditionally separate spheres of the aesthetic and political, as Neuber is infused with both the power of the aesthetic and the political power of a leader. The fu-

sion of these two positions into one figure gives her a status as *objet a* analogous to that of Schiller and other geniuses of Nazi cinema.

THE SUBTEXT OF FEMALE MOBILIZATION

How—given the role of woman under National Socialism—can one anchor the social and historical triumph of woman depicted in the woman-as-leader figure in *Komödianten*? I do not believe this figure signifies a fundamental rupture in Nazism's subordination of the feminine to the masculine, nor the personal influence of Pabst, but a limited deviation from the domestication of women propagated by Nazi policies. World War II is an important subtext to the film (although unfortunately much scholarship on Nazi film never considers anything *but* the subtext), especially in 1941 when the involvement of Britain and the U.S. in the war began to make ever heavier demands on Germany's military. Many historians have pointed out the contradictions of women's position in Nazi Germany.[21] Early social policies aimed at removing women from the work force and promoting motherhood, which was rewarded by social benefits as well as by a hierarchy of medals bestowed upon prolific childbearing women. Nevertheless, the Nazis were never able to stop the trends toward small families (and a high illegal abortion rate) and the participation of women in the workplace. Even between 1933 and 1938 the number of working women rose from 4.24 to 5.2 million.[22] As the war progressed economic demands opened up new employment opportunities and generated changing attitudes toward women, who were employed increasingly in heavy labor. In 1941 Hitler spoke of the "additional contribution" women can make: "millions of German women are in the country on the fields, and need to replace men in the most laborious work. Millions of German women and girls are working in factories, workshops and offices, and measure up to men there, too [*stellen auch auch dort ihren Mann*]."[23] These were to serve as a "model" to other women. By 1943, Goebbels went so far as to state his conviction that ". . . the German woman is resolutely determined to quickly fill out the space left by the man who has gone to the front *not only half way,* but *all the way.*"[24] Goebbels cautiously assures in his speech that Germany "need not rely on the bolshevist example," thus implying the boundaries of the changed status of women. While it called upon women to sacrifice glamor and leisure to the war economy, Nazi Germany would never hide behind women's skirts—a metaphor Theweleit analyzes as embodying the fear of "dissipating, contagious lust," linking the "red flood" with bolshevism (a fear which *Komödianten*'s Russian episode reflects).[25]

Komödianten's focus on strong women seems less incongruous in light of these developments; it reflects the anticipation that women will necessarily assume an ever larger public role due to the involvement of the male population in the war. Indeed, cinema audiences in the last years of the Third Reich were largely female. Considering the ideological fortification provided by the male genius films made in the same years, it hardly seems surprising that some should be aimed at the mobilization of women. Seen from this perspective, the appearance in *Komödianten* of women dressed in clothing suggestive of the military uniform, as well as the lack of imposing "soldierly" men, gains a new significance.[26] The visual codification of the "public" woman with her masculine features ensures that the "public" service of a female is seen as the exception in times of need—for example, during war. The film's mirror image of existing social relations, in which women usurp the various roles played by men, also undermines attempts at a nostalgic feminist reading of the film. Ignoring for a moment developments within the characters, all components of social organization in *Komödianten* are represented by women: the Duchess as upholder of class hierarchy, Neuber as embodiment of cultural progress, Philine as representative of private harmony. Because the forces of community, alienation, and class are *all* embodied by females, the issue of gender in the film recedes, as suggested earlier, in favor of other concerns.

The absence of male leaders in *Komödianten* allows women to become the models to which Hitler appealed. Neuber's death in destitution may serve as such a model, preparing women for an analogous death for a "great cause" in accordance with the self-effacing tradition of motherhood. Like the mother of Theweleit's "soldierly man," she becomes an "example for me of the belief that there is nothing so hard that it cannot be endured!"[27] The film's implicit interpellation is analogous to the cover of the 1 April 1940 edition of the Nazi magazine *Frauen Warte* (*Woman's Watchtower*), which features a sketch of a peasant woman driving a plough against a background of factory smokestacks, above which hovers the superdimensional but transparent portrait of a soldier's head. The cover clearly depicts in iconic form the spiritual dominance of the absent male that both necessitates and fortifies the female labor under National Socialism. *Komödianten* synthesizes this ideological mobilization with elements of what Hitchcock termed the "novelette" with reference to his own *Rebecca*: an "old-fashioned" story from the "school of feminine literature."[28] The Harlequin-romance style of both the Philine subplot and the Russian episode were presumably designed to appeal to a female audience, allowing the film to work on the level of fantasy as well as ideology.

II

GENDERIZING 18TH-CENTURY AESTHETICS: THE TRIAD NEUBER-LESSING-GOTTSCHED

I would like to return to the film text to show how in its appropriation of 18th-century cultural history, *Komödianten* again undermines a feminist reading. In assuming its aesthetic position the film relies on a second, historically seminal triad, Gottsched-Neuber-Lessing, which reinstates gender as a social-historical category. *Komödianten* reshuffles 18th-century cultural history, transforming the early Enlightenment's struggle for bourgeois aesthetic forms (ca. 1730s) into a "high" Enlightenment debate between rationality and the "heart" (ca. 1770s-1780s). Be-

sides preempting the chronological development of this debate (displacing it from the second to the first half of the century), the film condenses the debate in the narrative struggle between Neuber and Gottsched. The historical Neuber was indeed instrumental in reforming the status of theater, which was crucial to the institution of a bourgeois vs. a courtly art form. But as Gottsched's contemporary and collaborator, she predated Sentimentality's stress on affective art. The film translates their historical coalition for the institutionalization of a genre into an ahistorical, personal conflict, in which Neuber represents the position that Schiller takes in Maisch's film: she defends the "heart," which is infused with a Nazified notion of community. By allowing a woman to serve as its central defender of the heart, of the community in defiance of mechanistic rationalism, *Komödianten* valorizes the feminine as a principle that encompasses the affective, the intuitive, the space of dissolution in the "dark" realm of the aesthetic. This celebration of the feminine is mediated, though, by the film's integration of the third member of the triad. While Gottsched as a male represents an adversarial rationalism that Neuber as a female must surmount, in order to achieve her historical mission Neuber must depend on another male, embodied in her spiritual offspring Lessing. In its historical dimension then, *Komödianten* at once exalts the feminine and depicts its limitations. While powerful as a principle of aesthetic dissolution, representing the loss of boundaries essential to a community of the "heart," the feminine as the beautiful is always subject to the sublime, which amounts to phallic mastery (even if both are valorized as essential components of art).

In its strategy of transforming a diachronic constellation into a synchronic, gender-based one, *Komödianten* resorts to several historical distortions; i.e., it surrenders chronology to ideology. First, the film lends a xenophobic dimension to the respective aesthetic positions (as it did to courtly art in the figure of the Duke), since the Gottsched/Neuber debate is also articulated in terms of a competition between French and German drama. The fact that the figures representing the "heart," Neuber and the young Lessing (whose aim is to write "real German" dramas for Neuber's theater), simultaneously fight for the "German" over the "French" posits the "German" as the People replacing the universally human, just as Sentimentality posited the bourgeois, the "heart," as universally human. The film's opposition of German/Neuber/Lessing (whose mother/son relationship also suggests "family") to French/Gottsched (who appears childless, seemingly impotent) is all the more fanciful given Lessing's actual rejection of Gottsched's French (aristocratic) dramatic model in favor of an English (bourgeois) rather than a German model. Indeed, the fear of the foreign which the film ascribes to Lessing was a historical product of the 19th, not the 18th century.

Second, the age of the adversaries is likewise adjusted in accordance with their aesthetic position. Although Gottsched, born in 1700, was three years younger than Neuber, he appears in the film as a bald old man, considerably her senior. The age difference between Gottsched and Neuber stands metaphorically for the old being superseded by the new, in this case early Enlightenment, the logocentric, being superseded by Sentimentality (albeit about 30 years too early and using somewhat incorrect figures). Not only does the film render Gottsched old and outdated with his "scissors and paste" adaptation of a foreign drama, *Sterbender Cato* (1730), but it depicts his attitude toward the public as one of arrogance toward "dull, stolid masses," whereas historically his condemnation of the masses' lack of taste was based on a (for its time) progressive faith in the ability of education to improve that taste. When Gottsched remarks in the film that "Theater is not the mirror of life. Life is filthy, only art is pure," he is at odds with the historical Gottsched's vision of art as a medium that could directly influence "life" for the better. Art as an autonomous sphere in itself would have had no legitimation for Gottsched; the words this film puts in his mouth would better suit a Novalis or a Schlegel.

Neuber's defense of the People's intuitive appreciation of art intermingles the discourse of late 18th-century aestheticians with Nazi Volk rhetoric, insinuating, like *Friedrich Schiller,* that aesthetic instinct cannot be taught rationally.[29] Again recalling Maisch's film, Neuber describes her art as an articulation of the People: "they sit down there and wait for you to illuminate their dark feeling, to sharpen their dull thoughts, to let their silent mouth speak the words it couldn't form until then. Through us, through the stage the Volk speaks to itself, to the world. I want the mute Germany to begin to speak." The idea that "speaking" is not only achieved discursively, but also through the "heart," which is always already present outside of discourse as "dark feeling," recalls the valorization of *cognitio intuitiva* by figures like Baumgarten and Lessing. Similarly, Neuber recalls thinkers like J. M. von Loen in her defense of the elision of class distinctions through art: "No one can express nobility who is not noble himself or portray the sublime if he has not the sublime within him. . . . The great artist is himself a high aristocrat."[30] From a historical perspective, these ideas should go hand in hand with the institutionalization of art as a medium for "practicing" the disposition of sympathy and virtue, rather than as a medium that could be dispensed with once society had received its (rational) message. This notion of art exercising a general disposition was an important component in the development from early Enlightenment to Sentimentality.[31]

If Neuber predates Sentimentality, in Lessing at least the film finds a historical representative of the development—though not this early in his career, when he was roughly four or five years of age. This collapsing of decades underlies the film's most amusing anachronism; at its conclusion after Neuber's death, Lessing appears with a new drama written for her, *Emilia Galotti.* Since Neuber stopped performing in 1750 and died in 1760 (which is also confused, since the film seems to erase this 10-year gap and to locate her death shortly after the St. Petersburg appearance, which occurred in 1740), it gives pause that a drama published in 1772 makes its way onto her stage. If it is off-balance chronologically, *Emilia Galotti* fits in ideologically, because it represents the "high" Enlightenment position with which the film as a whole aligns itself, as exemplified by the Philine narrative. Following a classic/romantic conception of art transcending life, Lessing bases his drama on Philine's "tragic destiny" and allows her remark "Pearls mean tears," which he overhears, to find its way into his manuscript—thus the film transforms its quotation of Lessing's famous line instead into the *source* of the phrase. Woman's value seems thus dependent on her disembodiment; she inspires but hardly creates autonomous art:

ARMIN:

You speak as though you loved her!

LESSING:

No—Yes! I love a shadow of her, more glowing than the live person. An image [*Abbild*] more blooming than the source [*Bild*]. . . . If I am successful, her destiny will become eternal destiny!

The portrayal of *Sterbender Cato* (1730) and *Emilia Galotti* (1772) as nearly contemporary dramas transfers a historical development that took some 40 years onto a synchronic level, rendering the rationality/"heart" debate more easily graspable. It is fun and comforting for the spectator to see a series of important events and people all wrapped up in a neat narrative package. This blending of biography and fiction lends the illusion of having understood what an epoch was all about, not to mention knowing who the "real" Emilia Galotti was. The subsumption of a great cultural heritage in a "meaningful" narrative explains and enhances the end result of that development: the mystification of art and genius.

Although Lessing's role within the narrative is peripheral (as a sidekick to Armin, a sympathetic observer of events, a fan of Neuber), his presence gains immensely in ideological significance within the film's hierarchical ordering of achievement. His presence on the sidelines as the "real" genius reminds us of the boundaries of the feminine. As forcefully as *Komödianten* demonstrates Lessing's dependency on Neuber's spiritual nurturance, it insists that Neuber is dependent on Lessing as well, although not necessarily on him personally. As the male writer, Lessing provides the "sperm"—the written word of creative genius that fertilizes Neuber's merely *reproductive* gift—just as the film's opening text promises. *Komödianten* implies that without this mating with the male, creative genius, Neuber's efforts would have been futile and the German stage would still be a hollow shell. As an actress, Neuber represents Sentimentality's valorization of the aesthetic, of the expression of feeling, both of which require traditional "feminine" traits of emotion and sensitivity. The film thus corroborates Alfred Rosenberg's remark that woman is "lyrical" by contrast to man who is "inventive, forming [*gestaltend, architektonisch*] and synthetic [*zusammenfassend, synthetisch*]."[32] Neuber's historical contribution remains within the "feminine" sphere of the intuitive and affective: "the theater in bourgeois society was one of the few spaces which allowed women a prime space in the arts, precisely because acting was seen as imitative and reproductive, rather than original and productive."[33] Hence, only Lessing is privileged by the kind of stylized framing commonly employed in the "genius" films to visualize the inspirational act, as when he appears at a desk discussing his attempts to capture Philine in fiction. The scene is foregrounded by the diagonal line of the room's wall, and light streams through the window behind him as if to illuminate his creative impetus.

Komödianten thus surreptitiously restores the belief that it is indeed men who "make history"—even within art—and that while females may be indispensable, they remain but nurturers. For all its role reversals, the film's tribute to a woman's historical role thus exemplifies Hitler's comment, "when I acknowledge Treitschke's statement that men make history, I'm not forgetting that it's women who raise our boys to be men."[34] The limitation of Neuber's historical role is already implicit in the film's primary thematization of the *institutionalization* of art, rather than a stylistic or political *content*. This focus is contained in the title ***Komödianten,*** which refers to 17th- and 18th-century traveling artists' troupes, the historical successors of the *comedia dell'arte,* who were excluded from respectable society. This non-status gains leitmotif character in the film, with Lessing praising Gottsched for even mentioning theater in the university, the Duchess insisting that actresses can only serve for personal *"plaisir,"* or Neuber warning Philine that actresses are "more disdained than bums and thieves." Neuber's historical feat is not one of productive genius, but a liberation of the institution of theater from earlier, courtly dramatic forms, a founding of *Heimat.* Hence the film constantly juxtaposes terms (often French) associated with the older institution of theater (*Komödiant* or *Actrice/Acteur*) with terms valorizing the genre, such as "artist" (*Künstler*) and "poet" (*Dichter*).

The celebration of historical models, male or female, was part of Nazism's consistent strategy of invoking history while suppressing any critical dialogue with it. The narrativization of Germany's historical heritage made it easier to grasp, allowing for the conscious or unconscious internalization of a normative set of values. Even where a Nazi film permits gender boundaries to gain an ambiguous dimension as does ***Komödianten,*** it never ceases to reinforce submission to the authoritative individual; it promotes the leader as the most genuine, most successful fill-in for the collective void. While conceding that—under certain conditions—women may assume a public role, the film affirms at once the Führer principle and the predominance of male creativity. Thus, ***Komödianten*** provides another example of Nazism's reorganization of history as narrative—a compensatory reorganization addressing the needs of the present.

Notes

1. Anke Gleber, "Das Fräulein von Teilheim: Die ideologische Funktion der Frau in der nationalsozialistischen Lessing-Adaption," *German Quarterly* 59.4 (Fall 1986): 547-568; Verena Leuken, "Zur Erzählstruktur des nationalsozialistischen Films," *MuK* 13 (Veröffentlichung des Forschungsschwerpunkts Massenmedien und Kommunikation an der Universität Siegen, 1981); Karsten Witte, "Visual Pleasure Inhibited: Aspects of the German Revue Film," *New German Critique* 24-25 (Fall/Winter 1981-2): 238-263, especially 253-59.

2. Leander often portrayed professional women, usually singers who forfeit their career for love and/or domesticity; cf. *Zu neuen Ufern* (1937), *Heimat* (1938), and especially *Die grosse Liebe* (1940). See also the many articles on women in Nazi film in *Frauen und Film,* issues e.g. 14 (December 1977), 38 (May 1985), 44/45 (October 1988).

3. Quoted in Wulf Wülfing, "Die heilige Luise von Preussen. Zur Mythisierung einer Figur der Geschichte in der deutschen Literatur des 19. Jahrhunderts," *Bewegung und Stillstand in Metaphern und Mythen* (Stuttgart: Klett-Cotta, 1984) 272.

4. Silvia Bovenschen, *Die imaginierte Weiblichkeit. Exemplarische Untersuchungen zu kulturgeschichtlichen und literarischen Präsentationsformen des Weiblichen* (Frankfurt: Suhrkamp, 1979).

5. In his sociological study of Nazi film, Gerd Albrecht discusses the relative infrequency with which the marital status of the male protagonist is even disclosed in what he calls "P-films" (films with a political function), while the marital status of females is always a central issue, reflecting woman's confinement to the private sphere. *Nationalsozialistische Filmpolitik* (Stuttgart: Ferdinand Enke, 1969) 147-154.

6. Cf. the juxtaposition of the feminized vs. the "natural" male in *The Scarlet Pimpernel,* as well as in the *Zorro* or *Superman* films.

7. The film's (and Johannes's) acceptance of Neuber's infidelity again breaks with the norms of the Nazi film narrative, which normally punishes the adulterous female at the least with guilt (cf. Harlan's *Das unsterbliche Herz* [1939], in which Peter Henlein's young wife feels guilty for her attraction to a younger man), but more typically with intense suffering or death (cf. Gründgens's *Der Schritt vom Wege* [1939], based on Fontane's *Effi Briest*; Willi Forst's *Mazurka* [1935], in which a woman falsely accused of infidelity loses her husband and daughter; or Käutner's *Romanze in Moll* [1942]). This is not to say that female infidelity is not occasionally portrayed with considerable sympathy, but only that the erotic titillation achieved by the theme is contained by the ultimate price paid by the female protagonist. Cf. also Goebbel's justification for having changed the ending of the original script of *Opfergang* (1944) in such a way as to spare the life of the adulterous husband: "The adulterous wife must die and not the husband,"

quoted in Francis Courtade and Pierre Cadars, *Geschichte des Films im dritten Reich,* trans. Florian Hopf (Munich/Vienna: Carl Hanser, 1975).

8. In an interesting recent reading of the film, Anke Gleber points out affinities between the Duke's remark and "ideological assumptions behind Nazi film." See "Masochism and Wartime Melodrama: *Komödianten* (1941)," *The Films of G. W. Pabst: An Extraterritorial Cinema,* ed. Eric Rentschler (New Brunswick, N.J.: Rutgers UP, 1990) 181. While the Duke's remarks indeed display a striking congruence with the Nazi project, it is important to note that the subject position created by the film rejects his cynicism in favor of Neuber's "Völkisch" stance.

9. I am using the term social fantasy as it has been introduced by Slavoj Zizek, as fantasy "invented" by a society to mask the impossibility of its posited utopian ideal: "At the stake of social-ideological fantasy is to construct a vision of society which *does* exist, a society which is not split by an antagonistic division, a society in which the relation between its parts is organic, complementary." *The Sublime Object of Ideology* (London and New York: Verso, 1989) 126. For Nazism the supreme social fantasy is the "Jew," who provides a positive embodiment of social *negativity,* fostering the illusion that eradication of the "Jew" will result in social harmony.

10. Cf. the visual relief to the massive, overpowering studio sets of the Russian sequence provided by Germany's "fresh air" in the subsequent sequence when the troupe returns home and is forced to perform outside. I am aware of the apparent contradiction between my reading of monumentalism in the Russian set as negative and Nazism's well-known endorsement of monumentalism in art and architecture. I know of no Nazi film, however, in which a grandiose, massive scale in an interior, private setting is associated with "positive" figures. Rather, grand-scale interiors tend to characterize the lifestyle of the self-aggrandizing and materialistic (the huge chest opened in *Komödianten*'s Russian sequence to reveal lavish costumes recalls the chest in which Süss Oppenheimer hides his wealth in Veit Harlan's 1940 film *Jew Süss.* In both cases the chests suggest excess and materialistic values). The grandiosity of Nazi art by contrast celebrates either the alleged perfection of the German race, or an embodiment of the Nazi state (which is by definition seen as a pure expression of the Volk), but remains confined to an exterior, public sphere. The collision of interiority and monumentality in Nazi cinema tends to disrupt the nurturance of the private sphere, ensured by a feminine presence.

11. Klaus Theweleit, *Male Fantasies,* trans. Steven Conway, vol. 1 (Minneapolis: U of Minnesota P, 1987). This is not to deny that Neuber's near dissolution is a source of pleasure to the (presumably female) spectator of 1941. On one level, then, the termination of the relationship elicits a sense of disappointment by denying the female spectator the Duke as an object of desire.

12. In the very first scene of the film Neuber appears on stage as Medea, lamenting the impending death of her daughter, who leans on her shoulder for support much as Philine will later in the film. Indeed, the lines Neuber recites prefigure her role as mother as well as the artist's "path of suffering" so central to the genius genre: "I gave many children life; death took many children from me. Sorrow heaps upon sorrow; a mountain of pain suffocates my heart."

13. Teresa de Lauretis, "Desire in Narrative," *Alice Doesn't* (Bloomington: Indiana UP, 1984) 103-157, especially 123. In remarking on precisely the tension between sympathy for and enjoyment of Philine's suffering, Anka Gleber repeatedly posits a disconcertingly clear-cut division between male and female spectators. Cf., for example, "Clearly, Philine's pain evokes identification in the female spectator. Simultaneously, the male spectator can readily align himself with the camera's explorations of Philine's face and figure" (177). While I agree with the conflicting reactions Gleber addresses, her ascription of reactions to individual genders oversimplifies the complexity of spectator response acknowledged in feminist scholarship today.

14. Cf. Miriam Hansen's discussion of the importance of the male hero initiating the gaze in classical cinema, and of how being looked *at* (vs. looking) serves as an indicator of a female's virtue; Miriam Hansen, "Pleasure, Ambivalence, Identification: Valentino and Female Spectatorship," *Cinema Journal* 25.4 (Summer 1986): 11-12.

15. Laura Mulvey, "Visual Pleasure and Narrative Cinema," *Screen* 16.3 (Autumn 1975): 19.

16. Linda Schulte-Sasse, "The Jew as Other under National Socialism: Veit Harlan's *Jud Süss* (1940)," *German Quarterly* 61.1 (Winter 1968): 22-49.

17. As in 18th-century dramas, particularly Schiller's *Kabale und Liebe, Komödianten* thematizes the issue of trust, especially when Armin's uncle persuades Philine that Armin is engaged to a woman of his own class. Philine possesses the absolute security of feeling characteristic of such figures as Luise Miller, thus initially refusing to believe Armin capable of leaving her. Yet like Ferdinand, whose aristocratic socialization permits him to more readily believe the falsified letter portraying Luise as promiscuous, Armin readily falls for the intrigue and castigates Philine as fickle. Both male figures have grown accustomed to hypocrisy and promiscuity through their aristocratic context.

18. See Jochen Schulte-Sasse, "Literarische Wertung: Zum unausweichlichen historischen Verfall einer literaturkritischen Praxis," *Lili* 18.71 (1988): 13-47.

19. See Theweleit's *Male Fantasies,* or Karl Prumm, *Die Literatur des soldatischen Nationalismus der zwanziger Jahre (1918-1933)* (Kronberg/Ts: Scriptor, 1974).

20. Laura Mulvey, "Afterthoughts inspired by Duel in the Sun," *Visual and Other Pleasures* (Bloomington: Indiana UP, 1989) 33-34.

21. See, for example, Renate Wiggershaus, *Frauen unterm Nationalsozialismus* (Wuppertal: Peter Hammer, 1984); Annette Kuhn and Valentine Rothe, *Frauen im deutschen Faschismus* (Düsseldorf: Schwann, 1983) 2 vols; Claudia Koonz, *Mothers in the Fatherland: Women, The Family, and Nazi Politics* (New York: St. Martin's, 1987); David Schoenbaum, *Hitler's Social Revolution. Class and Status in Nazi Germany 1933-39* (New York: Norton, 1980) esp. "The Third Reich and Women" 178-192.

22. Schoenbaum 185.

23. Quoted from a speech given by Hitler on 4 May 1941 to the Reichstag; reprinted in Kuhn and Rothe 117.

24. From Goebbel's speech on 18 February 1943 at a NSDAP rally in the Berlin Sport Palace; quoted in Wiggershaus 27.

25. Klaus Theweleit, *Male Fantasies,* trans. Erica Carter and Chris Turner, vol. 2 (Minneapolis: U of Minnesota P, 1989) 27-35.

26. Karen Ellwanger and Eva-Maria Warth's excellent reading of the film *The Woman of my Dreams* (*Die Frau meiner Träume,* 1943) regards the protagonist's manipulation of her own image through clothing as a sign of emancipation, warning against the "ahistorical" tendency of some feminist scholarship to regard all Nazi films under a one-dimensional perspective of the image of woman propagated in the thirties, thus ignoring "changed social reality of the forties with its modified role expectations for women." "Die Frau meiner Träume. Weiblichkeit und Maskerade: eine Untersuchung zu Form und Funktion von Kleidung als Zeichensystem im Film," *Frauen und Film* 38 (May 1985): 67.

27. Paul von Lettow-Vorbeck, *Mein Leben* (Bilderbach a.d. Riss, 1957) 58ff; quoted in Theweleit, vol. 1, 102.

28. See Tanja Modleski's discussion of how Hitchcock dismisses *Rebecca* based on its genre tradition in *The Women Who Knew Too Much. Hitchcock and Feminist Theory* (New York: Methuen, 1988) 43-55.

29. In a transparent reference to National Socialist biologism, Schiller insists in an argument with the Duke of Württemburg that genius can only be "born," never "trained." Cf. Linda Schulte-Sasse, "National Socialism's Aestheticization of Genius. The Case of Herbert Maisch's *Friedrich Schiller—Triumph eines Ge-*

nies," forthcoming in *Germanic Review*'s special film edition, 1990.

30. Cf. von Loen's *Aristocracy*: "[Virtue] alone is of noble birth, because it stems from heaven. . . . This nobility is possessed by all pious and wise people" (Ulm 1752); quoted in Jochen Schulte-Sasse, *Literarische Struktur und historisch-sozialer Kontext: Zum Beispiel Lessings "Emilia Galotti"* (Paderborn: Schöningh, 1975) 23.

31. See Jochen Schulte-Sasse, ed., *Briefwechsel über das Trauerspiel: Lessing, Nicolai, Mendelssohn* (Munich: Winkler, 1972) especially 52-57, 76-85, and 207-215.

32. Alfred Rosenberg, *Der Mythos des 20, Jahrhunderts* (Munich: Hoheneichen Verlag, 1930) 508. Nazi cinema's portrayals of such "inventive" spirits focus on male biographies, as in *Andreas Schlüter* (architecture), *Diesel* (technology), *Paracelsus, Robert Koch,* or Steinhoff's *Der Volksfeind* (medicine).

33. Andreas Huyssen, "Mass Culture as Woman: Modernism's Other," *After the Great Divide* (Bloomington: Indiana UP, 1986) 51.

34. From Hitler's speech opening the exhibit "Die Frau" on 18 March 1933; quoted in Wiggershaus 15.

Thomas Elsaesser (essay date 1990)

SOURCE: Elsaesser, Thomas. "Transparent Duplicities: The Threepenny Opera (1931)." In *The Films of G. W. Pabst: An Extraterritorial Cinema,* edited by Eric Rentschler, pp. 103-15. New Brunswick: Rutgers University Press, 1990.

[*In the following essay, Elsaesser argues in favor of* The Threepenny Opera*'s merits as a great achievement in Weimar cinema despite a lawsuit filed against Pabst by Bertolt Brecht—the author of the opera upon which Pabst's film is based.*]

PRELIMINARIES

To write about Pabst's **The Threepenny Opera** (**Die 3-Groschen-Oper,** 1931) is to venture into a minefield of received opinions. Even if one sidesteps the boobytraps of literary adaptations and refrains from debating the faithfulness of filmed classics, one ends up frying on the barbed wire of Bertolt Brecht's powerfully polemical defense of his intellectual property in *The Threepenny Trial* (*Der Dreigroschenprozess*). Finally, Pabst's ambivalent role within the Nazi film industry seems to weigh the arguments in favor of assuming that the filmmaker had necessarily "betrayed" Brecht.[1] Any assessment of the film in its own right is therefore likely to be seen as a case of special pleading. But since the film is most often discussed in the context of Brecht,[2] I propose to dispose as quickly as possible of the question of the lawsuit and the circumstances of the production. Instead, I want to concentrate on whether, in light of the film itself, Pabst's approach to the material has a coherence of its own. This should allow some conclusions about Pabst, and also put the case of *The Threepenny Opera* for being considered a major work of Weimar Cinema.

The Lawsuit and its Legacy

On the merits of the lawsuit and trial, commentators usually attend to Brecht's version. This seems reasonable, especially since his purpose in writing up his experiences with the film industry are interesting for two reasons. First, it will be remembered that Brecht, from about 1928 onwards, was practicing what one might call a strategy of cultural intervention, wanting to make his presence felt in virtually every debate and through every existing medium of artistic production. Brecht, in Walter Benjamin's words, sought "never to supply the apparatus without trying to change it."[3] Not only did he work in the theater, he wrote radio plays, participated in musical life through his collaborations with Kurt Weill, Paul Hindemith, and Hanns Eisler. He was active in proletarian associations such as the *Rote Wedding* and wrote learning plays for factories and workers' clubs. He involved himself in filmmaking via Prometheus Film, and with Slatan Dudow and Eisler made *Kuhle Wampe*.[4] For the theater he wrote such different plays for such different publics (or non-publics) as *The Mother* (*Die Mutter*) and *St. Joan of the Stockyards* (*Die heilige Johanna der Schlachthöfe*). All this made the years between 1928 and 1933 among the most productive of his life.[5] *The Threepenny Trial* must be seen in this context.

Second, Brecht (who lost his case—whereas Weill accepted an out-of-court settlement and did rather well financially) was able to take the legal debate onto the high ground of political theory and ideological critique. By focusing on the contradictions between bourgeois notions of artistic autonomy, on the one hand, and capitalist notions of property, on the other, Brecht demonstrated that bourgeois law, though called upon to defend intellectual rights of ownership, cannot in practice legislate against a material concept of ownership, even if this leaves bourgeois ideology in tatters as a result.[6] Since Brecht believed neither in artistic autonomy nor in the capitalist mode of production, he could claim to have instigated the lawsuit in order for the system to reveal its own contradictions: hence the subtitle "Sociological Experiment," a prime example of Brecht's "interventionist thinking (*eingreifendes Denken*)."[7] *The Threepenny Trial* was a sociological experiment not only about individual authorship under capitalism, but a materialist account of how the structure of the film industry itself determines the nature of the products.

Pabst, in an interview with A. Kraszna-Krausz (not quoted as often as Brecht) given on becoming the Head of Dacho (the independent union of German film-workers), implicitly comments on the controversy and points to one of the historical reasons for the ambivalent position of the creative personnel in filmmaking: "A process [of production developed during stormy commercial prosperity means that] the originators of mental-creative work were (and are) not able to decide sufficiently for themselves. They are used as *material* nearly always." Pabst is here astutely political, especially when he goes on to make the case not only on behalf of (relatively privileged) writers, but of others active in the industry, including technicians. Pabst stressed, for instance, the importance of unionization. He concluded: "The social question of the film-worker remains unsolved as long as the film is the exclusive property, that is to say: 'good' in the hands of the manufacturer and his renters."[8]

Brecht and Weill, when taking out proceedings against Nero, knew that they could count on maximum publicity. The whole affair attracted much press coverage, well beyond the film industry trade journals and the culture section of daily papers, because *The Threepenny Opera* was "hot property" at the time, the hottest there was, in fact.[9] As a consequence, the lawsuit was personalized and publicized to an extraordinary degree, with every critic feeling he had to take a stand. Thus, when writing up *The Threepenny Trial,* Brecht had a fat clipping file to draw on.[10] There is some doubt whether he ever saw the film, either then, or subsequently.[11]

The Circumstances of Production

What did the situation look like from the point of view of Nero Film, and by extension, the German film industry? Kurt Weill had sold the film rights of *The Threepenny Opera* to the Berlin representative of Warner Brothers, who went into coproduction with Tobis Klangfilm[12] and Seymour Nebenzahl as owner of Nero Film. On May 21, 1930, Brecht signed a contract with Nero Film-AG, giving him "consultation rights" (*Mitbestimmung*) on the script, but no powers of a veto.[13] The film was to be shot in three versions: German, French and English, as was common practice for major productions in the brief period between the coming of sound and the invention of dubbing.[14] This already indicates that the companies involved were not only hoping for worldwide distribution, but from the start conceived of it as a major production,[15] indeed, it was said to have had the "biggest set that had ever been made for a German movie up to that time."[16]

Nero, with its aggressive production policy (other major Nero films during these years included Pabst's *Kameradschaft* and Fritz Lang's *M*), wanted to break into the international market, and also to strengthen its hand against Ufa, the distribution giant in the German and European market. For Warner Brothers, teaming up with a German independent producer was a way of keeping a foot in the door. Much, therefore, was riding on the success of the project and its smooth realization. In the Kraszna-Krausz interview Pabst is aware of the wider economic implications and also of his own dilemma as creative artist and representative of a professional body within the film industry:

G.W.P.:

> Once already, eight years ago, Germany was able to determine the development of the silent film. Then Germany like the whole rest of the world succumbed to the American film. Now for the second time the fate of the European film is lying in the hands of Germany. France, England have already succumbed afresh to American money. Russia has not yet succeeded in finding a productive attitude to the sound-film. America's production however has driven into a blind alley, out of which the way will scarcely be found alone [*sic*]. Germany is uncommonly enabled by its literary and musical past to determine the shape of the sound-film of to-morrow, if . . .

A.K.K.:

> . . . if the German industry will not be Americanized in spite of all that. If the Russia of the silent film won't remain eternally the 'Mekka' of the German critics.

G.W.P.:

> . . . and if the German film-workers will at last determine their fate—and with it the fate of the German film—all by themselves.[17]

The Threepenny Trial was, in this respect, a minor episode in the international struggle of the major companies to sew up the European market, with mixed results. It may have been good box-office publicity for the international release of the film, but there is evidence to suggest that the delays and the terms of the eventual settlement foiled the plans for an English-language version.[18]

Weill sued Warner/Nero because of the music, rather than any alterations in the text, nor for fearing that the social message of the play had been blunted.[19] In the contract he was guaranteed exclusive control over the music to be used. The grounds on which he was able to litigate successfully were apparently that in the scene of the beggars' final march on Trafalgar Square, one trumpet call was inserted that Weill had not composed.[20] Weill's settlement is, so to speak, a counter-example of a Brechtian brass trade (*Messingkauf*): Nero bought from Weill the trumpet call he had not composed.

BRECHT AND PABST: TWO DIFFERENT APPROACHES TO THE CINEMA?

When considering how "faithful" the film is to Brecht, one is looking at two sources, rather than simply at the original Brecht-Weill opera: Brecht wrote a fairly detailed treatment for the film, as stipulated by his contract. Since the publication of this treatment,[21] several critics have tried to extrapolate from it Brecht's implicit conception of the film, comparing it to Pabst's realization.[22] Most of them take the view that the film is somehow "fatal to Brecht."[23] The exception is Jan-Christopher Horak, who in a careful assessment of Brecht's treatment of the film script by Leo Lania, Béla Balázs and Ladislaus Vajda,[24] and of Pabst's actual realization of both, comes to the conclusion that "Pabst's film is ideologically more correct from a Marxist point of view" than the opera, Brecht's treatment, and the script.[25] The argument generally revolves around two basic issues: first, whether Pabst's concern for a more classical continuity style—integrating the songs into the narrative and leaving out as many as he did (from the "Ballad of Sexual Dependency" and the "Tango Ballad," to the "Executioner's Ballad" and Mack's prison song)—constituted a betrayal of Brecht's epic form and undermined the role of the street singer and various other protagonists, who in the original step in and out of their fictional roles. Second, whether the changes made to Brecht's treatment by the scriptwriters somehow inverted, attenuated, or otherwise falsified the political message Brecht wanted to convey. On the first issue, Horak maintains that Pabst's direction of the actors (many, such as Ernst Busch, Lotte Lenya, Carola Neher, drawn from the first or second stage production) "comes closest to the Brechtian conception of 'epic' theater,"[26] insofar as dialogue is pared down and sparingly used. (This, of course, is also due to the technical difficulties of combining music, camera movement and spoken word in one take.[27]) The characters, in the love scenes for instance, look straight into the camera, breaking the illusionistic space of the diegesis.

Discussions of the second point—alterations to the story line—have focused mainly on the ending, and the motivation for the rivalry between Peachum and Macheath. In the opera, Peachum puts pressure on Tiger Brown, the police chief, to avenge Macheath's seduction of and elopement with Peachum's daughter Polly. In Brecht's treatment, the sexual shenanigans are secondary and the rivalry is between the bosses of two competing businesses, both leeching on the middle class: Macheath's gang of professional thieves and fences (the "Platte," numbering around 120 men), and Peachum's beggar syndicate. Lania, Vajda and Balázs's script once again personalizes the antagonism between Peachum and Macheath and sends Peachum to a dismal fate after his beggars have turned upon him. The finished film represents a compromise, or rather, a skillful synchro-meshing of the two narrative motors driving the conflicting interests, notably by making Polly a much stronger character. At first a typically "romantic" figure, lovestruck, vain, and innocent, Polly turns herself into a hardheaded businesswoman: she is the one who, during Macheath's stint in jail, leads the gang into going legitimate, and sets the terms on which both Tiger Brown and old Peachum join the Bank—the ironic twist being that she does it "out of love," as if running a bank were no different from keeping the house tidy for her husband's return. Brecht, in his film treatment, is mainly interested in working out the logic of capitalist dog-eat-dog-or-join-the-pack, making the play more like *Arturo Ui* by introducing a gradient of move and counter-move into the linear flow. The transition from opera to film gave Brecht a chance to maximize the cinema's ability to suggest through editing new connections and new chains of cause, effect, and consequence.

Reading *The Bruise* (*Die Beule*), one cannot help feeling that Brecht was having fun being hard-boiled and cynical.

He must have known the problems his ideas would encounter in production. Some scenes are more dada than epic theater, with sketches of the dramatic situation and characterization that are broad caricature.[28] Montage sequences underline the didactic gestus of the whole. Brecht tried to use film as a medium that "reduces" lines of dramatic development, intent to get from A to B in the shortest possible time. At worst, Brecht is trying to sabotage the project from the start; at best, *The Bruise* is a critique of the dominant modes of the silent "author's film" prevalent during the 1920s.

Brecht creates causal relationships; Weimar cinema dissolves causal relationships. Brecht is elliptical in order to force issues into contradictions, whereas expressionist cinema uses ellipsis to suspend causality, to introduce ambiguity, and to open up parentheses. Where Brecht is interested in metonymy, the German cinema employs metaphor; Brecht goes for satire, pastiches, irony, the German cinema for pathos, self-tormented psychology, primary process imagery. Brecht's is a text of verbal aggression, the Weimar cinema revels in texts of mute repression. Brecht's affectivity is all invested in punning and "Witz" (the saving of psychic energy) whereas the Weimar cinema's psychic economy is more like dreamwork: it, too, shifts the burden of representation onto figures of condensation and displacement, but without the semiotic or comic payoffs.

What is generally missing in German films is not an attention to detail or objects, but their concretization within the image, and also within the intellectual movement of a scene. Expressionist abstraction is, as Brecht recognized, the very opposite of the kind of reduction or foreshortening ("*Verkürzung*") he was after. It is a form of symbolic generalization which opens the event to its contamination by the categories of the imaginary: reversible, inward, existential, psychoanalytical. The historical specificity and social gestus are almost always absent.

Yet Pabst's work, too, provides a critique of Weimar cinema while at the same time exploiting to the full what had made the German cinema internationally famous in the 1920s. He parodies, for instance, the expressionist mania for charging objects with a life of their own. In one of the night scenes, as the gang steals the furnishings for Mackie's wedding, we see an armchair scurrying through the streets, shot at and followed by a policeman. Here Surrealism is invoked to deflate Expressionism.[29] More importantly, though, Pabst has rethought in terms of his medium the issues that Brecht raises in the original and in his film treatment.[30] *The Threepenny Opera,* as we have it, is not so much a film about the contradictions between moral codes and business practices (the theme of capitalism's own betrayal of the ideology that supports it, also taken up in *The Threepenny Trial*). Instead, Pabst concentrates on the duplicity of representation itself, and of filmic representation in particular.

To phrase the contrast between Brecht and Pabst in these terms may seem paradoxical, given that Brecht, too, criticized bourgeois modes of representation, and above all, the canons of realism and verisimilitude. But Brecht's notion of representation was language-based, and in his film work he seems to show little interest in the crises of representation brought about by the new culture of the image (however perceptive he was about photography).[31] For Brecht, the primacy of language always remained the writer's hope, coupled with an enlightenment belief in the demystifying powers of the word.[32]

Before exploring this point further, it is worth mentioning that *The Threepenny Opera* is also "Brechtian" in ways perhaps different from those mentioned above. To the extent that it engages with a recognizable fictional scenario, the narrative is a standard Weimar Oedipal situation: a man steals a daughter from a father, who becomes violent and homicidal but is essentially powerless to intervene, since in the process, the daughter emancipates herself from both father and lover. This scenario, which is similar to, say, a *Heimatfilm* like *Vulture Wally* (*Die Geier-Wally,* E. A. Dupont, 1921), is deconstructed by Pabst, who lets the material interests ("business") triumph over blood ties and family interests—except that in the end, family interests and business interests are made to coincide perfectly. What in other Weimar films gives rise to melodrama (or comedy) becomes here a parody for the purpose of a materialist critique of the bourgeois family. Rather than depicting a story of betrayal and jealousy (Macheath, unfaithful to Jenny, is betrayed by her to Peachum, who betrays him to the police) which would amount to psychologizing the Brechtian plot, the film is true to Brecht's consistent de-Oedipalizing of family relationships: as in *Mother Courage (Mutter Courage und ihre Kinder), Galileo,* and even *The Caucasian Chalk Circle (Der kaukasische Kreidekreis).*

PABST'S POWERPLAY OF APPEARANCES

Pabst's cinema, and especially where it deals with political or social issues, has always supported its dramatic conflicts by underpinning them with another structure altogether: that of visual fascination, the treachery and irony of appearances.[33] Revolution, as in *The Love of Jeanne Ney,* or the turmoil of postwar inflation, as in *The Joyless Street,* are grist to the same mill, where power is defined across its hold on the machineries of make-believe. In this, of course, he is not alone among the major Weimar directors: Fritz Lang and Ernst Lubitsch, too, work with the very structures of the cinema as the powerplay of appearances.

Pabst's obsession with the shifting configurations produced by the false ontology of the filmic image can, I think, be usefully compared to that of Lang: the logic of *The Threepenny Opera* as a film rests on its place within this wider, also typically Weimar preoccupation. Pabst's Mackie Messer (and especially as incarnated by Rudolf Forster) is above all, the hero of many disguises: the opening song, already in Brecht, emphasizes his ubiquity and invisibility. But the way the film introduces him, leaving the brothel in Drury Lane, emphasizes another point. One of the girls passes him his cane through the window, he tugs at it, she playfully refuses to let go and the cane unsheathes to reveal a lethal dagger, the "teeth" from the song. No object that Mackie is associated with is what it appears to be and yet each becomes a metaphor of his personality. In this respect, he is a second cousin to Dr. Mabuse, equally dandified, though Mabuse is more darkly intelligent and tormented than Macheath. But whereas Mabuse connotes the mesmerizing power of capitalism itself with its breathtaking manipulation of the mass media and public institutions, Mackie Messer's power is founded on erotic power, the register of seduction, which in Mabuse is a mere by-product, a consequence of deploying the kind of intellect needed to wield social power. The Mackie of the film seems incapable of the deeds attributed to him in the Mack the Knife song, however much we see him actively encouraging the legend, and, indeed, being a slave to its claims.

Thus, apart from keeping certain epic elements already mentioned (the songs, the street singer-presenter), Pabst retains a typical ambivalence. In the guise of a critique of "moonshine and romanticism," the opera had romanticized the proletarian demimonde of the brothel, the pimp, sexual libertinage, and antibourgeois moral sentiment. Brecht's film treatment goes some way towards excising this lumpen sentimentality. Pabst returns to the element that undoubtedly had made the opera such a hit, but adds a telling nuance, in that he uses the performative cabaret mode to redefine the main protagonist's social status as a celebrity. For instance, the first time we see Mackie Messer head-on is when he joins the crowd listening to Ernst Busch singing the Mack the Knife song. His look into the camera introduces a point of view of the crowd and initiates his search for Polly and her mother. Pabst cuts to the crowds moving closer to Ernst Busch singing, then to Mackie entering the frame, followed by a policeman. Mackie twirls his cane in response to the line about the teeth no one can see. A tracking shot from a high angle (the level of Ernst Busch standing on a platform) follows the crowd milling about before it identifies with the diagonal movement of Polly and Mrs. Peachum.

Here the camera, at first moved by Macheath in pursuit of Polly, turns out to be the delegate of the singer's narrative, weaving the character of Mackie and the setting into the song, and constructing a narrational en-abyme effect rather than a distancing device, by its complex shift in focalization.[34] Macheath, distracted from his quest for Polly, gets caught up in listening to the song that celebrates his exploits, which introduces both the motif of vanity and self-display, and the extent that he, too, is implicated in the universe of the "show" which so completely dominates the world of the brothel, but also that of Peachum's beggars. The young man through whom the audience is introduced to Peachum's business and whose real poverty lacks credibility until he is kitted out in rags, looks at himself in the mirror, gazing at his image in wonderment and awe. The scene is similar to an earlier one at the wedding, where the pastor, anxious to get away, catches sight of himself in a mirror and is rooted to the spot by his reflection. Later, at a moment of great danger, with the police in hot pursuit, Macheath looks at himself on a "Wanted" poster, and encouraged by this boost to his ego, sets about seducing another female passerby. In these instances of recognition/miscognition, the characters lose themselves to the phenomenon of fascination itself: but only Macheath, captivated by his own image, makes narcissism the chief resource of his power over others.

Eroticism as seduction has in Pabst's cinema much to do with the characters' ability to control the image, which in turn is a control of one's own appearance and disappearance: witness Mackie's compulsive Thursday visits to the "whores at Tunbridge," elaborate charades of regularity and surprise, geared not toward the sensuous extension of moments of pleasure, but the *mise en scène* of an ever more skillful vanishing artist. From this it would seem that the power of fascination is ambivalent in respect of gender. In *The Threepenny Opera,* Mackie, phallic hero par excellence, is "feminized" by his flaunted narcissism, assuming the function of a fetish, and becoming the love object of both males and females: of the masculinized Jenny, the ultra-feminine Polly, and of Tiger Brown, his buddy from the wars. In his dependence on this circulation of desire and its frustration (and the social machinations which result from it), Mackie's position is similar to the role occupied by Lulu in *Pandora's Box.*[35] No doubt his eroticism brings into Pabst's text a subversion quite different from that intended by Brecht and makes Mackie an ambivalent narrative agent, halfway between possessor of the look that furthers the plot and the look that acknowledges being-looked-at-ness: longingly, suspiciously, angrily, admiringly.

Yet Pabst's reworking of the central figure is, as it were, only the localized instance, the evidence of a structure of perversity and narrational reversibility which allows the director to bracket it with another structure of fascination, also perhaps erotic, but in the first instance directed towards the social world: the fascination emanating from the different sham worlds which vie for the spectator's attention. There is the world of Peachum's beggars, that of Tiger Brown's forces of law and order, of capitalist business practices, of respectability, and of Jenny's sexuality, all of them dominated by display and masquerade, which find their corollaries in the wedding feast and the brothel visit and culminate in the crowd scenes and the sham revolution of the beggars' procession.

UNIFORMS AND DUMMIES, WINDOWS AND DOORS

One of the criticisms leveled against *The Threepenny Opera* is that Pabst allowed it to become the set designer's and art director's film.[36] But the evident emphasis on textures and materials, decor, and props rather underlines the inner logic of Pabst's conception, and the continuity that exists between "classical" Weimar cinema of the 1920s and the sound films of the early 1930s. For a distinctive feature of German silent cinema, and part of its pioneering role in film history, is the "designed" look of so many of the films, based as they were on the close collaboration between director, scriptwriter, cameraman, art director, and editor. This labor-intensive and costly production method allowed directors to pre-design each shot or set-up, and to integrate characters, setting, figure movement, and editing in a way Hollywood had to acquire by importing the star talents from Germany in the 1920s—Lubitsch, Murnau, Pommer, among others.[37]

Thus, here is a further reason why the collaboration with Brecht was bound to be difficult, given Brecht's unwillingness to subject himself to this apparatus and Pabst's habit of planning set-ups very carefully but improvising story details and dialogue material to fit in with the visual conception:

> In framing a scene from the pictorial point of view and in understanding how to use the camera for pictorial effect, he is probably one of the greatest. . . . What makes it rather difficult for a writer to work with Pabst [is that] he has to supply the whole structure and at the same time he has to creep, as it were, into Pabst's personality in order to present a story to him, a story which Pabst always sees in pictures, not in scenes. . . . Pabst is certainly not a disciplined person, in the sense of being able to organize a story, to construct. And so if the other man, like Brecht, is just the opposite, but also unable to tell a story, darting from point to point, then you have no counter balance and no force that supplies the structure, the skeleton for the story.[38]

To the extent, therefore, that Pabst's *Threepenny Opera* coheres around a unity of style,[39] it is still very much an example of a "cinema of metaphor" in the tradition of the 1920s.[40] Two metaphoric chains run through the film. One is centered on puppets and dummies, statues and objets d'art; the second on windows, partitions, doors, and Mackie's prison cell. Scenes are not only frequently marked off by a fade-out or black leader (thereby minimizing narrational contiguity), but stand under a different master image: for instance, the window of the brothel and the milliner's shop window are "condensed" in the scene where Jenny opens the window to signal to Mrs. Peachum and the police; the mirrors in the dance hall anticipate those at the wedding and in Peachum's house; the stairs at the warehouse serve as altar for the wedding ceremony, allow Macheath to do his dictation and office work, and "rhyme" Tiger Brown's entrance with the gang's exit; at Peachum's the stairs dramatize the family quarrel, and in the brothel, they show Mackie making his escape.

Both metaphoric series function either in tandem or as counterpoints and both are integral to locating the film in a play of the human and the mechanical, of inside and outside, open and closed, of mirrors and walls, light and darkness—in short, a play of doubles and oppositional pairs entirely focused on sight, illusionism, and imaginary space: a combination which fairly defines that intensification of visual pleasure in Weimar cinema which one might call the fascination of the false.

The subject of puppets is introduced very early on. Before the film properly begins, and over the chorus from the Threepenny song, doll-like stand-ins of the leading characters parade in the round like Seven Deadly Sins or Foolish Virgins on a medieval cathedral clock. Besides preparing for the narrational effects described above, which place Mackie both inside and outside the double fiction of the song and the narrative, the playful sarcasm of the figurines raises the question of who controls the mechanism activating the power politics, of who, finally, pulls the strings on whom and is thus in charge of the show.[41] The motif is taken up when we see the dummy bride in the shop window, stripped bare by Mackie's "bachelors" a few scenes further on, with one of the thieves tipping his hat to her— very nearly the same hat that was tipped to Mackie in the dance hall, and then to Tiger Brown. His is the character most closely associated with the metaphoric chain that goes from dress-dummies to dress uniforms, from bowler hats and etiquette to the imposture of office and authority most graphically shown in the scene where one of Macheath's men lets himself be caught "redhanded" by the police in order to deliver the wedding invitation—hidden in his deferentially lowered hat—directly to Tiger Brown. Visually, the bowler hats and their self-importance are echoed in the grotesquely inflated barrels dominating Macheath's warehouse.[42] Morally, the motif leads to Peachum, his dummies as beggars, and his beggars as the rent-a-mob dummies of the powers-that-be. Yet so aware is the film of its play on reversal and ironic inversions that Pabst not only introduces a slave motif in the brothel, shown full of statues of negresses, but they form a rhyming contrast to the white plaster goddesses with Greek pretensions in the warehouse, shown most prominently after Polly sings her ballad of the man with the dirty collar who doesn't know how to treat a lady, and Mackie admonishes his men who find the song "very nice": "You call this nice, you fools— it's art."

The metaphoric chain that links the many windows, trapdoors, partitions, and skylights first of all draws attention to the sets themselves. In the warehouse, a slow pan reveals the whole brilliant display, but the scene is actually constructed as a series of rapidly changing passages to different fantasy worlds. The backdrop to the wedding, for instance, is the harbor and the moon, in keeping with Mackie and Polly's "Moon over Soho" duet. But its character as a stage (or movie) set, now in keeping with the intensely felt phoniness of the sentiments expressed, is underscored by the fact that we first see it as a steel door, before it is hung with Chinese embroidery. After another song, announced by Polly and applauded by the guests as a performance, a curtain is pulled, the marital bed revealed and a drawbridge raised. The atmosphere of a country fair combines with the sophisticated illusionism of a backstage musical, and as in *Pandora's Box,* the stage and the mechanics of putting on a show serve as a metaphor for the deceptiveness of representation, but also the pleasure of that very deceptiveness. The warehouse, Aladdin's cave of capitalist production, here a surrealist accumulation of stolen goods and a hideous clash of styles, gives not only the wedding an air of unreality: by celebrating the false bottom of the world it depicts, it turns the human players, but especially the figures of morality and law (the pastor and Tiger Brown) into mere props and objects, obsolete mementos of a bygone age.

This scene stands in a structural contrast to the one in the brothel, which is built very similarly around the foregrounded architectural elements of the decor. Jenny's entrance is lit explicitly to recall that of Tiger Brown when he stepped through the skylight of the warehouse. But what is highlighted here are the different acts of transfer and exchange: framed in the window, Jenny stuffs Mrs. Peachum's bribe in her stocking, the same window that Mackie steps through immediately after. Jenny then opens the window making the fatal sign to Mrs. Peachum and the policemen, before closing it again, while other girls draw the curtains. The window makes this drama of entrapment and betrayal into a scene where money, glances, and bodies become interchangeable signs of transaction and transgression.

Thus, even motifs that relate more directly to the political issues, such as the constant references to ledgers and accounts, bills, papers, lists, bail money, and bank business are, as it were, introduced via references to visual exchanges. Conspicuous at the bank, for instance, is a sliding door with frosted glass, giving rise to a kind of shadow play, where each "board member" takes a bow without the spectator seeing the object of their deference. It is through this very door that Tiger Brown comes, as he slips from one high office to another, strutting into the room with his guard-officer's uniform.

The Charm and Charisma of Mackie Messer

One reason why the film contains so many sets with partitions, panes of clear or frosted glass, blinds and curtains, windows half-lifted and suddenly dropped, is that they play a key role in defining Mackie Messer's mode of authority, based as his attraction is on his image as a show-value. Noticeable from the opening scene—sash windows are raised, objects like a glove, a cane are passed through, linking the inside with the outside—is that entrances, exits, and internal frames establish the paradigm of communicating vessels so important for the movement of the film as a whole. In this respect, transparency and transport are the secrets of Mackie's success, and his power (of fascination, of attraction) resides in an ability to penetrate walls and summon people through windows. The scene where Mackie takes Polly to the dance hall, persuades her to marry him, and organizes the wedding all at the same time is Pabst's way of showing a form of power in action, based, it seems, entirely on the glance and the gesture, on shadows spied through partitions and messages passed as if by magic. Mackie looks at the camera (an incompletely sutured point-of-view shot towards the two crooks), Polly looks at Mackie, while between them is a spherical wall-mounted light, announcing the full moon later on. This set-up is repeated many times: the spectator is drawn into

the imaginary space to the front of the screen, and witnessing the consequences of Mackie's look, experiences the power of that look. Thus Mackie does not have to do anything to win Polly: he is the man who makes things happen by simply being seen. In the dance hall full of mirrors reflecting other couples dancing, everything organizes itself around Mackie—source of a power that is economic, logistic, and erotic—but in this scene framed, himself, as a spectator.

This play on vision establishes a double mode of control on the level of the narrative, Macheath's power is defined as active but the mode in which this power is exercised and visualized is passive. A male character defined as phallic but also narcissistic, and the many scenes staged around windows, apertures, and partitions, dramatize a mode in which seeing and being seen are the two aggregate states of the same resource of power and control.

If Mackie is an ambiguous character in relation to gender, since he is not only erotic object, but also both producer and product of the narrative, a similar ambiguity surrounds the female characters—with one important proviso. While the film's image of masculinity is embodied in Mackie, that of femininity is split between Polly and Jenny. Pabst has always been recognized as an exceptional director of actresses and the creator of memorable women characters:

> Pabst has [in each of his films] displayed an interest in the mental and physical make-up of his feminine players, with the result that he has often brought to the screen women who have been unusually attractive in a bizarre, neurotic manner, very different from the brilliantly turned out, sophisticated but stereotyped women of American pictures, or the dreary young ladies favoured by British directors.[43]

Paul Rotha goes on to single out the chance meeting of Mackie and the girl in the street immediately after his escape from the brothel, which, indeed has the sort of eroticism Baudelaire first captured in his eros-and-the-city poem "To a Passerby." But more crucial to the narrative as a whole is the transformation of Polly, and how she translates the aggressive eroticism of Jenny into a specifically masculine power potential. Polly's mode of subjectivity is emblematically introduced in the scene in front of the milliner's shop. Mackie's desire in the opening scene is born out of a division: the frame is split, as it were, between him catching a disappearing glimpse of Polly and him separating from Jenny. Polly's desire is depicted more classically—for a female character—through the narcissistic doubling of an image. As the song ends on "Mackie, what was your price," we see Polly in front of the shop window with the wedding dress. The camera is inside the window for this shot, then reverses the angle, and Mackie enters into the frame, but appears on the same side as the dummy in the window display.[44] Polly sees the reflection and smiles. Only then does she turn around and, with an expression of shock, sees the "real" Mackie Messer standing next to her. From being the imaginary dummy groom next to the dummy bride he becomes the spy who has seen her see her fantasy. These are the terms around which the seduction in the dance hall and the consent to marriage play themselves out across the screen of Polly's romantic double vision: glance/glance into camera by Polly/Mackie Messer, implicating the spectator into their erotic space. But Polly's narrative trajectory is, of course, the total transformation of this feminine imaginary: it ends with her assuming phallic power over both father and husband, staged in that extraordinary scene already mentioned, where all the thieves turned bank managers bow before an invisible presence, which we infer before we know it, is Polly. Her desire, overinscribed in the register of vision during the first scene, has become that ultimate of male power in the German cinema (of both Lang and Pabst)—invisibility.

DUPLICITY: THE POWER OF THE FALSE

Recent criticism of *The Threepenny Opera* has drawn attention to the fact that duplicity is one of the film's central preoccupations. Tony Rayns even speaks of "frank duplicity."[45] In one sense, of course, this is in keeping with Brecht's original, and indeed his film treatment. Whereas the opera had insisted on the moral duplicity, the film treatment wanted to focus on the economic and political implications of such duplicity. What makes the film appear at one level a retrograde step is that Pabst seems to celebrate the same duplicity which in Brecht is the moral of the fable, and which the verbal wit, and the logic of the dramatic conflicts are called upon to expose. However, Pabst has recognized that the kind of duplicity which the opera had seized upon is the more difficult to focus critically, since its effects are multiple. First, duplicity energizes. Contradictions create differentials, and differentials are the very lifeblood of capitalism, its source of profit and power. Second, duplicity eroticizes. In the play Mackie is attractive to women because he plays hot and cold, because of his double standards, making explicit the duplicity of bourgeois morals by holding a mirror up to it. Finally, duplicity is the source of humor and wit. Pabst has, consistent with his project of translating all these issues into the terms appropriate to the cinema, made a film in which the false is not criticized by the true, but by the false, raised to its nth power.

This he does, essentially, by contrasting distinct forms of cinematic space, all of them imaginary. There is the use of offscreen space to the side of the frame, mostly used for comic effects, and to underscore the social hypocrisy, cynicism, and double morality enacted by the dialogue. Then there is the space to the front of the action, into the camera, and thus toward the spectator, in a manner apparently "estranging" (breaking the illusion) while also implicating us through its performative dimension. But the most typical space of the film, a kind of meta- or hyper-space of representation, is that constructed in the form of an infinite regress, *en-abyme,* in which a show appears within a show, a frame framing a frame. It is these cinematic markings of spatial relationships which create that constant awareness of the differentiations and degrees operating on the reality

status of the image. They structure the intrigue and its logic more decisively than other, more directly social issues, and they would allow one to investigate further the fascination emanating from duplicity.

If one were to read *The Threepenny Opera*—analogous to so many German films of the early 1930s, and especially those of Lang—as a statement about the nature of power in the age of the mediated images and the manipulation of appearances, then the elaborate *mise en scène* of Mackie Messer's charisma could be seen, by itself, as a mystification of the source of power. But one might argue that what was at issue for Pabst was first and foremost to preserve the popularity—the original opera's social truth value—and that which had made it commercial, in short, a "hot property."[46] For by emphasizing Mackie's and Polly's narcissism, Pabst enacts and also deconstructs them as role models. It is not so much, as Jean Oser jokingly put it, that "every girl wanted to be Polly . . . every fellow wanted to be Mackie,"[47] but that every spectator, male and female, wants to be in love with their self-image, across the desire of the other. Mackie and Polly have what to this day characterizes the successful consumer of mass-entertainment: "style."

The German cinema thus contributed to world cinema not so much a new psychological language, a new inwardness, nor even the cinema's own self-reflexivity, but perhaps a different mode of displacing the technology of filmic production into an intensification of the erotic aspect of the filmic reality, which became the heightening of the commodity—the glamour, seizing not only the men or the women characters, but all objects, including the decor. Here lies the peculiar achievement of Pabst's *mise en scène* in *The Threepenny Opera*: he was able to imbue every aspect of the filmic process with value in itself, as an added attraction to the commodity status of the artifact which was the opera and became the film.

Notes

1. Even John Willett, who admits to liking the film, thinks that Pabst and Brecht were antagonistic in their outlook. "Gersch, like other students of Brecht, on the whole takes Brecht's view and argues that Nero . . . had political objections to the new material. . . . Personally, I doubt whether this was due to anyone but Pabst, whose divergences from Brecht's views . . . were surely predictable from the start." See John Willett, *Brecht in Context* (London: Methuen, 1984), 115.

2. See, for instance, *Europe* (January-February 1957), special Brecht issue, 14-21; *Ecran,* No. 73 (March 1973): 2-29; *Screen* 16.4 (Winter 1975-1976): 16-33; *Cinématographe* (Paris), No. 125 (December 1986): 38-39, 42-44.

3. Walter Benjamin, "The Artist as Producer," in *Reflections,* ed. Peter Demetz, trans. Edmund Jephcott (New York and London: Harcourt Brace Jovanovich, 1978), 220-238.

4. See "Interview with George Höllering," *Screen* 15.2 (Summer 1974): 41-73 and *Screen* 15.4 (Winter 1974-1975): 71-79.

5. See Willett, *Brecht in Context,* 180-184.

6. "Capitalism in its practice is cogent (*konsequent*), because it has to be. But if it is cogent in practice, it has to be ideologically contradictory (*inkonsequent*). . . . Reality has developed to a point where the only obstacle to the progress of capitalism is capitalism itself." Bertolt Brecht, *Gesammelte Werke in 20 Bänden* (Frankfurt: Suhrkamp, 1967), 18:204.

7. Willett calls it "a classic early media study to set alongside some of Benjamin's and subsequently Enzensberger's writings" (*Brecht in Context,* 116).

8. A. Kraszna-Krausz, "G. W. Pabst Before the Microphone of German Broadcasting," *Close Up* 8.2 (June 1931): 122.

9. According to Jean Oser, who worked on the film as editor: "When *Dreigroschenoper* came out, it formed the entire pre-Hitler generation until 1933; for about five years . . . every girl wanted to be [like Polly, talk like Polly, and every fellow] like Mackie Messer. Apparently the ideal man was a pimp." See Interview with Oser by Gideon Bachmann, reprinted in *Masterworks of the German Cinema,* introduced by Dr. Roger Manvell (London: Lorrimer, 1973), 299. (Line in [] missing from original; see microfiche file *Die Dreigroschenoper* in British Film Institute Library, London.)

10. See *Bertolt Brechts Dreigroschenbuch* (Frankfurt: Suhrkamp, 1973), 271-336, for a selection of contemporary reviews.

11. John Willett seems to think he did (*Brecht in Context,* 117).

12. "Tobis had a monopoly on all sound film production in Germany because they had bought up all the Swiss, Danish and German patents. They were the only ones who could actually make sound films. You had to rent the sound crew and equipment from them. I was working for Tobis, and so when Pabst wanted to make a sound film . . . I became editor for him" (Oser interview, 298).

13. See Wolfgang Gersch, *Film bei Brecht* (Berlin/GDR: Henschel, 1975), 48, and Willett, *Brecht in Context,* 114.

14. See Ginette Vincendeau, "Hollywood Babel," *Screen* 29.2 (Spring 1988): 24-39.

15. "I agree with Brecht, because you don't make a million-dollar movie out of a story which should practically be shot in a backyard" (Oser interview, 299).

16. Ibid., 300. This may be something of an exaggeration, considering the sets for "*Grossfilme*" of the 1920s such as *Metropolis* or *Faust.*

17. A. Kraszna-Krausz, "Pabst Before the Microphone," 125-126.

18. "An English version, *The Threepennies Opera* [*sic*], was also supposed to have been shot. But it appears that essentially this became a straightforward dubbing of the German version." Claude Beylie, "Quelques notes sur l'opéra de quat'sous," *L'Avant-Scène du Cinéma,* No. 177 (1 December 1976): 4. "The film was released in France . . . and was a tremendous success. In Germany it was not such a success and it was attacked quite often by the critics" (Oser interview, 299). *The Threepenny Opera* premiered in Berlin on February 19, 1931 and was banned by the *Filmprüfstelle* on August 10, 1933. After a press show in Paris in March 1931, the French version was banned by the censors and only opened in November 1931, with some minor cuts, at the famous Studio des Ursulines. The cinema also showed the uncut German version.

19. See Lee Atwell, *G. W. Pabst* (Boston: Twayne, 1977), 83: "Although the Theater am Schiffbauerdamm production was carried out strictly according to Brecht's directions, it would be a mistake to assume that critics or audiences were captivated by Brecht's bitter cynicism about the human condition. Rather, they were taken with Kurt Weill's jazz-influenced, easily singable score and songs."

20. This information according to the interview with Jean Oser. Willett maintains that it was the music in the wedding scene Weill objected to (115).

21. "Die Beule." See bibliography for publication data.

22. See Arlene Croce, "*The Threepenny Opera,*" *Film Quarterly* 6.1 (Fall 1960): 43-45; Alan Stanbrook, "Great Films of the Century No. 10: *Die Dreigroschenoper,*" *Films and Filming* 7.7 (April 1961): 15-17, 38; Wolfgang Gersch, *Film bei Brecht,* 48-71; Willett, 113-116. These may usefully be compared to some of the original reviews of the film, such as those by Lotte Eisner, Siegfried Kracauer, and Paul Rotha.

23. Arlene Croce, 45.

24. Reprinted in full (with indications of cuts and alterations made during the shooting) in *Masterworks of the German Cinema,* 179-276.

25. Jan-Christopher Horak, "*Threepenny Opera*: Brecht vs. Pabst," *Jump Cut,* No. 15 (July 1977): 20.

26. Ibid. Willett takes a similar view: "At all events, the finished film is as distinctively a Brecht work as are his other collective works of the time, starting perhaps with the *Threepenny Opera* and not excluding *Happy End* of which he chose to wash his hands; and so far as is now known he was satisfied with it" (117).

27. Paul Rotha, in his very favorable review of the film, draws special attention "to the prevalence of moving

camera work in *Die Dreigroschenoper.* Since the introduction of the spoken word into film-making, there has been a growing tendency to decrease the number of direct cuts in a picture, partly because of the desire to minimize the amount of different camera setups and partly on account of the difficulties attendant on cutting and joining the sound strip" (repr. in *Masterworks of the German Cinema,* 296).

28. The central idea, namely that Peachum keeps in peak condition the bruise on one of his beggar's heads, received from Macheath's men when they punish him for grassing on a robbery, may be good enough for a cabaret sketch, but is plainly silly as the dramatic premise for the "multi-million movie." Erwin Leiser, who knew Brecht personally in the 1950s and occasionally went to the cinema with him, speaks of Brecht's "hair-raising ideas of what was feasible in a feature film" ("'Schlecht genug?'—Brecht und der Film," *Neue Zürcher Zeitung,* 16 June 1983, 45).

29. "If the director has subverted the play's subversiveness, it is to the end of a poetic anarchy, irrational, beautiful and precise, where surrealism, expressionism and Marxism find a remarkable if fleeting common ground" (Tony Rayns, *Monthly Film Bulletin,* July 1974, 162).

30. In this he is within Brechtian thinking, according to which an adaptation ought to constitute the "deconstruction of the work, according to the vantage point of keeping its social function within a new apparatus." Bertolt Brecht, *"Der Dreigroschenprozess,"* in *Schriften zur Literatur und Kunst,* 2 vols. (Frankfurt: Suhrkamp, 1966), 1:30; also quoted in Gersch, *Film bei Brecht,* 51.

31. See the famous remark in *The Threepenny Trial,* about a photo of the Krupp works or A.E.G. not telling anything about the reality of such institutions (*Bertolt Brechts Dreigroschenbuch,* 135).

32. See Josette Féral, "Distanciation et multi-media, ou Brecht inversé," in *Brecht Thirty Years After,* ed. P. Kleber and C. Visser (Cambridge: Cambridge University Press, forthcoming).

33. Barthélemy Amengual goes so far as to claim that the favorite Pabst shot is the low-angle, and it functions as a kind of matrix or mastershot, because it concretizes the attitude of fascination. See *Georg Wilhelm Pabst* (Paris: Seghers, 1966), 57, n. 33.

34. The narrational complexity of the scene is even more of a technical tour de force when one considers the difficulties of setting up such a scene with the sound equipment then available.

35. See my "Lulu and the Meter Man," *Screen* 24.4-5 (July-October 1983): 4-36.

36. Andrey Andreyev is often mentioned as being responsible for its look, along with Fritz Arno Wagner, the chief cameraman. A sumptuous volume dedicated to Hans Casparius, edited by Hans-Michael Bock and Jürgen Berger, *Photo: Casparius* (West Berlin: Stiftung Deutsche Kinemathek, 1978), gives the fullest visual record of the making of *The Threepenny Opera* and also contains a wealth of contemporary material, documenting the lawsuit, trade journal reports, press comments, production notes, and Pabst's shooting script (165-431).

37. See Barry Salt, "From Caligari to Who?," *Sight and Sound* 48.2 (Spring 1979): 119-123, for a useful discussion of set design in Weimar cinema; also my "Secret Affinities: F. W. Murnau," *Sight and Sound* 58.1 (Winter 1988-1989): 33-39. One of the most astute commentators on this feature of Pabst's style is still Paul Rotha, who talks of the film's "dovetailed workmanship": "Not solely on account of their individual merit as design do I draw attention to these sets, but because they are the envelope, as it were, of the film. Without the self-contained world that they create, a world of dark alleys, hanging rigging and twisting stairways, without their decorative yet realistic values, without the air of finality and completeness which they give, this film-operetta would not have been credible. . . . This is due not only to the settings in themselves, but the very close relationship maintained between the players and their surroundings, which has come about because the director and the architect have to all intents and purposes worked with one mind. Each corner and each doorway is conceived in direct relationship to the action played within its limits. This factor, together with the cooperation of the camerawork, builds the film into a solid, well-informed unity" (*Masterworks of the German Cinema,* 295).

38. Leo Lania, interviewed by Gideon Bachmann, "Six Talks on G. W. Pabst," *Cinemages* (New York) 1.3 (1955).

39. Pabst shows his sense of humor also in this respect: when Mackie is in prison, even his socks match the bars of his cell.

40. See Michael Henry, *Le cinéma expressioniste allemand* (Fribourg: Edition du Signe, 1971), 41-58, for the notion of metaphoric space in relation to German films. I am using the term here as shorthand for a rather complex narratological issue which I discuss further in "National Cinema and Subject-Construction" (unpub. paper, Society for Cinema Studies Conference, New York, June 1985).

41. "It looks forward (in the integration of characters and setting) to *Le Crime de M. Lange* rather than backwards to *The Joyless Street*" (Rayns, 162). Rotha also commented on how Pabst emphasized "the relationship between the players and their surroundings" (*Masterworks of the German Screen,* 295).

42. They were noted with amazement by Paul Rotha, ibid.: "On all sides of the set rise up great barrels, ridiculous barrels of absurd height and girth, yet how

admirably original. Mackie's dressing-room consists of smaller barrels placed slightly apart, behind each of which he vanishes in turn to complete his toilet."

43. Ibid., 297.

44. Very similar shots can be found in Lang's *M,* at the beginning and end of *Fury,* and in R. W. Fassbinder's *Berlin Alexanderplatz.*

45. Rayns, 162.

46. See note 30.

47. See note 9.

Anne Friedberg (essay date 1990)

SOURCE: Friedberg, Anne. "An *Unheimlich* Maneuver between Psychoanalysis and the Cinema: *Secrets of a Soul.*" In *The Films of G. W. Pabst: An Extraterritorial Cinema,* edited by Eric Rentschler, pp. 41-51. New Brunswick: Rutgers University Press, 1990.

[*In the following essay, Friedberg explores the relationship between cinema and psychoanalysis in light of Pabst's experiences making* Secrets of a Soul.]

"Mass culture is psychoanalysis in reverse."

—Leo Löwenthal

The coincident birthdates of psychoanalysis and the cinema have frequently been celebrated as "no accident." Freud's theory of the unconscious, his "science" of the psyche (*die Seele*),[1] was, from the start, a theory in search of an apparatus. Yet the cinema, an apparatus which could reproduce and project specular images, was, from its beginnings, an apparatus in search of a theory. Historians who accept metaphors of incipience, birth, parturition, and infancy for the two quite separate "bodies" of psychoanalysis and cinema—one a theoretical "body," the other an apparatical corpus which only developed its theoretical parasites when well into adolescence—might also want to chart a further history of these figures. As both "bodies" developed, there were moments of mutual attraction, occasions of intercourse and isolation, in what has remained a frequently ambivalent and largely undocumented affair. Freud, who sired and literally engendered his theories, was a protective and possessive father. The cinema, polymorphously conceived, a culmination of inventions and marketing strategies on an international scale, was much more promiscuous in its outreach.

In this context, G. W. Pabst's 1926 film, *Secrets of a Soul* (*Geheimnisse einer Seele*), is one such moment of encounter, a chapter in the still unwritten and untheorized metahistory of psychoanalysis and cinema.[2] Shown at Freud's seventieth birthday celebration in Berlin, *Secrets of a Soul* was an occasion for an unprecedented collaboration between the quite separate worlds of film production and psychoanalysis. In working on *Secrets of a Soul,* the filmmaker Pabst was pulled into the carefully-guarded realm of psychoanalysis. Karl Abraham and Hanns Sachs, both members of Freud's exclusive "circle" of seven, were pulled into the brash mass-cultural world of the cinema.[3] The exchange between them, a transference of sorts, provides a unique case study of the reactions of one institution to another.

A CASE STUDY

The production circumstances for *Secrets of a Soul* provide rare insight into Freud's own attitude toward the cinema: a reaction-formation of defense and suspicion. It was not Freud's first encounter. The much-celebrated exchange between Freud and the master of *Fehlleistung* himself, Hollywood producer and self-styled studio mogul, Samuel Goldwyn, provides an earlier indication of Freud's dismissiveness toward any cinematic attempts to appropriate his theories. Goldwyn offered Freud $100,000 to cooperate on a film "depicting scenes from the famous love scenes of history, beginning with Antony and Cleopatra."[4] Freud refused to discuss Goldwyn's offer. According to Hanns Sachs, who reported their exchange in a letter circulated to Freud's official circle, Freud's telegram of refusal created more of a furor in New York than the publication of *The Interpretation of Dreams.*[5]

In contrast to the Goldwyn proposal, the project which became *Secrets of a Soul* involved a more substantial confrontation. The proposition came from Hans Neumann of Ufa—from Berlin, then, not from Hollywood. Whether or not the original impetus for the film stemmed from Ernö Metzner (a point obscured in most accounts),[6] it was Hans Neumann who approached Karl Abraham, the founder of the Berlin Psychoanalytic Society and the recently elected President of the International Association of Psychoanalysis, with a detailed project for a film about psychoanalysis. Ufa, at this point in the mid-twenties, was certainly engaged in the campaign to have the cinema considered as a legitimate art, a product of high culture. (The Ufa division responsible for *Secrets of a Soul* was the Kulturfilm-Abteilung.) Significantly coincident with the legitimation crusade by cinema enthusiasts, psychoanalysts also campaigned for the legitimacy of the "science" of the unconscious. In February 1925, Karl Abraham wrote to Freud that a lecture he would give at the Berlin Society for Gynecology and Obstetrics would be the "first official recognition of psychoanalysis in Germany."[7]

The correspondence of Freud and Karl Abraham between June and December of 1925, details, along with news of Abraham's progressing illness, Freud's vehement distrust of the cinema. The timing here may not quite be coincidental: Abraham took to his bed just after his visit from Hans Neumann, as if the film idea, not the bronchitis he caught on his lecture tour in Holland, were the agent of fatal infection. Abraham died that year on Christmas Day, and the disagreements he had with Freud, particularly about the "film matter" [*Filmsache*], were never resolved. But one thing from the letters seems evident: the structure of the disagreement between Freud and Abraham was not new to them. The "film affair," as Abraham called it, was indeed a repetition of earlier interactions, of previous disputes about discipleship. Whereas Abraham had been the first to label Jung and Rank as "deviants," Freud had to be convinced to distrust them. The "film affair" reversed this structure. Freud was suspicious and Abraham reassuring. The cinema project was, to Freud, an unquestionable betrayal of his theories. A brief précis of their exchange bears this out.

On June 7, 1925, Abraham wrote a long letter to Freud explaining Neumann's proposal. Laced with his own doubts about the project, Abraham's letter defensively anticipates Freud's sense of protective custody.

> I need hardly mention that this kind of thing is not really up my street; nor that this type of project is typical of our times and that it is sure to be carried out, if not with us, then with other people who know nothing about it.[8]

Abraham outlines the offer:

> The difference between this straightforward offer compared with the American Goldwyn is obvious. The plan for the film is as follows: the first part is to serve as an introduction and will give impressive examples illustrating repression, the unconscious, the dream, parapraxis, anxiety, etc. The director of the company who knows some of your papers is, for instance, very enthusiastic about the analogy of the invader used in the lectures to illustrate repression and resistance. The second part will present a life history from the viewpoint of psychoanalysis and will show the treatment and cure of neurotic symptoms.[9]

"The analogy of the invader" was taken from the lectures that Freud gave at Clark University in 1909, lectures that were intended to explain the theory of the unconscious in simple language to an American audience. Freud metaphorized the unconscious as a lecture hall and illustrated repression as the need to kick out an audience member who makes a disturbance. If Neumann was "enthusiastic" about this analogy, it was because it had proved so successful in translating Freud's theories to an easily understood, accessible level. If the Clark lectures helped establish Freud's reputation in America, Neumann must have calculated that the "Worcester-simile," as it came to be known, would work for an equally simple-minded film audience.

In addition to the film, Neumann proposed an accompanying pamphlet, "easily comprehensible and non-scientific," to be sold through the *Internationaler Psychoanalytischer Verlag*. Despite his avowed hesitancies, Abraham seemed somewhat seduced by the idea. He includes his own plans for the film.

> My idea is not to describe psychoanalysis systematically but to give examples from everyday life and to develop the theory around them. . . . Our influence should extend into every detail in order to avoid anything that might discredit us in any way.[10]

Freud's reply was swift and uncompromising. On June 9th, he wrote back quite directly: "I do not feel happy about your magnificent project." The following succinct statement of hesitation illustrates Freud's attitude toward the cinema:

> *My chief objection is still that I do not believe that satisfactory plastic representation of our abstractions is at all possible. . . .* The small example that you mentioned, the representation of repression by means of my Worcester simile, would make an absurd rather than an instructive impact.[11]

> (emphasis mine)

Freud frequently sought topological metaphors to describe and make more tangible the otherwise abstract concept of the unconscious, but he never appealed to the cinema as an apt analog.

Freud's "A Note Upon the 'Mystic Writing Pad'" (written in the fall of 1924, published in the *Internationale Zeitschrift für Psychoanalyse* in 1925) is curiously coincident with these debates about a film project.[12] In this short piece, Freud chooses the model of the "Mystic-Writing-Pad" (*der Wunderblock*), a recently marketed writing contraption with a thin layer of celluloid over a waxed surface, as a "concrete representation" of the perceptual apparatus of the mind. He dismisses auxiliary apparatuses intended to substitute for "the improvement or intensification of our sensory functions . . . spectacles, photographic cameras, ear trumpets."[13] Devices used to aid memory, a category which could include the cinema, are, Freud claims, similarly imperfect, "since our mental apparatus accomplishes precisely what they cannot: it has an unlimited receptive capacity for new perceptions and nevertheless lays down as permanent—even though not unalterable—memory traces of them."[14] While Freud's prompt response to Abraham illustrates his vehement distrust of the cinema to represent his abstractions, "A Note Upon the 'Mystic Writing Pad'" seems to demonstrate that he was still thrashing about for suitable concrete illustrations.

As the correspondence between Freud and Abraham continued, the positions solidified. Abraham supplied progress reports in July. By then it was clear that Sachs, the Berlin-based, Vienna-born analyst, was as involved as Abraham.

> Sachs and I believe that we have every guarantee that the matter will be carried out with genuine seriousness. In particular, we think we have succeeded in principle in presenting even the most abstract concepts. Each of us had an idea concerning these and they complemented each other in the most fortunate way.[15]

And in August:

> The work on the film is progressing well. Sachs is devoting himself to it and is proving very competent, and I am also trying to do my share.[16]

The last letters between Freud and Abraham, in October and November, address their differences directly:

You know, dear Professor, that I am unwilling to enter once again into a discussion of the film affair [*Filmangelegenheit*]. But because of your reproach of harshness (in your circular letter), I find myself once more in the same position as on several previous occasions. . . . I advanced an opinion which is basically yours as well but which you did not admit to consciousness.[17]

Freud, although he does not agree that he is in unconscious concordance with Abraham, is conciliatory in what was his last letter to Abraham.

It does not make a deep impression on me that I cannot convert myself to your point of view in the film affair [*Filmsache*]. There are a good many things that I see differently and judge differently. . . . With that let us close the argument about something that you yourself describe as a trifle.[18]

If the differences between Abraham and Freud were not enough of a disturbance to Sachs and Abraham as co-scenarists, Sachs also was distraught by an article by R. J. Storfer, the director of the *Verlag*, which had criticized the film project. Sachs had discovered that Storfer and Siegfried Bernfeld, another Viennese analyst, had also written a film script that they were trying to interest other film companies in. Storfer and Bernfeld discussed their project with Abraham who informed them that his contract with Ufa stipulated that no other "official" *Verlag*-supported film could be made within a period of three years.[19]

The opening titles of **Secrets of a Soul** credit the manuscript as a collaboration between two film-world talents, Hans Neumann and Colin Ross, with technical advice from two psychoanalysts, Dr. Karl Abraham and Dr. Hanns Sachs. Sachs wrote the monograph to accompany the film. The thirty-one-page pamphlet describes the case study in the film and provides an introduction to many of the psychoanalytic concepts it attempts to illustrate. The pamphlet has separate sections to explain: I. *Fehlhandlungen* ("slips" or parapraxes); II. *Die Neurose*—in this case, a phobia and a compulsion (*Zwangsimpuls*); and III. *Die Traumdeutung*—the theoretical background to dream interpretation. In his closing commentary, Sachs acknowledges Freud's objections and admits:

No single film can explain the entire scope of psychoanalysis, nor can a single case be used to illustrate all clinical manifestations. A great deal was discarded from the presentation when it was too difficult or too scientific for the general public, or unsuitable for film portrayal.[20]

Nicht Freudlos: A Film with Freud

Secrets of a Soul was not the first film to deal with serious psychological problems nor the first to attempt cinematic representation of dreams or mental phenomena, but it *was* the first film that directly tried to represent *psychoanalytic* descriptions of the etiology of a phobia and the method of psychoanalysis as treatment.

In the early fall of 1925, Hans Neumann asked G. W. Pabst to direct the project on psychoanalysis.[21] Pabst had just completed **The Joyless Street—Die freudlose Gasse**—to mixed critical acclaim. He was now being asked to direct, indirectly, a film "mit Freud."

Aside from this rather obvious intertextual pun on Pabst's own filmography,[22] **Secrets of a Soul** also had a number of unintentional but nevertheless significant linguistic twists in casting. Werner Krauss, who had played the Döppelganger in *The Cabinet of Dr. Caligari* (*Das Cabinet des Dr. Caligari,* 1920)—madman in the inner story, benevolent doctor in the framing story—was now cast as the neurotic analysand.[23] Krauss's career trajectory, initially at least, took him from Caligari to Freud.[24] The doctor-to-patient transference in Krauss's filmography seems further ironized by the choice of actor who was to play the analyst[25] in the film: an actor from the Moscow Art Theatre, Pavel Pavlov.[26] Pabst's assistant director, Mark Sorkin, took classes from Sachs on psychoanalysis so that he could tutor Pavlov.[27] That same year, in the Soviet Union, Vsevold Pudovkin was at work on a film that also attempted a straightforward cinematic appropriation of psychological theories. Yet Pudovkin's film, *Mechanics of the Brain,* was about the work of Freud's mightiest theoretical opponent, the physiologist Ivan Pavlov.

Abraham and Sachs's script had to contend with the essential problem of translating a "talking cure" into a silent series of images. *Secrets* presents a case study—the origins of a knife phobia and its treatment through analysis. Pabst's own relation to knives also seems to demand some analysis. Instead of a phobia of knives, Pabst seems to have had an obsessive fixation on them, a genuine *Messerzwang*. Knives play significant roles not only in **Secrets,** but in a number of Pabst films, including **Pandora's Box, The Threepenny Opera,** and **Paracelsus.**

Secrets of a Soul is a film narrative with the structure of a detective film, the psychoanalyst as a sort-of Sherlock Jr. who witnesses each image as the analysand retells the events leading up to his nightmare and his resulting phobia. The analyst must then deduce and decode the origins of the client's phobia. *Geheimnisse* uses dream analysis as the central hermeneutical tool of its narrative; the dream is a cinematic attempt at direct pictorial transcription of psychic mechanisms, a key to the locked room of the unconscious.

A quick comparison with Buster Keaton's 1924 film, *Sherlock Junior,* illustrates how such analytic narratives entail the skills of film analysis. In the diegetic world of *Sherlock Junior,* Sherlock is an actual film spectator, a movie projectionist who studies to become a detective. He falls asleep and "dreams" the solution to his case. Keaton, more directly, dreams a film in which he *projects* himself as the heroic protagonist. The film he views is a wish-fulfillment, from which he could conduct his own deductions about behavior. The dream in *Sherlock Junior* is structured like a film, the spatial discontinuities of each abrupt shot change become the source of comedy. Each cut displaces the hero from one setting to another. He sits on a park bench, the shot changes, Keaton is suddenly in a landscape without a bench and falls to the ground. *Secrets of a Soul,* unlike the Keaton film, makes no direct reference to the apparatical construction of the cinema. But both films use the dream as a key to unlock the narrative mysteries. Just as Keaton doubles for the film spectator who deduces a conclusion from a series of images, the psychoanalyst in *Secrets* doubles for the role of a film analyst who rereads and hence interprets the film-dream image.

A brief description of the film's narrative and its construction demonstrates that it addresses its spectator in a quite sophisticated fashion.[28] *Secrets* can be separated into the following sections: Pre-dream—coincident events that lead up to the nightmare; The Dream; Post-dream—the series of parapraxes which demonstrate the phobia and compulsion; The Analysis; and The Epilogue/Cure.

I. Pre-Dream

The opening shot (in the German print) is of Werner Krauss's face distorted in a small round shaving mirror. In crosscut fashion, a spatial separation is established between the husband's bedroom, where he shaves by the window, and the wife's bedroom, where she brushes her hair in front of her vanity. After some crosscutting and matched continuity on the door between their rooms, the man exits his room and enters hers. The wife playfully attempts to kiss her husband and is rebuffed by the shaving cream on his face. She shows him a straggly tuft of hair on her neck, indicating that she needs it to be trimmed. As he applies shaving cream and begins to shave his wife's neck, they are interrupted. The interruption occurs literally as this chain of images is abruptly intercut with an image from a third space of the neighbor opening her shutters and screaming. This is followed by the first intertitle: "Help!!!"[29] Although the film is silent, the scream for help is vividly demonstrated. As the man begins to reapply the razor, he notices that he has cut his wife's neck.

Circumstances continue to conspire toward the husband's disturbance: on his way to work, he sees a crowd has gathered across the street, ambulances and police. His neighbors are talking, a title indicates: "Last night, with the razorblade he————."[30] The husband goes to his workplace, a chemical laboratory, and registers some distress in reaction to a point-of-view shot of his letter opener, the blade of which he avoids using. A woman and her young daughter visit the laboratory; after he gets up from his desk to give the little girl some candy, the girl's mother and the female lab assistant exchange knowing glances, as if to laugh at him. That evening when he returns home, his wife shows him an article in the newspaper, which we assume has to do with the crime next door. It upsets him and he throws the newspaper into the fire.

A police inspector comes to their house to inquire about the crime. The man answers that he only learned about it

when he heard the "help" cry that morning. After the inspector leaves, the wife shows her husband an exotic gift and a letter sent by her cousin to announce his imminent arrival. The cousin's letter is accompanied by photos and another gift, a saber-like sheathed sword. The photos of the cousin show him standing quite erect wearing a pith helmet of phallic proportions. The husband's attention to the saber is intensified by a point-of-view shot of the sword. He brandishes the sword briefly and then puts it down hastily.

When they retire for bed that evening, the wife seems disappointed when her husband bids her good night at the door to her bedroom and then retires to his room. A series of crosscut shots of the husband-in-his-bed and the wife-in-her-bed are intercut with images of a storm that is brewing outside on their patio. Then a title indicates: "The Dream."[31]

In terms of Freudian dream analysis, all of the narrative events that have happened up until this dream, furnish day-residues which contribute to the logic of the husband's disturbance. Each of these circumstances—the murder, his guilt over cutting his wife's neck, the gossiping neighbors, the two women laughing at him in his workplace, the visit by the police inspector, the imminent arrival of his wife's cousin, and the gifts of the fertility statue and the sword—all become part of the dreamwork.

The images from the dream are intercut with images of the man sleeping fitfully as lightning flashes over his face. There is a linguistic significance to the coincidence of the storm and the cousin's arrival that is apparent only in the German-language print or to those familiar with the sounds of German. Later as the man is describing the dream to the analyst, he says: During the night before the outbreak of my illness, there was a bad storm [*ein schweres Unwetter*].[32] Here, *ein schweres Unwetter* becomes easily conflated with the disturbing arrival of the cousin, *der Vetter.*

II. The Dream

The dream sequence was designed by Ernö Metzner and shows off the cinematography of Guido Seeber. This sequence of seventy-five shots uses many camera-tricks—superimpositions, model-shots, stop-action and reverse-motion—to illustrate the condensations and displacements of the dreamwork.[33] Unlike the previous progression of images, the dream is not constructed with the logic of continuity editing, but follows a purely associative sequence, associations that are not immediately apparent. Lotte Eisner maintains that the dream sequence would not have been possible were it not for the lessons of expressionism: "In this style Pabst discovered a means of giving a luminous and unreal relief to objects or people, of deforming architectural perspective, and of distorting the relative proportion of objects."[34]

While only a shot-by-shot breakdown of the seventy-five shots in the dream would completely describe its structure, it can be reduced to its basic elements: four associative sequences interrupted by shots of the husband sleeping fitfully. In this sequence, all of the images have dark backgrounds. We will see many of these images again later in the film when the dream is retold to the analyst, but they are repeated with a whitened background, the actions made more visible.

The first eighteen shots of the dream establish, through crosscutting, an image of the cousin sitting in a tree wearing his pith helmet. The husband looks up to him from the patio to his house and frantically tries to get back inside the house. The cousin aims an imaginary gun at the husband and, through stop-action dissolve, a real gun appears. The husband then jumps into the black space of the air, and, in point-of-view shots, we see the patio getting smaller as the husband floats upward. The cousin aims and shoots and in point-of-view shots the patio gets larger as the husband falls to the ground. Shot 19 shows the husband in bed fitfully tossing and turning.

The dream resumes (shots 20-43) with a crosscut of three images: a cave-like space filled with a large version of the cousin's fertility statue gift; the husband against a black background as a crossing gate comes down, preventing him from moving forward; and a superimposition of two electric trains, crossing in perpendicular directions, with, in another layer of superimposition, the cousin waving from the window of a moving train. This sequence concludes as the crossing gate goes up and the man walks toward us dressed in a bowler hat with a cane. An expressionistic cardboard town pops up from an empty black space. A tower spirals upward in front of the town. The tower is shaped as a phallus, with its top resembling the cousin's helmet. The husband looks up to the top of the tower where bells are ringing. The ringing bells become superimposed with the heads of the three women—his wife, his lab assistant, and the woman who visited with her child.[35]

This second dream segment is interrupted with shots (44-47) of the husband tossing and turning; the wife asleep and then waking; the husband tossing and turning. The dream resumes with an intercut sequence (shots 48-64) of another complex superimposition (a courtroom-like trial superimposing a shadow of drums, the wife showing the cut-mark on her neck, a group of men) with shots of the husband hanging from the bars of another gate which prevents him from moving forward.

The dream is interrupted again (shots 65-67 show the husband in bed) and then resumes (shots 68-76) with its final segment. The husband, in a laboratory-like room, goes to a high window to look out. In counter-shot, the husband sees a dark pool with lily pads. Then, in reverse angle, we see the husband looking through barred windows. In the counter-shot, a small boat with the wife and the cousin floats into the darkened pool. The wife pulls a baby doll out of the water—a somewhat unnatural movement because it is pulled out of the water in reverse motion. The husband watches this through the barred window. The wife and cousin then embrace and the wife gives the cousin the doll. In the lab the husband runs for a knife, flails about and then begins stabbing at a superimposed image of his wife. He repeats the rutting gestures of this stabbing until she disappears.

III. POST-DREAM

After the dream, the husband begins to exhibit a variety of paraparaxes. The next morning when he begins to shave he "accidentally" drops his razor on the floor and decides instead to go to the barber. Then, while he is at the laboratory demonstrating something with a test tube, the phone rings. His female assistant answers it and when she informs him that his wife wants him to know that her cousin has arrived, he abruptly drops the test tube and it shatters on the floor.

When he returns home that evening, the wife and cousin show him some old photos. In a reaction shot to one of the photographs, of the three of them as children, the husband is visibly troubled. As they dine, he is afraid to touch his knife, asking his wife to carve the roast. Disturbed by the knives, he suddenly excuses himself, leaves the house and goes to his club. After several drinks, he exits without his key. He is observed by the doctor who follows him home, and in front of his gate tells him: "You have a reason for not wishing to enter your house." And as if to explain how he knows this: "It is part of my profession."[36] When the husband returns home, his wife greets him but as he embraces her he stares repeatedly at the knife on the table and at the back of her neck. His hand reaches out for the knife, and only with great effort does he resist the urge to pick it up. Quite distraught, he again leaves the house.

As the evidence of his disturbance accumulates, it has become apparent that, since his dream, the husband has a fear of knives and also a compulsion to kill his wife. For refuge, he goes to his mother's house. His concerned mother asks: "Don't you know anybody who could help you?" As if in response, her question is followed by an image of the smiling doctor with a superimposed key. After locating the doctor through his club, the man goes to the doctor to confess his compulsion to kill his wife. The doctor tells him it is only a symptom of a more complicated malady and that there is a method—*Psychoanalyse*—that can treat this kind of disease.

Before the analysis officially begins, the husband is told he must move out of his house and in with his mother. (As soon as it becomes apparent that the husband has left his wife, the cousin also moves to a hotel.) When the film was first shown at the Berlin Psychoanalytic Society's celebration of Freud's seventieth birthday in May 1926, a member of the Society objected to this part of the film's portrait of psychoanalytic treatment. If every man must leave his wife and live with his mother, as the character in the film is told to do, the analyst worried, no one would consent to psychoanalysis.[37]

IV. The Analysis

The hundred or so shots that compose the scene in the doctor's office, intercutting dream, symbolic representation, early childhood memories, and the retelling of everyday events with the interaction between the analyst and analysand, form a montage strategy quite unlike the "invisible editing" that had been applauded in Pabst's *The Joyless Street.* This alteration between couch-based shots and the pictorial renditions of the husband's dream and memories, creates for the viewer an entry into complex character subjectivity.

A brief analysis of the shot sequence of the retold dream illustrates that Pabst was employing one of his most complicated uses of montage, a strategy that would have been applauded by Eisenstein, if not in ideological terms, at least in formal ones. Yet many of the images from the dream and retold narrative are left unanalyzed, and this excess of meaning forms, almost, an intellectual overtone.

An enumeration of the variety of shot types will help clarify the montage alternation between: 1) Symbolic representations, fantasies, or perhaps figures of speech: for example, as if to symbolize their marriage and desire for children, we see the husband and wife against a white background, planting a small tree. A dark and empty room becomes, through stop-action dissolve, filled with nursery furniture. The husband also tells of imagining his wife in compromising positions and we see shots of her in a harem-like place, reclining with the helmeted cousin, smoking on a long pipe. 2) Childhood memories: the photograph that upset the husband triggers his memory of a childhood Christmas with an electric train, the occasion when his wife, as a young girl, gave her baby doll to the cousin. 3) Retold dream images: repetitions of the dream, but altered slightly in sequence. 4) Retold narrative events: some of the earlier events or interactions repeated—the cry for help, the neighbors talking, the woman laughing in the lab—are shown now isolated against a white background.

In the sequencing of these images, the analyst is being "told" what we as spectators "see." The analyst is positioned as a fictional surrogate for the film spectator who performs an interpretation of the logic of each image and its sequence. But it is not apparent until the psychoanalytic sessions begin that there is an implicit equation between dream analysis and film analysis in this repetition of images from the dream and from otherwise quotidian events. As film spectators, we have just seen these images. This analytic repetition, rereading, is not unlike the critical-theoretical activity of film analysis, in which one interprets images and the associative logic of their sequence. Yet the equation remains implicit. *Secrets of a Soul* does not make the activity of film analysis at all explicit to the viewer who reviews the dream and narrative images and must recontextualize and reanalyze their significance.

What seems most striking about this implicit equation is how many of the images remain unanalyzed and uninterpreted. This overload of signification creates a curious excess in the film, perhaps more like a semiotic undertow than an intellectual overtone. While it suggests that the viewer must resee what has been seen before, the absence of analysis of some of the images also becomes a striking repression. Many elements that are made quite explicit in the visual language of the film—the phallic nature of the cousin's helmet and the shattered test-tube, the shadow of the cousin's phallic helmet on the wife's womb—are not analyzed in the verbal exchange between the analyst and analysand. But these elements are apparent to the film spectator who is also deducing the logic behind the man's phobia. The spectator of *Secrets of a Soul* is positioned as a more astute psychoanalyst than the fictional surrogate. The narrative pleasure offered by the film is in the act of hermeneutical detection, the act of psychoanalysis. In short, it is a film which equates the boons of psychoanalytic treatment and cure with the skills of film analysis.

Certainly, *Secrets* did not attempt to contend with some of the more controversial foundations of Freud's theories of infantile psycho-sexual development, and chose instead to depict the concept of the unconscious and the therapeutic powers of psychoanalysis to treat mild neuroses such as this case of phobia and compulsion. The analysis demonstrated is classically Freudian; the film embodies the structure of dream analysis as Freud intended it to be performed. Yet here the "talking cure" is successfully reduced to silent images. An analysis is conducted, not on the speech of the analysand but on images that Pabst provides. Ironically, the American critic, Harry Alan Potamkin, would write of Pabst's "psychologism" that "his own 'suppressed desire' was more social than Freudian."[38]

V. Epilogue/Cure

The "cure" achieved at the end of the film, is not unlike the cure supplied by other film narrative endings—a final frame in which the family unit, here with the addition of a child, embraces happily. The epilogue is idyllically set in a countryside more reminiscent of a tranquil landscape in German romanticism than the twisted chiaroscuro of expressionism. The ending functions as straightforward wish-fulfillment, not unlike the tacked-on conclusion of F. W. Murnau's *The Last Laugh (Der letzte Mann,* 1924) a compensation for all that has been suffered in the course of the narrative. Here the endangered marriage has been repaired, consummated—and, indeed, blessed with a child. If *Secrets of a Soul* was to be an advertising film for psychoanalysis, this final image of the happy family unit was the product being sold.

Secrets Made Public

For Hanns Sachs and Karl Abraham, the ambition behind *Secrets of a Soul* was to make public the secrets of psychoanalysis, to extol its curative virtues. For Hans Neumann and G. W. Pabst, the film provided an occasion to use a psychoanalytic case study as a cinematic narrative, to exploit the hermeneutic similarities between the work of psychoanalysis and the act of cinema spectatorship. While

Freud's reaction to *Secrets of a Soul* remains unknown (it was not recorded by Jones, nor mentioned in any of Freud's own papers), his hostility toward the cinematic appropriation of his theories suggests a vigorous, almost Luddite, resistance to the tools of modernity. Nevertheless, *Secrets of a Soul* remains the first film to use psychoanalysis as a narrative device and it was, if not Freud's first, certainly his last *unheimlich* maneuver with the cinema.

Notes

1. As Bruno Bettelheim points out in "Freud and the Soul" (an essay which first appeared in *The New Yorker,* 1 March 1982, and later became part of *Freud and Man's Soul* [New York: Knopf, 1983]), English translations of Freud excise most of his references to the *soul* (70-78). Both Strachey and Brill translate the German word *Seele* as *psyche* or as "mind," rather than *soul,* eliminating much of its associative meaning. In all Standard Edition translations, for example, *der seelische Apparat,* is translated as *mental* apparatus. If Freud had meant "of the intellect" or "of the mind," Bettelheim asserts, he would have used the word "*geistig*" (72). "Freud never faltered in his conviction that it was important to think in terms of the soul when trying to comprehend his system, because no other concept would make equally clear what he meant; nor can there be any doubt that he meant soul, and not the mind, when he wrote '*seelisch*'" (73). The German word *Seele* carries the spiritual connotations of the word "*soul,*" a word that is generally omitted from more scientific-sounding English translations of Freud.

2. The English-language title of the film retains much of what Bettelheim claims is lost from most translations of Freud. However, the title seems to give little indication of these psychoanalytic references to English-language viewers who are unaware of Freud's emphasis on the "soul." *Geheimnisse* also contains the root word *Heim,* as in *heimlich* (the concealed, the withheld, the PRIVATE), a key word in Freud's lengthy analysis of "*Das Unheimliche.*" This 1919 essay explored the similarities in signification between *heimlich* and *unheimlich,* words that should have opposite contradictory meanings, but instead come to mean the same thing—familiar and yet concealed. Translated as "The Uncanny," the essay becomes another example of the linguistic loss of root words and connotations in translation. There are two previous English-language articles on the film: Bernard Chodorkoff and Seymour Baxter, "*Secrets of a Soul*: An Early Psychoanalytic Film Venture," *American Imago* 31.4 (Winter 1974): 319-334; Nick Browne and Bruce McPherson, "Dream and Photography in a Psychoanalytic Film: *Secrets of a Soul,*" *Dreamworks* 1.1 (Spring 1980): 35-45.

3. Freud had given six of his disciples—Rank, Eitingon, Ferenczi, Jones, Abraham, Sachs—each a ring set with a semiprecious stone. The seven became a cabal-like group of intimates, corresponding regularly with circulating letters. By 1926, Rank and Ferenczi had broken with the circle, Abraham had died, and only Jones, Sachs, Eitingon, and Freud were left. While Sachs describes the protocols of the circle of seven, he makes no mention of the *Geheimnisse* project in his memoir of Freud, *Freud, Master and Friend* (Cambridge: Harvard University Press, 1944).

4. See Ernest Jones, *The Life and Work of Sigmund Freud,* 3 vols. (New York: Basic Books, 1957), 3:114. Jones gets a few of the details wrong in his account. Perhaps as evidence of his faint knowledge of the film world, he refers to Goldwyn as a film director. Jones also writes that the finished film was screened in Berlin in January 1926, but it was not screened until 24 March 1926 at the Gloria-Palast in Berlin.

5. Ibid., 114.

6. Chodorkoff and Baxter claim (319) that Ernö Metzner suggested the idea to Hans Neumann, who intended to direct the film himself. Their source for this information was the unpublished biography by Michael Pabst. They also describe how "documentary department officials" at Ufa felt that Neumann had "insufficient experience" and instead chose Pabst because *The Joyless Street* had impressed them.

7. *A Psychoanalytic Dialogue: The Letters of Sigmund Freud and Karl Abraham 1907-1926,* ed. Hilda C. Abraham and Ernst L. Freud (New York: Basic Books, 1964), 380. The German edition of the correspondence can be found in: *Sigmund Freud, Karl Abraham, Briefe 1907-1926,* ed. Hilda C. Abraham und Ernst L. Freud (Frankfurt am Main: Fischer, 1965), 355-371.

8. *Letters of Freud and Abraham,* 380.

9. Ibid., 382-383.

10. Ibid., 383.

11. Ibid., 384.

12. "A Note Upon the 'Mystic-writing-pad,'" *The Standard Edition of the Complete Psychological Works of Sigmund Freud,* 24 vols., trans. and ed. James Strachey et al. (London: Hogarth, 1953-1973), 19:227-232. ["Notiz über den 'Wunderblock,'" *Gesammelte Werke* (London: Imago, 1940-1952), 14:3-8.]

13. Ibid., 228.

14. Ibid., 228.

15. *Letters of Freud and Abraham,* 389.

16. Ibid., 392.

17. Ibid., 398.

18. Ibid., 399. Freud refers to the matter as the "*Filmsache.*" While Abraham's term in his letter of October 27, 1925, "*die Filmangelegenheit,*" more directly

meant "affair." In the English translation, the translators continue to refer to it as "film affair."

19. See Jones, *Life and Work,* 3:115.

20. Hanns Sachs, *Psychoanalyse. Rätsel des Unbewussten* (Berlin: Lichtbild-Bühne, 1926), 29. Translation by A. F.

21. Lee Atwell's account in *G. W. Pabst* (Boston: Twayne, 1977), 37-42, describes the origin of the project without mentioning the correspondence between Abraham and Freud. Atwell attributes the project's origin to Pabst, who out of his interest in Freud's work, and his acquaintance with a Dr. Nicholas Kaufmann, contacted Neumann and met Sachs and Abraham. Atwell also places Pabst in collaboration with Colin Ross and Neumann, as if Pabst had been involved in the scriptwriting stage of the production. The Chodorkoff and Baxter account (in *American Imago*), places Pabst's entrance to the project much later, in the fall of 1925, after, as the summer of correspondence between Freud and Abraham indicates, the script had been written.

22. The American critic and correspondent for *Close Up,* Harry Alan Potamkin, made this pun in his 1933 article, "Pabst and the Social Film," published in the literary journal *Hound and Horn.* Of Pabst he wrote: "He was as yet the humanitarian, and not the 'psychologist,' in the '*freudlose Gasse*' (the street without Freud.)" This essay is reprinted in *The Compound Cinema,* ed. Lewis Jacobs (New York and London: Teachers College, 1977), 410-421.

23. In the German-language version, the man is not given a name. In the English-language version, his name is Martin Fellman.

24. Kracauer's well-known account of German cinema in the Weimar years is titled *From Caligari to Hitler.* In this case, Werner Krauss went from playing the duplicitous Doctor Caligari, both benevolent and mad, to playing, in *Secrets,* a man maddened and sent to a benevolent doctor. Both films are narratives of cure, with a similar hermeneutic structure, detective work that involves the interpretation of data as symptoms and clues.

25. In the German-language version of the film, the doctor remains unnamed, while in the English-language version, the doctor is named Dr. Orth. Orth in Greek means correction of deformities, as in orthodontia, orthopedics; in short, Dr. Cure.

26. "Pawel Pawlow" in the German print. Atwell (41) maintains that Pabst had been impressed with Pavlov especially in Robert Wiene's *Raskolnikow* (1923).

27. Mark Sorkin was assistant director for numerous Pabst films. Sorkin, who spoke fluent Russian, translated his lessons from Sachs for Pavlov, who spoke only Russian and knew nothing of Freud's work. Pavlov performed so convincingly that, according to

Atwell, a group of American therapists contacted him for a lecture (Atwell, 41-42).

28. A few minor differences in the available English-language and German-language prints also bear some description. In the English version of *Secrets,* the film opens with an image of Freud, as if his silent outward gaze provided indication of his sanction. The second image in the English print is of Dr. Orth, writing case notes at his desk. These shots are not unlike the shots in *Caligari* as Werner Krauss sits at his desk writing case notes. They are designed to place the analyst-character as a fictional surrogate, sponsored by Freud. The German print opens without the direct visual appeal to Freud's authorization. Both prints begin with explanatory titles which mention psychoanalysis and the teachings of "Universität Prof. Dr. Sigmund Freud." The first image in the German print is the razor being sharpened. Although the variance between these two versions is relatively small, the difference between them amounts to whether there is a framing story or not. The English-language opening recalls the framing story of *The Cabinet of Doctor Caligari.* Dr. Orth writes case notes, framing the inner story of a disturbed man and securing the narrative agency of the Doctor as storyteller. If we begin the film without a framing structure, there is no narrating agency. While the German print refers to "Der Mann" and "Die Frau" throughout, the English-language print assigns names to its characters. Also, instead of using intertitles, the English-language print superimposes its titles as subtitles over the image. An analysis of the film must take into account the variance in these prints because narrative information is presented in a more redundant manner in the English-language print. For example, while the German print begins directly with the bedroom shaving scene, the English-language print not only establishes the framing "case history," but follows with explicit subtitles over the shots of Werner Krauss shaving his wife's neck: "Facts of the case: Martin Fellman, a chemist, one morning while trimming the hair on the back of his wife's neck . . ."

29. In the English-language print, there is no separate intertitle to interrupt the images. Instead, the subtitle, "Help! Murder! Help!" appears over the image of the woman screaming.

30. Again, the narrative information in the English print is not supplied by a separate intertitle, but by a subtitle over the image: "He did it with a razor—."

31. In the English print, the subtitle "Martin dreamed that . . ." appears over a shot of the husband in his bed.

32. This is a translation of the intertitle in the German print. In the English print: "The day before my disorder became apparent, a terrible storm raged."

33. Atwell (42) says the optical effects in the dream sequence took six weeks to produce.

34. Lotte H. Eisner, *The Haunted Screen,* trans. Roger Greaves (Berkeley and Los Angeles: University of California Press, 1969), 31. Eisner seems to attribute these aspects of the dream sequence to Pabst, not to Metzner or Seeber.

35. The superimposition of the three tower bells with the three women's faces suggests a French-English pun on *belle* and *bell,* a visual pun that would later be used by Luis Buñuel in *Tristana* (1970).

36. The English-language print is more explicit about his profession. The subtitle reads: "I am a psychoanalyst; it is part of my work."

37. This account is given in Chodorkoff and Baxter, 321, quoted from the unpublished biography.

38. *The Compound Cinema,* 412.

Michael Geisler (essay date 1990)

SOURCE: Geisler, Michael. "The Battleground of Modernity: *Westfront 1918* (1930)." In *The Films of G. W. Pabst: An Extraterritorial Cinema,* edited by Eric Rentschler, pp. 91-102. New Brunswick: Rutgers University Press, 1990.

[*In the following essay, Geisler examines the ways in which Pabst's film* Westfront 1918 *reflects Germany at the end of the Weimar Republic rather than the events of World War I depicted in the film.*]

A number of major texts in film history have never been accorded their due because more popular contemporary releases have pre-empted the audience's as well as the critics' attention and interest. Pabst was twice unlucky in this respect. *The Joyless Street* (1925) had had to compete with D. W. Griffith's 1924 release, *Isn't Life Wonderful?,* which dealt with inflation-ridden post-World War I Germany. Likewise, when *Westfront 1918* premiered on May 23, 1930 at the Berlin Capitol Theater, it was soon superseded by Lewis Milestone's slicker and technically more sophisticated *All Quiet on the Western Front* (released in Germany in December of 1930). Milestone's film benefited from the spectacular international success of Erich Maria Remarque's novel of 1929,[1] whereas Pabst had adapted a relatively obscure narrative by Ernst Johannsen, *Vier von der Infanterie.*[2]

Although present-day critics tend to see *Westfront* as an achievement of equal value to, or perhaps even surpassing *All Quiet on the Western Front,* the canon will not be corrected quite so easily.[3] In 1961, thirty filmmakers, theorists, critics, and historians were asked the curious question, which films were "most effective" in addressing the problems of war and peace. *All Quiet on the Western Front* showed up on twelve lists, while *Westfront* was named only twice.[4] Given this kind of reception history, my primary goal in this essay is to open up an access route to the film by exploring how it interacts with the immediate socio-historical and cultural environment, the final crisis-ridden years of the Weimar Republic, and not, as one might expect, its narrative referent, the end of World War I.

THE TEXT

Pabst wanted his first "talkie" to reflect the aesthetic potential of sound.[5] Both *All Quiet on the Western Front* and *Westfront 1918* established a basic convention of the war film genre; the relentless assault on the acoustic nerves of the audience through the verisimilitudinous reproduction of artillery noise, machine-gun fire, and the screams of the wounded and dying has become a stock component of (most) combat war films, part of a calculated synthesis intended to shock the viewer into reliving the experience of battle.

The film's opening sequence introduces three of the four central characters in a genre picture, or, as Aubry and Pétat call it, an "image d'Epinal."[6] Behind the German front lines, a group of soldiers, billeted in a French house, are shown flirting with a young French woman, Yvette, who lives in the house with her grandfather. We are introduced to the scene through the subjective perspective of "the student." The jovial "Bavarian" is playing cards with Karl, the only one of the foursome introduced by name and in some ways the film's protagonist. A friendly, but serious and reserved character, Karl is apparently a white-collar worker (in the book he is an engineer). The idyllic scene is suddenly disrupted by a short burst of artillery shelling, during which the student and Yvette discover their mutual attraction.

A brief transition introduces the lieutenant and takes us to the front lines. Shelled by their own artillery, Karl and the Bavarian are buried alive beneath the rubble, but saved by fellow soldiers in a dramatic rescue operation. Since the telephone lines are down, the lieutenant sends the student, as a volunteer, to relay the message that the German trenches are being shelled by 'friendly fire.' The student uses the opportunity to sneak back to the village for a brief reunion with Yvette. Returning to the front, he runs into Karl, who is on leave visiting his wife for the first time in eighteen months. Resting on the edge of a shell crater, in the middle of a vast, empty, war-torn landscape, the two soldiers have a chat, with the student telling Karl he is in love with Yvette.

A long transitional sequence follows in which we see a chanteuse and two music hall clowns perform for hundreds of soldiers at a front theater. Besides bridging the gap in narrated time created by Karl's journey home, this sequence gives Pabst a chance to show off the production values of the new sound film.[7]

Coming home, Karl first runs into a local businessman who asks why they haven't taken Paris yet. Meanwhile, Karl's mother has been standing in line for hours at the butcher's. A neighbor discovers Karl crossing the line to get to his apartment, but the mother, although desperate to see her son, cannot afford to wait for days or weeks for another chance to get a piece of meat. In the end, the store is sold out just as she reaches the entrance.

Entering his apartment, Karl finds his wife in bed with a lover—the butcher's son, who has bought her affections with food. Dumbfounded, Karl stumbles back to the kitchen, picks up his rifle, and returns to the bedroom, where he forces his wife and the lover to kiss at gunpoint, but then his anger gives way to resignation. Dropping the weapon, he sees a draft notice on the table. "You too?" he asks the lover. The man nods and quietly leaves. Karl's wife blames the hunger at home for her actions, repeating stereotypically, "Ich kann doch nichts dafür" ("It isn't my fault"). Karl does not reproach his wife any further, but refuses to show (or accept) any signs of affection during his entire leave, departing without a gesture of reconciliation.

The scenes at home are contrastively interspersed with sequences at the front where, during a sudden attack by French troops, the student is killed in hand-to-hand combat. Her house destroyed by artillery shelling, Yvette is relocated by the German army. She does not want to leave her village, for fear that the student will never find her; she has not heard of his death yet.

Returning to the front, Karl, in an obviously suicidal gesture, volunteers for a dangerous mission ahead of the German front. Although fully aware of the danger, the Bavarian nevertheless goes with him. The lieutenant has been informed that the French are planning a major attack and that he has to hold the line at all cost. What follows are the film's most spectacular sequences, a crescendo of increasingly heavy shelling and massive infantry combat scenes, culminating in a tank attack. In the course of the onslaught, the Bavarian is killed by a French hand grenade, and Karl fatally wounded. In what is probably the best-known shot of the film, the lieutenant, his mind cracked from the insanity of the slaughter, slowly rises from a heap of dead bodies to offer a final, lunatic salute to his unseen superiors.

The final sequence shows the aftermath of battle. A transition shot takes us, along with the mad lieutenant, into an army hospital filled with the screams and groans of the wounded and dying. Before dying himself, Karl experiences a hallucinatory vision of his wife, accusing him of having left her without a reconciliation. "It isn't my fault," she says. "We are all guilty," Karl responds in a mumble. Without realizing that Karl is already dead, a wounded French soldier lying next to him takes his hand, and, caressing it slowly, assures him, "Moi, camarade . . . pas enemie, pas enemie . . ."

Westfront 1918 was shot during the spring of 1930, after Pabst's return from England, where he had familiarized himself with the new sound technology. Having seen a number of Hollywood sound productions in London, he was very dissatisfied with the way they immobilized camera and crew inside stationary soundproof booths. For

Westfront, he chose instead to opt for the far more mobile "blimps," a soundproof casing which encloses only the body of the camera (with the controls extended through the casing), leaving it free to roam the soundstage. This was all the more important because of the new continuity problems presented by sound. German sound production at the time was still fairly primitive and sound mixing technology was not yet available.

For the combat sequences, Pabst and his editors Hans (later Jean) Oser and Paul Falkenberg inserted pieces of sound track containing the explosions by hand between lines of dialogue, sometimes between words, to match the visuals. The resulting synchronization problems were enormous, since the slightest mistake would make the explosions obscure the dialogue.[8] Pabst realized that he could not employ the "invisible cutting" which had become his directorial trademark since *The Joyless Street.* Relying on the mobility of the blimp camera to the fullest, Pabst used a visual technique he had tried successfully in *The Love of Jeanne Ney,* a mode of internal montage sometimes referred to as editing-within-the-shot. A pan or travelling shot of very long duration is subdivided by the arrangement and composition of movement within the frame. The careful coordination of camera movement and blocking conveys the impression of a series of different shots organized around a natural dramatic progression.

The first shot of the initial trench sequence demonstrates this technique. Lasting a total of sixty-five seconds, it opens with a "marker": a not very high-angle view of barbed wire covering the trenches. From the lower border of the frame emerges a group of soldiers led by the lieutenant; tracking with the group, the camera travels to the right along the line of the trench. Hesitating briefly when the lieutenant stops to receive the report, it then leaves him to pick up a group of soldiers entering the frame from behind the officer and follows them to their stations along the battle line. Another halt is motivated by two groups of soldiers who have been waiting in a connecting trench. Again emerging from the lower border of the frame, one troop moves to the left, one to the right; the camera, as if uncertain where to go, first follows the troop moving to the left, but then, reconsidering, resumes its previous track to the right, finally stopping and tilting up to open the view to the area in front of the German lines. In doing so, it defines the stage for the first major explosions which cloud up the image, providing a logical point for a cut.[9]

Along with the creative use of the long take and the traveling shot, Pabst also exploited the creative tension between sound and image. Characteristically, he used sound as a bridge between sequences. The idyllic scene in Yvette's house ends with an older soldier playfully spanking a younger comrade; at that precise moment, a grenade explodes, thrusting the house into darkness and setting the stage for the war sequences to follow. Similarly, at the end of the front theater sequence, the band plays a marching song which dissolves into another march (Ludwig Uhland's "Ich hatt' einen Kameraden") played by the band of a troop of young recruits who are leaving Karl's home town for the front. The audio overlap links the two heterogeneous sequences, bridging the time/space ellipsis. Audiovisual counterpoint creates ironic tension and provides a sense of foreboding. As Karl ascends the stairs to his apartment (where he will find his wife in the embrace of another man), the soldiers in the streets sing, "In der Heimat . . . da gibt's ein Wiedersehen" ("Someday, coming home, we will meet again").

According to his collaborators, Pabst actively solicited advice from his production team. One of the more impressive shots of the final sequence is said to have been suggested by the cinematographer Fritz Arno Wagner. To cover up Gustav Diessl's consummate overacting in his death scene, Pabst told him to simply lie perfectly still, with his eyes open, while Wagner slowly turned a light away from his face. The result is an eerily underplayed, highly suggestive impression of death.

Pabst's editor on **Westfront,** Hans Oser, claims that Pabst, under pressure from the producers, excised an important scene:

> During the last days of World War I it was pretty quiet: the French were living in their trenches, and the Germans in theirs, and really they didn't have a war going between them anymore. And somehow they even had fun with each other; they yelled at each other and all. And there is one sequence then where the French are on their parapets—they are lying in the sun; and the Germans on theirs. And suddenly a German general comes to visit the Front. He comes in, looks through his binoculars, and says: "Are you crazy? Look at them all exposed! Come on! Load! Shoot!" So the Germans start shooting. Naturally, the French immediately make an attack which leads to the end of the movie and the entire slaughter scene.[10]

If Oser's account is correct, this would be a significant omission. The scene would have been one of the very few moments where Pabst (and scenarists Ladislaus Vajda and Peter Martin Lampel) would have broken through the restrictive perspective of simply showing the sufferings of the common soldier; it might even have been one of the few points where the film would have hinted at an answer to Karl's final self-accusation. As described by Oser, the omitted sequence suggests an allusion to Germany's attack on neutral Belgium at the beginning of World War I and thus could have been interpreted as an admission of guilt.

CONTEMPORARY RECEPTION

Summarizing contemporary response to **Westfront,** Lee Atwell claims: "Although acknowledging Pabst's artistry, the press found little to praise in a work that so graphically showed German military defeat, especially at a time when the country was already primed for another war for the Fatherland."[11] Apart from the historical inaccuracy—in 1930 few Germans were interested in fighting another war—a survey of leading film critics contradicts Atwell's account. With the obvious exception of the Hugenberg

press and the fascist papers, most contemporary critics liked the film. Writing in the *Berliner Tageblatt,* Eugen Szatmari extolled the film's realistic portrayal of the horrors of war, while at the same time pointing to Pabst's refusal of Hollywood-style "realism," which permits special effects to dominate the narrative. He saw the significance of the principal characters in their function as types, representatives for the millions of soldiers who died in the front lines. Although he criticized Pabst for his inadequate portrayal of the misery and hunger at home, Szatmari concluded: "In the fight against war, this film is . . . worth more than thousands of books, pamphlets, and articles."[12] In the journal *Die literarische Welt,* Ernst Blass compared the film to the greatest achievements of the Russian filmmakers, calling it "the first sound film that justifies this invention" and "the most important German film in years."[13] According to Herbert Ihering, the influential critic of the *Berliner Börsen-Courier,* the film's very strength—the realistic representation of the chaos of war—also provides its central weakness. The chaos is simply duplicated, instead of becoming an integral part of an organized, unified idea. The film "lacks a consistent effect, because it is not based on a specific point of view, because it lacks a guiding idea." Yet Ihering also praises Pabst for his use of sound, adding that "one can only criticize any aspect of this film after having emphasized that it towers high above the average German production."[14]

In his *Frankfurter Zeitung* review, Siegfried Kracauer, like Szatmari, faulted the film's portrayal of the conditions at home, but he praised Pabst's creativity in handling sound and the film's authentic presentation of the war experience. He strongly recommended **Westfront** as a historical document: "Already a generation has reached the age of maturity which does not know those years from personal experience. They have to see, and see time and again, what they have not seen for themselves. It is unlikely that the things they see will work as a deterrent, but they must at least know about them."[15] At the time, Kracauer still seems to have believed that works of art might serve as instruments of *raisonnement,* if not as agents of political change—enough so, at any rate, to recommend the film as a catalyst for the construction of public memory. Sixteen years later, as he settled accounts with Weimar cinema in *From Caligari to Hitler,* he would reverse his 1930 evaluation. Kracauer now charged **Westfront** with the same shortcomings traditionally held against texts of the *Neue Sachlichkeit* (New Objectivity), a weakness consisting in

> not transgressing the limits of pacifism itself. This indictment of war is not supported by the slightest hint of its causes, let alone by insight into them. . . . **Westfront 1918** amounts to a noncommittal survey of war horrors. Their exhibition is a favorite weapon of the many pacifists who indulge in the belief that the mere sight of such horrors suffices to deter people from war.[16]

Not unpredictably, *Die Rote Fahne,* the Communist Party newspaper, attacked the film's "pacifist obfuscation" which avoided any true criticism of the imperialist war. As Michael Gollbach has pointed out in his analysis of anti-war novels of the Weimar Republic, this was standard procedure: the Communists attacked pacifism even more vehemently than they attacked the militarists on the Right. They considered pacifism a dangerous delusion, since it kept people from thinking about the real causes of war.[17] Against this backdrop it is all the more remarkable that *Die Rote Fahne*'s anonymous reviewer, having made his anti-pacifist point, proceeded to commend the film for its "courageous realism" and its lack of sentimentality.[18]

General audience response seems to have been mixed: several critics report that moviegoers were shocked by the realistic depiction of the slaughter,[19] and the Nazis apparently tried to disrupt the premiere, but were shouted down by war veterans.[20] Eight months later when *All Quiet on the Western Front* opened in Berlin, the Nazis succeeded, through riots and mass demonstrations, in effecting the banning of Milestone's film until September of 1931, when a heavily censored version was released. Eventually, of course, the Nazis would get their way with *Westfront* as well. On April 27, 1933, after Hitler's ascension to power, the film was banned in Germany.

Westfront was widely distributed in France (in a French version and in the original German), and was highly acclaimed by critics there as well as in England, where it circulated on a smaller scale.[21] In the United States, the film was handicapped by its release after the spectacular success of *All Quiet* and James Whale's screen adaptation of Robert C. Sherriff's *Journey's End,* and by the fact that no English-language version seems to have been available. While the reviewer for *Variety,* reporting from Berlin in May 1930, enthusiastically extolled "this overwhelming picture with its clear and true to life view on the horrors of war," the *New Yorker,* after the American release of early 1931, showed signs of battle fatigue: "It's the horrors of war again, and there are some bits as truly agonizing as anything we have seen of the sort. If you don't know German, however, you are going to be floored by the story."[22] Mordaunt Hall, in the *New York Times,* conceded that "this film is undoubtedly another good argument against war," but went on to complain that it was "not a good entertainment," since "many of the interesting phases of battles are excluded."[23] *Time,* however, hailed the film as "one of the best directed and most gruesome of War pictures," noting especially that Pabst was less of a moralizer than Milestone. And in what has since turned out to be the blueprint for nearly every German production successfully distributed in the United States, the reviewer gave Pabst credit for creating, with small resources, "a picture that in every technical respect except sound can compete with the best Hollywood product."[24]

Although it could never seriously compete with the popularity of *All Quiet, Westfront* managed to establish itself as one of the premier anti-war films and a brilliant example of a director's optimal use of a new cinematic code, even while the technology still lay in its infancy. In 1960, it was included in a series of articles focussing on "Great Films of the Century,"[25] and in 1981, it was one of four

Pabst works to be re-released in Paris.[26] While it is often grouped with *The Threepenny Opera* and *Kameradschaft* as part of Pabst's "Social Trilogy," this classification is somewhat misleading.[27] If there are similar concerns in Pabst's texts of this period, they are to be found in *Westfront* and *Kameradschaft,* and not so much in *The Threepenny Opera.* The two films address a common issue through very different but obviously complementary narratives. *Kameradschaft* picks up exactly where *Westfront* leaves off. The fraternization between the French soldier and the dying Karl ("Moi, camarade . . . pas enemie") anticipates the solidarity of the German workers overcoming the ideology of the "arch enemy" to come to the rescue of their French comrades. The opening sequence of the two boys, one French, one German, fighting over marbles in *Kameradschaft* relegates the atrocities of *Westfront* to the realm of immature behavior. In one often-cited scene of *Kameradschaft,* an old French miner, seeing the German rescuer approaching with his gas mask over his face, experiences a hallucinatory flashback to the war. And the ironic final sequence, cut from some contemporary versions, returns us to the world of *Westfront 1918* with the inscription over the border gate reading "Frontière 1919." *Kameradschaft* thus works as a companion piece to *Westfront,* pointing to the possibility of positive action where the earlier film had been content to show the relatively passive suffering of the soldiers.

In contrast, *The Threepenny Opera* looks more like a throwback to the chiaroscuro, the decor, and the romantic netherworld of the expressionist phase.[28] The painted sets and dreamlike streets of Macheath's Soho have little in common with the documentary realism of the trench scenes in *Westfront* or the shower room sequence in *Kameradschaft.* And the steamy intrigues of Polly, Macheath, and Peachum are more reminiscent of the liaisons dangereuses of *Pandora's Box* than of the cool, detached group portraits of both *Westfront* and *Kameradschaft*—which are, ironically, much less illusionist, since the lack of a central identification figure undermines empathy for the sake of a concentration, however distracted, on the narrative itself. I would therefore, as Aubry and Pétat do,[29] group *Westfront* and *Kameradschaft* together as a diptych which shares with *The Threepenny Opera* little more than the same moment in Pabst's life.[30]

The one feature of *Westfront* that almost all reviewers and critics seem to agree on is the "near-documentary realism" of its portrayal of the war. In fact, the word "documentary" crops up in nearly every article or book written on the film.[31] Applied to the context of 1929, "documentary" does more than describe a particular style. It points to a specific period in German cultural history and the aesthetics associated with it, namely the *Neue Sachlichkeit.*

NEUE SACHLICHKEIT AND THE WAR NOVEL

Westfront 1918 was the first major feature film from Germany to portray life at the front and combat in the trenches, and, apparently, one of the first anti-war features on the international scene.³² Thus, while there were at the time no preestablished patterns of cinematic reception (hence the strong reactions to the vivid battle scenes), the film nevertheless inserted itself into the contemporary discourse of war novels in the late twenties and early thirties. Arnold Zweig's *The Case of Sergeant Grischa* (*Der Streit um den Sergeanten Grischa*, (1927), Ludwig Renn's *War* (*Krieg*, 1928), Remarque's *All Quiet on the Western Front* (*Im Western nichts Neues*, 1929), Theodor Plivier's *The Kaiser's Coolies* (*Des Kaisers Kulis*, (1930), Edlef Köppen's *Higher Command* (*Heeresbericht*, 1930), and Adam Scharrer's *Renegades* (*Vaterlandslose Gesellen*, 1930) are notable examples of a wave of anti-war novels, most of them thinly fictionalized diaries, that swept Germany during the late Weimar years. They stood in contrast to an equally strong reaction from the Right which valorized the war experience, following the early example set by Ernst Jünger's *Storm of Steel* (*In Stahlgewittern*, 1920). While few of these works except for Jünger's diaries have achieved a permanent place in the literary canon, it is important to keep in mind that, at least after 1930, they far outstripped the pacifist literature in terms of quantity (even though none of them attained the popularity of Remarque's book).³³ In the years immediately following the war there was, in fact, a surge of books dealing with World War I in which the militaristic perspective dominated.³⁴ Against these uncritical glorifications of the German military, the few critical books that came out during this period could not prevail, particularly since very few of them had the literary qualities of Egon Erwin Kisch's reportage *Soldier in the Prague Korps* (*Soldat im Prager Korps*, 1922).

For the first ten years of the Weimar Republic, the interpretation of events as provided by the military thus became the official view of the war. This contributed significantly to the eventual acceptance of the "stab-in-the-back" legend, the myth, promoted by the German General Staff, that the army, undefeated on the battlefield, had been cut down from behind by a war-weary home front.³⁵ These were the specific historical developments to which the *neusachlichen* war narratives reacted. Among the many radically different, and sometimes even contradictory currents of the *Neue Sachlichkeit*, the most obviously fallacious, yet most intriguing and influential one, is grounded in the persuasive power of documentary authenticity and factual reportage.³⁶ In an effort to create a critical public sphere through documentary drama and film, through the new techniques of collage and montage, through the newspaper editorial, the muckraking investigation, and the new genre of literary reportage developed by Egon Erwin Kisch and others, critical realists attempted to provide information that would otherwise be restricted to a small circle of industrialists and militarists.

In this light, the pathetic irony of the end of *All Quiet on the Western Front* assumes an added, political dimension: "He fell in October 1918, on a day that was so quiet and still on the whole front that the army report confined itself to the single sentence: All Quiet on the Western Front."³⁷ Hard to translate into English, the original conveys a subtle, yet important variance between the title and the way the line is quoted at the end of the novel: "im Westen *sei* nichts Neues zu melden" (my italics).³⁸ In the indirect speech, the subjunctive form "sei" contains a basic tension, a claim to put the record straight by telling things as they really were, a claim that informs not only Remarque's book, but most of the anti-war novels and diaries of the time. In Edlef Köppen's *Higher Command*, the juxtaposition of the official war reports issued by the Army High Command (long documentary inserts taken from official army news releases), and the actual experiences of the soldiers is not only thematized, it becomes the structural basis for a complex narrative montage.³⁹ The documentary realism of the *Neue Sachlichkeit*, especially in the anti-war novels of 1929-1930, thus seeks to establish a counter-history from below, to undermine the dominant historiography by confronting it with the facts.⁴⁰

In retrospect, the naiveté of this strategy is apparent. It took the operative fiction of the bourgeois public sphere—the free flow of information as a corollary to the free exchange of other commodities—at face value, as if it existed in historical reality. At the time, however, things may have looked different. The Weimar constitution gave Germany, for the first time in history, something akin to freedom of expression. With the advent of the stabilization period, when it appeared that the fragile Republic might be more robust than any of its supporters had dared to hope, the time seemed right to try and set the record straight. Given the tremendous ideological smokescreens thrown up by the militant Right for more than a decade, was it really such a farfetched idea to think that the public, once confronted with the facts, would stop believing fairy tales? Yet this only partially explains the sudden boom in war narratives and the record-breaking sales of Remarque's novel. What had changed in the fabric of German society to bring about this renewed interest in war narratives in 1929-1930?

No doubt the world economic crisis that began with the New York stock market crash on October 25, 1929 is of importance here. While the crisis hit most Western nations hard enough, the German situation was exacerbated by the fact that people had just barely gained confidence in the economic and political stability of the Republic, based on a mere five years of relative calm and prosperity. Most Germans remembered the decade between 1914 and 1923-1924 as a continuity of war, terror in the streets, massive inflation and unemployment, and national humiliation—this in contrast to a Wilhelmine Empire which, along with authoritarian rule, had brought Germans an unprecedented half century of peace and relative prosperity.⁴¹ The crisis reignited the debate about the lost war and its aftermath, for both the Left and the Right, the "root cause" of Weimar's economic and societal woes.⁴² On a psychological level, the return to World War I went beyond the goal of establishing a cause-and-effect relationship between 1918-1919 and 1928-1929. Rather, the renewed debate amounted to a displaced attempt at coming to terms with the problems of 1929-1930. Besides being its possible "root cause," the war also provided a convincing metaphor for widespread economic anxieties, feelings of undeserved victimization, and general fears that the fabric of society was coming apart at the seams.[43]

Many of the literary texts associated with the *Neue Sachlichkeit* share common thematic and political concerns with the war novels—concerns that go beyond similarities in form and style. The randomization of life (and death) in the city, as expressed in such diverse works as Hermann Hesse's *Steppenwolf* (1927), Alfred Döblin's *Berlin Alexanderplatz* (1929), or Erich Kästner's *Fabian* (1931), closely resembles the experience of random injury and death in the trenches as related by the war novels and films, with the big city replacing the war as the impersonal agent of fate. The protagonists of these novels—and here one could add Hans Fallada's *Little Man—What Now?* (*Kleiner Mann—was nun?*, 1932)—are largely passive individuals, clearly not in control of their own lives, exactly the predicament of the nonheroes of the anti-war novels. Helmut Lethen writes of the death of Erich Kästner's civilian hero Fabian that "the demise of the moralist condemns the survival strategies of all the other characters in the novel as immoral" (and hence, by implication, those of Weimar society as a whole).[44] Analogously, the deaths of the four protagonists of *Westfront 1918*, like the death of Remarque's Paul Bäumer, are not merely an indictment of Prussian militarism, but *also* an accusation of contemporary society in the late Weimar Republic.[45]

Against this backdrop, several of the episodes in *Westfront* take on additional significance: the vagaries of the soldiers' lives, the unexpected strokes of luck which have to be enjoyed with a carpe diem mentality before they dissipate into thin air, as well as the completely unpredictable misfortunes, including sudden death, mirror the incidental perspective in the novels of the *Neue Sachlichkeit*. This *neusachliche* mentality is visualized by Pabst in the brief sequence where the student, returning from his short reunion with Yvette, runs into Karl, who is going home on leave. We first see Karl in a long shot as a small figure silhouetted against an expansive wasteland of charcoaled tree trunks, brush wood, and bomb craters. The two then sit down on the edge of a large shell crater, their legs dangling over the side, and share their experiences, chatting happily, quite unperturbed by their incommodious accommodations. Reinforced by the framing (a two shot which excludes the desolate background), this scene recalls Walter Benjamin's classic characterization of the *neusachliche* mentality: "Never have people made themselves more at home in an uncomfortable situation."[46]

The short-lived relationship between the student and Yvette originates during his brief stay at her house. They are separated when the student is called to the front, but he finds his way back, twice risking his life for the chance to spend one night with her. Their eventual separation contains a typically *neusachliche* sense of irony. As Yvette screams from offscreen for fear that the student might not be able to find her again, the audience knows that she

need not bother: he has already been killed. The only difference between their affair and the many nearly identical ones in the 'civilian' novels of *Neue Sachlichkeit* is that here the protagonists' completely randomized existence can "still" be traced back to an identifiable, plausible, if insane, cause: the war. The lieutenant's crazed salute at the end is not merely an accusation of Wilhelmine militarism; it is also an allegorical reflection of the desperate, cynical irony of a middle class and its intelligentsia uprooted not by the war, but by its progressive proletarianization, which became particularly virulent during the world economy crisis.[47] Since one is unable (or unwilling) to comprehend the economic forces underlying this process, one must either capitulate to a totally randomized experience (speaking of *Neue Sachlichkeit*'s cynical resignation) or displace the problem to another plane, where a more transparent cause-effect relationship can be substituted. War, being the classic repository of chance existence, is still one step away from complete randomness.

For the writers and filmmakers of the late Weimar Republic, war became a non-synchronous, but identifiable metaphor to express their experience of lost values and identities, their social, economic, and political anxieties. This rhetoric of war is by no means confined to the war novel proper. The protagonist of Kästner's *Fabian* finds himself in a dream in which he observes scores of people standing on an endless stairwell, each with his or her hand in the pockets of the person on the next higher rung of the ladder, while simultaneously being robbed by the people behind them. Fabian's idealistic friend Labude announces that advent of the age of reason, cheered on by the people, who nevertheless continue to pick each other's pockets. The scene now turns into one of bloody civil war reminiscent of the Spartacus uprising, with figures shooting from windows and roof tops. The people on the stairwell take cover, but continue to steal from each other; they are killed with their hands still in each other's pockets.[48] Kästner's text foregrounds the interrelationship between economic exploitation, the failure of the German Enlightenment, and apocalyptic violence, doubly displaced, however, onto the level of moral exhortation and the realm of dreams. Similarly, Pabst thematizes, in the scenes between Karl, his wife, and her lover, the interdependence of economic reification (she sleeps with the butcher because he provides her with food), political events (the draft notice), and ethical values (Karl is admonished by his mother and his wife not to apply the yardstick of "normal" moral behavior to extreme situations). Karl's subsequent death in battle is the direct result of his inability to adapt to a system of ethics predicated on the commodification of values. The privileged position Pabst grants to the homecoming scene suggests that the discussion of value commodification is the film's hidden center—a reading already established in the preceding scene when the mother must suppress her desire to welcome her returning son in the interest of keeping her place in line at the butcher's.

This interpretation would go beyond a reading of war as a displaced metaphor for the general uncertainty of the times.

It would align **Westfront** with the concerns expressed by Pabst in such apparently different texts as ***The Joyless Street*** and ***Pandora's Box*** by revealing, at the heart of the text, a reflection on the reification of ethics and human relationships, an issue which is one of the central themes of the *Neue Sachlichkeit*. Pabst throws Karl's character into higher relief by giving him a name rather than a simple designation like "The Bavarian," "The Student," "The Lieutenant."[49] This underscores the importance of the character in the narrative's overall configuration. Together, the three types constitute a microcosm of the German class system: the proletarian, the officer, and the academic (who doubles as the youth). Karl's brief encounter with the capitalist adds a crucial social type. Pabst thus gives, on the one hand, a dispassionately "objective" account of the war, taking pains to relate it to all facets of German society, which is offset, on the other hand, by a subjectivized approach showing the dehumanizing effect of the war on the personal sphere. The overall impression is one of pervasive destruction.

CHATTING ON THE EDGE OF A SHELL HOLE

The operative limits of **Westfront** are circumscribed by the limits of liberal opposition to war, a framework in which war is understood and presented as a natural disaster, inexorable, incalculable, inescapable. As Richard Whitehall puts it, Pabst's preoccupations "are not those of a man running counter to popular thought," but instead have to be seen as "the reliable reflection of liberal European thought in general."[50]

However, it is this seismographic consciousness (along with Pabst's undisputed directorial skills) which makes **Westfront** such an extremely intriguing text after all. By keeping viewers at arm's length from most of the character types, Pabst denies them genuine identification, avoiding the empathic short-circuit so characteristic of many war films. This effect is further enhanced by the contradictions in Karl's personality; in collapsing the barriers between public sphere (front) and private domain (home), the film transcends both its own dichotomous vision and the limitations of the war film genre. War is shown as an overwhelmingly destructive social force which cannot be contained either geographically (at the front) or psychologically (by seeking salvation in interpersonal relationships unaffected by the war experience).

The only real escape from war is incidental, ephemeral, and bracketed in time and space (as in the student's brief, risky reunion with his lover). When projected against the portrayal of war as all-encompassing destruction, affecting every aspect of human interaction, the film's vignettes of evanescent happiness, culled from the surrounding chaos, are precise visual analogues to their counterparts in *Steppenwolf* or *Fabian*, with war, in **Westfront,** replacing less clearly defined agents (the Big City, modernism, vague notions of objectification) as the displaced cause for the destruction of values and lives. These surprising analogies between a classic war film and key texts of the *Neue Sa-*

chlichkeit point to underlying affinities extending far beyond the pale of the war novels proper.

However, the dominance of the war metaphor in texts of the *Neue Sachlichkeit,* at least on the left-liberal side of its spectrum, cannot be explained in terms of a particular Weimar predisposition towards militarism. Nor is Peter Sloterdijk's interpretation of Weimar culture's use of "the front" as a metaphor for the Republic's modernist cynicism entirely convincing.[51] I would instead suggest that the pervasive rhetoric of war, even on the Left, points to an awareness among Weimar intellectuals of living in an uncertain peace beneath which the real conflicts behind World War I remained unresolved. In a recent book on the Holocaust, Arno J. Mayer calls the time between 1914 and 1945 "the second Thirty Years War," referring to the continuing tensions and armed conflicts in Central Europe.[52] It is this sensibility, the feeling of existing in a temporal no-man's-land somewhere between undeclared peace and undeclared war, which finds its most characteristic expression in the texts of the *Neue Sachlichkeit*. **Westfront** supplies the key visual image for this sensibility: the meeting between the student and Karl, in the middle of a wasteland, where the two sit on the edge of a crater. The quintessential expression of the *neusachliche* perspective on life—"chatting on the edge of a shell hole"—is the Weimar Republic's equivalent to Paris dancing on a volcano.

Notes

1. In Germany, Remarque's *All Quiet on the Western Front* (*Im Westen nichts Neues*) sold more than one million copies within sixteen months of its first publication by Ullstein Verlag in January of 1929; by the end of 1929, the book had been translated into twelve languages. See Michael Gollbach, *Die Wiederkehr des Weltkrieges in der Literatur* (Kronberg/Taunus: Scriptor, 1978), 42. It is probably to this day the single most popular book ever published by a German author.

2. Translations of *Vier von der Infanterie* (Hamburg: Fackelreiter-Verlag, 1929) supplied some of the various alternative titles of the film in foreign releases: *Four Infantry Men, Comrades of 1918, Shame of A Nation.* In France, the film is generally known as *Quatre de l'infanterie.*

3. "The controversy over the superiority of *All Quiet* or *Westfront* continues today. Both are distinguished movies, but Pabst's film is probably the better." See Jack Spears, "World War I on the Screen," *Films in Review* 17 (May-June/July 1966): 361. Spears argues that Pabst's film has "more sustained realism" and "less sentimentality" than Milestone's. Compare also William Uricchio, "*Westfront 1918,*" in *Magill's Survey of Cinema. Foreign Language Films,* 8 vols., ed. Frank N. Magill (Englewood Cliffs, N. J.: Salem, 1985), 7:3350: "Unlike the more successful *All Quiet on the Western Front, Westfront 1918* avoids sensationalist pathos and emotionalism, providing instead a sober *exposé* of the consequences of war."

4. Robert Hughes, ed., *Film: Book 2. Films of War and Peace* (New York: Grove, 1962), 154-202.

5. See Noël Carroll, "Lang, Pabst, and Sound," *Cinétracts* (Montreal) 2.1 (Fall 1978): 15-23.

6. Yves Aubry and Jacques Pétat, *G. W. Pabst* (Paris: Editions l'Avant-Scène, 1968), 333. This is an apt comparison, as it links the sequence to the rich but largely neglected tradition of popular visual narrative. In the eighteenth and nineteenth centuries, the French city of Epinal was the center of the illustrated print, a medium, which, at that time, played a similar role in the popular imagination as film and television have in this century.

7. Here, as in other parts of the film, Pabst takes great care to expose the viewer to a variety of German dialects. This is a feature the film shares with much of the contemporary war literature, a reminder that, for many of the soldiers, the encounter in the trenches with comrades from all over Germany was also the first physical experience of their country as a united body, the German nation-state being less than fifty years old.

8. Gideon Bachmann, "Interview with Marc Sorkin," in "Six Talks on G. W. Pabst," *Cinemages* (New York) 1.3 (1955): 39.

9. This kind of precision work within the frame was possible because Pabst, according to his assistant director, editor, and long-time collaborator Paul Falkenberg, usually set up, blocked, and shot entire sequences with the final edited product already firmly in mind. See "Six Talks on Pabst," *Cinemages*: 44.

10. Bachmann, "Interview with Jean Oser," in "Six Talks on Pabst," *Cinemages*: 60.

11. Lee Atwell, *G. W. Pabst* (Boston: Twayne, 1977), 80.

12. Eugen Szatmari, "*Westfront 1918,*" *Berliner Tageblatt,* 25 May 1930.

13. Ernst Blass, "Neue Filme," *Die literarische Welt* 6.23 (6 June 1930): 7.

14. Herbert Ihering, "*Westfront* und *Cyankali,*" *Berliner Börsen-Courier,* 24 May 1930. Reprinted in Herbert Ihering, *Von Reinhardt bis Brecht. Vier Jahrzehnte Theater und Film* (Berlin/GDR: Aufbau, 1961), 3:308-309.

15. Siegfried Kracauer, "*Westfront 1918,*" *Frankfurter Zeitung,* 27 May 1930.

16. Siegfried Kracauer, *From Caligari to Hitler: A Psychological History of the German Film* (Princeton: Princeton University Press, 1947), 234-235.

17. Gollbach, *Die Wiederkehr,* 309ff.

18. "*Westfront 1918.* Ein pazifistischer Tonfilm," *Die Rote Fahne,* 27 May 1930.

19. See Kracauer's review and the one in *Die Rote Fahne.* According to some accounts, up to twenty people are supposed to have fainted during the premiere.

20. Richard Whitehall, "*Westfront 1918*—Great Films of the Century No. 5," *Films and Filming,* 6 (September 1960): 34.

21. Whitehall, 34, and Atwell, 80-81.

22. "Mag.," "*Four Infantry Men,*" *Variety,* 18 June 1930, 55; "J. C. M.," "The Current Cinema," *The New Yorker,* 28 February 1931, 59.

23. Mordaunt Hall, "The Screen," *The New York Times,* 20 February 1931, 18.

24. "The New Pictures," *Time,* 2 March 1931, 26.

25. Compare Whitehall.

26. Along with *The Joyless Street, Kameradschaft,* and the French production *Salonique, nid d'espions (Mademoiselle Docteur).* For contemporary reevaluations, see Renaud Bezombes, "Les perdants de l'histoire," *Cinématographe* (Paris) No. 65 (February 1981): 57-59; and Daniel Sauvaget, "Quatre films de G. W. Pabst," *La Revue du Cinéma,* No. 359 (March 1981): 43-48.

27. See Atwell, 75.

28. See Lotte H. Eisner, *The Haunted Screen,* trans. Roger Greaves (Berkeley and Los Angeles: University of California Press, 1969), 317.

29. Aubry and Pétat, 333.

30. If one insists on looking for a trilogy, I would suggest that, had he been given a chance to do it, Pabst's unrealized script, *War is Declared,* sold to Paramount in 1934, might have been a more likely candidate than *The Threepenny Opera.* Peter Lorre was to have played a wireless operator on an ocean liner who, as a hoax, tells the passengers that war has broken out: "The tranquil, friendly atmosphere of the ship becomes divided into combative camps along nationalist lines. When they ultimately learn of the hoax, they are shocked into a realization of their folly and are made to realize their common humanity" (Atwell, 116).

31. Aubry and Pétat speak of "cet aspect documentaire" (333); Falkenberg mentions Pabst's "penchant for the documentary touch" (50); Bezombes singles out "la veine documentaire" (57); and Sauvaget talks of "les charactères réalistes, quasi documentaires" (46).

32. Although not conceived as an anti-war film, King Vidor's *The Big Parade* seems to have been the first American production to be received as one—due mostly to its realistic trench sequences.

33. Gollbach, *Die Wiederkehr,* 276.

34. Hans-Harald Müller, *Der Krieg und die Schriftsteller. Der Kriegsroman der Weimarer Republik* (Stuttgart: Metzler, 1986), 20-35.

35. This was the almost inevitable result of the rigorous censorship exercised by the German Army High

Command throughout the entire war, particularly after the Marne battle. See Kurt Koszyk, *Deutsche Presse 1914-1945* (Berlin: Colloquium, 1972), 21. See also W. Nicolai, *Nachrichtendienst, Presse und Volksstimmung im Weltkrieg* (Berlin: Mittler und Sohn, 1920). Nicolai's report is a revealing, if obviously biased, insider account by the officer in charge of public relations and censorship.

36. For a critique of the *Neue Sachlichkeit* as a coherent movement comparable to, for instance, Expressionism, see Jost Hermand and Frank Trommler, *Die Kultur der Weimarer Republik* (Munich: Nymphenburger Verlagshandlung, 1978), 119.

37. Erich Maria Ramarque, *All Quiet on the Western Front,* trans. A. W. Wheen (New York: Fawcett, 1987), 296.

38. Erich Maria Remarque, *Im Westen nichts Neues* (Berlin: Ullstein, 1976 [orig. 1929]), 204.

39. For an in-depth analysis of *Higher Command,* see Martin Patrick and Anthony Travers, *German Novels on the First World War and Their Ideological Implications, 1918-1933* (Stuttgart: Akademischer Verlag Heinz, 1982), 129ff.

40. I am speaking here of only *one* of a number of rather heterogeneous currents within the *Neue Sachlichkeit.* Edmund Gruber's attempt to synthesize all the various types of war novels under the common label of 'objectivism' is highly problematic, given the political and aesthetic contradictions within the movement. See *"Neue Sachlichkeit* and the World War," *German Life and Letters* 20 (1966-1967): 138-149. See also Müller, 306n.

41. See Walter Laqueur, *Weimar. A Cultural History 1918-1933* (New York: Putnam, 1974), 2-3.

42. Gollbach, 2.

43. The documentary pull of the naturalistic descriptions of combat scenes and the seemingly autobiographical first-person narration has been so strong that Remarque's book, even today, is read in introductory social science courses as reportage on World War I, rather than as a comment on the contemporary Germany of 1929 (at, for example, Boston University). I am indebted to Michael Kaern for this reference.

44. Helmut Lethen, *Neue Sachlichkeit 1924-1932. Studien zur Literatur des "weissen Sozialismus"* (Stuttgart: Metzler, 1970), 143.

45. Compare Remarque, *Im Westen nichts Neues,* 184-185: "What will our fathers do when we will stand up and come forward and demand that they justify their actions? What do they expect us to do when the time comes where there won't be any war? . . . What will happen afterwards? And what is to become of us?" (My translation—M.G.)

46. Walter Benjamin, "Linke Melancholie," *Gesammelte Schriften,* 4 vols., ed. Hella Tiedemann-Bartels (Frankfurt am Main: Suhrkamp, 1972), 3:281.

47. Compare Ernst Bloch's concept of nonsynchronicity, developed against the historical backdrop of the late Weimar Republic, and first outlined in his *Heritage of Our Times.* See the German original, *Erbschaft dieser Zeit* (Zurich: Obrecht und Helbling, 1935).

48. Erich Kästner, *Fabian,* in *Gesammelte Schriften für Erwachsene,* 8 vols. (Munich and Zurich: Droemer Knaur, 1969), 2:124-126.

49. This is a significant departure from Johannsen's story, where only "The Student" is typified. "The Bavarian" has a name, and "The Lieutenant" of the film replaces another (named) character. Although he appears in the book, the Lieutenant plays only a minor role.

50. Whitehall, *"Westfront 1918,"* 34.

51. Peter Sloterdijk, *Kritik der zynischen Vernunft,* 2 vols. (Frankfurt am Main: Suhrkamp, 1983), 2:748-754.

52. Arno J. Mayer, *Why Did the Heavens Not Darken?* (New York: Pantheon, 1989).

Eric Rentschler (essay date 1990)

SOURCE: Rentschler, Eric. "The Problematic Pabst: An *Auteur* Directed by History." In *The Films of G. W. Pabst: An Extraterritorial Cinema,* edited by Eric Rentschler, pp. 1-23. New Brunswick: Rutgers University Press, 1990.

[*In the following essay, Rentschler discusses Pabst as a "problematic" figure in cinema.*]

"None of us who knew Pabst well felt that we ever knew him at all. He was all things to all men, and nothing consistently. He would argue any side of the question with apparent complete conviction and sincerity, but to see this happen over and over was to suspect that he had no convictions at all. He worked like a scientist, presenting stimuli to his actors and watching their reactions with a cold-blooded detachment. He never made any comment, never explained himself. I always felt he lived his life completely alone."

—Louise Brooks, in conversation with Richard Griffith[1]

"Whereas the greatest artists carry their times, Pabst, as a passive contemporary, is carried by the times. He follows. Expressionism, naturalism, sexualism, Freudianism, internationalism, anti-Nazism, exoticism, Nazism, de-Nazification, mysticism, agnosticism; all of the phases experienced by his nation and his class appear again during his artistic career. This is not to say that he was a man without faith. On the contrary. But he received his faith and strength from the current trends, being too susceptible and too irresolute to find them in himself."

—Barthélemy Amengual[2]

"Whether dealing with 'content' or 'form,' Pabst operated as a *metteur en scène*. He lacked a bold conception of film language, and was never the radical agitator some mistook him for."

—Edgardo Cozarinsky[3]

An Extraterritorial Life, an Extraterritorial Career

G. W. Pabst is film history's ultimate nowhere man. An ambiguous figure, he remains a director whose biography and oeuvre do not readily lend themselves to fixed paradigms or comfortable generalizations. To speak of him as "problematic" seems warranted, given the word's multiple connotations: unresolved, hard to place, somewhat suspicious. Critics describing Pabst and his films invariably resort to formulations involving vacillation, oscillation, and uncertainty,[4] to evaluations marked by frustration, disappointment, and anger.[5] At one time an artist with a solid position in the canon of international cinema, he has been increasingly displaced, reduced to a tragic case, an instance of an individual compromised by his own lack of substance and subjectivity.[6] Karsten Witte, echoing a phrase used by Harry Alan Potamkin to describe *The Threepenny Opera,* locates the "extraterritorial" as the privileged site in Pabst's *Shanghai Drama,* a space that in fact governs his work over many epochs in quite different settings.[7] The term is an apposite one, I think, in the way it characterizes not only Pabst's films, but indeed his life, not only the content of his texts, but their formal shape as well, not only his curious relation to contemporaries, but also his disenfranchisement by film historians.[8]

The extraterritorial citizen is both a representative and an outsider, someone whose real place is elsewhere, a person who lives in one country while subject to the laws of another. Pabst, without a doubt, embodies this dialectical condition, a suspended state in both time and space. He never seemed to be identical with where he was: during the Weimar Republic, Pabst gained the reputation of a "red" and an internationalist, someone given to the seductions of foreign models, be they Soviet or American.[9] When he went into exile, he was not able to adapt to foreign situations, to escape the suspicion that, deep down, he was a German after all.[10] (He was, of course, Austrian by birth.) It is difficult to speak of Pabst as a German director with the same conviction used to discuss valorized figures in that national film history. Indeed, other famous emigrants like F. W. Murnau and Fritz Lang, despite similar changes of locale, remained true to themselves in the face of challenges to their integrity and vision.[11] Flexibility and lack of fixity, both in his life and in his work, become recurring themes in approaches to Pabst. It stands to reason that his favorite actor, Werner Krauss, and his most striking female persona, Louise Brooks, have so often been eulogized as chameleon-like spirits and ambiguous entities, in keeping with a director who himself was a creature of many masks and, so his critics would have us believe, a man without qualities.[12]

Perhaps, though, there is a more profound logic to this seeming indeterminateness, to this constant state of personal and textual instability, of not being quite at one with one's place, in one's life, in one's fictions. To be sure, Pabst's narratives feature a continuing cast of nomads, exiles, transients: the wayfaring apprentice Arno (*The Treasure*), a man not at home in his own household, whose greatest fear is his own dreams (*Secrets of a Soul*), treacherous and slippery Khalibiev (*The Love of Jeanne Ney*), fugitives from the Law like Lulu (*Pandora's Box*), inner emigrants (*Don Quixote*), a social climber never happy with his station, never secure in his place (*A Modern Hero*), individuals on the run from contemporaries, misunderstood by their times (*Komödianten* and *Paracelsus*), Carl Maria von Weber on the way to Prague (*Through the Forests, through the Fields*). These films, for all of Pabst's ostensible "realism" and social authenticity, seem more convincing in dissolving spaces, collapsing borders, leading the viewer inevitably and inexorably into singular, frenzied, indeed extraterrestrial milieux: the exotic climes of a dreamer, the brothel as an Arcadian site, the subterranean realm of desire in Atlantis, the eerie laboratory of Paracelsus where one searches for an elixir of life, the expansive bowels of the earth in *Kameradschaft* and *Mysterious Depths,* networks of trenches and corridors (*Westfront, The Last Ten Days*), an imaginary city inhabited by spies, collaborators, foreign interests (*Shanghai Drama*), make-believe London on whose streets walk Jack the Ripper and Mack the Knife.

The logic of extraterritoriality inheres in the formal shape of Pabst's films as well. He would enter film history as the master of fluid editing, whose continuity cutting would break down class borders and transcend spatial demarcations, unsettling, confusing, and recasting, a textual strategy that makes transitions unnoticeable and at the same time renders conventional distinctions inoperative.[13] The knife serves as the dismemberer's privileged instrument; the tool figures as a conspicuous and continuing preoccupation throughout Pabst's work, as a motif, an obsession, an objective correlative to a mind interested in segmenting and reassembling, dissecting and undoing. Social observer, scientist, and sadist, the director captures his audience in a calculated play of distance and suspense, dispassion and identification, a game commingling displeasure and fascination. Blades sever links and create new boundaries. Mirrors, likewise, fix identities and confound the self. It is fitting that Pabst's early study of male anxiety, *Secrets of a Soul,* introduces both props into the opening sequence as pliers of uncertainty. Mirrors shatter with regularity in Pabst's cinema (as in *The Love of Jeanne Ney* or *The Trial*); they reveal images of our worst presentiments (the husband's self-denigrating travesty in *Komödianten*); they show us an askew world for what it is (the tilted frame we see in reflection in *Shanghai Drama*). These reflections, like Pabst's continuities, are spurious ones, in keeping with a cinema of false identities and unfixed borders, a place where spectators never really feel at home.

Pabst, too, is a homeless person, consigned by most film historians to the lesser lodgings of those who have lost their once considerable fortune. In the early thirties, Paul

Rotha spoke of Pabst as "perhaps the one great genius of the film outside Soviet Russia, approached, though in an entirely different manner, by Carl Dreyer, Chaplin, and René Clair."[14] His career interrupted and sidetracked by exile, ultimately betrayed by re-emigration, Pabst would never find firm footing or regain his directorial hand after first leaving Germany.[15] He is considered a seminal figure in Weimar cinema who, unfortunately, continued making films after 1931. The major studies of the director concentrate on the pre-1932 work as the only examples worthy of sustained discussion, as if the subjectivity (never a stable one at that) we associate with the signifier "Pabst" broke down, becoming an increasingly moot and, in the end, all but indistinct entity. The later films destroyed Pabst's reputation, causing us to relativize the importance of even his most revered efforts: Pabst appears now to have never been all there—a director without conviction, someone bound by circumstance and context. Had he died after completing *Kameradschaft,* he would, no doubt, figure much more centrally in our notions of international film history.[16]

THE UNCERTAINTY PRINCIPLE

At one time an ambassador for film art held in high international esteem, Pabst, was subsequently perceived as a betrayer of realism, an apostate and accommodator.[17] Declared persona non grata, he was expelled from the Pantheon of cinema. His work flopped in France, failed miserably in America, hit moral rock bottom in Nazi Germany, and never recovered in a host of postwar sites. The espouser of a social film, the unrelenting observer, the progressive activist dissolved and disappeared, causing much concern, bewilderment, and irritation among his former defenders; Pabst, the "failed realist" remained the governing paradigm in film historiography into the fifties.[18] With the rise of auteurism and a different inflection in standards of critical measure, Pabst now came under attack for his lack of a persistent vision, for his thematic meandering and his overall *uncertainty.* Present-day notions still feed on this image of the *auteur manqué*: "The Zeitgeist," claims Edgardo Cozarinsky, "if anything, speaks through his work and makes it refractory to any *politique des auteurs* approach."[19] More virulent yet, David Thomson views Pabst as a prime example of authorial incapacity: "Few careers probe the theory of the director's influence on film more embarrassingly than Pabst's."[20] Even at his best (prior to 1932), Pabst still suffered from impersonality, contentism, and superficiality; his social studies and authentic dramas do not lend themselves well to searches for creative volition behind the text. Oddly enough, ideologically encumbered artists like Leni Riefenstahl would find a more sympathetic reception among auteurists. Her formal achievements and aesthetic will outweighed the blatant political inscriptions of her films, it seemed. As the sixties progressed, Riefenstahl would enjoy increasing critical favor; at the same time, Pabst all but fell out of sight.

To a degree, then, the ostensible discourse *of* Pabst is a function of discourse *about* Pabst. The harshness of recent reckonings extends not only to the post-Weimar output that had troubled Pabst's contemporaries and caused his erstwhile champions to despair. The fierce taking of stock exerts a retrospective force as well, neutralizing the entire corpus, rendering the figure as a lesser light, a surveyor of social surfaces, a craftsman whose talents were ones of organization and instrumentation—and definitely not *mise en scène.* A cinema of extraterritoriality and an extraterritorial career, Pabst's work and life fail to impress with a first person. If we choose, as the *politique des auteurs* did, "the personal factor in artistic creation as a standard of reference" and assume "that it continues and even progresses from one film to the next,"[21] then Pabst does not stand up well to his competitors.

The cards have been stacked against him, to be sure. Even his most uncontested films—*The Joyless Street, The Love of Jeanne Ney, Diary of Lost Girl*—underwent substantial revisions at the hands of censors and foreign distributors, making them at times all but incomprehensible. A director lauded for his invisible editing, he found his carefully crafted work recut, indeed mutilated. Other films simply no longer exist and can only be discussed on the basis of contemporary reviews. In the United States, only a bare dozen of Pabst's thirty-three films—many in questionable versions—are presently available, all of them either Weimar or Nazi films.[22] In this way, our images of Pabst accord to a very limited access to his work, a quite circumscribed notion of his career as a whole, a critical methodology that posits his lack of directorial personality, and a current situation that, by and large, does not allow us ready opportunity to test these notions on the basis of his entire work. What is uncertain here is not only Pabst's presence, but the presence of his films—and present-day images of him and his oeuvre which derive from partial evidence and superannuated paradigms.

The present collection of essays seeks to rethink Pabst's films as a textual body and to reconsider his career as a whole. An important element in these approaches is an examination of how Pabst has been imaged by contemporaries and subsequent historians and the way in which these portraits involve insight and oversight. The contributors here have a variety of motivations and clearly different agendas. Some revisit Pabst to establish links between the discourses of the films and the social discourses in which they are embedded. Others use his films to actualize or dramatize certain current debates about such matters as spectatorship, gender, and subjectivity. In several instances we find appreciations of works obscured by the passage of time as well as research offering missing information. And, in the case of the Nazi films, we encounter the first substantial attempts to engage (but not indulge) Pabst's output at its most problematic. The following comments provide a backdrop for the volume as a whole, setting the individual essays within the life's script of one of film history's premier displaced persons.

SHAKY FOUNDATIONS

The first shot of Pabst's first film fixes on an edifice, a house, the dwelling of a bell-founder somewhere in Southern Styria, Pabst's homeland. This is a precarious structure: it has once before burned to the ground and will come crashing down at the end of the film. The film explores the foundations of the house, offering glimpses of the space's interior topography on a map, revealing hidden secrets as its inhabitants skulk through dark corridors and labyrinthine passages. The initial sequence contrasts images of apparent domestic stability (a craftsman, his wife and daughter, an assistant) with ones of wandering. The final scene will picture a couple disappearing into the distance, their goal uncertain, at best an undefined away-from-here: flight from a site of greed and calamity, escape from a home that no longer exists. Beate and Arno move down a road into the receding spaces before them, away from the camera in a deep-focus composition, from a full foreground into the uncertainties of a vanishing point. If Pabst's cinema is one of extraterritoriality, *The Treasure* (1923) stands as a compelling founding text, a debut film that points ahead in various directions.

Bernhard Riff does much to rethink popular notions of the film as simple fantastic indulgence couched in a fairy-tale world, insisting that the studio-bound production involves constructive energies from different directions, a curious mix of expressionism, impressionism, and naturalism which makes the film hard to place. As Riff points out, critics, oddly enough, tend to locate the film in a medieval setting, despite clear markers that fix it in a much later period. Riff initially clarifies our understanding of the film's own relation to its textual basis, the egregious blood-and-soil fustian of Rudolf Hans Bartsch, as well as the manner in which it addresses a contemporary context of inflation and anti-Semitism. Seen in this light, *The Treasure* ceases to be an example of "classical expressionism," a film "set in an imaginary medieval locale . . . against an architecture of bizarrely distorted forms."[23] Instead of concentrating on composition and set design alone, Riff scrutinizes the film's play of oppositions at both a thematic and a stylistic level. *The Treasure* suggests the way to *The Joyless Street,* from a rudimentary cinema of contrast and obvious formal dialectic to a more ambiguous exploration of space, a less certain mode of providing spatial orientation, a finding he demonstrates with a scene near the film's end. Breaking out of a pattern of contrasts, of cross-cuts between frenzied gold-seekers and innocent romantics, a schematic textuality, Pabst surprises us by dispersing the camera eye, displacing it into an unseen space that opens up when the couple enter a room. If there is a logic in Pabst's development, suggests Riff, it has to do with a movement towards a cinema which denies us easy fixities and collapses firm foundations.

WOMEN WAITING

The Joyless Street (1925) explores an equally tenuous space, a locale without orientation, a site of aimlessness and anxiety: the street. In Pabst's film, big city avenues do not offer succor to the flâneur and serve as semiotic playgrounds which inspire reveries and dream-images.[24] Here one does not walk; one waits. Unlike Kracauer's "War-

tende," however, spirits living in abeyance, devoid of religious sustenance, plagued by feelings of alienation, bereft of hope and orientation, Pabst's protagonists seem frantic, possessed, and angry.[25] It is not *horror vacui* or *temps morts* they face, but rather the urgency of the most immediate material concerns. The author of *From Caligari to Hitler* would chide the director for his insufficient depiction of the inflation era and its ambience of economic chaos and moral ambiguity. Many progressive contemporaries nevertheless viewed the film as a stirring "moral protest, if not a socialist manifestation." Pabst, according to Kracauer, did not go far enough, even if he clearly grasped the social dimensions of the predicament. His realism was undermined by both the film's melodramatic schematics and his infatuation with his female players.[26]

Patrice Petro's discussion of *The Joyless Street,* part of her lengthier study on Weimar cinema and photojournalism, stresses an extra territory worthy of exploration and explanation: the place of women.[27] Petro suggests a similarity between the way female figures are positioned in this film and how they were positioned by the cinematic institution in the mid-twenties. Put another way, we find a convergence between the women who wait and the women who watch: both harbor an intense anger and dramatic potential, an excess that spills over into the filmic fiction and—censor officials feared—activates latent energies averse to patriarchy. Pabst's recourse to melodrama here, according to Petro, does not vitiate the film's realism; it heightens the value of *The Joyless Street* as a document telling multiple stories and reflecting the non-simultaneity between male and female responses to modernity. The film features two dramas, that of Grete Rumfort and that of Maria Lechner. The first is a tale of virtue rewarded, the second one is less reassuring. Rather, it exudes "guilt, desire, and repression," incorporating a woman's frightful recognition of her lover's betrayal (in a shot taken from behind a patterned window which evokes a similar scene in *Secrets of a Soul*) and her murderous impulse—and deed. Maria acts out a repressed female anger, an anger that returns with a vengeance in the film's closing sequence, despite the seeming neatness with which Grete's destiny has just been resolved.

The denouement betrays signs of editorial intervention which render it seemingly incoherent and yet strikingly emphatic. Petro sees the passage as the manifestation of an uncontained female ire, drawing attention to a singular motif to essentialize the dynamics: the images of Maria's friend, who stands outside the butcher's shop and demands entry, "knocking, then pounding, as if to express the force of an ineffable desire and anger."[28] The final version of the film depicts the result of this unleashed potential (the butcher's bloodied face) even if the actual murder scene has been excised, apparently by the censors. In this reading, Pabst becomes a filmmaker who surveys the same site and reveals its different realities, engaging both the male anxiety of the *Angestellten* class as well as acknowledging female rage, supplying in the end two resolutions, one comforting in its patriarchal logic, the other transgressive in its expression of repressed female desire.[29]

THE UNEXPLORED SPACES OF DREAM ANALYSIS

Secrets of a Soul (1926) is both symptomatic and ironic, a text that reflects the double concern of many important Weimar films. It interrogates male subjectivity and, likewise, the nature of cinema itself, providing a scintillating metafilmic inquiry. Focussing on a troubled psyche, the film discloses an unacceptable identity, an alternative person and unbearable self, a man who can no longer direct his own actions. The protagonist slips from the symbolic into the imaginary, regressing from the head of a household to a dependent child and mother's boy. The film's dynamics will allow him to reassume, in a hyperbolic and overdetermined way, a position of authority and control over himself, his household, and his wife. Cinema, likewise, appears here as a medium whose task it is to order images, to provide pleasing self-images, to harness the seemingly irrational and arbitrary. The impetus of film and psychoanalysis is a common one: both involve a medium, both have to do with a quest for narrative, both also employ similar mechanisms, acting as institutions, dream factories, indeed textual apparatuses, as Anne Friedberg points out in her contribution. Pabst, argues Friedberg, succeeded—despite Freud's own misgivings and hostilities—in translating a talking cure into a silent film. In so doing, Pabst created a dynamics wherein the analyst in the text corresponds to the analyst outside the text, placing the spectator in a discursive relation to the onscreen exchange.

In Friedberg's discussion of the suggested equation "between dream analysis and film analysis," it becomes apparent that *Secrets of a Soul* presents much that remains, in the end, unanalyzed and left out of the psychoanalyst's closing statement. In essence, we find an element of repression in the doctor's account. What results is an ironic tension between the exclusions of the inscribed explanation and our knowledge as onlookers of what it leaves out.[30] As Friedberg puts it: "The spectator of *Secrets of a Soul* is positioned as a more astute psychoanalyst than the fictional surrogate." It would seem, then, that Pabst's cinema calls into question the power of simple answers and straightforward solutions. The psychoanalytical treatment will exorcise the impossible self, banish the man's feelings of insufficiency and trace them back to a childhood trauma, and enable him once again to wield the phallus. Nonetheless, certain excess baggage remains: we can never really dispel the possibility of a liaison between the cousin and the wife. He lurks offscreen with the wife when the husband returns home, suggesting another scene in keeping with the patient's worst dreams. And, to be sure, the wish-fulfilling final sequence provides an all too neat bit of closure; the resolution is overly emphatic, almost hysterically thorough. The doctor urges his subject at one juncture to tell him everything that passes before his mental eye. Later, he prompts the troubled man in no uncertain terms: "Do not repress a single thought, even if you think it is unimportant or absurd." In this way, the film establishes certain standards that are not fully met by the would-be practitioner. The film analyst is challenged to do better.

Secrets of a Soul, from its very first shots, provides the spectator with an admonition not to be deluded by initial impressions, not to be fooled by spurious connections. The opening image shows a strip of material being used to sharpen a blade, suggesting a strip of celluloid and the hand and tool that cuts it. The introductory passage makes it clear just how convincingly editing can manipulate and distort. A number of shots lead us to believe the husband and wife are in the same room; eyeline matches and directionals deceive, though, for the two inhabit separate spaces and are hardly as intimate as it would seem: a wall stands between them, in fact. The editing creates a false image that we come to recognize as such after we regain our bearings. In the same way, the psychoanalyst edits a story derived from his patient's mental images, a "final cut" that seems to edify. If the psychoanalyst entered the man's life by returning a key, it is significant that the object both opens *and* closes, just as the ultimate explanation privileges certain moments and memories while blocking out others. The epilogue, which otherwise would be superfluous, provides a further perspective beyond the initial closure, one both ironic and unsettling.[31]

The final sequence contains a fair bit of residue from the main body of the film: we see the now vigorous man pulling fish out of a stream, recalling the dream image of his wife pulling a doll from the water. During analysis, the doctor "read" the image as one suggesting "an imminent or desired birth." The moment is pregnant with possibility, but the undeniable link between the two "scenes" is immediately disavowed as the man dumps the bucket of fish back into the water, thus aborting meaning, graphically depressing any recall of the disturbing premonition of his wife's infidelity. The ensuing handheld shot of him bounding up the incline to his wife recalls the first shots with an outside perspective—glimpses of onlookers and police running toward the house of murder—echoing again in all the apparent exuberance another previous instance of disquiet. What about his fears of a woman with an independent gaze (something the film confirms as not his projection alone) and a sexuality that excludes him? (Is their child also his child—or his cousin's?) The film deals with secrets of his soul; it also suggests that his wife may have ones of her own. As he rejoins his spouse on the hilltop and lifts their child, we remember an earlier fantasy image of togetherness and fertility against a white screen backdrop. There is no trace now of the cousin; that disturbing factor has departed. The pair exists in a no-place, a utopia of wishful thinking, a dreamscape. Once again, certain footing gives way to precarious ground and here the film ends.

STORY OUTSIDE OF HISTORY

In Pabst's rendering of Ilya Ehrenburg's novel, the love of Jeanne Ney takes precedence over the forces of revolution and history. The adaptation enraged the author, who protested that Ufa had depoliticized and trivialized his book: "With what moving idiocy do they latch onto foreign names and props in order to fabricate yet another bit of nonsense with the best of all happy ends!"³² Do the happy end and the overall affirmative dynamics of *The Love of Jeanne Ney* (1927) substantiate the claims that Pabst compromised Ehrenburg, buckling under studio pressure to fulfill Babelsberg's desire to emulate Hollywood, to make a film about Soviet experience, but in the American style? David Bathrick remains sensitive to the film's many determinants, its inherently contradictory project "as an attempt to negotiate precisely the conflicting discourses of Soviet and American styles . . . as they influenced Weimar cinema." A progressive film artist working for a studio hardly sympathetic to his politics, Pabst steered a cinematic course that maneuvered between differing notions of montage and divergent approaches to the representation of history. Both a social document and a melodrama, the film provides a striking sense of milieux, place, and time, yet likewise privileges a character and an aesthetics working in opposition to "the film's understanding of itself as an historical or social document of twentieth-century life." Pabst empowers Jeanne's gaze and allows her focus ultimately to determine how the narrative will unfold: namely, as "an inexorably forward-moving love story which subordinated history to the overriding imperatives of melodrama." As in *The Joyless Street*, Pabst studies a historical setting and supplies multiple "fixes" on a time and its places. Jeanne stands as a curious expression of extraterritoriality, a variation on Pabst's cinema of life in the elsewhere: her perspective freely dispenses time, granting us access to the past (three flashbacks) and disposing over the future (two flashforwards). She administers story—and yet she embodies a force whose personal volition militates against history at large. In a manner similar to the epilogue of *Secrets of a Soul,* her happiness comes at the cost of the film's ultimate retreat from the world of social reality and historical process, a private triumph in a sphere determined above all by generic dictates.

THE STAKES OF SEXUALITY, SEXUALITY AT STAKE

Woman's position in *The Love of Jeanne Ney* at once activates story and enervates history. A circumscribed frame of reference, Jeanne, like other female protagonists in Pabst's narratives, is a source of control and disturbance. The dominion of Louise Brooks exerts an even more compelling power; her fascination as a screen presence and a fictional character threatens the very authority of the director himself. Critics have repeatedly suggested that the ultimate energy fueling *Pandora's Box* (1929) comes from an actress's sterling performance and persona rather than Pabst's directorial intelligence, in essence recasting the *auteur* in a secondary role as recorder; if he showed any talent here, it was above all his aplomb with a found subject.³³ The two essays in this volume devoted to Pabst's films with Louise Brooks, *Pandora's Box* and *Diary of a Lost Girl* (1929), remain much more skeptical about the ostensible sovereignty ascribed to women in Pabst's films and Weimar cinema as a whole.

Mary Ann Doane and Heide Schlüpmann both agree with Thomas Elsaesser that Pabst represents "sexuality *in* the cinema as the sexuality *of* the cinema."³⁴ Sexuality stands out as a remarkable zone of disturbance both in Pabst's works and the discussions of them. In his reading of *Pandora's Box,* Elsaesser stresses Lulu's androgyny and indeterminacy, seeing her as image incarnate, as an embodiment of cinema and its imaginary arsenal; if Lulu, as he claims "is forever image," she represents the hopes vested in filmic modernism.³⁵ Doane scrutinizes the same image and, likewise, recognizes how Lulu's countenance interrupts narrative flow in an otherwise classical continuity and fragments space by dint of its eroticism. In fact: "In her most desirous (and disruptive) state, Lulu is *outside of* the *mise en scène*. There is a somewhat fantastic hallucinatory quality attached to her image." This image fascinates and frightens, existing above all in the space of male projection, both for the needy men in the text and for smitten male critics outside the film.³⁶ If Lulu exists as an embodiment of male lack, she bears a Pabstian inflection: despatialized and ahistoricized, a freefloating signifier, circulating in a sphere of desire and obsession, subject to the Law of an endangered subjectivity. Contrary to Elsaesser, Doane sees the sexuality of Pabst's cinema, at least in the case of *Pandora's Box,* as a lethal one. Lulu may fascinate, captivate, and scintillate; in the end, she—and every other trace of femininity in the film—"constitutes a danger which must be systematically eradicated." Pabst's modernism of disjunctive cuts and disturbed identifications places woman in an extra territory governed nonetheless by conventional notions of sexual difference.

Heide Schlüpmann's article on *Diary of a Lost Girl* likewise insists that the enigma of woman in cinema is that of male projection. As an institution among others in Weimar Germany, cinema served to assist in the reconstruction of a mortally wounded patriarchy, participating in a larger project of restoring certain privileges and powers. This, in Schlüpmann's account, explains the particularly strained and precarious position of woman within Pabst's narrative as well as the problematic situation of the actress before the camera and the female spectator in the cinema. Pabst's second film with Louise Brooks involves a lost girl—and a lost diary, a personal voice present in the literary source not incorporated in the adaptation and ultimately abandoned as a prop in the film (it simply disappears without explanation). A floundering personage, Thymian is cast out of her home, separated from her father, and deposited in a brutal reform school. Distraught and disaffected, she escapes into a brothel, finding there what would seem to be a modicum of stability in a scenario that otherwise denies her happiness and succor. Throughout it all, and even in the apparently Arcadian bordello, Thymian is the object of an everpresent monitoring institutional gaze. The would-be kind madame with her eyeglasses replicates the workings of the filmic apparatus as a whole; just as she oversees the goings-on in her house, so too does the enunciator behind the camera exercise a specular omnipotence. *Diary of a Lost Girl* offers the male spectator a position similar to the filmmaker's imagined control over his objects. Female suffering corresponds to lacking male presence; in this way, the absent-present male viewer "can always imagine himself to be the basis and fulfillment of this erotic long-ing." Male fantasy finds its ideal partner in a sadistic ap-paratus with which the male spectator can readily identify, for it restores lost power and authority. The female specta-tor retains at best a secondary identification with the Brooks character, an alignment with a self-denying and di-minished image of woman.

A REALISM OF THE HYPERBOLICALLY FALSE

No matter the gender, claims Thomas Elsaesser in his study of *The Threepenny Opera* (1931), identification does not come easily in Pabst's cinema or in Weimar film. Contrary to what previous critics have maintained, *The Threepenny Opera* does not compromise Brecht's anti-illusionist impetus, relativizing "epic" subversion and un-dermining the play's critical impact. Employing a strategy similar to David Bathrick's, Elsaesser views the adaptation on its own terms, instead of reiterating the well-known brouhaha about putative creative and political violence wreaked by the director on a progressive author. Rather than chide the director for his betrayal of Brecht's discur-sive endeavors, for his atmospheric effects, artificial sets, precious camera work and impressionistic lighting, his fe-tishization of female physiognomies, Elsaesser glimpses in the film a remarkably incisive attack on social reality and established authority.[37] Pabst, unlike Brecht, did not stop at exposing the gap between bourgeois illusions and bour-geois institutions, revealing the bankruptcy, immorality, and ruthlessness of middle-class ideology.[38] The filmmaker addressed power at its base and traced the appeal of au-thority to its source, namely "the duplicity of representa-tion" itself, refunctionalizing the cinematic medium—in a way not contemplated by Brecht—as a means to depict and dismantle the modern machinery of false images and affirmative culture.

As an artist, Pabst, so it would seem, wavered between re-alistic impulse and fantastic indulgence; his films move back and forth between social surfaces and exotic depths, traversing alternatively gritty streets and artificial interiors, peregrinating from concrete settings to imaginary loca-tions. In a related way, Pabst is identified as a filmmaker caught between a reverence for the classical continuities (seamless editing, cause-and-effect narrative construction) and an attraction to certain modernist techniques, endeav-oring to be both popular and progressive, accessible and transgressive.[39] Elsaesser sees these oppositions as spe-cious, unequal to the textual challenges of *The Three-penny Opera,* whose hero, Mackie Messer—like Lang's Mabuse and Haghi—is a man of many guises, a figure who exists, above all, as an illusive, fascinating, and se-ductive image. Macheath dramatizes and embodies We-imar film's awareness of the "fascination of the false," as-suming (how could it be different?) a curious status and eccentric position as pure surface, show value, fetish, as gaze and gesture which control the narrative and yet be-come the ultimate objects of on- and offscreen spectators as well. The most telling space of the film, avers Elsaesser, is a no-man's-land of imaginary effects which reveals sym-

bolic functions, "a kind of meta- or hyper-space of repre-sentation . . . constructed in the form of an infinite re-gress, en-abyme, in which a show appears within a show, a frame framing a frame."

Elsaesser's conclusions illustrate a basic variance in recent discussions of gender in Weimar cinema.[40] *The Three-penny Opera* revolves around illusionary appearances and imaginary spaces, disclosing the appeal and dominion of sham organizations (beggars, police, criminals, banks, en-tertainment apparatuses) in a play of props, dummies, and doubles. Macheath, according to Elsaesser, bears out the fact that in matters of gender "the power of fascination is ambivalent." The character assumes a position redolent of Lulu, both center of attention and producer/product of the narrative action. (Doane would stress, however, the differ-ent ways in which the two narratives ultimately dispose over these images.) Pabst's film grants Polly at one point the definitive enabling power in German film, that of in-visibility. She stands as an unseen authority to which thieves-turned-bankers defer. If the illusion of the image triumphs in *The Threepenny Opera,* it appears here in the guise of a woman who assumes the power of the image defined in male terms.

BREAKING DOWN BORDERS

Polly's sovereignty might, of course, be read differently, as a mirror reflection of a precarious subjectivity that ex-ists as a shell and an empty signifier, or as the appearance of an illusion, every bit as much of a void as her male counterpart, Macheath, for whom she acts as a stand-in during the bank scene. Her reign is of short duration, at any rate: the final sequence will show her looking at the returned Mackie in rapture as he performs with his old war comrade, Tiger Brown. Viewed as a whole, Pabst's films feature men with deficient egos and indeterminate identities governed by frenzy, anxiety, irresolution. Cad-dish bon vivants and avuncular lechers abound, from Khalibiev and Raymond Ney to Meinert and Henning (*Diary of a Lost Girl*), the forsaken and betrayed lover in *Shanghai Drama,* Philine's would-be rapist in *Komödi-anten,* or the effete abductor of *Through the Forests, through the Fields. Westfront 1918* (1930) and *Kamerad-schaft* (1931), quite conspicuously demonstrate the dy-namics of the male bond and, as social documents, articu-late the fluidity between men's self-images and their images of women.[41]

Michael Geisler shows how *Westfront* breaks down bor-ders, spatial and temporal ones. Perhaps because the film destroyed boundaries in such a thoroughgoing way, it was criticized for its lack of "consistent effect" and a "guiding idea" (Herbert Ihering) amounting to, at best, "a noncom-mittal survey of war horrors" (Kracauer). As a pacifist ex-clamation, it situates soldiers, regardless of homeland, as inherent allies, as brothers under the uniform. The vicissi-tudes on the battlefield extend to the homefront where starvation and desperation also take their toll. Geisler ex-plores how Pabst's war film displaces the bewilderment and chaos of late twenties Weimar onto the historical site of World War I, replacing the city of New Objectivity with the horrors of modern warfare and suggesting a perceived affinity between metropolis, modernity, and apocalypse. A further transgressed border, as Barthélemy Amengual indicates, is that between the realism of the trenches and combat and Pabst's visual expressionism of markers and signs, a function not so much of aesthetic zeal as of a will to capture dynamics that reduce the natural to mere raw material, the human shape to abstract form.[42] At the center of the film, in Geisler's account, is an idyllic moment of repose in a barren landscape which *in nuce* characterizes the *neusachliche* condition. Karl and the student recline at the edge of a bomb crater and make themselves comfortable. They speak of plentiful food in Brussels, a joyful return home, and, to be certain, of their mutual desire for missing women. The intimate moment ends in a shared gaze, a pat on the back, and laughter. We then cut to a large hall and watch a lively audience partake of a revue whose first offering is a song by "Miss Forget-Me-Not." The camera fixes longingly on her legs and her performance, not for a moment allowing one to forget the special place of women, even in the revelry of the male bond.

Kameradschaft contains many links to *Westfront* and can, as Geisler says, be seen as a continuation of the earlier film: the opening agonistic struggle between two boys over marbles reasserts as puerile the oppositions overcome by *Westfront*. The closing sequence of *Kameradschaft* celebrates international worker solidarity—but appearances deceive. The jubilation of the moment is undermined by a scene which reinstates the underground border between France and Germany—the "Frontière 1919" the narrative had sought to render inoperative. The old arrangement is put back in place as government officials look on; a document passes from one side of the barrier to the other, representatives sign and stamp it. For Russell Berman, this is not just an ironic epilogue. It corresponds to the hollowness of the film's overall message, essentializing the manner in which the text breaks down national borders only to erect others. The workers of the world, in Berman's provocative allegorical reading, unite—not against management or political oppression, but rather in a struggle against nature itself, against subterranean powers beneath the earth's surface and in their own persons. Male solidarity, in fact, seems grounded in a conspicuous exclusion of women, having as its criterion an embrace of one's like with decidedly homoerotic overtones. *Kameradschaft,* as a historical document, provides in retrospect an etiology and a pathology, unwittingly presaging the collapse of internationalist ideals and demonstrating why working-class comradeship would succumb to the forces of reaction. In this vein, the film offers insights into "the libidinal economy" of instrumental rationality as internalized by the proletariat. If anything prevails, it is repression, denial, and discipline, the powers of technology and organization. Women no doubt play a diminished role in this scenario, a subordinate element on the margins of the narrative; they wait before the mine gates and demand entry. They embody a potentially disruptive energy we have seen explode

in *The Joyless Street,* an energy restrained in *Kameradschaft* in a way that makes it all the more conspicuous.

EXPEDITION INTO THE IMAGINARY

In keeping with tendencies in German cinema prompted by the switchover to sound technology, Pabst's career became an increasingly international one, with a single production like *The Threepenny Opera* encompassing two language versions with different casts and variant running times; critics began to voice suspicions that Pabst, like many of his peers, was escaping into a world of elaborate sets, high production values, and artificial effects. (Thomas Elsaesser has addressed how we might come to different conclusions.) While conservative and nationalist sensibilities exercised a growing grip on film production in the Germany of the early thirties, one found fewer outspoken and engaged films and a larger number of generic effusions that, in Rudolf Arnheim's description, took flight "from the horrors of reality into the horrors of irreality." According to Arnheim, *The Mistress of Atlantis* (1932) demonstrated how a once politically correct, intellectually ambitious, if not artistically overendowed, filmmaker had fallen prey to outside pressures and run for cover.[43]

Karl Sierek's analysis of selected fragments from the relatively unknown film presents it not as a document of artistic ambiguity lacking authorship, or a spiritual impasse, but rather as a work that interrogates the cinematic apparatus itself, revealing the processes of representation, enunciation, and spectatorship in the guise of a crazed man's retrospective tale of search and desire. Saint-Avit's peregrination into an imaginary realm, into the world of Antinea and Atlantis, involves a quest to find his missing friend, Morhange—and more. In Sierek's essay, *The Mistress of Atlantis* amounts to a subterranean fantasy, an allegory of a cave, indeed a film about cinema, whose narrative gaps open up the functionings of meaning construction, whose breaks in patterned identification (matching eyelines and directionals) divulge other spaces and different sites, allowing the (male) viewer at once to study his onscreen surrogate and recognize the pathological constitution of the subject by a projection mechanism. Treading a nether world of dream and fantasy, *The Mistress of Atlantis* offers a modernist experiment. Here "the screen no longer presents the world of film, but rather the world of cinema," a primal realm in which male desire becomes intoxicated with the image of a woman, but above all recognizes itself as a split entity, as a subject whose ultimate object is the image of its own self.

HERR PABST GOES TO HOLLYWOOD

A Modern Hero, so runs common consensus, marks the downfall of the once modernist filmmaker/hero, the director repeatedly celebrated in the journal *Close Up* and lauded as late as 1933 as Europe's "strongest director" and a source of continuing hope. In the words of Harry Alan Potamkin: "To find in the bourgeois cinema, within its commercial realm, as socially conscientious an artist as Pabst is indeed a discovery!"[44] Unlike Lubitsch or Murnau,

Pabst did not travel well. Contrary to Lang, he lacked the will to assert himself, "the arrogant, hard-nosed tenacity and ruthlessness to survive in the Hollywood studio."[45] The sojourn in the United States (Pabst's second one) would prove traumatic, resulting in what seems to have been a compromised film by a filmmaker who would never recover from the experience. This is a narrative shared by a wide spectrum of commentators, from Leni Riefenstahl[46] to Lee Atwell.[47]

Jan-Christopher Horak has done thorough detective work, tracking down correspondence, documents, and press releases, offering a more exact account of what transpired during this period. In looking through Pabst's correspondence with Warner Bros. officials about *A Modern Hero,* we indeed bear witness to a tense exchange; the director received repeated admonitions to respect the script, to heed editing conventions, to provide more close-ups and backup footage. It is indeed an instance of a foreigner being forced to toe the line; as Hal B. Wallis insisted to his employee, "You will have to get used to our way of shooting pictures."

Horak goes on to scrutinize the final product and recognizes much that would suggest a not utterly compromised endeavor. We find a trajectory quite in keeping with other Pabst films: an ever-wanting male subject rises in the world on the shirt tails of women, ultimately capitulating in the wake of financial ruin and domestic catastrophe, retreating to a domineering mother and contemplating a return to Europe, in a conclusion that replicates Kracauer's privileged Weimar scenario, wherein a thwarted son takes refuge in a maternal lap. As Horak observes, Paul Rader is a problematic figure, a questionable focus for spectator identification. The precarious happy end involves an overdetermined regression, an Oedipal fixation with incestuous underpinnings. More than just a critique of capitalism, a disillusioned rendering of the American dream, a film about the signifying chain love, sex, and money, Pabst's sole Hollywood film is a distinctly perverse text that despite differences of place and production can be read within the logic of his previous—and subsequent work.

THE EMIGRATION TRILOGY

The pre-1933 films of Pabst have a consistent cast and an insistent dynamics. They feature the obsessed, the dispossessed, the displaced, the placeless, figures without shelter, individuals orphaned, women waiting and men on the run, a cinema of extraterritorial uncertainty in which characters exist on dangerous ground, where history provides the most uncommodious sanctuary, where utopian dreams betray above all a will to renounce the real. Pabst respected, confronted, and reflected upon the constructive potential of a machinery anchored in a harsh reality and circumscribed by inhospitable constellations. Despite imposing circumstances, he gained world renown and wide admiration during the Weimar years, standing as a role model for a cinema of the future, an individual admired for his courage and conviction. He would pay the price of these convictions, leaving Germany as the nation journeyed into night, recognizing that the country had no place for his like.

An exile by choice, Pabst once again (he had been imprisoned in a P.O.W. camp during World War I) became an extraterritorial citizen, crafting films that turned on this dilemma. One might call *Don Quixote* (1933), *High and Low* (1933), and *Shanghai Drama* (1938) his "Emigration Trilogy," films that, despite their differences of time and place, explore the problematics of exile. A tri-lingual production in Pabst's rendering, *Don Quixote* offers a tale of a man who takes flight from mercenary contemporaries and changing conditions into a realm of enchantment and adventure. It is likewise a tale of male desire for an idealized image of woman; if any obsession sustains the hero's readings, it is an unrequited erotic energy. The drama unfolds as an episodic, indeed epic, construction.[48] The film's opening sequence shows the printed words of the Cervantes novel, leafing through the volume as words give rise to moving images, the animated figures of Lotte Reiniger. We then see the transfixed reader as he declaims an epic romance and we watch a film portraying the mental images that come of these encounters. The final shots picture a broken man, incarcerated and disenfranchised, his treasured tomes burning in a public square. (Pabst finished the film late in 1932 prior to similar demonstrations in Nazi Germany.) We hear the knight's funeral dirge and watch the apparatus reconstitute his story from the flames, the reverse-motion photography reclaiming, in an act of discursive resistance, the pages with which the film began.

High and Low, the trilogy's second leg, is not just a failed comedy of manners, a jejune example of French Poetic Realism, as is commonly maintained. Does it make sense to read this film within the contexts of generic convention or a national cinema? asks Gertrud Koch. Is there not something inherently eccentric and singular about a German-language crew filming a Hungarian play about a Viennese apartment house in a Paris studio with a cast of French players and German emigrant actors? In her reevaluation of *High and Low,* Koch discovers a document about "social rupture and displacement," a work that lacks local color and folkloric detail precisely because its emphasis lies elsewhere. *High and Low,* the product of an exile ensemble, portrays the destiny of emigrants, "stranded souls, rising and descending, individuals whose cards have been reshuffled, who lack the security of social fixity." A comedy about an unbalanced world, it destabilizes—without putting things back into place in the end. Even the male icon, Jean Gabin, undergoes a transformation, an education at the hands of a woman. Emancipation and sexuality, it would seem, do not have to be mutually exclusive. The pert schoolteacher and the sensitized soccer player escape convention and a closed community, although the film denies us easy confirmation that paradise is near; as Koch concludes, "Whether they have arrived in a lovers' seventh heaven remains anyone's guess."

Shanghai Drama seems to issue from an opium den. It supplies a hyperbolic extension of the Pabstian topography: more imaginary than *The Threepenny Opera* or *The Mistress of Atlantis*; a sultry space of intrigue and excess which rivals *The Love of Jeanne Ney*; a hallucinatory dreamscape similar in its punitive surrealism to *Secrets of a Soul*; a sphere of melodrama, noir, and spies whose prime locations are streets, a night club, and a torture chamber, whose leading players are both conspirators and performers. Contemporary critics laughed it off as a crude spy thriller, an absurd genre film that demonstrates "the exigencies of exile and the stupidity of producers," whose director "isn't really here at all, except for a few seconds in a neat knifing," as Graham Greene wrote in 1939.[49] A film whose plot is confused, indeed obscure, this would seem to be, as James Agee opined, André Malraux's *Human Condition* "redone for the pulps."[50]

In Karsten Witte's analysis, the film makes conceptual and narrative sense if one discerns the historical inscriptions and grasps the text as not just pure escapism or a romantic potboiler, but takes its neon-light promise as its premise. The film, quite literally, portrays "le rêve de Shanghai," a spectacle of estrangement and displacement, thematizing exile as a continent and a condition. *Shanghai Drama* unfolds as a melodrama about dislocation where exiles seek escape to yet another station, where local inhabitants breathe uneasily in an ambience of foreign opportunism and imported cabal, where all involved remain subject to a constantly shifting and arbitrary Law. Shanghai stands as an emblem for the exotic, a cipher of the emigrant's uncertainty; *Shanghai Drama,* observes Witte, provides an interesting station in a directional career increasingly on the run from history, evidence that the filmmaker was quite conscious of his fugitive status and its precarious terms.

ANOTHER KIND OF FUGITIVE CINEMA

For complex reasons, the prodigal Pabst visited Austria and, as World War II broke out, found himself a captive of circumstance, as in 1914, in the wrong place at an unpropitious moment.[51] He would later deny he had collaborated or conformed in his return to the German film industry, now under the tutelage of National Socialism. He is reputed to have kept a diary during these years, although it has thus far not been made available for public scrutiny.[52] The completed films Pabst did leave behind have done irreparable damage to his image. Depending on one's perspective, they amount to aesthetic bankruptcy, redeemed at best by hints of a former mastery, on the one hand, or signs of opportunism and accommodation, proof of the director's inherent lack of volition. Anke Gleber's contribution on *Komödianten* (1941) and Regine Mihal Friedman's analysis of *Paracelsus* (1943) do not seek to point fingers and condemn Pabst, nor do they skirt difficult questions catalyzed by problematic films. Eluding sweeping judgments and avoiding neat cubbyholes, the two look at Pabst's costume dramas in the discursive context out of which they arose and in which they functioned.

Pabst's NS-films involve misunderstood geniuses, individuals whose great contributions to German culture re-

ceive retrospective tribute by a modern state film machinery. Caroline Neuber, actress and activist, envisions the German drama of the future and a more mature national audience, although she will see neither within her lifetime. *Komödianten* offers a monument to a failed genius, a woman whose triumph would consist of having given birth to a national theater. According to Anke Gleber, the film portrays Neuber as a self-denying and masochistic facilitator, a maternal figure who relinquishes her own desire for the sake of a larger calling. Quite literally, we will see how a dying woman becomes the material for the edifice celebrated in the closing sequence: the camera dissolves from a shot of Caroline's mid-body to the exterior of the National Theater where young Lessing's play is to premiere. With its cast of Käthe Dorsch, Hilde Krahl, and Henny Porten, an actresses' film for a female audience, *Komödianten* might at first glance be mistaken for an anomaly, a Nazi film that empowers women. An exchange between Neuber's surrogate daughter, Philine, and her protectoress, the Duchess, is crucial. Philine describes Caroline as "a great woman who had the stuff to be a great man!" The Duchess protests: "Stop! Neuberin should remain a woman and prove what we women are capable of!" The ideological mission of the film, claims Gleber, lay in addressing women left on the homefront of 1941 while their husbands were away at war. *Komödianten* is a Nazi woman's film, offering figures of identification and, ultimately, positions one was meant, by implication, to assume. Not so much a genius as an object lesson, Caroline Neuber, the activist and midwife, became the stuff for a Nazi film that evoked passions and freed feelings, "all the better to serve as a model of female submission for wartime female spectators."

Where we can locate Pabst in these texts remains difficult: *Komödianten* and *Paracelsus* maintain a thematic consistency, it is true, and contain episodic structures and nomadic narratives typical of previous films. Still, even if Pabst apparently resisted the State film apparatus, greeting certain projects with uneasiness, it remains hard to find ambiguity in these quite tendentious productions.[53] What one can fix is the position these films assumed in a larger discourse, in Nazi culture and German cinemas, in Pabst's career and subsequent discussions of his work. *Paracelsus* is generally read as a curious blend of *Autorenkino* and Nazi film, one of Pabst's "most brilliant films" (Lee Atwell)[54] and yet, "not quite so politically innocent as some would have it" (David Stewart Hull).[55] Clearly the film reflects Nazi cinema's penchant for reaching into the grab bag of history and ransacking it for political purposes, transforming past events and personages into myth—the "tamed richness" spoken of by Roland Barthes which one alternately evokes and dismisses. One takes liberties with the past for a good reason: what really is at issue are present-day agendas. Paracelsus is a surrogate *Führer,* a genius ahead of his time, someone in touch with the elements, nature, and folk, a thinker who eschews narrow categories and embraces a wider view of things.

Regine Mihal Friedman shows how the sixteenth-century scientist was pressed into the service of Nazi hagiography, going on then to look more closely at the film's formal dynamics beyond blatant ideological histrionics. She concentrates on what she terms a "zone of disturbance" at the film's center, a moment of textual excess—a dance of death followed by a procession of flagellants—which serves no narrative purpose, but stands out markedly, so much so that most commentators have singled out these scenes as striking and noteworthy. This sequence, in Friedman's mind, serves a *mise en abyme* function, at once essentializing the film's own workings and yet turning in on the film as well, offering a glimpse at the ambiguities of its construction. The images of possessed dancers and tormented bodies present a discourse on the "manipulation of the human" and "the mechanization of the living," expressing "the frenzied desires of bodies to be liberated, but also to be disciplined and punished." Herein rest energies harnessed by National Socialism and inscribed in this film, a work that ultimately ruptures into a stunning "commentary on the present in the form of a grotesque tableau."

THE POSTWAR ODYSSEY

The films Pabst made after 1945, with several exceptions, came under even harsher criticism than his Nazi output. The postwar work bears the label of genre and formula: costume dramas, literary adaptations, sappy melodramas, historical reconstructions, and even a bit of *Heimat* sentimentality. Hopelessly out of step with history, behind the times and unable to catch up, Pabst had lost all incisiveness. "In fact, the former advocate of social realism moved increasingly toward a position of mysticism or romantic evasion."[56] The career of the late Pabst is a study in desperation: a bombastic attempt at rehabilitation (*The Trial*, 1948),[57] a subsequent casting about in the international scene (a failed production company in Vienna, Italian coproductions of little note), an odyssey that even included the ultimately forsaken plan to film Homer's epic about the long return home of a warrior. Pabst's own return to German-language productions hardly found admiring audiences and enthused critics. His melodramas, *The Confession of Ina Kahr* (1954) and *Roses for Bettina* (1955), appeared as recourses to the Ufa entertainments of the Nazi era, virulent manifestations of his own artistic deterioration. The two retrospective readings of the Third Reich, *The Last Ten Days* and *The Jackboot Mutiny* (both released in 1955) betrayed Pabst's predilection for wallowing in effects and obscuring causes. The historical portraits revisited the attempt on Hitler's life and the Führer's final days in the bunker, replicating a wider mythology of the Adenauer period which displaced guilt onto an inexorable destiny, portraying National Socialism as evil incarnate, a plague upon mankind. Freddy Buache castigated Pabst in no uncertain terms: "As a loyal servant to official morality, he makes excuses and provides the regime with alibis, or rather, he takes refuge in comfortable melodrama. He has become a zombie-director. His death, no doubt, occurred in 1932-33."[58]

These harsh judgments seem to obviate any need to scrutinize the later films more carefully. Yet when we do look at them with more attention and less impatience, we find much that warrants interest and extended discussion, even if these films hardly recommend themselves as misunderstood hallmarks of postwar European cinema. Based on a novel by Rudolf Brunngraber, *The Trial* is about a son who bears false witness against his father. A Jewish boy, cajoled, hounded, and seduced by mercenary opportunists, serves reactionary forces in their anti-Semitic campaign, a reenactment of an actual court case in late nineteenth-century Hungary. (Pabst had already contemplated a similar project early in the thirties.) The chauvinists conspire to force the youngster to claim he saw his elders commit the ritual murder of a village girl, prompting the boy to describe a fictional scene of violence allegedly glimpsed through a keyhole. Point of view becomes a prime issue in this primal scenario about an errant son made by German cinema's premier prodigal spirit. In his attempt to resurrect a forsaken legacy of social criticism and realistic resolve, Pabst placed the Jewish community between the fronts, at the mercy of larger political interests, a plaything for parties on both sides of the ideological spectrum. In a study of projections and false images, as Karl Prümm makes clear, we see precious few glimpses of the Jewish citizenry except from an outside perspective. Unlike Pabst's most compelling dramas about the disenfranchised, the ostensible objects of his sympathy do not enjoy a convincing presence—either as voice or gaze—in *The Trial.* For all of Pabst's great ambitions, Prümm concludes, the film disappoints because its critical viewpoint remains so short-sighted.

Pabst's postwar melodramas involve sadomasochistic dynamics that abound with excess and perversion. ***Roses for Bettina*** might be productively compared to R. W. Fassbinders's *Martha* (1973): both end with female protagonists paralyzed and dependent, bound to weelchairs and subservient to dominant—and creepy—males. There is a similar logic and common strategy at work in ***Diary of a Lost Girl, Shanghai Drama, Komödianten, The Confession of Ina Kahr,*** and ***Roses for Bettina,*** where "the structures of melodrama preside with such triumphant aggressiveness, excess, and imperialism that one thinks Pabst . . . is making an anti-melodrama."[59] Tormented and destructive males (especially the self-effacingly sinister Paul of *Ina Kahr* portrayed by Curt Jürgens), jealous father figures, sacrificial heroines—and outbreaks of textual hysteria (what Amengual calls Pabst's "fêtes"[60]) mark these shrill and overdetermined narratives, films one could well reconsider in terms of a shrewd *mise en scène* that undermines trivial stories.

Marc Silberman views Pabst's final years and his creative decline in the context of postwar German cinema as a whole. Adenauer's Federal Republic was a time and a place not beholden to creative impulse, stylistic zeal, and alternative endeavor. The film apparatus of the fifties in Germany did not allow authorship to flourish: think of the directorial fates of returned exiles like Fritz Lang and Robert Siodmak and the difficulties experienced by outspoken spirits such as Wolfgang Staudte. In this way, *The*

Last Ten Days becomes a function of an era's tunnel vision, a spectacle of history made with a documentary zeal and told from a melodramatic perspective, serving in the end to mystify fascism and cloud memories of that past, while participating in a larger collective desire to ward off traumatic and unpleasant recollections. History becomes melodrama, a tale of disintegration and male hysteria, an account of a demented figure's fantasies and fantasms in a subterranean setting. Here, too, we find one of Pabst's famous celebrations, a delirious scene where people become grotesque marionettes, mechanical bodies. Human beings succumb to an abandon that renders them frenzied apparatuses caught up in a dance of death. With visual attention and spectator interest bound in a fascination with a madman's delusions and his minions' desperate final hours, it makes sense, as Silberman argues, that the voices of resistance, conscience, and morality ring hollow and do not convince.

Several words about Pabst's final film, **Through the Forests, through the Fields** (1956), are in order. Its first shot provides an almost ironic textual allegory, essentializing the dialectical relationship between male self-images and men's images of women we find in so many of Pabst's films. The miniature of a woman, the famous opera singer, Caroline Brandt, rests on a Count's phallic soldierly headdress, suggesting her surrender and his conquest—an illusion on both counts, we will soon learn, a fraud and a fantasy. The Count has in fact acquired the portrait through a ruse. The film unfolds as a struggle between two men for the woman's favor. Count Schwarzenbrünn, a dandy and an idler, lacks a steady presence in his moribund existence. His competitor, the composer Carl Maria von Weber, needs his lover's voice and person as a medium for his music. In the end, the musician will triumph as his "Romantic Fantasy" is performed in a village square. What triumphs above all is the composer's own romantic fantasy—the phantasm of a woman. The last shot of Pabst's last film is striking: an artist looks offscreen during a moment of seeming victory, seeking the affirmative gaze of a woman who stands outside of the image, invisible, yet potent, the source of recognition the man needs if his success is to be complete. If the first image of Pabst's cinema showed us a house with questionable foundations, the last shot of his work fades out from a subject whose identity rests on equally precarious ground.

Notes

1. Paul Rotha and Richard Griffith, *The Film Till Now: A Survey of World Cinema* (London: Spring, 1967), 584n.

2. Barthélemy Amengual, *G. W. Pabst* (Paris: Seghers, 1966), 16. Amengual goes on to quote Glauco Viazzi's appraisal of Pabst from 1949: "Pabst is a director who, bound to history, always wanted to answer questions posed by history. But first, he *submits* to history."

3. Edgardo Cozarinsky, "G. W. Pabst," in *Cinema: A Critical Dictionary,* 2 vols., ed. Richard Roud (New York: Viking, 1980), 2:752.

4. A preferred locution is the phrase "between," a measure of Pabst's allegedly mercurial disposition, his constant indecision. In the end, one often simply speaks of him as someone whose mind and person pose an unsolvable riddle. See, for instance, Eric Rhode, *A History of the Cinema from Its Origins to 1970* (New York: Hill and Wang, 1976), 190: "He is the most impassive of directors, the cold surface of his films being about as yielding as the monocled eye of a Junker officer. He remains enigmatic at every level; and whether or not he intended to be so, or was in fact ingenuous, is part of the Pabst enigma."

5. See Rotha and Griffith, *Film Till Now,* 582ff. Griffith, in his reckoning with Pabst's career, shares Kracauer's analysis that the so-called social trilogy—*Westfront, The Threepenny Opera, Kameradschaft*—manifests a fatal political ignorance and ultimately "showed unmistakable symptoms of immaturity" in lacking awareness of one's historical spectatorship (582). "Pabst's case," Griffith observes, "is a subtle, knotty and perhaps an insoluble one. . . . It is an all too significant commentary on film commentators, including the present writer. Our record has been for too long one of absorption in technique for its own sake, or alternatively of accepting sociological intentions at their face value" (584-585).

6. See, for example, the career assessment in *rororo Film lexikon,* ed. Liz-Anne Bawden and Wolfram Tichy (Reinbek: Rowohlt, 1978), 1246. Alexandre Arnoux, "Un déjeuner avec Pabst," *Pour Vous,* 29 January 1931 (quoted in Amengual, *Pabst,* 17), traces, in the director's own words, this instability to the trauma experienced in World War I. "We belong," Pabst explains, "to a sacrificed generation, cut in two. Our rhythm of life was broken; our generation carries within itself a rupture, an abyss between its youth and maturity. This explains the uncertainty and gasping of our works, their broken line, the difficulty we experience in finding a style."

7. Harry Alan Potamkin, "Pabst and the Social Film," in *The Compound Cinema,* ed. Lewis Jacobs (New York and London: Teachers College, 1977), 416. The article originally appeared in *Hound and Horn,* January-March 1933.

8. Ulrich Gregor and Enno Patalas, *Geschichte des Films. 1: 1895-1939,* 2 vols. (Reinbek: Rowohlt, 1976), 61: Pabst is superficial, someone who glosses over surfaces and fails to penetrate them, taking recourse to the most obvious forms of melodrama and kitsch even in his Weimar films.

9. In his contribution, David Bathrick discusses this very dilemma in terms of Pabst's *The Love of Jeanne Ney.* The films of the early thirties in particular provoked this criticism on the Right.

10. See Cornelius Schnauber, *Fritz Lang in Hollywood* (Vienna, Munich and Zürich: Europaverlag, 1986), 147. Fritz Lang allegedly complained in a letter of

12 October 1966 to Lotte Eisner that Pabst, during his American sojourn, had spread rumors that Lang was in fact a secret agent for the National Socialists. Schnauber implicitly claims that Pabst (who returned to Vienna in 1939 and made "party line films") was a more likely suspect.

11. In this light it makes sense that the nomadic German director of Wim Wenders's *The State of Things* (*Der Stand der Dinge,* 1982), a filmmaker whose quest for images shipwrecks on Hollywood's narrative bulwarks, is seen as sharing the fate of Fritz Lang and F. W. Murnau. The film makes no mention of Pabst. Compare as well Lotte Eisner's treatment of Lang and Murnau (about whom she wrote exhaustive books) to her more problematical relationship to Pabst.

12. See Willi Forst's characterization of Krauss's talents of transformation in Robert Dachs, *Willi Forst. Eine Biographie* (Vienna: Kremayr & Scherlau, 1986), 81. Krauss, likewise, is reputed to have had a famous fear of close-ups. William Shawn, in his introduction to Louise Brooks's *Lulu in Hollywood* (New York: Knopf, 1983), ix, talks about how the actress's person became one with her screen image: "It is difficult to believe that Louise Brooks exists apart from her creation. Pabst himself identified the two, and even Louise Brooks has had her moments of confusion."

13. See Karel Reisz and Gavin Millar, *The Technique of Film Editing* (New York: Hastings House, 1968), 48: "Pabst may have been one of the first film-makers to time most of his cuts on specific movements within the picture in an attempt to make the transitions as unnoticeable as possible."

14. Rotha and Griffith, 263. See as well Potamkin's utopian document, "A Proposal for a School of the Motion Picture," reprinted in *The Compound Cinema,* 587-592. Among the faculty to be responsible for "Theory of Direction" were Pabst, Eisenstein, Pudovkin, Milestone, Flaherty, Howard, Clair, and Asquith. The proposal first appeared in *Hound and Horn,* October 1933.

15. Using organic metaphors, Langlois maintains that Pabst's fate bears out how a national hero languishes when uprooted from his native soil. The statement appears in the unpaginated brochure, *Der Regisseur G. W. Pabst* (Munich: Photo- und Filmmuseum, 1963).

16. Compare Amengual, 12: "In nine years, from 1923 to 1932, Pabst made fifteen films. His best work, or rather, *all* of his work is there." Even more explicit is Warren French's "Editor's Foreword" to Lee Atwell, *G. W. Pabst* (Boston: Twayne, 1977), 7: "One cannot suppress the distressing thought that if Pabst had died, like Murnau, during his American visit in the 1930s, he would probably have a far more glorious reputation today."

17. Rotha and Griffith, 582: Pabst presents "the most extraordinary and baffling case of the 'accommodators,'" i.e. filmmakers who fell in with the National Socialists.

18. See Georges Sadoul's characterization of Pabst in *Histoire de l'art du Cinéma des origines à nos jours,* 4th ed. (Paris: Flammarion, 1955).

19. Cozarinsky in *Cinema: A Critical Dictionary,* 1: 752.

20. David Thomson, *A Biographical Dictionary of Film,* 2nd rev. ed. (New York: Morrow, 1981), 455.

21. André Bazin, "La politique des auteurs," as rendered in *Theories of Authorship,* ed. John Caughie (London, Boston and Henley: Routledge & Kegan Paul, 1981), 45.

22. For particulars on the present availability of Pabst films in the United States, see *Feature Films: A Directory of Feature Films on 16mm and Videotape Available for Rental, Sale, and Lease,* ed. James L. Limbacher, 8th ed. (New York and London: Bowker, 1985).

23. Atwell, *G. W. Pabst,* 21.

24. Pabst seems aware of the distinctly gender-bound logic of the street. Loitering, wandering, and idle gazing when practiced by a male have an altogether different significance than when exercised by a woman. Pabst does not replicate the "street film" rhetoric of the metropolis as a phantasmagoria which we find, for instance, in Karl Grune's *The Street* (*Die Strasse,* 1923). Cf. Klaus Kreimeier, "Die Strasse im deutschen Film vor 1933," *epd Kirche und Film* (December 1972): 10-16.

25. Compare the essay of 1922, "Die Wartenden," reprinted in Siegfried Kracauer, *Das Ornament der Masse,* ed. Karsten Witte (Frankfurt am Main: Suhrkamp, 1977), 106-119.

26. Siegfried Kracauer, *From Caligari to Hitler: A Psychological History of the German Film* (Princeton: Princeton University Press, 1947), 170.

27. Patrice Petro, *Joyless Streets: Women and Melodramatic Representation in Weimar Germany* (Princeton: Princeton University Press, 1989).

28. This motif—one that recurs throughout Weimar productions, as Petro points out—is not considered in Kracauer's study, which he describes as "a history of motifs pervading films of all levels" (8).

29. See Kracauer's significant and regrettably still untranslated reportage, *Die Angestellten. Aus dem neuesten Deutschland.* The study first ran in 1929 and 1930 as a continuing serial in the *Frankfurter Zeitung*; the initial book edition appeared in 1930 (Frankfurt am Main: Frankfurter Societäts-Druckerei, Abteilung Buchverlag).

30. Compare Nick Browne and Bruce McPherson, "Dream and Photography in a Psychoanalytic Film: *Secrets of a Soul,*" *Dreamworks* 1:1 (Spring 1980):

36-37: One of the problems posed here, claim the authors, has to do with the "disjunction in the film between the precise and voluminous psychological detail and the paucity, even disingenuousness, of its psychoanalytic explanation," something that "calls for a more thoroughgoing analysis of the case than either the film or its commentators provide."

31. Compare the more conventional interpretation of the epilogue as an entity, according to Kracauer (172), "which drags the whole plot into the sphere of melodrama, thus definitely nullifying its broader implications."

32. This quotation is taken from Ehrenburg's flier, *Protest gegen die Ufa* (Stuttgart: Rhein, 1928).

33. See Lotte H. Eisner's incisive commentary in *The Haunted Screen,* trans. Roger Greaves (Berkeley and Los Angeles: University of California Press, 1969), 296: "In *Pandora's Box* and *Diary of a Lost Girl* we have the miracle of Louise Brooks. Her gifts of profound intuition may seem purely passive to an inexperienced audience, yet she succeeded in stimulating an otherwise unequal director's talent to the extreme. Pabst's remarkable evolution must thus be seen as an encounter with an actress who needed no directing, but could move across the screen causing the work of art to be born by her mere presence."

34. Thomas Elsaesser, "Lulu and the Meter Man," *Screen* 24.4-5 (July-October 1983): 33.

35. Ibid., 36: "What Pabst could not prevent, in any case, was the momentous shift, whereby the film industry, seizing on the woman's body, and focusing gratification so much on the voyeuristic look, turned the cinema into an obsessional, fetishistic instrument, and thus betrayed in some sense its Modernist promise, by making this modernism instrumental and subservient to the logic of capital and the commodity."

36. For an inventory of such celebrations, see Doane's essay. Compare Andrew Sarris, *The American Cinema* (New York: Dutton, 1968), 151: The author remembers Pabst's work not because of its directorial presence, "but rather for the retroactive glory of Louise Brooks. . . . The preeminence of Miss Brooks as the beauty of the twenties indicates the classic nature of the cinema, and its built-in machinery for an appeal to the verdict of history."

37. Compare Eisner's appraisal, 316: "In his adaptation for the cinema Pabst diluted the original [*Threepenny Opera*] by his attachment to chiaroscuro and *Stimmung.*" For a more favorable evaluation of the film's social dimension, see Potamkin, "Pabst and the Social Film," 415f.

38. See Brecht's notes to *The Threepenny Opera,* "The Literarization of the Theatre," in *Brecht on Theatre,* ed. and trans. John Willett (New York: Hill and Wang, 1964), 43: "The *Threepenny Opera* is concerned with bourgeois conceptions not only as con-

tent, by representing them, but also through the manner in which it does."

39. In this reading, Pabst would seem to span the boundaries of film as mass culture and modernism. For an articulation of this dialectic in the wider context of Weimar cinema, see Petro, *Joyless Streets,* 4-9.

40. Petro maintains that Kracauer posits a male subject as the object and spectator of Weimar films. Elsaesser, she goes on to say, circumvents "questions of sexual ambiguity and androgyny as they relate to the female spectator, in favor of a sliding or unstable identification, one that remains bound to a male spectator position" (17).

41. Compare Freddy Buache's indictment of the two films in *G. W. Pabst* (Lyon: Serdoc, 1965), 50: In *Westfront,* "the author . . . due to weakness of character or lack of conscience, abandons restating the sociological moment in the historic totalization. *Westfront* depicts war as a runaway Evil, descended from an unforeseeable Destiny, without economic and political origins." In essence, then, Pabst "deliberately ignores the motives and horrible mechanics."

42. Compare Amengual's comments on *Westfront,* 42: "Pabst, powerless to create the real in its blatancy here, tries to recover it in the fantastic by turning to expressionism. More than the war, he depicts the nightmare of war."

43. Rudolf Arnheim, *Kritiken und Aufsätze zum Film,* ed. Helmut H. Diederichs (Frankfurt am Main: Fischer, 1979), 259-260. Arnheim's notice originally appeared in *Die Weltbühne* on 13 September 1932 as "Flucht in die Kulisse." Kracauer, in *From Caligari to Hitler,* 242, calls the film "an outright retrogression from 'social conclusiveness' into pure escapism."

44. "Pabst and the Social Film," 420.

45. Atwell, 116-117. Compare Herman F. Weinberg, "The Case of Pabst," in *Saint Cinema: Writings on Film, 1929-1970,* 2nd rev. ed. (New York: Ungar, 1980), 19: "Pabst floundered about the studios of France and Hollywood without being able to adjust himself to the terrible nightmare of this shocking reality, namely that the integrity of the artist was a myth so far as the world is concerned, that art is not universal, nor above the bickerings of politicians and dictators, that money rules all, and that this is pretty much the worst of all possible worlds. How else to explain the abortion made in Hollywood which carried his name as director?"

46. Riefenstahl describes her work with Pabst (who assisted in some scenes of *Tiefland*) in her *Memoiren* (Munich and Hamburg: Knaus, 1987), 369: Pabst "was no longer the man I had known twelve years before when we had worked so well on *Piz Palü.* His personality had changed. . . . Nothing remained of what had once been such a good eye for visual matters. Hollywood apparently had no positive influence

on him, his approach now was perfunctory and seemed more in keeping with what one might expect for commercial films."

47. Atwell, 116: "Pabst was bitterly disillusioned by the repressive system of Hollywood's assembly-line methods where he had virtually no creative control and was regarded primarily as a functionary rather than an artist." Pabst reflected on how Hollywood had compromised his authorial endeavors in an essay of 1937, "Servitude et grandeur à Hollywood."

48. Compare Edgardo Cozarinsky, "Foreign Filmmakers in France," in *Rediscovering French Film,* ed. Mary Lea Bandy (New York: Museum of Modern Art, 1983), 140: "Though Jacques Ibert's score and Paul Morand's lyrics in *Don Quichotte* dilute into Parisian chic an approach obviously inspired by Brecht and Weill . . . , the 'epic theater' treatment of a selection of episodes from Cervantes suggests a possible reading of the classic that is as unexpected as it is engaging." The epic treatment may well explain the disappointment experienced by critics like Otis Ferguson. See his review of 9 January 1935, reprinted in *The Film Criticism of Otis Ferguson,* ed. Robert Wilson (Philadelphia: Temple University Press, 1971), 64: "As far as such central matters as the dominant idea and its execution are concerned, the picture is a pretty straight flop. A few attitudes, a few big tableaux, and no flowing of one small thing into another."

49. Review in *The Spectator,* 28 July 1939, reprinted in *Graham Greene on Film. Collected Film Criticism 1935-1940,* ed. John Russell Taylor (New York: Simon and Schuster, 1972), 235.

50. Agee's notice appeared on 3 February 1945 in *The Nation.* It is reprinted in *Agee on Film,* 2 vols. (New York: Grosset & Dunlap, 1969), 1: 140.

51. For a lengthy account, see the materials gathered in Atwell, 121-123, including a recollection by Pabst's widow. See as well Boguslaw Drewniak, *Der deutsche Film 1938-1945. Ein Gesamtüberblick* (Düsseldorf: Droste, 1987), 66. Drewniak speaks of Pabst as Nazi Germany's most prominent re-emigrant: "After Pabst's return, the public was astonished. Every reader of the *Philo Lexikon* (Berlin, 1935) knew that the director Pabst was of pure Jewish descent."

52. Michael Pabst related this fact in a recent conversation with Hans-Michael Bock.

53. For more particulars, see Hans-Michael Bock's essay in this volume. For a rather lame attempt to vindicate Pabst's wartime work, see Leo Lania, "In Defense of Pabst," letter in *The New York Times,* 2 April 1950.

54. Atwell, 126. The author's account of the film, here as elsewhere, abounds with infelicities and errors. Renata, Pfefferkorn's daughter, is referred to as "the merchant's wife." Fritz Rasp, the *Magister,* is called the "Schoolmaster" and characterized as "subdued"

(!). The famous publisher Froben becomes "an invalid who is suffering from a leg injury." Atwell goes on to confuse two central scenes, namely the visit of the ailing Ulrich von Hutten to Paracelsus and the fatal treatment of Froben by Paracelsus's assistant. In Atwell, we read: "When Ulrich von Hutten, a prominent citizen [!], is seized by the illness [presumably the plague, but in fact, syphilis, as the film makes clear], Paracelsus administers a potion that momentarily effects a miraculous cure, but when the man dies, Paracelsus is roughly expelled" (127).

55. David Stewart Hull, *Film in the Third Reich* (Berkeley: University of California Press, 1969), 246.

56. Atwell, 135.

57. See Eisner, 329. She describes the persistence of the "mawkish perfection of the 'Ufa style'" above all in the "pseudo-historical film." "It introduces a false note into all the costume film productions made during the Third Reich, from *Jud Süss* (1940) and *Rembrandt* (1942) to Pabst's *Paracelsus* (1943) and Riefenstahl's *Tiefland* (1944)." This style "is still there to mar Pabst's post-Nazi film *Prozess.*"

58. Buache, 94.

59. Amengual, 40. The phrase is meant to describe *Diary of a Lost Girl*; Amengual likens it to Luis Buñuel's Mexican films.

60. These celebrations are ubiquitous in Pabst's work. According to Amengual, they both exalt and condemn eros (35). For an eloquent and expressive account of this motif and its larger significance in the Pabstian corpus, see Amengual, 78ff., esp. 81: "Celebrations, theatrical representations, dreams—few of Pabst's films ignore them. From the spectacle of Frau Greifer among her angels in *Joyless Street,* from the troupe's travels in *Komödianten,* to the cancan in *Mistress of Atlantis* and the café concerts in *Mademoiselle Docteur,* from the *Shanghai Drama,* from Peachum's revolutionary 'masquerade' to Michel Simon's pseudo-suicide in *High and Low,* not to mention the 'opera' diffused by images in *The Threepenny Opera,* love and life reveal themselves to be a universal conspiracy in which each brings its stone without being aware of it, a gigantic machine for conditioning reflexes."

Russell A. Berman (essay date 1993)

SOURCE: Berman, Russell. "A Solidarity of Repression: Pabst and the Proletariat." In *Cultural Studies of Modern Germany: History, Representation, and Nationhood,* pp. 123-33. Madison: The University of Wisconsin Press, 1993.

[*In the following essay, Berman contends that Pabst's allegedly left-wing film Kameradschaft is actually ambivalent on the issue of proletarian liberties.*]

The lesson of Nolde's vicissitudes in Nazi Germany involves the limits of intentionality: the painter's desire to identify with the fascist state was unable to influence the state's rejection of the painter. A similar disjunction operates in the case of Pabst's *Kameradschaft* (1931), one of the most explicitly political films of the late Weimar Republic. For the ostensibly leftist celebration of proletarian solidarity betrays, under scrutiny, a much more ambivalent agenda. True, the final sequence of the film seems to demonstrate unambiguously the establishment of the solidarity promised by the title. The last of the German mine workers, who volunteered to rescue their French comrades trapped in an underground disaster, return to the border after the successful conclusion of the operation. The thronging mass that greets them is in a festive mood, explained by a French worker who leaps onto a platform and, framed by the French and German flags, delivers a rousing speech proclaiming proletarian unity, pacifism, and internationalism. With appropriate symmetry, the German worker who initiated the rescue movement, Wittkopp (Ernst Busch), responds with a parallel address in German: workers are the same everywhere—"Kumpel ist Kumpel"—and will refuse to be pushed into war; even if "the people on top" are caught in disputes, the miners have learned the importance of solidarity and *Kameradschaft.*

Yet despite the uplifting assertions of an international working-class community of interest, what appears to be unambiguously conclusive at the end of the film is in fact open to some considerable doubt. An epilogue (which is missing in the versions generally available in the United States) shows German and French guards in the mine shaft reconstructing the border barrier that had been broken through during the rescue efforts. Several explanations for the omission of this sequence have been offered, ranging from the "derisive howls and hisses from audiences" when it was first screened in Berlin, to objections from German censors. According to Siegfried Kracauer, Pabst intended the coda as a critique of nationalism, but it was misunderstood as an attack on the Treaty of Versailles (as the document which established the postwar boundaries) and therefore very much part of the nationalist agenda.[1]

Whatever the significance of this sequence and its excision, the ideals announced in the double speeches are in fact undermined by more than the epilogue's fiction of a reerected fence. As the epigraph proudly asserts, *Kameradschaft* is "founded on fact," in particular on the factual past of the mine disaster at Courrières in 1906, when German workers did indeed rush to the aid of the trapped French miners. While maintaining a camera style designed to evoke the realist authenticity of a documentary, Pabst shifts the event to the postwar era and to Lorraine—the border runs right through the mine—in order better to stage the issue of national divisions and working-class internationalism. The film is consequently able to produce the message of the final speeches and their optimistic ring. Yet that message rings hollow, as soon as the source of the ostensibly documentary material is taken into account: if the solidarity of 1906 could not prevent 1914, why should

the viewer in 1931 trust an unreflected repetition of that solidarity to prevent a new war?[2] Therefore the ambiguity of *Kameradschaft* is by no means dependent on a subversive epilogue, missing or not, but is rather a consequence of the historical construction of the foregrounded message of solidarity. The concluding ideals turn out to have little plausibility on their own merit, which is to say that *Kameradschaft* has less value as a vehicle of internationalism than as evidence with which to study the failure of internationalisms and the weakness of working-class solidarity on the eve of National Socialism.

In fact, the very manner with which the film attempts to assert its message of solidarity turns out to demonstrate its instability. The lengthy encounter in the mines, so profoundly intense, intimate, and, as will be discussed in a moment, full of sexual and mythic undertones, is seemingly summed up in two sloganeering speeches, as if the public language of political leaders were adequate to articulate a collective identity or a socialist hegemony.[3] The concluding sequence enacts, one might say, a linguistic turn in the much richer analysis carried out by the text, privileging the speech of the cadre over both the preceding material experience, the substance of the extended narrative, and the concrete multiplicity of the assembled workers. Yet speech, to which the film ascribes the power to assert the identity of comradeship, turns out to be inadequate, as Wittkopp is forced to announce at the commencement of his address: "What the French comrade said, I could not understand; what he meant, we could all understand." Thus even in the context of this political speech, which announces the self-evident socialist message of the film, speech itself is presented as insufficient and relegated to a secondary status vis-à-vis a more effective mode of expression—*meinen* rather than *sagen*—and the construction of the collective is thereby shifted from rational communication into an irrational domain of opinion and a nonverbal semiosis.

This contradiction—Wittkopp's speech insisting on the limits of speech—obviously undermines the plausibility of the solidarity which is the central message of his own speech, i.e., Pabst's proletarian community is stillborn. To the extent that this failure has to do with the structure of language and, in particular, the hierarchical relationship between cadre and collective, the final sequence of *Kameradschaft* could well be contrasted with another document of Franco-German peacemaking, the Strassburg Oath of 842; in the latter case, both the Carolingian leaders and their military followers participate in speech, producing presumably a more complex network of loyalties and collective identities. In contrast, the modern film silences the collectives and permits only the leaders to speak. By presenting two separate speeches, one in French and one in German, it effectively reproduces the national division that the speakers themselves want to deny.

However, the ambiguity of politics in *Kameradschaft* and the failure of Pabst's ideals are not solely a result of this distorted communicative structure at the end of the film.

From its very outset, the film presents a critique of nationalism that never thoroughly measures up to the values of pacifism and socialism that are so urgently underscored. *Kameradschaft* begins with a game between two boys, one German and one French; the opening shot shows a marble rolling across the ground. Through a montage of editing, the boys, who quickly begin to quarrel, are set in relation to tensions between France and Germany along the border in the context of the growing German unemployment. The point of the gaming commencement is, however, not simply that adults are behaving like children but, more important, the suggestion that the wrong game is being played since the aleatory moment of free play, the rolling marble, has been displaced by an inappropriate game of agonistic embattlement.

The gaming that follows in the film is exclusively agonistic: the muted class struggle between workers and management; the heroic struggle with nature; and, especially, the reminiscence of the wartime struggle in the single flashback of the movie. Even aspects of the celebrated solidarity are tied closely to images of combat: the procession of the German rescuers leaving their town recalls soldiers leaving for war, they have to smash through the border and survive a volley of shots, and when they arrive at the gates of the French mine they are initially mistaken for troops. The images of comity depend ultimately on an iconography of enmity, since the body of the film presents no alternative to a confrontational agonistics, i.e., the struggle with the national enemy—which is ostensibly rejected—is preserved in the militarization of the vocabulary of solidarity and is displaced into another terrain of struggle: interestingly, less the struggle with another class than the struggle to master a threatening nature.

None of these permutations returns to the utopian moment of aleatory play with which the film opened, the rolling marble; nothing has retracted the fall into agonistics, and the film's initial problem, the need to return to a nonrepressive *homo ludens,* is never solved.[4] Clearly the solidarity envisioned by the film is not a solution, since it is very much implicated in processes of struggle and mastery, despite the rosy rhetoric of the concluding speeches. Given this discrepancy between the end of the cinematic text with its message of socialist harmony and the opening assertion of an ontology of struggle and repression, it is crucial to pay close attention to the nature of the social bonds represented in the course of the film and not only to the terms of the social contract announced at its conclusion. Is the comradeship of *Kameradschaft* a matter less of a pacifist internationalism than a comradeship-in-arms of men conquering nature? What are the grounds for the collective identity of the workers? If it is true that the proletariat has no fatherland and, as Wittkopp puts it, all the workers are the same—"Kumpel ist Kumpel"—then one has to ask what force holds the community of comrades together.

A likely answer is some considerable homosocial attraction: the decision to launch the rescue expedition is made as part of a spectacular shower room sequence replete with glistening nude male bodies, and a fight with a delirious French miner (who has succumbed to the haunting memories of the war) concludes when the victorious German affectionately strokes the cheek of his now unconscious and prostrate opponent. Yet more important than these examples of an ostensible male eroticism, extensive evidence points to the exclusion of women as a crucial aspect of the construction of the male collective.[5]

The point is not that there are no women working in the mines (that, presumably, is a moment of verisimilitude in the film) but that both the German and French miners, all men, are constructed as groups from whom women have been emphatically separated. Phrased another way, the separation which has been caused by women can be healed only when the women are separated away and the men come together in the dark, deep inside the earth. The origin of this problematic is the dance-hall scene which follows immediately on the initial exposition. Three German miners enter the music-filled *Kursaal* on the French side of the border. The film cuts to an attractive young couple, Emile and Françoise, dancing with obvious affection for each other. When one of the Germans asks her for a dance, she refuses, which is taken for a nationalist affront, and a melee is only narrowly avoided when the German withdraws from the woman.

This separation of a male collective from a female sphere is repeated on the French side as well. On their way home, the couple overhears an engineer commenting on the fire in the mine; Françoise insists that Emile give up his job, and when he refuses, she decides to leave. The following morning, we see Emile enter the mine, and Françoise departs on a train just as the disaster strikes. By now, however, a network of sexual imagery has become apparent: Emile chooses the fire in the phallic mine shaft over Françoise's female sexuality, just as the three Germans retreat from Françoise into the conviviality of an infantile eroticism (one of his companions pleads with the rejected suitor to "leave the women alone and come back to the rabbit," a reference to the pet they have inexplicably brought with them: an indication of both childishness and genital renunciation, since the alternative to the woman is the genderless neuter of the *Kaninchen*). Furthermore Françoise's path back to the mining town is marked first by her abandonment of her suitcase—a sign perhaps of her renunciation of an independent life but certainly for Freud a standard symbol of female genitalia.[6] This latter association is confirmed by the fact that Françoise proceeds back to the mine by taking a ride with a nun, an incontrovertible indication of the denial of female sexuality.

The underlying sexual economy turns out to be one in which male solidarity is produced in response to a threat by women (the encounter in the dance hall) and is preserved through the negation and subordination of women (Emile prefers the mine to Françoise). Precisely this logic is played out outside the gates of the mine. In the belief that the mine management has prematurely given up the search for the buried workers, the crowd, composed mainly of women and led by Françoise, tries to storm the gates. Françoise is in the front of the surging mass and is shot in a slightly elevated position, calling to those behind her, not unlike the famous iconography of the figure of the revolutionary *Liberté*. Yet just at this moment of radical confrontation, the German rescue company arrives with all its military demeanor. This unexpected turn of events quiets the crowd and bewilders Françoise, who can only mutter, "Les Allemands, c'est pas possible."

Even the moment of rescue, therefore, is constructed through the ostentatious displacement of women: instead of the radical crowd led by the female allegory of liberty, the heroic role is reserved for the uniformed German volunteers, fresh from the showers. The price of the male bonding turns out to be a simultaneous displacement of a radical alternative—the impassioned crowd led by Françoise—by a more disciplined and hierarchical group. Excluded from the male discipline of the socialist organization, the anarchic energy of the unruly mass presumably could eventually be occupied by antisocialist, especially fascist movements that more effectively articulated values of spontaneity and a populist antipatriarchy.[7] It follows then that the apparent shallowness of the ideals of *Kameradschaft* and the weakness of working-class solidarity had to do with the implicit misogyny in the symbolism and political practice of the working-class movement. To the extent that the collective of proletarian solidarity was de facto a matter of male bonding, it could not be a radical one. On the contrary, this reading of the film should show how, despite the rhetoric of socialist revolution, such male bonding was implicated in an establishmentarian defense of the status quo from a putative female threat—the threat at the borders, the imminence of separation and castration—and the need to sublate the wound in the healing collective of a male whole.

These sexual politics of the community are explored in the overriding iconographic concern: the construction of identity through the establishment of division and the anxiety over an impending disruption of the border. At the outset, the borders are of course treated as evidence of unnecessary enmity and belligerence: the border drawn between the two children or blocking the passage of the unemployed workers. These images are obviously fully compatible with the message of internationalism illustrated by the German miners' breaking through the underground wall marking the 1919 border. Yet the miners are not the only force to break through walls: the catastrophe first appears as the eruption of a flaming explosion tearing through the brick containment wall and setting off the collapse of the sides of a mine shaft. Masses of stones, flooding water, and impenetrable smoke pour into various frames, obscuring the images of the figures and threatening their lives. So despite the different evaluations of a positive socialist internationalism and a murderously brute force of nature, both appear on the screen as the activity of masses challenging borders. *Kameradschaft*'s judgment of the mass is therefore intriguingly ambivalent. Proletarian solidarity is applauded as an alternative to the divisiveness of national borders, but the homologous power of the elements, breaking down the divisions erected by technology, is portrayed as the ultimate danger.

The radical crowd storming the gates of the mine can arguably be associated with a position of class struggle: the enemy is the owner or, at least, the manager. The genuine lesson of the film, however, is a different one: workers of the world unite, not in a struggle with the bourgeoisie but in a struggle to control nature. The ambivalent portrayals of the sublime mass—never-ending solidarity and the infinite elements—are resolved to the extent that the film sets the two against each other: proletarian solidarity of the masses overcoming the threat of the masses of the elements. The pacifist theme provides an excuse to redirect an initial aggression pointed at a foreign enemy (across the national border) toward nature in the form of technological mastery.

Yet this redirection of aggression is also an introversion; the mass (of workers) is turned against the mass (of nature), and one is forced to ask to what extent it is in effect turned against itself. Is the conquest of nature, which the film portrays as a struggle with external nature, in fact a displacement of a repression of an internal nature? *Kameradschaft* explores the viability of mechanisms to control the masses, who appear in their full spontaneity at the moment of catastrophe. As the train carrying Françoise pulls out of the station, the alarm whistle sounds at the mine, and suddenly, in a series of shots, the otherwise placid pedestrians of the city break into a frantic run. This sudden transformation is the genuine crisis of the film: the crowd is born, perhaps the only convincing echo of the aleatory chaos of the game of marbles, and the film suggests several competing analyses of this origin—the moment of terror that disrupts the petit bourgeois routine of everyday life as well as the undeniable concern and compassion for the endangered workers.

However, one shot in particular is crucial, showing the panicked crowd rushing off but reflected in a store window displaying a series of indistinguishable caps. If there is a radical moment in *Kameradschaft,* this is it, although it is not the moral intended by Pabst. The shot sets up a relationship between, on the one hand, a commodified culture—the exhibition of wares—whose ultimate product, however, is the spectacle, the reflection in the window, and, on the other, the emergence of the crowd. Yet this crowd of consumers, *flaneurs,* and dislocated individuals has the propensity to explode in the spontaneous combustion of a Luxemburgian anarchy, culminating in the riot at the mine gate.[8] This radical threat to the society of commodities is averted by the discipline of a male socialism that arrives in the nick of time to save the capitalist organization. Proletarian solidarity appears to be a version of crowd control. The mass is turned against the mass, and this self-negation unfolds in two different ways: the sequences within the mine, representing an effort to master nature, are both a metaphor for the repression of the masses outside the gates and a displacement of the control of an internal nature necessary for the establishment of the promised comradeship.

While the displacement of the radical crowd is an important indication of the political underbelly of socialist solidarity, the film ultimately places greater emphasis on the second trajectory of self-negation, the instinctual archeology of the male bond. The workers conquer nature and thereby conquer themselves. This dialectic of technological progress is staged in a primitive setting, with man pitted against elementary forces of fire and water gushing through elongated shafts. *Kameradschaft* therefore seems to display some remarkable similarity with Freud's reading of the myth of Prometheus. Both explore the libidinal economy of technology, and both pose the problem in terms of male collectives mastering fire (both, by the way, are works of 1931). Most important, however, is the shared recognition of a homoerotic or homosocial foundation for the technological community of men.

Freud begins his comments on the myth with a consideration of the hollow stick in which Prometheus transports the fire; he interprets it as a penis symbol with reference to the oneiric rhetoric of inversion: "What a man harbours in his penis-tube is not fire. On the contrary, it is the means of *quenching* fire; it is the water of his stream of urine." By associating fire furthermore with the heat of erotic desire, Freud can suggest "that to primal man the attempt to quench fire with his own water had the meaning of a pleasurable struggle with another phallus."[9] The elementary ambivalence of fire and water is clearly present in the iconography of the catastrophe in *Kameradschaft*: both push through the shaft, presumably a threatening resurgence of libidinal energy which it is the labor of the film to master in the interest of civilization and technological progress.

As for Freud, the film too suggests that this progress requires a reorganization of homoeroticism, i.e., a renunciation of the pleasurable play with another phallus and the consequent establishment of a homosocial community: the handclasp of the German and French rescuers in the darkness of the mine. Simultaneously this male community of self-repression can itself function as a mechanism of repression vis-à-vis the threat of the female crowd. Yet in Freud's reading the myth also preserves a knowledge of the costs of progress and the suffering caused by repression: Prometheus' deed is a crime for which he is punished, that is, the crime against nature inherent in any denial of libido. On this point, the film diverges markedly: the conquest of nature, internal and external, is presented as unambiguously positive, and suffering is relegated to a past characterized as lacking adequate control. This refusal to identify and critique the experience of repression means that, for all its progressive self-presentation, *Kameradschaft* boils down to a lesson in discipline and self-control. This conservative apology for civilizational repression belies the socialist aspirations of the film's conclusion and is an important symptom of the sort of weakness that prevented the working-class movement from mounting a plausible response to the challenge of an antirationalist fascism.

The negativity that adheres to the Promethean myth, which insists on the criminal and even blasphemous character of progress, is preserved in classical psychoanalysis as the notion of a necessary discontent in civilization. Historical development has been paid for with an enormously painful repression and instinctual denial: in particular, Freud discusses the sublimation of homoeroticism in the taming of fire as the initiation of technology.[10] That same process of libidinal repression is staged in *Kameradschaft* which, however, refuses to treat repression as an object of criticism. Instead repression, denial, discipline, and technological progress are celebrated and presented as unambiguously positive. One consequence of this affirmative stance is the extraordinarily timid character of the political message, a strangely meek socialism without class struggle, as if the excessive repression of nature robbed the movement of any real spunk.

A second consequence is the importance of technology, which overshadows any vestigial romanticism of the worker as producer, and the crucial technology for *Kameradschaft* is ultimately the film itself. The anxiety about borders which the film thematizes is no doubt a consequence of the relatively new use of the moving camera, which was so central to Pabst's exploration of a realist cinema. Despite the considerable editing and montage in the film, innovative camera movement contributed to a redefinition of the frame of the shot, and, as Noel Carroll has commented, "The feeling engendered is that the cameraman is pursuing an unstaged action, shifting his point of view as the event develops. . . . Throughout the film, camera movement has the look of following the action rather than delimiting it."[11] This spontaneity and movement, however, like the obliteration of the borders within the film, set off a crisis: the organization of space has gone out of control, and in both cases, the formal construction of the film and the content of its narrative, the answer to the crisis is technological progress, in particular the technology of the sound film.

Sound, and not proletarian solidarity, is arguably the real hero of *Kameradschaft.* The sound of the factory whistle calls the workers, and the alarm siren announces the disaster. Pabst uses sound to indicate explosions taking place elsewhere than in a particular shot, and Françoise and Emile can overhear, without seeing, a conversation regarding the underground fire. More important, certainly, is the role of sound in the rescue operation, when a stranded French miner attracts the attention of a German volunteer by banging on a metal pipe with his wrench. Finally the intended message of the film is presented in the concluding oratorical performances of the double speeches.

The central role of sound—in 1931 still very much a new technology—is in fact announced in the film itself in a way that indicates its complicity in the network of sexual politics and repression. Renouncing her plans for independence, Françoise rushes back to the site of the mine disaster by hitching a ride with a nun; the imagery of sexual denial has already been mentioned. When asked if she has a relative in the mine, Françoise replies, "my brother," then pauses, and adds, "son ami," his friend, i.e., not her own friend or lover, but her brother's colleague. This reply is compatible with the analysis of the construction of the homoerotic collective. Yet the pause in the middle of the phrase draws attention to another ambiguity: the ambiguity not of the relationship but of the phoneme itself, which can be taken either as a possessive adjective or as an independent noun, in which case "son, ami" turns into "sound, friend." In this version, then, Françoise's cryptic answer identifies the mine less as the locus of male solidarity than as the site of an innovation having to do with the technological reproduction of acoustic phenomena.

This account might well appear plausible if one keeps in mind the uses of sound already enumerated. It turns out to be irresistible if one reexamines the final rescue episode, which can be treated as the climax of the film. The three Germans from the dance-hall sequence did not join the rescue crew, but instead set off on their own to dig their way through from the German side of the mine to the French side, where they eventually end up trapped together with two French men, a young miner and his grandfather. Finding their escape route blocked, they give up all hope, and one of the Germans comments, "Well, we'll take the electric tram to heaven," at which point a telephone rings; earlier shots have indicated that a telephone operator in the mine office has been trying to determine if and where anyone was still caught below, i.e., the five remaining victims have literally been saved by the bell or, in other words, by friend sound, the electric tram to heaven.

Friend sound, "son, ami," is electrically reproduced sound, itself the technological innovation of *Kameradschaft* as well as the result of the technological progress which *Kameradschaft* records: the control of fire. Although the film refuses to explore the dialectic inherent in the mastery of nature, it does in fact draw attention to alternative appropriations of technology. The telephone, which is the actual agent of rescue, has already made a number of appearances in the film: forced to allow his employees to set off on their rescue expedition, the manager of the German mine rings up his French opposite number and suggests that he deserves credit for what was in fact an act of spontaneous solidarity; and when the German workers crash across the French border, the border guards call ahead. That is, in the two earlier cases, the telephone, as a cipher of the new technology of acoustic reproduction, is deeply involved in the structures of control and domination, while in the final sequence it works as a tool of emancipation.

This investigation of the technologically most advanced means of communication is located within a historical theory of the media. Like many texts of the Weimar period, *Kameradschaft* suggests that a culture of verbal literacy—individual reading in a bourgeois private sphere—belongs to an increasingly distant past. The metaphor for such anachronistic reading, indeed the only text genuinely "read" in the course of the film, is a poster on the wall outside of the dance hall; in addition, a thermometer em-

bedded in a containment wall is read just before the explosion occurs. The location of reading on exterior walls is indicative of the dissolution of traditional bourgeois notions of privacy (a development underscored by the single shot of a domestic interior in the center of which one sees the gaping speaker of a victrola for the reproduction of sound). The insistence on the writing on the wall is moreover evidence of the proximity of an impending catastrophe, since *Kameradschaft* is so much about the tumbling down of walls and, therefore, the obsolescence of an older media culture.

The catastrophe is the explosion of the masses: the masses of commodities in the shop window, the masses of the crowd, and the masses of a threatening nature. *Kameradschaft* describes an inadequate response by tracing the journey of the grandfather who sneaks into the mine and searches on his own for his beloved grandson. With little equipment, he signifies a technologically backward mode of operation; with his tiny lamp in the cavernous darkness, all he can do is light up the imagery, take shots, so to speak, but his abilities, a metaphor for the silent film, prove insufficient for the task at hand. Only with the successful and collective repression of nature, the conquest of fire, and its metamorphosis into the electricity of the telephone can the project of retrieval be completed.

The success of that project and the recognition of the potentially progressive use of technology do not fully obscure the simultaneous regressive potential, i.e., the manipulative use of the new technology. Nevertheless *Kameradschaft,* with its unbroken historical optimism, indisputably emphasizes the positive developments, just as it fully conceals the pain and suffering of the *via dolorosa* of progress. As an analysis of a profound restructuring of the organization of the media, it therefore too naively insists on the beneficial role of the electric reproduction of sound. The telephone as a tram to heaven does not only anticipate the role of sound in subsequent cinematic realism, including Pabst's own; it also prefigures the use of sound in propaganda and the function of the radio in National Socialist Germany. *Kameradschaft,* like much of the contemporary workers' movement, fails to understand that a solidarity based on repression cannot be progressive and that technology as a blind domination of nature is bound to prevent solidarity.

Notes

1. "A Mine Disaster," *New York Times,* November 9, 1932; Lee Atwell, *G. Pabst* (Boston: Twayne, 1977), 101; Siegfried Kracauer, *From Caligari to Hitler: A Psychological History of the German Film* (Princeton: Princeton University Press, 1971) 240.

2. "As the film stands now, to accept the accord which effected the rescue as permanent in proletarian fraternity would be a delusive irony, especially when we recall that the actual event at Courrières did not prevent that war of 1914." Harry Alan Potamkin, "Pabst and the Social Film," in *Horn and Hounds,* January-

March, 1933, 303. Cf. "Kameradschaft," in *Deutsche Filmzeitung,* no. 51/52 (1931): 14-16, rpt. in *Erobert den Film!* (Berlin: Neue Gesellschaft für bildende Kunst, 1977), 171.

3. Cf. the discussion of politics and language in Ernesto Laclau and Chantal Mouffe, *Hegemony and Socialist Strategy: Towards a Radical Democratic Politics* (London: Verso, 1985).

4. Cf. Nancy Webb-Kelly, *Homo Ludens, Homo Aestheticus: The Transformation of "Free Play" in the Rise of Literary Criticism,* Diss., Stanford University, 1988.

5. Cf. Michael Rohrwasser, *Saubere Mädel, Starke Genossen: Proletarische Massenliteratur?* (Frankfurt: Roter Stern, 1977); Klaus Theweleit, *Male Fantasies* (Minneapolis: University of Minnesota Press, 1987).

6. Sigmund Freud, *The Interpretation of Dreams,* in *The Standard Edition of the Complete Psychological Works,* Vol. 5 (London: Hogarth Press, 1953), 354.

7. Cf. Alice Yaeger Kaplan, *Reproductions of Banality: Fascism, Literature, and French Intellectual Life* (Minneapolis: University of Minnesota Press, 1986), and Peter Brückner et al., "Perspectives on the Fascist Public Sphere," *New German Critique,* no. 11 (Spring 1977):94-132.

8. Cf. Rosa Luxemburg, *Selected Political Writings,* ed. Dick Howard (New York: Monthly Review Press, 1971).

9. Sigmund Freud, "The Acquisition and Control of Fire," *Standard Edition,* Vol. 22 (London: Hogarth Press, 1964), 188, 190.

10. "It is as though primal man had the habit, when he came in contact with fire, of satisfying an infantile desire connected with it, by putting it out with a stream of his urine. The legends that we possess leave no doubt about the originally phallic view taken of tongues of flames as they shoot upwards. Putting out fire by micturating—a theme to which modern giants, Gulliver in Liliput and Rabelais' Gargantua, still hark back—was therefore a kind of sexual act with a male, an enjoyment of sexual potency in a homosexual competition. The first person to renounce this desire and spare the fire was able to carry it off with him and subdue it to his own use. By damping down the fire of his own sexual excitation, he had tamed the natural force of fire. This great cultural conquest was thus the reward for his renunciation of instinct." Sigmund Freud, *Civilization and Its Discontents, Standard Edition,* Vol. 21 (London: Hogarth Press, 1921), 90.

11. Noel Carroll, "Lang, Pabst, and Sound," *Cine-Tracte* 2, no. 1 (1978):22.

Ira Konigsberg (essay date fall 1995)

SOURCE: Konigsberg, Ira. "Cinema, Psychoanalysis, and Hermeneutics: G. W. Pabst's *Secrets of a Soul.*" *Michigan Quarterly Review* 34, no. 4 (fall 1995): 519-47.

[*In the following essay, Konigsberg examines* Secrets of the Soul *in the context of films that feature psychoanalysts as either saviors or demons.*]

In the 1948 film *The Snake Pit,* a psychiatrist (played by Leo Genn) has a long therapeutic session with a patient (played by Olivia de Havilland) in which he slowly opens up to her two earlier traumas that have resulted in her nervous breakdown and incarceration in a mental institution. A photograph of Sigmund Freud prominently appears on the wall behind them throughout much of the scene. *The Snake Pit* was Hollywood's fifth highest box-office success for the year and earned an impressive list of Academy Award nominations. Freud and psychoanalysis have on occasion been good box office and have also been treated with a certain amount of reverence in commercial cinema. We should remember that many Hollywood film-makers were under the influence of psychoanalysts at the time, an influence evident in the many films of the 1950s and 1960s that employ psychotherapists, and here I mean both analysts and nonanalysts, as an important and positive element in their plots. One looks back with nostalgia to a time when psychotherapists were not fools like Richard Dreyfuss in *What About Bob* (1991), lovesick fools like Dudley Moore in *Lovesick* (1983), corrupt lovesick fools like Richard Gere in *Final Analysis* (1991), or cannibals like Anthony Hopkins in *The Silence of the Lambs* (1991).

Psychotherapists were certainly portrayed as comic or horrific figures in earlier films, but they were also treated with a good deal more respect than in recent years. The number of relatively high-profile films during the past decade with depraved, demented, dysfunctional, or simply incompetent therapists, however, seems to be making a statement—a statement, perhaps, about the way psychotherapy is currently perceived in the public mind. Psychotherapists are receiving their share of abuse in film along with other professional types like lawyers or doctors—there has always been a democratic undercurrent of disdain for authority figures in our popular culture (more so, I might add, than for our wealthy class) and the times are ripe for disdaining authority. But we are talking about the movies, a popular art form that establishes a historical context and a set of conventions in which professional types are caught: for example, Richard Gere's role as the duped psychotherapist is certainly a spinoff from William Hurt's performance as the incompetent lawyer in *Body Heat* (1981). Hannibal Lecter in *The Silence of the Lambs* is the modern equivalent of the deranged scientist or doctor in the earlier horror film—only in this case we have moved from the attempts of the earlier figure to control the human body to an attempt to control the mind, from Dr. Frankenstein putting together the parts of dead bodies to Hannibal disassembling the layers of the human psyche. His cannibalism is a metaphor for his wish to devour the mind of the heroine—he is our culture's ultimate depiction of the "shrink."

These contemporary portrayals of the "shrink" in cinema may also be a defensive reaction of our culture against the truth that our time is in considerable need of psychotherapy, that the psychotherapist potentially carries significant power. An important essay by Claude Lévi-Strauss, "The Sorcerer and his Magic," demonstrates apparent differences and interesting correspondences between the shamans of primitive cultures and the psychoanalyst in ours, especially in their role of causing a "conversion" in an individual and thus integrating his or her "contradictory elements" into more acceptable "systems of reference" (178). I would like to take this parallel in another direction and add to the shaman and psychoanalyst such figures from a variety of cultures as the psychotherapist in general, the witch doctor, the alchemist, the priest, the artist, and the scientist, and claim that they all perform a similar role in the popular minds of their respective cultures, acting as both an intermediary and a transitional object between this world and another, between everyday reality and some other type of reality, between the known and the unknown. *The Exorcist* (1973) combines the priest and psychiatrist in the figure of Father Karas. In such films as *The Cabinet of Dr. Caligari* (1919), *I Was a Teenage Werewolf* (1957), *Dressed to Kill* (1980), *The Howling* (1981), *Manhunter* (1986), and *The Silence of the Lambs,* the psychiatrist becomes a focal point for the fears and terrors we associate with unknown worlds, but, interestingly, none of these figures are analysts.

The 1926 silent film *Secrets of a Soul*[1] is the first of a different group of films in which the psychoanalyst specifically becomes our savior from such fears and terrors. I am referring to a group of salvational films in which Freud hovers in the background—in one version of *Secrets of a Soul* a portrait of Freud appears on the screen after the opening titles that praise his contributions[2]—in which psychiatry and psychotherapy are considerably influenced by psychoanalysis, in which the unconscious and the methodology of psychoanalysis that discloses that unconscious are treated with reverence and fascination.[3] I shall mention as examples four films in this category after the Pabst film: Alfred Hitchcock's *Spellbound* in 1945, a film that in spite of all its outrages finds most of its suspense and twists of plot in the unconscious mind of its hero and that brings the surrealistic images of Salvador Dali to its dream sequence; *Mine Own Executioner,* a British film about a lay analyst that appeared in 1947 and that has been totally forgotten;[4] *The Snake Pit* in 1948; John Huston's well-intentioned if misguided *Freud* in 1962 that focuses on the great man's early life and theories. We might do better to concentrate on these films than the counter-transference films in which we have met the enemy, who also happens to be a psychotherapist, and he is us. Aggression and violence have generally been film's particular forte, satisfying the public's id as a type of socially acceptable pornography; and films about psychotherapy have been quick to tap into film's romance with violence, to exploit and explore the death instinct more than other aspects of the psyche in order to satisfy the audience's vicarious taste for thrills. Though some of the salvational films fall into this vast category, all of them present the analyst not as the perpetrator of violence but as our savior from self-destructive impulses.

The opening titles to *Secrets of A Soul* immediately identify the film as salvational in nature while also placing it in a historical context.

> In everyone's life, there are desires and passions that remain unknown to our conscious minds. In dark hours of emotional conflict, such unconscious drives try to assert themselves. Such struggles engender mysterious illnesses, the explanation and healing of which are the professional province of psychoanalysis. The teachings of university professor Dr. Sigmund Freud signify an important development in the training of doctors schooled in psychoanalysis who treat such emotional illnesses.[5]

Freud's relation to *Secrets of a Soul* was cautious.[6] Ernest Jones in his biography of Freud relates that Samuel Goldwyn, "the well-known film director [*sic*], approached Freud with an offer of $100,000 if he would cooperate in making a film depicting scenes from the famous love stories of history, beginning with Antony and Cleopatra." Jones tells us that Freud was "amused" at Goldwyn's "ingenious way of exploiting the association between psychoanalysis and love," but declined the offer. Jones goes on to describe how Hans Neumann approached Karl Abraham about consultation for a film to be made by Germany's famous UFA film company concerning "the mechanisms of psychoanalysis" (114). Abraham wrote Freud about the offer on 7 June 1925, stating that the film company wanted Freud's authorization and that Abraham himself was to make suggestions on behalf of Freud's colleagues. He also mentioned a "comprehensible and non-scientific pamphlet on psychoanalysis" that he was to write and that would be published in conjunction with the film. Abraham argued for the project on the basis that it would be better to have such a film supervised by those in the know than any of "the wild analysts in Berlin" and also mentioned the possibility of publishing the pamphlet through their psychoanalytic press, the *Verlag,* and thus helping its fortunes (382-83). Freud's reactions were not at all positive, and his comments on film and psychoanalysis have been quoted many times over: "My chief objection is still that I do not believe that satisfactory plastic representation of our abstractions is at all possible." His following remark is also worth quoting: "We do not want to give our consent to anything insipid. Mr. Goldwyn was at any rate clever enough to stick to the aspect of our subject that can be plastically represented very well, that is to say, love." Freud went on to say that since Abraham seemed "not disinclined to engage in the matter," they should both wait and see if the script was good, and, if so, he would later give his authorization, though he preferred not to have his name associated with the project at all (384).

Hanns Sachs worked with Abraham as a consultant on the film and ultimately became the chief advisor when Abraham withdrew because of ill health. Both Abraham and Sachs are designated as "fellow workers" on the cover of the screenplay, with Colin Ross and Hans Neumann listed as writers.[7] The title page reads, *The Secrets of the Soul, A Psychoanalytical Film Project,* followed by *Part Two: The Secret of a Soul, A Psychoanalytical Chamberplay.* It seems unlikely that part one refers to the pamphlet that was to be written, since that publication was to be an exegesis of the film itself. One can only wonder at this time about the overall scope of the project originally intended. At some point in late summer or early fall of 1925, G. W. Pabst became the director of the film—Pabst had recently directed **Joyless Street,** certainly the most famous of the German street films and a work that shows Pabst extending his expressionistic film technique into the realm of realistic social problems. *Secrets of a Soul* was his fourth film and demonstrates a logical solution to the tension in his earlier work between expressionism and naturalism by using the former technique for the dream and memory sequences and the latter for the events taking place in the conscious, everyday world. The husband in the film is played by Werner Krauss, who played the role of the psychiatrist Dr. Caligari in the first German expressionist film, *The Cabinet of Dr. Caligari*—recall that in the interior story he is a mad doctor who controls the mind and actions of the somnambulist Cesare and in the frame story he appears to be the kind and healing figure who is about to bring Francis back to sanity, both roles indicative of the ambiguous psychiatrist in future film. There is some irony and perhaps some significance in the fact that the first major psychiatrist and first actual analysand in cinema were played by the same actor. The role of the analyst in *Secrets of a Soul,* Dr. Charles Orth, was played by Pavel Pavlov, an actor from the Moscow Art Theater who spoke only Russian and at first knew nothing about psychoanalysis.

Jones tells us that Freud later complained to Abraham that "the film company were announcing without his consent, that the film was being made and presented 'with Freud's cooperation'" (114). Indeed, *Time* magazine in this country even stated that "every foot of the film . . . will be planned and scrutinized by Dr. Freud." Abraham became upset at attempts by A. S. Storfer, director of the *Verlag,* and Siegfried Bernfeld to sell a script for another psychoanalytic film. But Sachs clearly became central in the making of *Secrets of a Soul* and wrote the short monograph on the film called *Psychoanalysis: Riddle of the Unconscious,*[8] which was intended as an explanation of some basic psychoanalytic concepts and as an explication of the film. The film was screened at a psychoanalytic congress held in Berlin to celebrate Freud's seventieth birthday in 1926 and was well received after its opening in Europe and the United States.

Freud's prejudice against cinema is curious, especially since his theories and the film medium were born at virtually the same time and both offered entries into the human mind. At the end of *The Interpretation of Dreams,* Freud compares the psyche "to a compound microscope or photographic apparatus, or something of the kind [in which] . . . psychical locality will correspond to a point inside that apparatus at which one of the preliminary stages of an image comes into being" (V. 5, 536); yet in his "A Note Upon the Mystic Writing Pad" (1925),[9] some twenty-five years later and published only a year before the appearance of *Secrets of a Soul,* when he again seems to be in earnest search for some kind of apparatus that will act as a metaphor for the operations of the mind, he rejects devices such as the "photographic camera" because they cannot receive new impressions while holding onto memory traces of earlier perceptions. The writing pad with its thin plastic layer on top of a wax base seems a much better representative of the mental process he wishes to suggest. It is interesting to speculate why Freud was so resistant to the film medium and its potential for dealing with the human mind, especially since this is the direction that some of the earliest theorizing on film was to take. Perhaps his distrust was due to the newness of the medium in general and its appeal to a wide public—there has always been a certain vulgarity associated with film because of its popularity, its tendency to simplify human nature, and its exploitative appeal to the audience's less civilized emotions. But, ironically, was not this dark, emotional world the very landscape of the human psyche that Freud himself explored, and was not this the reason for Goldwyn's offer to him? Freud might also have been resistant to film because he was still unaware of its imagistic potential, its capacity to use superimpositions, split screens, dissolves, models, matting shots and other special effects to create a mental time and space, as it was to do in *Secrets of a Soul.*

Ten years before the appearance of *Secrets of a Soul,* Hugo Münsterberg, a German psychologist teaching at Harvard, published *The Photoplay: A Psychological Study,* a significant attempt to show the correspondence of film to the human mind, at least in its conscious aspects:[10] "We recognize that in every case the objective world of outer events had been shaped and molded until it became adjusted to the subjective movements of the mind. The mind develops memory ideas and imaginative ideas; in the moving picture they become reality" (58). As early as 1916, someone is noticing how the motion picture, with its use of close-ups, flashbacks and flashforwards, and movement in space "obeys the laws of the mind rather than those of the outer world" (41). At the same time as the production of *Secrets of a Soul* in Germany, a group of avant-garde filmmakers in France was beginning to use film as an expression of the unconscious. Although we can find various theoreticians in later years discussing film as a psychological art form, the most significant advance in this direction took place in the 1960s, especially with the writing of Jean-Louis Baudry and Christian Metz in France. Baudry and Metz were influential in laying upon film theory the burden of Jacques Lacan and his concept of the mirror phase, but they are especially interesting in their use of Freud to explicate the viewer's response to the film medium. The relation between film and dream has often been suggested in film theory, but Baudry and Metz are the first writers to make the correspondence seem convincing. I have no time to go into the analogy but let me say that sitting in a darkened area, passive in an immobile state, with images appearing before their consciousness, viewers loosen their hold on reality and undergo a type of regressive experience that puts them in a state akin to that of dreaming and day-dreaming. The fact that the images themselves are signifiers without any reality, are a two-dimensional imprint of a world that does not exist in reality, reminds us of the images of our dreams that also have no actuality. The crucial mechanism here is the way, in a state of reverie, we project our fantasies into the images on the screen, the way in which our fantasies interact with those on the screen so that what we see seems to emanate from ourselves, just the way the dream images are a creation of our own psyches.

If viewing a film is akin to the dream experience, if the special power of film is to give presence to a fantasy world, a film such as *Secrets of A Soul,* which offers a dream as a central portion of its narrative, is creating for us the experience of viewing a dream within a dream. Just as the play within the play discloses some hidden truth about what takes place in the outer world of the literary text, so does the dream within the film, itself experienced as a dream, disclose a similar hidden truth about the world that surrounds it. Freud comments that "What is dreamt in a dream after waking from the 'dream within the dream' is what the dream-wish seeks to put in the place of an obliterated reality. It is safe to suppose, therefore, that what has been 'dreamt' in the dream is a representation of the reality, the true recollection, while the continuation of the dream, on the contrary, merely represents what the dreamer wishes" (338). Freud's point is that the inner dream discloses some reality, some truth that the outer dream hides. *Secrets of a Soul,* therefore, indicates that films about psychoanalysis, and psychoanalysis itself in its reading and use of dreams, function according to already-established practices and rules of narrative art and are influenced by the same basic strategies of interpretation.

Psychoanalysis in general functions according to methodologies similar to those we use when analyzing both a literary and film text, when we first understand the manifest content while searching for a latent meaning, but when we also put all of our information, manifest and latent, into some type of structure or developmental order.[11] The Russian formalists have given us a set of terms that help us better understand the second part of this interpretive strategy, the "sujet" and the "fabula"—the first term referring to the text in the order that we find it, and the second referring to the text that we both discover and rearrange in our own mind so that we finally have a logically ordered sequence of events that tell the larger story.[12] Interpreting texts according to their "sujet" and "fabula" is close to the analytical method where the material as it is given and then deciphered is put into some type of logical ordering, some kind of cause and effect relationship, some kind of sequence and development that also tells the larger story. I am discussing what in psychoanalytic terms is referred to as "construction" or, more accurately, "reconstruction," concepts that I shall turn to in more detail later in this essay, after we look at Pabst's film and are ready to make some larger cultural generalizations. The most obvious type of narrative text that fits the "sujet/fabula" and "reconstruction" paradigms is the mystery, where the reader or viewer is impelled to discover some hidden events that will explain the present situation, some hidden cause and effect relationship between events, some logical and chronological order that transcends the material as presented. This may explain why psychotherapy is often presented in film in the context of a mystery. In such works there seem to be two mysteries—the mystery involving the external events and the mystery of one of the character's psyches, often some trauma or traumatic event that explains the outer mystery or contributes to its explanation.[13] Indeed, what also takes place in a number of these films is the conflation of both aggressor and victim so that the mysteries we seek to answer are explained by such characters' self-victimizations—so that these characters are, indeed, their own executioners.[14]

Let me specify how most of the psychoanalytic salvational films fit into this general category. In the psychoanalytic films, where the focus is usually on a character's self-victimization, we seem to resolve a mystery about the character that only covers up another mystery; we seem to discover something that answers to the course of present events only to discover that there is another mystery to be answered, another level of psychic events that is a truer explanation of what has taken place—it is as if these films are never satisfied with what they at first explain, as if they are suggesting that the mystery of the mind goes deeper and deeper. In *Mine Own Executioner,* a man nearly strangles his wife and, with the help of his analyst, is able to remember a traumatic experience in which he killed a guard while escaping from a camp for prisoners of war. But while the patient feels grateful that he now understands the buried past that has led to his irrational behavior, the analyst feels that the patient is still dangerous because some earlier traumatic experience remains buried and unrecognized. This other trauma is only hinted at and never fully exposed before the tragic ending of the film. In *The Snake Pit,* the therapist, through the use of truth serum, encourages the patient to remember the car accident that caused the death of her male friend, but immediately we discover some interior, earlier experience, an event when as a young girl she wished for the death of her father just before he actually died.[15] This backward direction of the *sujet* in order to propose the forward direction of a larger *fabula* is most obvious in *Freud,* a work that dramatizes Sigmund Freud's self-analysis and his parallel analysis of the composite character Cecily, showing him pushing further and further into the psyche, back in time, until his discovery of childhood sexuality which is the first step in the development of the oedipal complex that explains his, Cecily's, and our present mental states.

In a curious way, *Secrets of A Soul* satisfies the type of structure I am describing—the mystery behind the mystery, the explanation behind the explanation, the psychic trauma behind the psychic trauma. On the surface, the film's story is quite simple. A husband and wife live together congenially, but are unable to have children. A murder next door and the announced visit of the wife's cousin, a childhood friend of the couple, precipitate in the husband an emotional reaction and strange dream, at the end of which he repeatedly stabs his wife. The actual visit of the cousin and a childhood photograph exacerbate his condition to the point where he is unable to hold a knife because of his fear of stabbing his wife. He undergoes psychoanalysis, while living apart from his wife with his mother, and is finally cured when he and the analyst, with the help of the dream and photograph, trace his present emotional state back to an event in his childhood that caused him to become jealous of his wife's relationship with her cousin. The cousin goes off and the couple go on to parenthood and a happy life. But the explanation that the film puts forth for the husband's knife phobia, for his present irrational actions, cannot possibly be the full reason—the events from the past recounted in the film suggest earlier events that are a truer explanation for the patient's present behavior, though these earlier events are not articulated in the film itself.

The structure of the film indicates the kind of inward movement that I am referring to as a series of frames—of frames within frames. The titles that begin the film, the statement concerning Dr. Sigmund Freud and his teaching as well as Freud's photograph (everything that appears on the screen is part of the film's *sujet* and also part of its fiction) create for us a level of "reality" in which the film's narrative action is to be embedded. The portrait of Freud appears in the Rohauer print of the film, where it is immediately followed by a brief scene showing Dr. Orth writing, "Facts of the case of Martin Fellman, a chemist . . . ," a scene paralleled in the final shots of this version when we see him writing,

> Case History #326
> Martin Fellman
> Illness: Knife Phobia[16]

The framing device of Dr. Orth writing his case history not only encloses the narrative actions in another frame, but also attempts to place them in a larger context of which they are only a part—case #326 means that there have been 325 other cases for this particular psychoanalyst. In this version of the film, then, the narration of the husband, his wife, and her cousin actually begins within two frames, the first, that of Freud and psychoanalysis; the second, that of Dr. Orth and his case histories. But the narrative itself is obviously the frame for the larger and more significant action and imagery of the husband's dream, which itself becomes a frame for the story of the childhood event that led to the dream—and, I wish to argue, this childhood event is only a frame for a deeper configuration and dynamics that we must figure out for ourselves.

The pamphlet that Hanns Sachs wrote as a guide to the film is of help to us now. In this pamphlet Sachs attempts to write a primer concerning psychoanalysis and an explication of the film in psychoanalytic terms. An opening explanation of parapraxis[17] (a misaction like a slip of the tongue or misplacing an object that results from unconscious motives) leads to a discussion of the hero's breaking of the test tube in the film and then an extensive explication of the film, with citations of other examples of parapraxis. Sachs also provides explanations of phobia and compulsion to explain the behavior of the film's protagonist. The central portion of the explication is an analysis of the husband's dream. For the most part Sachs' explication of the film is no more satisfying than the analyst's explication within the film, but Sachs lets us in on the secret of *Secrets of a Soul* toward the end of his pamphlet when he tells us that "Erotic problems, which have been especially important for psychoanalysis, are touched upon at various points but could be clarified only to a certain degree" (29).

A good deal in the film is not clarified. I suppose we can say that even though the film is dealing with a talking cure, the images must speak for themselves, tell us more than the film's titles—logically this must be the case since this is a motion picture and a silent one at that, but more is suggested and hidden in the narrative than in even the most ambiguous and subtle of silent narrative films. The explanation that the husband's desire to kill his wife and the resulting knife phobia are the products of a jealousy that can be traced back to the childhood event in which his wife gave a doll to her cousin might cure the husband in the film, but it hardly satisfies the viewer. I will suggest briefly what I believe the film wants us to interpret for ourselves. When the husband shaves the back of his wife's neck, at the start of the narrative, and then cuts her as the result of a shout of "Murder" from a neighboring house, his act is clearly connected to the actual murder announced by the shout, which, we later learn, was committed with a razor and "prompted by jealousy." His accidental injury of his wife is thus made to suggest his own jealousy and the possibility of his committing some greater violence on her; but it also suggests an act of violence that we cannot yet perceive, one that seems to disturb and threaten the characters in the film. The razor and the gash on the wife's neck suggest from the start that on some still unrecognizable level we are dealing with violent sexuality.

We soon find out that the couple is childless, that their childlessness is the product of their dysfunctional sexual life which we are led to attribute to the husband. There is a telling moment when a little girl, to whom the husband has just given a piece of candy in his laboratory, is told by her mother, "Come, Daddy is waiting for us," as if to indicate to us that the husband is not the little girl's Daddy or a Daddy in general, that Daddy is elsewhere, and that, by not being a Daddy, the husband is still a child. We should note at this point that Daddy is also missing from the interior story of the film, that though the husband's mother is alive, apparently his father is not, and that in his memories of the past, only his mother appears.

The absence of the husband's father allows for the ready identification of the wife's cousin with this figure. The cousin had sent them a statue of Kwanon, the Japanese mother-goddess, with a child in her lap, and a Japanese dagger. The dagger is both phallic and destructive, yet it is important that the statue with which it is associated is a statue of maternity and not fertility. The statue stands for the wife who is potentially a mother and the dagger for the husband's phallic desires but also for the fact that his impotence has murdered life. But we must, of course, relate the dagger to the razor with which he lacerated his wife's neck and see it as a symbol for the rage and destructive impulses that he seems to hold for the woman (and, perhaps, for women in general). The husband slowly pulls the dagger out of its scabbard and then throws it down with repulsion. His later inability to hold either razor or knife, after his dream and the scene the following night when he feels a compulsion to plunge the dagger into his wife's neck, indicates that the razor and knife have become instruments of potential destruction for him personally, in part as instruments of aggression to overcome his own phallic weakness, but also, we begin to surmise, because of his jealousy of his wife and her cousin. But the film is starting to force us to surmise something else, that, on some level, the husband associates his wife and her cousin with his mother and father, and that the razor and dagger represent his own feared punishment of castration by his father for his oedipal wishes for his mother.

Earlier in the film, when the analyst asks the husband why he and his wife cannot have babies, the husband describes to him "wild fantasies" in which he sees himself looking unhappily through some kind of trellis while his erotically clad wife makes love with her cousin. What is constantly hinted at, then, through the film's very apparent suggestion of violence in the interactions of the men and women, in the phallic symbols of the razor and knife, in the female symbol of the slash, in the closed bedrooms and separating doors, is the primal scene and the child's association of violence both with the sexual act performed between the parents, but also the punishment with which he is threatened by the father for sexually desiring his mother. No wonder the husband is unable to consummate his relationship with his wife. In his adult life, he has taken the place of the father by becoming a husband; but in his inhibition to take the place of his father he has taken upon himself a symbolic castration in his inability to have sex with his wife. Thus as castrated husband he also assumes the role of the punished son.

All of this is carefully suggested by the events in the dream, replete with sexual imagery. The large tower, shaped like a penis, for example, that suddenly arises in the middle of the Italian village indicates the sexual nature of the husband's own inadequacy but also the threatening penis of both the cousin and the father whom he represents. The husband's sexual inadequacy and his fear of castration are indicated both by the anxious way in which he rushes up the tower (three times we see the same middle-long shot of him running up the steps on the side of the tall structure), frantically leans out and gestures, and

then drops his hat; and by the faces of three women—his servant, wife, and assistant—superimposed over the tolling bells, laughing at him derisively for his impotence.

The husband's guilt, not only for cutting his wife's neck and for his murderous impulses toward her, but also guilt from early childhood for his feelings toward his mother, lead to a court trial with his father-surrogate, the cousin as prosecutor. The wife bares her neck and points to the slash from her husband's razor. The storm outside melts into the world of his dreams and produces the drum rolls that announce his guilt and his execution but also announce the key sequence of the film.

The husband's laboratory has become his cell; he rushes to the window, lifts himself to the bars, and down below sees a boat with his wife and her cousin. Close-up shots of the husband frantically screaming are interspersed throughout the scene viewed in a high-angle, point-of-view shot from the husband's perspective. His wife catches a doll that is meant to represent a baby and that seems to leap into her arms from the water. She cuddles the baby and then gives it to her cousin, waving to her husband as the boat moves off. The dream ends violently, with the husband, over and over, thrusting the dagger into an image of his wife, thrusting it as if performing a savage act of intercourse. Later, during his therapy, when the analyst tells him that the baby coming from the water signifies "impending" or "desired" birth, the husband has the clue that weakens his defenses and allows him to find the episode in his past that can explain his present phobia and compulsion. The solution he works out falls short of the solution that we are supposed to read into the film, partly because the husband has not realized whose birth he has been witnessing in his dream—that his wife and her cousin as stand-ins for his parents have actually given birth to him,[18] that he has witnessed the primal scene responsible for his own existence, that his screaming throughout the scene has been his screaming as a baby first entering the world, that the savage thrusts of his dagger into his wife were his angry reaction to his parents' copulation and an act of desire for his own mother.

Another psychodynamic element that ought to be noted is the strong attraction that the husband feels for his wife's cousin.[19] I have suggested that in his unconscious, the husband sees in this man the usurping and threatening figure of the father who has taken his mother from him and who threatens him with castration. But though the husband may feel anger toward this man, he is strongly drawn to him. Their embraces are worth noting, but so is that moment when the two meet after so many years and the cousin pats the husband on the stomach, an action that suggests a fond husband patting the swollen belly of his pregnant wife. The screenplay for the film strongly implies that such feelings exist especially for the husband when it describes his nervous tension while he continuously and demonstratively strokes the cousin's face during their greetings. The film, then, very much suggests that part of the husband's problem may also be the strong attraction he feels for his wife's cousin, an attraction that may draw its source from his unconscious identification of this figure with his father—or perhaps I should say unconscious substitution of this figure for his father since the latter never appears in the film nor in the husband's memories. It is conceivable that the husband is also angry with his wife for taking her cousin's affections from him. The child never shakes loose of the attraction it feels for the father, a buried attraction that in the male child leaves a residue of homosexual feelings that can in later years fix on a male replacement for the father.

I shall explain this relationship further in a moment, but first I must turn to the final scene to complete our survey of the work and introduce one more interpretive level. The final scene in *Secrets of A Soul* always reminds me of the penultimate scene of Ingmar Bergman's *Wild Strawberries* (1957). The scene in the later film is dreamed by Isak Borg, but the conclusion of *Secrets* is also dreamlike and unreal. In Bergman's film Isak redreams and revises the primal scene, nay sets it right by fantasizing the pastoral scene in which his parents sit by the lake, his father fishing with a long pole, and wave to him to join them. The film ends with the seventy-six year-old man smiling as he falls into a deep sleep, smiling because he has substituted for his original fantasy of the primal scene this ideal vision which now includes him. The final scene in *Secrets* celebrates the husband's successful psychotherapy by demonstrating that he has overcome his impotence and become a father. He fishes with a long pole in a rich pastoral setting and then rushes to his wife who holds their baby. But the husband's passionate rush to his wife, the fact that he throws his basket of fish into the water, the wavering handheld shot of him as he rushes up the hill suggest another level, another story for us to discover—the husband still acts like a child at the conclusion of the film, acts like he is rushing to his mother.

Although Abraham had written on the oral stage and made an important contribution with his work on oral sadism, I think that the advisors to the film intended us to interpret it largely on an oedipal level; but in dealing so fully with this level of the psyche, they inevitably, though unwittingly, opened up the husband's soul to other levels of interpretation. Immediately before viewing the photographs of himself, his wife, and her cousin, the husband views one of himself and his mother, suggesting, I believe, another subtext in the film and another level to his psychic conflicts. The husband feels both a bonding with and rage for his mother that seem to derive from an earlier time of his childhood than that which we have been discussing. Hanns Sachs, in his pamphlet, describes a scene that appears in the screenplay but in none of the versions of the film now available. Overwhelmed by his compulsion and the feeling that he will never be able to control it, the husband rushes to his laboratory to take poison. About to end his life, his eyes focus on a picture of his mother, and he realizes "that yet another woman plays a role in his life, one with a love that reaches farther back and is deeper than the one which joins him to his wife" (10). Bringing

the picture of his mother to his lips for a parting kiss, he knocks over the bottle of poison and is saved. Sachs means the incident to indicate the saving power of his love for his mother, but this love may also be regressive and paralyzing. In the Rohauer print of the film we read the title, "In mental distress, Martin's mind turned to his mother." Unable to live at home with his wife because of his compulsion to mutilate her with a sharp instrument, the husband goes to live with his mother while he is in therapy. There is an especially impressive scene in which his mother cuts his food before hiding the knife upon his arrival. The husband then sits at the table, eating his meat with a spoon with obvious childish pleasure. A considerable reversal and regression has taken place in his life—in this instance it is his mother who wields the phallic knife and it is the husband who regresses to helpless childhood. The husband's relationship with his mother might also further explain his homosexual feelings for the cousin in a psychoanalytic context. Freud discusses the process whereby young boys with such maternal attachments, after puberty, internalize the mother and identify with her to the point of taking on her love objects. Although he at first suggests that such a process satisfies the boy's narcissism since the love-object becomes a substitute for his childish self, he later argues that the object can also be identified with the mother's other love, the father.[20] I would argue that at the same time that the child feels this excessive love for the mother, he also feels a rage at this dependency and attachment.

Indeed, the husband seems to feel rage at all the women in the film, as we can see in the dream—the derisive laughter of the three women with their heads superimposed upon the tolling bells is an indication of the shame and inadequacy he feels from his relationship with women in general. His behavior in his dream when he slashes wildly with the knife at the image of his wife, a slashing repeated at the end of his therapy as a type of abreaction that is supposed to indicate his cure,[21] reminds me of Melanie Klein's terrible infant, venting its rage on the body of its mother in its fantasies (128-30). Part of the husband's rage may derive from the fact that he will never be able to father a baby with his mother; but the rage seems to date from a more primitive time, when he saw the woman as giving but also depriving—as a totally controlling figure. The husband's regression to childhood when he dines with his mother suggests that he has not yet been able to separate from her in a healthy way—she remains an internalized object that controls his dreams, his memories, and his marriage. The statue of Kwanon that the cousin has sent to the husband and his wife is more than a symbol of maternity; she also represents the powerful mother who still holds control over the husband's emotional life. The dagger that the cousin has sent them, then, and all the razors and knives in the film, take on another level of meaning. The husband stabbing wildly with a knife at the image of his wife, who, in his unconscious has come to represent his mother, is the husband attempting symbolically to cut the umbilical cord that still has him connected to this powerful figure. The husband's dream, his phobia and compulsion in the film, are all symptoms of his struggle for separation and individuation.

Secrets of a Soul, then, is a far more subtle and complex work than film history has allowed.[22] The dream-sequence, an innovative and bold attempt to use the spatial and temporal flexibilities of the film medium to portray the labyrinthine and many-leveled workings of the mind, is worth the price of admission and certainly seems no less effective than dream sequences in later psychoanalytic films that were to have far more technical advantages from special-effects cinematography. But what is most compelling for the modern viewer is the film's openness to multiple interpretations, none of them contradictory. To read the film is an experience akin to reading the psyche of an individual—levels of meaning overlay one another and fuse together at the same time.[23] Although we discern some kind of developmental order when viewing the film, some type of *fabula,* this type of ordering imposed upon the film is largely theoretical and tentative, and exists beyond the text and the immediate presence of the main character who remains a complex amalgam. The multivalenced quality to the film that I am describing achieves a significant connection with hermeneutics and interpretation in general as they have developed in the twentieth century. It is not *Secrets of a Soul* that has changed but the ways in which we read it. Even though the makers of the film had already undermined any clear and unequivocal meaning by compromising on what would be manifest through explicit explanation in the film and what would remain latent in the film's visual imagery, they still were certain about the work's ultimate meaning.

We might, at this point in our discussion, be more sympathetic to Freud's ultimate rejection of the motion-picture camera in his search for some kind of mechanical metaphor for the operations of the mind. Certainly film can project images on a screen in such a fashion that they resemble thought, fantasy, and dream; but Freud wished to find a sufficiently complex metaphor to describe the way the brain operates. We must admit that he was right about the limitation of film emulsion as a metaphor for the storing power of the brain, about its inability to repress and store an endless series of images of reality. The filmic process is a good metaphor for the way in which the brain registers and then recalls to consciousness at a later time some series of events—but the emulsion is limited, normally, to only one such registration. The mystic writing pad at least has the virtue of countless registrations, even though the images cannot again be reconfigured. It has the virtue of suggesting the layers of "memory-traces" that can be received, absorbed, and fused together by the mind. Freud's writing pad is an apt metaphor for the multivalenced and complex network of representations and significations of the "mnemic systems" stored in the mind (1925, 230).

An ambivalence about the validity and authenticity of any single psychoanalytic interpretation in analysis in general may be suggested by the way in which Freud seems to minimize the difference between the the terms "construction" and "reconstruction" (between putting together something for the first time and putting together something that has already existed in the past) in his essay "Construction in Analysis." He claims that "interpretation" is something "one does to a single element of the material while "construction" is "when one lays before the subject of the analysis a piece of his early history that he has forgotten." But he also writes, "We do not pretend that an individual construction is anything more than a conjecture which awaits examination, confirmation or rejection" (259-65). Construction, then, is dependent upon both individual interpretations of isolated elements in the analysis but also upon a broader conjecture or interpretation of the material that awaits confirmation on the part of the analysand. Freud seems fairly certain, however, that the past, for the analyst, is recoupable: "His work of construction or, if it is preferred, of reconstruction, resembles to a great extent the archaeologist's excavation of some dwelling-place that has been destroyed and buried of some ancient edifice." Both the analyst and archeologist must "reconstruct by means of supplementing and combining the surviving remains" and both are "subject to many of the same difficulties and sources of error"; but the analyst works under better conditions since he is dealing with material, none of which is permanently destroyed and all of which is finally accessible. In spite of the partial story that *Secrets of a Soul* explicitly unfolds, its screenplay, like the film itself, demonstrates the same confidence we find in Freud's essay for reassembling the past when it tells us that at one point, during the analytic sessions, the Doctor's eyes light up— "the reconstruction has worked for him" (107). From then on the analytic sessions in the screenplay are divided between the husband's memories of events and sections marked "Picture of the Doctor's Reconstruction."

Such confidence in interpretation and the recuperation of the past has been undermined in recent years in the psychoanalytic literature. Donald P. Spence, for example, has argued that the creation of the patient's life into a logical narrative is "evidence more of a general preference for closure and good fit than for the effectiveness of the technique or the usefulness of the theory" (123).[24] Harold P. Blum's balanced work on the subject, *Reconstruction in Psychoanalysis: Childhood Revisited and Recreated,* states that reconstruction is a dynamic, contextual, and developing process that "is never 'what really happened,' as might be proposed by external observers or historians" (37).

This shift in analytical thinking resembles a similar change that has taken place in literary interpretation, a movement from the interpretive strategy that E. D. Hirsch, Jr. argues for in *Validity in Interpretation,* first published in 1967, when he says that "even though we can never be certain that our interpretive guesses are correct, we know that they *can* be correct and that the goal of interpretation as a discipline is constantly to increase the probability that they are correct" (207), to the type of thinking by such deconstructionists as Paul de Man and J. Hillis Miller in the 1970s and 1980s and represented by Jonathan Culler's statement in *On Deconstruction: Theory and Criticism after Structuralism*: "In reading particular works and rereadings of these works, deconstruction attempts to understand these phenomena of textuality—the relations of language and metalanguage, for example, or effects of externality and internality, or the possible interaction of conflicting logics" (225). The group of salvational films I am discussing are structured to produce the type of reading suggested by Culler. They are mystery films *par excellence* and their multiple mysteries concern the human psyche and our ability and inability to understand that psyche. These films are ultimately about processes, the process of the psychotherapist and his patient to solve the mysteries of the soul but also the process of the viewer to understand the mysteries—the various textualities and logics—of the film. If one thinks of these films as finished artifacts, as finitely definable and describable, then they must fail—*Secrets of A Soul* in this context would be a most unsatisfactory film.

The non-existence of any single work of art called *Secrets of a Soul,* the fact that there are differing versions at this time and no authorative, original version, emphasizes the impossibility of placing any closure on our attempt to get at the work's meaning. Nor do I think that we shall ever "reconstruct" such an original and definitive print. When I began researching this film, I was advised by a distinguished scholar of German film that I could not possibly write on *Secrets of a Soul* without using the restored print available at the Film Museum in Munich. When I finally was able to view this print, I was struck by a number of important shots and titles missing from it and available in the Rohauer print—and also impressed by a number of shots in the Munich print not present in either the Rohauer or West-Glen versions. My letter to the present director of the Film Museum in Munich, questioning why shots clearly filmed during production were not used in the original release, resulted in a reply admitting that the "restored" print must not be fully restored and asking for information on the location of the missing material. We may ultimately have a print that puts together all of the available shots, but I doubt we shall ever know the version exactly the way Pabst released it—especially since there are also some major discrepancies between the subtitles and intertitles of the available prints. Any hermeneutics concerning *Secrets of a Soul* must satisfy the poststructuralist and deconstructive scriptures about interpretation and meaning in general—lacking both the author's presence and any single originary visual or verbal text, the film offers instead a play of texts and meanings.

Secrets of a Soul also raises questions about the privileged status given to language in the theory of interpretation. It does so by asking us to consider whether the film's titles tell us the whole story—or even a piece of one. And it also asks us why its language, the titles we see on the screen, is to be given privileged status, is to be seen as an outside intervention and transcendent truth, and is not to be seen instead as part of the film, as another of the images that we see on the screen, as another element in the secrets and mysteries of the soul, as another text. The un-

certain state of the verbal text to the film reinforces this point about the circumscribed nature of language. In the West-Glen version available in this country and in the "restored" version in Munich, which seems to be a fuller version of the former, the all-powerful analyst has disappeared from the opening and closing—we no longer see him framing the film with his act of writing. We must relate to this omission the fact that the West-Glen print has fewer titles than both the "restored" version and the one available in this country from the Rohauer Collection, and that both the West-Glen and Munich prints are missing a long series of titles that convey Dr. Orth's explanation to the husband of the nature of his illness at the end of the therapy.[25] *Secrets of a Soul* seems to demonstrate a struggle with language through the differences between its available versions—a struggle exacerbated, nay motivated by the simple fact that the film is silent, silent of spoken language. If psychoanalysis is dependent on language, if language is the passage to the unconscious, what we have in this film is a futile struggle to get to that unconscious. But I must also connect the missing shots of the analyst writing in both the West-Glen and "restored" versions to the missing father in the film as well as to the missing language. I borrow, at this point, a bit of Lacan that reinforces my matriarchal interpretation of this film. What we find in the form and substance of *Secrets of a Soul* is the struggle to move from the imaginary to the symbolic, the imaginary that fosters a feeling of oneness to the mother, the symbolic that is the realm of the prohibiting language that belongs to the father. If film is truly an oral experience, a taking in of the images and sounds emanating from the screen, and if the screen is itself a residual memory of the dream screen, then it follows that the very nature of film is matriarchal, and the struggle of film to move into the realm of language must be doomed.

The missing language and missing father inevitably lead us back to the role of Dr. Orth in the film. Significantly missing from his interaction with the husband are the issues of transference and, concomitantly, counter-transference—issues not absent from such later salvational films as *Mine Own Executioner* and *Freud*. The missing transference and counter-transference become especially obvious in the film's problematic handling of the husband's neurosis and cure, forcing us to impose them on the film ourselves. While we are making, for ourselves, a host of interpretations from the husband's life and dream, the analyst is creating a very limited and circumscribed story, one that emphasizes his own control over the material and over the husband. The powerful analyst has himself become an author in the act of reading, and the patient for him is a "readerly text" on which to inscribe his own meaning, a process we see in the behavior of a large number of the therapists we meet in non-comic films about psychotherapy—a process that savagely erupts in the portrayal of Hannibal Lecter in *The Silence of the Lambs*.

At one point in *Secrets of a Soul,* the husband looks at some photos that his wife has been showing to her cousin. The husband looks fondly at the picture of himself as a young boy and his mother, then one of himself, his wife, and her cousin as children, but appears disturbed when he next views a photograph of the three of them from the same period evidently taken at a Christmas celebration.[26] During his psychotherapy the husband remembers the time during the Christmas party when the disturbing photograph was taken—there are two interesting aspects to his memory. The first is the doll held by the little girl since in the actual photograph we have viewed earlier in the film she is empty-handed.[27] We must ponder, then, whether events took place exactly as the husband remembers them—or what we are seeing, and what he and the analyst are taking for reality, have instead been changed by projections from the husband's unconscious, altered by his own fantasies. The second interesting element in this memory is the photographer taking the picture, who seems to be aiming his camera right at us, the audience, with a mirror behind him showing his own reflection.[28] The presence of the photographer almost seems to authenticate the scene of the three children the way we now see it, but this photographer appears in the husband's memory and is, therefore, only as reliable a recorder of reality as that memory itself—the photographer's reflection in the mirror specifically suggests the separation of memory from reality, the fact that memory shows us a version and reflection of actual events. The shot of the photographer, however, is also a self-reflexive image that makes us ponder more than the mind as a recorder of reality—makes us ponder the issue of art and representation, especially cinema as photography, as moving pictures with the ability and inability to represent reality, both external and internal.

But the photographer is also aiming his camera at us, involving us in his picture-making process and in the world of the film as well, involving us in the impossible search for some original source and original meaning to all these images. Both the uncertainty about the visual representations and the failure of language in the film put the burden of meaning on our interpretive faculties. *Secrets of a Soul* is ultimately a self-reflexive film about hermeneutics, about interpretation in general, about the process of looking for meaning. The film becomes a "readerly text" for us, an analysand, and we become the empowered analyst. We are invited to play this role, to get into this process, so long as we remember the openness of the film to multiple readings but also to our own counter-transference, the infusion of our own fantasies and defenses. Or perhaps I might say that the film on the screen becomes a unique transitional object for each of us. In analyzing the film I watch it over and over—in fact, it is the nature of film to be seen over and over, pretending to be fixed with the same images, the same titles, the same sequence. But the very act of viewing, the fact that I watch the film each time in a different frame of mind and with a different day's residue, the fact that each print will be seen in a different theater, with a different quality of image and sound, by a different audience, and by different individuals in the audience means that it can never be fixed or determinate in meaning.

And here is the final lesson we learn from viewing *Secrets of a Soul*: searching the film for any single neurotic pattern or pathology that explains the husband's behavior, like searching for any original or authoritative print of the film, can only be a partial success at best—meaning does not ultimately reside in the work itself but in the person making the interpretation. The three versions of the film (four if we include the one referred to in Sachs' publication) and the multiple interpretations inherent in the text open up the work to contemporary deconstructive readings, reader-response theory, and psychoanalytic concepts of counter-transference and reconstruction. Perhaps now we can understand the natural and increasing appeal of film for psychoanalysts:[29] its presentation of images that create an experience not far from dreaming or daydreaming, that provoke us to interpret them not only in terms of what the film presents to us as its meaning but also in terms of something hidden and subversive; our attempt to put image into language and to fix the meaning of image through language; the fact that we are always interpreting in spite of the fact that we are always misremembering; and the fact that our discovery of the latent in the manifest and our construction of the *fabula* from the *sujet* are together a creative act that is part of the entire work's development. Films may pretend to have their own meanings, but there can be no meanings without someone doing the interpreting and, I must add, taking part in the fantasy— the viewing experience is the experience of analysis, but the true film critic realizes that he or she is both analyst and analysand. The frequent appearance of psychotherapists in film, the frequent stories that involve psychotherapy, are a tautology because film viewing, to begin with, is an analytic process—but because all tautologies are self-reflexive, such films draw attention to what the film medium is all about.

Notes

1. The German title is *Geheimnisse einer Seele*. Translated as "Soul" in the English title, "Seele" maintains its original meaning rather than being deprived of its spiritual significance as when Strachey translates Freud's use of the word as "psyche" or "mind" in the *Standard Edition of the Complete Psychological Works of Sigmund Freud*. See Bettelheim for a discussion of the English translations of Freud's works.

2. The portrait appears in an English-language version of the film available in this country as part of the Rohauer Collection. The Filmmuseum of the Münchner Stadtmuseum claims that its version of the film is "restored," even though the print is missing the photograph of Freud as well as a number of other shots available in the Rohauer print. Also missing the portrait, and somewhat close to the "restored" print in Munich but without all the titles, is an English version of the film available in this country through West-Glen. I shall have something more to say on these various prints of the film below.

3. I am excluding from this category several films in which psychotherapists perform similar ameliorative roles, but which do not quite fit the category I am defining. I exclude, most notably, *The Three Faces of*

Eve (1957) because the focus is more on the sensational issue of multiple personalities than the therapeutic alliance, *David and Lisa* (1963) because the film is most concerned with the pathologies and relationship of the two main characters, and *I Never Promised You a Rose Garden* (1973) because the film, though certainly about the therapeutic alliance, does not follow the particular narrative structure of mystery and discovery that I will be describing in the following pages.

4. No mention of the film appears in a recent history of the psychiatrist in cinema by Gabbard and Gabbard.

5. I shall directly translate the German titles from the Munich print since they are likely to be the original titles and since the English translation in the Rohauer print seems to me more discursive and melodramatic. *Spellbound* begins with similar titles extolling the merits of psychoanalysis in "open[ing] the locked doors of [the] mind."

6. The story of the genesis of the film from the perspective of Freud and his circle is told in detail in Chodorkoff and Baxter. Friedberg also gives an account of the film's genesis.

7. I am grateful to Jan-Christopher Horak, Director of the Filmmuseum in the Münchner Stadtmuseum, for making a copy of the screenplay available, and to my colleague Peter Bauland for his help in translating the German.

8. I am grateful to the Deutsches Institut For Filmkunde in Wiesbaden-Biebrich, Germany, for a photocopy of this work.

9. Browne and McPherson cite this quotation from *The Interpretation of Dreams* and then refer to Derrida's "Freud and the Scene of Writing" in which the French philosopher discusses Freud's discovery of an adequate model for the operations of the mind in "Note on the Mystic Writing Pad" (36).

10. In *Psychotherapy,* published in 1909, Münsterberg clearly argued against the unconscious as developed by Freud and argued instead for one filled with memories and learning, one directly connected to but unnoticed by the conscious mind (15-26).

11. Interpretation as the single most important activity in literary criticism received much emphasis from the New Criticism that was so pervasive in the years following the second world war, an emphasis that was not diminished by the deconstructive movement. Indeed, deconstruction itself became an interpretive strategy, e.g., the work's meaning was the difficulty or impossibility of meaning (see Culler for a discussion of interpretation in the context of the New Criticism and deconstruction, 3-17). The New Criticism can be seen as part of the development of hermeneutics in Western thought from the writing of the German philosopher Wilhelm Dilthey in the late nineteenth century. Paul Ricoeur's *Freud and Philosophy:*

An Essay on Interpretation is essential reading for understanding the relationship of Freud's thinking to hermeneutics.

12. See especially Tomashevsky's "Thématique," 267-69.

13. An obvious example of this process takes place in Alfred Hitchcock's *Psycho* (1960) when the psychiatrist at the end of the film explains the mystery and the pathology of Norman Bates that has been responsible for that mystery; but in such films as Robert Siodmak's *The Dark Mirror* (1946) and Robert Benton's *Still of the Night* (1982) the psychotherapy plays a more pervasive and crucial role in solving an external mystery.

14. Variations on this theme appear in Stanley Kramer's *Home of the Brave* (1949) and Barbra Streisand's *Prince of Tides* (1991).

15. There is an interesting variation on this type of double exposure in *Spellbound* when the hero discovers his earliest trauma, his reaction as a young boy to his accidental killing of his brother, and, as a result, then remembers the more recent trauma that has caused his present amnesia, his reaction to the murder of the doctor. In this film the solving of the two internal mysteries frees the character from suspicion and allows for the solution to an external mystery.

16. The "restored" version in the Munich Museum and the West-Glen print begin with the opening titles concerning psychoanalysis followed by the narrative itself, which begins with a shot of the husband sharpening his razor and then a mirror shot of him shaving himself—this entire shaving sequence is missing from the narrative proper in the Rohauer print, which begins with the husband entering his wife's bedroom. While the husband is identified as Martin Fellman in Dr. Orth's notebook as well as on two occasions during the film and his wife's cousin is identified as Erich at the end of his letter to the couple in the Rohauer print, their names are totally missing from both the Munich and West-Glen prints.

17. Sachs uses the word "Fehlhandlung" or faulty action instead of Freud's "Fehlleistung" or faulty function. The editor of the *Standard Edition* of Freud's works tells us that no equivalent term to "Fehlleistung" existed in English and the word "parapraxis" had to be invented (1901, viii).

18. A point also made by Browne and McPherson in their discussion of the film's oedipal theme.

19. A relationship first touched upon by Chodorkoff and Baxter.

20. Freud at first identified the loved object with the self because his theory of homosexuality was partly based on the life of Leonardo da Vinci, who was raised for the first three years of his life without a father (1910,

98-100). Since the husband's father is totally absent in *Secrets of A Soul* such an interpretation has some credence, but the oedipal elements in the film clearly show the husband's identification of the cousin with his father. It is certainly possible that the strong mother and the absence of the father in early childhood can later produce a homosexual configuration where the love object represents both the self and the missing father, a fusion that further compensates for the parental absence. Later, in "Some Neurotic Mechanisms in Jealousy, Paranoia, and Homosexuality," Freud argued that homosexuality may be induced by the high regard for the male organ and also by either regard for the father or fear of him (in the later case his danger is removed by making him the loved object). Both "the clinging to a condition of the penis in the object, as well as the retiring in favor of the father—may be ascribed to the castration complex" (231).

21. The analyst points out that the husband is cured because he is now holding a knife. Abreaction is a type of catharsis, normally achieved through language, that frees the patient from an affect that is the product of some early trauma. The concept is associated with Freud's early work on hysteria and was frequently achieved through hypnosis, though some form of abreaction continued to be sought in psychoanalytic treatment under certain conditions. Many films featuring psychotherapy, including most of the salvational psychoanalytic films, use abreaction as the denouement of their plots because of its dramatic nature.

22. The work has generally been judged as visually interesting but intellectually superficial (see, for example, Kracauer's assessment, 170-72).

23. There are obviously more interpretive possibilities than the series I have outlined here, each dependent on one's psychoanalytic leanings. In addition to 1) Dr. Orth's logical, though incomplete narrative; 2) the oedipal interpretation as suggested by the film's visual imagery; 3) the implications of homosexual feelings between the two male figures from their interactions; and 4) my pre-oedipal reading, the film can easily support 5) an object-relations approach in terms of the husband's relationships with his mother and father as projected onto his involvement with his wife and her cousin; 6) a self-psychology interpretation through a focus on the husband's narcissistic injuries and the structure of his self.

24. He also states that "The preferred explanation for a series of symptoms tends to be cast in terms of single events—the primal scene is the outstanding example" (144).

25. The titles in this portion of the Rohauer version appear as subtitles, except for the last part of this explanation that appears as intertitles. The West-Glen and "restored" versions use only subtitles for the analyst's explanation.

26. In the screenplay, the oedipal significance of this photograph is underscored when the wife and her cousin are described as playing husband and wife with a cradle and doll while the husband watches sadly from a distance. Later that night, the husband again looks at the photograph which seems to undergo a strange transformation before his eyes: both his wife and cousin grow older continuing to play mother and father, while he remains the young child looking sadly on.

27. The husband remembers that at this Christmas celebration his mother gave him her new baby to hold. In his mind, he must have felt that he was no longer the play father, but his own father, and his little sibling was his and his mother's child. When his wife, as the little girl, felt deserted by him as a result of his mother's action and gave the doll to her cousin, the husband conflated the two women in his mind and felt rejected by his mother. Because the husband associated the little girl with his mother, he, in fact, also became the doll that she gave to the cousin, and the girl and her cousin his parents. The doll in his memory is related to the doll that his wife holds while in the boat with her cousin at the end of the husband's dream, when he dreams his own birth.

28. August Ruhs suggests that the man with the camera is the husband's father reminding us of the filmmaker with his constant cinematic references to the primal scene beneath the sublimated events of the film itself (31). Browne and McPherson also relate the primal scene to this photograph and the husband's memory of the photograph being shot (44).

29. I refer not only to the large number of classes on film now part of psychoanalytic training and the multitude of lectures on films given by psychoanalysts, but also to such groups as The Forum for the Psychoanalytic Study of Film in Washington, D.C., which promote these activities as well as further communication between analysts and film scholars on the subject of film.

References

Abraham, Karl. 1924. "A Short Study of the Development of the Libido, Viewed in the Light of Mental Disorders." *Selected Papers*. London: Hogarth Press, 1927. 418-501.

Baudry, Jean Louis. 1970. "Ideological Effects of the Basic Cinematographic Apparatus." Trans. Alan Williams. *Film Quarterly* 28 (1974-75). 39-47.

Bettelheim, Bruno. *Freud and Man's Soul*. New York: Alfred Knopf, 1983.

Blum, Harold P. *Reconstruction in Psychoanalysis: Childhood Revisited and Recreated*. Madison, Conn.: International Universities Press, 1994.

Browne, Nick and Bruce McPherson. "Dream and Photography in a Psychoanalytic Film: *Secrets of A Soul*." *Dreamworks* 1 (Spring 1980): 35-45.

Chodorkoff, Bernard and Seymour Baxter. "*Secrets of a Soul*: An Early Psychoanalytic Film Venture." *American Imago* 31 (Winter 1974): 319-34.

Culler, Jonathan. *The Pursuit of Signs: Semiotics, Literature, Deconstruction.* Ithaca: Cornell University Press, 1981.

Eberwein, Robert T. *Film and the Dream Screen: A Sleep and a Forgetting.* Princeton: Princeton University Press, 1984.

Freud, Sigmund and Karl Abraham. *A Psycho-Analytic Dialogue: The Letters of Sigmund Freud and Karl Abraham.* Ed. Hilda C. Abraham and Ernst L. Freud. Trans. Bernard Marsh and Hilda C. Abraham. London: The Hogarth Press, 1965.

Freud, Sigmund. 1900. *The Interpretation of Dreams. The Standard Edition of the Complete Psychological Works of Sigmund Freud.* Ed. James Strachey. London: Hogarth Press, 1953-74. Vols. 4 and 5.

———. 1901. *The Psychopathology of Everyday Life. Standard Edition.* Vol. 6.

———. 1910. "Leonardo da Vinci and a Memory of his Childhood." *Standard Edition.* 11: 59-137.

———. 1922. "Some Neurotic Mechanisms in Jealousy, Paranoia, and Homosexuality." *Standard Edition.* 18: 221-32.

———. 1925. "A Note Upon a Mystic Writing Pad." *Standard Edition.* 19: 226-232.

———. 1937. "Construction in Analysis." *Standard Edition.* 23: 256-269.

Friedberg, Anne. "An *Unheimlich* Maneuver between Psychoanalysis and the Cinema: *Secrets of a Soul (1926)*." *The Films of G. W. Pabst: An Extraterritorial Cinema.* 1990. Ed. Eric Rentschler. New Brunswick: Rutgers University Press, 1990. 41-51.

Gabbard, Krin and Glen O. Gabbard. *Psychiatry and the Cinema.* Chicago: The University of Chicago Press, 1987.

Hirsch, E. D., Jr. *Validity in Interpretation.* New Haven: Yale University Press, 1967.

Jones, Ernest. *The Life and Work of Sigmund Freud.* Vol. 3: *The Last Phase, 1919-39.* New York: Basic Books, 1957.

Klein, Melanie. 1932. *The Psycho-Analysis of Children.* Trans. Alix Strachey. Revised H. A. Thorner. New York: Delacorte, 1975.

Kracauer, Siegfried. *From Caligari to Hitler: A Psychological History of the German Film.* Princeton: Princeton University Press, 1947.

Lévi-Strauss, Claude. "The Sorcerer and his Magic." *Structural Anthropology.* Trans. Clair Jacobson and Brooke Grudfest Shoepf. Anchor Books. New York: Doubleday, 1967. 161-80.

Metz, Christian. *The Imaginary Signifier: Psychoanalysis and the Cinema.* Trans. Celia Britton, Annwyl Williams, Ben Brewster and Alfred Guzzetti. Bloomington: Indiana University Press, 1982.

Münsterberg, Hugo. *Psychotherapy.* New York: Moffat, Yard and Co., 1912.

———. *The Photoplay: A Psychological Study.* New York: D. Appleton, 1916.

Ricoeur, Paul. *Freud and Philosophy: An Essay on Interpretation.* Trans. Denis Savage. New Haven: Yale University Press, 1970.

Ross, Colin and Hans Neumann. Manuscript. *Die Geheimnisse der Seele, Psychoanalytisches Filmwerk. Zweiter Teil: Das Geheimnis einer Seele, Ein Psychoalytisches Kammerspiel.* Berlin: Kulturabteilung der UFA, n.d.

Ruhs, August. "Geheimnisse Einer Seele: Ein Freud-Loses Projekt." *G. W. Pabst.* Ed. Gottfried Schlemmer, Bernard Riff, and Georg Haberl. Münster: Maks Publikationen, 1990. 20-32.

Sachs, Hanns. *Psychoanalyse: Rätsel des Unbewussten.* Berlin: Lichtbild-Bühne, 1926.

Spence, Donald P. *Narrative Truth and Historical Truth: Meaning and Interpretation in Psychoanalysis.* New York: W. W. Norton & Company, 1982.

Tomashevsky, Boris. "Thématique." *Théorie de la littérature.* Ed. Tzvetan Todorov. Paris: Éditions du Seuil, 1965. 263-307.

Additional coverage of Pabst's life and career is contained in the following source published by the Gale Group: *International Dictionary of Films and Filmmakers: Directors,* **Vol. 2.**

How to Use This Index

Literary Criticism Series
Cumulative Author Index

Astley, William 1855-1911
  See Warung, Price
Aston, James
  See White, T(erence) H(anbury)
Asturias, Miguel Angel 1899-1974 .... **CLC 3, 8, 13; HLC 1**
  See also CA 25-28; 49-52; CANR 32; CAP 2; CDWLB 3; DA3; DAM MULT, NOV; DLB 113; HW 1; LAW; MTCW 1, 2; RGWL 2; WLIT 1
Atares, Carlos Saura
  See Saura (Atares), Carlos
Athanasius c. 295-c. 373 .... **CMLC 48**
Atheling, William
  See Pound, Ezra (Weston Loomis)
Atheling, William, Jr.
  See Blish, James (Benjamin)
Atherton, Gertrude (Franklin Horn)
  1857-1948 .... **TCLC 2**
  See also CA 104; 155; DLB 9, 78, 186; HGG; RGAL 4; SUFW; TCWW 2
Atherton, Lucius
  See Masters, Edgar Lee
Atkins, Jack
  See Harris, Mark
Atkinson, Kate 1951- .... **CLC 99**
  See also CA 166; CANR 101; DLB 267
Attaway, William (Alexander)
  1911-1986 .... **CLC 92; BLC 1**
  See also BW 2, 3; CA 143; CANR 82; DAM MULT; DLB 76
Atticus
  See Fleming, Ian (Lancaster); Wilson, (Thomas) Woodrow
Atwood, Margaret (Eleanor) 1939- ... **CLC 2, 3, 4, 8, 13, 15, 25, 44, 84, 135; PC 8; SSC 2, 46; WLC**
  See also AAYA 12; BEST 89:2; BPFB 1; CA 49-52; CANR 3, 24, 33, 59, 95; CN 7; CP 7; CPW; CWP; DA; DA3; DAB; DAC; DAM MST, NOV, POET; DLB 53, 251; EXPN; FW; INT CANR-24; LAIT 5; MTCW 1, 2; NFS 4, 12, 13, 14; PFS 7; RGSF 2; SATA 50; SSFS 3, 13; TWA; YAW
Aubigny, Pierre d'
  See Mencken, H(enry) L(ouis)
Aubin, Penelope 1685-1731(?) .... **LC 9**
  See also DLB 39
Auchincloss, Louis (Stanton) 1917- .. **CLC 4, 6, 9, 18, 45; SSC 22**
  See also AMWS 4; CA 1-4R; CANR 6, 29, 55, 87; CN 7; DAM NOV; DLB 2, 244; DLBY 1980; INT CANR-29; MTCW 1; RGAL 4
Auden, W(ystan) H(ugh) 1907-1973 . **CLC 1, 2, 3, 4, 6, 9, 11, 14, 43, 123; PC 1; WLC**
  See also AAYA 18; AMWS 2; BRW 7; BRWR 1; CA 9-12R; 45-48; CANR 5, 61, 105; CDBLB 1914-1945; DA; DA3; DAB; DAC; DAM DRAM, MST, POET; DLB 10, 20; EXPP; MTCW 1, 2; PAB; PFS 1, 3, 4, 10; TUS; WP
Audiberti, Jacques 1900-1965 .... **CLC 38**
  See also CA 25-28R; DAM DRAM
Audubon, John James 1785-1851 . **NCLC 47**
  See also ANW; DLB 248
Auel, Jean M(arie) 1936- .... **CLC 31, 107**
  See also AAYA 7; BEST 90:4; BPFB 1; CA 103; CANR 21, 64; CPW; DA3; DAM POP; INT CANR-21; NFS 11; RHW; SATA 91
Auerbach, Erich 1892-1957 .... **TCLC 43**
  See also CA 118; 155
Augier, Emile 1820-1889 .... **NCLC 31**
  See also DLB 192; GFL 1789 to the Present
August, John
  See De Voto, Bernard (Augustine)

Augustine, St. 354-430 .... **CMLC 6; WLCS**
  See also DA; DA3; DAB; DAC; DAM MST; DLB 115; EW 1; RGWL 2
Aunt Belinda
  See Braddon, Mary Elizabeth
Aunt Weedy
  See Alcott, Louisa May
Aurelius
  See Bourne, Randolph S(illiman)
Aurelius, Marcus 121-180 .... **CMLC 45**
  See also Marcus Aurelius
  See also RGWL 2
Aurobindo, Sri
  See Ghose, Aurabinda
Austen, Jane 1775-1817 ...... **NCLC 1, 13, 19, 33, 51, 81, 95; WLC**
  See also AAYA 19; BRW 4; BRWR 2; BYA 3; CDBLB 1789-1832; DA; DA3; DAB; DAC; DAM MST, NOV; DLB 116; EXPN; LAIT 2; NFS 1, 14; TEA; WLIT 3; WYAS 1
Auster, Paul 1947- .... **CLC 47, 131**
  See also CA 69-72; CANR 23, 52, 75; CMW 4; CN 7; DA3; DLB 227; MTCW 1
Austin, Frank
  See Faust, Frederick (Schiller)
  See also TCWW 2
Austin, Mary (Hunter) 1868-1934 . **TCLC 25**
  See also Stairs, Gordon
  See also ANW; CA 109; 178; DLB 9, 78, 206, 221; FW; TCWW 2
Averroes 1126-1198 .... **CMLC 7**
  See also DLB 115
Avicenna 980-1037 .... **CMLC 16**
  See also DLB 115
Avison, Margaret 1918- .... **CLC 2, 4, 97**
  See also CA 17-20R; CP 7; DAC; DAM POET; DLB 53; MTCW 1
Axton, David
  See Koontz, Dean R(ay)
Ayckbourn, Alan 1939- ...... **CLC 5, 8, 18, 33, 74; DC 13**
  See also BRWS 5; CA 21-24R; CANR 31, 59; CBD; CD 5; DAB; DAM DRAM; DFS 7; DLB 13, 245; MTCW 1, 2
Aydy, Catherine
  See Tennant, Emma (Christina)
Ayme, Marcel (Andre) 1902-1967 ... **CLC 11; SSC 41**
  See also CA 89-92; CANR 67; CLR 25; DLB 72; EW 12; GFL 1789 to the Present; RGSF 2; RGWL 2; SATA 91
Ayrton, Michael 1921-1975 .... **CLC 7**
  See also CA 5-8R; 61-64; CANR 9, 21
Azorin .... **CLC 11**
  See also Martinez Ruiz, Jose
  See also EW 9
Azuela, Mariano 1873-1952 .. **TCLC 3; HLC 1**
  See also CA 104; 131; CANR 81; DAM MULT; HW 1, 2; LAW; MTCW 1, 2
Baastad, Babbis Friis
  See Friis-Baastad, Babbis Ellinor
Bab
  See Gilbert, W(illiam) S(chwenck)
Babbis, Eleanor
  See Friis-Baastad, Babbis Ellinor
Babel, Isaac
  See Babel, Isaak (Emmanuilovich)
  See also EW 11; SSFS 10
Babel, Isaak (Emmanuilovich)
  1894-1941(?) .... **TCLC 2, 13; SSC 16**
  See also Babel, Isaac
  See also CA 104; 155; MTCW 1; RGSF 2; RGWL 2; TWA
Babits, Mihaly 1883-1941 .... **TCLC 14**
  See also CA 114; CDWLB 4; DLB 215

Babur 1483-1530 .... **LC 18**
Babylas 1898-1962
  See Ghelderode, Michel de
Baca, Jimmy Santiago 1952- .... **PC 41**
  See also CA 131; CANR 81, 90; CP 7; DAM MULT; DLB 122; HLC 1; HW 1, 2
Baca, Jose Santiago
  See Baca, Jimmy Santiago
Bacchelli, Riccardo 1891-1985 .... **CLC 19**
  See also CA 29-32R; 117; DLB 264
Bach, Richard (David) 1936- .... **CLC 14**
  See also AITN 1; BEST 89:2; BPFB 1; BYA 5; CA 9-12R; CANR 18, 93; CPW; DAM NOV, POP; FANT; MTCW 1; SATA 13
Bache, Benjamin Franklin
  1769-1798 .... **LC 74**
  See also DLB 43
Bachman, Richard
  See King, Stephen (Edwin)
Bachmann, Ingeborg 1926-1973 .... **CLC 69**
  See also CA 93-96; 45-48; CANR 69; DLB 85; RGWL 2
Bacon, Francis 1561-1626 .... **LC 18, 32**
  See also BRW 1; CDBLB Before 1660; DLB 151, 236, 252; RGEL 2; TEA
Bacon, Roger 1214(?)-1294 .... **CMLC 14**
  See also DLB 115
Bacovia, George 1881-1957 .... **TCLC 24**
  See also Vasiliu, Gheorghe
  See also CDWLB 4; DLB 220
Badanes, Jerome 1937- .... **CLC 59**
Bagehot, Walter 1826-1877 .... **NCLC 10**
  See also DLB 55
Bagnold, Enid 1889-1981 .... **CLC 25**
  See also BYA 2; CA 5-8R; 103; CANR 5, 40; CBD; CWD; CWRI 5; DAM DRAM; DLB 13, 160, 191, 245; FW; MAICYA 1, 2; RGEL 2; SATA 1, 25
Bagritsky, Eduard 1895-1934 .... **TCLC 60**
Bagrjana, Elisaveta
  See Belcheva, Elisaveta Lyubomirova
Bagryana, Elisaveta -1991 .... **CLC 10**
  See also Belcheva, Elisaveta Lyubomirova
  See also CA 178; CDWLB 4; DLB 147
Bailey, Paul 1937- .... **CLC 45**
  See also CA 21-24R; CANR 16, 62; CN 7; DLB 14; GLL 2
Baillie, Joanna 1762-1851 .... **NCLC 71**
  See also DLB 93; RGEL 2
Bainbridge, Beryl (Margaret) 1934- . **CLC 4, 5, 8, 10, 14, 18, 22, 62, 130**
  See also BRWS 6; CA 21-24R; CANR 24, 55, 75, 88; CN 7; DAM NOV; DLB 14, 231; MTCW 1, 2
Baker, Carlos (Heard)
  1909-1987 .... **TCLC 119**
  See also CA 5-8R; 122; CANR 3, 63; DLB 103
Baker, Elliott 1922- .... **CLC 8**
  See also CA 45-48; CANR 2, 63; CN 7
Baker, Jean H. .... **TCLC 3, 10**
  See also Russell, George William
Baker, Nicholson 1957- .... **CLC 61**
  See also CA 135; CANR 63; CN 7; CPW; DA3; DAM POP; DLB 227
Baker, Ray Stannard 1870-1946 .... **TCLC 47**
  See also CA 118
Baker, Russell (Wayne) 1925- .... **CLC 31**
  See also BEST 89:4; CA 57-60; CANR 11, 41, 59; MTCW 1, 2
Bakhtin, M.
  See Bakhtin, Mikhail Mikhailovich
Bakhtin, M. M.
  See Bakhtin, Mikhail Mikhailovich
Bakhtin, Mikhail
  See Bakhtin, Mikhail Mikhailovich

Boyle, Kay 1902-1992 .... **CLC 1, 5, 19, 58, 121; SSC 5**
See also CA 13-16R; 140; CAAS 1; CANR 29, 61, 110; DLB 4, 9, 48, 86; DLBY 1993; MTCW 1, 2; RGAL 4; RGSF 2; SSFS 10, 13, 14

Boyle, Mark
See Kienzle, William X(avier)

Boyle, Patrick 1905-1982 .... **CLC 19**
See also CA 127

Boyle, T. C.
See Boyle, T(homas) Coraghessan
See also AMWS 8

Boyle, T(homas) Coraghessan
1948- .... **CLC 36, 55, 90; SSC 16**
See also Boyle, T. C.
See also BEST 90:4; BPFB 1; CA 120; CANR 44, 76, 89; CN 7; CPW; DA3; DAM POP; DLB 218; DLBY 1986; MTCW 2; SSFS 13

Boz
See Dickens, Charles (John Huffam)

Brackenridge, Hugh Henry
1748-1816 .... **NCLC 7**
See also DLB 11, 37; RGAL 4

Bradbury, Edward P.
See Moorcock, Michael (John)
See also MTCW 2

Bradbury, Malcolm (Stanley)
1932-2000 .... **CLC 32, 61**
See also CA 1-4R; CANR 1, 33, 91, 98; CN 7; DA3; DAM NOV; DLB 14, 207; MTCW 1, 2

Bradbury, Ray (Douglas) 1920- .... **CLC 1, 3, 10, 15, 42, 98; SSC 29, 53; WLC**
See also AAYA 15; AITN 1, 2; AMWS 4; BPFB 1; BYA 4, 5, 11; CA 1-4R; CANR 2, 30, 75; CDALB 1968-1988; CN 7; CPW; DA; DA3; DAB; DAC; DAM MST, NOV, POP; DLB 2, 8; EXPN; EXPS; HGG; LAIT 3, 5; MTCW 1, 2; NFS 1; RGAL 4; RGSF 2; SATA 11, 64, 123; SCFW 2; SFW 4; SSFS 1; SUFW; TUS; YAW

Braddon, Mary Elizabeth
1837-1915 .... **TCLC 111**
See also Aunt Belinda
See also BRWS 8; CA 108; 179; CMW 4; DLB 18, 70, 156; HGG

Bradford, Gamaliel 1863-1932 .... **TCLC 36**
See also CA 160; DLB 17

Bradford, William 1590-1657 .... **LC 64**
See also DLB 24, 30; RGAL 4

Bradley, David (Henry), Jr. 1950- ... **CLC 23, 118; BLC 1**
See also BW 1, 3; CA 104; CANR 26, 81; CN 7; DAM MULT; DLB 33

Bradley, John Ed(mund, Jr.) 1958- . **CLC 55**
See also CA 139; CANR 99; CN 7; CSW

Bradley, Marion Zimmer
1930-1999 .... **CLC 30**
See also Chapman, Lee; Dexter, John; Gardner, Miriam; Ives, Morgan; Rivers, Elfrida
See also AAYA 40; BPFB 1; CA 57-60; 185; CAAS 10; CANR 7, 31, 51, 75, 107; CPW; DA3; DAM POP; DLB 8; FANT; FW; MTCW 1, 2; SATA 90; SATA-Obit 116; SFW 4; YAW

Bradshaw, John 1933- .... **CLC 70**
See also CA 138; CANR 61

Bradstreet, Anne 1612(?)-1672 ...... **LC 4, 30; PC 10**
See also AMWS 1; CDALB 1640-1865; DA; DA3; DAC; DAM MST, POET; DLB 24; EXPP; FW; PFS 6; RGAL 4; TUS; WP

Brady, Joan 1939- .... **CLC 86**
See also CA 141

Bragg, Melvyn 1939- .... **CLC 10**
See also BEST 89:3; CA 57-60; CANR 10, 48, 89; CN 7; DLB 14; RHW

Brahe, Tycho 1546-1601 .... **LC 45**

Braine, John (Gerard) 1922-1986 . **CLC 1, 3, 41**
See also CA 1-4R; 120; CANR 1, 33; CD-BLB 1945-1960; DLB 15; DLBY 1986; MTCW 1

Bramah, Ernest 1868-1942 .... **TCLC 72**
See also CA 156; CMW 4; DLB 70; FANT

Brammer, William 1930(?)-1978 ...... **CLC 31**
See also CA 77-80

Brancati, Vitaliano 1907-1954 .... **TCLC 12**
See also CA 109; DLB 264

Brancato, Robin F(idler) 1936- .... **CLC 35**
See also AAYA 9; BYA 6; CA 69-72; CANR 11, 45; CLR 32; JRDA; MAICYA 2; MAICYAS 1; SAAS 9; SATA 97; WYA; YAW

Brand, Max
See Faust, Frederick (Schiller)
See also BPFB 1; TCWW 2

Brand, Millen 1906-1980 .... **CLC 7**
See also CA 21-24R; 97-100; CANR 72

Branden, Barbara .... **CLC 44**
See also CA 148

Brandes, Georg (Morris Cohen)
1842-1927 .... **TCLC 10**
See also CA 105; 189

Brandys, Kazimierz 1916-2000 .... **CLC 62**

Branley, Franklyn M(ansfield)
1915- .... **CLC 21**
See also CA 33-36R; CANR 14, 39; CLR 13; MAICYA 1, 2; SAAS 16; SATA 4, 68

Brathwaite, Edward Kamau 1930- . **CLC 11; BLCS**
See also BW 2, 3; CA 25-28R; CANR 11, 26, 47, 107; CDWLB 3; CP 7; DAM POET; DLB 125

Brathwaite, Kamau
See Brathwaite, Edward Kamau

Brautigan, Richard (Gary)
1935-1984 ..... **CLC 1, 3, 5, 9, 12, 34, 42**
See also BPFB 1; CA 53-56; 113; CANR 34; DA3; DAM NOV; DLB 2, 5, 206; DLBY 1980, 1984; FANT; MTCW 1; RGAL 4; SATA 56

Brave Bird, Mary
See Crow Dog, Mary (Ellen)
See also NNAL

Braverman, Kate 1950- .... **CLC 67**
See also CA 89-92

Brecht, (Eugen) Bertolt (Friedrich)
1898-1956 ..... **TCLC 1, 6, 13, 35; DC 3; WLC**
See also CA 104; 133; CANR 62; CDWLB 2; DA; DA3; DAB; DAC; DAM DRAM, MST; DFS 4, 5, 9; DLB 56, 124; EW 11; IDTP; MTCW 1, 2; RGWL 2; TWA

Brecht, Eugen Berthold Friedrich
See Brecht, (Eugen) Bertolt (Friedrich)

Bremer, Fredrika 1801-1865 .... **NCLC 11**
See also DLB 254

Brennan, Christopher John
1870-1932 .... **TCLC 17**
See also CA 117; 188; DLB 230

Brennan, Maeve 1917-1993 .... **CLC 5**
See also CA 81-84; CANR 72, 100; TCLC 124

Brent, Linda
See Jacobs, Harriet A(nn)

Brentano, Clemens (Maria)
1778-1842 .... **NCLC 1**
See also DLB 90; RGWL 2

Brent of Bin Bin
See Franklin, (Stella Maria Sarah) Miles (Lampe)

Brenton, Howard 1942- .... **CLC 31**
See also CA 69-72; CANR 33, 67; CBD; CD 5; DLB 13; MTCW 1

Breslin, James 1930-
See Breslin, Jimmy
See also CA 73-76; CANR 31, 75; DAM NOV; MTCW 1, 2

Breslin, Jimmy .... **CLC 4, 43**
See also Breslin, James
See also AITN 1; DLB 185; MTCW 2

Bresson, Robert 1901(?)-1999 .... **CLC 16**
See also CA 110; 187; CANR 49

Breton, Andre 1896-1966 .. **CLC 2, 9, 15, 54; PC 15**
See also CA 19-20; 25-28R; CANR 40, 60; CAP 2; DLB 65, 258; EW 11; GFL 1789 to the Present; MTCW 1, 2; RGWL 2; TWA; WP

Breytenbach, Breyten 1939(?)- .. **CLC 23, 37, 126**
See also CA 113; 129; CANR 61; CWW 2; DAM POET; DLB 225

Bridgers, Sue Ellen 1942- .... **CLC 26**
See also AAYA 8; BYA 7, 8; CA 65-68; CANR 11, 36; CLR 18; DLB 52; JRDA; MAICYA 1, 2; SAAS 1; SATA 22, 90; SATA-Essay 109; WYA; YAW

Bridges, Robert (Seymour)
1844-1930 .... **TCLC 1; PC 28**
See also BRW 6; CA 104; 152; CDBLB 1890-1914; DAM POET; DLB 19, 98

Bridie, James .... **TCLC 3**
See also Mavor, Osborne Henry
See also DLB 10

Brin, David 1950- .... **CLC 34**
See also AAYA 21; CA 102; CANR 24, 70; INT CANR-24; SATA 65; SCFW 2; SFW 4

Brink, Andre (Philippus) 1935- . **CLC 18, 36, 106**
See also AFW; BRWS 6; CA 104; CANR 39, 62, 109; CN 7; DLB 225; INT CA-103; MTCW 1, 2; WLIT 2

Brinsmead, H. F.
See Brinsmead, H(esba) F(ay)

Brinsmead, H. F(ay)
See Brinsmead, H(esba) F(ay)

Brinsmead, H(esba) F(ay) 1922- ...... **CLC 21**
See also CA 21-24R; CANR 10; CLR 47; CWRI 5; MAICYA 1, 2; SAAS 5; SATA 18, 78

Brittain, Vera (Mary) 1893(?)-1970 . **CLC 23**
See also CA 13-16; 25-28R; CANR 58; CAP 1; DLB 191; FW; MTCW 1, 2

Broch, Hermann 1886-1951 .... **TCLC 20**
See also CA 117; CDWLB 2; DLB 85, 124; EW 10; RGWL 2

Brock, Rose
See Hansen, Joseph
See also GLL 1

Brod, Max 1884-1968 .... **TCLC 115**
See also CA 5-8R; 25-28R; CANR 7; DLB 81

Brodkey, Harold (Roy) 1930-1996 ... **CLC 56**
See also CA 111; 151; CANR 71; CN 7; DLB 130; TCLC 123

Brodskii, Iosif
See Brodsky, Joseph
See also RGWL 2

Brodsky, Iosif Alexandrovich 1940-1996
See Brodsky, Joseph
See also AITN 1; CA 41-44R; 151; CANR 37, 106; DA3; DAM POET; MTCW 1, 2

Brodsky, Joseph . **CLC 4, 6, 13, 36, 100; PC 9**
See also Brodsky, Iosif Alexandrovich
See also AMWS 8; CWW 2; MTCW 1

Buchan, John 1875-1940 .... **TCLC 41**
See also CA 108; 145; CMW 4; DAB; DAM POP; DLB 34, 70, 156; HGG; MSW; MTCW 1; RGEL 2; RHW; YABC 2

Buchanan, George 1506-1582 .... **LC 4**
See also DLB 132

Buchanan, Robert 1841-1901 .... **TCLC 107**
See also CA 179; DLB 18, 35

Buchheim, Lothar-Guenther 1918- .... **CLC 6**
See also CA 85-88

Buchner, (Karl) Georg 1813-1837 . **NCLC 26**
See also CDWLB 2; DLB 133; EW 6; RGSF 2; RGWL 2; TWA

Buchwald, Art(hur) 1925- .... **CLC 33**
See also AITN 1; CA 5-8R; CANR 21, 67, 107; MTCW 1, 2; SATA 10

Buck, Pearl S(ydenstricker) 1892-1973 .... **CLC 7, 11, 18, 127**
See also AAYA 42; AITN 1; AMWS 2; BPFB 1; CA 1-4R; 41-44R; CANR 1, 34; CDALBS; DA; DA3; DAB; DAC; DAM MST, NOV; DLB 9, 102; LAIT 3; MTCW 1, 2; RGAL 4; RHW; SATA 1, 25; TUS

Buckler, Ernest 1908-1984 .... **CLC 13**
See also CA 11-12; 114; CAP 1; CCA 1; DAC; DAM MST; DLB 68; SATA 47

Buckley, Vincent (Thomas) 1925-1988 .... **CLC 57**
See also CA 101

Buckley, William F(rank), Jr. 1925- . **CLC 7, 18, 37**
See also AITN 1; BPFB 1; CA 1-4R; CANR 1, 24, 53, 93; CMW 4; CPW; DA3; DAM POP; DLB 137; DLBY 1980; INT CANR-24; MTCW 1, 2; TUS

Buechner, (Carl) Frederick 1926- . **CLC 2, 4, 6, 9**
See also BPFB 1; CA 13-16R; CANR 11, 39, 64; CN 7; DAM NOV; DLBY 1980; INT CANR-11; MTCW 1, 2

Buell, John (Edward) 1927- .... **CLC 10**
See also CA 1-4R; CANR 71; DLB 53

Buero Vallejo, Antonio 1916-2000 ... **CLC 15, 46, 139; DC 18**
See also CA 106; 189; CANR 24, 49, 75; DFS 11; HW 1; MTCW 1, 2

Bufalino, Gesualdo 1920(?)-1990 ...... **CLC 74**
See also CWW 2; DLB 196

Bugayev, Boris Nikolayevich 1880-1934 .... **TCLC 7; PC 11**
See also Bely, Andrey; Belyi, Andrei
See also CA 104; 165; MTCW 1

Bukowski, Charles 1920-1994 ... **CLC 2, 5, 9, 41, 82, 108; PC 18; SSC 45**
See also CA 17-20R; 144; CANR 40, 62, 105; CPW; DA3; DAM NOV, POET; DLB 5, 130, 169; MTCW 1, 2

Bulgakov, Mikhail (Afanas'evich) 1891-1940 .... **TCLC 2, 16; SSC 18**
See also BPFB 1; CA 105; 152; DAM DRAM, NOV; NFS 8; RGSF 2; RGWL 2; SFW 4; TWA

Bulgya, Alexander Alexandrovich 1901-1956 .... **TCLC 53**
See also Fadeyev, Alexander
See also CA 117; 181

Bullins, Ed 1935- ... **CLC 1, 5, 7; BLC 1; DC 6**
See also BW 2, 3; CA 49-52; CAAS 16; CAD; CANR 24, 46, 73; CD 5; DAM DRAM, MULT; DLB 7, 38, 249; MTCW 1, 2; RGAL 4

Bulwer-Lytton, Edward (George Earle Lytton) 1803-1873 .... **NCLC 1, 45**
See also DLB 21; RGEL 2; SFW 4; SUFW; TEA

Bunin, Ivan Alexeyevich 1870-1953 .... **TCLC 6; SSC 5**
See also CA 104; RGSF 2; RGWL 2; TWA

Bunting, Basil 1900-1985 ...... **CLC 10, 39, 47**
See also BRWS 7; CA 53-56; 115; CANR 7; DAM POET; DLB 20; RGEL 2

Bunuel, Luis 1900-1983 ... **CLC 16, 80; HLC 1**
See also CA 101; 110; CANR 32, 77; DAM MULT; HW 1

Bunyan, John 1628-1688 ..... **LC 4, 69; WLC**
See also BRW 2; BYA 5; CDBLB 1660-1789; DA; DAB; DAC; DAM MST; DLB 39; RGEL 2; TEA; WCH; WLIT 3

Buravsky, Alexandr .... **CLC 59**

Burckhardt, Jacob (Christoph) 1818-1897 .... **NCLC 49**
See also EW 6

Burford, Eleanor
See Hibbert, Eleanor Alice Burford

Burgess, Anthony . **CLC 1, 2, 4, 5, 8, 10, 13, 15, 22, 40, 62, 81, 94**
See also Wilson, John (Anthony) Burgess
See also AAYA 25; AITN 1; BRWS 1; CD-BLB 1960 to Present; DAB; DLB 14, 194, 261; DLBY 1998; MTCW 1; RGEL 2; RHW; SFW 4; YAW

Burke, Edmund 1729(?)-1797 .... **LC 7, 36; WLC**
See also BRW 3; DA; DA3; DAB; DAC; DAM MST; DLB 104, 252; RGEL 2; TEA

Burke, Kenneth (Duva) 1897-1993 ... **CLC 2, 24**
See also AMW; CA 5-8R; 143; CANR 39, 74; DLB 45, 63; MTCW 1, 2; RGAL 4

Burke, Leda
See Garnett, David

Burke, Ralph
See Silverberg, Robert

Burke, Thomas 1886-1945 .... **TCLC 63**
See also CA 113; 155; CMW 4; DLB 197

Burney, Fanny 1752-1840 .... **NCLC 12, 54, 107**
See also BRWS 3; DLB 39; RGEL 2; TEA

Burney, Frances
See Burney, Fanny

Burns, Robert 1759-1796 ... **LC 3, 29, 40; PC 6; WLC**
See also BRW 3; CDBLB 1789-1832; DA; DA3; DAB; DAC; DAM MST, POET; DLB 109; EXPP; PAB; RGEL 2; TEA; WP

Burns, Tex
See L'Amour, Louis (Dearborn)
See also TCWW 2

Burnshaw, Stanley 1906- .... **CLC 3, 13, 44**
See also CA 9-12R; CP 7; DLB 48; DLBY 1997

Burr, Anne 1937- .... **CLC 6**
See also CA 25-28R

Burroughs, Edgar Rice 1875-1950 . **TCLC 2, 32**
See also AAYA 11; BPFB 1; BYA 4, 9; CA 104; 132; DA3; DAM NOV; DLB 8; FANT; MTCW 1, 2; RGAL 4; SATA 41; SCFW 2; SFW 4; TUS; YAW

Burroughs, William S(eward) 1914-1997 .. **CLC 1, 2, 5, 15, 22, 42, 75, 109; WLC**
See also Lee, William; Lee, Willy
See also AITN 2; AMWS 3; BPFB 1; CA 9-12R; 160; CANR 20, 52, 104; CN 7; CPW; DA; DA3; DAB; DAC; DAM MST, NOV, POP; DLB 2, 8, 16, 152, 237; DLBY 1981, 1997; HGG; MTCW 1, 2; RGAL 4; SFW 4; TCLC 121

Burton, Sir Richard F(rancis) 1821-1890 .... **NCLC 42**
See also DLB 55, 166, 184

Burton, Robert 1577-1640 .... **LC 74**
See also DLB 151; RGEL 2

Buruma, Ian 1951- .... **CLC 163**
See also CA 128; CANR 65

Busch, Frederick 1941- .... **CLC 7, 10, 18, 47**
See also CA 33-36R; CAAS 1; CANR 45, 73, 92; CN 7; DLB 6, 218

Bush, Ronald 1946- .... **CLC 34**
See also CA 136

Bustos, F(rancisco)
See Borges, Jorge Luis

Bustos Domecq, H(onorio)
See Bioy Casares, Adolfo; Borges, Jorge Luis

Butler, Octavia E(stelle) 1947- .... **CLC 38, 121; BLCS**
See also AAYA 18; AFAW 2; BPFB 1; BW 2, 3; CA 73-76; CANR 12, 24, 38, 73; CLR 65; CPW; DA3; DAM MULT, POP; DLB 33; MTCW 1, 2; NFS 8; SATA 84; SCFW 2; SFW 4; SSFS 6; YAW

Butler, Robert Olen, (Jr.) 1945- ...... **CLC 81, 162**
See also BPFB 1; CA 112; CANR 66; CSW; DAM POP; DLB 173; INT CA-112; MTCW 1; SSFS 11

Butler, Samuel 1612-1680 ...... **LC 16, 43**
See also DLB 101, 126; RGEL 2

Butler, Samuel 1835-1902 .... **TCLC 1, 33; WLC**
See also BRWS 2; CA 143; CDBLB 1890-1914; DA; DA3; DAB; DAC; DAM MST, NOV; DLB 18, 57, 174; RGEL 2; SFW 4; TEA

Butler, Walter C.
See Faust, Frederick (Schiller)

Butor, Michel (Marie Francois) 1926- .... **CLC 1, 3, 8, 11, 15, 161**
See also CA 9-12R; CANR 33, 66; DLB 83; EW 13; GFL 1789 to the Present; MTCW 1, 2

Butts, Mary 1890(?)-1937 .... **TCLC 77**
See also CA 148; DLB 240

Buxton, Ralph
See Silverstein, Alvin; Silverstein, Virginia B(arbara Opshelor)

Buzo, Alexander (John) 1944- .... **CLC 61**
See also CA 97-100; CANR 17, 39, 69; CD 5

Buzzati, Dino 1906-1972 .... **CLC 36**
See also CA 160; 33-36R; DLB 177; RGWL 2; SFW 4

Byars, Betsy (Cromer) 1928- .... **CLC 35**
See also AAYA 19; BYA 3; CA 33-36R, 183; CAAE 183; CANR 18, 36, 57, 102; CLR 1, 16, 72; DLB 52; INT CANR-18; JRDA; MAICYA 1, 2; MAICYAS 1; MTCW 1; SAAS 1; SATA 4, 46, 80; SATA-Essay 108; WYA; YAW

Byatt, A(ntonia) S(usan Drabble) 1936- .... **CLC 19, 65, 136**
See also BPFB 1; BRWS 4; CA 13-16R; CANR 13, 33, 50, 75, 96; DA3; DAM NOV, POP; DLB 14, 194; MTCW 1, 2; RGSF 2; RHW; TEA

Byrne, David 1952- .... **CLC 26**
See also CA 127

Byrne, John Keyes 1926-
See Leonard, Hugh
See also CA 102; CANR 78; INT CA-102

Byron, George Gordon (Noel) 1788-1824 ..... **NCLC 2, 12, 109; PC 16; WLC**
See also BRW 4; CDBLB 1789-1832; DA; DA3; DAB; DAC; DAM MST, POET; DLB 96, 110; EXPP; PAB; PFS 1, 14; RGEL 2; TEA; WLIT 3; WP

Byron, Robert 1905-1941 .... **TCLC 67**
See also CA 160; DLB 195

C. 3. 3.
See Wilde, Oscar (Fingal O'Flahertie Wills)

Caballero, Fernan 1796-1877 .... **NCLC 10**
Cabell, Branch
  See Cabell, James Branch
Cabell, James Branch 1879-1958 .... **TCLC 6**
  See also CA 105; 152; DLB 9, 78; FANT;
  MTCW 1; RGAL 4; SUFW
Cabeza de Vaca, Alvar Nunez
  1490-1557(?) .... **LC 61**
Cable, George Washington
  1844-1925 .... **TCLC 4; SSC 4**
  See also CA 104; 155; DLB 12, 74; DLBD
  13; RGAL 4; TUS
Cabral de Melo Neto, Joao
  1920-1999 .... **CLC 76**
  See also CA 151; DAM MULT; LAW;
  LAWS 1
Cabrera Infante, G(uillermo) 1929- . **CLC 5,
  25, 45, 120; HLC 1; SSC 39**
  See also CA 85-88; CANR 29, 65, 110; CD-
  WLB 3; DA3; DAM MULT; DLB 113;
  HW 1, 2; LAW; LAWS 1; MTCW 1, 2;
  RGSF 2; WLIT 1
Cade, Toni
  See Bambara, Toni Cade
Cadmus and Harmonia
  See Buchan, John
Caedmon fl. 658-680 .... **CMLC 7**
  See also DLB 146
Caeiro, Alberto
  See Pessoa, Fernando (Antonio Nogueira)
Caesar, Julius .... **CMLC 47**
  See also Julius Caesar
  See also AW 1; RGWL 2
Cage, John (Milton, Jr.) 1912-1992 . **CLC 41**
  See also CA 13-16R; 169; CANR 9, 78;
  DLB 193; INT CANR-9
Cahan, Abraham 1860-1951 .... **TCLC 71**
  See also CA 108; 154; DLB 9, 25, 28;
  RGAL 4
Cain, G.
  See Cabrera Infante, G(uillermo)
Cain, Guillermo
  See Cabrera Infante, G(uillermo)
Cain, James M(allahan) 1892-1977 .. **CLC 3,
  11, 28**
  See also AITN 1; BPFB 1; CA 17-20R; 73-
  76; CANR 8, 34, 61; CMW 4; DLB 226;
  MSW; MTCW 1; RGAL 4
Caine, Hall 1853-1931 .... **TCLC 97**
  See also RHW
Caine, Mark
  See Raphael, Frederic (Michael)
Calasso, Roberto 1941- .... **CLC 81**
  See also CA 143; CANR 89
Calderon de la Barca, Pedro
  1600-1681 .... **LC 23; DC 3; HLCS 1**
  See also EW 2; RGWL 2; TWA
Caldwell, Erskine (Preston)
  1903-1987 .... **CLC 1, 8, 14, 50, 60; SSC
  19**
  See also AITN 1; AMW; BPFB 1; CA 1-4R;
  121; CAAS 1; CANR 2, 33; DA3; DAM
  NOV; DLB 9, 86; MTCW 1, 2; RGAL 4;
  RGSF 2; TCLC 117; TUS
Caldwell, (Janet Miriam) Taylor (Holland)
  1900-1985 .... **CLC 2, 28, 39**
  See also BPFB 1; CA 5-8R; 116; CANR 5;
  DA3; DAM NOV, POP; DLBD 17; RHW
Calhoun, John Caldwell
  1782-1850 .... **NCLC 15**
  See also DLB 3, 248
Calisher, Hortense 1911- ..... **CLC 2, 4, 8, 38,
  134; SSC 15**
  See also CA 1-4R; CANR 1, 22; CN 7;
  DA3; DAM NOV; DLB 2, 218; INT
  CANR-22; MTCW 1, 2; RGAL 4; RGSF 2

Callaghan, Morley Edward
  1903-1990 .... **CLC 3, 14, 41, 65**
  See also CA 9-12R; 132; CANR 33, 73;
  DAC; DAM MST; DLB 68; MTCW 1, 2;
  RGEL 2; RGSF 2
Callimachus c. 305 B.C.-c. 240
  B.C. .... **CMLC 18**
  See also AW 1; DLB 176; RGWL 2
Calvin, Jean
  See Calvin, John
  See also GFL Beginnings to 1789
Calvin, John 1509-1564 .... **LC 37**
  See also Calvin, Jean
Calvino, Italo 1923-1985 .... **CLC 5, 8, 11, 22,
  33, 39, 73; SSC 3, 48**
  See also CA 85-88; 116; CANR 23, 61;
  DAM NOV; DLB 196; EW 13; MTCW 1,
  2; RGSF 2; RGWL 2; SFW 4; SSFS 12
Camden, William 1551-1623 .... **LC 77**
  See also DLB 172
Cameron, Carey 1952- .... **CLC 59**
  See also CA 135
Cameron, Peter 1959- .... **CLC 44**
  See also CA 125; CANR 50; DLB 234;
  GLL 2
Camoens, Luis Vaz de 1524(?)-1580
  See also EW 2; HLCS 1
Camoes, Luis de 1524(?)-1580 .... **LC 62;
  HLCS 1; PC 31**
  See also RGWL 2
Campana, Dino 1885-1932 .... **TCLC 20**
  See also CA 117; DLB 114
Campanella, Tommaso 1568-1639 .... **LC 32**
  See also RGWL 2
Campbell, John W(ood, Jr.)
  1910-1971 .... **CLC 32**
  See also CA 21-22; 29-32R; CANR 34;
  CAP 2; DLB 8; MTCW 1; SCFW; SFW 4
Campbell, Joseph 1904-1987 .... **CLC 69**
  See also AAYA 3; BEST 89:2; CA 1-4R;
  124; CANR 3, 28, 61, 107; DA3; MTCW
  1, 2
Campbell, Maria 1940- .... **CLC 85**
  See also CA 102; CANR 54; CCA 1; DAC;
  NNAL
Campbell, Paul N. 1923-
  See hooks, bell
  See also CA 21-24R
Campbell, (John) Ramsey 1946- ..... **CLC 42;
  SSC 19**
  See also CA 57-60; CANR 7, 102; DLB
  261; HGG; INT CANR-7; SUFW
Campbell, (Ignatius) Roy (Dunnachie)
  1901-1957 .... **TCLC 5**
  See also AFW; CA 104; 155; DLB 20, 225;
  MTCW 2; RGEL 2
Campbell, Thomas 1777-1844 .... **NCLC 19**
  See also DLB 93, 144; RGEL 2
Campbell, Wilfred .... **TCLC 9**
  See also Campbell, William
Campbell, William 1858(?)-1918
  See Campbell, Wilfred
  See also CA 106; DLB 92
Campion, Jane .... **CLC 95**
  See also AAYA 33; CA 138; CANR 87
Campion, Thomas 1567-1620 .... **LC 78**
  See also CDBLB Before 1660; DAM POET;
  DLB 58, 172; RGEL 2
Camus, Albert 1913-1960 ...... **CLC 1, 2, 4, 9,
  11, 14, 32, 63, 69, 124; DC 2; SSC 9;
  WLC**
  See also AAYA 36; AFW; BPFB 1; CA 89-
  92; DA; DA3; DAB; DAC; DAM DRAM,
  MST, NOV; DLB 72; EW 13; EXPN;
  EXPS; GFL 1789 to the Present; MTCW
  1, 2; NFS 6; RGSF 2; RGWL 2; SSFS 4;
  TWA
Canby, Vincent 1924-2000 .... **CLC 13**
  See also CA 81-84; 191

Cancale
  See Desnos, Robert
Canetti, Elias 1905-1994 .. **CLC 3, 14, 25, 75,
  86**
  See also CA 21-24R; 146; CANR 23, 61,
  79; CDWLB 2; CWW 2; DA3; DLB 85,
  124; EW 12; MTCW 1, 2; RGWL 2; TWA
Canfield, Dorothea F.
  See Fisher, Dorothy (Frances) Canfield
Canfield, Dorothea Frances
  See Fisher, Dorothy (Frances) Canfield
Canfield, Dorothy
  See Fisher, Dorothy (Frances) Canfield
Canin, Ethan 1960- .... **CLC 55**
  See also CA 131; 135
Cankar, Ivan 1876-1918 .... **TCLC 105**
  See also CDWLB 4; DLB 147
Cannon, Curt
  See Hunter, Evan
Cao, Lan 1961- .... **CLC 109**
  See also CA 165
Cape, Judith
  See Page, P(atricia) K(athleen)
  See also CCA 1
Capek, Karel 1890-1938 .... **TCLC 6, 37; DC
  1; SSC 36; WLC**
  See also CA 104; 140; CDWLB 4; DA;
  DA3; DAB; DAC; DAM DRAM, MST,
  NOV; DFS 7, 11 !**; DLB 215; EW 10;
  MTCW 1; RGSF 2; RGWL 2; SCFW 2;
  SFW 4
Capote, Truman 1924-1984 . **CLC 1, 3, 8, 13,
  19, 34, 38, 58; SSC 2, 47; WLC**
  See also AMWS 3; BPFB 1; CA 5-8R; 113;
  CANR 18, 62; CDALB 1941-1968; CPW;
  DA; DA3; DAB; DAC; DAM MST, NOV,
  POP; DLB 2, 185, 227; DLBY 1980,
  1984; EXPS; GLL 1; LAIT 3; MTCW 1,
  2; NCFS 2; RGAL 4; RGSF 2; SATA 91;
  SSFS 2; TUS
Capra, Frank 1897-1991 .... **CLC 16**
  See also CA 61-64; 135
Caputo, Philip 1941- .... **CLC 32**
  See also CA 73-76; CANR 40; YAW
Caragiale, Ion Luca 1852-1912 ...... **TCLC 76**
  See also CA 157
Card, Orson Scott 1951- .... **CLC 44, 47, 50**
  See also AAYA 11, 42; BPFB 1; BYA 5, 8;
  CA 102; CANR 27, 47, 73, 102, 106;
  CPW; DA3; DAM POP; FANT; INT
  CANR-27; MTCW 1, 2; NFS 5; SATA
  83, 127; SCFW 2; SFW 4; YAW
Cardenal, Ernesto 1925- .... **CLC 31, 161;
  HLC 1; PC 22**
  See also CA 49-52; CANR 2, 32, 66; CWW
  2; DAM MULT, POET; HW 1, 2; LAWS
  1; MTCW 1, 2; RGWL 2
Cardozo, Benjamin N(athan)
  1870-1938 .... **TCLC 65**
  See also CA 117; 164
Carducci, Giosue (Alessandro Giuseppe)
  1835-1907 .... **TCLC 32**
  See also CA 163; EW 7; RGWL 2
Carew, Thomas 1595(?)-1640 . **LC 13; PC 29**
  See also BRW 2; DLB 126; PAB; RGEL 2
Carey, Ernestine Gilbreth 1908- ...... **CLC 17**
  See also CA 5-8R; CANR 71; SATA 2
Carey, Peter 1943- .... **CLC 40, 55, 96**
  See also CA 123; 127; CANR 53, 76; CN
  7; INT CA-127; MTCW 1, 2; RGSF 2;
  SATA 94
Carleton, William 1794-1869 .... **NCLC 3**
  See also DLB 159; RGEL 2; RGSF 2
Carlisle, Henry (Coffin) 1926- .... **CLC 33**
  See also CA 13-16R; CANR 15, 85
Carlsen, Chris
  See Holdstock, Robert P.

Carlson, Ron(ald F.) 1947- .... **CLC 54**
See also CA 105; CAAE 189; CANR 27; DLB 244

Carlyle, Thomas 1795-1881 ..... **NCLC 22, 70**
See also BRW 4; CDBLB 1789-1832; DA; DAB; DAC; DAM MST; DLB 55, 144, 254; RGEL 2; TEA

Carman, (William) Bliss
1861-1929 .... **TCLC 7; PC 34**
See also CA 104; 152; DAC; DLB 92; RGEL 2

Carnegie, Dale 1888-1955 .... **TCLC 53**

Carossa, Hans 1878-1956 .... **TCLC 48**
See also CA 170; DLB 66

Carpenter, Don(ald Richard)
1931-1995 .... **CLC 41**
See also CA 45-48; 149; CANR 1, 71

Carpenter, Edward 1844-1929 .... **TCLC 88**
See also CA 163; GLL 1

Carpenter, John (Howard) 1948- ... **CLC 161**
See also AAYA 2; CA 134; SATA 58

Carpentier (y Valmont), Alejo
1904-1980 . **CLC 8, 11, 38, 110; HLC 1; SSC 35**
See also CA 65-68; 97-100; CANR 11, 70; CDWLB 3; DAM MULT; DLB 113; HW 1, 2; LAW; RGSF 2; RGWL 2; WLIT 1

Carr, Caleb 1955(?)- .... **CLC 86**
See also CA 147; CANR 73; DA3

Carr, Emily 1871-1945 .... **TCLC 32**
See also CA 159; DLB 68; FW; GLL 2

Carr, John Dickson 1906-1977 .... **CLC 3**
See also Fairbairn, Roger
See also CA 49-52; 69-72; CANR 3, 33, 60; CMW 4; MSW; MTCW 1, 2

Carr, Philippa
See Hibbert, Eleanor Alice Burford

Carr, Virginia Spencer 1929- .... **CLC 34**
See also CA 61-64; DLB 111

Carrere, Emmanuel 1957- .... **CLC 89**
See also CA 200

Carrier, Roch 1937- .... **CLC 13, 78**
See also CA 130; CANR 61; CCA 1; DAC; DAM MST; DLB 53; SATA 105

Carroll, James P. 1943(?)- .... **CLC 38**
See also CA 81-84; CANR 73; MTCW 1

Carroll, Jim 1951- .... **CLC 35, 143**
See also AAYA 17; CA 45-48; CANR 42

Carroll, Lewis ... **NCLC 2, 53; PC 18; WLC**
See also Dodgson, Charles L(utwidge)
See also AAYA 39; BRW 5; BYA 5, 13; CD-BLB 1832-1890; CLR 2, 18; DLB 18, 163, 178; DLBY 1998; EXPN; EXPP; FANT; JRDA; LAIT 1; NFS 7; PFS 11; RGEL 2; SUFW; TEA; WCH

Carroll, Paul Vincent 1900-1968 ...... **CLC 10**
See also CA 9-12R; 25-28R; DLB 10; RGEL 2

Carruth, Hayden 1921- ..... **CLC 4, 7, 10, 18, 84; PC 10**
See also CA 9-12R; CANR 4, 38, 59, 110; CP 7; DLB 5, 165; INT CANR-4; MTCW 1, 2; SATA 47

Carson, Rachel Louise 1907-1964 .... **CLC 71**
See also AMWS 9; ANW; CA 77-80; CANR 35; DA3; DAM POP; FW; LAIT 4; MTCW 1, 2; NCFS 1; SATA 23

Carter, Angela (Olive) 1940-1992 ...... **CLC 5, 41, 76; SSC 13**
See also BRWS 3; CA 53-56; 136; CANR 12, 36, 61, 106; DA3; DLB 14, 207, 261; EXPS; FANT; FW; MTCW 1, 2; RGSF 2; SATA 66; SATA-Obit 70; SFW 4; SSFS 4, 12; WLIT 4

Carter, Nick
See Smith, Martin Cruz

Carver, Raymond 1938-1988 ..... **CLC 22, 36, 53, 55, 126; SSC 8, 51**
See also AMWS 3; BPFB 1; CA 33-36R; 126; CANR 17, 34, 61, 103; CPW; DA3; DAM NOV; DLB 130; DLBY 1984, 1988; MTCW 1, 2; RGAL 4; RGSF 2; SSFS 3, 6, 12, 13; TCWW 2; TUS

Cary, Elizabeth, Lady Falkland
1585-1639 .... **LC 30**

Cary, (Arthur) Joyce (Lunel)
1888-1957 .... **TCLC 1, 29**
See also BRW 7; CA 104; 164; CDBLB 1914-1945; DLB 15, 100; MTCW 2; RGEL 2; TEA

Casanova de Seingalt, Giovanni Jacopo
1725-1798 .... **LC 13**

Casares, Adolfo Bioy
See Bioy Casares, Adolfo
See also RGSF 2

Casas, Bartolome de las 1474-1566
See Las Casas, Bartolome de
See also WLIT 1

Casely-Hayford, J(oseph) E(phraim)
1866-1903 .... **TCLC 24; BLC 1**
See also BW 2; CA 123; 152; DAM MULT

Casey, John (Dudley) 1939- .... **CLC 59**
See also BEST 90:2; CA 69-72; CANR 23, 100

Casey, Michael 1947- .... **CLC 2**
See also CA 65-68; CANR 109; DLB 5

Casey, Patrick
See Thurman, Wallace (Henry)

Casey, Warren (Peter) 1935-1988 .... **CLC 12**
See also CA 101; 127; INT 101

Casona, Alejandro .... **CLC 49**
See also Alvarez, Alejandro Rodriguez

Cassavetes, John 1929-1989 .... **CLC 20**
See also CA 85-88; 127; CANR 82

Cassian, Nina 1924- .... **PC 17**
See also CWP; CWW 2

Cassill, R(onald) V(erlin) 1919- ... **CLC 4, 23**
See also CA 9-12R; CAAS 1; CANR 7, 45; CN 7; DLB 6, 218

Cassiodorus, Flavius Magnus c. 490(?)-c.
583(?) .... **CMLC 43**

Cassirer, Ernst 1874-1945 .... **TCLC 61**
See also CA 157

Cassity, (Allen) Turner 1929- .... **CLC 6, 42**
See also CA 17-20R; CAAS 8; CANR 11; CSW; DLB 105

Castaneda, Carlos (Cesar Aranha)
1931(?)-1998 .... **CLC 12, 119**
See also CA 25-28R; CANR 32, 66, 105; DNFS 1; HW 1; MTCW 1

Castedo, Elena 1937- .... **CLC 65**
See also CA 132

Castedo-Ellerman, Elena
See Castedo, Elena

Castellanos, Rosario 1925-1974 .... **CLC 66; HLC 1; SSC 39**
See also CA 131; 53-56; CANR 58; CD-WLB 3; DAM MULT; DLB 113; FW; HW 1; LAW; MTCW 1; RGSF 2; RGWL 2

Castelvetro, Lodovico 1505-1571 .... **LC 12**

Castiglione, Baldassare 1478-1529 ...... **LC 12**
See also Castiglione, Baldesar
See also RGWL 2

Castiglione, Baldesar
See Castiglione, Baldassare
See also EW 2

Castillo, Ana (Hernandez Del)
1953- .... **CLC 151**
See also AAYA 42; CA 131; CANR 51, 86; CWP; DLB 122, 227; DNFS 2; FW; HW 1

Castle, Robert
See Hamilton, Edmond

Castro (Ruz), Fidel 1926(?)-
See also CA 110; 129; CANR 81; DAM MULT; HLC 1; HW 2

Castro, Guillen de 1569-1631 .... **LC 19**

Castro, Rosalia de 1837-1885 ... **NCLC 3, 78; PC 41**
See also DAM MULT

Cather, Willa (Sibert) 1873-1947 .... **TCLC 1, 11, 31, 99, 125; SSC 2, 50; WLC**
See also AAYA 24; AMW; AMWR 1; BPFB 1; CA 104; 128; CDALB 1865-1917; DA; DA3; DAB; DAC; DAM MST, NOV; DLB 9, 54, 78, 256; DLBD 1; EXPN; EXPS; LAIT 3; MAWW; MTCW 1, 2; NFS 2; RGAL 4; RGSF 2; RHW; SATA 30; SSFS 2, 7; TCWW 2; TUS

Catherine II
See Catherine the Great
See also DLB 150

Catherine the Great 1729-1796 .... **LC 69**
See also Catherine II

Cato, Marcus Porcius 234 B.C.-149
B.C. .... **CMLC 21**
See also Cato the Elder

Cato, Marcus Porcius, the Elder
See Cato, Marcus Porcius

Cato the Elder
See Cato, Marcus Porcius
See also DLB 211

Catton, (Charles) Bruce 1899-1978 . **CLC 35**
See also AITN 1; CA 5-8R; 81-84; CANR 7, 74; DLB 17; SATA 2; SATA-Obit 24

Catullus c. 84 B.C.-54 B.C. .... **CMLC 18**
See also AW 2; CDWLB 1; DLB 211; RGWL 2

Cauldwell, Frank
See King, Francis (Henry)

Caunitz, William J. 1933-1996 .... **CLC 34**
See also BEST 89:3; CA 125; 130; 152; CANR 73; INT 130

Causley, Charles (Stanley) 1917- .... **CLC 7**
See also CA 9-12R; CANR 5, 35, 94; CLR 30; CWRI 5; DLB 27; MTCW 1; SATA 3, 66

Caute, (John) David 1936- .... **CLC 29**
See also CA 1-4R; CAAS 4; CANR 1, 33, 64; CBD; CD 5; CN 7; DAM NOV; DLB 14, 231

Cavafy, C(onstantine) P(eter) ... **TCLC 2, 7; PC 36**
See also Kavafis, Konstantinos Petrou
See also CA 148; DA3; DAM POET; EW 8; MTCW 1; RGWL 2; WP

Cavalcanti, Guido c. 1250-c.
1300 .... **CMLC 54**

Cavallo, Evelyn
See Spark, Muriel (Sarah)

Cavanna, Betty .... **CLC 12**
See also Harrison, Elizabeth (Allen) Cavanna
See also JRDA; MAICYA 1; SAAS 4; SATA 1, 30

Cavendish, Margaret Lucas
1623-1673 .... **LC 30**
See also DLB 131, 252; RGEL 2

Caxton, William 1421(?)-1491(?) .... **LC 17**
See also DLB 170

Cayer, D. M.
See Duffy, Maureen

Cayrol, Jean 1911- .... **CLC 11**
See also CA 89-92; DLB 83

Cela, Camilo Jose 1916-2002 .... **CLC 4, 13, 59, 122; HLC 1**
See also BEST 90:2; CA 21-24R; CAAS 10; CANR 21, 32, 76; DAM MULT; DLBY 1989; EW 13; HW 1; MTCW 1, 2; RGSF 2; RGWL 2

Celan, Paul -1970 .... **CLC 10, 19, 53, 82; PC 10**
See also Antschel, Paul
See also CDWLB 2; DLB 69; RGWL 2

Celine, Louis-Ferdinand .. **CLC 1, 3, 4, 7, 9, 15, 47, 124**
See also Destouches, Louis-Ferdinand
See also DLB 72; EW 11; GFL 1789 to the Present; RGWL 2

Cellini, Benvenuto 1500-1571 .... **LC 7**

Cendrars, Blaise .... **CLC 18, 106**
See also Sauser-Hall, Frederic
See also DLB 258; GFL 1789 to the Present; RGWL 2; WP

Centlivre, Susanna 1669(?)-1723 .... **LC 65**
See also DLB 84; RGEL 2

Cernuda (y Bidon), Luis 1902-1963 . **CLC 54**
See also CA 131; 89-92; DAM POET; DLB 134; GLL 1; HW 1; RGWL 2

Cervantes, Lorna Dee 1954- .... **PC 35**
See also CA 131; CANR 80; CWP; DLB 82; EXPP; HLCS 1; HW 1

Cervantes (Saavedra), Miguel de 1547-1616 .... **LC 6, 23; HLCS; SSC 12; WLC**
See also BYA 1, 14; DA; DAB; DAC; DAM MST, NOV; EW 2; LAIT 1; NFS 8; RGSF 2; RGWL 2; TWA

Cesaire, Aime (Fernand) 1913- . **CLC 19, 32, 112; BLC 1; PC 25**
See also BW 2, 3; CA 65-68; CANR 24, 43, 81; DA3; DAM MULT, POET; GFL 1789 to the Present; MTCW 1, 2; WP

Chabon, Michael 1963- .... **CLC 55, 149**
See also AMWS 11; CA 139; CANR 57, 96

Chabrol, Claude 1930- .... **CLC 16**
See also CA 110

Challans, Mary 1905-1983
See Renault, Mary
See also CA 81-84; 111; CANR 74; DA3; MTCW 2; SATA 23; SATA-Obit 36; TEA

Challis, George
See Faust, Frederick (Schiller)
See also TCWW 2

Chambers, Aidan 1934- .... **CLC 35**
See also AAYA 27; CA 25-28R; CANR 12, 31, 58; JRDA; MAICYA 1, 2; SAAS 12; SATA 1, 69, 108; WYA; YAW

Chambers, James 1948-
See Cliff, Jimmy
See also CA 124

Chambers, Jessie
See Lawrence, D(avid) H(erbert Richards)
See also GLL 1

Chambers, Robert W(illiam) 1865-1933 .... **TCLC 41**
See also CA 165; DLB 202; HGG; SATA 107; SUFW

Chamisso, Adelbert von 1781-1838 .... **NCLC 82**
See also DLB 90; RGWL 2; SUFW

Chance, John T.
See Carpenter, John (Howard)

Chandler, Raymond (Thornton) 1888-1959 .... **TCLC 1, 7; SSC 23**
See also AAYA 25; AMWS 4; BPFB 1; CA 104; 129; CANR 60, 107; CDALB 1929-1941; CMW 4; DA3; DLB 226, 253; DLBD 6; MSW; MTCW 1, 2; RGAL 4; TUS

Chang, Eileen 1921-1995 .... **SSC 28**
See also CA 166; CWW 2

Chang, Jung 1952- .... **CLC 71**
See also CA 142

Chang Ai-Ling
See Chang, Eileen

Channing, William Ellery 1780-1842 .... **NCLC 17**
See also DLB 1, 59, 235; RGAL 4

Chao, Patricia 1955- .... **CLC 119**
See also CA 163

Chaplin, Charles Spencer 1889-1977 .... **CLC 16**
See also Chaplin, Charlie
See also CA 81-84; 73-76

Chaplin, Charlie
See Chaplin, Charles Spencer
See also DLB 44

Chapman, George 1559(?)-1634 .... **LC 22**
See also BRW 1; DAM DRAM; DLB 62, 121; RGEL 2

Chapman, Graham 1941-1989 .... **CLC 21**
See also Monty Python
See also CA 116; 129; CANR 35, 95

Chapman, John Jay 1862-1933 .... **TCLC 7**
See also CA 104; 191

Chapman, Lee
See Bradley, Marion Zimmer
See also GLL 1

Chapman, Walker
See Silverberg, Robert

Chappell, Fred (Davis) 1936- .... **CLC 40, 78, 162**
See also CA 5-8R; CAAE 198; CAAS 4; CANR 8, 33, 67, 110; CN 7; CP 7; CSW; DLB 6, 105; HGG

Char, Rene(-Emile) 1907-1988 .... **CLC 9, 11, 14, 55**
See also CA 13-16R; 124; CANR 32; DAM POET; DLB 258; GFL 1789 to the Present; MTCW 1, 2; RGWL 2

Charby, Jay
See Ellison, Harlan (Jay)

Chardin, Pierre Teilhard de
See Teilhard de Chardin, (Marie Joseph) Pierre

Chariton fl. 1st cent. (?)- .... **CMLC 49**

Charlemagne 742-814 .... **CMLC 37**

Charles I 1600-1649 .... **LC 13**

Charriere, Isabelle de 1740-1805 .. **NCLC 66**

Chartier, Emile-Auguste
See Alain

Charyn, Jerome 1937- .... **CLC 5, 8, 18**
See also CA 5-8R; CAAS 1; CANR 7, 61, 101; CMW 4; CN 7; DLBY 1983; MTCW 1

Chase, Adam
See Marlowe, Stephen

Chase, Mary (Coyle) 1907-1981 .... **DC 1**
See also CA 77-80; 105; CAD; CWD; DFS 11; DLB 228; SATA 17; SATA-Obit 29

Chase, Mary Ellen 1887-1973 .... **CLC 2**
See also CA 13-16; 41-44R; CAP 1; SATA 10; TCLC 124

Chase, Nicholas
See Hyde, Anthony
See also CCA 1

Chateaubriand, Francois Rene de 1768-1848 .... **NCLC 3**
See also DLB 119; EW 5; GFL 1789 to the Present; RGWL 2; TWA

Chatterje, Sarat Chandra 1876-1936(?)
See Chatterji, Saratchandra
See also CA 109

Chatterji, Bankim Chandra 1838-1894 .... **NCLC 19**

Chatterji, Saratchandra .... **TCLC 13**
See also Chatterje, Sarat Chandra
See also CA 186

Chatterton, Thomas 1752-1770 .... **LC 3, 54**
See also DAM POET; DLB 109; RGEL 2

Chatwin, (Charles) Bruce 1940-1989 .... **CLC 28, 57, 59**
See also AAYA 4; BEST 90:1; BRWS 4; CA 85-88; 127; CPW; DAM POP; DLB 194, 204

Chaucer, Daniel
See Ford, Ford Madox
See also RHW

Chaucer, Geoffrey 1340(?)-1400 .. **LC 17, 56; PC 19; WLCS**
See also BRW 1; BRWR 2; CDBLB Before 1660; DA; DA3; DAB; DAC; DAM MST, POET; DLB 146; LAIT 1; PAB; PFS 14; RGEL 2; TEA; WLIT 3; WP

Chavez, Denise (Elia) 1948-
See also CA 131; CANR 56, 81; DAM MULT; DLB 122; FW; HLC 1; HW 1, 2; MTCW 2

Chaviaras, Strates 1935-
See Haviaras, Stratis
See also CA 105

Chayefsky, Paddy .... **CLC 23**
See also Chayefsky, Sidney
See also CAD; DLB 7, 44; DLBY 1981; RGAL 4

Chayefsky, Sidney 1923-1981
See Chayefsky, Paddy
See also CA 9-12R; 104; CANR 18; DAM DRAM

Chedid, Andree 1920- .... **CLC 47**
See also CA 145; CANR 95

Cheever, John 1912-1982 ..... **CLC 3, 7, 8, 11, 15, 25, 64; SSC 1, 38; WLC**
See also AMWS 1; BPFB 1; CA 5-8R; 106; CABS 1; CANR 5, 27, 76; CDALB 1941-1968; CPW; DA; DA3; DAB; DAC; DAM MST, NOV, POP; DLB 2, 102, 227; DLBY 1980, 1982; EXPS; INT CANR-5; MTCW 1, 2; RGAL 4; RGSF 2; SSFS 2, 14; TUS

Cheever, Susan 1943- .... **CLC 18, 48**
See also CA 103; CANR 27, 51, 92; DLBY 1982; INT CANR-27

Chekhonte, Antosha
See Chekhov, Anton (Pavlovich)

Chekhov, Anton (Pavlovich) 1860-1904 . **TCLC 3, 10, 31, 55, 96; DC 9; SSC 2, 28, 41, 51; WLC**
See also BYA 14; CA 104; 124; DA; DA3; DAB; DAC; DAM DRAM, MST; DFS 1, 5, 10, 12; EW 7; EXPS; LAIT 3; RGSF 2; RGWL 2; SATA 90; SSFS 5, 13, 14; TWA

Cheney, Lynne V. 1941- .... **CLC 70**
See also CA 89-92; CANR 58

Chernyshevsky, Nikolai Gavrilovich
See Chernyshevsky, Nikolay Gavrilovich
See also DLB 238

Chernyshevsky, Nikolay Gavrilovich 1828-1889 .... **NCLC 1**
See also Chernyshevsky, Nikolai Gavrilovich

Cherry, Carolyn Janice 1942-
See Cherryh, C. J.
See also CA 65-68; CANR 10

Cherryh, C. J. .... **CLC 35**
See also Cherry, Carolyn Janice
See also AAYA 24; BPFB 1; DLBY 1980; FANT; SATA 93; SCFW 2; SFW 4; YAW

Chesnutt, Charles W(addell) 1858-1932 .... **TCLC 5, 39; BLC 1; SSC 7, 54**
See also AFAW 1, 2; BW 1, 3; CA 106; 125; CANR 76; DAM MULT; DLB 12, 50, 78; MTCW 1, 2; RGAL 4; RGSF 2; SSFS 11

Chester, Alfred 1929(?)-1971 .... **CLC 49**
See also CA 196; 33-36R; DLB 130

Chesterton, G(ilbert) K(eith) 1874-1936 . **TCLC 1, 6, 64; PC 28; SSC 1, 46**
See also BRW 6; CA 104; 132; CANR 73; CDBLB 1914-1945; CMW 4; DAM NOV, POET; DLB 10, 19, 34, 70, 98, 149, 178;

Connelly, Marc(us Cook) 1890-1980 . **CLC 7**
See also CA 85-88; 102; CANR 30; DFS 12; DLB 7; DLBY 1980; RGAL 4; SATA-Obit 25

Connor, Ralph .... **TCLC 31**
See also Gordon, Charles William
See also DLB 92; TCWW 2

Conrad, Joseph 1857-1924 .... **TCLC 1, 6, 13, 25, 43, 57; SSC 9; WLC**
See also AAYA 26; BPFB 1; BRW 6; BRWR 2; BYA 2; CA 104; 131; CANR 60; CDBLB 1890-1914; DA; DA3; DAB; DAC; DAM MST, NOV; DLB 10, 34, 98, 156; EXPN; EXPS; LAIT 2; MTCW 1, 2; NFS 2; RGEL 2; RGSF 2; SATA 27; SSFS 1, 12; TEA; WLIT 4

Conrad, Robert Arnold
See Hart, Moss

Conroy, (Donald) Pat(rick) 1945- ... **CLC 30, 74**
See also AAYA 8; AITN 1; BPFB 1; CA 85-88; CANR 24, 53; CPW; CSW; DA3; DAM NOV, POP; DLB 6; LAIT 5; MTCW 1, 2

Constant (de Rebecque), (Henri) Benjamin 1767-1830 .... **NCLC 6**
See also DLB 119; EW 4; GFL 1789 to the Present

Conway, Jill K(er) 1934- .... **CLC 152**
See also CA 130; CANR 94

Conybeare, Charles Augustus
See Eliot, T(homas) S(tearns)

Cook, Michael 1933-1994 .... **CLC 58**
See also CA 93-96; CANR 68; DLB 53

Cook, Robin 1940- .... **CLC 14**
See also AAYA 32; BEST 90:2; BPFB 1; CA 108; 111; CANR 41, 90, 109; CPW; DA3; DAM POP; HGG; INT CA-111

Cook, Roy
See Silverberg, Robert

Cooke, Elizabeth 1948- .... **CLC 55**
See also CA 129

Cooke, John Esten 1830-1886 .... **NCLC 5**
See also DLB 3, 248; RGAL 4

Cooke, John Estes
See Baum, L(yman) Frank

Cooke, M. E.
See Creasey, John

Cooke, Margaret
See Creasey, John

Cooke, Rose Terry 1827-1892 ...... **NCLC 110**
See also DLB 12, 74

Cook-Lynn, Elizabeth 1930- .... **CLC 93**
See also CA 133; DAM MULT; DLB 175; NNAL

Cooney, Ray .... **CLC 62**
See also CBD

Cooper, Douglas 1960- .... **CLC 86**

Cooper, Henry St. John
See Creasey, John

Cooper, J(oan) California (?)- .... **CLC 56**
See also AAYA 12; BW 1; CA 125; CANR 55; DAM MULT; DLB 212

Cooper, James Fenimore 1789-1851 .... **NCLC 1, 27, 54**
See also AAYA 22; AMW; BPFB 1; CDALB 1640-1865; DA3; DLB 3, 183, 250, 254; LAIT 1; NFS 9; RGAL 4; SATA 19; TUS; WCH

Coover, Robert (Lowell) 1932- ...... **CLC 3, 7, 15, 32, 46, 87, 161; SSC 15**
See also AMWS 5; BPFB 1; CA 45-48; CANR 3, 37, 58; CN 7; DAM NOV; DLB 2, 227; DLBY 1981; MTCW 1, 2; RGAL 4; RGSF 2

Copeland, Stewart (Armstrong) 1952- .... **CLC 26**

Copernicus, Nicolaus 1473-1543 .... **LC 45**

Coppard, A(lfred) E(dgar) 1878-1957 .... **TCLC 5; SSC 21**
See also BRWS 8; CA 114; 167; DLB 162; HGG; RGEL 2; RGSF 2; SUFW; YABC

Coppee, Francois 1842-1908 .... **TCLC 25**
See also CA 170; DLB 217

Coppola, Francis Ford 1939- ... **CLC 16, 126**
See also AAYA 39; CA 77-80; CANR 40, 78; DLB 44

Corbiere, Tristan 1845-1875 .... **NCLC 43**
See also DLB 217; GFL 1789 to the Present

Corcoran, Barbara (Asenath) 1911- .... **CLC 17**
See also AAYA 14; CA 21-24R; CAAE 191; CAAS 2; CANR 11, 28, 48; CLR 50; DLB 52; JRDA; MAICYA 2; MAICYAS 1; RHW; SAAS 20; SATA 3, 77, 125

Cordelier, Maurice
See Giraudoux, Jean(-Hippolyte)

Corelli, Marie .... **TCLC 51**
See also Mackay, Mary
See also DLB 34, 156; RGEL 2; SUFW

Corman, Cid .... **CLC 9**
See also Corman, Sidney
See also CAAS 2; DLB 5, 193

Corman, Sidney 1924-
See Corman, Cid
See also CA 85-88; CANR 44; CP 7; DAM POET

Cormier, Robert (Edmund) 1925-2000 .... **CLC 12, 30**
See also AAYA 3, 19; BYA 1, 2, 6, 8, 9; CA 1-4R; CANR 5, 23, 76, 93; CDALB 1968-1988; CLR 12, 55; DA; DAB; DAC; DAM MST, NOV; DLB 52; EXPN; INT CANR-23; JRDA; LAIT 5; MAICYA 1, 2; MTCW 1, 2; NFS 2; SATA 10, 45, 83; SATA-Obit 122; WYA; YAW

Corn, Alfred (DeWitt III) 1943- .... **CLC 33**
See also CA 179; CAAE 179; CAAS 25; CANR 44; CP 7; CSW; DLB 120; DLBY 1980

Corneille, Pierre 1606-1684 .... **LC 28**
See also DAB; DAM MST; DLB 268; EW 3; GFL Beginnings to 1789; RGWL 2; TWA

Cornwell, David (John Moore) 1931- .... **CLC 9, 15**
See also le Carre, John
See also CA 5-8R; CANR 13, 33, 59, 107; DA3; DAM POP; MTCW 1, 2

Cornwell, Patricia (Daniels) 1956- . **CLC 155**
See also AAYA 16; BPFB 1; CA 134; CANR 53; CMW 4; CPW; CSW; DAM POP; MSW; MTCW 1

Corso, (Nunzio) Gregory 1930-2001 . **CLC 1, 11; PC 33**
See also CA 5-8R; 193; CANR 41, 76; CP 7; DA3; DLB 5, 16, 237; MTCW 1, 2; WP

Cortazar, Julio 1914-1984 ... **CLC 2, 3, 5, 10, 13, 15, 33, 34, 92; HLC 1; SSC 7**
See also BPFB 1; CA 21-24R; CANR 12, 32, 81; CDWLB 3; DA3; DAM MULT, NOV; DLB 113; EXPS; HW 1, 2; LAW; MTCW 1, 2; RGSF 2; RGWL 2; SSFS 3; TWA; WLIT 1

Cortes, Hernan 1485-1547 .... **LC 31**

Corvinus, Jakob
See Raabe, Wilhelm (Karl)

Corvo, Baron
See Rolfe, Frederick (William Serafino Austin Lewis Mary)
See also GLL 1; RGEL 2

Corwin, Cecil
See Kornbluth, C(yril) M.

Cosic, Dobrica 1921- .... **CLC 14**
See also CA 122; 138; CDWLB 4; CWW 2; DLB 181

Costain, Thomas B(ertram) 1885-1965 .... **CLC 30**
See also BYA 3; CA 5-8R; 25-28R; DLB 9; RHW

Costantini, Humberto 1924(?)-1987 . **CLC 49**
See also CA 131; 122; HW 1

Costello, Elvis 1955- .... **CLC 21**

Costenoble, Philostene 1898-1962
See Ghelderode, Michel de

Costenoble, Philostene 1898-1962
See Ghelderode, Michel de

Cotes, Cecil V.
See Duncan, Sara Jeannette

Cotter, Joseph Seamon Sr. 1861-1949 .... **TCLC 28; BLC 1**
See also BW 1; CA 124; DAM MULT; DLB 50

Couch, Arthur Thomas Quiller
See Quiller-Couch, Sir Arthur (Thomas)

Coulton, James
See Hansen, Joseph

Couperus, Louis (Marie Anne) 1863-1923 .... **TCLC 15**
See also CA 115; RGWL 2

Coupland, Douglas 1961- .... **CLC 85, 133**
See also AAYA 34; CA 142; CANR 57, 90; CCA 1; CPW; DAC; DAM POP

Court, Wesli
See Turco, Lewis (Putnam)

Courtenay, Bryce 1933- .... **CLC 59**
See also CA 138; CPW

Courtney, Robert
See Ellison, Harlan (Jay)

Cousteau, Jacques-Yves 1910-1997 .. **CLC 30**
See also CA 65-68; 159; CANR 15, 67; MTCW 1; SATA 38, 98

Coventry, Francis 1725-1754 .... **LC 46**

Coverdale, Miles c. 1487-1569 .... **LC 77**
See also DLB 167

Cowan, Peter (Walkinshaw) 1914- .... **SSC 28**
See also CA 21-24R; CANR 9, 25, 50, 83; CN 7; DLB 260; RGSF 2

Coward, Noel (Peirce) 1899-1973 . **CLC 1, 9, 29, 51**
See also AITN 1; BRWS 2; CA 17-18; 41-44R; CANR 35; CAP 2; CDBLB 1914-1945; DA3; DAM DRAM; DFS 3, 6; DLB 10, 245; IDFW 3, 4; MTCW 1, 2; RGEL 2; TEA

Cowley, Abraham 1618-1667 .... **LC 43**
See also BRW 2; DLB 131, 151; PAB; RGEL 2

Cowley, Malcolm 1898-1989 .... **CLC 39**
See also AMWS 2; CA 5-8R; 128; CANR 3, 55; DLB 4, 48; DLBY 1981, 1989; MTCW 1, 2

Cowper, William 1731-1800 ..... **NCLC 8, 94; PC 40**
See also BRW 3; DA3; DAM POET; DLB 104, 109; RGEL 2

Cox, William Trevor 1928-
See Trevor, William
See also CA 9-12R; CANR 4, 37, 55, 76, 102; DAM NOV; INT CANR-37; MTCW 1, 2; TEA

Coyne, P. J.
See Masters, Hilary

Cozzens, James Gould 1903-1978 . **CLC 1, 4, 11, 92**
See also AMW; BPFB 1; CA 9-12R; 81-84; CANR 19; CDALB 1941-1968; DLB 9; DLBD 2; DLBY 1984, 1997; MTCW 1, 2; RGAL 4

Dacey, Philip 1939- .... **CLC 51**
See also CA 37-40R; CAAS 17; CANR 14, 32, 64; CP 7; DLB 105

Dagerman, Stig (Halvard)
1923-1954 .... **TCLC 17**
See also CA 117; 155; DLB 259

D'Aguiar, Fred 1960- .... **CLC 145**
See also CA 148; CANR 83, 101; CP 7; DLB 157

Dahl, Roald 1916-1990 .... **CLC 1, 6, 18, 79**
See also AAYA 15; BPFB 1; BRWS 4; BYA 5; CA 1-4R; 133; CANR 6, 32, 37, 62; CLR 1, 7, 41; CPW; DA3; DAB; DAC; DAM MST, NOV, POP; DLB 139, 255; HGG; JRDA; MAICYA 1, 2; MTCW 1, 2; RGSF 2; SATA 1, 26, 73; SATA-Obit 65; SSFS 4; TEA; YAW

Dahlberg, Edward 1900-1977 .. **CLC 1, 7, 14**
See also CA 9-12R; 69-72; CANR 31, 62; DLB 48; MTCW 1; RGAL 4

Daitch, Susan 1954- .... **CLC 103**
See also CA 161

Dale, Colin .... **TCLC 18**
See also Lawrence, T(homas) E(dward)

Dale, George E.
See Asimov, Isaac

Dalton, Roque 1935-1975(?) .... **PC 36**
See also CA 176; HLCS 1; HW 2

Daly, Elizabeth 1878-1967 .... **CLC 52**
See also CA 23-24; 25-28R; CANR 60; CAP 2; CMW 4

Daly, Maureen 1921- .... **CLC 17**
See also AAYA 5; BYA 6; CANR 37, 83, 108; JRDA; MAICYA 1, 2; SAAS 1; SATA 2, 129; WYA; YAW

Damas, Leon-Gontran 1912-1978 .... **CLC 84**
See also BW 1; CA 125; 73-76

Dana, Richard Henry Sr.
1787-1879 .... **NCLC 53**

Daniel, Samuel 1562(?)-1619 .... **LC 24**
See also DLB 62; RGEL 2

Daniels, Brett
See Adler, Renata

Dannay, Frederic 1905-1982 .... **CLC 11**
See also Queen, Ellery
See also CA 1-4R; 107; CANR 1, 39; CMW 4; DAM POP; DLB 137; MTCW 1

D'Annunzio, Gabriele 1863-1938 ... **TCLC 6, 40**
See also CA 104; 155; EW 8; RGWL 2; TWA

Danois, N. le
See Gourmont, Remy(-Marie-Charles) de

Dante 1265-1321 .... **CMLC 3, 18, 39; PC 21; WLCS**
See also DA; DA3; DAB; DAC; DAM MST, POET; EFS 1; EW 1; LAIT 1; RGWL 2; TWA; WP

d'Antibes, Germain
See Simenon, Georges (Jacques Christian)

Danticat, Edwidge 1969- .... **CLC 94, 139**
See also AAYA 29; CA 152; CAAE 192; CANR 73; DNFS 1; EXPS; MTCW 1; SSFS 1; YAW

Danvers, Dennis 1947- .... **CLC 70**

Danziger, Paula 1944- .... **CLC 21**
See also AAYA 4, 36; BYA 6, 7, 14; CA 112; 115; CANR 37; CLR 20; JRDA; MAICYA 1, 2; SATA 36, 63, 102; SATA-Brief 30; WYA; YAW

Da Ponte, Lorenzo 1749-1838 .... **NCLC 50**

Dario, Ruben 1867-1916 ... **TCLC 4; HLC 1; PC 15**
See also CA 131; CANR 81; DAM MULT; HW 1, 2; LAW; MTCW 1, 2; RGWL 2

Darley, George 1795-1846 .... **NCLC 2**
See also DLB 96; RGEL 2

Darrow, Clarence (Seward)
1857-1938 .... **TCLC 81**
See also CA 164

Darwin, Charles 1809-1882 .... **NCLC 57**
See also BRWS 7; DLB 57, 166; RGEL 2; TEA; WLIT 4

Darwin, Erasmus 1731-1802 .... **NCLC 106**
See also DLB 93; RGEL 2

Daryush, Elizabeth 1887-1977 ...... **CLC 6, 19**
See also CA 49-52; CANR 3, 81; DLB 20

Das, Kamala 1934- .... **PC 43**
See also CA 101; CANR 27, 59; CP 7; CWP; FW

Dasgupta, Surendranath
1887-1952 .... **TCLC 81**
See also CA 157

Dashwood, Edmee Elizabeth Monica de la Pasture 1890-1943
See Delafield, E. M.
See also CA 119; 154

da Silva, Antonio Jose
1705-1739 .... **NCLC 114**
See also Silva, Jose Asuncion

Daudet, (Louis Marie) Alphonse
1840-1897 .... **NCLC 1**
See also DLB 123; GFL 1789 to the Present; RGSF 2

Daumal, Rene 1908-1944 .... **TCLC 14**
See also CA 114

Davenant, William 1606-1668 .... **LC 13**
See also DLB 58, 126; RGEL 2

Davenport, Guy (Mattison, Jr.)
1927- .... **CLC 6, 14, 38; SSC 16**
See also CA 33-36R; CANR 23, 73; CN 7; CSW; DLB 130

David, Robert
See Nezval, Vitezslav

Davidson, Avram (James) 1923-1993
See Queen, Ellery
See also CA 101; 171; CANR 26; DLB 8; FANT; SFW 4; SUFW

Davidson, Donald (Grady)
1893-1968 .... **CLC 2, 13, 19**
See also CA 5-8R; 25-28R; CANR 4, 84; DLB 45

Davidson, Hugh
See Hamilton, Edmond

Davidson, John 1857-1909 .... **TCLC 24**
See also CA 118; DLB 19; RGEL 2

Davidson, Sara 1943- .... **CLC 9**
See also CA 81-84; CANR 44, 68; DLB 185

Davie, Donald (Alfred) 1922-1995 .... **CLC 5, 8, 10, 31; PC 29**
See also BRWS 6; CA 1-4R; 149; CAAS 3; CANR 1, 44; CP 7; DLB 27; MTCW 1; RGEL 2

Davie, Elspeth 1919-1995 .... **SSC 52**
See also CA 120; 126; 150; DLB 139

Davies, Ray(mond Douglas) 1944- ... **CLC 21**
See also CA 116; 146; CANR 92

Davies, Rhys 1901-1978 .... **CLC 23**
See also CA 9-12R; 81-84; CANR 4; DLB 139, 191

Davies, (William) Robertson
1913-1995 .... **CLC 2, 7, 13, 25, 42, 75, 91; WLC**
See also Marchbanks, Samuel
See also BEST 89:2; BPFB 1; CA 33-36R; 150; CANR 17, 42, 103; CN 7; CPW; DA; DA3; DAB; DAC; DAM MST, NOV, POP; DLB 68; HGG; INT CANR-17; MTCW 1, 2; RGEL 2; TWA

Davies, Walter C.
See Kornbluth, C(yril) M.

Davies, William Henry 1871-1940 ... **TCLC 5**
See also CA 104; 179; DLB 19, 174; RGEL 2

Da Vinci, Leonardo 1452-1519 ..... **LC 12, 57, 60**
See also AAYA 40

Davis, Angela (Yvonne) 1944- .... **CLC 77**
See also BW 2, 3; CA 57-60; CANR 10, 81; CSW; DA3; DAM MULT; FW

Davis, B. Lynch
See Bioy Casares, Adolfo; Borges, Jorge Luis

Davis, Gordon
See Hunt, E(verette) Howard, (Jr.)

Davis, H(arold) L(enoir) 1896-1960 . **CLC 49**
See also ANW; CA 178; 89-92; DLB 9, 206; SATA 114

Davis, Rebecca (Blaine) Harding
1831-1910 .... **TCLC 6; SSC 38**
See also CA 104; 179; DLB 74, 239; FW; NFS 14; RGAL 4; TUS

Davis, Richard Harding
1864-1916 .... **TCLC 24**
See also CA 114; 179; DLB 12, 23, 78, 79, 189; DLBD 13; RGAL 4

Davison, Frank Dalby 1893-1970 ..... **CLC 15**
See also CA 116; DLB 260

Davison, Lawrence H.
See Lawrence, D(avid) H(erbert Richards)

Davison, Peter (Hubert) 1928- .... **CLC 28**
See also CA 9-12R; CAAS 4; CANR 3, 43, 84; CP 7; DLB 5

Davys, Mary 1674-1732 .... **LC 1, 46**
See also DLB 39

Dawson, (Guy) Fielding (Lewis)
1930-2002 .... **CLC 6**
See also CA 85-88; 202; CANR 108; DLB 130

Dawson, Peter
See Faust, Frederick (Schiller)
See also TCWW 2, 2

Day, Clarence (Shepard, Jr.)
1874-1935 .... **TCLC 25**
See also CA 108; DLB 11

Day, John 1574(?)-1640(?) .... **LC 70**
See also DLB 62, 170; RGEL 2

Day, Thomas 1748-1789 .... **LC 1**
See also DLB 39; YABC 1

Day Lewis, C(ecil) 1904-1972 . **CLC 1, 6, 10; PC 11**
See also Blake, Nicholas
See also BRWS 3; CA 13-16; 33-36R; CANR 34; CAP 1; CWRI 5; DAM POET; DLB 15, 20; MTCW 1, 2; RGEL 2

Dazai Osamu .... **TCLC 11; SSC 41**
See also Tsushima, Shuji
See also CA 164; DLB 182; MJW; RGSF 2; RGWL 2; TWA

de Andrade, Carlos Drummond
See Drummond de Andrade, Carlos

de Andrade, Mario 1892-1945
See Andrade, Mario de
See also CA 178; HW 2

Deane, Norman
See Creasey, John

Deane, Seamus (Francis) 1940- ...... **CLC 122**
See also CA 118; CANR 42

de Beauvoir, Simone (Lucie Ernestine Marie Bertrand)
See Beauvoir, Simone (Lucie Ernestine Marie Bertrand) de

de Beer, P.
See Bosman, Herman Charles

de Brissac, Malcolm
See Dickinson, Peter (Malcolm)

de Campos, Alvaro
See Pessoa, Fernando (Antonio Nogueira)

de Chardin, Pierre Teilhard
See Teilhard de Chardin, (Marie Joseph) Pierre

Dee, John 1527-1608 .... **LC 20**
See also DLB 136, 213

DA3; DAM MULT, NOV; DLB 175; LAIT 5; MTCW 2; NFS 3; NNAL; RGAL 4; SATA 75; SATA-Obit 94; TCWW 2; YAW

Dorris, Michael A.
See Dorris, Michael (Anthony)

Dorsan, Luc
See Simenon, Georges (Jacques Christian)

Dorsange, Jean
See Simenon, Georges (Jacques Christian)

Dos Passos, John (Roderigo)
1896-1970 ... **CLC 1, 4, 8, 11, 15, 25, 34, 82; WLC**
See also AMW; BPFB 1; CA 1-4R; 29-32R; CANR 3; CDALB 1929-1941; DA; DA3; DAB; DAC; DAM MST, NOV; DLB 4, 9; DLBD 1, 15; DLBY 1996; MTCW 1, 2; NFS 14; RGAL 4; TUS

Dossage, Jean
See Simenon, Georges (Jacques Christian)

Dostoevsky, Fedor Mikhailovich
1821-1881 . **NCLC 2, 7, 21, 33, 43; SSC 2, 33, 44; WLC**
See also Dostoevsky, Fyodor
See also AAYA 40; DA; DA3; DAB; DAC; DAM MST, NOV; EW 7; EXPN; NFS 3, 8; RGSF 2; RGWL 2; SSFS 8; TWA

Dostoevsky, Fyodor
See Dostoevsky, Fedor Mikhailovich
See also DLB 238

Doughty, Charles M(ontagu)
1843-1926 .... **TCLC 27**
See also CA 115; 178; DLB 19, 57, 174

Douglas, Ellen .... **CLC 73**
See also Haxton, Josephine Ayres; Williamson, Ellen Douglas
See also CN 7; CSW

Douglas, Gavin 1475(?)-1522 .... **LC 20**
See also DLB 132; RGEL 2

Douglas, George
See Brown, George Douglas
See also RGEL 2

Douglas, Keith (Castellain)
1920-1944 .... **TCLC 40**
See also BRW 7; CA 160; DLB 27; PAB; RGEL 2

Douglas, Leonard
See Bradbury, Ray (Douglas)

Douglas, Michael
See Crichton, (John) Michael

Douglas, (George) Norman
1868-1952 .... **TCLC 68**
See also BRW 6; CA 119; 157; DLB 34, 195; RGEL 2

Douglas, William
See Brown, George Douglas

Douglass, Frederick 1817(?)-1895 .. **NCLC 7, 55; BLC 1; WLC**
See also AFAW 1, 2; AMWS 3; CDALB 1640-1865; DA; DA3; DAC; DAM MST, MULT; DLB 1, 43, 50, 79, 243; FW; LAIT 2; NCFS 2; RGAL 4; SATA 29

Dourado, (Waldomiro Freitas) Autran
1926- .... **CLC 23, 60**
See also CA 25-28R, 179; CANR 34, 81; DLB 145; HW 2

Dourado, Waldomiro Autran
See Dourado, (Waldomiro Freitas) Autran
See also CA 179

Dove, Rita (Frances) 1952- .... **CLC 50, 81; BLCS; PC 6**
See also AMWS 4; BW 2; CA 109; CAAS 19; CANR 27, 42, 68, 76, 97; CDALBS; CP 7; CSW; CWP; DA3; DAM MULT, POET; DLB 120; EXPP; MTCW 1; PFS 1, 15; RGAL 4

Doveglion
See Villa, Jose Garcia

Dowell, Coleman 1925-1985 .... **CLC 60**
See also CA 25-28R; 117; CANR 10; DLB 130; GLL 2

Dowson, Ernest (Christopher)
1867-1900 .... **TCLC 4**
See also CA 105; 150; DLB 19, 135; RGEL 2

Doyle, A. Conan
See Doyle, Sir Arthur Conan

Doyle, Sir Arthur Conan
1859-1930 .... **TCLC 7; SSC 12; WLC**
See also Conan Doyle, Arthur
See also AAYA 14; BRWS 2; CA 104; 122; CDBLB 1890-1914; CMW 4; DA; DA3; DAB; DAC; DAM MST, NOV; DLB 18, 70, 156, 178; EXPS; HGG; LAIT 2; MSW; MTCW 1, 2; RGEL 2; RGSF 2; RHW; SATA 24; SCFW 2; SFW 4; SSFS 2; TEA; WCH; WLIT 4; WYA; YAW

Doyle, Conan
See Doyle, Sir Arthur Conan

Doyle, John
See Graves, Robert (von Ranke)

Doyle, Roddy 1958(?)- .... **CLC 81**
See also AAYA 14; BRWS 5; CA 143; CANR 73; CN 7; DA3; DLB 194

Doyle, Sir A. Conan
See Doyle, Sir Arthur Conan

Dr. A
See Asimov, Isaac; Silverstein, Alvin; Silverstein, Virginia B(arbara Opshelor)

Drabble, Margaret 1939- ...... **CLC 2, 3, 5, 8, 10, 22, 53, 129**
See also BRWS 4; CA 13-16R; CANR 18, 35, 63; CDBLB 1960 to Present; CN 7; CPW; DA3; DAB; DAC; DAM MST, NOV, POP; DLB 14, 155, 231; FW; MTCW 1, 2; RGEL 2; SATA 48; TEA

Drapier, M. B.
See Swift, Jonathan

Drayham, James
See Mencken, H(enry) L(ouis)

Drayton, Michael 1563-1631 .... **LC 8**
See also DAM POET; DLB 121; RGEL 2

Dreadstone, Carl
See Campbell, (John) Ramsey

Dreiser, Theodore (Herman Albert)
1871-1945 .... **TCLC 10, 18, 35, 83; SSC 30; WLC**
See also AMW; CA 106; 132; CDALB 1865-1917; DA; DA3; DAC; DAM MST, NOV; DLB 9, 12, 102, 137; DLBD 1; LAIT 2; MTCW 1, 2; NFS 8; RGAL 4; TUS

Drexler, Rosalyn 1926- .... **CLC 2, 6**
See also CA 81-84; CAD; CANR 68; CD 5; CWD

Dreyer, Carl Theodor 1889-1968 ...... **CLC 16**
See also CA 116

Drieu la Rochelle, Pierre(-Eugene)
1893-1945 .... **TCLC 21**
See also CA 117; DLB 72; GFL 1789 to the Present

Drinkwater, John 1882-1937 .... **TCLC 57**
See also CA 109; 149; DLB 10, 19, 149; RGEL 2

Drop Shot
See Cable, George Washington

Droste-Hulshoff, Annette Freiin von
1797-1848 .... **NCLC 3**
See also CDWLB 2; DLB 133; RGSF 2; RGWL 2

Drummond, Walter
See Silverberg, Robert

Drummond, William Henry
1854-1907 .... **TCLC 25**
See also CA 160; DLB 92

Drummond de Andrade, Carlos
1902-1987 .... **CLC 18**
See also Andrade, Carlos Drummond de
See also CA 132; 123; LAW

Drury, Allen (Stuart) 1918-1998 .... **CLC 37**
See also CA 57-60; 170; CANR 18, 52; CN 7; INT CANR-18

Dryden, John 1631-1700 ..... **LC 3, 21; DC 3; PC 25; WLC**
See also BRW 2; CDBLB 1660-1789; DA; DAB; DAC; DAM DRAM, MST, POET; DLB 80, 101, 131; EXPP; IDTP; RGEL 2; TEA; WLIT 3

Duberman, Martin (Bauml) 1930- ..... **CLC 8**
See also CA 1-4R; CAD; CANR 2, 63; CD 5

Dubie, Norman (Evans) 1945- .... **CLC 36**
See also CA 69-72; CANR 12; CP 7; DLB 120; PFS 12

Du Bois, W(illiam) E(dward) B(urghardt)
1868-1963 ... **CLC 1, 2, 13, 64, 96; BLC 1; WLC**
See also AAYA 40; AFAW 1, 2; AMWS 2; BW 1, 3; CA 85-88; CANR 34, 82; CDALB 1865-1917; DA; DA3; DAC; DAM MST, MULT, NOV; DLB 47, 50, 91, 246; EXPP; LAIT 2; MTCW 1, 2; NCFS 1; PFS 13; RGAL 4; SATA 42

Dubus, Andre 1936-1999 ..... **CLC 13, 36, 97; SSC 15**
See also AMWS 7; CA 21-24R; 177; CANR 17; CN 7; CSW; DLB 130; INT CANR-17; RGAL 4; SSFS 10

Duca Minimo
See D'Annunzio, Gabriele

Ducharme, Rejean 1941- .... **CLC 74**
See also CA 165; DLB 60

Duchen, Claire .... **CLC 65**

Duclos, Charles Pinot- 1704-1772 .... **LC 1**
See also GFL Beginnings to 1789

Dudek, Louis 1918- .... **CLC 11, 19**
See also CA 45-48; CAAS 14; CANR 1; CP 7; DLB 88

Duerrenmatt, Friedrich 1921-1990 ... **CLC 1, 4, 8, 11, 15, 43, 102**
See also Durrenmatt, Friedrich
See also CA 17-20R; CANR 33; CMW 4; DAM DRAM; DLB 69, 124; MTCW 1, 2

Duffy, Bruce 1953(?)- .... **CLC 50**
See also CA 172

Duffy, Maureen 1933- .... **CLC 37**
See also CA 25-28R; CANR 33, 68; CBD; CN 7; CP 7; CWD; DFS 15; DLB 14; FW; MTCW 1

Du Fu
See Tu Fu
See also RGWL 2

Dugan, Alan 1923- .... **CLC 2, 6**
See also CA 81-84; CP 7; DLB 5; PFS 10

du Gard, Roger Martin
See Martin du Gard, Roger

Duhamel, Georges 1884-1966 .... **CLC 8**
See also CA 81-84; 25-28R; CANR 35; DLB 65; GFL 1789 to the Present; MTCW 1

Dujardin, Edouard (Emile Louis)
1861-1949 .... **TCLC 13**
See also CA 109; DLB 123

Duke, Raoul
See Thompson, Hunter S(tockton)

Dulles, John Foster 1888-1959 .... **TCLC 72**
See also CA 115; 149

Dumas, Alexandre (pere)
1802-1870 .... **NCLC 11, 71; WLC**
See also AAYA 22; BYA 3; DA; DA3; DAB; DAC; DAM MST, NOV; DLB 119, 192; EW 6; GFL 1789 to the Present; LAIT 1, 2; NFS 14; RGWL 2; SATA 18; TWA; WCH

Dumas, Alexandre (fils)
1824-1895 .... **NCLC 9; DC 1**
See also DLB 192; GFL 1789 to the Present;
RGWL 2

Dumas, Claudine
See Malzberg, Barry N(athaniel)

Dumas, Henry L. 1934-1968 .... **CLC 6, 62**
See also BW 1; CA 85-88; DLB 41; RGAL
4

du Maurier, Daphne 1907-1989 .. **CLC 6, 11,
59; SSC 18**
See also AAYA 37; BPFB 1; BRWS 3; CA
5-8R; 128; CANR 6, 55; CMW 4; CPW;
DA3; DAB; DAC; DAM MST, POP;
DLB 191; HGG; LAIT 3; MSW; MTCW
1, 2; NFS 12; RGEL 2; RGSF 2; RHW;
SATA 27; SATA-Obit 60; SSFS 14; TEA

Du Maurier, George 1834-1896 ..... **NCLC 86**
See also DLB 153, 178; RGEL 2

Dunbar, Paul Laurence 1872-1906 . **TCLC 2,
12; BLC 1; PC 5; SSC 8; WLC**
See also AFAW 1, 2; AMWS 2; BW 1, 3;
CA 104; 124; CANR 79; CDALB 1865-
1917; DA; DA3; DAC; DAM MST,
MULT, POET; DLB 50, 54, 78; EXPP;
RGAL 4; SATA 34

Dunbar, William 1460(?)-1520(?) .... **LC 20**
See also BRWS 8; DLB 132, 146; RGEL 2

Duncan, Dora Angela
See Duncan, Isadora

Duncan, Isadora 1877(?)-1927 .... **TCLC 68**
See also CA 118; 149

Duncan, Lois 1934- .... **CLC 26**
See also AAYA 4, 34; BYA 6, 8; CA 1-4R;
CANR 2, 23, 36, 111; CLR 29; JRDA;
MAICYA 1, 2; MAICYAS 1; SAAS 2;
SATA 1, 36, 75, 133; WYA; YAW

Duncan, Robert (Edward)
1919-1988 .... **CLC 1, 2, 4, 7, 15, 41, 55;
PC 2**
See also CA 9-12R; 124; CANR 28, 62;
DAM POET; DLB 5, 16, 193; MTCW 1,
2; PFS 13; RGAL 4; WP

Duncan, Sara Jeannette
1861-1922 .... **TCLC 60**
See also CA 157; DLB 92

Dunlap, William 1766-1839 .... **NCLC 2**
See also DLB 30, 37, 59; RGAL 4

Dunn, Douglas (Eaglesham) 1942- .... **CLC 6,
40**
See also CA 45-48; CANR 2, 33; CP 7;
DLB 40; MTCW 1

Dunn, Katherine (Karen) 1945- .... **CLC 71**
See also CA 33-36R; CANR 72; HGG;
MTCW 1

Dunn, Stephen (Elliott) 1939- .... **CLC 36**
See also AMWS 11; CA 33-36R; CANR
12, 48, 53, 105; CP 7; DLB 105

Dunne, Finley Peter 1867-1936 ...... **TCLC 28**
See also CA 108; 178; DLB 11, 23; RGAL
4

Dunne, John Gregory 1932- .... **CLC 28**
See also CA 25-28R; CANR 14, 50; CN 7;
DLBY 1980

Dunsany, Lord .... **TCLC 2, 59**
See also Dunsany, Edward John Moreton
Drax Plunkett
See also DLB 77, 153, 156, 255; FANT;
IDTP; RGEL 2; SFW 4; SUFW

**Dunsany, Edward John Moreton Drax
Plunkett** 1878-1957
See Dunsany, Lord
See also CA 104; 148; DLB 10; MTCW 1

du Perry, Jean
See Simenon, Georges (Jacques Christian)

Durang, Christopher (Ferdinand)
1949- .... **CLC 27, 38**
See also CA 105; CAD; CANR 50, 76; CD
5; MTCW 1

Duras, Marguerite 1914-1996 . **CLC 3, 6, 11,
20, 34, 40, 68, 100; SSC 40**
See also BPFB 1; CA 25-28R; 151; CANR
50; CWW 2; DLB 83; GFL 1789 to the
Present; IDFW 4; MTCW 1, 2; RGWL 2;
TWA

Durban, (Rosa) Pam 1947- .... **CLC 39**
See also CA 123; CANR 98; CSW

Durcan, Paul 1944- .... **CLC 43, 70**
See also CA 134; CP 7; DAM POET

Durkheim, Emile 1858-1917 .... **TCLC 55**

Durrell, Lawrence (George)
1912-1990 ..... **CLC 1, 4, 6, 8, 13, 27, 41**
See also BPFB 1; BRWS 1; CA 9-12R; 132;
CANR 40, 77; CDBLB 1945-1960; DAM
NOV; DLB 15, 27, 204; DLBY 1990;
MTCW 1, 2; RGEL 2; SFW 4; TEA

Durrenmatt, Friedrich
See Duerrenmatt, Friedrich
See also CDWLB 2; EW 13; RGWL 2

Dutt, Toru 1856-1877 .... **NCLC 29**
See also DLB 240

Dwight, Timothy 1752-1817 .... **NCLC 13**
See also DLB 37; RGAL 4

Dworkin, Andrea 1946- .... **CLC 43, 123**
See also CA 77-80; CAAS 21; CANR 16,
39, 76, 96; FW; GLL 1; INT CANR-16;
MTCW 1, 2

Dwyer, Deanna
See Koontz, Dean R(ay)

Dwyer, K. R.
See Koontz, Dean R(ay)

Dwyer, Thomas A. 1923- .... **CLC 114**
See also CA 115

Dybek, Stuart 1942- .... **CLC 114; SSC 55**
See also CA 97-100; CANR 39; DLB 130

Dye, Richard
See De Voto, Bernard (Augustine)

Dyer, Geoff 1958- .... **CLC 149**
See also CA 125; CANR 88

Dylan, Bob 1941- .... **CLC 3, 4, 6, 12, 77; PC
37**
See also CA 41-44R; CANR 108; CP 7;
DLB 16

Dyson, John 1943- .... **CLC 70**
See also CA 144

E. V. L.
See Lucas, E(dward) V(errall)

Eagleton, Terence (Francis) 1943- .. **CLC 63,
132**
See also CA 57-60; CANR 7, 23, 68; DLB
242; MTCW 1, 2

Eagleton, Terry
See Eagleton, Terence (Francis)

Early, Jack
See Scoppettone, Sandra
See also GLL 1

East, Michael
See West, Morris L(anglo)

Eastaway, Edward
See Thomas, (Philip) Edward

Eastlake, William (Derry)
1917-1997 .... **CLC 8**
See also CA 5-8R; 158; CAAS 1; CANR 5,
63; CN 7; DLB 6, 206; INT CANR-5;
TCWW 2

Eastman, Charles A(lexander)
1858-1939 .... **TCLC 55**
See also CA 179; CANR 91; DAM MULT;
DLB 175; NNAL; YABC 1

Eberhart, Richard (Ghormley)
1904- .... **CLC 3, 11, 19, 56**
See also AMW; CA 1-4R; CANR 2;
CDALB 1941-1968; CP 7; DAM POET;
DLB 48; MTCW 1; RGAL 4

Eberstadt, Fernanda 1960- .... **CLC 39**
See also CA 136; CANR 69

**Echegaray (y Eizaguirre), Jose (Maria
Waldo)** 1832-1916 .... **TCLC 4; HLCS 1**
See also CA 104; CANR 32; HW 1; MTCW
1

Echeverria, (Jose) Esteban (Antonino)
1805-1851 .... **NCLC 18**
See also LAW

Echo
See Proust, (Valentin-Louis-George-Eugene-
)Marcel

Eckert, Allan W. 1931- .... **CLC 17**
See also AAYA 18; BYA 2; CA 13-16R;
CANR 14, 45; INT CANR-14; MAICYA
2; MAICYAS 1; SAAS 21; SATA 29, 91;
SATA-Brief 27

Eckhart, Meister 1260(?)-1327(?) ... **CMLC 9**
See also DLB 115

Eckmar, F. R.
See de Hartog, Jan

Eco, Umberto 1932- .... **CLC 28, 60, 142**
See also BEST 90:1; BPFB 1; CA 77-80;
CANR 12, 33, 55, 110; CPW; CWW 2;
DA3; DAM NOV, POP; DLB 196, 242;
MSW; MTCW 1, 2

Eddison, E(ric) R(ucker)
1882-1945 .... **TCLC 15**
See also CA 109; 156; DLB 255; FANT;
SFW 4; SUFW

Eddy, Mary (Ann Morse) Baker
1821-1910 .... **TCLC 71**
See also CA 113; 174

Edel, (Joseph) Leon 1907-1997 .. **CLC 29, 34**
See also CA 1-4R; 161; CANR 1, 22; DLB
103; INT CANR-22

Eden, Emily 1797-1869 .... **NCLC 10**

Edgar, David 1948- .... **CLC 42**
See also CA 57-60; CANR 12, 61; CBD;
CD 5; DAM DRAM; DFS 15; DLB 13,
233; MTCW 1

Edgerton, Clyde (Carlyle) 1944- ...... **CLC 39**
See also AAYA 17; CA 118; 134; CANR
64; CSW; INT 134; YAW

Edgeworth, Maria 1768-1849 .... **NCLC 1, 51**
See also BRWS 3; DLB 116, 159, 163; FW;
RGEL 2; SATA 21; TEA; WLIT 3

Edmonds, Paul
See Kuttner, Henry

Edmonds, Walter D(umaux)
1903-1998 .... **CLC 35**
See also BYA 2; CA 5-8R; CANR 2; CWRI
5; DLB 9; LAIT 1; MAICYA 1, 2; RHW;
SAAS 4; SATA 1, 27; SATA-Obit 99

Edmondson, Wallace
See Ellison, Harlan (Jay)

Edson, Russell 1935- .... **CLC 13**
See also CA 33-36R; DLB 244; WP

Edwards, Bronwen Elizabeth
See Rose, Wendy

Edwards, G(erald) B(asil)
1899-1976 .... **CLC 25**
See also CA 201; 110

Edwards, Gus 1939- .... **CLC 43**
See also CA 108; INT 108

Edwards, Jonathan 1703-1758 .... **LC 7, 54**
See also AMW; DA; DAC; DAM MST;
DLB 24; RGAL 4; TUS

Efron, Marina Ivanovna Tsvetaeva
See Tsvetaeva (Efron), Marina (Ivanovna)

Egoyan, Atom 1960- .... **CLC 151**
See also CA 157

Ehle, John (Marsden, Jr.) 1925- ...... **CLC 27**
See also CA 9-12R; CSW

Ehrenbourg, Ilya (Grigoryevich)
See Ehrenburg, Ilya (Grigoryevich)

Ehrenburg, Ilya (Grigoryevich)
1891-1967 .... **CLC 18, 34, 62**
See also CA 102; 25-28R

Ehrenburg, Ilyo (Grigoryevich)
See Ehrenburg, Ilya (Grigoryevich)

Epstein, Jacob 1956- .... **CLC 19**
 See also CA 114
Epstein, Jean 1897-1953 .... **TCLC 92**
Epstein, Joseph 1937- .... **CLC 39**
 See also CA 112; 119; CANR 50, 65
Epstein, Leslie 1938- .... **CLC 27**
 See also CA 73-76; CAAS 12; CANR 23,
 69
Equiano, Olaudah 1745(?)-1797 .... **LC 16;
 BLC 2**
 See also AFAW 1, 2; CDWLB 3; DAM
 MULT; DLB 37, 50; WLIT 2
Erasmus, Desiderius 1469(?)-1536 ...... **LC 16**
 See also DLB 136; EW 2; RGWL 2; TWA
Erdman, Paul E(mil) 1932- .... **CLC 25**
 See also AITN 1; CA 61-64; CANR 13, 43,
 84
Erdrich, Louise 1954- .... **CLC 39, 54, 120**
 See also AAYA 10; AMWS 4; BEST 89:1;
 BPFB 1; CA 114; CANR 41, 62;
 CDALBS; CN 7; CP 7; CPW; CWP;
 DA3; DAM MULT, NOV, POP; DLB 152,
 175, 206; EXPP; LAIT 5; MTCW 1; NFS
 5; NNAL; PFS 14; RGAL 4; SATA 94;
 SSFS 14; TCWW 2
Erenburg, Ilya (Grigoryevich)
 See Ehrenburg, Ilya (Grigoryevich)
Erickson, Stephen Michael 1950-
 See Erickson, Steve
 See also CA 129; SFW 4
Erickson, Steve .... **CLC 64**
 See also Erickson, Stephen Michael
 See also CANR 60, 68
Ericson, Walter
 See Fast, Howard (Melvin)
Eriksson, Buntel
 See Bergman, (Ernst) Ingmar
Ernaux, Annie 1940- .... **CLC 88**
 See also CA 147; CANR 93; NCFS 3
Erskine, John 1879-1951 .... **TCLC 84**
 See also CA 112; 159; DLB 9, 102; FANT
Eschenbach, Wolfram von
 See Wolfram von Eschenbach
Eseki, Bruno
 See Mphahlele, Ezekiel
Esenin, Sergei (Alexandrovich)
 1895-1925 .... **TCLC 4**
 See also CA 104; RGWL 2
Eshleman, Clayton 1935- .... **CLC 7**
 See also CA 33-36R; CAAS 6; CANR 93;
 CP 7; DLB 5
Espriella, Don Manuel Alvarez
 See Southey, Robert
Espriu, Salvador 1913-1985 .... **CLC 9**
 See also CA 154; 115; DLB 134
Espronceda, Jose de 1808-1842 ..... **NCLC 39**
Esquivel, Laura 1951(?)- ... **CLC 141; HLCS
 1**
 See also AAYA 29; CA 143; CANR 68;
 DA3; DNFS 2; LAIT 3; MTCW 1; NFS
 5; WLIT 1
Esse, James
 See Stephens, James
Esterbrook, Tom
 See Hubbard, L(afayette) Ron(ald)
Estleman, Loren D. 1952- .... **CLC 48**
 See also AAYA 27; CA 85-88; CANR 27,
 74; CMW 4; CPW; DA3; DAM NOV,
 POP; DLB 226; INT CANR-27; MTCW
 1, 2
Etherege, Sir George 1636-1692 .... **LC 78**
 See also BRW 2; DAM DRAM; DLB 80;
 PAB; RGEL 2
Euclid 306 B.C.-283 B.C. .... **CMLC 25**
Eugenides, Jeffrey 1960(?)- .... **CLC 81**
 See also CA 144

Euripides c. 484 B.C.-406 B.C. .... **CMLC 23,
 51; DC 4; WLCS**
 See also AW 1; CDWLB 1; DA; DA3;
 DAB; DAC; DAM DRAM, MST; DFS 1,
 4, 6; DLB 176; LAIT 1; RGWL 2
Evan, Evin
 See Faust, Frederick (Schiller)
Evans, Caradoc 1878-1945 ... **TCLC 85; SSC
 43**
 See also DLB 162
Evans, Evan
 See Faust, Frederick (Schiller)
 See also TCWW 2
Evans, Marian
 See Eliot, George
Evans, Mary Ann
 See Eliot, George
Evarts, Esther
 See Benson, Sally
Everett, Percival
 See Everett, Percival L.
 See also CSW
Everett, Percival L. 1956- .... **CLC 57**
 See also Everett, Percival
 See also BW 2; CA 129; CANR 94
Everson, R(onald) G(ilmour)
 1903-1992 .... **CLC 27**
 See also CA 17-20R; DLB 88
Everson, William (Oliver)
 1912-1994 .... **CLC 1, 5, 14**
 See also CA 9-12R; 145; CANR 20; DLB
 5, 16, 212; MTCW 1
Evtushenko, Evgenii Aleksandrovich
 See Yevtushenko, Yevgeny (Alexandrovich)
 See also RGWL 2
Ewart, Gavin (Buchanan)
 1916-1995 .... **CLC 13, 46**
 See also BRWS 7; CA 89-92; 150; CANR
 17, 46; CP 7; DLB 40; MTCW 1
Ewers, Hanns Heinz 1871-1943 ..... **TCLC 12**
 See also CA 109; 149
Ewing, Frederick R.
 See Sturgeon, Theodore (Hamilton)
Exley, Frederick (Earl) 1929-1992 .... **CLC 6,
 11**
 See also AITN 2; BPFB 1; CA 81-84; 138;
 DLB 143; DLBY 1981
Eynhardt, Guillermo
 See Quiroga, Horacio (Sylvestre)
Ezekiel, Nissim 1924- .... **CLC 61**
 See also CA 61-64; CP 7
Ezekiel, Tish O'Dowd 1943- .... **CLC 34**
 See also CA 129
Fadeyev, A.
 See Bulgya, Alexander Alexandrovich
Fadeyev, Alexander .... **TCLC 53**
 See also Bulgya, Alexander Alexandrovich
Fagen, Donald 1948- .... **CLC 26**
Fainzilberg, Ilya Arnoldovich 1897-1937
 See Ilf, Ilya
 See also CA 120; 165
Fair, Ronald L. 1932- .... **CLC 18**
 See also BW 1; CA 69-72; CANR 25; DLB
 33
Fairbairn, Roger
 See Carr, John Dickson
Fairbairns, Zoe (Ann) 1948- .... **CLC 32**
 See also CA 103; CANR 21, 85; CN 7
Fairfield, Flora
 See Alcott, Louisa May
Fairman, Paul W. 1916-1977
 See Queen, Ellery
 See also CA 114; SFW 4
Falco, Gian
 See Papini, Giovanni
Falconer, James
 See Kirkup, James

Falconer, Kenneth
 See Kornbluth, C(yril) M.
Falkland, Samuel
 See Heijermans, Herman
Fallaci, Oriana 1930- .... **CLC 11, 110**
 See also CA 77-80; CANR 15, 58; FW;
 MTCW 1
Faludi, Susan 1959- .... **CLC 140**
 See also CA 138; FW; MTCW 1; NCFS 3
Faludy, George 1913- .... **CLC 42**
 See also CA 21-24R
Faludy, Gyoergy
 See Faludy, George
Fanon, Frantz 1925-1961 .... **CLC 74; BLC 2**
 See also BW 1; CA 116; 89-92; DAM
 MULT; WLIT 2
Fanshawe, Ann 1625-1680 .... **LC 11**
Fante, John (Thomas) 1911-1983 ..... **CLC 60**
 See also AMWS 11; CA 69-72; 109; CANR
 23, 104; DLB 130; DLBY 1983
Farah, Nuruddin 1945- .. **CLC 53, 137; BLC
 2**
 See also AFW; BW 2, 3; CA 106; CANR
 81; CDWLB 3; CN 7; DAM MULT; DLB
 125; WLIT 2
Fargue, Leon-Paul 1876(?)-1947 .... **TCLC 11**
 See also CA 109; CANR 107; DLB 258
Farigoule, Louis
 See Romains, Jules
Farina, Richard 1936(?)-1966 .... **CLC 9**
 See also CA 81-84; 25-28R
Farley, Walter (Lorimer)
 1915-1989 .... **CLC 17**
 See also BYA 14; CA 17-20R; CANR 8,
 29, 84; DLB 22; JRDA; MAICYA 1, 2;
 SATA 2, 43, 132; YAW
Farmer, Philip Jose 1918- .... **CLC 1, 19**
 See also AAYA 28; BPFB 1; CA 1-4R;
 CANR 4, 35, 111; DLB 8; MTCW 1;
 SATA 93; SCFW 2; SFW 4
Farquhar, George 1677-1707 .... **LC 21**
 See also BRW 2; DAM DRAM; DLB 84;
 RGEL 2
Farrell, J(ames) G(ordon)
 1935-1979 .... **CLC 6**
 See also CA 73-76; 89-92; CANR 36; DLB
 14; MTCW 1; RGEL 2; RHW; WLIT 4
Farrell, James T(homas) 1904-1979 . **CLC 1,
 4, 8, 11, 66; SSC 28**
 See also AMW; BPFB 1; CA 5-8R; 89-92;
 CANR 9, 61; DLB 4, 9, 86; DLBD 2;
 MTCW 1, 2; RGAL 4
Farrell, Warren (Thomas) 1943- ...... **CLC 70**
 See also CA 146
Farren, Richard J.
 See Betjeman, John
Farren, Richard M.
 See Betjeman, John
Fassbinder, Rainer Werner
 1946-1982 .... **CLC 20**
 See also CA 93-96; 106; CANR 31
Fast, Howard (Melvin) 1914- ... **CLC 23, 131**
 See also AAYA 16; BPFB 1; CA 1-4R, 181;
 CAAE 181; CAAS 18; CANR 1, 33, 54,
 75, 98; CMW 4; CN 7; CPW; DAM NOV;
 DLB 9; INT CANR-33; MTCW 1; RHW;
 SATA 7; SATA-Essay 107; TCWW 2;
 YAW
Faulcon, Robert
 See Holdstock, Robert P.
Faulkner, William (Cuthbert)
 1897-1962 .... **CLC 1, 3, 6, 8, 9, 11, 14,
 18, 28, 52, 68; SSC 1, 35, 42; WLC**
 See also AAYA 7; AMW; AMWR 1; BPFB
 1; BYA 5; CA 81-84; CANR 33; CDALB
 1929-1941; DA; DA3; DAB; DAC; DAM
 MST, NOV; DLB 9, 11, 44, 102; DLBD
 2; DLBY 1986, 1997; EXPN; EXPS;

Fitzgerald, Zelda (Sayre)
1900-1948 .... **TCLC 52**
See also AMWS 9; CA 117; 126; DLBY
1984

Flanagan, Thomas (James Bonner)
1923- .... **CLC 25, 52**
See also CA 108; CANR 55; CN 7; DLBY
1980; INT 108; MTCW 1; RHW

Flaubert, Gustave 1821-1880 .... **NCLC 2, 10,**
19, 62, 66; SSC 11; WLC
See also DA; DA3; DAB; DAC; DAM
MST, NOV; DLB 119; EW 7; EXPS; GFL
1789 to the Present; LAIT 2; NFS 14;
RGSF 2; RGWL 2; SSFS 6; TWA

Flavius Josephus
See Josephus, Flavius

Flecker, Herman Elroy
See Flecker, (Herman) James Elroy

Flecker, (Herman) James Elroy
1884-1915 .... **TCLC 43**
See also CA 109; 150; DLB 10, 19; RGEL
2

Fleming, Ian (Lancaster) 1908-1964 . **CLC 3,**
30
See also AAYA 26; BPFB 1; CA 5-8R;
CANR 59; CDBLB 1945-1960; CMW 4;
CPW; DA3; DAM POP; DLB 87, 201;
MSW; MTCW 1, 2; RGEL 2; SATA 9;
TEA; YAW

Fleming, Thomas (James) 1927- ...... **CLC 37**
See also CA 5-8R; CANR 10, 102; INT
CANR-10; SATA 8

Fletcher, John 1579-1625 .... **LC 33; DC 6**
See also BRW 2; CDBLB Before 1660;
DLB 58; RGEL 2; TEA

Fletcher, John Gould 1886-1950 .... **TCLC 35**
See also CA 107; 167; DLB 4, 45; RGAL 4

Fleur, Paul
See Pohl, Frederik

Flooglebuckle, Al
See Spiegelman, Art

Flora, Fletcher 1914-1969
See Queen, Ellery
See also CA 1-4R; CANR 3, 85

Flying Officer X
See Bates, H(erbert) E(rnest)

Fo, Dario 1926- .... **CLC 32, 109; DC 10**
See also CA 116; 128; CANR 68; CWW 2;
DA3; DAM DRAM; DLBY 1997; MTCW
1, 2

Fogarty, Jonathan Titulescu Esq.
See Farrell, James T(homas)

Follett, Ken(neth Martin) 1949- .... **CLC 18**
See also AAYA 6; BEST 89:4; BPFB 1; CA
81-84; CANR 13, 33, 54, 102; CMW 4;
CPW; DA3; DAM NOV, POP; DLB 87;
DLBY 1981; INT CANR-33; MTCW 1

Fontane, Theodor 1819-1898 .... **NCLC 26**
See also CDWLB 2; DLB 129; EW 6;
RGWL 2; TWA

Fontenot, Chester .... **CLC 65**

Fonvizin, Denis Ivanovich
1744(?)-1792 .... **LC 81**
See also DLB 150; RGWL 2

Foote, Horton 1916- .... **CLC 51, 91**
See also CA 73-76; CAD; CANR 34, 51,
110; CD 5; CSW; DA3; DAM DRAM;
DLB 26, 266; INT CANR-34

Foote, Mary Hallock 1847-1938 .. **TCLC 108**
See also DLB 186, 188, 202, 221

Foote, Shelby 1916- .... **CLC 75**
See also AAYA 40; CA 5-8R; CANR 3, 45,
74; CN 7; CPW; CSW; DA3; DAM NOV,
POP; DLB 2, 17; MTCW 2; RHW

Forbes, Cosmo
See Lewton, Val

Forbes, Esther 1891-1967 .... **CLC 12**
See also AAYA 17; BYA 2; CA 13-14; 25-
28R; CAP 1; CLR 27; DLB 22;
MAICYA 1, 2; RHW; SATA 2, 100; YAW

Forche, Carolyn (Louise) 1950- .... **CLC 25,**
83, 86; PC 10
See also CA 109; 117; CANR 50, 74; CP 7;
CWP; DA3; DAM POET; DLB 5, 193;
INT CA-117; MTCW 1; RGAL 4

Ford, Elbur
See Hibbert, Eleanor Alice Burford

Ford, Ford Madox 1873-1939 ... **TCLC 1, 15,**
39, 57
See also Chaucer, Daniel
See also BRW 6; CA 104; 132; CANR 74;
CDBLB 1914-1945; DA3; DAM NOV;
DLB 34, 98, 162; MTCW 1, 2; RGEL 2;
TEA

Ford, Henry 1863-1947 .... **TCLC 73**
See also CA 115; 148

Ford, John 1586-1639 .... **LC 68; DC 8**
See also BRW 2; CDBLB Before 1660;
DA3; DAM DRAM; DFS 7; DLB 58;
IDTP; RGEL 2

Ford, John 1895-1973 .... **CLC 16**
See also CA 187; 45-48

Ford, Richard 1944- ..... **CLC 46, 99; SSC 57**
See also AMWS 5; CA 69-72; CANR 11,
47, 86; CN 7; CSW; DLB 227; MTCW 1;
RGAL 4; RGSF 2

Ford, Webster
See Masters, Edgar Lee

Foreman, Richard 1937- .... **CLC 50**
See also CA 65-68; CAD; CANR 32, 63;
CD 5

Forester, C(ecil) S(cott) 1899-1966 ... **CLC 35**
See also CA 73-76; 25-28R; CANR 83;
DLB 191; RGEL 2; RHW; SATA 13

Forez
See Mauriac, Francois (Charles)

Forman, James
See Forman, James D(ouglas)

Forman, James D(ouglas) 1932- .... **CLC 21**
See also AAYA 17; CA 9-12R; CANR 4,
19, 42; JRDA; MAICYA 1, 2; SATA 8,
70; YAW

Forman, Milos 1932- .... **CLC 164**
See also CA 109

Fornes, Maria Irene 1930- . **CLC 39, 61; DC**
10; HLCS 1
See also CA 25-28R; CAD; CANR 28, 81;
CD 5; CWD; DLB 7; HW 1, 2; INT
CANR-28; MTCW 1; RGAL 4

Forrest, Leon (Richard) 1937-1997 .. **CLC 4;**
BLCS
See also AFAW 2; BW 2; CA 89-92; 162;
CAAS 7; CANR 25, 52, 87; CN 7; DLB
33

Forster, E(dward) M(organ)
1879-1970 ...... **CLC 1, 2, 3, 4, 9, 10, 13,**
15, 22, 45, 77; SSC 27; WLC
See also AAYA 2, 37; BRW 6; BRWR 2;
CA 13-14; 25-28R; CANR 45; CAP 1;
CDBLB 1914-1945; DA; DA3; DAB;
DAC; DAM MST, NOV; DLB 34, 98,
162, 178, 195; DLBD 10; EXPN; LAIT
3; MTCW 1, 2; NCFS 1; NFS 3, 10, 11;
RGEL 2; RGSF 2; SATA 57; SUFW;
TCLC 125; TEA; WLIT 4

Forster, John 1812-1876 .... **NCLC 11**
See also DLB 144, 184

Forster, Margaret 1938- .... **CLC 149**
See also CA 133; CANR 62; CN 7; DLB
155

Forsyth, Frederick 1938- .... **CLC 2, 5, 36**
See also BEST 89:4; CA 85-88; CANR 38,
62; CMW 4; CN 7; CPW; DAM NOV,
POP; DLB 87; MTCW 1, 2

Forten, Charlotte L. 1837-1914 .... **TCLC 16;**
BLC 2
See also Grimke, Charlotte L(ottie) Forten
See also DLB 50, 239

Foscolo, Ugo 1778-1827 .... **NCLC 8, 97**
See also EW 5

Fosse, Bob .... **CLC 20**
See also Fosse, Robert Louis

Fosse, Robert Louis 1927-1987
See Fosse, Bob
See also CA 110; 123

Foster, Hannah Webster
1758-1840 .... **NCLC 99**
See also DLB 37, 200; RGAL 4

Foster, Stephen Collins
1826-1864 .... **NCLC 26**
See also RGAL 4

Foucault, Michel 1926-1984 . **CLC 31, 34, 69**
See also CA 105; 113; CANR 34; DLB 242;
EW 13; GFL 1789 to the Present; GLL 1;
MTCW 1, 2; TWA

Fouque, Friedrich (Heinrich Karl) de la
Motte 1777-1843 .... **NCLC 2**
See also DLB 90; RGWL 2; SUFW

Fourier, Charles 1772-1837 .... **NCLC 51**

Fournier, Henri Alban 1886-1914
See Alain-Fournier
See also CA 104; 179

Fournier, Pierre 1916- .... **CLC 11**
See also Gascar, Pierre
See also CA 89-92; CANR 16, 40

Fowles, John (Robert) 1926- . **CLC 1, 2, 3, 4,**
6, 9, 10, 15, 33, 87; SSC 33
See also BPFB 1; BRWS 1; CA 5-8R;
CANR 25, 71, 103; CDBLB 1960 to
Present; CN 7; DA3; DAB; DAC; DAM
MST; DLB 14, 139, 207; HGG; MTCW
1, 2; RGEL 2; RHW; SATA 22; TEA;
WLIT 4

Fox, Paula 1923- .... **CLC 2, 8, 121**
See also AAYA 3, 37; BYA 3, 8; CA 73-76;
CANR 20, 36, 62, 105; CLR 1, 44; DLB
52; JRDA; MAICYA 1, 2; MTCW 1; NFS
12; SATA 17, 60, 120; WYA; YAW

Fox, William Price (Jr.) 1926- .... **CLC 22**
See also CA 17-20R; CAAS 19; CANR 11;
CSW; DLB 2; DLBY 1981

Foxe, John 1517(?)-1587 .... **LC 14**
See also DLB 132

Frame, Janet .. **CLC 2, 3, 6, 22, 66, 96; SSC**
29
See also Clutha, Janet Paterson Frame
See also CN 7; CWP; RGEL 2; RGSF 2;
TWA

France, Anatole .... **TCLC 9**
See also Thibault, Jacques Anatole Francois
See also DLB 123; GFL 1789 to the Present;
MTCW 1; RGWL 2; SUFW

Francis, Claude .... **CLC 50**
See also CA 192

Francis, Dick 1920- .... **CLC 2, 22, 42, 102**
See also AAYA 5, 21; BEST 89:3; BPFB 1;
CA 5-8R; CANR 9, 42, 68, 100; CDBLB
1960 to Present; CMW 4; CN 7; DA3;
DAM POP; DLB 87; INT CANR-9;
MSW; MTCW 1, 2

Francis, Robert (Churchill)
1901-1987 .... **CLC 15; PC 34**
See also AMWS 9; CA 1-4R; 123; CANR
1; EXPP; PFS 12

Francis, Lord Jeffrey
See Jeffrey, Francis
See also DLB 107

Frank, Anne(lies Marie)
1929-1945 .... **TCLC 17; WLC**
See also AAYA 12; BYA 1; CA 113; 133;
CANR 68; DA; DA3; DAB; DAC; DAM
MST; LAIT 4; MAICYA 2; MAICYAS 1;

CLR 62; CN 7; CSW; DA3; DAM MULT;
DLB 2, 33, 152; DLBY 1980; EXPN;
LAIT 5; MTCW 1, 2; NFS 5, 7; RGAL 4;
RGSF 2; RHW; SATA 86; SSFS 5; YAW

Gaitskill, Mary 1954- .... **CLC 69**
See also CA 128; CANR 61; DLB 244

Galdos, Benito Perez
See Perez Galdos, Benito
See also EW 7

Gale, Zona 1874-1938 .... **TCLC 7**
See also CA 105; 153; CANR 84; DAM
DRAM; DLB 9, 78, 228; RGAL 4

Galeano, Eduardo (Hughes) 1940- . **CLC 72;**
HLCS 1
See also CA 29-32R; CANR 13, 32, 100;
HW 1

Galiano, Juan Valera y Alcala
See Valera y Alcala-Galiano, Juan

Galilei, Galileo 1564-1642 .... **LC 45**

Gallagher, Tess 1943- .... **CLC 18, 63; PC 9**
See also CA 106; CP 7; CWP; DAM POET;
DLB 120, 212, 244

Gallant, Mavis 1922- . **CLC 7, 18, 38; SSC 5**
See also CA 69-72; CANR 29, 69; CCA 1;
CN 7; DAC; DAM MST; DLB 53;
MTCW 1, 2; RGEL 2; RGSF 2

Gallant, Roy A(rthur) 1924- .... **CLC 17**
See also CA 5-8R; CANR 4, 29, 54; CLR
30; MAICYA 1, 2; SATA 4, 68, 110

Gallico, Paul (William) 1897-1976 ..... **CLC 2**
See also AITN 1; CA 5-8R; 69-72; CANR
23; DLB 9, 171; FANT; MAICYA 1, 2;
SATA 13

Gallo, Max Louis 1932- .... **CLC 95**
See also CA 85-88

Gallois, Lucien
See Desnos, Robert

Gallup, Ralph
See Whitemore, Hugh (John)

Galsworthy, John 1867-1933 .... **TCLC 1, 45;**
SSC 22; WLC
See also BRW 6; CA 104; 141; CANR 75;
CDBLB 1890-1914; DA; DA3; DAB;
DAC; DAM DRAM, MST, NOV; DLB
10, 34, 98, 162; DLBD 16; MTCW 1;
RGEL 2; SSFS 3; TEA

Galt, John 1779-1839 .... **NCLC 1, 110**
See also DLB 99, 116, 159; RGEL 2; RGSF
2

Galvin, James 1951- .... **CLC 38**
See also CA 108; CANR 26

Gamboa, Federico 1864-1939 .... **TCLC 36**
See also CA 167; HW 2; LAW

Gandhi, M. K.
See Gandhi, Mohandas Karamchand

Gandhi, Mahatma
See Gandhi, Mohandas Karamchand

Gandhi, Mohandas Karamchand
1869-1948 .... **TCLC 59**
See also CA 121; 132; DA3; DAM MULT;
MTCW 1, 2

Gann, Ernest Kellogg 1910-1991 ..... **CLC 23**
See also AITN 1; BPFB 2; CA 1-4R; 136;
CANR 1, 83; RHW

Garber, Eric 1943(?)-
See Holleran, Andrew
See also CANR 89

Garcia, Cristina 1958- .... **CLC 76**
See also AMWS 11; CA 141; CANR 73;
DNFS 1; HW 2

Garcia Lorca, Federico 1898-1936 . **TCLC 1,**
7, 49; DC 2; HLC 2; PC 3; WLC
See also Lorca, Federico Garcia
See also CA 104; 131; CANR 81; DA;
DA3; DAB; DAC; DAM DRAM, MST,
MULT, POET; DFS 10; DLB 108; HW 1,
2; MTCW 1, 2; TWA

Garcia Marquez, Gabriel (Jose)
1928- .... **CLC 2, 3, 8, 10, 15, 27, 47, 55,**
68; HLC 1; SSC 8; WLC
See also AAYA 3, 33; BEST 89:1, 90:4;
BPFB 2; BYA 12; CA 33-36R; CANR 10,
28, 50, 75, 82; CDWLB 3; CPW; DA;
DA3; DAB; DAC; DAM MST, MULT,
NOV, POP; DLB 113; DNFS 1, 2; EXPN;
EXPS; HW 1, 2; LAIT 2; LAW; LAWS
1; MTCW 1, 2; NCFS 3; NFS 1, 5, 10;
RGSF 2; RGWL 2; SSFS 1, 6; TWA;
WLIT 1

Garcilaso de la Vega, El Inca 1503-1536
See also HLCS 1; LAW

Gard, Janice
See Latham, Jean Lee

Gard, Roger Martin du
See Martin du Gard, Roger

Gardam, Jane (Mary) 1928- .... **CLC 43**
See also CA 49-52; CANR 2, 18, 33, 54,
106; CLR 12; DLB 14, 161, 231; MAI-
CYA 1, 2; MTCW 1; SAAS 9; SATA 39,
76, 130; SATA-Brief 28; YAW

Gardner, Herb(ert) 1934- .... **CLC 44**
See also CA 149; CAD; CD 5

Gardner, John (Champlin), Jr.
1933-1982 ...... **CLC 2, 3, 5, 7, 8, 10, 18,**
28, 34; SSC 7
See also AITN 1; AMWS 6; BPFB 2; CA
65-68; 107; CANR 33, 73; CDALBS;
CPW; DA3; DAM NOV, POP; DLB 2;
DLBY 1982; FANT; MTCW 1; NFS 3;
RGAL 4; RGSF 2; SATA 40; SATA-Obit
31; SSFS 8

Gardner, John (Edmund) 1926- .... **CLC 30**
See also CA 103; CANR 15, 69; CMW 4;
CPW; DAM POP; MTCW 1

Gardner, Miriam
See Bradley, Marion Zimmer
See also GLL 1

Gardner, Noel
See Kuttner, Henry

Gardons, S. S.
See Snodgrass, W(illiam) D(e Witt)

Garfield, Leon 1921-1996 .... **CLC 12**
See also AAYA 8; BYA 1, 3; CA 17-20R;
152; CANR 38, 41, 78; CLR 21; DLB
161; JRDA; MAICYA 1, 2; MAICYAS 1;
SATA 1, 32, 76; SATA-Obit 90; TEA;
WYA; YAW

Garland, (Hannibal) Hamlin
1860-1940 .... **TCLC 3; SSC 18**
See also CA 104; DLB 12, 71, 78, 186;
RGAL 4; RGSF 2; TCWW 2

Garneau, (Hector de) Saint-Denys
1912-1943 .... **TCLC 13**
See also CA 111; DLB 88

Garner, Alan 1934- .... **CLC 17**
See also AAYA 18; BYA 3, 5; CA 73-76,
178; CAAE 178; CANR 15, 64; CLR 20;
CPW; DAB; DAM POP; DLB 161, 261;
FANT; MAICYA 1, 2; MTCW 1, 2; SATA
18, 69; SATA-Essay 108; SUFW; YAW

Garner, Hugh 1913-1979 .... **CLC 13**
See also Warwick, Jarvis
See also CA 69-72; CANR 31; CCA 1; DLB
68

Garnett, David 1892-1981 .... **CLC 3**
See also CA 5-8R; 103; CANR 17, 79; DLB
34; FANT; MTCW 2; RGEL 2; SFW 4;
SUFW

Garos, Stephanie
See Katz, Steve

Garrett, George (Palmer) 1929- .. **CLC 3, 11,**
51; SSC 30
See also AMWS 7; BPFB 2; CA 1-4R;
CAAE 202; CAAS 5; CANR 1, 42, 67,
109; CN 7; CP 7; CSW; DLB 2, 5, 130,
152; DLBY 1983

Garrick, David 1717-1779 .... **LC 15**
See also DAM DRAM; DLB 84, 213;
RGEL 2

Garrigue, Jean 1914-1972 .... **CLC 2, 8**
See also CA 5-8R; 37-40R; CANR 20

Garrison, Frederick
See Sinclair, Upton (Beall)

Garro, Elena 1920(?)-1998
See also CA 131; 169; CWW 2; DLB 145;
HLCS 1; HW 1; LAWS 1; WLIT 1

Garth, Will
See Hamilton, Edmond; Kuttner, Henry

Garvey, Marcus (Moziah, Jr.)
1887-1940 .... **TCLC 41; BLC 2**
See also BW 1; CA 120; 124; CANR 79;
DAM MULT

Gary, Romain .... **CLC 25**
See also Kacew, Romain
See also DLB 83

Gascar, Pierre .... **CLC 11**
See also Fournier, Pierre

Gascoyne, David (Emery)
1916-2001 .... **CLC 45**
See also CA 65-68; 200; CANR 10, 28, 54;
CP 7; DLB 20; MTCW 1; RGEL 2

Gaskell, Elizabeth Cleghorn
1810-1865 .... **NCLC 5, 70, 97; SSC 25**
See also BRW 5; CDBLB 1832-1890; DAB;
DAM MST; DLB 21, 144, 159; RGEL 2;
RGSF 2; TEA

Gass, William H(oward) 1924- . **CLC 1, 2, 8,**
11, 15, 39, 132; SSC 12
See also AMWS 6; CA 17-20R; CANR 30,
71, 100; CN 7; DLB 2, 227; MTCW 1, 2;
RGAL 4

Gassendi, Pierre 1592-1655 .... **LC 54**
See also GFL Beginnings to 1789

Gasset, Jose Ortega y
See Ortega y Gasset, Jose

Gates, Henry Louis, Jr. 1950- .... **CLC 65;**
BLCS
See also BW 2, 3; CA 109; CANR 25, 53,
75; CSW; DA3; DAM MULT; DLB 67;
MTCW 1; RGAL 4

Gautier, Theophile 1811-1872 .. **NCLC 1, 59;**
PC 18; SSC 20
See also DAM POET; DLB 119; EW 6;
GFL 1789 to the Present; RGWL 2;
SUFW; TWA

Gawsworth, John
See Bates, H(erbert) E(rnest)

Gay, John 1685-1732 .... **LC 49**
See also BRW 3; DAM DRAM; DLB 84,
95; RGEL 2; WLIT 3

Gay, Oliver
See Gogarty, Oliver St. John

Gay, Peter (Jack) 1923- .... **CLC 158**
See also CA 13-16R; CANR 18, 41, 77;
INT CANR-18

Gaye, Marvin (Pentz, Jr.)
1939-1984 .... **CLC 26**
See also CA 195; 112

Gebler, Carlo (Ernest) 1954- .... **CLC 39**
See also CA 119; 133; CANR 96

Gee, Maggie (Mary) 1948- .... **CLC 57**
See also CA 130; CN 7; DLB 207

Gee, Maurice (Gough) 1931- .... **CLC 29**
See also AAYA 42; CA 97-100; CANR 67;
CLR 56; CN 7; CWRI 5; MAICYA 2;
RGSF 2; SATA 46, 101

Gelbart, Larry (Simon) 1928- .... **CLC 21, 61**
See also Gelbart, Larry
See also CA 73-76; CANR 45, 94

Gelbart, Larry 1928-
See Gelbart, Larry (Simon)
See also CAD; CD 5

Gelber, Jack 1932- .... **CLC 1, 6, 14, 79**
See also CA 1-4R; CAD; CANR 2; DLB 7,
228

Gellhorn, Martha (Ellis)
1908-1998 .... **CLC 14, 60**
See also CA 77-80; 164; CANR 44; CN 7;
DLBY 1982, 1998

Genet, Jean 1910-1986 .. **CLC 1, 2, 5, 10, 14, 44, 46**
See also CA 13-16R; CANR 18; DA3;
DAM DRAM; DFS 10; DLB 72; DLBY
1986; EW 13; GFL 1789 to the Present;
GLL 1; MTCW 1, 2; RGWL 2; TWA

Gent, Peter 1942- .... **CLC 29**
See also AITN 1; CA 89-92; DLBY 1982

Gentile, Giovanni 1875-1944 .... **TCLC 96**
See also CA 119

Gentlewoman in New England, A
See Bradstreet, Anne

Gentlewoman in Those Parts, A
See Bradstreet, Anne

Geoffrey of Monmouth c.
1100-1155 .... **CMLC 44**
See also DLB 146; TEA

George, Jean
See George, Jean Craighead

George, Jean Craighead 1919- .... **CLC 35**
See also AAYA 8; BYA 2, 4; CA 5-8R;
CANR 25; CLR 1; 80; DLB 52; JRDA;
MAICYA 1, 2; SATA 2, 68, 124; WYA;
YAW

George, Stefan (Anton) 1868-1933 . **TCLC 2, 14**
See also CA 104; 193; EW 8

Georges, Georges Martin
See Simenon, Georges (Jacques Christian)

Gerhardi, William Alexander
See Gerhardie, William Alexander

Gerhardie, William Alexander
1895-1977 .... **CLC 5**
See also CA 25-28R; 73-76; CANR 18;
DLB 36; RGEL 2

Gerson, Jean 1363-1429 .... **LC 77**
See also DLB 208

Gersonides 1288-1344 .... **CMLC 49**
See also DLB 115

Gerstler, Amy 1956- .... **CLC 70**
See also CA 146; CANR 99

Gertler, T. .... **CLC 134**
See also CA 116; 121

Ghalib .... **NCLC 39, 78**
See also Ghalib, Asadullah Khan

Ghalib, Asadullah Khan 1797-1869
See Ghalib
See also DAM POET; RGWL 2

Ghelderode, Michel de 1898-1962 ..... **CLC 6, 11; DC 15**
See also CA 85-88; CANR 40, 77; DAM
DRAM; EW 11; TWA

Ghiselin, Brewster 1903-2001 .... **CLC 23**
See also CA 13-16R; CAAS 10; CANR 13;
CP 7

Ghose, Aurabinda 1872-1950 .... **TCLC 63**
See also CA 163

Ghose, Zulfikar 1935- .... **CLC 42**
See also CA 65-68; CANR 67; CN 7; CP 7

Ghosh, Amitav 1956- .... **CLC 44, 153**
See also CA 147; CANR 80; CN 7

Giacosa, Giuseppe 1847-1906 .... **TCLC 7**
See also CA 104

Gibb, Lee
See Waterhouse, Keith (Spencer)

Gibbon, Lewis Grassic .... **TCLC 4**
See also Mitchell, James Leslie
See also RGEL 2

Gibbons, Kaye 1960- .... **CLC 50, 88, 145**
See also AAYA 34; AMWS 10; CA 151;
CANR 75; CSW; DA3; DAM POP;
MTCW 1; NFS 3; RGAL 4; SATA 117

Gibran, Kahlil 1883-1931 . **TCLC 1, 9; PC 9**
See also CA 104; 150; DA3; DAM POET,
POP; MTCW 2

Gibran, Khalil
See Gibran, Kahlil

Gibson, William 1914- .... **CLC 23**
See also CA 9-12R; CAD 2; CANR 9, 42,
75; CD 5; DA; DAB; DAC; DAM
DRAM, MST; DFS 2; DLB 7; LAIT 2;
MTCW 2; SATA 66; YAW

Gibson, William (Ford) 1948- ... **CLC 39, 63; SSC 52**
See also AAYA 12; BPFB 2; CA 126; 133;
CANR 52, 90, 106; CN 7; CPW; DA3;
DAM POP; DLB 251; MTCW 2; SCFW
2; SFW 4

Gide, Andre (Paul Guillaume)
1869-1951 ..... **TCLC 5, 12, 36; SSC 13; WLC**
See also CA 104; 124; DA; DA3; DAB;
DAC; DAM MST, NOV; DLB 65; EW 8;
GFL 1789 to the Present; MTCW 1, 2;
RGSF 2; RGWL 2; TWA

Gifford, Barry (Colby) 1946- .... **CLC 34**
See also CA 65-68; CANR 9, 30, 40, 90

Gilbert, Frank
See De Voto, Bernard (Augustine)

Gilbert, W(illiam) S(chwenck)
1836-1911 .... **TCLC 3**
See also CA 104; 173; DAM DRAM, POET;
RGEL 2; SATA 36

Gilbreth, Frank B(unker), Jr.
1911-2001 .... **CLC 17**
See also CA 9-12R; SATA 2

Gilchrist, Ellen (Louise) 1935- .. **CLC 34, 48, 143; SSC 14**
See also BPFB 2; CA 113; 116; CANR 41,
61, 104; CN 7; CPW; CSW; DAM POP;
DLB 130; EXPS; MTCW 1, 2; RGAL 4;
RGSF 2; SSFS 9

Giles, Molly 1942- .... **CLC 39**
See also CA 126; CANR 98

Gill, Eric 1882-1940 .... **TCLC 85**

Gill, Patrick
See Creasey, John

Gillette, Douglas .... **CLC 70**

Gilliam, Terry (Vance) 1940- .... **CLC 21, 141**
See also Monty Python
See also AAYA 19; CA 108; 113; CANR
35; INT 113

Gillian, Jerry
See Gilliam, Terry (Vance)

Gilliatt, Penelope (Ann Douglass)
1932-1993 .... **CLC 2, 10, 13, 53**
See also AITN 2; CA 13-16R; 141; CANR
49; DLB 14

Gilman, Charlotte (Anna) Perkins (Stetson)
1860-1935 ..... **TCLC 9, 37, 117; SSC 13**
See also AMWS 11; BYA 11; CA 106; 150;
DLB 221; EXPS; FW; HGG; LAIT 2;
MAWW; MTCW 1; RGAL 4; RGSF 2;
SFW 4; SSFS 1

Gilmour, David 1946- .... **CLC 35**

Gilpin, William 1724-1804 .... **NCLC 30**

Gilray, J. D.
See Mencken, H(enry) L(ouis)

Gilroy, Frank D(aniel) 1925- .... **CLC 2**
See also CA 81-84; CAD; CANR 32, 64,
86; CD 5; DLB 7

Gilstrap, John 1957(?)- .... **CLC 99**
See also CA 160; CANR 101

Ginsberg, Allen 1926-1997 .... **CLC 1, 2, 3, 4, 6, 13, 36, 69, 109; PC 4; WLC**
See also AAYA 33; AITN 1; AMWS 2; CA
1-4R; 157; CANR 2, 41, 63, 95; CDALB
1941-1968; CP 7; DA; DA3; DAB; DAC;
DAM MST, POET; DLB 5, 16, 169, 237;
GLL 1; MTCW 1, 2; PAB; PFS 5; RGAL
4; TCLC 120; TUS; WP

Ginzburg, Eugenia .... **CLC 59**

Ginzburg, Natalia 1916-1991 .... **CLC 5, 11, 54, 70**
See also CA 85-88; 135; CANR 33; DFS
14; DLB 177; EW 13; MTCW 1, 2;
RGWL 2

Giono, Jean 1895-1970 .... **CLC 4, 11**
See also CA 45-48; 29-32R; CANR 2, 35;
DLB 72; GFL 1789 to the Present; MTCW
1; RGWL 2; TCLC 124

Giovanni, Nikki 1943- .... **CLC 2, 4, 19, 64, 117; BLC 2; PC 19; WLCS**
See also AAYA 22; AITN 1; BW 2, 3; CA
29-32R; CAAS 6; CANR 18, 41, 60, 91;
CDALBS; CLR 6, 73; CP 7; CSW; CWP;
CWRI 5; DA; DA3; DAB; DAC; DAM
MST, MULT, POET; DLB 5, 41; EXPP;
INT CANR-18; MAICYA 1, 2; MTCW 1,
2; RGAL 4; SATA 24, 107; TUS; YAW

Giovene, Andrea 1904-1998 .... **CLC 7**
See also CA 85-88

Gippius, Zinaida (Nikolayevna) 1869-1945
See Hippius, Zinaida
See also CA 106

Giraudoux, Jean(-Hippolyte)
1882-1944 .... **TCLC 2, 7**
See also CA 104; 196; DAM DRAM; DLB
65; EW 9; GFL 1789 to the Present;
RGWL 2; TWA

Gironella, Jose Maria 1917-1991 ..... **CLC 11**
See also CA 101; RGWL 2

Gissing, George (Robert)
1857-1903 .... **TCLC 3, 24, 47; SSC 37**
See also BRW 5; CA 105; 167; DLB 18,
135, 184; RGEL 2; TEA

Giurlani, Aldo
See Palazzeschi, Aldo

Gladkov, Fyodor (Vasilyevich)
1883-1958 .... **TCLC 27**
See also CA 170

Glanville, Brian (Lester) 1931- .... **CLC 6**
See also CA 5-8R; CAAS 9; CANR 3, 70;
CN 7; DLB 15, 139; SATA 42

Glasgow, Ellen (Anderson Gholson)
1873-1945 .... **TCLC 2, 7; SSC 34**
See also AMW; CA 104; 164; DLB 9, 12;
MAWW; MTCW 2; RGAL 4; RHW;
SSFS 9; TUS

Glaspell, Susan 1882(?)-1948 . **TCLC 55; DC 10; SSC 41**
See also AMWS 3; CA 110; 154; DFS 8;
DLB 7, 9, 78, 228; MAWW; RGAL 4;
SSFS 3; TCWW 2; TUS; YABC 2

Glassco, John 1909-1981 .... **CLC 9**
See also CA 13-16R; 102; CANR 15; DLB
68

Glasscock, Amnesia
See Steinbeck, John (Ernst)

Glasser, Ronald J. 1940(?)- .... **CLC 37**

Glassman, Joyce
See Johnson, Joyce

Gleick, James (W.) 1954- .... **CLC 147**
See also CA 131; 137; CANR 97; INT CA-
137

Glendinning, Victoria 1937- .... **CLC 50**
See also CA 120; 127; CANR 59, 89; DLB
155

Glissant, Edouard (Mathieu)
1928- .... **CLC 10, 68**
See also CA 153; CANR 111; CWW 2;
DAM MULT

Gloag, Julian 1930- .... **CLC 40**
See also AITN 1; CA 65-68; CANR 10, 70;
CN 7

Glowacki, Aleksander
See Prus, Boleslaw

Griffith, D(avid Lewelyn) W(ark)
1875(?)-1948 .... **TCLC 68**
See also CA 119; 150; CANR 80

Griffith, Lawrence
See Griffith, D(avid Lewelyn) W(ark)

Griffiths, Trevor 1935- .... **CLC 13, 52**
See also CA 97-100; CANR 45; CBD; CD
5; DLB 13, 245

Griggs, Sutton (Elbert)
1872-1930 .... **TCLC 77**
See also CA 123; 186; DLB 50

Grigson, Geoffrey (Edward Harvey)
1905-1985 .... **CLC 7, 39**
See also CA 25-28R; 118; CANR 20, 33;
DLB 27; MTCW 1, 2

Grillparzer, Franz 1791-1872 . **NCLC 1, 102;**
DC 14; SSC 37
See also CDWLB 2; DLB 133; EW 5;
RGWL 2; TWA

Grimble, Reverend Charles James
See Eliot, T(homas) S(tearns)

Grimke, Charlotte L(ottie) Forten
1837(?)-1914
See Forten, Charlotte L.
See also BW 1; CA 117; 124; DAM MULT,
POET

Grimm, Jacob Ludwig Karl
1785-1863 .... **NCLC 3, 77; SSC 36**
See also DLB 90; MAICYA 1, 2; RGSF 2;
RGWL 2; SATA 22; WCH

Grimm, Wilhelm Karl 1786-1859 .. **NCLC 3,**
77; SSC 36
See also CDWLB 2; DLB 90; MAICYA 1,
2; RGSF 2; RGWL 2; SATA 22; WCH

Grimmelshausen, Hans Jakob Christoffel
von
See Grimmelshausen, Johann Jakob Christoffel von
See also RGWL 2

Grimmelshausen, Johann Jakob Christoffel
von 1621-1676 .... **LC 6**
See also Grimmelshausen, Hans Jakob
Christoffel von
See also CDWLB 2; DLB 168

Grindel, Eugene 1895-1952
See Eluard, Paul
See also CA 104; 193

Grisham, John 1955- .... **CLC 84**
See also AAYA 14; BPFB 2; CA 138;
CANR 47, 69; CMW 4; CN 7; CPW;
CSW; DA3; DAM POP; MSW; MTCW 2

Grossman, David 1954- .... **CLC 67**
See also CA 138; CWW 2

Grossman, Vasily (Semenovich)
1905-1964 .... **CLC 41**
See also CA 124; 130; MTCW 1

Grove, Frederick Philip .... **TCLC 4**
See also Greve, Felix Paul (Berthold
Friedrich)
See also DLB 92; RGEL 2

Grubb
See Crumb, R(obert)

Grumbach, Doris (Isaac) 1918- . **CLC 13, 22,**
64
See also CA 5-8R; CAAS 2; CANR 9, 42,
70; CN 7; INT CANR-9; MTCW 2

Grundtvig, Nicolai Frederik Severin
1783-1872 .... **NCLC 1**

Grunge
See Crumb, R(obert)

Grunwald, Lisa 1959- .... **CLC 44**
See also CA 120

Guare, John 1938- .... **CLC 8, 14, 29, 67**
See also CA 73-76; CAD; CANR 21, 69;
CD 5; DAM DRAM; DFS 8, 13; DLB 7,
249; MTCW 1, 2; RGAL 4

Gubar, Susan (David) 1944- .... **CLC 145**
See also CA 108; CANR 45, 70; FW;
MTCW 1; RGAL 4

Gudjonsson, Halldor Kiljan 1902-1998
See Laxness, Halldor
See also CA 103; 164; CWW 2

Guenter, Erich
See Eich, Guenter

Guest, Barbara 1920- .... **CLC 34**
See also CA 25-28R; CANR 11, 44, 84; CP
7; CWP; DLB 5, 193

Guest, Edgar A(lbert) 1881-1959 ... **TCLC 95**
See also CA 112; 168

Guest, Judith (Ann) 1936- .... **CLC 8, 30**
See also AAYA 7; CA 77-80; CANR 15,
75; DA3; DAM NOV, POP; EXPN; INT
CANR-15; LAIT 5; MTCW 1, 2; NFS 1

Guevara, Che .... **CLC 87; HLC 1**
See also Guevara (Serna), Ernesto

Guevara (Serna), Ernesto
1928-1967 .... **CLC 87; HLC 1**
See also Guevara, Che
See also CA 127; 111; CANR 56; DAM
MULT; HW 1

Guicciardini, Francesco 1483-1540 ..... **LC 49**

Guild, Nicholas M. 1944- .... **CLC 33**
See also CA 93-96

Guillemin, Jacques
See Sartre, Jean-Paul

Guillen, Jorge 1893-1984 . **CLC 11; HLCS 1;**
PC 35
See also CA 89-92; 112; DAM MULT,
POET; DLB 108; HW 1; RGWL 2

Guillen, Nicolas (Cristobal)
1902-1989 .... **CLC 48, 79; BLC 2; HLC**
1; PC 23
See also BW 2; CA 116; 125; 129; CANR
84; DAM MST, MULT, POET; HW 1;
LAW; RGWL 2; WP

Guillen y Alvarez, Jorge
See Guillen, Jorge

Guillevic, (Eugene) 1907-1997 .... **CLC 33**
See also CA 93-96; CWW 2

Guillois
See Desnos, Robert

Guillois, Valentin
See Desnos, Robert

Guimaraes Rosa, Joao
See Rosa, Joao Guimaraes
See also LAW

Guimaraes Rosa, Joao 1908-1967
See also CA 175; HLCS 2; LAW; RGSF 2;
RGWL 2

Guiney, Louise Imogen
1861-1920 .... **TCLC 41**
See also CA 160; DLB 54; RGAL 4

Guinizelli, Guido c. 1230-1276 ...... **CMLC 49**

Guiraldes, Ricardo (Guillermo)
1886-1927 .... **TCLC 39**
See also CA 131; HW 1; LAW; MTCW 1

Gumilev, Nikolai (Stepanovich)
1886-1921 .... **TCLC 60**
See also CA 165

Gunesekera, Romesh 1954- .... **CLC 91**
See also CA 159; CN 7; DLB 267

Gunn, Bill .... **CLC 5**
See also Gunn, William Harrison
See also DLB 38

Gunn, Thom(son William) 1929- .. **CLC 3, 6,**
18, 32, 81; PC 26
See also BRWS 4; CA 17-20R; CANR 9,
33; CDBLB 1960 to Present; CP 7; DAM
POET; DLB 27; INT CANR-33; MTCW
1; PFS 9; RGEL 2

Gunn, William Harrison 1934(?)-1989
See Gunn, Bill
See also AITN 1; BW 1, 3; CA 13-16R;
128; CANR 12, 25, 76

Gunn Allen, Paula
See Allen, Paula Gunn

Gunnars, Kristjana 1948- .... **CLC 69**
See also CA 113; CCA 1; CP 7; CWP; DLB
60

Gunter, Erich
See Eich, Guenter

Gurdjieff, G(eorgei) I(vanovich)
1877(?)-1949 .... **TCLC 71**
See also CA 157

Gurganus, Allan 1947- .... **CLC 70**
See also BEST 90:1; CA 135; CN 7; CPW;
CSW; DAM POP; GLL 1

Gurney, A. R.
See Gurney, A(lbert) R(amsdell), Jr.
See also DLB 266

Gurney, A(lbert) R(amsdell), Jr.
1930- .... **CLC 32, 50, 54**
See also Gurney, A. R.
See also AMWS 5; CA 77-80; CAD; CANR
32, 64; CD 5; DAM DRAM

Gurney, Ivor (Bertie) 1890-1937 ... **TCLC 33**
See also BRW 6; CA 167; PAB; RGEL 2

Gurney, Peter
See Gurney, A(lbert) R(amsdell), Jr.

Guro, Elena 1877-1913 .... **TCLC 56**

Gustafson, James M(oody) 1925- ... **CLC 100**
See also CA 25-28R; CANR 37

Gustafson, Ralph (Barker)
1909-1995 .... **CLC 36**
See also CA 21-24R; CANR 8, 45, 84; CP
7; DLB 88; RGEL 2

Gut, Gom
See Simenon, Georges (Jacques Christian)

Guterson, David 1956- .... **CLC 91**
See also CA 132; CANR 73; MTCW 2;
NFS 13

Guthrie, A(lfred) B(ertram), Jr.
1901-1991 .... **CLC 23**
See also CA 57-60; 134; CANR 24; DLB 6,
212; SATA 62; SATA-Obit 67

Guthrie, Isobel
See Grieve, C(hristopher) M(urray)

Guthrie, Woodrow Wilson 1912-1967
See Guthrie, Woody
See also CA 113; 93-96

Guthrie, Woody .... **CLC 35**
See also Guthrie, Woodrow Wilson
See also LAIT 3

Gutierrez Najera, Manuel 1859-1895
See also HLCS 2; LAW

Guy, Rosa (Cuthbert) 1925- .... **CLC 26**
See also AAYA 4, 37; BW 2; CA 17-20R;
CANR 14, 34, 83; CLR 13; DLB 33;
DNFS 1; JRDA; MAICYA 1, 2; SATA 14,
62, 122; YAW

Gwendolyn
See Bennett, (Enoch) Arnold

H. D. .... **CLC 3, 8, 14, 31, 34, 73; PC 5**
See also Doolittle, Hilda

H. de V.
See Buchan, John

Haavikko, Paavo Juhani 1931- .. **CLC 18, 34**
See also CA 106

Habbema, Koos
See Heijermans, Herman

Habermas, Juergen 1929- .... **CLC 104**
See also CA 109; CANR 85; DLB 242

Habermas, Jurgen
See Habermas, Juergen

Hacker, Marilyn 1942- . **CLC 5, 9, 23, 72, 91**
See also CA 77-80; CANR 68; CP 7; CWP;
DAM POET; DLB 120; FW; GLL 2

Hadrian 76-138 .... **CMLC 52**

Haeckel, Ernst Heinrich (Philipp August)
1834-1919 .... **TCLC 83**
See also CA 157

Hafiz c. 1326-1389(?) .... **CMLC 34**
See also RGWL 2

Haggard, H(enry) Rider
1856-1925 .... **TCLC 11**
See also BRWS 3; BYA 4, 5; CA 108; 148;
DLB 70, 156, 174, 178; FANT; MTCW
2; RGEL 2; RHW; SATA 16; SCFW; SFW
4; SUFW; WLIT 4

Hagiosy, L.
See Larbaud, Valery (Nicolas)

Hagiwara, Sakutaro 1886-1942 .... **TCLC 60;
PC 18**
See also CA 154

Haig, Fenil
See Ford, Ford Madox

Haig-Brown, Roderick (Langmere)
1908-1976 .... **CLC 21**
See also CA 5-8R; 69-72; CANR 4, 38, 83;
CLR 31; CWRI 5; DLB 88; MAICYA 1,
2; SATA 12

Hailey, Arthur 1920- .... **CLC 5**
See also AITN 2; BEST 90:3; BPFB 2; CA
1-4R; CANR 2, 36, 75; CCA 1; CN 7;
CPW; DAM NOV, POP; DLB 88; DLBY
1982; MTCW 1, 2

Hailey, Elizabeth Forsythe 1938- ..... **CLC 40**
See also CA 93-96; CAAE 188; CAAS 1;
CANR 15, 48; INT CANR-15

Haines, John (Meade) 1924- .... **CLC 58**
See also CA 17-20R; CANR 13, 34; CSW;
DLB 5, 212

Hakluyt, Richard 1552-1616 .... **LC 31**
See also DLB 136; RGEL 2

Haldeman, Joe (William) 1943- .... **CLC 61**
See also Graham, Robert
See also AAYA 38; CA 53-56, 179; CAAE
179; CAAS 25; CANR 6, 70, 72; DLB 8;
INT CANR-6; SCFW 2; SFW 4

Hale, Sarah Josepha (Buell)
1788-1879 .... **NCLC 75**
See also DLB 1, 42, 73, 243

Halevy, Elie 1870-1937 .... **TCLC 104**

Haley, Alex(ander Murray Palmer)
1921-1992 .... **CLC 8, 12, 76; BLC 2**
See also AAYA 26; BPFB 2; BW 2, 3; CA
77-80; 136; CANR 61; CDALBS; CPW;
CSW; DA; DA3; DAB; DAC; DAM MST,
MULT, POP; DLB 38; LAIT 5; MTCW
1, 2; NFS 9

Haliburton, Thomas Chandler
1796-1865 .... **NCLC 15**
See also DLB 11, 99; RGEL 2; RGSF 2

Hall, Donald (Andrew, Jr.) 1928- ...... **CLC 1,
13, 37, 59, 151**
See also CA 5-8R; CAAS 7; CANR 2, 44,
64, 106; CP 7; DAM POET; DLB 5;
MTCW 1; RGAL 4; SATA 23, 97

Hall, Frederic Sauser
See Sauser-Hall, Frederic

Hall, James
See Kuttner, Henry

Hall, James Norman 1887-1951 ..... **TCLC 23**
See also CA 123; 173; LAIT 1; RHW 1;
SATA 21

Hall, (Marguerite) Radclyffe
1880-1943 .... **TCLC 12**
See also BRWS 6; CA 110; 150; CANR 83;
DLB 191; MTCW 2; RGEL 2; RHW

Hall, Rodney 1935- .... **CLC 51**
See also CA 109; CANR 69; CN 7; CP 7

Hallam, Arthur Henry
1811-1833 .... **NCLC 110**
See also DLB 32

Halleck, Fitz-Greene 1790-1867 .... **NCLC 47**
See also DLB 3, 250; RGAL 4

Halliday, Michael
See Creasey, John

Halpern, Daniel 1945- .... **CLC 14**
See also CA 33-36R; CANR 93; CP 7

Hamburger, Michael (Peter Leopold)
1924- .... **CLC 5, 14**
See also CA 5-8R; CAAE 196; CAAS 4;
CANR 2, 47; CP 7; DLB 27

Hamill, Pete 1935- .... **CLC 10**
See also CA 25-28R; CANR 18, 71

Hamilton, Alexander
1755(?)-1804 .... **NCLC 49**
See also DLB 37

Hamilton, Clive
See Lewis, C(live) S(taples)

Hamilton, Edmond 1904-1977 .... **CLC 1**
See also CA 1-4R; CANR 3, 84; DLB 8;
SATA 118; SFW 4

Hamilton, Eugene (Jacob) Lee
See Lee-Hamilton, Eugene (Jacob)

Hamilton, Franklin
See Silverberg, Robert

Hamilton, Gail
See Corcoran, Barbara (Asenath)

Hamilton, Mollie
See Kaye, M(ary) M(argaret)

Hamilton, (Anthony Walter) Patrick
1904-1962 .... **CLC 51**
See also CA 176; 113; DLB 10, 191

Hamilton, Virginia (Esther)
1936-2002 .... **CLC 26**
See also AAYA 2, 21; BW 2, 3; BYA 1, 2,
8; CA 25-28R; CANR 20, 37, 73; CLR 1,
11, 40; DAM MULT; DLB 33, 52; DLBY
01; INT CANR-20; JRDA; LAIT 5; MAI-
CYA 1, 2; MAICYAS 1; MTCW 1, 2;
SATA 4, 56, 79, 123; SATA-Obit 132;
WYA; YAW

Hammett, (Samuel) Dashiell
1894-1961 .... **CLC 3, 5, 10, 19, 47; SSC
17**
See also AITN 1; AMWS 4; BPFB 2; CA
81-84; CANR 42; CDALB 1929-1941;
CMW 4; DA3; DLB 226; DLBD 6; DLBY
1996; LAIT 3; MSW; MTCW 1, 2; RGAL
4; RGSF 2; TUS

Hammon, Jupiter 1720(?)-1800(?) . **NCLC 5;
BLC 2; PC 16**
See also DAM MULT, POET; DLB 31, 50

Hammond, Keith
See Kuttner, Henry

Hamner, Earl (Henry), Jr. 1923- ...... **CLC 12**
See also AITN 2; CA 73-76; DLB 6

Hampton, Christopher (James)
1946- .... **CLC 4**
See also CA 25-28R; CD 5; DLB 13;
MTCW 1

Hamsun, Knut .... **TCLC 2, 14, 49**
See also Pedersen, Knut
See also EW 8; RGWL 2

Handke, Peter 1942- .... **CLC 5, 8, 10, 15, 38,
134; DC 17**
See also CA 77-80; CANR 33, 75, 104;
CWW 2; DAM DRAM, NOV; DLB 85,
124; MTCW 1, 2; TWA

Handy, W(illiam) C(hristopher)
1873-1958 .... **TCLC 97**
See also BW 3; CA 121; 167

Hanley, James 1901-1985 ..... **CLC 3, 5, 8, 13**
See also CA 73-76; 117; CANR 36; CBD;
DLB 191; MTCW 1; RGEL 2

Hannah, Barry 1942- .... **CLC 23, 38, 90**
See also BPFB 2; CA 108; 110; CANR 43,
68; CN 7; CSW; DLB 6, 234; INT CA-
110; MTCW 1; RGSF 2

Hannon, Ezra
See Hunter, Evan

Hansberry, Lorraine (Vivian)
1930-1965 ... **CLC 17, 62; BLC 2; DC 2**
See also AAYA 25; AFAW 1, 2; AMWS 4;
BW 1, 3; CA 109; 25-28R; CABS 3;
CANR 58; CDALB 1941-1968; DA;
DA3; DAB; DAC; DAM DRAM, MST,
MULT; DFS 2; DLB 7, 38; FW; LAIT 4;
MTCW 1, 2; RGAL 4; TUS

Hansen, Joseph 1923- .... **CLC 38**
See also Brock, Rose; Colton, James
See also BPFB 2; CA 29-32R; CAAS 17;
CANR 16, 44, 66; CMW 4; DLB 226;
GLL 1; INT CANR-16

Hansen, Martin A(lfred)
1909-1955 .... **TCLC 32**
See also CA 167; DLB 214

Hansen and Philipson eds. .... **CLC 65**

Hanson, Kenneth O(stlin) 1922- .... **CLC 13**
See also CA 53-56; CANR 7

Hardwick, Elizabeth (Bruce) 1916- . **CLC 13**
See also AMWS 3; CA 5-8R; CANR 3, 32,
70, 100; CN 7; CSW; DA3; DAM NOV;
DLB 6; MAWW; MTCW 1, 2

Hardy, Thomas 1840-1928 .. **TCLC 4, 10, 18,
32, 48, 53, 72; PC 8; SSC 2; WLC**
See also BRW 6; BRWR 1; CA 104; 123;
CDBLB 1890-1914; DA; DA3; DAB;
DAC; DAM MST, NOV, POET; DLB 18,
19, 135; EXPN; EXPP; LAIT 2; MTCW
1, 2; NFS 3, 11, 15; PFS 3, 4; RGEL 2;
RGSF 2; TEA; WLIT 4

Hare, David 1947- .... **CLC 29, 58, 136**
See also BRWS 4; CA 97-100; CANR 39,
91; CBD; CD 5; DFS 4, 7; DLB 13;
MTCW 1; TEA

Harewood, John
See Van Druten, John (William)

Harford, Henry
See Hudson, W(illiam) H(enry)

Hargrave, Leonie
See Disch, Thomas M(ichael)

Harjo, Joy 1951- .... **CLC 83; PC 27**
See also CA 114; CANR 35, 67, 91; CP 7;
CWP; DAM MULT; DLB 120, 175;
MTCW 2; NNAL; PFS 15; RGAL 4

Harlan, Louis R(udolph) 1922- .... **CLC 34**
See also CA 21-24R; CANR 25, 55, 80

Harling, Robert 1951(?)- .... **CLC 53**
See also CA 147

Harmon, William (Ruth) 1938- .... **CLC 38**
See also CA 33-36R; CANR 14, 32, 35;
SATA 65

Harper, F. E. W.
See Harper, Frances Ellen Watkins

Harper, Frances E. W.
See Harper, Frances Ellen Watkins

Harper, Frances E. Watkins
See Harper, Frances Ellen Watkins

Harper, Frances Ellen
See Harper, Frances Ellen Watkins

Harper, Frances Ellen Watkins
1825-1911 ..... **TCLC 14; BLC 2; PC 21**
See also AFAW 1, 2; BW 1, 3; CA 111; 125;
CANR 79; DAM MULT, POET; DLB 50,
221; MAWW; RGAL 4

Harper, Michael S(teven) 1938- ... **CLC 7, 22**
See also AFAW 2; BW 1; CA 33-36R;
CANR 24, 108; CP 7; DLB 41; RGAL 4

Harper, Mrs. F. E. W.
See Harper, Frances Ellen Watkins

Harpur, Charles 1813-1868 .... **NCLC 114**
See also DLB 230; RGEL 2

Harris, Christie (Lucy) Irwin
1907-2002 .... **CLC 12**
See also CA 5-8R; CANR 6, 83; CLR 47;
DLB 88; JRDA; MAICYA 1, 2; SAAS 10;
SATA 6, 74; SATA-Essay 116

Harris, Frank 1856-1931 .... **TCLC 24**
See also CA 109; 150; CANR 80; DLB 156,
197; RGEL 2

Harris, George Washington
1814-1869 .... **NCLC 23**
See also DLB 3, 11, 248; RGAL 4

Harris, Joel Chandler 1848-1908 ... **TCLC 2; SSC 19**
See also CA 104; 137; CANR 80; CLR 49; DLB 11, 23, 42, 78, 91; LAIT 2; MAICYA 1, 2; RGSF 2; SATA 100; WCH; YABC 1

Harris, John (Wyndham Parkes Lucas) Beynon 1903-1969
See Wyndham, John
See also CA 102; 89-92; CANR 84; SATA 118; SFW 4

Harris, MacDonald .... **CLC 9**
See also Heiney, Donald (William)

Harris, Mark 1922- .... **CLC 19**
See also CA 5-8R; CAAS 3; CANR 2, 55, 83; CN 7; DLB 2; DLBY 1980

Harris, Norman .... **CLC 65**

Harris, (Theodore) Wilson 1921- .... **CLC 25, 159**
See also BRWS 5; BW 2, 3; CA 65-68; CAAS 16; CANR 11, 27, 69; CDWLB 3; CN 7; CP 7; DLB 117; MTCW 1; RGEL 2

Harrison, Barbara Grizzuti 1934- . **CLC 144**
See also CA 77-80; CANR 15, 48; INT CANR-15

Harrison, Elizabeth (Allen) Cavanna 1909-2001
See Cavanna, Betty
See also CA 9-12R; 200; CANR 6, 27, 85, 104; MAICYA 2; YAW

Harrison, Harry (Max) 1925- .... **CLC 42**
See also CA 1-4R; CANR 5, 21, 84; DLB 8; SATA 4; SCFW 2; SFW 4

Harrison, James (Thomas) 1937- ...... **CLC 6, 14, 33, 66, 143; SSC 19**
See also Harrison, Jim
See also CA 13-16R; CANR 8, 51, 79; CN 7; CP 7; DLBY 1982; INT CANR-8

Harrison, Jim
See Harrison, James (Thomas)
See also AMWS 8; RGAL 4; TCWW 2; TUS

Harrison, Kathryn 1961- .... **CLC 70, 151**
See also CA 144; CANR 68

Harrison, Tony 1937- .... **CLC 43, 129**
See also BRWS 5; CA 65-68; CANR 44, 98; CBD; CD 5; CP 7; DLB 40, 245; MTCW 1; RGEL 2

Harriss, Will(ard Irvin) 1922- .... **CLC 34**
See also CA 111

Harson, Sley
See Ellison, Harlan (Jay)

Hart, Ellis
See Ellison, Harlan (Jay)

Hart, Josephine 1942(?)- .... **CLC 70**
See also CA 138; CANR 70; CPW; DAM POP

Hart, Moss 1904-1961 .... **CLC 66**
See also CA 109; 89-92; CANR 84; DAM DRAM; DFS 1; DLB 7, 266; RGAL 4

Harte, (Francis) Bret(t) 1836(?)-1902 .... **TCLC 1, 25; SSC 8; WLC**
See also AMWS 2; CA 104; 140; CANR 80; CDALB 1865-1917; DA; DA3; DAC; DAM MST; DLB 12, 64, 74, 79, 186; EXPS; LAIT 2; RGAL 4; RGSF 2; SATA 26; SSFS 3; TUS

Hartley, L(eslie) P(oles) 1895-1972 ... **CLC 2, 22**
See also BRWS 7; CA 45-48; 37-40R; CANR 33; DLB 15, 139; HGG; MTCW 1, 2; RGEL 2; RGSF 2; SUFW

Hartman, Geoffrey H. 1929- .... **CLC 27**
See also CA 117; 125; CANR 79; DLB 67

Hartmann, Sadakichi 1869-1944 ... **TCLC 73**
See also CA 157; DLB 54

Hartmann von Aue c. 1170-c. 1210 .... **CMLC 15**
See also CDWLB 2; DLB 138; RGWL 2

Hartog, Jan de
See de Hartog, Jan

Haruf, Kent 1943- .... **CLC 34**
See also CA 149; CANR 91

Harwood, Ronald 1934- .... **CLC 32**
See also CA 1-4R; CANR 4, 55; CBD; CD 5; DAM DRAM, MST; DLB 13

Hasegawa Tatsunosuke
See Futabatei, Shimei

Hasek, Jaroslav (Matej Frantisek) 1883-1923 .... **TCLC 4**
See also CA 104; 129; CDWLB 4; DLB 215; EW 9; MTCW 1, 2; RGSF 2; RGWL 2

Hass, Robert 1941- ... **CLC 18, 39, 99; PC 16**
See also AMWS 6; CA 111; CANR 30, 50, 71; CP 7; DLB 105, 206; RGAL 4; SATA 94

Hastings, Hudson
See Kuttner, Henry

Hastings, Selina .... **CLC 44**

Hathorne, John 1641-1717 .... **LC 38**

Hatteras, Amelia
See Mencken, H(enry) L(ouis)

Hatteras, Owen .... **TCLC 18**
See also Mencken, H(enry) L(ouis); Nathan, George Jean

Hauptmann, Gerhart (Johann Robert) 1862-1946 .... **TCLC 4; SSC 37**
See also CA 104; 153; CDWLB 2; DAM DRAM; DLB 66, 118; EW 8; RGSF 2; RGWL 2; TWA

Havel, Vaclav 1936- ..... **CLC 25, 58, 65, 123; DC 6**
See also CA 104; CANR 36, 63; CDWLB 4; CWW 2; DA3; DAM DRAM; DFS 10; DLB 232; MTCW 1, 2

Haviaras, Stratis .... **CLC 33**
See also Chaviaras, Strates

Hawes, Stephen 1475(?)-1529(?) .... **LC 17**
See also DLB 132; RGEL 2

Hawkes, John (Clendennin Burne, Jr.) 1925-1998 .. **CLC 1, 2, 3, 4, 7, 9, 14, 15, 27, 49**
See also BPFB 2; CA 1-4R; 167; CANR 2, 47, 64; CN 7; DLB 2, 7, 227; DLBY 1980, 1998; MTCW 1, 2; RGAL 4

Hawking, S. W.
See Hawking, Stephen W(illiam)

Hawking, Stephen W(illiam) 1942- . **CLC 63, 105**
See also AAYA 13; BEST 89:1; CA 126; 129; CANR 48; CPW; DA3; MTCW 2

Hawkins, Anthony Hope
See Hope, Anthony

Hawthorne, Julian 1846-1934 .... **TCLC 25**
See also CA 165; HGG

Hawthorne, Nathaniel 1804-1864 ... **NCLC 2, 10, 17, 23, 39, 79, 95; SSC 3, 29, 39; WLC**
See also AAYA 18; AMW; AMWR 1; BPFB 2; BYA 3; CDALB 1640-1865; DA; DA3; DAB; DAC; DAM MST, NOV; DLB 1, 74, 183, 223; EXPN; EXPS; HGG; LAIT 1; NFS 1; RGAL 4; RGSF 2; SSFS 1, 7, 11, 15; SUFW; TUS; WCH; YABC 2

Haxton, Josephine Ayres 1921-
See Douglas, Ellen
See also CA 115; CANR 41, 83

Hayaseca y Eizaguirre, Jorge
See Echegaray (y Eizaguirre), Jose (Maria Waldo)

Hayashi, Fumiko 1904-1951 .... **TCLC 27**
See also Hayashi Fumiko
See also CA 161

Hayashi Fumiko
See Hayashi, Fumiko
See also DLB 180

Haycraft, Anna (Margaret) 1932-
See Ellis, Alice Thomas
See also CA 122; CANR 85, 90; MTCW 2

Hayden, Robert E(arl) 1913-1980 . **CLC 5, 9, 14, 37; BLC 2; PC 6**
See also AFAW 1, 2; AMWS 2; BW 1, 3; CA 69-72; 97-100; CABS 2; CANR 24, 75, 82; CDALB 1941-1968; DA; DAC; DAM MST, MULT, POET; DLB 5, 76; EXPP; MTCW 1, 2; PFS 1; RGAL 4; SATA 19; SATA-Obit 26; WP

Hayek, F(riedrich) A(ugust von) 1899-1992 .... **TCLC 109**
See also CA 93-96; 137; CANR 20; MTCW 1, 2

Hayford, J(oseph) E(phraim) Casely
See Casely-Hayford, J(oseph) E(phraim)

Hayman, Ronald 1932- .... **CLC 44**
See also CA 25-28R; CANR 18, 50, 88; CD 5; DLB 155

Hayne, Paul Hamilton 1830-1886 . **NCLC 94**
See also DLB 3, 64, 79, 248; RGAL 4

Hays, Mary 1760-1843 .... **NCLC 114**
See also DLB 142, 158; RGEL 2

Haywood, Eliza (Fowler) 1693(?)-1756 .... **LC 1, 44**
See also DLB 39; RGEL 2

Hazlitt, William 1778-1830 ...... **NCLC 29, 82**
See also BRW 4; DLB 110, 158; RGEL 2; TEA

Hazzard, Shirley 1931- .... **CLC 18**
See also CA 9-12R; CANR 4, 70; CN 7; DLBY 1982; MTCW 1

Head, Bessie 1937-1986 .... **CLC 25, 67; BLC 2; SSC 52**
See also AFW; BW 2, 3; CA 29-32R; 119; CANR 25, 82; CDWLB 3; DA3; DAM MULT; DLB 117, 225; EXPS; FW; MTCW 1, 2; RGSF 2; SSFS 5, 13; WLIT 2

Headon, (Nicky) Topper 1956(?)- ..... **CLC 30**

Heaney, Seamus (Justin) 1939- ..... **CLC 5, 7, 14, 25, 37, 74, 91; PC 18; WLCS**
See also BRWR 1; BRWS 2; CA 85-88; CANR 25, 48, 75, 91; CDBLB 1960 to Present; CP 7; DA3; DAB; DAM POET; DLB 40; DLBY 1995; EXPP; MTCW 1, 2; PAB; PFS 2, 5, 8; RGEL 2; TEA; WLIT 4

Hearn, (Patricio) Lafcadio (Tessima Carlos) 1850-1904 .... **TCLC 9**
See also CA 105; 166; DLB 12, 78, 189; HGG; RGAL 4

Hearne, Vicki 1946-2001 .... **CLC 56**
See also CA 139; 201

Hearon, Shelby 1931- .... **CLC 63**
See also AITN 2; AMWS 8; CA 25-28R; CANR 18, 48, 103; CSW

Heat-Moon, William Least .... **CLC 29**
See also Trogdon, William (Lewis)
See also AAYA 9

Hebbel, Friedrich 1813-1863 .... **NCLC 43**
See also CDWLB 2; DAM DRAM; DLB 129; EW 6; RGWL 2

Hebert, Anne 1916-2000 .... **CLC 4, 13, 29**
See also CA 85-88; 187; CANR 69; CCA 1; CWP; CWW 2; DA3; DAC; DAM MST, POET; DLB 68; GFL 1789 to the Present; MTCW 1, 2

Hecht, Anthony (Evan) 1923- ...... **CLC 8, 13, 19**
See also AMWS 10; CA 9-12R; CANR 6, 108; CP 7; DAM POET; DLB 5, 169; PFS 6; WP

Heyward, (Edwin) DuBose
1885-1940 .... **TCLC 59**
See also CA 108; 157; DLB 7, 9, 45, 249;
SATA 21

Heywood, John 1497(?)-1580(?) .... **LC 65**
See also DLB 136; RGEL 2

Hibbert, Eleanor Alice Burford
1906-1993 .... **CLC 7**
See also Holt, Victoria
See also BEST 90:4; CA 17-20R; 140;
CANR 9, 28, 59; CMW 4; CPW; DAM
POP; MTCW 2; RHW; SATA 2; SATA-
Obit 74

Hichens, Robert (Smythe)
1864-1950 .... **TCLC 64**
See also CA 162; DLB 153; HGG; RHW;
SUFW

Higgins, George V(incent)
1939-1999 .... **CLC 4, 7, 10, 18**
See also BPFB 2; CA 77-80; 186; CAAS 5;
CANR 17, 51, 89, 96; CMW 4; CN 7;
DLB 2; DLBY 1981, 1998; INT CANR-
17; MSW; MTCW 1

Higginson, Thomas Wentworth
1823-1911 .... **TCLC 36**
See also CA 162; DLB 1, 64, 243

Higgonet, Margaret ed. .... **CLC 65**

Highet, Helen
See MacInnes, Helen (Clark)

Highsmith, (Mary) Patricia
1921-1995 .... **CLC 2, 4, 14, 42, 102**
See also Morgan, Claire
See also BRWS 5; CA 1-4R; 147; CANR 1,
20, 48, 62, 108; CMW 4; CPW; DA3;
DAM NOV, POP; MSW; MTCW 1, 2

Highwater, Jamake (Mamake)
1942(?)-2001 .... **CLC 12**
See also AAYA 7; BPFB 2; BYA 4; CA 65-
68; 199; CAAS 7; CANR 10, 34, 84; CLR
17; CWRI 5; DLB 52; DLBY 1985;
JRDA; MAICYA 1, 2; SATA 32, 69;
SATA-Brief 30

Highway, Tomson 1951- .... **CLC 92**
See also CA 151; CANR 75; CCA 1; CD 5;
DAC; DAM MULT; DFS 2; MTCW 2;
NNAL

Hijuelos, Oscar 1951- .... **CLC 65; HLC 1**
See also AAYA 25; AMWS 8; BEST 90:1;
CA 123; CANR 50, 75; CPW; DA3; DAM
MULT, POP; DLB 145; HW 1, 2; MTCW
2; RGAL 4; WLIT 1

Hikmet, Nazim 1902(?)-1963 .... **CLC 40**
See also CA 141; 93-96

Hildegard von Bingen 1098-1179 . **CMLC 20**
See also DLB 148

Hildesheimer, Wolfgang 1916-1991 .. **CLC 49**
See also CA 101; 135; DLB 69, 124

Hill, Geoffrey (William) 1932- ...... **CLC 5, 8, 18, 45**
See also BRWS 5; CA 81-84; CANR 21,
89; CDBLB 1960 to Present; CP 7; DAM
POET; DLB 40; MTCW 1; RGEL 2

Hill, George Roy 1921- .... **CLC 26**
See also CA 110; 122

Hill, John
See Koontz, Dean R(ay)

Hill, Susan (Elizabeth) 1942- ...... **CLC 4, 113**
See also CA 33-36R; CANR 29, 69; CN 7;
DAB; DAM MST, NOV; DLB 14, 139;
HGG; MTCW 1; RHW

Hillard, Asa G. III .... **CLC 70**

Hillerman, Tony 1925- .... **CLC 62**
See also AAYA 40; BEST 89:1; BPFB 2;
CA 29-32R; CANR 21, 42, 65, 97; CMW
4; CPW; DA3; DAM POP; DLB 206;
MSW; RGAL 4; SATA 6; TCWW 2; YAW

Hillesum, Etty 1914-1943 .... **TCLC 49**
See also CA 137

Hilliard, Noel (Harvey) 1929-1996 ... **CLC 15**
See also CA 9-12R; CANR 7, 69; CN 7

Hillis, Rick 1956- .... **CLC 66**
See also CA 134

Hilton, James 1900-1954 .... **TCLC 21**
See also CA 108; 169; DLB 34, 77; FANT;
SATA 34

Himes, Chester (Bomar) 1909-1984 .. **CLC 2,
4, 7, 18, 58, 108; BLC 2**
See also AFAW 2; BPFB 2; BW 2; CA 25-
28R; 114; CANR 22, 89; CMW 4; DAM
MULT; DLB 2, 76, 143, 226; MSW;
MTCW 1, 2; RGAL 4

Hinde, Thomas .... **CLC 6, 11**
See also Chitty, Thomas Willes

Hine, (William) Daryl 1936- .... **CLC 15**
See also CA 1-4R; CAAS 15; CANR 1, 20;
CP 7; DLB 60

Hinkson, Katharine Tynan
See Tynan, Katharine

Hinojosa(-Smith), Rolando (R.) 1929-
See also CA 131; CAAS 16; CANR 62;
DAM MULT; DLB 82; HLC 1; HW 1, 2;
MTCW 2; RGAL 4

Hinton, S(usan) E(loise) 1950- .. **CLC 30, 111**
See also AAYA 2, 33; BPFB 2; BYA 2, 3;
CA 81-84; CANR 32, 62, 92; CDALBS;
CLR 3, 23; CPW; DA; DA3; DAB; DAC;
DAM MST, NOV; JRDA; LAIT 5; MAI-
CYA 1, 2; MTCW 1, 2; NFS 5, 9, 15;
SATA 19, 58, 115; WYA; YAW

Hippius, Zinaida .... **TCLC 9**
See also Gippius, Zinaida (Nikolayevna)

Hiraoka, Kimitake 1925-1970
See Mishima, Yukio
See also CA 97-100; 29-32R; DA3; DAM
DRAM; MTCW 1, 2

Hirsch, E(ric) D(onald), Jr. 1928- .... **CLC 79**
See also CA 25-28R; CANR 27, 51; DLB
67; INT CANR-27; MTCW 1

Hirsch, Edward 1950- .... **CLC 31, 50**
See also CA 104; CANR 20, 42, 102; CP 7;
DLB 120

Hitchcock, Alfred (Joseph)
1899-1980 .... **CLC 16**
See also AAYA 22; CA 159; 97-100; SATA
27; SATA-Obit 24

Hitchens, Christopher (Eric)
1949- .... **CLC 157**
See also CA 152; CANR 89

Hitler, Adolf 1889-1945 .... **TCLC 53**
See also CA 117; 147

Hoagland, Edward 1932- .... **CLC 28**
See also ANW; CA 1-4R; CANR 2, 31, 57,
107; CN 7; DLB 6; SATA 51; TCWW 2

Hoban, Russell (Conwell) 1925- ... **CLC 7, 25**
See also BPFB 2; CA 5-8R; CANR 23, 37,
66; CLR 3, 69; CN 7; CWRI 5; DAM
NOV; DLB 52; FANT; MAICYA 1, 2;
MTCW 1, 2; SATA 1, 40, 78; SFW 4

Hobbes, Thomas 1588-1679 .... **LC 36**
See also DLB 151, 252; RGEL 2

Hobbs, Perry
See Blackmur, R(ichard) P(almer)

Hobson, Laura Z(ametkin)
1900-1986 .... **CLC 7, 25**
See also Field, Peter
See also BPFB 2; CA 17-20R; 118; CANR
55; DLB 28; SATA 52

Hoccleve, Thomas c. 1368-c. 1437 ...... **LC 75**
See also DLB 146; RGEL 2

Hoch, Edward D(entinger) 1930-
See Queen, Ellery
See also CA 29-32R; CANR 11, 27, 51, 97;
CMW 4; SFW 4

Hochhuth, Rolf 1931- .... **CLC 4, 11, 18**
See also CA 5-8R; CANR 33, 75; CWW 2;
DAM DRAM; DLB 124; MTCW 1, 2

Hochman, Sandra 1936- .... **CLC 3, 8**
See also CA 5-8R; DLB 5

Hochwaelder, Fritz 1911-1986 .... **CLC 36**
See also Hochwalder, Fritz
See also CA 29-32R; 120; CANR 42; DAM
DRAM; MTCW 1

Hochwalder, Fritz
See Hochwaelder, Fritz
See also RGWL 2

Hocking, Mary (Eunice) 1921- .... **CLC 13**
See also CA 101; CANR 18, 40

Hodgins, Jack 1938- .... **CLC 23**
See also CA 93-96; CN 7; DLB 60

Hodgson, William Hope
1877(?)-1918 .... **TCLC 13**
See also CA 111; 164; CMW 4; DLB 70,
153, 156, 178; HGG; MTCW 2; SFW 4;
SUFW

Hoeg, Peter 1957- .... **CLC 95, 156**
See also CA 151; CANR 75; CMW 4; DA3;
DLB 214; MTCW 2

Hoffman, Alice 1952- .... **CLC 51**
See also AAYA 37; AMWS 10; CA 77-80;
CANR 34, 66, 100; CN 7; CPW; DAM
NOV; MTCW 1, 2

Hoffman, Daniel (Gerard) 1923- . **CLC 6, 13, 23**
See also CA 1-4R; CANR 4; CP 7; DLB 5

Hoffman, Stanley 1944- .... **CLC 5**
See also CA 77-80

Hoffman, William 1925- .... **CLC 141**
See also CA 21-24R; CANR 9, 103; CSW;
DLB 234

Hoffman, William M(oses) 1939- ..... **CLC 40**
See also CA 57-60; CANR 11, 71

Hoffmann, E(rnst) T(heodor) A(madeus)
1776-1822 .... **NCLC 2; SSC 13**
See also CDWLB 2; DLB 90; EW 5; RGSF
2; RGWL 2; SATA 27; SUFW; WCH

Hofmann, Gert 1931- .... **CLC 54**
See also CA 128

Hofmannsthal, Hugo von
1874-1929 .... **TCLC 11; DC 4**
See also CA 106; 153; CDWLB 2; DAM
DRAM; DFS 12; DLB 81, 118; EW 9;
RGWL 2

Hogan, Linda 1947- .... **CLC 73; PC 35**
See also AMWS 4; ANW; BYA 12; CA 120;
CANR 45, 73; CWP; DAM MULT; DLB
175; NNAL; SATA 132; TCWW 2

Hogarth, Charles
See Creasey, John

Hogarth, Emmett
See Polonsky, Abraham (Lincoln)

Hogg, James 1770-1835 .... **NCLC 4, 109**
See also DLB 93, 116, 159; HGG; RGEL 2;
SUFW

Holbach, Paul Henri Thiry Baron
1723-1789 .... **LC 14**

Holberg, Ludvig 1684-1754 .... **LC 6**
See also RGWL 2

Holcroft, Thomas 1745-1809 .... **NCLC 85**
See also DLB 39, 89, 158; RGEL 2

Holden, Ursula 1921- .... **CLC 18**
See also CA 101; CAAS 8; CANR 22

Holderlin, (Johann Christian) Friedrich
1770-1843 .... **NCLC 16; PC 4**
See also CDWLB 2; DLB 90; EW 5; RGWL
2

Holdstock, Robert
See Holdstock, Robert P.

Holdstock, Robert P. 1948- .... **CLC 39**
See also CA 131; CANR 81; DLB 261;
FANT; HGG; SFW 4

Holinshed, Raphael fl. 1580- .... **LC 69**
See also DLB 167; RGEL 2

Author Index

Jaynes, Roderick
  See Coen, Ethan
Jeake, Samuel, Jr.
  See Aiken, Conrad (Potter)
Jean Paul 1763-1825 .... **NCLC 7**
Jefferies, (John) Richard
  1848-1887 .... **NCLC 47**
  See also DLB 98, 141; RGEL 2; SATA 16;
  SFW 4
Jeffers, (John) Robinson 1887-1962 .. **CLC 2,**
  3, 11, 15, 54; PC 17; WLC
  See also AMWS 2; CA 85-88; CANR 35;
  CDALB 1917-1929; DA; DAC; DAM
  MST, POET; DLB 45, 212; MTCW 1, 2;
  PAB; PFS 3, 4; RGAL 4
Jefferson, Janet
  See Mencken, H(enry) L(ouis)
Jefferson, Thomas 1743-1826 .. **NCLC 11, 103**
  See also ANW; CDALB 1640-1865; DA3;
  DLB 31, 183; LAIT 1; RGAL 4
Jeffrey, Francis 1773-1850 .... **NCLC 33**
  See also Francis, Lord Jeffrey
Jelakowitch, Ivan
  See Heijermans, Herman
Jellicoe, (Patricia) Ann 1927- .... **CLC 27**
  See also CA 85-88; CBD; CD 5; CWD;
  CWRI 5; DLB 13, 233; FW
Jemyma
  See Holley, Marietta
Jen, Gish .... **CLC 70**
  See also Jen, Lillian
Jen, Lillian 1956(?)-
  See Jen, Gish
  See also CA 135; CANR 89
Jenkins, (John) Robin 1912- .... **CLC 52**
  See also CA 1-4R; CANR 1; CN 7; DLB
  14
Jennings, Elizabeth (Joan)
  1926-2001 .... **CLC 5, 14, 131**
  See also BRWS 5; CA 61-64; 200; CAAS
  5; CANR 8, 39, 66; CP 7; CWP; DLB 27;
  MTCW 1; SATA 66
Jennings, Waylon 1937- .... **CLC 21**
Jensen, Johannes V. 1873-1950 ...... **TCLC 41**
  See also CA 170; DLB 214
Jensen, Laura (Linnea) 1948- .... **CLC 37**
  See also CA 103
Jerome, Jerome K(lapka)
  1859-1927 .... **TCLC 23**
  See also CA 119; 177; DLB 10, 34, 135;
  RGEL 2
Jerrold, Douglas William
  1803-1857 .... **NCLC 2**
  See also DLB 158, 159; RGEL 2
Jewett, (Theodora) Sarah Orne
  1849-1909 .... **TCLC 1, 22; SSC 6, 44**
  See also AMW; CA 108; 127; CANR 71;
  DLB 12, 74, 221; EXPS; FW; MAWW;
  NFS 15; RGAL 4; RGSF 2; SATA 15;
  SSFS 4
Jewsbury, Geraldine (Endsor)
  1812-1880 .... **NCLC 22**
  See also DLB 21
Jhabvala, Ruth Prawer 1927- . **CLC 4, 8, 29,**
  94, 138
  See also BRWS 5; CA 1-4R; CANR 2, 29,
  51, 74, 91; CN 7; DAB; DAM NOV; DLB
  139, 194; IDFW 3, 4; INT CANR-29;
  MTCW 1, 2; RGSF 2; RGWL 2; RHW;
  TEA
Jibran, Kahlil
  See Gibran, Kahlil
Jibran, Khalil
  See Gibran, Kahlil
Jiles, Paulette 1943- .... **CLC 13, 58**
  See also CA 101; CANR 70; CWP

Jimenez (Mantecon), Juan Ramon
  1881-1958 .... **TCLC 4; HLC 1; PC 7**
  See also CA 104; 131; CANR 74; DAM
  MULT, POET; DLB 134; EW 9; HW 1;
  MTCW 1, 2; RGWL 2
Jimenez, Ramon
  See Jimenez (Mantecon), Juan Ramon
Jimenez Mantecon, Juan
  See Jimenez (Mantecon), Juan Ramon
Jin, Ha .... **CLC 109**
  See also Jin, Xuefei
  See also CA 152; DLB 244
Jin, Xuefei 1956-
  See Jin, Ha
  See also CANR 91
Joel, Billy .... **CLC 26**
  See also Joel, William Martin
Joel, William Martin 1949-
  See Joel, Billy
  See also CA 108
John, Saint 107th cent. -100 .... **CMLC 27**
John of the Cross, St. 1542-1591 .... **LC 18**
  See also RGWL 2
John Paul II, Pope 1920- .... **CLC 128**
  See also CA 106; 133
Johnson, B(ryan) S(tanley William)
  1933-1973 .... **CLC 6, 9**
  See also CA 9-12R; 53-56; CANR 9; DLB
  14, 40; RGEL 2
Johnson, Benjamin F., of Boone
  See Riley, James Whitcomb
Johnson, Charles (Richard) 1948- .... **CLC 7,**
  51, 65, 163; BLC 2
  See also AFAW 2; AMWS 6; BW 2, 3; CA
  116; CAAS 18; CANR 42, 66, 82; CN 7;
  DAM MULT; DLB 33; MTCW 2; RGAL
  4
Johnson, Denis 1949- . **CLC 52, 160; SSC 56**
  See also CA 117; 121; CANR 71, 99; CN
  7; DLB 120
Johnson, Diane 1934- .... **CLC 5, 13, 48**
  See also BPFB 2; CA 41-44R; CANR 17,
  40, 62, 95; CN 7; DLBY 1980; INT
  CANR-17; MTCW 1
Johnson, Eyvind (Olof Verner)
  1900-1976 .... **CLC 14**
  See also CA 73-76; 69-72; CANR 34, 101;
  DLB 259; EW 12
Johnson, J. R.
  See James, C(yril) L(ionel) R(obert)
Johnson, James Weldon
  1871-1938 . **TCLC 3, 19; BLC 2; PC 24**
  See also AFAW 1, 2; BW 1, 3; CA 104;
  125; CANR 82; CDALB 1917-1929; CLR
  32; DA3; DAM MULT, POET; DLB 51;
  EXPP; MTCW 1, 2; PFS 1; RGAL 4;
  SATA 31; TUS
Johnson, Joyce 1935- .... **CLC 58**
  See also CA 125; 129; CANR 102
Johnson, Judith (Emlyn) 1936- .... **CLC 7, 15**
  See also Sherwin, Judith Johnson
  See also CA 25-28R; 153; CANR 34
Johnson, Lionel (Pigot)
  1867-1902 .... **TCLC 19**
  See also CA 117; DLB 19; RGEL 2
Johnson, Marguerite (Annie)
  See Angelou, Maya
Johnson, Mel
  See Malzberg, Barry N(athaniel)
Johnson, Pamela Hansford
  1912-1981 .... **CLC 1, 7, 27**
  See also CA 1-4R; 104; CANR 2, 28; DLB
  15; MTCW 1, 2; RGEL 2
Johnson, Paul (Bede) 1928- .... **CLC 147**
  See also BEST 89:4; CA 17-20R; CANR
  34, 62, 100
Johnson, Robert .... **CLC 70**
Johnson, Robert 1911(?)-1938 .... **TCLC 69**
  See also BW 3; CA 174

Johnson, Samuel 1709-1784 .... **LC 15, 52;**
  WLC
  See also BRW 3; BRWR 1; CDBLB 1660-
  1789; DA; DAB; DAC; DAM MST; DLB
  39, 95, 104, 142, 213; RGEL 2; TEA
Johnson, Uwe 1934-1984 .. **CLC 5, 10, 15, 40**
  See also CA 1-4R; 112; CANR 1, 39; CD-
  WLB 2; DLB 75; MTCW 1; RGWL 2
Johnston, George (Benson) 1913- .... **CLC 51**
  See also CA 1-4R; CANR 5, 20; CP 7; DLB
  88
Johnston, Jennifer (Prudence)
  1930- .... **CLC 7, 150**
  See also CA 85-88; CANR 92; CN 7; DLB
  14
Joinville, Jean de 1224(?)-1317 ..... **CMLC 38**
Jolley, (Monica) Elizabeth 1923- ..... **CLC 46;**
  SSC 19
  See also CA 127; CAAS 13; CANR 59; CN
  7; RGSF 2
Jones, Arthur Llewellyn 1863-1947
  See Machen, Arthur
  See also CA 104; 179; HGG
Jones, D(ouglas) G(ordon) 1929- ..... **CLC 10**
  See also CA 29-32R; CANR 13, 90; CP 7;
  DLB 53
Jones, David (Michael) 1895-1974 .... **CLC 2,**
  4, 7, 13, 42
  See also BRW 6; BRWS 7; CA 9-12R; 53-
  56; CANR 28; CDBLB 1945-1960; DLB
  20, 100; MTCW 1; PAB; RGEL 2
Jones, David Robert 1947-
  See Bowie, David
  See also CA 103; CANR 104
Jones, Diana Wynne 1934- .... **CLC 26**
  See also AAYA 12; BYA 6, 7, 9, 11, 13; CA
  49-52; CANR 4, 26, 56; CLR 23; DLB
  161; FANT; JRDA; MAICYA 1, 2; SAAS
  7; SATA 9, 70, 108; SFW 4; YAW
Jones, Edward P. 1950- .... **CLC 76**
  See also BW 2, 3; CA 142; CANR 79; CSW
Jones, Gayl 1949- ...... **CLC 6, 9, 131; BLC 2**
  See also AFAW 1, 2; BW 2, 3; CA 77-80;
  CANR 27, 66; CN 7; CSW; DA3; DAM
  MULT; DLB 33; MTCW 1, 2; RGAL 4
Jones, James 1921-1977 ...... **CLC 1, 3, 10, 39**
  See also AITN 1, 2; AMWS 11; BPFB 2;
  CA 1-4R; 69-72; CANR 6; DLB 2, 143;
  DLBD 17; DLBY 1998; MTCW 1; RGAL
  4
Jones, John J.
  See Lovecraft, H(oward) P(hillips)
Jones, LeRoi .... **CLC 1, 2, 3, 5, 10, 14**
  See also Baraka, Amiri
  See also MTCW 2
Jones, Louis B. 1953- .... **CLC 65**
  See also CA 141; CANR 73
Jones, Madison (Percy, Jr.) 1925- ...... **CLC 4**
  See also CA 13-16R; CAAS 11; CANR 7,
  54, 83; CN 7; CSW; DLB 152
Jones, Mervyn 1922- .... **CLC 10, 52**
  See also CA 45-48; CAAS 5; CANR 1, 91;
  CN 7; MTCW 1
Jones, Mick 1956(?)- .... **CLC 30**
Jones, Nettie (Pearl) 1941- .... **CLC 34**
  See also BW 2; CA 137; CAAS 20; CANR
  88
Jones, Preston 1936-1979 .... **CLC 10**
  See also CA 73-76; 89-92; DLB 7
Jones, Robert F(rancis) 1934- .... **CLC 7**
  See also CA 49-52; CANR 2, 61
Jones, Rod 1953- .... **CLC 50**
  See also CA 128
Jones, Terence Graham Parry
  1942- .... **CLC 21**
  See also Jones, Terry; Monty Python
  See also CA 112; 116; CANR 35, 93; INT
  116; SATA 127

Kazakov, Yuri Pavlovich 1927-1982 . **SSC 43**
　　See also CA 5-8R; CANR 36; MTCW 1;
　　RGSF 2
Kazan, Elia 1909- .... **CLC 6, 16, 63**
　　See also CA 21-24R; CANR 32, 78
Kazantzakis, Nikos 1883(?)-1957 .... **TCLC 2,**
　　5, 33
　　See also BPFB 2; CA 105; 132; DA3; EW
　　9; MTCW 1, 2; RGWL 2
Kazin, Alfred 1915-1998 ..... **CLC 34, 38, 119**
　　See also AMWS 8; CA 1-4R; CAAS 7;
　　CANR 1, 45, 79; DLB 67
Keane, Mary Nesta (Skrine) 1904-1996
　　See Keane, Molly
　　See also CA 108; 114; 151; CN 7; RHW
Keane, Molly .... **CLC 31**
　　See also Keane, Mary Nesta (Skrine)
　　See also INT 114
Keates, Jonathan 1946(?)- .... **CLC 34**
　　See also CA 163
Keaton, Buster 1895-1966 .... **CLC 20**
　　See also CA 194
Keats, John 1795-1821 ... **NCLC 8, 73; PC 1;**
　　WLC
　　See also BRW 4; BRWR 1; CDBLB 1789-
　　1832; DA; DA3; DAB; DAC; DAM MST,
　　POET; DLB 96, 110; EXPP; PAB; PFS 1,
　　2, 3, 9; RGEL 2; TEA; WLIT 3; WP
Keble, John 1792-1866 .... **NCLC 87**
　　See also DLB 32, 55; RGEL 2
Keene, Donald 1922- .... **CLC 34**
　　See also CA 1-4R; CANR 5
Keillor, Garrison .... **CLC 40, 115**
　　See also Keillor, Gary (Edward)
　　See also AAYA 2; BEST 89:3; BPFB 2;
　　DLBY 1987; SATA 58; TUS
Keillor, Gary (Edward) 1942-
　　See Keillor, Garrison
　　See also CA 111; 117; CANR 36, 59; CPW;
　　DA3; DAM POP; MTCW 1, 2
Keith, Carlos
　　See Lewton, Val
Keith, Michael
　　See Hubbard, L(afayette) Ron(ald)
Keller, Gottfried 1819-1890 .... **NCLC 2; SSC**
　　26
　　See also CDWLB 2; DLB 129; EW; RGSF
　　2; RGWL 2
Keller, Nora Okja 1965- .... **CLC 109**
　　See also CA 187
Kellerman, Jonathan 1949- .... **CLC 44**
　　See also AAYA 35; BEST 90:1; CA 106;
　　CANR 29, 51; CMW 4; CPW; DA3;
　　DAM POP; INT CANR-29
Kelley, William Melvin 1937- .... **CLC 22**
　　See also BW 1; CA 77-80; CANR 27, 83;
　　CN 7; DLB 33
Kellogg, Marjorie 1922- .... **CLC 2**
　　See also CA 81-84
Kellow, Kathleen
　　See Hibbert, Eleanor Alice Burford
Kelly, M(ilton) T(errence) 1947- ...... **CLC 55**
　　See also CA 97-100; CAAS 22; CANR 19,
　　43, 84; CN 7
Kelly, Robert 1935- .... **SSC 50**
　　See also CA 17-20R; CAAS 19; CANR 47;
　　CP 7; DLB 5, 130, 165
Kelman, James 1946- .... **CLC 58, 86**
　　See also BRWS 5; CA 148; CANR 85; CN
　　7; DLB 194; RGSF 2; WLIT 4
Kemal, Yashar 1923- .... **CLC 14, 29**
　　See also CA 89-92; CANR 44; CWW 2
Kemble, Fanny 1809-1893 .... **NCLC 18**
　　See also DLB 32
Kemelman, Harry 1908-1996 .... **CLC 2**
　　See also AITN 1; BPFB 2; CA 9-12R; 155;
　　CANR 6, 71; CMW 4; DLB 28
Kempe, Margery 1373(?)-1440(?) ... **LC 6, 56**
　　See also DLB 146; RGEL 2

Kempis, Thomas a 1380-1471 .... **LC 11**
Kendall, Henry 1839-1882 .... **NCLC 12**
　　See also DLB 230
Keneally, Thomas (Michael) 1935- ... **CLC 5,**
　　8, 10, 14, 19, 27, 43, 117
　　See also BRWS 4; CA 85-88; CANR 10,
　　50, 74; CN 7; CPW; DA3; DAM NOV;
　　MTCW 1, 2; RGEL 2; RHW
Kennedy, Adrienne (Lita) 1931- ..... **CLC 66;**
　　BLC 2; DC 5
　　See also AFAW 2; BW 2, 3; CA 103; CAAS
　　20; CABS 3; CANR 26, 53, 82; CD 5;
　　DAM MULT; DFS 9; DLB 38; FW
Kennedy, John Pendleton
　　1795-1870 .... **NCLC 2**
　　See also DLB 3, 248, 254; RGAL 4
Kennedy, Joseph Charles 1929-
　　See Kennedy, X. J.
　　See also CA 1-4R; CAAE 201; CANR 4,
　　30, 40; CP 7; CWRI 5; MAICYA 2; MAI-
　　CYAS 1; SATA 14, 86; SATA-Essay 130
Kennedy, William 1928- ... **CLC 6, 28, 34, 53**
　　See also AAYA 1; AMWS 7; BPFB 2; CA
　　85-88; CANR 14, 31, 76; CN 7; DA3;
　　DAM NOV; DLB 143; DLBY 1985; INT
　　CANR-31; MTCW 1, 2; SATA 57
Kennedy, X. J. .... **CLC 8, 42**
　　See also Kennedy, Joseph Charles
　　See also CAAS 9; CLR 27; DLB 5; SAAS
　　22
Kenny, Maurice (Francis) 1929- ...... **CLC 87**
　　See also CA 144; CAAS 22; DAM MULT;
　　DLB 175; NNAL
Kent, Kelvin
　　See Kuttner, Henry
Kenton, Maxwell
　　See Southern, Terry
Kenyon, Robert O.
　　See Kuttner, Henry
Kepler, Johannes 1571-1630 .... **LC 45**
Ker, Jill
　　See Conway, Jill K(er)
Kerkow, H. C.
　　See Lewton, Val
Kerouac, Jack 1922-1969 ...... **CLC 1, 2, 3, 5,**
　　14, 29, 61; WLC
　　See also Kerouac, Jean-Louis Lebris de
　　See also AAYA 25; AMWS 3; BPFB 2;
　　CDALB 1941-1968; CPW; DLB 2, 16,
　　237; DLBD 3; DLBY 1995; GLL 1;
　　MTCW 2; NFS 8; RGAL 4; TCLC 117;
　　TUS; WP
Kerouac, Jean-Louis Lebris de 1922-1969
　　See Kerouac, Jack
　　See also AITN 1; CA 5-8R; 25-28R; CANR
　　26, 54, 95; DA; DA3; DAB; DAC; DAM
　　MST, NOV, POET, POP; MTCW 1, 2
Kerr, Jean 1923- .... **CLC 22**
　　See also CA 5-8R; CANR 7; INT CANR-7
Kerr, M. E. .... **CLC 12, 35**
　　See also Meaker, Marijane (Agnes)
　　See also AAYA 2, 23; BYA 1, 7, 8; CLR
　　29; SAAS 1; WYA
Kerr, Robert .... **CLC 55**
Kerrigan, (Thomas) Anthony 1918- .. **CLC 4,**
　　6
　　See also CA 49-52; CAAS 11; CANR 4
Kerry, Lois
　　See Duncan, Lois
Kesey, Ken (Elton) 1935-2001 ... **CLC 1, 3, 6,**
　　11, 46, 64; WLC
　　See also AAYA 25; BPFB 2; CA 1-4R; 204;
　　CANR 22, 38, 66; CDALB 1968-1988;
　　CN 7; CPW; DA; DA3; DAB; DAC;
　　DAM MST, NOV, POP; DLB 2, 16, 206;
　　EXPN; LAIT 4; MTCW 1, 2; NFS 2;
　　RGAL 4; SATA 66; SATA-Obit 131; TUS;
　　YAW

Kesselring, Joseph (Otto)
　　1902-1967 .... **CLC 45**
　　See also CA 150; DAM DRAM, MST
Kessler, Jascha (Frederick) 1929- ...... **CLC 4**
　　See also CA 17-20R; CANR 8, 48, 111
Kettelkamp, Larry (Dale) 1933- .... **CLC 12**
　　See also CA 29-32R; CANR 16; SAAS 3;
　　SATA 2
Key, Ellen (Karolina Sofia)
　　1849-1926 .... **TCLC 65**
　　See also DLB 259
Keyber, Conny
　　See Fielding, Henry
Keyes, Daniel 1927- .... **CLC 80**
　　See also AAYA 23; BYA 11; CA 17-20R,
　　181; CAAE 181; CANR 10, 26, 54, 74;
　　DA; DA3; DAC; DAM MST, NOV;
　　EXPN; LAIT 4; MTCW 2; NFS 2; SATA
　　37; SFW 4
Keynes, John Maynard
　　1883-1946 .... **TCLC 64**
　　See also CA 114; 162, 163; DLBD 10;
　　MTCW 2
Khanshendel, Chiron
　　See Rose, Wendy
Khayyam, Omar 1048-1131 ... **CMLC 11; PC**
　　8
　　See also Omar Khayyam
　　See also DA3; DAM POET
Kherdian, David 1931- .... **CLC 6, 9**
　　See also AAYA 42; CA 21-24R; CAAE 192;
　　CAAS 2; CANR 39, 78; CLR 24; JRDA;
　　LAIT 3; MAICYA 1, 2; SATA 16, 74;
　　SATA-Essay 125
Khlebnikov, Velimir .... **TCLC 20**
　　See also Khlebnikov, Viktor Vladimirovich
　　See also EW 10; RGWL 2
Khlebnikov, Viktor Vladimirovich 1885-1922
　　See Khlebnikov, Velimir
　　See also CA 117
Khodasevich, Vladislav (Felitsianovich)
　　1886-1939 .... **TCLC 15**
　　See also CA 115
Kielland, Alexander Lange
　　1849-1906 .... **TCLC 5**
　　See also CA 104
Kiely, Benedict 1919- .... **CLC 23, 43**
　　See also CA 1-4R; CANR 2, 84; CN 7;
　　DLB 15
Kienzle, William X(avier)
　　1928-2001 .... **CLC 25**
　　See also CA 93-96; 203; CAAS 1; CANR
　　9, 31, 59, 111; CMW 4; DA3; DAM POP;
　　INT CANR-31; MSW; MTCW 1, 2
Kierkegaard, Soren 1813-1855 ..... **NCLC 34,**
　　78
　　See also EW 6; TWA
Kieslowski, Krzysztof 1941-1996 .... **CLC 120**
　　See also CA 147; 151
Killens, John Oliver 1916-1987 .... **CLC 10**
　　See also BW 2; CA 77-80; 123; CAAS 2;
　　CANR 26; DLB 33
Killigrew, Anne 1660-1685 .... **LC 4, 73**
　　See also DLB 131
Killigrew, Thomas 1612-1683 .... **LC 57**
　　See also DLB 58; RGEL 2
Kim
　　See Simenon, Georges (Jacques Christian)
Kincaid, Jamaica 1949- ..... **CLC 43, 68, 137;**
　　BLC 2
　　See also AAYA 13; AFAW 2; AMWS 7;
　　BRWS 7; BW 2, 3; CA 125; CANR 47,
　　59, 95; CDALBS; CDWLB 3; CLR 63;
　　CN 7; DA3; DAM MULT, NOV; DLB
　　157, 227; DNFS 1; EXPS; FW; MTCW
　　2; NCFS 1; NFS 3; SSFS 5, 7; TUS; YAW

King, Francis (Henry) 1923- .... **CLC 8, 53, 145**
See also CA 1-4R; CANR 1, 33, 86; CN 7; DAM NOV; DLB 15, 139; MTCW 1

King, Kennedy
See Brown, George Douglas

King, Martin Luther, Jr.
1929-1968 .... **CLC 83; BLC 2; WLCS**
See also BW 2, 3; CA 25-28; CANR 27, 44; CAP 2; DA; DA3; DAB; DAC; DAM MST, MULT; LAIT 5; MTCW 1, 2; SATA 14

King, Stephen (Edwin) 1947- .... **CLC 12, 26, 37, 61, 113; SSC 17, 55**
See also AAYA 1, 17; AMWS 5; BEST 90:1; BPFB 2; CA 61-64; CANR 1, 30, 52, 76; CPW; DA3; DAM NOV, POP; DLB 143; DLBY 1980; HGG; JRDA; LAIT 5; MTCW 1, 2; RGAL 4; SATA 9, 55; SUFW; WYAS 1; YAW

King, Steve
See King, Stephen (Edwin)

King, Thomas 1943- .... **CLC 89**
See also CA 144; CANR 95; CCA 1; CN 7; DAC; DAM MULT; DLB 175; NNAL; SATA 96

Kingman, Lee .... **CLC 17**
See also Natti, (Mary) Lee
See also CWRI 5; SAAS 3; SATA 1, 67

Kingsley, Charles 1819-1875 .... **NCLC 35**
See also CLR 77; DLB 21, 32, 163, 178, 190; FANT; MAICYA 2; MAICYAS 1; RGEL 2; WCH; YABC 2

Kingsley, Henry 1830-1876 .... **NCLC 107**
See also DLB 21, 230; RGEL 2

Kingsley, Sidney 1906-1995 .... **CLC 44**
See also CA 85-88; 147; CAD; DFS 14; DLB 7; RGAL 4

Kingsolver, Barbara 1955- . **CLC 55, 81, 130**
See also AAYA 15; AMWS 7; CA 129; 134; CANR 60, 96; CDALBS; CPW; CSW; DA3; DAM POP; DLB 206; INT CA-134; LAIT 5; MTCW 2; NFS 5, 10, 12; RGAL 4

Kingston, Maxine (Ting Ting) Hong
1940- .... **CLC 12, 19, 58, 121; AAL; WLCS**
See also AAYA 8; AMWS 5; BPFB 2; CA 69-72; CANR 13, 38, 74, 87; CDALBS; CN 7; DA3; DAM MULT; DLB 173, 212; DLBY 1980; FW; INT CANR-13; LAIT 5; MAWW; MTCW 1, 2; NFS 6; RGAL 4; SATA 53; SSFS 3

Kinnell, Galway 1927- ..... **CLC 1, 2, 3, 5, 13, 29, 129; PC 26**
See also AMWS 3; CA 9-12R; CANR 10, 34, 66; CP 7; DLB 5; DLBY 1987; INT CANR-34; MTCW 1, 2; PAB; PFS 9; RGAL 4; WP

Kinsella, Thomas 1928- .... **CLC 4, 19, 138**
See also BRWS 5; CA 17-20R; CANR 15; CP 7; DLB 27; MTCW 1, 2; RGEL 2; TEA

Kinsella, W(illiam) P(atrick) 1935- . **CLC 27, 43**
See also AAYA 7; BPFB 2; CA 97-100; CAAS 7; CANR 21, 35, 66, 75; CN 7; CPW; DAC; DAM NOV, POP; FANT; INT CANR-21; LAIT 5; MTCW 1, 2; NFS 15; RGSF 2

Kinsey, Alfred C(harles)
1894-1956 .... **TCLC 91**
See also CA 115; 170; MTCW 2

Kipling, (Joseph) Rudyard
1865-1936 ... **TCLC 8, 17; PC 3; SSC 5, 54; WLC**
See also AAYA 32; BRW 6; BYA 4; CA 105; 120; CANR 33; CDBLB 1890-1914; CLR 39, 65; CWRI 5; DA; DA3; DAB; DAC; DAM MST, POET; DLB 19, 34,

141, 156; EXPS; FANT; LAIT 3; MAICYA 1, 2; MTCW 1, 2; RGEL 2; RGSF 2; SATA 100; SFW 4; SSFS 8; SUFW; TEA; WCH; WLIT 4; YABC 2

Kirk, Russell (Amos) 1918-1994 .. **TCLC 119**
See also AITN 1; CA 1-4R; 145; CAAS 9; CANR 1, 20, 60; HGG; INT CANR-20; MTCW 1, 2

Kirkland, Caroline M. 1801-1864 . **NCLC 85**
See also DLB 3, 73, 74, 250, 254; DLBD 13

Kirkup, James 1918- .... **CLC 1**
See also CA 1-4R; CAAS 4; CANR 2; CP 7; DLB 27; SATA 12

Kirkwood, James 1930(?)-1989 .... **CLC 9**
See also AITN 2; CA 1-4R; 128; CANR 6, 40; GLL 2

Kirshner, Sidney
See Kingsley, Sidney

Kis, Danilo 1935-1989 .... **CLC 57**
See also CA 109; 118; 129; CANR 61; CDWLB 4; DLB 181; MTCW 1; RGSF 2; RGWL 2

Kissinger, Henry A(lfred) 1923- ..... **CLC 137**
See also CA 1-4R; CANR 2, 33, 66, 109; MTCW 1

Kivi, Aleksis 1834-1872 .... **NCLC 30**

Kizer, Carolyn (Ashley) 1925- ... **CLC 15, 39, 80**
See also CA 65-68; CAAS 5; CANR 24, 70; CP 7; CWP; DAM POET; DLB 5, 169; MTCW 2

Klabund 1890-1928 .... **TCLC 44**
See also CA 162; DLB 66

Klappert, Peter 1942- .... **CLC 57**
See also CA 33-36R; CSW; DLB 5

Klein, A(braham) M(oses)
1909-1972 .... **CLC 19**
See also CA 101; 37-40R; DAB; DAC; DAM MST; DLB 68; RGEL 2

Klein, Joe
See Klein, Joseph

Klein, Joseph 1946- .... **CLC 154**
See also CA 85-88; CANR 55

Klein, Norma 1938-1989 .... **CLC 30**
See also AAYA 2, 35; BPFB 2; BYA 6, 7, 8; CA 41-44R; 128; CANR 15, 37; CLR 2, 19; INT CANR-15; JRDA; MAICYA 1, 2; SAAS 1; SATA 7, 57; WYA; YAW

Klein, T(heodore) E(ibon) D(onald)
1947- .... **CLC 34**
See also CA 119; CANR 44, 75; HGG

Kleist, Heinrich von 1777-1811 ...... **NCLC 2, 37; SSC 22**
See also CDWLB 2; DAM DRAM; DLB 90; EW 5; RGSF 2; RGWL 2

Klima, Ivan 1931- .... **CLC 56**
See also CA 25-28R; CANR 17, 50, 91; CDWLB 4; CWW 2; DAM NOV; DLB 232

Klimentov, Andrei Platonovich
1899-1951 .... **TCLC 14; SSC 42**
See also CA 108

Klinger, Friedrich Maximilian von
1752-1831 .... **NCLC 1**
See also DLB 94

Klingsor the Magician
See Hartmann, Sadakichi

Klopstock, Friedrich Gottlieb
1724-1803 .... **NCLC 11**
See also DLB 97; EW 4; RGWL 2

Knapp, Caroline 1959-2002 .... **CLC 99**
See also CA 154

Knebel, Fletcher 1911-1993 .... **CLC 14**
See also AITN 1; CA 1-4R; 140; CAAS 3; CANR 1, 36; SATA 36; SATA-Obit 75

Knickerbocker, Diedrich
See Irving, Washington

Knight, Etheridge 1931-1991 . **CLC 40; BLC 2; PC 14**
See also BW 1, 3; CA 21-24R; 133; CANR 23, 82; DAM POET; DLB 41; MTCW 2; RGAL 4

Knight, Sarah Kemble 1666-1727 .... **LC 7**
See also DLB 24, 200

Knister, Raymond 1899-1932 .... **TCLC 56**
See also CA 186; DLB 68; RGEL 2

Knowles, John 1926-2001 ... **CLC 1, 4, 10, 26**
See also AAYA 10; BPFB 2; BYA 3; CA 17-20R; 203; CANR 40, 74, 76; CDALB 1968-1988; CN 7; DA; DAC; DAM MST, NOV; DLB 6; EXPN; MTCW 1, 2; NFS 2; RGAL 4; SATA 8, 89; SATA-Obit 134; YAW

Knox, Calvin M.
See Silverberg, Robert

Knox, John c. 1505-1572 .... **LC 37**
See also DLB 132

Knye, Cassandra
See Disch, Thomas M(ichael)

Koch, C(hristopher) J(ohn) 1932- .... **CLC 42**
See also CA 127; CANR 84; CN 7

Koch, Christopher
See Koch, C(hristopher) J(ohn)

Koch, Kenneth 1925-2002 .... **CLC 5, 8, 44**
See also CA 1-4R; CAD; CANR 6, 36, 57, 97; CD 5; CP 7; DAM POET; DLB 5; INT CANR-36; MTCW 2; SATA 65; WP

Kochanowski, Jan 1530-1584 .... **LC 10**
See also RGWL 2

Kock, Charles Paul de 1794-1871 . **NCLC 16**

Koda Rohan
See Koda Shigeyuki

Koda Rohan
See Koda Shigeyuki
See also DLB 180

Koda Shigeyuki 1867-1947 .... **TCLC 22**
See also Koda Rohan
See also CA 121; 183

Koestler, Arthur 1905-1983 ... **CLC 1, 3, 6, 8, 15, 33**
See also BRWS 1; CA 1-4R; 109; CANR 1, 33; CDBLB 1945-1960; DLBY 1983; MTCW 1, 2; RGEL 2

Kogawa, Joy Nozomi 1935- ...... **CLC 78, 129**
See also CA 101; CANR 19, 62; CN 7; CWP; DAC; DAM MST, MULT; FW; MTCW 2; NFS 3; SATA 99

Kohout, Pavel 1928- .... **CLC 13**
See also CA 45-48; CANR 3

Koizumi, Yakumo
See Hearn, (Patricio) Lafcadio (Tessima Carlos)

Kolmar, Gertrud 1894-1943 .... **TCLC 40**
See also CA 167

Komunyakaa, Yusef 1947- .... **CLC 86, 94; BLCS**
See also AFAW 2; CA 147; CANR 83; CP 7; CSW; DLB 120; PFS 5; RGAL 4

Konrad, George
See Konrad, Gyorgy
See also CWW 2

Konrad, Gyorgy 1933- .... **CLC 4, 10, 73**
See also Konrad, George
See also CA 85-88; CANR 97; CDWLB 4; CWW 2; DLB 232

Konwicki, Tadeusz 1926- .... **CLC 8, 28, 54, 117**
See also CA 101; CAAS 9; CANR 39, 59; CWW 2; DLB 232; IDFW 3; MTCW 1

Koontz, Dean R(ay) 1945- .... **CLC 78**
See also AAYA 9, 31; BEST 89:3, 90:2; CA 108; CANR 19, 36, 52, 95; CMW 4; CPW; DA3; DAM NOV, POP; HGG; MTCW 1; SATA 92; SFW 4; YAW

Kopernik, Mikolaj
See Copernicus, Nicolaus

Kopit, Arthur (Lee) 1937- ...... **CLC 1, 18, 33**
See also AITN 1; CA 81-84; CABS 3; CD
5; DAM DRAM; DFS 7, 14; DLB 7;
MTCW 1; RGAL 4
Kopitar, Jernej (Bartholomaus)
1780-1844 .... **NCLC 117**
Kops, Bernard 1926- .... **CLC 4**
See also CA 5-8R; CANR 84; CBD; CN 7;
CP 7; DLB 13
Kornbluth, C(yril) M. 1923-1958 .... **TCLC 8**
See also CA 105; 160; DLB 8; SFW 4
Korolenko, V. G.
See Korolenko, Vladimir Galaktionovich
Korolenko, Vladimir
See Korolenko, Vladimir Galaktionovich
Korolenko, Vladimir G.
See Korolenko, Vladimir Galaktionovich
Korolenko, Vladimir Galaktionovich
1853-1921 .... **TCLC 22**
See also CA 121
Korzybski, Alfred (Habdank Skarbek)
1879-1950 .... **TCLC 61**
See also CA 123; 160
Kosinski, Jerzy (Nikodem)
1933-1991 .... **CLC 1, 2, 3, 6, 10, 15, 53,
70**
See also AMWS 7; BPFB 2; CA 17-20R;
134; CANR 9, 46; DA3; DAM NOV;
DLB 2; DLBY 1982; HGG; MTCW 1, 2;
NFS 12; RGAL 4; TUS
Kostelanetz, Richard (Cory) 1940- .. **CLC 28**
See also CA 13-16R; CAAS 8; CANR 38,
77; CN 7; CP 7
Kostrowitzki, Wilhelm Apollinaris de
1880-1918
See Apollinaire, Guillaume
See also CA 104
Kotlowitz, Robert 1924- .... **CLC 4**
See also CA 33-36R; CANR 36
Kotzebue, August (Friedrich Ferdinand) von
1761-1819 .... **NCLC 25**
See also DLB 94
Kotzwinkle, William 1938- ..... **CLC 5, 14, 35**
See also BPFB 2; CA 45-48; CANR 3, 44,
84; CLR 6; DLB 173; FANT; MAICYA
1, 2; SATA 24, 70; SFW 4; YAW
Kowna, Stancy
See Szymborska, Wislawa
Kozol, Jonathan 1936- .... **CLC 17**
See also CA 61-64; CANR 16, 45, 96
Kozoll, Michael 1940(?)- .... **CLC 35**
Kramer, Kathryn 19(?)- .... **CLC 34**
Kramer, Larry 1935- .... **CLC 42; DC 8**
See also CA 124; 126; CANR 60; DAM
POP; DLB 249; GLL 1
Krasicki, Ignacy 1735-1801 .... **NCLC 8**
Krasinski, Zygmunt 1812-1859 .... **NCLC 4**
See also RGWL 2
Kraus, Karl 1874-1936 .... **TCLC 5**
See also CA 104; DLB 118
Kreve (Mickevicius), Vincas
1882-1954 .... **TCLC 27**
See also CA 170; DLB 220
Kristeva, Julia 1941- .... **CLC 77, 140**
See also CA 154; CANR 99; DLB 242; FW
Kristofferson, Kris 1936- .... **CLC 26**
See also CA 104
Krizanc, John 1956- .... **CLC 57**
See also CA 187
Krleza, Miroslav 1893-1981 .... **CLC 8, 114**
See also CA 97-100; 105; CANR 50; CD-
WLB 4; DLB 147; EW 11; RGWL 2
Kroetsch, Robert 1927- .. **CLC 5, 23, 57, 132**
See also CA 17-20R; CANR 8, 38; CCA 1;
CN 7; CP 7; DAC; DAM POET; DLB 53;
MTCW 1
Kroetz, Franz
See Kroetz, Franz Xaver

Kroetz, Franz Xaver 1946- .... **CLC 41**
See also CA 130
Kroker, Arthur (W.) 1945- .... **CLC 77**
See also CA 161
Kropotkin, Peter (Aleksieevich)
1842-1921 .... **TCLC 36**
See also CA 119
Krotkov, Yuri 1917-1981 .... **CLC 19**
See also CA 102
Krumb
See Crumb, R(obert)
Krumgold, Joseph (Quincy)
1908-1980 .... **CLC 12**
See also BYA 1, 2; CA 9-12R; 101; CANR
7; MAICYA 1, 2; SATA 1, 48; SATA-Obit
23; YAW
Krumwitz
See Crumb, R(obert)
Krutch, Joseph Wood 1893-1970 ..... **CLC 24**
See also ANW; CA 1-4R; 25-28R; CANR
4; DLB 63, 206
Krutzch, Gus
See Eliot, T(homas) S(tearns)
Krylov, Ivan Andreevich
1768(?)-1844 .... **NCLC 1**
See also DLB 150
Kubin, Alfred (Leopold Isidor)
1877-1959 .... **TCLC 23**
See also CA 112; 149; CANR 104; DLB 81
Kubrick, Stanley 1928-1999 .... **CLC 16**
See also AAYA 30; CA 81-84; 177; CANR
33; DLB 26; TCLC 112
Kueng, Hans 1928-
See Kung, Hans
See also CA 53-56; CANR 66; MTCW 1, 2
Kumin, Maxine (Winokur) 1925- ..... **CLC 5,
13, 28, 164; PC 15**
See also AITN 2; AMWS 4; ANW; CA
1-4R; CAAS 8; CANR 1, 21, 69; CP 7;
CWP; DA3; DAM POET; DLB 5; EXPP;
MTCW 1, 2; PAB; SATA 12
Kundera, Milan 1929- . **CLC 4, 9, 19, 32, 68,
115, 135; SSC 24**
See also AAYA 2; BPFB 2; CA 85-88;
CANR 19, 52, 74; CDWLB 4; CWW 2;
DA3; DAM NOV; DLB 232; EW 13;
MTCW 1, 2; RGSF 2; SSFS 10
Kunene, Mazisi (Raymond) 1930- ... **CLC 85**
See also BW 1, 3; CA 125; CANR 81; CP
7; DLB 117
Kung, Hans .... **CLC 130**
See also Kueng, Hans
Kunikida Doppo 1869(?)-1908
See Doppo, Kunikida
See also DLB 180
Kunitz, Stanley (Jasspon) 1905- .. **CLC 6, 11,
14, 148; PC 19**
See also AMWS 3; CA 41-44R; CANR 26,
57, 98; CP 7; DA3; DLB 48; INT CANR-
26; MTCW 1, 2; PFS 11; RGAL 4
Kunze, Reiner 1933- .... **CLC 10**
See also CA 93-96; CWW 2; DLB 75
Kuprin, Aleksander Ivanovich
1870-1938 .... **TCLC 5**
See also CA 104; 182
Kureishi, Hanif 1954(?)- .... **CLC 64, 135**
See also CA 139; CBD; CD 5; CN 7; DLB
194, 245; GLL 2; IDFW 4; WLIT 4
Kurosawa, Akira 1910-1998 ..... **CLC 16, 119**
See also AAYA 11; CA 101; 170; CANR
46; DAM MULT
Kushner, Tony 1957(?)- .... **CLC 81; DC 10**
See also AMWS 9; CA 144; CAD; CANR
74; CD 5; DA3; DAM DRAM; DFS 5;
DLB 228; GLL 1; LAIT 5; MTCW 2;
RGAL 4
Kuttner, Henry 1915-1958 .... **TCLC 10**
See also CA 107; 157; DLB 8; FANT;
SCFW 2; SFW 4

Kutty, Madhavi
See Das, Kamala
Kuzma, Greg 1944- .... **CLC 7**
See also CA 33-36R; CANR 70
Kuzmin, Mikhail 1872(?)-1936 ...... **TCLC 40**
See also CA 170
Kyd, Thomas 1558-1594 .... **LC 22; DC 3**
See also BRW 1; DAM DRAM; DLB 62;
IDTP; RGEL 2; TEA; WLIT 3
Kyprianos, Iossif
See Samarakis, Antonis
Labrunie, Gerard
See Nerval, Gerard de
La Bruyere, Jean de 1645-1696 .... **LC 17**
See also DLB 268; EW 3; GFL Beginnings
to 1789
Lacan, Jacques (Marie Emile)
1901-1981 .... **CLC 75**
See also CA 121; 104; TWA
Laclos, Pierre Ambroise Francois
1741-1803 .... **NCLC 4, 87**
See also EW 4; GFL Beginnings to 1789;
RGWL 2
La Colere, Francois
See Aragon, Louis
Lacolere, Francois
See Aragon, Louis
La Deshabilleuse
See Simenon, Georges (Jacques Christian)
Lady Gregory
See Gregory, Lady Isabella Augusta (Persse)
Lady of Quality, A
See Bagnold, Enid
**La Fayette, Marie-(Madelaine Pioche de la
Vergne)** 1634-1693 .... **LC 2**
See also Lafayette, Marie-Madeleine
See also GFL Beginnings to 1789; RGWL
2
Lafayette, Marie-Madeleine
See La Fayette, Marie-(Madelaine Pioche
de la Vergne)
See also DLB 268
Lafayette, Rene
See Hubbard, L(afayette) Ron(ald)
La Fontaine, Jean de 1621-1695 .... **LC 50**
See also DLB 268; EW 3; GFL Beginnings
to 1789; MAICYA 1, 2; RGWL 2; SATA
18
Laforgue, Jules 1860-1887 . **NCLC 5, 53; PC
14; SSC 20**
See also DLB 217; EW 7; GFL 1789 to the
Present; RGWL 2
Layamon
See Layamon
See also DLB 146
Lagerkvist, Paer (Fabian)
1891-1974 .... **CLC 7, 10, 13, 54**
See also Lagerkvist, Par
See also CA 85-88; 49-52; DA3; DAM
DRAM, NOV; MTCW 1, 2; TWA
Lagerkvist, Par .... **SSC 12**
See also Lagerkvist, Paer (Fabian)
See also DLB 259; EW 10; MTCW 2;
RGSF 2; RGWL 2
Lagerloef, Selma (Ottiliana Lovisa)
1858-1940 .... **TCLC 4, 36**
See also Lagerlof, Selma (Ottiliana Lovisa)
See also CA 108; MTCW 2; SATA 15
Lagerlof, Selma (Ottiliana Lovisa)
See Lagerloef, Selma (Ottiliana Lovisa)
See also CLR 7; SATA 15
La Guma, (Justin) Alex(ander)
1925-1985 .... **CLC 19; BLCS**
See also AFW; BW 1, 3; CA 49-52; 118;
CANR 25, 81; CDWLB 3; DAM NOV;
DLB 117, 225; MTCW 1, 2; WLIT 2
Laidlaw, A. K.
See Grieve, C(hristopher) M(urray)

Lainez, Manuel Mujica
See Mujica Lainez, Manuel
See also HW 1

Laing, R(onald) D(avid) 1927-1989 . **CLC 95**
See also CA 107; 129; CANR 34; MTCW 1

Lamartine, Alphonse (Marie Louis Prat) de
1790-1869 .... **NCLC 11; PC 16**
See also DAM POET; DLB 217; GFL 1789
to the Present; RGWL 2

Lamb, Charles 1775-1834 ..... **NCLC 10, 113;
WLC**
See also BRW 4; CDBLB 1789-1832; DA;
DAB; DAC; DAM MST; DLB 93, 107,
163; RGEL 2; SATA 17; TEA

Lamb, Lady Caroline 1785-1828 ... **NCLC 38**
See also DLB 116

Lamming, George (William) 1927- ... **CLC 2,
4, 66, 144; BLC 2**
See also BW 2, 3; CA 85-88; CANR 26,
76; CDWLB 3; CN 7; DAM MULT; DLB
125; MTCW 1, 2; NFS 15; RGEL 2

L'Amour, Louis (Dearborn)
1908-1988 .... **CLC 25, 55**
See also Burns, Tex; Mayo, Jim
See also AAYA 16; AITN 2; BEST 89:2;
BPFB 2; CA 1-4R; 125; CANR 3, 25, 40;
CPW; DA3; DAM NOV, POP; DLB 206;
DLBY 1980; MTCW 1, 2; RGAL 4

Lampedusa, Giuseppe (Tomasi) di
.... **TCLC 13**
See also Tomasi di Lampedusa, Giuseppe
See also CA 164; EW 11; MTCW 2; RGWL
2

Lampman, Archibald 1861-1899 ... **NCLC 25**
See also DLB 92; RGEL 2; TWA

Lancaster, Bruce 1896-1963 .... **CLC 36**
See also CA 9-10; CANR 70; CAP 1; SATA
9

Lanchester, John 1962- .... **CLC 99**
See also CA 194; DLB 267

Landau, Mark Alexandrovich
See Aldanov, Mark (Alexandrovich)

Landau-Aldanov, Mark Alexandrovich
See Aldanov, Mark (Alexandrovich)

Landis, Jerry
See Simon, Paul (Frederick)

Landis, John 1950- .... **CLC 26**
See also CA 112; 122

Landolfi, Tommaso 1908-1979 .... **CLC 11, 49**
See also CA 127; 117; DLB 177

Landon, Letitia Elizabeth
1802-1838 .... **NCLC 15**
See also DLB 96

Landor, Walter Savage
1775-1864 .... **NCLC 14**
See also BRW 4; DLB 93, 107; RGEL 2

Landwirth, Heinz 1927-
See Lind, Jakov
See also CA 9-12R; CANR 7

Lane, Patrick 1939- .... **CLC 25**
See also CA 97-100; CANR 54; CP 7; DAM
POET; DLB 53; INT 97-100

Lang, Andrew 1844-1912 .... **TCLC 16**
See also CA 114; 137; CANR 85; DLB 98,
141, 184; FANT; MAICYA 1, 2; RGEL 2;
SATA 16; WCH

Lang, Fritz 1890-1976 .... **CLC 20, 103**
See also CA 77-80; 69-72; CANR 30

Lange, John
See Crichton, (John) Michael

Langer, Elinor 1939- .... **CLC 34**
See also CA 121

Langland, William 1332(?)-1400(?) ..... **LC 19**
See also BRW 1; DA; DAB; DAC; DAM
MST, POET; DLB 146; RGEL 2; TEA;
WLIT 3

Langstaff, Launcelot
See Irving, Washington

Lanier, Sidney 1842-1881 .... **NCLC 6**
See also AMWS 1; DAM POET; DLB 64;
DLBD 13; EXPP; MAICYA 1; PFS 14;
RGAL 4; SATA 18

Lanyer, Aemilia 1569-1645 .... **LC 10, 30**
See also DLB 121

Lao-Tzu
See Lao Tzu

Lao Tzu c. 6th cent. B.C.-3rd cent.
B.C. .... **CMLC 7**

Lapine, James (Elliot) 1949- .... **CLC 39**
See also CA 123; 130; CANR 54; INT 130

Larbaud, Valery (Nicolas)
1881-1957 .... **TCLC 9**
See also CA 106; 152; GFL 1789 to the
Present

Lardner, Ring
See Lardner, Ring(gold) W(ilmer)
See also BPFB 2; CDALB 1917-1929; DLB
11, 25, 86, 171; DLBD 16; RGAL 4;
RGSF 2

Lardner, Ring W., Jr.
See Lardner, Ring(gold) W(ilmer)

Lardner, Ring(gold) W(ilmer)
1885-1933 .... **TCLC 2, 14; SSC 32**
See also Lardner, Ring
See also AMW; CA 104; 131; MTCW 1, 2;
TUS

Laredo, Betty
See Codrescu, Andrei

Larkin, Maia
See Wojciechowska, Maia (Teresa)

Larkin, Philip (Arthur) 1922-1985 ... **CLC 3,
5, 8, 9, 13, 18, 33, 39, 64; PC 21**
See also BRWS 1; CA 5-8R; 117; CANR
24, 62; CDBLB 1960 to Present; DA3;
DAB; DAM MST, POET; DLB 27;
MTCW 1, 2; PFS 3, 4, 12; RGEL 2

**Larra (y Sanchez de Castro), Mariano Jose
de** 1809-1837 .... **NCLC 17**

Larsen, Eric 1941- .... **CLC 55**
See also CA 132

Larsen, Nella 1893-1963 ...... **CLC 37; BLC 2**
See also AFAW 1, 2; BW 1; CA 125; CANR
83; DAM MULT; DLB 51; FW

Larson, Charles R(aymond) 1938- ... **CLC 31**
See also CA 53-56; CANR 4

Larson, Jonathan 1961-1996 .... **CLC 99**
See also AAYA 28; CA 156

Las Casas, Bartolome de 1474-1566 . **LC 31;
HLCS**
See also Casas, Bartolome de las
See also LAW

Lasch, Christopher 1932-1994 .... **CLC 102**
See also CA 73-76; 144; CANR 25; DLB
246; MTCW 1, 2

Lasker-Schueler, Else 1869-1945 ... **TCLC 57**
See also CA 183; DLB 66, 124

Laski, Harold J(oseph) 1893-1950 . **TCLC 79**
See also CA 188

Latham, Jean Lee 1902-1995 .... **CLC 12**
See also AITN 1; BYA 1; CA 5-8R; CANR
7, 84; CLR 50; MAICYA 1, 2; SATA 2,
68; YAW

Latham, Mavis
See Clark, Mavis Thorpe

Lathen, Emma .... **CLC 2**
See also Hennissart, Martha; Latsis, Mary
J(ane)
See also BPFB 2; CMW 4

Lathrop, Francis
See Leiber, Fritz (Reuter, Jr.)

Latsis, Mary J(ane) 1927(?)-1997
See Lathen, Emma
See also CA 85-88; 162; CMW 4

Lattany, Kristin
See Lattany, Kristin (Elaine Eggleston)
Hunter

Lattany, Kristin (Elaine Eggleston) Hunter
1931- .... **CLC 35**
See also AITN 1; BW 1; BYA 3; CA 13-
16R; CANR 13, 108; CLR 3; CN 7; DLB
33; INT CANR-13; MAICYA 1, 2; SAAS
10; SATA 12, 132; YAW

Lattimore, Richmond (Alexander)
1906-1984 .... **CLC 3**
See also CA 1-4R; 112; CANR 1

Laughlin, James 1914-1997 .... **CLC 49**
See also CA 21-24R; 162; CAAS 22; CANR
9, 47; CP 7; DLB 48; DLBY 1996, 1997

Laurence, (Jean) Margaret (Wemyss)
1926-1987 . **CLC 3, 6, 13, 50, 62; SSC 7**
See also BYA 13; CA 5-8R; 121; CANR
33; DAC; DAM MST; DLB 53; FW;
MTCW 1, 2; NFS 11; RGEL 2; RGSF 2;
SATA-Obit 50; TCWW 2

Laurent, Antoine 1952- .... **CLC 50**

Lauscher, Hermann
See Hesse, Hermann

Lautreamont 1846-1870 .. **NCLC 12; SSC 14**
See also Lautreamont, Isidore Lucien Du-
casse
See also GFL 1789 to the Present; RGWL 2

Lautreamont, Isidore Lucien Ducasse
See Lautreamont
See also DLB 217

Laverty, Donald
See Blish, James (Benjamin)

Lavin, Mary 1912-1996 . **CLC 4, 18, 99; SSC
4**
See also CA 9-12R; 151; CANR 33; CN 7;
DLB 15; FW; MTCW 1; RGEL 2; RGSF
2

Lavond, Paul Dennis
See Kornbluth, C(yril) M.; Pohl, Frederik

Lawler, Raymond Evenor 1922- .... **CLC 58**
See also CA 103; CD 5; RGEL 2

Lawrence, D(avid) H(erbert Richards)
1885-1930 .... **TCLC 2, 9, 16, 33, 48, 61,
93; SSC 4, 19; WLC**
See also Chambers, Jessie
See also BPFB 2; BRW 7; BRWR 2; CA
104; 121; CDBLB 1914-1945; DA; DA3;
DAB; DAC; DAM MST, NOV, POET;
DLB 10, 19, 36, 98, 162, 195; EXPP;
EXPS; LAIT 2, 3; MTCW 1, 2; PFS 6;
RGEL 2; RGSF 2; SSFS 2, 6; TEA; WLIT
4; WP

Lawrence, T(homas) E(dward)
1888-1935 .... **TCLC 18**
See also Dale, Colin
See also BRWS 2; CA 115; 167; DLB 195

Lawrence of Arabia
See Lawrence, T(homas) E(dward)

Lawson, Henry (Archibald Hertzberg)
1867-1922 .... **TCLC 27; SSC 18**
See also CA 120; 181; DLB 230; RGEL 2;
RGSF 2

Lawton, Dennis
See Faust, Frederick (Schiller)

Laxness, Halldor .... **CLC 25**
See also Gudjonsson, Halldor Kiljan
See also EW 12; RGWL 2

Layamon fl. c. 1200- .... **CMLC 10**
See also Layamon
See also RGEL 2

Laye, Camara 1928-1980 ... **CLC 4, 38; BLC
2**
See also AFW; BW 1; CA 85-88; 97-100;
CANR 25; DAM MULT; MTCW 1, 2;
WLIT 2

Layton, Irving (Peter) 1912- .... **CLC 2, 15,
164**
See also CA 1-4R; CANR 2, 33, 43, 66; CP
7; DAC; DAM MST, POET; DLB 88;
MTCW 1, 2; PFS 12; RGEL 2

Lazarus, Emma 1849-1887 ...... NCLC **8, 109**

Lazarus, Felix
See Cable, George Washington

Lazarus, Henry
See Slavitt, David R(ytman)

Lea, Joan
See Neufeld, John (Arthur)

Leacock, Stephen (Butler)
1869-1944 .... TCLC **2**; SSC **39**
See also CA 104; 141; CANR 80; DAC; DAM MST; DLB 92; MTCW 2; RGEL 2; RGSF 2

Lead, Jane Ward 1623-1704 .... LC **72**
See also DLB 131

Leapor, Mary 1722-1746 .... LC **80**
See also DLB 109

Lear, Edward 1812-1888 .... NCLC **3**
See also BRW 5; CLR 1, 75; DLB 32, 163, 166; MAICYA 1, 2; RGEL 2; SATA 18, 100; WCH; WP

Lear, Norman (Milton) 1922- .... CLC **12**
See also CA 73-76

Leautaud, Paul 1872-1956 .... TCLC **83**
See also CA 203; DLB 65; GFL 1789 to the Present

Leavis, F(rank) R(aymond)
1895-1978 .... CLC **24**
See also BRW 7; CA 21-24R; 77-80; CANR 44; DLB 242; MTCW 1, 2; RGEL 2

Leavitt, David 1961- .... CLC **34**
See also CA 116; 122; CANR 50, 62, 101; CPW; DA3; DAM POP; DLB 130; GLL 1; INT 122; MTCW 2

Leblanc, Maurice (Marie Emile)
1864-1941 .... TCLC **49**
See also CA 110; CMW 4

Lebowitz, Fran(ces Ann) 1951(?)- ... CLC **11, 36**
See also CA 81-84; CANR 14, 60, 70; INT CANR-14; MTCW 1

Lebrecht, Peter
See Tieck, (Johann) Ludwig

le Carre, John .... CLC **3, 5, 9, 15, 28**
See also Cornwell, David (John Moore)
See also AAYA 42; BEST 89:4; BPFB 2; BRWS 2; CDBLB 1960 to Present; CMW 4; CN 7; CPW; DLB 87; MSW; MTCW 2; RGEL 2; TEA

Le Clezio, J(ean) M(arie) G(ustave)
1940- .... CLC **31, 155**
See also CA 116; 128; DLB 83; GFL 1789 to the Present; RGSF 2

Leconte de Lisle, Charles-Marie-Rene
1818-1894 .... NCLC **29**
See also DLB 217; EW 6; GFL 1789 to the Present

Le Coq, Monsieur
See Simenon, Georges (Jacques Christian)

Leduc, Violette 1907-1972 .... CLC **22**
See also CA 13-14; 33-36R; CANR 69; CAP 1; GFL 1789 to the Present; GLL 1

Ledwidge, Francis 1887(?)-1917 .... TCLC **23**
See also CA 123; 203; DLB 20

Lee, Andrea 1953- .... CLC **36**; BLC **2**
See also BW 1, 3; CA 125; CANR 82; DAM MULT

Lee, Andrew
See Auchincloss, Louis (Stanton)

Lee, Chang-rae 1965- .... CLC **91**
See also CA 148; CANR 89

Lee, Don L. .... CLC **2**
See also Madhubuti, Haki R.

Lee, George W(ashington)
1894-1976 .... CLC **52**; BLC **2**
See also BW 1; CA 125; CANR 83; DAM MULT; DLB 51

Lee, (Nelle) Harper 1926- .... CLC **12, 60**; WLC
See also AAYA 13; AMWS 8; BPFB 2; BYA 3; CA 13-16R; CANR 51; CDALB 1941-1968; CSW; DA; DA3; DAB; DAC; DAM MST, NOV; DLB 6; EXPN; LAIT 3; MTCW 1, 2; NFS 2; SATA 11; WYA; YAW

Lee, Helen Elaine 1959(?)- .... CLC **86**
See also CA 148

Lee, John .... CLC **70**

Lee, Julian
See Latham, Jean Lee

Lee, Larry
See Lee, Lawrence

Lee, Laurie 1914-1997 .... CLC **90**
See also CA 77-80; 158; CANR 33, 73; CP 7; CPW; DAB; DAM POP; DLB 27; MTCW 1; RGEL 2

Lee, Lawrence 1941-1990 .... CLC **34**
See also CA 131; CANR 43

Lee, Li-Young 1957- .... CLC **164**; PC **24**
See also CA 153; CP 7; DLB 165; PFS 11, 15

Lee, Manfred B(ennington)
1905-1971 .... CLC **11**
See also Queen, Ellery
See also CA 1-4R; 29-32R; CANR 2; CMW 4; DLB 137

Lee, Shelton Jackson 1957(?)- .... CLC **105**; BLCS
See also Lee, Spike
See also BW 2, 3; CA 125; CANR 42; DAM MULT

Lee, Spike
See Lee, Shelton Jackson
See also AAYA 4, 29

Lee, Stan 1922- .... CLC **17**
See also AAYA 5; CA 108; 111; INT 111

Lee, Tanith 1947- .... CLC **46**
See also AAYA 15; CA 37-40R; CANR 53, 102; DLB 261; FANT; SATA 8, 88, 134; SFW 4; SUFW; YAW

Lee, Vernon .... TCLC **5**; SSC **33**
See also Paget, Violet
See also DLB 57, 153, 156, 174, 178; GLL 1; SUFW

Lee, William
See Burroughs, William S(eward)
See also GLL 1

Lee, Willy
See Burroughs, William S(eward)
See also GLL 1

Lee-Hamilton, Eugene (Jacob)
1845-1907 .... TCLC **22**
See also CA 117

Leet, Judith 1935- .... CLC **11**
See also CA 187

Le Fanu, Joseph Sheridan
1814-1873 .... NCLC **9, 58**; SSC **14**
See also CMW 4; DA3; DAM POP; DLB 21, 70, 159, 178; HGG; RGEL 2; RGSF 2; SUFW

Leffland, Ella 1931- .... CLC **19**
See also CA 29-32R; CANR 35, 78, 82; DLBY 1984; INT CANR-35; SATA 65

Leger, Alexis
See Leger, (Marie-Rene Auguste) Alexis Saint-Leger

Leger, (Marie-Rene Auguste) Alexis Saint-Leger 1887-1975 .. CLC **4, 11, 46**; PC **23**
See also Perse, Saint-John; Saint-John Perse
See also CA 13-16R; 61-64; CANR 43; DAM POET; MTCW 1

Leger, Saintleger
See Leger, (Marie-Rene Auguste) Alexis Saint-Leger

Le Guin, Ursula K(roeber) 1929- ..... CLC **8, 13, 22, 45, 71, 136**; SSC **12**
See also AAYA 9, 27; AITN 1; BPFB 2; BYA 5, 8, 11, 14; CA 21-24R; CANR 9, 32, 52, 74; CDALB 1968-1988; CLR 3, 28; CN 7; CPW; DA3; DAB; DAM MST, POP; DLB 8, 52, 256; EXPS; FANT; FW; INT CANR-32; JRDA; LAIT 5; MAICYA 1, 2; MTCW 1, 2; NFS 6, 9; SATA 4, 52, 99; SCFW; SFW 4; SSFS 2; SUFW; WYA; YAW

Lehmann, Rosamond (Nina)
1901-1990 .... CLC **5**
See also CA 77-80; 131; CANR 8, 73; DLB 15; MTCW 2; RGEL 2; RHW

Leiber, Fritz (Reuter, Jr.)
1910-1992 .... CLC **25**
See also BPFB 2; CA 45-48; 139; CANR 2, 40, 86; DLB 8; FANT; HGG; MTCW 1, 2; SATA 45; SATA-Obit 73; SCFW 2; SFW 4; SUFW

Leibniz, Gottfried Wilhelm von
1646-1716 .... LC **35**
See also DLB 168

Leimbach, Martha 1963-
See Leimbach, Marti
See also CA 130

Leimbach, Marti .... CLC **65**
See also Leimbach, Martha

Leino, Eino .... TCLC **24**
See also Loennbohm, Armas Eino Leopold

Leiris, Michel (Julien) 1901-1990 ..... CLC **61**
See also CA 119; 128; 132; GFL 1789 to the Present

Leithauser, Brad 1953- .... CLC **27**
See also CA 107; CANR 27, 81; CP 7; DLB 120

Lelchuk, Alan 1938- .... CLC **5**
See also CA 45-48; CAAS 20; CANR 1, 70; CN 7

Lem, Stanislaw 1921- ...... CLC **8, 15, 40, 149**
See also CA 105; CAAS 1; CANR 32; CWW 2; MTCW 1; SCFW 2; SFW 4

Lemann, Nancy 1956- .... CLC **39**
See also CA 118; 136

Lemonnier, (Antoine Louis) Camille
1844-1913 .... TCLC **22**
See also CA 121

Lenau, Nikolaus 1802-1850 .... NCLC **16**

L'Engle, Madeleine (Camp Franklin)
1918- .... CLC **12**
See also AAYA 28; AITN 2; BPFB 2; BYA 2, 4, 5, 7; CA 1-4R; CANR 3, 21, 39, 66, 107; CLR 1, 14, 57; CPW; CWRI 5; DA3; DAM POP; DLB 52; JRDA; MAICYA 1, 2; MTCW 1, 2; SAAS 15; SATA 1, 27, 75, 128; SFW 4; WYA; YAW

Lengyel, Jozsef 1896-1975 .... CLC **7**
See also CA 85-88; 57-60; CANR 71; RGSF 2

Lenin 1870-1924
See Lenin, V. I.
See also CA 121; 168

Lenin, V. I. .... TCLC **67**
See also Lenin

Lennon, John (Ono) 1940-1980 .. CLC **12, 35**
See also CA 102; SATA 114

Lennox, Charlotte Ramsay
1729(?)-1804 .... NCLC **23**
See also DLB 39; RGEL 2

Lentricchia, Frank, (Jr.) 1940- .... CLC **34**
See also CA 25-28R; CANR 19, 106; DLB 246

Lenz, Gunter .... CLC **65**

Lenz, Siegfried 1926- .... CLC **27**; SSC **33**
See also CA 89-92; CANR 80; CWW 2; DLB 75; RGSF 2; RGWL 2

Leon, David
See Jacob, (Cyprien-)Max

MacLean, Alistair (Stuart)
1922(?)-1987 .... **CLC 3, 13, 50, 63**
See also CA 57-60; 121; CANR 28, 61;
CMW 4; CPW; DAM POP; MTCW 1;
SATA 23; SATA-Obit 50; TCWW 2

Maclean, Norman (Fitzroy)
1902-1990 .... **CLC 78; SSC 13**
See also CA 102; 132; CANR 49; CPW;
DAM POP; DLB 206; TCWW 2

MacLeish, Archibald 1892-1982 ... **CLC 3, 8, 14, 68**
See also AMW; CA 9-12R; 106; CAD;
CANR 33, 63; CDALBS; DAM POET;
DFS 15; DLB 4, 7, 45; DLBY 1982;
EXPP; MTCW 1, 2; PAB; PFS 5; RGAL
4; TUS

MacLennan, (John) Hugh
1907-1990 .... **CLC 2, 14, 92**
See also CA 5-8R; 142; CANR 33; DAC;
DAM MST; DLB 68; MTCW 1, 2; RGEL
2; TWA

MacLeod, Alistair 1936- .... **CLC 56**
See also CA 123; CCA 1; DAC; DAM
MST; DLB 60; MTCW 2; RGSF 2

Macleod, Fiona
See Sharp, William
See also RGEL 2; SUFW

MacNeice, (Frederick) Louis
1907-1963 .... **CLC 1, 4, 10, 53**
See also BRW 7; CA 85-88; CANR 61;
DAB; DAM POET; DLB 10, 20; MTCW
1, 2; RGEL 2

MacNeill, Dand
See Fraser, George MacDonald

Macpherson, James 1736-1796 .... **LC 29**
See also Ossian
See also BRWS 8; DLB 109; RGEL 2

Macpherson, (Jean) Jay 1931- .... **CLC 14**
See also CA 5-8R; CANR 90; CP 7; CWP;
DLB 53

Macrobius fl. 430- .... **CMLC 48**

MacShane, Frank 1927-1999 .... **CLC 39**
See also CA 9-12R; 186; CANR 3, 33; DLB
111

Macumber, Mari
See Sandoz, Mari(e Susette)

Madach, Imre 1823-1864 .... **NCLC 19**

Madden, (Jerry) David 1933- .... **CLC 5, 15**
See also CA 1-4R; CAAS 3; CANR 4, 45;
CN 7; CSW; DLB 6; MTCW 1

Maddern, Al(an)
See Ellison, Harlan (Jay)

Madhubuti, Haki R. 1942- . **CLC 6, 73; BLC 2; PC 5**
See also Lee, Don L.
See also BW 2, 3; CA 73-76; CANR 24,
51, 73; CP 7; CSW; DAM MULT, POET;
DLB 5, 41; DLBD 8; MTCW 2; RGAL 4

Maepenn, Hugh
See Kuttner, Henry

Maepenn, K. H.
See Kuttner, Henry

Maeterlinck, Maurice 1862-1949 ..... **TCLC 3**
See also CA 104; 136; CANR 80; DAM
DRAM; DLB 192; EW 8; GFL 1789 to
the Present; RGWL 2; SATA 66; TWA

Maginn, William 1794-1842 .... **NCLC 8**
See also DLB 110, 159

Mahapatra, Jayanta 1928- .... **CLC 33**
See also CA 73-76; CAAS 9; CANR 15,
33, 66, 87; CP 7; DAM MULT

Mahfouz, Naguib (Abdel Aziz Al-Sabilgi)
1911(?)- .... **CLC 153**
See also Mahfuz, Najib (Abdel Aziz al-
Sabilgi)
See also BEST 89:2; CA 128; CANR 55,
101; CWW 2; DA3; DAM NOV; MTCW
1, 2; RGWL 2; SSFS 9

Mahfuz, Najib (Abdel Aziz al-Sabilgi)
.... **CLC 52, 55**
See also Mahfouz, Naguib (Abdel Aziz Al-
Sabilgi)
See also AFW; DLBY 1988; RGSF 2;
WLIT 2

Mahon, Derek 1941- .... **CLC 27**
See also BRWS 6; CA 113; 128; CANR 88;
CP 7; DLB 40

Maiakovskii, Vladimir
See Mayakovski, Vladimir (Vladimirovich)
See also IDTP; RGWL 2

Mailer, Norman 1923- ... **CLC 1, 2, 3, 4, 5, 8, 11, 14, 28, 39, 74, 111**
See also AAYA 31; AITN 2; AMW; BPFB
2; CA 9-12R; CABS 1; CANR 28, 74, 77;
CDALB 1968-1988; CN 7; CPW; DA;
DA3; DAB; DAC; DAM MST, NOV,
POP; DLB 2, 16, 28, 185; DLBD 3;
DLBY 1980, 1983; MTCW 1, 2; NFS 10;
RGAL 4; TUS

Maillet, Antonine 1929- .... **CLC 54, 118**
See also CA 115; 120; CANR 46, 74, 77;
CCA 1; CWW 2; DAC; DLB 60; INT
120; MTCW 2

Mais, Roger 1905-1955 .... **TCLC 8**
See also BW 1, 3; CA 105; 124; CANR 82;
CDWLB 3; DLB 125; MTCW 1; RGEL 2

Maistre, Joseph 1753-1821 .... **NCLC 37**
See also GFL 1789 to the Present

Maitland, Frederic William
1850-1906 .... **TCLC 65**

Maitland, Sara (Louise) 1950- .... **CLC 49**
See also CA 69-72; CANR 13, 59; FW

Major, Clarence 1936- . **CLC 3, 19, 48; BLC 2**
See also AFAW 2; BW 2, 3; CA 21-24R;
CAAS 6; CANR 13, 25, 53, 82; CN 7;
CP 7; CSW; DAM MULT; DLB 33; MSW

Major, Kevin (Gerald) 1949- .... **CLC 26**
See also AAYA 16; CA 97-100; CANR 21,
38; CLR 11; DAC; DLB 60; INT CANR-
21; JRDA; MAICYA 1, 2; MAICYAS 1;
SATA 32, 82, 134; WYA; YAW

Maki, James
See Ozu, Yasujiro

Malabaila, Damiano
See Levi, Primo

Malamud, Bernard 1914-1986 .. **CLC 1, 2, 3, 5, 8, 9, 11, 18, 27, 44, 78, 85; SSC 15; WLC**
See also AAYA 16; AMWS 1; BPFB 2; CA
5-8R; 118; CABS 1; CANR 28, 62;
CDALB 1941-1968; CPW; DA; DA3;
DAB; DAC; DAM MST, NOV, POP;
DLB 2, 28, 152; DLBY 1980, 1986;
EXPS; LAIT 4; MTCW 1, 2; NFS 4, 9;
RGAL 4; RGSF 2; SSFS 8, 13; TUS

Malan, Herman
See Bosman, Herman Charles; Bosman,
Herman Charles

Malaparte, Curzio 1898-1957 .... **TCLC 52**
See also DLB 264

Malcolm, Dan
See Silverberg, Robert

Malcolm X .... **CLC 82, 117; BLC 2; WLCS**
See also Little, Malcolm
See also LAIT 5

Malherbe, Francois de 1555-1628 .... **LC 5**
See also GFL Beginnings to 1789

Mallarme, Stephane 1842-1898 ...... **NCLC 4, 41; PC 4**
See also DAM POET; DLB 217; EW 7;
GFL 1789 to the Present; RGWL 2; TWA

Mallet-Joris, Francoise 1930- .... **CLC 11**
See also CA 65-68; CANR 17; DLB 83;
GFL 1789 to the Present

Malley, Ern
See McAuley, James Phillip

Mallowan, Agatha Christie
See Christie, Agatha (Mary Clarissa)

Maloff, Saul 1922- .... **CLC 5**
See also CA 33-36R

Malone, Louis
See MacNeice, (Frederick) Louis

Malone, Michael (Christopher)
1942- .... **CLC 43**
See also CA 77-80; CANR 14, 32, 57

Malory, Sir Thomas 1410(?)-1471(?) . **LC 11; WLCS**
See also BRW 1; BRWR 2; CDBLB Before
1660; DA; DAB; DAC; DAM MST; DLB
146; EFS 2; RGEL 2; SATA 59; SATA-
Brief 33; TEA; WLIT 3

Malouf, (George Joseph) David
1934- .... **CLC 28, 86**
See also CA 124; CANR 50, 76; CN 7; CP
7; MTCW 2

Malraux, (Georges-)Andre
1901-1976 .... **CLC 1, 4, 9, 13, 15, 57**
See also BPFB 2; CA 21-22; 69-72; CANR
34, 58; CAP 2; DA3; DAM NOV; DLB
72; EW 12; GFL 1789 to the Present;
MTCW 1, 2; RGWL 2; TWA

Malzberg, Barry N(athaniel) 1939- ... **CLC 7**
See also CA 61-64; CAAS 4; CANR 16;
CMW 4; DLB 8; SFW 4

Mamet, David (Alan) 1947- .. **CLC 9, 15, 34, 46, 91; DC 4**
See also AAYA 3; CA 81-84; CABS 3;
CANR 15, 41, 67, 72; CD 5; DA3; DAM
DRAM; DFS 15; DLB 7; IDFW 4;
MTCW 1, 2; RGAL 4

Mamoulian, Rouben (Zachary)
1897-1987 .... **CLC 16**
See also CA 25-28R; 124; CANR 85

Mandelshtam, Osip
See Mandelstam, Osip (Emilievich)
See also EW 10; RGWL 2

Mandelstam, Osip (Emilievich)
1891(?)-1943(?) .... **TCLC 2, 6; PC 14**
See also Mandelshtam, Osip
See also CA 104; 150; MTCW 2; TWA

Mander, (Mary) Jane 1877-1949 ... **TCLC 31**
See also CA 162; RGEL 2

Mandeville, Bernard 1670-1733 .... **LC 82**
See also DLB 101

Mandeville, Sir John fl. 1350- ...... **CMLC 19**
See also DLB 146

Mandiargues, Andre Pieyre de .... **CLC 41**
See also Pieyre de Mandiargues, Andre
See also DLB 83

Mandrake, Ethel Belle
See Thurman, Wallace (Henry)

Mangan, James Clarence
1803-1849 .... **NCLC 27**
See also RGEL 2

Maniere, J.-E.
See Giraudoux, Jean(-Hippolyte)

Mankiewicz, Herman (Jacob)
1897-1953 .... **TCLC 85**
See also CA 120; 169; DLB 26; IDFW 3, 4

Manley, (Mary) Delariviere
1672(?)-1724 .... **LC 1, 42**
See also DLB 39, 80; RGEL 2

Mann, Abel
See Creasey, John

Mann, Emily 1952- .... **DC 7**
See also CA 130; CAD; CANR 55; CD 5;
CWD; DLB 266

Mann, (Luiz) Heinrich 1871-1950 ... **TCLC 9**
See also CA 106; 164, 181; DLB 66, 118;
EW 8; RGWL 2

Mann, (Paul) Thomas 1875-1955 ... **TCLC 2, 8, 14, 21, 35, 44, 60; SSC 5; WLC**
See also BPFB 2; CA 104; 128; CDWLB 2;
DA; DA3; DAB; DAC; DAM MST, NOV;

DLB 66; EW 9; GLL 1; MTCW 1, 2;
RGSF 2; RGWL 2; SSFS 4, 9; TWA

Mannheim, Karl 1893-1947 .... **TCLC 65**
See also CA 204

Manning, David
See Faust, Frederick (Schiller)
See also TCWW 2

Manning, Frederic 1887(?)-1935 ... **TCLC 25**
See also CA 124; DLB 260

Manning, Olivia 1915-1980 .... **CLC 5, 19**
See also CA 5-8R; 101; CANR 29; FW;
MTCW 1; RGEL 2

Mano, D. Keith 1942- .... **CLC 2, 10**
See also CA 25-28R; CAAS 6; CANR 26,
57; DLB 6

Mansfield, Katherine ... **TCLC 2, 8, 39; SSC
9, 23, 38; WLC**
See also Beauchamp, Kathleen Mansfield
See also BPFB 2; BRW 7; DAB; DLB 162;
EXPS; FW; GLL 1; RGEL 2; RGSF 2;
SSFS 2, 8, 10, 11

Manso, Peter 1940- .... **CLC 39**
See also CA 29-32R; CANR 44

Mantecon, Juan Jimenez
See Jimenez (Mantecon), Juan Ramon

Mantel, Hilary (Mary) 1952- .... **CLC 144**
See also CA 125; CANR 54, 101; CN 7;
RHW

Manton, Peter
See Creasey, John

Man Without a Spleen, A
See Chekhov, Anton (Pavlovich)

Manzoni, Alessandro 1785-1873 ... **NCLC 29,
98**
See also EW 5; RGWL 2; TWA

Map, Walter 1140-1209 .... **CMLC 32**

Mapu, Abraham (ben Jekutiel)
1808-1867 .... **NCLC 18**

Mara, Sally
See Queneau, Raymond

Marat, Jean Paul 1743-1793 .... **LC 10**

Marcel, Gabriel Honore 1889-1973 . **CLC 15**
See also CA 102; 45-48; MTCW 1, 2

March, William 1893-1954 .... **TCLC 96**

Marchbanks, Samuel
See Davies, (William) Robertson
See also CCA 1

Marchi, Giacomo
See Bassani, Giorgio

Marcus Aurelius
See Aurelius, Marcus
See also AW 2

Marguerite
See de Navarre, Marguerite

Marguerite d'Angouleme
See de Navarre, Marguerite
See also GFL Beginnings to 1789

Marguerite de Navarre
See de Navarre, Marguerite
See also RGWL 2

Margulies, Donald 1954- .... **CLC 76**
See also CA 200; DFS 13; DLB 228

Marie de France c. 12th cent. - ..... **CMLC 8;
PC 22**
See also DLB 208; FW; RGWL 2

Marie de l'Incarnation 1599-1672 ...... **LC 10**

Marier, Captain Victor
See Griffith, D(avid Lewelyn) W(ark)

Mariner, Scott
See Pohl, Frederik

Marinetti, Filippo Tommaso
1876-1944 .... **TCLC 10**
See also CA 107; DLB 114, 264; EW 9

Marivaux, Pierre Carlet de Chamblain de
1688-1763 .... **LC 4; DC 7**
See also GFL Beginnings to 1789; RGWL
2; TWA

Markandaya, Kamala .... **CLC 8, 38**
See also Taylor, Kamala (Purnaiya)
See also BYA 13; CN 7

Markfield, Wallace 1926- .... **CLC 8**
See also CA 69-72; CAAS 3; CN 7; DLB
2, 28

Markham, Edwin 1852-1940 .... **TCLC 47**
See also CA 160; DLB 54, 186; RGAL 4

Markham, Robert
See Amis, Kingsley (William)

Marks, J
See Highwater, Jamake (Mamake)

Marks, J.
See Highwater, Jamake (Mamake)

Marks-Highwater, J
See Highwater, Jamake (Mamake)

Marks-Highwater, J.
See Highwater, Jamake (Mamake)

Markson, David M(errill) 1927- .... **CLC 67**
See also CA 49-52; CANR 1, 91; CN 7

Marley, Bob .... **CLC 17**
See also Marley, Robert Nesta

Marley, Robert Nesta 1945-1981
See Marley, Bob
See also CA 107; 103

Marlowe, Christopher 1564-1593 ...... **LC 22,
47; DC 1; WLC**
See also BRW 1; BRWR 1; CDBLB Before
1660; DA; DA3; DAB; DAC; DAM
DRAM, MST; DFS 1, 5, 13; DLB 62;
EXPP; RGEL 2; TEA; WLIT 3

Marlowe, Stephen 1928- .... **CLC 70**
See also Queen, Ellery
See also CA 13-16R; CANR 6, 55; CMW
4; SFW 4

Marmontel, Jean-Francois 1723-1799 .. **LC 2**

Marquand, John P(hillips)
1893-1960 .... **CLC 2, 10**
See also AMW; BPFB 2; CA 85-88; CANR
73; CMW 4; DLB 9, 102; MTCW 2;
RGAL 4

Marques, Rene 1919-1979 .. **CLC 96; HLC 2**
See also CA 97-100; 85-88; CANR 78;
DAM MULT; DLB 113; HW 1, 2; LAW;
RGSF 2

Marquez, Gabriel (Jose) Garcia
See Garcia Marquez, Gabriel (Jose)

Marquis, Don(ald Robert Perry)
1878-1937 .... **TCLC 7**
See also CA 104; 166; DLB 11, 25; RGAL
4

Marric, J. J.
See Creasey, John
See also MSW

Marryat, Frederick 1792-1848 .... **NCLC 3**
See also DLB 21, 163; RGEL 2; WCH

Marsden, James
See Creasey, John

Marsh, Edward 1872-1953 .... **TCLC 99**

Marsh, (Edith) Ngaio 1899-1982 .. **CLC 7, 53**
See also CA 9-12R; CANR 6, 58; CMW 4;
CPW; DAM POP; DLB 77; MSW;
MTCW 1, 2; RGEL 2; TEA

Marshall, Garry 1934- .... **CLC 17**
See also AAYA 3; CA 111; SATA 60

Marshall, Paule 1929- .. **CLC 27, 72; BLC 3;
SSC 3**
See also AFAW 1, 2; AMWS 11; BPFB 2;
BW 2, 3; CA 77-80; CANR 25, 73; CN 7;
DA3; DAM MULT; DLB 33, 157, 227;
MTCW 1, 2; RGAL 4; SSFS 15

Marshallik
See Zangwill, Israel

Marsten, Richard
See Hunter, Evan

Marston, John 1576-1634 .... **LC 33**
See also BRW 2; DAM DRAM; DLB 58,
172; RGEL 2

Martha, Henry
See Harris, Mark

Marti (y Perez), Jose (Julian)
1853-1895 .... **NCLC 63; HLC 2**
See also DAM MULT; HW 2; LAW; RGWL
2; WLIT 1

Martial c. 40-c. 104 .... **CMLC 35; PC 10**
See also AW 2; CDWLB 1; DLB 211;
RGWL 2

Martin, Ken
See Hubbard, L(afayette) Ron(ald)

Martin, Richard
See Creasey, John

Martin, Steve 1945- .... **CLC 30**
See also CA 97-100; CANR 30, 100;
MTCW 1

Martin, Valerie 1948- .... **CLC 89**
See also BEST 90:2; CA 85-88; CANR 49,
89

Martin, Violet Florence
1862-1915 .... **TCLC 51**

Martin, Webber
See Silverberg, Robert

Martindale, Patrick Victor
See White, Patrick (Victor Martindale)

Martin du Gard, Roger
1881-1958 .... **TCLC 24**
See also CA 118; CANR 94; DLB 65; GFL
1789 to the Present; RGWL 2

Martineau, Harriet 1802-1876 .... **NCLC 26**
See also DLB 21, 55, 159, 163, 166, 190;
FW; RGEL 2; YABC 2

Martines, Julia
See O'Faolain, Julia

Martinez, Enrique Gonzalez
See Gonzalez Martinez, Enrique

Martinez, Jacinto Benavente y
See Benavente (y Martinez), Jacinto

Martinez de la Rosa, Francisco de Paula
1787-1862 .... **NCLC 102**
See also TWA

Martinez Ruiz, Jose 1873-1967
See Azorin; Ruiz, Jose Martinez
See also CA 93-96; HW 1

Martinez Sierra, Gregorio
1881-1947 .... **TCLC 6**
See also CA 115

Martinez Sierra, Maria (de la O'LeJarraga)
1874-1974 .... **TCLC 6**
See also CA 115

Martinsen, Martin
See Follett, Ken(neth Martin)

Martinson, Harry (Edmund)
1904-1978 .... **CLC 14**
See also CA 77-80; CANR 34; DLB 259

Martyn, Edward 1859-1923 .... **TCLC 121**
See also CA 179; DLB 10; RGEL 2

Marut, Ret
See Traven, B.

Marut, Robert
See Traven, B.

Marvell, Andrew 1621-1678 .... **LC 4, 43; PC
10; WLC**
See also BRW 2; BRWR 2; CDBLB 1660-
1789; DA; DAB; DAC; DAM MST,
POET; DLB 131; EXPP; PFS 5; RGEL 2;
TEA; WP

Marx, Karl (Heinrich)
1818-1883 .... **NCLC 17, 114**
See also DLB 129; TWA

Masaoka, Shiki .... **TCLC 18**
See also Masaoka, Tsunenori

Masaoka, Tsunenori 1867-1902
See Masaoka, Shiki
See also CA 117; 191; TWA

Masefield, John (Edward)
1878-1967 .... **CLC 11, 47**
See also CA 19-20; 25-28R; CANR 33;
CAP 2; CDBLB 1890-1914; DAM POET;

DLB 10, 19, 153, 160; EXPP; FANT;
MTCW 1, 2; PFS 5; RGEL 2; SATA 19

Maso, Carole 19(?)- .... **CLC 44**
See also CA 170; GLL 2; RGAL 4

Mason, Bobbie Ann 1940- ... **CLC 28, 43, 82,
154; SSC 4**
See also AAYA 5, 42; AMWS 8; BPFB 2;
CA 53-56; CANR 11, 31, 58, 83;
CDALBS; CN 7; CSW; DA3; DLB 173;
DLBY 1987; EXPS; INT CANR-31;
MTCW 1, 2; NFS 4; RGAL 4; RGSF 2;
SSFS 3,8; YAW

Mason, Ernst
See Pohl, Frederik

Mason, Hunni B.
See Sternheim, (William Adolf) Carl

Mason, Lee W.
See Malzberg, Barry N(athaniel)

Mason, Nick 1945- .... **CLC 35**

Mason, Tally
See Derleth, August (William)

Mass, Anna .... **CLC 59**

Mass, William
See Gibson, William

Massinger, Philip 1583-1640 .... **LC 70**
See also DLB 58; RGEL 2

Master Lao
See Lao Tzu

Masters, Edgar Lee 1868-1950 .... **TCLC 2,
25; PC 1, 36; WLCS**
See also AMWS 1; CA 104; 133; CDALB
1865-1917; DA; DAC; DAM MST,
POET; DLB 54; EXPP; MTCW 1, 2;
RGAL 4; TUS; WP

Masters, Hilary 1928- .... **CLC 48**
See also CA 25-28R; CANR 13, 47, 97; CN
7; DLB 244

Mastrosimone, William 19(?)- .... **CLC 36**
See also CA 186; CAD; CD 5

Mathe, Albert
See Camus, Albert

Mather, Cotton 1663-1728 .... **LC 38**
See also AMWS 2; CDALB 1640-1865;
DLB 24, 30, 140; RGAL 4; TUS

Mather, Increase 1639-1723 .... **LC 38**
See also DLB 24

Matheson, Richard (Burton) 1926- .. **CLC 37**
See also AAYA 31; CA 97-100; CANR 88,
99; DLB 8, 44; HGG; INT 97-100; SCFW
2; SFW 4

Mathews, Harry 1930- .... **CLC 6, 52**
See also CA 21-24R; CAAS 6; CANR 18,
40, 98; CN 7

Mathews, John Joseph 1894-1979 .... **CLC 84**
See also CA 19-20; 142; CANR 45; CAP 2;
DAM MULT; DLB 175; NNAL

Mathias, Roland (Glyn) 1915- .... **CLC 45**
See also CA 97-100; CANR 19, 41; CP 7;
DLB 27

Matsuo Basho 1644-1694 .... **LC 62; PC 3**
See also Basho, Matsuo
See also DAM POET; PFS 2, 7

Mattheson, Rodney
See Creasey, John

Matthews, (James) Brander
1852-1929 .... **TCLC 95**
See also DLB 71, 78; DLBD 13

Matthews, Greg 1949- .... **CLC 45**
See also CA 135

Matthews, William (Procter III)
1942-1997 .... **CLC 40**
See also AMWS 9; CA 29-32R; 162; CAAS
18; CANR 12, 57; CP 7; DLB 5

Matthias, John (Edward) 1941- .... **CLC 9**
See also CA 33-36R; CANR 56; CP 7

Matthiessen, F(rancis) O(tto)
1902-1950 .... **TCLC 100**
See also CA 185; DLB 63

Matthiessen, Peter 1927- ... **CLC 5, 7, 11, 32,
64**
See also AAYA 6, 40; AMWS 5; ANW;
BEST 90:4; BPFB 2; CA 9-12R; CANR
21, 50, 73, 100; CN 7; DA3; DAM NOV;
DLB 6, 173; MTCW 1, 2; SATA 27

Maturin, Charles Robert
1780(?)-1824 .... **NCLC 6**
See also BRWS 8; DLB 178; HGG; RGEL
2; SUFW

Matute (Ausejo), Ana Maria 1925- .. **CLC 11**
See also CA 89-92; MTCW 1; RGSF 2

Maugham, W. S.
See Maugham, W(illiam) Somerset

Maugham, W(illiam) Somerset
1874-1965 .. **CLC 1, 11, 15, 67, 93; SSC
8; WLC**
See also BPFB 2; BRW 6; CA 5-8R; 25-
28R; CANR 40; CDBLB 1914-1945;
CMW 4; DA; DA3; DAB; DAC; DAM
DRAM, MST, NOV; DLB 10, 36, 77, 100,
162, 195; LAIT 3; MTCW 1, 2; RGEL 2;
RGSF 2; SATA 54

Maugham, William Somerset
See Maugham, W(illiam) Somerset

Maupassant, (Henri Rene Albert) Guy de
1850-1893 .... **NCLC 1, 42, 83; SSC 1;
WLC**
See also BYA 14; DA; DA3; DAB; DAC;
DAM MST; DLB 123; EW 7; EXPS; GFL
1789 to the Present; LAIT 2; RGSF 2;
RGWL 2; SSFS 4; SUFW; TWA

Maupin, Armistead (Jones, Jr.)
1944- .... **CLC 95**
See also CA 125; 130; CANR 58, 101;
CPW; DA3; DAM POP; GLL 1; INT 130;
MTCW 2

Maurhut, Richard
See Traven, B.

Mauriac, Claude 1914-1996 .... **CLC 9**
See also CA 89-92; 152; CWW 2; DLB 83;
GFL 1789 to the Present

Mauriac, Francois (Charles)
1885-1970 .... **CLC 4, 9, 56; SSC 24**
See also CA 25-28; CAP 2; DLB 65; EW
10; GFL 1789 to the Present; MTCW 1,
2; RGWL 2; TWA

Mavor, Osborne Henry 1888-1951
See Bridie, James
See also CA 104

Maxwell, William (Keepers, Jr.)
1908-2000 .... **CLC 19**
See also AMWS 8; CA 93-96; 189; CANR
54, 95; CN 7; DLB 218; DLBY 1980; INT
CA-93-96; SATA-Obit 128

May, Elaine 1932- .... **CLC 16**
See also CA 124; 142; CAD; CWD; DLB
44

Mayakovski, Vladimir (Vladimirovich)
1893-1930 .... **TCLC 4, 18**
See also Maiakovskii, Vladimir; Mayak-
ovsky, Vladimir
See also CA 104; 158; MTCW 2; SFW 4;
TWA

Mayakovsky, Vladimir
See Mayakovski, Vladimir (Vladimirovich)
See also EW 11; WP

Mayhew, Henry 1812-1887 .... **NCLC 31**
See also DLB 18, 55, 190

Mayle, Peter 1939(?)- .... **CLC 89**
See also CA 139; CANR 64, 109

Maynard, Joyce 1953- .... **CLC 23**
See also CA 111; 129; CANR 64

Mayne, William (James Carter)
1928- .... **CLC 12**
See also AAYA 20; CA 9-12R; CANR 37,
80, 100; CLR 25; FANT; JRDA; MAI-
CYA 1, 2; MAICYAS 1; SAAS 11; SATA
6, 68, 122; YAW

Mayo, Jim
See L'Amour, Louis (Dearborn)
See also TCWW 2

Maysles, Albert 1926- .... **CLC 16**
See also CA 29-32R

Maysles, David 1932-1987 .... **CLC 16**
See also CA 191

Mazer, Norma Fox 1931- .... **CLC 26**
See also AAYA 5, 36; BYA 1, 8; CA 69-72;
CANR 12, 32, 66; CLR 23; JRDA; MAI-
CYA 1, 2; SAAS 1; SATA 24, 67, 105;
WYA; YAW

Mazzini, Guiseppe 1805-1872 .... **NCLC 34**

McAlmon, Robert (Menzies)
1895-1956 .... **TCLC 97**
See also CA 107; 168; DLB 4, 45; DLBD
15; GLL 1

McAuley, James Phillip 1917-1976 .. **CLC 45**
See also CA 97-100; DLB 260; RGEL 2

McBain, Ed
See Hunter, Evan
See also MSW

McBrien, William (Augustine)
1930- .... **CLC 44**
See also CA 107; CANR 90

McCabe, Patrick 1955- .... **CLC 133**
See also CA 130; CANR 50, 90; CN 7;
DLB 194

McCaffrey, Anne (Inez) 1926- .... **CLC 17**
See also AAYA 6, 34; AITN 2; BEST 89:2;
BPFB 2; BYA 5; CA 25-28R; CANR 15,
35, 55, 96; CLR 49; CPW; DA3; DAM
NOV, POP; DLB 8; JRDA; MAICYA 1,
2; MTCW 1, 2; SAAS 11; SATA 8, 70,
116; SFW 4; WYA; YAW

McCall, Nathan 1955(?)- .... **CLC 86**
See also BW 3; CA 146; CANR 88

McCann, Arthur
See Campbell, John W(ood, Jr.)

McCann, Edson
See Pohl, Frederik

McCarthy, Charles, Jr. 1933-
See McCarthy, Cormac
See also CANR 42, 69, 101; CN 7; CPW;
CSW; DA3; DAM POP; MTCW 2

McCarthy, Cormac .... **CLC 4, 57, 59, 101**
See also McCarthy, Charles, Jr.
See also AAYA 41; AMWS 8; BPFB 2; CA
13-16R; CANR 10; DLB 6, 143, 256;
TCWW 2

McCarthy, Mary (Therese)
1912-1989 .. **CLC 1, 3, 5, 14, 24, 39, 59;
SSC 24**
See also AMW; BPFB 2; CA 5-8R; 129;
CANR 16, 50, 64; DA3; DLB 2; DLBY
1981; FW; INT CANR-16; MAWW;
MTCW 1, 2; RGAL 4; TUS

McCartney, (James) Paul 1942- . **CLC 12, 35**
See also CA 146; CANR 111

McCauley, Stephen (D.) 1955- .... **CLC 50**
See also CA 141

McClaren, Peter .... **CLC 70**

McClure, Michael (Thomas) 1932- ... **CLC 6,
10**
See also CA 21-24R; CAD; CANR 17, 46,
77; CD 5; CP 7; DLB 16; WP

McCorkle, Jill (Collins) 1958- .... **CLC 51**
See also CA 121; CSW; DLB 234; DLBY
1987

McCourt, Frank 1930- .... **CLC 109**
See also CA 157; CANR 97; NCFS 1

McCourt, James 1941- .... **CLC 5**
See also CA 57-60; CANR 98

McCourt, Malachy 1932- .... **CLC 119**
See also SATA 126

McCoy, Horace (Stanley)
1897-1955 .... **TCLC 28**
See also CA 108; 155; CMW 4; DLB 9

Murfree, Mary Noailles 1850-1922 ... **SSC 22**
See also CA 122; 176; DLB 12, 74; RGAL 4

Murnau, Friedrich Wilhelm
See Plumpe, Friedrich Wilhelm

Murphy, Richard 1927- .... **CLC 41**
See also BRWS 5; CA 29-32R; CP 7; DLB 40

Murphy, Sylvia 1937- .... **CLC 34**
See also CA 121

Murphy, Thomas (Bernard) 1935- ... **CLC 51**
See also CA 101

Murray, Albert L. 1916- .... **CLC 73**
See also BW 2; CA 49-52; CANR 26, 52, 78; CSW; DLB 38

Murray, James Augustus Henry
1837-1915 .... **TCLC 117**

Murray, Judith Sargent
1751-1820 .... **NCLC 63**
See also DLB 37, 200

Murray, Les(lie Allan) 1938- .... **CLC 40**
See also BRWS 7; CA 21-24R; CANR 11, 27, 56, 103; CP 7; DAM POET; DLBY 01; RGEL 2

Murry, J. Middleton
See Murry, John Middleton

Murry, John Middleton
1889-1957 .... **TCLC 16**
See also CA 118; DLB 149

Musgrave, Susan 1951- .... **CLC 13, 54**
See also CA 69-72; CANR 45, 84; CCA 1; CP 7; CWP

Musil, Robert (Edler von)
1880-1942 .... **TCLC 12, 68; SSC 18**
See also CA 109; CANR 55, 84; CDWLB 2; DLB 81, 124; EW 9; MTCW 2; RGSF 2; RGWL 2

Muske, Carol .... **CLC 90**
See also Muske-Dukes, Carol (Anne)

Muske-Dukes, Carol (Anne) 1945-
See Muske, Carol
See also CA 65-68; CAAE 203; CANR 32, 70; CWP

Musset, (Louis Charles) Alfred de
1810-1857 .... **NCLC 7**
See also DLB 192, 217; EW 6; GFL 1789 to the Present; RGWL 2; TWA

Mussolini, Benito (Amilcare Andrea)
1883-1945 .... **TCLC 96**
See also CA 116

My Brother's Brother
See Chekhov, Anton (Pavlovich)

Myers, L(eopold) H(amilton)
1881-1944 .... **TCLC 59**
See also CA 157; DLB 15; RGEL 2

Myers, Walter Dean 1937- .. **CLC 35; BLC 3**
See also AAYA 4, 23; BW 2; BYA 6, 8, 11; CA 33-36R; CANR 20, 42, 67, 108; CLR 4, 16, 35; DAM MULT, NOV; DLB 33; INT CANR-20; JRDA; LAIT 5; MAICYA 1, 2; MAICYAS 1; MTCW 2; SAAS 2; SATA 41, 71, 109; SATA-Brief 27; WYA; YAW

Myers, Walter M.
See Myers, Walter Dean

Myles, Symon
See Follett, Ken(neth Martin)

Nabokov, Vladimir (Vladimirovich)
1899-1977 .... **CLC 1, 2, 3, 6, 8, 11, 15, 23, 44, 46, 64; SSC 11; WLC**
See also AMW; AMWR 1; BPFB 2; CA 5-8R; 69-72; CANR 20, 102; CDALB 1941-1968; DA; DA3; DAB; DAC; DAM MST, NOV; DLB 2, 244; DLBD 3; DLBY 1980, 1991; EXPS; MTCW 1, 2; NCFS 4; NFS 9; RGAL 4; RGSF 2; SSFS 6, 15; TCLC 108; TUS

Naevius c. 265 B.C.-201 B.C. .... **CMLC 37**
See also DLB 211

Nagai, Kafu .... **TCLC 51**
See also Nagai, Sokichi
See also DLB 180

Nagai, Sokichi 1879-1959
See Nagai, Kafu
See also CA 117

Nagy, Laszlo 1925-1978 .... **CLC 7**
See also CA 129; 112

Naidu, Sarojini 1879-1949 .... **TCLC 80**
See also RGEL 2

Naipaul, Shiva(dhar Srinivasa)
1945-1985 .... **CLC 32, 39**
See also CA 110; 112; 116; CANR 33; DA3; DAM NOV; DLB 157; DLBY 1985; MTCW 1, 2

Naipaul, V(idiadhar) S(urajprasad)
1932- .... **CLC 4, 7, 9, 13, 18, 37, 105; SSC 38**
See also BPFB 2; BRWS 1; CA 1-4R; CANR 1, 33, 51, 91; CDBLB 1960 to Present; CDWLB 3; CN 7; DA3; DAB; DAC; DAM MST, NOV; DLB 125, 204, 207; DLBY 1985, 2001; MTCW 1, 2; RGEL 2; RGSF 2; TWA; WLIT 4

Nakos, Lilika 1899(?)- .... **CLC 29**

Narayan, R(asipuram) K(rishnaswami)
1906-2001 . **CLC 7, 28, 47, 121; SSC 25**
See also BPFB 2; CA 81-84; 196; CANR 33, 61; CN 7; DA3; DAM NOV; DNFS 1; MTCW 1, 2; RGEL 2; RGSF 2; SATA 62; SSFS 5

Nash, (Frediric) Ogden 1902-1971 . **CLC 23; PC 21**
See also CA 13-14; 29-32R; CANR 34, 61; CAP 1; DAM POET; DLB 11; MAICYA 1, 2; MTCW 1, 2; RGAL 4; SATA 2, 46; TCLC 109; WP

Nashe, Thomas 1567-1601(?) .... **LC 41**
See also DLB 167; RGEL 2

Nathan, Daniel
See Dannay, Frederic

Nathan, George Jean 1882-1958 .... **TCLC 18**
See also Hatteras, Owen
See also CA 114; 169; DLB 137

Natsume, Kinnosuke
See Natsume, Soseki

Natsume, Soseki 1867-1916 .... **TCLC 2, 10**
See also Natsume Soseki; Soseki
See also CA 104; 195; RGWL 2; TWA

Natsume Soseki
See Natsume, Soseki
See also DLB 180

Natti, (Mary) Lee 1919-
See Kingman, Lee
See also CA 5-8R; CANR 2

Navarre, Marguerite de
See de Navarre, Marguerite

Naylor, Gloria 1950- . **CLC 28, 52, 156; BLC 3; WLCS**
See also AAYA 6, 39; AFAW 1, 2; AMWS 8; BW 2, 3; CA 107; CANR 27, 51, 74; CN 7; CPW; DA; DA3; DAC; DAM MST, MULT, NOV; DLB 173; FW; MTCW 1, 2; NFS 4, 7; RGAL 4; TUS

Neff, Debra .... **CLC 59**

Neihardt, John Gneisenau
1881-1973 .... **CLC 32**
See also CA 13-14; CANR 65; CAP 1; DLB 9, 54, 256; LAIT 2

Nekrasov, Nikolai Alekseevich
1821-1878 .... **NCLC 11**

Nelligan, Emile 1879-1941 .... **TCLC 14**
See also CA 114; DLB 92

Nelson, Willie 1933- .... **CLC 17**
See also CA 107

Nemerov, Howard (Stanley)
1920-1991 .... **CLC 2, 6, 9, 36; PC 24**
See also AMW; CA 1-4R; 134; CABS 2; CANR 1, 27, 53; DAM POET; DLB 5, 6;

DLBY 1983; INT CANR-27; MTCW 1, 2; PFS 10, 14; RGAL 4; TCLC 124

Neruda, Pablo 1904-1973 .. **CLC 1, 2, 5, 7, 9, 28, 62; HLC 2; PC 4; WLC**
See also CA 19-20; 45-48; CAP 2; DA; DA3; DAB; DAC; DAM MST, MULT, POET; DNFS 2; HW 1; LAW; MTCW 1, 2; PFS 11; RGWL 2; TWA; WLIT 1; WP

Nerval, Gerard de 1808-1855 ... **NCLC 1, 67; PC 13; SSC 18**
See also DLB 217; EW 6; GFL 1789 to the Present; RGSF 2; RGWL 2

Nervo, (Jose) Amado (Ruiz de)
1870-1919 .... **TCLC 11; HLCS 2**
See also CA 109; 131; HW 1; LAW

Nesbit, Malcolm
See Chester, Alfred

Nessi, Pio Baroja y
See Baroja (y Nessi), Pio

Nestroy, Johann 1801-1862 .... **NCLC 42**
See also DLB 133; RGWL 2

Netterville, Luke
See O'Grady, Standish (James)

Neufeld, John (Arthur) 1938- .... **CLC 17**
See also AAYA 11; CA 25-28R; CANR 11, 37, 56; CLR 52; MAICYA 1, 2; SAAS 3; SATA 6, 81; SATA-Essay 131; YAW

Neumann, Alfred 1895-1952 .... **TCLC 100**
See also CA 183; DLB 56

Neumann, Ferenc
See Molnar, Ferenc

Neville, Emily Cheney 1919- .... **CLC 12**
See also BYA 2; CA 5-8R; CANR 3, 37, 85; JRDA; MAICYA 1, 2; SAAS 2; SATA 1; YAW

Newbound, Bernard Slade 1930-
See Slade, Bernard
See also CA 81-84; CANR 49; CD 5; DAM DRAM

Newby, P(ercy) H(oward)
1918-1997 .... **CLC 2, 13**
See also CA 5-8R; 161; CANR 32, 67; CN 7; DAM NOV; DLB 15; MTCW 1; RGEL 2

Newcastle
See Cavendish, Margaret Lucas

Newlove, Donald 1928- .... **CLC 6**
See also CA 29-32R; CANR 25

Newlove, John (Herbert) 1938- .... **CLC 14**
See also CA 21-24R; CANR 9, 25; CP 7

Newman, Charles 1938- .... **CLC 2, 8**
See also CA 21-24R; CANR 84; CN 7

Newman, Edwin (Harold) 1919- ...... **CLC 14**
See also AITN 1; CA 69-72; CANR 5

Newman, John Henry 1801-1890 . **NCLC 38, 99**
See also BRWS 7; DLB 18, 32, 55; RGEL 2

Newton, (Sir) Isaac 1642-1727 ...... **LC 35, 53**
See also DLB 252

Newton, Suzanne 1936- .... **CLC 35**
See also BYA 7; CA 41-44R; CANR 14; JRDA; SATA 5, 77

New York Dept. of Ed. .... **CLC 70**

Nexo, Martin Andersen
1869-1954 .... **TCLC 43**
See also CA 202; DLB 214

Nezval, Vitezslav 1900-1958 .... **TCLC 44**
See also CA 123; CDWLB 4; DLB 215

Ng, Fae Myenne 1957(?)- .... **CLC 81**
See also CA 146

Ngema, Mbongeni 1955- .... **CLC 57**
See also BW 2; CA 143; CANR 84; CD 5

Ngugi, James T(hiong'o) .... **CLC 3, 7, 13**
See also Ngugi wa Thiong'o

Ngugi wa Thiong'o
See Ngugi wa Thiong'o
See also DLB 125

Ngugi wa Thiong'o 1938- .... **CLC 36; BLC 3**
See also Ngugi, James T(hiong'o); Ngugi wa Thiong'o
See also AFW; BRWS 8; BW 2; CA 81-84; CANR 27, 58; CDWLB 3; DAM MULT, NOV; DNFS 2; MTCW 1, 2; RGEL 2

Nichol, B(arrie) P(hillip) 1944-1988 . **CLC 18**
See also CA 53-56; DLB 53; SATA 66

Nicholas of Cusa 1401-1464 .... **LC 80**
See also DLB 115

Nichols, John (Treadwell) 1940- .... **CLC 38**
See also CA 9-12R; CAAE 190; CAAS 2; CANR 6, 70; DLBY 1982; TCWW 2

Nichols, Leigh
See Koontz, Dean R(ay)

Nichols, Peter (Richard) 1927- .... **CLC 5, 36, 65**
See also CA 104; CANR 33, 86; CBD; CD 5; DLB 13, 245; MTCW 1

Nicholson, Linda ed. .... **CLC 65**

Ni Chuilleanain, Eilean 1942- .... **PC 34**
See also CA 126; CANR 53, 83; CP 7; CWP; DLB 40

Nicolas, F. R. E.
See Freeling, Nicolas

Niedecker, Lorine 1903-1970 ..... **CLC 10, 42; PC 42**
See also CA 25-28; CAP 2; DAM POET; DLB 48

Nietzsche, Friedrich (Wilhelm) 1844-1900 .... **TCLC 10, 18, 55**
See also CA 107; 121; CDWLB 2; DLB 129; EW 7; RGWL 2; TWA

Nievo, Ippolito 1831-1861 .... **NCLC 22**

Nightingale, Anne Redmon 1943-
See Redmon, Anne
See also CA 103

Nightingale, Florence 1820-1910 ... **TCLC 85**
See also CA 188; DLB 166

Nijo Yoshimoto 1320-1388 .... **CMLC 49**
See also DLB 203

Nik. T. O.
See Annensky, Innokenty (Fyodorovich)

Nin, Anais 1903-1977 ..... **CLC 1, 4, 8, 11, 14, 60, 127; SSC 10**
See also AITN 2; AMWS 10; BPFB 2; CA 13-16R; 69-72; CANR 22, 53; DAM NOV, POP; DLB 2, 4, 152; GLL 2; MAWW; MTCW 1, 2; RGAL 4; RGSF 2

Nisbet, Robert A(lexander) 1913-1996 .... **TCLC 117**
See also CA 25-28R; 153; CANR 17; INT CANR-17

Nishida, Kitaro 1870-1945 .... **TCLC 83**

Nishiwaki, Junzaburo 1894-1982 .... **PC 15**
See also Nishiwaki, Junzaburo
See also CA 194; 107; MJW

Nishiwaki, Junzaburo 1894-1982
See Nishiwaki, Junzaburo
See also CA 194

Nissenson, Hugh 1933- .... **CLC 4, 9**
See also CA 17-20R; CANR 27, 108; CN 7; DLB 28

Niven, Larry .... **CLC 8**
See also Niven, Laurence Van Cott
See also AAYA 27; BPFB 2; BYA 10; DLB 8; SCFW 2

Niven, Laurence Van Cott 1938-
See Niven, Larry
See also CA 21-24R; CAAS 12; CANR 14, 44, 66; CPW; DAM POP; MTCW 1, 2; SATA 95; SFW 4

Nixon, Agnes Eckhardt 1927- .... **CLC 21**
See also CA 110

Nizan, Paul 1905-1940 .... **TCLC 40**
See also CA 161; DLB 72; GFL 1789 to the Present

Nkosi, Lewis 1936- .... **CLC 45; BLC 3**
See also BW 1, 3; CA 65-68; CANR 27, 81; CBD; CD 5; DAM MULT; DLB 157, 225

Nodier, (Jean) Charles (Emmanuel) 1780-1844 .... **NCLC 19**
See also DLB 119; GFL 1789 to the Present

Noguchi, Yone 1875-1947 .... **TCLC 80**

Nolan, Christopher 1965- .... **CLC 58**
See also CA 111; CANR 88

Noon, Jeff 1957- .... **CLC 91**
See also CA 148; CANR 83; DLB 267; SFW 4

Norden, Charles
See Durrell, Lawrence (George)

Nordhoff, Charles (Bernard) 1887-1947 .... **TCLC 23**
See also CA 108; DLB 9; LAIT 1; RHW 1; SATA 23

Norfolk, Lawrence 1963- .... **CLC 76**
See also CA 144; CANR 85; CN 7; DLB 267

Norman, Marsha 1947- .... **CLC 28; DC 8**
See also CA 105; CABS 3; CAD; CANR 41; CD 5; CSW; CWD; DAM DRAM; DFS 2; DLB 266; DLBY 1984; FW

Normyx
See Douglas, (George) Norman

Norris, (Benjamin) Frank(lin, Jr.) 1870-1902 .... **TCLC 24; SSC 28**
See also AMW; BPFB 2; CA 110; 160; CDALB 1865-1917; DLB 12, 71, 186; NFS 12; RGAL 4; TCWW 2; TUS

Norris, Leslie 1921- .... **CLC 14**
See also CA 11-12; CANR 14; CAP 1; CP 7; DLB 27, 256

North, Andrew
See Norton, Andre

North, Anthony
See Koontz, Dean R(ay)

North, Captain George
See Stevenson, Robert Louis (Balfour)

North, Captain George
See Stevenson, Robert Louis (Balfour)

North, Milou
See Erdrich, Louise

Northrup, B. A.
See Hubbard, L(afayette) Ron(ald)

North Staffs
See Hulme, T(homas) E(rnest)

Northup, Solomon 1808-1863 ...... **NCLC 105**

Norton, Alice Mary
See Norton, Andre
See also MAICYA 1; SATA 1, 43

Norton, Andre 1912- .... **CLC 12**
See also Norton, Alice Mary
See also AAYA 14; BPFB 2; BYA 4, 10, 12; CA 1-4R; CANR 68; CLR 50; DLB 8, 52; JRDA; MAICYA 2; MTCW 1; SATA 91; SUFW; YAW

Norton, Caroline 1808-1877 .... **NCLC 47**
See also DLB 21, 159, 199

Norway, Nevil Shute 1899-1960
See Shute, Nevil
See also CA 102; 93-96; CANR 85; MTCW 2

Norwid, Cyprian Kamil 1821-1883 .... **NCLC 17**

Nosille, Nabrah
See Ellison, Harlan (Jay)

Nossack, Hans Erich 1901-1978 .... **CLC 6**
See also CA 93-96; 85-88; DLB 69

Nostradamus 1503-1566 .... **LC 27**

Nosu, Chuji
See Ozu, Yasujiro

Notenburg, Eleanora (Genrikhovna) von
See Guro, Elena

Nova, Craig 1945- .... **CLC 7, 31**
See also CA 45-48; CANR 2, 53

Novak, Joseph
See Kosinski, Jerzy (Nikodem)

Novalis 1772-1801 .... **NCLC 13**
See also CDWLB 2; DLB 90; EW 5; RGWL 2

Novick, Peter 1934- .... **CLC 164**
See also CA 188

Novis, Emile
See Weil, Simone (Adolphine)

Nowlan, Alden (Albert) 1933-1983 ... **CLC 15**
See also CA 9-12R; CANR 5; DAC; DAM MST; DLB 53; PFS 12

Noyes, Alfred 1880-1958 ...... **TCLC 7; PC 27**
See also CA 104; 188; DLB 20; EXPP; FANT; PFS 4; RGEL 2

Nunn, Kem .... **CLC 34**
See also CA 159

Nwapa, Flora 1931-1993 .... **CLC 133; BLCS**
See also BW 2; CA 143; CANR 83; CD-WLB 3; CWRI 5; DLB 125; WLIT 2

Nye, Robert 1939- .... **CLC 13, 42**
See also CA 33-36R; CANR 29, 67, 107; CN 7; CP 7; CWRI 5; DAM NOV; DLB 14; FANT; HGG; MTCW 1; RHW; SATA 6

Nyro, Laura 1947-1997 .... **CLC 17**
See also CA 194

Oates, Joyce Carol 1938- .. **CLC 1, 2, 3, 6, 9, 11, 15, 19, 33, 52, 108, 134; SSC 6; WLC**
See also AAYA 15; AITN 1; AMWS 2; BEST 89:2; BPFB 2; BYA 11; CA 5-8R; CANR 25, 45, 74; CDALB 1968-1988; CN 7; CP 7; CPW; CWP; DA; DA3; DAB; DAC; DAM MST, NOV, POP; DLB 2, 5, 130; DLBY 1981; EXPS; FW; HGG; INT CANR-25; LAIT 4; MAWW; MTCW 1, 2; NFS 8; RGAL 4; RGSF 2; SSFS 1, 8; TUS

O'Brian, E. G.
See Clarke, Arthur C(harles)

O'Brian, Patrick 1914-2000 .... **CLC 152**
See also CA 144; 187; CANR 74; CPW; MTCW 2; RHW

O'Brien, Darcy 1939-1998 .... **CLC 11**
See also CA 21-24R; 167; CANR 8, 59

O'Brien, Edna 1936- ..... **CLC 3, 5, 8, 13, 36, 65, 116; SSC 10**
See also BRWS 5; CA 1-4R; CANR 6, 41, 65, 102; CDBLB 1960 to Present; CN 7; DA3; DAM NOV; DLB 14, 231; FW; MTCW 1, 2; RGSF 2; WLIT 4

O'Brien, Fitz-James 1828-1862 ..... **NCLC 21**
See also DLB 74; RGAL 4; SUFW

O'Brien, Flann .... **CLC 1, 4, 5, 7, 10, 47**
See also O Nuallain, Brian
See also BRWS 2; DLB 231; RGEL 2

O'Brien, Richard 1942- .... **CLC 17**
See also CA 124

O'Brien, (William) Tim(othy) 1946- . **CLC 7, 19, 40, 103**
See also AAYA 16; AMWS 5; CA 85-88; CANR 40, 58; CDALBS; CN 7; CPW; DA3; DAM POP; DLB 152; DLBD 9; DLBY 1980; MTCW 2; RGAL 4; SSFS 5, 15

Obstfelder, Sigbjoern 1866-1900 .... **TCLC 23**
See also CA 123

O'Casey, Sean 1880-1964 .... **CLC 1, 5, 9, 11, 15, 88; DC 12; WLCS**
See also BRW 7; CA 89-92; CANR 62; CBD; CDBLB 1914-1945; DA3; DAB; DAC; DAM DRAM, MST; DLB 10; MTCW 1, 2; RGEL 2; TEA; WLIT 4

O'Cathasaigh, Sean
See O'Casey, Sean

Osbourne, Lloyd 1868-1947 .... **TCLC 93**

Oshima, Nagisa 1932- .... **CLC 20**
See also CA 116; 121; CANR 78

Oskison, John Milton 1874-1947 ... **TCLC 35**
See also CA 144; CANR 84; DAM MULT;
DLB 175; NNAL

Ossian c. 3rd cent. - .... **CMLC 28**
See also Macpherson, James

Ossoli, Sarah Margaret (Fuller)
1810-1850 .... **NCLC 5, 50**
See also Fuller, Margaret; Fuller, Sarah
Margaret
See also CDALB 1640-1865; FW; SATA 25

Ostriker, Alicia (Suskin) 1937- .... **CLC 132**
See also CA 25-28R; CAAS 24; CANR 10,
30, 62, 99; CWP; DLB 120; EXPP

Ostrovsky, Alexander 1823-1886 .. **NCLC 30,
57**

Otero, Blas de 1916-1979 .... **CLC 11**
See also CA 89-92; DLB 134

Otto, Rudolf 1869-1937 .... **TCLC 85**

Otto, Whitney 1955- .... **CLC 70**
See also CA 140

Ouida .... **TCLC 43**
See also De La Ramee, (Marie) Louise
See also DLB 18, 156; RGEL 2

Ouologuem, Yambo 1940- .... **CLC 146**
See also CA 111; 176

Ousmane, Sembene 1923- ... **CLC 66; BLC 3**
See also Sembene, Ousmane
See also BW 1, 3; CA 117; 125; CANR 81;
CWW 2; MTCW 1

Ovid 43 B.C.-17 .... **CMLC 7; PC 2**
See also AW 2; CDWLB 1; DA3; DAM
POET; DLB 211; RGWL 2; WP

Owen, Hugh
See Faust, Frederick (Schiller)

Owen, Wilfred (Edward Salter)
1893-1918 ... **TCLC 5, 27; PC 19; WLC**
See also BRW 6; CA 104; 141; CDBLB
1914-1945; DA; DAB; DAC; DAM MST,
POET; DLB 20; EXPP; MTCW 2; PFS
10; RGEL 2; WLIT 4

Owens, Rochelle 1936- .... **CLC 8**
See also CA 17-20R; CAAS 2; CAD;
CANR 39; CD 5; CP 7; CWD; CWP

Oz, Amos 1939- ..... **CLC 5, 8, 11, 27, 33, 54**
See also CA 53-56; CANR 27, 47, 65;
CWW 2; DAM NOV; MTCW 1, 2; RGSF
2

Ozick, Cynthia 1928- .... **CLC 3, 7, 28, 62,
155; SSC 15**
See also AMWS 5; BEST 90:1; CA 17-20R;
CANR 23, 58; CN 7; CPW; DA3; DAM
NOV, POP; DLB 28, 152; DLBY 1982;
EXPS; INT CANR-23; MTCW 1, 2;
RGAL 4; RGSF 2; SSFS 3, 12

Ozu, Yasujiro 1903-1963 .... **CLC 16**
See also CA 112

Pabst, G. W. 1885-1967 .... **TCLC 127**

Pacheco, C.
See Pessoa, Fernando (Antonio Nogueira)

Pacheco, Jose Emilio 1939-
See also CA 111; 131; CANR 65; DAM
MULT; HLC 2; HW 1, 2; RGSF 2

Pa Chin .... **CLC 18**
See also Li Fei-kan

Pack, Robert 1929- .... **CLC 13**
See also CA 1-4R; CANR 3, 44, 82; CP 7;
DLB 5; SATA 118

Padgett, Lewis
See Kuttner, Henry

Padilla (Lorenzo), Heberto
1932-2000 .... **CLC 38**
See also AITN 1; CA 123; 131; 189; HW 1

Page, Jimmy 1944- .... **CLC 12**

Page, Louise 1955- .... **CLC 40**
See also CA 140; CANR 76; CBD; CD 5;
CWD; DLB 233

Page, P(atricia) K(athleen) 1916- ...... **CLC 7,
18; PC 12**
See also Cape, Judith
See also CA 53-56; CANR 4, 22, 65; CP 7;
DAC; DAM MST; DLB 68; MTCW 1;
RGEL 2

Page, Stanton
See Fuller, Henry Blake

Page, Stanton
See Fuller, Henry Blake

Page, Thomas Nelson 1853-1922 .... **SSC 23**
See also CA 118; 177; DLB 12, 78; DLBD
13; RGAL 4

Pagels, Elaine Hiesey 1943- .... **CLC 104**
See also CA 45-48; CANR 2, 24, 51; FW;
NCFS 4

Paget, Violet 1856-1935
See Lee, Vernon
See also CA 104; 166; GLL 1; HGG

Paget-Lowe, Henry
See Lovecraft, H(oward) P(hillips)

Paglia, Camille (Anna) 1947- .... **CLC 68**
See also CA 140; CANR 72; CPW; FW;
GLL 2; MTCW 2

Paige, Richard
See Koontz, Dean R(ay)

Paine, Thomas 1737-1809 .... **NCLC 62**
See also AMWS 1; CDALB 1640-1865;
DLB 31, 43, 73, 158; LAIT 1; RGAL 4;
RGEL 2; TUS

Pakenham, Antonia
See Fraser, (Lady) Antonia (Pakenham)

Palamas, Kostes 1859-1943 .... **TCLC 5**
See also CA 105; 190; RGWL 2

Palazzeschi, Aldo 1885-1974 .... **CLC 11**
See also CA 89-92; 53-56; DLB 114, 264

Pales Matos, Luis 1898-1959
See Pales Matos, Luis
See also HLCS 2; HW 1; LAW

Paley, Grace 1922- .. **CLC 4, 6, 37, 140; SSC
8**
See also AMWS 6; CA 25-28R; CANR 13,
46, 74; CN 7; CPW; DA3; DAM POP;
DLB 28, 218; EXPS; FW; INT CANR-
13; MAWW; MTCW 1, 2; RGAL 4;
RGSF 2; SSFS 3

Palin, Michael (Edward) 1943- .... **CLC 21**
See also Monty Python
See also CA 107; CANR 35, 109; SATA 67

Palliser, Charles 1947- .... **CLC 65**
See also CA 136; CANR 76; CN 7

Palma, Ricardo 1833-1919 .... **TCLC 29**
See also CA 168; LAW

Pancake, Breece Dexter 1952-1979
See Pancake, Breece D'J
See also CA 123; 109

Pancake, Breece D'J .... **CLC 29**
See also Pancake, Breece Dexter
See also DLB 130

Panchenko, Nikolai .... **CLC 59**

Pankhurst, Emmeline (Goulden)
1858-1928 .... **TCLC 100**
See also CA 116; FW

Panko, Rudy
See Gogol, Nikolai (Vasilyevich)

Papadiamantis, Alexandros
1851-1911 .... **TCLC 29**
See also CA 168

Papadiamantopoulos, Johannes 1856-1910
See Moreas, Jean
See also CA 117

Papini, Giovanni 1881-1956 .... **TCLC 22**
See also CA 121; 180; DLB 264

Paracelsus 1493-1541 .... **LC 14**
See also DLB 179

Parasol, Peter
See Stevens, Wallace

Pardo Bazan, Emilia 1851-1921 .... **SSC 30**
See also FW; RGSF 2; RGWL 2

Pareto, Vilfredo 1848-1923 .... **TCLC 69**
See also CA 175

Paretsky, Sara 1947- .... **CLC 135**
See also AAYA 30; BEST 90:3; CA 125;
129; CANR 59, 95; CMW 4; CPW; DA3;
DAM POP; INT CA-129; MSW; RGAL 4

Parfenie, Maria
See Codrescu, Andrei

Parini, Jay (Lee) 1948- .... **CLC 54, 133**
See also CA 97-100; CAAS 16; CANR 32,
87

Park, Jordan
See Kornbluth, C(yril) M.; Pohl, Frederik

Park, Robert E(zra) 1864-1944 ..... **TCLC 73**
See also CA 122; 165

Parker, Bert
See Ellison, Harlan (Jay)

Parker, Dorothy (Rothschild)
1893-1967 .. **CLC 15, 68; PC 28; SSC 2**
See also AMWS 9; CA 19-20; 25-28R; CAP
2; DA3; DAM POET; DLB 11, 45, 86;
EXPP; FW; MAWW; MTCW 1, 2; RGAL
4; RGSF 2; TUS

Parker, Robert B(rown) 1932- .... **CLC 27**
See also AAYA 28; BEST 89:4; BPFB 3;
CA 49-52; CANR 1, 26, 52, 89; CMW 4;
CPW; DAM NOV, POP; INT CANR-26;
MSW; MTCW 1

Parkin, Frank 1940- .... **CLC 43**
See also CA 147

Parkman, Francis, Jr. 1823-1893 .. **NCLC 12**
See also AMWS 2; DLB 1, 30, 183, 186,
235; RGAL 4

Parks, Gordon (Alexander Buchanan)
1912- .... **CLC 1, 16; BLC 3**
See also AAYA 36; AITN 2; BW 2, 3; CA
41-44R; CANR 26, 66; DA3; DAM
MULT; DLB 33; MTCW 2; SATA 8, 108

Parks, Tim(othy Harold) 1954- ...... **CLC 147**
See also CA 126; 131; CANR 77; DLB 231;
INT CA-131

Parmenides c. 515 B.C.-c. 450
B.C. .... **CMLC 22**
See also DLB 176

Parnell, Thomas 1679-1718 .... **LC 3**
See also DLB 95; RGEL 2

Parra, Nicanor 1914- ... **CLC 2, 102; HLC 2;
PC 39**
See also CA 85-88; CANR 32; CWW 2;
DAM MULT; HW 1; LAW; MTCW 1

Parra Sanojo, Ana Teresa de la 1890-1936
See de la Parra, (Ana) Teresa (Sonojo)
See also HLCS 2; LAW

Parrish, Mary Frances
See Fisher, M(ary) F(rances) K(ennedy)

Parshchikov, Aleksei .... **CLC 59**

Parson, Professor
See Coleridge, Samuel Taylor

Parson Lot
See Kingsley, Charles

Parton, Sara Payson Willis
1811-1872 .... **NCLC 86**
See also DLB 43, 74, 239

Partridge, Anthony
See Oppenheim, E(dward) Phillips

Pascal, Blaise 1623-1662 .... **LC 35**
See also DLB 268; EW 3; GFL Beginnings
to 1789; RGWL 2; TWA

Pascoli, Giovanni 1855-1912 .... **TCLC 45**
See also CA 170; EW 7

Pasolini, Pier Paolo 1922-1975 .. **CLC 20, 37,
106; PC 17**
See also CA 93-96; 61-64; CANR 63; DLB
128, 177; MTCW 1; RGWL 2

Pasquini
See Silone, Ignazio

Pastan, Linda (Olenik) 1932- .... **CLC 27**
See also CA 61-64; CANR 18, 40, 61; CP
7; CSW; CWP; DAM POET; DLB 5; PFS
8

Pasternak, Boris (Leonidovich)
1890-1960 ...... **CLC 7, 10, 18, 63; PC 6;
SSC 31; WLC**
See also BPFB 3; CA 127; 116; DA; DA3;
DAB; DAC; DAM MST, NOV, POET;
EW 10; MTCW 1, 2; RGSF 2; RGWL 2;
TWA; WP

Patchen, Kenneth 1911-1972 .... **CLC 1, 2, 18**
See also CA 1-4R; 33-36R; CANR 3, 35;
DAM POET; DLB 16, 48; MTCW 1;
RGAL 4

Pater, Walter (Horatio) 1839-1894 . **NCLC 7,
90**
See also BRW 5; CDBLB 1832-1890; DLB
57, 156; RGEL 2; TEA

Paterson, A(ndrew) B(arton)
1864-1941 .... **TCLC 32**
See also CA 155; DLB 230; RGEL 2; SATA
97

Paterson, Katherine (Womeldorf)
1932- .... **CLC 12, 30**
See also AAYA 1, 31; BYA 1, 2, 7; CA 21-
24R; CANR 28, 59, 111; CLR 7, 50;
CWRI 5; DLB 52; JRDA; LAIT 4; MAI-
CYA 1, 2; MAICYAS 1; MTCW 1; SATA
13, 53, 92, 133; WYA; YAW

Patmore, Coventry Kersey Dighton
1823-1896 .... **NCLC 9**
See also DLB 35, 98; RGEL 2; TEA

Paton, Alan (Stewart) 1903-1988 ...... **CLC 4,
10, 25, 55, 106; WLC**
See also AAYA 26; AFW; BPFB 3; BRWS
2; BYA 1; CA 13-16; 125; CANR 22;
CAP 1; DA; DA3; DAB; DAC; DAM
MST, NOV; DLB 225; DLBD 17; EXPN;
LAIT 4; MTCW 1, 2; NFS 3, 12; RGEL
2; SATA 11; SATA-Obit 56; TWA; WLIT
2

Paton Walsh, Gillian 1937- .... **CLC 35**
See also Paton Walsh, Jill; Walsh, Jill Paton
See also AAYA 11; CANR 38, 83; CLR 2,
65; DLB 161; JRDA; MAICYA 1, 2;
SAAS 3; SATA 4, 72, 109; YAW

Paton Walsh, Jill
See Paton Walsh, Gillian
See also BYA 1, 8

Patton, George S(mith), Jr.
1885-1945 .... **TCLC 79**
See also CA 189

Paulding, James Kirke 1778-1860 ... **NCLC 2**
See also DLB 3, 59, 74, 250; RGAL 4

Paulin, Thomas Neilson 1949-
See Paulin, Tom
See also CA 123; 128; CANR 98; CP 7

Paulin, Tom .... **CLC 37**
See also Paulin, Thomas Neilson
See also DLB 40

Pausanias c. 1st cent. - .... **CMLC 36**

Paustovsky, Konstantin (Georgievich)
1892-1968 .... **CLC 40**
See also CA 93-96; 25-28R

Pavese, Cesare 1908-1950 .. **TCLC 3; PC 13;
SSC 19**
See also CA 104; 169; DLB 128, 177; EW
12; RGSF 2; RGWL 2; TWA

Pavic, Milorad 1929- .... **CLC 60**
See also CA 136; CDWLB 4; CWW 2; DLB
181

Pavlov, Ivan Petrovich 1849-1936 . **TCLC 91**
See also CA 118; 180

Payne, Alan
See Jakes, John (William)

Paz, Gil
See Lugones, Leopoldo

Paz, Octavio 1914-1998 . **CLC 3, 4, 6, 10, 19,
51, 65, 119; HLC 2; PC 1; WLC**
See also CA 73-76; 165; CANR 32, 65, 104;
CWW 2; DA; DA3; DAB; DAC; DAM
MST, MULT, POET; DLBY 1990, 1998;
DNFS 1; HW 1, 2; LAW; LAWS 1;
MTCW 1, 2; RGWL 2; SSFS 13; TWA;
WLIT 1

p'Bitek, Okot 1931-1982 ..... **CLC 96; BLC 3**
See also AFW; BW 2, 3; CA 124; 107;
CANR 82; DAM MULT; DLB 125;
MTCW 1, 2; RGEL 2; WLIT 2

Peacock, Molly 1947- .... **CLC 60**
See also CA 103; CAAS 21; CANR 52, 84;
CP 7; CWP; DLB 120

Peacock, Thomas Love
1785-1866 .... **NCLC 22**
See also BRW 4; DLB 96, 116; RGEL 2;
RGSF 2

Peake, Mervyn 1911-1968 .... **CLC 7, 54**
See also CA 5-8R; 25-28R; CANR 3; DLB
15, 160, 255; FANT; MTCW 1; RGEL 2;
SATA 23; SFW 4

Pearce, Philippa
See Christie, Philippa
See also CA 5-8R; CANR 4, 109; CWRI 5;
FANT; MAICYA 2

Pearl, Eric
See Elman, Richard (Martin)

Pearson, T(homas) R(eid) 1956- .... **CLC 39**
See also CA 120; 130; CANR 97; CSW;
INT 130

Peck, Dale 1967- .... **CLC 81**
See also CA 146; CANR 72; GLL 2

Peck, John (Frederick) 1941- .... **CLC 3**
See also CA 49-52; CANR 3, 100; CP 7

Peck, Richard (Wayne) 1934- .... **CLC 21**
See also AAYA 1, 24; BYA 1, 6, 8, 11; CA
85-88; CANR 19, 38; CLR 15; INT
CANR-19; JRDA; MAICYA 1, 2; SAAS
2; SATA 18, 55, 97; SATA-Essay 110;
WYA; YAW

Peck, Robert Newton 1928- .... **CLC 17**
See also AAYA 3, 43; BYA 1, 6; CA 81-84,
182; CAAE 182; CANR 31, 63; CLR 45;
DA; DAC; DAM MST; JRDA; LAIT 3;
MAICYA 1, 2; SAAS 1; SATA 21, 62,
111; SATA-Essay 108; WYA; YAW

Peckinpah, (David) Sam(uel)
1925-1984 .... **CLC 20**
See also CA 109; 114; CANR 82

Pedersen, Knut 1859-1952
See Hamsun, Knut
See also CA 104; 119; CANR 63; MTCW
1, 2

Peeslake, Gaffer
See Durrell, Lawrence (George)

Peguy, Charles (Pierre)
1873-1914 .... **TCLC 10**
See also CA 107; 193; DLB 258; GFL 1789
to the Present

Peirce, Charles Sanders
1839-1914 .... **TCLC 81**
See also CA 194

Pellicer, Carlos 1900(?)-1977
See also CA 153; 69-72; HLCS 2; HW 1

Pena, Ramon del Valle y
See Valle-Inclan, Ramon (Maria) del

Pendennis, Arthur Esquir
See Thackeray, William Makepeace

Penn, William 1644-1718 .... **LC 25**
See also DLB 24

PEPECE
See Prado (Calvo), Pedro

Pepys, Samuel 1633-1703 ... **LC 11, 58; WLC**
See also BRW 2; CDBLB 1660-1789; DA;
DA3; DAB; DAC; DAM MST; DLB 101,
213; NCFS 4; RGEL 2; TEA; WLIT 3

Percy, Thomas 1729-1811 .... **NCLC 95**
See also DLB 104

Percy, Walker 1916-1990 .... **CLC 2, 3, 6, 8,
14, 18, 47, 65**
See also AMWS 3; BPFB 3; CA 1-4R; 131;
CANR 1, 23, 64; CPW; CSW; DA3;
DAM NOV, POP; DLB 2; DLBY 1980,
1990; MTCW 1, 2; RGAL 4; TUS

Percy, William Alexander
1885-1942 .... **TCLC 84**
See also CA 163; MTCW 2

Perec, Georges 1936-1982 .... **CLC 56, 116**
See also CA 141; DLB 83; GFL 1789 to the
Present

**Pereda (y Sanchez de Porrua), Jose Maria
de** 1833-1906 .... **TCLC 16**
See also CA 117

Pereda y Porrua, Jose Maria de
See Pereda (y Sanchez de Porrua), Jose
Maria de

Peregoy, George Weems
See Mencken, H(enry) L(ouis)

Perelman, S(idney) J(oseph)
1904-1979 .. **CLC 3, 5, 9, 15, 23, 44, 49;
SSC 32**
See also AITN 1, 2; BPFB 3; CA 73-76;
89-92; CANR 18; DAM DRAM; DLB 11,
44; MTCW 1, 2; RGAL 4

Peret, Benjamin 1899-1959 .... **TCLC 20; PC
33**
See also CA 117; 186; GFL 1789 to the
Present

Peretz, Isaac Loeb 1851(?)-1915 ... **TCLC 16;
SSC 26**
See also CA 109

Peretz, Yitzkhok Leibush
See Peretz, Isaac Loeb

Perez Galdos, Benito 1843-1920 ... **TCLC 27;
HLCS 2**
See also Galdos, Benito Perez
See also CA 125; 153; HW 1; RGWL 2

Peri Rossi, Cristina 1941- .. **CLC 156; HLCS
2**
See also CA 131; CANR 59, 81; DLB 145;
HW 1, 2

Perlata
See Peret, Benjamin

Perloff, Marjorie G(abrielle)
1931- .... **CLC 137**
See also CA 57-60; CANR 7, 22, 49, 104

Perrault, Charles 1628-1703 ... **LC 2, 56; DC
12**
See also BYA 4; CLR 79; DLB 268; GFL
Beginnings to 1789; MAICYA 1, 2;
RGWL 2; SATA 25; WCH

Perry, Anne 1938- .... **CLC 126**
See also CA 101; CANR 22, 50, 84; CMW
4; CN 7; CPW

Perry, Brighton
See Sherwood, Robert E(mmet)

Perse, St.-John
See Leger, (Marie-Rene Auguste) Alexis
Saint-Leger

Perse, Saint-John
See Leger, (Marie-Rene Auguste) Alexis
Saint-Leger
See also DLB 258

Perutz, Leo(pold) 1882-1957 .... **TCLC 60**
See also CA 147; DLB 81

Peseenz, Tulio F.
See Lopez y Fuentes, Gregorio

Pesetsky, Bette 1932- .... **CLC 28**
See also CA 133; DLB 130

Peshkov, Alexei Maximovich 1868-1936
See Gorky, Maxim
See also CA 105; 141; CANR 83; DA;
DAC; DAM DRAM, MST, NOV;
MTCW 2

Pessoa, Fernando (Antonio Nogueira)
1898-1935 ..... **TCLC 27; HLC 2; PC 20**
See also CA 125; 183; DAM MULT; EW
10; RGWL 2; WP

Peterkin, Julia Mood 1880-1961 ...... **CLC 31**
See also CA 102; DLB 9

Peters, Joan K(aren) 1945- .... **CLC 39**
See also CA 158; CANR 109

Peters, Robert L(ouis) 1924- .... **CLC 7**
See also CA 13-16R; CAAS 8; CP 7; DLB
105

Petofi, Sandor 1823-1849 .... **NCLC 21**
See also RGWL 2

Petrakis, Harry Mark 1923- .... **CLC 3**
See also CA 9-12R; CANR 4, 30, 85; CN 7

Petrarch 1304-1374 .... **CMLC 20; PC 8**
See also DA3; DAM POET; EW 2; RGWL
2

Petronius c. 20-66 .... **CMLC 34**
See also AW 2; CDWLB 1; DLB 211;
RGWL 2

Petrov, Evgeny .... **TCLC 21**
See also Kataev, Evgeny Petrovich

Petry, Ann (Lane) 1908-1997 ... **CLC 1, 7, 18**
See also AFAW 1, 2; BPFB 3; BW 1, 3;
BYA 2; CA 5-8R; 157; CAAS 6; CANR
4, 46; CLR 12; CN 7; DLB 76; JRDA;
LAIT 1; MAICYA 1, 2; MAICYAS 1;
MTCW 1; RGAL 4; SATA 5; SATA-Obit
94; TCLC 112; TUS

Petursson, Halligrimur 1614-1674 .... **LC 8**

Peychinovich
See Vazov, Ivan (Minchov)

Phaedrus c. 15 B.C.-c. 50 .... **CMLC 25**
See also DLB 211

Phelps (Ward), Elizabeth Stuart
See Phelps, Elizabeth Stuart
See also FW

Phelps, Elizabeth Stuart
1844-1911 .... **TCLC 113**
See also Phelps (Ward), Elizabeth Stuart
See also DLB 74

Philips, Katherine 1632-1664 . **LC 30; PC 40**
See also DLB 131; RGEL 2

Philipson, Morris H. 1926- .... **CLC 53**
See also CA 1-4R; CANR 4

Phillips, Caryl 1958- .... **CLC 96; BLCS**
See also BRWS 5; BW 2; CA 141; CANR
63, 104; CBD; CD 5; CN 7; DA3; DAM
MULT; DLB 157; MTCW 2; WLIT 4

Phillips, David Graham
1867-1911 .... **TCLC 44**
See also CA 108; 176; DLB 9, 12; RGAL 4

Phillips, Jack
See Sandburg, Carl (August)

Phillips, Jayne Anne 1952- .... **CLC 15, 33,
139; SSC 16**
See also BPFB 3; CA 101; CANR 24, 50,
96; CN 7; CSW; DLBY 1980; INT
CANR-24; MTCW 1, 2; RGAL 4; RGSF
2; SSFS 4

Phillips, Richard
See Dick, Philip K(indred)

Phillips, Robert (Schaeffer) 1938- .... **CLC 28**
See also CA 17-20R; CAAS 13; CANR 8;
DLB 105

Phillips, Ward
See Lovecraft, H(oward) P(hillips)

Piccolo, Lucio 1901-1969 .... **CLC 13**
See also CA 97-100; DLB 114

Pickthall, Marjorie L(owry) C(hristie)
1883-1922 .... **TCLC 21**
See also CA 107; DLB 92

Pico della Mirandola, Giovanni
1463-1494 .... **LC 15**

Piercy, Marge 1936- .... **CLC 3, 6, 14, 18, 27,
62, 128; PC 29**
See also BPFB 3; CA 21-24R; CAAE 187;
CAAS 1; CANR 13, 43, 66, 111; CN 7;

CP 7; CWP; DLB 120, 227; EXPP; FW;
MTCW 1, 2; PFS 9; SFW 4

Piers, Robert
See Anthony, Piers

Pieyre de Mandiargues, Andre 1909-1991
See Mandiargues, Andre Pieyre de
See also CA 103; 136; CANR 22, 82; GFL
1789 to the Present

Pilnyak, Boris 1894-1938 . **TCLC 23; SSC 48**
See also Vogau, Boris Andreyevich

Pinchback, Eugene
See Toomer, Jean

Pincherle, Alberto 1907-1990 ...... **CLC 11, 18**
See also Moravia, Alberto
See also CA 25-28R; 132; CANR 33, 63;
DAM NOV; MTCW 1

Pinckney, Darryl 1953- .... **CLC 76**
See also BW 2, 3; CA 143; CANR 79

Pindar 518(?) B.C.-438(?) B.C. .... **CMLC 12;
PC 19**
See also AW 1; CDWLB 1; DLB 176;
RGWL 2

Pineda, Cecile 1942- .... **CLC 39**
See also CA 118; DLB 209

Pinero, Arthur Wing 1855-1934 .... **TCLC 32**
See also CA 110; 153; DAM DRAM; DLB
10; RGEL 2

Pinero, Miguel (Antonio Gomez)
1946-1988 .... **CLC 4, 55**
See also CA 61-64; 125; CAD; CANR 29,
90; DLB 266; HW 1

Pinget, Robert 1919-1997 .... **CLC 7, 13, 37**
See also CA 85-88; 160; CWW 2; DLB 83;
GFL 1789 to the Present

Pink Floyd
See Barrett, (Roger) Syd; Gilmour, David;
Mason, Nick; Waters, Roger; Wright, Rick

Pinkney, Edward 1802-1828 .... **NCLC 31**
See also DLB 248

Pinkwater, Daniel
See Pinkwater, Daniel Manus

Pinkwater, Daniel Manus 1941- .... **CLC 35**
See also AAYA 1; BYA 9; CA 29-32R;
CANR 12, 38, 89; CLR 4; CSW; FANT;
JRDA; MAICYA 1, 2; SAAS 3; SATA 8,
46, 76, 114; SFW 4; YAW

Pinkwater, Manus
See Pinkwater, Daniel Manus

Pinsky, Robert 1940- .... **CLC 9, 19, 38, 94,
121; PC 27**
See also AMWS 6; CA 29-32R; CAAS 4;
CANR 58, 97; CP 7; DA3; DAM POET;
DLBY 1982, 1998; MTCW 2; RGAL 4

Pinta, Harold
See Pinter, Harold

Pinter, Harold 1930- .. **CLC 1, 3, 6, 9, 11, 15,
27, 58, 73; DC 15; WLC**
See also BRWR 1; BRWS 1; CA 5-8R;
CANR 33, 65; CBD; CD 5; CDBLB 1960
to Present; DA; DA3; DAB; DAC; DAM
DRAM, MST; DFS 3, 5, 7, 14; DLB 13;
IDFW 3, 4; MTCW 1, 2; RGEL 2; TEA

Piozzi, Hester Lynch (Thrale)
1741-1821 .... **NCLC 57**
See also DLB 104, 142

Pirandello, Luigi 1867-1936 ...... **TCLC 4, 29;
DC 5; SSC 22; WLC**
See also CA 104; 153; CANR 103; DA;
DA3; DAB; DAC; DAM DRAM, MST;
DFS 4, 9; DLB 264; EW 8; MTCW 2;
RGSF 2; RGWL 2

Pirsig, Robert M(aynard) 1928- ... **CLC 4, 6,
73**
See also CA 53-56; CANR 42, 74; CPW 1;
DA3; DAM POP; MTCW 1, 2; SATA 39

Pisarev, Dmitry Ivanovich
1840-1868 .... **NCLC 25**

Pix, Mary (Griffith) 1666-1709 .... **LC 8**
See also DLB 80

Pixerecourt, (Rene Charles) Guilbert de
1773-1844 .... **NCLC 39**
See also DLB 192; GFL 1789 to the Present

Plaatje, Sol(omon) T(shekisho)
1878-1932 .... **TCLC 73; BLCS**
See also BW 2, 3; CA 141; CANR 79; DLB
125, 225

Plaidy, Jean
See Hibbert, Eleanor Alice Burford

Planche, James Robinson
1796-1880 .... **NCLC 42**
See also RGEL 2

Plant, Robert 1948- .... **CLC 12**

Plante, David (Robert) 1940- . **CLC 7, 23, 38**
See also CA 37-40R; CANR 12, 36, 58, 82;
CN 7; DAM NOV; DLBY 1983; INT
CANR-12; MTCW 1

Plath, Sylvia 1932-1963 ..... **CLC 1, 2, 3, 5, 9,
11, 14, 17, 50, 51, 62, 111; PC 1, 37;
WLC**
See also AAYA 13; AMWS 1; BPFB 3; CA
19-20; CANR 34, 101; CAP 2; CDALB
1941-1968; DA; DA3; DAB; DAC; DAM
MST, POET; DLB 5, 6, 152; EXPN;
EXPP; FW; LAIT 4; MAWW; MTCW 1,
2; NFS 1; PAB; PFS 1, 15; RGAL 4;
SATA 96; TUS; WP; YAW

Plato c. 428 B.C.-347 B.C. . **CMLC 8; WLCS**
See also AW 1; CDWLB 1; DA; DA3;
DAB; DAC; DAM MST; DLB 176; LAIT
1; RGWL 2

Platonov, Andrei
See Klimentov, Andrei Platonovich

Platt, Kin 1911- .... **CLC 26**
See also AAYA 11; CA 17-20R; CANR 11;
JRDA; SAAS 17; SATA 21, 86; WYA

Plautus c. 254 B.C.-c. 184 B.C. .... **CMLC 24;
DC 6**
See also AW 1; CDWLB 1; DLB 211;
RGWL 2

Plick et Plock
See Simenon, Georges (Jacques Christian)

Plieksans, Janis
See Rainis, Janis

Plimpton, George (Ames) 1927- .... **CLC 36**
See also AITN 1; CA 21-24R; CANR 32,
70, 103; DLB 185, 241; MTCW 1, 2;
SATA 10

Pliny the Elder c. 23-79 .... **CMLC 23**
See also DLB 211

Plomer, William Charles Franklin
1903-1973 .... **CLC 4, 8**
See also AFW; CA 21-22; CANR 34; CAP
2; DLB 20, 162, 191, 225; MTCW 1;
RGEL 2; RGSF 2; SATA 24

Plotinus 204-270 .... **CMLC 46**
See also CDWLB 1; DLB 176

Plowman, Piers
See Kavanagh, Patrick (Joseph)

Plum, J.
See Wodehouse, P(elham) G(renville)

Plumly, Stanley (Ross) 1939- .... **CLC 33**
See also CA 108; 110; CANR 97; CP 7;
DLB 5, 193; INT 110

Plumpe, Friedrich Wilhelm
1888-1931 .... **TCLC 53**
See also CA 112

Po Chu-i 772-846 .... **CMLC 24**

Poe, Edgar Allan 1809-1849 ..... **NCLC 1, 16,
55, 78, 94, 97, 117; PC 1; SSC 1, 22,
34, 35, 54; WLC**
See also AAYA 14; AMW; BPFB 3; BYA 5,
11; CDALB 1640-1865; CMW 4; DA;
DA3; DAB; DAC; DAM MST, POET;
DLB 3, 59, 73, 74, 248, 254; EXPP;
EXPS; HGG; LAIT 2; MSW; PAB; PFS
1, 3, 9; RGAL 4; RGSF 2; SATA 23;
SCFW 2; SFW 4; SSFS 2, 4, 7, 8; SUFW;
WP; WYA

Poet of Titchfield Street, The
　See Pound, Ezra (Weston Loomis)
Pohl, Frederik 1919- .... **CLC 18; SSC 25**
　See also AAYA 24; CA 61-64; CAAE 188;
　CAAS 1; CANR 11, 37, 81; CN 7; DLB
　8; INT CANR-11; MTCW 1, 2; SATA 24;
　SCFW 2; SFW 4
Poirier, Louis 1910-
　See Gracq, Julien
　See also CA 122; 126; CWW 2
Poitier, Sidney 1927- .... **CLC 26**
　See also BW 1; CA 117; CANR 94
Polanski, Roman 1933- .... **CLC 16**
　See also CA 77-80
Poliakoff, Stephen 1952- .... **CLC 38**
　See also CA 106; CBD; CD 5; DLB 13
Police, The
　See Copeland, Stewart (Armstrong); Sum-
　mers, Andrew James; Sumner, Gordon
　Matthew
Polidori, John William 1795-1821 . **NCLC 51**
　See also DLB 116; HGG
Pollitt, Katha 1949- .... **CLC 28, 122**
　See also CA 120; 122; CANR 66, 108;
　MTCW 1, 2
Pollock, (Mary) Sharon 1936- .... **CLC 50**
　See also CA 141; CD 5; CWD; DAC; DAM
　DRAM, MST; DFS 3; DLB 60; FW
Polo, Marco 1254-1324 .... **CMLC 15**
Polonsky, Abraham (Lincoln)
　1910-1999 .... **CLC 92**
　See also CA 104; 187; DLB 26; INT 104
Polybius c. 200 B.C.-c. 118 B.C. ... **CMLC 17**
　See also AW 1; DLB 176; RGWL 2
Pomerance, Bernard 1940- .... **CLC 13**
　See also CA 101; CAD; CANR 49; CD 5;
　DAM DRAM; DFS 9; LAIT 2
Ponge, Francis 1899-1988 .... **CLC 6, 18**
　See also CA 85-88; 126; CANR 40, 86;
　DAM POET; GFL 1789 to the Present;
　RGWL 2
Poniatowska, Elena 1933- . **CLC 140; HLC 2**
　See also CA 101; CANR 32, 66, 107; CD-
　WLB 3; DAM MULT; DLB 113; HW 1,
　2; LAWS 1; WLIT 1
Pontoppidan, Henrik 1857-1943 .... **TCLC 29**
　See also CA 170
Poole, Josephine .... **CLC 17**
　See Helyar, Jane Penelope Josephine
　See also SAAS 2; SATA 5
Popa, Vasko 1922-1991 .... **CLC 19**
　See also CA 112; 148; CDWLB 4; DLB
　181; RGWL 2
Pope, Alexander 1688-1744 ...... **LC 3, 58, 60,**
　64; PC 26; WLC
　See also BRW 3; BRWR 1; CDBLB 1660-
　1789; DA; DA3; DAB; DAC; DAM MST,
　POET; DLB 95, 101, 213; EXPP; PAB;
　PFS 12; RGEL 2; WLIT 3; WP
Popov, Yevgeny .... **CLC 59**
Poquelin, Jean-Baptiste
　See Moliere
Porter, Connie (Rose) 1959(?)- .... **CLC 70**
　See also BW 2, 3; CA 142; CANR 90, 109;
　SATA 81, 129
Porter, Gene(va Grace) Stratton .. **TCLC 21**
　See also Stratton-Porter, Gene(va Grace)
　See also BPFB 3; CA 112; CWRI 5; RHW
Porter, Katherine Anne 1890-1980 ... **CLC 1,**
　3, 7, 10, 13, 15, 27, 101; SSC 4, 31, 43
　See also AAYA 42; AITN 2; AMW; BPFB
　3; CA 1-4R; 101; CANR 1, 65; CDALBS;
　DA; DA3; DAB; DAC; DAM MST, NOV;
　DLB 4, 9, 102; DLBD 12; DLBY 1980;
　EXPS; LAIT 3; MAWW; MTCW 1, 2;
　NFS 14; RGAL 4; RGSF 2; SATA 39;
　SATA-Obit 23; SSFS 1, 8, 11; TUS

Porter, Peter (Neville Frederick)
　1929- .... **CLC 5, 13, 33**
　See also CA 85-88; CP 7; DLB 40
Porter, William Sydney 1862-1910
　See Henry, O.
　See also CA 104; 131; CDALB 1865-1917;
　DA; DA3; DAB; DAC; DAM MST; DLB
　12, 78, 79; MTCW 1, 2; TUS; YABC 2
Portillo (y Pacheco), Jose Lopez
　See Lopez Portillo (y Pacheco), Jose
Portillo Trambley, Estela 1927-1998
　See Trambley, Estela Portillo
　See also CANR 32; DAM MULT; DLB
　209; HLC 2; HW 1
Posse, Abel .... **CLC 70**
Post, Melville Davisson
　1869-1930 .... **TCLC 39**
　See also CA 110; 202; CMW 4
Potok, Chaim 1929-2002 ... **CLC 2, 7, 14, 26,**
　112
　See also AAYA 15; AITN 1, 2; BPFB 3;
　BYA 1; CA 17-20R; CANR 19, 35, 64,
　98; CN 7; DA3; DAM NOV; DLB 28,
　152; EXPN; INT CANR-19; LAIT 4;
　MTCW 1, 2; NFS 4; SATA 33, 106;
　SATA-Obit 134; TUS; YAW
Potter, Dennis (Christopher George)
　1935-1994 .... **CLC 58, 86, 123**
　See also CA 107; 145; CANR 33, 61; CBD;
　DLB 233; MTCW 1
Pound, Ezra (Weston Loomis)
　1885-1972 .. **CLC 1, 2, 3, 4, 5, 7, 10, 13,**
　18, 34, 48, 50, 112; PC 4; WLC
　See also AMW; AMWR 1; CA 5-8R; 37-
　40R; CANR 40; CDALB 1917-1929; DA;
　DA3; DAB; DAC; DAM MST, POET;
　DLB 4, 45, 63; DLBD 15; EFS 2; EXPP;
　MTCW 1, 2; PAB; PFS 2, 8; RGAL 4;
　TUS; WP
Povod, Reinaldo 1959-1994 .... **CLC 44**
　See also CA 136; 146; CANR 83
Powell, Adam Clayton, Jr.
　1908-1972 .... **CLC 89; BLC 3**
　See also BW 1, 3; CA 102; 33-36R; CANR
　86; DAM MULT
Powell, Anthony (Dymoke)
　1905-2000 .... **CLC 1, 3, 7, 9, 10, 31**
　See also BRW 7; CA 1-4R; 189; CANR 1,
　32, 62, 107; CDBLB 1945-1960; CN 7;
　DLB 15; MTCW 1, 2; RGEL 2; TEA
Powell, Dawn 1896(?)-1965 .... **CLC 66**
　See also CA 5-8R; DLBY 1997
Powell, Padgett 1952- .... **CLC 34**
　See also CA 126; CANR 63, 101; CSW;
　DLB 234; DLBY 01
Powell, (Oval) Talmage 1920-2000
　See Queen, Ellery
　See also CA 5-8R; CANR 2, 80
Power, Susan 1961- .... **CLC 91**
　See also BYA 14; CA 160; NFS 11
Powers, J(ames) F(arl) 1917-1999 ..... **CLC 1,**
　4, 8, 57; SSC 4
　See also CA 1-4R; 181; CANR 2, 61; CN
　7; DLB 130; MTCW 1; RGAL 4; RGSF
　2
Powers, John J(ames) 1945-
　See Powers, John R.
　See also CA 69-72
Powers, John R. .... **CLC 66**
　See also Powers, John J(ames)
Powers, Richard (S.) 1957- .... **CLC 93**
　See also AMWS 9; BPFB 3; CA 148;
　CANR 80; CN 7
Pownall, David 1938- .... **CLC 10**
　See also CA 89-92; 180; CAAS 18; CANR
　49, 101; CBD; CD 5; CN 7; DLB 14

Powys, John Cowper 1872-1963 ... **CLC 7, 9,**
　15, 46, 125
　See also CA 85-88; CANR 106; DLB 15,
　255; FANT; MTCW 1, 2; RGEL 2; SUFW
Powys, T(heodore) F(rancis)
　1875-1953 .... **TCLC 9**
　See also BRWS 8; CA 106; 189; DLB 36,
　162; FANT; RGEL 2; SUFW
Prado (Calvo), Pedro 1886-1952 ... **TCLC 75**
　See also CA 131; HW 1; LAW
Prager, Emily 1952- .... **CLC 56**
　See also CA 204
Pratolini, Vasco 1913-1991 .... **TCLC 124**
　See also DLB 177; RGWL 2
Pratt, E(dwin) J(ohn) 1883(?)-1964 . **CLC 19**
　See also CA 141; 93-96; CANR 77; DAC;
　DAM POET; DLB 92; RGEL 2; TWA
Premchand .... **TCLC 21**
　See also Srivastava, Dhanpat Rai
Preussler, Otfried 1923- .... **CLC 17**
　See also CA 77-80; SATA 24
Prevert, Jacques (Henri Marie)
　1900-1977 .... **CLC 15**
　See also CA 77-80; 69-72; CANR 29, 61;
　DLB 258; GFL 1789 to the Present;
　IDFW 3, 4; MTCW 1; RGWL 2; SATA-
　Obit 30
Prevost, (Antoine Francois)
　1697-1763 .... **LC 1**
　See also EW 4; GFL Beginnings to 1789;
　RGWL 2
Price, (Edward) Reynolds 1933- ... **CLC 3, 6,**
　13, 43, 50, 63; SSC 22
　See also AMWS 6; CA 1-4R; CANR 1, 37,
　57, 87; CN 7; CSW; DAM NOV; DLB 2,
　218; INT CANR-37
Price, Richard 1949- .... **CLC 6, 12**
　See also CA 49-52; CANR 3; DLBY 1981
Prichard, Katharine Susannah
　1883-1969 .... **CLC 46**
　See also CA 11-12; CANR 33; CAP 1; DLB
　260; MTCW 1; RGEL 2; RGSF 2; SATA
　66
Priestley, J(ohn) B(oynton)
　1894-1984 .... **CLC 2, 5, 9, 34**
　See also BRW 7; CA 9-12R; 113; CANR
　33; CDBLB 1914-1945; DA3; DAM
　DRAM, NOV; DLB 10, 34, 77, 100, 139;
　DLBY 1984; MTCW 1, 2; RGEL 2; SFW
　4
Prince 1958(?)- .... **CLC 35**
Prince, F(rank) T(empleton) 1912- .. **CLC 22**
　See also CA 101; CANR 43, 79; CP 7; DLB
　20
Prince Kropotkin
　See Kropotkin, Peter (Aleksieevich)
Prior, Matthew 1664-1721 .... **LC 4**
　See also DLB 95; RGEL 2
Prishvin, Mikhail 1873-1954 .... **TCLC 75**
Pritchard, William H(arrison)
　1932- .... **CLC 34**
　See also CA 65-68; CANR 23, 95; DLB
　111
Pritchett, V(ictor) S(awdon)
　1900-1997 ... **CLC 5, 13, 15, 41; SSC 14**
　See also BPFB 3; BRWS 3; CA 61-64; 157;
　CANR 31, 63; CN 7; DA3; DAM NOV;
　DLB 15, 139; MTCW 1, 2; RGEL 2;
　RGSF 2; TEA
Private 19022
　See Manning, Frederic
Probst, Mark 1925- .... **CLC 59**
　See also CA 130
Prokosch, Frederic 1908-1989 ...... **CLC 4, 48**
　See also CA 73-76; 128; CANR 82; DLB
　48; MTCW 2

Propertius, Sextus c. 50 B.C.-c. 16
B.C. .... **CMLC 32**
See also AW 2; CDWLB 1; DLB 211;
RGWL 2

Prophet, The
See Dreiser, Theodore (Herman Albert)

Prose, Francine 1947- .... **CLC 45**
See also CA 109; 112; CANR 46, 95; DLB
234; SATA 101

Proudhon
See Cunha, Euclides (Rodrigues Pimenta)
da

Proulx, Annie
See Proulx, E(dna) Annie

Proulx, E(dna) Annie 1935- ...... **CLC 81, 158**
See also AMWS 7; BPFB 3; CA 145;
CANR 65, 110; CN 7; CPW 1; DA3;
DAM POP; MTCW 2

Proust,
(Valentin-Louis-George-Eugene-)Marcel
1871-1922 .... **TCLC 7, 13, 33; WLC**
See also BPFB 3; CA 104; 120; CANR 110;
DA; DA3; DAB; DAC; DAM MST, NOV;
DLB 65; EW 8; GFL 1789 to the Present;
MTCW 1, 2; RGWL 2; TWA

Prowler, Harley
See Masters, Edgar Lee

Prus, Boleslaw 1845-1912 .... **TCLC 48**
See also RGWL 2

Pryor, Richard (Franklin Lenox Thomas)
1940- .... **CLC 26**
See also CA 122; 152

Przybyszewski, Stanislaw
1868-1927 .... **TCLC 36**
See also CA 160; DLB 66

Pteleon
See Grieve, C(hristopher) M(urray)
See also DAM POET

Puckett, Lute
See Masters, Edgar Lee

Puig, Manuel 1932-1990 .... **CLC 3, 5, 10, 28,**
65, 133; HLC 2
See also BPFB 3; CA 45-48; CANR 2, 32,
63; CDWLB 3; DA3; DAM MULT; DLB
113; DNFS 1; GLL 1; HW 1, 2; LAW;
MTCW 1, 2; RGWL 2; TWA; WLIT 1

Pulitzer, Joseph 1847-1911 .... **TCLC 76**
See also CA 114; DLB 23

Purchas, Samuel 1577(?)-1626 .... **LC 70**
See also DLB 151

Purdy, A(lfred) W(ellington)
1918-2000 .... **CLC 3, 6, 14, 50**
See also CA 81-84; 189; CAAS 17; CANR
42, 66; CP 7; DAC; DAM MST, POET;
DLB 88; PFS 5; RGEL 2

Purdy, James (Amos) 1923- .... **CLC 2, 4, 10,**
28, 52
See also AMWS 7; CA 33-36R; CAAS 1;
CANR 19, 51; CN 7; DLB 2, 218; INT
CANR-19; MTCW 1; RGAL 4

Pure, Simon
See Swinnerton, Frank Arthur

Pushkin, Aleksandr Sergeevich
See Pushkin, Alexander (Sergeyevich)
See also DLB 205

Pushkin, Alexander (Sergeyevich)
1799-1837 .... **NCLC 3, 27, 83; PC 10;**
SSC 27, 55; WLC
See also Pushkin, Aleksandr Sergeevich
See also DA; DA3; DAB; DAC; DAM
DRAM, MST, POET; EW 5; EXPS; RGSF
2; RGWL 2; SATA 61; SSFS 9; TWA

P'u Sung-ling 1640-1715 .... **LC 49; SSC 31**

Putnam, Arthur Lee
See Alger, Horatio, Jr.

Puzo, Mario 1920-1999 .... **CLC 1, 2, 6, 36,**
107
See also BPFB 3; CA 65-68; 185; CANR 4,
42, 65, 99; CN 7; CPW; DA3; DAM
NOV, POP; DLB 6; MTCW 1, 2; RGAL
4

Pygge, Edward
See Barnes, Julian (Patrick)

Pyle, Ernest Taylor 1900-1945
See Pyle, Ernie
See also CA 115; 160

Pyle, Ernie .... **TCLC 75**
See also Pyle, Ernest Taylor
See also DLB 29; MTCW 2

Pyle, Howard 1853-1911 .... **TCLC 81**
See also BYA 2, 4; CA 109; 137; CLR 22;
DLB 42, 188; DLBD 13; LAIT 1; MAI-
CYA 1, 2; SATA 16, 100; WCH; YAW

Pym, Barbara (Mary Crampton)
1913-1980 .... **CLC 13, 19, 37, 111**
See also BPFB 3; BRWS 2; CA 13-14; 97-
100; CANR 13, 34; CAP 1; DLB 14, 207;
DLBY 1987; MTCW 1, 2; RGEL 2; TEA

Pynchon, Thomas (Ruggles, Jr.)
1937- ... **CLC 2, 3, 6, 9, 11, 18, 33, 62,**
72, 123; SSC 14; WLC
See also AMWS 2; BEST 90:2; BPFB 3;
CA 17-20R; CANR 22, 46, 73; CN 7;
CPW 1; DA; DA3; DAC; DAM
MST, NOV, POP; DLB 2, 173; MTCW 1,
2; RGAL 4; SFW 4; TUS

Pythagoras c. 582 B.C.-c. 507
B.C. .... **CMLC 22**
See also DLB 176

Q
See Quiller-Couch, Sir Arthur (Thomas)

Qian, Chongzhu
See Ch'ien, Chung-shu

Qian Zhongshu
See Ch'ien, Chung-shu

Qroll
See Dagerman, Stig (Halvard)

Quarrington, Paul (Lewis) 1953- ..... **CLC 65**
See also CA 129; CANR 62, 95

Quasimodo, Salvatore 1901-1968 ..... **CLC 10**
See also CA 13-16; 25-28R; CAP 1; DLB
114; EW 12; MTCW 1; RGWL 2

Quatermass, Martin
See Carpenter, John (Howard)

Quay, Stephen 1947- .... **CLC 95**
See also CA 189

Quay, Timothy 1947- .... **CLC 95**
See also CA 189

Queen, Ellery .... **CLC 3, 11**
See also Dannay, Frederic; Davidson,
Avram (James); Deming, Richard; Fair-
man, Paul W.; Flora, Fletcher; Hoch, Ed-
ward D(entinger); Kane, Henry; Lee,
Manfred B(ennington); Marlowe, Stephen;
Powell, (Oval) Talmage; Sheldon, Walter
J(ames); Sturgeon, Theodore (Hamilton);
Tracy, Don(ald Fiske); Vance, John Hol-
brook
See also BPFB 3; CMW 4; MSW; RGAL 4

Queen, Ellery, Jr.
See Dannay, Frederic; Lee, Manfred
B(ennington)

Queneau, Raymond 1903-1976 ..... **CLC 2, 5,**
10, 42
See also CA 77-80; 69-72; CANR 32; DLB
72, 258; EW 12; GFL 1789 to the Present;
MTCW 1, 2; RGWL 2

Quevedo, Francisco de 1580-1645 .... **LC 23**

Quiller-Couch, Sir Arthur (Thomas)
1863-1944 .... **TCLC 53**
See also CA 118; 166; DLB 135, 153, 190;
HGG; RGEL 2; SUFW

Quin, Ann (Marie) 1936-1973 .... **CLC 6**
See also CA 9-12R; 45-48; DLB 14, 231

Quinn, Martin
See Smith, Martin Cruz

Quinn, Peter 1947- .... **CLC 91**
See also CA 197

Quinn, Simon
See Smith, Martin Cruz

Quintana, Leroy V. 1944- .... **PC 36**
See also CA 131; CANR 65; DAM MULT;
DLB 82; HLC 2; HW 1, 2

Quiroga, Horacio (Sylvestre)
1878-1937 .... **TCLC 20; HLC 2**
See also CA 117; 131; DAM MULT; HW
1; LAW; MTCW 1; RGSF 2; WLIT 1

Quoirez, Francoise 1935- .... **CLC 9**
See also Sagan, Francoise
See also CA 49-52; CANR 6, 39, 73; CWW
2; MTCW 1, 2; TWA

Raabe, Wilhelm (Karl) 1831-1910 . **TCLC 45**
See also CA 167; DLB 129

Rabe, David (William) 1940- .. **CLC 4, 8, 33;**
DC 16
See also CA 85-88; CABS 3; CAD; CANR
59; CD 5; DAM DRAM; DFS 3, 8, 13;
DLB 7, 228

Rabelais, Francois 1494-1553 .... **LC 5, 60;**
WLC
See also DA; DAB; DAC; DAM MST; EW
2; GFL Beginnings to 1789; RGWL 2;
TWA

Rabinovitch, Sholem 1859-1916
See Aleichem, Sholom
See also CA 104

Rabinyan, Dorit 1972- .... **CLC 119**
See also CA 170

Rachilde
See Vallette, Marguerite Eymery

Racine, Jean 1639-1699 .... **LC 28**
See also DA3; DAB; DAM MST; DLB 268;
EW 3; GFL Beginnings to 1789; RGWL
2; TWA

Radcliffe, Ann (Ward) 1764-1823 ... **NCLC 6,**
55, 106
See also DLB 39, 178; HGG; RGEL 2;
SUFW; WLIT 3

Radclyffe-Hall, Marguerite
See Hall, (Marguerite) Radclyffe

Radiguet, Raymond 1903-1923 ...... **TCLC 29**
See also CA 162; DLB 65; GFL 1789 to the
Present; RGWL 2

Radnoti, Miklos 1909-1944 .... **TCLC 16**
See also CA 118; CDWLB 4; DLB 215;
RGWL 2

Rado, James 1939- .... **CLC 17**
See also CA 105

Radvanyi, Netty 1900-1983
See Seghers, Anna
See also CA 85-88; 110; CANR 82

Rae, Ben
See Griffiths, Trevor

Raeburn, John (Hay) 1941- .... **CLC 34**
See also CA 57-60

Ragni, Gerome 1942-1991 .... **CLC 17**
See also CA 105; 134

Rahv, Philip .... **CLC 24**
See also Greenberg, Ivan
See also DLB 137

Raimund, Ferdinand Jakob
1790-1836 .... **NCLC 69**
See also DLB 90

Raine, Craig (Anthony) 1944- .. **CLC 32, 103**
See also CA 108; CANR 29, 51, 103; CP 7;
DLB 40; PFS 7

Raine, Kathleen (Jessie) 1908- ..... **CLC 7, 45**
See also CA 85-88; CANR 46, 109; CP 7;
DLB 20; MTCW 1; RGEL 2

Rainis, Janis 1865-1929 .... **TCLC 29**
See also CA 170; CDWLB 4; DLB 220

Rhys, Jean 1894(?)-1979 ...... **CLC 2, 4, 6, 14, 19, 51, 124; SSC 21**
See also BRWS 2; CA 25-28R; 85-88; CANR 35, 62; CDBLB 1945-1960; CD-WLB 3; DA3; DAM NOV; DLB 36, 117, 162; DNFS 2; MTCW 1, 2; RGEL 2; RGSF 2; RHW; TEA

Ribeiro, Darcy 1922-1997 .... **CLC 34**
See also CA 33-36R; 156

Ribeiro, Joao Ubaldo (Osorio Pimentel)
1941- .... **CLC 10, 67**
See also CA 81-84

Ribman, Ronald (Burt) 1932- .... **CLC 7**
See also CA 21-24R; CAD; CANR 46, 80; CD 5

Ricci, Nino 1959- .... **CLC 70**
See also CA 137; CCA 1

Rice, Anne 1941- .... **CLC 41, 128**
See also Rampling, Anne
See also AAYA 9; AMWS 7; BEST 89:2; BPFB 3; CA 65-68; CANR 12, 36, 53, 74, 100; CN 7; CPW; CSW; DA3; DAM POP; GLL 2; HGG; MTCW 2; YAW

Rice, Elmer (Leopold) 1892-1967 ...... **CLC 7, 49**
See also CA 21-22; 25-28R; CAP 2; DAM DRAM; DFS 12; DLB 4, 7; MTCW 1, 2; RGAL 4

Rice, Tim(othy Miles Bindon)
1944- .... **CLC 21**
See also CA 103; CANR 46; DFS 7

Rich, Adrienne (Cecile) 1929- ... **CLC 3, 6, 7, 11, 18, 36, 73, 76, 125; PC 5**
See also AMWS 1; CA 9-12R; CANR 20, 53, 74; CDALBS; CP 7; CSW; CWP; DA3; DAM POET; DLB 5, 67; EXPP; FW; MAWW; MTCW 1, 2; PAB; PFS 15; RGAL 4; WP

Rich, Barbara
See Graves, Robert (von Ranke)

Rich, Robert
See Trumbo, Dalton

Richard, Keith .... **CLC 17**
See also Richards, Keith

Richards, David Adams 1950- .... **CLC 59**
See also CA 93-96; CANR 60, 110; DAC; DLB 53

Richards, I(vor) A(rmstrong)
1893-1979 .... **CLC 14, 24**
See also BRWS 2; CA 41-44R; 89-92; CANR 34, 74; DLB 27; MTCW 2; RGEL 2

Richards, Keith 1943-
See Richard, Keith
See also CA 107; CANR 77

Richardson, Anne
See Roiphe, Anne (Richardson)

Richardson, Dorothy Miller
1873-1957 .... **TCLC 3**
See also CA 104; 192; DLB 36; FW; RGEL 2

Richardson (Robertson), Ethel Florence Lindesay 1870-1946
See Richardson, Henry Handel
See also CA 105; 190; DLB 230; RHW

Richardson, Henry Handel .... **TCLC 4**
See also Richardson (Robertson), Ethel Florence Lindesay
See also DLB 197; RGEL 2; RGSF 2

Richardson, John 1796-1852 .... **NCLC 55**
See also CCA 1; DAC; DLB 99

Richardson, Samuel 1689-1761 ...... **LC 1, 44; WLC**
See also BRW 3; CDBLB 1660-1789; DA; DAB; DAC; DAM MST, NOV; DLB 39; RGEL 2; TEA; WLIT 3

Richler, Mordecai 1931-2001 .... **CLC 3, 5, 9, 13, 18, 46, 70**
See also AITN 1; CA 65-68; 201; CANR 31, 62, 111; CCA 1; CLR 17; CWRI 5; DAC; DAM MST, NOV; DLB 53; MAI-CYA 1, 2; MTCW 1, 2; RGEL 2; SATA 44, 98; SATA-Brief 27; TWA

Richter, Conrad (Michael)
1890-1968 .... **CLC 30**
See also AAYA 21; BYA 2; CA 5-8R; 25-28R; CANR 23; DLB 9, 212; LAIT 1; MTCW 1, 2; RGAL 4; SATA 3; TCWW 2; TUS; YAW

Ricostranza, Tom
See Ellis, Trey

Riddell, Charlotte 1832-1906 .... **TCLC 40**
See also Riddell, Mrs. J. H.
See also CA 165; DLB 156

Riddell, Mrs. J. H.
See Riddell, Charlotte
See also HGG; SUFW

Ridge, John Rollin 1827-1867 .... **NCLC 82**
See also CA 144; DAM MULT; DLB 175; NNAL

Ridgeway, Jason
See Marlowe, Stephen

Ridgway, Keith 1965- .... **CLC 119**
See also CA 172

Riding, Laura .... **CLC 3, 7**
See also Jackson, Laura (Riding)
See also RGAL 4

Riefenstahl, Berta Helene Amalia 1902-
See Riefenstahl, Leni
See also CA 108

Riefenstahl, Leni .... **CLC 16**
See also Riefenstahl, Berta Helene Amalia

Riffe, Ernest
See Bergman, (Ernst) Ingmar

Riggs, (Rolla) Lynn 1899-1954 .... **TCLC 56**
See also CA 144; DAM MULT; DLB 175; NNAL

Riis, Jacob A(ugust) 1849-1914 ..... **TCLC 80**
See also CA 113; 168; DLB 23

Riley, James Whitcomb
1849-1916 .... **TCLC 51**
See also CA 118; 137; DAM POET; MAI-CYA 1, 2; RGAL 4; SATA 17

Riley, Tex
See Creasey, John

Rilke, Rainer Maria 1875-1926 .. **TCLC 1, 6, 19; PC 2**
See also CA 104; 132; CANR 62, 99; CD-WLB 2; DA3; DAM POET; DLB 81; EW 9; MTCW 1, 2; RGWL 2; TWA; WP

Rimbaud, (Jean Nicolas) Arthur
1854-1891 .... **NCLC 4, 35, 82; PC 3; WLC**
See also DA; DA3; DAB; DAC; DAM MST, POET; DLB 217; EW 7; GFL 1789 to the Present; RGWL 2; TWA; WP

Rinehart, Mary Roberts
1876-1958 .... **TCLC 52**
See also BPFB 3; CA 108; 166; RGAL 4; RHW

Ringmaster, The
See Mencken, H(enry) L(ouis)

Ringwood, Gwen(dolyn Margaret) Pharis
1910-1984 .... **CLC 48**
See also CA 148; 112; DLB 88

Rio, Michel 1945(?)- .... **CLC 43**
See also CA 201

Ritsos, Giannes
See Ritsos, Yannis

Ritsos, Yannis 1909-1990 .... **CLC 6, 13, 31**
See also CA 77-80; 133; CANR 39, 61; EW 12; MTCW 1; RGWL 2

Ritter, Erika 1948(?)- .... **CLC 52**
See also CD 5; CWD

Rivera, Jose Eustasio 1889-1928 ... **TCLC 35**
See also CA 162; HW 1, 2; LAW

Rivera, Tomas 1935-1984
See also CA 49-52; CANR 32; DLB 82; HLCS 2; HW 1; RGAL 4; SSFS 15; TCWW 2; WLIT 1

Rivers, Conrad Kent 1933-1968 .... **CLC 1**
See also BW 1; CA 85-88; DLB 41

Rivers, Elfrida
See Bradley, Marion Zimmer
See also GLL 1

Riverside, John
See Heinlein, Robert A(nson)

Rizal, Jose 1861-1896 .... **NCLC 27**

Roa Bastos, Augusto (Antonio)
1917- .... **CLC 45; HLC 2**
See also CA 131; DAM MULT; DLB 113; HW 1; LAW; RGSF 2; WLIT 1

Robbe-Grillet, Alain 1922- .... **CLC 1, 2, 4, 6, 8, 10, 14, 43, 128**
See also BPFB 3; CA 9-12R; CANR 33, 65; DLB 83; EW 13; GFL 1789 to the Present; IDFW 3, 4; MTCW 1, 2; RGWL 2; SSFS 15

Robbins, Harold 1916-1997 .... **CLC 5**
See also BPFB 3; CA 73-76; 162; CANR 26, 54; DA3; DAM NOV; MTCW 1, 2

Robbins, Thomas Eugene 1936-
See Robbins, Tom
See also CA 81-84; CANR 29, 59, 95; CN 7; CPW; CSW; DA3; DAM NOV, POP; MTCW 1, 2

Robbins, Tom .... **CLC 9, 32, 64**
See also Robbins, Thomas Eugene
See also AAYA 32; AMWS 10; BEST 90:3; BPFB 3; DLBY 1980; MTCW 2

Robbins, Trina 1938- .... **CLC 21**
See also CA 128

Roberts, Charles G(eorge) D(ouglas)
1860-1943 .... **TCLC 8**
See also CA 105; 188; CLR 33; CWRI 5; DLB 92; RGEL 2; RGSF 2; SATA 88; SATA-Brief 29

Roberts, Elizabeth Madox
1886-1941 .... **TCLC 68**
See also CA 111; 166; CWRI 5; DLB 9, 54, 102; RGAL 4; RHW; SATA 33; SATA-Brief 27; WCH

Roberts, Kate 1891-1985 .... **CLC 15**
See also CA 107; 116

Roberts, Keith (John Kingston)
1935-2000 .... **CLC 14**
See also CA 25-28R; CANR 46; DLB 261; SFW 4

Roberts, Kenneth (Lewis)
1885-1957 .... **TCLC 23**
See also CA 109; 199; DLB 9; RGAL 4; RHW

Roberts, Michele (Brigitte) 1949- ..... **CLC 48**
See also CA 115; CANR 58; CN 7; DLB 231; FW

Robertson, Ellis
See Ellison, Harlan (Jay); Silverberg, Robert

Robertson, Thomas William
1829-1871 .... **NCLC 35**
See also Robertson, Tom
See also DAM DRAM

Robertson, Tom
See Robertson, Thomas William
See also RGEL 2

Robeson, Kenneth
See Dent, Lester

Robinson, Edwin Arlington
1869-1935 .... **TCLC 5, 101; PC 1, 35**
See also AMW; CA 104; 133; CDALB 1865-1917; DA; DAC; DAM MST, POET; DLB 54; EXPP; MTCW 1, 2; PAB; PFS 4; RGAL 4; WP

Rousseau, Jean-Baptiste 1671-1741 ...... **LC 9**

Rousseau, Jean-Jacques 1712-1778 .... **LC 14, 36; WLC**
See also DA; DA3; DAB; DAC; DAM MST; EW 4; GFL Beginnings to 1789; RGWL 2; TWA

Roussel, Raymond 1877-1933 .... **TCLC 20**
See also CA 117; 201; GFL 1789 to the Present

Rovit, Earl (Herbert) 1927- .... **CLC 7**
See also CA 5-8R; CANR 12

Rowe, Elizabeth Singer 1674-1737 ..... **LC 44**
See also DLB 39, 95

Rowe, Nicholas 1674-1718 .... **LC 8**
See also DLB 84; RGEL 2

Rowlandson, Mary 1637(?)-1678 .... **LC 66**
See also DLB 24, 200; RGAL 4

Rowley, Ames Dorrance
See Lovecraft, H(oward) P(hillips)

Rowling, J(oanne) K(athleen)
1965- .... **CLC 137**
See also AAYA 34; BYA 13, 14; CA 173; CLR 66, 80; SATA 109

Rowson, Susanna Haswell
1762(?)-1824 .... **NCLC 5, 69**
See also DLB 37, 200; RGAL 4

Roy, Arundhati 1960(?)- .... **CLC 109**
See also CA 163; CANR 90; DLBY 1997

Roy, Gabrielle 1909-1983 .... **CLC 10, 14**
See also CA 53-56; 110; CANR 5, 61; CCA 1; DAB; DAC; DAM MST; DLB 68; MTCW 1; RGWL 2; SATA 104

Royko, Mike 1932-1997 .... **CLC 109**
See also CA 89-92; 157; CANR 26, 111; CPW

Rozanov, Vassili 1856-1919 .... **TCLC 104**

Rozewicz, Tadeusz 1921- ...... **CLC 9, 23, 139**
See also CA 108; CANR 36, 66; CWW 2; DA3; DAM POET; DLB 232; MTCW 1, 2

Ruark, Gibbons 1941- .... **CLC 3**
See also CA 33-36R; CAAS 23; CANR 14, 31, 57; DLB 120

Rubens, Bernice (Ruth) 1923- .... **CLC 19, 31**
See also CA 25-28R; CANR 33, 65; CN 7; DLB 14, 207; MTCW 1

Rubin, Harold
See Robbins, Harold

Rudkin, (James) David 1936- .... **CLC 14**
See also CA 89-92; CBD; CD 5; DLB 13

Rudnik, Raphael 1933- .... **CLC 7**
See also CA 29-32R

Ruffian, M.
See Hasek, Jaroslav (Matej Frantisek)

Ruiz, Jose Martinez .... **CLC 11**
See also Martinez Ruiz, Jose

Rukeyser, Muriel 1913-1980 . **CLC 6, 10, 15, 27; PC 12**
See also AMWS 6; CA 5-8R; 93-96; CANR 26, 60; DA3; DAM POET; DLB 48; FW; GLL 2; MTCW 1, 2; PFS 10; RGAL 4; SATA-Obit 22

Rule, Jane (Vance) 1931- .... **CLC 27**
See also CA 25-28R; CAAS 18; CANR 12, 87; CN 7; DLB 60; FW

Rulfo, Juan 1918-1986 .. **CLC 8, 80; HLC 2; SSC 25**
See also CA 85-88; 118; CANR 26; CD-WLB 3; DAM MULT; DLB 113; HW 1, 2; LAW; MTCW 1, 2; RGSF 2; RGWL 2; WLIT 1

Rumi, Jalal al-Din 1207-1273 .... **CMLC 20**
See also RGWL 2; WP

Runeberg, Johan 1804-1877 .... **NCLC 41**

Runyon, (Alfred) Damon
1884(?)-1946 .... **TCLC 10**
See also CA 107; 165; DLB 11, 86, 171; MTCW 2; RGAL 4

Rush, Norman 1933- .... **CLC 44**
See also CA 121; 126; INT 126

Rushdie, (Ahmed) Salman 1947- .... **CLC 23, 31, 55, 100; WLCS**
See also BEST 89:3; BPFB 3; BRWS 4; CA 108; 111; CANR 33, 56, 108; CN 7; CPW 1; DA3; DAB; DAC; DAM MST, NOV, POP; DLB 194; FANT; INT CA-111; MTCW 1, 2; RGEL 2; RGSF 2; TEA; WLIT 4

Rushforth, Peter (Scott) 1945- .... **CLC 19**
See also CA 101

Ruskin, John 1819-1900 .... **TCLC 63**
See also BRW 5; BYA 5; CA 114; 129; CD-BLB 1832-1890; DLB 55, 163, 190; RGEL 2; SATA 24; TEA; WCH

Russ, Joanna 1937- .... **CLC 15**
See also BPFB 3; CA 5-28R; CANR 11, 31, 65; CN 7; DLB 8; FW; GLL 1; MTCW 1; SCFW 2; SFW 4

Russell, George William 1867-1935
See A.E.; Baker, Jean H.
See also BRWS 8; CA 104; 153; CDBLB 1890-1914; DAM POET; RGEL 2

Russell, Jeffrey Burton 1934- .... **CLC 70**
See also CA 25-28R; CANR 11, 28, 52

Russell, (Henry) Ken(neth Alfred)
1927- .... **CLC 16**
See also CA 105

Russell, William Martin 1947-
See Russell, Willy
See also CA 164; CANR 107

Russell, Willy .... **CLC 60**
See also Russell, William Martin
See also CBD; CD 5; DLB 233

Rutherford, Mark .... **TCLC 25**
See also White, William Hale
See also DLB 18; RGEL 2

Ruyslinck, Ward .... **CLC 14**
See also Belser, Reimond Karel Maria de

Ryan, Cornelius (John) 1920-1974 .... **CLC 7**
See also CA 69-72; 53-56; CANR 38

Ryan, Michael 1946- .... **CLC 65**
See also CA 49-52; CANR 109; DLBY 1982

Ryan, Tim
See Dent, Lester

Rybakov, Anatoli (Naumovich)
1911-1998 .... **CLC 23, 53**
See also CA 126; 135; 172; SATA 79; SATA-Obit 108

Ryder, Jonathan
See Ludlum, Robert

Ryga, George 1932-1987 .... **CLC 14**
See also CA 101; 124; CANR 43, 90; CCA 1; DAC; DAM MST; DLB 60

S. H.
See Hartmann, Sadakichi

S. S.
See Sassoon, Siegfried (Lorraine)

Saba, Umberto 1883-1957 .... **TCLC 33**
See also CA 144; CANR 79; DLB 114; RGWL 2

Sabatini, Rafael 1875-1950 .... **TCLC 47**
See also BPFB 3; CA 162; RHW

Sabato, Ernesto (R.) 1911- .... **CLC 10, 23; HLC 2**
See also CA 97-100; CANR 32, 65; CD-WLB 3; DAM MULT; DLB 145; HW 1, 2; LAW; MTCW 1, 2

Sa-Carneiro, Mario de 1890-1916 . **TCLC 83**

Sacastru, Martin
See Bioy Casares, Adolfo
See also CWW 2

Sacher-Masoch, Leopold von
1836(?)-1895 .... **NCLC 31**

Sachs, Marilyn (Stickle) 1927- .... **CLC 35**
See also AAYA 2; BYA 6; CA 17-20R; CANR 13, 47; CLR 2; JRDA; MAICYA 1, 2; SAAS 2; SATA 3, 68; SATA-Essay 110; WYA; YAW

Sachs, Nelly 1891-1970 .... **CLC 14, 98**
See also CA 17-18; 25-28R; CANR 87; CAP 2; MTCW 2; RGWL 2

Sackler, Howard (Oliver)
1929-1982 .... **CLC 14**
See also CA 61-64; 108; CAD; CANR 30; DFS 15; DLB 7

Sacks, Oliver (Wolf) 1933- .... **CLC 67**
See also CA 53-56; CANR 28, 50, 76; CPW; DA3; INT CANR-28; MTCW 1, 2

Sadakichi
See Hartmann, Sadakichi

Sade, Donatien Alphonse Francois
1740-1814 .... **NCLC 3, 47**
See also EW 4; GFL Beginnings to 1789; RGWL 2

Sadoff, Ira 1945- .... **CLC 9**
See also CA 53-56; CANR 5, 21, 109; DLB 120

Saetone
See Camus, Albert

Safire, William 1929- .... **CLC 10**
See also CA 17-20R; CANR 31, 54, 91

Sagan, Carl (Edward) 1934-1996 .... **CLC 30, 112**
See also AAYA 2; CA 25-28R; 155; CANR 11, 36, 74; CPW; DA3; MTCW 1, 2; SATA 58; SATA-Obit 94

Sagan, Francoise .... **CLC 3, 6, 9, 17, 36**
See also Quoirez, Francoise
See also CWW 2; DLB 83; GFL 1789 to the Present; MTCW 2

Sahgal, Nayantara (Pandit) 1927- .... **CLC 41**
See also CA 9-12R; CANR 11, 88; CN 7

Said, Edward W. 1935- .... **CLC 123**
See also CA 21-24R; CANR 45, 74, 107; DLB 67; MTCW 2

Saint, H(arry) F. 1941- .... **CLC 50**
See also CA 127

St. Aubin de Teran, Lisa 1953-
See Teran, Lisa St. Aubin de
See also CA 118; 126; CN 7; INT 126

Saint Birgitta of Sweden c.
1303-1373 .... **CMLC 24**

Sainte-Beuve, Charles Augustin
1804-1869 .... **NCLC 5**
See also DLB 217; EW 6; GFL 1789 to the Present

Saint-Exupery, Antoine (Jean Baptiste Marie Roger) de 1900-1944 .... **TCLC 2, 56; WLC**
See also BPFB 3; BYA 3; CA 108; 132; CLR 10; DA3; DAM NOV; DLB 72; EW 12; GFL 1789 to the Present; LAIT 3; MAICYA 1, 2; MTCW 1, 2; RGWL 2; SATA 20; TWA

St. John, David
See Hunt, E(verette) Howard, (Jr.)

St. John, J. Hector
See Crevecoeur, Michel Guillaume Jean de

Saint-John Perse
See Leger, (Marie-Rene Auguste) Alexis Saint-Leger
See also EW 10; GFL 1789 to the Present; RGWL 2

Saintsbury, George (Edward Bateman)
1845-1933 .... **TCLC 31**
See also CA 160; DLB 57, 149

Sait Faik .... **TCLC 23**
See also Abasiyanik, Sait Faik

Sheridan, Richard Brinsley
  1751-1816 .... NCLC **5**, **91**; DC **1**; WLC
  See also BRW 3; CDBLB 1660-1789; DA;
  DAB; DAC; DAM DRAM, MST; DFS
  15; DLB 89; WLIT 3
Sherman, Jonathan Marc .... CLC **55**
Sherman, Martin 1941(?)- .... CLC **19**
  See also CA 116; 123; CANR 86
Sherwin, Judith Johnson
  See Johnson, Judith (Emlyn)
  See also CANR 85; CP 7; CWP
Sherwood, Frances 1940- .... CLC **81**
  See also CA 146
Sherwood, Robert E(mmet)
  1896-1955 .... TCLC **3**
  See also CA 104; 153; CANR 86; DAM
  DRAM; DFS 15; DLB 7, 26, 249; IDFW
  3, 4; RGAL 4
Shestov, Lev 1866-1938 .... TCLC **56**
Shevchenko, Taras 1814-1861 .... NCLC **54**
Shiel, M(atthew) P(hipps)
  1865-1947 .... TCLC **8**
  See also Holmes, Gordon
  See also CA 106; 160; DLB 153; HGG;
  MTCW 2; SFW 4; SUFW
Shields, Carol 1935- .... CLC **91**, **113**
  See also AMWS 7; CA 81-84; CANR 51,
  74, 98; CCA 1; CN 7; CPW; DA3; DAC;
  MTCW 2
Shields, David 1956- .... CLC **97**
  See also CA 124; CANR 48, 99
Shiga, Naoya 1883-1971 ..... CLC **33**; SSC **23**
  See also Shiga Naoya
  See also CA 101; 33-36R; MJW
Shiga Naoya
  See Shiga, Naoya
  See also DLB 180
Shilts, Randy 1951-1994 .... CLC **85**
  See also AAYA 19; CA 115; 127; 144;
  CANR 45; DA3; GLL 1; INT 127; MTCW
  2
Shimazaki, Haruki 1872-1943
  See Shimazaki Toson
  See also CA 105; 134; CANR 84
Shimazaki Toson .... TCLC **5**
  See also Shimazaki, Haruki
  See also DLB 180
Sholokhov, Mikhail (Aleksandrovich)
  1905-1984 .... CLC **7**, **15**
  See also CA 101; 112; MTCW 1, 2; RGWL
  2; SATA-Obit 36
Shone, Patric
  See Hanley, James
Shreve, Susan Richards 1939- .... CLC **23**
  See also CA 49-52; CAAS 5; CANR 5, 38,
  69, 100; MAICYA 1, 2; SATA 46, 95;
  SATA-Brief 41
Shue, Larry 1946-1985 .... CLC **52**
  See also CA 145; 117; DAM DRAM; DFS
  7
Shu-Jen, Chou 1881-1936
  See Lu Hsun
  See also CA 104
Shulman, Alix Kates 1932- .... CLC **2**, **10**
  See also CA 29-32R; CANR 43; FW; SATA
  7
Shusaku, Endo
  See Endo, Shusaku
Shuster, Joe 1914-1992 .... CLC **21**
Shute, Nevil .... CLC **30**
  See also Norway, Nevil Shute
  See also BPFB 3; DLB 255; NFS 9; RHW;
  SFW 4
Shuttle, Penelope (Diane) 1947- .... CLC **7**
  See also CA 93-96; CANR 39, 84, 92, 108;
  CP 7; CWP; DLB 14, 40
Sidney, Mary 1561-1621 .... LC **19**, **39**
  See also Sidney Herbert, Mary

Sidney, Sir Philip 1554-1586 . LC **19**, **39**; PC
32
  See also BRW 1; BRWR 2; CDBLB Before
  1660; DA; DA3; DAB; DAC; DAM MST,
  POET; DLB 167; EXPP; PAB; RGEL 2;
  TEA; WP
Sidney Herbert, Mary
  See Sidney, Mary
  See also DLB 167
Siegel, Jerome 1914-1996 .... CLC **21**
  See also CA 116; 169; 151
Siegel, Jerry
  See Siegel, Jerome
Sienkiewicz, Henryk (Adam Alexander Pius)
  1846-1916 .... TCLC **3**
  See also CA 104; 134; CANR 84; RGSF 2;
  RGWL 2
Sierra, Gregorio Martinez
  See Martinez Sierra, Gregorio
Sierra, Maria (de la O'LeJarraga) Martinez
  See Martinez Sierra, Maria (de la
  O'LeJarraga)
Sigal, Clancy 1926- .... CLC **7**
  See also CA 1-4R; CANR 85; CN 7
Sigourney, Lydia H.
  See Sigourney, Lydia Howard (Huntley)
  See also DLB 73, 183
Sigourney, Lydia Howard (Huntley)
  1791-1865 .... NCLC **21**, **87**
  See also Sigourney, Lydia H.; Sigourney,
  Lydia Huntley
  See also DLB 1
Sigourney, Lydia Huntley
  See Sigourney, Lydia Howard (Huntley)
  See also DLB 42, 239, 243
Siguenza y Gongora, Carlos de
  1645-1700 .... LC **8**; HLCS **2**
  See also LAW
Sigurjonsson, Johann 1880-1919 ... TCLC **27**
  See also CA 170
Sikelianos, Angelos 1884-1951 ...... TCLC **39**;
PC 29
  See also RGWL 2
Silkin, Jon 1930-1997 .... CLC **2**, **6**, **43**
  See also CA 5-8R; CAAS 5; CANR 89; CP
  7; DLB 27
Silko, Leslie (Marmon) 1948- .... CLC **23**, **74**,
  114; SSC **37**; WLCS
  See also AAYA 14; AMWS 4; ANW; BYA
  12; CA 115; 122; CANR 45, 65; CN 7;
  CP 7; CPW 1; CWP; DA; DA3; DAC;
  DAM MST, MULT, POP; DLB 143, 175,
  256; EXPP; EXPS; LAIT 4; MTCW 2;
  NFS 4; NNAL; PFS 9; RGAL 4; RGSF 2;
  SSFS 4, 8, 10, 11
Sillanpaa, Frans Eemil 1888-1964 ... CLC **19**
  See also CA 129; 93-96; MTCW 1
Sillitoe, Alan 1928- .. CLC **1**, **3**, **6**, **10**, **19**, **57**,
  148
  See also AITN 1; BRWS 5; CA 9-12R;
  CAAE 191; CAAS 2; CANR 8, 26, 55;
  CDBLB 1960 to Present; CN 7; DLB 14,
  139; MTCW 1, 2; RGEL 2; RGSF 2;
  SATA 61
Silone, Ignazio 1900-1978 .... CLC **4**
  See also CA 25-28; 81-84; CANR 34; CAP
  2; DLB 264; EW 12; MTCW 1; RGSF 2;
  RGWL 2
Silone, Ignazione
  See Silone, Ignazio
Silva, Jose Asuncion
  See da Silva, Antonio Jose
  See also LAW
Silver, Joan Micklin 1935- .... CLC **20**
  See also CA 114; 121; INT 121
Silver, Nicholas
  See Faust, Frederick (Schiller)
  See also TCWW 2

Silverberg, Robert 1935- .... CLC **7**, **140**
  See also AAYA 24; BPFB 3; BYA 7, 9; CA
  1-4R, 186; CAAE 186; CAAS 3; CANR
  1, 20, 36, 85; CLR 59; CN 7; CPW; DAM
  POP; DLB 8; INT CANR-20; MAICYA
  1, 2; MTCW 1, 2; SATA 13, 91; SATA-
  Essay 104; SCFW 2; SFW 4
Silverstein, Alvin 1933- .... CLC **17**
  See also CA 49-52; CANR 2; CLR 25;
  JRDA; MAICYA 1, 2; SATA 8, 69, 124
Silverstein, Virginia B(arbara Opshelor)
  1937- .... CLC **17**
  See also CA 49-52; CANR 2; CLR 25;
  JRDA; MAICYA 1, 2; SATA 8, 69, 124
Sim, Georges
  See Simenon, Georges (Jacques Christian)
Simak, Clifford D(onald) 1904-1988 . CLC **1**,
  55
  See also CA 1-4R; 125; CANR 1, 35; DLB
  8; MTCW 1; SATA-Obit 56; SFW 4
Simenon, Georges (Jacques Christian)
  1903-1989 .... CLC **1**, **2**, **3**, **8**, **18**, **47**
  See also BPFB 3; CA 85-88; 129; CANR
  35; CMW 4; DA3; DAM POP; DLB 72;
  DLBY 1989; EW 12; GFL 1789 to the
  Present; MSW; MTCW 1, 2; RGWL 2
Simic, Charles 1938- .... CLC **6**, **9**, **22**, **49**, **68**,
  130
  See also AMWS 8; CA 29-32R; CAAS 4;
  CANR 12, 33, 52, 61, 96; CP 7; DA3;
  DAM POET; DLB 105; MTCW 2; PFS 7;
  RGAL 4; WP
Simmel, Georg 1858-1918 .... TCLC **64**
  See also CA 157
Simmons, Charles (Paul) 1924- .... CLC **57**
  See also CA 89-92; INT 89-92
Simmons, Dan 1948- .... CLC **44**
  See also AAYA 16; CA 138; CANR 53, 81;
  CPW; DAM POP; HGG
Simmons, James (Stewart Alexander)
  1933- .... CLC **43**
  See also CA 105; CAAS 21; CP 7; DLB 40
Simms, William Gilmore
  1806-1870 .... NCLC **3**
  See also DLB 3, 30, 59, 73, 248, 254;
  RGAL 4
Simon, Carly 1945- .... CLC **26**
  See also CA 105
Simon, Claude 1913-1984 ... CLC **4**, **9**, **15**, **39**
  See also CA 89-92; CANR 33; DAM NOV;
  DLB 83; EW 13; GFL 1789 to the Present;
  MTCW 1
Simon, Myles
  See Follett, Ken(neth Martin)
Simon, (Marvin) Neil 1927- ... CLC **6**, **11**, **31**,
  39, **70**; DC **14**
  See also AAYA 32; AITN 1; AMWS 4; CA
  21-24R; CANR 26, 54, 87; CD 5; DA3;
  DAM DRAM; DFS 2, 6, 12; DLB 7, 266;
  LAIT 4; MTCW 1, 2; RGAL 4; TUS
Simon, Paul (Frederick) 1941(?)- ..... CLC **17**
  See also CA 116; 153
Simonon, Paul 1956(?)- .... CLC **30**
Simonson, Rick ed. .... CLC **70**
Simpson, Harriette
  See Arnow, Harriette (Louisa) Simpson
Simpson, Louis (Aston Marantz)
  1923- .... CLC **4**, **7**, **9**, **32**, **149**
  See also AMWS 9; CA 1-4R; CAAS 4;
  CANR 1, 61; CP 7; DAM POET; DLB 5;
  MTCW 1, 2; PFS 7, 11, 14; RGAL 4
Simpson, Mona (Elizabeth) 1957- ... CLC **44**,
  146
  See also CA 122; 135; CANR 68, 103; CN
  7
Simpson, N(orman) F(rederick)
  1919- .... CLC **29**
  See also CA 13-16R; CBD; DLB 13;
  RGEL 2

Thames, C. H.
    See Marlowe, Stephen
Tharoor, Shashi 1956- .... **CLC 70**
    See also CA 141; CANR 91; CN 7
Thelwell, Michael Miles 1939- .... **CLC 22**
    See also BW 2; CA 101
Theobald, Lewis, Jr.
    See Lovecraft, H(oward) P(hillips)
Theocritus c. 310 B.C.- .... **CMLC 45**
    See also AW 1; DLB 176; RGWL 2
Theodorescu, Ion N. 1880-1967
    See Arghezi, Tudor
    See also CA 116
Theriault, Yves 1915-1983 .... **CLC 79**
    See also CA 102; CCA 1; DAC; DAM
    MST; DLB 88
Theroux, Alexander (Louis) 1939- .... **CLC 2,
    25**
    See also CA 85-88; CANR 20, 63; CN 7
Theroux, Paul (Edward) 1941- ..... **CLC 5, 8,
    11, 15, 28, 46**
    See also AAYA 28; AMWS 8; BEST 89:4;
    BPFB 3; CA 33-36R; CANR 20, 45, 74;
    CDALBS; CN 7; CPW 1; DA3; DAM
    POP; DLB 2, 218; HGG; MTCW 1, 2;
    RGAL 4; SATA 44, 109; TUS
Thesen, Sharon 1946- .... **CLC 56**
    See also CA 163; CP 7; CWP
Thespis fl. 6th cent. B.C. .... **CMLC 51**
Thevenin, Denis
    See Duhamel, Georges
Thibault, Jacques Anatole Francois
    1844-1924
    See France, Anatole
    See also CA 106; 127; DA3; DAM NOV;
    MTCW 1, 2; TWA
Thiele, Colin (Milton) 1920- .... **CLC 17**
    See also CA 29-32R; CANR 12, 28, 53,
    105; CLR 27; MAICYA 1, 2; SAAS 2;
    SATA 14, 72, 125; YAW
Thistlethwaite, Bel
    See Wetherald, Agnes Ethelwyn
Thomas, Audrey (Callahan) 1935- .... **CLC 7,
    13, 37, 107; SSC 20**
    See also AITN 2; CA 21-24R; CAAS 19;
    CANR 36, 58; CN 7; DLB 60; MTCW 1;
    RGSF 2
Thomas, Augustus 1857-1934 .... **TCLC 97**
Thomas, D(onald) M(ichael) 1935- . **CLC 13,
    22, 31, 132**
    See also BPFB 3; BRWS 4; CA 61-64;
    CAAS 11; CANR 17, 45, 75; CDBLB
    1960 to Present; CN 7; CP 7; DA3; DLB
    40, 207; HGG; INT CANR-17; MTCW 1,
    2; SFW 4
Thomas, Dylan (Marlais)
    1914-1953 ... **TCLC 1, 8, 45, 105; PC 2;
    SSC 3, 44; WLC**
    See also BRWS 1; CA 104; 120; CANR 65;
    CDBLB 1945-1960; DA; DA3; DAB;
    DAC; DAM DRAM, MST, POET; DLB
    13, 20, 139; EXPP; LAIT 3; MTCW 1, 2;
    PAB; PFS 1, 3, 8; RGEL 2; RGSF 2;
    SATA 60; TEA; WLIT 4; WP
Thomas, (Philip) Edward
    1878-1917 .... **TCLC 10**
    See also BRW 6; BRWS 3; CA 106; 153;
    DAM POET; DLB 19, 98, 156, 216; PAB;
    RGEL 2
Thomas, Joyce Carol 1938- .... **CLC 35**
    See also AAYA 12; BW 2, 3; CA 113; 116;
    CANR 48; CLR 19; DLB 33; INT CA-
    116; JRDA; MAICYA 1, 2; MTCW 1, 2;
    SAAS 7; SATA 40, 78, 123; WYA; YAW
Thomas, Lewis 1913-1993 .... **CLC 35**
    See also ANW; CA 85-88; 143; CANR 38,
    60; MTCW 1, 2
Thomas, M. Carey 1857-1935 .... **TCLC 89**
    See also FW

Thomas, Paul
    See Mann, (Paul) Thomas
Thomas, Piri 1928- .... **CLC 17; HLCS 2**
    See also CA 73-76; HW 1
Thomas, R(onald) S(tuart)
    1913-2000 .... **CLC 6, 13, 48**
    See also CA 89-92; 189; CAAS 4; CANR
    30; CDBLB 1960 to Present; CP 7; DAB;
    DAM POET; DLB 27; MTCW 1; RGEL
    2
Thomas, Ross (Elmore) 1926-1995 .. **CLC 39**
    See also CA 33-36R; 150; CANR 22, 63;
    CMW 4
Thompson, Francis (Joseph)
    1859-1907 .... **TCLC 4**
    See also BRW 5; CA 104; 189; CDBLB
    1890-1914; DLB 19; RGEL 2; TEA
Thompson, Francis Clegg
    See Mencken, H(enry) L(ouis)
Thompson, Hunter S(tockton)
    1937(?)- .... **CLC 9, 17, 40, 104**
    See also BEST 89:1; BPFB 3; CA 17-20R;
    CANR 23, 46, 74, 77, 111; CPW; CSW;
    DA3; DAM POP; DLB 185; MTCW 1, 2;
    TUS
Thompson, James Myers
    See Thompson, Jim (Myers)
Thompson, Jim (Myers)
    1906-1977(?) .... **CLC 69**
    See also BPFB 3; CA 140; CMW 4; CPW;
    DLB 226; MSW
Thompson, Judith .... **CLC 39**
    See also CWD
Thomson, James 1700-1748 .... **LC 16, 29, 40**
    See also BRWS 3; DAM POET; DLB 95;
    RGEL 2
Thomson, James 1834-1882 .... **NCLC 18**
    See also DAM POET; DLB 35; RGEL 2
Thoreau, Henry David 1817-1862 .. **NCLC 7,
    21, 61; PC 30; WLC**
    See also AAYA 42; AMW; ANW; BYA 3;
    CDALB 1640-1865; DA; DA3; DAB;
    DAC; DAM MST; DLB 1, 183, 223;
    LAIT 2; NCFS 3; RGAL 4; TUS
Thorndike, E. L.
    See Thorndike, Edward L(ee)
Thorndike, Edward L(ee)
    1874-1949 .... **TCLC 107**
    See also CA 121
Thornton, Hall
    See Silverberg, Robert
Thubron, Colin (Gerald Dryden)
    1939- .... **CLC 163**
    See also CA 25-28R; CANR 12, 29, 59, 95;
    CN 7; DLB 204, 231
Thucydides c. 455 B.C.-c. 395
    B.C. .... **CMLC 17**
    See also AW 1; DLB 176; RGWL 2
Thumboo, Edwin Nadason 1933- .... **PC 30**
    See also CA 194
Thurber, James (Grover)
    1894-1961 .. **CLC 5, 11, 25, 125; SSC 1,
    47**
    See also AMWS 1; BPFB 3; BYA 5; CA
    73-76; CANR 17, 39; CDALB 1929-1941;
    CWRI 5; DA; DA3; DAB; DAC; DAM
    DRAM, MST, NOV; DLB 4, 11, 22, 102;
    EXPS; FANT; LAIT 3; MAICYA 1, 2;
    MTCW 1, 2; RGAL 4; RGSF 2; SATA
    13; SSFS 1, 10; SUFW; TUS
Thurman, Wallace (Henry)
    1902-1934 .... **TCLC 6; BLC 3**
    See also BW 1, 3; CA 104; 124; CANR 81;
    DAM MULT; DLB 51
Tibullus c. 54 B.C.-c. 18 B.C. .... **CMLC 36**
    See also AW 2; DLB 211; RGWL 2
Ticheburn, Cheviot
    See Ainsworth, William Harrison

Tieck, (Johann) Ludwig
    1773-1853 .... **NCLC 5, 46; SSC 31**
    See also CDWLB 2; DLB 90; EW 5; IDTP;
    RGSF 2; RGWL 2; SUFW
Tiger, Derry
    See Ellison, Harlan (Jay)
Tilghman, Christopher 1948(?)- .... **CLC 65**
    See also CA 159; CSW; DLB 244
Tillich, Paul (Johannes)
    1886-1965 .... **CLC 131**
    See also CA 5-8R; 25-28R; CANR 33;
    MTCW 1, 2
Tillinghast, Richard (Williford)
    1940- .... **CLC 29**
    See also CA 29-32R; CAAS 23; CANR 26,
    51, 96; CP 7; CSW
Timrod, Henry 1828-1867 .... **NCLC 25**
    See also DLB 3, 248; RGAL 4
Tindall, Gillian (Elizabeth) 1938- ...... **CLC 7**
    See also CA 21-24R; CANR 11, 65, 107;
    CN 7
Tiptree, James, Jr. .... **CLC 48, 50**
    See also Sheldon, Alice Hastings Bradley
    See also DLB 8; SCFW 2; SFW 4
Tirso de Molina
    See Tirso de Molina
    See also RGWL 2
Tirso de Molina 1580(?)-1648 ..... **LC 73; DC
    13; HLCS 2**
    See also Tirso de Molina
Titmarsh, Michael Angelo
    See Thackeray, William Makepeace
**Tocqueville, Alexis (Charles Henri Maurice
    Clerel Comte) de** 1805-1859 .. **NCLC 7,
    63**
    See also EW 6; GFL 1789 to the Present;
    TWA
Toibin, Colm 1955- .... **CLC 162**
    See also CA 142; CANR 81
Tolkien, J(ohn) R(onald) R(euel)
    1892-1973 .... **CLC 1, 2, 3, 8, 12, 38;
    WLC**
    See also AAYA 10; AITN 1; BPFB 3;
    BRWS 2; CA 17-18; 45-48; CANR 36;
    CAP 2; CDBLB 1914-1945; CLR 56;
    CPW 1; CWRI 5; DA; DA3; DAB; DAC;
    DAM MST, NOV, POP; DLB 15, 160,
    255; EFS 2; FANT; JRDA; LAIT 1; MAI-
    CYA 1, 2; MTCW 1, 2; NFS 8; RGEL 2;
    SATA 2, 32, 100; SATA-Obit 24; SFW 4;
    SUFW; TEA; WCH; WYA; YAW
Toller, Ernst 1893-1939 .... **TCLC 10**
    See also CA 107; 186; DLB 124; RGWL 2
Tolson, M. B.
    See Tolson, Melvin B(eaunorus)
Tolson, Melvin B(eaunorus)
    1898(?)-1966 .... **CLC 36, 105; BLC 3**
    See also AFAW 1, 2; BW 1, 3; CA 124; 89-
    92; CANR 80; DAM MULT, POET; DLB
    48, 76; RGAL 4
Tolstoi, Aleksei Nikolaevich
    See Tolstoy, Alexey Nikolaevich
Tolstoi, Lev
    See Tolstoy, Leo (Nikolaevich)
    See also RGSF 2; RGWL 2
Tolstoy, Alexey Nikolaevich
    1882-1945 .... **TCLC 18**
    See also CA 107; 158; SFW 4
Tolstoy, Leo (Nikolaevich)
    1828-1910 .. **TCLC 4, 11, 17, 28, 44, 79;
    SSC 9, 30, 45, 54; WLC**
    See also Tolstoi, Lev
    See also CA 104; 123; DA; DA3; DAB;
    DAC; DAM MST, NOV; DLB 238; EFS
    2; EW 7; EXPS; IDTP; LAIT 2; NFS 10;
    SATA 26; SSFS 5; TWA
Tolstoy, Count Leo
    See Tolstoy, Leo (Nikolaevich)

Turgenev, Ivan (Sergeevich) 1818-1883 .... **NCLC 21, 37; DC 7; SSC 7; WLC**
See also DA; DAB; DAC; DAM MST, NOV; DFS 6; DLB 238; EW 6; RGSF 2; RGWL 2; TWA

Turgot, Anne-Robert-Jacques 1727-1781 .... **LC 26**

Turner, Frederick 1943- .... **CLC 48**
See also CA 73-76; CAAS 10; CANR 12, 30, 56; DLB 40

Turton, James
See Crace, Jim

Tutu, Desmond M(pilo) 1931- .... **CLC 80; BLC 3**
See also BW 1, 3; CA 125; CANR 67, 81; DAM MULT

Tutuola, Amos 1920-1997 ...... **CLC 5, 14, 29; BLC 3**
See also AFW; BW 2, 3; CA 9-12R; 159; CANR 27, 66; CDWLB 3; CN 7; DA3; DAM MULT; DLB 125; DNFS 2; MTCW 1, 2; RGEL 2; WLIT 2

Twain, Mark .... **TCLC 6, 12, 19, 36, 48, 59; SSC 34; WLC**
See also Clemens, Samuel Langhorne
See also AAYA 20; AMW; BPFB 3; BYA 2, 3, 11, 14; CLR 58, 60, 66; DLB 11; EXPN; EXPS; FANT; LAIT 2; NFS 1, 6; RGAL 4; RGSF 2; SFW 4; SSFS 1, 7; SUFW; TUS; WCH; WYA; YAW

Tyler, Anne 1941- . **CLC 7, 11, 18, 28, 44, 59, 103**
See also AAYA 18; AMWS 4; BEST 89:1; BPFB 3; BYA 12; CA 9-12R; CANR 11, 33, 53, 109; CDALBS; CN 7; CPW; CSW; DAM NOV, POP; DLB 6, 143; DLBY 1982; EXPN; MAWW; MTCW 1, 2; NFS 2, 7, 10; RGAL 4; SATA 7, 90; TUS; YAW

Tyler, Royall 1757-1826 .... **NCLC 3**
See also DLB 37; RGAL 4

Tynan, Katharine 1861-1931 .... **TCLC 3**
See also CA 104; 167; DLB 153, 240; FW

Tyutchev, Fyodor 1803-1873 .... **NCLC 34**

Tzara, Tristan 1896-1963 ..... **CLC 47; PC 27**
See also CA 153; 89-92; DAM POET; MTCW 2

Uhry, Alfred 1936- .... **CLC 55**
See also CA 127; 133; CAD; CD 5; CSW; DA3; DAM DRAM, POP; DFS 15; INT CA-133

Ulf, Haerved
See Strindberg, (Johan) August

Ulf, Harved
See Strindberg, (Johan) August

Ulibarri, Sabine R(eyes) 1919- .... **CLC 83; HLCS 1**
See also CA 131; CANR 81; DAM MULT; DLB 82; HW 1, 2; RGSF 2

Unamuno (y Jugo), Miguel de 1864-1936 . **TCLC 2, 9; HLC 2; SSC 11**
See also CA 104; 131; CANR 81; DAM MULT, NOV; DLB 108; EW 8; HW 1, 2; MTCW 1, 2; RGSF 2; RGWL 2; TWA

Undercliffe, Errol
See Campbell, (John) Ramsey

Underwood, Miles
See Glassco, John

Undset, Sigrid 1882-1949 ..... **TCLC 3; WLC**
See also CA 104; 129; DA; DA3; DAB; DAC; DAM MST, NOV; EW 9; FW; MTCW 1, 2; RGWL 2

Ungaretti, Giuseppe 1888-1970 ... **CLC 7, 11, 15**
See also CA 19-20; 25-28R; CAP 2; DLB 114; EW 10; RGWL 2

Unger, Douglas 1952- .... **CLC 34**
See also CA 130; CANR 94

Unsworth, Barry (Forster) 1930- .... **CLC 76, 127**
See also BRWS 7; CA 25-28R; CANR 30, 54; CN 7; DLB 194

Updike, John (Hoyer) 1932- . **CLC 1, 2, 3, 5, 7, 9, 13, 15, 23, 34, 43, 70, 139; SSC 13, 27; WLC**
See also AAYA 36; AMW; AMWR 1; BPFB 3; BYA 12; CA 1-4R; CABS 1; CANR 4, 33, 51, 94; CDALB 1968-1988; CN 7; CP 7; CPW 1; DA; DA3; DAB; DAC; DAM MST, NOV, POET, POP; DLB 2, 5, 143, 218, 227; DLBD 3; DLBY 1980, 1982, 1997; EXPP; HGG; MTCW 1, 2; NFS 12; RGAL 4; RGSF 2; SSFS 3; TUS

Upshaw, Margaret Mitchell
See Mitchell, Margaret (Munnerlyn)

Upton, Mark
See Sanders, Lawrence

Upward, Allen 1863-1926 .... **TCLC 85**
See also CA 117; 187; DLB 36

Urdang, Constance (Henriette) 1922-1996 .... **CLC 47**
See also CA 21-24R; CANR 9, 24; CP 7; CWP

Uriel, Henry
See Faust, Frederick (Schiller)

Uris, Leon (Marcus) 1924- .... **CLC 7, 32**
See also AITN 1, 2; BEST 89:2; BPFB 3; CA 1-4R; CANR 1, 40, 65; CN 7; CPW 1; DA3; DAM NOV, POP; MTCW 1, 2; SATA 49

Urista, Alberto H. 1947- .... **PC 34**
See also Alurista
See also CA 45-48, 182; CANR 2, 32; HLCS 1; HW 1

Urmuz
See Codrescu, Andrei

Urquhart, Guy
See McAlmon, Robert (Menzies)

Urquhart, Jane 1949- .... **CLC 90**
See also CA 113; CANR 32, 68; CCA 1; DAC

Usigli, Rodolfo 1905-1979
See also CA 131; HLCS 1; HW 1; LAW

Ustinov, Peter (Alexander) 1921- .... **CLC 1**
See also AITN 1; CA 13-16R; CANR 25, 51; CBD; CD 5; DLB 13; MTCW 2

U Tam'si, Gerald Felix Tchicaya
See Tchicaya, Gerald Felix

U Tam'si, Tchicaya
See Tchicaya, Gerald Felix

Vachss, Andrew (Henry) 1942- .... **CLC 106**
See also CA 118; CANR 44, 95; CMW 4

Vachss, Andrew H.
See Vachss, Andrew (Henry)

Vaculik, Ludvik 1926- .... **CLC 7**
See also CA 53-56; CANR 72; CWW 2; DLB 232

Vaihinger, Hans 1852-1933 .... **TCLC 71**
See also CA 116; 166

Valdez, Luis (Miguel) 1940- ..... **CLC 84; DC 10; HLC 2**
See also CA 101; CAD; CANR 32, 81; CD 5; DAM MULT; DFS 5; DLB 122; HW 1; LAIT 4

Valenzuela, Luisa 1938- .... **CLC 31, 104; HLCS 2; SSC 14**
See also CA 101; CANR 32, 65; CDWLB 3; CWW 2; DAM MULT; DLB 113; FW; HW 1, 2; LAW; RGSF 2

Valera y Alcala-Galiano, Juan 1824-1905 .... **TCLC 10**
See also CA 106

Valery, (Ambroise) Paul (Toussaint Jules) 1871-1945 .... **TCLC 4, 15; PC 9**
See also CA 104; 122; DA3; DAM POET; DLB 258; EW 8; GFL 1789 to the Present; MTCW 1, 2; RGWL 2; TWA

Valle-Inclan, Ramon (Maria) del 1866-1936 .... **TCLC 5; HLC 2**
See also CA 106; 153; CANR 80; DAM MULT; DLB 134; EW 8; HW 2; RGSF 2; RGWL 2

Vallejo, Antonio Buero
See Buero Vallejo, Antonio

Vallejo, Cesar (Abraham) 1892-1938 .... **TCLC 3, 56; HLC 2**
See also CA 105; 153; DAM MULT; HW 1; LAW; RGWL 2

Valles, Jules 1832-1885 .... **NCLC 71**
See also DLB 123; GFL 1789 to the Present

Vallette, Marguerite Eymery 1860-1953 .... **TCLC 67**
See also CA 182; DLB 123, 192

Valle Y Pena, Ramon del
See Valle-Inclan, Ramon (Maria) del

Van Ash, Cay 1918- .... **CLC 34**

Vanbrugh, Sir John 1664-1726 .... **LC 21**
See also BRW 2; DAM DRAM; DLB 80; IDTP; RGEL 2

Van Campen, Karl
See Campbell, John W(ood, Jr.)

Vance, Gerald
See Silverberg, Robert

Vance, Jack .... **CLC 35**
See also Vance, John Holbrook
See also DLB 8; FANT; SCFW 2; SFW 4; SUFW

Vance, John Holbrook 1916-
See Queen, Ellery; Vance, Jack
See also CA 29-32R; CANR 17, 65; CMW 4; MTCW 1

Van Den Bogarde, Derek Jules Gaspard Ulric Niven 1921-1999 .... **CLC 14**
See also Bogarde, Dirk
See also CA 77-80; 179

Vandenburgh, Jane .... **CLC 59**
See also CA 168

Vanderhaeghe, Guy 1951- .... **CLC 41**
See also BPFB 3; CA 113; CANR 72

van der Post, Laurens (Jan) 1906-1996 .... **CLC 5**
See also AFW; CA 5-8R; 155; CANR 35; CN 7; DLB 204; RGEL 2

van de Wetering, Janwillem 1931- ... **CLC 47**
See also CA 49-52; CANR 4, 62, 90; CMW 4

Van Dine, S. S. .... **TCLC 23**
See also Wright, Willard Huntington
See also MSW

Van Doren, Carl (Clinton) 1885-1950 .... **TCLC 18**
See also CA 111; 168

Van Doren, Mark 1894-1972 .... **CLC 6, 10**
See also CA 1-4R; 37-40R; CANR 3; DLB 45; MTCW 1, 2; RGAL 4

Van Druten, John (William) 1901-1957 .... **TCLC 2**
See also CA 104; 161; DLB 10; RGAL 4

Van Duyn, Mona (Jane) 1921- ...... **CLC 3, 7, 63, 116**
See also CA 9-12R; CANR 7, 38, 60; CP 7; CWP; DAM POET; DLB 5

Van Dyne, Edith
See Baum, L(yman) Frank

van Itallie, Jean-Claude 1936- .... **CLC 3**
See also CA 45-48; CAAS 2; CAD; CANR 1, 48; CD 5; DLB 7

Van Loot, Cornelius Obenchain
See Roberts, Kenneth (Lewis)

van Ostaijen, Paul 1896-1928 .... **TCLC 33**
See also CA 163

Van Peebles, Melvin 1932- .... **CLC 2, 20**
See also BW 2, 3; CA 85-88; CANR 27, 67, 82; DAM MULT

EXPS; LAIT 4; MTCW 1, 2; NFS 3; RGAL 4; SCFW; SFW 4; SSFS 5; TUS; YAW

Von Rachen, Kurt
See Hubbard, L(afayette) Ron(ald)

von Rezzori (d'Arezzo), Gregor
See Rezzori (d'Arezzo), Gregor von

von Sternberg, Josef
See Sternberg, Josef von

Vorster, Gordon 1924- .... **CLC 34**
See also CA 133

Vosce, Trudie
See Ozick, Cynthia

Voznesensky, Andrei (Andreievich)
1933- .... **CLC 1, 15, 57**
See also CA 89-92; CANR 37; CWW 2; DAM POET; MTCW 1

Wace, Robert c. 1100-c. 1175 .... **CMLC 55**
See also DLB 146

Waddington, Miriam 1917- .... **CLC 28**
See also CA 21-24R; CANR 12, 30; CCA 1; CP 7; DLB 68

Wagman, Fredrica 1937- .... **CLC 7**
See also CA 97-100; INT 97-100

Wagner, Linda W.
See Wagner-Martin, Linda (C.)

Wagner, Linda Welshimer
See Wagner-Martin, Linda (C.)

Wagner, Richard 1813-1883 .... **NCLC 9**
See also DLB 129; EW 6

Wagner-Martin, Linda (C.) 1936- .... **CLC 50**
See also CA 159

Wagoner, David (Russell) 1926- .... **CLC 3, 5, 15; PC 33**
See also AMWS 9; CA 1-4R; CAAS 3; CANR 2, 71; CN 7; CP 7; DLB 5, 256; SATA 14; TCWW 2

Wah, Fred(erick James) 1939- .... **CLC 44**
See also CA 107; 141; CP 7; DLB 60

Wahloo, Per 1926-1975 .... **CLC 7**
See also BPFB 3; CA 61-64; CANR 73; CMW 4; MSW

Wahloo, Peter
See Wahloo, Per

Wain, John (Barrington) 1925-1994 . **CLC 2, 11, 15, 46**
See also CA 5-8R; 145; CAAS 4; CANR 23, 54; CDBLB 1960 to Present; DLB 15, 27, 139, 155; MTCW 1, 2

Wajda, Andrzej 1926- .... **CLC 16**
See also CA 102

Wakefield, Dan 1932- .... **CLC 7**
See also CA 21-24R; CAAS 7; CN 7

Wakefield, Herbert Russell
1888-1965 .... **TCLC 120**
See also CA 5-8R; CANR 77; HGG; SUFW

Wakoski, Diane 1937- ...... **CLC 2, 4, 7, 9, 11, 40; PC 15**
See also CA 13-16R; CAAS 1; CANR 9, 60, 106; CP 7; CWP; DAM POET; DLB 5; INT CANR-9; MTCW 2

Wakoski-Sherbell, Diane
See Wakoski, Diane

Walcott, Derek (Alton) 1930- .... **CLC 2, 4, 9, 14, 25, 42, 67, 76, 160; BLC 3; DC 7**
See also BW 2; CA 89-92; CANR 26, 47, 75, 80; CBD; CD 5; CDWLB 3; CP 7; DA3; DAB; DAC; DAM MST, MULT, POET; DLB 117; DLBY 1981; DNFS 1; EFS 1; MTCW 1, 2; PFS 6; RGAL 2; TWA

Waldman, Anne (Lesley) 1945- .... **CLC 7**
See also CA 37-40R; CAAS 17; CANR 34, 69; CP 7; CWP; DLB 16

Waldo, E. Hunter
See Sturgeon, Theodore (Hamilton)

Waldo, Edward Hamilton
See Sturgeon, Theodore (Hamilton)

Walker, Alice (Malsenior) 1944- ... **CLC 5, 6, 9, 19, 27, 46, 58, 103; BLC 3; PC 30; SSC 5; WLCS**
See also AAYA 3, 33; AFAW 1, 2; AMWS 3; BEST 89:4; BPFB 3; BW 2, 3; CA 37-40R; CANR 9, 27, 49, 66, 82; CDALB 1968-1988; CN 7; CPW; CSW; DA; DA3; DAB; DAC; DAM MST, MULT, NOV, POET, POP; DLB 6, 33, 143; EXPN; EXPS; FW; INT CANR-27; LAIT 3; MAWW; MTCW 1, 2; NFS 5; RGAL 4; RGSF 2; SATA 31; SSFS 2, 11; TUS; YAW

Walker, David Harry 1911-1992 ...... **CLC 14**
See also CA 1-4R; 137; CANR 1; CWRI 5; SATA 8; SATA-Obit 71

Walker, Edward Joseph 1934-
See Walker, Ted
See also CA 21-24R; CANR 12, 28, 53; CP 7

Walker, George F. 1947- .... **CLC 44, 61**
See also CA 103; CANR 21, 43, 59; CD 5; DAB; DAC; DAM MST; DLB 60

Walker, Joseph A. 1935- .... **CLC 19**
See also BW 1, 3; CA 89-92; CAD; CANR 26; CD 5; DAM DRAM, MST; DFS 12; DLB 38

Walker, Margaret (Abigail)
1915-1998 .... **CLC 1, 6; BLC; PC 20**
See also AFAW 1, 2; BW 2, 3; CA 73-76; 172; CANR 26, 54, 76; CN 7; CP 7; CSW; DAM MULT; DLB 76, 152; EXPP; FW; MTCW 1, 2; RGAL 4; RHW

Walker, Ted .... **CLC 13**
See also Walker, Edward Joseph
See also DLB 40

Wallace, David Foster 1962- ..... **CLC 50, 114**
See also AMWS 10; CA 132; CANR 59; DA3; MTCW 2

Wallace, Dexter
See Masters, Edgar Lee

Wallace, (Richard Horatio) Edgar
1875-1932 .... **TCLC 57**
See also CA 115; CMW 4; DLB 70; MSW; RGEL 2

Wallace, Irving 1916-1990 .... **CLC 7, 13**
See also AITN 1; BPFB 3; CA 1-4R; 132; CAAS 1; CANR 1, 27; CPW; DAM NOV, POP; INT CANR-27; MTCW 1, 2

Wallant, Edward Lewis 1926-1962 ... **CLC 5, 10**
See also CA 1-4R; CANR 22; DLB 2, 28, 143; MTCW 1, 2; RGAL 4

Wallas, Graham 1858-1932 .... **TCLC 91**

Walley, Byron
See Card, Orson Scott

Walpole, Horace 1717-1797 .... **LC 2, 49**
See also BRW 3; DLB 39, 104, 213; HGG; RGEL 2; SUFW; TEA

Walpole, Hugh (Seymour)
1884-1941 .... **TCLC 5**
See also CA 104; 165; DLB 34; HGG; MTCW 2; RGEL 2; RHW

Walser, Martin 1927- .... **CLC 27**
See also CA 57-60; CANR 8, 46; CWW 2; DLB 75, 124

Walser, Robert 1878-1956 .... **TCLC 18; SSC 20**
See also CA 118; 165; CANR 100; DLB 66

Walsh, Gillian Paton
See Paton Walsh, Gillian

Walsh, Jill Paton .... **CLC 35**
See also Paton Walsh, Gillian
See also CLR 2, 65; WYA

Walter, Villiam Christian
See Andersen, Hans Christian

Walton, Izaak 1593-1683 .... **LC 72**
See also BRW 2; CDBLB Before 1660; DLB 151, 213; RGEL 2

Wambaugh, Joseph (Aloysius, Jr.)
1937- .... **CLC 3, 18**
See also AITN 1; BEST 89:3; BPFB 3; CA 33-36R; CANR 42, 65; CMW 4; CPW 1; DA3; DAM NOV, POP; DLB 6; DLBY 1983; MSW; MTCW 1, 2

Wang Wei 699(?)-761(?) .... **PC 18**
See also TWA

Ward, Arthur Henry Sarsfield 1883-1959
See Rohmer, Sax
See also CA 108; 173; CMW 4; HGG

Ward, Douglas Turner 1930- .... **CLC 19**
See also BW 1; CA 81-84; CAD; CANR 27; CD 5; DLB 7, 38

Ward, E. D.
See Lucas, E(dward) V(errall)

Ward, Mrs. Humphry 1851-1920
See Ward, Mary Augusta
See also RGEL 2

Ward, Mary Augusta 1851-1920 ... **TCLC 55**
See also Ward, Mrs. Humphry
See also DLB 18

Ward, Peter
See Faust, Frederick (Schiller)

Warhol, Andy 1928(?)-1987 .... **CLC 20**
See also AAYA 12; BEST 89:4; CA 89-92; 121; CANR 34

Warner, Francis (Robert le Plastrier)
1937- .... **CLC 14**
See also CA 53-56; CANR 11

Warner, Marina 1946- .... **CLC 59**
See also CA 65-68; CANR 21, 55; CN 7; DLB 194

Warner, Rex (Ernest) 1905-1986 ...... **CLC 45**
See also CA 89-92; 119; DLB 15; RGEL 2; RHW

Warner, Susan (Bogert)
1819-1885 .... **NCLC 31**
See also DLB 3, 42, 239, 250, 254

Warner, Sylvia (Constance) Ashton
See Ashton-Warner, Sylvia (Constance)

Warner, Sylvia Townsend
1893-1978 .... **CLC 7, 19; SSC 23**
See also BRWS 7; CA 61-64; 77-80; CANR 16, 60, 104; DLB 34, 139; FANT; FW; MTCW 1, 2; RGEL 2; RGSF 2; RHW

Warren, Mercy Otis 1728-1814 ..... **NCLC 13**
See also DLB 31, 200; RGAL 4; TUS

Warren, Robert Penn 1905-1989 .. **CLC 1, 4, 6, 8, 10, 13, 18, 39, 53, 59; PC 37; SSC 4; WLC**
See also AITN 1; AMW; BPFB 3; BYA 1; CA 13-16R; 129; CANR 10, 47; CDALB 1968-1988; DA; DA3; DAB; DAC; DAM MST, NOV, POET; DLB 2, 48, 152; DLBY 1980; 1989; INT CANR-10; MTCW 1, 2; NFS 13; RGAL 4; RGSF 2; RHW; SATA 46; SATA-Obit 63; SSFS 8; TUS

Warshofsky, Isaac
See Singer, Isaac Bashevis

Warton, Thomas 1728-1790 .... **LC 15, 82**
See also DAM POET; DLB 104, 109; RGEL 2

Waruk, Kona
See Harris, (Theodore) Wilson

Warung, Price .... **TCLC 45**
See also Astley, William
See also DLB 230; RGEL 2

Warwick, Jarvis
See Garner, Hugh
See also CCA 1

Washington, Alex
See Harris, Mark

Washington, Booker T(aliaferro)
1856-1915 .... **TCLC 10; BLC 3**
See also BW 1; CA 114; 125; DA3; DAM MULT; LAIT 2; RGAL 4; SATA 28

Wojciechowska, Maia (Teresa)
1927-2002 .... **CLC 26**
See also AAYA 8; BYA 3; CA 9-12R, 183;
CAAE 183; CANR 4, 41; CLR 1; JRDA;
MAICYA 1, 2; SAAS 1; SATA 1, 28, 83;
SATA-Essay 104; SATA-Obit 134; YAW

Wojtyla, Karol
See John Paul II, Pope

Wolf, Christa 1929- .... **CLC 14, 29, 58, 150**
See also CA 85-88; CANR 45; CDWLB 2;
CWW 2; DLB 75; FW; MTCW 1; RGWL
2; SSFS 14

Wolf, Naomi 1962- .... **CLC 157**
See also CA 141; CANR 110; FW

Wolfe, Gene (Rodman) 1931- .... **CLC 25**
See also AAYA 35; CA 57-60; CAAS 9;
CANR 6, 32, 60; CPW; DAM POP; DLB
8; FANT; MTCW 1; SATA 118; SCFW 2;
SFW 4

Wolfe, George C. 1954- .... **CLC 49; BLCS**
See also CA 149; CAD; CD 5

Wolfe, Thomas (Clayton)
1900-1938 ...... **TCLC 4, 13, 29, 61; SSC
33; WLC**
See also AMW; BPFB 3; CA 104; 132;
CANR 102; CDALB 1929-1941; DA;
DA3; DAB; DAC; DAM MST, NOV;
DLB 9, 102, 229; DLBD 2, 16; DLBY
1985, 1997; MTCW 1, 2; RGAL 4; TUS

Wolfe, Thomas Kennerly, Jr.
1930- .... **CLC 147**
See also Wolfe, Tom
See also CA 13-16R; CANR 9, 33, 70, 104;
DA3; DAM POP; DLB 185; INT
CANR-9; MTCW 1, 2; TUS

Wolfe, Tom .... **CLC 1, 2, 9, 15, 35, 51**
See also Wolfe, Thomas Kennerly, Jr.
See also AAYA 8; AITN 2; AMWS 3; BEST
89:1; BPFB 3; CN 7; CPW; CSW; DLB
152; LAIT 5; RGAL 4

Wolff, Geoffrey (Ansell) 1937- .... **CLC 41**
See also CA 29-32R; CANR 29, 43, 78

Wolff, Sonia
See Levitin, Sonia (Wolff)

Wolff, Tobias (Jonathan Ansell)
1945- .... **CLC 39, 64**
See also AAYA 16; AMWS 7; BEST 90:2;
BYA 12; CA 114; 117; CAAS 22; CANR
54, 76, 96; CN 7; CSW; DA3; DLB 130;
INT CA-117; MTCW 2; RGAL 4; RGSF
2; SSFS 4, 11

Wolfram von Eschenbach c. 1170-c.
1220 .... **CMLC 5**
See also CDWLB 2; DLB 138; EW 1;
RGWL 2

Wolitzer, Hilma 1930- .... **CLC 17**
See also CA 65-68; CANR 18, 40; INT
CANR-18; SATA 31

Wollstonecraft, Mary 1759-1797 ..... **LC 5, 50**
See also BRWS 3; CDBLB 1789-1832;
DLB 39, 104, 158, 252; FW; LAIT 1;
RGEL 2; TEA; WLIT 3

Wonder, Stevie .... **CLC 12**
See also Morris, Steveland Judkins

Wong, Jade Snow 1922- .... **CLC 17**
See also CA 109; CANR 91; SATA 112

Woodberry, George Edward
1855-1930 .... **TCLC 73**
See also CA 165; DLB 71, 103

Woodcott, Keith
See Brunner, John (Kilian Houston)

Woodruff, Robert W.
See Mencken, H(enry) L(ouis)

Woolf, (Adeline) Virginia
1882-1941 .. **TCLC 1, 5, 20, 43, 56, 101,
123; SSC 7; WLC**
See also BPFB 3; BRW 7; BRWR 1; CA
104; 130; CANR 64; CDBLB 1914-1945;
DA; DA3; DAB; DAC; DAM MST, NOV;
DLB 36, 100, 162; DLBD 10; EXPS; FW;

LAIT 3; MTCW 1, 2; NCFS 2; NFS 8,
12; RGEL 2; RGSF 2; SSFS 4, 12; TEA;
WLIT 4

Woollcott, Alexander (Humphreys)
1887-1943 .... **TCLC 5**
See also CA 105; 161; DLB 29

Woolrich, Cornell .... **CLC 77**
See also Hopley-Woolrich, Cornell George
See also MSW

Woolson, Constance Fenimore
1840-1894 .... **NCLC 82**
See also DLB 12, 74, 189, 221; RGAL 4

Wordsworth, Dorothy 1771-1855 .. **NCLC 25**
See also DLB 107

Wordsworth, William 1770-1850 .. **NCLC 12,
38, 111; PC 4; WLC**
See also BRW 4; CDBLB 1789-1832; DA;
DA3; DAB; DAC; DAM MST, POET;
DLB 93, 107; EXPP; PAB; PFS 2; RGEL
2; TEA; WLIT 3; WP

Wotton, Sir Henry 1568-1639 .... **LC 68**
See also DLB 121; RGEL 2

Wouk, Herman 1915- .... **CLC 1, 9, 38**
See also BPFB 2, 3; CA 5-8R; CANR 6,
33, 67; CDALBS; CN 7; CPW; DA3;
DAM NOV, POP; DLBY 1982; INT
CANR-6; LAIT 4; MTCW 1, 2; NFS 7;
TUS

Wright, Charles (Penzel, Jr.) 1935- .. **CLC 6,
13, 28, 119, 146**
See also AMWS 5; CA 29-32R; CAAS 7;
CANR 23, 36, 62, 88; CP 7; DLB 165;
DLBY 1982; MTCW 1, 2; PFS 10

Wright, Charles Stevenson 1932- ... **CLC 49;
BLC 3**
See also BW 1; CA 9-12R; CANR 26; CN
7; DAM MULT, POET; DLB 33

Wright, Frances 1795-1852 .... **NCLC 74**
See also DLB 73

Wright, Frank Lloyd 1867-1959 .... **TCLC 95**
See also AAYA 33; CA 174

Wright, Jack R.
See Harris, Mark

Wright, James (Arlington)
1927-1980 .... **CLC 3, 5, 10, 28; PC 36**
See also AITN 2; AMWS 3; CA 49-52; 97-
100; CANR 4, 34, 64; CDALBS; DAM
POET; DLB 5, 169; EXPP; MTCW 1, 2;
PFS 7, 8; RGAL 4; TUS; WP

Wright, Judith (Arundell)
1915-2000 .... **CLC 11, 53; PC 14**
See also CA 13-16R; 188; CANR 31, 76,
93; CP 7; CWP; DLB 260; MTCW 1, 2;
PFS 8; RGEL 2; SATA 14; SATA-Obit
121

Wright, L(aurali) R. 1939- .... **CLC 44**
See also CA 138; CMW 4

Wright, Richard (Nathaniel)
1908-1960 .... **CLC 1, 3, 4, 9, 14, 21, 48,
74; BLC 3; SSC 2; WLC**
See also AAYA 5, 42; AFAW 1, 2; AMW;
BPFB 3; BW 1; BYA 2; CA 108; CANR
64; CDALB 1929-1941; DA; DA3; DAB;
DAC; DAM MST, MULT, NOV; DLB 76,
102; DLBD 2; EXPN; LAIT 3, 4; MTCW
1, 2; NCFS 1; NFS 1, 7; RGAL 4; RGSF
2; SSFS 3, 9, 15; TUS; YAW

Wright, Richard B(ruce) 1937- .... **CLC 6**
See also CA 85-88; DLB 53

Wright, Rick 1945- .... **CLC 35**

Wright, Rowland
See Wells, Carolyn

Wright, Stephen 1946- .... **CLC 33**

Wright, Willard Huntington 1888-1939
See Van Dine, S. S.
See also CA 115; 189; CMW 4; DLBD 16

Wright, William 1930- .... **CLC 44**
See also CA 53-56; CANR 7, 23

Wroth, Lady Mary 1587-1653(?) .... **LC 30;
PC 38**
See also DLB 121

Wu Ch'eng-en 1500(?)-1582(?) .... **LC 7**

Wu Ching-tzu 1701-1754 .... **LC 2**

Wurlitzer, Rudolph 1938(?)- .... **CLC 2, 4, 15**
See also CA 85-88; CN 7; DLB 173

Wyatt, Sir Thomas c. 1503-1542 . **LC 70; PC
27**
See also BRW 1; DLB 132; EXPP; RGEL
2; TEA

Wycherley, William 1640-1716 .... **LC 8, 21**
See also BRW 2; CDBLB 1660-1789; DAM
DRAM; DLB 80; RGEL 2

Wylie, Elinor (Morton Hoyt)
1885-1928 .... **TCLC 8; PC 23**
See also AMWS 1; CA 105; 162; DLB 9,
45; EXPP; RGAL 4

Wylie, Philip (Gordon) 1902-1971 ... **CLC 43**
See also CA 21-22; 33-36R; CAP 2; DLB
9; SFW 4

Wyndham, John .... **CLC 19**
See also Harris, John (Wyndham Parkes
Lucas) Beynon
See also DLB 255; SCFW 2

Wyss, Johann David Von
1743-1818 .... **NCLC 10**
See also JRDA; MAICYA 1, 2; SATA 29;
SATA-Brief 27

Xenophon c. 430 B.C.-c. 354
B.C. .... **CMLC 17**
See also AW 1; DLB 176; RGWL 2

Yakumo Koizumi
See Hearn, (Patricio) Lafcadio (Tessima
Carlos)

Yamamoto, Hisaye 1921- .... **SSC 34; AAL**
See also DAM MULT; LAIT 4; SSFS 14

Yanez, Jose Donoso
See Donoso (Yanez), Jose

Yanovsky, Basile S.
See Yanovsky, V(assily) S(emenovich)

Yanovsky, V(assily) S(emenovich)
1906-1989 .... **CLC 2, 18**
See also CA 97-100; 129

Yates, Richard 1926-1992 .... **CLC 7, 8, 23**
See also AMWS 11; CA 5-8R; 139; CANR
10, 43; DLB 2, 234; DLBY 1981, 1992;
INT CANR-10

Yeats, W. B.
See Yeats, William Butler

Yeats, William Butler 1865-1939 .... **TCLC 1,
11, 18, 31, 93, 116; PC 20; WLC**
See also BRW 6; BRWR 1; CA 104; 127;
CANR 45; CDBLB 1890-1914; DA; DA3;
DAB; DAC; DAM DRAM, MST, POET;
DLB 10, 19, 98, 156; EXPP; MTCW 1,
2; NCFS 3; PAB; PFS 1, 2, 5, 7, 13, 15;
RGEL 2; TEA; WLIT 4; WP

Yehoshua, A(braham) B. 1936- .. **CLC 13, 31**
See also CA 33-36R; CANR 43, 90; RGSF
2

Yellow Bird
See Ridge, John Rollin

Yep, Laurence Michael 1948- .... **CLC 35**
See also AAYA 5, 31; BYA 7; CA 49-52;
CANR 1, 46, 92; CLR 3, 17, 54; DLB 52;
FANT; JRDA; MAICYA 1, 2; MAICYAS
1; SATA 7, 69, 123; WYA; YAW

Yerby, Frank G(arvin) 1916-1991 . **CLC 1, 7,
22; BLC 3**
See also BPFB 3; BW 1, 3; CA 9-12R; 136;
CANR 16, 52; DAM MULT; DLB 76;
INT CANR-16; MTCW 1; RGAL 4; RHW

Yesenin, Sergei Alexandrovich
See Esenin, Sergei (Alexandrovich)

Literary Criticism Series
Cumulative Topic Index

This index lists all topic entries in Gale's *Classical and Medieval Literature Criticism, Contemporary Literary Criticism, Drama Criticism, Literature Criticism from 1400 to 1800, Nineteenth-Century Literature Criticism,* and *Twentieth-Century Literary Criticism.*

Topic Index

Topic Index

TCLC Cumulative Nationality Index

AMERICAN

Adams, Andy **56**
Adams, Brooks **80**
Adams, Henry (Brooks) **4, 52**
Addams, Jane **76**
Agee, James (Rufus) **1, 19**
Aldrich, Bess (Genevra) Streeter **125**
Allen, Fred **87**
Anderson, Maxwell **2**
Anderson, Sherwood **1, 10, 24, 123**
Anthony, Susan B(rownell) **84**
Atherton, Gertrude (Franklin Horn) **2**
Austin, Mary (Hunter) **25**
Baker, Ray Stannard **47**
Baker, Carlos (Heard) **119**
Bambara, Toni Cade **116**
Barry, Philip **11**
Baum, L(yman) Frank **7**
Beard, Charles A(ustin) **15**
Becker, Carl (Lotus) **63**
Belasco, David **3**
Bell, James Madison **43**
Benchley, Robert (Charles) **1, 55**
Benedict, Ruth (Fulton) **60**
Benét, Stephen Vincent **7**
Benét, William Rose **28**
Bierce, Ambrose (Gwinett) **1, 7, 44**
Biggers, Earl Derr **65**
Bishop, Elizabeth **121**
Bishop, John Peale **103**
Black Elk **33**
Boas, Franz **56**
Bodenheim, Maxwell **44**
Bok, Edward W. **101**
Bourne, Randolph S(illiman) **16**
Boyd, James **115**
Boyd, Thomas (Alexander) **111**
Bradford, Gamaliel **36**
Brennan, Christopher John **17**
Brennan, Maeve **124**
Brodkey, Harold (Roy) **123**
Bromfield, Louis (Brucker) **11**
Broun, Heywood **104**
Bryan, William Jennings **99**
Burroughs, Edgar Rice **2, 32**
Burroughs, William S(eward) **121**
Cabell, James Branch **6**
Cable, George Washington **4**
Cahan, Abraham **71**
Caldwell, Erskine (Preston) **117**
Cardozo, Benjamin N(athan) **65**
Carnegie, Dale **53**
Cather, Willa (Sibert) **1, 11, 31, 99, 125**
Chambers, Robert W(illiam) **41**
Chandler, Raymond (Thornton) **1, 7**
Chapman, John Jay **7**
Chase, Mary Ellen **124**
Chesnutt, Charles W(addell) **5, 39**
Childress, Alice **116**
Chopin, Katherine **5, 14, 127**
Cobb, Irvin S(hrewsbury) **77**
Coffin, Robert P(eter) Tristram **95**

Cohan, George M(ichael) **60**
Comstock, Anthony **13**
Cotter, Joseph Seamon Sr. **28**
Cram, Ralph Adams **45**
Crane, (Harold) Hart **2, 5, 80**
Crane, Stephen (Townley) **11, 17, 32**
Crawford, F(rancis) Marion **10**
Crothers, Rachel **19**
Cullen, Countée **4, 37**
Darrow, Clarence (Seward) **81**
Davis, Rebecca (Blaine) Harding **6**
Davis, Richard Harding **24**
Day, Clarence (Shepard Jr.) **25**
Dent, Lester **72**
De Voto, Bernard (Augustine) **29**
Dewey, John **95**
Dreiser, Theodore (Herman Albert) **10, 18, 35, 83**
Dulles, John Foster **72**
Dunbar, Paul Laurence **2, 12**
Duncan, Isadora **68**
Dunne, Finley Peter **28**
Eastman, Charles A(lexander) **55**
Eddy, Mary (Ann Morse) Baker **71**
Einstein, Albert **65**
Erskine, John **84**
Faust, Frederick (Schiller) **49**
Fenollosa, Ernest (Francisco) **91**
Fields, W. C. **80**
Fisher, Dorothy (Frances) Canfield **87**
Fisher, Rudolph **11**
Fitzgerald, F(rancis) Scott (Key) **1, 6, 14, 28, 55**
Fitzgerald, Zelda (Sayre) **52**
Fletcher, John Gould **35**
Foote, Mary Hallock **108**
Ford, Henry **73**
Forten, Charlotte L. **16**
Freeman, Douglas Southall **11**
Freeman, Mary E(leanor) Wilkins **9**
Fuller, Henry Blake **103**
Futrelle, Jacques **19**
Gale, Zona **7**
Garland, (Hannibal) Hamlin **3**
Gilman, Charlotte (Anna) Perkins (Stetson) **9, 37, 117**
Ginsberg, Allen **120**
Glasgow, Ellen (Anderson Gholson) **2, 7**
Glaspell, Susan **55**
Goldman, Emma **13**
Green, Anna Katharine **63**
Grey, Zane **6**
Griffith, D(avid Lewelyn) W(ark) **68**
Griggs, Sutton (Elbert) **77**
Guest, Edgar A(lbert) **95**
Guiney, Louise Imogen **41**
Hall, James Norman **23**
Handy, W(illiam) C(hristopher) **97**
Harper, Frances Ellen Watkins **14**
Harris, Joel Chandler **2**
Harte, (Francis) Bret(t) **1, 25**
Hartmann, Sadakichi **73**
Hatteras, Owen **18**

Hawthorne, Julian **25**
Hearn, (Patricio) Lafcadio (Tessima Carlos) **9**
Hecht, Ben **101**
Hellman, Lillian (Florence) **119**
Hemingway, Ernest (Miller) **115**
Henry, O. **1, 19**
Hergesheimer, Joseph **11**
Heyward, (Edwin) DuBose **59**
Higginson, Thomas Wentworth **36**
Holley, Marietta **99**
Holly, Buddy **65**
Holmes, Oliver Wendell Jr. **77**
Hopkins, Pauline Elizabeth **28**
Horney, Karen (Clementine Theodore Danielsen) **71**
Howard, Robert E(rvin) **8**
Howe, Julia Ward **21**
Howells, William Dean **7, 17, 41**
Huneker, James Gibbons **65**
Hurston, Zora Neale **121**
Ince, Thomas H. **89**
James, Henry **2, 11, 24, 40, 47, 64**
James, William **15, 32**
Jewett, (Theodora) Sarah Orne **1, 22**
Johnson, James Weldon **3, 19**
Johnson, Robert **69**
Kerouac, Jack **117**
Kinsey, Alfred C(harles) **91**
Kirk, Russell (Amos) **119**
Kornbluth, C(yril) M. **8**
Korzybski, Alfred (Habdank Skarbek) **61**
Kubrick, Stanley **112**
Kuttner, Henry **10**
Lardner, Ring(gold) W(ilmer) **2, 14**
Lewis, (Harry) Sinclair **4, 13, 23, 39**
Lewisohn, Ludwig **19**
Lewton, Val **76**
Lindsay, (Nicholas) Vachel **17**
Locke, Alain (Le Roy) **43**
Lockridge, Ross (Franklin) Jr. **111**
London, Jack **9, 15, 39**
Lovecraft, H(oward) P(hillips) **4, 22**
Lowell, Amy **1, 8**
Mankiewicz, Herman (Jacob) **85**
March, William **96**
Markham, Edwin **47**
Marquis, Don(ald Robert Perry) **7**
Masters, Edgar Lee **2, 25**
Matthews, (James) Brander **95**
Matthiessen, F(rancis) O(tto) **100**
McAlmon, Robert (Menzies) **97**
McCoy, Horace (Stanley) **28**
Mead, George Herbert **89**
Mencken, H(enry) L(ouis) **13**
Micheaux, Oscar (Devereaux) **76**
Millay, Edna St. Vincent **4, 49**
Mitchell, Margaret (Munnerlyn) **11**
Mitchell, S(ilas) Weir **36**
Mitchell, William **81**
Monroe, Harriet **12**
Moody, William Vaughan **105**
Morley, Christopher (Darlington) **87**
Morris, Wright **107**

Nationality Index

TCLC-127 Title Index

493

ISBN 0-7876-5941-X

90000

9 780787 659417